MILLER'S
Antiques
PRICE GUIDE

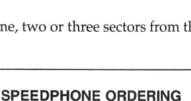

MILLER'S
Antiques
PRICE GUIDE

Consultants
Judith and Martin Miller

General Editor
Josephine Davis

1996
Volume XVII

MILLER'S ANTIQUES PRICE GUIDE 1996

Created and designed by
Miller's
The Cellars, High Street,
Tenterden, Kent, TN30 6BN
Tel: 01580 766411

Consultants: Judith & Martin Miller

General Editor: Josephine Davis
Editorial and Production Co-ordinator: Sue Boyd
Editorial Assistants: Marion Rickman, Jo Wood, Gillian Judd
Production Assistants: Gillian Charles, Karen Taylor
Advertising Executive: Elizabeth Smith
Advertising Assistants: Melinda Williams, Joanne Daniels
Index compiled by: DD Editorial Services, Beccles
Design: Jody Taylor, Kari Reeves, Matthew Leppard, Shirley Reeves
Additional photography: Ian Booth, Robin Saker

First published in Great Britain in 1995
by Miller's, an imprint of
Reed Consumer Books Limited,
Michelin House, 81 Fulham Road,
London SW3 6RB
and Auckland, Melbourne, Singapore and Toronto

A CIP catalogue record for this book is
available from the British Library

ISBN 1-85732-616-4

Bromide output by Perfect Image, Hurst Green, E. Sussex
Illustrations by G.H. Graphics, St. Leonard's-on-Sea
Colour origination by Scantrans, Singapore
Printed and bound in England by William Clowes Ltd.,
Beccles and London

Front cover illustrations:
Top l. *A 'Tulip' delftware charger, London, late 17thC, 16in (41cm) diam. S*
Centre. *A Wedgwood copy of the Portland or Barberini vase, c1850, 10in (25cm) high. S*
Top r. *A bronze figure, 'Fan Dancer', by Marcel Bouraine, c1920, 23½in (60cm) high. S*
Below. *A Regency ebonised oak chaise longue, c1815, 78½in (200cm) long. S*

KEY TO ILLUSTRATIONS

Each illustration and descriptive caption is accompanied by a letter code. By reference to the following list of Auctioneers (denoted by *) and Dealers (•) the source of any item may be immediately determined. In no way does this constitute or imply a contract or binding offer on the part of any of our contributors to supply or sell the goods illustrated, or similar articles, at the prices stated. Advertisers in this year's directory are denoted by †.

AAV * Academy Auctioneers & Valuers, Northcote House, Northcote Avenue, Ealing, London, W5 3UR. Tel: 0181 579 7466

AG * Anderson & Garland (Auctioneers), Marlborough House, Marlborough Crescent, Newcastle-upon-Tyne, Tyne & Wear, NE1 4EE. Tel: 0191 232 6278

AH *† Andrew Hartley, Victoria Salerooms, Little Lane, Ilkley, Yorkshire, LS29 8EA. Tel: 01943 816363

AL •† Ann Lingard, Ropewalk Antiques, Ropewalk, Rye, Sussex, TN31 7NA. Tel: 01797 223486

ALS •† Allan Smith Clocks, Amity Cottage, 162 Beechcroft Road, Upper Stratton, Swindon, Wiltshire, SN2 6QE. Tel: 01793 822977

AMH • Amherst Antiques, 23 London Road, Riverhead, Sevenoaks, Kent, TN13 2BU. Tel: 01732 455047

AnE • The Antiques Emporium, The Old Chapel, Long Street, Tetbury, Glos., GL8 8AA. Tel: 01666 505281

AP *† Andrew Pickford, The Hertford Saleroom, 42 St Andrew Street, Hertford, Hertfordshire, SG14 1JA. Tel: 01992 583508

ASA •† A S Antiques, 26 Broad Street, Pendleton, Salford, Gt. Manchester, M6 5BY. Tel: 0161 737 5938

ASH •† Ashburton Marbles, Grate Hall, North Street, Ashburton, Devon, TQ13 7QD. Tel: 01364 653189

Bea * Bearnes, Avenue Road, Torquay, Devon, TQ2 5TG. Tel: 01803 296277

BEN • 20th Century Glass, 291 Westbourne Grove, London, W11 2QB. Tel: 0181 806 7068

Ber • Berry Antiques, The Old Butcher's Shop, Goudhurst, Kent, TN17 1AE. Tel: 01580 212115

BHA • Beaubush House Antiques, 95 High Street, Sandgate, Folkestone, Kent, CT20 3BY. Tel: 01303 249099

BIG * Bigwood Auctioneers Ltd, The Old School, Tiddington, Stratford-upon-Avon, Warwickshire, CV37 7AW. Tel: 01789 269415

BKK •† Bona Arts Decorative Ltd, 19 Princes Mead Shopping Centre, Farnborough, Hampshire, GU14 7TJ. Tel: 01252 372188/544130

Bon *† Bonhams, Montpelier Galleries, Montpelier Street, London, SW7 1HH. Tel: 0171 584 9161

BRA •† Billiard Room Antiques, The Old School, Church Lane, Chilcompton, Bath, Somerset, BA3 4HP. Tel: 01761 232839

BRD • Birdham Antiques, The Old Bird & Ham, Main Road, Birdham, Chichester, Sussex, PO20 7HS. Tel: 01243 51141

Bri * Bristol Auction Rooms, St John's Place, Apsley Road, Clifton, Bristol, Avon, BS8 2ST. Tel: 0117 973 7201

BWe * Biddle & Webb Ltd, Ladywood Middleway, Birmingham, West Midlands, B16 0PP. Tel: 0121 455 8042

C * Christie, Manson & Woods Ltd, 8 King Street, St James's, London, SW1Y 6QT. Tel: 0171 839 9060

C(G) * Christie's (International) S.A., 8 Place de la Taconnerie, 1204 Geneva, Switzerland. Tel: 00 4122 311 17 66

C(S) * Christie's Scotland Ltd, 164-166 Bath Street, Glasgow, Scotland, G2 4TG. Tel: 0141 332 8134

CAG *† Canterbury Auction Galleries, 40 Station Road West, Canterbury, Kent, CT2 8AN. Tel: 01227 763337

CB •† Christine Bridge Antiques, 78 Castelnau, London, SW13 9EX. Tel: 0181 741 5501

CCP •† Campden Country Pine Antiques, High Street, Chipping Campden, Glos., GL55 6HN. Tel: 01386 840315

CNY * Christie, Manson & Woods International Inc., 502 Park Avenue, (including Christie's East), New York, U.S.A., NY 10022. Tel: 001 212 546 1000

Cou • Country Homes, 61 Long Street, Tetbury, Glos., GL8 8AA. Tel: 01666 502342

CPA • Country Pine Antiques, The Barn, Upper Bush Farm, Upper Bush, Rochester, Kent, ME2 1HQ. Tel: 01634 717982.

CPi • Classic Pianos, 1B Park Terrace, East Horsham, Sussex, RH13 5DJ. Tel: 01403 241344

CS •† Christopher Sykes Antiques, The Old Parsonage, Woburn, Bucks., MK17 9QM. Tel: 01525 290259

CSK * Christie's South Kensington Ltd, 85 Old Brompton Road, London, SW7 3LD. Tel: 0171 581 7611

DA *† Dee Atkinson & Harrison, The Exchange Saleroom, Driffield, Yorkshire, YO25 7LJ. Tel: 01377 253151

DaD * David Dockree, 224 Moss Lane, Bramhall, Stockport, Cheshire, SK7 1BD. Tel: 0161 485 1258

DMa • David Masters Antiques, Elm Tree Farm, High Halden, Ashford, Kent, TN26 3BP. Tel: 01233 850551

DN * Dreweatt-Neate, Donnington Priory, Donnington, Newbury, Berkshire, RG13 2JE. Tel: 01635 31234

DUN • Richard Dunton, 920 Christchurch Road, Boscombe, Bournemouth, Dorset, BH7 6DL. Tel: 01202 425963

E * Ewbank Auctioneers, Burnt Common Auction Rooms, London Road, Send, Woking, Surrey, GU23 7LN. Tel: 01483 223101

EL * Eldred's, Robert C Eldred Co Inc, 1475 Route 6A, East Dennis, Massachusetts 0796, U.S.A., 02641. Tel: 001 508 385 3116

EP *† Evans & Partridge, Agriculture House, High Street, Stockbridge, Hampshire, SO20 6HF. Tel: 01264 810702

FAG • Fagins Antiques, The Old Whiteways Cider Factory, Hele, Exeter, Devon, EX5 4PW. Tel: 01392 882062

FBG * Frank H Boos Gallery, 420 Enterprise Court, Bloomfield Hills, Michigan, U.S.A., 48302.

FD • Frank Dux Antiques, 33 Belvedere, Bath, Avon, BA1 5HR. Tel: 01225 312367

FFAP * Freeman Fine Art Of Philadelphia Inc, 1808 Chestnut Street, Philadelphia, U.S.A., PA 19103. Tel: 001 215 563 9275

FOX • Foxhole Antiques, High Street, Goudhurst, Kent, TN17 1AE. Tel: 01580 212025

G&CC•† Goss & Crested China Ltd, 62 Murray Road, Horndean, Hampshire, PO8 9JL. Tel: 01705 597440

GAL • Gale & Sons, 52 Long Street, Tetbury, Glos., GL8 8AQ. Tel: 01666 502686

GAS • Gasson Antiques, PO Box 11, Cranleigh, Surrey, GU6 8YY. Tel: 01483 277476

GeC •† Gerard Campbell, Maple House, Market Place, Lechlade-on-Thames, Glos., GL7 3AB. Tel: 01367 252267

GH * Giles Haywood, The Auction House, St John's Road, Stourbridge, West Midlands, DY8 1EW. Tel: 01384 370891

GHA •† Garden House Antiques, 116-118 High Street, Tenterden, Kent, TN30 6HT. Tel: 01580 763664

GJC • G & J Claessens, George Street, Buxton, Derbyshire, SK17 6AT. Tel: 01298 72198/25597

GN •† Gillian Neale Antiques, PO Box 247, Aylesbury, Bucks, HP20 1JZ.

GRG • Gordon Reece Gallery, Finkle Street, Knaresborough, Yorkshire, HG5 8AA. Tel: 01423 866219

HAB •† Hamilton Billiards & Games Co, Park Lane, Knebworth, Hertfordshire, SG3 6PJ. Tel: 01438 811995

HAH • Hayman & Hayman, Antiquarius M15/L3, 135/7 Kings Road, London, SW3 4PW. Tel: 0171 351 6568/0181 741 0959

HCC *† Chapman & Son, H C, The Auction Mart, North Street, Scarborough, Yorkshire, YO11 1DL. Tel: 01723 372424

HCH * Hobbs & Chambers, Market Place, Cirencester, Glos., GL7 1QQ. Tel: 01285 654736

HEA •† Peter Hearnden, Corn Exchange Antiques Centre, 64 The Pantiles, Tunbridge Wells, Kent, TN2 5TN. Tel: 01892 539652

HEM •† The Hemswell Antiques Centre, Caenby Corner Estate, Hemswell Cliff, Gainsborough, Lincolnshire, DN21 5TJ. Tel: 01427 668389

HeR • Heritage Restorations, Maes Y Glydfa, Llanfair Caereinion, Welshpool, Powys, Wales, SY21 0HD. Tel: 01938 810384

HEW •† Muir Hewitt, Halifax Antiques Centre, Queens Road Mills, Queen's Road/Gibbet Street, Halifax, Yorkshire, HX1 4LR. Tel: 01422 366657

HOA •† Bob Hoare Pine Antiques, Unit Q, Phoenix Place, North Street, Lewes, Sussex, BN7 2DQ. Tel: 01273 480557

HOLL*† Holloways, 49 Parsons Street, Banbury, Oxfordshire, OX16 8PF. Tel: 01295 253197

HSS * Spencer and Sons, Henry (Phillips), 20 The Square, Retford, Notts, DN22 6BX. Tel: 01777 708633

JBL • Judi Bland, Durham House Antique Centre, Sheep Street, Stow-on-the-Wold, Glos., GL54 1AA. Tel: 01451 870404

JC • J Collins & Son, The Studio, 63 High Street, Bideford, Devon, EX39 2AN. Tel: 01237 473103

JH * Jacobs & Hunt, Lavant Street, Petersfield, Hampshire, GU32 3EF. Tel: 01730 62744/5

JHa • Jeanette Hayhurst Fine Glass, 32a Kensington Church Street, London, W8 4HA. Tel: 0171 938 1539

JHo •† Jonathan Horne (Antiques) Ltd, 66C Kensington Church Street, London, W8 4BY. Tel: 0171 221 5658

JHW • John Howkins, 1 Dereham Road, Norwich, Norfolk. Tel: 01603 627832

JL • Joy Luke, The Gallery, 300E Grove Street, Bloomington, U.S.A., IL 61701. Tel: 001 309 828 5533

JPr • Joanna Proops Antiques and Textiles, 3 Saville Row, Bath, Avon, BA1 2QP. Tel: 01225 310795

KEY •† Key Antiques, 11 Horse Fair, Chipping Norton, Oxfordshire, OX7 5AL. Tel: 01608 643777

L * Lawrence Fine Art Auctioneers, South Street, Crewkerne, Somerset, TA18 8AB. Tel: 01460 73041

L&E * Locke & England, Black Horse Agencies, 18 Guy Street, Leamington Spa, Warwickshire, CV32 4RT. Tel: 01926 889100

LB • The Lace Basket, 116 High Street, Tenterden, Kent. Tel: 01580 763923/763664

LHA * Lesley Hindman Auctioneers, 215 West Ohio Street, Chicago, Illinois, U.S.A., IL 60610. Tel: 001 312 670 0010

LRG * Lots Road Chelsea Auction Galleries, 71 Lots Road, Worldsend, Chelsea, London, SW10 0RN. Tel: 0171 351 7771

LT *† Louis Taylor Auctioneers & Valuers, Britannia House, 10 Town Road, Hanley, Stoke-on-Trent, Staffordshire, ST1 2QG. Tel: 01782 214111

M * Morphets of Harrogate, 4-6 Albert Street, Harrogate, Yorkshire, HG1 1JL. Tel: 01423 502282

MAT * Matthews, Christopher, 23 Mount Street, Harrogate, Yorkshire, HG2 8DQ. Tel: 01423 871756

MCA * Mervyn Carey, Twysden Cottage, Benenden, Cranbrook, Kent. Tel: 01580 240283

McC *† McCartneys, Portcullis Salerooms, Ludlow, Shropshire, SY8 1PZ. Tel: 01584 872636

MIL Milverton Antiques, Fore Street, Milverton, Taunton, Somerset, TA4 1JU. Tel: 01823 400592

Mit * Mitchells, Fairfield House, Station Road, Cockermouth, Cumbria, CA13 9PY. Tel: 01900 827800

MJB * Bowman, Michael J, 6 Haccombe House, Netherton, Newton Abbot, Devon, TQ 12 4SJ. Tel: 01626 872890

MJW • Mark J West, Cobb Antiques Ltd, 39a High Street, Wimbledon Village, London, SW19 5JX. Tel: 0181 946 2811

MofC • Millers of Chelsea Antiques Ltd, Netherbrook House, 86 Christchurch Road, Ringwood, Hampshire, BH24 1DR. Tel: 01425 472062

MSA •† M S Antiques, 25a Holland Street, London, W8 4JF. Tel: 0171 937 0793

MST * Martin Spencer-Thomas, Bicton Street Auction Rooms, Exmouth, Devon, EX8 2RT. Tel: 01395 267403

MSW *† Swain Auctions, Marilyn, The Old Barracks, Sandon Road, Grantham, Lincolnshire, NG31 9AS. Tel: 01476 68861

N * Neales, 192-194 Mansfield Road, Nottingham, Notts, NG1 3HU. Tel: 0115 962 4141

Nor •† Sue Norman, L4 Antiquarius, 135 King's Road, London, SW3. Tel: 0171 352 7217

OCA •† The Old Cinema, 160 Chiswick High Road, London, W4 1PR. Tel: 0181 995 4166

OO •† Pieter Oosthuizen, 1st Floor, Georgian Village, Camden Passage, London, N1. Tel: 0171 359 3322/376 3852

OPH • The Old Pine House, 16 Warwick Street, Royal Leamington Spa, Warwickshire, CV32 5LL. Tel: 01926 470477

P *† Phillips, Blenstock House, 7 Blenheim Street, New Bond Street, London, W1Y 0AS. Tel: 0171 629 6602

P(B) * Phillips, 1 Old King Street, Bath, Avon, BA1 2JT. Tel: 01225 310609
P(EA)* Phillips, Dover House, Wolsey Street, Ipswich, Suffolk, IP1 1UD. Tel: 01473 255137
P(NE)* Phillips North East, St Mary's, Oakwellgate, Gateshead, Tyne & Wear, NE8 2AX. Tel: 0191 477 6688
PAO •† P A Oxley, The Old Rectory, Cherhill, Calne, Wiltshire, SN11 8UX. Tel: 01249 816227
PC Private Collection.
PCh *† Cheney, Peter, Western Road Auction Rooms, Western Road, Littlehampton, Sussex, BN17 5NP. Tel: 01903 722264/713418
PHA •† Paul Hopwell Antiques, 30 High Street, West Haddon, Northants., NN6 7AP. Tel: 01788 510636
PHay• Peggy Hayden, Lincolnshire. Tel: 01507 343261
PSG • Patrick & Susan Gould, Stand L17 Gray's Mews Antique Market, Davies Mews, Davies Street, London, W1. Tel: 0171 408 0129
PT •† Pieces of Time, 1-7 Davies Mews, London, W1Y 1AR. Tel: 0171 629 2422
PUR • The Purple Shop, Antiquarius, 135 Kings Road, Chelsea, London, SW3 5ST. Tel: 0171 352 1127
PWh •† Thomas Mercer (Chronometers) Ltd, 32 Bury Street, St James, London, SW1Y 6AU. Tel: 0171 321 0353
RA • Roberts Antiques, Lancashire. Tel: 01253 827794
RBB *† Russell Baldwin & Bright, Ryelands Road, Leominster, Hereford & Worcs., HR6 8NZ. Tel: 01568 611166
RdeR•† Rogers de Rin, 76 Royal Hospital Road, London, SW3 4HN. Tel: 0171 352 9007
RHa • Robert Hall, 15c Clifford Street, London, W1X 1RF. Tel: 0171 734 4008
RIT * Ritchie Inc., D & J Auctioneers & Appraisers of Antiques & Fine Arts, 288 King Street East, Toronto, Ontario, Canada, M5A 1K4. Tel: (416) 364 1864
RP • Robert Pugh, Avon. Tel: 01225 314713
RUM •† Rumours Decorative Arts, 10 The Mall, Upper Street, Camden Passage, Islington, London. Tel: 01582 873561/0171 704 6549
RYA • Robert Young Antiques, 68 Battersea Bridge Road, London, SW11. Tel: 0171 228 7847
S * Sotheby's, 34-35 New Bond Street, London, W1A 2AA. Tel: 0171 493 8080
S(Am)* Sotheby's Amsterdam, Rokin 102, Amsterdam, Netherlands, 1012 KZ. Tel: 31 (20) 627 5656
S(G) * Sotheby's, 13 Quai du Mont Blanc, CH-1201 Geneva, Switzerland. Tel: 41 (22) 732 8585
S(HK)* Sotheby's, 502-503 Exchange Square Two, 8 Connaught Place Central, Hong Kong, China. Tel: 852 524 8121
S(NY)* Sotheby's, 1334 York Avenue, New York NY 10021, U.S.A. Tel: 212 606 7000
S(S) * Sotheby's Sussex, Summers Place, Billingshurst, Sussex, RH14 9AD. Tel: 01403 783933
SAS •† Special Auction Services, Andrew Hilton, The Coach House, Midgham Park, Reading, Berkshire, RG7 5UG. Tel: 01734 712949
SIG • Sigma Antiques, Water Skellgate, Ripon, Yorkshire, HG4 1BQ. Tel: 01765 603163
SK(B)* Skinner Inc, 357 Main Street, Bolton, U.S.A., MA 01740. Tel: 0101 508 779 6241
SLN * Sloan's, C G Sloan & Company Inc, 4920 Wyaconda Road, North Bethesda, MD 20852 , U.S.A. Tel: 0101 301 468 4911/669 5066
Som •† Somervale Antiques, 6 Radstock Road, Midsomer Norton, Bath, Avon, BA3 2AJ. Tel: 01761 412686
SP • Sue Pearson, 13 Prince Albert Street, Brighton, Sussex. Tel: 01273 329247
STA • Michelina & George Stacpoole, Main St, Adare, Co Limerick, Ireland. Tel: 00 353 61396409
SUL • Sullivan Antiques (Chantal O'Sullivan), 43-44 Francis Street, Dublin 8, Ireland. Tel: 00 3531 4541143/4539659
SWN • Swan Antiques, Kent. Tel: 01580 712720
SWO *† Sworder & Sons, G E, 15 Northgate End, Bishops Stortford, Hertfordshire, CM23 2ET. Tel: 01279 651388
Tem •† Temeraire, 11a Higher Street, Brixham, Devon, TQ5 8HW. Tel: 01803 851523
TOZ • Bruce Tozer, 14a Margaret's Buildings, Bath, Avon, BA1 2LP. Tel: 01225 420875
TP •† The Collector, 9 Church Street, Marylebone, London, NW8 8DT. Tel: 0171 706 4586
TPC •† The Pine Cellars, 39 Jewry Street, Winchester, Hampshire, SO23 8RY. Tel: 01962 777546
TVM •† Teresa Vanneck-Murray, Vanneck House, 22 Richmond Hill, Richmond-Upon-Thames, Surrey, TW10 6QX. Tel: 0181 940 2035
UC •† Up Country, The Old Corn Stores, 68 St John's Road, Tunbridge Wells, Kent, TN4 9PE. Tel: 01892 523341
VS *† Vennett-Smith, T, 11 Nottingham Road, Gotham, Nottingham, Notts, NG11 OHE. Tel: 0115 983 0541
W * Walter's, No 1 Mint Lane, Lincoln, Lincolnshire, LN1 1UD. Tel: 01522 525454
Wad * Waddingtons, 189 Queen Street East, Toronto, Ontario , Canada, M5A 1SZ. Tel: (416) 362 1678
WAL *† Wallis & Wallis, West Street Auction Galleries, Lewes, Sussex, BN7 2NJ. Tel: 01273 480208
WAT • Waterloo Antiques, 20 The Waterloo, Cirencester, Glos., GL7 2PZ. Tel: 01285 644887
WBB •† Sir William Bentley Billiards, Standen Manor Farm, Hungerford, Berkshire, RG17 0RB. Tel: 01488 681711/01672 870629
WEL • Wells Reclamation & Co, The Old Cider Farm, Coxley, Nr Wells, Somerset, BA5 1RQ. Tel: 01749 677087/677484
WL * Wintertons Ltd, Lichfield Auction Centre, Wood End Lane, Fradley, Lichfield, Staffordshire, WS13 8NF. Tel: 01543 263256
WN • What Now, Cavendish Arcade, The Crescent, Buxton, Derbyshire, SK17 6BQ. Tel: 01298 27178/23417
WRe • Walcot Reclamations, 108 Walcot Street, Bath, Avon, BA1 5BG. Tel: 01225 444404
WTA •† Witney and Airault, Prinny's Gallery, 3 Meeting House Lane, The Lanes, Brighton, Sussex, BN1 1HB. Tel: 01273 204554
WW *† Woolley & Wallis, Salisbury Salerooms, 51-61 Castle Street, Salisbury, Wiltshire, SP1 3SU. Tel: 01722 411422
YY • Yesteryear, 24D Magdalen Street, Norwich, Norfolk, NH3 1HU. Tel: 01603 622908

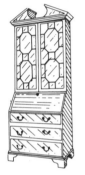

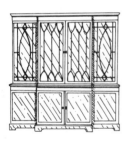

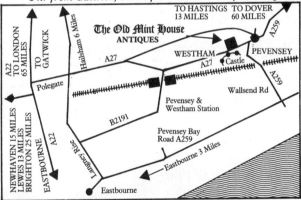

LAKESIDE
A CASE FOR FINE QUALITY

Whether you are looking for an individual piece or high volume, at Lakeside both quality and attention to detail are foremost. Lakeside furniture can also be adapted to suit the needs of the individual by varying the dimensions or materials used. An established firm with customers worldwide, our reputation precedes us.

QUALITY FURNITURE • AT GOOD PRICES • Quality

For more information see our colour advertisement at the back of this guide

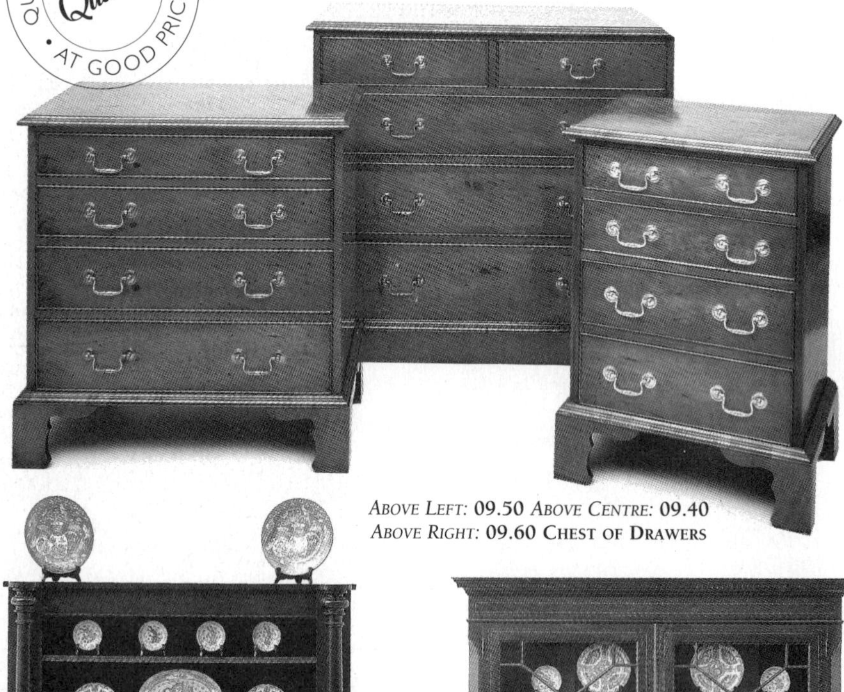

Above Left: 09.50 *Above Centre:* 09.40
Above Right: 09.60 Chest of Drawers

Above: 05.30T
Small Open Bookcase
Below: 21.75-7
2 Pillar Table Yew

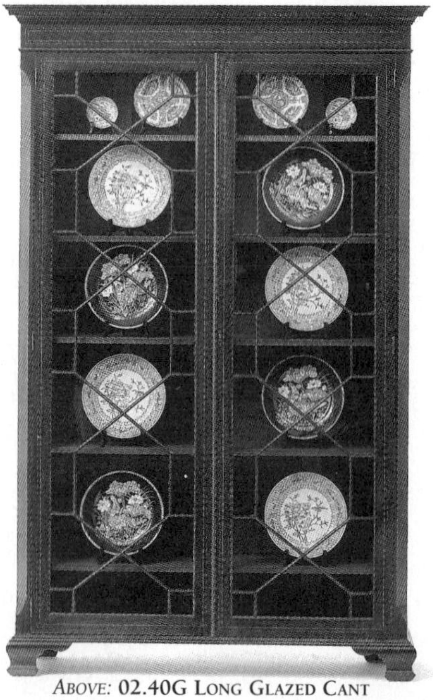

Above: 02.40G Long Glazed Cant

21.MC
Mahogany Two Door Cant

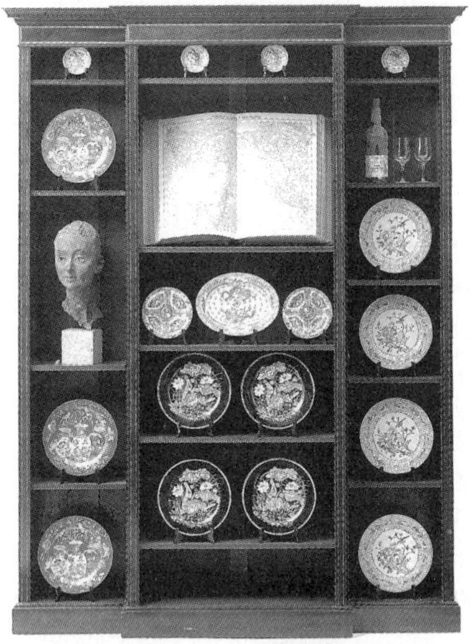

05.25H
Tall Open Breakfront

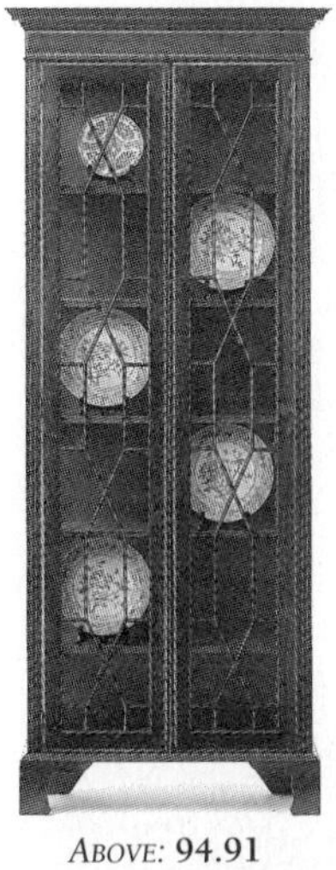

Above: 94.91
Glazed Sided Cabinet
Above Right: 05.10H
Small open Bookcase

LAKESIDE
limited

Old Cement Works, South Heighton,
Newhaven, East Sussex BN9 0HS
Tel 01273 513326 Fax 01273 515528

Mc Bains of Exeter

Adjacent Exeter Airport, Exeter, Devon EX5 2BA
Tel: (01392) 366261 Fax: (01392) 365572

★ 40,000 SQUARE FEET OF SHOWROOMS ★
★ QUALITY GEORGIAN, VICTORIAN & EDWARDIAN FURNITURE ★
★ BEST POSSIBLE TRADE PRICES ★
★ LARGE STOCK OF 'SHIPPING' FURNITURE ★
★ FURNITURE ARRIVING DAILY ★
★ CONTAINERS PACKED FREE ★
★ SHIPPING ARRANGED WORLDWIDE ★
★ EXPORT ADVICE & DOCUMENTATION ★
★ EASY ACCESS FROM M5 MOTORWAY ★
★ PERSONAL & COURTEOUS SERVICE ★
★ LONG ESTABLISHED FAMILY BUSINESS ★

A FRENCH WAREHOUSE IN ENGLAND

-Country Armoires, Tables, Dressers
-Louis XV Bedroom, Dining, Lounge Suites
-Large Selection of French Decorative Furniture

Regular Packing & Shipping To U.S

PIERRE of L P Antiques

Short Acre Street (A34)
Walsall Midlands
(1 Mile Off J.10, - M6)

TEL/FAX 01922 746764
01922 495155
0860 249097

WE ALSO NOW IMPORT SPANISH FURNITURE

INTERNATIONAL FURNITURE

TEL: 01273 611251
FAX: 01273 611574

Makers of English Traditional Furniture and custom built to your own requirements.

INTERNATIONAL FURNITURE EXPORTERS
Old Cement Works
South Heighton
Newhaven
East Sussex BN9 0HS
U.K.

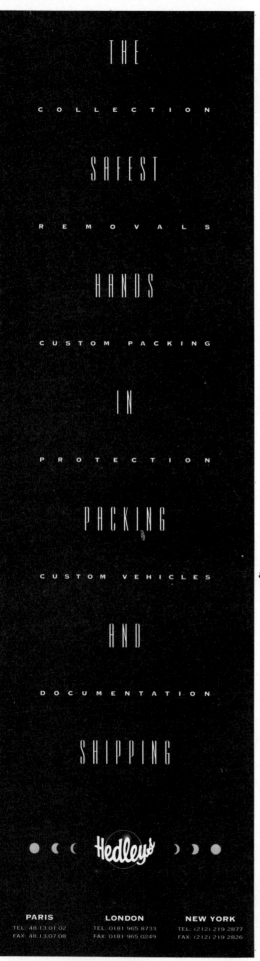

ACKNOWLEDGEMENTS

The publishers would like to acknowledge the great assistance given by our consultants:

OAK & COUNTRY FURNITURE:	**Phillip Johnson,** Bentley Antiques, Willow View, Station Road, Bentley, Surrey, GU10 5JY
BEDS:	**Richard Gold, FRICS,** Lawrence Fine Art Auctioneers, South Street, Crewkerne, Somerset TA18 8AB.
ARCHITECTURAL ANTIQUES:	**Jackie Rees,** Sotheby's, Summers Place, Billingshurst, West Sussex RH14 9AD
SPECTACLES:	**Stephen James,** 4 The Cherry Orchard, Hadlow, Tonbridge, Kent TN11 OHU
SILVER & WINE ANTIQUES:	**Henry Willis,** 38 Cheap Street, Sherborne, Dorset, DT9 3PX
DOLLS' HOUSES:	**Clare Fletcher,** Phillips Bath, 1 Old King Street, Bath, Avon, BA1 2JT.
GLASS:	**Christine Bridge,** 78 Castlenau, Barnes, London SW13 9EX
BLUE & WHITE TRANSFER WARE:	**Gillian Neale,** PO Box 247, Aylesbury, Bucks, HP20 1JZ
DECORATIVE ARTS:	**Audrey Sternshine,** 26 Broad Street, Pendleton, Salford 6, Manchester M6 5BY.
ARMS & ARMOUR:	**Roy Butler,** Wallis & Wallis, West Street Auction Galleries, Lewes, E. Sussex BN7 2NJ.

CONTENTS

MILLER'S 1996

The Granary Galleries
Fine Antiques

Specialists in
18th & 19th century furniture

COMPREHENSIVE STOCKS
AVAILABLE FOR THE HOME
AND OVERSEAS MARKET

COURT HOUSE
ASH PRIORS, NR. BISHOPS
LYDEARD, TAUNTON TA4 3NQ
TELEPHONE BISHOPS LYDEARD
(01823) 432402 & 432816

Also at

Bramble Cross Antiques

EXETER ROAD, HONITON EX14 8AL
TELEPHONE (01404) 47085

REFERENCE BOOKS ON ANTIQUES AND COLLECTING

1000's of titles in stock -
including scarce items

Send for latest catalogue

John Ives (MG)

5 Normanhurst Drive
Twickenham
Middlesex TW1 1NA
Tel: 0181-892 6265
Fax: 0181-744 3944

Hemswell Antiques Centres

270 SHOPS IN THREE ADJACENT BUILDINGS

Selling: Period Furniture • Shipping Furniture
Pine Furniture • Oriental Rugs • Long Case Clocks
Jewellery • Prints • Books • Silver • Pictures
Ceramics and many Collectables

Tel: Hemswell (01427) 668389
Fax: (01427) 668935
Open Daily 10.00 am to 5.00 pm
Licensed Restaurant

- Nationwide Deliveries Arranged
- Container Packing Service
- Single Items Shipping Arranged

Hemswell Antiques Centre, Caenby Corner Estate,
Hemswell Cliff, Gainsborough, Lincs. DN21 5TJ

INTRODUCTION

'Royal hair sold for a snip' reported the *Daily Telegraph* when an American collector paid £3,910 for a lock of Charles I's hair at auction earlier this year. The world of antiques and collectables continues to provide wonderful stories for the press. We are always inspired by tales of people finding rare items in their gardens or attics. Bonhams recently sold the earliest recorded piece of British creamware when one of their directors discovered a 1743 teapot amongst some cardboard boxes in his garage. It fetched £39,100, against an estimate of £10,000–20,000.

These discoveries always intrigue the collector but what is happening in the more day-to-day world of the antiques trade? The slow but sure recovery of the trade following the recession continues, with all dealers and auctioneers reporting that collectors are willing to pay good prices for quality pieces. Derek Roberts of Tonbridge, who specialises in clocks, told Miller's that 'fine carriage clocks' were getting good prices and that there is actually a shortage of good mahogany longcase clocks, particularly those made in London at the end of the 18thC, with pretty painted faces. Georgian bracket clocks remain very popular but as they become more expensive and harder to find, elegant Regency bracket clocks are finding popularity. Mediocre material has been tougher to sell.

Furniture sales are always a good indication of the health of the market. Once again, the story is that quality sells. Robert Young (who specialises in traditional oak and country furniture) told Miller's that the best material has sold throughout the recession and continues to do so – particularly painted furniture with the original paint (even if rather battered, it is key that home restoration is not attempted!). Garden antiques (statuary, benches, etc.) are a growing market but, reported Robert Young, many of his customers are buying wrought iron furniture for use in urban flats rather than gardens. This trend for putting items to alternative uses can be found elsewhere: Martin Hanness of The Old Cinema reported that oak office furniture from the 1920s and 1930s.

In the ever popular field of rugs and carpets 'the market is strong in good sized decorative carpets' Andrew Middleton at Bonhams told Miller's with Ushaks, Agras and Zeigler Mahals selling well. Another core area is pottery. The much-respected dealer, Jonathan Horne, was in optimistic mood when Miller's spoke to him. The market is 'definitely more lively,' he said although he also commented that quality pieces sold throughout the recession. While conditions still favour the buyer he advocates buying in areas which have traditionally been slower, such as salt-glazed stoneware which should prove a good investment.

Audrey Sternshine of AS Antique Galleries told Miller's 'There is a refreshing buoyancy in the Decorative Arts market. Much of the finite output of the Art Nouveau and Deco periods has already found its way into private collections. Sustained interest from an increasing body of discerning collectors, particularly for bronze and bronze and ivory figures, Arts and Crafts furniture, metalware, Studio Pottery and silver, is resulting in a noticeable surge in prices.'

So now that Art Deco is an established part of the antiques market, with many pieces fetching very high prices, what is the next big thing? The Bonhams Twentieth Century Furniture and Design sale held in February highlighted the desirability of many designers from the mid-1930s to the 1970s. The selection ranged from Bauhaus chairs to 1950s toasters, Murano glass in dazzling gem-like colours to moulded plastic furniture from the 1970s. The sale made almost £96,000. The star lot was Marcel Breuer's Isokon Long Chair from 1935 which fetched £6,670 (see below). Chairs in this style have appeared at auction before, but as Alexander Payne of Bonhams pointed out, this version is a rare model both in construction and materials. Unusual pieces apart, this is certainly an area to watch as collectors turn with great interest to the domestic interiors of this century. Much is still very affordable (indeed you may find it already in your home) and this is an area where boot fairs and junk shops will still provide rich pickings.

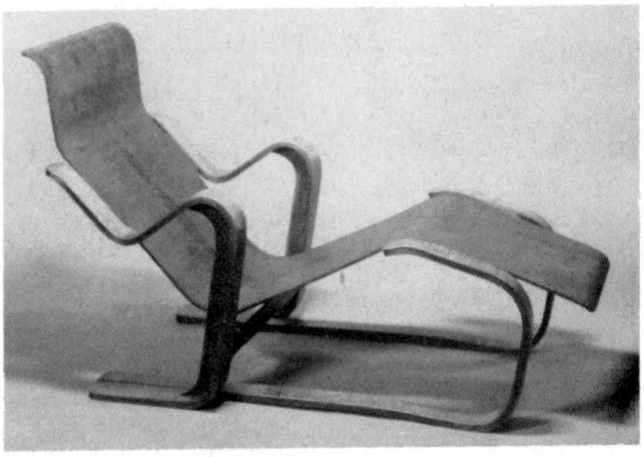

It is our aim to make the Guide easy to use. In order to find a particular item, consult the contents on page 23 to find the main heading, for example, Silver. Having located your area of interest, you will find that larger sections have been sub-divided. If you are looking for a particular factory, designer or craftsmen, consult the index which starts on page 798. For the first time we have included a *Miller's Compares* feature which highlights and explains the difference between two pieces that look, to the untrained eye, almost identical.

Please remember Miller's pricing policy: we provide you with a price GUIDE not a price LIST. Our price ranges are worked out by a team of trade and auction house experts, and are based on actual prices realised. They reflect variables, such as condition, location, desirability and so on. Don't forget that if you are selling it is quite likely you will be offered less than the price range.

Lastly, we are always keen to improve the Guide. If you feel that we have left something important out, or have any other comments about the book, please write and let us know; we always value feedback from our readers.

Dates	British Monarch	British Period	French Period
1558-1603	Elizabeth I	Elizabethan	Renaissance
1603-1625	James I	Jacobean	
1625-1649	Charles I	Carolean	Louis XIII (1610-1643)
1649-1660	Commonwealth	Cromwellian	Louis XIV (1643-1715)
1660-1685	Charles II	Restoration	
1685-1689	James II	Restoration	
1689-1694	William & Mary	William & Mary	
1694-1702	William III	William III	
1702-1714	Anne	Queen Anne	
1714-1727	George I	Early Georgian	Régence (1715-1723)
1727-1760	George II	Early Georgian	Louis XV (1723-1774)
1760-1811	George III	Late Georgian	Louis XVI (1774-1793) Directoire (1793-1799) Empire (1799-1815)
1812-1820	George III	Regency	Restauration (1815-1830)
1820-1830	George IV	Regency	
1830-1837	William IV	William IV	Louis Philippe (1830-1848) 2nd Empire (1848-1870) 3rd Republic (1871-1940)
1837-1901	Victoria	Victorian	
1901-1910	Edward VII	Edwardian	

German Period	U.S. Period	Style	Woods
		Gothic	Oak Period (to c1670)
Renaissance	Early Colonial		
		Baroque (c1620-1700)	
Renaissance/ Baroque (c1650-1700)			
			Walnut period (c1670-1735)
	William & Mary		
	Dutch Colonial	Rococo (c 1695-1760)	
Baroque (c1700-1730)	Queen Anne		
			Early mahogany period (c1735-1770)
Rococo (c1730-1760)	Chippendale (from 1750)		
Neo-classicism (c1760-1800)		Neo-classical (c1755-1805)	Late mahogany period (c1770-1810)
	Early Federal (1790-1810)		
Empire (c1800-1815	American Directoire (1798-1804)	Empire (c1799-1815)	
	American Empire (1804-1815)		
Biedermeier (c1815-1848	Late Federal (1810-1830)	Regency (c1812-1830)	
Revivale (c1830-1880)		Eclectic (c1830-1880)	
	Victorian		
Jugendstil (c1880-1920)		Arts & Crafts (c1880-1900)	
	Art Nouveau (c1900-1920)	Art Nouveau (c1900-1920)	

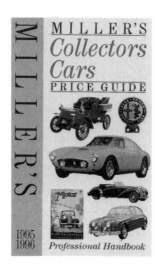

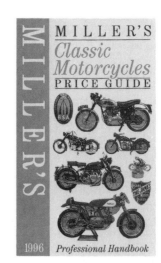

FURNITURE

Auction houses are reporting that good quality and original pieces of furniture are making far in excess of their pre-sale estimates, despite the fact that foreign buyers are not spending as much as they were. Recently in Canterbury, Kent a functional William IV mahogany table, in good condition, fetched £4,200 against an estimate of £1,250–1,700. Decorative furniture, whose popularity is influenced by fashion, is selling well as long as it is genuine and original. Beds of all types and from all periods have also continued making good prices at auction, if criterea based on condition and originality are met. This trend can be seen throughout the bed sections in several catagories in *Miller's Antiques Price Guide*, such as Oak and Country Furniture, and Pine.

HISTORY OF THE BED

The typical enclosed bed of the late 16th and early 17thC was often incorrectly called a 'four-poster'. Beds of this period had a roof or a tester and, in fact, only had two poles at the foot of the bed to support the tester, as the other end was supported by the headboard. The four-poster did not actually appear until the 18thC.

Initially only the head of very rich households enjoyed the luxury of a bed while other family members slept on straw mattresses on the floor. Many early beds are still in their original home and genuine articles rarely appear on the market. Beds that were removed were often dismantled as they were considered too big and unfashionable. Consequently many 'Elizabethan' tester beds that do appear on the market have been made up from the parts of older beds.

The tester was added to beds to provide a platform from which to hang curtains. This provided the occupants with a means to fully enclose the bed, not only to keep out cold draughts but also to ensure privacy from their servants. Tester beds were a prized family possession and were frequently passed down from generation to generation.

As well as testers, the Jacobeans made fabric covered beds. These beds, still made for the wealthy classes, were entirely covered in material, with the wooden frame used only to support and suspend heavier fabrics. They would have holes drilled in the bed frame through which ropes would have been interwoven from side to side to support the mattress.

By the William and Mary period the fabric covered bed had become very popular. Hardly any wood would have shown, with the possible exception of an ornate, walnut veneered and mitred cornice. Queen Anne period beds were generally two post full testers with a fabric covered headboard which provided the support for the tester.

By Georgian times the fashion for wooden beds had returned. The choice of wood, the carving, decoration and style reflected the influence of the Chippendale period. All the materials and techniques of the day, including gilding and lacquering, were employed.

Fabrics varied from wonderful handmade embroideries to the plushest velvets and silks. Mattresses were now supported with wooden slats rather than interwoven ropes. Beds of the Hepplewhite, Adam, and Sheraton periods would have been of the open four-poster type, with the show posts mirroring the woods, carving, fluting and turning of the classical style. The rear posts were made of inferior woods, pine and beech, for example, and would remain virtually unfinished as they were entirely fabric covered and would not have been seen. The cornice at this time would, more often than not, have been fabric covered as well.

By 1800, half-tester beds had become both fashionable and popular. They were large, impressive structures with deep carvings and mouldings on the show wood and with magnificent drapes, swags and hangings. However, their popularity diminished as the century progressed and by mid-Victorian times they had become virtually no more than large-framed bedheads.

The brass bedstead appeared from about 1870 and was made entirely from metal tubing with brass posts, finials and rods. The more mundane brass beds would have been cast iron with brass plated or perhaps solid brass adornments. Square section brass beds always enjoyed greater popularity than round tubed sectioned beds and consequently have a higher value. Iron bedsteads can still be bought for reasonable prices and can be easily cleaned, repaired and painted by even the most amateur restorer.

Pine beds are also available in all shapes, designs and sizes. The Scandinavian boat-type bed is very popular. Although some of these beds will be genuine, many have been improved or even totally reconstructed from old pine timbers.

When considering the purchase of an antique bed, bear in mind that not many were made and only a few have survived intact. Look carefully for signs of re-used timber and panels such as oddly placed keyholes and old joints in the wrong place as an indication that odd pieces of furniture may have been used in the construction.

Georgian period beds in particular should be closely examined under the fabrics to reveal dry rot, unfinished surfaces and old darkened nail holes. Beds of this period were generally bolted together so it is another good sign to look for when establishing authenticity. Metal bedsteads are too numerous at present to attract the faker and it is very easy to identify the modern reproduction.

Finally, if you are lucky enough to find a genuine, unaltered period bed, remember to keep enough funds in reserve for the custom-built mattress you will need.

Richard Gold

COLLECTING EARLY OAK & COUNTRY FURNITURE

Collecting early oak furniture that would have furnished a simple home rather than a stately house remains a largely unexploited area of investment. This furniture, steeped in 300 years of colourful history, is Britain's heritage. As a collector of 17th and 18thC country furniture, one is preserving this heritage for future generations.

For anyone wanting to start a collection of early oak and country furniture, buying an oak chest is a good item with which to begin. Readily available, they represent good value for money especially if you are collecting within the confines of a limited budget. Other items, such as joint stools, gateleg tables, bureaux, sets of chairs, settles, cupboards and dressers command considerably higher prices.

The oak chest was one of the most common pieces of furniture of the medieval period. The craftsmen at the time fitted elaborate open tracery iron straps, hinges and locks and the carving was predominantly in the Gothic style. Few genuine pieces of medieval domestic furniture remain today, and most that have are kept in museums for all to appreciate and enjoy.

After the restoration of Charles II to the throne in 1660, furniture became more sophisticated in design and of lighter construction. For example, the butt nailed plank chest gave way to the panelled chest which had a jointed framework secured by wooden pegs. Carving became more stylised and reflected the architecture, the floral and geometric patterns of that period. Walnut, pine and elm were among the woods used in that period, but oak remained the principal timber for furniture in northern Europe and the one which best withstood the ravages of time.

Although tastes and styles changed with the Restoration period (1660–89) and with the introduction of new techniques, oak and the old functional styles were still favoured by less affluent people throughout the 18th and early 19thC, especially in rural areas. No doubt this is where the somewhat misleading definition of 'country furniture' was derived.

As with all areas of collecting it is best to arm yourself in advance with as much information as possible about the item you wish to buy. This will not only help you identify what you are looking for but it will also enable you to ask knowledgeable questions from the dealer or auction house. Below are terms and explanations regarding chests that will help you on your way.

Chests can be subdivided into two general categories: the coffer shown *above*, and the mule chest.

The term 'coffer' is used quite freely to describe chests of all kinds. However, they are, strictly speaking, a travelling trunk which is banded with metalwork and covered with leather or other fabrics. Coffers are usually constructed from oak planks or panels, but are occasionally comprised from elm.

Plank coffers consist of five planks nailed together to form a box with a sixth plank as a lid, and the end planks extending to form legs. The carving tends to be simple, usually concentrated on the front, and to a lesser extent on the sides. Occasionally the planks have a scalloped finish to the exposed end grain.

Panelled coffers have a mortice and tenon, peg jointed framework with planked infill panels. Lids were usually two planks battened together or constructed in panel form. The legs were a continuation of the stiles. The panels are either flat in cross-section or fielded, with the chamfered edges having the effect of a raised centre.

Internally, both types of coffers were frequently fitted with a full depth shallow box attached at lid level to one of the end frames. Inaccurately termed the candle box, this shallow box was used for storing fragrant herbs to freshen clothing and blankets which were kept in the coffer.

The mule chest, shown *below,* is the stage between the coffer and the chest of drawers, the upper section being a chest, with one, two or three drawers beneath. For these reasons this piece of hybrid furniture has acquired the name mule chest.

The alternative name of 'dower chest' is applied when the chest is used to store the trousseau of a bride to be.

The basic construction of the mule chest is similar to that of the coffer. The drawers, sometimes referred to as 'tills', are usually hung from runners that locate into rebates positioned centrally on the thick drawer sides. The grain in the base of the drawer runs front to back. However, with extra wide single drawers the grain runs side-to-side. Drawer joints are either butt nailed or dovetailed. The front panel of the drawer is either plain or decorated with applied geometric mouldings or cockbeading. Mule chests made in the 18thC tended to have fielded panels or false upper front panels to resemble drawers. They also had brass handles and escutcheons, less carving and shaped feet.

Carving on chests is not always prevalent, but many have their front framework carved with repeating geometric patterns based on a variety of designs such as linked circles and semi-circles, see *below*.

These patterns can be found interspersed with chip carvings, achieved by stabbing a chisel vertically and then at a 45 degree angle to form a chip, and various shapes of punched decoration also achieved with a chisel punching the wood to form a design. Floral designs, especially trailing vines and leaves, miniature rows of carved arches or flutes are also popular. Chests decorated with such carvings have a higher value.

The carving of figures and dates, animals, an owner's name or initials, *below,* can significantly increase saleroom prices, and at the other end of the scale a coffer with only shallow chip carving and punched decoration will fetch considerably less at auction.

Inlay is another example of ornamentation. Shown *below* is a banding of segments of holly wood and ebony set into the frame in a herringbone pattern.

Original wire loops or strap hinges on chests, which were fixed with handmade nails, have often worn away and been replaced, with machine-made hinges of more conventional styles. The simple iron locks, which were also fixed by nails, have fared slightly better, although keys are invariably missing.

Once you have become familiar with the different types of chests, the next step in collecting is to investigate where to find chests and determine what one would pay for an oak and country chest.

Expect to find the more common pieces of 17th and 18thC country furniture in provincial auction houses, fairs and local antiques shops, with specialist shops stocking finer or more elaborate examples. Antiques magazines and local papers often give notice of forthcoming auctions, and larger antiques fairs or towns with multi-dealerships are well worth a visit. Prices will vary substantially owing to condition and quality. They will also vary from area to area.

Finally, to become really acquainted with the beauty of old furniture, there is no substitute for handling and touching genuine items. Visit auctions and antiques shops, feel the textures of the wood, even smell the distinctive aromas. Discuss your requirements with reputable dealers who will always welcome your enquiries and give invaluable advice.

Phillip Johnson

OAK & COUNTRY FURNITURE

Beds

A carved oak tester bed, restored, 17thC, 74in (188cm) long.
£4,600–5,200 *B*

Beds

Beds have often been altered, the most common change being in length – we are simply much taller now!

Size can account for considerable differences in price – a good Charles II four poster of, say, 55in (139.5cm) wide by 72in (182.5cm) long might well be less desirable than a poorer quality bed measuring 66in (167.5cm) wide by 84in (213cm) long.

Most bed buyers want to use their 'fantasy' furniture while retaining their modern day comforts.

An oak tester bed, with panelled canopy and well carved headboard, the front of the canopy supported by 2 bulbous turned supports united by a panelled front of 3 lozenge decorated panels, original rope holes to sides, 17thC, 76in (193cm) high, with modern mattress, 54in (137cm) wide.
£4,000–4,500 *B*

Bookcases

A George III oak bureau bookcase, with moulded cornice above a pair of astragal glazed doors, the lower part with fall front enclosing a fitted interior above 3 long drawers, on bracket feet, 36in (91.5cm).
£1,200–1,700 *DN*

A late 17thC style oak bookcase, with elaborate acanthus leaf carved cavetto cornice above a pair of astragal glazed doors, enclosing shelves, glazed sides, the lower part with further glazed doors above a leaf and flower carved moulded frieze, on a foliate carved base, 50in (127cm).
£3,500–4,000 *DN*

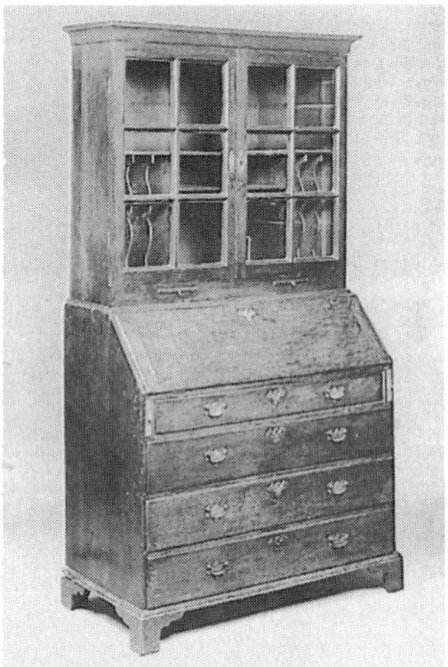

An oak bureau bookcase, the upper section with fitted interior, a pair of astragal glazed doors above candlestands, the sloping fall also with fitted interior, on bracket feet, possibly Welsh, c1800, 46½in (118cm).
£1,800–2,500 *CSK*

Bureaux

A Queen Anne oak bureau, the fall enclosing a stepped interior of drawers and pigeonholes above a well, on bracket feet, c1700, 38in (96.5cm).
£2,400–2,800 *Bon*

An oak bureau, applied throughout with double ovolo mouldings, the sloping flap with reading rest, on later bracket feet, early 18thC, 37½in (95cm).
£2,000–2,500 *Bea*

An oak bureau, the sloping front with a book rest, early 18thC, 30in (76cm).
£1,700–2,200 *L*

A George III oak bureau, 28in (71cm) wide.
£850–1,200 *DN*

An oak Eton bureau cabinet, damaged feet, late 19thC, 30in (76cm).
£950–1,100 *C*

A George III oak bureau, the fall front enclosing a fitted interior, on bracket feet, 36in (91.5cm).
£700–1,000 *DN*

Chairs

An Elizabethan oak wainscot chair, with solid seat and turned front supports united by a stretcher, c1700.
£2,500–3,000 *B*

In the Furniture section when there is only one measurement it refers to the width of the piece, unless otherwise stated.

r. A child's oak wainscot chair, with carved crest rail, c1650, 22in (55.5cm) high.
£2,200–2,500 *RYA*

An oak side chair, c1695.
£600–800 *KEY*

An oak side chair, with panelled back, c1700.
£600–700 *KEY*

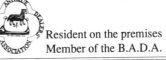

An oak wainscot chair, 17thC.
£900–1,200 *MAT*

An oak wainscot armchair, with carved scrolls to the central panel and lunette borders, turned frame, 17thC.
£650–750 *RBB*

An oak armchair, with a carved shaped rail above a diaper carved panelled back, solid seat and turned legs, restored, 17thC.
£900–1,200 *DN*

An oak wainscot chair, 17thC.
£1,100–1,500 *MAT*

A joined oak armchair, on turned legs tied by bobbin turned stretchers, restored, c1680.
£600–800 *Bon*

A pair of Charles II oak chairs, with fielded panelled backs above solid seats, on baluster turned legs tied by similar front stretchers, c1680.
£900–1,200 *Bon*

A joined oak armchair, with a plain fielded panelled back and scrolled arms, above a solid seat, on baluster turned legs tied by a block stretcher, restored, late 17thC.
£800–1,200 *Bon*

An oak chair, with shaped, carved and heart-pierced cresting, North Country, c1710.
£600–700 *RYA*

An oak armchair, the panelled back inlaid with bog oak and fruitwood, on ring turned baluster legs joined by stretchers, restored, Yorkshire, late 17thC.
£1,000–1,500 *C*

A comb backed primitive armchair, with saddle seat and reduced pad feet, c1750.
£1,200–1,500 *RYA*

A Welsh oak splat-backed primitive armchair, c1770.
£300–350 *RYA*

A set of 8 oak upholstered dining chairs, including 2 armchairs, each with studded back, padded seat, block and turned legs joined by stretchers, parts 17thC.
£4,000–6,000 *CSK*

A child's elm plank chair, c1780.
£1,000–1,200 *RYA*

A child's comb back Windsor armchair, in good original condition, c1790, 24in (61cm) high.
£1,000–1,250 *RYA*

A comb back primitive Windsor armchair, with traces of original paint, 18thC, 40in (101.5cm) high.
£1,200–1,500 *RYA*

A low back Windsor armchair, with old painted surface, c1800, 26in (66cm) high.
£400–500 *RYA*

A spindle backed garden chair, dark stained and varnished but still retaining original dark green paint, on baluster turned legs, united by a plain stretcher, 18thC.
£700–900 *WL*

A Welsh oak box seat open armchair, with panel back and wavy toprail, the arms with flattened terminals and hinged solid seat, on square legs enclosed by fielded panels, late 18thC.
£800–900 *CSK*

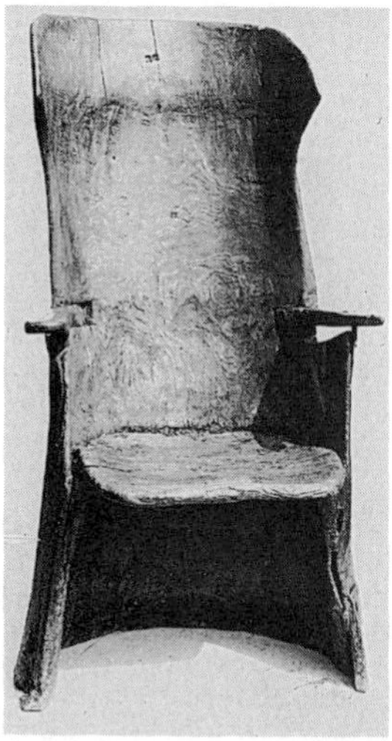

A dug-out ash armchair, the well raked back constructed from a single hollowed ash trunk, the shaped flat arms with iron handwrought supports above a circular seat, of original untouched patination, 18thC.
£5,000–5,500 *B*

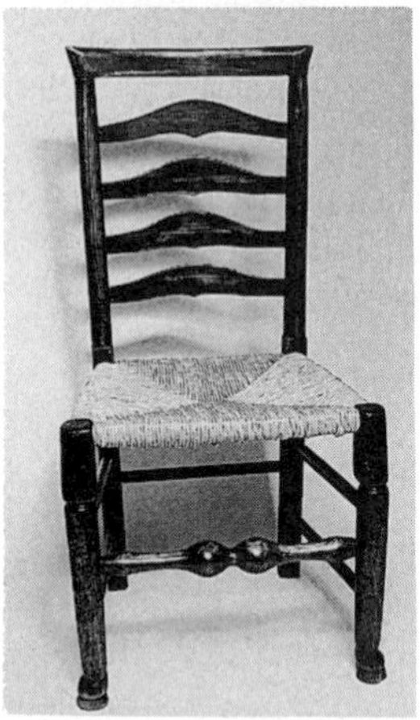

A harlequin set of 6 chairs, comprising 2 carvers and 4 singles, c1840.
£1,500–1,850 *RYA*

A set of 6 yew and elm Windsor low back armchairs, each with pierced central splat, ring turned arm supports and ring turned legs joined by crinoline stretchers, one oak front leg, one arm support and one stretcher replaced, early 19thC.
£3,500–4,500 *CSK*

A miniature fan back primitive Windsor stick chair, with traces of original green paint, c1780, 22in (56cm) high.
£1,200–1,500 *RYA*

A pair of dark oak hall chairs, with pierced leaf carved central splat, flanked by barley-twist supports, 19thC.
£150–250 *BWe*

An oak armchair, with straw work back and sides, downswept arm supports, solid seat and square chamfered legs enclosed by panels, upper rows of straw work missing, Orkneys, late 19thC.
£250–350 *CSK*

A fruitwood, ash, elm and beechwood Windsor armchair, with central pierced wheel splat, incurved arm supports and turned legs joined by stretchers, Thames Valley, early 19thC.
£450–650 *CSK*

A child's yew, fruitwood, elm and oak Windsor armchair, with pierced vertical splat, baluster turned arm supports, ring turned legs and crinoline stretcher, repaired, early 19thC.
£450–550 *CSK*

A hawthorn primitive low chair, with 2 pieces of naturally shaped cleft timber joined by sticks, the legs joined by stick stretchers, inscribed beneath '1490', Sutherland, early 19thC.
£1,000–1,200 *CSK*

Settles

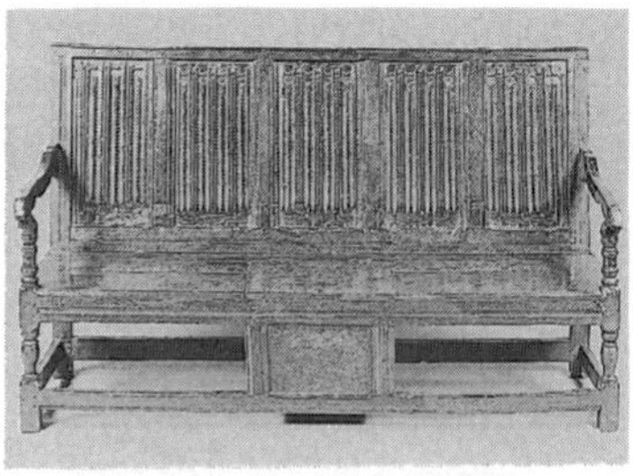

An oak settle, the back with linenfold panels and undulating arms, supported on turned columns, the seat with a central well and hinged cover, on inverted baluster turned legs joined by moulded stretchers with a central fascia panel, early 17thC, 65½in (166cm).
£1,700–2,200 *P*

Two French oak choir stalls, each with individual seats, flanked by Ionic style columns and carved with figures and animals, some raised on octagonal columns, one with 5 seats, the other with 6, late 19thC, 129 and 159in (328 and 404cm) wide.
£2,800–3,500 *CSK*

A carved oak hall settle, carved with rococo motifs and portrait heads, the arms with lions' mask terminals, 19thC, 56½in (143cm).
£550–600 *WL*

An elm high backed settle, with shaped sides and arm rests on turned supports, slightly bowed seat and moulded facing uprights, West Country, early 19thC, 65in (165cm) long.
£1,500–2,000 *CSK*

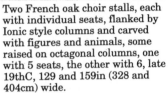

An oak triple section settle/table, with plank top, arms with baluster turned supports, the box seat with 3 hinged lids, 2 with locks, above a panelled front and sides, on sleigh feet, stamped 'W.B.' twice around the central lock, mid-17thC, 75in (190.5cm).
£4,700–5,500 *CSK*

Chests

An oak chest, the hinged top with moulded decoration cut from the solid, the front and back panels clamped into wide stile feet, lockplate replaced, c1500, 36in (91.5cm) long.
£4,000–5,000 *CSK*

An oak boarded chest, the hinged top and front with 2 vertical lines of gouged decoration, the sides extending to feet, projecting to the front and carved on the sides with a cross, ironwork replaced, minor repairs, early 17thC, 18in (46cm).
£5,000–6,000 *CSK*

An oak chest, the hinged lid above a triple panelled front, scratch carved with geometrical patterns and centred with swirling hearts, the drawer below carved with scrolling foliage, on stile feet, drawer damaged, West Country, restored, late 17thC, 46½in (118cm).
£400–600 *CSK*

A chest with similar scratch carved uprights and rails is illustrated in Victor Chinnery's, Oak Furniture - The British Tradition, *Antique Collectors' Club, 1979.*

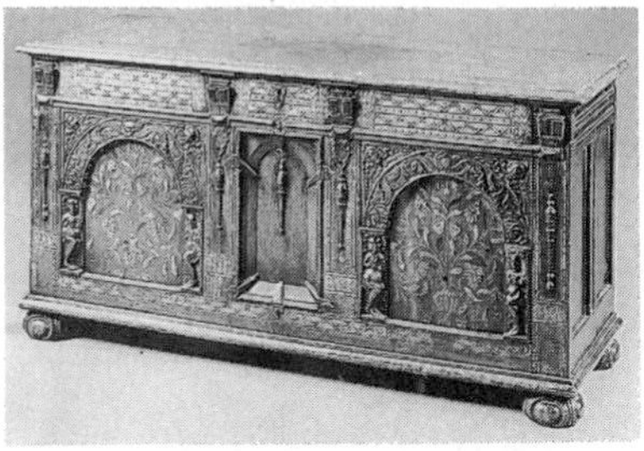

l. An oak and inlaid chest, with parquetry frieze, on later bun feet, North Country, early 17thC, 59in (150cm) wide.
£6,000–7,000 *CSK*

An inlaid oak dower chest, 17thC.
£650–700 *MAT*

A fruitwood mule chest of small proportions, with hinged top and panelled front above a drawer, on stump feet, early 18thC.
£1,000–1,200 *DN*

Two late Stuart period oak chests:
l. With 4 graduated raised cushion moulded drawers with turned handles, on split baluster ornament block feet, 38½in (97cm).
£1,400–1,800
r. With 4 long graduated drawers, each applied with geometric mouldings, with brass pear drop handles, on block legs, 33in (84cm).
£1,000–1,500 *WL*

An oak chest, with a moulded edged top and 4 moulded panelled drawers, on later bun feet, mid-17thC, 40in (102cm).
£1,500–2,000 *CSK*

An oak chest of drawers, with dentil frieze, fitted with a deep drawer with boxwood strapwork, flanked by elm panels, above 2 shallow drawers, each with panelled front veneered in oyster cut laburnum, 17thC, 38½in (97cm) wide.
£1,700–2,200 *L*

An oak and crossbanded tallboy, the upper section with a moulded cornice and 7 drawers, above 2 short and 2 long drawers, on later bun feet, early 18thC, 38in (96.5cm) wide.
£900–1,200 *CSK*

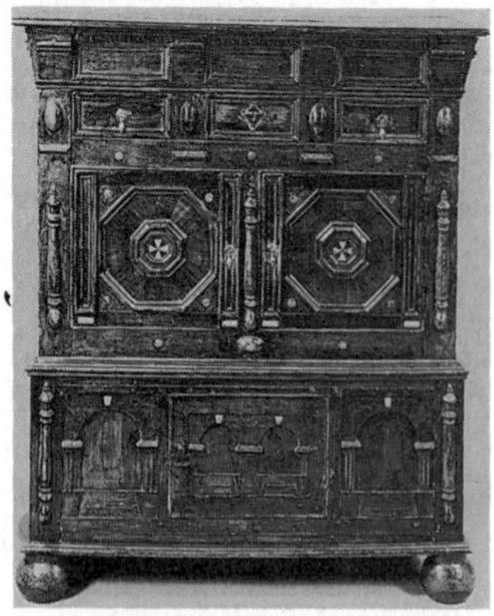

An oak chest in 2 parts, on bun feet, the upper part basically 17thC with later parts, 47½in (120cm) wide.
£1,800–2,000 *P*

An oak chest-on-chest, with brass loop handles, on shaped bracket feet, 18thC.
£650–1,000 *BWe*

An oak chest-on-stand, the 2 short and 3 long drawers to the upper part with featherbanding, the lower part with a single shallow drawer and 5 turned legs to a flat shaped stretcher, 18thC, 37in (94cm).
£1,800–2,200 *B*

A William and Mary style oak chest-on-stand, on barley-twist legs united by concave stretchers, with replacement brasses, 37½in (96cm) wide.
£2,000–2,500 *WL*

An oak and chequer banded chest-on-stand, with moulded cornice and later frieze drawer, ogee arched apron, cabriole legs and pad feet, repaired and with later parts, mid-18thC, 43½in (110cm).
£1,500–2,000 *CSK*

The residue of a 16thC oak coffer, the panelled front carved with urns, stylised birds and foliage, sides missing, 63in (160cm) wide.
£400–600 *L*

Miller's is a price GUIDE not a price LIST

An oak coffer, with channel moulded stiles and muntins throughout, the hinged top divided into 3 panels, the front and sides with nulled panels, on chip-carved stiles, mid-17thC, 28in (71cm) wide.
£3,000–3,500 *Bea*

An inlaid oak coffer, the rising plank top of good patination above a 3 panel front decorated with arcades and a surround of chequered inlay in bog oak and holly, 17thC, 60in (152cm).
£700–800 *B*

A Charles II oak coffer, enclosing a candle box, restored, c1680, 48in (122cm) wide.
£400–500 *Bon*

In the Furniture section when there is only one measurement it refers to the width of the piece, unless otherwise stated.

Coffers

A carved oak and marquetry inlaid coffer, with a guilloche carved apron, on block feet, restored, early 17thC, 61in (155cm) wide.
£1,000–1,200 *Bon*

An oak coffer of panelled construction, with a hinged top and moulded and lozenge decorated front, on stile feet, mid-17thC, 35in (89cm) wide.
£1,600–2,000 *CSK*

An oak coffer, on block feet, late 17thC, 48½in (123cm).
£800–1,000 *Bon*

An oak coffer, the rising 4 panel top above a front of 3 panels with stylised tree-of-life and tulip decoration raised from an ebonised background, a carved surround and a shallow single drawer beneath, 17thC, 57in (144.5cm) wide.
£400–600 *B*

Cupboards

A French Provincial oak buffet, with a bead decorated frieze, enclosed by a pair of decorated shaped arched panel doors and undulating apron, on scroll feet, restored, late 18thC, 50in (127cm) wide.
£1,400–1,800 *CSK*

An oak cupboard, with fluted frieze above a carved fielded panelled door, with a guilloche carved apron, on sledge feet, 17thC, 36½in (93cm) wide.
£1,300–1,800 *Bon*

An oak corner cupboard, with architecturally moulded cornice above a fielded panelled door enclosing shaped shelves, with 3 deep drawers below, flanked by canted angles, on a plinth, late 18thC, 38½in (98cm) wide.
£1,500–2,000 *CSK*

A George III oak standing corner cupboard, with a moulded cornice above a pair of panelled doors, the lower part now with a drop panel, on bracket feet, 48in (122cm) wide.
£700–1,000 *DN*

An oak three-section buffet, 17thC.
£1,200–1,600 *MAT*

An oak corner cupboard, with fitted interior, later backboards, late 18thC, 42in (106.5cm).
£1,900–2,500 *CSK*

A French Provincial fruitwood and chestnut buffet, on cabriole feet, formerly with a superstructure, early 19thC, 57½in (146cm) wide.
£1,100–1,500 *CSK*

A oak credence cupboard, 17thC.
£2,100–2,700 *MAT*

A carved dark oak hanging wall cupboard, the hutch doors with bobbin turned finials set between 4 corner shelves to either side and foliate carved side pieces, 19thC, 53½in (136cm) wide.
£350–500 *DA*

An oak press cupboard, the carved frieze dated '1687' and initialled 'M.M.', on stile feet, replacements, Lake District, late 17thC, 64in (162.5cm) wide.
£2,000–2,500 *CSK*

A North German oak cupboard, on fluted stile feet, repaired, c1600, 47in (119cm) wide.
£2,200–3,000 *CSK*

An oak press cupboard, with trailing foliage and rosette carved frieze, on stile feet, some later mouldings, late 17thC, 56in (142cm) wide.
£1,800–2,200 *CSK*

An oak press cupboard, decorated with flowers, restorations and replacements, Lake District, late 17thC, 54in (137cm) wide.
£1,200–1,800 *CSK*

An oak press cupboard, with a frieze carved with rosettes and guilloche, on turned column supports, the central arcaded panel with diamond lozenge, dated '1616' and initialled 'D.H.', on stile feet, replacements and repairs, early 17thC, 56in (142cm).
£2,200–2,800 *CSK*

An oak press cupboard, with moulded cornice and central panel flanked by panelled doors and projecting column supports, above a pair of large panelled doors, on channelled stile feet, part of cornice loose, early 18thC, 50in (127cm) wide.
£3,500–4,500 *CSK*

An oak linen press, in 2 parts, the top with a pair of panelled doors, carved above 'J:1729:H', the bottom part with 4 short drawers, on plank feet, 57in (145cm) wide.
£1,300–1,700 *P*

An oak press cupboard, the projecting frieze carved with the date '1680' above a recessed panelled front with 2 doors, the base with 2 panelled doors on channel moulded stiles, some alterations, 65in (165cm) wide.
£1,700–2,000 *Bea*

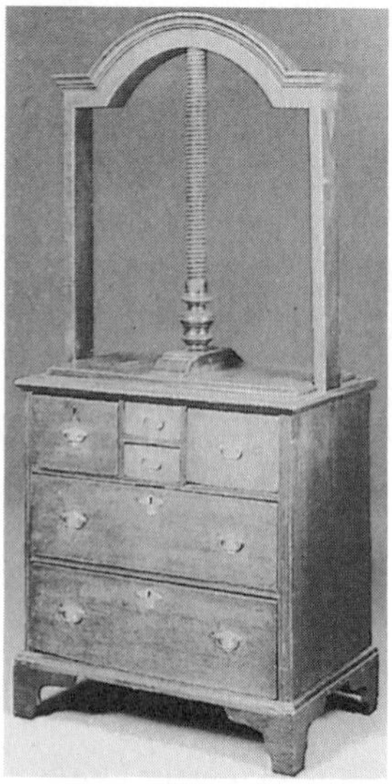

An oak linen press, the arched superstructure with spirally threaded press, now worn, above an arrangement of 6 variously sized drawers, on bracket feet, repairs, late 18thC, 31½in (80cm).
£900–1,200 *CSK*

A George III oak press cupboard, with moulded top above a pair of ogee fielded panelled doors, the base with dummy drawers, on cabriole legs with pad feet, 50in (127cm) wide.
£1,500–2,000 *DN*

A George III oak press cupboard, with moulded cornice above a reeded frieze and a pair of panelled doors flanked by similar fluted canted angles, on bracket feet, 49in (124.5cm) wide.
£2,500–3,000 *DN*

In the Furniture section when there is only one measurement it refers to the width of the piece, unless otherwise stated.

r. A George III oak linen press, on short block feet, 54½in (138cm).
£2,000–2,500 *WL*

A Welsh oak tridarn, the upper section with turned front column supports and slatted sides, the panelled back with stained foliate decoration, on block feet, the upper section possibly associated, early 18thC, 55½in (141cm) wide.
£4,500–5,500 *Bon*

A Welsh oak tridarn, on block feet, early 18thC, 50in (127cm).
£4,000–5,000 *L&E*

A French Provincial oak armoire, with a pair of cartouche-shaped panelled doors on shaped feet, late 18thC, 62in (157cm) wide.
£1,000–1,500 *CSK*

A French Provincial oak armoire, on projecting stile legs, early 19thC, 56in (142cm) wide.
£600–900 *CSK*

Dressers

A Dutch/Flemish elm dresser, with moulded and canted top, on a later plinth base, 17thC, with an oak superstructure, c1920, 58in (147cm) wide.
£1,300–1,800 *P*

An oak low dresser, with 3 frieze drawers, serpentine underframe, on cabriole front legs with pointed pad feet, mid-18thC, 74in (188cm).
£2,500–3,000 *Bea*

An oak dresser, on lyre shaped upright supports joined by a pine potboard, south Wales, early 18thC, 59in (150cm).
£3,500–4,500 *CSK*

An oak low dresser, on solid end supports, 17thC, 60in (153cm).
£3,000–4,000 *P*

An oak dresser, with 3 crossbanded frieze drawers above a shaped apron, associated cabriole legs with pad feet, re-toed, West Midlands, mid-18thC, 79in (201cm).
£3,000–4,000 *CSK*

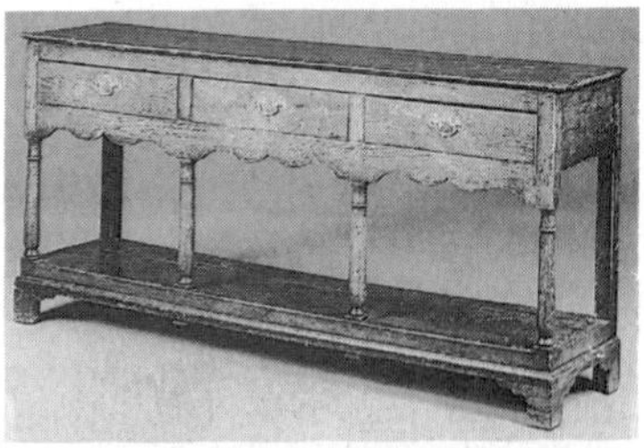

An oak dresser, with ogee shaped aprons, on turned column supports joined by a potboard, on bracket feet, south Wales, early 18thC, 69½in (177cm).
£4,000–5,000 *CSK*

A oak canopied dresser, the upper part with original backed oak boards and 2 shelves, early 18thC, 61in (155cm).
£6,000–6,500 *B*

This type of dresser is attributed to the Conwy Valley, North Wales, in The Welsh Dresser, *by T. Alun Davies, published by The National Museum of Wales.*

An oak dresser, the boarded rack with 3 shelves, 3 frieze drawers below, 4 turned front legs and potboard beneath, south Wales, 18thC, 55in (139.5cm).
£3,500–4,000 *B*

A Cumberland oak dresser, the shelved rack with spice drawers, the base with 2 long drawers and central cutlery drawer, 2 moulded panel cupboard doors beneath, 18thC, 57in (144.5cm) wide.
£3,000–3,500 *B*

This dresser has its original receipt for ten guineas, from W. H. Mawson, Keswick, signed upon a penny stamp.

An oak dresser, with moulded top, 3 drawers crossbanded in yew, shaped aprons, on cabriole legs with pad feet, replacements to legs, mid-18thC, 78in (198cm).
£3,500–4,000 *CSK*

An oak dresser, the top with a later ledge back, above 3 frieze drawers and ogee arched aprons, on cabriole legs, re-toed, replacements, mid-18thC, 77in (196cm).
£2,000–2,500 *CSK*

Miller's is a price GUIDE not a price LIST

An oak dresser, crossbanded and inlaid, on cabriole legs, late 18thC, 78in (198cm).
£4,000–4,500 *B*

An oak cupboard dresser base, the 3 frieze drawers above 2 cupboard doors and centre fielded panel, on bracket feet, 18thC, 72in (182.5cm).
£4,000–4,500 *B*

An oak dresser, on stile feet, restored, top and base possibly associated, mid-18thC, 64½in (164cm) wide.
£2,200–3,200 *Bea*

A George III oak 3 drawer dresser base, on square legs with inside chamfer, handles missing and escutcheons damaged, 78in (198cm).
£1,500–2,000 *L&E*

An oak and mahogany crossbanded dresser, with moulded and key pattern cornice, wavy canopy, 2 shelves, side niches, cupboards with small doors, 3 drawers, on cabriole front legs with pad feet, c1800, 83in (210.5cm).
£2,800–3,500 *HOLL*

A George III oak dresser, the raised plate rack with moulded cornice above 3 open shelves, 3 frieze drawers and 3 central dummy drawers flanked by 2 cupboard doors, on bracket feet, the rack possibly associated, 67in (170cm) wide.
£2,500–3,000 *CSK*

A Georgian oak dresser, top and bottom probably associated, 56in (142cm).
£2,000–2,500 *L*

A George III oak dresser, with shaped apron, on bracket feet, 70in (177.5cm) wide.
£3,000–3,500 *L&E*

l. A George III oak Swansea Valley dresser base, with 5 small drawers to back, and 3 deep and 4 shallow drawers to the shaped frieze, turned supports to potboard and stile feet, 61in (155cm) wide.
£3,500–4,000 *Bri*

l. An oak dresser, the frieze with two geometrically panelled drawers, raised on turned and square legs, 18thC, 65in (165cm) long.
£2,000–2,500 *AG*

A sycamore dresser, with figured top above 3 frieze drawers and square tapering legs, c1800, 72in (182.5cm) wide.
£1,700–2,200 *CSK*

An oak dresser, the doors with geometric mouldings, 18thC, 61½in (157cm).
£1,800–2,200 *L*

An oak dresser, the boarded plate rack with moulded cornice, 3 shelves flanked by line inlaid and pilaster uprights, above 4 central drawers with a drawer and a cupboard to either side, flanked by quarter columns, on bracket feet, north Wales or Cheshire, early 19thC, 70in (177.5cm) wide.
£3,000–4,000 *CSK*

A George III oak dresser, with later top, the drawers with centred inlaid stars, on stump feet, 69in (175cm) wide.
£2,000–3,000 *DN*

An oak dresser, the panelled back with reeded mouldings and 2 open shelves, the base with 3 frieze drawers and 2 panelled doors, on block feet, early 19thC, 75in (190.5cm) wide.
£2,500–3,000 *Bea*

An oak dresser, with shaped apron and bracket feet, north Wales, early 19thC, later boarded plate rack, 67in (170cm) wide.
£3,000–3,500 *CSK*

An oak dresser, the later upper part with an arrangement of shelves and cupboards, the lower part with 2 short drawers and a pair of panelled cupboards, on stump feet, early 19thC, 53in (134.5cm) wide.
£900–1,200 *DN*

Stools

An oak joint stool, with moulded top, ogee arched panelled friezes and baluster legs joined by stretchers, one toe missing, early 17thC, 18in (46cm) wide.
£3,500–4,000 *CSK*

Miller's is a price GUIDE not a price LIST

A child's oak joint stool, initialled and dated '1643', 13in (33cm) high.
£2,000–2,200 *RYA*

An oak joint stool, with double moulded top, lunette carved friezes, reeded and stop fluted supports joined by moulded stretchers, early ownership initials 'I.W.' beneath seat, c1600, 18in (46cm).
£4,500–5,000 *CSK*

A miniature fruitwood three-legged stool, c1780, 6½in (16.5cm) high.
£100–150 *RYA*

A miniature barrel topped stool/candlestand, with traces of original green paint, c1800, 6in (15cm) diam.
£100–150 *RYA*

A Welsh oak slab topped stool, c1800, 12in (30.5cm) high.
£125–150 *RYA*

Two fruitwood stools:
l. With traces of original paint, c1800, 6in (15cm) high. **£100–130**
r. c1820, 7½in (19cm) high.
£75–85 *RYA*

l. An oak stool, c1800, 5in (12.5cm) high.
£75–100
r. A Norwegian pine stool, c1820, 10in (25cm) high.
£100–120 *RYA*

Tables

l. An oak gateleg table, on baluster turned end supports and gates on either side, early 18thC, 54in (137cm) long.
£1,500–2,000 *B*

A Charles II oak and yew centre table, with twelve-sided moulded top, above a cage formed of turned balusters flanking shaped arches, revolving around a central turned baluster, supported by 3 scrolling bracket feet, 24in (61cm) diam.
£1,500–1,750 *S(NY)*

A similar table is illustrated in Victor Chinnery's, Oak Furniture - The British Tradition, *Antique Collectors' Club, 1979. These tables were popular through the 1720s and took their inspiration from Italian baroque forms. They became prototypes for candlestands later in the 17thC.*

MILLER'S COMPARES . . .

I An oak gateleg table, with an oval top above 2 drawers, on baluster turned legs, early 18thC, 47in (119cm) wide.
£3,000–4,000 *DN*

II An oak gateleg table, the oval top on baluster and bobbin turned legs joined by stretchers, 18thC, 57in (144.5cm) wide.
£500–800 *DN*

Table I **realised a much higher price than** *table II* **despite the fact that they look similar. A closer look at the actual pieces would reveal that** *table II* **had been stripped and repolished whereas the colour and patina of** *table I* **are very good and original. The tips of the drop leaves have been replaced on** *table II* **while** *table I* **remains unrestored and in good condition.** *Table I* **has more elaborately turned legs and the craftsmanship is of a higher quality.** *DN*

A fruitwood gateleg table, with oval top on turned legs, possibly Anglo-Chinese, 18thC, 32½in (83cm) extended.
£800–1,200 *DN*

An oak ten-seater double gate dining table, with oval dropleaf top above barley-twist turned legs, stretchers, and double gates on each side, 19thC, 69in (175cm) wide extended.
£3,000–3,500 *B*

An oak gateleg table, c1920, 30in (76cm) wide extended.
£225–265 *MofC*

An oak gateleg table, with oval top, single drawer and cup-and-cover shaped turned legs, 18thC with some 19thC iron hinges, 54in (137cm) wide.
£750–850 *BWe*

A 17thC style oak refectory table, the overhanging top with canted corners, with moulded frieze, baluster turned legs joined by stretchers, on bun feet, 67in (170cm) long.
£2,200–2,500 *S(NY)*

An elm refectory table, the planked top with cleated ends, the trestle ends with cup-and-cover turned supports, splay feet, and a plank stretcher, 19thC, 100in (254cm) long.
£2,000–2,500 *WW*

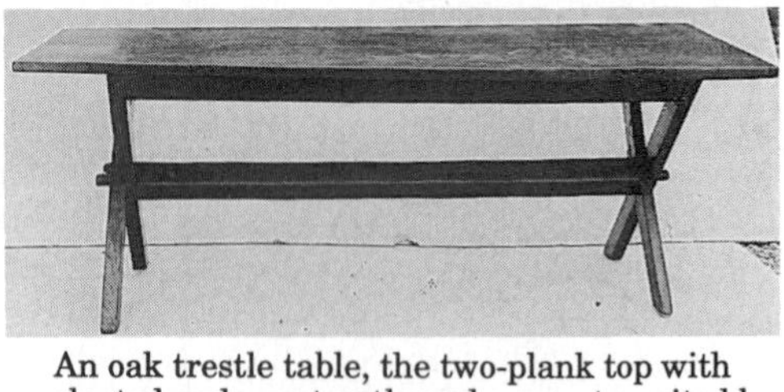

An oak trestle table, the two-plank top with cleated ends, on trestle end supports united by a central high stretcher, pegged at each end, 18thC, 77in (195.5cm) long.
£2,000–2,500 *B*

l. A Queen Anne oak side table, with shaped stretcher, early 18thC, 32in (81cm) wide.
£1,200–1,400
KEY

An oak side table, with a triple plank top, on slender baluster turned legs joined by square stretchers, 17thC, 78in (198cm) long, and a matching long stool, on slender baluster legs joined by flat stretchers, 71in (180cm) long.
£7,200–8,000 *L*

An oak side table, the moulded top above 2 short and one long drawer, on inverted baluster turned legs tied by a shaped X-shaped stretcher, early 18thC, 37in (94cm) wide.
£1,200–1,700 *Bon*

A French cherry wood occasional table, from Burgundy region, c1860, 24in (61cm) diam.
£300–350 *MofC*

A pale oak lowboy, with one long drawer above 2 side drawers, shaped frieze, on chamfered block legs, 18thC, 30in (76.5cm) wide.
£460–520 *WL*

An elm three-legged cricket table, c1800, 20in (50.5cm) diam.
£700–750 *RYA*

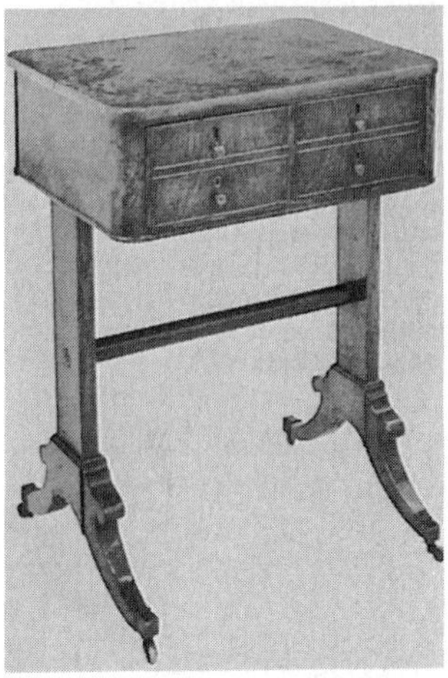

A George IV oak work table, the rounded top with a deep frieze fitted with 2 short drawers each simulating 2 drawers, the reverse with false drawers, on trestle legs and hipped downcurved feet, 21in (53cm) wide.
£500–700 *L*

Miscellaneous

In the Furniture section when there is only one measurement it refers to the width of the piece, unless otherwise stated.

A Victorian oak lectern in the form of an eagle perched on a ball, the stem carved with Gothic crosses, 63½in (162cm) high, and an associated platform, 24in (61cm) wide.
£550–600 *Bea*

A set of oak library steps, with a gallery and handrail above 7 treads, c1830, 85in (216cm) high.
£1,200–1,700 *CSK*

A Welsh oak candlestand, c1770, 25in (64cm) high.
£1,800–2,000 *RYA*

An oak candlestand, with stool base, c1740, 28½in (72.5cm) high.
£1,400–1,750 *RYA*

FURNITURE

Beds

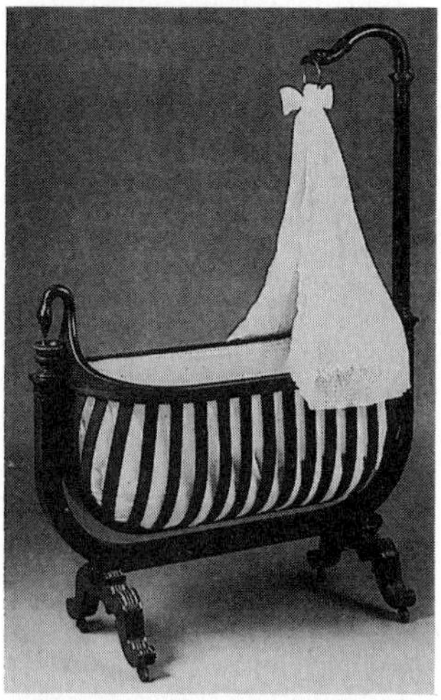

A French mahogany cradle, the crooked end support with an eagle's terminal and a brass ring in its beak, the boat-shaped crib with slatted sides and hooked beak end, on curved and reeded dual splayed legs with casters, 19thC, 49in (124cm) long.
£1,400–1,700 *CSK*

A brass bedstead, with lancet and Gothic style decoration, similarly decorated finials each end, mid-19thC, 52in (132cm) wide.
£1,600–1,900 *L&E*

An early Victorian pink painted double bed, the padded head and footboards covered in floral cotton, the headboard with rope-twist top and flowerhead centre, the foot with associated acorn finials joined by an arched clustered moulding, with boxspring and mattress, re-decorated, previously grained and parcel-gilt, possibly originally with posts, 71½in (182cm) wide.
£2,000–2,500 *C*

A George III mahogany four post tester bedstead, with foot posts carved to simulate bamboo, on block feet, 59in (149.5cm) wide.
£4,500–5,500 *S(NY)*

Beds

Tester beds are four poster beds surmounted by a wooden canopy. They were made during the 16thC, but most of those available today date from the second half of the 17thC. These heavily carved oak beds gave way to the more elegant mahogany beds of the 18thC. A heavier style of post re-emerged in the reign of George IV.

The half tester bed, which incorporated a half canopy, became very fashionable in the Victorian period. It had only two posts and was sometimes given additional support from the ceiling with the help of brackets concealed underneath the drapery.

Early American beds, made from oak, walnut and pine, are very simple in design. In the 18thC styles were based on beds from England, and during the early 19thC the influence of the French Empire bed is evident.

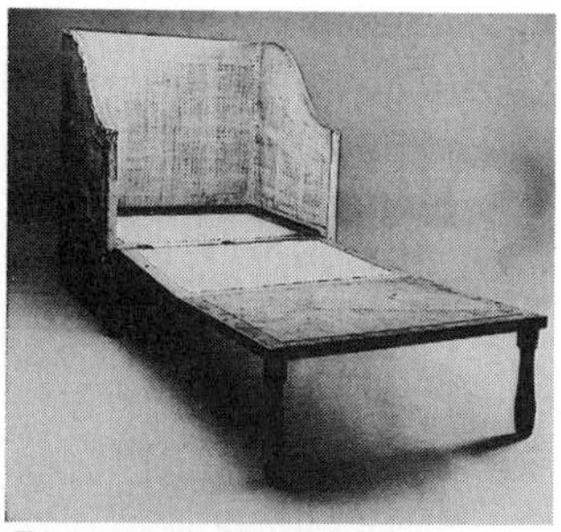

A Regency simulated rosewood folding bed, of bergère form, with solid back, scroll sides and fold-out seat, with removable baluster front legs, 77in (195.5cm) extended.
£6,000–7,000 *C*

An early Victorian mahogany half tester double bedstead, the serpentine cornice applied with foliate scrolls and hung with tasselled drapery, the footboard also carved with foliate scrolls, 67in (170cm) wide.
£3,200–4,000 *Bea*

A Victorian mahogany canopied double bed, the raised back with moulded framework for hanging fabric, the demi-lune tailboard with fielded panel flanked by carved and scrolled ornament, on bulbous feet.
£1,700–2,000 *WL*

l. A Victorian mahogany half tester bed, with moulded edged oblong half tester, arched panelled baseboard with carved scrolls and flowers, turned gadrooned columns with ball finials, turned feet and casters, with drapes, 59in (149.5cm) wide.
£1,500–2,000 *AH*

A Victorian mahogany half tester bed, with moulded edged serpentine half tester, the arched curving panelled baseboard with moulded crest, carved leaves, moulded base and casters, with drapes, 60in (152cm) wide.
£1,700–2,000 *AH*

A Victorian mahogany half tester bed, with arched and moulded crest, button upholstered headboard, arched panelled and curved baseboard with leaf and scroll carved pilasters, bun feet and casters, with drapes, 60in (152cm) wide.
£2,200–2,600 *AH*

A Victorian mahogany half tester bed, with moulded D-shaped half tester, the arched panelled baseboard carved with leaves, scrolls and central rosette, on moulded bracket feet and casters, with drapes, 65in (165cm) wide.
£2,000–2,500 *AH*

A Victorian brass bed.
£1,000–1,200 *DaD*

A Victorian satinwood half tester bed, with a moulded cornice and oval panel arched end with a moulded top rail, 72in (182.5cm) wide.
£1,100–1,500 *CSK*

A Victorian mahogany half tester bed, the ribbed canopy with Gothic tracery panels, the footboard with a running leaf frieze above similar tracery panels, 63in (160cm) wide.
£1,700–2,000 *DN*

An Edwardian mahogany and marquetry double bedstead, with crossbanded and line inlaid headboard and footboard, flanked by acanthus carved columns with flame finials, joined by panelled side rails with similar decoration, on tapered and gadrooned legs, 65in (165cm) wide.
£2,500–3,000 *CSK*

Styles of Bed Post

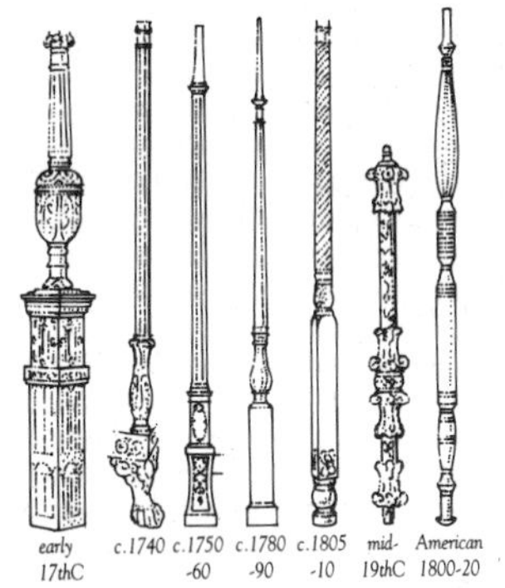

A Charles X line inlaid walnut lit en bateau, the head and footboard with outscrolled top rail above fluted column uprights joined by shaped burr veneered side rails, 84in (213cm) long.
£2,200–2,700 *CSK*

A Louis XVI style black and gilt japanned double bedstead, outlined with gilt foliate moulding decorated with chinoiserie scenes, on fluted supports with foliate finials, 63in (160cm) wide.
£1,500–2,000 *Bea*

A tester bed, the mahogany dentil moulded cornice with drapes, the front mahogany posts ribbed and carved with leaf petal collars above rosettes and swags, laurel leaf petal and turned supports, box spring with mattresss, 54in (137cm) wide.
£1,700–2,000 *WW*

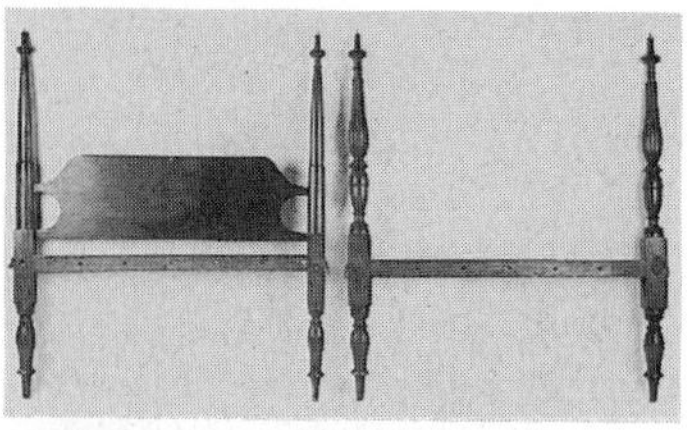

A Federal maple tall post canopy bed, New England, restored, c1820, 47in (119cm) wide.
£620–700 *SK(B)*

Beds

When oak tester beds became unfashionable during the 18thC, many were dismantled and put into storage, where they gradually fell into disrepair. Many were later rebuilt to suit Victorian tastes. Intact 17thC originals are rare.

The fluted footposts of the 18thC and early 19thC beds were sometimes converted into torchères (candle stands) during the early 20thC.

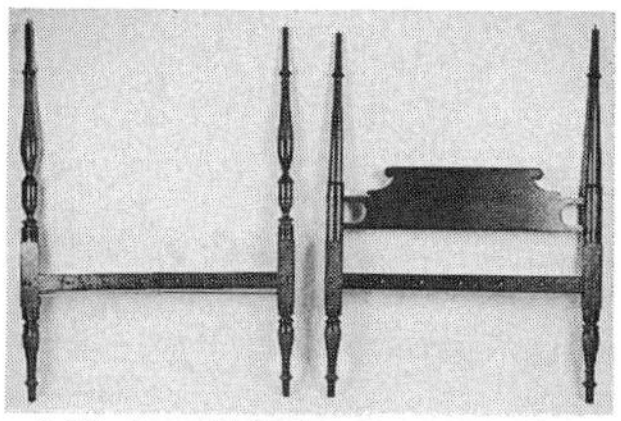

A Federal birch canopy bed, New England, restored, c1820, 55in (139.5cm) wide.
£1,250–1,300 *SK(B)*

Daybeds

A Regency grained and parcel gilt daybed, the ends overscrolled with floral rosette mounts, on scroll edged legs and brass mounted reeded tapering feet, with squab seat and bolsters, one leg loose, 88in (223.5cm) long.
£1,100–1,700 *CSK*

A Regency mahogany daybed, the outscrolled padded end with roundel terminals, above bolster and squab cushion covered in fringed striped material, on reeded sabre legs, restored, 71in (180cm) wide.
£1,000–1,500 *CSK*

An early Victorian rosewood daybed, by Boulnois, the curved padded back and serpentine seat covered in waved trellis pattern material, on turned tapering legs, brass caps and casters, one leg detached, the upholstery torn, the caps stamped 'Cope Collinson Patent Strong', with printed paper label 'From Boulnois/Upholsterer, & C.,/No. 44, Charlotte Street,/Rathbone Place, London'.
£1,000–1,400 *C*

Although his first name is not recorded, a number of labelled pieces survive by this maker. There is a labelled canterbury at Braybrooke Hall, Yorkshire.

A late Victorian walnut daybed, the single outswept padded end with scroll arms and padded seat, with loose cushion, on ring turned baluster legs, the casters stamped 'Howard & Sons Ltd., London', 56in (142cm) long.
£800–1,000 *C*

A late Victorian mahogany daybed, with buttoned arched chair back end and back rail, serpentine rounded seat, on turned tapering legs, 57in (145cm) long.
£550–800 *CSK*

A Victorian white painted and parcel gilt daybed, covered in a tropical patterned cotton with fringe, with baluster legs on brass caps and casters, 91in (232cm) long.
£1,300–1,700 *C*

An early Victorian rosewood daybed, the scrolled padded back, bolster and squab cushion covered in yellow floral damask, the back formed of joined scrolls, with panelled frieze, on tapering legs headed by scrolls and on later foliate gilt metal caps, 66in (167.5cm) long.
£1,400–1,800 *C*

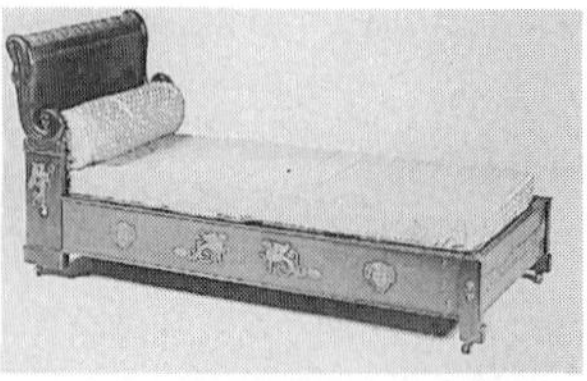

An Empire revival mahogany and gilt metal mounted daybed, the end with anthemion and cornucopiae mounted top rail between scrolling swan neck uprights, above a squab seat with bolster, the side rails and end with classical mounts, 69in (175cm) long.
£2,000–2,500 *CSK*

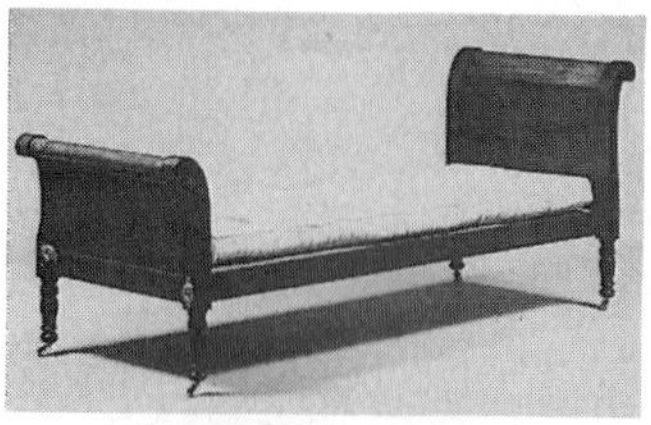

A Louis Philippe cherry wood daybed, with rolled head and footboard, on turned legs with brass casters, 19thC.
£2,000–2,500 *LHA*

Bonheur du Jour

A walnut, kingwood and satinwood inlaid bonheur du jour with ormolu mounts, the fall front revealing 3 drawers and 4 pigeon-holes, on cabriole legs, 31½in (80cm) wide.
£2,000–2,500 *HOLL*

A late Victorian mahogany bonheur du jour, the raised back with brass gallery, above 2 drawers and 2 foliate carved slides, above hinged leather lined writing surface, on square legs joined by shaped undertier, 29in (74cm) wide.
£600–900 *CSK*

A mahogany bonheur du jour, with overall chequer line inlay, on square tapering legs, 24½in (62cm) wide.
£800–1,000 *CSK*

Bonheur du Jour

The 'bonheur du jour' is a lady's small writing desk of delicate proportions. They were introduced in France during the last quarter of the 18thC.

Breakfront Bookcases

A George III style mahogany breakfront bookcase, on plinth base, 49in (124.5cm) wide.
£900–1,200 *CSK*

A Queen Anne style walnut breakfront bookcase, with a scrolling pediment decorated with florets and scallop motif, 2 pairs of glazed panelled doors below, enclosing adjustable shelves, raised on ogee bracket feet, 61½in (156cm) wide.
£4,000–4,500 *AG*

A George III style mahogany breakfront bookcase, with a dentil moulded and pedimented cornice centred with an urn finial, 4 glazed doors with applied astragals, on plinth base, 87in (221cm) wide.
£700–1,000 *CSK*

l. A satinwood banded mahogany breakfront bookcase, the simulated dentil moulded cornice above 3 geometrically astragal glazed doors, 3 frieze drawers and 3 cupboard doors, on a plinth base, labelled 'W. J. Mansell, Antique and Modern Furniture, 266 & 266a Fulham Road, and 2a Redcliffe Gardens, London SW', 71in (180cm) wide.
£3,000–3,500 *CSK*

Locate the source

The source of each illustration in* Miller's Antiques Price Guide *can easily be found by checking the code letters at the end of each caption with the Key to Illustrations located at the front of the book.

Bureau Bookcases

A Queen Anne style walnut bureau bookcase, with moulded edged domed top, 2 astragal glazed doors enclosing shelving, the fall front with fitted interior, with brass drop handles and bracket feet, 31in (78.5cm) wide.
£3,000–3,500 *AH*

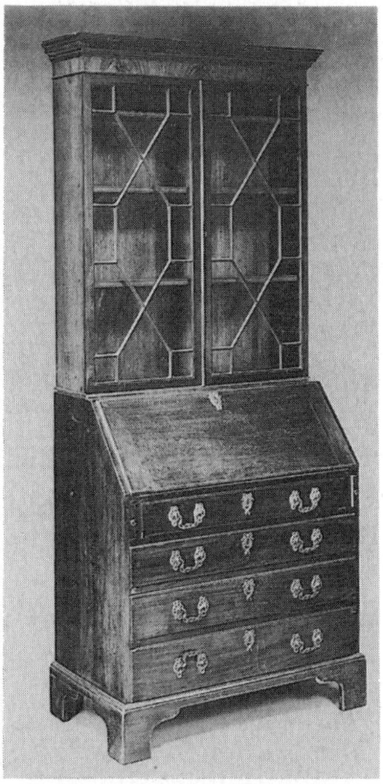

A George III mahogany bureau bookcase, the hinged fall front concealing a fitted interior of small drawers and pigeonholes, with 4 long graduated drawers below, on bracket feet, 38½in (98cm) wide.
£2,000–2,500 *P*

A mahogany bureau bookcase, on ogee bracket feet, the bureau 18thC, the top later, adapted, 57in (145cm) wide.
£2,000–2,500 *CSK*

Bureau Bookcases

To help determine if a bureau bookcase is comprised of its original parts, always check the following:

- The bookcase segment which sits on the bureau or cupboard base should be slightly smaller than the base.
- The retaining moulding should be fixed to the base rather than the top segement.
- It is unlikely that the top surface of the base would be veneered.

A bureau altered to take a bookcase on top will have a steeper angle to the fall front, in order to create a greater depth on top to accommodate the case or cabinet.

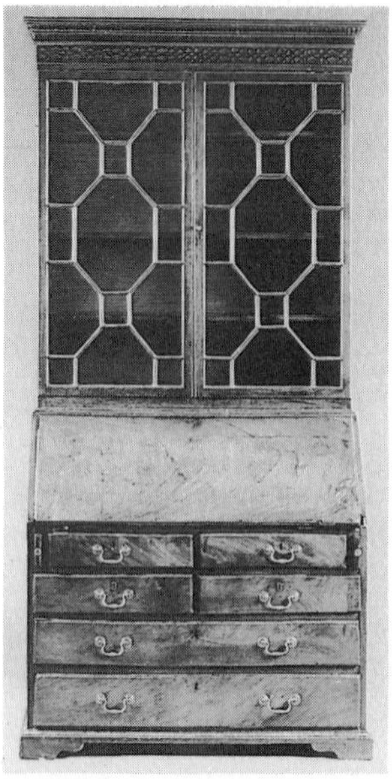

A George I walnut secrétaire bookcase, on bracket feet, early 18thC, 38½in (98cm) wide.
£4,000–4,500 *LHA*

A mahogany bureau bookcase, on bracket feet with ogee arched aprons, mainly early 19thC, the chequer stringing possibly later, 44½in (112cm) wide.
£2,500–3,000 *P*

l. A mahogany bureau bookcase, the base with 4 short and 2 long drawers, on bracket feet, associated, late 18thC.
£1,800–2,500 *CSK*

A late Victorian walnut cylinder bureau bookcase, with moulded cornice and a pair of glazed doors, the panelled roll-top enclosing fitted interior and with pull-out leather lined surface, each pedestal with 3 drawers and plinth, 41in (105cm) wide.
£2,000–2,500 *CSK*

Dwarf Bookcases

A set of mid-Victorian walnut open bookshelves, with adjustable shelves flanked by foliate corbels, on a plinth, 36in (92cm) wide.
£600–800 *CSK*

A Regency birchwood bookcase, inlaid with ebony lines above an inlaid frieze and 3 shelves, flanked by similarly inlaid borders, on turned acorn feet, 62in (157cm) wide.
£3,000–3,500 *DN*

A pair of mid-Victorian walnut open bookcases, each with a moulded edge, fitted with adjustable shelves, flanked by stiles with foliate scroll corbels, on a plinth base, 48in (122cm) wide.
£1,800–2,200 *CSK*

l. A mid-Victorian walnut dwarf bookcase, on a plinth base, 73½in (186.5cm) wide.
£2,000–2,500 *CSK*

A Victorian rosewood inverted breakfront bookcase, with shelves flanked by panelled cupboards with pilasters, on a plinth base, 84in (213cm) wide.
£1,200–1,700 *DN*

A mid-Victorian gilt metal mounted walnut and marquetry dwarf bookcase, with 3 glazed doors, on bracket feet, 65½in (166cm) wide.
£2,000–2,500 *CSK*

Secrétaire Bookcases

A George IV mahogany secrétaire bookcase, with a moulded and dentil cornice above a pair of doors with reeded glazing bars, the lower part with a fitted drawer and 3 long drawers, on splayed feet, 41½in (105cm) wide.
£2,000–2,500 *DN*

A mahogany secrétaire bookcase, with lined writing surface sliding to reveal compartmented interior, the kneehole with cupboard door flanked by 3 drawers to each side, on bracket feet, adapted, late 18thC, 47in (119cm) wide.
£1,700–2,200 *CSK*

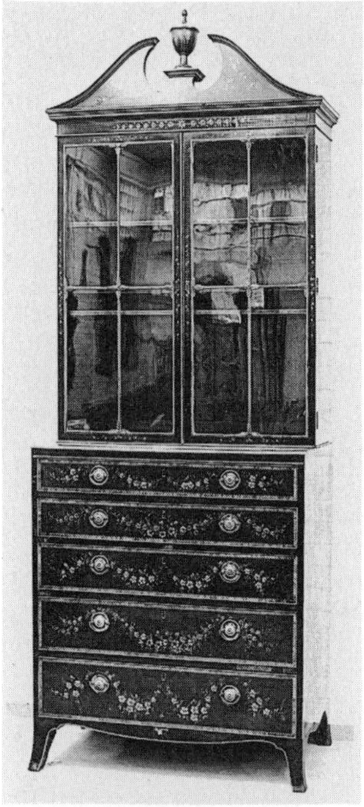

A mahogany secrétaire bookcase, crossbanded and painted with swags of flowers and cherubs, the side panels painted with Continental river landscapes, on splayed bracket feet, 19thC, 36in (91.5cm) wide.
£4,500–5,000 *HOLL*

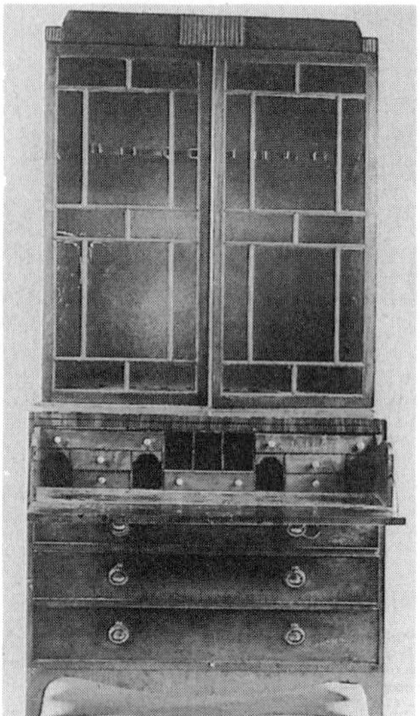

A Regency mahogany secrétaire bookcase, the upper section with arched cresting decorated with fluted panels, above a pair of geometrically glazed doors, enclosing a baize-lined gun cupboard interior, a fall front enclosing pigeonholes and satinwood fronted drawers, above 3 further long drawers, on bracket feet, 48in (122cm) wide.
£1,500–2,000 *CSK*

l. A George III mahogany secrétaire bookcase, with a cavetto cornice above a pair of astragal glazed doors, the lower part with tulipwood crossbanding and a fitted drawer above 3 long drawers, on splayed feet, 46in (116.5cm) wide.
£2,500–3,500 *DN*

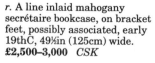

r. A line inlaid mahogany secrétaire bookcase, on bracket feet, possibly associated, early 19thC, 49½in (125cm) wide.
£2,500–3,000 *CSK*

A George III mahogany secrétaire bookcase, with a moulded cornice above a pair of astragal glazed doors, the base with a fitted drawer and 3 long drawers, on splayed feet, 41in (104cm) wide.
£3,000–4,000 *DN*

A line inlaid mahogany secrétaire bookcase, on bracket feet, restored, associated, parts early 19thC, 46in (117cm) wide.
£1,700–2,000 *CSK*

A Regency mahogany secrétaire bookcase, the fitted drawer with original acanthus decorated gilt handles, 49in (124.5cm) wide.
£4,500–5,000 *B*

Proportions

The proportions of any piece of furniture are important, both in determining its aesthetic value and in assessing authenticity. Quite often, when everything else appears to be correct, a fake may be detected simply by its uncharacteristic proportions – for example, bookcases are often reduced in depth to the point where they are no longer useful for shelving books.

A mahogany secrétaire cabinet, with associated top, on swept bracket feet, mainly early 19thC, 44½in (112cm) wide.
£1,000–1,500 *P*

A mahogany pedestal secrétaire bookcase, with fitted interior of drawers, pigeonholes and leather lined surface, each pedestal enclosed by an arched panelled door, plinth bases, possibly associated, early 19thC, 64in (162.5cm) wide.
£1,700–2,200 *CSK*

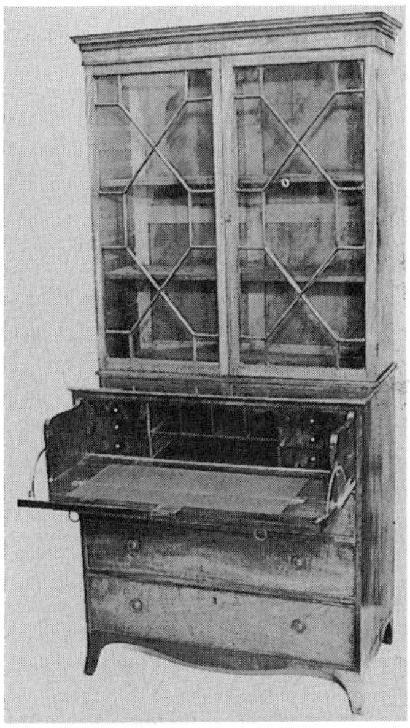

A Georgian mahogany secrétaire bookcase, the dummy drawer fall flap below enclosing a fitted interior of pigeonholes and small drawers, 3 long graduated drawers under with moulded ring handles, on splayed bracket feet, 40in (101.5cm) wide.
£2,500–3,000 *AG*

l. A George IV mahogany secrétaire bookcase, the associated upper part with a pair of astragal glazed doors above a fitted drawer and 3 further drawers, on splayed feet, 42½in (108cm) wide.
£2,500–3,000 *DN*

A pair of mahogany secrétaire alcove bookcases, each with dentil moulded cornice above a pair of astragal glazed doors, a fall front enclosing a fitted interior, above 2 panelled doors, 19thC, 37½in (97cm) wide.
£2,700–3,200 *CSK*

Library Bookcases

An early Victorian library bookcase, with a moulded cornice, 3 pairs of arched glazed doors, 3 pairs of conforming panelled doors to the projecting base, on a plinth, 114in (289.5cm).
£4,500–5,500 *Bea*

A Regency mahogany library bookcase, the cavetto cornice above a pair of glazed doors with scroll decorative edging, the base with conforming panel doors, on plinth base, 43½in (110cm) wide.
£1,500–2,000 *Bri*

A Canadian ash and butternut library bookcase, Ontario, c1880, 60in (152cm) wide.
£1,200–1,500 *RIT*

Revolving Bookcases

A mahogany and satinwood banded two-tier revolving bookcase, with 3 drawers, 18½in (47cm) square.
£1,000–1,200 *CSK*

A Victorian mahogany revolving bookcase, with 4 open shelves with spindles, stamped Danner's Revolving Bookcase Pat'd May 16, 1876, Feb 20, Dec 11, 1877, John Danner Canton Ohio', 25in (63.5cm).
£1,000–1,500 *SLN*

An Edwardian mahogany three-tiered revolving bookcase, the top with a moulded edge, slatted sides, on splayed feet with casters, 23in (59cm) wide.
£800–1,200 *CSK*

Miscellaneous Bookcases

A Georgian mahogany bookcase, on ogee bracket feet, 46½in (118cm) wide.
£1,500–2,000 *AG*

l. A George III style mahogany bookcase, with fluted and paterae decorated frieze above a pair of astragal glazed doors and a pair of cupboard doors, on plinth base, 51in (129.5cm) wide.
£1,000–1,500 *CSK*

Shelving

The earliest form of adjustable shelf on better quality bookcases was achieved by cutting rabbets (grooves) into the sides of the cabinet, into which the shelves could slide. In the early 18thC toothed ladders were introduced at each side, the removable rungs forming the shelf rests. By the end of the 18thC, movable pegs fitted into holes were used.

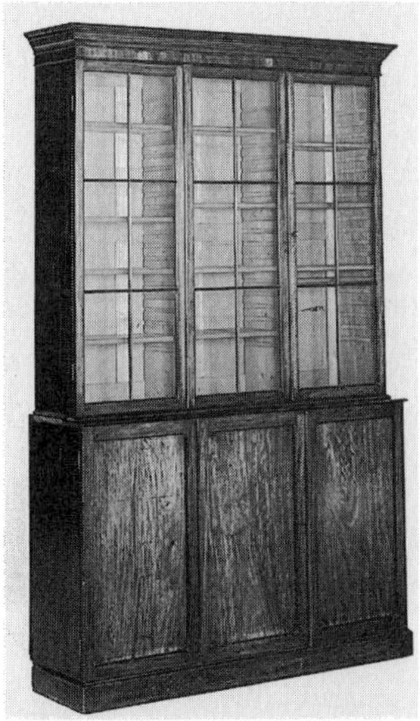

A George III mahogany bookcase, mounted on a plinth base, 65in (165cm) wide.
£4,500–5,000 *L&E*

Bookcases

Check that the glazing bars match the rest of the bookcase in quality, timber and age. Breakfront wardrobes of the mid- to late 19thC are often turned into bookcases by removing the solid panels to the doors and glazing the frames.

During the late 19thC many old glazed door cabinets were removed from their bureau or cupboard bases to have feet added and the tops fitted in to make 'Georgian' display cupboards or bookcases. This was not an 18thC form; the correct verson was much taller and often had drawers to the frieze base. The low 'dwarf' bookcases without doors became popular during the late 18thC.

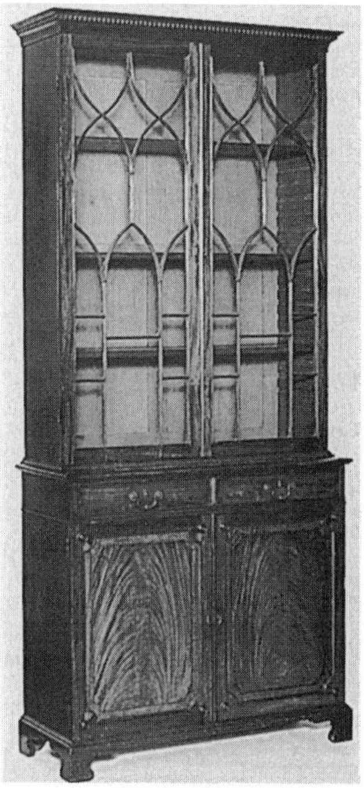

A George III mahogany bookcase, decorated with applied roundels, on bracket feet, 38in (96.5cm).
£2,000–2,500 *AG*

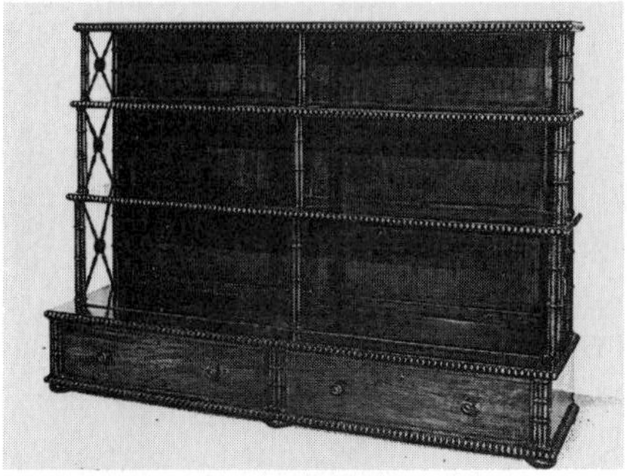

l. A mahogany and crossbanded open bookcase, comprising 4 graduated shelves with beaded edging, on cluster column supports, open X-framed sides, on box base with 2 drawers, brass knob handles, and bun feet, early 19thC, 61in (155cm).
£2,000–2,500 *AH*

A Georgian style mahogany bookcase, with arched cornice decorated with inlaid ebony stringing, 2 pairs of glazed panelled doors below enclosing adjustable shelves, on bracket feet, adapted, 43in (109cm) wide.
£1,200–1,700 *AG*

A Victorian mahogany bookcase, the moulded top above a pair of doors with carved glazing bars, the lower part with a frieze drawer and a pair of arched panelled doors, 39in (99cm).
£1,500–2,000 *DN*

A Victorian rosewood open bookcase, the top with a three-quarter gallery, on a plinth base, 66in (167.5cm).
£1,500–2,000 *CSK*

l. A Victorian mahogany bookcase, on turned feet, 41in (104cm) wide.
£1,300–1,700 *AG*

A Louis XV style burr walnut veneered bookcase on a table, applied with gilt metal foliate mounts, the serpentine base with a central frieze drawer, on cabriole legs, damaged, 36in (91.5cm) wide.
£800–1,200 *Bea*

Bureaux

A walnut and feather banded bureau, with brass drop handles and bracket feet, early 18thC, 38in (96.5cm).
£2,000–3,000 *AH*

A mahogany fall front bureau, with fitted interior above 4 graduated drawers, with ogee bracket feet, 18thC, 38in (95cms).
£600–800 *BWe*

Styles of Feet

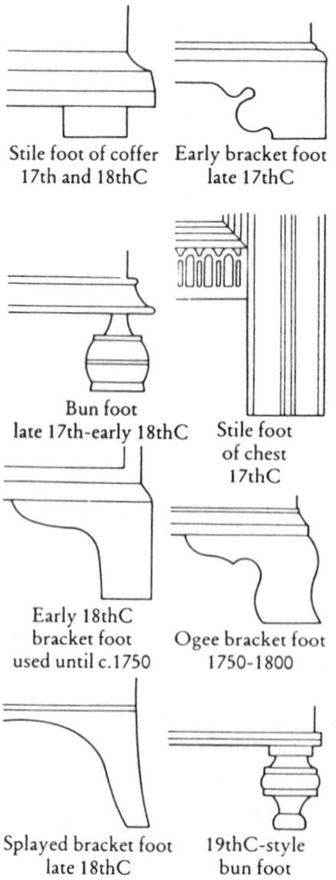

A George III mahogany bureau, the sloping fall front enclosing a fitted interior, on bracket feet, 46in (117cm).
£1,800–2,000 *CSK*

A George III mahogany bureau, the sloping flap enclosing a cupboard, drawers and pigeon-holes, 4 graduated long drawers below, on shaped bracket feet, 38in (96cm) wide.
£1,500–2,000 *Bea*

A George III mahogany bureau, on shaped bracket feet, restored, 38in (95cms) wide.
£2,000–2,500 *Bea*

A George III mahogany bureau, the fall front enclosing a fitted interior with drawers and pigeonholes, on bracket feet, 36in (92cm) wide.
£1,200–1,700 *CSK*

A George III mahogany bureau, the fall front enclosing a fitted interior of small pigeonholes and drawers flanking a central cupboard, above 4 long drawers, on bracket feet, 39in (99cm).
£1,700–2,200 *B*

A George III mahogany bureau, with a moulded crossbanded and boxwood strung fall front enclosing pigeonholes and small drawers, on bracket feet, 36in (91.5cm).
£1,500–2,000 *DN*

A George III crossbanded mahogany bureau, with leather lined writing surface, on ogee bracket feet, restorations, 44in (111.5cm)
£1,200–1,700 *CSK*

A George III mahogany bureau, 38in (96cm).
£1,200–1,800 *W*

Bureaux

Desirable points to look for:

- Good proportions
- Quality of construction
- Original handles and escutcheons
- Original feet
- Good colour and patination
- Small size - 36in (91.5cm) is about average
- Stepped interior and central cupboard
- Fitted 'well' and a slide
- Oak drawer linings
- Secret compartments

r. A George III mahogany bureau, with a fall front enclosing a fitted interior, on bracket feet, 40in (102cm) wide.
£900–1,200 *DN*

A George III mahogany bureau, on bracket feet, restorations, 2 feet loose, 34in (87cm).
£1,200–1,600 *CSK*

Miller's is a price GUIDE not a price LIST

A George III mahogany bureau, decorated with satinwood crossbanding and stringing, on square tapering legs and spade feet, 30in (77cm).
£1,200–1,700 *AG*

A George III mahogany bureau, the stepped interior with blind fret small drawers enclosed by the fall, above 4 long drawers with later brass handles, on bracket feet, 39in (99cm).
£1,200–1,500 *DN*

A George III mahogany bureau, the crossbanded and inlaid fall front enclosing an interior of small drawers and pigeonholes, flanking a central drawer with boxwood edging, on splayed bracket feet, 36in (91.5cm).
£1,500–2,000 *B*

A George III mahogany bureau, the sloping fall enclosing a fitted interior of drawers and pigeonholes around a central convex cupboard, with 2 short and 3 long drawers, on bracket feet, one missing, restored, 42in (107cm).
£1,200–1,700 *CSK*

A French walnut bureau, 19thC, 33in (83.5cm).
£1,600–2,000 *MR*

A George III mahogany bureau, the fall front enclosing an interior of small drawers and pigeonholes, 39in (99cm) wide.
£1,500–2,000 *B*

A Georgian walnut bureau, with brass swan neck handles, pierced shaped backplates, on bracket feet, 38in (96.5cm).
£1,500–2,000 *DA*

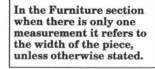

In the Furniture section when there is only one measurement it refers to the width of the piece, unless otherwise stated.

A late George III mahogany bureau, the sloping fall enclosing a fitted interior of bird's-eye maple veneered drawers and pigeonholes flanking a central cupboard, on bracket feet, 48in (122cm) wide.
£800–1,000 *CSK*

A George III mahogany bureau, on bracket feet, 38in (96.5cm).
£600–800 *DN*

An inlaid mahogany bureau, with chequer line inlay, on bracket feet, later inlaid, 19thC, 39in (98cm).
£1,600–2,000 *CSK*

A French mahogany bureau, with a superstructure of 3 panelled drawers, above a piano fall front enclosing a pull-out bird's-eye maple veneered interior of 3 drawers and leather lined surface, with 3 drawers under, on ring turned and reeded tapering legs, mid-19thC, 51in (130cm).
£1,400–1,700 *CSK*

r. A Regency ebonised line inlaid mahogany cylinder bureau, with hinged leather lined writing slope above 3 graduated drawers and shaped apron, on outswept bracket feet, 46in (117cm).
£1,600–2,000 *CSK*

A Syrian hardwood, ivory inlaid and strung bureau, decorated with chequer panels, stellar roundels and lozenge bands, meandering tendrils and stylised floral stems, with an open superstructure and sloping fall enclosing a writing slide, with an enclosed compartment to one side, fitted with two frieze drawers and hinged chequerboard with an open compartment below, on a plinth base, 46in (117cm).
£900–1,200 *CSK*

A Regency rosewood cylinder bureau, with brass inlaid front enclosing a sliding leather inset writing surface, on turned simulated rosewood legs, 40in (100cm).
£1,100–1,300 *DN*

A Continental walnut and marquetry bureau, surmounted by a cartouche-shaped back, with a hinged fall front enclosing a fitted interior, over 2 short and 2 long drawers, inlaid all-over with birds and classical urns amidst scrolling foliage, on bun feet, 18thC, 42in (106.5cm).
£3,500–4,500 *SLN*

l. A Sheraton style mahogany bureau de dame, with satinwood banded cylinder front, enclosing a writing slide and pigeonholes, on square tapering legs, 28in (71cm).
£1,200–1,700 *WL*

A Napoleon III walnut and gilt metal mounted bureau de dame, the top with a three-quarter foliate gallery, the shaped fall enclosing a tooled leather lined writing surface and fitted interior, with a frieze drawer, on cabriole legs headed with cabochon ornaments trailing to sabots, 34in (87cm) wide.
£1,600–2,000 *CSK*

A Swiss walnut secrétaire bureau, the fall front enclosing a leather lined fitted interior, above 3 further long drawers, on short cabriole legs, mid-19thC, 46in (117cm).
£1,500–2,000 *CSK*

Bureau Cabinets

A Queen Anne style walnut bureau cabinet, the double domed top section with 2 mirrored doors, the feather banded slope enclosing a fitted interior above 4 graduated long drawers, on ogee bracket feet, 35in (89cm).
£1,800–2,200 *C*

An Italian duck egg blue, floral painted and parcel gilt bureau cabinet, profusely decorated overall with floral sprays, on cabriole legs with hoof feet, 19thC, 32in (82cm) wide.
£1,700–2,200 *CSK*

A late George II mahogany bureau cabinet, the base with a sloping fall enclosing an interior with a central cupboard flanked by 8 pigeonholes and an arrangement of 12 drawers, with 2 short and 3 long drawers below, on bracket feet, one shelf and later back to bureau, 49in (124.5cm).
£1,700–2,200 *P*

Styles of Tops

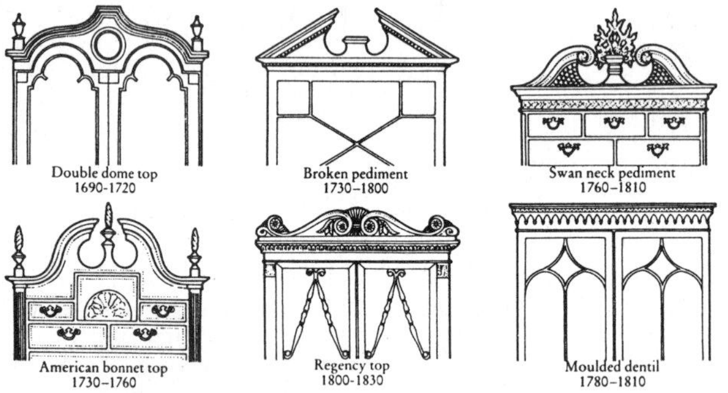

Miller's is a price GUIDE not a price LIST

A Continental painted bureau cabinet of small proportions, 28in (71cm) wide.
£1,800–2,200 *CAG*

A walnut and feather strung bureau cabinet, on bun feet, 29in (74cm) wide.
£3,000–4,000 *CSK*

A crossbanded and herringbone inlaid walnut bureau cabinet, with moulded cornice, 2 panelled doors enclosing shelves and small drawers, candleholders, the fall front enclosing fitted interior, with brass drop handles, on bracket feet, 18thC, 38in (96.5cm).
£5,500–6,000 *AH*

A George II oak cradle, with an arched hinged canopy and turned finials, on later rocker bases, 36in (92cm) long.
£1,400–1,800 *S(S)*

A Queen Anne oak and walnut banded bureau, 2 short and 3 long graduated drawers, on shaped bracket feet, interior restored, early 18thC, 35½in (91cm) wide.
£1,500–2,000 *S(S)*

A carved oak tester bed, the canopy with fluted panelling centred by geometric inlay, the headboard with 3 carved panels in the form of stylised arches with inlaid geometric borders, turned and fluted front posts, part 17thC, 79in (200.5cm) high.
£3,000–3,500 *S(S)*

An oak display cabinet, on S-scroll feet, bearing an ink mark on the reverse 'D.S. Normandy', mid-19thC, 57in (145cm) wide.
£3,400–4,000 *CSK*

An oak bureau cabinet, the fall front enclosing a fitted interior, 4 drawers beneath, c1740, 27in (69cm) wide.
£2,700–3,300 *Bon*

A George III oak bureau, with 4 long graduated drawers and fall revealing stationery compartments, late 18thC, 38in (96.5cm) wide.
£1,500–2,000 *S(S)*

A George III oak bureau, the fall revealing stationery compartments, late 18thC, damaged, 36in (92cm) wide.
£1,000–1,500 *S(S)*

A pair of William and Mary oak side chairs, with shaped top rails above moulded panelled splats, plank seats, on turned legs, restored, late 17thC.
£1,400–2,000 *S*

A Charles I carved oak panel back armchair, with foliate scroll cresting rail, stylised foliate tree flanked by scroll ears to back, later hinged seat, restored, c1620.
£1,500–2,500 *S(S)*

An oak armchair, the padded back and seat upholstered in floral Turkey work, the arms terminating in the masks of monkeys, on ring turned tapered column supports, on block feet, early 17thC.
£3,200–4,200 *C*

An ash and fruitwood spindle back armchair, with a bold central stretcher, c1830.
£800–1,000 *RYA*

A pair of elm and fruitwood dining chairs, c1780.
£800–900 *RYA*

A set of 6 ash and elm bow back Windsor dining chairs, c1780.
£1,500–1,650 *RYA*

A primitive ash and elm Windsor armchair, with fan and comb back, c1780.
£1,000–1,250 *RYA*

An Irish primitive ash comb back Windsor armchair, with shaped top rail, scroll arms and splayed legs, late 19thC.
£2,200–3,000 *C*

An ash dug-out chair, with pierced arm supports and elm seat with a shaped front seat rail, late 18thC.
£8,500–9,000 *C*

A primitive comb back armchair, with a figured ash seat, and narrow superstructure, West Country, c1800.
£2,000–2,500 *RYA*

An ash and elm Windsor bow backed carver chair, good patina, c1840.
£200–300 *RYA*

l. A pair of primitive Welsh comb back chairs, original paint, c1755.
£4,000–5,000 *RYA*

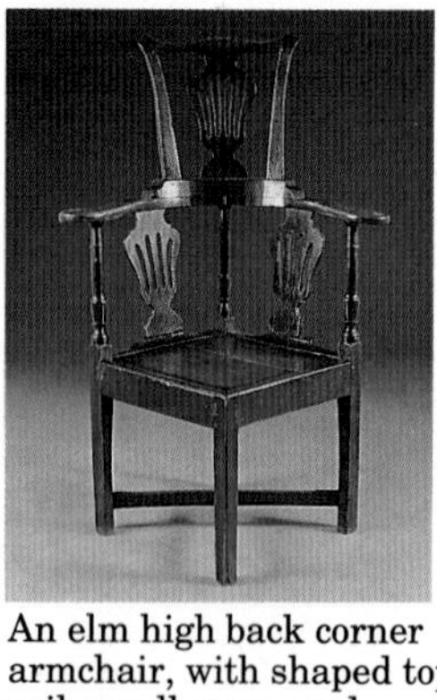

An elm high back corner armchair, with shaped top rail, scroll arms, and pierced vase splats, 18thC.
£4,000–4,500 *C*

A pair of fruitwood side chairs, with rush seats, c1900.
£200–240 *MofC*

A pair of fruitwood country chairs, with rush seats, c1890.
£100–125 *MofC*

A set of 4 Regency oak side chairs, attributed to George Bullock, with padded seats, covered in brown leather, damaged and repaired.
£12,000–14,000 *C*

An oak chest, the interior with a recess and 12 drawers, 17thC, 49½in (126cm) wide.
£2,000–3,000 *DN*

A child's oak joint chest, with plank top, 2 short drawers, mid-18thC, 24½in (62cm) wide.
£1,000–1,500 *Bon*

A George I oak bureau bookcase, with stepped interior and fitted top, c1720, 36in (91.5cm) wide.
£6,000–10,000 *PHA*

An oak coffer, with arched leaf-carved frieze, the front carved with leaves and strapwork, early 17thC, 58in (147cm) wide.
£2,000–2,500 *S*

An oak chest, inlaid with fruitwood and bog oak, the panels decorated with foliage, late 17thC, 53in (134.5cm) wide.
£2,500–3,000 *C*

An oak panelled coffer, inlaid with holly and bog oak, c1625, 52in (132cm) wide.
£5,250–5,750 *PHA*

An oak panelled coffer, inlaid with holly and bog oak, excellent condition and colour, c1625.
£3,000–5,000 *PHA*

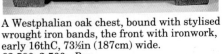

An oak coffer, inlaid with bog oak and holly, early 17thC, 57½in (146cm) long.
£1,000–1,200 *S*

The 'Thame' chest, oak, with iron hasp hinges, engraved horn plaques, c1575, 52in (132cm) long.
£6,400–7,000 *S(S)*

A Westphalian oak chest, bound with stylised wrought iron bands, the front with ironwork, early 16thC, 73½in (187cm) wide.
£2,500–3,500 *Bon*

A Welsh oak mule chest, with 2 drawers, on stile feet, mid-18thC, 55½in (141cm) long.
£500–800 *S(S)*

An oak coffer, probably Lake District, c1800, 61in (155cm) wide.
£400–500 *S(S)*

An oak coffer, the hinged top and panelled front with foliate and zig-zag decoration, 56½in (143.5cm) wide.
£1,400–2,000 *C*

A William and Mary oak chest of 3 drawers, on bun feet, c1695, 32in (81cm) wide.
£2,000–3,000 *PHA*

An oak cupboard,with louvred doors, mid-18thC, 27¼in (69cm) wide.
£7,500–8,000 *S*

A carved oak court cupboard, with panelled cupboards carved with masks, on turned legs, early 17thC.
£8,700–10,000 *S*

A George III oak press cupboard, on bracket feet, 53in (134.5cm) wide.
£1,500–2,500 *Bon*

An oak livery cupboard, the frieze inlaid with chequered stringing, mid-17thC, 67½in (171cm) wide.
£2,200–3,000 *Bon*

A James I carved oak court cupboard, early 17thC, 56¼in (143cm) wide.
£10,500–12,500 *S*

l. An oak dug-out cupboard, with twin plank door, on shaped stile feet, 18thC, 36in (91.5cm) wide.
£3,000–4,000 *C*

An oak joined press or aumbry, with central panel of pierced Gothic tracery, linenfold side panels, distressed, c1500.
£3,000–5,000 *Bon*

An oak wall cupboard, with arcaded frieze, 17thC and later, 30¼in (77cm) wide.
£1,700–2,000 *C*

A Welsh oak panelled livery cupboard, with 3 drawers below, c1750, 72in (182.5cm) high.
£2,000–4,000 *PHA*

An oak press cupboard in 2 parts, with a recessed panel flanked by decorated doors to either side, and a pair of panelled door cupboards below, 17thC, 62in (157cm) wide.
£2,300–3,300 *C*

A Welsh oak mural cupboard, incised 'T.E.', late 17thC, 24½in (62cm) wide.
£4,000–5,000 *C*

An oak dresser base, with associated moulded top, 5 drawers and a cupboard with later shelves, stile feet altered, late 17thC, 84½in (214cm) wide.
£8,000–9,000 *S(S)*

A Welsh oak cupboard dresser, with 2 small cupboards in the plate rack, c1700, 70in (177.5cm) high.
£5,000–10,000 *PHA*

An oak dresser, with moulded top, 3 short drawers above 2 cupboards, early 18thC, 70in (178cm) wide.
£2,000–3,000 *DN*

An oak dresser, restored, mid-18thC, 57in (145cm) wide.
£5,000–6,000 *Bon*

A Welsh oak dresser, with a potboard, c1790, 86in (218.5cm) wide.
£10,000–14,000 *PHA*

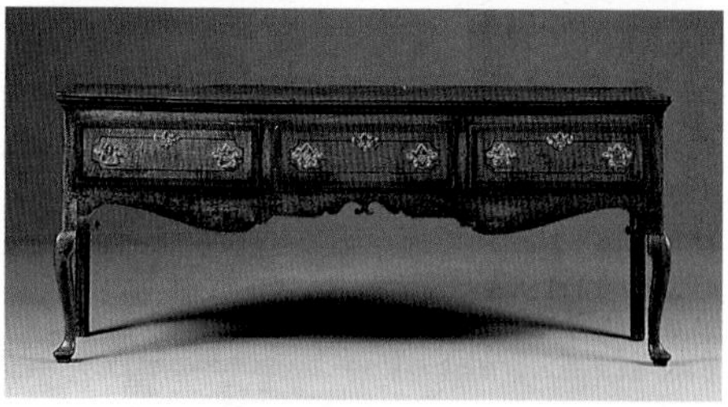

A George III oak dresser, crossbanded with mahogany, with 3 frieze drawers, on cabriole legs, restored, 78in (198cm) wide.
£10,000–12,000 *C*

A Welsh oak dresser, late 18thC, 71in (180cm) wide.
£2,200–2,700 *Bon*

A George III oak dresser base.
£4,500–5,500 *LT*

An oak dresser, with 6 drawers, mid-18thC, 70in (178cm) wide.
£4,700–5,200 *Bon*

An oak settle, the back with foliate scroll cresting, later solid seat, mid-17thC, 72in (182.5cm) long.
£2,000–2,500 *C*

An oak dresser, with dentilled cornice, possibly Cumbrian, late 18thC, 66in (167.5cm) wide.
£4,000–5,000 *S(S)*

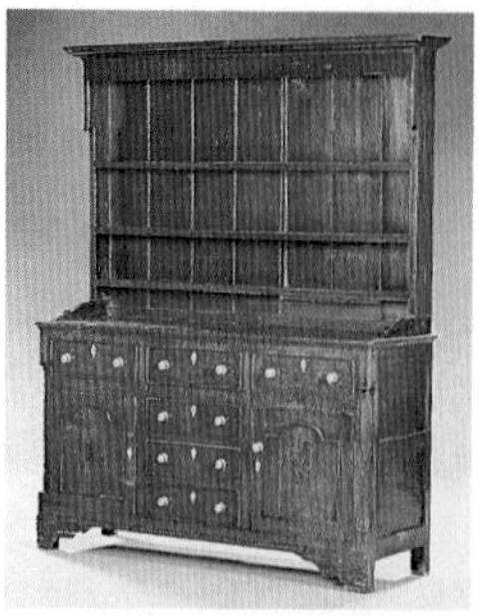

A Welsh oak dresser, with 3 frieze drawers above 3 dummy drawers, early 19thC, 63in (160cm) wide.
£4,000–5,000 *S(S)*

An elm settee, with leather padded back, close nailed scroll arms, solid seat, on square tapered legs, 18thC, 72in (183cm) long.
£6,000–6,500 *C*

A Welsh joint stool, with a secondary top, c1750, 20½in (52cm) high.
£350–450 *RYA*

A trestle-ended stool, with hand grip, c1820, 17in (43cm) high.
£85–120 *RYA*

A Spanish oak and walnut 2 drawer side table, c1640, 50in (127cm) wide.
£2,500–4,000 *PHA*

An elm slab-topped milking stool, c1780, 15in (38cm) high.
£100–150 *RYA*

A pair of oak joint stools, on columnar legs with block feet, 17thC, 20½in (52cm) high.
£6,000–6,500 *C*

An oak draw-leaf table, with parquetry frieze, foliate scroll carved moulded apron, on turned legs, parts 17thC.
£7,200–8,000 *CSK*

An oak dining table, on fret-carved end supports, joined by a shaped stretcher and dual splayed legs, 87½in (222cm) wide. **£4,000–5,000** *C*

A French burr ash side table, 19thC, 27in (68.5cm) wide.
£1,200–2,000 *PHA*

An oak refectory table, with spiral-twist supports, 19thC, 108in (274cm) wide.
£6,000–7,000 *CSK*

An oak table, early 18thC, 30in (76cm) high.
£5,000–6,000 *C*

An oak gateleg table, restored, c1680, 30½in (77cm) long.
£2,400–3,000 *Bon*

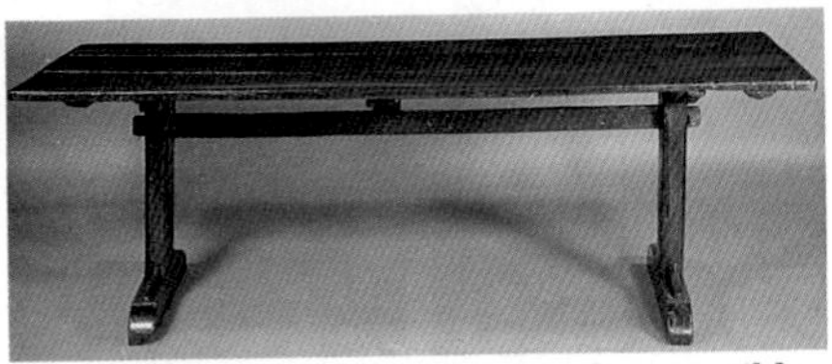

An oak trestle table, stretcher possibly altered, late 17thC, 96in (243.5cm) wide.
£5,000–6,000 *Bon*

A George III oak, yew, boxwood, ebony and burr elm sewing table, 28in (71cm) high.
£2,000–3,000 *PHA*

An oak refectory table, with forked end trestle supports, the top 17thC, the base 19thC, 113in (287cm) wide.
£7,800–8,500 *CSK*

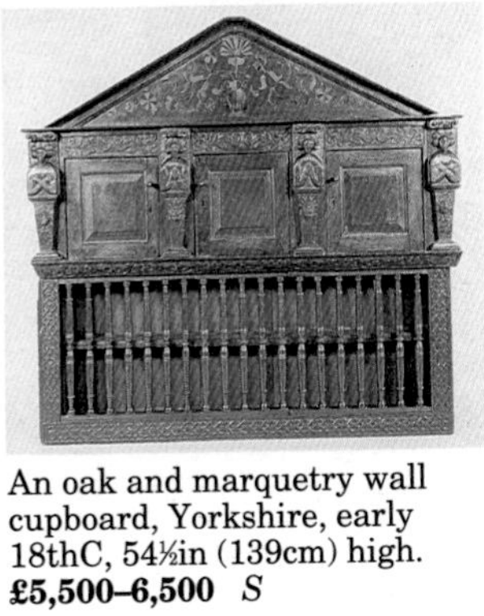

An oak and marquetry wall cupboard, Yorkshire, early 18thC, 54½in (139cm) high.
£5,500–6,500 *S*

A George IV bed, with later arcaded base, coronet possibly associated, box spring and fitted mattress, restored, re-decorated, 85in (214cm) wide.
£7,500–8,000 *C*

A bed tester, with moulded interior, fabric replaced, early 18thC, 66in (167.5cm) wide.
£2,000–2,500 *S*

An Edwardian mahogany, harewood and marquetry four poster bed, 41in (104cm) wide.
£1,700–2,500 *C*

A Louis XV style duchesse, with pierced foliate scroll carved top rail, on cabriole legs, 74½in (189cm) long.
£1,200–1,700 *CSK*

An early Victorian mahogany tester bed, with mattress, 83in (210.5cm) long.
£5,250–5,750 *C*

A mahogany tester bed, with floral needlework drapery frieze, c1800, 102in (259cm) high.
£8,000–9,000 *S(S)*

A French tulipwood, kingwood, mahogany lit en bateau, with porcelain plaques and gilt metal mounts, 19thC, 87in (221cm) wide.
£3,000–4,000 *C*

A late Victorian mahogany bed, the head and foot boards flanked by Egyptian caryatids, 88in (223.5cm) long.
£23,500–24,500 *C*

An early Victorian simulated rosewood tester bed, with mattress, 82in (208cm) long.
£11,000–11,250 *C*

A George III tester bed, with associated William IV turned front posts with later decoration, restored, 65in (165cm) wide.
£10,000–11,000 *C*

A William IV mahogany four poster bed, restored, c1835, 74in (188cm) wide.
£6,000–7,000 *S*

A pair of Charles X mahogany and ormolu mounted lits en bateaux, inscribed 'Brooke Baylis', various labels, later mattress, 79in (200.5cm) wide.
£2,500–3,500 *CSK*

A Regency brass mounted and parcel gilt rosewood bonheur du jour, banded with satinwood, restored, 36in (91.5cm) wide.
£3,000–5,000 *C*

An Edwardian rosewood and marquetry inlaid bonheur du jour, 24in (61cm) wide.
£1,200–1,700 *E*

Two Regency brass inlaid rosewood bonheur du jours, possibly by John Maclean, with brass trellis pattern panels, 33in (84cm) wide.
£12,000–15,000 *AG*

A late Victorian Gothic style walnut and parcel gilt decorated breakfront dwarf bookcase, 87in (221cm) wide.
£4,000–5,000 *CSK*

A French Empire mahogany bonheur du jour, the superstructure with a marble top, c1815, 32in (81cm) wide.
£2,500–3,500 *Bon*

A French kingwood parquetry and ormolu bonheur du jour, with bombé-shaped raised back, 32in (81cm) wide.
£5,000–5,500 *MAT*

A William IV satinwood open bookcase, with 4 adjustable shelves, on plinth base, 72in (182cm) wide.
£5,200–6,000 *C*

A pair of rosewood open bookcases, with brass grille sides, fitted with adjustable shelves, on a plinth base, 43in (109cm) wide.
£4,200–6,000 *CSK*

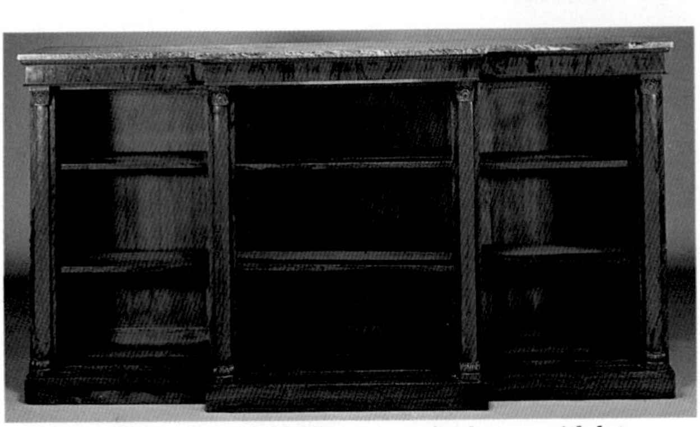

A William IV rosewood breakfront open bookcase, with later green marble slab, on plinth base, alterations, c1835, 85in (215cm) wide.
£1,500–2,500 *Bon*

A mid-Victorian burr walnut and parcel gilt dwarf open bookcase, with open adjustable shelves, 63in (160cm) wide.
£3,500–4,500 *CSK*

A rosewood inverted breakfront library bookcase, the 4 lower glazed doors set with brass trellis, c1825, 78½in (199cm) wide.
£7,000–9,000 *S*

A George III inlaid mahogany breakfront bookcase, some later inlay, 98in (249cm) wide.
£20,000–30,000 *Bon*

A 17thC style walnut and parcel gilt bookcase, 19thC, 68½in (174cm) wide.
£4,500–5,500 *C*

A mahogany double-sided book shelf, c1810, 33½in (85cm) wide.
£3,500–5,000 *S*

A George II mahogany bookcase, the base with fall front above a plinth base edged with foliage, the mask possibly later, 97½in (248cm) high.
£30,000–50,000 *C*

A George IV mahogany breakfront library bookcase, 146in (371cm) wide.
£17,000–20,000 *CSK*

r. A Regency mahogany breakfront bookcase, restored, 98in (249cm) high.
£3,000–4,000 *C*

A Victorian satin birch bookcase, restored.
£5,750–6,250 *C*

A satinwood breakfront display cabinet/bookcase, c1790, 89in (226cm) high.
£13,000–15,000 *S*

A walnut bookcase, the breakfront upper part with 4 Gothic arched glazed doors, 2 doors below, mid-19thC, 62½in (159cm) wide.
£12,000–16,000 *S*

An Edwardian mahogany and inlaid George III style library bookcase, 60in (152cm) wide.
£3,500–4,000 *Bri*

An early Victorian oak and holly bookcase, probably by George Morant, 47in (118cm) wide.
£2,400–2,600 *C*

A mahogany secrétaire bookcase, on splayed bracket feet, c1780, 37in (94cm) wide.
£6,000–7,000 *S*

A George III mahogany and brass bound peat bucket, restored.
£650–850 *C*

A George III mahogany peat bucket.
£1,300–1,600 *C*

A George II fruitwood bureau, restored, mid-18thC, 34in (86cm) wide.
£1,800–2,200 *Bon*

A George I japanned bureau cabinet, decorated with chinoiserie figures and trees in landscapes, the mirrored doors enclosing 3 adjustable shelves, restored, 41½in (105cm) wide.
£15,000–20,000 *C*

A walnut veneered cross and chevron banded bureau, c1720, 36½in (92cm) wide.
£4,000–4,500 *S*

A George I walnut bureau cabinet, the top and base possibly associated, restored, 28in (71cm) wide.
£29,000–35,000 *C*

A Queen Anne burr walnut bureau, slight damage, 18thC, 33in (83.5cm) wide.
£7,700–8,500 *S(NY)*

A Louis XVI style plum pudding mahogany and gilt brass mounted cylinder bureau, 36½in (93cm) wide.
£3,000–4,000 *CSK*

A William and Mary walnut, crossbanded and featherbanded bureau cabinet, with later bun feet, 41in (104cm) wide.
£12,000–16,000 *C*

A late Victorian walnut bureau de dame, inlaid with boxwood, 34in (86cm) wide.
£1,800–2,000 *E*

A French mahogany and ormolu mounted cylinder bureau, by Paul Sormani, brass lock plate signed, 19thC, 39in (99cm) wide.
£12,000–15,000 *CSK*

A mahogany architect's cabinet, c1830, 41½in (105cm) wide.
£14,500–16,000 *S*

An ebonised and cloisonné panelled credenza in the Chinese taste, late 19thC, 80½in (204cm) wide.
£4,000–5,000 *DN*

A Regency style rosewood side cabinet, the concave top above one long and 2 short frieze drawers, 63in (160cm) wide.
£3,000–4,000 *Bon*

A Victorian walnut credenza, inlaid with boxwood and ebony stringing, the central panelled doors with painted porcelain plaques.
£6,000–7,000 *SWO*

A German marquetry inlaid side cabinet, restored, early 17thC, 50in (127cm) wide.
£5,500–8,500 *Bon*

A pair of walnut side cabinets, inlaid with satinwood, with velvet lined interiors, 19thC, 33½in (85cm) wide.
£3,500–4,000 *MAT*

A Regency black japanned and parcel gilt side cabinet, with marble top, early 19thC, some restoration to decoration, 69in (175cm) wide.
£26,000–30,000 *S(NY)*

A late Victorian mahogany side cabinet, with gilt brass stringing, stamped 'Gillows', 41in (104cm) wide.
£2,500–3,500 *CSK*

A Tuscan walnut side cabinet, c1700, minor restoration, 30in (76cm) wide.
£3,000–4,000 *C*

An early Victorian rosewood breakfront side cabinet, with marble top, altered, c1840, 80in (203cm) wide.
£2,500–3,500 *Bon*

A pair of ebony side cabinets, with marble tops, each door centred by a mid-17thC Franco-Flemish carved panel, c1860, 42½in (108cm) wide.
£6,000–7,500 *S*

A Louis XVI ebony breakfront side cabinet, in the manner of Martin Carlin, with Sarancolin marble top, indistinctly stamped, c1780, 36in (90.5cm) wide.
£48,000–52,000 *S*

A George III giltwood and gilt composition display cabinet, 39in (99cm) wide.
£12,000–14,000 *C*

A Victorian walnut dwarf side cabinet, inlaid with lines and crossbanded in tulipwood, 75in (190.5cm) wide.
£3,000–4,000 *CSK*

A French ormolu mounted mahogany vitrine, by François Linke, signed, late 19thC, 63in (160cm) high.
£8,000–10,000 *C*

An early Georgian cabinet-on-stand, 39in (99cm) wide.
£2,500–3,000 *C*

A George III rosewood side cabinet, with crossbanded top, on later square tapering legs with spade feet, 45in (114cm) wide.
£7,500–10,000 *C*

A William and Mary walnut and marquetry cabinet-on-stand, replacement legs, 44in (112cm) wide.
£9,000–12,000 *S*

An Edwardian mahogany display cabinet, stamped 'Edwards and Roberts', 24½in (62.5cm) wide.
£3,500–4,000 *CSK*

A George II mahogany cabinet, with moulded cornice, the mirrored doors enclosing 20 short graduated drawers, repairs to feet, 46in (116.5cm) wide.
£14,000–16,000 *C*

Two Regency mahogany canterburies, c1810:
l. With X-shaped sides, 20in (50.5cm) wide.
r. With mahogany and pine lined drawer with brass knob handles, 22in (55.5cm) wide.
£2,000–2,500 each *JC*

A George III mahogany canterbury, with spindled divisions, c1790, 19½in (49cm) wide.
£5,000–6,000 *S*

A George IV mahogany canterbury, with turned pillars and legs, c1820, 19in (48cm) wide.
£3,000–4,000 *S*

A pair of George III mahogany armchairs, with needlepoint upholstery, downswept arms, on square chamfered legs, repaired.
£22,000–25,000 *S(NY)*

A Chippendale mahogany lolling chair, American, c1760.
£14,000–15,000 *CNY*

A George II mahogany library open armchair, restored.
£19,000–21,000 *C*

A pair of George III carved mahogany library armchairs, attributed to William Vile, some brackets and blocks replaced, c1760.
£500,000–550,000 *S*

A pair of George II mahogany library open armchairs, with cabriole legs, restored.
£15,000–20,000 *C*

A George III white painted and parcel gilt open armchair, restored.
£6,000–7,000 *C*

A set of 8 white painted 18thC style fauteuils, the padded backs and seats covered in patterned needlework.
£4,000–6,000 *C*

A pair of Regency mahogany armchairs, each with a scrolled panelled top rail, scrolled moulded arms, drop-in seats and sabre legs, c1810.
£4,000–5,000 *S*

A pair of Regency open armchairs, in the manner of Thomas Chippendale, all signed in ink 'W. Saul'.
£12,000–14,000 *C*

A set of 6 Regency ebonised armchairs, with padded backs and seats, ball finials and sabre legs, c1805.
£4,500–6,500 *S*

A pair of Louis XV beechwood fauteuils, with upholstered serpentine topped backs, loose cushioned seats, on leaf carved moulded supports and cabriole legs, c1730.
£11,000–15,000 *S*

A Regency ebonised and parcel gilt open armchair, stamped on seat rail 'MS' and paper label '112', restored and re-decorated.
£10,500–12,000 *C*

A pair of French giltwood armchairs, with ribbon carved frames, one c1780.
£1,700–2,500 *S*

A late Louis XVI painted and parcel gilt suite, stamped 'P. Achard', c1790.
£9,000–12,000 *S*

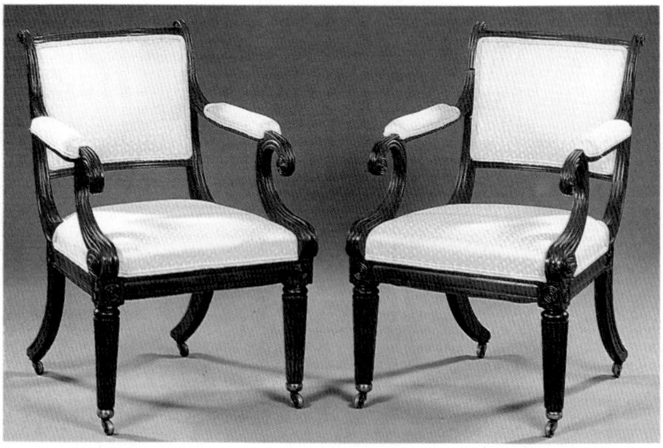

A pair of Regency rosewood library armchairs, with moulded padded concave backs, padded arms with scrolled supports, sprung seats, on reeded tapering legs headed by ringed bosses, brass casters, c1820. **£17,500–20,000** *S*

A set of 4 Louis XVI painted armchairs, stamped 'I. Lebas', covered in contemporary Aubusson tapestry, c1780.
£15,000–17,000 *S*

A pair of Italian walnut armchairs, the backs with carved finials, on carved sledge feet, restored, c1700.
£4,000–5,000 *Bon*

A pair of Napoleon III carved giltwood fauteuils, the frames with pierced ribbon tied floral and bowed cresting and thrysus finials, restored.
£3,000–4,000 *CSK*

A George II elm wing armchair, upholstered in leather, back legs replaced, c1740.
£2,500–3,500 *S*

A George III mahogany bergère, with square tapering front legs and casters, c1780.
£2,500–3,000 *S*

A George I elm wing armchair, upholstered in flame stitch, with shell carved cabriole legs and claw-and-ball feet.
£7,000–9,000 *C*

A George I walnut wing chair, on leaf carved cabriole legs and pad feet, repaired, early 18thC.
£5,500–6,000 *S(NY)*

A George III mahogany wing armchair, upholstered in leather, c1770.
£3,000–5,000 *Bon*

A late George III mahogany framed bergère library chair, with reeded framing and cane panels, the cushions and arm pads upholstered in corded cloth, on turned front supports with casters.
£1,800–2,200 *CAG*

A Queen Anne walnut wing armchair, frame and legs restored, c1705.
£3,000–4,000 *Bon*

A Regency caned mahogany bergère chair, with reeded top rail, stamped with maker's initials 'RW', c1810.
£4,000–6,000 *S*

A Regency bamboo armchair, with cushioned seat, early 19thC.
£1,200–1,700 *S*

A caned mahogany library bergère, with associated mahogany and brass adjustable book rest, c1820.
£7,000–9,000 *S*

A Regency mahogany library bergère, covered in close nailed leather, with brass claw feet and casters, restored.
£4,000–5,000 *C*

Two simulated calamander bergères, one William IV and the other later, with scrolled backs covered in silk and satin.
£4,500–5,000 *C*

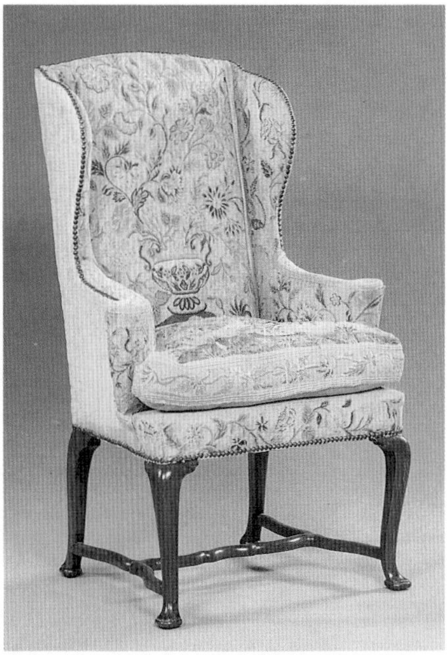

A George I walnut wing armchair, the back, arms and cushioned seat covered in associated 18thC floral wool needlework, the cabriole legs with pad feet and waved H-stretcher, c1720.
£19,000–21,000 *S*

A George IV stained beechwood bergère, with buttoned leather back, sides and seat, stamped 'B'.
£1,800–2,500 *CSK*

A Regency ebonised bergère, with curved arched back, squab seat, sabre legs, brass caps and casters.
£800–1,200 *CSK*

A pair of George III caned satinwood tub armchairs, possibly Colonial, late 18thC.
£4,000–5,000 *S(NY)*

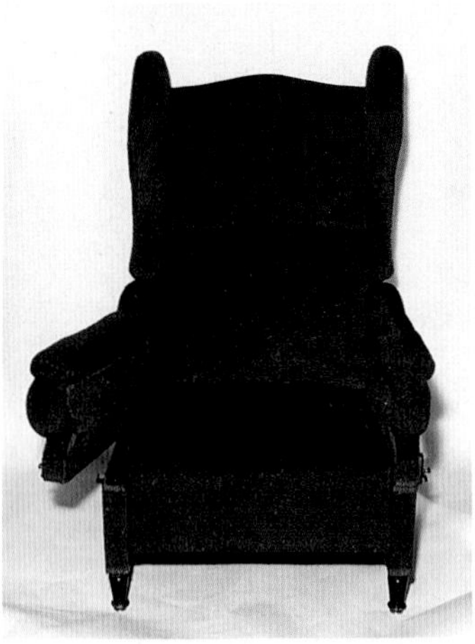

A library wing armchair, with reclining back and swing arm, late 19thC, 43in (109cm) high.
£1,200–1,400 *SIG*

A late Victorian easy armchair, with arched padded back, arms and seat, on turned tapered legs, with brass caps and casters stamped 'Howard & Sons, London'.
£900–1,200 *C*

A Louis XV caned beechwood fauteuil de bureau, with flower carved moulded frame, mid-18thC.
£11,000–14,000 *S*

A Restauration mahogany bergère, the back with terminals ending in stylised lotus leaves, c1825.
£3,500–4,500 *S*

A set of 4 Russian mahogany, painted and parcel gilt armchairs, with stuffed backs and seats, winged arm supports and paw feet, early 19thC.
£27,000–30,000 *S*

A set of 8 George II mahogany dining chairs, by Gillows of Lancaster, some with later blocks.
£50,000–52,000 *C*

A set of 8 George III mahogany dining chairs, restored, stamped 'ID'.
£11,000–13,000 *C*

A set of 12 Regency mahogany dining chairs, after a design by Thomas Sheraton, restored.
£465,000–500,000 *C*

A set of 8 Georgian mahogany dining chairs, comprising 6 singles and 2 armchairs, with slip-in seats.
£7,500–8,500 *JC*

A set of 6 Regency mahogany dining chairs, including 2 armchairs, re-railed, c1810.
£3,300–4,000 *S*

A set of 8 George III mahogany dining chairs, several with later blocks, restored.
£12,000–14,000 *C*

A late George III leather covered mahogany hall porter's chair, c1810.
£4,000–5,000 *S*

A set of 12 Regency beechwood dining chairs, comprising 6 armchairs and 6 side chairs, restored, early 19thC.
£16,500–17,000 *S(NY)*

A set of 12 Regency mahogany dining chairs, now fitted with loose cushions, stamped 'H', mid-19thC.
£13,500–£15,000 *S(NY)*

A set of 14 mahogany dining chairs, labelled 'Jetley, 52 South Audley St, London W, and stamped '2803' and '2804'.
£18,500–20,000 *S*

A pair of George I style japanned hall chairs.
£3,000–4,000 *C*

A pair of George I burr walnut side chairs, in the manner of Giles Grendey, upholstered in needlepoint, c1725.
£100,000–120,000 *S(NY)*

A pair of George II walnut side chairs, restored, some losses, accession number '21-1939-13', c1740.
£13,500–15,000 *S(NY)*

A set of 6 George IV mahogany hall chairs, repairs to seats.
£2,000–3,000 *C*

An Anglo-Indian ivory veneered caned side chair, the pierced splat carved with dragons' heads, on cabriole legs with claw-and-ball feet, joined by a stretcher, lacking ruby inset eyes, seat damaged, accession number '52.9.193', c1770.
£42,000–45,000 *S(NY)*

A set of 5 George II mahogany side chairs, 3 stamped 'B', repaired.
£10,500–12,000 *C*

A pair of George II gilt gesso side chairs, with front legs headed by lions' masks and acanthus carving, inner frame of the seats replaced.
£65,000–70,000 *C*

r. A set of 10 Italian painted chairs, Tuscan or Piedmontese, c1785.
£18,000–22,000 *S*

Two mid-Victorian buttoned back upholstered chairs, with original white china casters, c1870.
£800–1,200 each *JC*

A set of 8 Regency satinwood, fruitwood and mahogany side chairs.
£9,000–10,000 *C*

A George II mahogany side chair, covered in associated 18thC Mortlake tapestry, on cabriole legs, with later back blocks.
£27,000–30,000 *C*

A set of 8 Louis XV beechwood chairs, by F. Geny, formerly caned, c1775.
£9,500–10,500 *S*

An Empire painted chair, made for the Palace of Fontainebleau.
£1,700–2,500 *S*

A Queen Anne walnut bachelor's chest, the hinged top enclosing a panel with a well and drawers, metalwork and feet replaced, c1710, 36½in (93cm) wide.
£4,000–5,000 *S*

A Queen Anne walnut and maple chest of drawers, 37in (94cm) wide.
£2,000–3,000 *Bon*

A George III mahogany chest, moulded top, c1770, 38½in (98cm) wide.
£4,500–5,500 *S*

A Victorian mahogany double Wellington chest, c1840, 58½in (148cm) wide.
£6,000–7,000 *S*

A George III serpentine mahogany chest, with bracket feet, c1775, 36in (91.5cm) wide.
£7,500–8,500 *P*

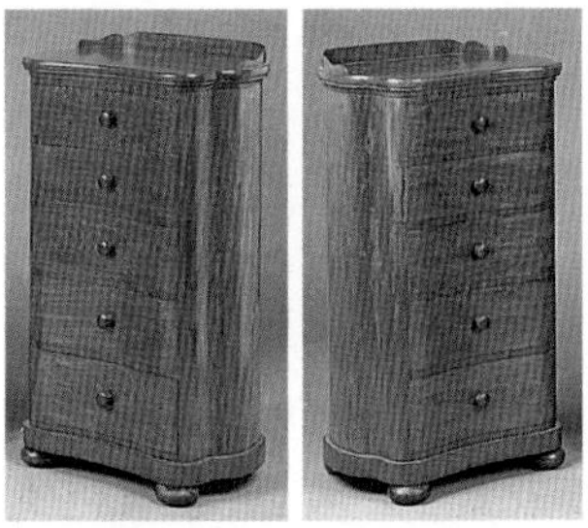

A pair of late Victorian pedestal chests, each with concave outline, undulating sides, half-galleried top, 5 drawers and bun feet, 39in (99cm) high.
£3,000–4,000 *CSK*

An early Georgian walnut tall chest, cross and feather banded overall, on later casters, 55in (139.5cm) high.
£4,700–5,200 *C*

A Queen Anne walnut chest of drawers, with crossbanded top, curvilinear inlay to drawers and top, handles and feet replaced, c1705, 38in (96.5cm) wide.
£8,000–9,000 *S*

A William and Mary inlaid burr walnut chest-on-stand, with quarter veneered crossbanded top, feather banded borders to drawers, the stand on trumpet-turned supports, c1680, 54in (137cm) high.
£8,000–10,000 *S(NY)*

An early 18thC veneered walnut and crossbanded chest-on-stand, with moulded edge top, 3 small over 3 long drawers, with brass drop handles, the later stand with a single shallow drawer flanked by deeper drawers, shaped apron and 6 turned supports, 41in (104cm) high.
£1,400–1,700 *AH*

A George III mahogany dressing chest, satinwood banded and inlaid with ebonised lines, 34in (86cm) wide.
£2,000–3,000 *C*

A walnut veneered tallboy, with chevron banded drawers, c1730, 66½in (169cm) high.
£6,500–7,500 *S*

A George III mahogany tallboy, with dentilled cornice and blind fret carved frieze, each drawer inscribed in gilt, on bracket feet, 75in (190.5cm) high.
£12,000–14,000 *C*

A George III mahogany tallboy, with sharks tooth inlay in boxwood and ebony, above an inlaid sycamore panel, 76in (193cm) high.
£2,500–3,000 *JC*

A William and Mary oyster veneered walnut chest-on-stand, c1690, 48in (122cm) high.
£10,000–12,000 *S*

A mahogany bedside cupboard, now with a leather lined panel, c1770, 21in (54cm) wide.
£1,900–2,200 *S*

A mahogany bedside cupboard, the lower part now baize lined, c1770, 20½in (52cm) wide.
£1,200–1,700 *S*

A George II mahogany linen press, with later sliding trays, carrying handles to the sides, on bracket feet, 51in (129.5cm) wide.
£2,500–3,500 *CSK*

A George II gilt decorated black japanned clothes press, attributed to Giles Grendey, the sides with later brass bail handles, c1740, 53in (183cm) wide.
£98,000–100,000 *S(NY)*

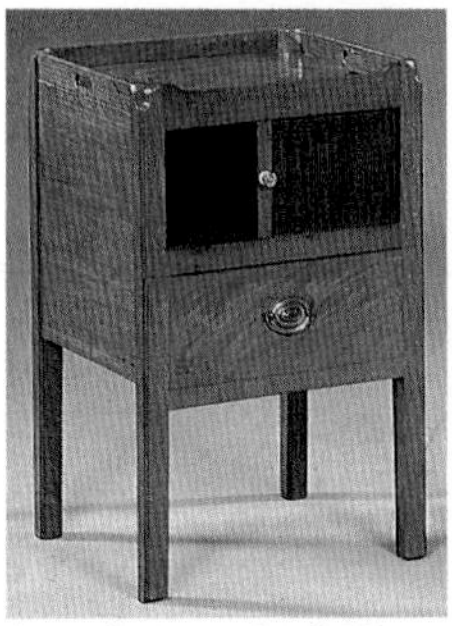

A mahogany bedside cupboard, originally with a pot, c1770, 19in (49cm) wide.
£1,400–1,700 *S*

A George III mahogany clothes press, attributed to Thomas Chippendale, 48in (122cm) wide.
£3,000–4,000 *C*

A mahogany bedside cupboard, now with leather lined panel, c1770, 21in (54cm) wide.
£1,800–2,500 *S*

Two matching mahogany dwarf wardrobes, c1800, 58in (148cm) high.
£2,000–3,000 *S*

A German parquetry armoire, with panels of Hungarian ash, surmounted by cherubs masks and flanked by pilasters, early 17thC, 83in (210.5cm) high.
£5,000–7,000 *S*

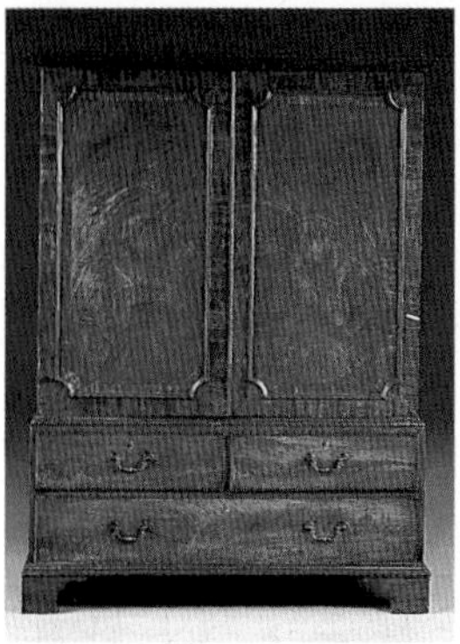

A George III mahogany linen press, the slides re-constructed, 51in (129.5cm) wide.
£3,700–4,200 *C*

A George III mahogany clothes press, drawer arrangement altered, 78in (198cm) high.
£1,200–1,700 *C*

A George III mahogany clothes press, inlaid with satinwood banding, 49in (124.5cm) wide.
£2,700–3,200 *C*

A George III mahogany linen press, with later cornice, adapted, the doors lengthened, and previously with further drawers, restored, 47½in (121cm) wide.
£300–500 *C*

A painted and parcel gilt Venetian early 18thC style wardrobe, with the Duchess of Portland's crest, English, late 19thC, 120in (306cm) wide.
£17,000–20,000 *CSK*

A Venetian painted serpentine commode, with marble top, decorated concave sides, on moulded cabriole legs, restored, c1760, 54½in (138cm) wide.
£5,000–6,000 *Bon*

A George III ormolu mounted satinwood serpentine commode, crossbanded in tulipwood and inlaid with ebonised boxwood lines, 51½in (130.5cm) wide.
£13,500–15,500 *C*

A Louis XVI tulipwood and amaranth commode, with breakfront marble top, c1785, 51½in (131cm) wide.
£8,500–12,000 *Bon*

A George III mahogany D-shaped commode, c1780, 33in (84cm) high.
£6,500–8,000 *S*

A Swedish Adolf Fredrick ormolu mounted kingwood, olivewood, amaranth and parquetry bombé commode, by Johan Gröndahl, mid-18thC, 44in (112cm) wide.
£22,000–25,000 *C*

An early Louis XV parquetry commode, attributed to Charles Cressent or Antoine Gaudreaus, with brèche d'Aleps marble top, c1740, 58½in (148cm) wide.
£180,000–200,000 *S*

A kingwood and marquetry bombé commode, 31in (79cm) wide.
£1,000–1,500 *CSK*

A Victorian burr walnut veneered and inlaid davenport, 22in (56cm) wide.
£1,000–1,500 *MAT*

Cabinets-on-Chests

A George II mahogany cabinet-on-chest, the top above a pair of panelled doors enclosing a slide, the lower section with a long drawer above 6 short drawers flanking a cupboard, on bracket feet, the top and base associated, the base extended in depth to accommodate the top, 47in (120cm).
£2,200–2,700 *C*

This cabinet-on-chest is a 'marriage' between a batchelor's chest and a clothes press.

A walnut and feather strung cabinet-on-chest, the upper part with a cushion frieze drawer and 11 drawers around a central enclosed compartment concealing 3 further drawers, all enclosed by a pair of panelled doors, on bracket feet, part early 18thC, 38in (96.5cm).
£3,000–4,000 *CSK*

An Anglo-Indian hardwood military cabinet-on-chest, in 3 sections, the upper part carved profusely with floral decoration and enclosed by a pair of arched glazed doors, above 2 short and 3 long drawers, cabochon carved apron, on turned feet, late 19thC, 36in (92cm) wide.
£1,000–1,500 *CSK*

Did you know?
MILLER'S* Antiques Price Guide *builds up year-by-year to form the most comprehensive antiques photo-reference library available.

r. A Dutch walnut floral marquetry display cabinet-on-chest, with velvet lined interior, pierced brass neo-classical handles and escutcheons, the deep shaped apron centred by an urn, inlaid throughout with flower trails, the side panels with flower-filled urns, on bold claw-and-ball feet, mid-18thC, marquetry 19thC, 41in (104cm).
£4,000–5,000 *N*

Cabinets-on-Stands

A William and Mary walnut and oyster olivewood cabinet on a later stand, the interior with 10 drawers around a central cupboard enclosing further drawers, the stand with spiral turned legs and stretchers, the latter centred with a finial, on turned legs, 43in (108cm).
£2,000–2,500 *P*

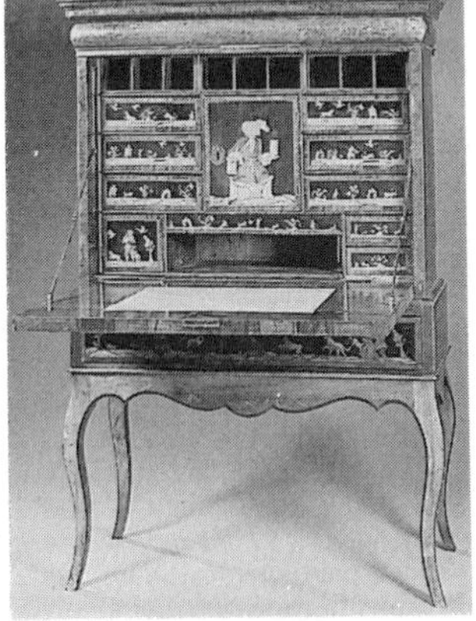

A walnut and pictorial marquetry cabinet-on-stand, with waved apron and cabriole legs, early 18thC and later, 42in (108cm).
£3,000–4,000 *C*

r. A black lacquered cabinet on giltwood and gesso stand, raised on paw feet, late 17thC, 42in (106.5cm).
£5,000–7,000 *HOLL*

A George II black japanned cabinet-on-stand, with a pair of doors decorated with Chinese buildings and figures, enclosing an interior with small drawers, veneered in purple heart and crossbanded, on a japanned stand with pivoted brackets, on square chamfered legs, 50in (127cm) high.
£2,000–3,000 *DN*

A late Victorian mahogany cabinet, with moulded cornice above a pair of glazed panelled doors, on slender scrolling claw-and-ball feet, 42in (106.5cm).
£850–1,000 *AG*

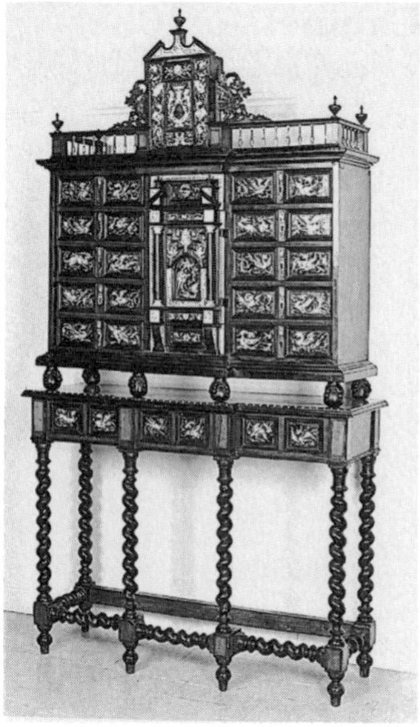

A Spanish cabinet-on-stand, veneered in walnut, rosewood and amboyna, with numerous front panels of bone and tortoiseshell marquetry, the matching base with twist-turned frame, 48in (122cm).
£6,500–7,000 *RBB*

Display Cabinets

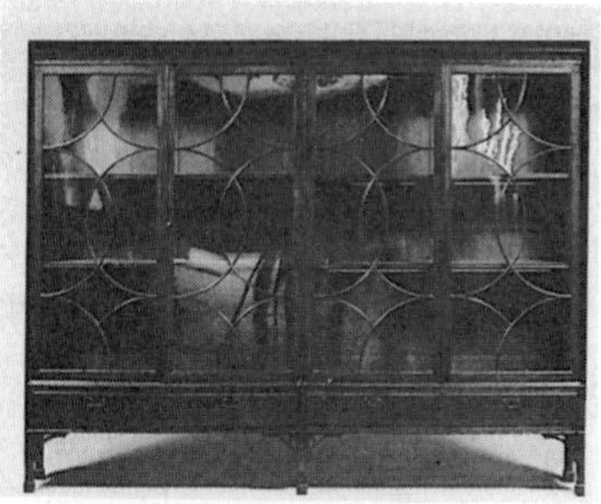

A George III style mahogany library cabinet, with moulded cornice over 4 mullion glazed doors, raised on a stand with 4 aligned fluted drawers, on block legs and feet, 19thC, 96in (243.5cm) wide.
£1,000–1,500 *LHA*

A George III style mahogany display cabinet, with pierced swan neck pediment above a pair of astragal glazed doors, raised on a stand with 2 small drawers and square tapering fluted legs, 96in (243.5cm) high.
£1,200–1,700 *DN*

A William IV mahogany breakfront display cabinet, on plinth base, 56in (142cm).
£1,200–1,700 *CSK*

l. A Georgian style mahogany display cabinet, with moulded cornice above 2 pairs of glazed panelled doors, enclosing mirror backed adjustable shelves, raised on a plinth base, 42½in (107cm).
£1,400–1,600 *AG*

An ebonised and brass display cabinet, on fluted tapering legs, 19thC, 42½in (108cm).
£800–1,000 *DN*

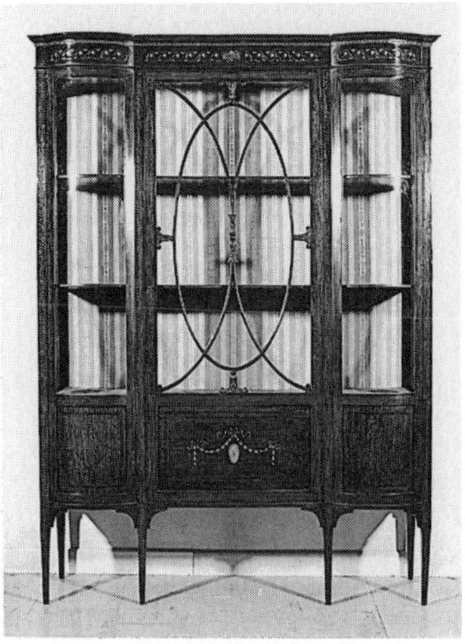

An Edwardian mahogany display cabinet, with inlaid floral and scroll decoration, on squared tapering supports, 56in (142cm) wide.
£1,500–2,000 *RBB*

A Continental mahogany cabinet, 19thC, 48in (122cm).
£1,200–1,700 *MAT*

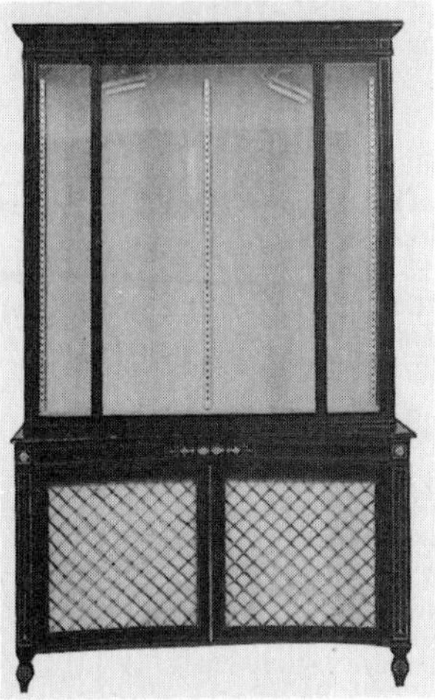

r. A Regency style ebonised wood and brass inlaid cabinet, with projecting moulded cornice above a glass cabinet door, revealing shelves, on an in-curving lower case inlaid with anthemion and paterae, over cupboard doors with brass trelliswork, on square tapering feet, 56in (142cm) wide.
£1,000–1,500 *LHA*

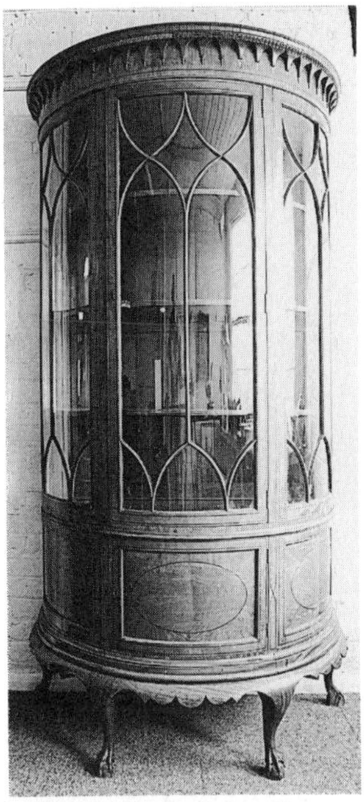

An Edwardian satinwood bowfront display cabinet, on cabriole supports with claw-and-ball feet, slight damage, 42in (106.5cm) wide.
£1,900–2,300 *CAG*

Miller's is a price GUIDE not a price LIST

An Edwardian mahogany breakfront display cabinet, with a moulded cornice above a glazed door, flanked by glazed sides, on square tapering legs with a platform stretcher, inlaid with boxwood lines throughout, 44½in (113cm) wide.
£400–600 *DN*

An Edwardian mahogany display cabinet, decorated with inlaid satinwood crossbanding, boxwood stringing and acanthus scrolls, raised on splay legs, 30in (77cm).
£2,200–2,700 *AG*

A French kingwood and ormolu mounted vitrine, with arched and moulded crest, the serpentine front with a central glazed door enclosing shelving, depicting 18thC figures in a pastoral setting, over Vernis Martin panels, shaped apron, and splayed feet, 19thC, 61in (155cm) wide.
£3,200–3,700 *AH*

Vernis Martin

Vernis Martin is the generic term used to describe the lacquers and varnishes used for decoration on furniture and French clocks made during the 18thC and 19thC.

It takes its name from the Martin brothers who, in 1730, were permitted to copy Japanese lacquer. It is found in many colours, but especially green.

A Napoleon III ebonised and gilt bronze mounted vitrine, on fluted tapering legs joined by a stretcher, marble top missing, 25in (63cm).
£4,500–5,000 *LHA*

An American carved and incised mahogany corner cabinet, 51in (129.5cm) wide.
£800–1,200 *SLN*

A French mahogany veneered half vitrine, with inlaid stringing, gilt bronze mounts and brass mouldings, the serpentine base with a drawer, gilt bronze rococo handles and mounts, on cabriole legs, 43in (109cm).
£5,200–5,700 *WW*

l. A Dutch oak display cabinet, veneered in walnut, with arched pediment, two glazed astragel doors and cushion frieze drawer.
£1,600–1,800 *DN*

In the Furniture section when there is only one measurement it refers to the width of the piece, unless otherwise stated.

Side Cabinets

A rosewood dwarf side cabinet, with a bead decorated edge, enclosed by 3 doors, with gros point needlework floral and scroll panels, between lotus carved stiles, on a plinth base, restored, 19thC, 78in (198cm).
£1,800–2,500 *CSK*

A Regency mahogany side cabinet, with pierced brass gallery, a pair of flame figured panelled doors with applied reeded mouldings and brass mounts, flanked by a pair of fluted tapering columns on baluster turned supports, 50in (127cm).
£6,200–6,800 *RBB*

A walnut marquetry and gilt metal mounted dwarf side cabinet, on turned feet, adapted, 19thC, 38½in (98cm).
£3,500–4,000 *CSK*

A walnut, tulipwood banded and gilt metal mounted dwarf cabinet, decorated with marquetry foliate scrolls between stiles, with Sèvres style floral plaques, on a shaped plinth base, stamped 'Wilkinson & Son, 8 Old Bond Street 10134', 19thC, 33in (83cm).
£1,600–2,000 *CSK*

A Victorian ebonised side cabinet, with boulle inlay, enclosing a single shelf, with ormulu cherub mounts, on a plinth base, 35in (89cm) wide.
£500–600 *WL*

A Victorian walnut breakfront side cabinet, with a pair of panelled doors enclosing small specimen drawers, flanked by shelves and barley-twist supports, on shaped plinth, 72in (182.5cm) wide.
£1,000–1,500 *DN*

A mahogany concave front cabinet, on turned and reeded legs with brass caps and casters, 19thC, 46½in (118cm).
£2,000–2,500 *CSK*

A Regency rosewood parcel gilt side cabinet, the raised mirror back with Carrara marble top on turned supports, open shelves and mirror back below, flanked by turned partly reeded columns, raised on a plinth base, 41in (104cm) wide.
£3,500–4,000 *AG*

l. A mid-Victorian rosewood serpentine dwarf side cabinet, on plinth, some veneer missing, 60in (153cm) wide.
£800–1,200 *CSK*

A mid-Victorian ebonised D-shaped side cabinet, applied with brass mouldings and agate insets, the frieze and central door inlaid with ivory and boxwood in Italian Mannerist style, a bowed glazed door and freestanding columns to each side, on a shaped plinth, 66in (167.5cm).
£1,000–1,500 *Bea*

A French mahogany chiffonier, the raised back with central armorial cresting surmounted by a coronet flanked by 2 carved foliate scrolling panels, with 2 shelves below, on carved and swagged scrolling supports, the top with a gadrooned border, 19thC, 63½in (161cm).
£1,800–2,200 *CSK*

A Victorian burr walnut credenza, with raised mirror back decorated with fruiting vines, the serpentine grey marble top above a central glazed panel door, decorated with fret carved brackets and applied fruiting vines, flowerheads and scrolls, flanked by a pair of glazed panelled doors enclosing shelves, raised on a serpentine-shaped base, with bun feet, 60in (152cm).
£2,000–2,500 *AG*

A mid-Victorian satin birch side cabinet, attributed to Holland & Sons, the lock stamped 'Hart & Son, London', 86½in (220cm).
£2,000–2,500 *CSK*

Chiffonier

A chiffonier is a low or side cabinet, with or without a drawer, with one or more shelves above.

Original 18thC pieces had solid doors which were often replaced in the 19thC with lattice or glass doors.

A William IV rosewood veneered chiffonier, the raised superstructure with a mirror back, a shelf with a pediment and leaf carved front pillars, the front with a roundel decorated frieze, a pair of domed glazed doors with pleated material behind, enclosing 2 shelves, leaf scroll capped side pilasters, on a plinth, 44in (111.5cm).
£1,200–1,700 *WW*

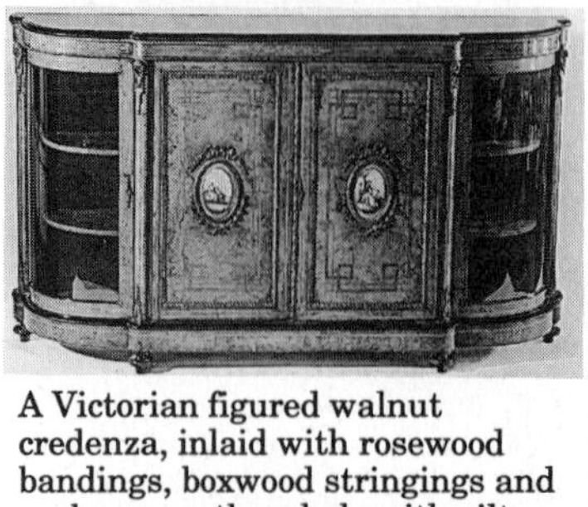

A Victorian figured walnut credenza, inlaid with rosewood bandings, boxwood stringings and arabesques, the whole with gilt metal mounts and mouldings, the panels with oval Sèvres style porcelain plaques painted with 'Lovers in a Garden' scenes within gilt metal wreathed ribbon pattern mounts, flanked by bowfronted display shelves, on turned feet, 72in (182.5cm).
£3,000–3,500 *CAG*

A French side cabinet, veneered in figured walnut, the top with a gilt bronze gallery, gilt bronze mounts to a central mirror door enclosing two shelves, on a shaped plinth, mid-19thC, 51in (129.5cm).
£2,700–3,200 *WW*

An early Victorian mahogany chiffonier, fitted with a cushion frieze drawer, a pair of recessed arched panelled doors below flanked by fluted stiles, on turned feet, 36in (91.5cm).
£750–1,000 *CSK*

A Victorian ebonised credenza, with boulle decoration and ormolu mounts, 48in (122cm).
£3,000–3,500 *BWe*

Credenza

- Side cabinets are often known as credenzas.
- A credenza normally implies a more ornate piece, in French or Italian style, which were very popular with the Victorians.
- Over-elaborate decoration or poor craftsmanship decrease their desirability.
- Serpentine shaped front and sides are always good features.

Canterburies

A George IV mahogany four-division canterbury, with central cut-out carrying handle, fitted drawer below, raised on turned tapering legs and brass casters, 18in (45.5cm).
£1,000–1,200 *AG*

A Regency mahogany four-division canterbury, the open compartments above a frieze drawer, on turned legs, restored, the drawers stamped 'J. Scott', 20in (51cm).
£800–1,200 *CSK*

A late Regency three-division canterbury, the dished slatted compartments with turned corner columns and an apron drawer below, on turned legs, brass cappings and casters, 19in (48cm).
£800–1,000 *P*

A Regency rosewood three-division canterbury, with carved and shaped rails, the base with a single drawer, on scrolled feet and small brass casters, 25in (65cm).
£1,200–1,700 *WL*

Canterburies

- A canterbury is movable item usually used for sheet music.
- Victorian examples with good carving fetch more than the earlier examples.
- Elegance is one of the major criteria in this small, expensive piece of furniture.

An early Victorian rosewood canterbury, with 3 open sections and wheel decoration, a fitted single drawer to the base, raised on turned tapering feet, 20½in (52cm).
£1,000–1,200 *AG*

A Victorian walnut canterbury, c1860, 26in (66cm).
£2,000–2,250 *GJC*

A Regency mahogany four-division canterbury, with a frieze drawer, on ring-turned tapering legs, 18in (46cm).
£700–1,000 *CSK*

An early Victorian mahogany canterbury, the slatted open compartments above a single drawer, on ring-turned legs, 22in (56cm).
£800–1,200 *CSK*

A Victorian burr walnut music canterbury, the straight top with spiral, ball turned and lyre shaped supports above one drawer, on turned feet with casters, 21in (53.5cm).
£950–1,200 *DN*

Open Armchairs

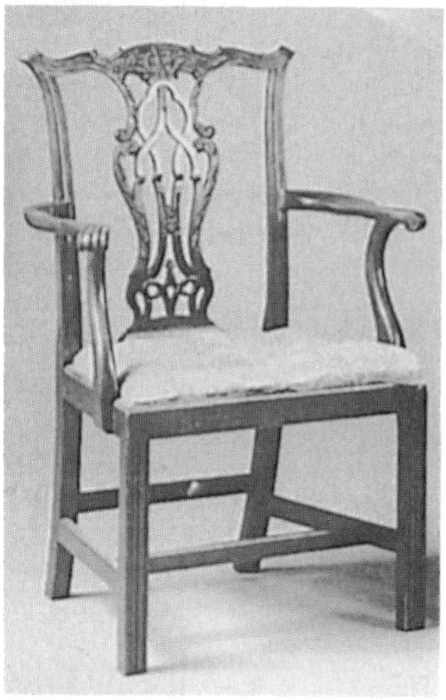

A George II style mahogany open armchair, the serpentine top rail above a pierced vase-shaped splat, flanked by outswept arms with scrolling terminals, the drop-in seat above square chamfered legs.
£300–400 *CSK*

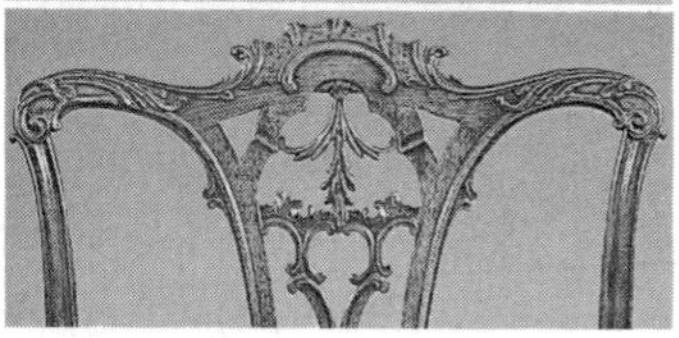

A George II mahogany armchair, with acanthus leaf and scroll carved top rail, a moulded, pierced scroll and leaf carved splat within moulded uprights, the shaped arms with cabochon carved handles and moulded supports, the padded seat with leaf and scroll carved aprons, on cabriole legs carved with leaves, flowers and scrolls on claw-and-ball feet, c1755.
£23,000–27,000 *S*

This armchair forms part of a distinguised and much published group. A very similar armchair, evidently by the same maker, is in the Untermyer Collection at the Metropolitan Museum of Art, New York.

A pair of George II mahogany cypher back armchairs, each with an elaborate splat interlaced with initials and reeded supports, the serpentine stuffed nailed leather seats on reeded cabriole legs with curved X-shaped stretches and scroll feet, c1755.
£123,000–125,000 *S*

These remarkable armchairs are of quite outstanding quality, distinguished by their superb colour and patination, their rarity and elegance of design, and a history which links them to a noted poet and a great British institution.

The splats of the chairs are carved with Cawthorne's own cypher, the initials 'JC'. Chairs of this kind, known originally as cypher back chairs, are of quite exceptional rarity. The cypher back chair enjoyed a brief vogue in England in the 1750s and 1760s and only a few examples are known to survive. This set is among the largest and finest in existence.

The chairs formed part of the historic furnishings of Tonbridge School, Kent, originally founded in the reign of Edward VI. They have remained at the school for almost 250 years, and were originally commissioned by the Rev. James Cawthorne, poet, scholar and Headmaster of Tonbridge from 1743–61.

A George III mahogany open armchair, covered in floral patterned green silk, on beaded fluted turned tapering legs and foliate carved ring turned feet.
£1,500–2,000 *C*

Miller's is a price GUIDE not a price LIST

A George III mahogany library armchair, the padded back, arms and seat covered in calico, on square chamfered legs.
£5,000–5,500 *C*

A George III armchair, in the neo-classical form, painted in duck egg blue and parcel gilt, the seat with two inverted insertions to the rear, c1775.
£3,000–3,500 *B*

A late George III mahogany armchair, with floral gros point needlework padded seat, on reeded turned tapering legs.
£400–500 *CSK*

A George III cream painted beechwood shield back armchair, in the Hepplewhite style.
£1,500–2,000 *CAG*

Whilst the decoration is somewhat rubbed in places it appears to be original and the construction method indicates a date of c1790.

Parts of a Chair

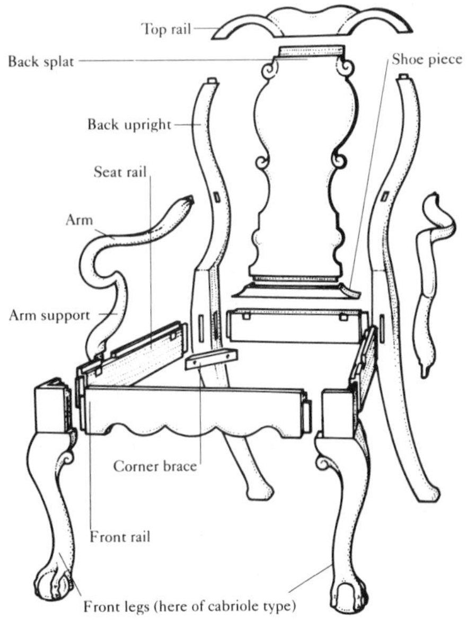

A George IV recumbent library armchair, the mahogany frame upholstered in leather with brass nails, on tulip petal carved turned front legs with brass casters, with a pull-out foot rest on a ratchet with turned legs, stamped 'R. Davis', followed by 'N.B.' G R patent, the underside with a trade label '17 Margaret Street, Cavendish Square, London'.
£5,000–5,500 *WW*

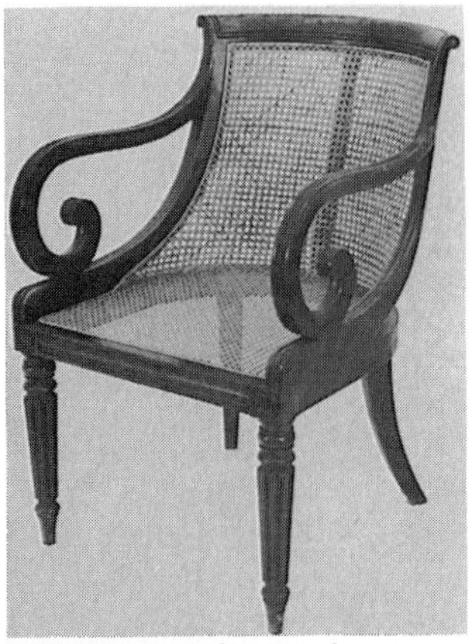

A Regency mahogany bergère chair, the spoon-shaped back with a scrolled top rail, reeded scrolled arms, caned seat, squab cushion, on turned lobed tapering legs.
£1,700–2,000 *L*

A mahogany reclining chair, with a padded hinged back, arms and seat, on turned legs, early 19thC.
£800–900 *DN*

A set of 4 Regency style mahogany open armchairs, each with spiral twist top rail, brass inlaid tablet, overswept arms, caned seat, on sabre legs, damaged.
£600–700 *CSK*

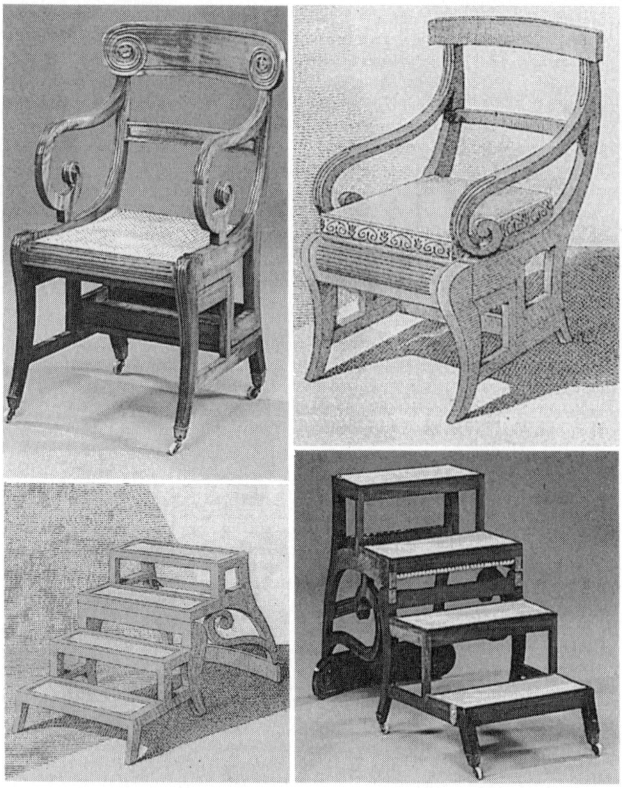

A Regency mahogany metamorphic armchair, in the manner of Morgan & Sanders, the curved top rail carved with paterae filled scrolls, the reeded frame with scroll arms, caned seat and sabre legs, opening to form 4 treads, c1815.
£9,000–12,000 *S*

The Regency period saw a particular fashion for furniture combining 2 or more functions. Known as 'patent metamorphic', or more simply 'metamorphic' furniture, pieces of this kind included a whole range of ingenious space saving features.

Metamorphic furniture had been known since the early 18thC, but from the turn of the 19thC pieces of this kind were produced in ever-growing numbers. The most popular model was the 'Patent Metamorphic Library Chair'. The chair tilts back on hinges to form a set of library steps and follows a pattern first introduced through a published design in Ackermann's Repository of the Arts *in July 1811. The design was credited to Morgan & Sanders, a major firm of Regency cabinet makers with extensive premises in Catherine Street, London.*

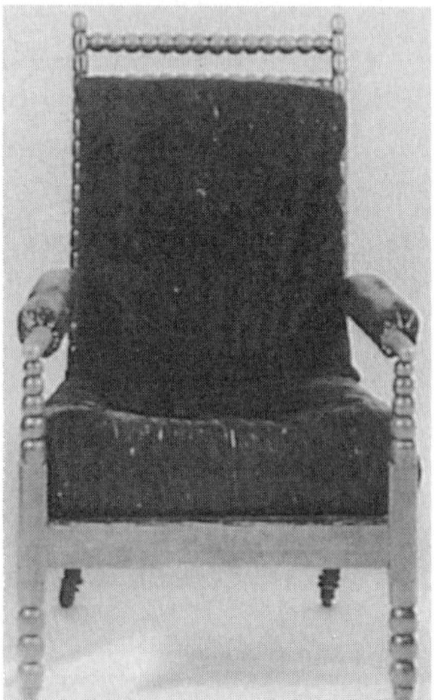

A George IV simulated rosewood, bobbin-turned armchair, with tapered turnings, vertical splats, padded arms and seat with cushion, on casters.
£500–600 *CSK*

A William IV mahogany armchair, the padded back within a moulded frame, padded elbow rests and scroll arms, on reeded legs.
£1,300–1,600 *DN*

A William IV mahogany open armchair, the arms carved with grotesque masks, strapwork and C-scrolls, on lambrequin headed monopodiae, possibly Irish.
£2,500–3,000 *C*

In the Furniture section when there is only one measurement it refers to the width of the piece, unless otherwise stated.

r. An early Victorian mahogany library armchair, on turned tapered legs with brass caps and casters.
£1,400–1,800 *CSK*

An early Victorian walnut armchair, with an elaborate leaf carved, pierced and scrolled top rail, padded back arms and seat, on turned leaf carved legs.
£500–700 *DN*

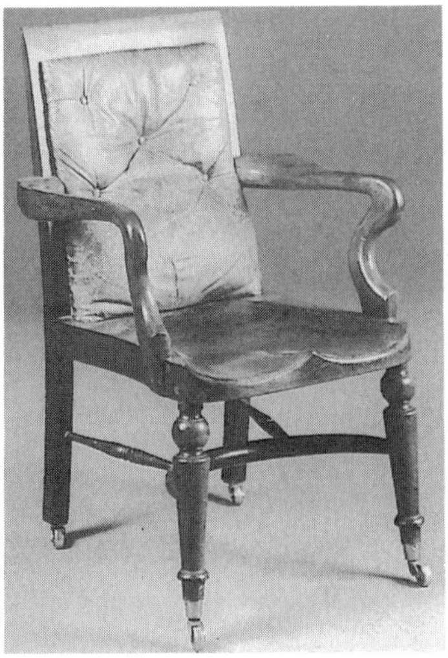

An early Victorian mahogany library chair, with a buttoned leather upholstered panelled back, scroll arm supports and shaped solid seat, on ring turned tapered legs joined by a crinoline stretcher terminating in brass cappings and casters, with a part label 'R. T. Rough, late Thos. Paul & Co. ...binet Maker and Upholstery, 5 Ludgate Hill, London', the cappings stamped 'Cope & Collinson Patent'.
£700–900 *CSK*

A bill of sale dated 1857 survives from this little known cabinet maker.

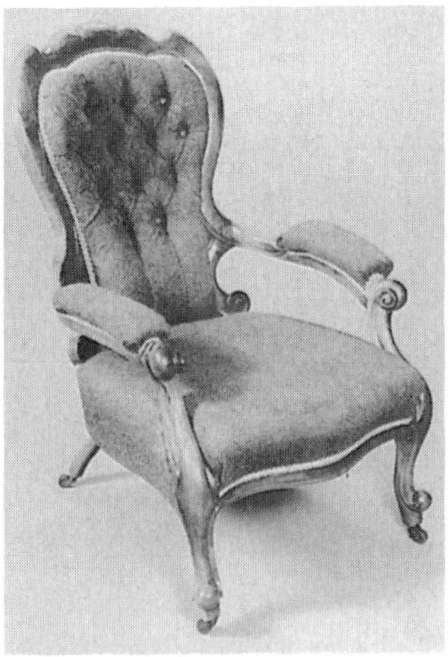

A Victorian walnut drawing room suite, comprising a chaise longue, an armchair and another chair, each with a shaped moulded frame, on cabriole legs.
£1,000–1,400 *DN*

Chair Seats

Seat rails are usually made in beech and are tenoned into the legs of the chair. Until c1840–50, corner braces were added for extra strength *(top)*. These fitted into slots in the seat rails and were simply glued. After c1840–50 corner brackets were used *(bottom)*. These were glued and screwed into the angle of the rails.

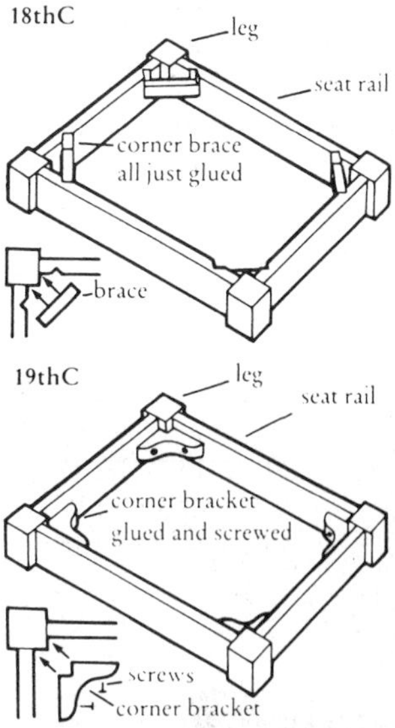

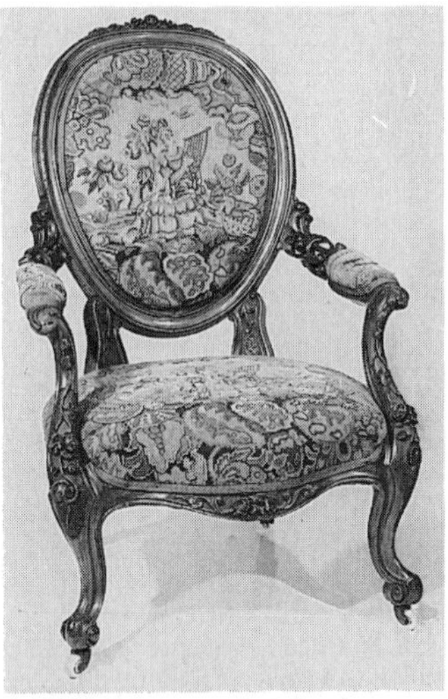

A Victorian carved walnut gentlemen's elbow chair, with flower carved crest on upholstered shield-shaped back, padded arms, overstuffed seat, carved frieze, cabriole legs with scrolled feet and china casters.
£1,200–1,400 *AH*

A Victorian walnut chair, on turned legs and casters.
£400–600 *DN*

A Victorian carved walnut open armchair.
£600–800 *DaD*

A pair of Victorian walnut spoon back salon chairs, with carved show frames and cabriole supports with casters, one with arms.
£800–900 *Bri*

A set of 14 Victorian walnut chairs, including 2 armchairs, each with a scoop back and padded embossed leather seat, on cabriole legs.
£3,000–4,000 *DN*

A Victorian lady's chair.
£700–900 *AH*

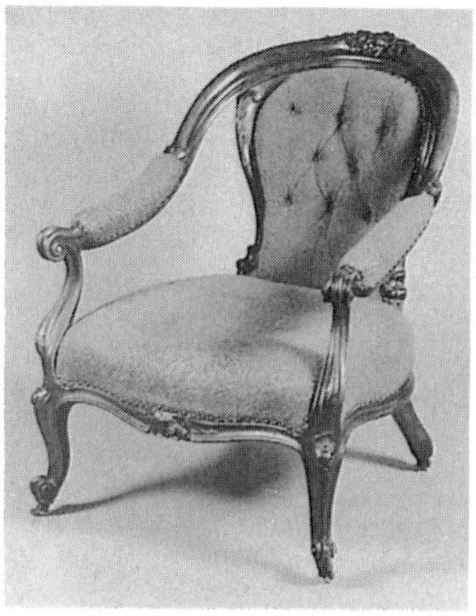

A Victorian rosewood armchair, with padded back within a moulded frame carved with flowerheads, a padded seat and elbow rests, on moulded cabriole legs.
£850–1,000 *DN*

A mid-Victorian walnut open armchair, on foliate headed cabriole legs with scroll feet.
£550–700 *CSK*

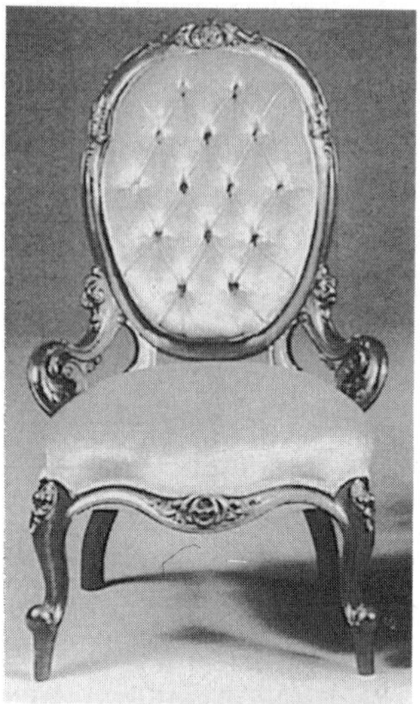

A mid-Victorian lady's walnut chair, the buttoned padded oval back with an interlaced foliate scroll cresting and pierced scroll supports, padded serpentine seat, on cabriole legs.
£600–700 *CSK*

A late Victorian ebonised armchair, with fluted mouldings, a close nailed leather top rail, arm supports and seat, on ring turned legs with casters, possibly an exercise chair.
£400–600 *CSK*

A German walnut library armchair, the arched padded back and arms with bold foliate terminals, above a padded seat and octagonal tapered legs, mid-19thC, later reading stand.
£800–1,200 *CSK*

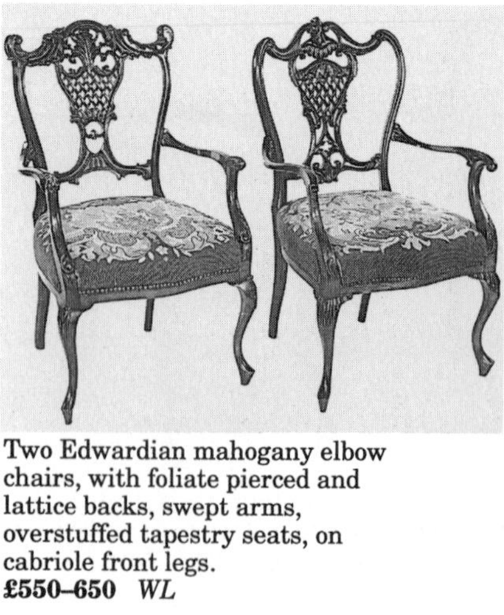

Two Edwardian mahogany elbow chairs, with foliate pierced and lattice backs, swept arms, overstuffed tapestry seats, on cabriole front legs.
£550–650 *WL*

A pair of Louis XVI carved beechwood fauteuils, re-toed.
£1,200–1,400 *CSK*

A set of 4 Italian rococo walnut armchairs, each with cartouche shaped backrest and patera carved crestrail, the moulded arms and serpentine seat raised on cabriole legs, minor repairs, c1760.
£3,500–4,800 *LHA*

A pair of stained beech framed open armchairs, on fluted tapering square legs, possibly Italian, late 18thC.
£1,500–2,000 *Bea*

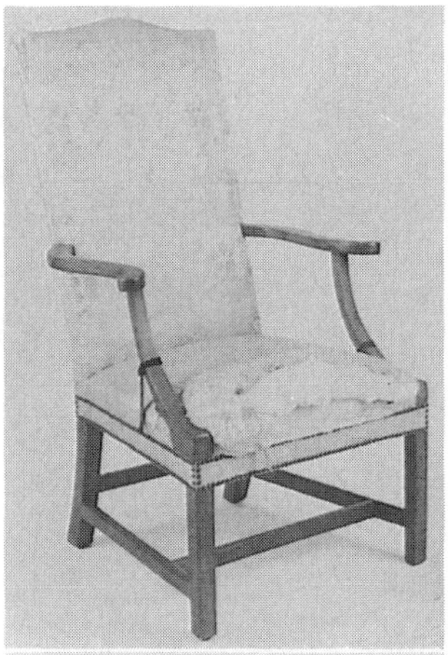

A mahogany inlaid open arm lolling chair, bears label 'Joseph Short', Newburyport, Massachusetts, slight damage, c1790, 44½in (113cm) high.
£17,000–18,000 *SK(B)*

Joseph Short (1771–1819) was a Newburyport cabinet maker.

Upholstered Armchairs

l. A William and Mary walnut high back armchair, now upholstered in brown velvet.
£1,700–2,000 *B*

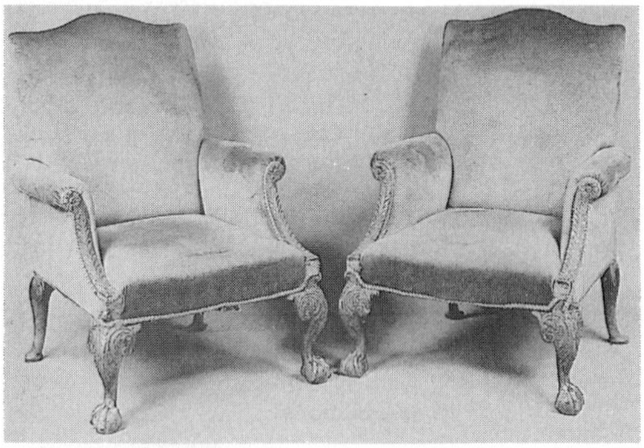

A pair of George II style mahogany armchairs, with padded serpentine backs, outswept arms and padded seats, foliate carved decoration to the arms, on cabriole legs terminating in claw-and-ball feet.
£1,500–2,000 *P*

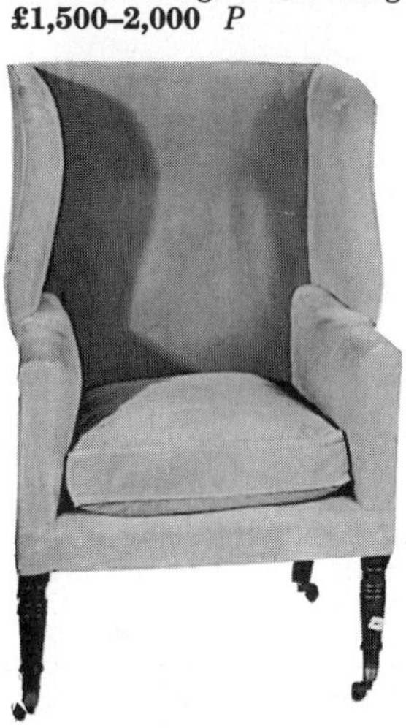

l. A George III mahogany wing armchair, upholstered in pale yellow velvet, the seat with a separate cushion, on ring turned tapering legs with brass box casters.
£1,200–1,500 *L&E*

A William IV mahogany library armchair, with a padded scoop back, the arms terminating in patera and scrolls, carved with stylised tulips, on turned reeded legs.
£3,500–4,000 *DN*

A Victorian rosewood armchair, with a scoop back, moulded frame and scroll arms, on moulded cabriole legs.
£900–1,200 *DN*

A late Victorian easy armchair, upholstered in green silk damask, with squab cushion, on ring turned legs, stamped 'Howard & Sons, Ltd., Berners Street, No. 1619969085i'.
£1,400–1,700 *CSK*

A pair of Louis XVI style white painted armchairs, each with arched padded back and foliate cresting flanked by pineapple finials, above padded arms with foliate terminals, squab seats and fluted tapering legs headed with rosettes.
£700–800 *CSK*

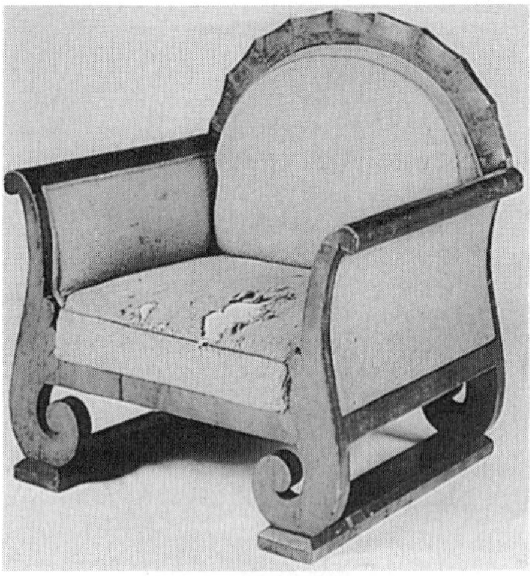

A Central European line inlaid walnut veneered three-piece suite, including 2 easy armchairs, with arched padded back and outswept arms, on scroll legs, and a matching sofa, 78in (198cm) wide.
£1,100–1,700 *CSK*

Bergère Chairs

A pair of Louis XV style mahogany bergères, each with an arched floral carved crest above a curved silk upholstered back and seat, on cabriole legs.
£2,250–2,750 *LHA*

A late George III mahogany framed bergère chair, with low moulded back inset with a cane panel, the drop-in seat upholstered in hide, on square moulded sabre front legs, with brass toes and casters.
£1,000–1,200 *CAG*

A Regency simulated rosewood and brass mounted bergère armchair, with inlaid horseshoe-shaped back rail, downswept arms with spherical finials, on downswept legs and casters.
£900–1,000 *CSK*

Bergère Chairs

Bergère, is the French name for an upholstered armchair with a rounded back and wide seat, differing from other armchairs in that it is upholstered between the arms and seat. These chairs were first made c1725 in France and soon after in other European countries. In England the term is applied to chairs with caned backs and sides.

A Regency mahogany bergère chair, the reeded curved scrolled top rail centred by a scroll and husk motif, with caned back and seat, on turned reeded tapering legs.
£1,500–1,700 *C*

A William IV walnut bergère chair, with a cane panel arched back, foliate scroll arms, serpentine seat, on acanthus carved turned tapering legs, with brass caps and casters.
£1,000–1,200 *CSK*

Children's Chairs

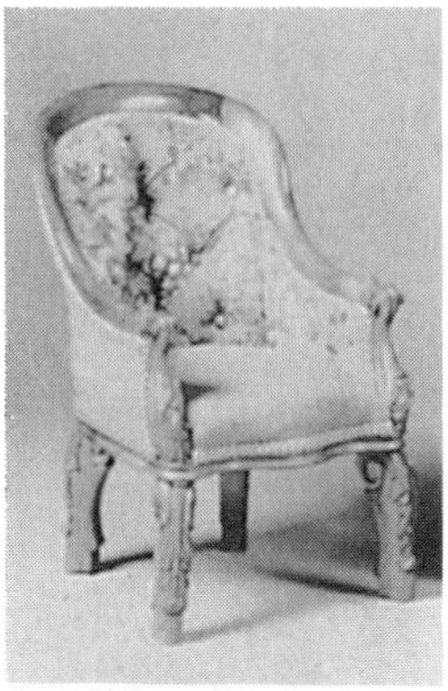

A child's walnut tub chair, the horseshoe shaped button back with scrolling terminals, serpentine padded seat and foliate carved legs, altered, 19thC.
£270–320 *CSK*

A set of 4 French children's walnut chairs, each with a gros point needlework padded arched back, on stylised lotus carved cabriole legs.
£250–300 *CSK*

A child's walnut fauteuil, in the Louis XV style, the cartouche shaped caned panel back with floral cresting, padded scroll arm supports, serpentine seat, on cabriole legs.
£200–250 *CSK*

Dining Chairs

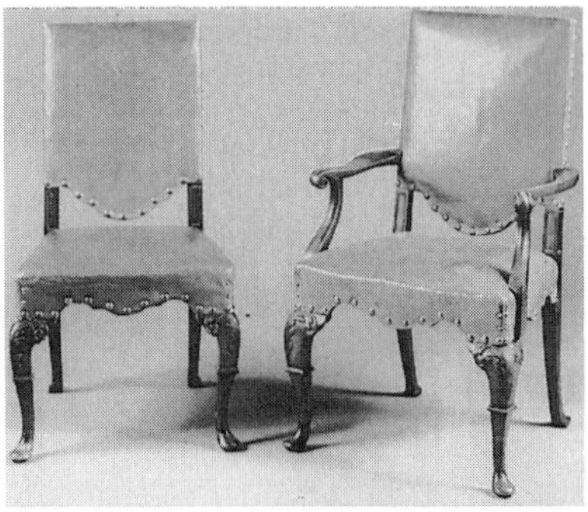

A set of 8 Queen Anne style beechwood dining chairs, 2 with arms, each with brass studded yellow leather back and seat, on foliate capped cabriole legs and pad feet.
£2,000–2,500 *CSK*

A pair of George I walnut ladderback dining chairs, with drop-in seats.
£1,000–1,200 *CSK*

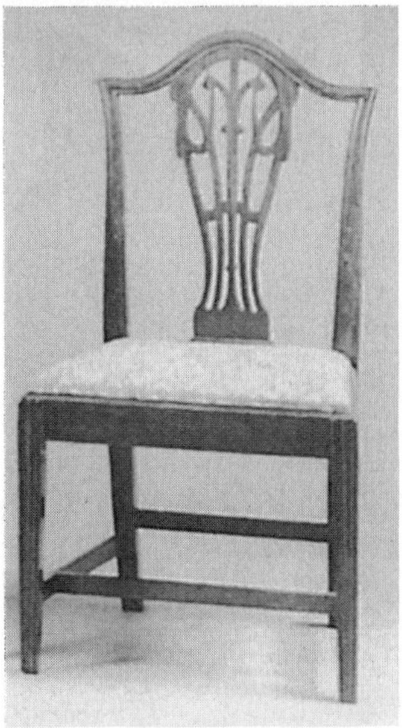

A set of 6 George III mahogany dining chairs, each with arched back and pierced vase splat, drop-in seat and square moulded tapering legs joined by stretchers.
£1,500–2,000 *CSK*

A set of 8 George III mahogany dining chairs.
£4,400–4,800 *DaD*

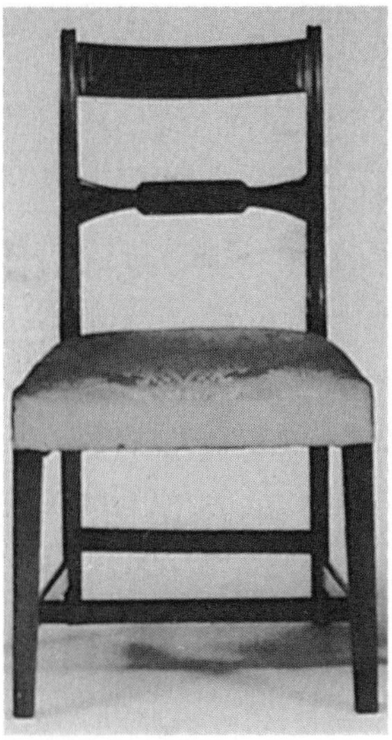

A set of 6 Provincial mahogany dining chairs, including one armchair, with replacements and restorations, early 19thC.
£1,200–1,800 *CSK*

A set of 8 Hepplewhite dining chairs, including 2 carvers, 19thC.
£3,000–3,850 *SUL*

A set of 12 mahogany dining chairs, with H-stretchers, comprising a pair of carver armchairs and 10 side chairs, some repairs, early 19thC.
£8,700–9,200 *WW*

Make the most of Miller's

Unless otherwise stated, any description which refers to 'a set' or 'a pair' includes a price guide for the entire set or the pair, even though the illustration may show only a single item.

A set of 10 George III style mahogany dining chairs, including 2 armchairs, each with a paper scroll rail and pierced splat, padded seats, on square moulded legs.
£1,600–2,000 *DN*

A set of 8 George III mahogany dining chairs including 2 armchairs, with stick backs, padded seats, on square tapering legs, some restoration.
£2,000–3,000 *DN*

l. A set of 8 George III style mahogany dining chairs, including 2 armchairs, each with an urn and Prince of Wales' feathers splat, drop-in seat, on moulded square legs.
£800–1,200 *DN*

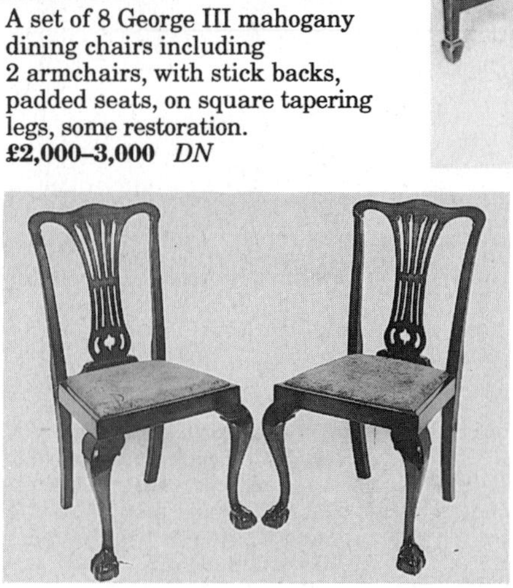

l. A set of 6 George III style mahogany dining chairs.
£650–750 *DaD*

A set of 8 George III style mahogany dining chairs, including a pair of armchairs, some stamped 'Hassan'.
£2,000–2,500 *CSK*

A set of 8 George III style mahogany dining chairs, each with bellflower decorated undulating top rail, pierced vase splat with central ribbon tie, above drop-in seats, on chamfered square legs joined by stretchers, repaired.
£2,000–2,500 *CSK*

A set of 8 mid-Georgian Chippendale style mahogany dining chairs, comprising 2 carvers and 6 standard chairs, overstuffed seats covered in brocade, on square chamfered legs, joined by square stretchers.
£7,500–8,000 *L&E*

A set of 6 George III style mahogany dining chairs, including 2 armchairs, each with a shield-shaped back with floral carved decoration, on square channelled legs joined by a stretcher, 19thC.
£1,600–2,000 *CSK*

A set of 8 George III style mahogany dining chairs, including one armchair, each with drop-in seat, on square tapering legs.
£2,000–2,500 *DN*

Miller's is a price GUIDE not a price LIST

A set of 6 George III style mahogany dining chairs, each with a pierced over-scrolled top rail, pierced vase splat, drop-in seat, on square chamfered legs joined by stretchers, 19thC.
£2,000–3,000 *CSK*

A set of 6 George III dining chairs, each with a shaped pierced splat, with padded seats, on square chamfered legs.
£3,500–4,000 *DN*

A set of 8 George III style walnut dining chairs, including two open armchairs.
£1,800–2,500 *CSK*

A set of 8 late George III mahogany dining chairs, with square shaped backs and pierced tapering splats, upholstered seats, raised on square tapering legs with spade feet.
£2,100–2,700 *AG*

A set of 16 George III mahogany dining chairs, including 2 armchairs.
£1,800–2,200 *L*

A set of 6 late George III mahogany dining chairs, including one armchair, with scroll arms, the seats upholstered in vinyl, on turned front legs.
£1,600–1,800 *CAG*

A set of 9 Georgian mahogany dining chairs, and 3 chairs of similar design, with moulded front legs and pierced stretchers, restored and re-railed.
£4,700–5,200 *CSK*

A set of 6 George IV mahogany dining chairs, including 2 armchairs, each with a shaped rail and anthemion splat, padded seats, on square moulded legs.
£1,700–2,000 *DN*

A set of 6 Regency rosewood dining chairs, including one armchair, the rectangular back rails with scrolling motifs and inlaid brass scrolling panels, the pierced horizontal splats with brass inlaid central entablature, with canework seats and squab cushions, on sabre legs.
£4,500–5,000 *AG*

A set of 6 Regency simulated rosewood dining chairs, with cane seats, loose squab cushions, on sabre legs, restored.
£2,000–3,000 *Bea*

A set of 6 Regency mahogany dining chairs, including a pair of carver chairs with scroll arms, the backs with veneered crests, pierced and reeded horizontal rails, over-stuffed seats, on front turned legs.
£2,800–3,200 *WW*

Make the most of Miller's

Unless otherwise stated, any description which refers to 'a set' or 'a pair' includes a price guide for the entire set or the pair, even though the illustration may show only a single item.

A set of 4 Regency simulated rosewood and decorated dining chairs, each with an anthemion and scroll decorated curved bar top rail and tablet splat, with the garter badge, caned seat, on ring turned tapering legs, stamped 'Gee'.
£800–1,200 *CSK*

John Gee, chair maker and turner, 1779–c1824, of 49 Wardour Street, Soho, was listed in the London Directories from 1779, and by 1803 was referred to as 'Chair Maker and Turner to His Majesty'.

l. A set of 6 Regency mahogany dining chairs, with leather drop-in seats, on ring turned legs.
£1,300–1,700 *L*

A set of 6 Regency mahogany dining chairs, including 2 carvers, with carved bar backs and moulded uprights, overstuffed seats, on turned tapering supports, restored.
£850–950 *Bri*

A set of 4 William IV mahogany dining chairs, each with curved and buttoned back, repairs.
£1,000–1,200 *CSK*

A set of 6 George IV mahogany dining chairs, possibly Scottish.
£1,700–2,000 *DN*

A set of 8 William IV style mahogany dining chairs, with oval backs and serpentine upholstered seats, on fluted tapering legs.
£1,400–2,000 *LHA*

A set of 8 William IV mahogany dining chairs, including an open armchair, with drop-in seats, on lotus lapeted turned legs.
£3,300–3,700 *CSK*

A set of 7 early Victorian mahogany dining chairs, including an armchair, each with a concave rail and horizontal carved splat, on turned tapering legs.
£2,000–2,500 *DN*

A pair of early Victorian Gothic style grained oak dining chairs, each with an arched traceried pierced back, above a padded seat covered in red material, on square tapering legs headed by panels, material worn.
£2,000–2,500 *C*

These chairs are contemporary with the oak grained bedroom furniture supplied in the 1840s for the new bedrooms created in the towers by William Burn. The bedroom furniture was generally supplied undecorated from London and grained in Darlington or Barnard Castle and this may also apply in the case of these chairs.

A set of 7 mahogany dining chairs, including one open armchair, with drop-in seats, on square tapering legs joined by H-stretchers, damaged, late 19thC.
£1,000–1,200 *CSK*

A set of 8 early Victorian oak dining chairs, with padded seats, on moulded turned tapering legs, one leg broken.
£800–1,200 *CSK*

r. A set of 10 dining chairs, including 2 armchairs, with square shaped pierced trellis pattern backs, the seats covered in hide, on moulded square tapering legs with spade feet, late 19thC.
£3,500–5,500 *AG*

A set of 6 early Victorian mahogany dining chairs, each with a concave rail and padded seats, on turned reeded legs.
£1,600–2,000 *DN*

A set of 8 mid-Victorian mahogany balloon back dining chairs.
£2,500–3,000 *CSK*

A set of 6 Victorian mahogany dining chairs.
£1,600–2,000 *DN*

l. A set of 6 Victorian dining chairs, each with a rail and horizontal splat, drop-in seat, on turned legs.
£850–1,000 *DN*

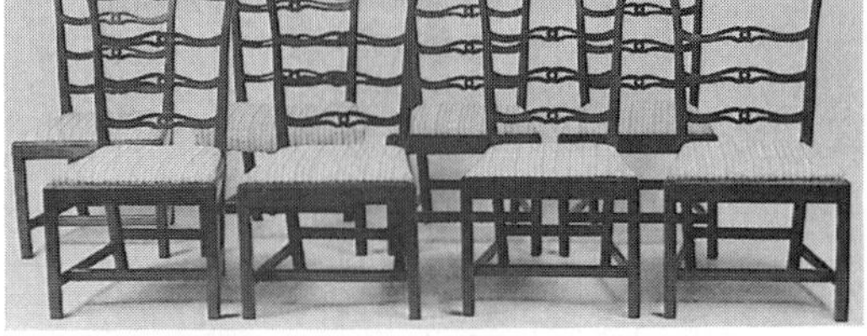

A set of 7 Chippendale side chairs, with moulded edge on seat rails and legs, North Shore, Massachusetts, old refinish, c1770, and one similar chair with over-upholstered seat.
£13,500–15,500 *SK(B)*

Hall Chairs

A pair of George III mahogany hall chairs, the shield-shaped backs painted with an heraldic crest, above fluted sprays, the seat on front reeded square tapering legs with H-stretchers, on spade feet.
£2,600–3,000 *WW*

A pair of George III mahogany hall chairs, the bell-shaped seats with ebony banding and roundels to the friezes, on front turned legs.
£1,200–1,700 *WW*

A pair of Regency mahogany hall chairs.
£700–900 *CSK*

A pair of early Victorian oak hall chairs, on ring turned legs.
£450–650 *CSK*

Locate the source

The source of each illustration in* Miller's Antiques Price Guide *can easily be found by checking the code letters at the end of each caption with the Key to Illustrations located at the front of the book.

A pair of Regency mahogany hall chairs, on ring turned tapering legs.
£900–1,200 *CSK*

A pair of mahogany hall chairs, the double scroll backs painted with the crest of Hardy of Dunstall Hall, Staffordshire, with solid seats, on reeded sabre front legs, early 19thC.
£650–750 *WL*

A pair of Victorian mahogany hall chairs, with shaped and pierced backs, the hard seats on turned legs and thimble feet.
£150–200 *DA*

Side Chairs

A walnut side chair, early 18thC with later parts.
£400–600 *CSK*

A George II walnut side chair, with a shell-carved rail and shaped solid splat, drop-in seat on shell-carved cabriole legs with claw-and-ball feet.
£600–800 *DN*

A Charles II ebonised and parcel gilt side chair, with a carved rail centred by a crown and cherubs, caned splat and seat on composite legs, joined by a carved pierced stretcher, with initials 'R.M.' on the reverse.
£300–400 *DN*

This chair could be the work of Robert Morris, who is recorded as making furniture for Charles II. It would be unusual for a maker to sign with initials on the reverse, especially someone appointed to the Monarch. However, the Earl of Harrington was connected to Charles II by marriage and there is a possibility that this chair came to the family in this way. Morris supplied chairs, couches, bedsteads, cushions, blankets, curtains and carpets to the Crown.

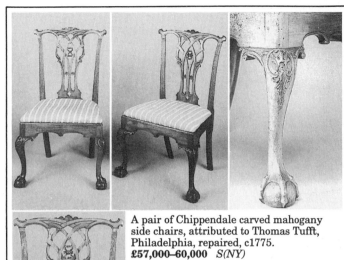

A pair of Chippendale carved mahogany side chairs, attributed to Thomas Tufft, Philadelphia, repaired, c1775.
£57,000–60,000 *S(NY)*

One chair bears the paper label on the inside back rail 'These two chairs were my Grandmother Lawrence's. Your Uncle Lawrence has the sofa that matches. It is in the big room'.
This pair of chairs is part of a large set of furniture made for Richard Edwards (1744–99) by Thomas Tufft.

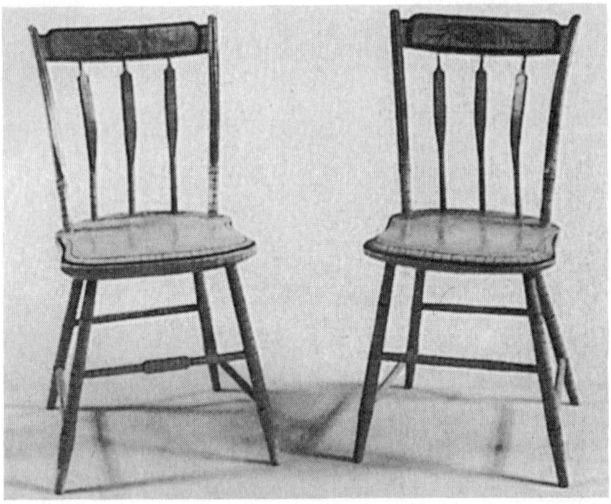

A pair of painted side chairs, New England, each painted yellow with brown and black detailing, front stretcher with tablet, 19thC.
£400–600 *CNY*

Miscellaneous Chairs

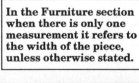

In the Furniture section when there is only one measurement it refers to the width of the piece, unless otherwise stated.

A pair of rosewood chairs, each with a shaped padded back within a leaf carved frame, padded seats, on fluted legs, early 19thC.
£400–600 *DN*

A harlequin set of 5 Queen Anne style single chairs, the seats and backs upholstered in old gold velvet, the legs carved with leafage and scrolled or pad feet.
£1,900–2,200 *RBB*

r. A pair of George III mahogany chairs, one partially re-railed.
£2,000–2,500 *C*

An early George III mahogany corner elbow chair, with curved back and arms, columnar and pierced vase splats, with a slip-in seat, on moulded square chamfered legs joined by stretchers.
£1,000–1,200 *CSK*

A Victorian walnut nursing chair, the upholstered back and bowed seat in a finialled, fluted frame, with turned tapered legs with studded collars.
£750–950 *C*

A set of 6 Victorian walnut chairs, each with a shaped rail and pierced carved back, on slender cabriole legs.
£1,200–1,800 *DN*

A George III mahogany corner chair, late 18thC.
£550–650 *LHA*

An early Victorian walnut chair, the padded panelled back with a C-scroll and rocaille cresting and surround, on spirally turned uprights, with a padded serpentine seat, on cabriole legs.
£200–250 *CSK*

A mid-Victorian walnut salon suite, comprising: a sofa, with buttoned curved ends and central oval, flanked by pierced foliate scrolling panels and with foliate cresting, scroll arm terminals, serpentine seat and cabriole legs headed with berried foliage, 82in (208cm) wide, a gentleman's armchair, a lady's armchair, and a set of 6 balloon back dining chairs.
£5,500–6,500 *CSK*

A set of 4 Regency mahogany chairs, each with a horizontal splat between reeded uprights, drop-in seats on moulded sabre legs, damaged.
£600–700 *DN*

A set of 6 early Victorian carved rosewood single chairs, with carved crest rail, pierced leaf decorated centre rail, drop-in seats, on turned tapered and decorated legs.
£2,000–2,500 *AH*

Four Dutch marquetry chairs, each with a shaped splat with vases of flowers and masks, padded seat, on cabriole legs, late 18thC.
£1,200–1,800 *DN*

Chests of Drawers

A Queen Anne bachelor's walnut chest, with hinged quarter veneered folding flap decorated with feather banding, 2 short and 3 long graduated drawers below with later pierced brass handles, bracket feet, 31in (79cm).
£1,800–2,400 *AG*

A George III mahogany chest of drawers, on outswept bracket feet, 33½in (85cm) wide.
£800–900 *CSK*

A George III mahogany chest of drawers, with a brushing slide, on bracket feet, restored, 35½in (91cm) wide.
£1,000–1,200 *CSK*

A mahogany chest of drawers, on ogee bracket feet, restored, 18thC, 37½in (95cm) wide.
£1,400–1,800 *CSK*

Styles of Feet

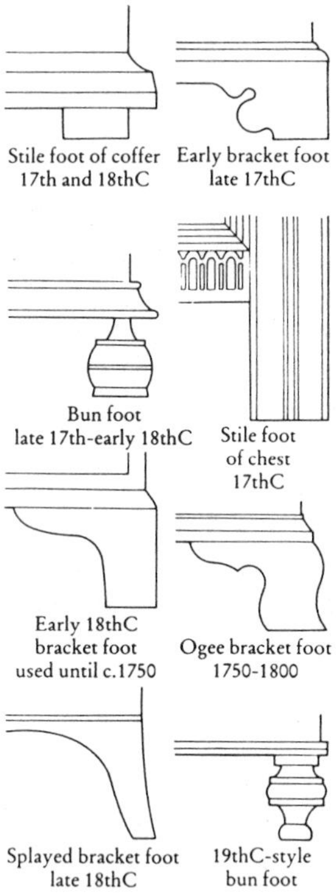

A George III mahogany chest of drawers, on bracket feet, 37in (94cm) wide.
£500–700 *DN*

l. A George III mahogany chest of drawers, on bracket feet, 36½in (93cm) wide.
£750–1,000 *DN*

A walnut and feather banded chest of drawers, with a quarter veneered crossbanded top, on later bracket feet, restored, early 18thC, 39in (99cm) wide.
£3,500–4,000 *CSK*

A George III small mahogany chest of drawers.
£500–600 *DaD*

A Georgian style mahogany bowfronted chest of drawers, decorated with reeded pilasters, on tapering feet, 34in (86cm).
£600–700 *AG*

A George III mahogany bowfronted chest, with brass plate handles, on splayed bracket feet, 40in (101.5cm) wide.
£2,400–2,800 *DN*

A George III mahogany chest, with rectangular top over two aligned and 3 graduated cockbeaded drawers, on ogee bracket feet, 19thC, 37in (94cm) wide.
£700–1,000 *LHA*

A George III mahogany bowfront chest, with 4 long drawers, on splayed feet, 40in (102cm) wide.
£400–600 *DN*

A George III mahogany chest of drawers, on later shaped bracket feet, 41in (104cm).
£1,700–2,000 *C*

A George III inlaid mahogany chest of drawers, on bracket feet, 37in (94cm) wide.
£1,200–1,500 *SLN*

A George III mahogany chest, with 4 long drawers flanked by outset pilasters, on turned feet, 35½in (91cm).
£1,300–1,700 *DN*

A George III mahogany chest of drawers.
£500–700 *DaD*

A George III mahogany bowfront chest, with a moulded top above 3 long drawers, on splay feet, 41in (104cm).
£500–700 *DN*

l. A George III mahogany chest of drawers, the moulded edge top with crossbanding, on shaped bracket feet, later veneered top, 40in (101cm) wide.
£1,000–1,200 *P*

A George III walnut chest of drawers, with a moulded top, on bracket feet, some alterations.
£400–500 *DN*

A George III mahogany bowfront chest, with 4 long drawers on bracket feet, 36in (91.5cm).
£900–1,200 *DN*

A George III mahogany chest, with moulded top edge, 2 short and 3 long graduated drawers, on ogee bracket feet and casters, 36in (92cm) wide.
£1,500–1,800 *P*

A George III mahogany serpentine chest of drawers, on bracket feet, 29½in (75cm).
£3,300–3,700 *CSK*

A George III mahogany chest, with original brass bail handles, on bracket feet, 31½in (80cm).
£2,700–3,200 *Bea*

A George III mahogany chest, the top with moulded foliate edge, above a brushing slide and 4 long drawers, on shaped bracket feet, restored, 30½in (77cm).
£1,700–2,000 *C*

A George IV mahogany bowfront chest of drawers, with 2 short and 3 long drawers flanked by inlaid boxwood lines, on turned feet, 35in (89cm).
£1,200–1,700 *DN*

r. A Regency mahogany bowfront chest of drawers, the graduated drawers with brass lions' mask ring handles, flanked by a pair of leaf carved reeded pilasters, on ball turned tapering feet, 47in (119cm).
£1,000–1,200 *MJB*

A walnut and featherbanded chest, with crossbanded and quarter veneered top, on scroll bracket feet, parts early 18thC, 35in (90cm).
£1,200–1,700 *P*

l. A Regency mahogany bowfront chest, with brushing slide and 3 graduated long drawers, on bracket feet, 35in (89cm).
£1,400–1,800 *CSK*

r. A mahogany chest, on ogee bracket feet, mid-18thC, 36in (91.5cm).
£2,700–3,000 *CSK*

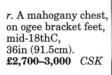

l. A mahogany and inlaid chest, with hinged top above a frieze with conch shells and central urn, above 2 dummy drawers and a further 6 drawers, all chequer strung, on ogee bracket feet, late c1800, 60in (152cm) wide.
£1,000–1,500 *CSK*

A William IV walnut miniature chest, the cockbeaded drawers with turned ivory handles, on splayed bracket feet, c1835, 10½in (26cm) wide.
£530–800 *LHA*

A Chippendale mahogany serpentine chest of drawers, Newport, Rhode Island, attributed to the Townsend-Goddard School, early surface, original brass handles, slight damage, c1775, 39in (99cm) wide.
£14,000–18,000 *SK(B)*

This chest has furnished the Thomas Robinson House, 64 Washington Street, Newport, Rhode Island, since the 18thC. The house was bought in 1760 by Thomas 'Quaker Tom' Robinson (1730–1817) a highly successful Newport merchant. The chest has remained in family ownership.

An early George III mahogany chest-on-chest, with blind fret frieze, the lower part with later handles, fluted pilasters and ogee bracket feet, 68in (172.5cm) high.
£3,500–4,000 *AH*

A miniature mahogany round cornered chest of drawers, c1885, 18in (45.5cm) high.
£220–260 *JHW*

A bird's-eye veneered figured maple chest, with quartering and crossbanding, the 4 serpentine front drawers with embossed decorative plate handles, the oak linings on side runners, scroll corner pilasters on bun feet, probably North German, 18thC, 35½in (90.5cm).
£2,000–2,500 *WW*

Authenticating Chests-on-Chests

While many chests-on-chests have been divided, some are the result of a 'marriage'.
A few simple checks are:

- The dovetailing in all drawers should match.
- The backboards of both top and bottom sections should be of similar timber and quality.
- Signs of handle changes (redundant holes inside the drawer fronts, marks on the drawer fronts themselves), should be the same on both sections.
- Both top and bottom sections may have canted corners, or possibly just the top section, but never the bottom section alone.
- Decorative details, such as crossbanding, should be consistant throughout the piece.
- The wood on both parts should match exactly.

A calamander chest, the 6 long drawers with ivory handles and escutcheons, on bracket feet, early 19thC, 38in (96.5cm).
£2,500–3,000 *DN*

Chests-on-Chests

A mahogany tallboy, on later ogee bracket feet, one central drawer coverted to secrétaire, upper section sides cut, mid-18thC, 70in (177.5cm) high.
£1,500–2,000 *Bea*

An early George III mahogany tallboy, on ogee bracket feet, damaged, cornice missing, 42in (106.5cm) wide.
£2,200–2,700 *CSK*

MILLER'S COMPARES . . .

I A walnut tallboy, with moulded cornice, the apron with sunburst inlay, on bracket feet, restored, early 18thC, 42½in (108cm) wide.
£2,200–3,000 *CSK*

II A mahogany tallboy, on bracket feet, restored, mid-18thC, 39in (99cm).
£900–1,200 *CSK*

Both tallboys look similar but *Item I* fetched a much higher price at auction, primarily due to the fact that it is made from walnut which is highly sought after and generally commands a higher price than mahogany. The colour of the walnut in *Item I* is particularly good and the sunburst detail, found at the base of the tallboy, adds an interesting feature to this piece. *Item II* lacks any such detail and the colour of the mahogany is not exceptional. *CSK*

A George III mahogany bowfront tallboy, the upper part with an arched cornice centred by a diced panel, the frieze inlaid with a boxwood trellis, fitted with 2 short and 3 long drawers, the lower part with 3 long drawers, on bracket feet, 46in (116.5cm) wide.
£2,000–2,500 *L*

Miller's is a price GUIDE not a price LIST

l. A George III mahogany chest-on-chest, 42in (106cm).
£2,000–2,500 *Bri*

A George III mahogany tallboy, on bracket feet, 42½in (108cm).
£1,500–2,000 *DN*

A George III mahogany chest-on-chest, on bracket feet, 43in (109cm) wide.
£1,000–1,500 *DN*

A George III mahogany tallboy, on bracket feet, later inlaid, 47in (119cm) wide.
£1,000–1,200 *CSK*

A mahogany veneered tallboy, oak lined, with chased brass ring paterae centred handles, on bracket feet, late 18thC, 47½in (121cm).
£1,500–2,000 *WW*

A George III mahogany tallboy, with moulded cornice and blind fret carved frieze, on bracket feet, associated, 45in (114cm) wide.
£1,800–2,200 *CSK*

A George III mahogany tallboy, the upper section flanked by chamfered and fluted corners, with brass handles and lock escutcheons, on bracket feet, 45in (114cm) wide.
£2,500–3,000 *AG*

A late George III mahogany tallboy, with chequer strung moulded cornice and stellar inlaid frieze, on bracket feet, restored, 44½in (113cm) wide.
£1,200–1,700 *CSK*

A George III mahogany tallboy, with Greek key moulded cornice, on bracket feet, 43½in (110cm).
£2,200–2,700 *CSK*

A George III mahogany tallboy, with moulded and dot decorated cornice, 2 short and 6 long drawers, on bracket feet, damaged, 47in (119cm) wide.
£1,200–1,700 *CSK*

A George III mahogany tallboy chest, the upper part with a moulded cornice, projecting canted angles, frieze inlaid with paterae, shells and oval panels with insects, on ogee bracket feet, 47in (119cm) wide.
£2,500–3,000 *CSK*

A George III provincial mahogany tallboy, on bracket feet.
£1,400–1,800 *CSK*

A mahogany tallboy, with shallow bracket feet, restored, late 18thC, 43½in (110cm).
£600–800 *CSK*

A walnut chest-on-chest, on bracket feet, 18thC, 40in (101.5cm) wide.
£1,600–2,000 *RBB*

A mahogany bowfront tallboy, on splayed bracket feet, early 19thC, 43in (109cms).
£1,500–2,000 *Bea*

l. A George III mahogany tallboy, later inlaid with boxwood and ebony lines, on ogee bracket feet, 49in (124.5cm) wide.
£1,500–2,000 *CSK*

In the Furniture section when there is only one measurement it refers to the width of the piece, unless otherwise stated.

A George II mahogany chest-on-chest, on ogee bracket feet, 44in (111cm) wide.
£2,200–2,700 *P*

Chests-on-Stands

A William and Mary floral marquetry chest-on-stand, inlaid in ivory and green stained ivory, the later stand on short turned legs, joined by ball turned stretchers, 37in (94cm).
£6,000–6,500 *L*

A Queen Anne maple tallboy, with projecting moulded cornice above 5 graduated drawers over lower case with long drawer, above 3 aligned drawers, on cabriole legs ending in pad feet, reconstructed, late 18thC, 36in (91.5cm) wide.
£1,700–2,200 *LHA*

A walnut chest-on-stand, featherbanded and line inlaid, on cabriole legs with pad feet, with oak sides, part 18thC, 41in (104cm) wide.
£2,000–2,500 *CSK*

r. A marquetry chest-on-stand, 18thC, 40in (101.5cm) wide.
£4,800–5,500 *JHW*

Dressing Chests

A George III harewood dressing chest, with satinwood inlay and banding, on splay feet, 36in (91.5cm) wide.
£17,000–20,000 *RBB*

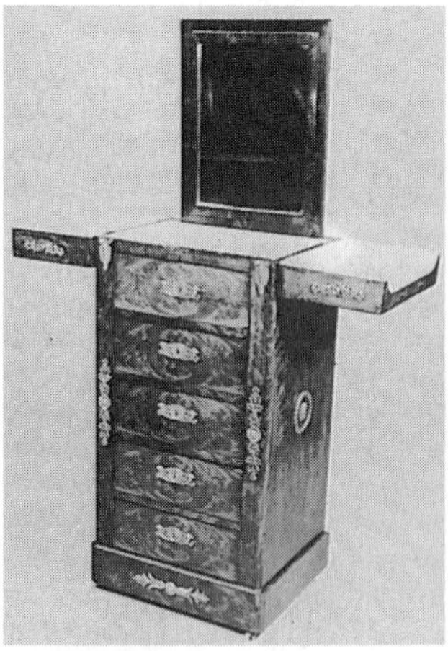

A French Empire mahagony enclosed dressing chest, the hinged divided top enclosing a rising mirror above one false and 4 real drawers, c1815, 21in (53.5cm) wide.
£2,200–2,700 *DN*

l. A Swiss walnut secrétaire dressing chest, the mirrored superstructure with 4 short drawers, above a Gothic arcaded fall front, enclosing a baize lined fitted interior, above 3 further long drawers, flanked by reeded column uprights, mid-19thC, 47in (199cm) wide.
£1,500–1,800 *CSK*

An American Federal ormolu mounted mahogany chest with dressing mirror, on tapering feet, c1825, 44in (111.5cm) wide.
£2,200–2,700 *SLN*

Military Chests

A mahogany and brass bound military chest, the top containing a secrétaire drawer, with carrying handles, on shaped bracket feet, 19thC, 43in (109cm).
£1,000–1,500 *P*

A brass bound mahogany military chest, with turned feet, early 19thC, 39in (99cm) wide.
£1,000–1,200 *CSK*

A Victorian teak military chest, walnut veneered and brass bound, in 2 parts, with 2 short and 3 long drawers, on turned feet, one drawer fitted with a Bramah lock, 39in (99cm) wide.
£800–1,200 *CSK*

Miscellaneous Chests

An Italian cedarwood chest, with hinged plank top, the later front decorated with foliage and dragon-type creatures, 17thC, 71in (180cm) long.
£2,000–2,500 *CSK*

Military Chests

The military chest is a set of drawers designed for travelling. It has no protruding parts and has metal mounts to protect the corners. It is made in strong woods such as teak and padouk.

A George III mahogany secrétaire chest, the moulded top above a fitted drawer and 3 long drawers, on splay feet, 36in (91.5cm).
£1,500–2,000 *DN*

A George III mahogany secrétaire chest, in 2 sections, the base with secrétaire drawer simulated as 2 short and one long drawer, enclosing a fitted interior, above 4 graduated long drawers, the lowest partially fitted, on shaped bracket feet, the feet possibly reduced in height, the top shelf section possibly associated, 30in (76cm) wide.
£3,300–4,000 *C*

A Dutch mahogany veneered chest, the hinged top with fan inlay and banding, with a later conversion to hinged ornamental shelves and side flaps, the drawers with embossed brass plate handles and escutcheons, outstanding front corners, inlaid dentil frieze, the apron with brass mounts, on square tapering fluted feet, 36in (91.5cm) wide.
£4,000–5,000 *WW*

Commodes

A pair of George III mahogany commodes, each with moulded top, 3 serpentine drawers with gilt brass mounts and handles, c1770, 40in (102cm) wide.
£167,000–170,000 *S*

A Louis XV style kingwood bombé commode, marquetry inlaid and applied with gilt metal mounts, the shaped streaked white marble top above 3 drawers, with a shaped apron, on downswept legs with gilt sabots, 45in (114cm).
£800–1,200 *CSK*

A Louis XV walnut and burr walnut serpentine commode, with shaped top above 4 graduating serpentine drawers, flanked by convex and concave doors, on ball feet, 34½in (87cm).
£3,000–3,500 *S(Am)*

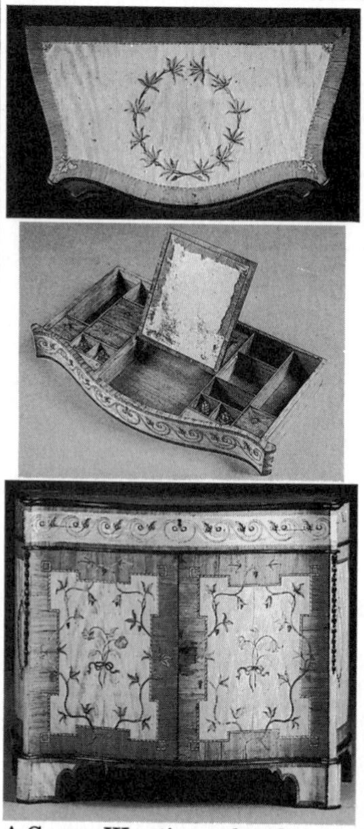

A George III satinwood and marquetry serpentine commode, the top inlaid with a foliate wreath within a geometric border and crossbanded in mahogany, the mahogany lined frieze drawer enclosing a fitted interior with a hinged mirror, lidded wells and associated glass bottles, above a pair of doors inlaid with trailing foliage, the sides inlaid with ribbon tied husk wreaths, shaped feet, attributed to Mayhew & Ince, restored, 42½in (108cm).
£33,000–35,000 *C*

On the evidence of quality and style, this commode can confidently be attributed to Messrs. Ince & Mayhew, cabinet makers and upholsterers. They publicised their establishment, based in Golden Square, Central London, in their pattern book, The Universal System of Household Furniture, *1762, which was dedicated to the 4th Duke of Marlborough, who was a member of King George III's household.*

r. A Louis XV black japanned serpentine commode, with a moulded marble top above a slide and 2 drawers, 26½in (68cm).
£3,000–3,500 *DN*

A Dutch mahogany commode, 18thC, 38in (96.5cm) wide.
£850–1,000 *L*

An Empire mahogany commode, with a black marble top, frieze drawer with 3 recessed drawers below, flanked by tapering column stiles extending to turned feet, 51½in (131cm) wide.
£1,500–2,000 *CSK*

A Louis XV style kingwood floral marquetry commode, the serpentine top with purple-brown marble slab, serpentine sides and bombé front, inlaid with floral sprays within gilt metal cartouches, the front divided to enclose 2 pull-out shelves, damaged, 46in (117cm) wide.
£2,300–2,700 *L*

A Louis XVI mahogany commode, with a later variegated marble top, 52in (132cm) wide.
£2,500–3,000 *CSK*

An Italian walnut commode, the top with re-entrant corners above 3 crossbanded drawers, flanked by spiral turned column uprights, the apron centred with a ribbon tied medallion, on paterae headed stop fluted tapering legs, 40in (101.5cm) wide.
£2,500–3,000 *CSK*

Cupboards

A George III mahogany tray top bedside commode, with panelled door and pull-out drawer below decorated with oval fruitwood stringing, enclosing a ceramic liner, cut-out side handles, on moulded square tapering legs, 18in (46cm) wide.
£650–750 *AG*

A George III mahogany tray top bedside commode, the pull-out front with shaped apron, on square chamfered legs, 19in (48cm) wide.
£500–700 *CSK*

In the Furniture section when there is only one measurement it refers to the width of the piece, unless otherwise stated.

l. A George III mahogany tray top bedside commode, the top above a tambour shutter, the pull-out front enclosing a ceramic bowl, on square legs, 20in (51cm).
£500–800 *CSK*

l. A George III mahogany bedside cupboard, the top with a waved gallery with carrying handles, above a drawer, 2 cupboards and a sliding commode drawer, 21in (53.5cm).
£1,200–1,700 *C*

A pair of mahogany bedside cupboards, in the form of Ionic columns, each with a drawer to one side, on fluted shafts, headed with egg-and-dart and scroll mouldings and enclosed by a panelled door, on plinth bases, 22in (56cm) wide.
£8,500–9,000 *CSK*

A pair of George III satinwood bedside cupboards, each with a D-breakfront top inlaid with a husk tipped circular patera, tulipwood crossbanding and ebonised mouldings, the tambour front of alternate staves of box wood and mahogany, each fitted with a drawer, one for a chamber pot recess, the drawer fronts inlaid with floral swags, on square tapering legs inlaid to simulate fluting, on block feet, 21in (54cm) wide.
£34,000–37,000 *L*

A walnut corner cupboard, crossbanded and herringbone inlaid, with moulded cornice to domed top, arched panelled and quarter veneered door enclosing shelving, on a moulded base, 18thC, 23½in (60cm).
£1,500–2,500 *AH*

A pair of Georgian mahogany bedside cupboards, each with a three-quarter gallery over a single panelled door, on square tapering legs, 34in (86cm) high.
£1,500–2,000 *AG*

A George III mahogany standing corner cupboard, with a pair of panelled doors enclosing shaped shelves, above a further pair of panelled doors, on a plinth base, 85in (216cm) high.
£1,200–1,500 *DN*

A mahogany and string inlaid corner cupboard, with scrolling and flower carved pediment, on a stand with 3 frieze drawers, shaped apron and 3 moulded square supports, 19thC, 40in (101.5cm) wide.
£1,000–1,500 *AH*

A George III mahogany corner cupboard, with a cavetto cornice above an astragal glazed door, a later lower part with a pair of panelled doors, on bracket feet, 81in (205.5cm) high.
£700–1,000 *DN*

A Georgian mahogany hanging corner cupboard, with turned handles, 30in (76cm).
£450–650 *DA*

A George III mahogany low clothes press, on bracket feet, 50in (127cm).
£1,500–2,000 *C*

A mahogany linen press, on bracket feet, parts possibly associated, early 19thC, 50in (127cm).
£1,500–2,000 *CSK*

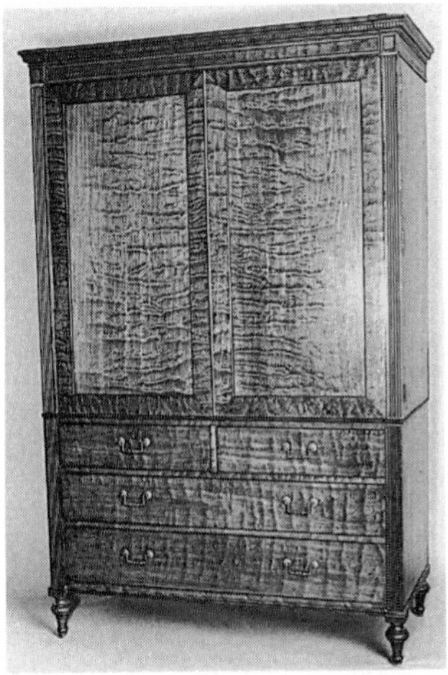

A mahogany linen press, with inlaid cornice above a pair of panelled doors enclosing trays, above 2 short and 2 long drawers, all flanked by fluted pilasters on turned feet, the locks stamped 'SW, SWD', and 'WWD Patent'.
£2,500–3,000 *DN*

A George III mahogany press, with a pair of simulated drawers above a long drawer, on shaped bracket feet, the doors possibly partially altered, 52in (132cm).
£1,700–2,200 *C*

A George III mahogany linen press, with a dentil cornice above a pair of doors with oval panels, enclosing trays, above 2 short and 2 long drawers, on splay feet, 48in (122cm).
£3,500–4,000 *DN*

A George III mahogany linen press, on splay feet, 51in (131cm).
£1,700–2,200 *DN*

A George III mahogany linen press, on turned bun feet, 51½in (129.5cm).
£1,100–1,400 *CSK*

A George III mahogany, crossbanded and string inlaid linen press, with moulded cornice, 51in (129.5cm).
£2,000–2,500 *AH*

A George III mahogany linen press, the drawers with brass drop handles, on moulded plinth and bracket feet, 52in (132cm).
£2,200–2,700 *AH*

A George III mahogany linen press, with a cavetto cornice above a pair of panelled doors, the lower part with 2 short and 2 long drawers, on splayed feet, 51in (130cm).
£1,200–1,800 *DN*

A George III small linen press, with moulded cornice, 2 panelled doors above 2 short and one long drawer, on shaped bracket feet, 46in (116cm).
£860–1,000 *WL*

A Georgian style mahogany linen press, by Maple and Company, with dentil cornice, with satinwood crossbanding and stringing overall, the drawers with brass handles, on ogee bracket feet, 49in (124.5cm).
£1,600–2,000 *AG*

A George IV mahogany small linen press, 41in (104cm).
£2,000–2,500 *P*

A George IV mahogany linen press, with a beaded triangular pediment flanked by reel turned mouldings, 2 panelled doors applied with acanthus carved columns, 54in (137cm).
£3,000–3,500 *Bea*

A Regency mahogany and ebonised low clothes press, on later turned feet, lacking one slide, later lock, 49in (124.5cm).
£650–850 *C*

A Regency mahogany linen press, the shaped cornice above 2 line inlaid panelled doors, 49in (124.5cm).
£1,600–2,000 *CSK*

In the Furniture section when there is only one measurement it refers to the width of the piece, unless otherwise stated.

A Regency mahogany clothes press, on turned feet, 54in (137cm).
£1,000–1,200 *CSK*

An early Victorian white painted linen press, the pediment cresting above a pair of panelled doors, with 3 long drawers, on plinth base, 51in (129.5cm).
£1,000–1,200 *C*

r. An early Victorian mahogany linen press, 50in (127cm).
£800–1,200 *CSK*

A late George III mahogany wardrobe, with moulded cornice, a pair of panelled doors above one long and 2 short drawers, on bracket feet, one panel warped, 45in (114cm).
£800–1,200 *CSK*

A late George III gentleman's mahogany wardrobe, with moulded cornice above a pair of satinwood crossbanded panelled doors, enclosing sliding shelves, 4 short and 2 long graduated drawers under, with brass handles, raised on bracket feet, 50in (127cm).
£2,600–3,000 *AG*

A mahogany breakfront wardrobe, early 19thC, 100in (254cm).
£1,600–2,000 *L*

An early Victorian mahogany breakfront wardrobe, the acorn moulded cornice above 2 panelled doors and 2 short and 2 long drawers, flanked by panelled and dummy drawer fronted long doors, on plinth base, 91in (231cm).
£1,800–2,200 *CSK*

A Victorian mahogany wardrobe, with a pair of panelled doors enclosing trays, above 2 drawers flanked by fluted outset pilasters, on a plinth base, 41in (104cm).
£1,500–2,000 *DN*

A French parquetry wardrobe, veneered in kingwood and rosewood, with fancy gilt metal mouldings and mounts, 19thC, 56in (142cm).
£1,400–1,800 *SWO*

Miller's is a price GUIDE not a price LIST

Davenports

A late George III mahogany davenport, with a pierced brass gallery above the leather lined writing slope, opening to reveal short drawers and storage space, the sliding top fitted with a pen drawer to the side with a slide, above 4 short graduated drawers with turned handles to one side and 4 false drawers to the other, raised on tapering bulbous feet, 20in (51cm).
£2,700–3,200 *AG*

Davenports

The quality of these compact writing tables, introduced in the late 18thC, can vary considerably. A high quality piece, provided that it is in good condition, will fetch double the price of one of lesser quality, and three times the price of one in need of restoration, even if it is of good quality.

An early Victorian rosewood davenport, the adjustable top with pierced three-quarter gallery and sloping leather lined fall, enclosing a fitted interior, with hinged pen drawer and 4 drawers below, with dummy drawers opposite, raised on scroll carved supports, on shaped plinth, damaged, 22½in (57cm).
£1,500–2,000 *CSK*

A Victorian burr walnut davenport, the superstructure fitted with pigeonholes flanking 3 short drawers, the piano roll front enclosing 2 short drawers above a rising pull-out leather lined slope, 4 drawers to the right, supported on leaf carved S-scrolls, 23in (58cm).
£2,500–3,000 *L*

A Victorian figured walnut davenport, with brass gallery above a leather inset slope enclosing a fitted interior, the base with 4 drawers opposed by dummy drawers, cabriole front supports, on bun feet with casters, 22in (56cm).
£1,400–1,800 *Bri*

A Victorian walnut davenport, raised on splay feet with ceramic casters, 22in (55.5cm).
£850–1,000 *AG*

A Victorian burr walnut davenport, with piano front and well fitted interior, a rising stationery compartment with fretwork frieze, 4 drawers and 4 false drawers to either side, 22in (56cm).
£2,500–3,500 *Bea*

A Victorian walnut davenport, with a hinged leather inset top enclosing a satin birch interior, above leaf carved supports, with 4 side drawers, 21in (53.5cm).
£600–800 *DN*

A Victorian walnut davenport, with rising stationery compartment, above a sloping front with hinged flap opening to reveal the pull-out writing surface, ink bottles, pen tray and 2 small drawers, 4 short drawers and 4 false drawers to the sides, raised on splay feet with carved bracket supports, 32½in (82.5cm).
£2,200–2,700 *AG*

An early Victorian rosewood davenport, with three-quarter baluster gallery, leather lined hinged slope, with turned feet, 20in (51cm).
£1,400–1,700 *CSK*

A Victorian crossbanded and boxwood strung walnut davenport, the raised back with a brass gallery, above a side door opening to reveal 4 drawers, with slender carved cabriole supports, 21½in (54.5cm).
£750–850 *DN*

A Victorian burr walnut and boxwood inlaid davenport, with an ogee outlined stationery compartment above a leather inset slope enclosing a fitted interior, the base with 4 drawers opposed by dummy drawers, twist front pilasters, on bun feet with casters, 21in (54cm).
£1,700–2,000 *Bri*

A Victorian walnut davenport, with rising top compartment, c1860, 22in (55.5cm).
£5,000–5,200 *GJC*

A late Victorian burr walnut davenport, brass mounted and ebonised, 22¼in (57cm).
£1,000–1,500 *CSK*

A Victorian walnut davenport.
£700–900 *DaD*

A mid-Victorian rosewood and walnut davenport, on foliate capped cabriole legs and bun feet, 22in (56cm).
£1,400–1,700 *CSK*

A Victorian davenport, veneered in Brazilian rosewood, the top with a gallery, the leather inset flap revealing a fitted interior with a hinged pull-out pen and ink drawer, with two brass lidded glass inkwells above two slides, 4 drawers with brass Bramah style locks, wooden handles, on moulded turned feet with brass casters, 22in (56cm).
£1,700–2,000 *WW*

Bramah Locks

Bramah locks were introduced in the late 18thC. They are set in a characteristic circular escutcheon and have patent cylindrical keys.

A late Victorian inlaid burr walnut davenport, with three-quarter brass gallery above inkwell, sloping leather lined fall enclosing fitted interior, with cupboard door to the side enclosing 4 drawers, on turned faceted legs, stamped 'From S & H Jewel, Furniture Warehouses 1, Great and 29, 30 & 31 Little Queen Street, Holborn'.
£2,200–2,700 *CSK*

Drawer Knobs and Escutcheons

Wooden knobs, favoured by the Victorians, and mother-of-pearl escutcheon plates (keyhole surrounds) are a sign of good quality. Both act as a good dating guide, as they were introduced c1850.

A late Victorian amboyna, walnut and rosewood davenport, 22¼in (57cm).
£1,500–1,700 *CSK*

Desks

A George III mahogany cylinder desk, 36in (91.5cm).
£3,000–3,500 *LT*

A Victorian mahogany twin pedestal cylinder desk, 48½in (123cm) wide.
£1,200–1,500 *Bri*

A Victorian mahogany cylinder-front desk, opening to reveal a fitted interior, the drawers with turned wooden knobs handles.
£900–1,200 *BWe*

An early George III mahogany kneehole pedestal desk, with a moulded edged top, a frieze drawer with a recessed enclosed cupboard below, flanked by 3 drawers to either side, on bracket feet, repaired, 35in (89cm).
£3,300–3,700 *CSK*

Kneehole Desk Conversions

It is not uncommon for a chest of drawers to be converted into a kneehole desk. Certain checks can be made for authenticity:

- The construction of the inner sides of the small drawers should correspond with the outer sides; the dovetails should match each other and look as if they were made by the same hand.
- The runners should have caused even wear to the carcass.
- The veneers used for the sides of the kneehole and for the recessed cupboard door should match the rest of the piece.

A George III mahogany kneehole desk, with moulded edged top, pierced drop drawer handles and bracket feet, 30in (76cm).
£1,500–2,000 *AH*

A George III mahogany kneehole desk, with a drawer to one side, brass drop drawer handles, on bracket feet, 30in (76cm).
£1,800–2,200 *AG*

A George III mahogany kneehole desk, the top inset with a panel of tooled leather, enclosed by recessed panelled door below, flanked by 3 drawers to either side, on outswept bracket feet, 43½in (110cm).
£2,000–2,500 *CSK*

A mahogany kneehole desk, on bracket feet and casters, late 18thC, 34½in (88cm).
£1,500–2,000 *P*

l. A mahogany secrétaire kneehole desk, the fall enclosing a fitted interior, with an arched apron drawer and enclosed recessed cupboard below, flanked by 3 drawers to either side, on bracket feet, restored, late 18thC, 33in (84cm) wide.
£1,600–2,000 *CSK*

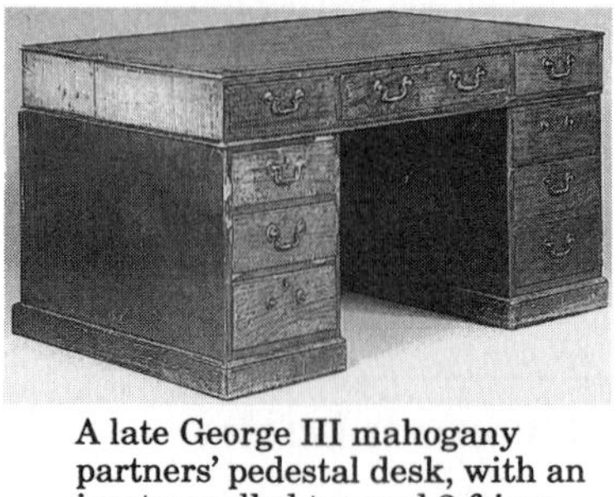

A late George III mahogany partners' pedestal desk, with an inset panelled top and 3 frieze drawers to either side, 3 drawers and an enclosed compartment to each pedestal, on plinth bases, 59in (150cm).
£3,300–4,000 *CSK*

l. A mahogany twin pedestal partners' desk, with tooled leather inset top, on plinth base with brass casters, early 19thC, 60in (152cm) wide.
£3,000–3,500 *L&E*

A Victorian mahogany partners' pedestal desk, the top inset with tooled red leather, the friezes with 3 drawers each side, oak lined, with brass Bramah locks some stamped 'J. T. Needs Late Bramah, 124 Piccadilly', the pedestals with drawers and sliding trays enclosed by panel doors, later embossed gilt brass ring handles, on plinths, 69in (175cm) wide.
£2,500–3,000 *WW*

A Victorian mahogany partners' desk, the moulded top with a tooled green leather inset, above 8 drawers, with 2 opposing cupboards, on a plinth base, 72½in (183cm).
£2,000–2,500 *P*

A large oak partners' desk, 19thC, 76in (193cm).
£1,700–2,000 *B*

In the Furniture section when there is only one measurement it refers to the width of the piece, unless otherwise stated.

l. A George II style walnut pedestal desk, with a leather inset top above 3 cushion moulded frieze drawers, on bracket feet, 46in (117cm) wide.
£1,200–1,800 *DN*

A mahogany pedestal desk, by Edwards & Roberts, the moulded edged top with maroon leather inset surface, the drawers with brass drop handles, 19thC, 48½in (123cm) wide.
£1,500–1,800 *AH*

A mahogany pedestal desk, the moulded leather inset top above 3 frieze drawers, on a plinth base, 19thC, 54in (137cm) wide.
£1,400–1,600 *DN*

A mahogany pedestal desk, with moulded leather inset top, 19thC, 47½in (121cm).
£1,200–1,600 *DN*

A Victorian mahogany pedestal desk, with reeded edged top, central frieze drawer with cupboard below, 8 pedestal drawers with brass ring handles, moulded base and bracket feet, 53½in (136cm) wide.
£1,000–1,500 *AH*

A Victorian mahogany writing desk, with raised gallery back and sloping front writing section, flanked by a series of drawers, on casters, 52in (132cm).
£1,400–1,700 *WL*

Casters

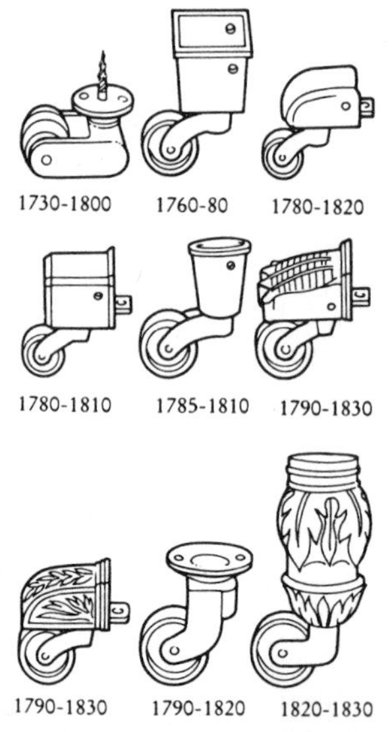

A Victorian mahogany pedestal desk, on a plinth base, 59in (150cm).
£1,500–2,000 *DN*

A late Victorian mahogany pedestal desk, the leather lined galleried top with writing slope, above 3 frieze drawers, on plinth base.
£1,600–2,000 *CSK*

An Italian ivory, walnut and boxwood inlaid slant-front desk-on-stand, the drawer with cast bronze handle, 38in (96.5cm).
£3,500–4,000 *CSK*

An Edwardian mahogany pedestal desk, with line inlay and satinwood banding, some bandings damaged ,54in (137cm).
£1,200–1,800 *CSK*

l. A George III mahogany enclosed travelling desk, with brass carrying handles, the hinged top opening to reveal a fitted interior of drawers and pigeonholes, adjustable baize writing surface, frieze drawer and recess beneath, on square tapering legs with brass toe caps and casters, 26in (66cm) wide.
£4,500–5,000 *RBB*

A walnut and kingwood veneered roll-top desk, of cylindrical form, inlaid with chequer lines, enclosing a fitted interior of drawers and cupboards, above a pull-out slide, with 2 drawers to the sides, on fluted tapering legs, 46in (116.5cm).
£700-1,000 *CSK*

A Regency mahogany and gilt brass mounted writing desk, the recessed superstructure with a high turned gallery, panelled fall enclosing alphabetically lettered pigeonholes, flanked by engine turned column stiles, the frieze drawer enclosing a tooled leather lined hinged ratcheted slope, flanked by a lidded compartment to either side and pen and inkwells, on turned reeded tapering legs with foliate brass caps and casters, stamped 'Wilkinson. Ludgate Hill 1335', the lock stamped 'Turners. W. Hampton. Patent', ratchet now lost, 48in (122cm) wide.
£3,000–5,000 CSK

William Wilkinson was trading from Ludgate Hill, City of London, from around 1808 and used this stamp until about 1820. Some of his furniture was given a serial number and that used here, 1335, is a low and early figure recorded in the Dictionary of English Furniture Makers, 1660–1840, *by G. Beard and T. Gilbert.*

A satinwood and marquetry desk, by Edwards and Roberts, the brass galleried back above 2 concave lidded compartments in the Carlton House manner, a shallow drawer beneath, with spade feet, brass toes and casters, the frieze drawer marked with maker's name, late 19thC, 48in (122cm) wide.
£4,000–4,500 *B*

A French parcel gilt and green decorated writing desk, on gadrooned and fluted tapering legs joined by stretchers, on toupie feet, 19thC, 33½in (85cm).
£1,200–1,700 *CSK*

In the Furniture section when there is only one measurement it refers to the width of the piece, unless otherwise stated.

r. A Victorian rosewood and inlaid writing desk, with cupboards enclosing slides, leather inset writing slope to top, 2 frieze drawers, on square tapering legs with casters, 42in (106.5cm) wide.
£1,000–1,200 *Bri*

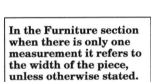

l. A gilt metal mounted tortoiseshell and brass inlaid writing desk, 42½in (108cm) wide.
£1,500–1,800 *CSK*

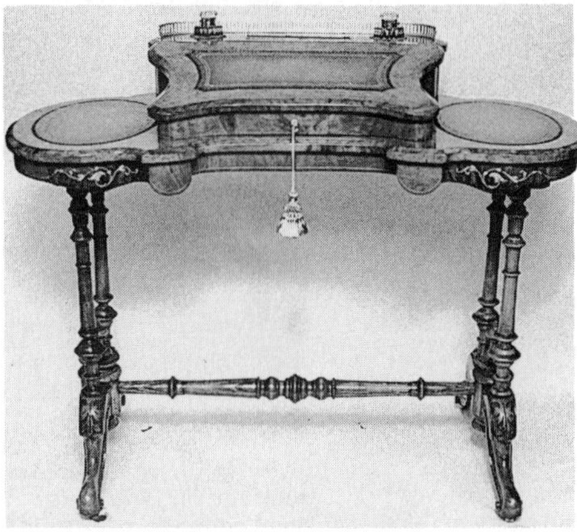

A Victorian walnut kidney-shaped writing desk, 38in (96.5cm) wide.
£3,250–3,500 *GJC*

Dumb Waiters

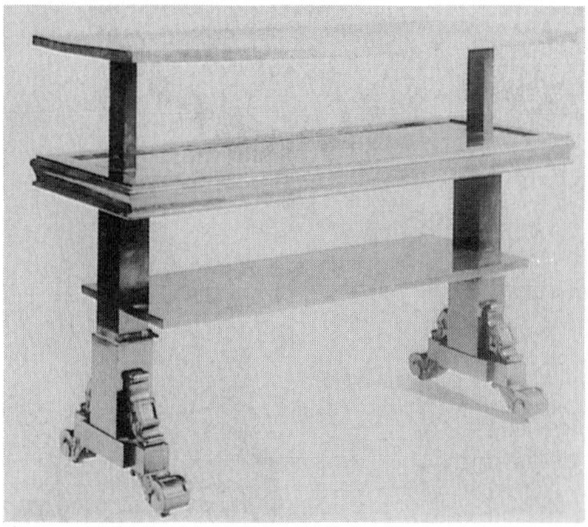

An early Victorian mahogany three-tier metamorphic dumb waiter, the adjustable tiers on square section end standards, on scroll bracket feet, 64in (162.5cm).
£2,000–2,300 *CSK*

A mahogany three-tier dumb waiter, on turned column and 3 cabriole legs with claw-and-ball feet, late 18thC, 22½in (57cm) diam.
£700–1,000 *CSK*

Dumb Waiters

The dumb waiter dates from the mid-18thC and continued to be produced until the Regency period. It was an English invention, consisting of 2 or 3 tiers on a stand, sometimes revolving, which was placed at the corner of a dining table and used to hold sauceboats, condiments and other dining accessories when servants were not present. More elaborate examples sometimes have special compartments for bottles and plates. A matching pair of dumb waiters is worth considerably more than two single ones.

A George III mahogany two-tier dumb waiter, on a turned central column, with 3 splay legs and brass casters, 35in (89cm) high.
£600–800 *AG*

Mirrors and Frames

A William and Mary oyster veneered cushion mirror, the plate within a moulded frame, 19½ by 17in (49.5 by 42.5cm).
£1,500–2,000 *C*

A convex mirror, with reeded ebonised slip to the glass, surmounted by a hippocampus and leaf sprays, the leaf spray base with a tied leaf tassel, 19thC, 37 by 27in (94 by 69cm).
£1,200–1,700 *WW*

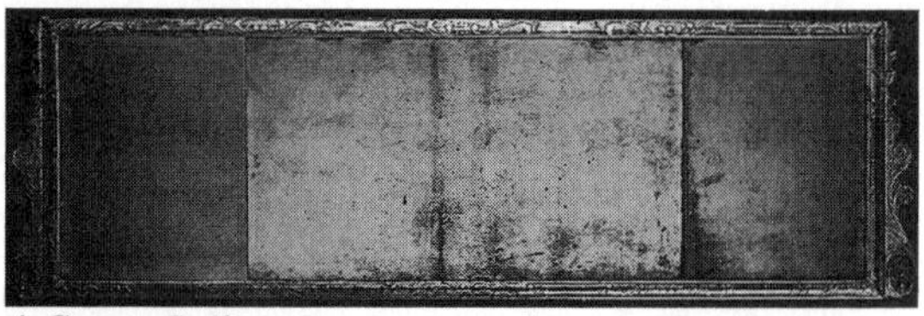

A George I gilt gesso overmantel mirror, the triple divided bevelled plate in a moulded frame decorated with elongated foliage on a pounced ground, with waved foliate sides and associated candle holders, 22 by 74in (56 by 188cm).
£2,500–3,500 *C*

r. A Queen Anne walnut and gilt gesso mirror, probably English, old refinish, slight damage, 18thC, 48½ by 24in (123 by 61cm).
£2,700–3,300 *SK(B)*

l. A carved and gilded frame, with scrolling acanthus leaf outer edge and rope twist inner edge, 18thC, 24½ by 31in (62.5 by 79cm).
£300–500 *CSK*

An early Georgian walnut toilet mirror, with later bevelled plate, raised on later bracket feet, 26 by 16in (66 by 41cm).
£500–700 *AG*

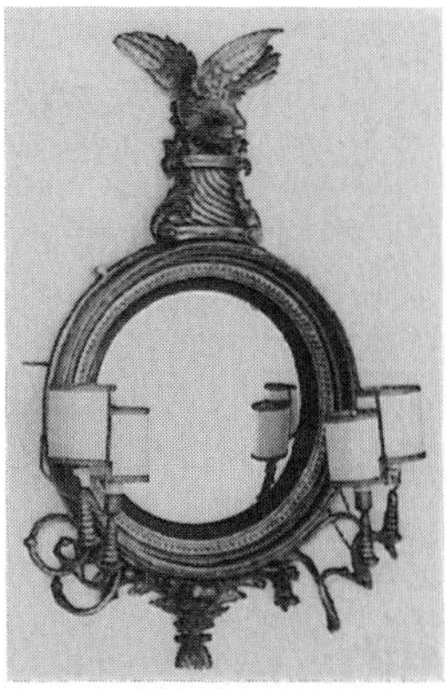

A convex wall mirror, surmounted by an eagle on an acanthus carved plinth, 2 pairs of candle sconces below on scrolling arms, now fitted for electricity, 19thC, 38in (96.5cm) high.
£800–1,000 *AG*

A pair of Chippendale style carved giltwood wall mirrors, each with cusped foliate cresting piece and acanthus scrolling borders, the bases carved with a crouching squirrel, 19thC,43 by 24in (109 by 61.5cm).
£6,200–7,000 *AG*

An early Georgian black and gilt japanned toilet mirror, the plate within a trellis and chinoiserie border, lacking adjustable support to the reverse, 21 by 18in (53 by 46cm).
£750–950 *C*

A carved wood mirror, the mirrored panels enclosed in a carved giltwood surround with scrolled foliate carved pine and gilt decoration, early 19thC, 84 by 36in (213 by 91.5cm).
£3,200–3,700 *B*

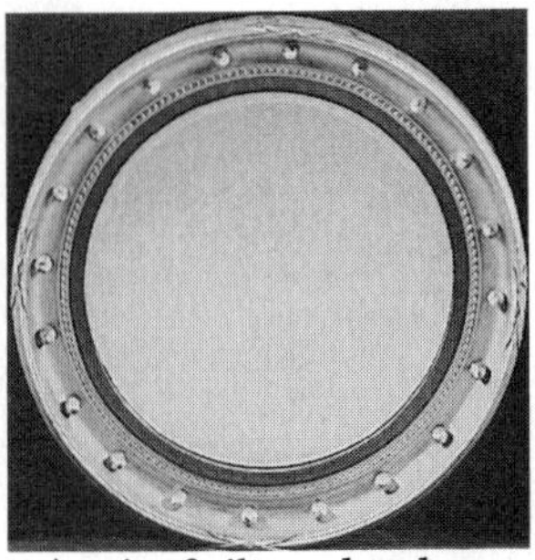

A pair of giltwood and gesso mirrors, each plate with a bevelled edge and ebonised reeded slip, with a ball decorated surround, 19thC, 25in (63.5cm) diam.
£600–900 *CSK*

Beware!

Be suspicious of any mirror in perfect condition. All old mirrors will have deteriorated to some extent and have non-reflective spots. Re-silvering reduces the value, particularly that of toilet and cheval mirrors. Mirror glass can be replaced, but the original glass should be retained and stored carefully.

A Regency white painted and parcel gilt cheval mirror, redecorated, 70 by 28in (177 by 71cm).
£2,000–3,000 *C*

A Regency giltwood over-mantel mirror, the later plate below a panel with a coloured print of putti playing blind man's buff, restored, 50 by 28in (127 by 71.5cm).
£1,000–1,500 *C*

A George III giltwood wall mirror, the plate with a pierced surround of C-scrolls with flowerheads and foliate clasps, with rocaille spray angles, some losses, 31 by 25in (78 by 64cm).
£800–1,200 *CSK*

A Regency giltwood mirror, the bevelled plate with ebonised slip surrounded by projecting spiral twist columns, with foliate clasps and corner rosettes, redecorated, 41½ by 35½in (105 by 90.5cm).
£800–1,200 *CSK*

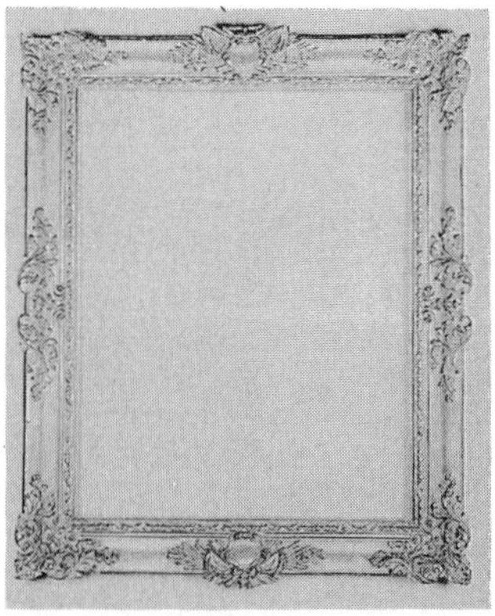

A carved and gilded frame, 19thC, 48 by 39in (122 by 99cm).
£600–800 *CSK*

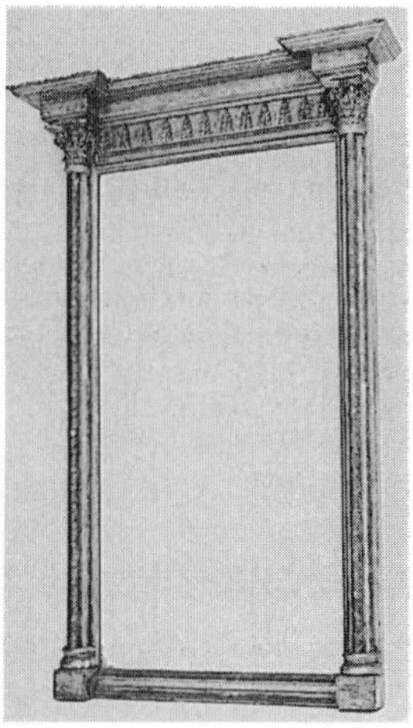

A Regency giltwood pier glass, the plate flanked by a ribbon band, cluster columns with Corinthian capitals, the frieze with stiff leaves, 63 by 43in (160 by 109cm).
£1,500–2,000 *L*

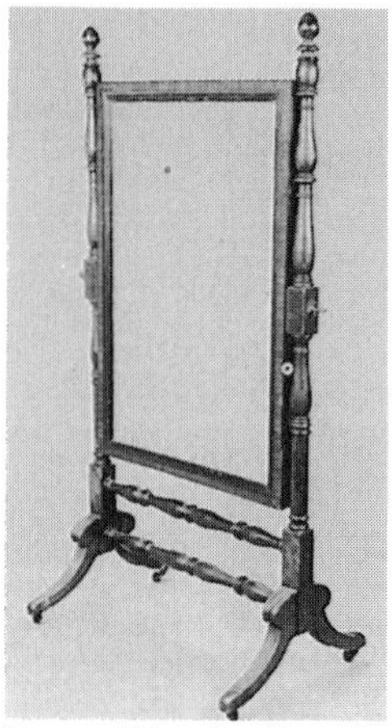

A George IV mahogany cheval mirror, the plate between turned uprights, on moulded splay legs, 70 by 35in (177.5 by 89cm).
£600–900 *DN*

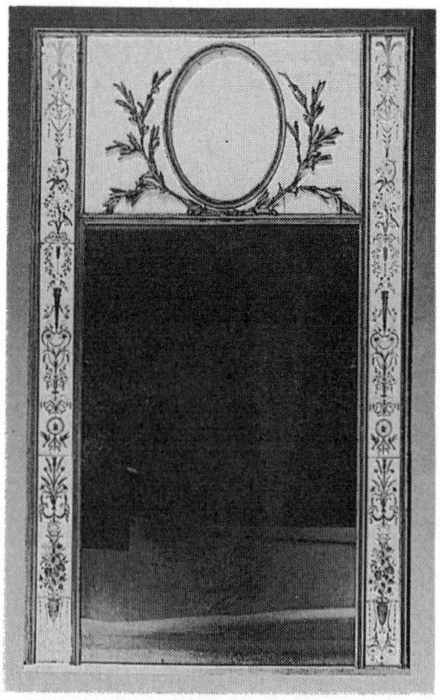

A Regency giltwood, white painted and verre églomisé mirror, the plate in beaded frame below a panel centred by a glazed oval framed with laurel, the sides with verre églomisé panels headed by Prince of Wales' feathers and decorated with pendant foliage and quivers of arrows, the plate inverted, 101 by 62½in (256.5 by 159cm).
£4,000–4,500 *C*

A Regency mahogany and boxwood strung cheval mirror, the hinged bevelled plate between ring turned uprights joined by a turned and reeded bar, on square tapering splayed legs, lacking candle sconces, 64in (163cm) high.
£1,700–2,200 *C*

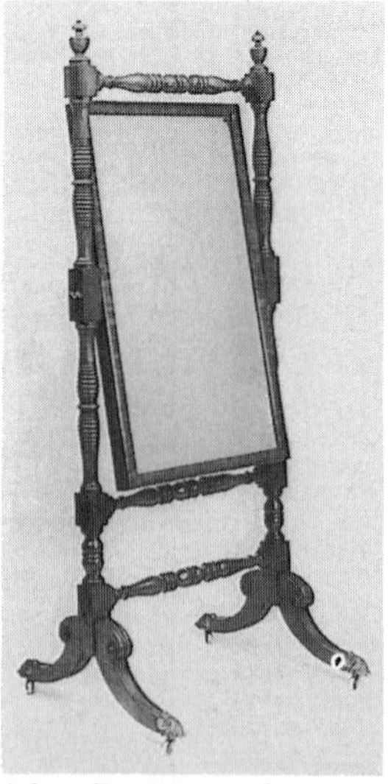

A late Regency mahogany cheval mirror, with a turned stretchered frame, reeded scroll legs, with chased brass sabots on casters.
£900–1,200 *WW*

A William IV walnut convex mirror, restored, 37 by 18in (94 by 46cm).
£1,500–2,000 *CSK*

A pair of giltwood silvered mirrors, each plate surmounted by a scrolling ribbon tied foliate cresting, late 19thC, 51 by 36½in (129.5 by 92cm).
£2,000–2,500 *CSK*

A Stuart style dressing mirror, with chinoiserie engraving to the silver cushion frame, backed on mahogany with easel support, probably late 19thC, 23 by 19½in (58.5 by 49.5cm).
£2,500–3,000 *WW*

Care!

Store original mirrors upright, never flat. Use 8 batons slightly larger than the plate, placing 6 upright and 2 across, to crate the mirror after wrapping with bubble paper.

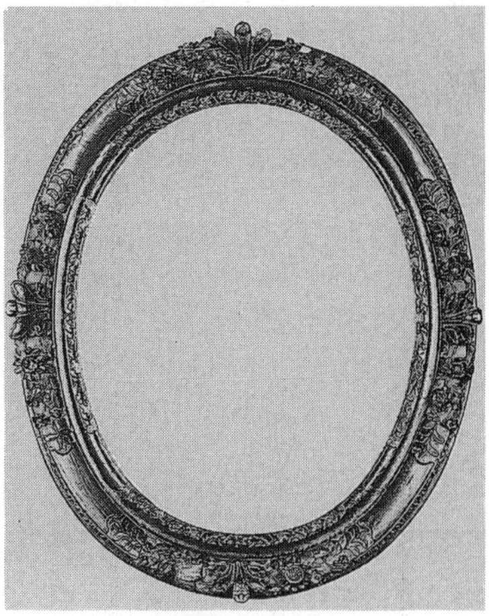

A Louis XIV carved frame, with panels of foliage and flowers in high profile, foliate outer and inner edge, 28½ by 23in (72.5 by 58.5cm).
£400–500 *CSK*

l. A Louis XIV style carved and gilded frame, with scallop shell corners and centres flanked by opposed C-scrolls, foliage and flowers on cross-hatched ground, sandwork and composition sight edge, 36 by 30in (91.5 by 76cm).
£2,500–3,000 *CSK*

l. A Louis XIV carved and gilded frame, with Metropolitan Museum label 'The Gilded Herman Doormer/Rembrandt', 29 by 21½in (73.5 by 54.5cm).
£250–350 *CSK*

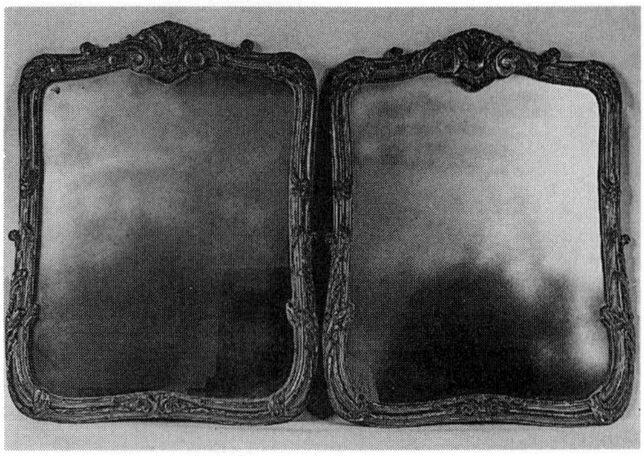

A pair of French gilded carved pier glasses, with acanthus scrolled frames, 30 by 24in (76 by 61cm).
£1,000–1,500 *HOLL*

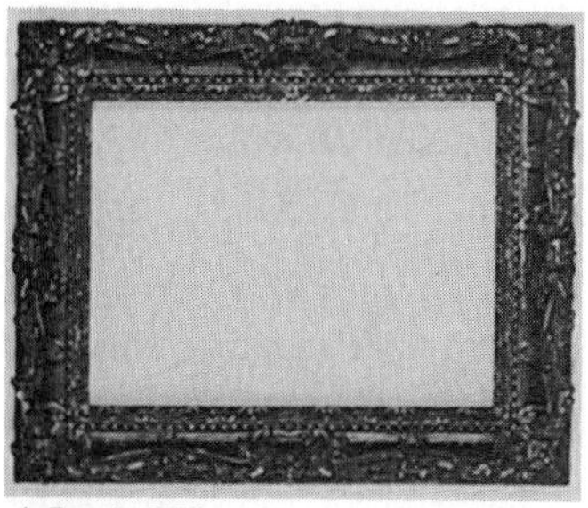

A Louis XV style carved and gilded frame, with beaded and foliate sight edge, 13 by 18½in (33 by 47cm).
£450–650 *CSK*

A Louis XV carved and gilded frame, with sandwork and foliate sight edge, 7 by 10in (20 by 26cm).
£500–800 *CSK*

An Italian 16thC style carved and gilded frame, with raised imbricated fruit border, 11in (28cm) diam.
£500–800 *CSK*

An Italian carved and gilded cassetta frame, with raised inner edge, 17thC, 36 by 49in (91.5 by 124.5cm).
£1,500–1,800 *CSK*

An Italian carved and gilded reverse profile frame, with scrolling foliate border, 17thC, 15 by 11in (38 by 28cm).
£850–1,000 *CSK*

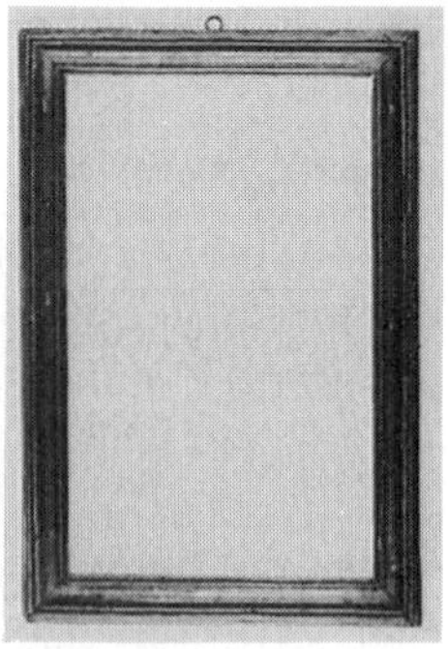

An Italian carved frame, with raised outer edge, 18thC, 18 by 12in (46 by 31cm).
£450–650 *CSK*

An Italian carved and gilded frame, with raised outer edge, 18thC, 24 by 20in (61 by 51cm).
£600–800 *CSK*

A pair of Swedish giltwood girandoles, each with a later plate within a beaded and moulded frame, surmounted by pierced ribbon tied cresting, with nozzles for candle branches, various pencil inscriptions to the reverse, later gold painted, c1800, 24 by 17in (62 by 17cm).
£1,500–2,000 *CSK*

l. An Italian carved giltwood wall mirror, with pierced and acanthus carved scrolling pediment, shell motif and scrolls to the base, mid-18thC, 44 by 21in (111.5 by 53cm).
£900–1,100 *AG*

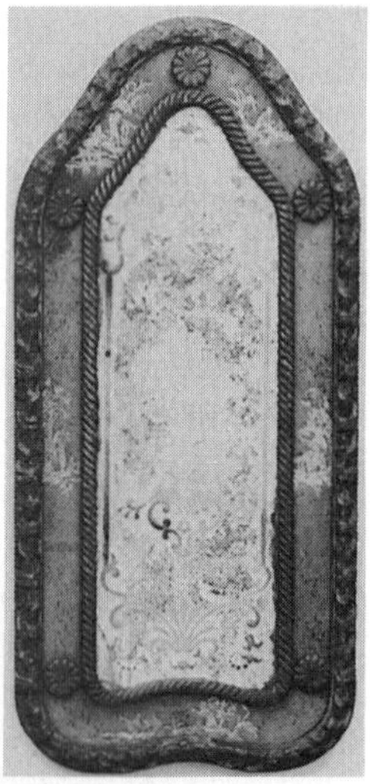

A pair of Italian carved wood and pale blue verre églomisé mirrored panels, each with a shaped arched top, the central plate engraved with a commedia dell'arte figure within a scrolling border, with silvered rope twist border and outer frame, late 18thC, 32 by 15in (81.5 by 38.5cm).
£2,500–3,000 *AG*

Screens

A George II style mahogany pole screen, the standard carved with foliage, on tripod supports, the needlework panel 18thC, 61in (155cm) high.
£2,000–2,500 *S(NY)*

A painted leather four-leaf screen, decorated overall with chinoiserie figures and buildings within foliage, late 19thC, 75½in (192cm) high.
£1,500–1,700 *C*

A George III style parcel gilt screen, centred by a wool and silk work panel depicting *Europa and the Bull*, surrounded by scrolling flowers on a dark blue field, the moulded frame carved with foliage, on moulded splay legs, 18thC, 45in (114cm) high.
£600–900 *DN*

An early Victorian rosewood screen, the Berlin needlework panel bordered by a spiral turned frame, on outswept scroll legs, 39in (99cm) wide.
£600–700 *CSK*

A mid-Victorian mahogany firescreen, the needlework panel within a foliate and scrolling surround, between spiral twist uprights joined by a similar stretcher, on arched foliate carved legs, 24in (61cm) wide.
£300–700 *CSK*

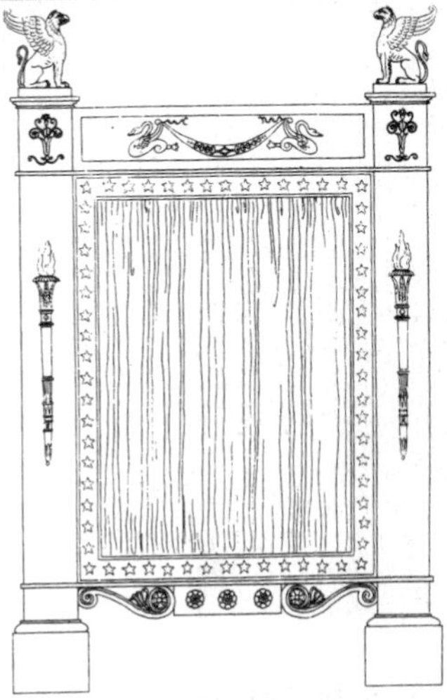

A Regency bronze mounted mahogany cheval firescreen, after a design by Thomas Hope, the frieze with classical bronze mounts, the front and back each with a pleated silk panel enclosed by ebony and brass bandings, and each side with a sliding panel, the apron and feet carved with anthemion scrolls, c1810, 43 by 30in (109 by 78cm).
£6,000–9,000 *S*

This firescreen was formerly at Knole in Kent, seat of the Dukes of Dorset, and is believed to have entered the collection through the marriage of Arabella Diana, widow of the 3rd Duke of Dorset, and Charles, 1st Earl Whitworth. It is based on an earlier model by Thomas Hope. Although less elaborate, with variations in the decorative detailing, the Knole firescreen retains the same distinctive form as that by Hope. The link is confirmed by the fact that the central frieze is taken from another of Hope's designs in Household Furniture and Interior Decoration, *illustrating a console table with the identical pattern of scrolling foliage and a central rosette.*

A Victorian rosewood screen, with a printed velvet panel, on a turned column with 3 moulded legs, 51in (130cm) high.
£300–400 *DN*

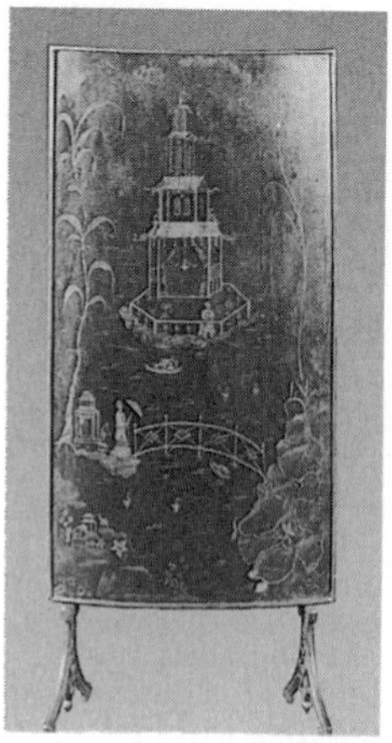

A Victorian cast iron and black and gilt japanned tôle firescreen, 49in (124.5cm) high.
£750–1,000 *C*

A pair of Victorian rosewood pole screens, the fret carved and barley-twist adjustable frames with glazed floral needlework panels.
£900–1,200 *MCA*

A Louis XVI style giltwood two-fold screen, with silk damask upholstered panels, late 19thC, 76in (193cm) high.
£1,000–1,200 *CSK*

l. A Victorian simulated rosewood pole screen, with an adjustable brass column, 58in (148cm) high.
£600–700 *WL*

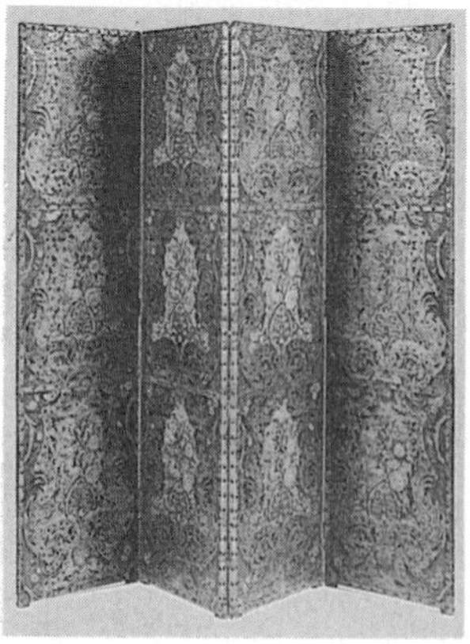

A Dutch cream painted, gilt and polychrome four-leaf screen, each leaf with poppies and roses in acanthus cartouche frames, 19thC, 78in (198cm) high.
£3,500–4,000 *C*

Sideboards

A satinwood, crossbanded mahogany and burr veneered breakfront sideboard, on square tapering legs, early 19thC, adapted, 90in (228.5cm).
£1,700–2,200 *CSK*

In the Furniture section when there is only one measurement it refers to the width of the piece, unless otherwise stated.

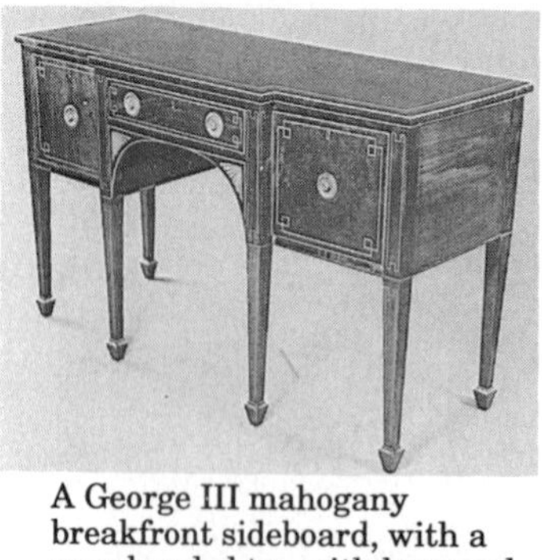

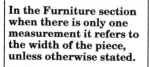

A George III mahogany breakfront sideboard, with a crossbanded top with boxwood lines, on 6 square tapering legs and block feet, 60in (152cm).
£2,000–3,000 *DN*

l. A mahogany breakfront sideboard, the foliate carved raised three-quarter gallery above a frieze drawer and arched apron drawer, flanked by a deep cellaret drawer and cupboard door, on ring turned legs with paw feet, early 19thC, the gallery later, 76in (193cm).
£1,400–2,000 *CSK*

A George III mahogany sideboard, with a crossbanded bowfronted top, on square tapering legs and spade feet, possibly reduced, 36in (91cm).
£2,000–3,000 *C*

A George III mahogany sideboard, with frieze drawer flanked by 2 deeper drawers, on square tapering legs, 58in (148cm).
£1,500–2,000 *DN*

A George III style mahogany sideboard, the crossbanded top with inlaid boxwood lines, 41in (104cm).
£1,700–2,300 *P*

A George III mahogany sideboard of bowfront outline, the boxwood strung top above a frieze drawer and two deep drawers, on square tapering legs with block feet, altered, 45½in (115cm).
£900–1,500 *DN*

A George III mahogany bowfront sideboard, the brass gallery with lions' paw feet and mounts, with pivotting right hand deep cellaret drawer, the left hand cupboard with internal drawer, flanked and centred by freestanding reeded pillars, on turned legs, 72in (182.5cm).
£3,500–4,500 *B*

A George III style mahogany sideboard, with a brass butler's rack, c1920, 72in (182.5cm).
£1,300–1,700 *LHA*

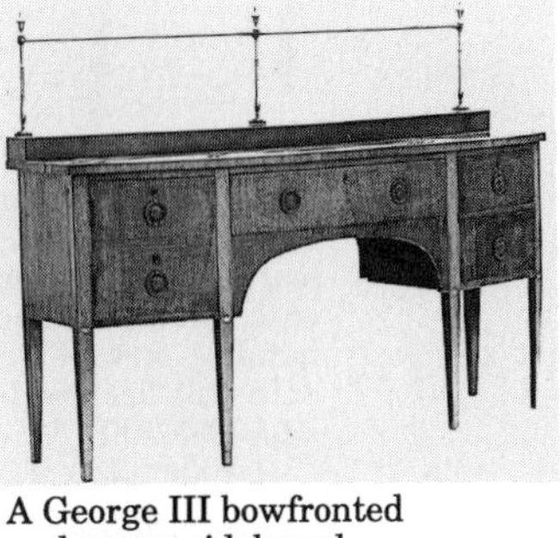

A George III bowfronted mahogany sideboard.
£1,400–1,700 *DaD*

l. A George III inlaid serpentine mahogany sideboard, with a non-matching mahogany back.
£5,000–5,500 *DaD*

A George III mahogany breakfront sideboard, with satinwood and tulipwood crossbanding, a long frieze drawer above an arch with fan spandrels, flanked by deep drawers each simulating 2 drawers, on square tapering legs and spade feet, 70in (178cm).
£2,700–3,200 *L*

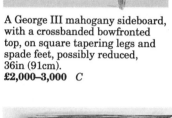

A George III bowfront sideboard, with dotted brass border to the top edge, cellaret drawer to one side and a cupboard to the other, with brass lions' mask ring handles and shaped ebony line inlay, 56in (142cm).
£2,500–3,000 *B*

A George III style satinwood crossbanded mahogany breakfront sideboard, 48½in (124cm).
£1,000–1,500 *CSK*

A George III mahogany bowfront sideboard, with feather banded inlay, stamped circular brass handles, on square tapering legs and spade feet, 57in (144.5cm).
£1,000–1,500 *WL*

A mahogany and inlaid bowfront sideboard, the crossbanded top above a frieze drawer and arched apron flanked by small drawers, on square tapering legs, 19thC, 36in (92cm).
£800–1,000 *CSK*

A late George III mahogany breakfront sideboard, on square tapering legs with spade feet, 66½in (169cm).
£1,200–1,700 *CSK*

A George IV mahogany sideboard, the triangular pediment with a pair of sliding panels to the superstructure below, the bowfronted base having 3 frieze drawers, on turned and fluted tapering legs, 62in (156cm).
£2,000–2,500 *P*

A Canadian walnut sideboard, c1880, 50in (127cm) wide.
£1,500–2,000 *RIT*

A Regency mahogany sideboard, with shaped three-quarter gallery applied with rosettes, a central frieze drawer and a pair of recessed panelled cupboard doors between spiral half columns, flanked by a drawer and cupboard door below, between multi-faceted uprights, on spiral twist legs and tapering feet, damaged, 73in (186cm) wide.
£1,700–2,200 *CSK*

A late Regency mahogany pedestal sideboard, fitted with a central frieze drawer, the pedestals fitted with drawers and adjustable shelves and enclosed by panelled doors, on plinth bases, 69in (175.5cm) wide.
£1,000–1,500 *CSK*

A Regency mahogany butler's sideboard, with galleried top, a single drawer above 2 panelled doors enclosing a cellaret drawer, on lobed bun feet, 38in (96.5cm).
£1,000–1,500 *WL*

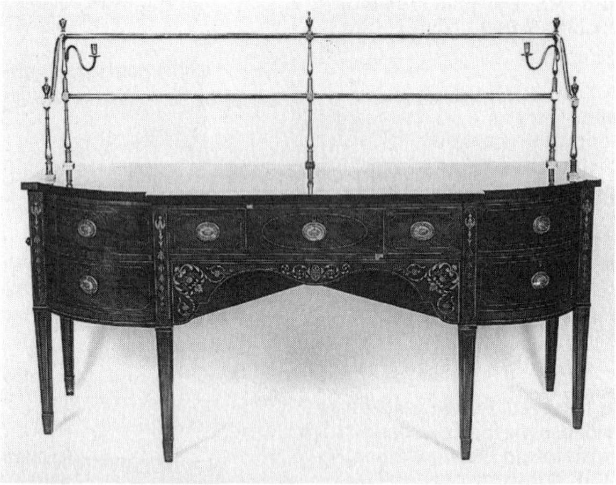

A Regency mahogany bow breakfront sideboard, outlined with boxwood stringing, inlaid with harewood classical leafy guilloche, pendants and scrollwork, brass gallery with urn finials and a pair of candle branches, brass oval handles, on tapered fluted legs and spade feet, c1820, 81in (205.5cm) wide.
£4,500–5,500 *N*

A German mahogany pedestal sideboard, with central slide drawer and panelled cupboard, each pedestal with 2 drawers and a panelled cupboard door enclosing fitted interiors, between reeded uprights with corbels, on bracket feet, mid-19thC, 75in (190cm).
£500–900 *CSK*

l. A William IV mahogany twin pedestal sideboard, the raised pedimented back with central laurel wreath in low relief, beaded moulded edged breakfront top, cushion frieze drawer, flanked on either side by a drawer with panelled cupboard door below, on a plinth base, 84in (213cm) wide.
£1,200–1,700 *AH*

Sofas

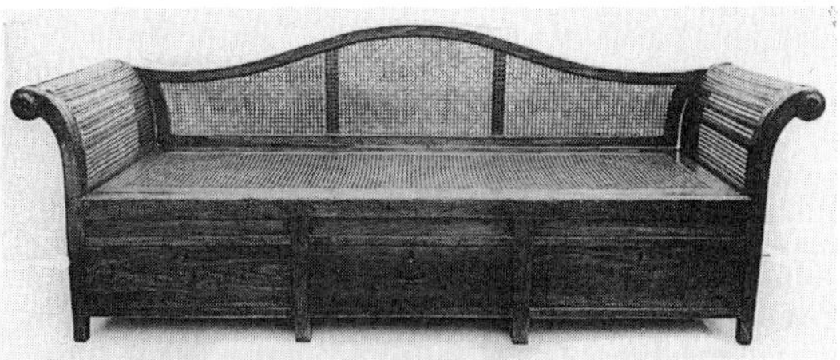

An officer's campaign or ship's captain's sofa bed, with scrolled arms at either end, the shaped back and seat with caning, above 3 drawers with brass flush handles and fastenings, the back removing to form a bed, now with modern cushions to form a settee, early 19thC, 89in (226cm) wide.
£3,500–4,000 *B*

l. A campaign settee, with removable outscrolled arms and rectangular back, with loose seat squab, on turned tapering mahogany legs with brass casters, early 19thC, 88in (223.5cm).
£2,500–3,500 *Bea*

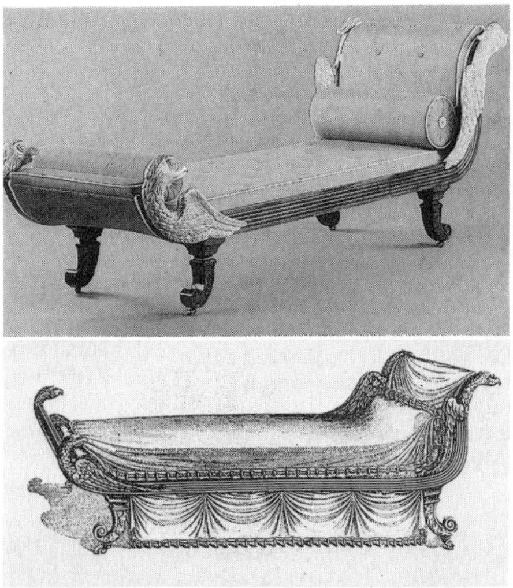

A parcel gilt mahogany couch, after a design by Thomas Sheraton, the ends with carved giltwood eagle supports and a reeded moulded frame, on moulded sabre legs carved with acanthus leaves, 86in (217cm) wide.
£29,000–32,000 *S*

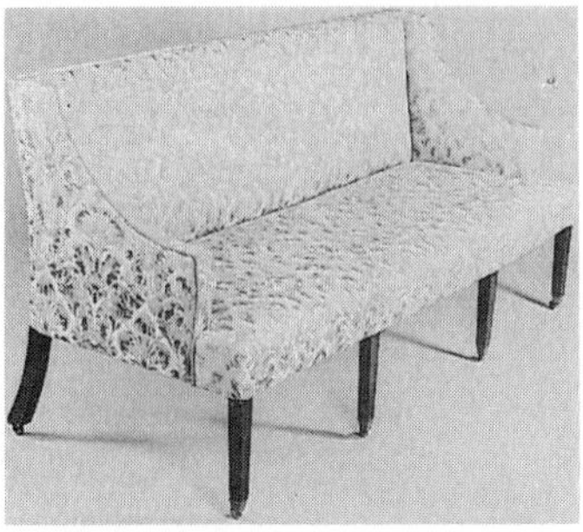

A George III mahogany sofa, with padded back, arms and seat, on square tapering legs with brass casters, restored, 76in (193cm).
£1,200–1,800 *DN*

A George III style mahogany serpentine sofa, the swept arms with rosette terminals, mid-19thC, 74in (188cm).
£1,000–1,200 *CSK*

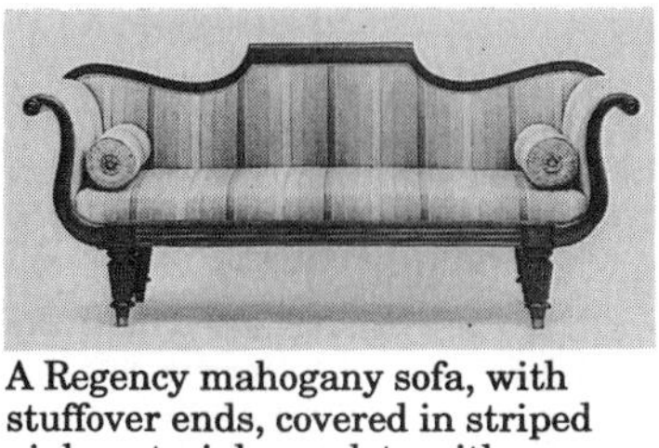

A Regency mahogany sofa, with stuffover ends, covered in striped pink material complete with bolsters, raised on reeded tapering legs and casters, 84in (213cm).
£900–1,200 *AG*

A George II carved walnut two chair-back settee, 62in (157cm).
£7,000–8,000 *SLN*

Did you know?
MILLER'S* Antiques Price Guide *builds up year-by-year to form the most comprehensive antiques photo-reference library available.

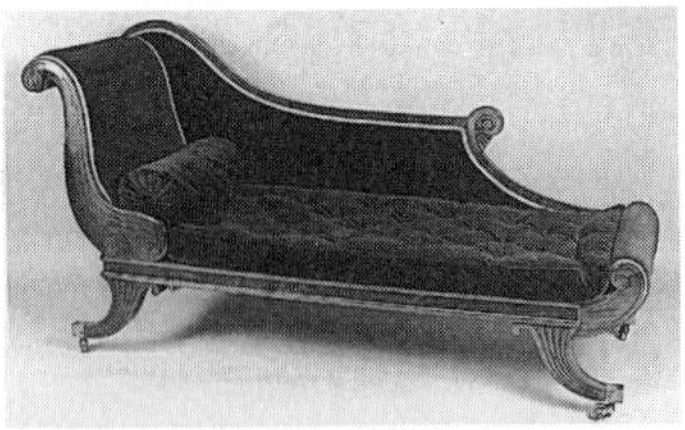

A Regency rosewood chaise longue.
£2,000–3,000 *SWO*

A Regency mahogany sofa, with foliate carved rectagular padded back, padded arms with stylised foliage and scroll carved fronts, squab seats and similar tapering legs, 85in (216cm).
£1,200–1,700 *CSK*

A walnut triple chair-back settee, in the Carolean manner, the carved cresting rails with cherubs, above caned centres and shaped surrounds, a caned seat with carved surround, scrolled arms and scrolling front legs united by turned stretchers, 19thC, 57in (144.5cm).
£800–1,200 *B*

A Regency giltwood sofa, the padded back, outscrolled arms and squab cushion covered in red and white striped silk and with cotton loose cover, on turned tapering legs, brass caps and casters, 89in (226cm) wide.
£5,200–5,500 *C*

This sofa was almost certainly supplied to William Harry (1792–1842), 3rd Earl of Darlington (and subsequently 1st Marquess and Duke of Cleveland) for Cleveland House, 19 St. James's Square, and was presumably moved to Raby on the sale and demolition of Cleveland House in 1892.

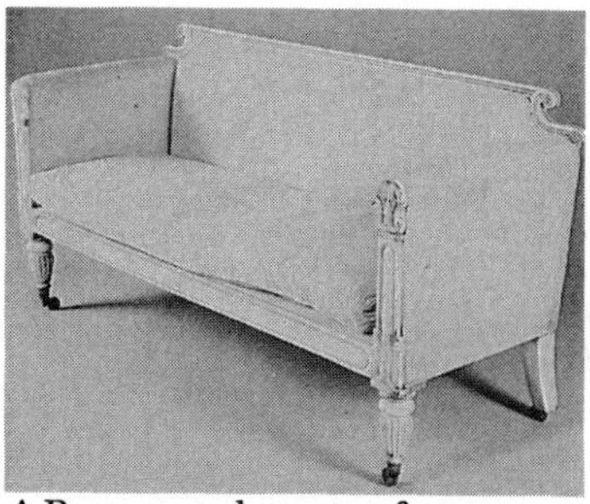

A Regency mahogany sofa, now white painted, the padded arms terminating in carved panelled ends, on reeded bulbous legs, 72in (183cm).
£700–1,000 *DN*

A Regency mahogany chaise longue, with scrolling padded back ends, padded seat, on ring turned tapering supports, brass cappings and casters, 75in (190cm).
£1,500–2,000 *P*

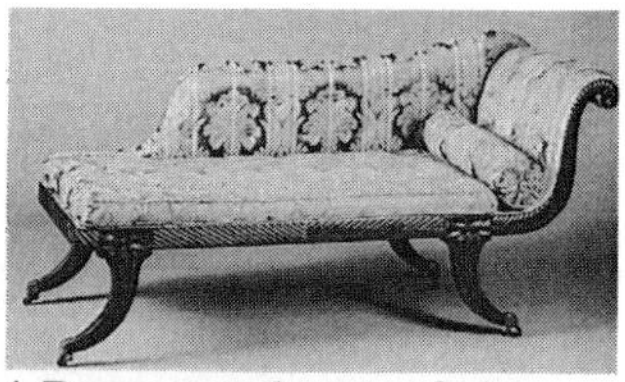

A Regency mahogany chaise longue, with squab seat and bolster, on reeded sabre legs, headed with large foliate tablets, restored, 70in (178cm).
£1,200–1,700 *CSK*

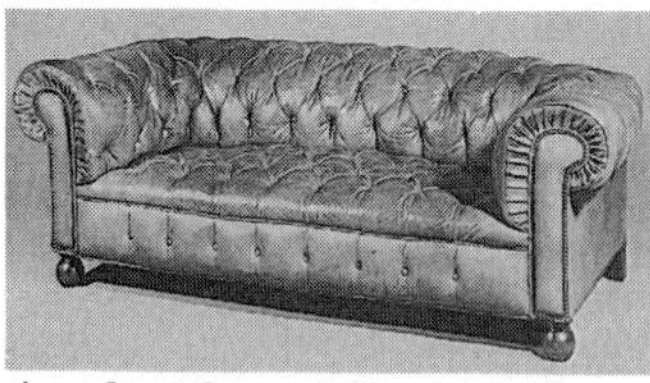

A walnut framed Chesterfield sofa, with ring turned legs, late 19thC, 78in (198cm).
£2,000–2,500 *CSK*

A William IV mahogany chaise longue, the outswept raised end and shaped downswept padded back above baluster and squab cushions, on paterae headed turned tapering reeded legs, 78in (198cm).
£600–900 *CSK*

An early Victorian rosewood framed sofa, with carved and scrolled arms, upholstered back, armrests and seat, on lions' paw feet, 90in (228.5cm).
£2,000–3,000 *Bea*

An early Victorian mahogany sofa, the padded arms with rosette terminals and foliate carved supports, on turned tapering legs with gadrooned collars, 96in (244cm) wide.
£1,200–1,500 *CSK*

A Victorian walnut cameo back settee.
£2,000–2,500 *LT*

An early Victorian mahogany settee, with a close nailed buttoned back, on turned lotus decorated legs, with brass caps and casters, possibly Scottish.
£2,000–2,500 *CSK*

An early Victorian rosewood double-ended settee, covered in buttoned fabric, requiring complete refurbishment.
£600–1,000 *L&E*

In the Furniture section when there is only one measurement it refers to the width of the piece, unless otherwise stated.

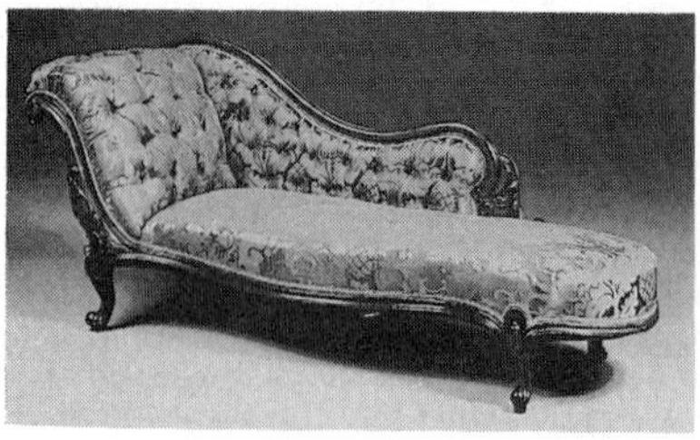

l. A mid-Victorian mahogany chaise longue, with green floral upholstery, on scroll carved cabriole legs, 74in (188cm) wide.
£1,200–1,700 *CSK*

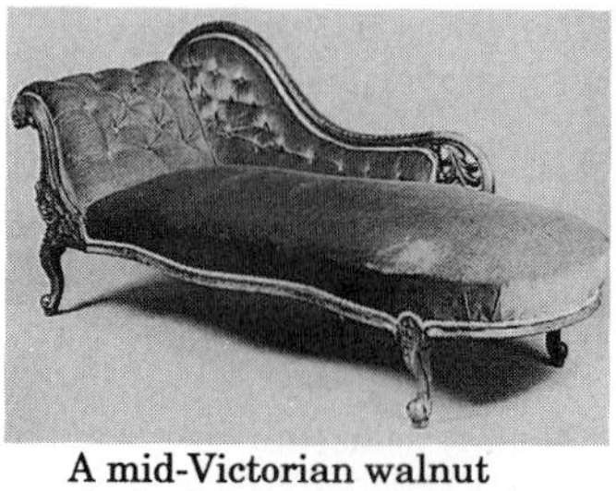

A mid-Victorian walnut chaise longue, with serpentine padded seat, on scroll feet, 74in (188cm).
£1,200–1,700 *CSK*

A Victorian walnut sofa, on flower carved cabriole legs, 71in (180cm).
£900–1,500 *DN*

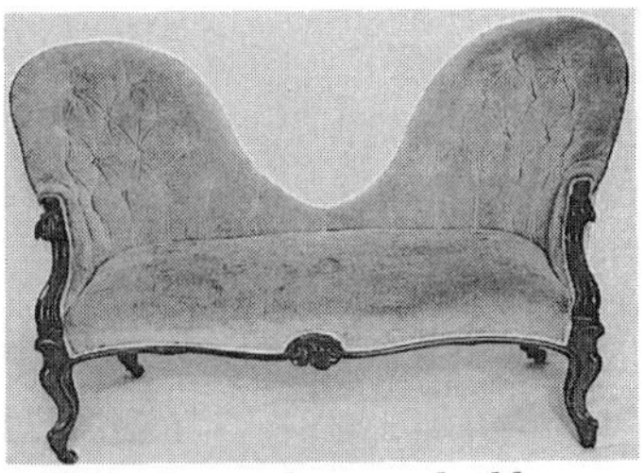

A Victorian mahogany double chair-back settee, covered in buttoned gold coloured velour, 69in (175cm).
£900–1,200 *AG*

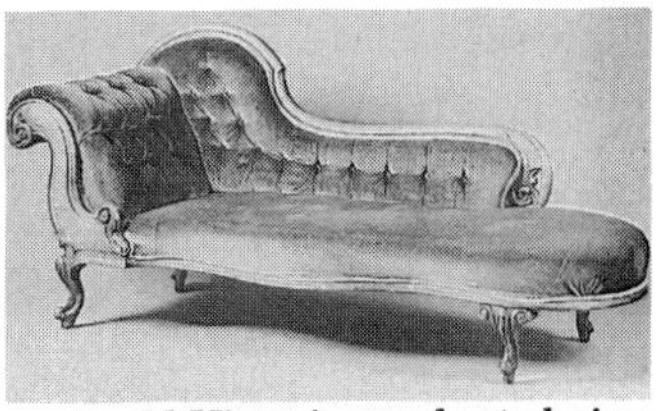

A mid-Victorian walnut chaise longue, upholstered in powder blue velvet, 80in (203cm).
£800–1,000 *CSK*

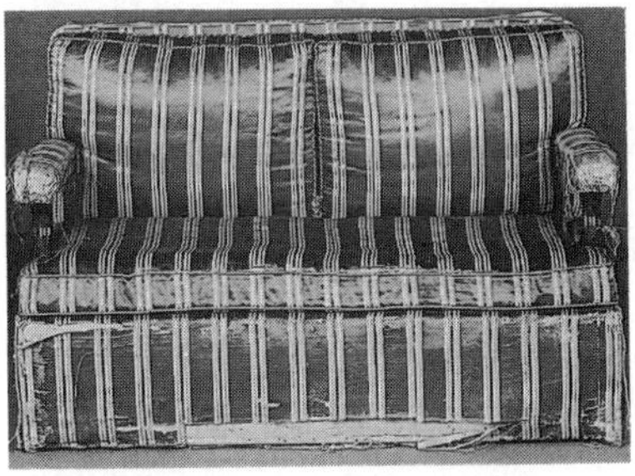

l. A Victorian walnut sofa, the padded back, armrests and squab cushion covered in red and white striped silk, the arms with panelled supports and key pattern bases with plinth, 53in (135cm) wide.
£1,500–2,000 *C*

A Victorian white painted and parcel gilt sofa, with arched padded back, sides and buttoned seat, on baluster legs, brass caps and casters, cover distressed, 87in (221cm).
£2,000–2,500 *C*

A late Victorian walnut scroll end settee, upholstered with buttoned faded pink fabric.
£600–1,000 *DA*

Miller's is a price GUIDE not a price LIST

A late Victorian mahogany serpentine chaise longue, on cabriole legs with scroll feet, 52in (183cm).
£700–900 *CSK*

An Edwardian rosewood sofa, on turned legs, 58in (148cm).
£400–600 *DN*

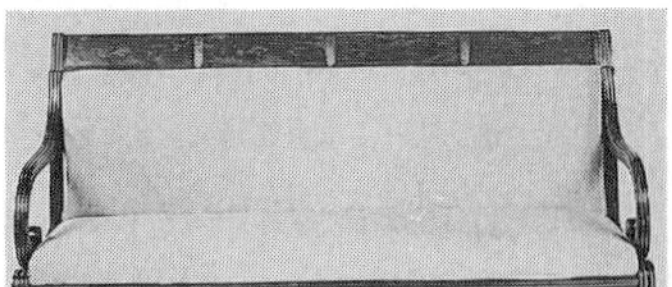

A Federal carved mahogany sofa, by William Camp, with brass lions' head feet, rose silk upholstery, Baltimore, c1820, 68in (172.5cm) wide.
£2,250–2,750 *SLN*

A Federal mahogany sofa, New England, c1815, 78in (198cm).
£800–1,200 *SK(B)*

A Louis XV style giltwood two-seater settee.
£1,000–1,500 *DA*

An Edwardian mahogany sofa, with a stuffover back, seat and scroll arms with sunflower and acanthus decorated supports, on spirally reeded and ring turned legs and casters.
£1,400–1,800 *CSK*

A Louis XV style walnut settee, with a moulded and foliate carved frame, tapestry upholstery, on cabriole legs, c1870, 86in (218.5cm).
£1,400–1,800 *SLN*

Stands

A line inlaid mahogany bookstand, the cane sided trough on turned support with central pierced decoration, on outswept legs and turned feet, 18in (46cm) wide.
£400–500 *CSK*

A George IV solid mahogany folio stand, the 2 railed hinged supports with solid rectangular end supports and panelled downswept legs with paw feet, restored, 29in (74cm) wide.
£1,800–2,200 *C*

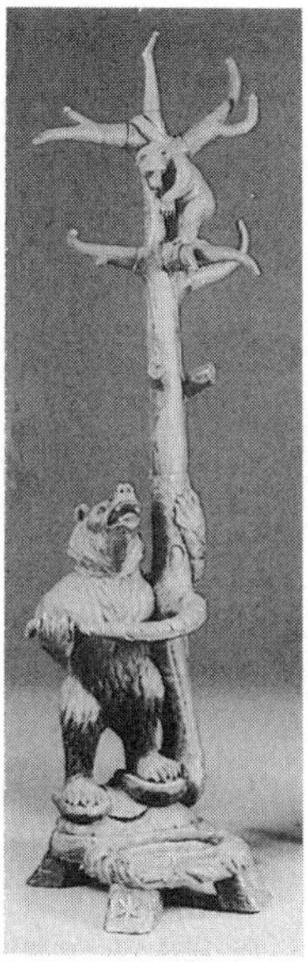

A carved hallstand, with a growling bear below and a cub in a branching tree, 79in (201cm) high.
£720–770 *CSK*

An early George III Chippendale style mahogany stand, the plain tray top with a slide, plain aprons, on square chamfered and moulded legs with fretted brackets, on casters, some brackets replaced, 25in high (63.5cm).
£1,300–1,600 *CAG*

A Dutch mahogany and satinwood kettle stand, with a brass liner, small drawer, on cabriole legs and pad feet, 18thC, 20in (51cm) wide.
£600–700 *DN*

A mahogany kettle stand, mid-18thC, 22in (56cm) high.
£900–1,200 *CSK*

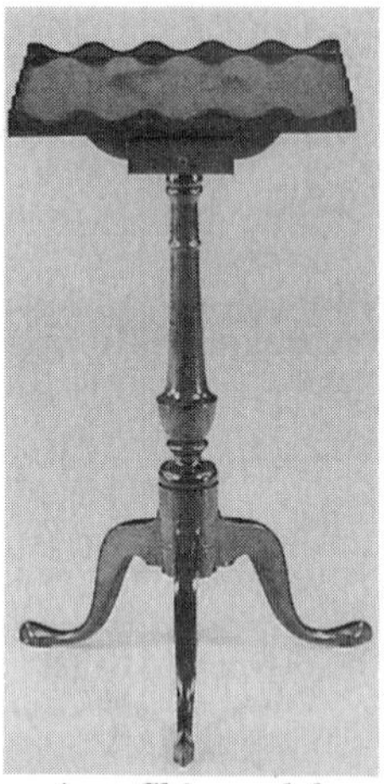

An American Chippendale cherrywood candlestand, on cabriole legs with snake feet, probably Connecticut, mid-18thC, 30in (76cm) high.
£700–1,000 *SLN*

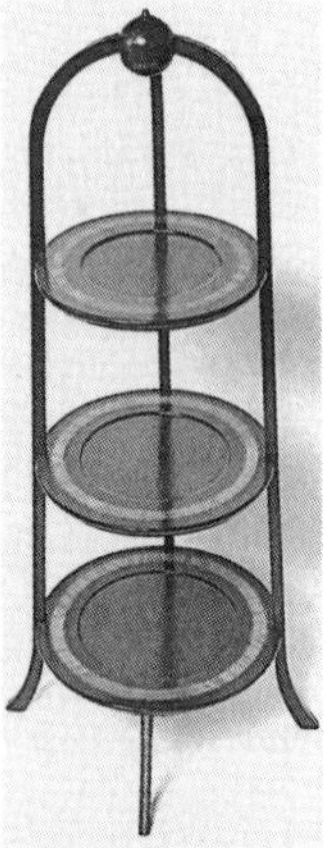

A mahogany inlaid cake stand, c1900, 35in (89cm) high.
£200–250 *JHW*

Steps

A set of George III mahogany library steps, with 2 extending steps on canted square legs, later canted square pole, 29in (73.5cm) high.
£1,800–2,200 *C*

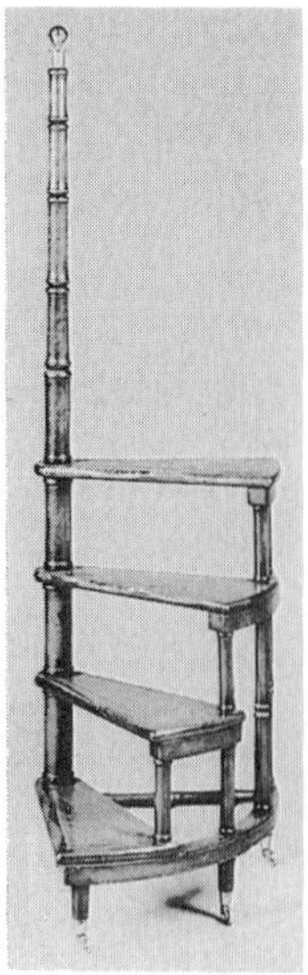

A set of yew and beech library steps, each leather lined tread linked by a ring turned pole with a brass ball finial, 67in (170cm) high.
£1,000–1,200 *CSK*

A set of yew folding four-tread library steps, with brass hinges, 15½in (39.5cm) wide.
£1,000–1,200 *C(S)*

A set of Victorian fruitwood and beech metamorphic library steps, the hinged green leather lined moulded top above a spindle galleried body incorporating 2 treads, on ring turned tapering legs, the top partially re-veneered, restored, 17in (43cm) wide.
£2,200–2,700 *C*

Stools

A George I style walnut stool, the caned seat with squab cushion, on shell headed cabriole legs and claw-and-ball feet, 45in (114cm).
£800–1,000 *CSK*

A George IV mahogany piano stool, with reeded legs joined by turned stretchers.
£300–350 *DN*

An ebonised and gilt revolving piano stool, by Gillows, 19thC, 20in (51cm) high.
£300–350 *JHW*

A carved mahogany revolving piano stool, with leather seat, early 19thC, 21in (53cm) high.
£180–230 *JHW*

A Regency rosewood piano stool, with padded green leather rising top, on a turned lotus leaf cast column and rounded concave sided triangular platform base, on tapering bun feet, 19in (48cm) high.
£800–1,200 *C*

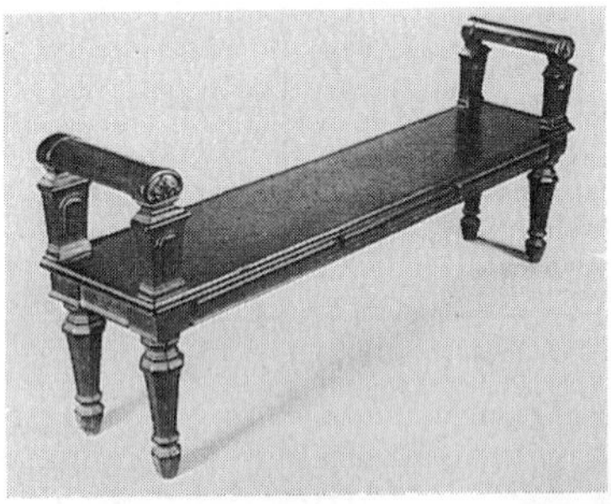

l. A William IV mahogany bench, with a leaf carved armrests, solid seat, on hexagonal tapering legs, 65in (165cm) long.
£1,800–2,000 *DN*

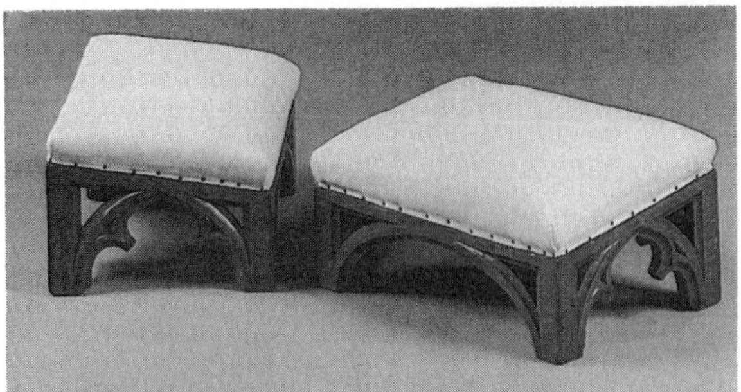

A pair of early Victorian oak stools, each with a sloping padded top, covered in calico, supported on canted square legs joined by pierced Gothic arches, 18in (46cm) wide.
£800–1,200 *C*

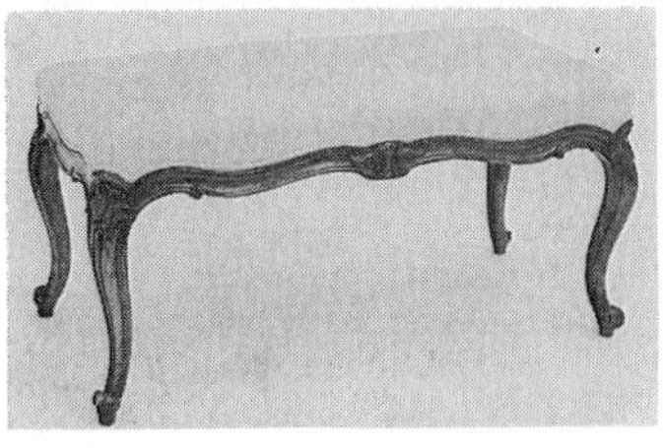

l. A Victorian walnut stool, with moulded cabriole legs and scrolled toes, 38in (96cm) wide.
£1,400–1,600 *L*

A Victorian brass mounted mahogany stool, the channelled top rail with pierced baluster frieze flanked by reeded downswept arms and moulded seat, on tapering reeded sabre legs joined by stretchers, stamped to the reverse 'JAS. SHOOLBRED & CO.', numbered '2724' and with registration mark for 13th December, 1883, 22in (56cm) wide.
£2,000–2,200 *C*

A mid-Victorian rosewood stool, the seat upholstered in tapestry, on foliate carved cabriole legs with scroll feet, damaged, 46½in (118cm).
£2,500–3,000 *CSK*

A walnut stool, the top covered in needlework, signed 'M.B. 1930', on cabriole legs joined by an H-shaped turned stretcher, on pad feet, 23in (58cm) wide.
£800–1,200 *C*

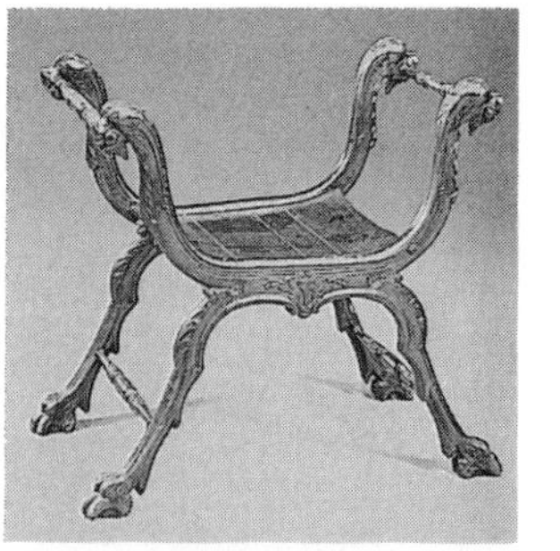

An Italian walnut X-frame stool, the terminals carved with animals' masks, with a solid seat, legs joined by a turned stretcher, late 19thC, 27in (69cm) wide.
£400–600 *C*

A French Empire style painted beechwood window bench, on sabre legs, mid-19thC, 56in (142cm).
£2,200–2,500 *LHA*

l. A Restauration giltwood footstool, in the manner of Marçion, on paw feet, with inventory No. '3096' and the mark of a label, c1820, 17½in (44.5cm) wide.
£3,500–5,000 *S*

The presence of fleurs-de-lys at the corners of this piece would suggest a Royal provenance.

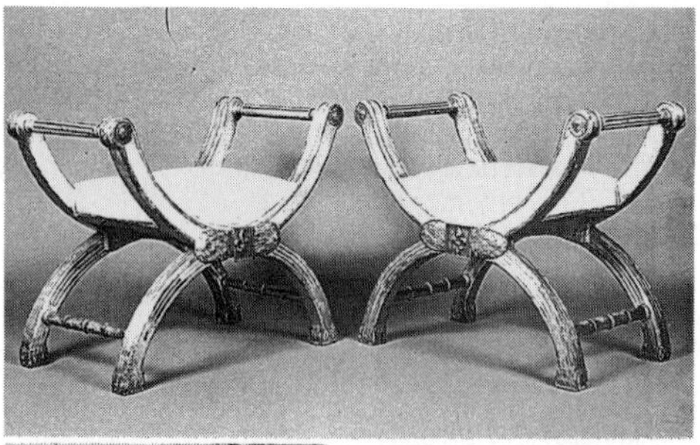

A pair of Italian Empire giltwood X-frame stools, marked on the underside with a crowned cypher, 34in (86cm) wide.
£10,000–12,000 *C*

The mark is possibly that of Caroline Bonaparte, Napoleon's sister, who married Joachim Murat, King of Naples,(1808–15).

Breakfast Tables

A George III mahogany breakfast table, the casters stamped 'New & Co', with depository label, 60in (152cm).
£2,000–3,000 *CSK*

l. A Regency mahogany breakfast table, the tilt-top on 4 ring turned uprights and ebonised line inlaid splayed legs, 48in (122cm) wide.
£600–800 *CSK*

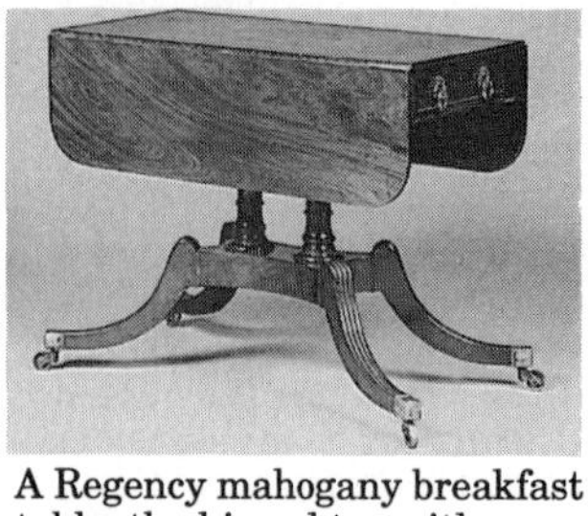

A Regency mahogany breakfast table, the hinged top with rounded corners and a reeded edge, fitted with a frieze drawer, 41in (104cm) extended.
£1,200–1,700 *CSK*

A Regency tulipwood breakfast table, on 4 squared moulded splayed legs joined by a platform stretcher, with brass casters, 48½in (123cm) diam.
£2,700–3,200 *DN*

A Regency mahogany tilt-top breakfast table, inlaid with rosewood, 53½in (135cm).
£1,700–2,000 *SLN*

A Regency mahogany breakfast table, the hinged top on a ring turned column and splayed quadruped supports, terminating in brass caps and casters, 65in (165cm) long.
£1,500–2,000 *CSK*

An early Victorian mahogany extending breakfast table, including one extra leaf, the oval top on turned lappeted column and circular platform, on scroll feet.
£2,000–3,000 *CSK*

A Victorian burr walnut breakfast table, with quartered veneered top, 4 moulded scroll supports, on bold scrolled outswept legs and casters, 60in (152cm) long.
£2,400–2,800 *CAG*

A Federal mahogany inlaid breakfast table, with drawers, New England, old refinish, damaged, c1800, 21½in (54cm).
£1,300–1,700 *SK(B)*

Did you know?
MILLER'S* Antiques Price Guide *builds up year-by-year to form the most comprehensive antiques photo-reference library available.

A William IV rosewood and brass inlaid breakfast table, on a square column base, with 4 downswept legs terminating in brass paw feet with casters, restored, 49in (124.5cm) diam.
£2,000–3,000 *DN*

An early Victorian mahogany circular breakfast table, on turned column and trefoil platform base with paw feet, 53½in (136cm) diam.
£1,700–2,200 *CSK*

A late Victorian inlaid burr walnut breakfast table, 53in (135cm).
£1,500–2,000 *CSK*

Card Tables

A George II mahogany metamorphic writing/card table, with fold-over top opening to a baize covered playing surface, further opening to reveal pigeonholes and small drawers, raised on scroll carved cabriole legs and pointed pad feet, 32in (81cm).
£2,800–3,400 *RBB*

A William IV pollard oak breakfast table, on a turned tapering and extended lotus column, with a stiff foliate base and trefoil platform with foliate bun feet with casters, 51½in (131cm) diam.
£1,500–2,000 *CSK*

A Victorian walnut breakfast table, the moulded top on a bulbous stem with splayed moulded legs, 37½in (95cm) diam.
£700–1,000 *DN*

A Louis Philippe mahogany breakfast table, on anthemion carved turned baluster column, quadripartite platform with 4 paw feet, 42in (106.5cm).
£700–1,000 *CSK*

A George II style mahogany card table, the top with a profusely foliate carved rim frieze, on square chamfered legs with trailing foliate carving, 37in (94cm).
£750–800 *CSK*

A George III demi-lune mahogany games table.
£650–750 *DaD*

Card Tables

Card tables were made by several different methods of construction to enable the folding flap to be supported. The earliest method was the same principle as the gateleg table, with both back legs swinging out on wooden hinges to 45° so that the back legs squared up with the front legs. From c1760 many card tables had a separate sliding frame, onto which the back legs were attached, and which pulled out on runners to extend to double the width, and so support the table top. From 1770 onwards many card tables had a single drawer without handles concealed in the frieze. From c1780 a novel hinged wooden concertina-action doubled back on itself to fold neatly into the underframe.

A mahogany card table, the folding baize lined top with candle stands, a single frieze drawer and 4 lappeted turned tapering supports with pad feet, 29in (74cm).
£900–1,400 *AH*

A mahogany and inlaid half-round card table, the top with radiating sunburst design, veneered radially, above serpentine friezes and square moulded legs headed with oval tablets, part 18thC, 36in (91.5cm).
£1,500–2,000 *CSK*

A George III crossbanded mahogany demi-lune card table, the hinged top enclosing a baize interior, on marquetry headed square tapering legs with spade feet, repaired, 36in (91.5cm).
£900–1,500 *CSK*

A George III mahogany card table with a tulipwood crossbanded top, on square tapering legs, 36in (91.5cm).
£1,300–1,700 *DN*

r. A George III mahogany card table, the crossbanded hinged top on square tapering legs headed by paterae and inlaid with boxwood lines, 36in (91.5cm) wide.
£700–1,000 *DN*

A George III mahogany and plum pudding mahogany card table, crossbanded overall and inlaid with boxwood lines, on turned tapering fluted legs and feet, brass caps and casters, 36in (91.5cm).
£1,800–2,200 *C*

A George III mahogany card table, on square moulded legs with pierced spandrels, adapted, 35in (89cm).
£1,500–2,000 *C*

A George III line inlaid demi-lune card table, the crossbanded hinged top on conch shell headed square tapering legs with block feet, restored, the top warped, 36in (91.5cm).
£500–800 *CSK*

A Regency rosewood card table, the folding top on turned column and circular platform, with paw feet, 37in (94cm).
£1,200–1,700 *CSK*

A George IV mahogany card table, with a hinged tulipwood crossbanded top, on turned reeded legs, 37in (94cm).
£900–1,200 *DN*

A Regency rosewood card table, the crossbanded top opening to reveal a baize lined surface and a games compartment beneath, 36in (91.5cm).
£1,800–2,500 *B*

A Regency burr veneered card table, with crossbanded D-shaped fold-over top on crossbanded sabre legs, 38in (96.5cm).
£1,800–2,200 *RBB*

Envelope Card Tables

The four-flap 'envelope' bridge table was a development of the Sheraton revival in the Edwardian period. The best examples are made of rosewood with fine inlay.
In view of their comparatively recent age, condition should be excellent to command a high price.

A late Regency period mahogany card table, with ebony inlay and stringing, baize lined D-shaped swivel top, 36in (91.5cm).
£1,500–2,000 *WW*

An early Victorian rosewood card table, with swivel top, bulbous octagonal column and concave-sided platform base, on paw feet, 36in (91.5cm).
£1,200–1,700 *CSK*

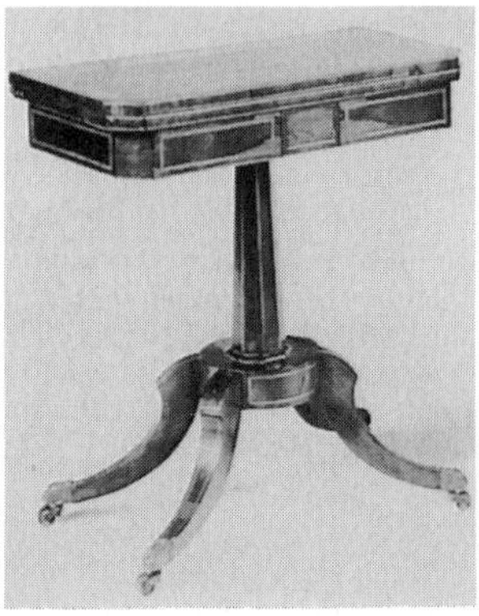

l. A Regency line inlaid rosewood card table, the canted hinged rectangular cross-banded top above a faceted column, on 4 hipped splayed legs, 28in (71cm) wide.
£1,500–2,000 *CSK*

r. A Victorian walnut card table, with moulded swivel hinged top, on 4 fluted columns and moulded square base with scroll feet, 36in (91.5cm).
£1,000–1,500 *DN*

l. An Edwardian mahogany envelope card table, with a floral carved frieze drawer, flanked by dot and dash decorated uprights, on channelled square tapering legs, with a galleried undertier.
£600–1,000 *CSK*

An Edwardian mahogany envelope card table, with inset wells and a single drawer, on cabriole legs with a cross stretcher, 22in (56cm) square.
£400–600 *M*

An Edwardian mahogany envelope card table, with a satinwood crossbanded swivel top above a small drawer, on square tapering legs inlaid with boxwood lines, 21½in (54cm).
£900–1,200 *DN*

An Edwardian satinwood and tulipwood crossbanded demi-lune card table, 36in (91.5cm).
£900–1,200 *CSK*

A mahogany card table, probably Massachusetts, old refinish, damaged, c1820, 35in (89.5cm).
£900–1,200 *SK(B)*

Centre Tables

A mahogany centre table, with reeded edges and root carved platform with paw feet, early 19thC, 35½in (90cm).
£750–1,000 *CSK*

Rosewood

Rosewood is an exotic hardwood, which is not rose coloured but blackish-brown, with an attractive stripe or ripple. It was commonly used for veneers from 18thC. When cut the wood has a rose-like fragrance.

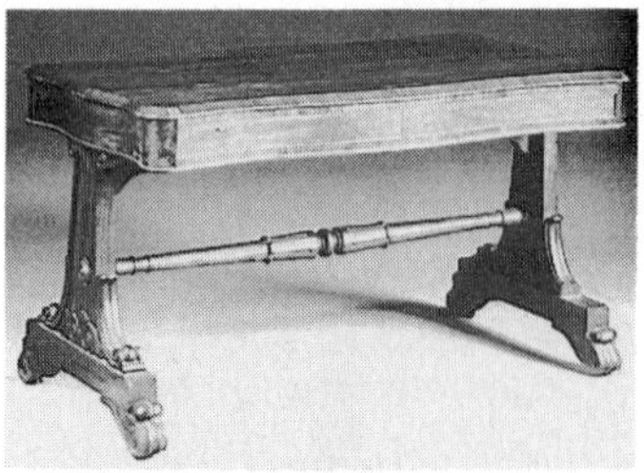

A George IV rosewood centre table, with 2 frieze drawers, on foliate carved end standards, joined by a turned stretcher, on scroll feet, 54in (137cm).
£1,600–2,000 *CSK*

An early Victorian pollard oak centre table, with 2 true and 4 false frieze drawers, on spiral turned legs, an X-shaped stretcher with central finial, on reeded feet, 47in (119cm).
£1,500–2,000 *CSK*

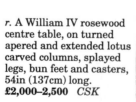

r. A William IV rosewood centre table, on turned apered and extended lotus carved columns, splayed legs, bun feet and casters, 54in (137cm) long.
£2,000–2,500 *CSK*

An early Victorian rosewood centre table, the top with 2 brushing slides, one inlaid for chess, the other upholstered for backgammon, on spiral turned twin end standards joined by a similar stretcher, on turned legs, 40½in (103cm).
£1,400–1,800 *CSK*

A Victorian walnut centre table, the octagonal top with 2 frieze drawers, on 4 turned tapered columns and quatrefoil base with curved feet, 48in (122cm) diam.
£800–1,200 *CSK*

A mid-Victorian oak centre table, possibly reduced, 44in (111.5cm).
£1,000–1,500 *CSK*

A Victorian walnut centre table.
£1,500–2,000 *DaD*

A Victorian walnut centre table, with a moulded and crossbanded top with scrolls, on turned fluted standard supports and splay legs, 48in (122cm).
£1,200–1,700 *DN*

An Edwardian walnut and marquetry centre table, the crossbanded top above a frieze drawer, on cabriole legs, stamped and labelled 'Edwards and Roberts, Wardour Street, 126 Piccadilly, 532 Oxford Street, London', 29in (73.5cm).
£1,400–1,700 *CSK*

An Edwardian mahogany and marquetry centre table, the crossbanded top with floral inlay, on square tapering legs with block feet, 37½in (95cm).
£900–1,400 *CSK*

A mahogany centre table, inlaid with mother-of-pearl, c1900, 30in (76cm).
£375–450 *JHW*

A Sheraton revival inlaid table, c1900, 29½in (74cm) diam.
£1,450–1,850 *JHW*

A Dutch mahogany and fruitwood centre table, the top divided into 4 fan-shaped panels inlaid with birds amidst foliage, 19thC, 38½in (98cm) diam.
£3,500–4,000 *LHA*

A boulle centre table, inlaid overall with panels of cut and engraved brass strapwork, on a red 'tortoiseshell' ground, ebonised borders, outlined with ormolu mouldings, the angular cabriole legs with satyrs' mask mounts, damaged, c1860, 38in (96.5cm) closed.
£1,000–1,400 *N*

A Louis XV style mahogany centre table, applied with gilt metal mounts, on foliate capped cabriole legs with gilt sabots, 42in (106.5cm).
£1,000–1,500 *CSK*

A French gilt metal mounted, brass inlaid and scarlet boulle decorated serpentine centre table, on cabriole legs with gilt sabots, late 19thC, 39½in (100cm) wide.
£800–1,200 *CSK*

A Spanish walnut centre table, the top above 2 frieze drawers, on baluster turned legs joined by similar turned stretchers, on bun feet, 19thC, 75½in (191.5cm).
£900–1,500 *CSK*

A Spanish walnut centre table, the top above a frieze drawer, on baluster turned legs joined by stretchers, c1800, 55½in (141cm).
£1,100–1,500 *CSK*

Console Tables

A George II style mahogany console table, with a later painted simulated marble banded top, the underneath with stencil mark '18' and letters 'L.D.R.', late 19thC, 63in (160cm).
£1,700–2,200 *CSK*

A Regency gilt composition console table, the top with a plain frieze mounted with palmettes, on a single caryatid support and monopodia, 16½in (42cm) wide.
£450–750 *C*

A William IV mahogany console table, with ledge back, associated white marble top, foliate edge and cushion moulded frieze drawer, on reeded foliate clasped supports joined by a concave sided undertier, 47½in (121cm).
£1,500–2,000 *CSK*

A Regency style gilt metal mounted serpentine console table, the mottled salmon marble top above a pierced rock work and foliate frieze on opposed scroll feet, joined by an undertier, repaired, mid-19thC, 35½in (90cm).
£800–1,200 *CSK*

Dining Tables

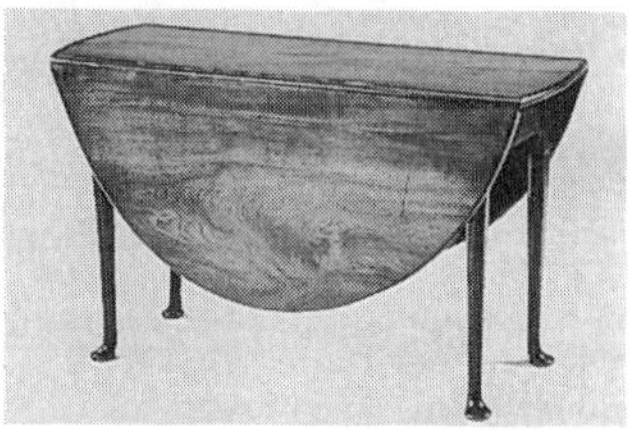

A Queen Anne mahogany drop-leaf dining table, 57in (144.5cm).
£1,200–1,500 *SLN*

A mahogany D-end dining table, with a drop-leaf centre section, part 18thC, 107in (272cm) extended.
£3,000–5,000 *CSK*

l. A red walnut drop-leaf dining table, with a pair of semi-circular hinged flaps, raised on turned tapering legs with club feet, mid-18thC, 50in (127cm).
£400–600 *AG*

A George II mahogany gateleg dining table, with club legs and pad feet, 77in (195.5cm) long.
£2,000–3,000 *C*

A mahogany D-end extending dining table, with one extra leaf, on square tapering legs, early 19thC, 75in (190.5cm) extended.
£2,000–2,500 *CSK*

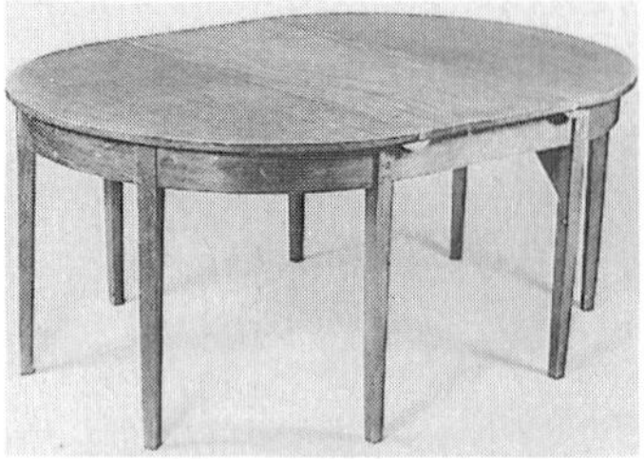

A George III mahogany D-end table, 67in (170cm) long, with one leaf.
£900–1,200 *DN*

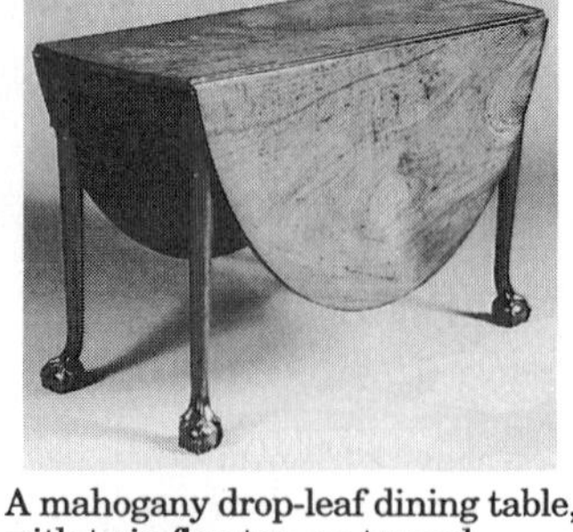

A mahogany drop-leaf dining table, with twin flap top, on turned tapering legs with claw-and-ball feet, mid-18thC, 46in (116.5cm).
£800–1,200 *CSK*

A mahogany extending dining table, with a moulded top, on an octagonal column and turned fluted legs, restored, 19thC, 131in (332.5cm) long, including 4 leaves.
£900–1,200 *DN*

A George III mahogany D-end dining table, the top above a boxwood strung frieze and a small drawer, on square tapering legs, restored, 93in (236cm) long, including 2 leaves.
£1,000–1,500 *DN*

A George III mahogany dining table, 60in (152cm).
£500–600 *DaD*

A William IV mahogany extending dining table, with brass caps and casters, 175in (445.5cm) long.
£6,000–7,000 *CSK*

A William IV mahogany twin pedestal dining table, 66in (167.5cm).
£1,200–1,700 *DaD*

A George IV mahogany pedestal dining table, with a segmentally veneered circular tip-up top, on a conforming platform and on semi-reeded bun feet, 48in (122cm) diam.
£2,500–3,500 *Bea*

A Regency mahogany twin pedestal dining table, with 2 D-shaped end sections and one associated leaf, possibly adapted, 69½in (176.5cm) long extended.
£3,200–5,000 *C*

A mahogany twin pillar dining table, on ring turned columns and splayed tripod supports with brass paw caps and casters, including 2 extra leaves, with later bearers, 19thC, 78in (198cm) long extended.
£4,500–5,000 *CSK*

An Irish Sheraton style dining table, with rosewood crossbanding, marquetry shell medallions and satinwood stringing, 19thC, 120in (304.5cm) extended.
£4,500–5,000 *RBB*

An early Victorian mahogany extending dining table, on tapering turned and reeded legs with china casters, 114in (289.5cm) long, including 3 leaves.
£2,200–2,700 *Bea*

An early Victorian mahogany extending dining table, on octagonal baluster and carved legs, terminating with brass toe caps and casters, 125½in (318cm) extended.
£3,000–4,000 *WL*

An early Victorian mahogany extending dining table, lacking leaves, 53½in (136cm) diam.
£2,000–3,000 *C*

An early Victorian mahogany extending dining table, the moulded top on turned carved legs with brass casters, 125½in (319cm), including 3 leaves.
£2,000–2,500 *DN*

A Victorian mahogany extending dining table, with moulded top, on a faceted stem and quadripartite base with reeded feet, 65in (165cm) long, including one leaf.
£2,000–2,500 *DN*

A Victorian mahogany dining table, 92in (233.5cm) long.
£2,000–2,500 *DaD*

l. A Victorian mahogany dining table, with 3 leaves, on 4 reeded tapering legs with casters, 119in (302cm) long extended.
£2,500–3,000 *Bri*

A Victorian mahogany extending dining table, with a moulded top, on turned fluted legs, 92in (234cm) including 2 leaves.
£1,500–2,000 *DN*

A Victorian faded mahogany dining table, with 2 leaves, 90in (228.5cm) extended.
£1,500–2,000 *MJB*

A Victorian mahogany dining table, with 3 leaves, on turned legs, 109½in (278cm) extended.
£2,500–3,500 *DN*

Display Tables

An Edwardian mahogany bijouterie table, the hinged top inlaid with brass lines and mouldings, with re-entrant corners, above 4 glazed panels, on similar square tapering legs, 25in (63.5cm).
£1,500–1,700 *DN*

An Italian silvered display table, the hinged glazed top and sides on squared baluster legs applied with husks, 19thC, 28½in (72cm).
£500–700 *DN*

Drum Tables

A George III mahogany drum table, with top above 4 frieze drawers alternativing with false drawers, on a turned stem with downswept legs and brass casters, 50in (127cm) diam.
£3,000–3,500 *DN*

Drum Tables

Drum tables, like centre tables, are used predominantly as decorative pieces in halls or large drawing rooms, although drum tables were initially used as writing tables. Drum tables date from as early as c1760 and were made in various forms until the middle of the 19thC. The top, supported on a pedestal base, is usually round and contains a series of drawers which are sometimes lettered alphabetically for filing papers. The top also rotates to give the user access to all the drawers without having to stand up.

A Regency satinwood drum table, ebonised and line inlaid, the leather lined top above 4 drawers and 4 false drawers, 48in (122cm) diam.
£2,500–3,000 *CSK*

A late Georgian mahogany drum top library table, with gilt tooled green leather lined surface, 2 drawers and 6 dummy drawers with brass ring handles, on a turned column and triple splay support having brass terminals and casters, 38in (96.5cm) diam.
£1,500–2,000 *MCA*

Dressing Tables

l. A mahogany dressing table, with raised bevelled toilet mirror on turned supports, with 6 small drawers below with turned ivory knob handles, one long drawer to the frieze, raised on turned columns with cut away platform undertier, on bun feet, mid-19thC, 35in (89cm) wide.
£700–1,000 *AG*

r. A Federal ormolu mounted marble top mahogany dressing table, c1825, 31½in (80cm) wide.
£3,500–5,000 *SLN*

Games Tables

l. Hepplewhite satinwood games table, with leather inset top over square tapering legs, ate 18thC, 35in (89cm) wide.
£1,200–1,500 *LHA*

r. A George III mahogany triple top games table, opening to reveal a plain surface, with a second section revealing counter wells, candle stands and a green baize lining, cabriole legs with claw-and-ball feet, 33in (84cm).
£1,500–2,000 *AG*

A Regency rosewood games/work table, the interior leather lined for backgammon, on dual ring turned columns joined by turned stretchers, on gilt bronze anthemion mounted downswept legs, work box missing, 30½in (77cm).
£2,000–2,500 *P*

A Regency brass inlaid rosewood games table, with felt lined playing surface, shaped standard and downswept legs ending in brass claw casters, 35½in (91cm).
£1,400–2,000 *LHA*

A Regency rosewood games/sewing table, with fold-over swivel top inlaid for backgammon, cribbage and chess, fitted single sewing drawer, on twin supports united by twin baluster turned stretchers, short scrolled feet, 30in (76cm) open.
£600–700 *WL*

Library Tables

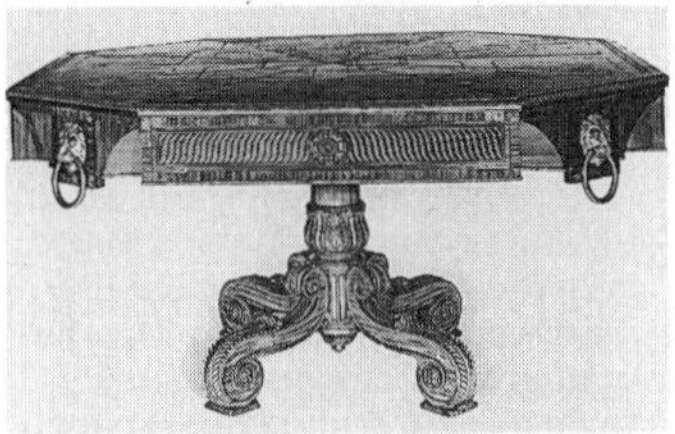

A Regency satinwood veneered library table, the original tooled leather top with ovolo ormolu moulding, the 4 drawers with mirror matched spiral fluting and central rosettes, the deeply canted corners with cupolated sections flanked by ormolu lions' mask rings, the painted and gilt base with an anthemion knop and 4 leaf capped S-scroll legs, c1815, 61in (155cm).
£110,000–120,000 *WW*

It is suggested that this table was inspired by Charles Heathcote Tatham, who worked closely with Henry Holland, and made by his brother's cabinet making firm of Marsh & Tatham. Drawings by C.H. Tatham in the RIBA Library in London of rosettes and lions' mask rings compare directly with those on this table.

A Victorian walnut games table, the moulded top inset for chess, on a baluster column and pierced legs, 29½in (75cm).
£500–700 *DN*

A mahogany double fold-over tea and games table, the baize lined games surface with recessed corners and counter dishes, crossbanded apron with single deep drawer, 5 cabriole legs with pad feet, 19thC, 32in (82cm).
£1,200–1,700 *AH*

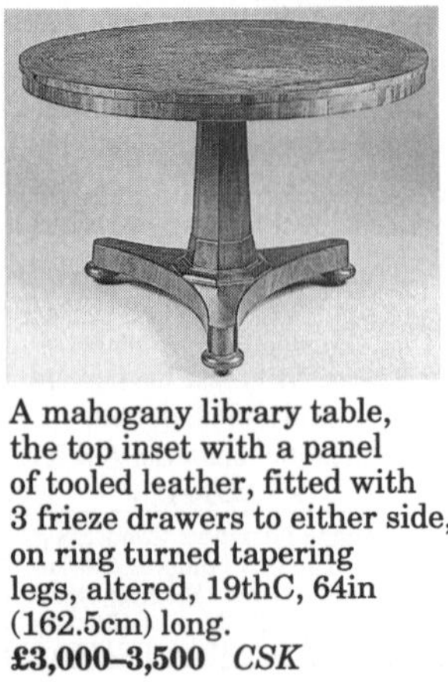

A mahogany library table, the top inset with a panel of tooled leather, fitted with 3 frieze drawers to either side, on ring turned tapering legs, altered, 19thC, 64in (162.5cm) long.
£3,000–3,500 *CSK*

MILLER'S COMPARES . . .

I A mahogany library table, the top inset with a panel of tooled leather, fitted with 3 frieze drawers to either side, on ring turned tapering legs, altered, 19thC, 41½in (105cm) wide.
£3,000–3,500 *CSK*

II A Regency style ebonised line inlaid mahogany library table, the top with green leather lining above 3 frieze drawers, on ring turned reeded tapering legs, 60in (152cm) wide.
£2,200–2,700 *CSK*

These library tables appear similar, however several factors contributed to *Table I* commanding a higher price at auction. *Table I* boasts a more finely tooled decorative top that is regarded as a very desirable feature. *Table I* also has elegantly turned legs and squared off corners as opposed to *Table II* which has reeded legs (small vertical columns) and rounded corners. The features comprising *Table I* make it a more stylish piece, with better proportions than those of *Table II*. *CSK*

The Tenterden Galleries

FLOWER HOUSE ANTIQUES

Flower House Antiques

FINE ENGLISH
& CONTINENTAL FURNITURE
AND COLLECTABLES

90 High Street, Tenterden,
Kent TN30 6JB

Telephone: 01580 763764

The Weald Antiques Gallery

Dealers specialising in furniture
Tunbridgeware - Ceramics - Dolls
Textiles - Prints - Paintings

We are always keen to purchase similar items
Open Monday - Saturday 10am - 5pm
106 High Street, Tenterden, Kent TN30 6HT

Shop: 01580 762939 Office: 01580 241960

Christine Antiques

Specialising in Oil Lamps,
Toilet Mirrors, Writing Slopes,
Needlework Boxes, Copperware.
In addition a wide selection
of Furniture and Oject D'Art.

Christine Antiques
4/6 Ashford Road, Tenterden
Kent. TN30 6AB.
Tenterden: 01580 764434

Sparks Antiques

English & Continental furniture, objects & collectors' items.

4, Manor Row,
Tenterden, Kent.
TN30 6HP

Tel: (01580) 766696

A George IV mahogany library table, fitted with 2 satinwood banded and strung frieze drawers, with dummy drawers to the sides and reverse, on ring turned tapering legs, with later casters, 49½in (126cm).
£2,400–3,200 *CSK*

An early Victorian oak library table, on spirally turned legs joined by similar stretchers, on bun feet with casters, 48in (122cm) wide.
£600–900 *CSK*

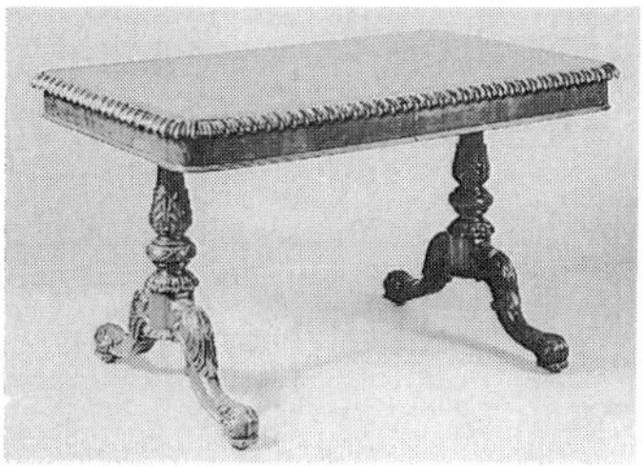

An early Victorian rosewood library table, the lined top with gadrooned border above 4 frieze drawers, on turned lotus lappeted and foliate carved end supports, with acanthus capped downswept legs and scrolling feet, stamped 'Gillows, Lancaster', 52in (132cm).
£3,000–3,500 *CSK*

A mid-Victorian rosewood library table, on pierced vase shaped standard end supports decorated with roundels and finials, joined by a spiral twist stretcher, on turned feet, 48in (122cm).
£1,000–1,200 *CSK*

A Victorian walnut tilt-top library table, the top inlaid with 6 floral marquetry cartouche panels, ebonised border, slightly damaged, 53½in (136cm) diam.
£5,200–6,000 *WL*

A mid-Victorian mahogany library table, 57in (144.5cm).
£2,500–4,000 *C*

A pair of mid-Victorian carved oak library tables, 51in (129.5cm).
£1,700–2,200 *CSK*

A North European mahogany library table, the leather lined top on bulbous column, with quadripartite platform, on bun feet, mid-19thC, 27in (69cm) wide.
£700–1,000 *CSK*

Loo Tables

l. A Victorian walnut loo table, 53in (135cm) wide.
£1,500–2,000 *DN*

r. A Victorian burr walnut loo table, the quarter-veneered serpentine shaped tip-up top with a carved scroll border, on a turned and carved column support and 4 splayed legs with scroll toes, 57in (144.5cm) long.
£1,200–1,500 *DN*

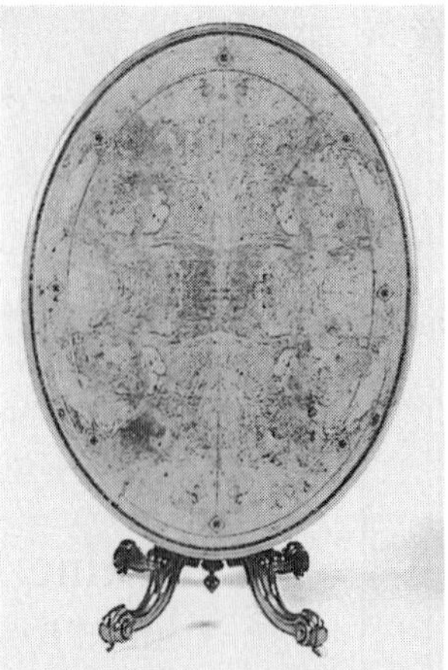

A mid-Victorian walnut, burr walnut and inlaid loo table, the quarter-veneered top with bands of thuya wood, rosewood and Tunbridge ware lozenges, 53in (135cm) wide.
£2,000–2,500 *CSK*

Nests of Tables

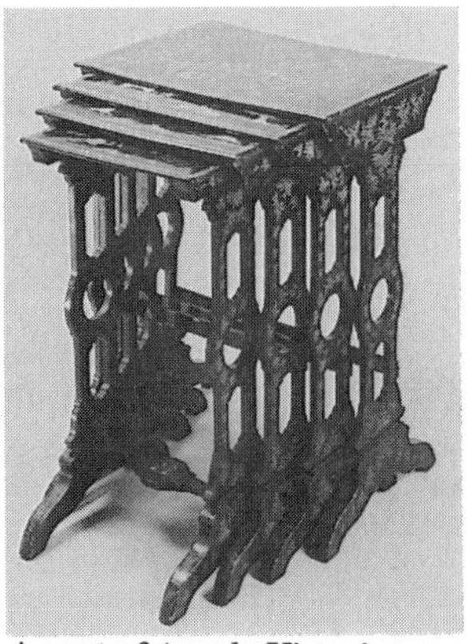

A nest of 4 early Victorian parcel gilt black lacquer tables, each top painted with chinoiserie and mother-of-pearl inlaid borders, on open trestle supports, largest 22in (56cm) wide.
£4,000–4,500 *S(NY)*

Occasional Tables

A Regency brass inlaid and gilt metal mounted rosewood occasional table, with rounded rectangular top above a turned column support, on tripartite base and scrolling feet, 18in (46cm) wide.
£700–900 *CSK*

Pembroke Tables

A laburnum parquetry veneered Pembroke table, with inlaid chequer stringing and banded in mahogany, the end friezes with an oak lined and a dummy drawer, with brass knob handles, square chamfered legs and block feet, pierced cross stretchers, 18thC, 27in (69cm) wide.
£6,500–7,000 *WW*

A nest of 4 mahogany tables, late 19thC.
£800–1,000 *DaD*

A Victorian walnut twin flap occasional table, the moulded edged serpentine-shaped top with single frieze drawer, on turned and fluted twin column trestle supports with scrolled feet, turned stretcher and china casters, 46in (116.5cm) long.
£900–1,200 *AH*

A George III Pembroke table, veneered in kingwood, the drop-leaf top crossbanded in ebony with satinwood outer bands, the bowed end friezes with one drawer and a dummy drawer, banded in ebony, the square tapering legs on brass casters, 30in (76cm) wide.
£3,000–4,000 *WW*

Did you know?

Pembroke tables became popular in the mid- to late 18thC, possibly designed and ordered by Henry Herbert, the Earl of Pembroke (1693–1751).

A nest of 3 Edwardian satinwood occasional tables, decorated with ebonised stringing and inlaid parquetry, largest 17½in (44cm) wide.
£400–600 *AG*

A late Victorian satinwood occasional table, on slender baluster turned legs and similar cross stretcher, on brass casters, 27½in (70cm) wide.
£250–300 *WL*

A George III fiddleback mahogany Pembroke table, by Daniel Elletson, crossbanded overall, the twin flap top with moulded edge above a deep frieze drawer and a dummy drawer, on square tapering legs with brass caps and casters, with maker's printed paper label, restored, 33in (84cm) wide.
£1,300–1,900 C

Daniel Elletson is recorded in the directories between 1792 and 1801. However, this is the first piece of labelled furniture by him to be recorded.

A George III mahogany Pembroke table, the twin flap top above a frieze drawer, on canted square legs joined by a concave-fronted undertier, restored, probably reduced in width, 35½in (91cm).
£1,000–1,500 *C*

A late Regency mahogany Pembroke table, with reeded mouldings, hinged top and frieze drawer, on turned tapering legs with brass caps and casters, 40½in (103cm) long extended.
£600–700 *CSK*

A William IV mahogany Pembroke table, the moulded top above 3 drawers, on a squared column applied with stylised lotus, on a quadripartite base and scroll feet, 33½in (85cm) wide.
£600–800 *DN*

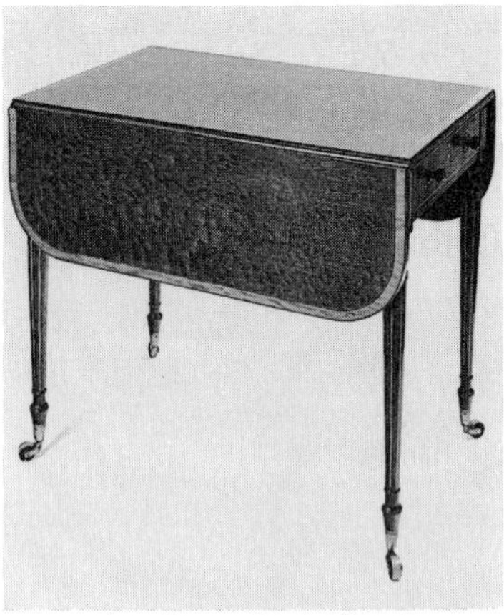

A satinwood inlaid mahogany Pembroke table, c1900, 41in (104cm) open.
£1,500–2,000 *MJB*

Reading Tables

A George III mahogany moulded snap-top reading table, on an adjustable column with a recessed manuscript support, 27½in (70cm) high.
£2,500–3,000 *DN*

A George III mahogany reading table, the hinged ratcheted adjustable top with a stay, on an adjustable column with splayed tripod legs and pad feet, 22in (56cm) wide.
£1,700–2,000 *CSK*

A Regency pale blue and ivory painted reading table, the hinged top with simulated marble centre, 29in (74cm) high.
£3,000–3,500 *AG*

Miller's is a price GUIDE not a price LIST

Serving Tables

A George III mahogany serving side table, 53in (134.5cm) long.
£5,200–6,000 *C*

A George III style mahogany breakfront serving table, on square tapering legs with spade feet, 54in (137cm) long.
£1,000–1,500 *CSK*

A mahogany D-shaped serving table, with recessed concave outline, shutter and reeded decoration, fitted with a frieze drawer, on polygonal and tapering legs terminating in claw feet, adapted, part early 19thC, 90in (228.5cm) long.
£2,000–3,000 *CSK*

A William IV mahogany serving table, the panelled frieze with a fall front drawer, on turned tapering reeded legs, 81in (205.5cm) long.
£1,700–2,200 *CSK*

A William IV mahogany serving table, with raised back and gadrooned border, on turned and reeded legs and turned feet, 58½in (148cm).
£1,200–1,700 *CSK*

A mahogany serpentine serving table, early 20thC, 60in (152cm).
£800–1,200 *MAT*

A William and Mary walnut and seaweed marquetry side table, the crossbanded top centred by a panel with a cartouche, smaller reserves and bandings above a drawer, on barley-twist legs joined by X-form stretchers, restored, 44in (111.5cm) wide.
£800–1,200 *DN*

Side Tables

A Georgian mahogany side table, with moulded Carrara marble top, on square chamfered legs with pierced arched brackets, 40in (101.5cm) wide.
£1,200–1,700 *AG*

A George III style mahogany side table, in the manner of Hicks of Dublin, segmentally veneered and centred by a demi-patera, satinwood crossbanded above a crossbanded frieze, 48in (122cm).
£1,000–1,500 *DN*

A Regency mahogany bowfront kneehole side table, inlaid with ebonised lines, 39in (99cm).
£1,400–2,000 *Bea*

l. A Regency rosewood side table, the platform base with claw feet, 42½in (108cm).
£500–600 *WL*

r. A William IV mahogany side table, with a plain three-quarter gallery, on turned and reeded tapering legs, 44in (111.5cm).
£550–650 *AG*

l. A silvered side table, with a marble top, early 20thC, 36in (91.5cm) wide.
£1,000–1,500
CSK

An Empire style mahogany ormolu mounted side table, with mottled brown and white marble top, 45in (114cm) wide.
£1,500–2,000 *AG*

A German side table, with a parquetry top, on 5 column legs, late 19thC, 25½in (65cm) wide.
£500–600 *DN*

A North Italian rosewood side table, the banded top inlaid with lines above a small drawer, on square tapering legs, late 18thC, 38in (96.5cm) wide.
£2,000–2,500 *DN*

Silver Tables

A George I Virginia walnut silver table, with a dished edge top, the curved frieze with an oak lined drawer and flared moulding, on cabriole legs and pad feet, 32in (81cm) wide.
£3,700–4,500 *WW*

A Dutch silver table, the dished edge top with protruding corners, oak lined frieze drawer with ornate brass swan neck handles and escutcheons, on cabriole legs, the toes on pad feet, 18thC, 33in (84cm).
£1,000–1,400 *WW*

Sofa Tables

A late George III mahogany sofa table, with 2 line inlaid frieze and opposing dummy drawers, on reeded end supports and downswept legs, one leaf chipped, 63in (160cm) wide.
£1,200–1,700 *CSK*

l. A Regency mahogany sofa table, the crossbanded top above 2 frieze and 2 dummy drawers, each with applied mouldings to the front, above 4 scrolling supports with a central turned column, on concave sided platform and 4 downswept legs with claw feet, 62in (157cm) extended.
£2,000–2,500 *CSK*

Sofa Tables

Sofa tables are sometimes marriages of a period top with a cheval mirror stand. Look out for the following tell-tale signs:

- Supports set too close.
- The colour of the stand must match the rest of the piece.
- Disguised screwholes.

Drawers should be shallow, but long drawers are better than those later cut down. Rosewood examples are especially desirable, as are lyre-end supports or those carved with Egyptian heads.

A Regency period mahogany sofa table, in the style of Gillows, the frieze with 2 mahogany lined and 2 dummy drawers with brass knob handles, flanked by carved florets, the quadruple ring turned end supports above scallop shells, 43in (109cm).
£2,500–3,000 *WW*

A Regency mahogany sofa table, the moulded edge top with rounded corners, 2 frieze drawers with brass knob handles and opposing dummy drawers, on square tapering trestle supports with scrolled feet, turned stretcher and brass casters, 60½in (154cm) long.
£1,400–1,800 *AH*

A rosewood sofa table, the twin flap top with burr crossbanding above 2 frieze drawers, on end standards and outswept legs, 59in (149.5cm) wide.
£2,000–2,500 *CSK*

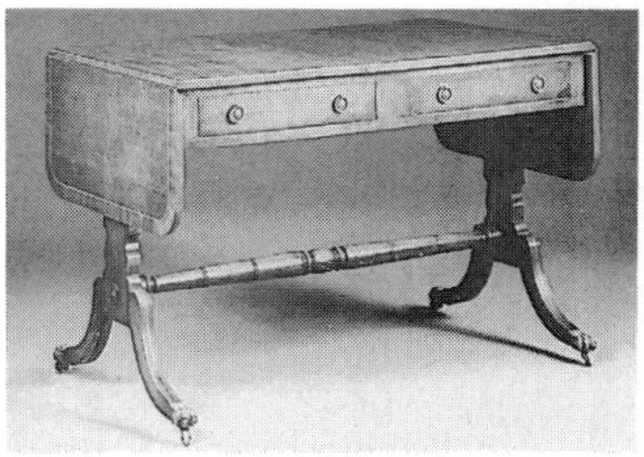

A Regency style mahogany sofa table, on standard end supports and reeded legs, top split, 65in (165cm) extended.
£700–1,200 *CSK*

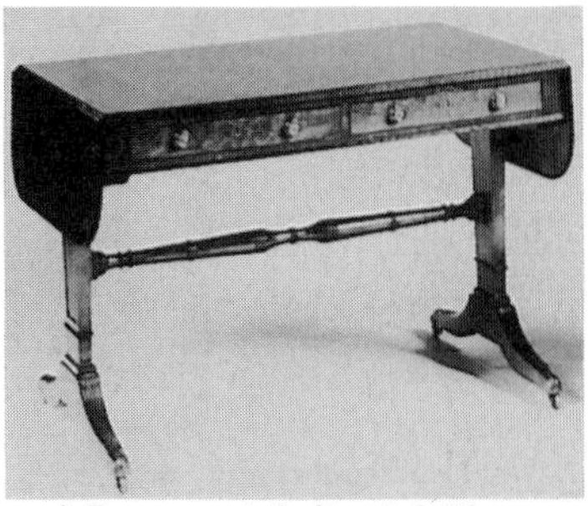

A Regency style line inlaid mahogany sofa table, with reeded end supports, joined by a stretcher and reeded outswept legs, 60in (152cm) extended.
£1,200–1,800 *CSK*

A Regency ebony line inlaid mahogany sofa table, with rectangular end standards and outswept legs, 60in (152cm).
£1,200–1,700 *CSK*

A Regency line inlaid rosewood and crossbanded mahogany pedestal sofa table, on twin standards and hipped splayed legs, 34in (86cm).
£900–1,200 *CSK*

A late Regency line inlaid and crossbanded mahogany sofa table, the rounded twin flap top above standard end supports, joined by a stretcher on outswept legs and claw feet, 57½in (146cm) extended.
£1,500–2,000 *CSK*

Tea Tables

l. A mahogany tea table, the hinged top with a foliate carved edge and concealed drawer in the gadrooned frieze, late 18thC and later, 33in (84cm) wide.
£1,000–1,200 *CSK*

r. A George II mahogany tea table, with a long frieze drawer, on lappet headed tapering turned legs with pad feet, 35in (89cm).
£1,000–1,200 *Bea*

l. A George III mahogany tea table, inlaid overall with an ebonised line, 34in (86cm).
£3,500–4,000 *C*

A George III mahogany tea table, carved overall with blind fretwork, on canted square legs headed by pierced angles, 33in (84cm) wide.
£1,700–2,200 *C*

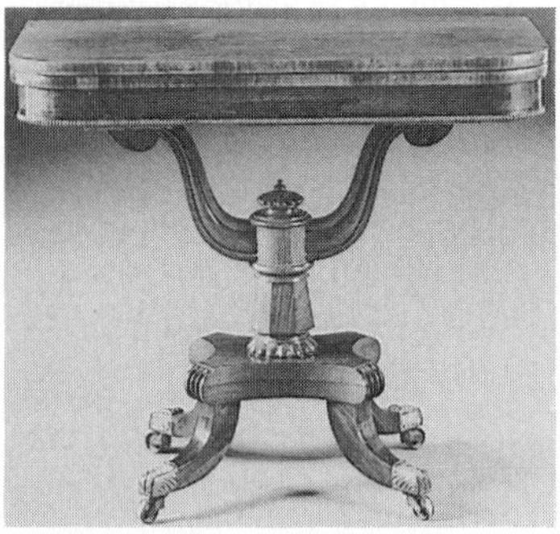

A William IV rosewood tea table, the top enclosing a baize lined interior, on a pierced U-shaped support and octagonal spreading shaft, on a concave sided platform and hipped downswept legs, brass caps and casters, 36in (91.5cm).
£1,000–1,500 *C*

An early Victorian mahogany tea table, with dolphin feet, 36in (91.5cm) wide.
£500–700 *M*

A George III satinwood inlaid mahogany fold-over top tea table, late 18thC, 32in (81cm).
£700-1,000 *LHA*

A George IV mahogany tea table, with reeded edge, a central tablet and corner paterae to the frieze, a turned stem and 4 hipped splayed legs with foliate cast brass caps and casters, 35in (89cm) wide.
£800–1,500 *Bea*

A George III mahogany tea table, with folding top and 2 frieze drawers, on square tapering legs, distressed, 42in (106cm).
£2,000–3,000 *C*

An early Victorian mahogany tea table, 36in (91.5cm).
£750–1,000 *CSK*

A French flame mahogany tea table, mid-19thC, 36in (91.5cm).
£900–1,200 *CSK*

Tip-Top Tables

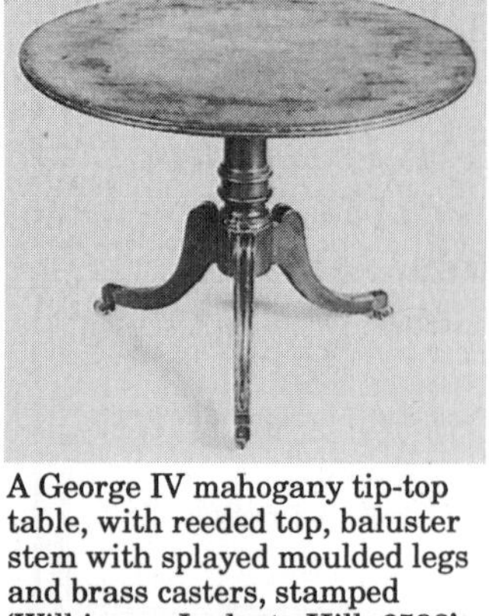

A George IV mahogany tip-top table, with reeded top, baluster stem with splayed moulded legs and brass casters, stamped 'Wilkinson, Ludgate Hill, 6538', 36in (91.5cm) diam.
£400–600 *DN*

An early Victorian rosewood table, the tilt-top on foliate column and trefoil platform with foliate bun feet, 29½in (75cm) diam.
£1,100–1,700 *CSK*

l. A Victorian papier mâché tilt-top tripod table, inlaid with mother-of-pearl and embellished in gilt, on shaped column and platform base, 22in (56cm) diam.
£250–500 *L&E*

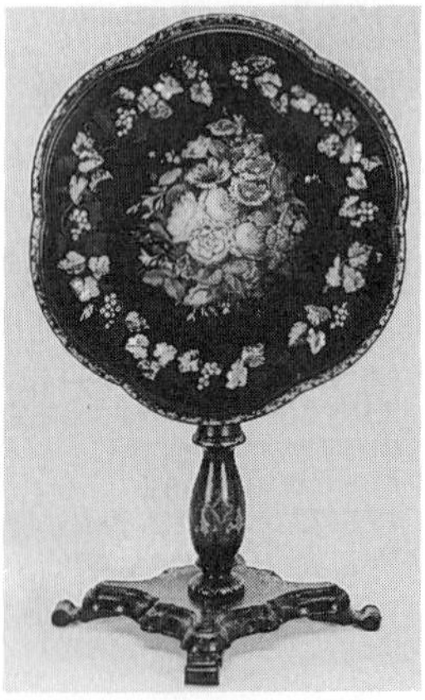

A Victorian papier mâché tilt-top table, edged with gilt, painted and inlaid with mother-of-pearl leaves and berries, on gilt embellished column support, platform base and 4 scroll feet, 41in (104cm) high.
£500–700 *L&E*

Tripod Tables

A George II mahogany tripod table, the oval top above a birdcage and turned column, on cabriole legs with pointed pad feet, 29in (73.5cm) diam.
£550–750 *CSK*

A George II mahogany tripod table, the dished tilt-top on turned column and cabriole legs with pad feet, 31½in (80cm) diam.
£500–800 *CSK*

An early George III mahogany tray-top tripod table, 22in (56cm) diam.
£3,000–4,000 *CAG*

l. A George III mahogany tripod table, on turned column and cabriole legs with pad feet, restored, 30in (76cm) diam.
£1,200–1,700 *CSK*

A George III mahogany tripod table, with a piecrust top on a turned column with downswept legs and claw-and-ball feet, 27½in (70cm) diam.
£1,800–2,200 *DN*

l. A George III mahogany tripod table, on birdcage support and leaf carved fluted baluster column, with acanthus carved downswept legs and claw-and-ball feet, 28in (71cm) diam.
£2,500–3,500 *DN*

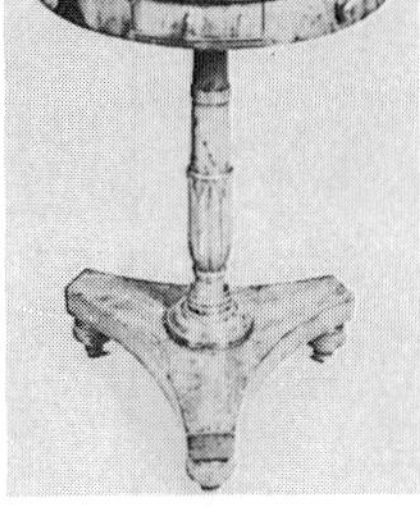

r. An olivewood tripod table, the segmentally veneered top centred by a star, above 4 small drawers, on a leaf carved stem and triform base, 19thC, 18in (46cm) diam.
£2,500–3,000 *DN*

A George III mahogany tripod table, with an octagonal top above a birdcage and column stem, on downswept legs with pad feet, 27½in (70cm) diam.
£900–1,200 *DN*

A Georgian mahogany tripod table, with a piecrust tip-up top, on a carved and turned column with acanthus carved legs, 24½in (62cm) diam.
£900–1,200 *AG*

A mid-Victorian walnut occasional table, with a circular dished top, carved with stylised foliate stems, on baluster column and splayed tripod supports, 16in (41cm) diam.
£400–600 *CSK*

Work Tables

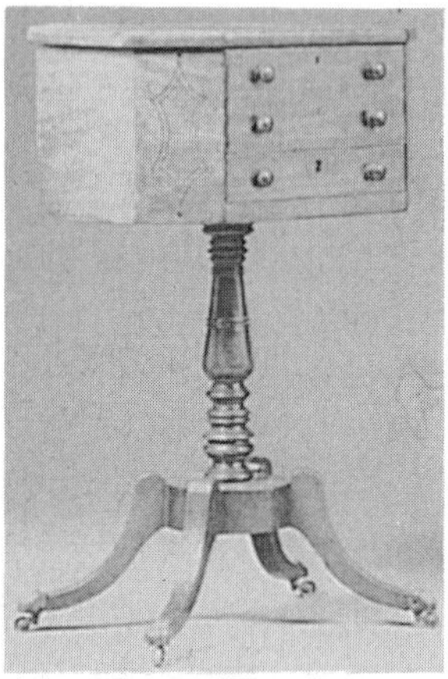

A late George III mahogany work table, the hinged top revealing a fitted interior, with 2 dummy drawers and one true drawer below, 19in (48cm) wide.
£600–800 *CSK*

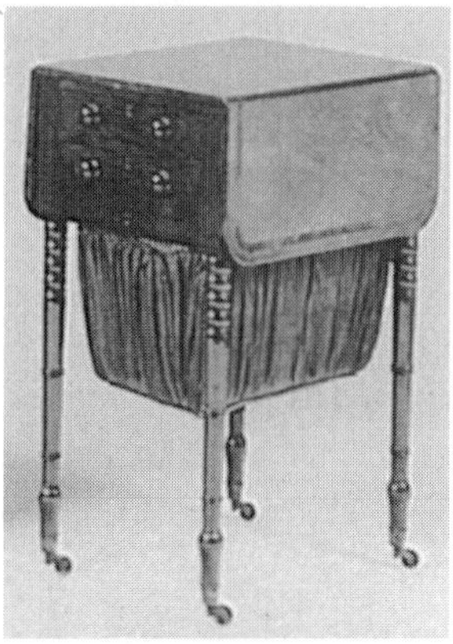

A late George III rosewood crossbanded line inlaid mahogany work table, with distressed silk upholstery, on ring turned tapering legs, 32in (81cm) wide.
£1,500–2,000 *CSK*

Miller's is a price GUIDE not a price LIST

A George IV mahogany work table, with tray top, a drawer at each end and carved pillar end supports, on carved cabriole legs, slide for workbag missing, by Gillow of Lancaster, for Ferguson & Co., c1825, 27½in (70cm).
£4,000–5,000 *S*

The design for this table is included among the Gillow Estimate Drawings and Costings for 1826 (number 3480). It was executed for a firm of cabinet makers and upholsterers named Ferguson & Co., recorded at 117 Oxford Street in Kelly's London Commercial Directory of 1822, *with which Gillow was closely associated throughout the 1820s and '30s. James William Ferguson served his apprenticeship with Gillows in Lancaster before moving to London and forming a partnership with another ex-employee of the firm, Henry Whiteside. Leonard Redman or Redmayne appears to have acted as backer for the partnership, which is recorded, between 1813 and 1840, as Ferguson, Whiteside & Redman or Ferguson, Redmayne & Co.*

A Regency rosewood sewing table, the fitted sliding drawer with well, 15¾in (40cm) wide.
£600–700 *WL*

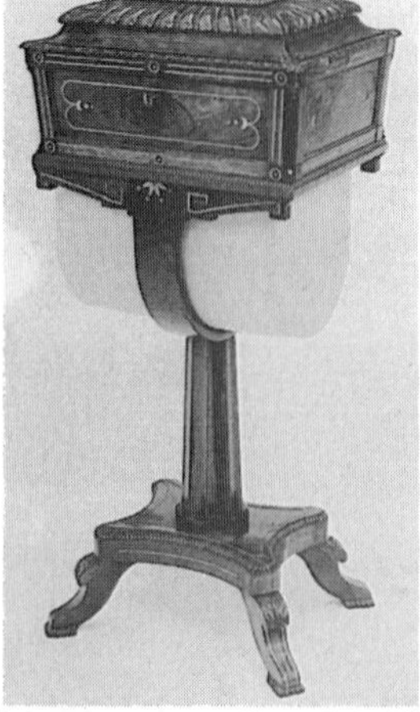

A Regency rosewood work table, of sarcophagus shape, all inlaid with brass lines, 14½in (37cm) wide.
£1,200–1,700 *L*

A George IV mahogany work table with one drop-leaf, one false drop-leaf fall front door and 2 false drawers to each end, on turned tapering legs, 19in (48cm).
£700–1,000 *DN*

A late Regency rosewood work and games table, the top inset with a sliding reversible inlaid chequerboard panel, a drawer pouch below, on U-support, quadruped beaded base, and carved claw feet, 19in (48.5cm).
£1,000–1,500 *HOLL*

A late Regency rosewood work table, 30in (76cm) wide.
£2,000–2,200 *GJC*

A Canadian figured maple work table, c1840.
£600–700 *RIT*

An early Victorian rosewood work table, 17½in (44.5cm).
£500–700 *CSK*

A Victorian burr walnut sewing table, with satinwood foliate inlay, 23in (59cm).
£900–1,500 *WL*

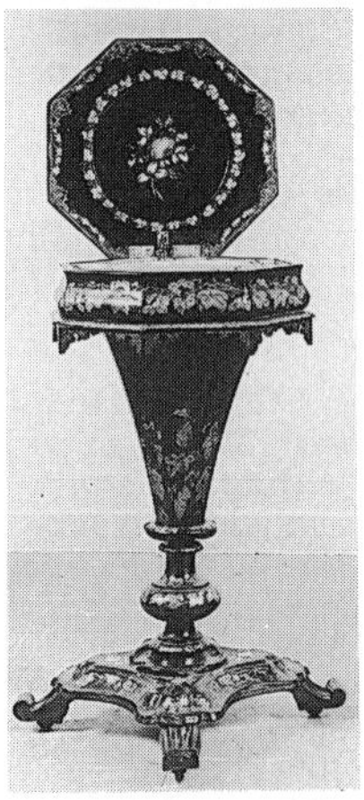

l. A Victorian papier-mâché work table, with interior compartments, on gilt leafage painted column and shaped platform base, 17in (43cm) diam.
£1,200–1,700 *RBB*

A late Victorian walnut and line inlaid work table, with fitted interior and basket below, on turned end supports joined by stretcher and foliate carved scrolling legs, 20in (51cm) wide.
£900–1,200 *CSK*

A Victorian walnut octagonal work/games table, the inlaid top with parquetry chess board, the tapering support on a carved tripod base, 17in (43cm).
£500–800 *Bea*

l. A Louis XV style kingwood and walnut work table with cross-banded top, the frieze inlaid with scrolling foliage, on squared cabriole legs, 12½in (32cm).
£600–900 *DN*

Use the Index!

Because certain items might fit easily into any number of categories, the quickest and surest method of locating any entry is by reference to the index at the back of the book.

This index has been fully cross-referenced for absolute simplicity.

A German mahogany work table, early 19thC, 19½in (49.5cm).
£800–1,000 *CSK*

A Federal mahogany work table, the top fitted for writing with a compartmented interior, old refinish, Philadelphia, c1815, 24in (62cm) wide.
£4,500–£5,500 *SK(B)*

A Federal carved mahogany work table, the top above 2 short drawers, over 4 leaf carved and baluster turned supports, centering a medial shaped shelf, New York, c1820, 22in (55.5cm).
£800–1,000 *CNY*

Writing Tables

A Louis XV style kingwood, marquetry inlaid and ormolu mounted writing table, 34in (86cm) wide.
£1,000–1,200 *AH*

A German walnut writing table with ebonised line inlay, early 18thC, 45in (114cm).
£1,200–1,700 *L&E*

An early Victorian mahogany writing table, with bowed ends, the leather lined top enclosing 2 ratcheted slopes, above 2 true and 2 frieze drawers, the end drawers missing, on ring turned reeded tapering legs, re-toed, 69in (175cm).
£6,000–7,000 *CSK*

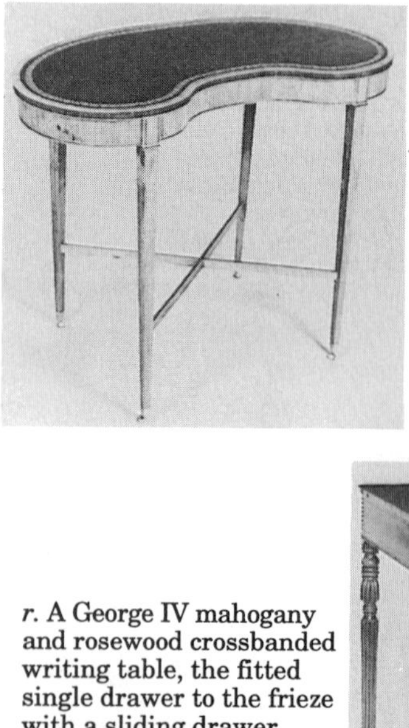

l. A George III tulipwood kidney-shaped writing table, with leather inset crossbanded top above a similarly banded frieze, on square tapering legs joined by an X-stretcher, 36in (91.5cm).
£1,200–1,700 *DN*

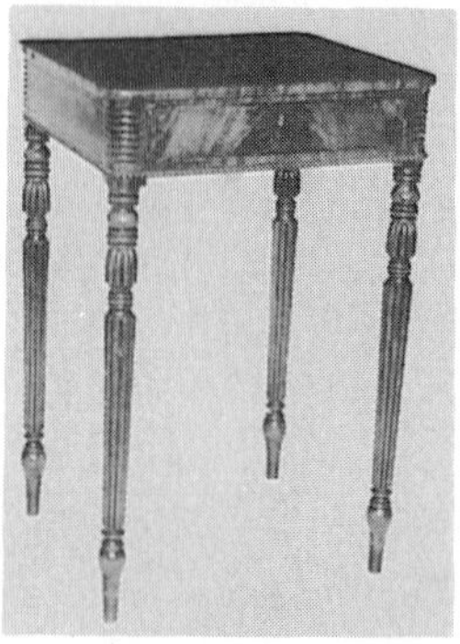

r. A George IV mahogany and rosewood crossbanded writing table, the fitted single drawer to the frieze with a sliding drawer enclosing a pen tray and inkwell, on fluted and turned tapering legs, 20½in (52cm) wide.
£700–1,000 *AG*

Miscellaneous Tables

A George III mahogany architect's table, the drawer front revealing a secrétaire compartment and pigeonholes, the 2 side flaps supported by hinged scroll brackets, 36in (91.5cm).
£1,000–1,500 *HOLL*

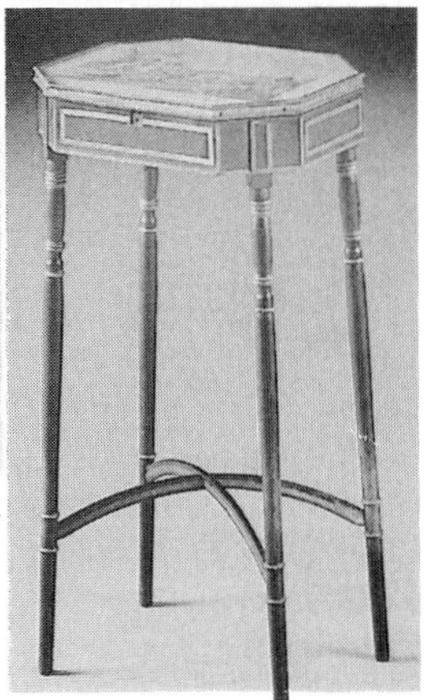

A late George III ormolu mounted painted lamp table, inset with a print of bathing putti, by F. Bartolozzi after G.B Cipriani, with panelled frieze, ring turned tapering legs, joined by a slightly arched X-shaped stretcher, and re-decorated base, formerly with pendant apron, 15in (38cm) wide.
£1,400–1,800 *C*

A George III mahogany spider's legs table, with hinged top, on turned supports joined by similar stretchers, on turned feet, 41½in (105cm) extended.
£800–1,100 *CSK*

A pair of George II style cream painted pier tables, each with Carrara marble top, 47½in (120.5cm) wide.
£3,400–4,000 *CSK*

A mid-Victorian oak Sutherland table, with twin flap top, on turned legs and splayed feet with casters, damaged, 45in (114cm) extended.
£500–800 *C*

A floral marquetry ebonised and amboyna salon table, the top with 4 semi-circular fall leaves, and brass classical borders and mounts, on tapered fluted legs joined by X-stretchers, c1860, 37½in (95cm).
£1,300–1,800 *N*

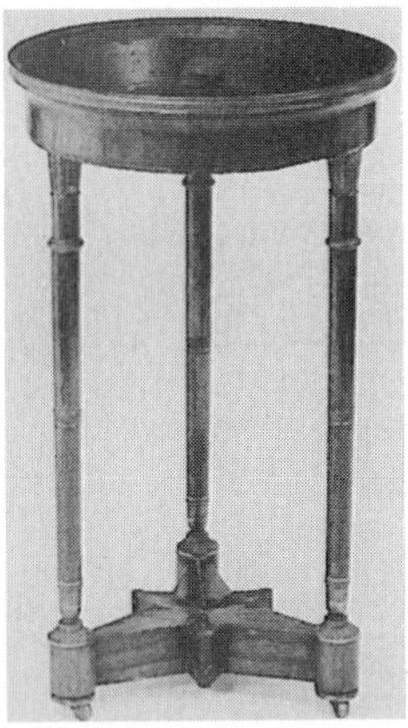

A Regency ormolu mounted rosewood plate table, the dished top lined in black American cloth, on 3 turned tapering supports with quiver-mounted gilt metal tops and star shaped platform base, 17in (43cm) diam.
£1,500–2,000 *AG*

l. A black walnut tavern table, with one long drawer, on square tapering legs, the whole grain-painted red over ochre, Pennsylvania, c1800, 35in (89cm) wide.
£1,500–2,000 *S(NY)*

Washstands

A pair of cream painted washstands, each with a shaped back painted with trailing ivy, simulated marble top and 2 small drawers, on standard supports with turned feet, 19thC, 37in (94cm) wide.
£800–1,200 *DN*

A George IV mahogany washstand, with reeded top, on ring turned legs, 36in (91.5cm) wide.
£800–1,000 *DN*

A George III mahogany enclosed washstand, the sloping fall enclosing a fitted interior with a mirror and sliding leather lined cistern with tap and recess below, an enclosed cupboard, 3 short and one long drawer, with a through drawer to the sides, on square tapering legs, on brass caps and casters, 26in (66cm) wide.
£1,000–1,500 *CSK*

A George IV mahogany washstand, with a gallery above a reeded top and 2 small drawers, 38½in (98cm).
£500–700 *DN*

A Regency mahogany washstand, 50½in (128.5cm) wide.
£1,100–1,800 *C*

A Regency mahogany washstand, with three-quarter solid gallery, above 4 openings, a panelled frieze and 3 simulated drawers, on ring turned tapering legs, 42in (107cm) wide.
£1,100–1,500 *C*

An early Victorian oak grained washstand, 46in (116.5cm).
£400–600 *C*

Whatnots

A George IV rosewood whatnot, with reeded finials above 4 tiers, divided by turned uprights, with a small drawer, on turned legs, 56½in (143cm) high.
£1,800–2,200 *DN*

A George IV mahogany whatnot with 4 tiers divided by turned balusters, the lower part with a small drawer, on turned legs, 56½in (143cm) high.
£1,000–1,500 *DN*

A Victorian burr walnut 2 tier whatnot, decorated with inlaid stringing, scrolls and medallions, the top with pierced brackets, on turned and fluted pilasters, a glazed panelled door under, enclosing lined shelves, on turned tapering legs with ceramic casters, 44in (111.5cm) high.
£1,100–1,700 *AG*

A Victorian walnut whatnot, with mirror top, c1860, 36in (91.5cm) high.
£1,500–1,700 *GJC*

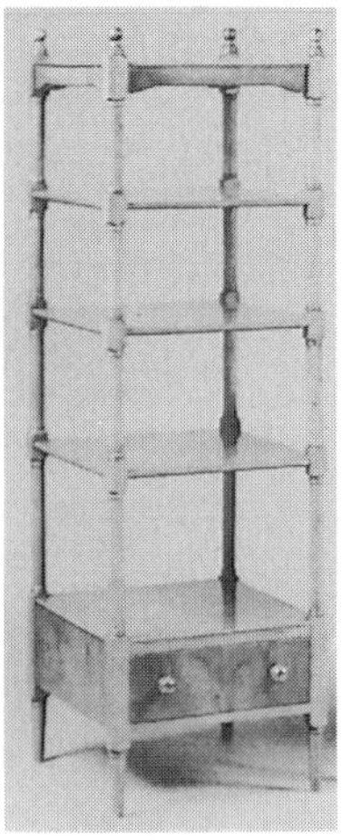

A yew wood veneered 5 tier whatnot, each joined by turned columns, with drawer below, on tapering feet, 16in (41cm) wide.
£300–500 *CSK*

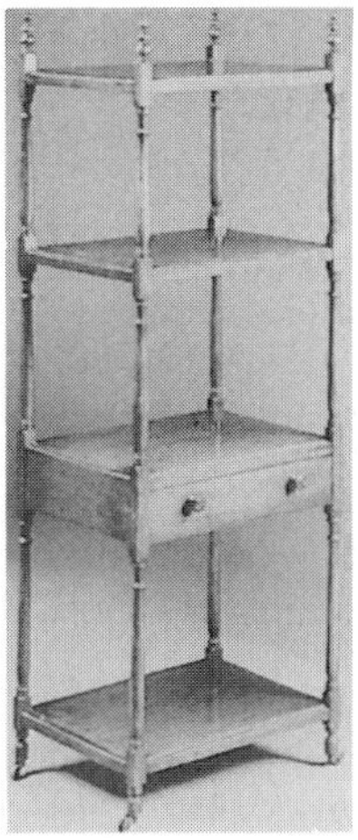

A mahogany 4 tier whatnot, with turned uprights above a frieze drawer, on turned legs, 18½in (47cm) wide.
£700–1,000 *CSK*

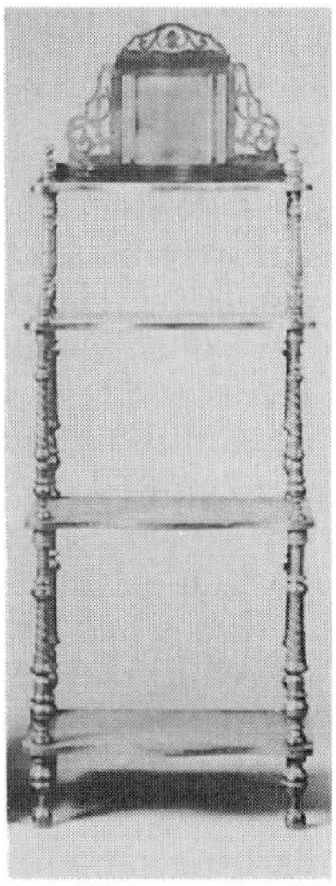

A late Victorian inlaid mahogany whatnot, the mirrored superstructure with pierced fret surround, above serpentine fronted shelf, with 3 similar tiers below, on turned supports, 21in (54cm) wide.
£200–400 *CSK*

Miscellaneous

A pair of teak hanging shelves, each with 3 graduated serpentine tiers, with pierced fret-carved galleries and hooked pendants, with ogee arched and scroll sides, 19thC, 22½in (57cm) high.
£1,200–1,700 *CSK*

These shelves were made for a member of the Wadia dynasty of Persian master shipbuilders whose ships were used by the East India Company during the 18th and 19thC.

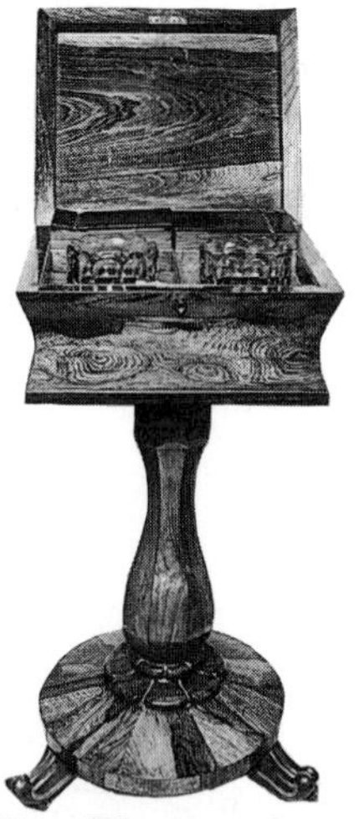

A William IV rosewood teapoy, with mixing bowls, on stand, c1840, 29in (74cm) high.
£1,200–1,400 *AnE*

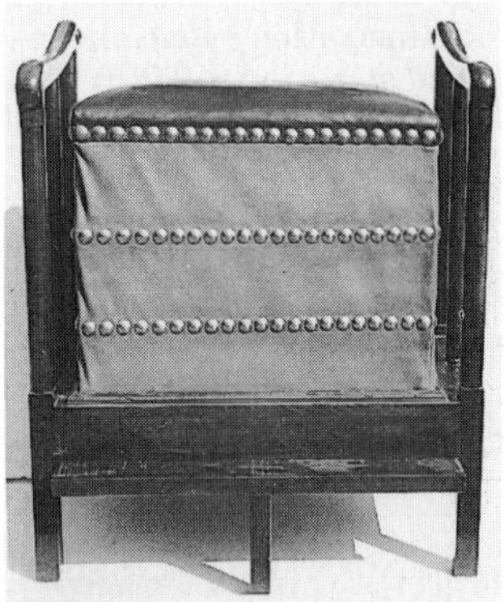

A George III mahogany chamber horse, with 2 arm supports, the rising sprung leather covered seat above a pull-out foot support, 30in (76cm) wide.
£700–1,000 *B*

A gentleman's exercising machine to simulate horseriding.

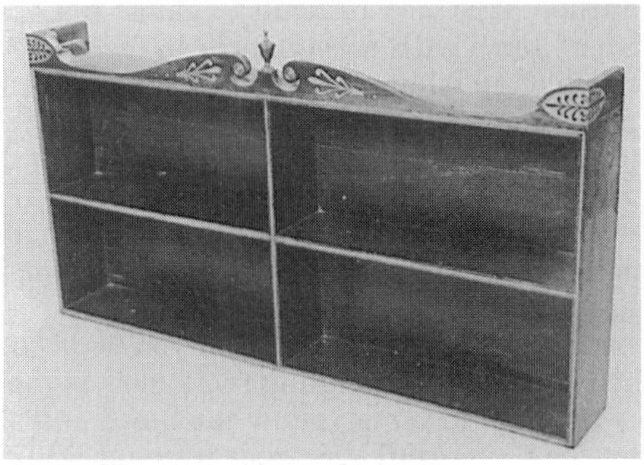

A set of Regency rosewood hanging shelves, the shaped cresting inlaid with anthemia and centred by an urn, above 4 divisions, 48in (122cm) wide.
£800–1,200 *DN*

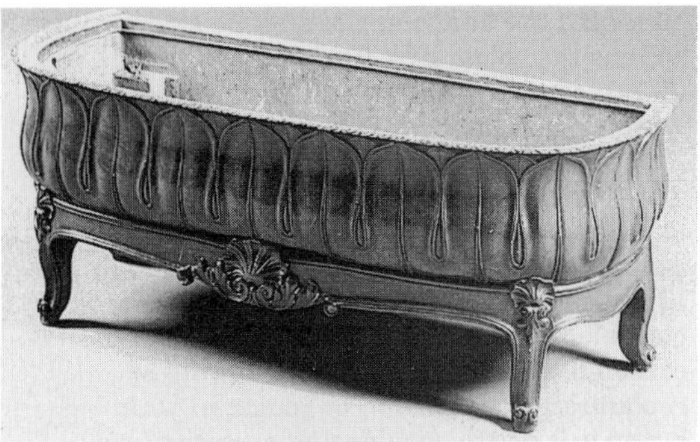

A carved mahogany D-shaped jardinière, with a lead liner and foliate lip, the bombé body with stiff-leaf carved decoration and scallop shell decorated frieze, on cabriole feet, late 19thC, 41in (104cm) long.
£3,000–3,500 *CSK*

ARCHITECTURAL ANTIQUES

Despite the recession, prices of architectural antiques have remained steady and, due to increased interest, all major salerooms now have auctions devoted to this field. Individual pieces can be found in most antique shops around the country, and there are now a number of specialist dealers. In response to the growing interest Sotheby's held its first auction devoted entirely to architectural antiques in May 1986.

Architectural antiques is a name which encompasses a vast array of items including garden statuary, garden furniture and architectural pieces such as old doors, bathtubs and fire surrounds. Modern reproductions of garden furniture tend to be more affordable and widely available, but do not compare with the originals. Aluminium copies of Coalbrookdale seats, for example, have the advantage of being less expensive and portable (it takes two men to lift the cast iron examples), but it is the original cast iron seats that will hold their value, whereas the modern copies will be worth very little in a few years time.

The same can be said for garden statuary. The illustration *below* shows one of a pair of carved stone urns, 21½in (54.5cm) high, which sold recently for £800.

It is evident that there is some damage but the colouring of the stone and the addition of various mosses and lichens make them more desirable to the collector than a pair of the modern composition stone urns. One of the charms of antique garden statuary and garden furniture is the patina of age which enhances the hard lines of a stone seat, softens the colour of a Bath stone urn and, in all cases, makes what is man-made harmonise with the natural beauty of a garden.

Whereas the popularity of garden statuary and garden furniture has not diminished over the past decade, the architectural side of such sales has taken longer to become established, and in some instances it is still possible to obtain interesting pieces at reasonable prices. If you are thinking of replanning your garden or rooms in your house it is worth considering architectural pieces. Anyone can place a seat under a tree or a fountain in a pond, but it takes imagination and flair to recycle stone balustrading, porticos and columns, balconies or old wood panelling.

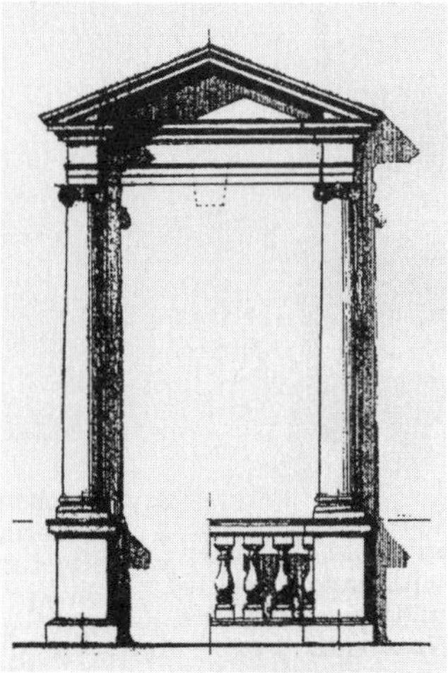

The illustration *above* shows one of a pair of stone balconies, now being used as components for a courtyard. If you look around, and let your imagination guide you, wonderful finds can be still be discovered among monumental architectural pieces.

For example, the white marble Corinthian capital, shown *above,* is early 20thC, measures 27 by 28in (69 by 71.5cm), and would make a good base for a table or pedestal for a fountain figure.

One-off items with an interesting provenance do occasionally come up for sale. The oak doors which were once the entrance to Sotheby's in Bond Street, dated 1900, were relatively ordinary doors but because of their provenance they fetched a high price of £690 at auction. It is very difficult to gauge the value of items with provenance, as their worth is often what the purchaser is willing to pay for the novelty of owning something special, and one would expect to spend a little extra.

Doors, windows and interior fittings such as panelling, are not easy to sell at the present time when the house market is still recovering from the recession. If you want to panel your library or dining room, now is the time to find and install solid hardwood doors, or put in a beautiful Victorian wrought iron spiral staircase. It is worth looking around antique shops while the prices of these items are still relatively attractive.

Jackie Rees.

Bronze

A bronze figure of a seated woman, by George John Lober, weathered patina, signed 'Otto Langman/Architecy, George Lober, Na. Sculptor 1935, Bedford Bronze Foundry, NY', 66in (168cm) high.
£15,500–17,000 *S(NY)*

A pair of bronze geese, 29in (73.5cm) high.
£2,800–3,000 *S(NY)*

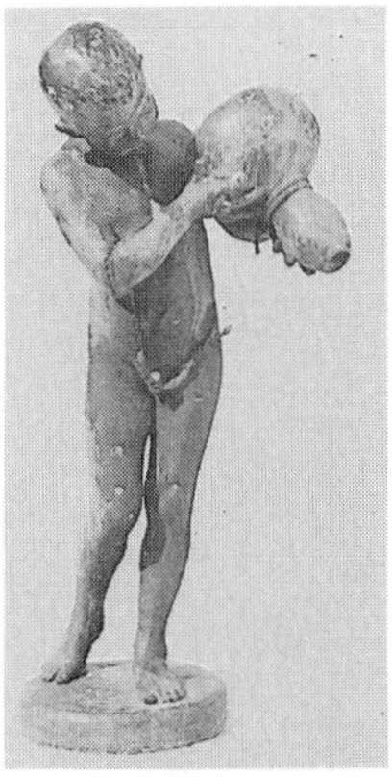

A bronze figure of a boy, with green/brown patination, late 19thC, 30in (76cm) high.
£1,000–1,200 *S(S)*

A bronze group of 3 boys, looking into water, rich green patination, signed 'REA', dated '1956–7', 25in (64cm) high.
£1,500–2,000 *S(S)*

A patinated bronze urn, by Emmanuel Fremiet, late 18thC, 48in (122cm) high.
£20,000–22,000 *S(NY)*

A pair of bronze urns, each on rising fluted circular foot and square base, weathered green patination, c1860, 36in (91.5cm) high.
£22,000–25,000 *S(S)*

This pair of bronze urns are copies of originals, believed to have been cast by Duval from designs by Louis XIV's goldsmith, Claude Ballin, and which remain today on short marble plinths separating the Parterre du Nord from the Parterre d'Eau at Versailles. They possibly originated from Bagatelle in the Bois du Boulogne, the estate of the Fourth Marquess of Hertford, 1800–67, who, through his friendship with Napoleon III, was allowed to make bronze copies of the originals. On the death of the Fourth Marquess in 1870 the estate passed to his son, Sir Richard Wallace and subsequently, on his death, to his secretary, Sir John Murray. All the urns were removed to England with the exception of 3 pairs, which were sold with the estate to the city of Paris in 1904.
These urns were later reproduced in cast iron by the Barbezat Foundry which was incorporated into the Société Anonyme des Hautes Fourneaux Fondeurs du Val d'Osne.

Clay

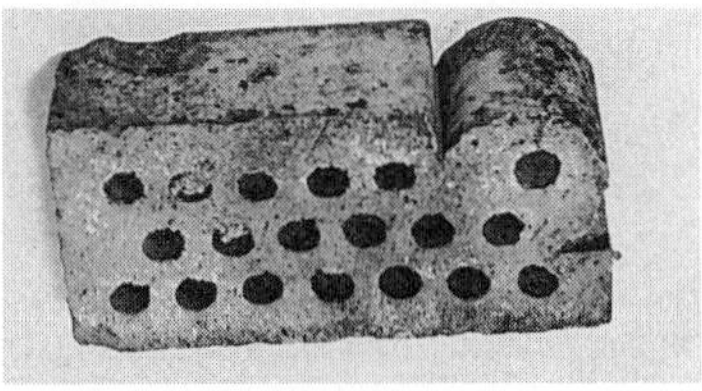

A brick corbel, 18thC, 9in (22.5cm) long.
£50–55 per 100 *WEL*

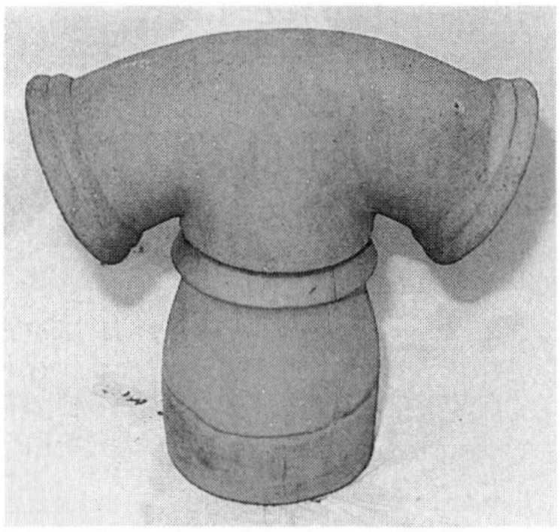

l. An H-shaped clay chimney pot, 19thC, 25in (63.5cm) high.
£45–55 *WEL*

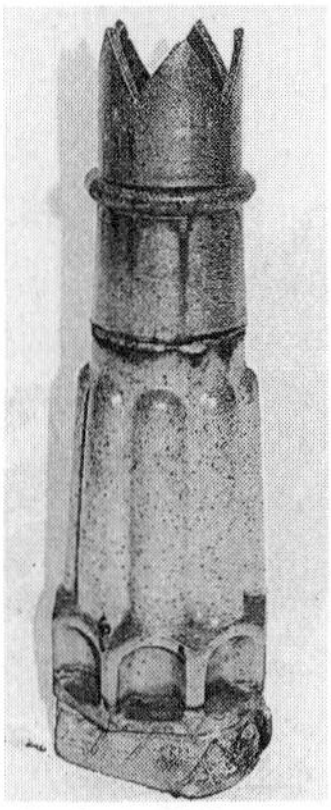

A glazed clay chimney pot, 19thC, 47½in (121cm) high.
£60–65 *WEL*

A clay chimney pot and cowl, 19thC, 33in (83.5cm) high.
£45–55 *WEL*

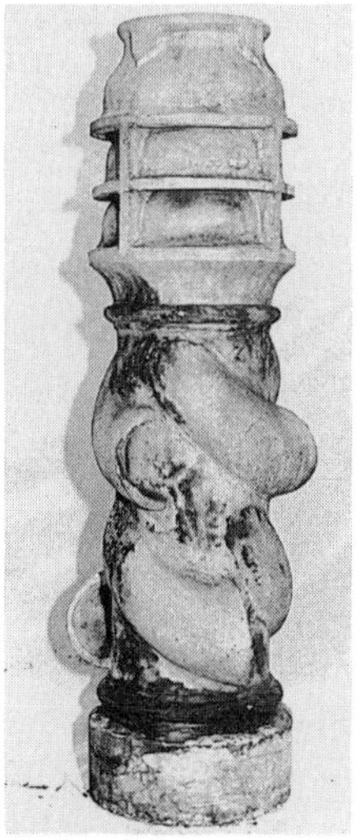

A clay chimney pot, c1870, 48in (122cm) high.
£145–200 *WEL*

A clay roof finial, 19thC, 24in (61cm) high.
£45–50 *WEL*

A clay roof finial, 19thC, 46in (116.5cm) high.
£85–90 *WEL*

A clay roof finial, 19thC, 27½in (70cm) high.
£45–50 *WEL*

A clay roof ridge tile, 19thC, 18in (45.5cm) long.
£4–5 *WEL*

A clay roof ridge tile, 19thC, 17in (43cm) high.
£8–10 *WEL*

A clay roof ridge tile, 19thC, 10in (25cm) high.
£4–5 *WEL*

A clay roof ridge tile, 19thC, 18½in (47cm) long.
£4–5 *WEL*

A clay roof ridge tile, 19thC, 10in (25cm) high.
£4–5 *WEL*

A clay roof ridge tile, 19thC, 12in (30.5cm) high.
£4–5 *WEL*

A clay roof ridge tile, 19thC, 18in (45.5cm) long.
£3–4 *WEL*

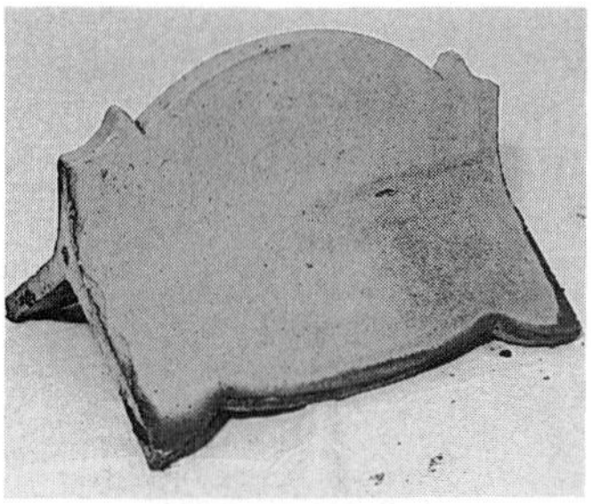

A clay roof ridge tile, 19thC, 10in (25cm) high.
£4–5 *WEL*

Iron

A wrought iron tunnel arch, incorporating 2 side entrances, 181in (459cm) long.
£950–1,200 *S(S)*

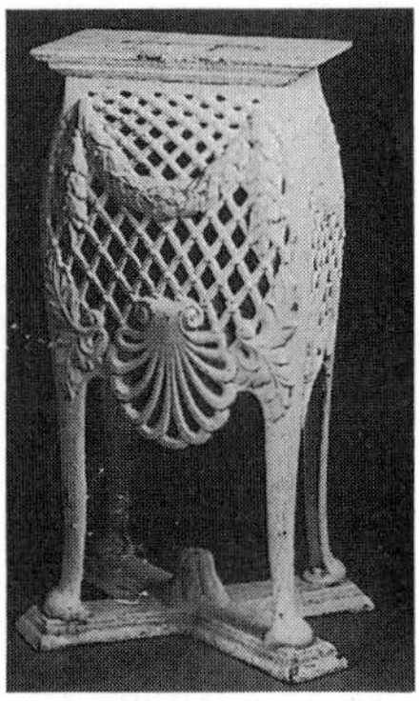

r. A pair of painted cast iron stands, each with a rectangular top over the trellis pattern, pierced bombé body with swag decoration, raised on bun feet and an X-shaped stand, 30in (76cm) high.
£3,500–4,000 *S(NY)*

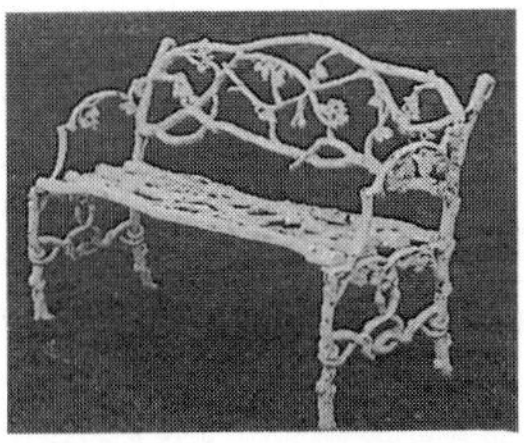

l. A rustic style cast iron seat, 19thC, 51in (129.5cm) wide.
£600–800 *S(S)*

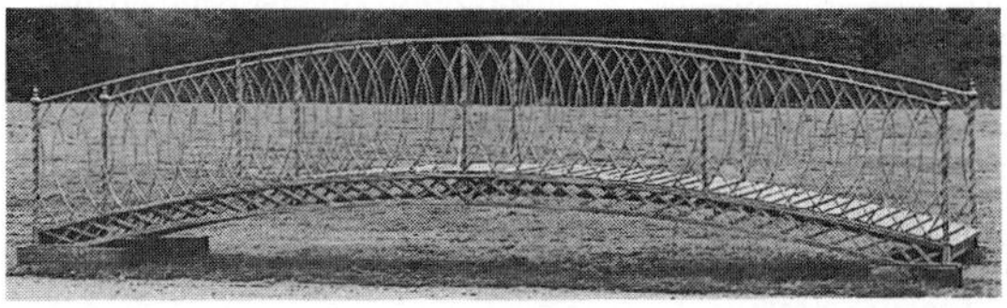

A wrought iron bridge, of shallow arched form, the sides with elliptical decoration above a trellis frieze, with a wooden slatted base, 20thC, 304in (772cm) long.
£5,200–6,500 *S(S)*

A Regency white painted cast iron garden seat, with integral foot rest, on wheels, 61in (155cm) wide.
£1,200–1,500 *WL*

A Handyside cast iron fountain, the scalloped bowl raised on 3 central entwined dolphins, 45in (114cm) high.
£5,700–6,200 *SWO*

A pair of French iron figures of reclining dogs, one on a lead base, the other on a cast stone base, 19thC, 19in (48cm) high.
£10,000–10,500 *CNY*

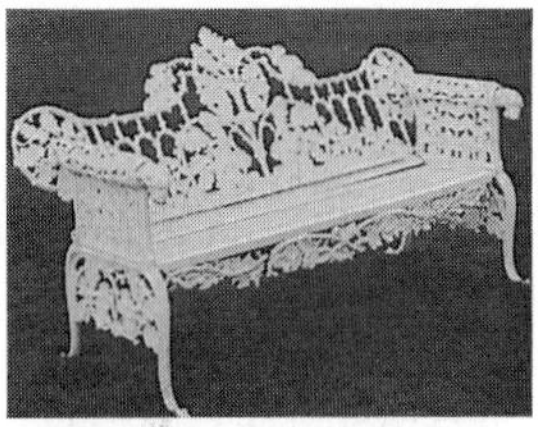

A Coalbrookdale Oak and Ivy pattern wrought iron seat, with a wooden slatted seat, the overscroll arms with dogs' head terminals, stamped 'C B Dale', registration No. '1392863, No. 30', with diamond registration stamp for 1859, 70in (178cm) wide.
£2,500–3,000 *S(S)*

A Regency wrought iron bench, 69in (175cm) wide.
£2,000–2,500 *C*

A Coalbrookdale cast iron seat, the arched rayed back above a slatted seat, registration marks obscured by paint, c1860, 47in (120cm) wide.
£800–1,200 *S(S)*

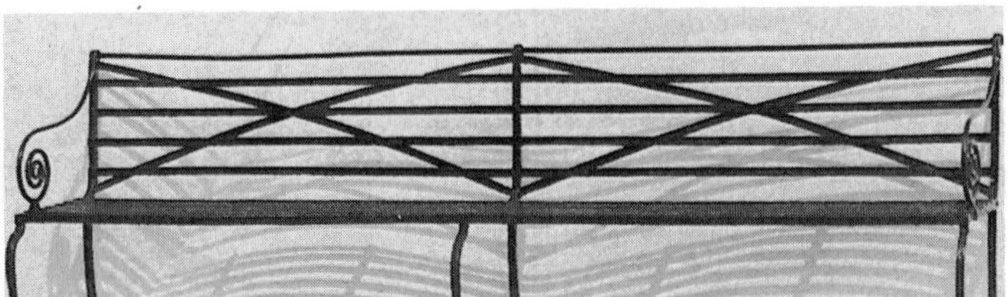

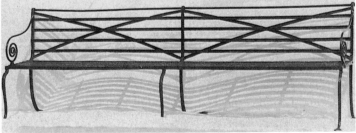

A Scottish wrought iron seat, the slatted seat and back with X-stretchers, overscroll arms, on cabriole legs, c1860, 120in (304cm) wide.
£1,200–1,700 *S(S)*

A cast iron seat, by John Finch, with a wooden slatted seat, the back and end supports pierced with foliage and strapwork, diamond registration stamp for 10th August 1866, No. 44, c1870, 64in (162.5cm) wide.
£1,800–2,300 *S(S)*

The original engraving for this seat is registered in the Public Records Office No. 199811 in 1866 with John Finch of Priory Street, Dudley, Worcestershire, as the manufacturer.

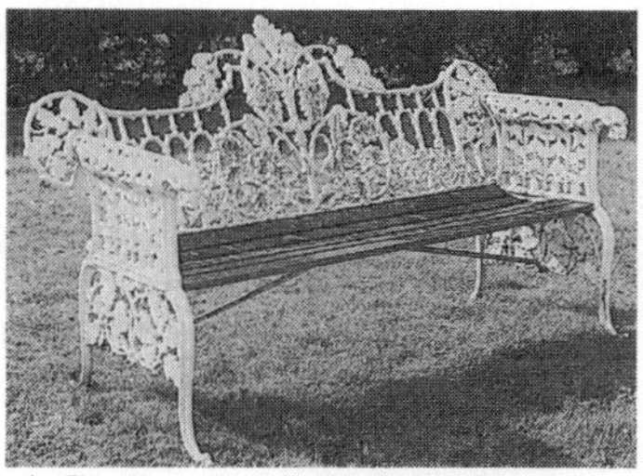

A Coalbrookdale Oak and Ivy pattern cast iron seat, with a wooden slatted seat, the end supports with diamond registration stamp for 8th January 1857, 72in (182cm) wide.
£2,700–3,200 *S(S)*

Miller's is a price GUIDE not a price LIST

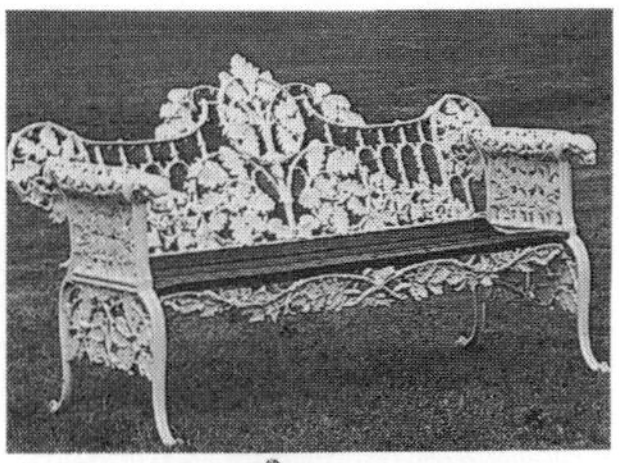

A Coalbrookdale Oak and Ivy pattern cast iron seat, with diamond registration stamp for 8th January 1857, 72in (183cm) wide.
£2,500–3,000 *S(S)*

A Coalbrookdale Oak and Ivy pattern cast iron seat, with a wooden slatted seat, the back stamped 'C B Dale & Co., No. 119253', and diamond registration stamp for 8th March 1859, 72in (182.5cm) wide.
£2,700–3,200 *S(S)*

This design is registered in the 1875 Coalbrookdale Catalogue, *Section III, page 256, number 30, The Oak and Ivy pattern was designed by the sculptor John Bell whose deerhound table, made for the 1855 Exhibition, is now in the Ironbridge Gorge Museum.*

A Coalbrookdale cast iron seat, with a wooden slatted seat, the back pierced with oval paterae, a diamond registration stamp for 5th May 1883, and registration No. '397749', numbered '71–2', 72in (182cm) wide.
£3,600–4,200 *S(S)*

The original signed engraving for this seat is registered in the Public Records Office and correspondingly numbered 397749 in 1883 under the Coalbrookdale Company Shropshire Ltd., and subsequently appears in the Coalbrookdale Catalogue of Garden and Park Furniture 1907.

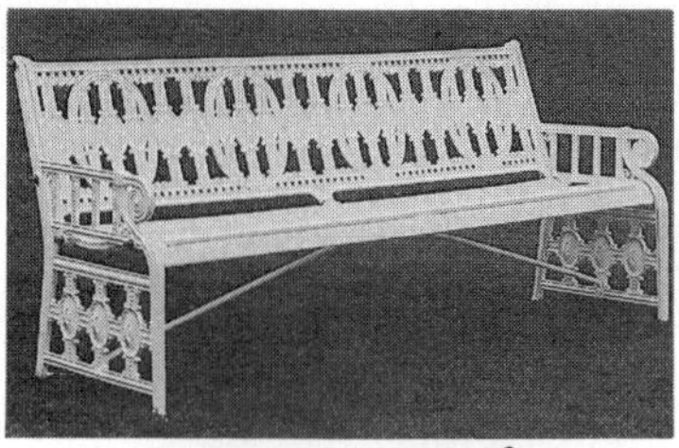

A wrought iron conversation seat, with an arcaded back and scrolled seat, the supports joined by stretchers, with scroll feet, 19thC, 53in (135cm) wide.
£2,000–2,500 *S(S)*

A cast iron Gothic style garden bench, late 19thC. 57½in (146cm) wide.
£1,600–1,800 *S(NY)*

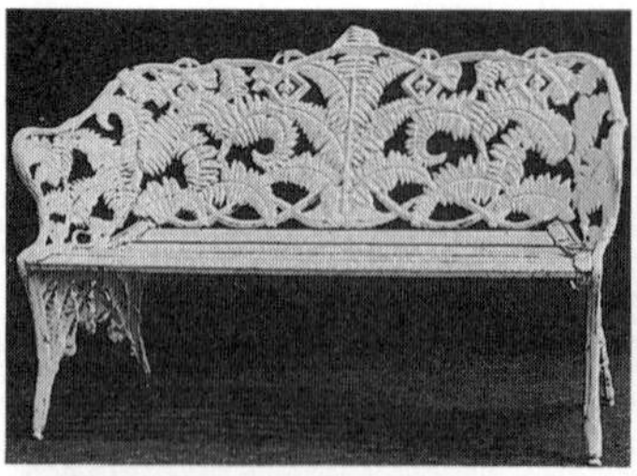

A Coalbrookdale Fern and Blackberry pattern cast iron seat, registration marks obscured by paint, late 19thC, 57in (145cm) wide.
£700–1,000 *S(S)*

A Coalbrookdale Nasturtium pattern cast iron seat, the back stamped 'C B DALE', with registration stamp for 1862, 71½in (182cm) wide.
£7,000–8,000 *S(S)*

A pair of cast iron chairs, from the Val d'Osne Foundry, c1860.
£3,000–4,000 *S(S)*

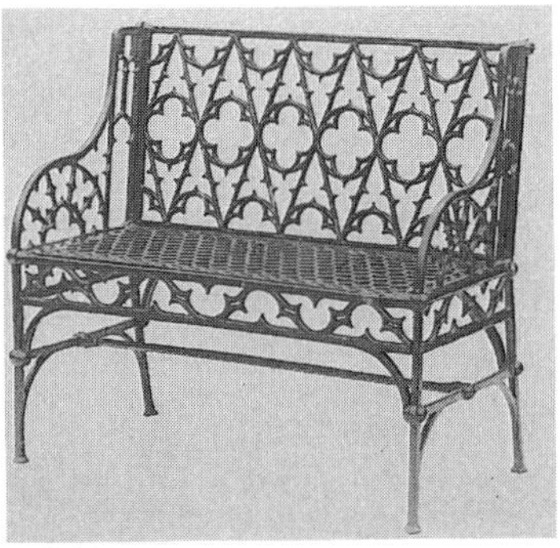

l. A cast iron seat, from the Val d'Osne Foundry, c1860, 56in (142cm) wide.
£1,500–2,000 *S(S)*

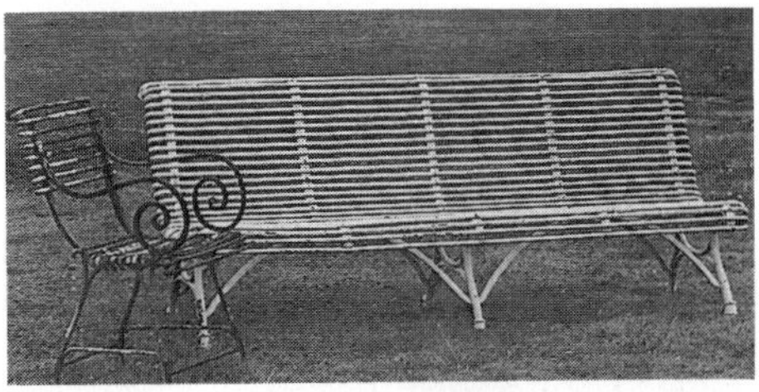

A French wrought iron seat, late 19thC, 77in (196cm), and an armchair, the back with a brass plate inscribed 'S. Sauveur'.
£450–700 *S(S)*

A neo-classical style cast iron garden suite, after a design by Karl Friedrich Schinkel, late 19thC.
£3,200–3,500 *S(NY)*

r. Three cast iron balcony panels, 19thC, each 19in (48cm) wide.
£100–140 *WEL*

Four cast iron balcony panels, 19thC, each 24½in (61cm) wide.
£225–250 *WEL*

A pair of wrought iron gates, the overscroll terminals with dragon masks, the lock plates stamped 'Chas. Smith & Sons, Birmingham', c1900, 142in (360cm) wide.
£6,500–8,500 *S(S)*

A cast iron foot scraper, 19thC, 20in (51cm) long.
£25–30 *WEL*

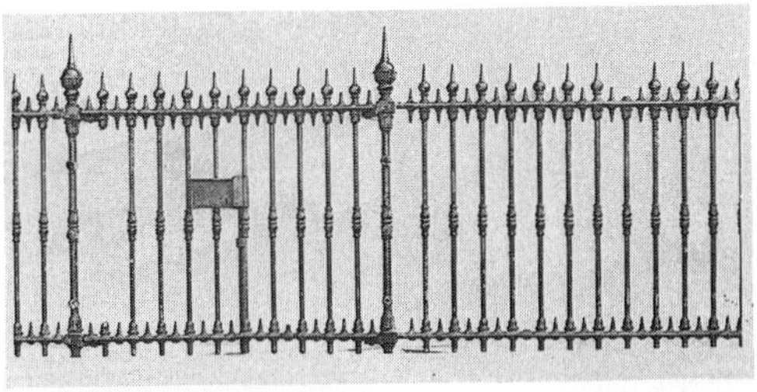

l. A quantity of cast iron railing panels, each with foliate cast upright and ball and point finial, 60in (152cm) high.
£550–900 *S(S)*

A French wire work and wrought iron plant stand, with zinc liner, late 19thC, 47in (119cm) wide.
£1,200–1,700 *S(S)*

A pair of cast iron urns, late 19thC, 30in (76cm) high.
£1,000–1,200 *S(S)*

l. A set of 4 cast iron urns, late 19thC, 24in (61cm) high.
£1,400–1,800 *S(S)*

A cast iron urn, late 19thC, 36in (91.5cm) diam.
£550–900 *S(S)*

A cast iron urn, late 19thC, 18in (45.5cm) high, on a square pedestal, 26in (66cm) high.
£700–1,100 *S(S)*

A pair of cast iron copies of the Borghese and Medici urns, each moulded with a frieze of figures and with loop handles, late 19thC, 20½in (52cm) high, on cast iron pedestals, 21in (53cm) high.
£650–750 *S(S)*

A pair of cast iron urns, each cast with leaf tips and flowers, stamped 'J. W. Fiske No. 21 and 23, Barclay Street, NY, Pat. May 12, 1874', late 19thC, 17in (43cm) high.
£2,700–3,000 *S(NY)*

A pair of cast iron urns, stamped 'M.F.G by Kramer Bros. F.D.Y Company, Dayton, Ohio', late 19thC, 34in (86.5cm) high.
£1,300–1,500 *S(NY)*

A blacksmith's wrought iron shop sign, the wall bracket supporting elaborate scrolls, an animal head and sign dated '1805', the terminal in the form of a key with elaborate handle, 19thC, 87in (221cm) high.
£1,200–1,700 *S(S)*

A wrought iron weather vane, the direction indicators on scrolled supports beneath a painted tin arrow and pennant pointer pierced with the initials 'VC' and dated '1778', 91in (231cm) high.
£500–700 *S(S)*

A pair of cast iron garden urns, the body flanked with loop handles, late 19thC, 28in (71cm) high.
£2,000–2,500 *S(NY)*

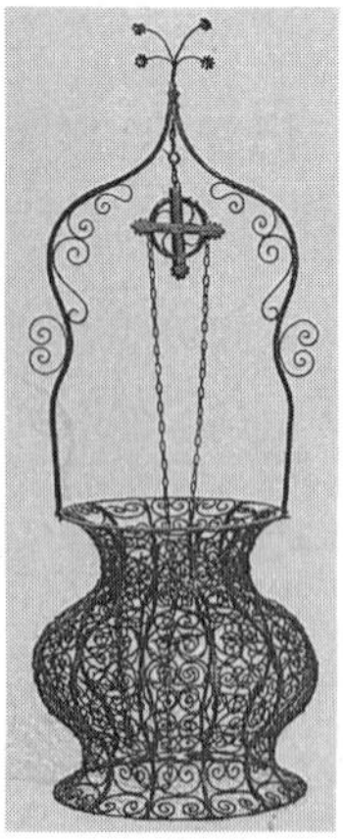

Miller's is a price GUIDE not a price LIST

l. A wrought iron wellhead, of baluster form above a collar-tied scroll and below ogee arched overthrow, c1900, 100in (254cm) high.
£1,200–1,700 *S(S)*

A selection of cast iron gratings, 19thC.
£8–30 per foot *WRe*

Lead

A Georgian lead cistern, of D-form, with strapwork and foliate decoration to the front and sides, the sides modelled with cherubs, the front with the initials 'W R' in a shaped cartouche and dated '1766', the side set with a bronze tap, 50in (127cm) wide.
£2,000–2,500 *S(S)*

A Stuart lead cistern, the panelled front dated '1677', with initials 'E B' inside a floral garland flanked by a portcullis and a coil of rope, one end decorated with a wreath enclosing a winged cherub mask, 54in (137cm) wide.
£4,500–5,000 *S(S)*

A lead fountain, in the form of 3 intertwined dolphins, their nostrils drilled for water, early 20thC, 38in (97cm) high.
£2,000–3,000 *S(S)*

A Carolean style lead urn, early 20thC, 25in (63cm) high.
£700–900 *S(S)*

A lead urn, early 20thC, 17in (43cm) high.
£200–225 *WRe*

A lead fountain depicting Neptune, signed 'Wheeler Williams, 1939 No. 36/Neptune'.
£3,500–4,000 *S(NY)*

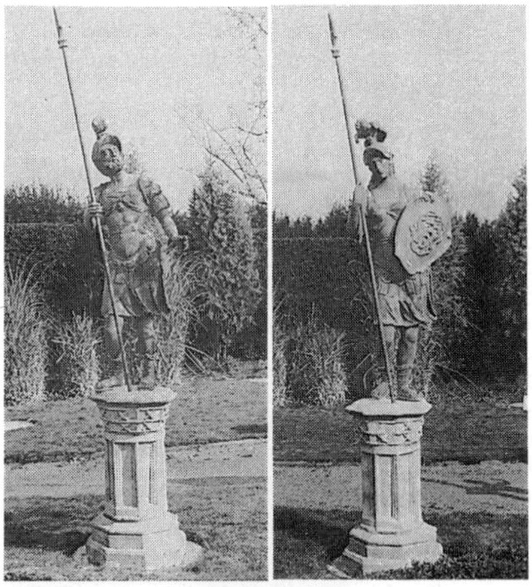

A pair of lead statues of Mars and Minerva, in the style of Andries Carpentière, each on panelled composition stone pedestal, c1730, 132in (335cm) high overall.
£9,000–11,000 *S(S)*

These statues were removed from the gardens of Ascoughfee Hall, Lincolnshire, which was acquired by the town of Spalding as a Jubilee Memorial at the turn of the century. Previously they had been been owned by the Johnson family, the most eminent of which, Maurice Johnson, was an antiquary and was amongst the 23 signatories of the Society of Antiquities when it was refounded in 1717–18.

Marble

l. A marble garden bench, the seat flanked by stylised lion supports, carved with masks and foliage, c1900, 86in (218.5cm) long.
£16,200–17,000 *S(NY)*

r. A pair of Italian veined pink marble brackets, each carved with volutes, stop fluting and with panelled sides, 19thC, 33in (83.5cm) high.
£1,200–1,700 *S(S)*

A French white marble bust of a priest, in clerical dress, 19thC, 34in (86cm) high.
£900–1,200 *S(S)*

An Indian white marble chair, with foliate pierced arched back and overscroll arms, 19thC.
£700–1,000 *S(S)*

A set of 4 white marble columns, 91in (231cm) high.
£3,600–5,000 *S(S)*

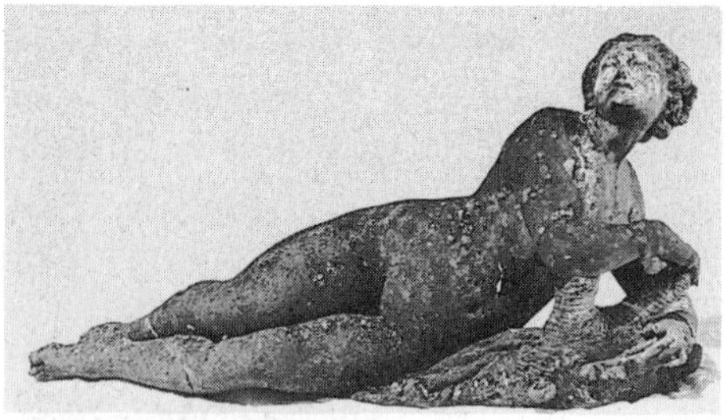

A white marble figure of a girl, 18thC, 37in (94cm) long.
£7,000–9,000 *S(S)*

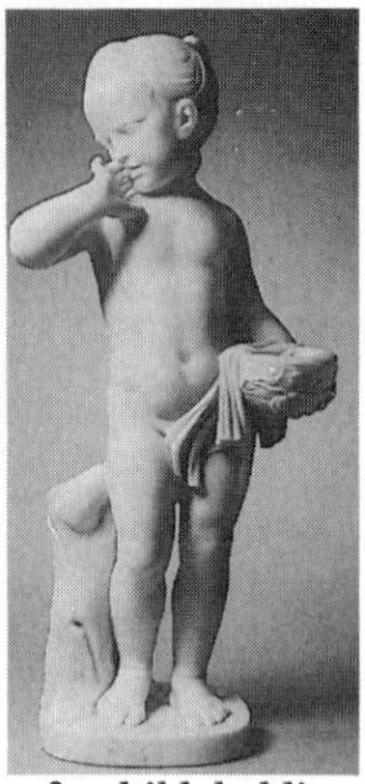

A marble figure of a child, holding a bird's nest, late 19thC, 30½in (77cm) high.
£1,400–1,600 *S(NY)*

A marble garden figural group, depicting a nude female figure astride a panther, 19thC, 35in (90cm) high.
£6,200–7,000 *S(NY)*

A Romanesque style marble figural column and sarcophagus, associated, 19thC.
£8,000–10,000 *S(NY)*

l. A marble wall font, signed 'A. Massi, Venezia', the pedestal headed by a satyr's mask, supporting a semi-circular font surmounted by a domed figural plaque, c1900, 60in (152cm) high.
£13,500–14,500 *S(NY)*

A marble planter, inset with a copper lining, raised on circular turned legs, late 19thC, 45in (114cm) high.
£15,000–16,000 *S(NY)*

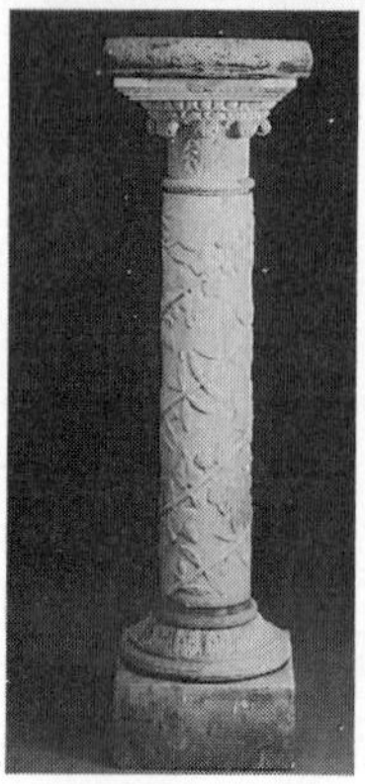

l. A marble pedestal, fitted with a bronze basin, the basin signed 'L. M. Sterling, 1916', damaged, 19thC, 62in (158cm) high.
£700–800 *S(NY)*

An Italian white marble fountain, with a boy seated astride a swan, on an associated oval veined marble bowl and stepped and carved square base, late 19thC, 61in (154cm) high.
£3,500–4,000 *S(S)*

A pair of marble garden planters, c1900.
£3,500–4,000 *S(NY)*

A marble garden plaque, carved with cherubs and satyrs, c1900, 45½in (116cm) long.
£7,000–7,500 *S(NY)*

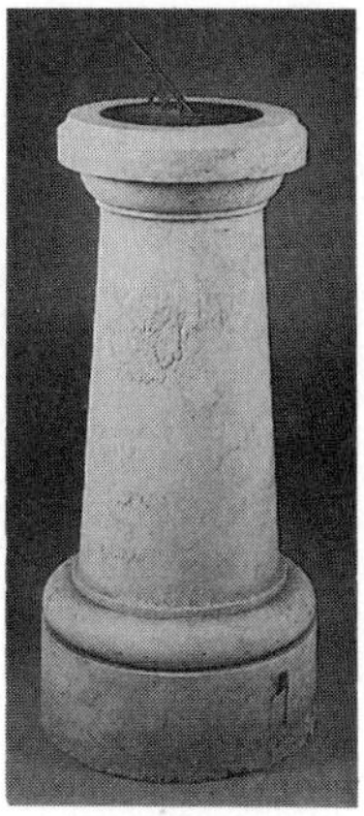

A marble sundial, the top inset with a bronze dial, 48in (122cm) high.
£1,000–1,200 *S(NY)*

A marble centre table, the top carved with scrolling foliage and geometric shapes, 37½in (95cm) diam.
£6,000–6,500 *S(NY)*

A pair of neo-classical marble urns, 19thC, 37in (94cm) high.
£29,000–31,000 *S(NY)*

A marble washstand, with 2 basins, c1930, 59in (149.5cm) wide.
£2,500–2,800 *WRe*

Stone

A French carved stone seat, the top with foliate carved borders on acanthus and valute carved supports, 19thC, 57in (144.5cm) long.
£2,000–2,500 *S(S)*

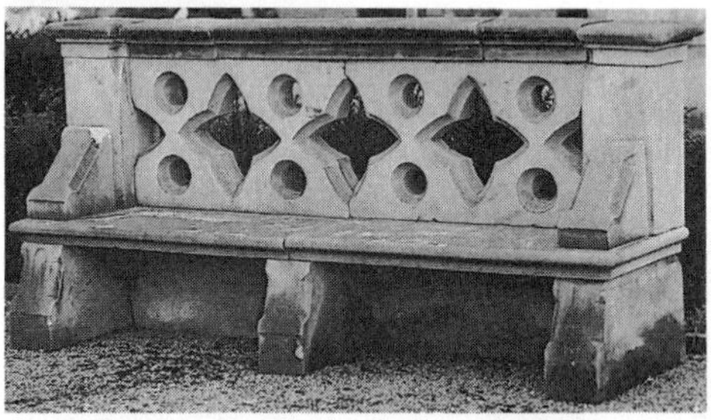

A sandstone seat, the back pierced with roundels and stars beneath moulded cappings, downswept arms and on shaped supports, 19thC, 77in (195.5cm) wide.
£1,400–2,000 *S(S)*

A pair of sandstone corbels, each carved in high relief with masks, 19thC, 9in (23cm) high.
£400–550 *S(S)*

A French carved stone bust of Turenne, with flowing hair, in classical dress, on a square base, 19thC, 35½in (90cm) high.
£4,000–4,500 *S(S)*

A Vicenza stone figure of a man, on a square base, 20thC, 62in (157cm) high, on a panelled composition stone pedestal, 34in (86cm) high.
£1,500–2,000 *S(S)*

A pair of carved stone columns, each of plain form with scroll carved capitals, 19thC, 115in (292cm) high.
£1,800–2,200 *S(S)*

r. A pair of large composition stone gate pier finials, in the form of pineapples, each on a rising circular foot and square base, damaged, 34½in (88cm) high.
£1,200–1,800 *S(S)*

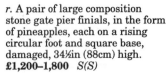

A set of 4 French carved stone child figures, representing the seasons, each scantily draped and holding an attribute, c1900, 34in (87cm) high.
£8,000–9,000 *S(S)*

A stoneware figure of a woman, early 20thC, 43½in (110cm) high.
£1,200–1,800 *S(S)*

A pair of composition stone horses, 20thC, 23in (58.5cm) high.
£450–500 *WRe*

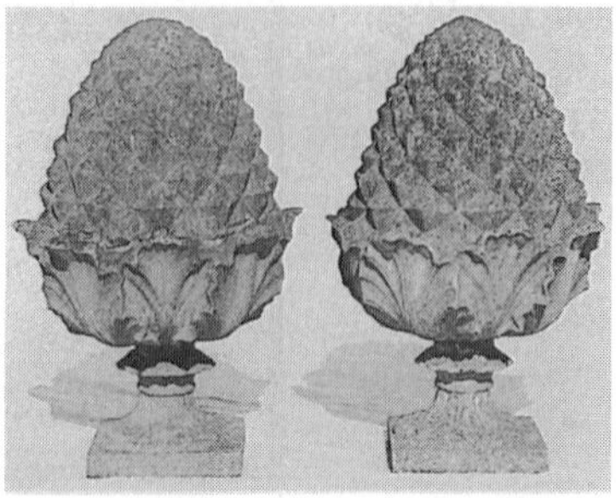

A pair of carved stone figures of putti, each standing holding aloft a fruiting urn, early 20thC, 59in (150cm) high.
£6,500–7,000 *S(S)*

A pair of stone lions, each seated with a paw perched on a cartouche shaped shield, 34in (86cm) high.
£12,000–13,000 *S(NY)*

A pair of Vicenza stone obelisks, 20thC, 62in (157cm) high, on similarly carved square pedestals, 19in (48cm) high.
£1,400–1,700 *S(S)*

A pair of carved stone gate pier balls, each on a rising square base, 19thC, 28in (71cm) high.
£2,000–2,500 *S(S)*

A George III mahogany double-sided pedestal desk, the moulded top lined in leather, the frieze and pedestals with 3 drawers in the front and back, c1800, 54in (137cm) wide.
£13,500–15,000 *S*

A William and Mary walnut kneehole desk, cross and feather banded overall, on later bun feet, restored, 31½in (80cm) wide.
£4,700–5,500 *C*

A George I walnut kneehole desk, the quartered moulded top with chevron and crossbandings, with 7 drawers round a shallow drawer and cupboard, on bracket feet, c1720, 30in (76cm) wide.
£18,000–22,000 *S*

A Queen Anne walnut kneehole desk, on bracket feet, c1715, 33in (84cm) wide.
£6,500–8,500 *Bon*

A mahogany pedestal desk, with green leather lined top and 9 drawers, mid-19thC, 47in (119cm) wide.
£3,000–3,500 *S*

A George III mahogany double-sided pedestal desk, with moulded leather lined top, each pedestal with 3 drawers one side and a door the other, c1800, 55in (139.5cm) wide.
£10,000–12,000 *S*

A George I walnut kneehole desk, with moulded quarter-veneered crossbanded top, a slide above a frieze drawer, 6 small drawers flanking a recessed cupboard, on bracket feet, c1720, 33½in (85cm) wide.
£10,500–12,000 *S*

A Queen Anne walnut kneehole desk, with herringbone and crossbanded top, on bracket feet, c1710, 32½in (82cm) wide.
£5,500–6,500 *Bon*

A George III mahogany pedestal desk, inlaid overall with ebonised line, the top lined in leather, on a plinth base, 54½in (138cm) wide.
£11,000–13,000 *C*

A George IV Gothic style mahogany pedestal library desk, probably designed by William Porden, the middle drawer centred by a quatrefoil, the top leather lined, 73in (185cm) wide.
£40,000–50,000 *C*

A George III mahogany library pedestal desk, with rounded rectangular blue leather lined top, the sides with carrying handles, on rounded plinth base, 55in (140cm) wide.
£51,000–55,000 *C*

A Victorian mahogany double-sided pedestal desk, one side with 9 drawers, the other with 3 drawers and a pair of doors, c1850, 60in (152cm) wide.
£4,500–5,500 *S*

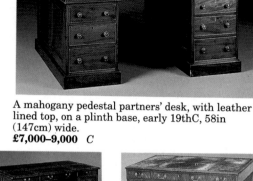

A mahogany pedestal partners' desk, with leather lined top, on a plinth base, early 19thC, 58in (147cm) wide.
£7,000–9,000 *C*

A Victorian inlaid amboyna partners' desk, with casters, 65½in (166cm) wide.
£42,000–45,000 *S(NY)*

A mahogany pedestal desk, the detachable two-part top with 6 replaced leather panels, early 19thC, 84in (213cm) wide.
£3,000–4,000 *S*

A mahogany double-sided pedestal desk, with 3 panels of crimson leather to the top, c1900, 59in (150cm) wide.
£4,000–5,000 *S*

A mahogany partners' pedestal desk, with leather lined top, c1900, 54in (137cm) wide.
£2,000–2,500 *S*

An Edwardian mahogany pedestal desk, with recessed D-shaped outline, crossbanded and inlaid, 48in (122cm) wide.
£2,500–3,000 *CSK*

An early Victorian satinwood pedestal desk, with Bramah locks, ivory bun handles and plain panelled back, 53½in (136cm) wide.
£7,500–8,500 *C*

A burr walnut veneered kidney-shaped pedestal desk in 3 parts, with leather top, 3 frieze and 3 drawers to each pedestal, 71¼in (181cm) wide.
£8,000–10,000 *CSK*

A Victorian mahogany pedestal partners' desk, each side with 3 frieze drawers and 3 drawers to each pedestal, on plinth base, restored, 72in (182.5cm) wide.
£9,000–12,000 *C*

An Edwardian mahogany and marquetry inlaid lady's writing desk, 48in (122cm) wide.
£3,000–4,000 *CSK*

A mahogany cylinder desk, with fitted interior, c1780, 40in (102cm) wide.
£5,000–6,000 *S*

A George IV rosewood desk, with baize lined fitted interior, 20in (50cm) wide.
£3,000–5,000 *S*

A Victorian mahogany desk, the superstructure with 8 drawers above a writing slope, 60in (152cm) wide.
£1,500–2,000 *E*

A mahogany three-tier dumb waiter, with tripod base, c1750, 42½in (108cm) high.
£2,000–2,500 *S*

A pair of Anglo-Irish mahogany dumb waiters, each with turned stem and tripod base, c1790, 59in (150cm) high.
£5,000–7,000 *S*

A William and Mary walnut and marquetry cushion mirror, later plate, 40½ by 29in (102 by 74cm).
£4,500–5,500 *C*

A parcel gilt walnut veneered wall mirror, c1730, 50 by 24in (127 by 61cm).
£2,000–3,000 *S*

A George I giltwood and gesso wall mirror, with original bevelled plate, scrolled leaf decorated pediment, shaped apron with scallop shell, 50½ by 26in (128 by 66.5cm).
£3,000–4,000 *AH*

A brass inlaid tortoiseshell mirror, the plate flanked by fluted pilasters and diaper panels, c1700, 56 by 34in (142 by 86cm).
£23,000–26,000 *S*

A late George II giltwood mirror, the arched plate with ribbon tied rosette band, re-gilded and restored, 50 by 34in (127 by 86cm).
£4,500–6,500 *C*

A giltwood pier mirror, the cresting with a Chinese glass painting of a man and a pair of ho-ho birds, c1760.
£10,500–12,500 *S*

A carved giltwood mirror, the ho-ho bird cresting above a later plate, re-gilded, c1760, 55½ by 27½in (141 by 70cm).
£3,000–4,500 *S(S)*

A George I gilt gesso mirror, with traces of original gilding, 61 by 29in (155 by 74cm).
£11,500–13,000 *C*

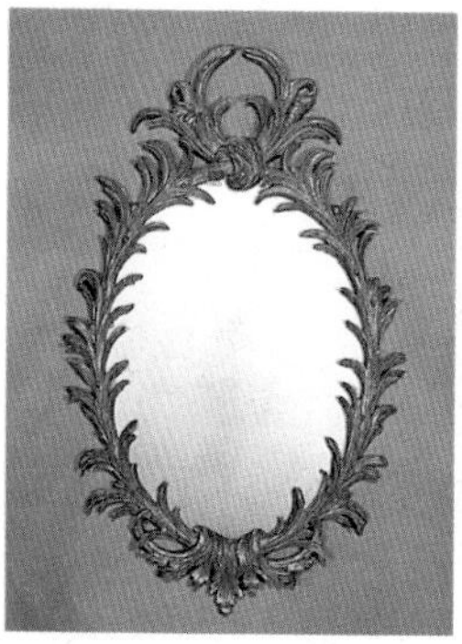

A George III giltwood mirror, the carved frame with a scrolling crest and foliate clasp, c1760, 39in (99cm) high.
£2,000–3,000 *Bon*

An early George III giltwood wall mirror, in the manner of John Linnell, c1765, 43in (109cm) high.
£4,000–6,000 *S*

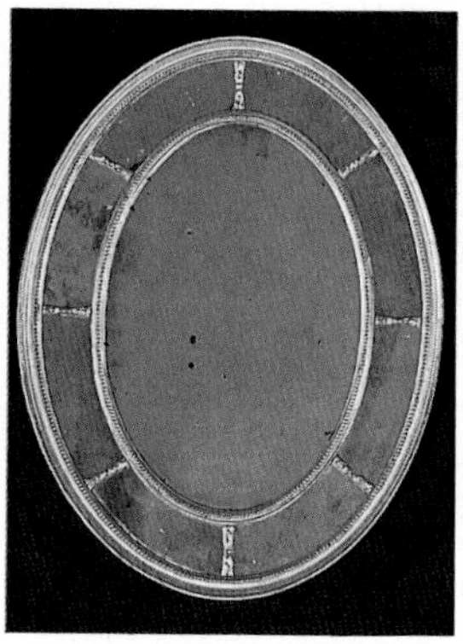

A George III giltwood wall mirror, with mirrored border and bead mouldings, c1770, 31½in (80cm) high.
£1,700–2,500 *S*

An Adam revival style giltwood wall mirror, 19thC, 54in (137cm) high.
£2,700–3,500 *S*

A George III carved mahogany cheval mirror, with adjustable swing mirror, c1790, 57½in (146cm) high.
£7,000–8,000 *S*

A Victorian giltwood mirror in early George III style, repaired.
£6,000–8,000 *C*

An Irish parcel gilt cut glass mirror, the plate within a reeded and star cushion frame, 23 by 15in (58.5 by 38cm).
£3,000–4,000 *C*

A William IV giltwood convex mirror, decorated with floral trelliswork, restored, 85in (216cm) high.
£22,000–27,000 *C*

A pair of Chippendale style giltwood pier mirrors, 20thC, 84 by 45in (213 by 114cm).
£10,500–12,500 *S*

A Régence giltwood mirror, with arched divided plate, the cresting carved with foliage and a female mask, restored, re-gilt, 68½ by 40in (174 by 101.5cm).
£7,000–10,000 *C*

A pair of walnut inlaid pedestals, with square tops, on plinth bases, 44½in (113cm) high.
£3,000–3,500 *CSK*

A tapestry, c1580, mounted as a mahogany firescreen.
£3,000–4,000 *C*

An early Louis XV eight-fold screen, possibly former wallpaper panels.
£6,000–7,000 *CSK*

An Empire revival mahogany and ormolu mounted pedestal, with marble top, 45in (114cm) high.
£900–1,100 *CSK*

l. A George III mahogany bowfront sideboard, with crossbanded top, c1780, 34in (86cm) wide.
£3,000–4,000 *S*

A mahogany serpentine sideboard, with pot cupboard, on plinth base with block feet, c1780, 76in (193cm) wide.
£10,000–12,000 *Bon*

A George IV mahogany sideboard, the arched centre and deep drawer flanked by a cellaret drawer and cupboard, on baluster legs, 78½in (199cm) wide.
£2,000–3,000 *C*

A George III mahogany bowfront sideboard, crossbanded and inlaid with boxwood lines, on square tapering legs, 57½in (146cm) wide.
£3,500–4,500 *DN*

A George III mahogany bowfront sideboard, banded and boxwood line inlaid, the central drawer flanked by a deep drawer with a secret drawer on one side, 66in (167.5cm) wide.
£1,800–2,200 *E*

A George III demi-lune sideboard, the central drawer flanked by 2 deep drawers, on square tapering legs with spade feet, c1780, 66½in (169cm) wide. **£4,500–5,500** *Bon*

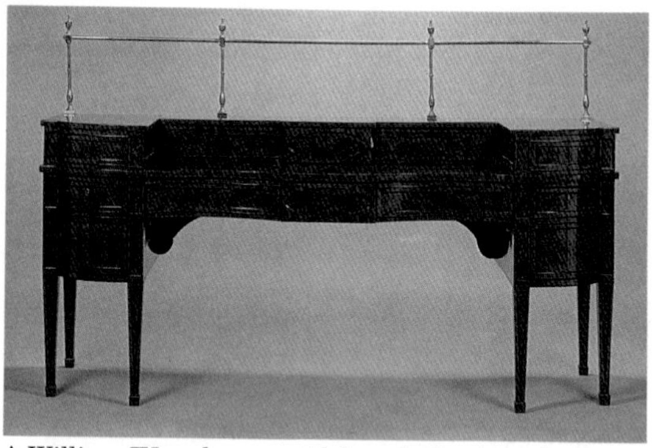

A William IV mahogany sideboard, the shaped top with a superstructure fitted with 2 drawers, a pair of slides and a brass splash rail, on square tapering legs and block feet, 19thC, 89in (226cm) long.
£6,500–8,000 *S(NY)*

A Regency mahogany pedestal sideboard, with later inlay, on square section feet, c1800, 55in (139.5cm) wide.
£1,700–2,200 *Bon*

A George III mahogany sideboard, crossbanded with boxwood and ebony stringing, on 6 square tapering supports, 60in (152cm) wide.
£1,700–2,200 *Bri*

A George IV brass inlaid mahogany sideboard, on turned reeded legs with casters, probably Northern Irish or Scottish, c1820, 70in (177.5cm) wide.
£2,500–3,500 *S*

A Regency mahogany sideboard, inlaid overall with ebony and boxwood lines, labelled 'Spearman 21-6-07/97', 56in (142cm) wide.
£6,000–7,000 *C*

A giltwood window seat, stamped 'C. Mellier & Co., 48, 49, 50 Margaret St, London' and '7611', c1890, 50in (127cm) wide.
£3,500–4,000 *S*

A pair of giltwood stools, each with a padded seat, on square fluted tapering legs with gadroon and foliate decoration, joined by an H-shaped stretcher, on foliate feet.
£3,000–3,500 *CSK*

A black painted and decorated window seat, the caned seat with squab cushion, 38½in (98cm) wide.
£2,000–3,000 *C*

A William and Mary walnut stool, with drop-in seat, moulded frieze and turned legs, 18in (46cm) diam.
£4,000–5,000 *S*

A George III painted and parcel gilt window bench, the seat with Vitruvian scroll carved apron, on square tapering legs headed by carved paterae, feet repaired, c1775, 55in (140cm) long.
£17,000–18,000 *S(NY)*

A James II giltwood stool, the top covered in silk floral damask, re-gilded and restored, 20in (51cm) high.
£10,000–11,000 *C*

A George II walnut stool, with padded top, on cabriole legs and pad feet, 21in (53cm) wide.
£4,000–4,500 *C*

A Louis XVI stool, the frieze carved with guilloche, stamped 'I. B. Sené', c1780, 19in (48cm) wide.
£3,000–3,500 *S*

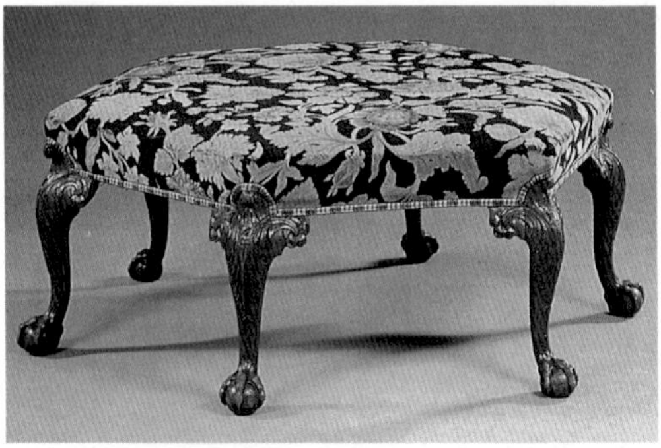

A mahogany stool, the top covered in machine needlework, on 6 leaf carved cabriole legs with claw-and-ball feet, possibly mid-18thC, 39½in (100cm) wide.
£14,000–15,000 *S*

A pair of grey painted stools, each with bead and reel-decorated friezes, on winged foliate-headed claw feet, with gadrooned bases, 35½in (91cm) wide.
£7,000–8,000 *CSK*

A giltwood stool, with moulded frieze and cabriole legs, 27in (69cm) wide.
£2,000–2,500 *S*

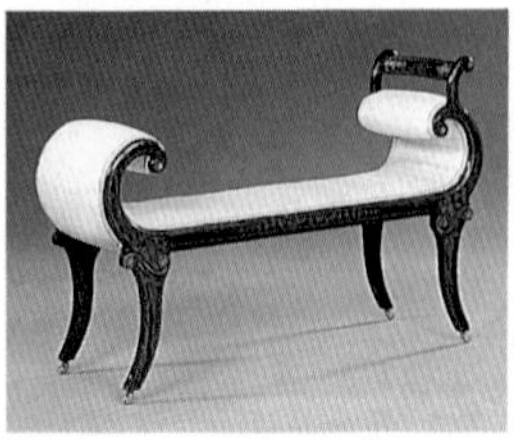

Two rosewood window seats, one c1815, one modern, 49in (124.5cm) long.
£3,500–4,500 *S*

A Regency ebonised window seat, with splayed legs headed by palmette angles and joined by a turned stretcher, restored, 41in (104cm) wide.
£3,500–4,500 *C*

An Edwardian Sheraton revival three-piece bergère suite, with painted floral satinwood frame and original cushions.
£5,000–5,500 *Bri*

A George II red walnut twin chairback settee, covered in later gros point floral needlework, 57in (145cm) wide.
£3,000–4,000 *C*

A Regency grained rosewood and parcel gilt sofa, with later caps, lacking back moulding, paper labels and seat rail inscribed 'Lord Darlington', 74in (188cm) long.
£11,000–12,000 *C*

A Louis XV walnut sofa, the back and seat rail centred by leafy scrollwork with a garland, mid-18thC, 70in (178cm) wide.
£2,000–3,000 *S*

A Regency ebonised sofa, with cushioned seat and sabre legs, c1810, 93in (236cm) long.
£5,000–6,000 *S*

An Edwardian Sheraton style satinwood settee, painted with classical figures and foliage, the tapering legs with brass casters, c1900, 72in (183cm) long.
£4,500–5,500 *S*

A pair of George IV mahogany chaise longues, the moulded end supports and seat rails on circular tapering reeded legs, c1825, 72in (183cm) long.
£9,000–10,000 *S*

An oak Gothic revival sofa, with padded back and overscrolled arms, the frame panelled with Gothic tracery, c1820, 96in (243.5cm) long.
£5,500–7,000 *S*

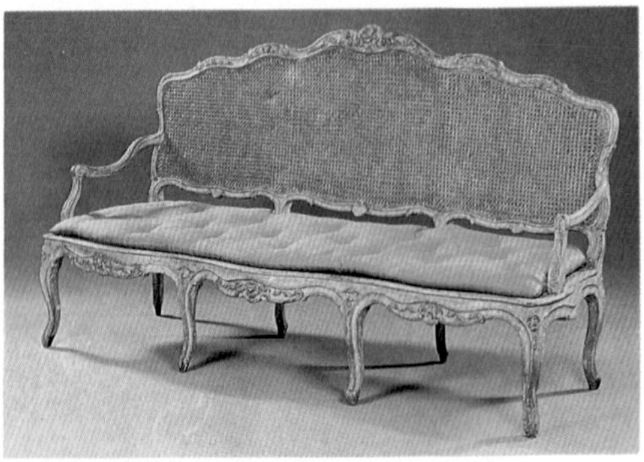

A Louis XV painted sofa, in the manner of Nogaret à Lyon, with caned loose cushioned seat, on cabriole legs, mid-18thC, 79in (200.5cm) long.
£3,500–5,500 *S*

A George II mahogany straight back sofa, the arms leaf carved all-over and with eagle head terminals, the base extensively carved, part re-made, 53in (134.5cm) wide.
£3,000–3,500 *Bri*

A George III style serpentine giltwood sofa, the moulded padded serpentine back headed by flowers, with serpentine cushioned seat, on tapering fluted legs, 67in (170cm) wide.
£6,000–7,000 *S*

A George III style serpentine giltwood sofa, with moulded arched padded back and padded arms, on leaf-capped front legs, 62½in (159cm) wide.
£5,000–6,500 *S*

A George III mahogany sofa, the arched curved padded back headed by ribbons, with fluted triple serpentine seat rail, on beaded cabriole front legs, c1775, 85in (216cm) wide.
£6,000–7,500 *S*

A George II mahogany architect's table, the adjustable top above a fitted drawer, c1755, 38½in (98cm) wide.
£3,000–4,000 *S*

A rosewood and brass inlaid breakfast table, the supports with foliate brass caps and casters, restored, early 19thC, 47in (119cm) diam.
£4,500–5,000 *CSK*

An early Victorian rosewood breakfast table, with pictorial centre, turned column, splayed supports, scroll feet, and casters, 49½in (126cm) diam.
£5,000–6,000 *CSK*

A Regency rosewood cross-banded breakfast table, with brass inlay and stringing, 50in (127cm) diam.
£3,700–4,200 *AG*

A Regency brass inlaid rosewood breakfast table, with hexagonal column and triform plinth, on gilt metal claw feet, c1810, 48in (122cm) diam.
£6,000–8,000 *Bon*

A George III mahogany draughtsman's table, with hinged ratcheted top, 35in (89cm) wide.
£1,500–2,000 *DN*

r. A Regency mahogany tilt-top crossbanded breakfast table, on turned shaft with gadrooned base with bead-and-reel edge, 47½in (121cm) diam.
£4,500–5,000 *C*

A Regency rosewood and brass inlaid breakfast table, on a triform base, with claw feet, c1830, 48in (122cm) diam.
£7,000–8,000 *Bon*

A Regency mahogany breakfast table, with a ringed baluster, c1815, 55in (140cm) diam.
£2,500–3,000 *S*

A late Regency rosewood breakfast table, with bead decoration, 56in (142cm) diam.
£10,000–11,000 *CSK*

A Queen Anne walnut veneered card table, with serpentine D-shaped top, the crossbanded interior with a central cypher, 3 frieze drawers, on 5 moulded legs with splayed pad feet, 33in (84cm) wide.
£16,000–17,500 *S*

A George II laburnum card table, the baize lined interior with counter wells, on lappeted club legs and club feet, 34½in (88cm) wide.
£6,000–7,000 *C*

A George II red walnut card table, with acanthus carved cabriole legs, restored, 35in (89cm) wide.
£1,700–2,000 *Bon*

A Regency mahogany and rosewood card table, with ormolu mounted frieze, 36in (91.5cm) wide.
£1,500–2,000 *Bon*

A pair of William IV rosewood and parcel gilt card tables, with baize lined interiors, and scroll decorated frieze, restored, 36in (91.5cm) wide.
£5,500–6,500 *CSK*

A marble topped mahogany centre table, the associated top with brass border and calamander crossbanding, early 19thC, 49in (124.5cm) wide.
£13,000–15,000 *S*

A Regency mahogany fold-over card table, with baize lined interior, on a central pillar with 4 concave legs and brass capped feet, 36in (91.5cm) wide.
£600–800 *JH*

A Viennese parcel gilt centre table, the ebonised support clasped by 3 serpents, c1810, 36in (91.5cm) diam.
£5,000–6,000 *S*

A Dutch marquetry folding card table, with profusely inlaid top, on square tapering legs, 19thC, 30in (76cm) wide.
£800–1,200 *E*

A George IV rosewood centre table, in the manner of Gillows, the top with bevelled edge above 2 frieze drawers, on baluster turned twin column end supports, c1825, 54in (137cm) wide.
£1,000–1,200 *Bon*

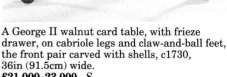

A George II walnut card table, with frieze drawer, on cabriole legs and claw-and-ball feet, the front pair carved with shells, c1730, 36in (91.5cm) wide.
£21,000–23,000 *S*

A George IV rosewood centre table, the hinged top with broad satinwood crossbanding and later neo-Adam griffin inlay, with gilt brass leaf scroll feet, c1825 and later, 54in (137cm) diam.
£8,000–9,000 *S*

An early Victorian satinwood centre table, the moulded top on a carved baluster and 4 fluted columns, on carved cabriole legs, 60in (152cm) wide.
£4,400–6,000 *S*

A French Empire mahogany and fruitwood console table, the marble top above a frieze drawer with ormolu mounts, on a plinth base, c1820, 59½in (151cm) wide.
£3,000–4,000 *Bon*

A Victorian rosewood and ivory elaborately inlaid centre table, stamped 'Collinson and Lock, London, 837', 32½in (83cm) wide.
£5,200–5,700 *S(S)*

A Charles X mahogany and parcel gilt centre table, with white marble top, on bun feet, re-gilded, 38in (96.5cm) diam.
£10,000–11,000 *C*

A George II style giltwood console table, with marble top, supported on a splayed eagle and marblised plinth, 35in (89.5cm) wide.
£5,000–6,000 *C*

A George II mahogany console table, with marble top, the plinth with rosette and ribbon moulding, with Victorian back legs, c1750, 27in (69cm) wide.
£4,000–5,000 *S*

A mid-Victorian ormolu mounted tortoiseshell and boulle marquetry centre table, inlaid with foliate scrolls, on scroll feet, 35in (89cm) diam.
£13,500–15,000 *C*

An Irish George IV giltwood console table, in the manner of del Vecchio, with later serpentine white marble top, 60½in (153.5cm) wide.
£7,500–9,500 *C*

A Napoleon III marquetry and gilt metal mounted centre table, the top decorated with foliate scrolls and musical trophies, on toupie feet, 54in (137cm) wide.
£5,000–6,000 *CSK*

A George II 'Irish' Cuban mahogany drop-leaf cottage dining table, with plain top, on cabriole legs with shell carving, 60in (152cm) wide.
£3,700–4,200 *CAG*

An early Victorian mahogany dining table, with 2 extra leaves, c1850, 121in (307cm) long extended.
£4,200–4,800 *S*

A mahogany capstan dining, with 8 numbered leaves, damaged, c1900, 96in (243.5cm) extended.
£10,000–12,000 *CSK*

l. A George III mahogany D-end dining table, with one extra leaf, on turned legs, 62½in (158cm) long extended.
£800–1,200 *E*

A mahogany dining table, with 2 leaves, on ring turned columns and fluted splayed supports with brass caps and casters, caps stamped 'Cocken', 94in (238cm) long extended. **£5,500–6,000** *CSK*

A George III mahogany dining table, with two plain pillars on reeded quadruple sabre legs, c1800, 74½in (189cm) long extended.
£8,300–9,000 *S*

A George III mahogany twin pillar dining table, the top with a later crossbanded edge, with one extra leaf, 75in (190.5cm) wide.
£4,200–5,000 *CSK*

A Regency style mahogany two-pillar dining table, on reeded sabre legs with brass casters, 20thC, 102½in (260cm) long extended.
£4,000–5,000 *S*

A mahogany dining table, with 4 outer leaves, base associated, early 19thC, 84in (213cm) long extended. **£15,000–16,500** *C*

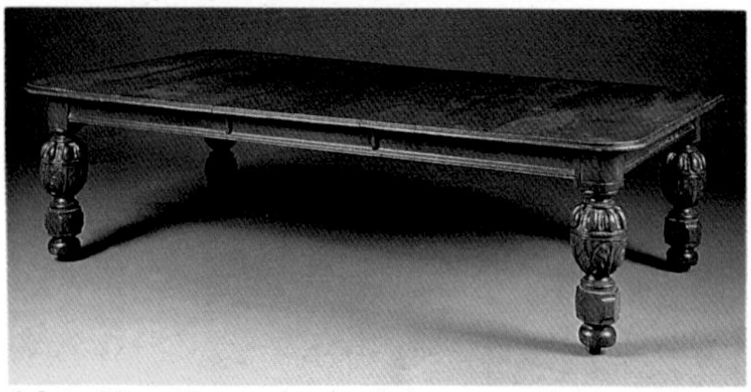

A late Victorian walnut wind system dining table, with 2 extra legs and 3 leaves, each with a drop hinged frieze, 155in (394cm) long extended.
£5,500–6,500 *CSK*

A Regency oak and holly dressing table, by George Bullock, on turned tapering legs, brass caps and casters, 48in (122cm) wide.
£3,500–5,000 *C*

An Edwardian satinwood bowfront dressing table, 50in (127cm) wide.
£1,700–2,200 *CSK*

A George II mahogany games table, with velvet lined and veneered fitted interior, on 5 turned legs and pad feet, c1740, 33in (83.5cm) wide.
£4,000–5,000 *S*

A George III mahogany drum table, with 4 real and 4 dummy drawers, revolving on a plain pillar and 4 reeded sabre legs, c1800, 42in (106.5cm) diam.
£6,400–7,000 *S*

A Regency mahogany drum dressing table, with leather lined divided hinged top, enclosing a fitted interior, c1800, 43½in (110cm) diam.
£6,000–7,000 *S*

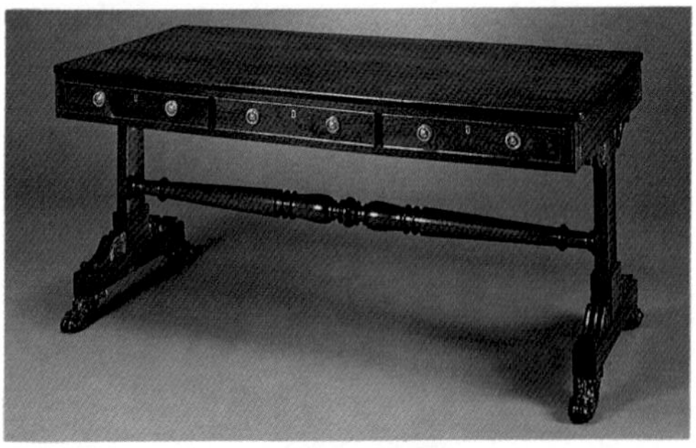

A Regency rosewood library table, with 3 real and 3 dummy drawers, on trestle supports joined by a turned stretcher, early 19thC, 59in (149.5cm) wide.
£8,500–10,000 *S(NY)*

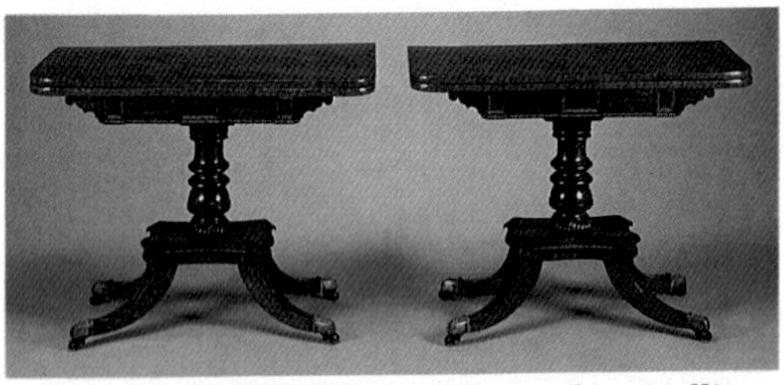

A pair of mahogany games tables, each swivelling top above a beaded frieze, a ring turned baluster standard, c1830, 36in (91.5cm) wide.
£7,500–9,000 *S(NY)*

A Dutch mahogany and inlaid games table, with fitted interior, mid-19thC, 30in (76cm) wide.
£2,000–3,000 *CSK*

A George IV rosewood drum table, with 4 real and 4 dummy drawers, the tricorn base with brass leaf scroll feet, restored, 49in (124.5cm) diam.
£25,500–27,000 *S*

A pair of Regency mahogany library tables, each with brass gallery and a pair of drawers, on sabre legs, repaired, c1810, 42½in (108cm) wide.
£9,000–10,000 *S*

A George IV carved and veneered rosewood double-sided library table, with curved ends and replaced brown leather top, carved end supports on claw feet, possibly Scottish, c1820, 57in (144.5cm) wide.
£8,000–9,500 *S*

A George IV rosewood library table, with cut brass inlay, plain end supports on beaded plinths and ball feet, c1820, 50½in (58cm) wide.
£5,000–6,000 *S*

A George IV mahogany double-sided library table, the tapering legs with lotus collars, 65in (165cm) wide.
£10,000–11,500 *S*

A Regency brass mounted rosewood library table, on brass claw feet, c1815, 39in (99cm) wide.
£9,000–10,000 *S*

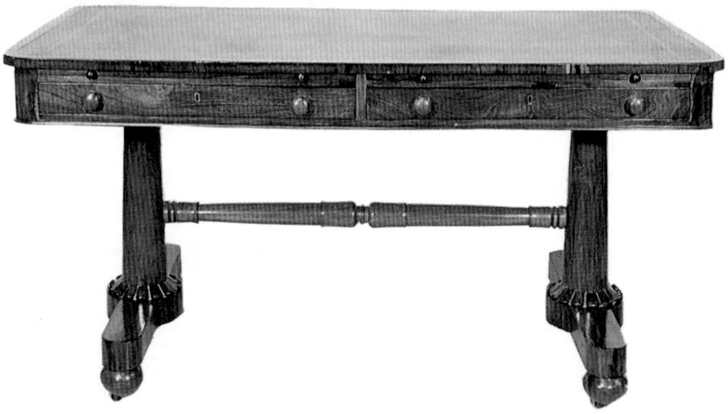

A rosewood library table, with inset leather top, 2 frieze slides and drawers with knob handles, 57in (144.5cm) wide.
£1,000–1,200 *AH*

A set of 4 Regency rosewood amboyna and maple quartetto tables, one with chessboard, largest 23in (58.5cm) wide.
£8,000–9,000 *C*

A Victorian walnut pedestal table, the tilt-top with satinwood inlay, c1855, 60in (152cm) wide.
£2,000–3,000 *S(S)*

An early Victorian rosewood library table, on scroll feet with concealed casters, c1840, 56in (142cm) wide.
£1,500–2,000 *S(S)*

A Regency mahogany and ebony line inlaid drum top library table, on a ring turned baluster column and reeded supports, 39½in (100cm) diam.
£5,500–6,500 *CSK*

A late George III nest of 3 rosewood tables, c1800, largest 19in (48cm) wide.
£2,000–3,000 *S*

A Victorian thuya wood and mahogany pedestal table, c1865, 56in (142cm) diam.
£8,000–9,000 *S(S)*

A George III satinwood veneered Pembroke table, c1775, 40in (101.5cm) wide.
£10,000–11,000 *S*

An Edwardian mahogany crossbanded Pembroke table, with string parquetry inlay, 30½in (77.5cm) wide.
£650–750 *AH*

A George III mahogany Pembroke table, c1775, 35½in (90cm) wide.
£3,500–4,500 *S*

A George III mahogany Pembroke table, c1780, 42in (106.5cm) diam.
£2,500–3,000 *S*

A George III mahogany 'spider's leg' Pembroke table, 42in (106.5cm) wide.
£800–1,000 *AH*

A pair of Regency mahogany serving tables, on acanthus carved cabriole legs with scroll feet, c1820, 60in (152cm) wide.
£12,000–13,000 *Bon*

An inlaid kingwood and rosewood side table, 18thC, 36in (92cm) wide.
£5,500–6,500 *SWO*

A George III mahogany Pembroke table, 31in (79cm) diam.
£2,500–3,500 *DN*

A George III satinwood secrétaire Pembroke table, c1800, 42in (106.5cm) diam.
£3,500–4,000 *S*

A Regency rosewood mirrored backed pier table, c1820, 30½in (77.5cm) wide.
£900–1,300 *Bon*

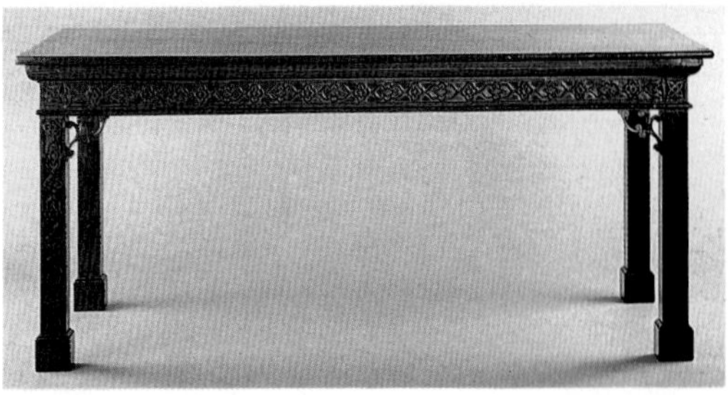

A George III mahogany serving table, with blind fret carved frieze, on square cut fretwork carved legs, on block feet, c1765, 78in (198cm) wide.
£10,000–11,000 *S*

A George II mahogany side table, the later marble top above a moulded cornice and plain frieze, previously with wooden top, with label inscribed 'Stanford', 54½in (138.5cm) wide.
£5,000–6,000 *C*

A Piedmontese giltwood side table, with serpentine verde antico marble top, above a frieze with 2 foliate carved drawers, 55½in (141cm) wide.
£8,000–9,000 *Bon*

A William and Mary simulated verde antico marble and part white-painted side table, with later double arched frieze, repaired, labelled, 39in (99cm) wide.
£11,000–12,000 *C*

An early George III mahogany silver table, with pierced Gothic fret gallery and pierced brackets, 32in (81.5cm) wide.
£11,000–12,000 *S*

A Regency rosewood and satinwood crossbanded sofa table, 64in (162.5cm) wide.
£2,500–3,500 *Bon*

A pair of Italian walnut demi-lune side tables, the tops inlaid alla certosina in bone and light wood, restored, c1680, 36in (91.5cm) wide.
£7,500–8,500 *Bon*

A Regency ivory mounted rosewood sofa table, crossbanded in satinwood, inlaid with boxwood and ebonised lines, later casters, 60in (152cm) wide.
£4,500–5,500 *C*

A Regency rosewood and giltwood sofa table, with burr yew crossbanding, giltwood pillars, down-curved legs and brass casters, c1810, 59in (150cm) wide.
£6,000–7,500 *S*

A George III mahogany sofa table, with crossbanded top later painted with a cartouche, embossed label 'E & H Jewell, High Holborn, London WC', 61½in (156cm) wide.
£5,500–6,500 *DN*

A carved mahogany tea table, the frieze and legs with blind Chinese fret, c1765, 32in (81cm) wide.
£3,700–4,200 *S*

A Regency rosewood sofa table, on ring turned column and outswept legs, c1815, 59in (150cm) long extended.
£3,000–4,000 *Bon*

A George II mahogany tripod table, the moulded top on a plain baluster and cabriole legs, c1740, 18in (45.5cm) high.
£4,000–5,000 *S*

A George II mahogany tripod table, with piecrust top, on a baluster stem, the tripod with claw-and-ball feet, restored, c1750, 21in (53cm) high.
£1,500–2,000 *S*

A George II mahogany tripod table, the top with waved edge, on leaf carved cabriole legs with carved leaf scroll feet, c1755, 26in (66cm) high.
£4,500–5,500 *S*

A George II mahogany tripod table, with waved top, fluted stem, leaf-carved cabriole legs, on hairy claw feet, 26½in (67.5cm) high.
£2,200–2,700 *S*

A Regency mahogany work table, the crossbanded canted top above a frieze drawer, c1810, 18in (45.5cm) wide.
£1,200–1,700 *Bon*

A Regency black and gold japanned tripod table, with figures and pavilions within a foliate border, on a decorated baluster column and outswept legs, c1815, 32in (81cm) diam.
£1,200–1,700 *Bon*

A George II mahogany tripod table, the hinged serpentine hexagonal top with a spindled gallery, with spirally moulded baluster on leaf-carved cabriole legs with pointed pad feet, c1755, 30in (76cm) high.
£22,000–24,000 *S*

A brass inlaid rosewood work table, with 4 canted sabre legs, c1815, 18½in (47cm) wide.
£2,000–2,500 *S*

A George II mahogany tripod table, the hinged top on a bird-cage support, plain stem and cabriole legs with pad feet, repaired, 27in (68.5cm) high.
£2,000–2,500 *S*

A mahogany tripod table, with hinged single plank top on a spirally reeded baluster and cabochon carved legs, c1750, 31in (78.5cm) high.
£3,000–4,000 *S*

A William IV rosewood work table, 28½in (72.5cm) high.
£1,000–1,400 *CSK*

A Victorian Tunbridge ware work table, by Edmund Nye, c1850, 17in (43cm) wide.
£1,500–2,000 *Bon*

A Regency laburnum writing table, with gilt tooled leather inset top, the frieze fitted with 3 cockbeaded drawers on each side, possibly Scottish, early 19thC, 46in (116.5cm) wide.
£9,500–10,500 *S(NY)*

A mahogany cleated top reading and writing table, c1750, 22½in (57cm) wide.
£3,000–3,500 *S*

A mahogany writing table, with candle stands, c1765, 35½in (90cm) wide.
£5,500–6,500 *S*

A pair of Louis Philippe ormolu mounted and brass inlaid tortoiseshell and boulle marquetry writing tables, the top with distressed red velvet panel and foliate corner clasps, 28in (71cm) wide.
£4,000–5,000 *C*

A mahogany double-sided writing table, the central drawer with a writing slide c1795, 65½in (166cm) wide.
£7,000–8,000 *S*

A Louis XVI tulipwood and amaranth writing table, c1780, 30in (76cm) wide.
£6,000–7,000 *S*

A Dutch mahogany and marquetry side table, 19thC, 29in (73.5cm) wide.
£3,000–4,000 *CSK*

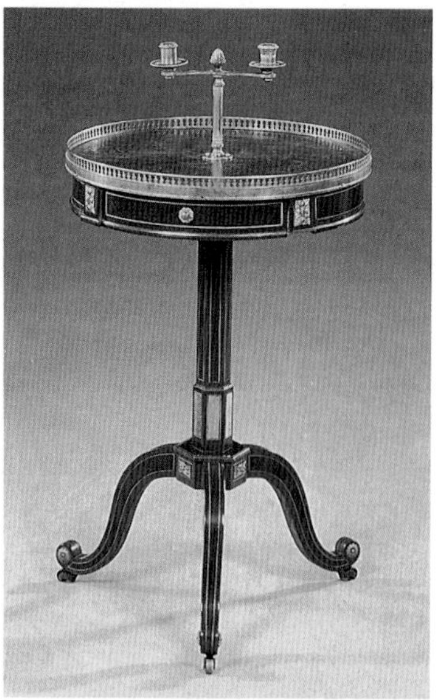

A Louis XVI mahogany and lacquer tripod writing table, stamped 'C. Mauter', with two-branch candelabrum, c1785, 29in (73.5cm) high.
£24,000–25,000 *S*

A set of 4 William IV mahogany torchères, each with tray-top on a turned stiff leaf carved shaft, slight variations, previously drilled for electricity, 48in (122cm) high.
£6,500–7,500 *C*

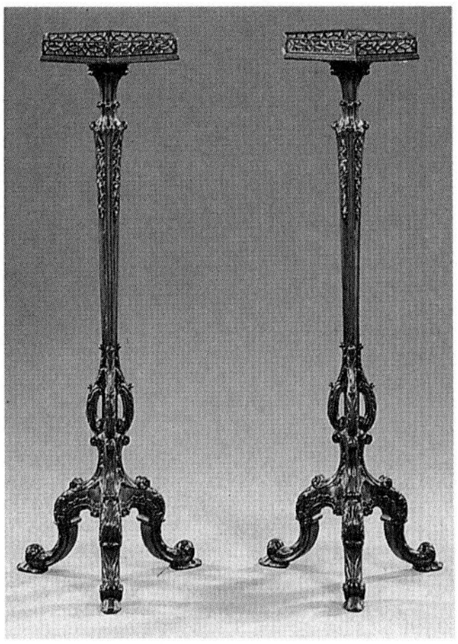

A pair of mahogany torchères, each with a carved stem and 3 rococo cabriole legs, c1920, 47½in (121cm) high.
£3,700–4,200 *S*

A George III mahogany four-tier whatnot, with square urn-topped pillars and a drawer, 66½in (169cm) high.
£2,200–2,700 *S*

A Regency coromandel wood whatnot, with four tiers and turned uprights, a drawer in lowest tier, 54in (137cm) high.
£5,000–6,000 *S*

A walnut and foliage inlaid four-tier whatnot, on turned supports, 19thC, 29in (73.5cm) high.
£700–900 *E*

A Regency mahogany four-tier whatnot, with adjustable reading slope, on turned tapering legs, 46in (116.5cm) high.
£1,800–2,500 *C*

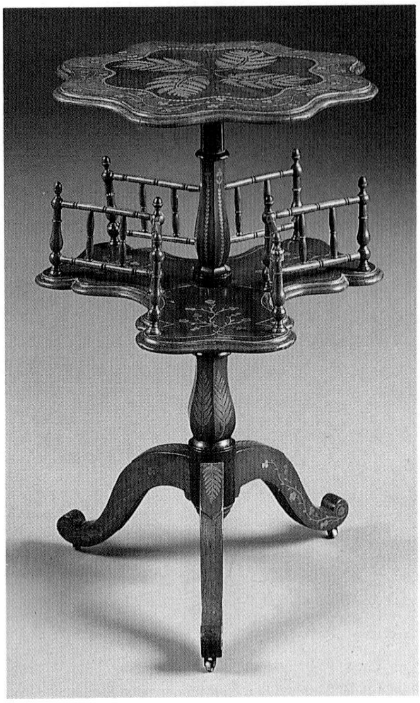

An Irish mid-Victorian Killarney yew and marquetry two-tier whatnot, on tripod base and scroll feet, 21in (53cm) wide.
£8,000–9,000 *C*

A Regency mahogany five-tier whatnot, with 2 drawers, on turned feet, repaired, 54½in (138.5cm) wide.
£3,000–4,000 *C*

A rosewood four-tier corner whatnot, with blind fret carved gallery, on spiral turned supports, 19thC, 18in (45.5cm) wide.
£750–1,000 *E*

A pair of painted jardinières, each with a large brass guilloche gallery and a tôle liner, on turned legs with casters, c1785, 30in (76cm) wide.
£24,000–26,000 *S*

A set of mahogany library steps, in the form of a table, with hinged treads, part 18thC, 32in (81cm) high.
£2,000–2,500 *CSK*

An early Louis XV metamorphic library step chair, the solid seat hinged to reveal 5 treads, parts later.
£3,000–4,000 *C*

A William IV rosewood library folio stand, with adjustable oblong slopes, on trestle supports with turned feet and casters, 27in (68.5cm) wide.
£2,500–3,000 *AH*

A set of mahogany and iron library steps, with 5 folding treads, 19thC, 59in (149.5cm) high.
£1,500–2,000 *S*

A Dutch mahogany jardinière, the slatted top with brass liner and swing handle, the concave-sided platform base with brass bun feet, 19thC, 19in (48cm) high.
£1,200–1,500 *AH*

A pair of Victorian bed steps, with caned backs and carpeted treads, on turned front legs, 17in (43cm) wide.
£1,400–1,700 *C*

A George III mahogany enclosed washstand, c1780, 19in (48cm) wide.
£1,300–1,700 *Bon*

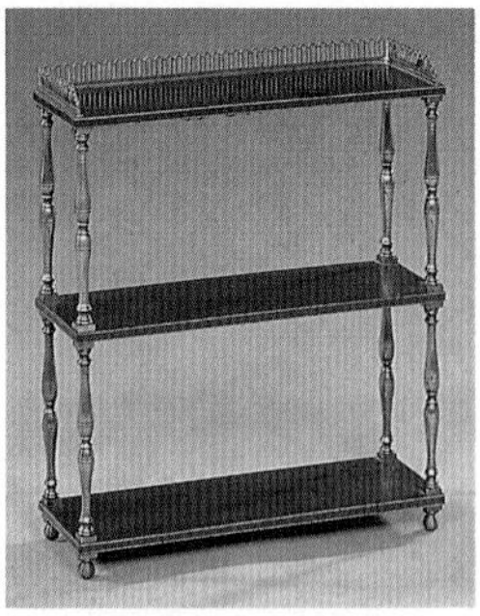

A mahogany and brass wall shelf, early 19thC, 19½in (50cm) wide.
£2,400–2,800 *S*

A pair of William IV mahogany three-tier hanging shelves, attributed to Gillows of Lancaster, 36in (91.5cm) wide.
£4,500–5,000 *C*

A set of Georgian bowfronted wall shelves, with mahogany shaped sides and polished pine shelves lipped with mahogany moulding, c1800, 30½in (77.5cm) wide.
£1,250–1,500 *JC*

A green painted tennis umpire's chair, with two-tier seat, 19thC.
£3,500–4,000 *C*

A Regency white painted wrought iron garden seat, with scroll feet, 43in (109cm) wide.
£2,500–3,000 *C*

A set of 4 white marble figures of the Seasons, by Professor Giuseppe Lazzerini, on signed square bases, c1862, 42½in (108cm) high.
£23,000–25,000 *S(S)*

A green painted wrought iron rocking chair, with interlaced seat, 18thC.
£2,800–3,200 *C*

A limestone font, with carved panels, mid-19thC, 32in (81cm) diam.
£1,500–2,000 *SWO*

A Vicenza stone fountain, with putti astride dolphins, mouths plumbed for water, 20thC, 84in (213cm) wide.
£10,000–12,000 *S(S)*

A pair of spelter figures of North American Indians, late 19thC, 72in (182.5cm) high.
£7,000–8,000 *S(S)*

A Regency white painted wrought iron garden bench, 73in (185cm) wide.
£1,500–2,000 *C*

A bronze lurcher and hare, by Victor Chemin, 44in (111.5cm) wide.
£10,000–11,000 *S(S)*

A pair of Bromsgrove Guild lead figures, c1908, 40in (101.5cm) high.
£12,000–13,000 *S(S)*

A Portland stone fountain, with 4 fountain heads, lobed pool surround with plinths and ogee sides, on plinth base, late 18thC, 216in (549cm) diam.
£11,000–12,500 *S(S)*

A white marble group, by Francesco Gajarini, signed, c1877, 38in (96.5cm) high.
£2,500–3,000 *S(S)*

A pair of stone lions, damage to plinths, each 14in (36cm) long.
£2,600–3,200 *C*

An Ogwell marble surround, with fluted jambs and frieze, c1840, 67in (170cm) wide.
£2,000–2,200 *ASH*

A set of steel and brass fire irons, with spiral twist shafts, mid-19thC.
£1,300–1,700 *S*

A marble and scagliola chimneypiece, in the style of Bossi, the tablet inlaid with a lidded urn hung with bellflowers flanked by stop-fluted decoration, 19thC, 70in (177.5cm) wide.
£12,000–13,500 *S(S)*

A golden oak fire surround, 1920s, 52in (132cm) wide.
£500–550 *ASH*

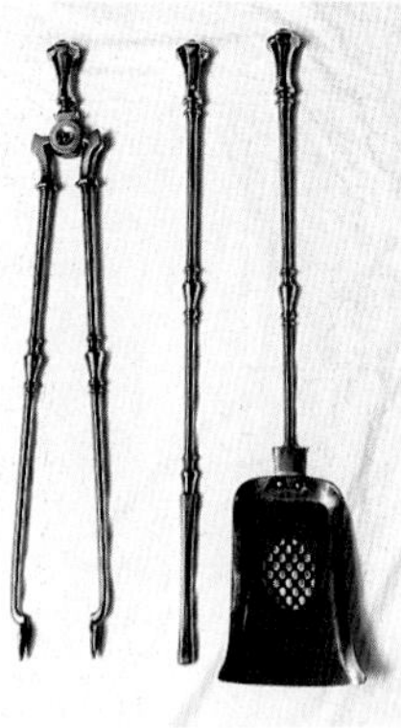

A set of Georgian steel fire irons, 28in (71cm) long.
£400–600 *ASH*

A George III white and jasper marble chimney surround, the frieze centred by a carved tablet of a woman flanked by inlaid Greek key pattern, 83in (210.5cm) wide.
£25,000–27,000 *S*

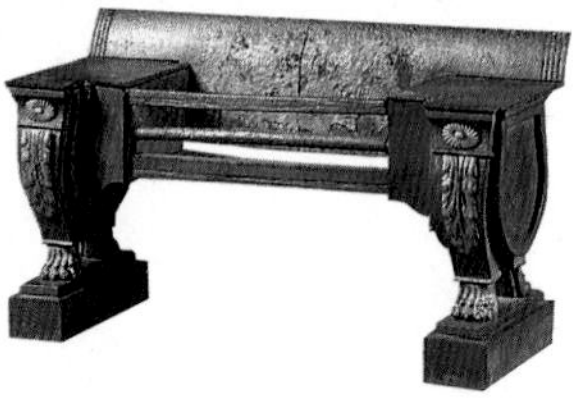

A Regency brass mounted iron sarcophagus basket grate, in the manner of George Bullock, 39in (99cm) wide.
£6,800–7,200 *C*

A Regency gilt metal mounted cast iron basket grate, in the manner of George Bullock, 36in (91.5cm) wide.
£7,500–8,500 *C*

A Victorian cast iron and brass fire basket, with a curved front, c1870, 19in (48cm) wide.
£350–450 *ASH*

A cast iron Empire style fire basket, with brass torchères, 1920s, 20in (50.5cm) wide.
£450–475 *ASH*

A Georgian cut steel fender, 42in (106.5cm) wide.
£200–230 *ASH*

A pair of copper and wrought iron fire iron rests, 19thC, 19in (48cm) high.
£100–150 *ASH*

A brass fender, with pierced and repoussé decoration, early 19thC, 53in (134.5cm) wide.
£400–600 *S*

A pair of cast brass and enamel andirons, modelled with the Stuart Arms, late 19thC, 23in (58.5cm) high.
£1,200–1,700 *CSK*

A pair of stone ball finials, 19thC, 16in (40.5cm) diam.
£60–80 *WEL*

A pair of composition stone gate pier finials, each in the form of a hound seated upright holding a shield, damaged, 19thC, 27in (68cm) high.
£1,700–2,200 *S(S)*

A milling stone, for crushing cider apples, 17th–18thC, 24in (61.5cm) diam.
£200–250 *WEL*

A wheelwright's stone, 17thC, 62in (157cm) diam.
£400–500 *WEL*

A carved sandstone pool surround, with 4 shaped square plinths, 156in (396cm) diam.
£3,500–5,500 *S(S)*

A Cotswold stone sundial, the baluster column on a square base supporting a circular dial, inscribed ' T. Rowley, Londini Fecit', beneath an armorial shield calibrated with hours, minutes, and with scroll pierced gnomen, c1730, 59in (150cm) high.
£6,000–7,000 *S(S)*

A composition stone sundial, the lobed and fluted column with square top, and an octagonal bronze dial calibrated with hours, bearing the date '1709', late 19thC, 45in (114cm) high.
£1,100–1,700 *S(S)*

A stoneware sundial pedestal, the lobed bulbous body and slender neck on a circular foot and square base, 51in (129.5cm) high, on lobed circular surround, early 20thC, 48in (122cm) diam, now set with a galvanised armillary sphere.
£1,000–1,300 *S(S)*

Two stone troughs, c1900.
£150–175 each *WEL*

A stone trough, 19thC, 23 by 19in (58.5 by 48cm).
£150–200 *WRe*

l. A composition stone urn, early 20thC, 15in (38cm) high.
£200–250 *WRe*

A staddle stone, 18thC, 30in (76cm) high.
£150–175 *WRe*

A Vicenza stone wellhead, carved in high relief with cherubs, swags of fruit and bellflower festoons, 20thC, 31in (79cm) high, on an octagonal base, 8in (20cm) high, with a later wrought iron overthrow, 73in (185cm) high.
£10,000–12,000 *S(S)*

A Coadestone royal coat-of-arms, the central panel with ribbon tied palms and inscribed 'Dieu Est Mon Droit', surmounted by a crown and flanked by a unicorn and lion, stamped 'Croggan 1831', 66in (167.5cm) wide.
£2,500–4,500 *S(S)*

A composition stone armorial coat-of-arms, the central shield with the arms of England flanked by a lion and unicorn, mid-19thC, 60in (152cm) high.
£1,800–2,200 *S(S)*

Terracotta

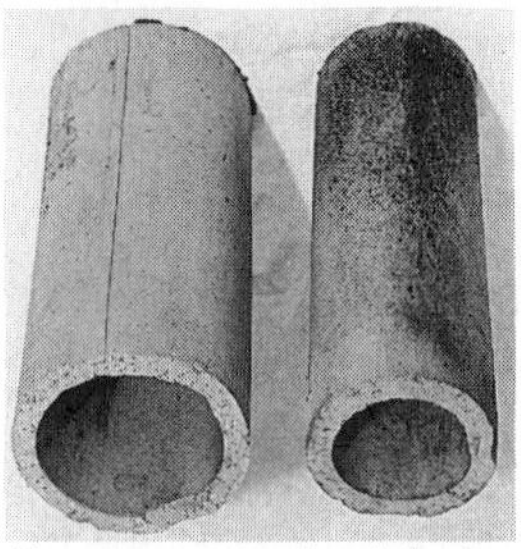

Two terracotta land drainage pipes, now used for storing wine, 12in (30.5cm) high.
£2–3 each *WEL*

A selection of glazed terracotta border tiles, 19thC.
£2–3 each *WEL*

A selection of terracotta floor tiles, 19thC, 6in (15cm) square.
£40–45 per 100 *WEL*

A pair of terracotta urns, early 20thC, 20in (50.5cm) high.
£125–150 *WRe*

A pair of terracotta garden seats, the arms formed as griffins, intertwining wings as backrests, circular stamp, early 20thC, 29in (74cm) high.
£6,250–6,750 *S(NY)*

Wirework

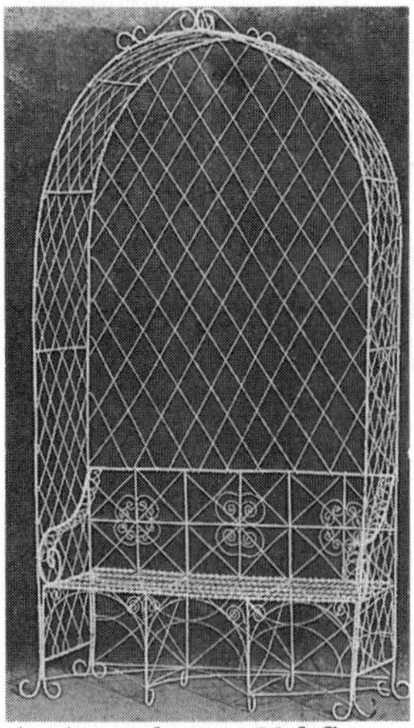

A wirework seat, 20thC, 54in (137cm) wide.
£1,400–1,800 *S(S)*

Fireplaces

A Victorian fireplace, comprising:
A Pettiton marble surround, 60in (152cm) wide.
£950–1,100
An Art Nouveau tiled insert.
£350–400
A cut brass fender, 36in (91.5cm).
£200–225 *ASH*

A Victorian fireplace, comprising:
A black marble surround, with fluted corbels, 62in (157cm) wide.
£1,450–1,650
A cast iron insert, with tiles by Minton depicting Aesop's Fables.
£500–600
A brass fender, with fire iron rests.
£300–350 *ASH*

A French rouge marble surround, inlaid with statuary marble panels with carved sunburst flowers, c1860, 67in (170cm) wide.
£3,000–3,250
A brass and steel fire grate, with lidded urns and claw feet, 38in (96.5cm) wide.
£1,600–1,800 *ASH*

An Edwardian oak fire surround, with 4 panels.
£500–600 *ASH*

A Carrara marble fire surround, with carved shell shaped corbels, 66in (167.5cm) wide.
£1,100–1,250
A Victorian tiled insert, with hand painted scenes, c1880, 38in (96.5cm) square.
£1,000–1,250
A Regency cut steel fender, 72in (182.5cm) wide.
£400–475 *ASH*

An Edwardian oak fire surround, c1900, 62in (157cm) wide.
£180–250 *ASH*

A Carrara marble chimneypiece, with carved shells to the capital, c1840, 65in (165cm) wide.
£2,200–2,400
A Victorian cast iron fender, 40in (101.5cm) wide.
£125–165
A Regency grate, c1840, 34in (86cm) wide.
£650–750 *ASH*

A Victorian stone fire surround, c1870, 64in (162.5cm) wide.
£950–1,100
A Victorian cast iron basket, with copper masks, 18in (45.5cm) wide.
£200–250
A cast iron fender, 30in (76cm) wide.
£100–150 *ASH*

A cast iron fire surround, 19thC.
£1,500–2,500 *BWe*

An Edwardian marble surround, with fluted jambs inlaid and decorated with Sienna marble.
£2,200–2,500
A Victorian tiled cast iron grate.
£400–450 *ASH*

A cast iron grate and fireback, the back with a double-headed eagle and lion mask front supports, 19thC, 30in (76cm) wide.
£400–600 *DN*

A Victorian Adam style fire grate, with a brass serpentine front, 24in (61cm) wide.
£600–700 *ASH*

A Victorian cast iron fire basket, with brass tapering legs and finials, 18in (45.5cm) wide.
£300–325 *ASH*

A Victorian cast iron fire basket, with large fire dogs, 36in (91.5cm) wide.
£500–650 *ASH*

An Edwardian brass canopied wrought iron grate, 28in (71cm) wide.
£700–800 *ASH*

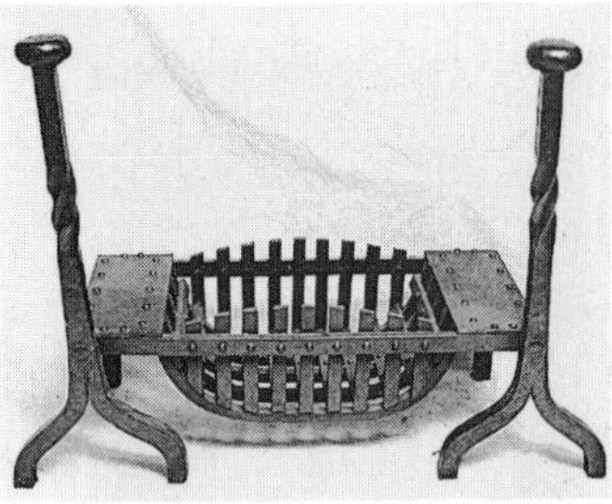

A cast iron fire basket, c1920, 24in (61cm) wide.
£250–300 *ASH*

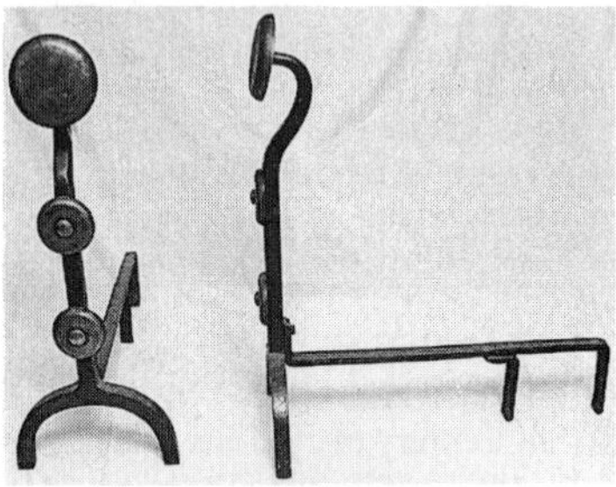

A pair of iron and steel andirons, 19thC, 24in (61cm) high.
£200–250 *ASH*

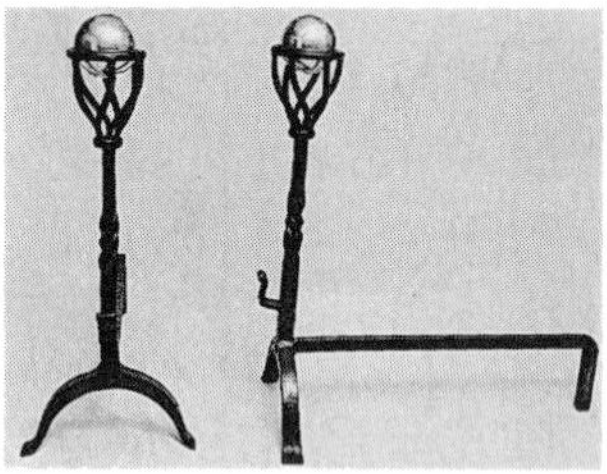

A pair of Victorian brass and wrought iron andirons, 23in (58.5cm) high.
£300–325 *ASH*

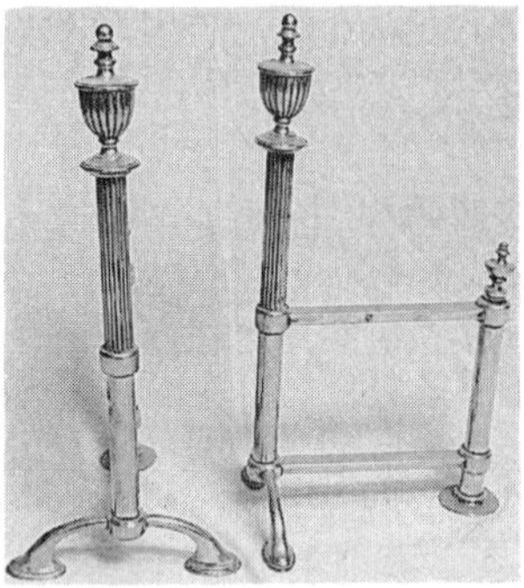

A pair of Victorian brass fire rests, 17½in (44cm) high.
£180–200 *ASH*

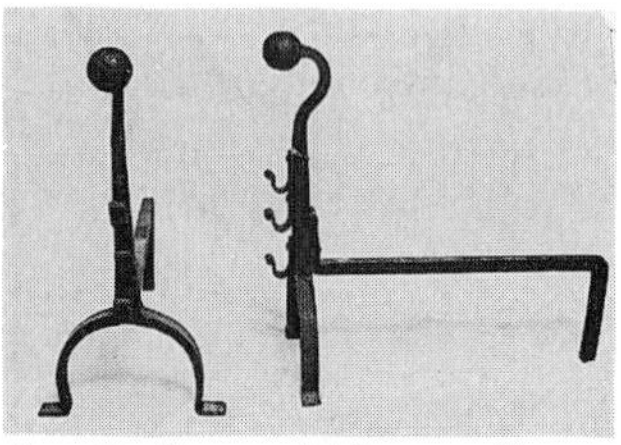

A pair of wrought iron andirons, country made, 19thC, 24in (61cm) high.
£150–180 *ASH*

A gilt brass fender, c1820, 55in (139.5cm) wide.
£400–600 *ASH*

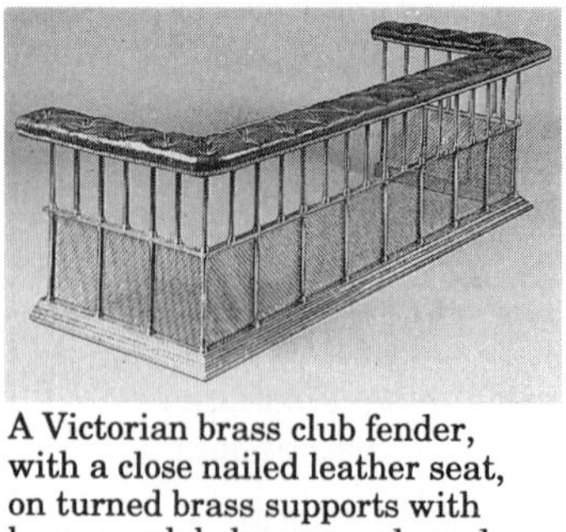

A Victorian brass club fender, with a close nailed leather seat, on turned brass supports with brass mesh below, on a shaped plinth, 78in (198cm) wide.
£2,500–3,000 *CSK*

A set of Victorian brass fire irons, 20in (50.5cm) wide.
£150–180 *ASH*

A steel and bronze fender, c1820, 59in (149.5cm) wide.
£300–400 *ASH*

r. A Victorian cast iron fender, 42in (106.5cm).
£80–120 *ASH*

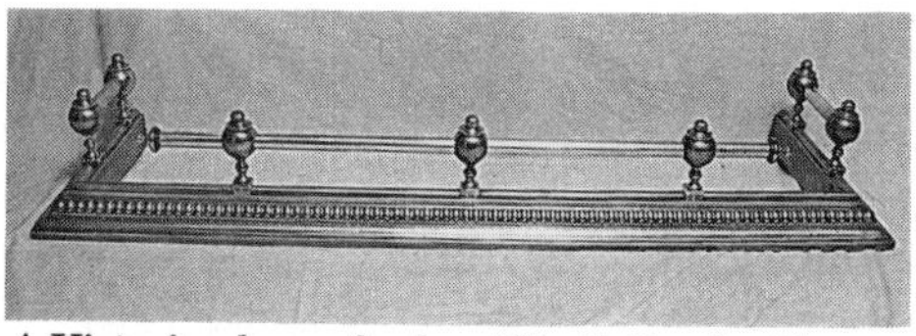
A Victorian brass fender, 56in (142cm) wide.
£300–400 *ASH*

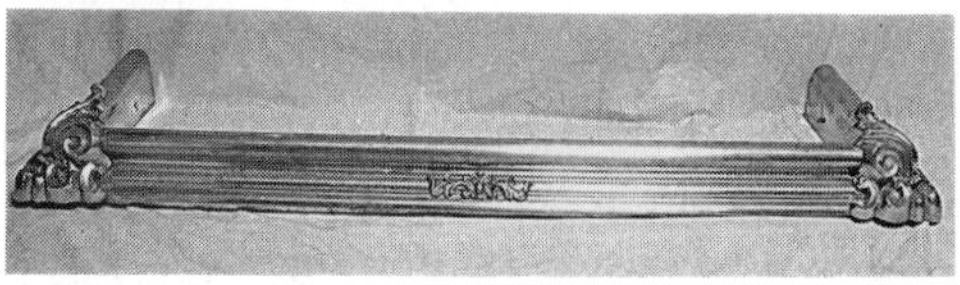
A brass fender, c1880, 55in (139.5cm) wide.
£300–325 *ASH*

An embossed copper fender, c1920, 56in (142cm) wide.
£150–175 *ASH*

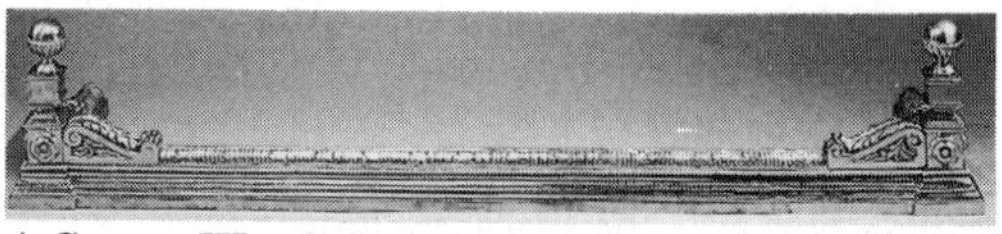
A George III polished steel and brass fire fender, cast with a beaded border, stylised flowerheads and scrolls, with ball finials, c1800, 62in (157cm) long.
£5,000–5,500 *S(NY)*

Miscellaneous

l. A Swinton Patent kitchen range, late 19thC, 47½in (120cm) wide.
£1,100–1,200 *WRe*

A bath/shower, with canopy, by Shanks & Co., c1920.
£6,800–7,000 *WRe*

A bellows, 19thC, 44in (111.5cm) high.
£400–500 *WRe*

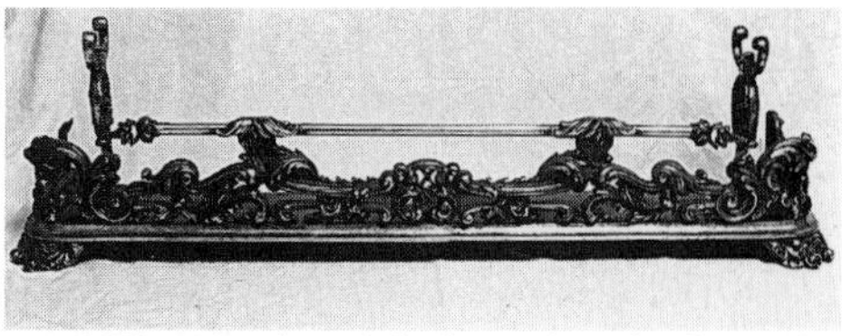
A Victorian burnished cast iron fender, 48in (122cm) wide.
£350–400 *ASH*

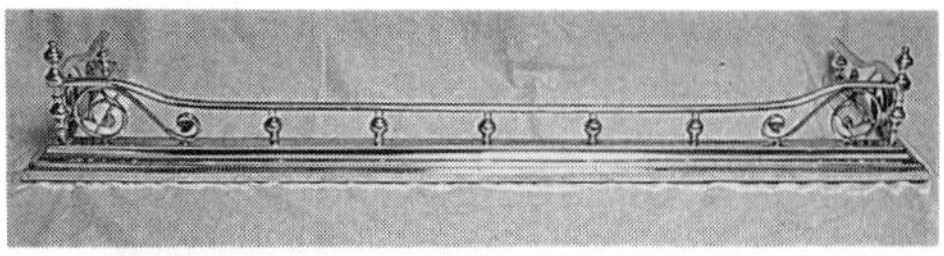
A brass fender, c1870, 53in (134.5cm) wide.
£300–350 *ASH*

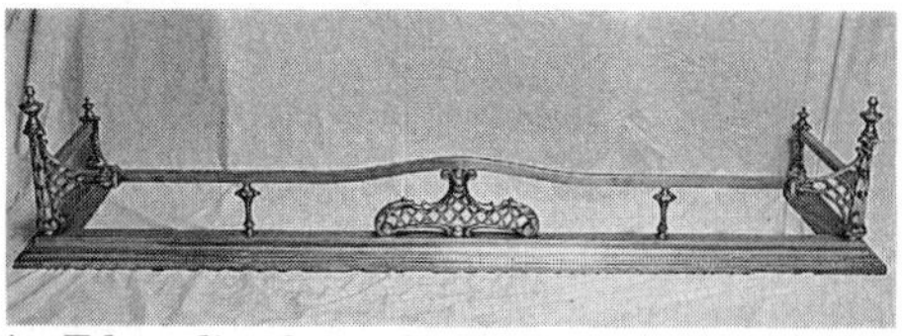
An Edwardian brass fender, 50in (127cm) wide.
£250–280 *ASH*

A Victorian rococo style cast iron fender, 45in (114cm) wide.
£280–350 *ASH*

POTTERY & PORCELAIN

COLLECTING BLUE & WHITE TRANSFER WARE

The pottery and porcelain market has improved steadily over the last year with dealers and collectors, particularly from America, once again eager to buy. The upper end of the market is strong whereas the collectables market has been slower to pick up. Those who buy and sell decorative pottery and porcelain, especially blue and white transfer wares, have reported that buyers know what they want and are, at the moment, paying a fair price.

Blue and white transfer printed pottery was introduced in the UK in about 1770. Transfers were made from copper engravings and then applied to the pottery. This process was perfected by potters such as Turner, Heath and Spode with other potters quickly following their methods. Cobalt blue became the popular colour, as cobalt could withstand the high temperatures necessary to fuse the porcelain glaze without altering the colour.

Many of the early patterns were copied from Chinese landscapes and chinoiserie patterns. By the 1820s other designs were introduced, such as rural scenes, botanical and animal subjects. Later, all-over sheet patterns which covered the whole piece of pottery were used. In the 1840s a series of paler blue 'romantic' type patterns became available with more white background visible.

Transfer printing was used on every conceivable item, such as plates, platters, dishes and jugs, bowls, footbaths, chamber pots and dressing table items. Sickroom and medical items, invalids' feeders, pap boats, infant feeding bottles, eye baths, ointment pots, commodes, bidets and bedpans were also decorated.

In this area of antiques, collections often take on a particular theme. For instance, several items may come from one particular factory, or consist of one pattern, shape or border, or they may originate from one particular country such as India.

The best way to start your own collection is to buy the pieces that you like and which you can afford from a reputable dealer or auction house. At auction it is the buyer's responsibility to satisfy himself as to the condition of the goods before purchase. When buying from a reputable dealer with specialist knowledge, more information about the item is usually available. Dealers belonging to a trade organization, such as BADA or LAPADA, are governed by a very strict code of trading practice which they must adopt, but always obtain a descriptive receipt for your purchase. This is necessary for your own protection againt loss, damage, fraudulent description and for insurance purposes. You should also include your collection on your household insurance listing the items carefully.

Antiques fairs usually offer a good supply of blue and white pottery, but do beware as not everything is as described on the label. If the fair states that all items exhibited are quality vetted then all the items have been inspected by a vetting committee to ensure that everything is as stated on the label. Still, beware of any restoration and look for changes in colour or variation in pattern. Run your fingers over the item, especially the edge of vulnerable parts such as plate edges, spouts and handles, to feel if the surface has altered, revealing possible restoration. If the item is restored, this need not deter you from purchasing it as long as the fact is pointed out to you and the price is right.

Not all pottery carries a mark on the underside, so experience is needed to tell original items from reproduction items. Antique pottery, with the exception of ironstone and stone china, is much lighter. The glaze has a blue rippled effect when held in the light. The presence of stilt marks on the underside, where the items were stacked in the kiln, indicates age. Older colours are softer and richer, with a depth of perspective, especially on pieces where the transfer depicts a view.

Reproduction items often have a dirty grey underside, to give the impression of use and age. Some reproductions are very decorative but should not, of course, be sold as genuine antiques.

The Spode factory has introduced a 'Blue Room Series' which are, in fact, copies of the original Spode plates, using transfers taken from the original copper plates. All this information is clearly printed on the back of each plate.

Collecting can be great fun, and as one becomes more experienced bargains can be spotted more easily. There are many books available on the subject and clubs to join, but remember 'hands on experience' is the best form of learning.

Good hunting and collecting.

Gillian Neale

POTTERY

Baskets

A Spode Net pattern chestnut basket, c1810, 10½in (26.5cm) wide.
£200–300 *GN*

A Spode chestnut basket and stand, decorated with the Gothic Castle pattern, c1810, the stand 9in (22.5cm) wide.
£400–500 *GN*

A Spode Italian pattern chestnut basket, c1820, 10in (25cm) wide.
£200–300 *GN*

Bottles

A creamware bottle or tea caddy, with 2 oval relief panels, one side inscribed 'Othello', the other with Shakespeare in the company of Muses, picked out in underglaze blue and green, damaged, impressed 'J. Voyez', c1770, 7in (18cm) high.
£700–900 *Bon*

Shakespeare is depicted in a fashionable Gothic interior worthy of Strawberry Hill. At his feet lie several folios, one clearly titled 'Henry', another 'Romeo'. While one muse sprinkles these works with floral offerings, the second stands in animated pose, flames flickering from her raised hand, recalling the opening lines from Henry V *'Oh for a Muse of Fire...'.*

A Ridgway female bed bottle, Humphrey's Clock Series, decorated with tales from *The Old Curiosity Shop*, c1835.
£500–600 *GN*

Bowls

A spongeware bowl, c1840, 4in (10cm) high.
£65–75 *RYA*

A Scottish earthenware basin, by John Marshall & Co., Bo'ness, Scotland, decorated in black with Canadian Sports pattern, c1880, 14in (35.5cm) diam.
£1,400–1,600 *RIT*

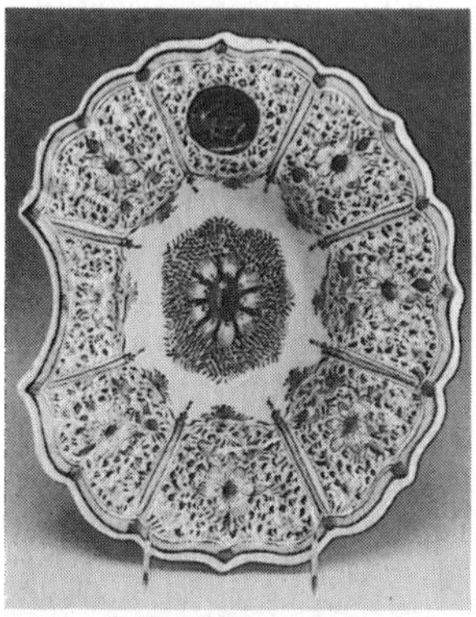

A Dutch Delft blue and white barber's bowl, with a soap depression on one side, minor glaze chips, mid-18thC, 11½in (29cm) long.
£700–750 *S(NY)*

Busts

A pair of pearlware busts of Princess Charlotte and Prince Leopold, each brightly decorated in coloured enamels, damaged, c1817, 9in (22.5cm) high.
£4,500–5,500 *DN*

A Staffordshire bust of the Earl of St. Vincent, c1795, 8in (20cm) high.
£400–450 *JHo*

A Staffordshire bust of Napoleon, c1820, 9½in (24cm) high.
£800–950 *MSA*

Candlesticks

A pair of Wedgwood lustre candlesticks, mid-19thC, 6in (15cm) high.
£500–550 *JHo*

r. A pair of three-light candelabra, by Richard Eckert & Co., in the form of a cobbler and his wife, decorated in coloured enamels, damaged, mark in blue, c1895, 10in (25cm) high.
£400–600 *DN*

Cow Creamers

A pearlware cow creamer and cover, sponged in brown and ochre, on a flat green glazed base, probably Yorkshire, restored, c1780, 5in (13cm) high.
£400–600 *DN*

A pearlware cow creamer and cover, sponged in brown and ochre, on a flat green glazed base, probably Yorkshire, restored, c1780, 5in (13cm) high.
£400–600 *DN*

A Pratt ware type cow creamer, patched in ochre and green against a powdered blue ground, horns chipped, late 18thC, 6in (15cm) high.
£250–300 *Bon*

A cow creamer, decorated in Pratt ware colours, c1810, 5in (12.5cm) high.
£400–450 *SWN*

Cradles

A Staffordshire cradle, c1800, 5in (12.5cm) long.
£400–450 *JHo*

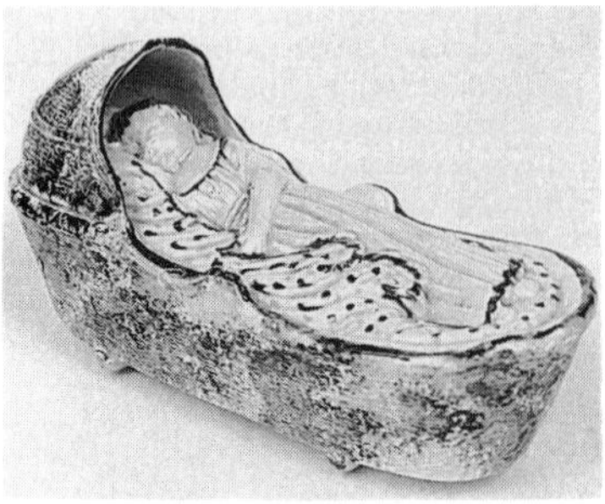

A Staffordshire cradle, c1800, 7½in (19cm) long.
£550–600 *JHo*

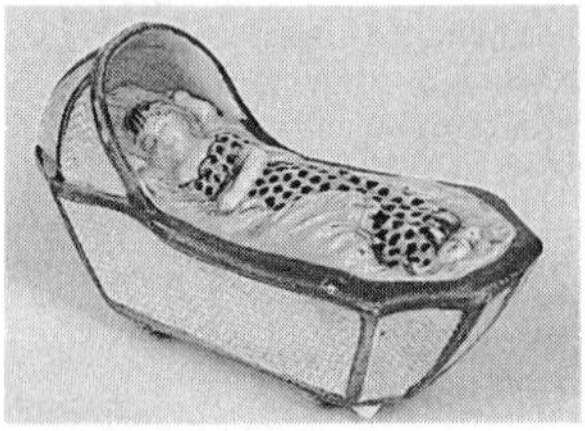

r. A Staffordshire cradle, early 19thC, 4½in (11.5cm) long.
£300–350 *JHo*

Cups

Two creamware bell-shaped cups, with reeded loop handles, each decorated in coloured enamels, with an iron red line rim, c1770, 2½in (6.5cm) high.
£300–350 *DN*

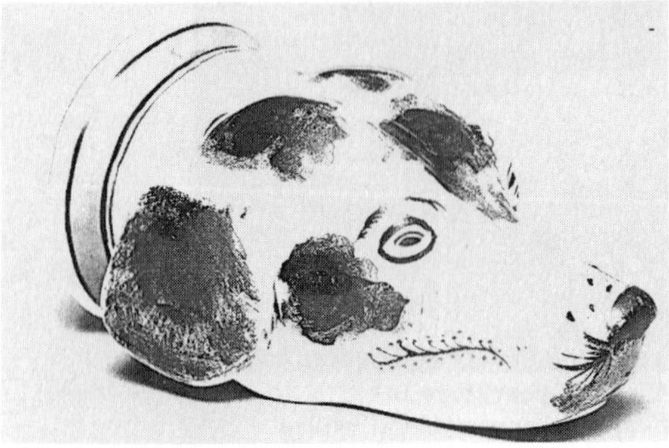

A Scottish pottery hound's head stirrup cup, decorated in black and puce, with green and black bands, hair crack, 19thC, 5in (12.5cm) long.
£250–350 *DN*

A Staffordshire slipware cup, dipped in maroon iron oxide, trailed in white, with 3 butterfly medallions, covered in a glutinous honey glaze, 17thC, 3in (7.5cm) high.
£2,000–3,000 *Bon*

This cup is attributed by the late Arnold Mountford to the Knypersley Kiln, South Staffordshire, and dated by him to the second quarter of the 17thC.

Feeders

A blue and white invalid's feeder, c1825, 3in (7.5cm) high.
£100–140 *GN*

An infant's feeding bottle, c1835, 7in (17.5cm) long.
£300–400 *GN*

An invalid's feeder, repaired, c1835, 2½in (6.5cm) high.
£80–100 *GN*

A Podmore & Walker pap feeder, decorated with an Italian scene, c1830, 4½in (11.5cm) long.
£100–130 *GN*

Figures – Animals

A Pratt type pearlware toy bear, moulded in 2 halves, with a moulded chain descending from the collar round its neck, spotted all over in ochre and green, late 18thC, 2½in (6.5cm) high.
£450–600 *Bon*

Pratt Ware

Pratt ware is a type of earthenware, decorated in vivid underglaze colours on a buff ground. It was first made in Staffordshire during the late 18thC and early 19thC, and named after the Pratt family.

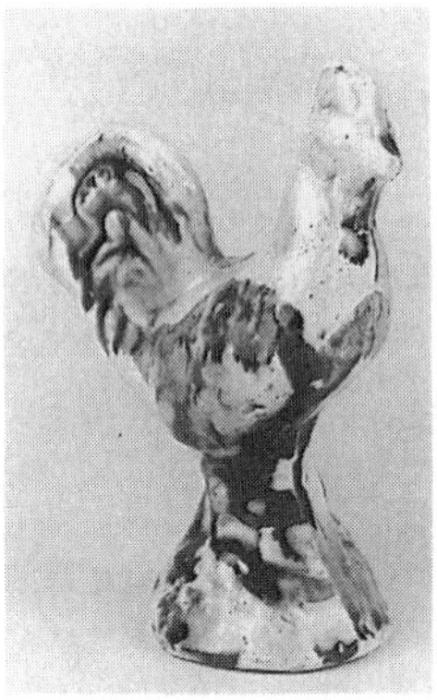

l. A creamware model of a cockerel, coloured with green and brown in-glaze oxides, c1760, 4in (10cm) high.
£200–250 *Bon*

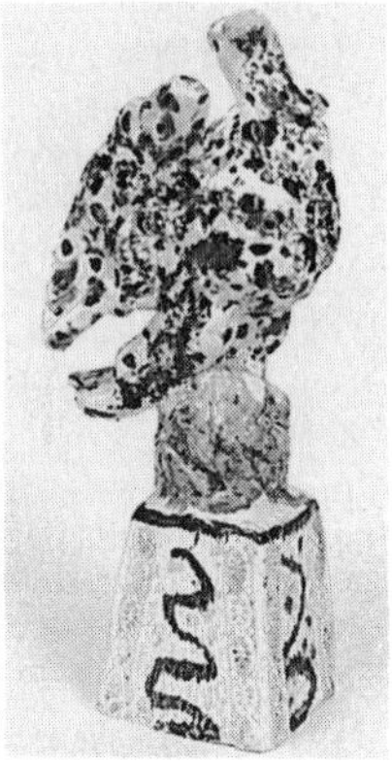

A Staffordshire Pratt type eagle, c1830, 10in (25cm) high.
£1,000–1,200 *JHo*

A Yorkshire bird whistle, early 19thC, 5in (13cm) high.
£500–550 *JHo*

A Staffordshire cow and calf, decorated with bocage, c1830, 5in (13cm) high.
£300–350 *MSA*

An in-glaze coloured creamware group of a bull and terrier, the brown dog snapping at the hooves of the large beast, its white hide patched in brown-black, the mound picked out in transparent greens, yellow and manganese, restored, c1790, 7in (18cm) wide.
£1,000–1,400 *Bon*

l. A pearlware bull baiting group, both animals splashed in light brown, on a green base edged in yellow between olive green lines, restored, Staffordshire or Yorkshire, c1790, 12in (30.5cm) wide.
£1,300–1,900 *C*

A Staffordshire cow and calf, decorated with bocage, c1830, 5½in (14cm) high.
£300–350 *MSA*

A pair of Staffordshire animals, depicting a deer and a doe, c1795, 5½in (14cm) high.
£850–950 *JHo*

A Staffordshire greyhound, c1850, 8in (20cm) high.
£150–180 *AnE*

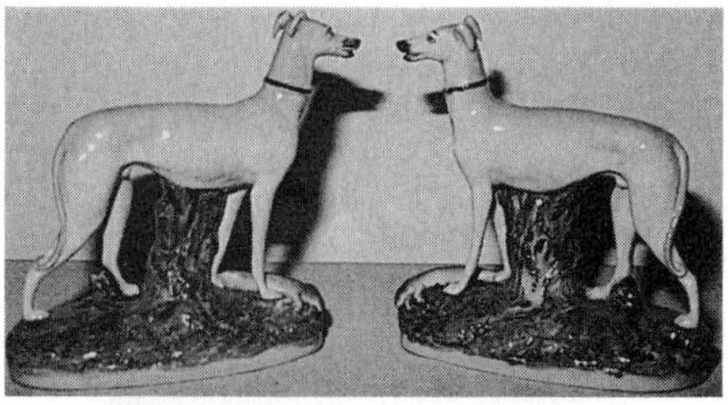

A pair of Staffordshire greyhounds, with rabbits, on green bases, 19thC, 10in (25cm) high.
£250–300 *JH*

A pearlware model of a setter, sponged in black, with floral bocage, the mound base titled in black beneath a puce scroll band, restored, c1830, 6in (15cm) high.
£700–800 *DN*

An enamelled pearlware spaniel, the base outlined in black, sparingly coloured with brown markings and tail, c1820, 8in (20cm) long.
£500–600 *Bon*

A pair of Staffordshire dogs, one seated on a barrel, c1860, 8½in (21cm) high.
£200–250 *AnE*

A pair of Staffordshire models of Indian elephants, shaded in tones of brown, the bases edged with gilt lines, damaged, late 19thC, 10in (25cm) high.
£1,300–1,700 *S*

An enamelled pearlware model of a hunting dog, before a flowering tree, wearing a yellow collar, with coat patched in black, restored, c1830, 6½in (16.5cm) high.
£900–1,000 *Bon*

This is possibly an otter hound.

A Staffordshire pottery dog and puppy, c1855, 5½in (14cm) high.
£750–850 *BHA*

A Ralph Wood type creamware figure of a fox, splashed in brown, on a mound base, damaged, c1780,3in (8cm) high.
£270–320 *DN*

l. A Staffordshire model of a fox carrying a goose, c1800, 6in (15cm) high.
£750–850 *JHo*

A Yorkshire model of a horse, damaged, early 19thC, 6in (15cm) high.
£2,000–2,500 *JHo*

A Yorkshire model of a horse, damaged, c1860, 6in (15cm) high.
£1,700–1,800 *JHo*

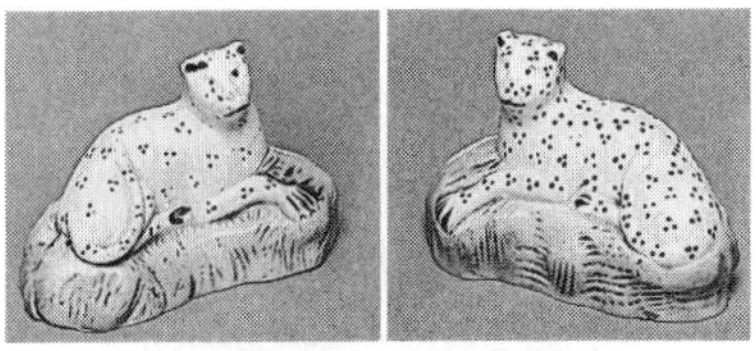

A pair of Staffordshire creamware figures of recumbent leopards, with black markings, each on a green glazed mound base, damaged, c1790, 3½in (9cm) wide.
£1,000–1,200 *DN*

A Staffordshire model of a lion, late 18thC, 7in (18cm) high.
£4,000–4,500 *JHo*

l. A Staffordshire creamware figure of a stag, repairs to antlers, c1800, 6in (15cm) high.
£350–450 *RA*

A pair of Walton enamelled models of a ram and a ewe, moulded banner marks 'Walton', c1820, 7in (18cm) high.
£1,200–1,700 *Bon*

A Yorkshire model of a rabbit, c1810, 5in (12.5cm) high.
£550–650 *JHo*

l. A Staffordshire model of a rabbit, repaired, early 19thC, 2½in (6cm) high.
£450–550 *JHo*

l. A Staffordshire pearlware model of a sheep, with bocage, c1830, 3½in (9cm) high.
£300–350 *MSA*

A pair of enamelled pearlware models of lions, each beast looking back to a snake emerging from a leafy tree, with scroll moulded bases picked out in blue, restored, c1820, 8in (20cm) high.
£1,700–2,200 *Bon*

A pair of Staffordshire models of lions, c1820, 2½in (6cm) high.
£1,200–1,300 *JHo*

Victorian Staffordshire Figures

A pair of figures of Robert Burns and Highland Mary, he wearing a plumed hat, turquoise jacket and tartan sash, his foot resting above a fountain, she wearing a simple dress, on oval gilt line bases, painted in colours and gilt, damaged, 19thC, 14½in (37cm) high, H50.
£400–500 *CSK*

Two equestrian figures of Napoleon Bonaparte, wearing blue capes and military uniform on piebald mounts, above rocky mounds applied with foliage on gilt line bases, painted in colours and gilt, worn, c1845, 6in (15cm) high, C42(a).
£400–500 *CSK*

A figure of Daniel O'Connell, his hand resting on a draped plinth, wearing a black coat and white trousers, on a grassy mound above an oval base, indistinctly titled in gilt 'Dan O'Connell', enriched in colours and gilt, c1875, 18in (46cm) high, B15.
£300–400 *CSK*

Figures – People

Staffordshire Figures

The letters and figures at the end of each caption refer to the cataloguing system used by P. D. Gordon Pugh, in his book *Staffordshire Portrait Figures*, published by Antique Collectors' Club Ltd., 1970.

A set of the Staffordshire Seasons, 3 dressed in blue coats, c1850, 8in (20cm) high.
£600–700 *JBL*

A Staffordshire figure, c1775, 4in (10cm) high.
£400–500 *JHo*

r. A Staffordshire figure, 'The Poor Laborer', early 19thC, 6in (15cm) high.
£250–300 *JHo*

A Staffordshire figure, c1740, 10in (25cm) high.
£700–800 *JHo*

A Staffordshire figure of a reclining man, c1880, 8in (20cm) high.
£300–350 *AnE*

A pearlware figure of recumbent Antony, his head raised, wearing a cuirass and cape, above a rocky moulded mound base, painted in colours, damaged, painted number, c1790, 12in (31cm) long.
£300–400 *CSK*

l. A pair of Staffordshire figures, 'Tenderness' and 'Friendship', c1800, 6½in (16cm) high.
£800–900 *JHo*

A Staffordshire group, 'Peter Restoring the Lame Man', c1820, 8in (20cm) high.
£750–850 *JHo*

A Staffordshire group, early 19thC, 8in (20cm) high.
£550–650 *JHo*

A Staffordshire group, early 19thC, 9in (23cm) high.
£600–700 *JHo*

r. A Staffordshire pearlware figure of a young girl, wearing a yellow and blue dress, holding a flower and an umbrella, seated before floral bocage, on a green glazed square base with black sponged border, restored, c1825, 10in (25cm) high.
£750–850 *DN*

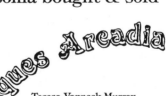

A pair of pearlware Staffordshire figures, 'Sheperd' and 'Sheperdess', early 19thC, 5½in (14cm) high.
£400–450 *TVM*

A Staffordshire group, early 19thC, 7½in (19cm) high.
£250–350 *JHo*

A Staffordshire pearlware group, Rural Pastimes, c1830, 9in (23cm) high.
£750–850 *MSA*

A group attributed to Obadiah Sherratt, The Baptism of Mary, one figure missing, c1820, 9½in (24cm) high.
£900–1,100 *JBL*

A pair of Staffordshire pearlware figures of young women, emblematic of Summer and Winter, each in contemporary costume and with a child at their side, decorated in green, blue, yellow and ochre, on oval scroll and shell-moulded mound bases, restored, c1825, 9in (23cm) high.
£1,200–1,400 *DN*

A pair of Staffordshire figures, The Shoemaker and His Wife, c1840, 13in (33cm) high.
£300–350 *AnE*

A Staffordshire figure of a reclining drummer boy, 19thC, 7in (18cm) high.
£280–320 *AnE*

A Staffordshire group, firing crack, c1850, 10in (25cm) high.
£100–150 *AnE*

A Staffordshire figure of Red Riding Hood, c1860, 9½in (24cm) high.
£160–185 *AnE*

A Staffordshire group of Victoria and Albert, c1860, 8in (20cm) high.
£200–225 *AnE*

A Staffordshire figure of a girl with a goat, c1870, 9in (23cm) high.
£300–340 *AnE*

r. A pair of Staffordshire figure groups, c1830, 7½in (19cm) high.
£1,000–1,100 *JHo*

A figure of John Liston as Sam Swipe, c1860, 6in (15cm) high.
£300–400 *JHo*

A Staffordshire figure group of Henry VIII and Anne Boleyn, c1800, 9in (23cm) high.
£400–500 *MSA*

A Staffordshire figure group, Giaffier and Zuleika from Byron's *The Bride of Abydos*, c1860, 13in (33cm) high.
£850–900 *MSA*

A pair of Staffordshire figures, Sancho Panza and Don Quixote, c1870, 9½in (24cm) high.
£450–500 *MSA*

A Staffordshire figure group, 'Charity', c1820, 9in (23cm) high.
£400–500 *MSA*

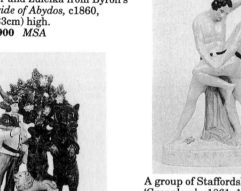

A group of Staffordshire figures, 'Grapplers', c1861, 11½in (29cm) high.
£2,500–2,900 *MSA*

A pair of Staffordshire figures of boxers, Molyneaux and Cribb, c1815, 9in (23cm) and 9½in (24cm) high.
£4,500–5,000 *MSA*

A Staffordshire pearlware group, of a Savoyard with a dancing bear and a lion, c1830, 9in (23cm) high.
£2,700–3,000 *MSA*

A pair of Staffordshire figures of horsemen, c1870, 7½in (19cm) high.
£450–500 *MSA*

l. A pair of Pratt type pearlware figures of a hunter and companion, a spotted dog pawing at the man standing with a gun under one arm, the companion holding a bird and spotted bag, both hollow figures picked out in greens, ochre and brown, late 18thC, 7in (18cm) high.
£850–1,000 *Bon*

A pair of enamelled pearlware figures of The Welsh Tailor and his Wife, each astride a goat, upon a scroll moulded base picked out in blue, restored, early 19thC, 6½in (16.5cm) high.
£850–1,000 *Bon*

A pearlware group of a musician and companion, she with a lute, he with a French horn, each decorated in brown, green, yellow and ochre, and before bocage, a monkey at their feet, on square plinth base with central anthemion, restored, c1810, 8in (20cm) high.
£650–800 *DN*

An enamelled pearlware group, entitled 'Widow and Orphan', the young woman gathering kindling with the help of 2 children, a baby on her back, wearing a headdress, green cape and patterned iron red dress, titled rustic base, c1810, 10½in (27cm) high.
£350–500 *Bon*

A figure of a lady, standing holding a posy in her left hand, wearing a feathered poke bonnet, a green neck scarf, long yellow gloves and a salmon coloured dress, with blue edging to the bodice, blue flowers on the skirt and a green and lilac ribbon border and green hem, early 19thC, 13½in (34cm) high.
£1,200–2,000 *P*

The figure, which is hollow cast, has been variously suggested to be Princess Charlotte, or Spring from a set of Seasons.

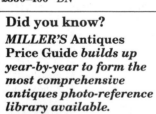

A pair of pearlware figures, inscribed 'Gardners', he with a spade and she with a watering can, each decorated in coloured enamels and standing before floral bocage, on titled mound bases, restored, c1825, 5in (13cm) high.
£350–400 *DN*

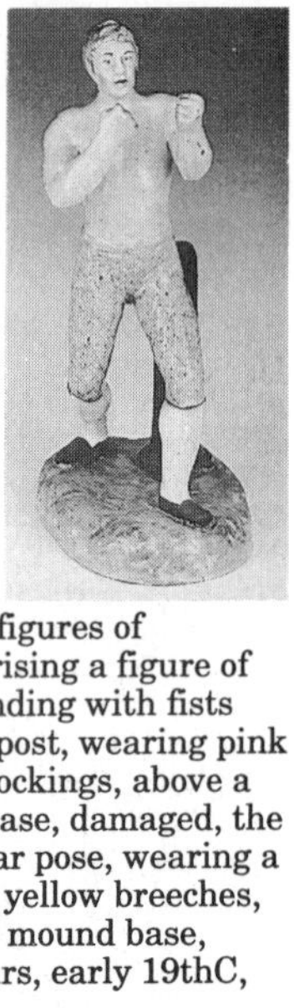

Two pearlware figures of pugilists, comprising a figure of Tom Cribb, standing with fists raised beside a post, wearing pink breeches and stockings, above a grassy mound base, damaged, the other in a similar pose, wearing a pink jacket and yellow breeches, on a tree stump mound base, painted in colours, early 19thC, 8in (20cm) high.
£2,000–2,200 *CSK*

Did you know?
MILLER'S* Antiques Price Guide *builds up year-by-year to form the most comprehensive antiques photo-reference library available.

A pair of equestrian figures of leopard hunters, each wearing a plumed hat, blue jacket, one wearing breeches, the other a kilt, each holding a spear above a cowering leopard, on rocky moulded mounds above oval gilt line bases, restored, 19thC, 10½in (27cm) high.
£900–1,100 *CSK*

r. A St. Peter's Pottery, Thomas Fell, figure of Apollo, wearing loose drapes painted with sprigs of flowers, above a shaped marblised plinth, damaged, impressed mark, c1820, 13½in (34cm) high.
£360–400 *CSK*

A set of 4 enamelled pearlware figures, The Four Apostles, each standing before a flowering tree, wearing predominantly orange coloured dress, on green rustic bases reserved with titles picked out in black, restored, c1830, 10in (25cm) high.
£1,200–1,600 *Bon*

Flatware

A Bristol charger, c1685, 13in (33.5cm) diam.
£3,000–4,500 *JHo*

A delft charger, London or Bristol, c1690, 13⅛in (34.5cm) diam.
£2,500–3,000 *JHo*

A Bristol delft charger, early 18thC, 13in (33.5cm) diam.
£3,500–4,000 *JHo*

Two Bristol blue and white delft dishes, painted within bianco sopra bianco borders, damaged, c1750, 8½in (21cm) diam.
£250–350 *CSK*

A pair of Liverpool delft octagonal plates, each centrally 'pencilled' with Cupid amidst flowers and leaves, the rims with a flowerhead panelled diaper band, damaged, c1765, 12½in (32cm) diam.
£400–550 *DN*

A Bristol delft blue and white charger, damaged, c1720, 14in (36cm) diam.
£250–300 *AnE*

A Liverpool delft plate, decorated in Fazackerly palette with buildings, bridges and a haystack in a river landscape, damaged, c1760, 8½in (21.5cm) diam.
£250–300 *DN*

A London delft blue and white punch bowl, the interior inscribed in the centre 'Success to Trade.', damaged, c1766, 10½in (26.5cm) diam.
£1,400–1,600 *S(NY)*

A London delft bowl inscribed 'Success to Trade No Stamps' provides proof that at least some of these delft punch bowls with 'Trade' inscriptions were made for the American market, or at least for British merchants involved in commerce with the American colonies.

A Liverpool delft plate, decorated in blue, green, orange and yellow with two swans, an insect, bamboo and rockwork, within an orange line rim, restored, c1760, 8½in (21.5cm) diam.
£350–400 *DN*

A Liverpool delft plate, decorated in Fazackerly palette with a central spray of flowers and leaves, the rim with 3 similar sprays, damaged, c1760, 9in (23cm) diam.
£270–320 *DN*

A pair of delft chargers, each white ground with green, blue, red, and brown decoration, 13½in (34.5cm) diam.
£1,800–2,000 *BHA*

l. Two London delft polychrome farmhouse deep plates, painted in blue, brown and green damaged, c1750, 9½in (24cm) diam.
£6,500–7,000 *C*

An Irish delft octagonal dish, painted in deep blue, the wide rim painted with a border of flowerheads, foliage and panels of trellis, 22½in (57.5cm) wide.
£600–700 *P*

Miller's is a price GUIDE not a price LIST

A delft blue and white armorial plate, the rim painted with stylised scrolling foliage, London or Dublin, damaged, 9in (23cm) diam.
£400–500 *CSK*

The arms are probably those of Cahusac of Languedoc, impaling those of Custers of Brabant.

A delft plate, painted in blue with a chinoiserie scene, 18thC, 15in (38cm) diam.
£300–400 *Bon*

r. A set of 6 Dutch Delft blue and white marriage plates, each decorated at the top of the rim in shades of blue delineated in black with the initials 'R^{G}R' above the date '1692', damaged, 10in (25cm) diam.
£2,200–2,500 *S(NY)*

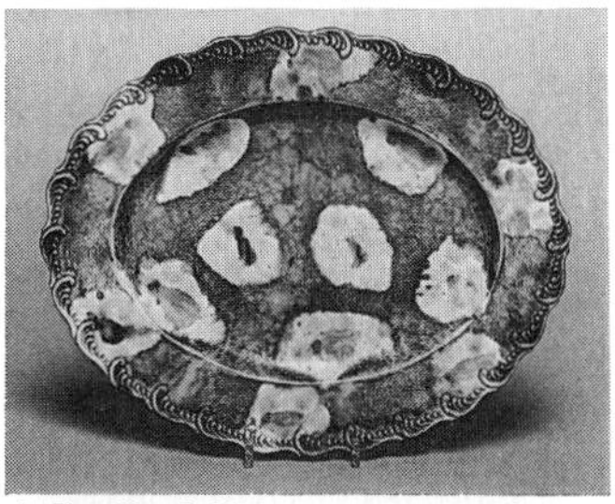

A Staffordshire creamware dish, with feather moulded border, splashed in green and yellow, on a grey sponged ground, the reverse sponged in brown, damaged, c1770, 14in (36cm) wide.
£250–350 *DN*

A Pratt ware plate, decorated with Christ in the Cornfield, with green border, inscribed and gilded, the reverse with 'Pratt/Prince Albert' stamp and overglaze print in purple.
£550–600 *SAS*

Presented to the Rev. G. Armitage. BA Camb., by the pupils of the Grammar School, Newcastle-under-Lyme as a mark of gratitude and esteem, Christmas 1853.

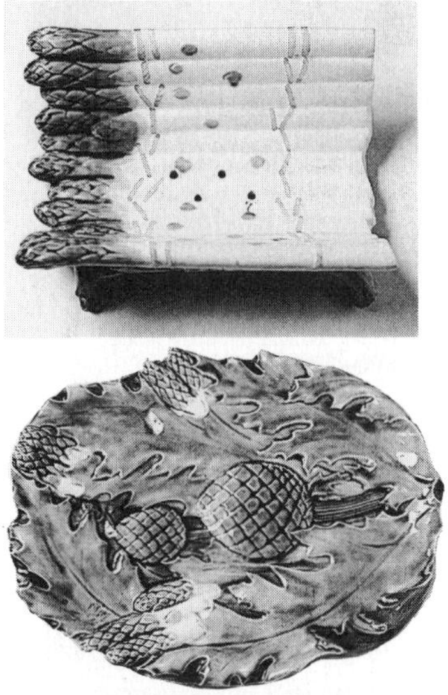

A Lunéville majolica asparagus and artichoke dish and cradle, c1880, 10in (25cm) long.
£350–375 *MofC*

A Staffordshire child's plate, black transfer decorated with 'Riddle' pattern, c1830, 6in (15cm) diam.
£50–60 *RP*

A Choisy-le-Roi majolica charger, French, c1900, 8in (20cm) diam.
£30–40 *MofC*

Six majolica plates, decorated with love birds, marked 'Salins', c1890, 8in (20cm) diam.
£250–275 *MofC*

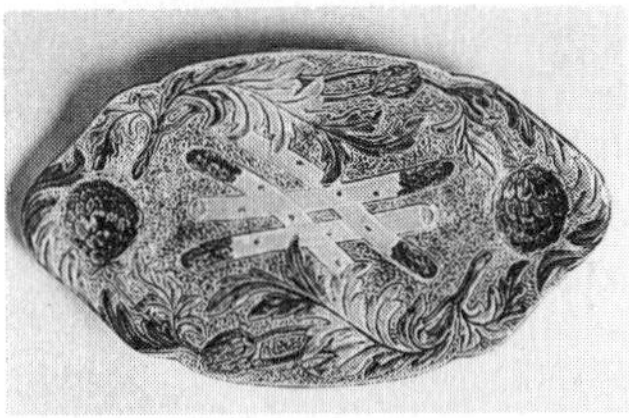

A French majolica asparagus dish, c1890, 17in (43.5cm) long.
£200–225 *MofC*

A child's plate, by Dillwyn, Swansea, decorated with a black transfer rural scene, c1830, 5½in (14cm) diam.
£65–75 *RP*

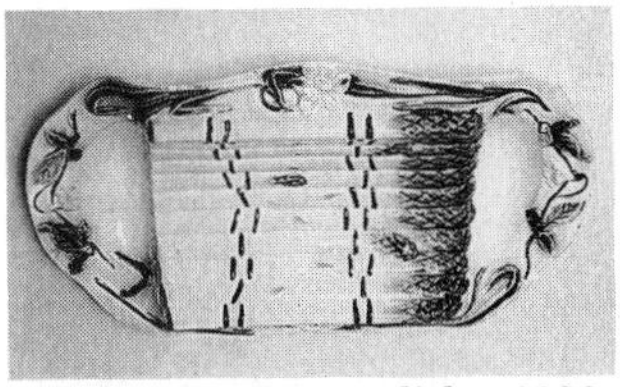

A Salins asparagus dish, c1890, 15in (38.5cm) long.
£250–265 *MofC*

A Savona blue and white dish, painted within a gadroon moulded well, the border painted with buildings on mounds and scattered flowers and foliage, damaged, blue shield mark, late 17thC, 18in (46cm) diam.
£2,200–2,700 *C*

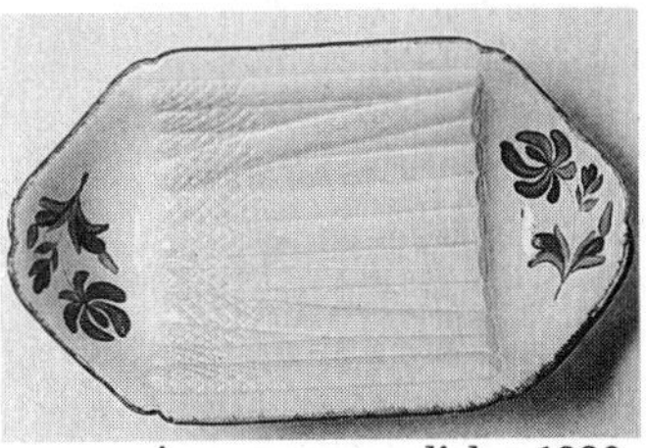

An asparagus dish, c1930, 13½in (34.5cm) long.
£150–175 *MofC*

r. A pair of Quimper plates, marked 'Henriot Quimper', c1920, 9½in (24cm) diam.
£125–150 *MofC*

A French majolica strawberry dish, c1890, 13in (33.5cm) wide.
£250–265 *MofC*

A Frankfurt faïence fluted charger, of silver shape, decorated in blue and manganese with Oriental figures in rocky landscapes, in Chinese Transitional style, damaged, early 18thC, 14in (35.5cm) diam.
£500–800 *DN*

An Italian maiolica istoriato dish, painted in Florentine style within a scrolling panel, the blue border painted with scrolling foliage below a gadrooned rim, damaged, 20thC, 20in (50.5cm) diam.
£200–300 *CSK*

An Italian maiolica istoriato dish, painted in a Castelli style with Venus and Mars, worn, 20thC, 20in (50.5cm) diam.
£420–500 *CSK*

Blue & White Transfer Ware

An oval plate, by Bevington & Co., Swansea, decorated with Monopteros pattern, c1820, 17in (43cm) wide.
£300–500 *GN*

A Davenport dessert dish, decorated with a scene of Bisham Abbey, c1810, 9½in (24cm) wide.
£150–200 *GN*

A blue and white dinner plate, Shipping series, maker unknown, c1815, 10in (25.5cm) diam).
£230–250 *Nor*

A Brameld dinner plate, Returning Woodman pattern, c1806, 10in (25.5cm) wide.
£160–180 *Nor*

A Thomas Godwin meat platter, decorated with a view of London, c1820, 18½in (47cm) wide.
£600–700 *GN*

Miller's is a price GUIDE not a price LIST

A dessert dish, by Andrew Stevenson, with ornithological scenes, c1820, 8in (20.5cm) high.
£180–200 *Nor*

A dessert dish, by Job Ridgway, Curling Palm Pattern, c1810, 8in (20.5cm) wide.
£180–200 *Nor*

A Ralph Hall plate, decorated with Sheltered Peasants pattern, c1820, 10in (25cm) diam.
£120–180 *GN*

A Rogers game dish, decorated with Greek Statue pattern, c1810, 9½in (24cm) wide.
£150–200 *GN*

A Wedgwood vegetable dish and cover, decorated with Hibiscus pattern, c1810, 18in (45.5cm) wide.
£200–300 *GN*

An Enoch Wood pie dish, London Views series, made for the US market, decorated with a view of the Bank of England, c1820, 11½in (29cm) wide.
£300–400 *GN*

A platter, Antique Scenery series, decorated with Craig Miller Castle, Scotland, c1825, 15in (38cm) wide.
£200–300 *GN*

A Spode Tower pattern well and tree platter, c1815, 21in (53.5cm) wide.
£350–550 *GN*

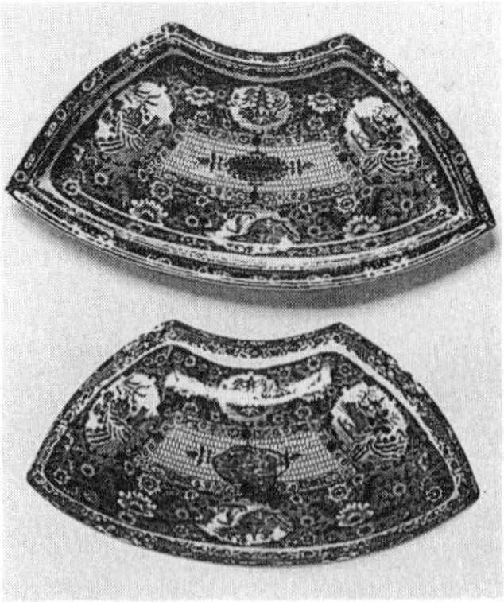

A Spode supper dish and cover, decorated with Net pattern, c1820, largest 14in (35.5cm) wide.
£200–300 *GN*

l. A British Marine series charger, c1835, 14½in (37cm) diam.
£400–500 *GN*

l. A Staffordshire British America pattern platter, by Podmore, Walker & Co., with a view of Montreal, c1850, 21in (53cm) wide.
£500–600 *RIT*

A drainer, by Edward and George Phillips, c1830, 13in (33cm) wide.
£320–360 *Nor*

Footbaths

A Copeland & Garrett footbath, the exterior printed in green, the interior rim with a similar band, mid-19thC, 21½in (55cm) diam, and a matching water jug, slight damage.
£600–700 *Bea*

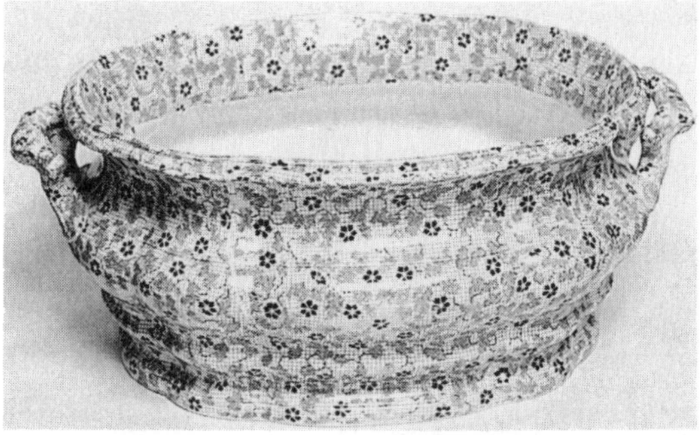

A Copeland & Garrett footbath, decorated with a sheet pattern, c1840, 20in (50.5cm) long.
£1,200–1,500 *GN*

A Minton floral patterned footbath, c1840, 19in (48cm) long.
£800–1,200 *GN*

Inkwells

A Liverpool delft inkwell, c1760, 4in (10cm) wide.
£350–400 *JHo*

A delft inkwell, probably Liverpool, the sides inscribed in blue 'William Whenell Lancaster 1764', chipped, 3in (7.5cm) diam.
£7,000–8,000 *S*

Jars

A Savona maiolica jar, 17thC, 7in (17.5cm) high.
£1,200–1,400 *RIT*

A Quimper jar, marked 'HB', 9in (22.5cm) high.
£120–140 *MofC*

A Montelupo oviform wet drug jar and cover, with dolphin handles, painted in blue, yellow, ochre, brown and green, damaged, mid-16thC, 18in (46cm) high.
£3,000–4,000 *C*

A Savona drug jar, with the drug label in dark manganese Gothic letters, dated on foot rim '1683', neck reduced, marked 'GT', 8in (20cm) high.
£300–400 *P*

An Italian maiolica 16thC style oviform jar, probably made in the Pesaro workshop of Ferrucio Mengarone, the reverse with a coat-of-arms flanked by the initials 'W.W.V.S.' and the date 'M.C.XLI' with 'W' below, enclosed by green bands, slight damage, late 19thC, 9½in (24cm) high.
£1,200–2,000 *C*

Make the most of Miller's

Condition is absolutely vital when assessing the value of an antique. Items in good condition are more likely to appreciate than less perfect examples. Rare, desirable items may command higher prices even when in need of restoration.

Jugs

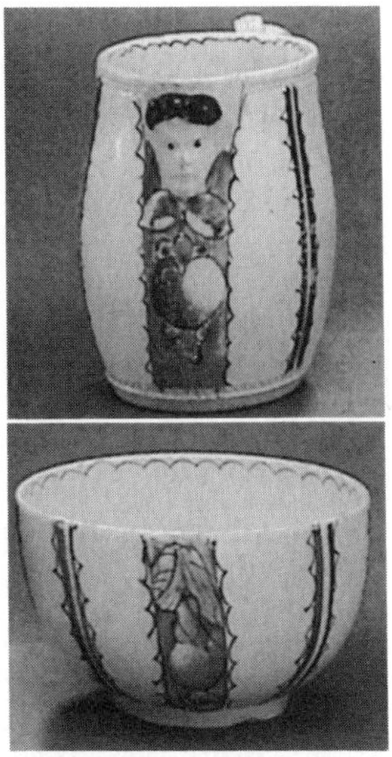

A creamware cream jug, probably Leeds, enamelled in the manner of David Rhodes, in black, iron red, puce, green and yellow, green enamel lines mark, Jacobs Collection No. 580, repaired, 3in (7.5cm) high, and a matching teabowl, Jacobs Collection No. 581, 3in (7.5cm) diam.
£600–800 *CNY*

A Staffordshire copper lustre clock face jug, c1840, 9½in (24cm) high.
£150–180 *RP*

A pearlware baluster-shaped harvest jug, painted in Pratt colours of green, yellow, ochre and brown, inscribed beneath the spout 'Thomas Mafsey Heaton Norris 1800' within a foliate cartouche, foliate swags below the rim, cracked, 10in (25cm) high.
£650–800 *C*

A Liverpool jug, dated '1801', 10in (25cm) high.
£800–1,000 *JHo*

A Staffordshire pearlware harvest jug, decorated with lustre bands, over-enamelled transfers of harvest and agricultural attributes, inscribed 'Uriah & Sarah Edge, 1824', 8in (20cm) high.
£500–600 *WL*

A Staffordshire copper lustre jug, with embossed portraits of Victoria and Albert, probably commemorating their wedding, c1840, 5in (12.5cm) high.
£160–200 *RP*

A creamware jug, inscribed 'Roger Rea 1772', 8½in (21.5cm) high.
£550–650 *P(EA)*

A Staffordshire pearlware mask jug, early 19thC.
£150–200 *W*

A pair of Staffordshire blue and white opaque jugs, printed with the 'Florentine' pattern, one impressed '6 quartz', blue printed marks within a scroll cartouche, damaged, c1840, 12in (31cm) high, and a similar jug, damaged, 10in (25cm) high.
£700–900 *C*

A Yorkshire blue and white jug, c1778, 8½in (21.5cm) high.
£2,000–2,500 *JHo*

A Pratt ware jug, decorated with The Sailor's Farewell, c1800, 6in (15cm) high.
£250–300 *RP*

A Pratt ware baluster-shaped jug, decorated with equestrian figures in low relief, early 19thC, 5½in (14cm) high.
£200–250 *AH*

An Onnaing majolica jug, marked '740 Frie', c1920, 7½in (19cm) high.
£100–145 *MofC*

A Portuguese 'Hamburg type' water jug, in the form of a sphinx with the tail forming the hollow handle, moulded in relief with leaf motifs, painted in yellow and blue, 9½in (24cm) high.
£5,000–6,000 *P*

These jugs were once thought to be of Hamburg manufacture, but are now attributed to Portugal.

A blue and white jug, by Dillwyn of Swansea, decorated in Women with Baskets pattern, c1820, 8in (20cm) high.
£250–300 *RP*

An Onnaing majolica jug, marked '834 Frie', c1920, 7½in (19cm) high.
£150–200 *MofC*

A majolica jug, decorated with grape pickers, c1900, 9in (22.5cm) high.
£250–280 *MofC*

A Quimper jug, marked 'Henriot Quimper', c1920, 8in (20cm) high.
£125–150 *MofC*

A blue and white jug and bowl set, by South Wales Pottery, Llanelly, decorated with Milan pattern, c1850, 12in (31cm) high.
£150–200 *RP*

A Sarreguemines majolica jug, marked 'No. 797', c1890, 9½in (24cm) high.
£200–250 *MofC*

A Nimy les Mous majolica jug, c1900, 8½in (21.5cm) high.
£250–270 *MofC*

Use the Index!

Because certain items might fit easily into any number of categories, the quickest and surest method of locating any entry is by reference to the index at the back of the book.

This index has been fully cross-referenced for absolute simplicity.

Character Jugs

A Ralph Wood type raised cup Toby jug, decorated with running glazes of blue and yellow, c1790, 10in (25cm) high.
£800–900 *JBL*

A Yorkshire Toby jug, decorated in Pratt ware colours, with an eight-sided glass and figurehead handle, c1790, 10in (25cm) high.
£600–700 *JBL*

A Pratt ware Toby jug, decorated in mainly yellow underglaze colours, c1790, 10in (25cm) high.
£650–750 *JBL*

A Collier Toby jug, decorated with blue running glazes, c1790, 10in (25cm) high.
£800–900 *JBL*

A Ralph Wood Toby jug, depicting Admiral Lord Howe, decorated with running glazes, restored, c1790, 10in (25cm) high.
£900–1,000 *JBL*

A Toby jug, decorated in blues and greys, with running glaze, c1800, 10in (25cm) high.
£400–500 *JBL*

A Neale Toby jug, decorated in red, brown and green, marked with a crown and 'C', c1820, 10in (25cm) high.
£900–1,000 *JBL*

A pearlware jug and cover, depicting a woman in a green and orange dress, white apron, and yellow hat, holding a bottle, on a vine moulded base, damaged, 19thC, 10in (25cm) high.
£600–800 *DN*

'The Landlord' Toby jug and cover, decorated in underglaze blue, red and green, inscribed 'Home Brewed Ale', c1855, 11in (28cm) high.
£400–500 *JBL*

A Walton 'Hearty Goodfellow' Toby jug, decorated in overglaze colours, with leaf design to small jug, c1820, 11in (28cm) high.
£700–800 *JBL*

A Staffordshire toby jug, with a tricorn hat, 19thC.
£150–200 *MR*

A Victorian Staffordshire jug, depicting Bacchus crowned with an ivy wreath, 8in (20cm) high.
£150–200 *AnE*

Mugs

A delft blue and white coffee can, possibly Liverpool, mid-18thC, 2½in (6.5cm) high.
£1,900–2,500 *S*

l. A Southwark delft blue and white mug, marked 'B/GW/1653', repaired, 7½in (19cm) high.
£34,000–40,000 *C*

A blue and white sponge decorated mug, with strap handle, c1830, 4in (10cm) high.
£65–75 *RYA*

Pottery or Porcelain?

Pottery includes anything made from baked clay. It embraces a large number of quite different materials, including earthenware and stoneware, covered in many different glazes.

Porcelain is a hard translucent white substance made from china clay and china stone. It has a clear ringing sound when struck.

Pots

A Davenport mustard pot, decorated with the Family and Mule pattern, c1820, 3in (7.5cm) diam.
£90–150 *GN*

A child's chamber pot, decorated with Arcadian Chariots pattern, c1835, 6in (15cm) diam.
£200–300 *GN*

A pair of pearlware pink lustre bough pots, c1820, 8½in (21.5cm) wide.
£1,000–1,200 *RP*

An Orchies cachepot, late 19thC, 8in (20cm) high.
£125–180 *MofC*

l. A Burmantofts jardinière, with moulded and coloured decoration depicting a royal coat-of-arms and floral panels, inscribed 'Victorian Diamond Jubilee', on a treacle glazed ground, impressed mark, small chips, c1897, 42½in (108cm) high.
£1,200–1,400 *SAS*

A Barbotine cachepot, c1900, 9in (22.5cm) high.
£200–250 *MofC*

Coffee Pots

A Staffordshire salt glazed coffee pot and cover, enamelled in colours with a Chinese lady in a blue and green robe, the rim and cover with a turquoise diaper border separated by shaped panels enclosing single flowerheads, the spout and handle enriched with iron red foliage, Jacobs Collection No. 527, cracked, c1755, 8in (21.5cm) high.
£1,200–1,500 *CNY*

A Staffordshire salt glazed coffee pot and cover, the front and back painted in iron red, the spout and handle enriched with iron red chevrons, Jacobs Collection No. 394, damaged, c1760, 9in (23cm) high.
£12,500–13,500 *CNY*

Teapots

A Staffordshire white salt glazed camel teapot and cover, the panelled domed cover attached to the handle with a metal chain mount, Jacobs Collection No. 656, c1750, 6in (15cm) high.
£6,000–7,000 *CNY*

A documentary creamware teapot, painted in brownish manganese outline, heightened in underglaze blue and green, all under a crackled greenish glaze, dated '1743', 7in (17.5cm) high.
£35,000–40,000 *Bon*

Until the discovery of this teapot, the earliest recorded piece of British creamware known has been the bowl in the British Museum inscribed 'EB 1743'. The 'EB' initials on the bowl have generally been taken to represent the Tunstall potter Enoch Booth. The newly discovered 'Tunstall' teapot supports this association, while the name 'F. Morgan', a name not hitherto known in a ceramic context, raises an interesting new thread of enquiry into the early history of Staffordshire creamwares, a tradition consolidated by Josiah Wedgwood.

A Staffordshire creamware globular teapot and cover, probably Wedgwood, with leaf moulded handle, spout and ball knop, brightly decorated in the manner of David Rhodes with a shepherdess, buildings and trees, cracked, c1770, 4½in (11.5cm) high.
£800–950 *DN*

l. A Staffordshire creamware teapot and cover, with scroll spout and notched rococo handle, on a diaper and trellis ground above the waisted section, with rouletted decoration, splashed in green, manganese and yellow, Jacobs Collection No. 604, restored, c1760, 5½in (13.5cm) high.
£6,250–7,000 *CNY*

l. A Staffordshire Liverpool transfer ware teapot, c1755, 5in (12.5cm) high.
£650–700 *JHo*

l. A Staffordshire teapot, c1765, 5in (12.5cm) high.
£1,500–1,800 *JHo*

A Staffordshire creamware pineapple teapot and cover, probably Wedgwood, restored, c1765, 5½in (13.5cm) high.
£6,000–7,000 *CNY*

A Staffordshire teapot, 19thC, 7in (17.5cm) high.
£80–110 *AnE*

A French provincial yellow glazed faïence teapot, c1880, 7in (17.5cm) high.
£80–100 *RYA*

A barge ware teapot, c1887, 13½in (34.5cm) high.
£250–350 *MSA*

A documentary Greatbatch creamware cylindrical teapot and cover, printed and painted with The Fortune Teller and The XII Houses of Heaven, restored, signed in the print, dated '1778', 5in (12.5cm) high.
£4,500–5,000 *CNY*

Another example of this documentary Greatbatch model but with gilt roulette bands in place of the present beading is in the collection of the City Museum and Art Gallery, Stoke-on-Trent.

Salts

A pair of polychrome delft capstan salts, the sides painted with flowers in red, green and blue, the flanged rims with blue false gadroons, the base with a blue zig-zag on a red herringbone ground, early 18thC, 2⅜in (6cm) high.
£12,000–15,000 *P*

A blue and white spongeware salt, rim chipped, c1820, 3in (7.5cm) diam.
£30–40 *RYA*

An Italian maiolica pedestal salt, the corners with winged female terms, on 4 feet, painted in colours with exotic birds, masks and foliage, damaged, 5in (12.5cm) high.
£300–400 *L*

Marks

Marks are found on the bases of many items. They may include factory marks, which changed periodically and can therefore help with dating. Maker's initials were also often used. Many marks were copied, faked or added retrospectively, so they should not be taken as an absolute guarantee of authenticity.

Services

l. A Ridgway's pottery dinner service, comprising 111 pieces, c1879.
£1,500–2,000 *WIL*

A French majolica fruit set, comprising 15 pieces, c1890, largest dish 10in (25cm) diam.
£850–900 *MofC*

A Whitehaven dinner service, decorated in Marseillaise pattern, early 19thC.
£1,500–2,000 *Mit*

Spill Vases

A Staffordshire spill vase, depicting a rustic scene, decorated in running glazes of browns and greens, c1820, 9in (23cm) high.
£700–900 *JBL*

A pair of Staffordshire pottery spill vases, with gold and brown lions and cubs on a white ground, interior of vase orange, c1860, 11½in (29cm) high.
£1,400–1,500 *BHA*

A Staffordshire gypsy group spill vase, c1850, 8in (20cm) high.
£150–185 *AnE*

A Staffordshire Ralph Wood spill vase, depicting a rural couple, c1810, 10½in (26.5cm) high.
£1,300–1,400 *MSA*

A Staffordshire spill vase, depicting a boy birds' nesting in a woodland setting, decorated in underglazed rustic colours and complex moulds, c1820, 9in (23cm) high.
£1,200–1,400 *JBL*

A mid-Victorian Staffordshire pottery rustic spill vase, depicting a cow and calf, on a stylised base.
£180–220 *MR*

A pair of Staffordshire spill vases, depicting children with foxes, c1860, 9in (23cm) high.
£450–550 *MSA*

Two spill vases, painted in colours, damaged, 19thC, 7in (17.5cm) high.
£1,000–1,200 *CSK*

A pair of spill vases, modelled as circus elephants, painted in colours and gilt, on shaped gilt lined bases, slight wear, 19thC, 6in (15cm) high.
£1,700–2,000 *CSK*

A Staffordshire spill vase, depicting a boy with sheep, c1830, 7in (17.5cm) high.
£600–700 *MSA*

Tankards

l. A Yorkshire tankard, c1775, 6½in (16.5cm) high.
£3,000–3,800 *JHo*

A Staffordshire tankard, probably Wedgwood, c1780, 6in (15cm) high.
£350–400 *JHo*

Tiles

A theatrical tile, depicting Mr Lee Lewis in the character of Harlequin', c1759, 5in (12.5cm) square.
£350–400 *JHo*

A Liverpool tile, depicting The Ape and the Fox, c1770, 5in (12.5cm) square.
£125–165 *JHo*

This design is also found on a set of creamware plates, printed in red with green enamelled borders, in the Victoria & Albert Museum.

A theatrical tile, depicting 'Mrs. Barry in the character of Athenais', in Nathaniel Lee's *Theodosius,* the print by Thornwaite after Roberts, from Bell's *British Theatre,* dated '12th December 1776', probably printed by Green, restored, 5in (12.5cm) square.
£200–260 *JHo*

A Liverpool tile, depicting The Sheep Biter, from *Aesop's Fables,* Croxall's edition, c1770, 5in (12.5cm) square.
£100–165 *JHo*

A tile depicting The Lark and Her Young Ones, from *Aesop's Fables,* c1770, 5in (12.5cm) square.
£150–185 *JHo*

Two Liverpool delft tiles, depicting 'The French Cook', and 'One lady in a chair accompanied by two gentlemen', printed in brick red, by Sadler, c1770, 5in (12.5cm) square, in a common frame.
£220–270 *DN*

The French Cook tile has satirical references to the famine in France caused by the Seven Years of War, 1756–63, showing a French cook preparing cats and dogs. Both from the Hodgkin Collection.

r. A theatrical tile of 'Mr. Lewis in the character of Douglas', in Home's *Douglas,* the print from Lowndes' *New English Theatre,* by Goldar after Dodd, dated '21st June 1777', 5in (12.5cm) square.
£350–400 *JHo*

A Liverpool tile, depicting The Sow and The Bitch, c1770, 5in (12.5cm) square.
£150–185 *JHo*

A theatrical tile of 'Mr. Garrick in the character of Abel Drugger', in Johnson's *The Alchemist,* the print from Sayer's *Dramatic Characters,* published in 1770, 5in (12.5cm) square.
£350–400 *JHo*

A set of 12 Dutch tiles, with puce weave basket and floral decoration, on a white ground, in a lacquered frame, 18thC, 20 by 16in (51 by 40.5cm).
£700–900 *GH*

Vases

A pair of Dutch Delft blue and white hexagonal pedestals for obelisk flower vases, painted with named figures of virtues within Doric columned cartouches, on claw-and-ball feet, damaged, blue 'AK' monogram for Adriaen Koeks, De Grieksche A factory, late 17thC, 15½in (39.5cm) high.
£4,700–5,200 *C*

A Dutch Delft hyacinth vase, in three sections, from the Adriaen Koeks' factory, painted in blue, damaged, 'AK' mongram marks, 28½in (72cm) high.
£112,000–120,000 *S*

The design originates in vases designed for Hampton Court and followed by members of the English Court.

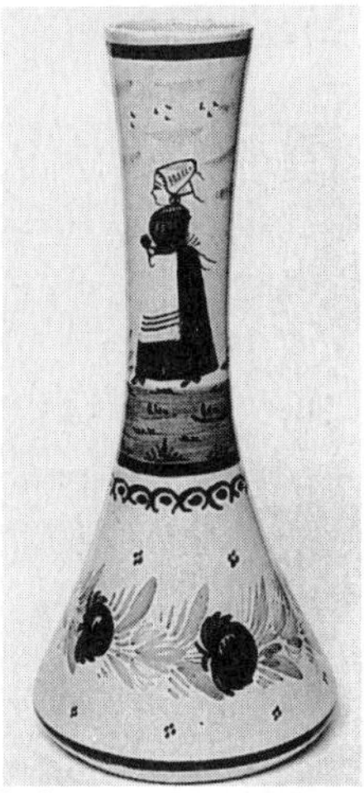

A Quimper vase, marked 'HB Quimper', c1920, 10in (25cm) high.
£125–160 *MofC*

An Italian maiolica vaso a palla, damaged, probably Sicilian, c1600, 12½in (32cm) high.
£500–700 *CSK*

Wall Pockets

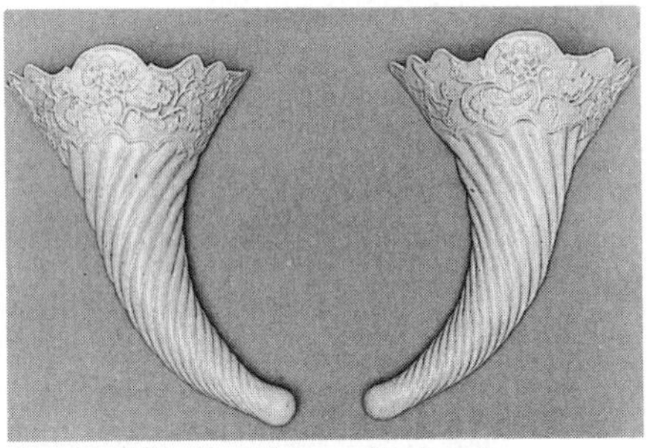

A pair of Staffordshire salt glazed stoneware spirally moulded cornucopia-shaped wall pockets, restored, c1750, 9½in (24cm) high.
£500–800 *DN*

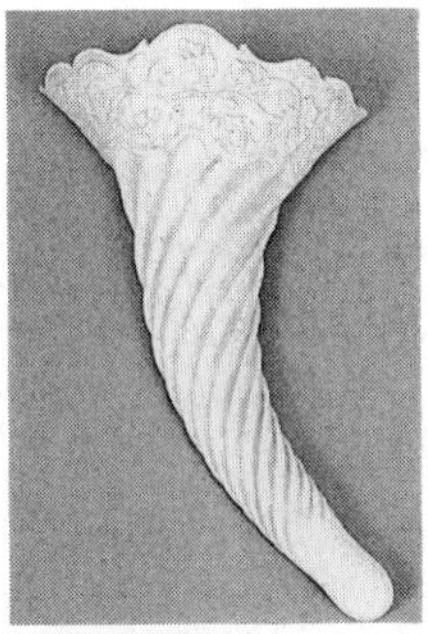

A Staffordshire cornucopia wall pocket, c1760, 9in (22.5cm) high.
£450–500 *JHo*

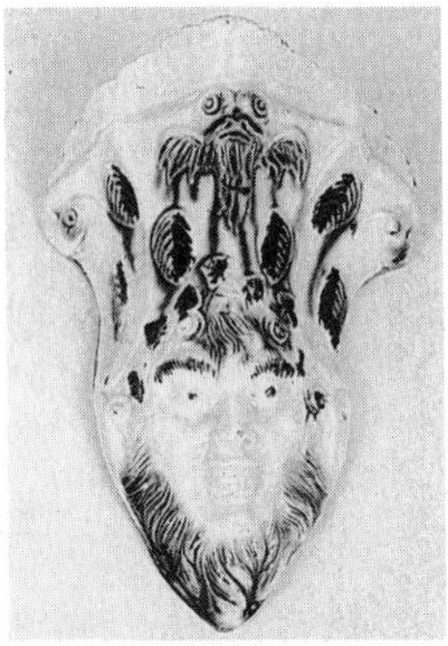

A Staffordshire wall pocket, c1765, 6½in (16.5cm) high.
£650–750 *JHo*

Miscellaneous

A Pratt ware box and screw cover, inscribed 'Christopher Parry', the base painted in brown, green and ochre with a garland of oak leaves and acorns, with brown borders and moulded beaded rims, small chip, 4in (10cm) diam.
£1,000–1,200 *S*

A Spode slop bucket, Italian pattern, c1820, 10in (25cm) wide.
£700–800 *GN*

l. A pair of delft blue and white flower bricks, painted with stylised flowers and foliage, London or Bristol, slightly damaged, c1745, 6in (15cm) wide.
£650–750 *CSK*

An early Staffordshire pastille burner, 19thC, 4in (10cm) high.
£200–265 *JHo*

A Pratt type pottery money box, with 3 money slots to the roof and chimneys, inscribed 'Salley Harper Hougate, March 16th, 1845', damaged, 7in (18cm) high.
£650–850 *CSK*

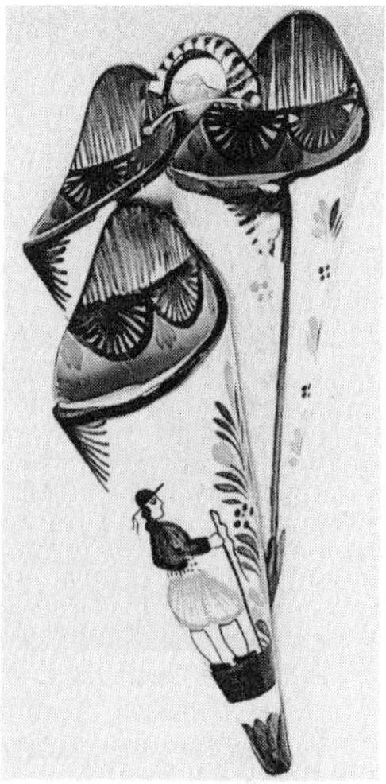

A Quimper posy holder, marked 'HB', c1920, 11in (28cm) high.
£70–80 *MofC*

A salt glazed stoneware scratch blue sauceboat, enriched in blue, restored, c1750, 6in (15cm) long.
£450–500 *DN*

An Obadiah Sherratt type enamelled pearlware tablet, inscribed 'Prepare to meet thy God', restored, c1830, 9½in (24cm) wide.
£600–900 *Bon*

A pair of Copeland garden seats, with yellow and red scrolling foliate and pierced diaper panels, on a grey ground with green banding, 19thC, 16½in (42cm) high.
£550–650 *AH*

r. A pottery barrel, decorated with Pratt ware colours, probably Bristol, c1810, 6in (15cm) high.
£350–450 *RP*

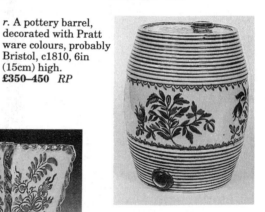

A pearlware model of a dovecote, pierced to the front with openings for the nesting birds before 5 rows of ledges supported on brackets, applied to the roof and reverse with sprigged decoration including representations of Toby Philpot, putti playing with a lion, Nelson and Lady Hamilton, Bacchus drawn in a chariot, Hamlet, Admiral Lord Rodney, Fame and bucolic hunting and drinking scenes, all enriched in colours, damaged, repaired, some pieces missing, c1800, 9in (23cm) high.
£3,000–3,500 *CSK*

A delft polychrome flower tub, the sides painted in blue and iron red, the angles and rim moulded with blue rope-twist, London or Bristol, damaged, c1700, 3½in (9cm) high.
£1,700–2,200 *C*

A delft blue and white tea caddy, metal mount to rim, cover missing, damaged, restored, 18thC, 6in (15cm) high.
£250–300 *CSK*

l. A creamware tea canister, moulded with panels of Oriental figures on cell diaper grounds, the rim with stiff leaf bands, damaged, c1770, 4½in (11.5cm) high.
£250–300 *DN*

A Staffordshire pottery clock, depicting the Lion and the Unicorn, white ground, decorated in pale green, black and brown, c1840, 10in (25cm) high.
£600–700 *BHA*

A clock face group of Daniel in the lion's den, painted in colours and gilt, on a gilt line base, slight wear, c1860, 10in (25cm) high.
£550–800 *CSK*

A Staffordshire pearlware watch stand, c1820, 9in (23cm) high.
£1,800–2,000 *MSA*

Mason's Ironstone

An early Mason's Ironstone jug, c1825, 9in (23cm) high.
£500–520 *AnE*

A Mason's Ironstone footbath, printed and painted in a famille rose palette, damaged, black printed mark, early 19thC, 19½in (49cm) wide.
£1,500–2,000 *CSK*

A Mason's Ironstone desk set, painted in the Imari palette, with blue ground and gilt borders, covers restored, gilt worn, black printed mark, 19thC, 12in (30.5cm) wide.
£600–700 *CSK*

Further Reading

For further reading on Mason's Ironstone, please refer to the article 'The Trading Methods of the Mason's Ironstone Factory', by Valerie Howard, in the June 1992 issue of *The Collector*, published by Barrington Publications. Tel: 0181 740 7020.

An early Mason's Ironstone dessert service, comprising 31 pieces, printed and coloured in green with a four-clawed dragon within panelled floral and pink diaper borders, gilt rims, damaged, tureens with impressed marks, plates and dishes with incised letter N, c1820, plates 9in (23cm) diam.
£1,200–1,700 *S*

A Mason's Ironstone part dinner service, painted in the Imari palette, damage and wear, printed and impressed marks, c1820.
£1,500–2,000 *CSK*

A Mason's patent Ironstone china part dinner service, comprising 61 pieces, transfer printed, coloured and enriched in gilding, damaged, brown printed marks, pattern No. 1379, c1850.
£3,500–4,500 *C*

Wedgwood

A Wedgwood yellow jasper dip salad bowl and servers, with black relief of grape vine festoons terminating at lions' masks, silver plated rim and utensils, impressed mark to bowl, 19thC, 8½in (21.5cm) diam.
£430–500 *SK(B)*

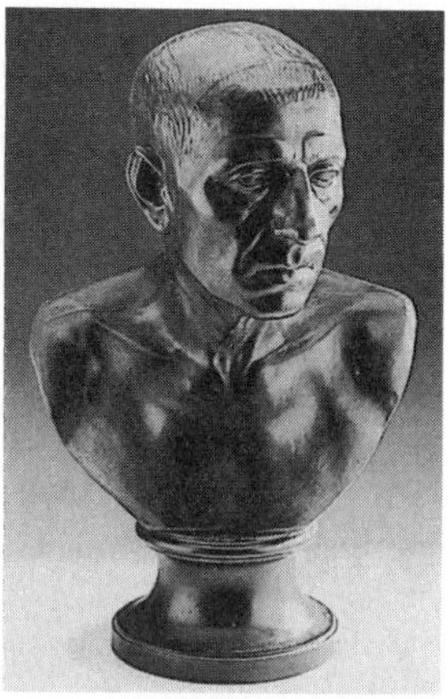

A Wedgwood black basalt library bust of Cicero, slight damage, impressed marks, late 18thC, 20in (51cm) high.
£1,500–2,000 *C*

A Wedgwood majolica centrepiece, the pierced basket top glazed in mottled green, yellow, and brown, the pedestal surrounded by 3 putti, restored, impressed date code 'CBX' for 1869, 16in (41cm) high.
£1,000–1,200 *MJB*

A Wedgwood pearlware jug, with loop handle,inscribed in black 'Robt. and Sah. Gould' and dated '1812', the orange ground decorated in green, puce, black and yellow with scrolling flowers and leaves, beneath a blue line border, impressed mark, 9in (23cm) high.
£400–600 *DN*

A Wedgwood creamware punch stand, on 3 scroll feet, restored, impressed mark, c1780, 7in (18cm) high.
£250–350 *DN*

A Wedgwood blue and white jasper portrait medallion of Admiral Lord Nelson, with a dipped bright blue ground, in a contemporary ebonised wood frame, damaged, impressed mark, c1798, 3½in (9cm) high.
£1,100–1,500 *C*

A Wedgwood dessert service, comprising 41 pieces, decorated with Shell and Seaweed pattern, c1785.
£3,500–4,500 *RIT*

A Wedgwood part tea service, printed in iron red within gilt line rims, comprising: 2 shaped square bread and butter plates, an oval milk jug, 12 teacups and saucers, and 12 side plates, damaged, impressed marks, blue printed Portland vase marks, c1885.
£800–900 *C*

A Wedgwood 3 colour jasper teapot and cover, on a white ground, restored, damaged, impressed 'Wedgwood', early 19thC, 4in (10cm) high, and a lilac jasper cup and saucer, the cup sprigged in white with putti and a dog on a lilac ground.
£1,000–1,200 *S*

l. A Wedgwood Fairyland plaque, decorated with Imps on a Bridge and Tree House pattern, Portland vase mark to the base, 13in (33cm) diam.
£2,500–3,000 *L*

A Wedgwood creamware dinner service, comprising 244 pieces, with bands of blue and gilt fern-like leaves and blue line borders.
£13,000–15,000 *P*

r. A Wedgwood Queen's ware miniature cabaret, comprising 11 pieces, damaged, some pieces with impressed upper case mark and/or painter's marks, c1800.
£1,000–1,500 *CNY*

A Wedgwood creamware part dessert service, comprising: a pair of ice pails, 3 oval dishes, 5 lobed dishes and 25 plates, each piece bearing a crest within a band of flowers and grasses and a gold rim, slight damage, plates 8½in (21.5cm) diam.
£1,100–1,500 *Bea*

A Wedgwood porcelain tricolour oviform urn and cover, applied in white with classically draped figures and trees within moulded stiff leaf paterae and anthemion borders on a blue ground, reserved on a peach ground, enriched in gilt, damaged, impressed upper case mark, 19thC, 7in (17.5cm) high.
£250–300 *CSK*

A Wedgwood 'Candlemas' Fairyland lustre vase, ovoid shape with short neck, decorated with witches' heads and gilt houses divided by light blue panels of imps, Portland Vase mark, pattern No. Z5157, 7½in (19cm) high.
£800–1,000 *P*

A pair of Wedgwood pottery blue and white urns and covers, damaged and repaired, impressed marks, date codes for 1875, 13in (33cm) high.
£1,000–1,500 *CSK*

Wemyss

r. A Wemyss three-handled tyg, painted with wild roses, c1900.
£800–1,000 *RdeR*

A Wemyss pig, decorated with roses, c1900, 20in (50.5cm) long.
£1,500–2,000 *RdeR*

A Wemyss plate, decorated with redcurrants, c1900, 5½in (14cm) diam.
£100–150 *RdeR*

A Wemyss plate, decorated with thistles, c1900, 5½in (14cm) diam.
£100–150 *RdeR*

l. & r. A pair of Wemyss hatpin holders, decorated with green painted rims and pink roses, chipped, impressed and black painted marks, c1900, 6in (15cm) high.
£250–300
c. A Wemyss loving cup, with green painted borders, the sides painted with pink roses, impressed and green painted marks, c1900, 8in (20cm) wide.
£300–350 *MJB*

A Wemyss basket, decorated with sweet peas, c1900, 11½in (29.5cm) wide.
£700–850 *RdeR*

A Wemyss mug, painted with black cockerels, c1900, 5½in (14cm) high.
£300–400 *RdeR*

A Wemyss egg cup, painted with cherries, c1900, 2½in (6.5cm) high.
£50–75 *RdeR*

A Wemyss bulb bowl, painted with crocuses, c1900, 8in (20cm) diam.
£400–500 *RdeR*

A Wemyss Gorden plate, painted with redcurrants, c1900, 8in (20cm) diam.
£250–300 *RdeR*

A Wemyss miniature dog bowl, c1900, 4½in (11.5cm) diam.
£300–400 *RdeR*

A Wemyss preserve pot, painted with raspberries, c1900, 5in (12.5cm) high.
£100–150 *RdeR*

A Wemyss biscuit jar, painted with strawberries, c1920, 4in (10cm) high.
£200–250 *RdeR*

A Wemyss vase, painted with peaches, signed, impressed mark, c1910, 11in (28cm) high.
£800–900 *CSA*

A Wemyss Gorden plate, painted with hairy gooseberries, c1900, 8in (20cm) diam.
£400–550 *RdeR*

A Wemyss three-handled tyg, painted with loganberries, c1925, 5in (12.5cm) high.
£300–400 *RdeR*

r. A Wemyss quaiche, painted with apples, c1920, 10in (25cm) wide.
£300–400 *RdeR*

A Wemyss cup and saucer, painted with roses, c1925, saucer 5in (12.5cm) diam.
£75–100 *RdeR*

A Wemyss Earlshall period mug, painted with a sampler design, handle restored, c1920, 5½in (14cm) high.
£800–1,000 *RdeR*

A Wemyss cauldron, painted with yellow roses, restored, c1920, 5in (12.5cm) high.
£250–300 *RdeR*

A pair of Wemyss candlesticks, painted with wild roses, c1920, 11½in (29.5cm) high.
£400–500 *RdeR*

A Wemyss pig, painted with shamrocks in green, impressed 'Wemyss Ware, RH & S', 6in (15cm) wide.
£320–380 *MJB*

A Wemyss gourd vase, painted with yellow roses, c1926, 9½in (24cm) high.
£150–200 *RdeR*

A Wemyss inkwell, painted with a brown hen and cockerel, c1920, 10in (25cm) wide.
£250–300 *RdeR*

r. A Wemyss pig, painted with pink flowering clover, green painted marks, c1930, 6in (15cm) wide.
£270–300 *MJB*

PORCELAIN

Baskets

A Bow pierced basket of garden flowers, applied with blue and yellow flowerheads, some damage and restoration, c1765, 3½in (9cm) wide.
£520–650 *C*

A Derby two-handled basket, by Stevenson & Hancock, with blue mark, c1850, 6in (15cm) high.
£220–270 *JHW*

A Derby reticulated basket, painted in iron red, purple, yellow, blue and green, with green rope-twist handles terminating in yellow, iron red and green floral clusters, damaged and restored, c1765, 8½in (21cm) wide.
£350–450 *S(NY)*

A Worcester basket, with blue ground, decorated in coloured enamels, a gilt scroll band and dentil rim, crescent mark, c1770, 8in (20cm) wide.
£750–850 *DN*

A Chamberlain's Worcester basket, painted with exotic birds, flowers and fruits, within a border of applied coloured shells and seaweed, moulded gilt rim, damaged and restored, iron red script mark, c1840, 10½in (27cm) wide.
£900–1,200 *CSK*

A Derby botanical basket, decorated in coloured enamels with angular stalked cranesbill within simple gilt borders, restored, inscribed verso, blue mark and pattern number '141', c1790, 10½in (26cm) wide.
£300–500 *DN*

A Worcester basket, printed in blue with the Pinecone pattern, crescent mark, c1770, 12in (30.5cm) diam.
£550–650 *DN*

A Worcester basket, decorated in coloured enamels, the exterior applied with flowerheads picked out in yellow and green, c1770, 7½in (19cm) diam.
£950–1,200 *DN*

Bowls

A Minton punchbowl, Sèvres mark, c1810, 10½in (27cm) diam.
£1,650–1,750 *AMH*

Two Worcester junket bowls, printed in blue with Pinecone pattern, wear and minor chips, crescent marks, c1770, 10in (25cm) diam.
£700–800 *CSK*

A Worcester bowl, printed in blue with the Marrow and Flower Sprays pattern, hatched crescent mark, c1780, 9in (23cm) diam.
£200–300 *DN*

A Meissen bowl, later decorated within shaped green borders edged with gilt lines, minor glaze chips, blue crossed swords mark, Pressnummer '23' gilt decorator's crown mark, a monogram, '32' and 3 stars, porcelain 18thC, decoration late 19thC, 8in (20cm) diam.
£1,300–1,700 *C*

A Sèvres blue ground pot pourri bowl and cover, with elaborate gilt interior, titled cameo bust medallions of Dante, Rossini and Raphael, against a red reserve and moulded putti, the elaborate mask-moulded stem above a domed foot, the pierced flat cover with putto finial, printed 'R.F. S53' in red, 'S.52' in green, 11½in (29cm) high.
£4,000–5,000 *S*

Boxes

A porcelain box and cover, possibly Russian, slight chips, 19thC, 14½in (37cm) wide, with associated white metal stand.
£850–950 *CSK*

A Sèvres casket and hinged cover, painted within a blue céleste border, gilt metal mounts, panel worn and re-gilded, signed 'Maugère', printed and painted marks, 19thC, 12in (30.5cm) wide.
£1,000–1,500 *CSK*

A German porcelain shaped snuff box, the hinged cover with painted en camaieu rose interior, restored and re-gilded, 18thC, 3in (7.5cm) wide.
£3,600–4,200 *CSK*

Candelabra & Candlesticks

A Meissen two-light candelabra, underglazed blue crossed swords and impressed '1129', c1870, 8in (19.5cm) high.
£550–650 *AG*

A pair of Bow candlesticks, the candle holders in the form of tulips, with pierced foliated mounts, on 3 scroll feet, c1765, 8in (20cm) high.
£2,200–2,700 *AG*

A pair of Meissen candelabra, with scrolling footed bases, painted in colours and gilt, minor damage, blue crossed swords mark, c1900, 13in (33cm) high.
£1,600–1,800 *CSK*

A pair of Meissen style candlesticks, representing the four Seasons, detailed in colours and gilt, crossed swords mark in blue and incised script numerals, 19thC, 13in (33cm) high.
£900–1,200 *RBB*

Miller's is a price GUIDE not a price LIST

A pair of Coalport candlesticks, with lime green ground, bases enriched with gilt, cracked and chipped, c1850, 12½in (32cm) high.
£400–500 *C*

Centrepieces

A Meissen table centrepiece, with 4 sweetmeat figures emblematic of the Seasons, the moulded details enriched in turquoise and gilding, chips and repairs, blue crossed swords mark, stand impressed 'H', c1755, 17in (43cm) high.
£10,000–11,000 *C*

A Berlin porcelain mantel clock, with enamel dial, the case painted with scenes of figures in 18thC dress, 2 handles modelled as cherubs' heads, surmounted by a draped urn and cover, standing on 4 scroll feet, enriched in colours and gilt, blue sceptre mark, 19thC, 13½in (34.5cm) high.
£900–1,200 *CSK*

Cups

A Meissen table centrepiece, with pierced panels printed with flowers in gilt foliated cartouches, on 4 encrusted floral scroll feet, underglazed blue crossed swords, 21in (53cm) high.
£1,800–2,200 *AG*

A Meissen clock case, minor chips, crossed swords in underglaze blue, incised numerals, c1870, 12in (30.5cm) high, with brass key.
£3,300–3,900 *S*

A Chelsea-Derby two-handled cup, cover and saucer, painted in colours between turquoise geometric pattern bands, gilt with beads below gilt dentil rims, slight wear, gilt mark, c1775, 5in (12.5cm) high.
£720–800 *CSK*

l. A Royal Crown Derby cup and saucer, decorated with Witches pattern, c1914, saucer 5in (12.5cm) diam.
£60–70 *YY*

Clocks

A Meissen clock and bracket, the dial set in a foliate scroll-moulded body encrusted with flowers and painted with a pair of lovers, the triangular scroll-moulded bracket with head and wings of Time and applied flowers, chipped and repaired, the bracket with crossed swords and dot in underglaze blue, c1770, 28in (71cm) high overall.
£3,700–5,000 *S*

A Chelsea tea bowl and saucer, painted within brown line rims, chipped, red anchor mark to tea bowl, c1756.
£250–300 *CSK*

Chelsea

Chelsea wares are divided into two groups according to the four marks used during the life of the factory.

- Triangle Period (1745–49).
- Raised Anchor Period (1749–52).
- Red Anchor Period (1752–57).
- Gold Anchor Period, (1757–69).

Glaze on early pieces is reasonably opaque, later becoming clearer and more 'glassy'; later still it becomes thicker with a tendency to craze.

A Worcester tea cup and saucer, c1755, 5in (12.5cm) diam.
£400–500 *BHA*

A Worcester large and small coffee cup and saucer, decorated in Kakiemon style with prunus, flowering branches and leaves, blue seal marks, c1770.
£300–400 *DN*

Two Vienna cups and saucers, painted with vignettes of figures at various pursuits in gardens among scattered sprigs of flowers between gilt bands, worn, blue beehive marks, Pressnummern, late 18thC.
£600–700 *CSK*

A Worcester tea bowl, coffee cup and saucer, decorated in iron red and gilt, within blue ground bands with flowerheads, blue seal marks, c1770.
£250–350 *DN*

A Worcester fluted two-handled cup, cover and stand, with flower knop, the C-scroll handles moulded with patera, decorated en grisaille with an interlinked band, on a turquoise ground frieze and gilt borders, c1780, cup 5in (12.5cm) high.
£300–400 *DN*

A Meissen blue ground cup and cover, painted in colours, within a shaped cartouche gilt with foliage, the rims gilt with scrolls, minor chip, blue crossed swords mark, 19thC, 5in (12.5cm) high.
£850–1,000 *CSK*

l. A Meissen yellow ground topographical cabinet cup, cover and stand, underglaze blue crossed swords mark, mid-19thC.
£700–800 *Bon*

A Worcester tea cup, coffee cup and saucer, brightly decorated in Japanese style, with shaped gilt cartouches, on a blue scale ground, blue seal marks, c1770.
£300–400 *DN*

A Worcester fluted tea cup and saucer, decorated in shades of green and gilt, within gilt zig-zag borders, c1775.
£200–300 *DN*

A Sèvres cabinet cup and saucer, painted with classical devices in blue ground panels, between gilt bands, on a green ground, the interior, handle and rims richly gilt, printed marks, 19thC.
£500–700 *CSK*

A Worcester cup and saucer, c1876, saucer 5in (12.5cm) diam.
£100–125 *YY*

Cutlery

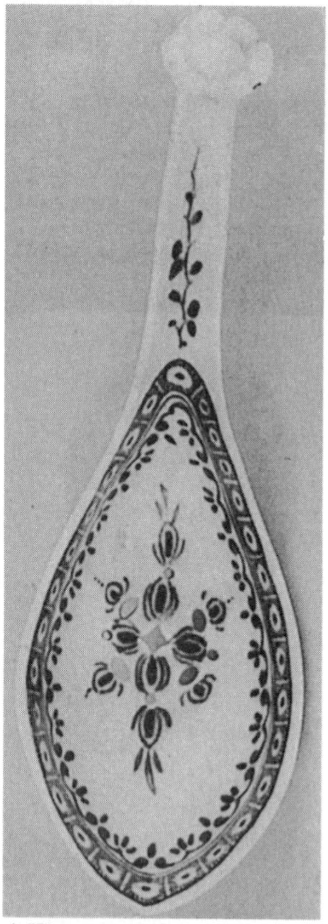

A Worcester blue and white pierced spoon, with flower form finial, painted with the Compass Flower pattern under a trellis border, c1765, 5in (12.5cm) long.
£700–800 *Bon*

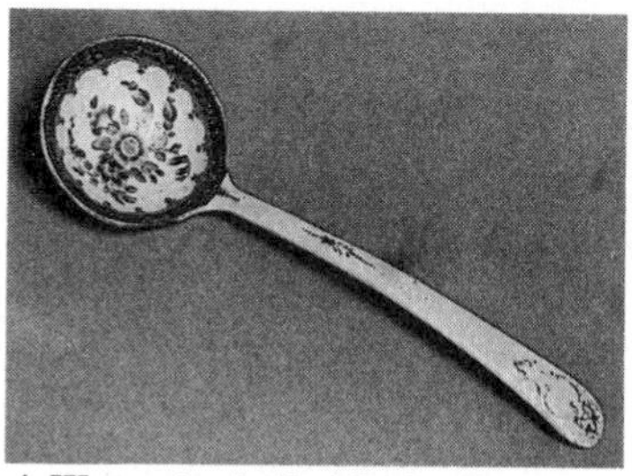

A Worcester ladle, the bowl decorated in coloured enamels, within blue and gilt flower and scroll borders, the tapering handle with scroll and leaf moulded terminal and picked out in gilt, chipped, c1775.
£300–400 *DN*

An assembled set of 24 French porcelain knife and fork handles, probably St. Cloud, each mounted with a reeded silver collar, 12 with a steel knife blade and 12 with a two-tined fork, slight damage, c1730, handles 3½ to 4in (9 to 10cm) long, together with an 18thC shagreen covered cutlery box, with a rose velvet lined and fitted interior and a brass bail handle and escutcheon.
£3,000–3,500 *S(NY)*

Handles of this type have been ascribed to the St. Cloud factory because, apart from the Rouen porcelain production from 1673 to c1696, the St Cloud factory appears to be the only significant French manufacturer producing soft paste porcelain in this 'lambrequin' style during the first half of the 18thC.

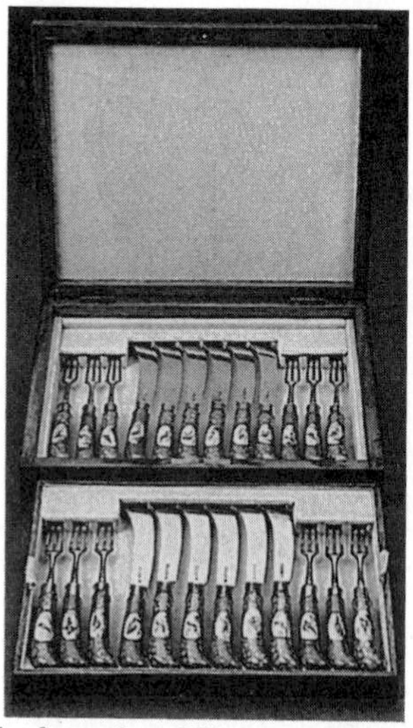

Twelve pairs of Sèvres pattern knife and fork handles, with silver gilt mounts, painted with bright colours within an oval gilt line cartouche, the grounds enriched with gilt caillouté pattern, some wear to gilding, the mounts with hallmarks for George Adams 1868, in a later fitted wooden box lined in beige fabric.
£2,500–3,500 *C*

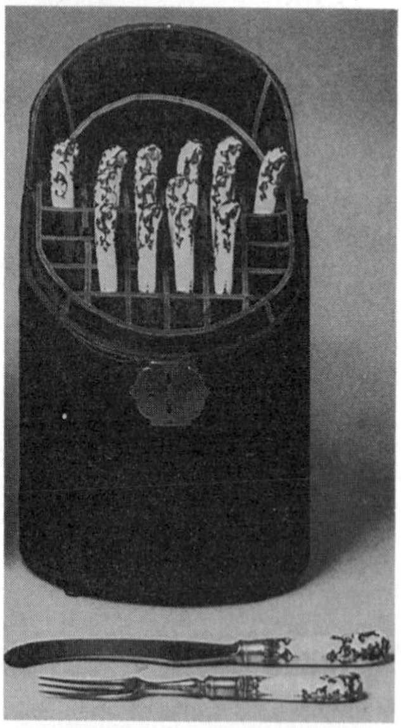

An assembled set of 16 French porcelain knife and fork handles, probably St. Cloud, each mounted with a silver collar and terminal tip, 7 with steel knife blades and 9 with a three-tined fork, c1730, handles 3½ to 4in (9 to 10cm) long, with an 18thC shagreen covered cutlery box with a rose velvet lined and fitted interior, brass bail handle and escutcheon.
£1,600–2,000 *S(NY)*

Figures – Animals

A pair of Bow white figures of buntings, on conical bases, the fronts applied with leafy branches, chipped and repaired, c1760, 4in (10cm) high.
£1,500–1,750 *S(NY)*

These birds were modelled after a pair of Meissen figures of canaries, c1745, but the Bow versions are generally enamelled as buntings.

A Bow model of a tawny owl, in shades of yellow and brown, enriched in green, chipped and restored, c1758, 7½in (19cm) high.
£3,500–4,000 *C*

A late Meissen model of a turkey, after a model by Kändler, with blue head, orange neck and brown and cream plumage, on rocky base, crossed swords mark, 23in (59cm) high.
£3,500–4,500 *P*

A Derby cow and calf group, c1800, 4½in (11cm) high.
£600–650 *RA*

Bow Porcelain c1745–76

- Probably the first porcelain factory in England.
- Early wares were mostly decorated in overglaze enamel colours.
- The clay body is of the phosphatic soft paste type, as used for Lowestoft, early Chaffers and early Derby wares.
- Painter's numerals were sometimes used on base or inside foot rings, as on Lowestoft (and occasionally Chaffers, Liverpool) wares.

r. A pair of Rockingham models of pugs, naturalistically coloured, impressed 'Rockingham Works Brameld', incised model number '76' and 'cl.2' in red, 2½in (6.5cm) high.
£1,100–1,600 *P*

A Chelsea model of a begging pug, after Meissen, naturalistically coloured, wearing a maroon collar applied with gilded bells and a flower, gold anchor mark, 3½in (9cm) high.
£750–950 *P*

A pair of Lowestoft models of pugs, decorated with sponged underglaze manganese, the eyes and collars in underglaze blue, one tail repaired, 3½in (9cm) high.
£4,200–4,800 *P*

Dogs of this type were formerly attributed to Longton Hall, but a Lowestoft origin is now generally accepted. A similar fragment was found near the factory site in 1968.

A Chelsea model of a hound, with light brown markings, wearing a black collar, red anchor mark, 2in (5cm) high.
£2,000–2,500 *P*

Porcelain

Porcelain can be sub-divided into hard and soft paste:

Hard Paste:
- Fired at a higher temperature than soft paste
- Cold feel to the touch
- Chip is flint- or glass-like
- Hard, glittery glaze which is fused to the paste

Soft Paste:
- A file will easily cut into soft paste (not a test to be recommended!)
- Chip is granular
- Warmer feeling to the touch
- Less stable in the kiln – figures in particular were difficult to fire. (No English soft paste figures can compare with Meissen and the other German factories.)
- The glaze was soft as it tended not to fuse into the body as much as glaze on hard paste and was prone to pooling and crazing
- Soft paste is more likely to discolour.

A Rockingham biscuit figure of a ratter and a detachable cage, the base applied with moss, chips and repairs, impressed griffin, 'Rockingham Works Brameld' and incised 'No. 89' marks, on an oval ebonised and plush stand with glass dome, 5in (12.5cm) long.
£1,500–2,000 *C*

This model is believed to be the only recorded example including a cage.

A Meissen model of a pug, wearing a blue collar with gilt bells, sparsely coloured, minor chips, blue crossed swords mark, late 19thC, 10in (25cm) high.
£1,700–2,200 *CSK*

A pair of Bow lions, painted in naturalistic polychrome enamels, on green washed bases, unmarked, c1750, 4in (10cm) wide.
£6,200–7,000 *WW*

A pair of Staffordshire porcelain cows, c1830, 4in (10cm) high.
£700–750 *BHA*

An early Meissen lioness, c1740, 3in (7.5cm) high.
£1,800–2,000 *BHA*

A Rockingham model of a rabbit, white with gilded details to the eyes and whiskers, gilt line to base, impressed 'Rockingham Works Brameld' and incised 'No. 106', 2½in (6cm) long.
£550–650 *P*

Four Meissen monkey figures, modelled as standing musicians wearing 18thC dress, painted and gilt, damaged and restored, blue crossed swords marks, Pressmumern, 19thC, 5½in (14cm) high.
£1,000–1,200 *CSK*

A Belleek biscuit porcelain group of a stag and hounds, damaged and restored, printed Belleek mark, First Period, c1865, 11½in (29cm) high.
£4,700–5,300 *S*

A pair of Derby, Duesbury & Co., stag and doe bocage figures, minor damage, c1770, 8in (20cm) high.
£600–800 *Bon*

Biscuit Porcelain

Biscuit porcelain is unglazed porcelain or earthenware that has been fired only once. The term also refers to white porcelain (especially figures) that has been left undecorated and unglazed.

Figures – People

A Bow figure of The Doctor, c1755, 6½in (16cm) high.
£900–1,200 *DMa*

A pair of Bow figures of New Dancers, on flower encrusted base with 4 scroll feet picked out in turquoise and gilt, damaged, restored, c1765, 9in (23cm) high.
£1,200–1,700 *DN*

Two Bow figures of Harlequin and Columbine, c1755, 5½in (14cm) high.
£2,000–2,500 *DMa*

A Bow figure of an hussar, wearing yellow cape, puce jacket enriched in gilding and iron red trousers, the plinth enriched in turquoise and puce, damaged, c1765, 6in (15cm) high.
£650–800 *C*

A pair of Bow male and female figures, each holding bunches of grapes, on square shaped encrusted floral bases with scroll feet, c1765, 7in (17.5cm) high.
£2,000–2,500 *AG*

A Chelsea group of 2 putti, emblematic of Spring and Summer, damaged, restored, red anchor mark, c1755, 7in (17.5cm) high.
£700–900 *CSK*

A Derby figure of a 'macaroni', with a dog, c1765, 6in (15cm) high.
£900–950 *BHA*

A pair of Chelsea chinoiserie bouquetière figures, enriched in gilding, restored, damage, c1756, 7in (17.5cm) high.
£4,000–6,000 *S*

A pair of Derby male and female figures, the bases encrusted with floral ornamentation, patch marks, c1765, 9in (23cm) high.
£1,200–1,700 *AG*

A set of 4 Derby figures, emblematic of the Continents, blue crossed swords and incised 'No. 200' marks, Robt. Bloor & Co., c1835, 8½in (21.5cm) high.
£1,300–1,800 *C*

A figure of a gladiator, probably Derby, picked out in yellow, turquoise, puce and gilding, patch marks, restored, late 18thC, 5in (12.5cm) high.
£400–500 *Bon*

A set of 4 Derby figures of children representing the Seasons, 2 girls with hats and baskets of flowers and fruit, and 2 boys with corn sheafs and braziers, restored, c1775, 5in (12.5cm) high.
£500–700 *Bon*

Two Derby groups of Procris and Cephalus, and Renaldo and Armida, painted in colours and gilt, incised numerals 'N75' and 'No 76', c1785, 7in (17.5cm) and 8in (20cm) high.
£900–1,200 *CSK*

A pair of Royal Worcester spill vase figures, after original models by James Hadley, sparsely coloured and gilt, slight wear, printed puce and impressed marks, date codes for 1889 and 1890, 9½in (24cm) high.
£1,000–1,300 *CSK*

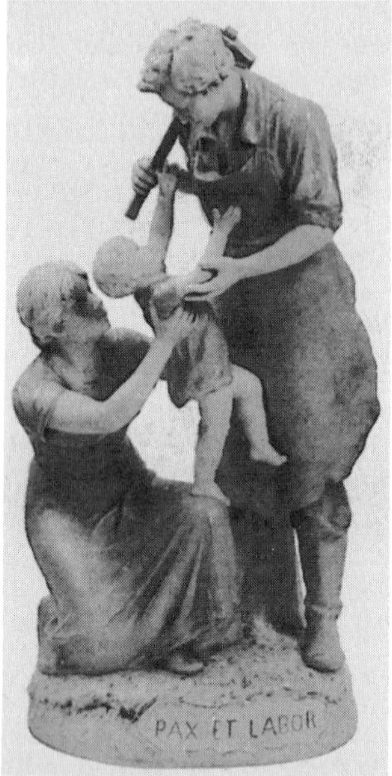

A large Royal Dux group of a mother and child welcoming the blacksmith home, he wearing a leather apron, carrying a hammer over his shoulder, inscribed 'Pax et Labor', 26in (66cm) high.
£2,000–3,000 *Bea*

A Derby set of the French Seasons, after the Tournai models by N. J. F. Gauron, painted with bright polychrome enamels, richly gilt details, scrolling gilt leaf trails to the circular bases, late 18thC, 10in (25cm) high.
£3,000–3,500 *WW*

r. A pair of Derby white biscuit groups of a shepherd and shepherdess, modelled by William-John Coffee and Jean-Jacques Spängler respectively, damaged, the shepherd with incised 'No 396', the shepherdess with incised crowned crossed batons and 'D' mark, 'N 395' and a '*' mark for the repairer, Isaac Farnsworth, 12in (31.5cm) and 10in (25cm) high.
£8,500–10,000 *S(NY)*

An experimental porcelain figure of an Oriental lady, in iron red lined, magenta-edged yellow mob cap, revealing her brown hair, in a long sleeved robe, the front decorated in underglaze blue with trailing foliage, and with overglaze turquoise blue enamel, damaged, probably late 1740s, 10½in (25.5cm) high.
£1,000–1,300 *C*

Although a definitive attribution for this figure is not possible, the likelihood of a Staffordshire origin with London connections should not be discounted. Joseph Wilson's recorded presence, first at Limehouse and then at Newcastle-under-Lyme, may perhaps provide a solution to this conundrum of attribution. No similar figure of this type would appear to be recorded. Apart from the paste and glaze which suggest an early experimental exercise, the underglaze blue decoration has some points of similarity with wares from the Limehouse factory, particularly the small berried foliage on the robe and scrolls about the base. The enamelling is reminiscent of the palette associated with Staffordshire salt glaze.

Make the most of Miller's

Unless otherwise stated, any description which refers to 'a set' or 'a pair' includes a price guide for the entire set or the pair, even though the illustration may show only a single item.

A pair of Berlin porcelain Malabar figures, painted with sprays of flowers, the lady holding a parrot, on square bases, damaged, underglaze blue marks, 19thC, 15in (38cm) and 16½in (42cm) high.
£1,400–1,800 *CSK*

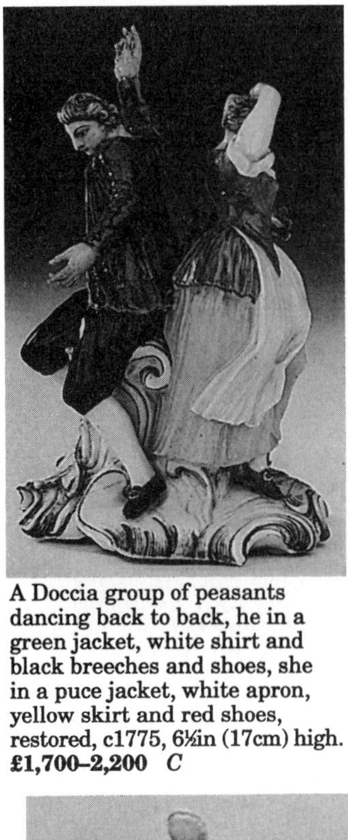

A Doccia group of peasants dancing back to back, he in a green jacket, white shirt and black breeches and shoes, she in a puce jacket, white apron, yellow skirt and red shoes, restored, c1775, 6½in (17cm) high.
£1,700–2,200 *C*

A Böttger figure of a seated Oriental gentleman, in a Böttger lustre gilt lined robe, restored, slight damage, c1720, 3in (7.5cm) high.
£3,400–4,000 *C*

A German porcelain figure of a putto, enriched in gilt, possibly Meissen, 18thC, 5in (12.5cm) high.
£300–400 *CSK*

A pair of Dresden groups, one of cherubic artists gathered around an easel on a rocky outcrop, the other of cherub sculptors gathered around a bust, blue crossed swords mark, one impressed '124' and incised number '4', the other impressed '110', incised '5', 6in (15cm) high.
£2,200–2,700 *L*

A pair of Meissen figures of duellists, modelled by J. J. Kändler, in black, puce, white, turquoise and yellow, restored, blue crossed swords marks at back of base, c1755, 8in (20cm) high.
£4,000–5,000 *C*

A Meissen figure of a child with chickens, c1860, 5in (12.5cm) high.
£650–750 *BHA*

A Meissen figure, The Woodcutter, c1880, 5½in (13.5cm) high.
£1,400–1,500 *BHA*

A pair of Meissen figures of a gardener and companion, damaged, blue crossed swords marks, Pressnummern '122' and '44', incised 'C72' and 'C73', c1880, 7in (17.5cm) and 6½in (16.5cm) high.
£1,400–1,800 *C*

A Meissen figure, The Water Carrier, c1880, 5½in (13.5cm) high.
£1,400–1,500 *BHA*

A pair of Meissen figures of a lady and gentleman, wearing simple 18thC dress, painted in colours and gilt, damaged, blue crossed swords mark, Pressnummern, late 19thC, 5in (12.5cm) high.
£1,000–1,400 *CSK*

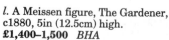

A pair of Meissen figures of a shepherd boy and shepherdess, painted in colours and gilt, restored, blue crossed swords mark, 19thC, 4½in (11cm) high.
£1,500–2,000 *CSK*

l. A Meissen figure, The Gardener, c1880, 5in (12.5cm) high.
£1,400–1,500 *BHA*

A Meissen figure of a lady card player, wearing pale blue lined flowered pink open robe, a striped and flowered skirt and yellow shoes, damaged, blue crossed swords mark, Pressummer '44', incised 'F.64', painted number '10', c1880, 6½in (16.5cm) high.
£1,000–1,400 *C*

A Meissen figure, possibly emblematic of Touch, enriched in colours and gilt, damaged, blue crossed swords marks, incised numerals and Pressnummern, c1900, 11in (28cm) high.
£800–1,200 *CSK*

l. A Meissen group of dancers, their arms interlinked, painted in colours and gilt, restored, slight wear, blue crossed swords mark, incised numerals and Pressnummer, c1880, 6in (15cm) high.
r. A group of dancers, damaged, blue crossed swords mark, incised numerals and Pressnummer, c1900, 6in (15cm) high.
£1,500–2,000 *CSK*

A Nymphenburg figure of Donna Martina, from the Italian Comedy series, modelled by Franz Anton Bustelli, wearing a purple flowered puce shawl, her skirt scattered with indianische Blumen, restored, impressed shield mark on foot, impressed '2, .iii.' in red, c1760, the decoration probably later, 7½in (19cm) high.
£1,800–2,200 *S*

A Vienna family group, decorated in coloured and flowered clothes, the rim with gilt scrolls, restored, blue beehive mark, c1780, 11½in (30cm) high.
£1,800–2,200 *C*

An Italian porcelain figure, emblematic of Winter, painted in bright colours, damaged, restored, painted blue mark, possibly Doccia, early 19thC, 9in (23cm) high.
£250–350 *CSK*

l. A pair of porcelain figures, modelled as a gardener leaning on a spade and his female companion, each on a gilt banded circular base, probably Russian, 19thC, 8½in (22cm) high.
£300–400 *P(EA)*

Flatware

A Bow blue and white plate, c1760, 9in (23cm) diam.
£400–475 *BHA*

A Derby porcelain plate, painted to the centre with a rose in full bloom and a bud, within a gilt rim, slight wear, titled to the reverse 'Moss Rose', iron red mark, c1810, 9in (23cm) diam.
£350–450 *CSK*

A Victorian Minton pierced plate, with floral decoration, ermine mark, c1851, 10½in (27cm) diam.
£600–650 *AMH*

A Chelsea plate from the Duke of Cambridge service, boldly painted in shades of rose, purple, iron red, yellow, green, blue and brown in the centre, with 5 scroll moulded cartouches edged in blue and gold, interrupting a border of gold feathering, within a turquoise green edge continuing to feathering on the underside, some damage, red anchor mark, c1765, 9in (23cm) diam.
£3,500–4,000 *S(NY)*

A Derby porcelain plate, painted to the centre with a single pink flower, within a blue ground border enriched in gilt with stylised foliate scrolls, titled to the reverse 'Seringapatum Hollyhock', slight wear, iron red marks, c1810, 9in (23cm) diam.
£270–320 *CSK*

A Victorian Minton pierced plate, painted by Thomas Kirkby, ermine mark, c1851, 10½in (27cm) diam.
£650–750 *AMH*

l. A Spode Imari pattern dish, c1880, 12in (30.5cm) wide.
£100–125 *YY*

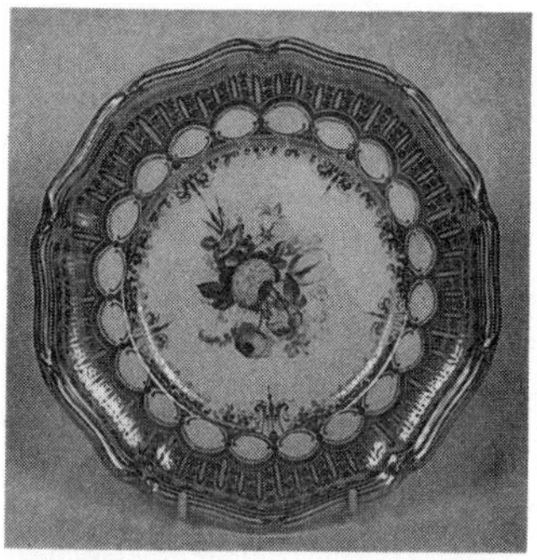

A Davenport plate, with heavily gilded flower decoration, c1860, 9in (23cm) diam.
£300–350 *BHA*

A Royal Crown Derby plate, decorated with Witches pattern, c1914, 9in (23cm) diam.
£70–80 *YY*

A Minton dessert plate, Albans pierced shape with cloisonné decoration, c1875, 10in (25cm) diam.
£800–900 *AMH*

A Worcester blue and white dish, of serrated outline, painted with the Pickle Leaf Vine pattern, crescent mark, c1760, 3in (7.5cm) wide.
£200–300 *Bon*

A Worcester blue and white pickle dish, painted in underglaze blue with the Transparent Rock pattern, c1760, 3in (7.5cm) wide.
£600–1,000 *Bon*

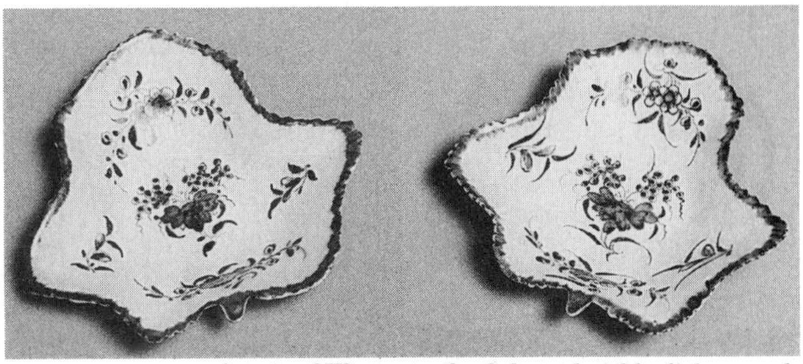

A pair of Worcester leaf-shaped pickle dishes, each painted in blue with the Pickle Leaf Vine pattern, within a blue line border, damaged, c1760, 4in (10cm) wide.
£300–500 *DN*

A Worcester plate, decorated in coloured enamels, the French green ground border with gilt scroll edge and suspending puce floral garlands, c1770, 8in (20cm) diam.
£300–400 *DN*

A Worcester plate, painted in blue with the K'ang H'si Lotus pattern, the reverse with two Chinese style flowersprays, damaged, emblem mark, c1775, 7in (17.5cm) diam.
£150–200 *DN*

A Worcester plate, with fluted rim, painted in blue with the Hundred Antiques pattern, seven-character Chinese style marks, c1775, 8in (20cm) diam.
£200–300 *DN*

A Worcester plate, centrally decorated in coloured enamels within a turquoise 'shagreen' and gilt scroll cartouche, the rim with trailing flowersprays, within blue and gilt borders, 8½in (21.5cm) diam.
£300–500 *DN*

A Worcester armorial plate, from the Duke of Clarence service, the centre painted in underglaze blue, iron red, gold and grisaille, with the arms of the Duke of Clarence and St. Andrew, encircled by the blue and gold Garter and motto 'Honi soit qui mal y pense', slight wear, crowned Flight and open crescent mark in underglaze blue, c1789, 9½in (24cm) diam.
£4,500–6,500 *S(NY)*

This rare plate is from the first of 2 services ordered from the Worcester factory of John and Joseph Flight in 1789 by H.R.H. Prince William Henry (1765–1837), who in 1830 became King William IV. It was most certainly commissioned to celebrate the new title of Duke of Clarence and St. Andrew, which he had received earlier that year.

A pair of creamware plates, possibly Dutch decorated, each painted in a limited palette, within a cell pattern border and moulded shaped and beaded rims, damaged, c1750, 9½in (24cm) diam.
£350–450 *CSK*

A Meissen tray, blue crossed swords mark, star and numeral '4', impressed 'I.33', Marcolini period, c1800, 11in (28cm) wide.
£150–200 *Bon*

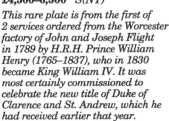

A Meissen plate, painted with a border of pendant flower garlands and an elaborately pierced rim, damaged, blue crossed swords and dot mark, Pressnummer '6', c1760, 9in (23cm) diam.
£450–550 *CSK*

A Meissen dish, with a moulded Dulong pattern border, the centre painted in a muted autumnal palette, the border enriched in pink lustre and gilding, damaged, cancelled blue crossed swords and star mark, Pressnummern '4' and '42', the porcelain late 18thC, the decoration late 19thC, 17½in (44.5cm) wide.
£700–800 *C*

A French plate, painted with blackberries and spider trompe l'oeil, factory unknown, late 19thC, 9in (23cm) diam.
£200–275 *BHA*

A set of 15 Berlin dessert plates, each centrally decorated in coloured enamels, border picked out in green, brown and gilt, damaged, marks in blue and stencilled mark in red, damaged, c1835, 9½in (24cm) diam.
£700–900 *DN*

A Vienna plate, the black centre with honeysuckle design, 19thC, 9½in (24cm) diam.
£300–350 *BHA*

A Vienna dish, painted with a titled classical scene of 'Peles u. Thetis', on a claret ground, minor rubbing, shield mark and 'P.' in blue, signed 'Knoeller', late 19thC, 16in (40.5cm) diam.
£2,000–2,700 *S*

A Vienna tray, painted with scene entitled 'Triumph Der Venus', signed Jäger, c1880, 15½in (40cm) high.
£1,500–1,600 *AMH*

A Vienna plaque, painted with a titled classical scene of Bacchus and Ariadne, within a gilt frame, flanked by panels of gilt scroll on a red ground, signed 'Knoeller', shield mark in underglaze blue, c1880, 13in (33cm) diam.
£2,000–2,700 *S*

Jugs

A Belleek jug, black transfer mark, 19thC, 7¼in (18.5cm) high.
£220–270 *JHW*

l. A large Sunderland lustre jug, inscribed with a verse 'The Sailor's Tear', also bearing transfers of the Bridge and 'Sailor's Farewell', with painted and pink lustre details, the presentation inscription dated '1841', 9in (23cm) high.
£350–450 *RBB*

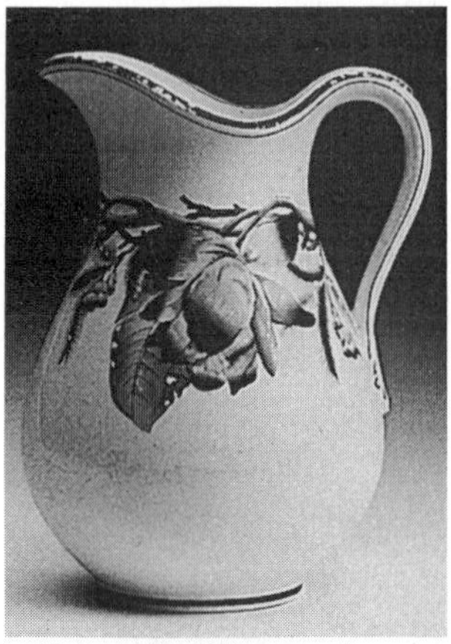

A Minton New Stone part washstand service, printed and coloured within green line rims, comprising a baluster jug, 2 circular bowls, a soap dish cover and liner, and a cover for a toothbrush holder, damaged, impressed marks and pattern 'A2534', date code for 1855, jug 12in (30.5cm) high.
£300–400 *C*

A Mintons part washstand service, printed with the Farley pattern, comprising a pear-shaped jug, 2 circular bowls, a sponge bowl and liner, and a toothbrush holder and cover, damaged, impressed and black printed marks, pattern number 'A3735', date codes for 1885, jug 10½in (27cm) high.
£750–900 *C*

A Worcester cabbage leaf-moulded mask jug, painted with exotic birds on an apple green ground, within shaped gilt C-scroll cartouches, beneath a border of moulded gilt stiff leaves, restored, slight damage, c1770, 8in (20cm) high.
£2,200–2,800 *C*

A Worcester blue and white mug, with a ribbed handle, painted with a fenced garden between an Oriental hut and a fisherman by an island below a crescent moon, small chip re-stuck to base, some firing faults, painter's mark, c1754, 2½in (6.5cm) high.
£2,200–2,900 *CSK*

A Worcester jug, with scroll handle and mask spout, painted in blue with the Dragon pattern, damaged, crescent mark, c1760, 7½in (19cm) high.
£200–300 *DN*

A Worcester jug, firing crack, c1760, 8in (20cm) high.
£1,000–1,250 *BHA*

A Lowestoft cylindrical mug, with scroll handle with thumb rest, painted in colours, with a border of stylised flower garlands above flowersprays, in the style of Thomas Curtis, 3in (7.5cm) high.
£800–1,000 *P*

The border is inspired by New Hall porcelain of similar date.

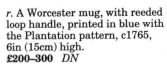

A Worcester jug, with scroll handle and mask spout, printed in blue with the Natural Sprays pattern, damaged, crescent mark, c1765, 6in (15cm) high.
£150–200 *DN*

Mugs

A Liverpool mug, Pennington's factory, with grooved loop handle, painted in blue with the 'Haymakers', misfired, c1760, 6in (15cm) high.
£1,700–2,200 *S*

There are 2 versions of the 'Haymakers' on porcelain. This example is the first version, taken from an engraving published by Robert Sayer in 1766. A Liverpool tile printed with the other scene is illustrated by Anthony Ray, Liverpool Printed Tiles, *fig. c3-5. That design is taken from an engraving entitled 'Harvest Home' by June, after Grimm.*

r. A Worcester mug, with reeded loop handle, printed in blue with the Plantation pattern, c1765, 6in (15cm) high.
£200–300 *DN*

A pair of Derby porter mugs, each painted with a rural scene within a gilded oval border, surrounded by bold acanthus leaf scrolling in orange and gilt, painted red marks and number '13', 4½in (11cm) high.
£950–1,200 *P*

Pastille Burners

A porcelain pastille burner and stand, perhaps Spode, modelled as a cottage, the interior of the base enriched in salmon pink, one pierced window with a face peering out, damaged, c1830, 5½in (14cm) high.
£600–800 *S*

A pair of Staffordshire porcelain cottage shaped pastille burners, windows picked out in gilt, applied with flowers and coloured granitic decoration, c1835, 3in (7.5cm) high.
£100–150 *DN*

A porcelain pastille burner, damaged, 4½in (11.5cm) high.
£120–170 *Bea*

A large porcelain pastille burner modelled as a multi-roofed thatched villa, painted, heightened in gilt and decorated with shredded clay and floral encrustation, on a shaped base, early 19thC, 6in (15cm) high.
£1,700–2,300 *P(EA)*

Plaques

A Berlin plaque, impressed sceptre mark, 'KPM' and 'H', 12½ by 7½in (31.5 by 19cm), in a carved and giltwood frame.
£4,000–5,000 *P*

A Continental plaque, painted by Mme. Palini, with Cardinal Richelieu in bright red habit and skull cap, dated '1840', 14½ by 13in (37 by 33cm), in a carved and giltwood frame.
£2,000–2,700 *P*

A German plaque, painted with a three-quarter figure of Ruth, after Landelle, 8½ by 6in (21.5 by 15cm), unframed.
£550–700 *P*

l. A German porcelain round plaque, decorated in coloured enamels with the Madonna and Child, after Raphael, 19thC, 4½in (11.5cm) diam, in a carved giltwood Florentine frame.
£200–250 *DN*

Pots

A pair of Derby two-handled flower pots and stands, painted in green, purple, iron red and enriched in gilding, with gilt rims and foot rims, damaged, crown, crossed batons, 'D' marks and No. '40' in iron red, Duesbury & Kean, c1810, 7in (17.5cm) high.
£7,000–8,000 *C*

A Pinxton yellow ground flared two-handled flower pot, painted in the manner of William Billingsley, with a landscape within a brown line and linked circle cartouches, enriched in brown and with brown line rim, slight damage, c1800, 5½in (13.5cm) high.
£2,200–2,900 *C*

Sauceboats

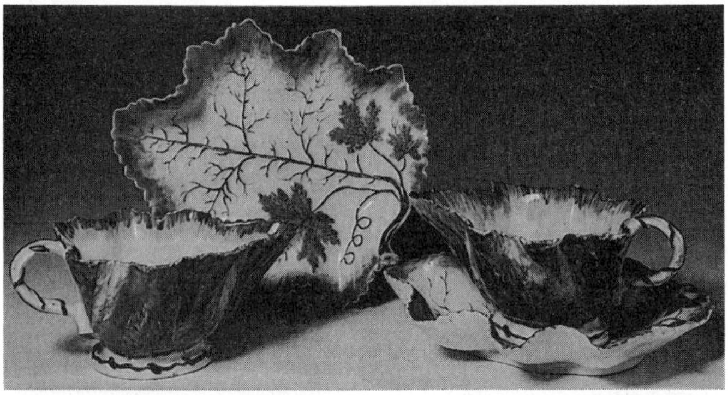

A pair of Bow sauceboats and stands, each with serrated green edges, with moulded veins and tendrils picked out in purple, the sauceboats moulded on the outside with overlapping leaves, stands 7½in (18.5cm) wide.
£3,500–4,000 *P*

A Worcester lobed sauceboat, with scroll handle, the interior painted in blue with the Sauceboat Peony pattern, within a cell diaper band, the exterior moulded with sprays of roses and leaves, crescent mark, c1770, 7in (17.5cm) wide.
£350–500 *DN*

A First Period Worcester sauceboat, painted in colours within moulded circular cartouches, iron red arrow and circle painter's mark, 7½in (19cm) wide.
£1,100–1,500 *L*

A Worcester yellow ground sauceboat, brightly decorated in coloured enamels, the fluted ground decorated in famille verte enamels with scattered flowers, restored, c1770, 7½in (19cm) wide.
£500–700 *DN*

Scent Bottles

A Chelsea scent bottle and stopper, the stopper with pink rose finial, the carnelian intaglio seal with a profile of a classical nobleman, gold mounts, slight damage, c1765, 3in (7.5cm) high.
£3,500–4,000 *S*

A gold mounted scent bottle, of a 'Girl in a Swing' type, decorated in yellow, white, puce, black and turquoise, the gold mount to the neck with chain attachment, slight damage, c1755, 4in (10cm) high.
£5,000–6,000 *C*

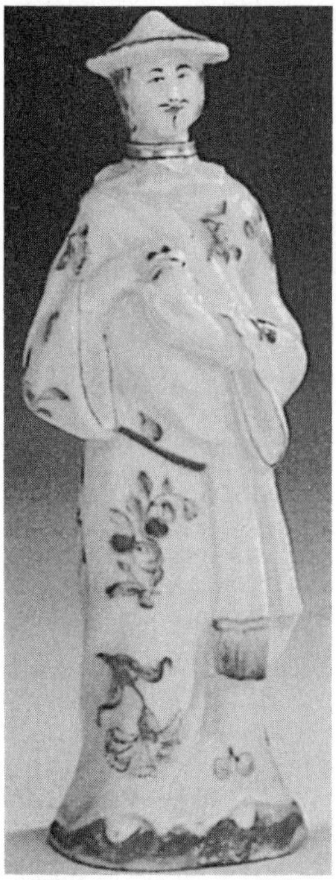

A 'Girl in a Swing' gold mounted scent bottle, modelled as an Oriental gentleman holding a brightly coloured dove, restored, c1755, 4in (10cm) high.
£5,000–6,000 *C*

A Meissen scent bottle and stopper, with metal mounts, modelled as a boy wearing 18thC dress, reaching around a tree stump grasping the horn of a goat, applied with fruiting vines, chipped, indistinct blue crossed swords mark, late 19thC, 3in (7.5cm) high.
£850–1,200 *CSK*

MILLER'S COMPARES . . .

I A 'Girl in a Swing' gold mounted scent bottle modelled as a squirrel, with iron red coat and black fur markings, the gilt mount to the neck with a chain attachment, the mount to the base with hinged gold cover and mirrored interior, minor chips, c1755, 2½in (6cm) high.
£7,200–8,000 *C*

II A 'Girl in a Swing' gold mounted scent bottle bottle modelled as a pug bitch, enriched in iron red and with a black muzzle, the gold mount to the neck with chain attachment, ribbed gold mount to the base, slight damage, c1755, 2½in (6cm) high.
£5,500–6,300 *C*

The descriptions of the scent bottles are very similar but *Item I* sold for considerably more at auction than *Item II*. This was due to the fact that *Item I's* theme (a squirrel) was rarer than *Item II's*. As a result bidding for *Item I* was fierce, driving the price upwards. If a few bidders are determined to own an object, such as in this instance, condition of an item can become a secondary consideration. *C*

Services

A Derby Ivy pattern part dinner service, comprising 99 pieces, crowned crossed batons, 'D' marks and '22' in iron red, the plates with incised size numbers, c1820.
£10,000–11,000 *S(NY)*

A Coalport tea service, comprising: a teapot, cover and stand, sucrier and cover, slop bowl, 2 cake plates, 9 tea cups and saucers and 6 coffee cans, all richly decorated with floral garlands on a solid gilt ground, damaged, c1810, teapot 8in (20cm) high.
£2,000–2,500 *S*

A Davenport Imari pattern dinner service, comprising 81 pieces, pattern No. 51, c1830.
£4,800–5,200 *RIT*

An Edwardian Royal Crown Derby tea set, comprising 16 pieces, and a lobed circular tray, decorated with red printed flowers, enriched with blue and gold, red printed marks, pattern No. 2712, tray 16½in (42cm) diam.
£600–800 *MJB*

A Royal Crown Derby miniature cabaret set, painted in Imari palette with panels of stylised flowers, comprising: a teapot and cover, sugar bowl and cover, cream jug, 2 cups and saucers and a quatrefoil tray, slight wear, printed marks, various date codes for 1915 and 1916.
£1,000–1,400 *CSK*

A New Hall Imari pattern part tea and coffee service, comprising: teapot and cover, sugar bowl and cover, milk jug, 2 cake dishes, 18 teacups, 12 coffee cans and 15 saucers, each painted in underglaze blue, iron red, black and gold with fruiting tree and other foliage within a gilt edged rim, the teapot, sugar bowl and milk jug with further gilt foliage, some damage, some pieces with pattern No. '446' and some with a painter's mark in iron red, c1800, teapot 6in (15cm) high.
£950–1,250 *S(NY)*

A Minton tea service, decorated in vivid colours and gilt, comprising: a teapot, cover and stand, sucrier and cover, saucer dish, milk jug, 8 tea cups, and 7 coffee cans and 6 saucers, some damage, mark and pattern No. '539' in blue, c1810.
£4,700–5,200 *S*

A porcelain miniature part tea service, encrusted with flowers within gilt flowerheads and scrolls, enriched in colours, comprising: a teapot and cover, sugar bowl and cover, milk jug and water jug, damaged, probably Minton, blue crossed swords mark, c1830.
£750–900 *CSK*

A composite Meissen, Dresden and Volkstedt Hausmaler chocolate service, painted within turquoise borders edged with pink lines and gilt dentil pattern rims, slight damage, cancelled blue crossed swords marks to sugar bowl and cups and saucers, blue crossed hayforks mark to chocolate pot and hot milk jug, slight damage, late 19thC, the tray 14in (36cm) wide.
£4,200–5,000 *C*

A Worcester Mansfield pattern part tea service, painted with a trellised baroque border, comprising: teapot and cover, sparrowbeak jug, slop bowl, and 6 teabowls and saucers, some damage, hollow crescent marks, c1770.
£700–1,000 *Bon*

A Paris black printed tea service, each piece decorated with figures in domestic settings or with characters in national costume, comprising: teapot and cover, smaller pot and cover, 2 sucriers and covers, slop basin, and 11 cups and saucers, minor cracks, mid-19thC.
£600–900 *Bon*

A Sèvres bleu céleste tête à tête, painted with pink roses within gilt foliage garlands, comprising: a milk jug, sugar bowl and cover, 2 cups and saucers and a tray, some damage and repair, blue and green interlaced 'L' marks enclosing date letter 'P' for 1768, painter's mark 'P', various incised marks, the bleu céleste ground probably later.
£4,500–5,000 *C*

Tea, Coffee & Chocolate Pots

A Chelsea Documentary hexagonal teapot and cover, decorated in puce monochrome, attributed to Jefferyes Hamett O'Neale, damaged, replacement metal spout and finial, c1752, 6in (15cm) high.
£5,200–6,000 *S*

A Worcester teapot and cover, with flower knop, printed in blue with the Birds in Branches pattern, small chip to spout, hatched crescent mark, c1775, 5in (12.5cm) high.
£400–500 *DN*

A pair of Meissen teapots and covers, modelled by J. J. Kändler, as a cockerel and hen with chicks, the tail feathers of the cockerel forming the handle, the chick forming the cover on the hen, both with iron red combs and wattles, black and brown feather markings, restored, the hen with blue crossed swords mark, the cockerel with Pressnummer '15' twice, c1740, 6½ and 8in (16 and 20cm) long.
£9,500–11,000 *C*

A Lowestoft teapot, with rose design, c1765, 6in (15cm) high.
£875–975 *BHA*

A Böttger white porcelain teapot and cover, decorated in low relief with sprays of chrysanthemums on each side and cover, the interior fitted with metal strainer, 4½in (11.5cm) high.
£10,000–12,000 *P*

A Meissen Kakiemon bullet-shaped teapot and cover, the spout and handle enriched in iron red, damaged, blue crossed swords mark, c1735, 4in (10cm) high.
£750–900 *CSK*

A Worcester baluster-shaped coffee pot and domed cover, printed in blue with the Fence pattern, hatched crescent mark, c1770, 10in (25cm) high.
£300–400 *DN*

A Meissen chocolate pot, 18thC, 4½in (11.5cm) high.
£650–700 *RA*

Miller's is a price GUIDE not a price LIST

Tureens

A Meissen blue and white tureen and cover, with moulded strapwork handles and Frauenkopf terminals, damaged, blue crossed swords mark and 'K', c1730, 9in (23cm) high.
£3,000–4,000 *C*

A Chamberlain's Worcester armorial tureen, cover and stand, the body painted with 2 coats-of-arms below a pale blue ground band, reserved with panels painted with exotic birds amongst branches between gilt C-scrolls and foliage, below a gilt beaded band, minor firing faults, painted mark to cover, c1820, the stand 12in (30.5cm) diam.
£1,700–2,200 *CSK*

The arms are those of the Prescot family.

A pair of Worcester tureens, covers and stands, the rustic handles and finial with flower terminals, printed in blue with the Pinecone pattern and allied prints, gadroon moulded rims, crescent marks.
£800–1,200 *P*

A Meissen Schneeballen tureen and cover, with stag trophy finial and scroll handles, chipped and repaired, crossed swords in underglaze blue, 14in (36cm) high.
£4,200–5,000 *S*

Urns

A pair of urns, painted with landscapes and filled with bouquets of flowers, of rococo-scroll outline, enriched in turquoise and gilt, above square plinth bases, damaged, possibly Coalbrookdale, c1825, 6in (15cm) high.
£550–650 *CSK*

Vases

A pair of Chelsea vases, gold anchor, c1760, 6½in (16cm) high.
£2,000–2,500 *BHA*

A Worcester Flight and Barr flared jardinière and stand, decorated in coloured enamels, within an oval gilt cartouche and titled 'Adelaide', on a bright yellow ground, the stand inscribed beneath in brown, painted marks in brown, c1800, 9in (23cm) high.
£400–600 *DN*

A 'Warwick' vase and cover, possibly Derby, colourfully painted, the rim decorated in relief and gilt, some wear, c1820, 10in (25cm) high.
£1,200–1,700 *S*

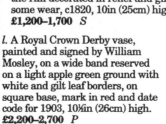

l. A Royal Crown Derby vase, painted and signed by William Mosley, on a wide band reserved on a light apple green ground with white and gilt leaf borders, on square base, mark in red and date code for 1903, 10¼in (26cm) high.
£2,200–2,700 *P*

A Chamberlain's Worcester jardinière, c1820, 7½in (19cm) high.
£1,300–1,400 *AMH*

A Royal Crown Derby vase and cover, by Desire Leroy, signed, painted within gilt surrounds with turquoise jewelling, on a pink ground, supported on quartrelobed oval foot, marks in red and date code for 1901, 6in (15cm) wide.
£3,500–4,000 *P*

A pair of Royal Crown Derby vases, painted and gilt in the Imari palette, slight wear, printed and incised marks, date codes for 1904, 8½in (21.5cm) high.
£1,000–1,200 *CSK*

A garniture of Derby 'Long Tom' vases, decorated and gilt in a vivid Imari palette, with a design of alternating panels of flowers and foliage, damaged and restored, red printed marks and '24', c1830, 21 and 24½in (53 and 62cm) high.
£5,000–5,500 *S*

A Royal Crown Derby jewelled vase and cover, painted and signed by Albert Gregory, on a dark blue ground, with gilt handles, the cover with gilt pinecone finial, on square base, marks in red and date code for 1911, 13½in (34.5cm) high.
£5,700–6,200 *P*

A pair of Vauxhall vases, painted in bright colours, with gilt footrims, 4in (10cm) high.
£2,000–2,500 *P*

A Minton pâte sur pâte decorated vase, c1891, 8½in (21.5cm) high.
£1,100–1,200 *AMH*

A pair of Minton blue ground 'Dresden scroll' vases and pierced covers, painted within leaf moulded sections enriched in gilt, damaged and restored, c1835, 12½in (32cm) high.
£450–550 *CSK*

A Royal Worcester vase and cover, with Renaissance style scroll borders and animal head handles shaded in blush ivory and coral, painted on a matt blue ground with 2 polar bears on a stepped glacier with mountains in the distance, signed H. Davis, shape No. 1764, date code for 1903, 16in (40.5cm) high.
£6,000–8,000 *P*

A Minton flower encrusted vase and cover, design No. 219, the base heightened in turquoise and gilt, c1838.
£900–1,100 *Bon*

A Worcester vase, with 2 scroll-moulded pistol-shaped handles, printed in blue with Pinecone pattern, damaged and restored, c1770, 11½in (29cm) high.
£300–500 *CSK*

A garniture of 3 Worcester Barr, Flight and Barr vases, painted with buildings in rural landscapes, with white beaded borders, the reverse with gilt foliate and scrollwork motifs, restored, impressed marks, c1810, 5½and 3½in (14 and 9cm) high.
£1,500–2,000 *S*

A Meissen Augustus Rex vase, painted and heightened in gilding, minor wear, 'AR' monogram in underglaze blue, c1730, 13in (33cm) high.
£12,000–15,000 *S*

Miscellaneous

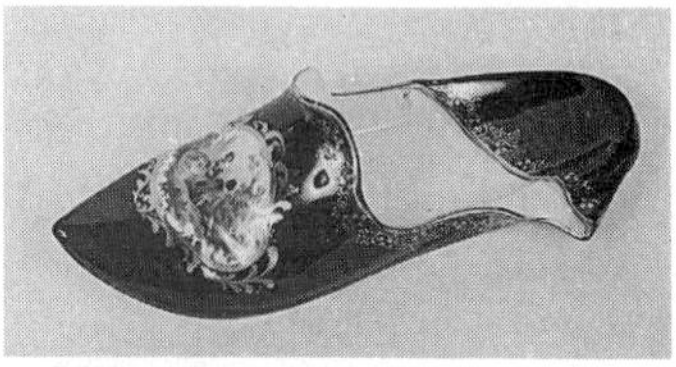

A Meissen slipper, the dark blue ground gilded with hand painted country scene, 19thC, 6½in (16.5cm) long.
£300–400 *BHA*

An early Bow six-shell sweeetmeat stand, painted in famille rose style, 8in (20cm) high.
£800–900 *P*

A Royal Worcester vase and cover, painted with a basket of fruit on a table, signed R. Sebright, reserved on a dark blue ground gilt with cailloutė design in French style, on circular foot, shape No. 2247, date code for 1921, 9in (23cm) high.
£2,500–3,000 *P*

A Meissen vase, the dark blue ground with gilt and floral decoration, 20thC, 6½in (16.5cm) high.
£375–475 *BHA*

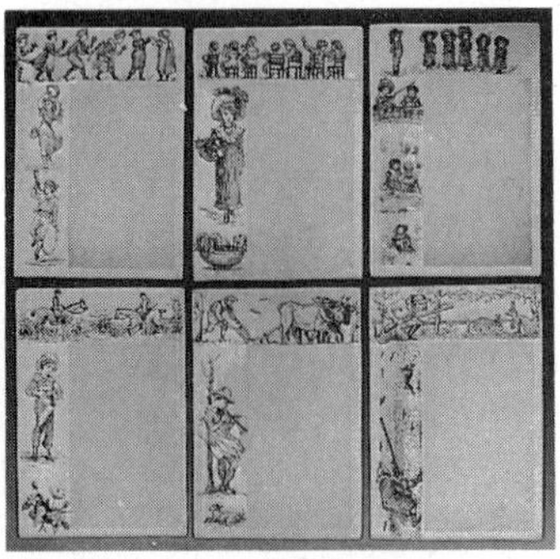

Six Mintons porcelain menu tablets, painted in sepia tones, slight wear and restoration, impressed factory mark, registration lozenge and date code for 1879, each 6 by 4in (15 by 10cm).
£450–650 *CSK*

A pair of Royal Worcester vases and covers, painted and signed by Harry Stinton, minor chip, shape No. 2425, printed mark in puce, date cypher for 1911, initialled 'CE' in burnt orange, some damage, 11in (28cm) high.
£3,000–3,500 *HSS*

A pair of Sèvres style blue celeste vases, with gilt metal mounts, painted with couples wearing 18thC dress, damaged, 19thC, 12in (30.5cm) high.
£1,000–1,200 *CSK*

A Victorian porcelain inkwell on tray, unmarked, c1900, 9in (23cm) wide.
£170–220 *JHW*

A Caughley inkwell, with separate central well fitting with 4 holes for quills, printed in blue with fruit and flower sprigs, traces of 'C' mark, 10in (25cm) diam.
£700–750 *P*

A Caughley tapering sided tea cannister and cover, printed in blue with the Fenced Garden pattern, with monogram 'EW', c1780, 5in (12.5cm) high.
£450–500 *DN*

A Frankenthal salt cellar, decorated in yellow and puce, blue mark, c1765, 6in (15cm) high.
£450–550 *DN*

A Grainger's Worcester candle extinguisher, modelled as a lady's head, in white glazed parian with gilded highlights, shape 204, printed shield mark, 3½in (9cm) high.
£400–450 *P*

A pair of Paris porcelain flasks and stoppers, modelled as seated Highland figures, enriched in gilt, chipped and restored, possibly Jacob Petit, mid-19thC, 7in (17.5cm) high.
£420–500 *CSK*

A Worcester Jabberwocky pattern jar and cover, c1765, 6in (15cm) high.
£1,250–1,450 *BHA*

Goss & Crested China

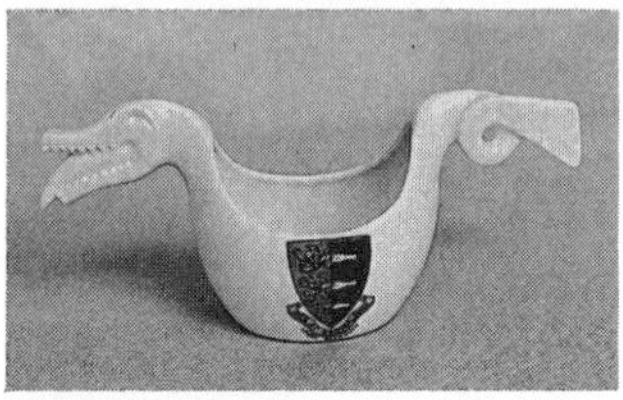

A Norwegian dragon-shaped beer bowl, by W. H. Goss, c1910, 6in (15cm) long.
£25–30 *G&CC*

A fireplace, by Willow, with some colouring, c1920, 2½in (6cm) high.
£18–20 *G&CC*

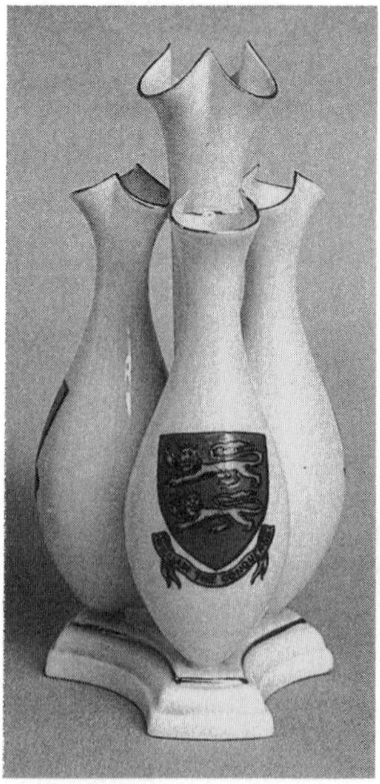

A Pompeian centrepiece, by W. H. Goss, c1910, 5in (12.5cm) high.
£70–80 *G&CC*

An Aylesbury duck, by W. H. Goss, c1925, 4in (10cm) long.
£275–300 *G&CC*

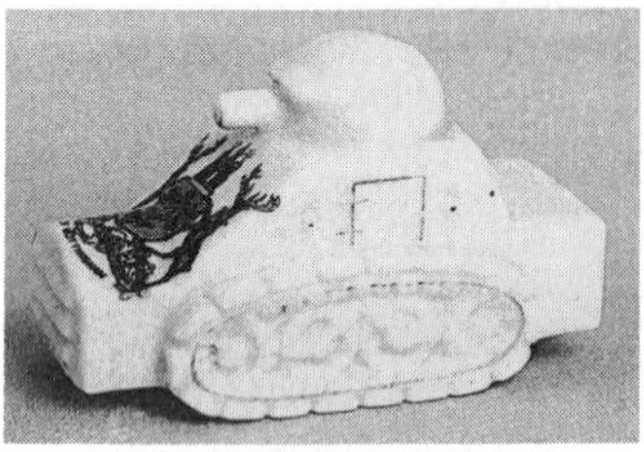

An Arcadian model of an armoured car, c1916, 3½in (9cm) long.
£35–45 *G&CC*

A WWI cannon shell, by Corona, c1916, 2½in (6.5cm) high.
£10–12 *G&CC*

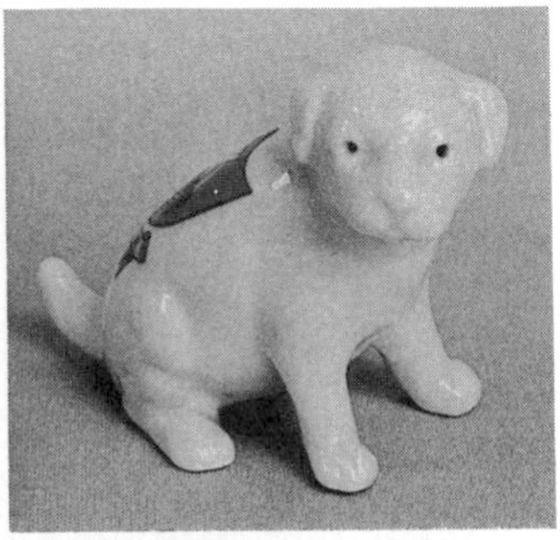

A Labrador puppy, by Grafton, c1920, 2½in (6cm) high.
£18–20 *G&CC*

An egg, by Arcadian, inscribed 'A Little Bird from Boxford', c1925, 2in (5.5cm) high.
£30–40 *G&CC*

A Devon oak pitcher, by W. H. Goss, c1910, 6in (15cm) high.
£5–6 *G&CC*

A black cat in a boot, by Arcadian, c1925, 2in (5.5cm) high.
£65–75 *G&CC*

A rabbit, by Carlton, c1910, 2½in (6cm) long.
£10–12 *G&CC*

l. A Portland vase, by W. H. Goss, c1910, 2in (5.5cm) high.
£5–7 *G&CC*

Did you know?
MILLER'S* Antiques Price Guide *builds up year-by-year to form the most comprehensive antiques photo-reference library available.

l. An Ostend Flemish bottle, by W. H. Goss, c1910, 2½in (6cm) high.
£8–10 *G&CC*

l. A Saffron Walden covered urn, by W. H. Goss, c1910, 4½in (11.5cm) high.
£30–40 *G&CC*

A cheese dish, by Gemma, c1910, 3in (7.5cm) long.
£6–8 *G&CC*

A basket of milk, with brown tops, by Arcadian, c1925, 2½in (6.5cm) high.
£18–22 *G&CC*

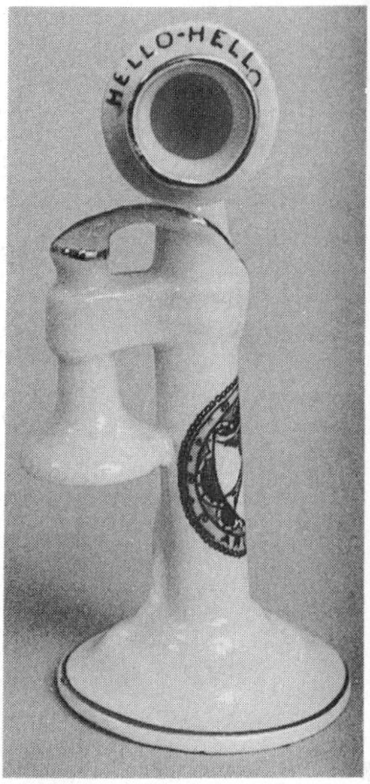

A stick telephone, by Carlton, c1925, 7in (17.5cm) high.
£25–30 *G&CC*

A model of a WWI hand grenade, by Arcadian, c1916, 2½in (6.5cm) high.
£15–20 *G&CC*

A Maltese vase à canard, by W. H. Goss, c1920, 1½in (4cm) high.
£15–20 *G&CC*

r. A Gravesend Oriental water cooler, by W. H. Goss, c1925, 3in (7.5cm) high.
£20–25 *G&CC*

r. A comical dog, by Gemma, c1920, 3½in (9cm) high.
£30–40 *G&CC*

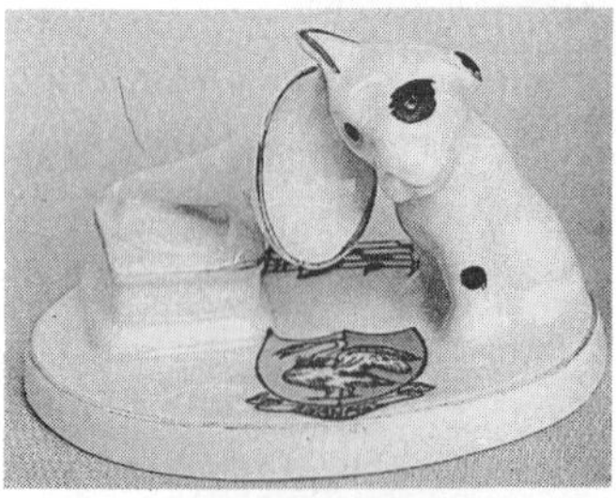

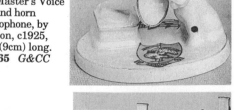

r. A model of the His Master's Voice dog and horn gramophone, by Carlton, c1925, 3½in (9cm) long.
£60–65 *G&CC*

r. A nightlight, in the form of Shakespeare's house, by W. H. Goss, 7½in (18.5cm) long.
£80–100 *SAS*

A creamware botanical part dinner service, comprising 109 pieces, each piece painted with a named specimen flower, perhaps Staffordshire, some damage, c1805.
£35,000–40,000 *C*

A set of 6 St. Clément plates, painted with different fruits, c1900, 8½in (21cm) diam.
£250–285 *MofC*

A Pratt-type commemorative flask, with moulded portraits of George III and Queen Charlotte, c1780, 5in (12.5cm) high.
£300–350 *Bon*

A double-faced St. Clément jug, with impressed mark, c1900, 9in (23cm) high.
£75–115 *MofC*

A Lambeth delft Persian blue posset pot, glaze chips, late 17thC, 4½in (11cm) high.
£10,000–12,000 *Bea*

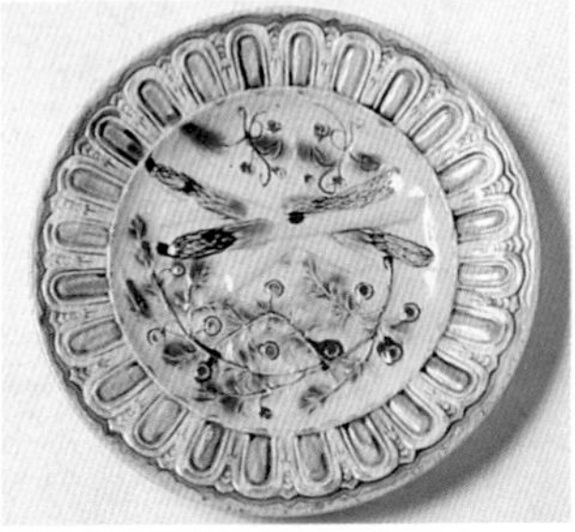

An asparagus plate, c1890, 9½in (24cm) diam.
£30–35 *MofC*

A pair of Staffordshire salt glazed stoneware marriage mugs, mid-18thC, largest 6½in (16.5cm) high.
£1,000–1,500 *DN*

A majolica Neptune vase, c1885, 17in (43cm) high.
£450–485 *MofC*

A Pratt ware tea caddy, probably by Gordon's Pottery, Prestonpans, late 18thC, 8in (20cm) high.
£200–220 *RA*

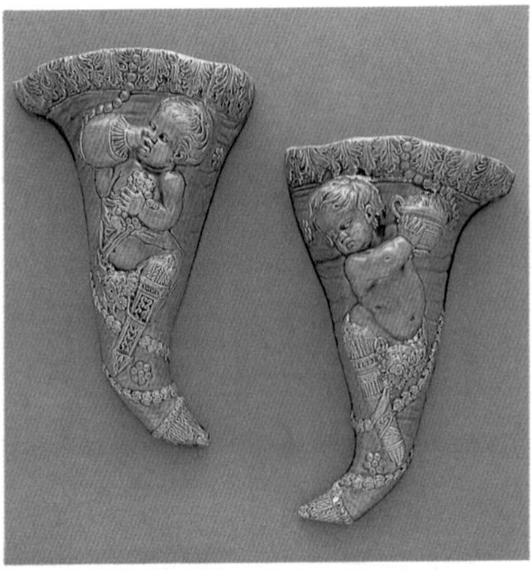

A pair of Staffordshire Ralph Wood type creamware wall pockets, emblematic of Autumn and Winter, gilding worn, c1780, 9½in (24cm) high.
£1,500–2,000 *CNY*

A delft charger, Bristol or London, c1700, 13½in (34.5cm) diam.
£3,000–3,300 *JHo*

A Casteldurante albarello, painted with a portrait, chip to foot, c1530, 8½in (21.5cm) high.
£7,000–8,000 *C*

A Castelli portrait wet drug jar of 'Orsini-Colonna' type, some damage, early 16thC, 10in (25cm) high.
£12,000–14,000 *C*

Two Montelupo dishes, painted in ochre, blue and manganese with equestrian figures in landscapes, minor rim chips and glaze flaking, the second restored, mid-17thC, 12½in (31.5cm) diam.
£7,500–8,000 *C*

A Gubbio lustred maiolica dish, painted with the Judgement of Solomon, Urbino or possibly Casteldurante, dated '1534', 10in (25cm) diam.
£32,000–34,000 *S*

A Castelli documentary plaque, painted by Francesco Antonio Saverio Grue, with initials 'DR/F.A.X.G/S', in a giltwood frame, early 18thC, 8½in (21.5cm) diam.
£14,000–16,000 *C*

A Casteldurante armorial pharmacy vase, slight damage, mid-16thC, 8in (20.5cm) high.
£5,500–6,500 *C*

A Faenza globular pharmacy jar, named for 'R.C. de Cosoli', minor rim flaking and chips to footrim, c1550, 8in (20.5cm) high.
£9,000–11,000 *C*

A pair of Venice oviform jars, painted in the workshop of Maestro Domenico, with portraits of St. Francis and St. Anthony, minor glaze flaking to rims, c1570, 10½in (26.5cm) high.
£19,000–21,000 *C*

An Urbino istoriato dish, painted in the manner of the Milan Marsyas painter, damaged, c1535, 10in (25.5cm) diam.
£9,500–11,000 *C*

A Gubbio lustred istoriato dish, painted with the story of Apollo and Marsyas, c1540, later frame, 9in (23cm) diam.
£8,000–9,000 *C*

An Urbino istoriato dish, painted in the Fontana workshop, c1550, 9½in (24cm) diam.
£7,000–8,500 *C*

An Urbino istoriato tondino, painted in the workshop of Guido Durantino, c1535, 10½in (26.5cm) diam.
£9,000–10,000 *C*

A pair of Siena pot pourri bowls and pierced covers, painted in the manner of Bartolomeo Terchi, damaged and repaired, c1730, 13in (33cm) diam.
£12,000–14,000 *C*

A Carey blue and white transfer ware dessert plate, with a view of Woburn Abbey, c1820, 9in (23cm) diam.
£150–250 *GN*

A Spode blue and white foot bath, transfer decorated with the Tower pattern, c1820, 18in (46cm) diam.
£1,200–1,500 *GN*

A Durlach fluted two-handled tureen, cover and stand, damaged, c1750, stand 15½in (40cm) wide.
£8,500–9,500 *C*

A Spode platter, transfer decorated with The Grasshopper pattern, c1812, 19in (48cm) wide.
£300–400 *GN*

A Spode blue and white transfer ware plate, decorated with view of the Bridge of Lugano, c1820, 10in (25cm) diam.
£70–90 *GN*

An English delft ware blue and white charger, c1720, 13½in (34cm) diam.
£250–300 *AnE*

A Staffordshire figure group, 'Courtship', c1820, 7in (17.5cm) high.
£2,000–2,200 *JHo*

A creamware group of St. George and the Dragon, restored, impressed 'Ra. Wood, Burslem', c1770, 11in (28cm) high. **£900–1,200** *Bon*

A Tittensor cow creamer, c1820, 6½in (16cm) high.
£875–975 *BHA*

A pair of Staffordshire pearlware figures of a stag and hind, on oval mound bases, restored, c1800, 6in (15cm) high.
£700–800 *DN*

A Quimper swan-shaped vase, c1920, 8in (20.5cm) high.
£175–200 *MofC*

A Staffordshire pearlware allegorical group of Sacred and Profane Love, c1810, 17in (43cm) high.
£1,000–1,200 *CNY*

A pair of Staffordshire figures, depicting Earth and Water, c1820, 7in (17.5cm) high.
£750–850 *JHo*

A Staffordshire peacock spill vase, 19thC, 7½in (18.5cm) high.
£200–250 *TVM*

A pair of pearlware groups of cows, one with a farmer, the other with his wife, the bases with sponged borders, restored, probably Yorkshire, c1815, 6in (15cm) high.
£2,000–2,500 *DN*

A Staffordshire group of mother and child, by Enoch Wood, c1790, 12½in (32cm) high.
£1,600–1,800 *BHA*

A pair of Staffordshire stags, with bocage, c1830, 7 and 8in (17.5 and 20cm) high.
£650–750 *MSA*

A Staffordshire figure The Drayman, c1820, 7in (17.5cm) high.
£400–450 *JHo*

A Derby figure of Harlequin, c1770, 6in (15cm) high.
£800–1,200 *DMa*

A Chelsea figure of a seated hare, some damage, c1755, 5in (12.5cm) high.
£11,000–12,000 *S(NY)*

A pair of Chelsea groups of gallants and companions, emblematic of the Seasons, some damage, restored, gold anchor marks, c1765, 13in (33cm) high.
£8,500–9,000 *C*

A Nymphenburg model of a monkey, restored, impressed shield, Pressnummer '5', 20thC, 11in (28cm) wide.
£450–650 *C*

A Meissen figure, by Acier, c1775, 6½in (16.5cm) high.
£1,400–1,500 *BHA*

A Meissen figure of Empress Catherine II of Russia's favourite dog, some damage, blue crossed swords mark, c1880, 17in (43cm) long.
£5,200–6,000 *C*

A Meissen pagoda figure pastille burner, modelled by J. F. Eberlein, damaged, marked, c1735, 6in (15.5cm).
£5,000–6,000 *C*

A Meissen group of Empress Catherine II, damaged, restored, marked, c1880, 10in (25cm) high.
£3,000–3,500 *C*

A Bow box and cover, naturalistically modelled, some damage, c1756, 5in (12.5cm) long.
£18,500–20,000 *S(NY)*

A Bow box and cover, modelled as a duck, some damage, c1756, 5in (12.5cm) long.
£11,000–12,000 *S(NY)*

A Meissen model of a monkey, modelled by J. G. Kirchner, restored, blue crossed swords mark, c1735, 10in (25cm) high.
£5,500–6,500 *C*

A Meissen figure of a foot soldier, some damage, restored, crossed swords mark, c1750, 9in (23cm) high.
£2,000–3,000 *Bon*

A pair of Meissen figures of parakeets, modelled after J. J. Kändler, perched on tree stumps, some damage, restored, crossed swords mark in blue, incised '63' and impressed '34', 13in (33cm) high.
£1,500–2,000 *CAG*

A Meissen group of Mezzetin and Columbine, modelled by J. J. Kändler, she holding a birdcage, some damage, c1740, 7¼in (18.5cm) high.
£9,500–10,000 *C*

A Meissen group of The Handkiss, modelled by J. J. Kändler, the lady with a pug on her lap, minor chips and restoration, c1740, 6in (15cm) high.
£32,000–35,000 *C*

A Meissen figure of Columbine, modelled by Kändler and Reinicke, c1744, 5¼in (13.5cm) high.
£4,800–5,500 *C*

A Bow group of 'The Fortune Teller', by the Muses modeller, minor chips, c1752, 7in (17.5cm) high.
£6,500–7,500 *S*

A Bow figure of Pierrot, c1755, 6in (15cm) high.
£900–1,200 *DMa*

A Derby group, restored, c1765, 11½in (29cm) high.
£2,000–3,000 *DMa*

A Bow figure of James Quin as 'Falstaff', chipped and repaired, c1750, 9in (23cm) high.
£2,000–2,200 *S(NY)*

A Meissen group of Augustus III and his wife, modelled by J. J. Kändler, c1744, 8¼in (21cm) high. **£20,000–22,000** *C*

A Meissen group, modelled by Paul Scheurich, blue crossed swords and dot mark, incised signature, 'Pressnummer 42', c1924, 11in (28cm) high.
£7,000–7,500 *C*

A pair of Derby figures, allegorical of Liberty and Matrimony, damaged and restored, c1765, 8¼in (21cm) high.
£2,200–2,500 *S(NY)*

A Chelsea figure of Dr. Boloardo, modelled by J.J. Kändler, damaged, c1754, 6in (15cm) high.
£9,500–10,000 *C*

A pair of Derby figures, chipped, c1760, 7in (17.5cm) high.
£1,600–1,800 *BHA*

A Worcester cabbage leaf moulded jug, painted in the manner of N. van Berchem, c1760, 8in (20.5cm) high.
£700–900 *Bon*

A set of 7 Meissen wall sconces, marked, converted for electricity, damaged, c1880, 22½in (57cm) high.
£6,500–7,500 *S*

A Sèvres teapot and cover, minor chips, marked, c1757, 4½in (11.5cm) high.
£6,000–7,000 *C*

A Meissen gold-mounted snuff box, marked, c1723, 2½in (6.5cm) wide.
£38,000–45,000 *S*

A Meissen tea caddy and cover, blue crossed swords mark, c1730, 4in (11cm) high.
£8,000–9,000 *C*

A Caughley mug, painted by Fidelle Duvivier, c1792, 5½in (14cm) high.
£10,000–11,000 *S(NY)*

A Chelsea jug, some damage, incised mark, c1745, 4½in (11cm) high.
£13,000–14,000 *C*

A Dresden clock case, in the Meissen style, chipped, crossed swords mark, late 19thC, 28in (71cm) high.
£3,500–5,000 *S*

An early Worcester 'Wigornia' type cream boat, slight damage, c1752, 2½in (6.5cm) high.
£12,000–13,000 *S(NY)*

Twelve Meissen knife and fork handles, painted in the manner of A. F. von Löwenfinck, c1735, 3in (7.5cm) long, in velvet lined box.
£4,000–5,000 *C*

A Böttger boordaloue, crossed swords mark, c1725, 8in (20cm) wide.
£7,000–9,000 *C*

A Meissen cup and saucer, caduceus and pseudo Chinese mark, c1725.
£23,000–25,000 *S*

A Minton heavily decorated double inkstand, Meissen mark, c1830, 10in (25cm) wide.
£1,700–1,800 *BHA*

Three Minton new stone candlesticks, repaired, impressed marks, c1860, 8in (20cm) high.
£350–450 *C*

A Meissen cabinet plate, painted with a scene of Badagosse *(sic)*, crossed swords mark and 'I', c1814, 9in (23cm) diam.
£4,000–5,000 *P*

A Nympenburg dish, from the Hof service, slight rubbing, blue star mark and impressed shield mark, c1765, 13½in (34cm) wide.
£3,500–4,000 *C*

A Sèvres plate, the centre painted with a landscape, indistinct lustre signature, various marks, c1825, 9in (23cm) diam.
£9,000–10,000 *C*

A Chelsea sunflower dish, damaged, red anchor mark, c1755, 9in (23cm) wide.
£4,200–4,800 *S(NY)*

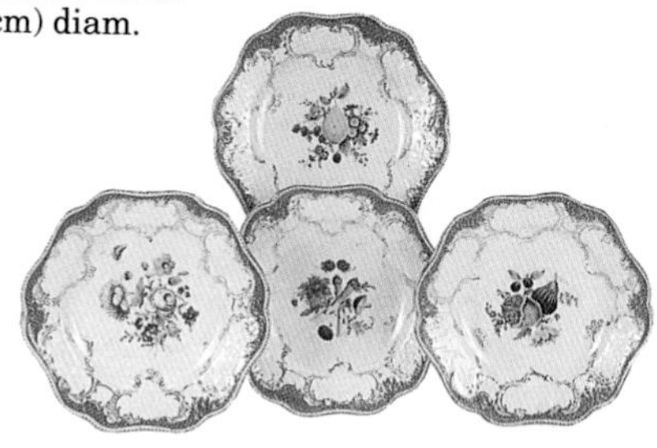

Twenty four Meissen plates, painted with fruit, vegetables, flowers and insects within scroll borders and gilt cartouches, slight damage, blue crossed swords marks, Pressnummer '8', incised '13', c1880, 10½in (27cm) diam.
£6,500–7,500 *C*

A Meissen gilt metal mounted dish, blue crossed swords mark, c1890, 18in (46cm) diam.
£6,000–7,000 *C*

A Chelsea fable decorated plate, probably painted by Jefferyes Hamett O'Neale, small chips, c1755, 9in (23cm) diam.
£25,000–27,000 *S(NY)*

A Worcester dish, decorated in enamels with sprays of flowers and leaves, within blue and gilt borders, crescent mark, c1775, 11in (28cm) wide.
£400–500 *DN*

A Worcester platter, some damage, gold crescent mark, c1775, 13½in (34cm) wide.
£26,000–28,000 *S(NY)*

A Vienna porcelain set of 5 chargers and a pair of urns, 'Antoinette and Famille', late 19thC, 12½in (32cm) diam.
£4,000–5,000 *JHW*

A Chelsea dish, painted in the manner of Jefferyes Hamett O'Neale, red anchor mark, c1752, 17in (43cm) diam.
£11,000–12,000 *S*

A Worcester plate, from the Duke of Gloucester service, painted with fruit, slight rubbing, gold crescent mark, c1770, 9in (22.5cm) diam.
£9,000–10,000 *C*

A Meissen part dinner service, comprising 71 pieces, painted with loose bouquets and scattered sprigs within gadroon moulded borders and gilt line rims, blue crossed swords mark, late 19thC.
£8,000–9,000 *C*

A Meissen part dinner service, comprising 75 pieces, painted with clusters of fruit, some chips, blue crossed swords mark, various Pressnummern and incised marks, c1870.
£9,000–10,000 *C*

A Derby pink ground part service, comprising 27 pieces, painted in rich colours in pattern No. 212 by William Pegg, blue crossed batons and 'D' mark, c1800.
£9,000–10,000 *C(NY)*

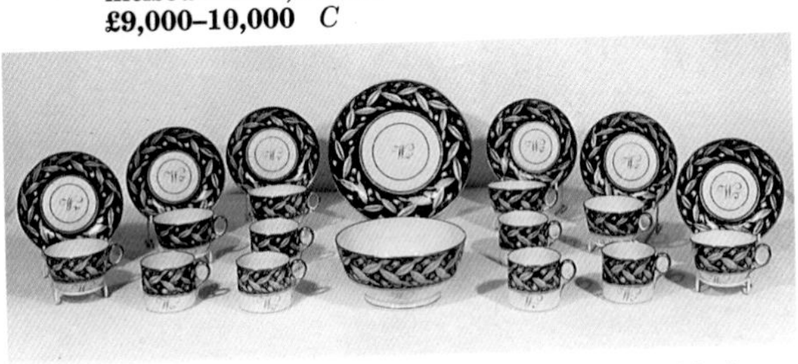

A New Hall porcelain part tea service, comprising 26 pieces, with gilded mazarine blue banding over-decorated with white leaves and harebells, Pattern No. 540, 18thC.
£1,500–2,000 *AH*

A Höchst part tea and coffee service, comprising 13 pieces, chips and repairs, c1765, coffee pot 9½in (24cm) high.
£3,000–4,000 *S*

A Coalport composite part service for dinner and dessert, comprising 76 pieces, damaged, c1815.
£6,500–7,500 *C*

A Derby part dinner service, comprising 91 pieces, some damage, crowned crossed batons and 'D' marks in iron red, various painter's numerals, tureen 14½in (37cm) long.
£2,500–3,500 *S(NY)*

A Worcester Barr, Flight and Barr part dessert service, painted in the Imari palette, some rubbing to gilt rims, script, incised and impressed marks, c1815.
£11,000–12,000 *C*

A Minton bamboo moulded part washstand service, comprising 14 pieces, painted with leaves, impressed marks and date codes for 1866, chamber pot 5in (12.5cm) high.
£3,500–4,500 *C*

A pair of Derby two-handled vases and covers, painted en grisaille, minor wear, each incised '62', c1770, 10in (25cm) high.
£4,000–4,500 *CNY*

A Meissen vase and cover, some damage, restored, Dreher's mark, c1740, 14½in (37cm) high.
£7,500–8,500 *C*

A pair of Paris vases, painted with Dutch peasants, the handles with satyrs' masks, covers lacking, some damage and wear, restored, c1835, 14½in (37cm) high.
£2,000–3,000 *C*

A Höchst vase and cover, some damage and restoration, c1780, 12½in (31cm) high.
£2,500–3,000 *C*

A Berlin campana vase, foot restored, various marks, c1840, 10in (25cm) high.
£18,500–20,000 *S*

A pair of Sèvres two-handled vases, with detachable flared collars, some damage, various marks, 1837, 12in (30.5cm) high.
£13,500–14,500 *C*

A pair of Sèvres ormolu mounted vases, signed 'Leber', c1880, 33½in (84cm) high.
£9,500–11,000 *S*

A pair of Meissen vases and covers, damage, marked, c1880, 15in (38cm) high.
£5,500–6,500 *C*

A Vienna two-handled vase and cover, painted with cherubs at play, signed 'Neumann'.
£350–400 *AAV*

A Minton pot pourri vase and cover, c1830, 11in (28cm) high.
£500–600 *BHA*

A pair of Meissen pot pourri vases and pierced covers, applied with foliage scrolls enriched with gilding, some damage and repairs, one with blue crossed swords mark, c1750, 11in (28cm) high.
£5,500–6,500 *C*

A pair of Sèvres hand painted vases, signed 'Lyset', early 20thC, 12in (31.5cm) high.
£300–350 *JHW*

A gilt metal mounted Sèvres pattern vase and cover, c1920 50½in (128cm) high.
£7,000–8,000 *C*

A painted famille rose bowl and cover, the interior and cover each painted in iron red, some damage and repairs, Qianlong seal marks and of the period, 4½in (11.5cm) diam.
£35,000–37,000 *S*

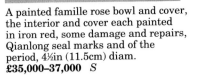

A dragon dish, restored, Jiaqing seal mark and of period, 10in (25.5cm) diam.
£2,000–2,500 *C*

A doucai bowl, painted and enamelled with an Immortal drifting on a branch, Kangxi six-character mark and of the period, 3½in (9cm) diam.
£42,000–44,000 *C*

A teapot stand, painted with figures, Ch'ien Lung, 5in (12.5cm) diam.
£200–240 *AnE*

A doucai painted and enamelled bowl, Daoguang seal mark and of the period, 6½in (16.5cm) diam.
£8,000–10,000 *C*

A pair of doucai dishes and a pair of blue and white dishes, Guangxu six-character marks and of the period, 8in (20.5cm) diam.
£1,800–2,200 *C*

A pair of saucers, painted in underglaze blue and enamels, slight damage, Wanli marks and of the period, 4in (10.5cm) diam.
£2,500–3,500 *S*

A dragon vase and cover, some damage, Daoguang seal mark and of the period, 8in (20.5cm) diam.
£4,000–5,000 *S*

A Canton famille rose punchbowl, enamelled with dignitaries, 19thC, 21in (53cm) diam.
£10,000–12,000 *C*

A pair of underglaze blue and yellow enamelled dragon dishes, some damage, one rim polished, Qianlong seal marks and of the period, 10in (25cm) diam.
£3,000–4,000 *C*

Five saucer dishes, painted and enamelled, one with Qianlong seal mark and 4 with Daoguang seal marks and of the period, 7½in (18cm) diam. **£6,500–7,000** *C*

A pair of famille rose yellow ground butterfly bowls, with flaring rims, cracked, iron red Tongzhi four-character marks and of the period, 10in (25cm) diam.
£2,000–2,500 *C*

A dragon dish, painted with a dragon pursuing a flaming pearl, restored, mark and period of Yongzheng, restored, 18½in (47cm) diam.
£11,000–13,000 *S*

A famille rose Mandarin palette tankard, Ch'ien Lung period, c1770, 4in (10cm) high.
£350–400 *AnE*

A famille verte armorial ewer, made for the Portuguese market, restored, Kangxi, c1720, 12½in (32cm) high.
£9,000–10,000 *S*

An enamelled doucai bowl, the sides with slightly flaring rim, restored, Yongzheng six-character mark and of the period, 9½in (24cm) diam.
£6,000–8,000 *C*

A Ko-Imari ewer, decorated with a wide band of plum blossom, slight chips and restoration, late 17thC, 9in (23cm) high.
£26,000–28,000 *C*

A Fahua garden seat, with a central band of rampant lions grasping ribbons, Ming Dynasty, 16thC, 12½in (32cm) diam.
£3,000–4,000 *S*

A Dutch beaker and saucer, painted with flowerheads, Ch'ien Lung, c1740, saucer 5½in (14cm) diam.
£200–245 *AnE*

A famille rose tea service, comprising 13 pieces, decorated with floral panels on a gold diaper ground, gilding rubbed, some restoration, Qianlong.
£2,000–3,000 *S*

A pair of assembled gilt metal and Chinese porcelain candlesticks, painted in famille verte and famille rose, on 2 inverted Arita saucer dishes, 19thC, 10½in (26.5cm) high.
£4,500–5,500 *C*

A pair of dragon bowls, the interior decorated with a shou medallion, marks and period of Kangxi, 4in (10cm) high, on wood stands.
£13,500–15,000 *S*

A pair of pottery guardians, standing on rock plinths, restoration to some sections, Tang Dynasty, 33½in (85cm) high.
£2,000–3,000 *S*

A pair of warriors, Northern Sung Dynasty, 22½in (57.5cm) high.
£3,000–4,000 *MA*

A pair of court attendants, in green and amber glaze, Ming Dynasty, 18in (45.5cm) high.
£600–900 *GHa*

A famille rose figure of a boy, Yongzheng/ Qianlong, c1735, mounted on a painted wooden stand.
£64,000–68,000 *S*

A pair of pottery Immortals, Sung Dynasty, c1300, 18½in (47cm) high.
£2,000–3,000 *MA*

A famille rose cistern, Qianlong, restored, 13in (33cm) high.
£25,000–35,000 *S*

A famille rose cistern, Qianlong, hat re-gilded, 13in (33cm) high.
£25,000–30,000 *S*

A Ming Fahua figure of a luohan, reign and date mark and of period, c1577, 18in (45.5cm) high.
£7,000–8,000 *C*

A matched pair of Sancai pottery figures of lokapala, each standing on a recumbent bull, the heads unglazed, Tang Dynasty, restored, 36in (91.5cm) high.
£18,500–22,000 *C*

A famille rose figure of a courtier, holding a sceptre, body cracked, Qianlong, 24in (61cm) high.
£25,000–28,000 *S*

A painted pottery figure of a lokapala, Tang Dynasty, restored, 30in (76cm) high.
£4,000–6,000 *S*

A tureen and cover, modelled as a crouching hawk, the feathers detailed in sepia with gilding, restored, Qing Dynasty, Qianlong, 8½in (21.5cm) wide.
£6,000–7,000 *S*

A pair of hawks, each perched on a jagged pierced rock and with one claw raised and clenched, the feathers heightened with gilding, restored, Qing Dynasty, Qianlong, 11in (28cm) high.
£48,000–52,000 *S*

A pair of ormolu mounted glazed parrots, each perched on pierced rockwork bases, Qing Dynasty, Kangxi, 8½in (21.5cm) high.
£10,000–12,000 *S*

A Sancai figure of a horse, tail restuck, Tang Dynasty, 14in (35.5cm) high.
£8,000–9,000 *S*

A Sancai glazed pottery horse, with an unglazed saddle, on wood stand, restoration to legs, neck, saddle and ears, Tang Dynasty, 19¼in (49cm) high.
£8,000–9,000 *S*

A Sancai figure of a horse, restored, Tang Dynasty, 12½in (32cm) high.
£4,500–5,500 *C*

A Ming glazed horse, c1600, 11¼in (29cm) high.
£600–650 *AnE*

A glazed pottery figure of a horse, the rump with aperture for the tail, restored, Tang Dynasty, 25½in (65cm) high.
£65,000–70,000 *C*

A pair of Kakiemon cockerels, standing on rockwork bases, slight restoration, late 17thC, 9 and 9¾in (23 and 24.5cm) high.
£57,000–65,000 *C*

A famille rose five-piece garniture, some rim chips repaired, Yongzheng, 10½in (26cm) high.
£7,000–8,000 *C*

A pair of Chinese ginger jars and covers, Qianlong seal marks, 8½in (22cm) high.
£1,600–2,000 *CSK*

A Kakiemon vase, with band of chrysanthemums, minute chips, late 17thC, 8in (20.5cm) high.
£32,000–34,000 *C*

A famille verte rouleau vase, Kangxi, 18in (46cm) high.
£22,000–24,000 *S*

A famille rose five-piece garniture, covers non-matching and one restored, Qianlong, c1740, tallest 11in (28cm) high.
£6,000–7,000 *C*

A pair of famille rose baluster vases, with applied dragon handles, 19thC, 28½in (72.5cm) high.
£6,800–7,200 *C*

A Korean underglaze blue and copper red jar, 19th/20thC, 11in (28cm) high.
£5,000–6,000 *C*

A famille verte yenyen vase, Kangxi, 18in (46cm) high.
£33,000–35,000 *S*

A pair of Sung glazed vases, 13th/14thC, 8in (20.5cm) high.
£1,500–2,000 *MA*

An enamelled moon flask, restored, Yongzheng seal mark, 16½in (42.5cm) high.
£11,000–13,000 *C*

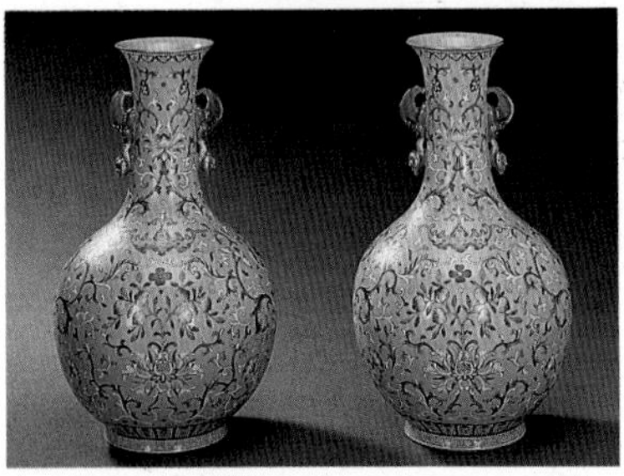

A pair of famille rose vases, restored, Qianlong seal marks and of the periods, 11in (28cm) high.
£15,000–17,000 *S*

A late Ming dynasty double gourd vase, repaired, Tianqi, 11in (28cm) high.
£1,500–2,000 *S*

A pair of Japanese vases, one chipped, 18thC, 4½in (12cm) high.
£900–1,200 *CSK*

A famille rose five-piece garniture, lids restored, one beaker restored, Qianlong, largest 11½in (29.5cm) high.
£4,000–5,000 *S*

A yenyen vase, decorated with deer and 2 cranes, Qing Dynasty, Kangxi, 18½in (47cm) high.
£5,000–6,000 *S(HK)*

A tripod ewer and cover, the spout in the form of a chicken's head, chipped, Qing Dynasty, Qianlong, 6in (15cm) wide.
£3,000–4,000 *S(HK)*

A pair of Lotus Pond saucers, each with low rounded sides, painted with a band of mandarin ducks, spots on rim, marks and period of Yongzheng, 4½in (11.5cm) diam.
£14,500–16,000 *S(HK)*

A pair of underglaze blue bowls, each decorated with cranes, the interior with a medallion enclosing a fruiting peach tree, one with short firing mark under glaze, marks and period of Yongzheng, 6in (15cm) diam.
£38,000–42,000 *S(HK)*

A blue and white bowl, the exterior painted with the 'Three Friends' and branches, light wear, mark and period of Yongzheng, 7½in (19cm) diam.
£2,500–3,500 *S(HK)*

A pair of dragon jardinières, each decorated with dragons amid cloud and flame scrolls, small glaze cracks, mark and period of Daoguang, 8½in (21.5cm) diam.
£7,500–8,500 *S(HK)*

A Ming dish, the interior painted with a Daoist scene of an Immortal, attendants and Shoulao, the exterior with floral sprigs, kiln grit and glaze pooling, Wanli period, 6½in (17cm) diam.
£2,500–3,500 *S(HK)*

An underglaze blue jar, decorated with lotus flowers and stems, mark and period of Yongzheng, 4½in (11.5cm) high.
£9,500–10,500 *S(HK)*

A soft paste vase, painted with a temple hall and buildings, Qing Dynasty, 15½in (40cm) high.
£2,000–2,500 *S(HK)*

A pair of blue and white butter lamps, the interiors decorated with lotus flower medallions, the exteriors with lança characters, lotus flowers and leafy stems, seal marks and period of Qianlong, 6in (15cm) diam.
£15,000–16,000 *S(HK)*

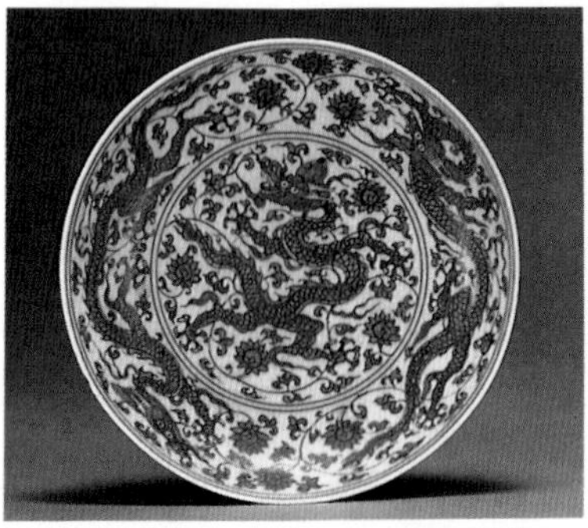

A Ming blue and white saucer dish, painted with a dragon leaping among scrolling lotus, rim chip, mark and period of Zhengde, 8in (20cm) diam.
£7,000–8,000 *S(HK)*

A Ming provincial storage jar, glaze damage and small chip, 16thC, 6in (15cm) high.
£70–80 *AnE*

A Ming provincial bowl, painted with a pair of sinuous dragons, c1600, 5in (12.5cm) diam.
£100–115 *AnE*

Two kraak porselein bottle vases, cracked, Wanli, tallest 12¼in (31cm) high.
£1,500–2,000 *C*

A rose-water sprinkler, with brass mounted top, made for the middle Eastern market, 18thC, 8½in (21.5cm) high.
£550–600 *AnE*

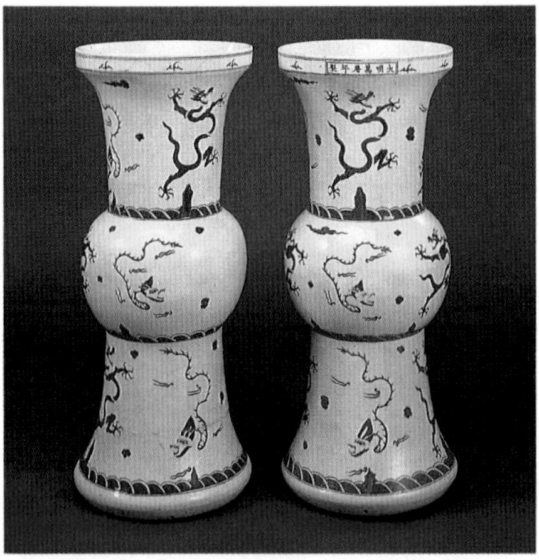

Two Ming style gu vases, painted with dragons amidst clouds, Wanli six-character marks, 19thC, 32½in (83cm) high.
£6,500–7,000 *C*

A Chinese Willow pattern spoon tray, applied with gilt in Europe, mid-19thC, 5in (12.5cm) wide.
£75–80 *AnE*

A Ming 'Karonic' vase, with Islamic inscription, Zhengde mark and of period, 3½in (9cm) high, and a vase, 17thC.
£4,500–5,000 *C*

A pair of Ming style hu vases, with moulded taotie mask handles, one restored, Qianlong seal mark, 19thC, 19½in (50cm) high.
£7,000–8,000 *C*

A baluster vase and cover, restored, Kangxi, on a European giltwood stand, damaged, c1840, 61½in (156cm) high.
£11,000–13,000 *S*

A bulb planter, painted with a continuous scene of scholars and attendants in a mountain and river landscape, Kangxi, 9in (23cm) diam.
£450–500 *AnE*

An Arita garniture, comprising 3 jars and covers and 2 beaker vases, each painted with a continuous scene of trailing clouds and ho-o birds on rocks, peonies and pomegranates, damaged and restored, late 17thC, jars 21½in (54.5cm) high.
£34,000–36,000 *C*

A Ban Chiang culture burial urn, from Thailand, circa 1000 B.C., 7in (17.5cm) high.
£200–300 *GRG*

A celadon glazed bowl, from the Si Sarchanarhi kiln, Thailand, made for export to Indonesia, recovered from a marine excavation in 1993, 14th/15thC, 11in (28cm) diam.
£300–360 *GRG*

A Yangshao culture neolithic painted pottery cup/bowl, 1st half 3rd millenium B.C., 3in (7.5cm) high.
£600–700 *GRG*

A Yangshao culture neolithic painted pottery bowl, with hatched diamond motifs and deep black bands, lst half 3rd century B.C., 7½in (19cm) high.
£1,200–1,400 *GRG*

A Ming horse and rider tomb figure, 14th/17thC, 11in (28cm) high.
£350–400 *SIG*

A crackle glazed bottle, with narrow neck, Chinese or Thai, 16thC, 10in (25cm) high.
£175–210 *GRG*

A Ban Chiang culture vessel, from Thailand, circa 1000 B.C., 14in (36cm) high.
£400–500 *GRG*

A Ming horse, 14th/17thC, 14½in (37cm) high.
£1,400–1,600 *SIG*

A Yangshao culture neolithic painted vessel, with narrow neck and 2 handles, 3rd century B.C., 4in (10cm) high.
£600–700 *GRG*

A Yangshao culture neolithic pottery vessel, early 3rd century B.C., 11½in (29cm) high.
£2,400–2,600 *GRG*

A Thai bowl, from the old Sukhon kiln, with underglazed fish design, 16thC, 9in (23cm) diam.
£250–300 *GRG*

A Thai coiled pot storage jar, 14thC, 10in (25.5cm) high.
£100–120 *GRG*

A Clichy faceted double overlay close concentric millefiori mushroom weight, small chips, mid-19thC, 3in (7.5cm) diam.
£3,000–3,500 *C*

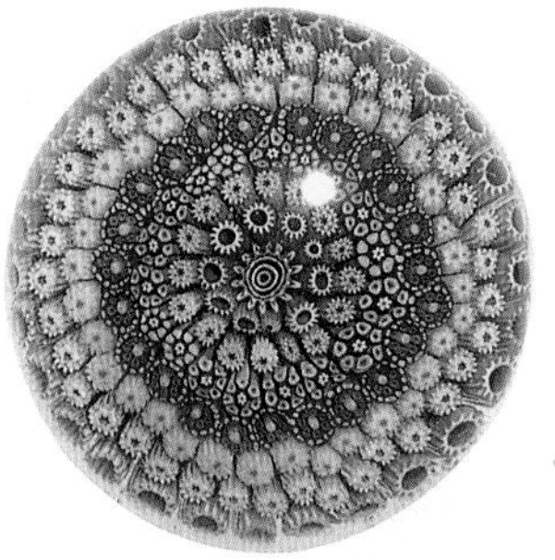

A St. Louis close concentric millefiori weight, with large central pink cogwheel cane, mid-19thC, 3in (7.5cm) diam.
£2,200–2,500 *C*

A Baccarat faceted garlanded blue camomile weight, with star cut base, slight chip to footrim, mid-19thC, 3in (7.5cm) diam.
£1,700–2,000 *C*

A Baccarat garlanded yellow buttercup weight, the flower with 2 rows of recessed petal around a white centre, scratched, mid-19thC, 2½in (6.5cm) diam.
£2,600–3,000 *C*

A St. Louis carpet-ground patterned millefiori weight, mid-19thC, 2¾in (7cm) diam.
£3,000–3,500 *C*

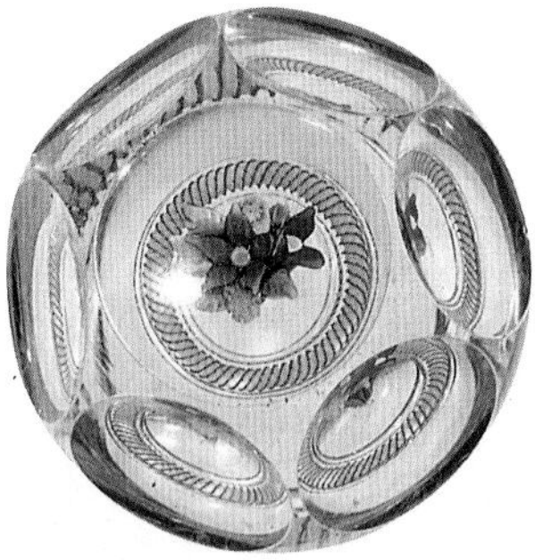

A St. Louis faceted upright bouquet weight, slight chip to edge of one printy, mid-19thC, 3¼in (8cm) diam.
£1,700–2,000 *C*

A green mercury glass vase, c1880, 9½in (23cm) high.
£500–650 *DUN*

A petal-moulded wine goblet, c1840, 6in (15cm) high.
£150–200 *CB*

A set of 4 wine glasses, with flute cut cup-shaped bowls, on cut knopped stems and plain conical feet, c1850, 5½in (13.5cm) high.
£250–300 *Som*

An amethyst glass roemer, with hollow stem, prunts and trailed foot, c1880, 5in (12.5cm) high.
£75–95 *CB*

A wine glass, with ribbed ogee bowl and bladed knop, c1800, 5in (12.5cm) high.
£80–90 *CB*

A wine glass, with cup bowl and knopped incised twist stem, c1800, 5½in (14cm) high.
£400–500 *CB*

A Bohemian engraved goblet, attributed to Franz Zach, depicting a pair of fighting stags in a woodland scene, the flared cut foot with a band of flutes, the reverse cut with a lens, c1860, 6in (15cm) high.
£3,200–3,500 *S*

A set of 8 amber wine glasses, the cup-shaped bowls with engraved fruiting vine decoration, on plain drawn stems and conical feet, c1840, 4½in (11.5cm) high.
£340–380 *Som*

l. A wine glass, with opaque spiral thread stem, c1765, 7in (17cm) high.
£1,300–1,600
r. An air-twist wine glass, c1760, 7¼in (18.5cm) high.
£3,300–3,700 *C*

A mercury glass vase, c1800, 11½in (29.5cm) high.
£750–950 *DUN*

A Bristol wine glass, with ribbed cup bowl, c1790, 5in (12.5cm) high.
£120–150 *CB*

A set of 12 wine glasses, the conical bowls on bladed knopped stems, plain conical feet, c1820, 5in (12.5cm) high.
£900–1,100 *Som*

A Potsdam-Zechlin engraved and gilt armorial goblet, the beaded faceted knopped stem heightened in gilding, the foot cut with radiating petals, c1740, 8½in (21.5cm) high.
£11,000–12,000 *S*

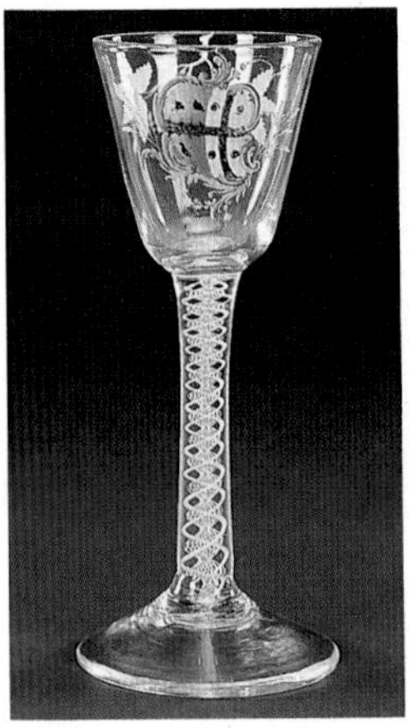

A Beilby armorial wine glass, attributed to William Beilby, on a double series opaque twist stem and conical foot, gilding rubbed, c1765, 6in (15cm) high.
£10,000–11,000 *S*

A Bohemian engraved blue stained footed bowl, with scalloped rim, signed 'F. Zach', c1850, 11in (28cm) high.
£9,500–11,000 *S*

An engraved wine glass, with inscription 'De Goede Negootie', mid-18thC, 8in (20cm) high.
£1,200–1,500 *Bon*

A Jacobite cordial glass, the small trumpet bowl engraved with a Jacobite rose, on a drawn multiple spiral air-twist stem and plain conical foot, c1745, 5½in (14cm) high.
£1,400–2,000 *Som*

A carafe, gilt in the atelier of James Giles, the slender neck with ogee upper part and dentil border, c1770, 8½in (21.5cm) high.
£800–1,200 *C*

A set of 6 roemer type wine glasses, with cup-shaped bowls, hollow stems and raspberry prunts, on trailed concial feet, c1825, 4in (10cm) high.
£640–700 *Som*

A set of 7 wine glasses, each with conical bowls on stems with bladed knops, c1800, 5in (12.5cm) high.
£450–550 *Som*

A pair of Bohemian Zwischengoldglas carafes, with faceted spire stoppers and screw threads, c1740, 12½in (31.5cm) high.
£2,200–2,700 *S*

A spirit decanter, with lozenge stopper, c1780, 8in (20cm) high.
£550–650 *Som*

A set of 8 wine glasses, the trumpet bowls with base collars, on stems with shoulder ball knops and plain conical feet, c1840, 5in (12.5cm) high.
£740–800 *Som*

A pink opalescent basket, with 'rustic' spurs, 9in (22.5cm) high.
£200–220 *CB*

An amethyst globular decanter, engraved with a band of thistles and roses, c1860, 9½in (24cm) high.
£200–300 *CB*

A cut and gilded green glass bowl, c1790, 3½in (9cm) high.
£500–650 *CB*

A pink threaded glass jam dish, in an electroplated frame, with a thistle finial, 5½in (14cm) high.
£60–85 *CB*

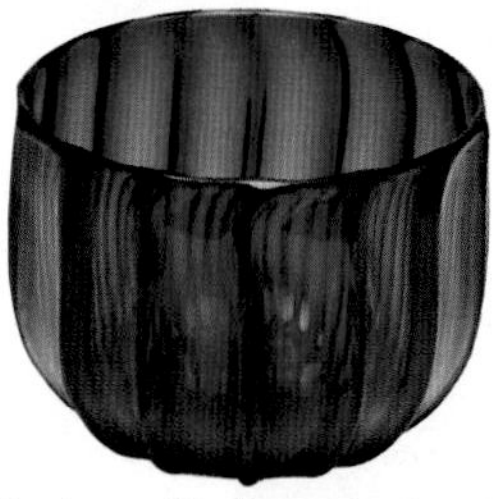

A ribbed moulded green glass bowl, c1820, 4in (10cm) diam.
£60–90 *CB*

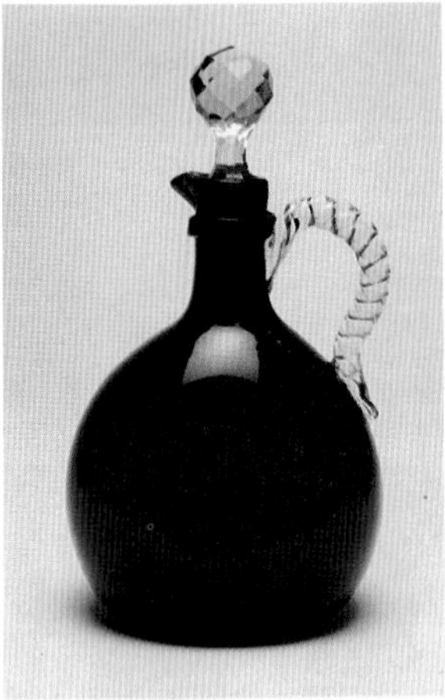

A blue claret jug, with barley-twist clear handle and facet cut stopper, c1820, 6in (15cm) high.
£100–150 *CB*

A set of 6 green condiment bottles, with gilded cartouche, in a papier mâché frame, c1800, 9in (22.5cm) wide.
£1,600–2,000 *CB*

A cameo vase, decorated in white over blue satin glass, by T. Webb, Stourbridge, c1890, 6in (15cm) high.
£500–600 *CB*

A cranberry glass bowl, with clear frill, in a silver plated stand, 7in (17.5cm) high.
£100–120 *CB*

A blue glass cream jug, decorated with white stripes, with a clear handle and foot, c1860, 4in (10cm) high.
£150–200 *CB*

An amber glass claret jug, engraved with flowers and ferns, with a clear glass handle and stopper, c1870, 9in (22.5cm) high.
£150–170 *CB*

A yellow and white swirl glass casket, with gilded brass mounts, c1890, 6in (15cm) wide.
£450–550 *CB*

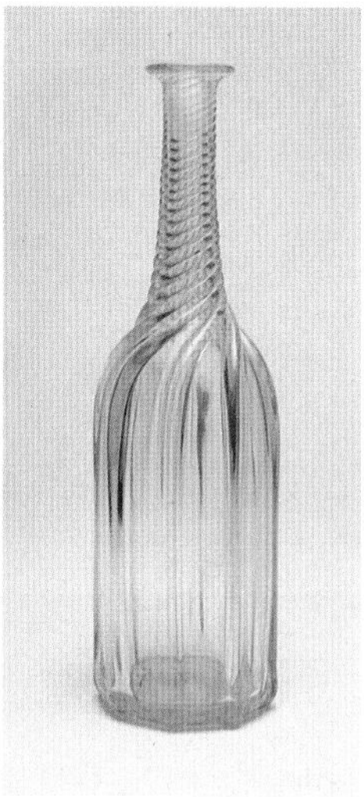

A ribbed yellow uranium glass serving bottle,c1840, 11½in (29.5cm) high.
£90–130 *CB*

A green claret jug, with barley twist handle, 1870, 9in (22.5cm) high.
£100–150 *CB*

An amethyst glass cream jug and bowl, with wrythen moulding, c1830, 3½in (9cm) high.
£250–300 *CB*

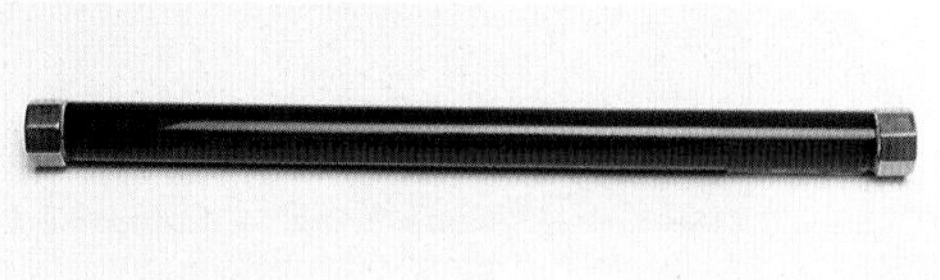

A blue glass ruler, with hexagonal brass mounts, c1860, 10in (25cm) long.
£90–120 *CB*

A cranberry glass pink-to-pale 'ice glass' jug, c1890, 7½in (19cm) high.
£100–150 *CB*

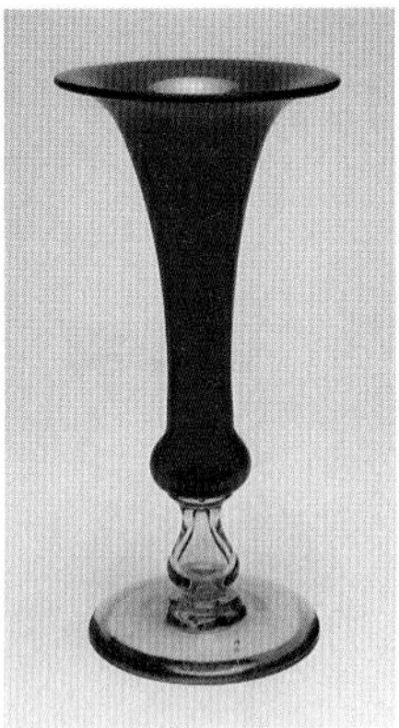

A cranberry glass tulip vase, with clear foot, c1890, 13in (33cm) high.
£250–300 *CB*

Two cameo glass scent bottles, hallmarked London 1887:
l. with flattened, gadrooned body, 3in (7.5cm) diam.
£1,300–1,500
r. Webb's, 5in (12.5cm) long.
£550–650 *Som*

An amethyst jug and basin, jug inscribed 'Be canny with the cream', basin inscribed 'And be canny with the sugar', c1800, jug 3⅛in (8.5cm) high.
£480–520 *Som*

A blue tea mixing bowl, engraved with a band of vesica decoration, possibly Irish, c1810, 6in (15cm) high.
£250–350 *Som*

A pair of cut glass trumpet-shaped vases, on compressed onion-shaped bases with circular star base stands, 16½in (42cm) high.
£140–180 *PCh*

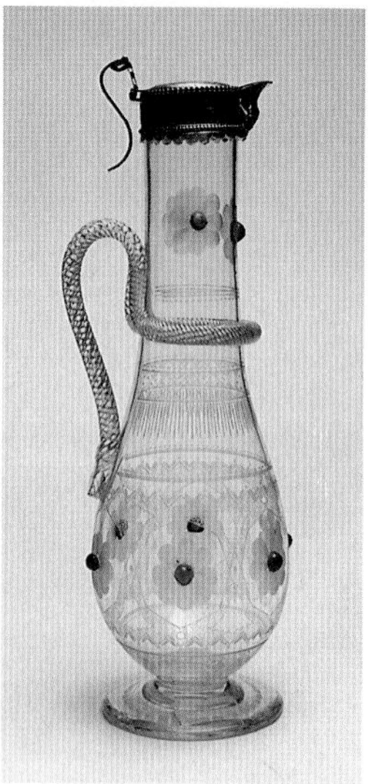

An claret jug, with snake handle, and silver plated lid and rim, c1870, 12in (30.5cm) high.
£650–700 *MJW*

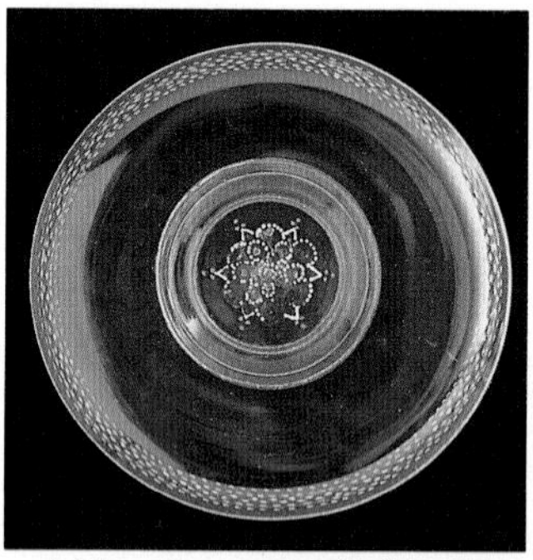

A Venetian enamelled low tazza, painted with a stylised rosette, on a spreading conical foot, early 16thC, 10in (25cm) diam.
£5,000–5,500 *S*

A cameo vase, carved with scrolling leaves, the foot in the form of a chrysanthemum, probably by Thomas Webb, c1885, 4in (10.5cm) diam.
£1,200–1,700 *S*

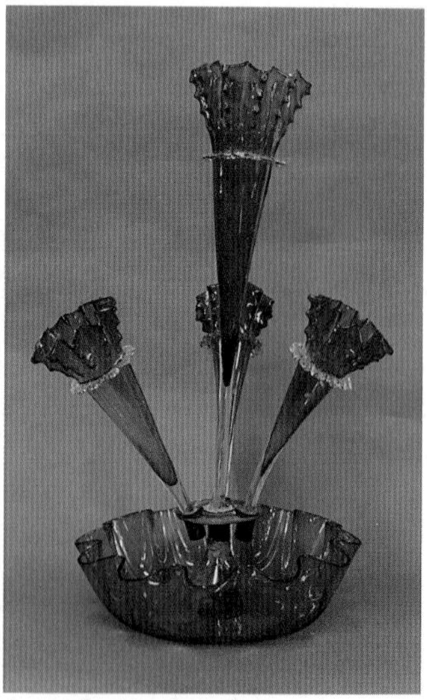

A cranberry glass flower épergne, late 19thC, 19in (48.5cm) high.
£200–250 *PCh*

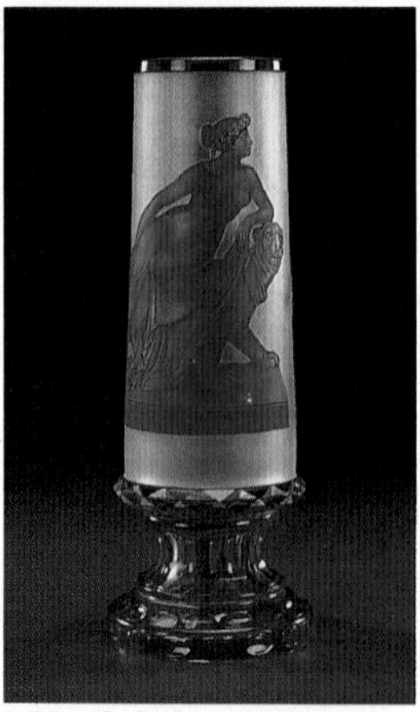

A North Bohemian blue overlay vase, attributed to Franz Zach, c1860, 12½in (32cm) high.
£10,000–11,000 *S*

A blue glass cream jug, with ribbed body, c1790, 4in (20cm) high, and a goblet, with knopped stem and petal moulded base, c1830, 6in (15cm) high.
£200–300 each *Som*

Chinese Dynasties and Marks

Earlier Dynasties

Shang Yin	c1532–1927 B.C.	Wei	386–557
Western Zhou	1027–770 B.C.	Sui	589–617
Spring and Autumn Annals	770–480 B.C.	Tang (T'ang)	618–906
Warring States	484–221 B.C.	Five Dynasties	907–960
Qin (Ch'in)	221–206 B.C.	Liao	907–1125
Western Han	206 B.C.–24 A.D.	Sung	960–1280
Eastern Han	25–220	Chin	1115–1260
Three Kingdoms	221–265	Yüan	1280–1368
Six Dynasties	265–589		

Ming Dynasty

Hongwu (Hung Wu)
1368-1398

Yongle (Yung Lo)
1403-1424

Xuande (Hsüan Té)
1426-1435

Chenghua (Ch'éng Hua)
1465-1487

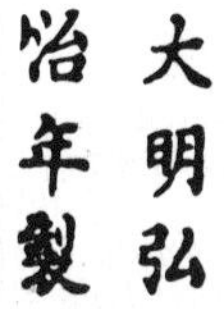
Hongzhi
(Hung Chih)
1488-1505)

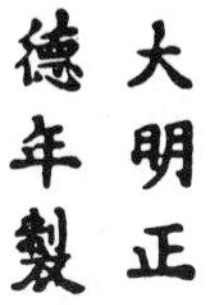
Zhengde
(Chéng Té)
1506-1521

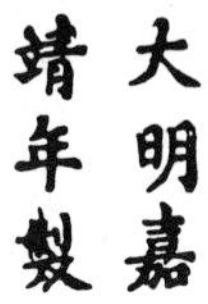
Jiajing
(Chia Ching)
1522-1566

Longqing
(Lung Ching)
1567-1572

Wanli (Wan Li)
1573-1620

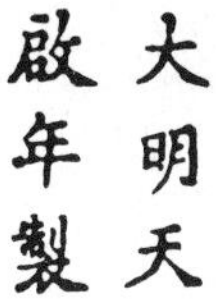
Tianqi
(Tien Chi)
1621-1627

Chongzhen
(Ch'ung Chêng)
1628-1644

Qing (Ch'ing) Dynasty

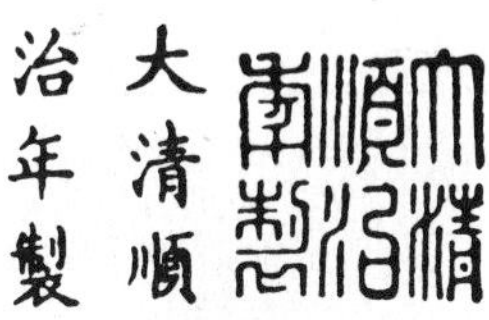
Shunzhi
(Shun Chih)
1644-1661

Kangxi (K'ang Hsi)
1662-1722

Yongzheng (Yung Chêng)
1723-1735

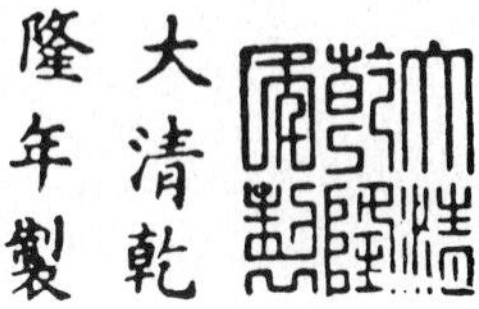
Qianlong (Ch'ien Lung)
1736-1795'

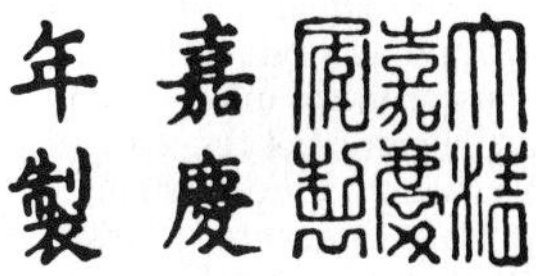
Jiaqing (Chia Ch'ing)
1796-1820

Daoguang (Tao Kuang)
1821-1850

Xianfeng (Hsien Féng)
1851-1861

Tongzhi (T'ung Chih)
1862-1874

Guangxu (Kuang Hsu)
1875-1908

Xuantong
(Hsuan T'ung)
1909-1911

Hongxian
(Hung Hsien)
1916

CHINESE CERAMICS
Bowls

A red earthenware single-handled bowl, with green glaze, Eastern Han Dynasty, 8in (20cm) wide.
£400–500 *GRG*

A blue and white dragon and phoenix bowl, Kangxi six-character mark and of the period, 5½in (14cm) diam.
£4,500–5,000 *C*

A blue and white bowl, painted with a continuous scene, restored, 17thC, 14in (35.5cm) diam.
£720–800 *CSK*

A pair of incised yellow ground famille rose bowls, each with flared rounded sides supported on a small slightly flared foot, decorated with 9 red bats, each carrying a double gourd tied with a blue ribbon, flying amidst green clouds above a band of lappets and below a cloud collar at the rim, all picked out in enamels with outlines incised on the yellow enamel ground, the interior enamelled yellow, slight damage, marks and period of Yongzheng, 5in (12.5cm) diam, on wood stands.
£20,000–25,000 *S*

The small group of Yongzheng bowls made in this design are surprisingly varied in the carving of the clouds and the position of the bats on each individual bowl. It is unusual to find these engraved yellow ground bowls decorated in enamels other than green.

A bowl and cover, the body carved with overlapping bands of lotus petals, the cover with carved sgraffito, covered with a greenish white glaze, Northern Song Dynasty, 3½in (9cm) diam.
£1,000–1,200 *GRG*

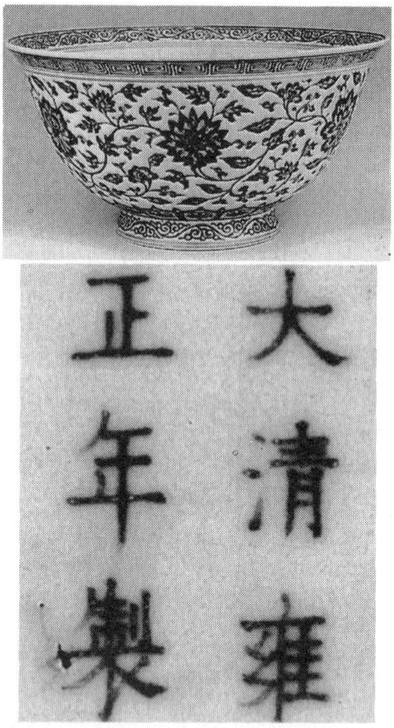

A blue and white bowl, chip repaired, Yongzheng six-character mark and of the period, 9½in (24cm) diam.
£1,400–1,800 *CSK*

A liver red glazed bowl, with widely flaring sides, the interior plain, rim rubbed, underglaze blue Qianlong seal mark and of the period, 7in (17.5cm) diam, on a wood stand.
£500–800 *CSK*

r. A Cantonese punch bowl, with painted friezes of figure groups in famille rose enamels and gilt, 19thC, 16in (41cm) diam.
£1,800–2,000 *RBB*

A blue and white fruit bowl, the exterior painted in strong underglaze blue, with darker 'heaping and piling' effect, the interior glazed white, frit on rim, mark and period of Xuande, the mark written in a line below the rim, 11½in (29.5cm) diam.
£82,000–90,000 *S*

These distinctive Ming bowls, whose exact use is uncertain, appear to have been made only for a very short time, as they all have the Xuande reign marks below the rim. They were painted in a number of different designs, including flower scrolls such as tree peony, rose, stylised lotus or 'lingzhi' fungus.
Although experts are uncertain of their exact use it has been it has been suggested that these shallow bowls with 'finger thick' walls served scholars as brush washers. They may also have been used for playing dice in the palace, or for cricket fights, popular in the Ming dynasty, for which the extreme thickness of the bowls would render them an ideal battlefield!

A famille rose eggshell porcelain bowl, painted and gilt with a continuous scene of officials and ladies at leisure on a fenced rocky terrace, cracked, blue enamel Qianlong four-character mark, 5½in (14cm) diam, in a fitted tin box.
£150–200 *CSK*

Decorative Symbols

An interest in Chinese porcelain is greatly enhanced by a knowledge of the many decorative symbols used.

A dragon symbolized authority, strength, wisdom, goodness – and, by association, the Emperor.

Ducks in pairs symbolize a long and happy marriage.

The peony denotes love, beauty, harmony, happiness and honour.

The Three Friends of Winter (pine, prunus and bamboo) symbolize spiritual harmony.

Cranes are emblems of longevity – and transport for Immortals.

A pair of wucai dragon and phoenix bowls, Daoguang seal marks and of the period, 6in (15.5cm) diam.
£6,500–7,500 *C*

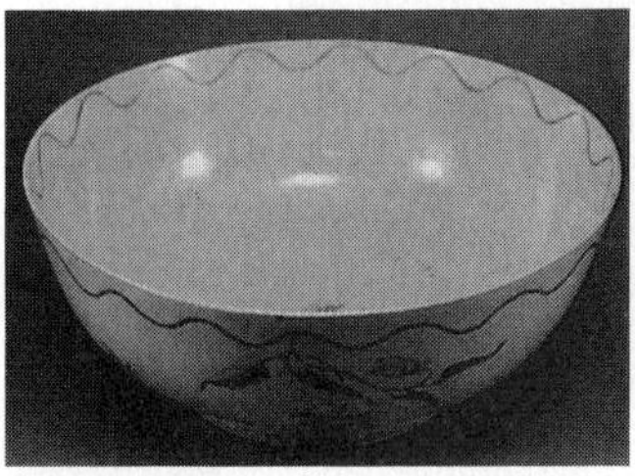

An export porcelain rouge-de-fer punchbowl, Qianlong period, c1750, 11in (28cm) diam.
£1,500–2,000 *RIT*

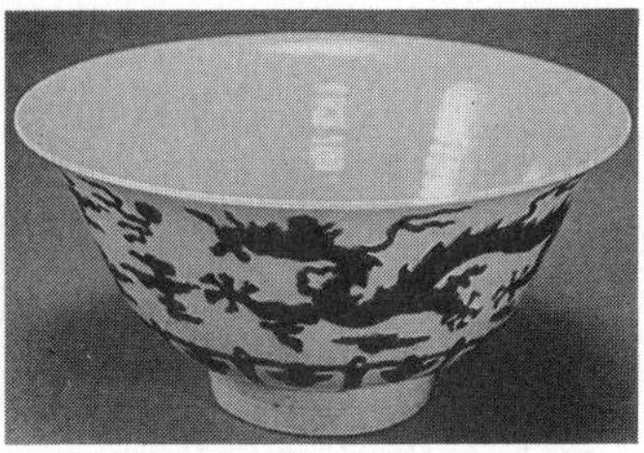

An Imperial yellow ground dragon bowl, with overglaze green enamel decoration, Guangxu mark and period, 6in (15cm) diam.
£750–800 *RIT*

Cups & Tea Bowls

A Fujian Ware tea bowl, with Temmokh or hare foot glaze, Southern Sung Dynasty, 4in (10cm) diam.
£600–700 *GRG*

A Fujian Ware dark brown stoneware tea bowl, with thick brown and blue hare's fur glaze, Southern Sung Dynasty, 4in (10cm) diam.
£1,000–1,200 *GRG*

A famille rose tea bowl and saucer, painted with blossoming plants, Yongzheng period, saucer 5in (12.5cm) diam.
£550–650 *CSK*

A famille rose cup, painted with a continuous scene of chrysanthemums on a yellow ground, blue enamel Qianlong seal mark, 2½in (6cm) diam.
£250–300 *CSK*

l. **A famille rose barrel-shaped mug, painted and gilt, Qianlong, 4½in (11.5cm) high.**
£450–550 *CSK*

A set of 12 famille rose flaring cups, each enamelled around the exterior, one cracked, blue enamel Qianlong four-character mark, 3⅓in (8.5cm) diam, in a fitted box.
£19,000–22,000 *C*

An export armorial part tea service, comprising: 4 custard cups and 6 covers, 6 tea bowls, 5 saucers, 6 plates and a saucer dish, all painted in underglaze blue famille rose enamels and gilt with a central coat-of-arms and the motto 'Non Desidia' above the monogram 'ML', crest of Loch, all within spearhead borders, damaged, c1790, 4in (10cm) high.
£1,500–2,000 *CSK*

A tea bowl and saucer, Ch'ien Lung period, saucer 4in (10cm) diam.
£40–45 *AnE*

An export blue and white tea bowl and saucer, painted with Neptune and attendants, 18thC, saucer 4½in (11.5cm) diam.
£400–500 *CSK*

Ewers

A Yingqing lobed ewer, with flaring neck, curved spout and ribbed handle, Song Dynasty, 8in (20cm) high.
£350–550 *CSK*

A blue and white ewer, with short spout and 4 lug mask handles, restored, cover missing, Transitional, 14in (35.5cm) high.
£1,100–1,500 *CSK*

Figures

An unglazed horse, with signs of paintwork, Tang Dynasty, 24in (61.5cm) wide.
£10,000–11,000 *GRG*

This is a magnificent example of a well-modelled form, with one leg raised and a finely modelled head, turned slightly.

A horse's grey earthenware head, with some natural pigment, Han Dynasty, decorations Western Han, 6in (15cm) high.
£400–500 *GRG*

A Fereghan horse, with painted details, Tang Dynasty 618–906 A.D., 16in (40.5cm) high.
£2,000–2,500 *RIT*

A buff pottery figure of a recumbent lion dog, traces of pigment remaining, possibly restored, probably Han Dynasty, 19in (48cm) wide.
£1,500–2,000 *Bon*

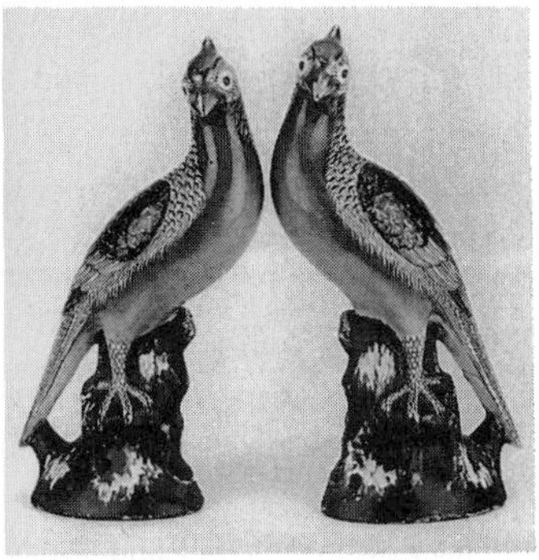

A pair of famille rose models of pheasants, perched on pierced rockwork, 14in (35.5cm) high.
£1,600–2,000 *CSK*

A pair of famille rose cockerels, standing on pierced rockwork, minor enamel rubbing, 6½in (16.5cm) high.
£1,200–1,700 *CSK*

A blanc-de-chine model of Guanyin, wearing flowing robes and a high cowl, seated beside rockwork, damaged, 17th/18thC, 7½in (19cm) high.
£720–800 *CSK*

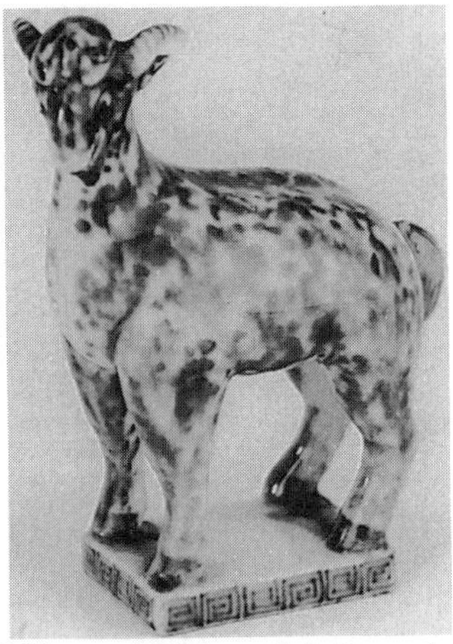

A blue and white model of a goat, Jiaqing six-character mark, 4in (10cm) high.
£350–400 *CSK*

A famille rose model of Buddha, seated leaning against his sack, wearing flowing robes and holding a necklace, the clothes decorated with butterflies among flowers, 12in (30.5cm) high, on a wood stand.
£1,800–2,200 *CSK*

Flasks

A pair of blue and white reticulated moonflasks, with stylised lappet handles, painted with bands of scrolling lotus and foliage, damaged, Daoguang seal marks and of the period, 11in (28cm) high.
£700–900 *CSK*

r. A celadon glazed moonflask, with a bulbous neck, raised on a splayed foot, all under an even pale greyish green glaze, some surface crackle, one side later enamelled in Europe, Yongzheng seal mark and of the period, 21½in (54cm) high.
£6,000–8,000 *C*

A pair of famille rose figures of ho ho birds, the brightly decorated figures perched on rockwork, 11in (28cm) high.
£500–600 *DN*

Five green and ochre glazed pottery attendants, some red and black pigments remaining, all with detachable heads, damaged, Ming Dynasty, 16in (40.5cm) high.
£500–650 *CSK*

A pair of clobbered flasks, painted in underglaze blue, coloured enamels and gilt, the porcelain 18thC, 11in (28cm) high.
£1,700–2,200 *CSK*

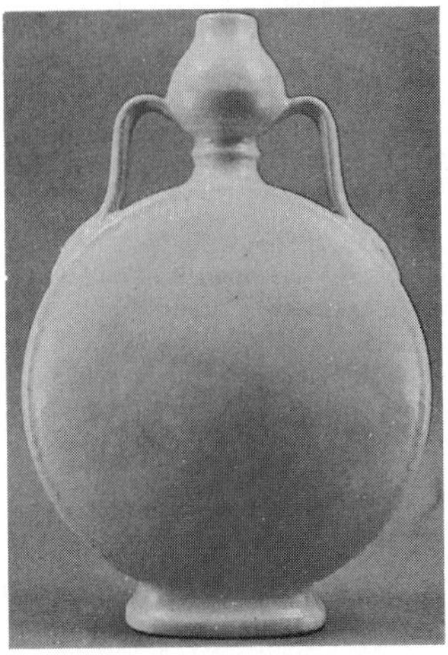

Flatware

A Yingqing conical dish, with rounded sides and flaring rim divided by 6 notches, the interior showing a flower with leaves under a greenish-blue glaze, Song Dynasty, 7½in (19cm) diam.
£1,400–1,600 *GRG*

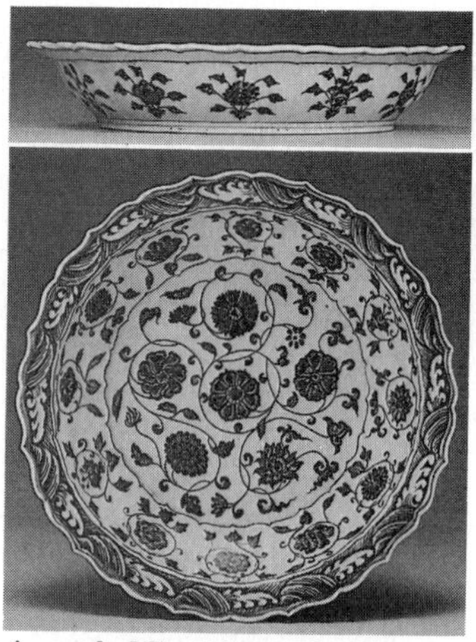

An early Ming blue and white lobed foliate rim dish, bright underglaze blue with 'heaped and piling' highlighting the design, the base unglazed, Yongle, 13in (33cm) diam, boxed.
£112,000–120,000 *C*

A Ming blue and white dragon dish, with rounded sides and flaring rim, painted in strong tones with a five-clawed dragon amidst a lotus meander and flame scrolls, surrounded by 2 striding dragons among lotus meander and flame scrolls, the reverse with 2 similar dragons above ruyi lappets around the base, slight damage, Zhengde four-character mark and of the period, 9½in (24cm) diam.
£28,000–33,000 *C*

It is rare to find a Zhengde dish of this size, painted with this design, which is seen as one of the trademarks of this period.

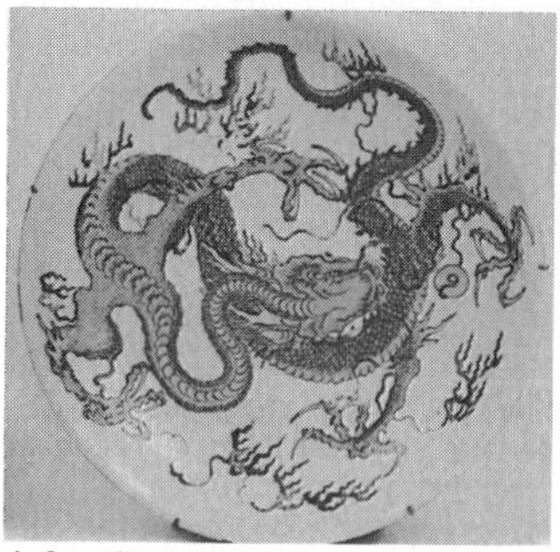

A famille verte saucer dish, the interior painted in aubergine, yellow and green, with a dragon pursuing a flaming pearl, double foot rim, rim chips, Kangxi blue six-character mark within double circle, and of the period, 13in (33cm) diam.
£950–1,200 *L*

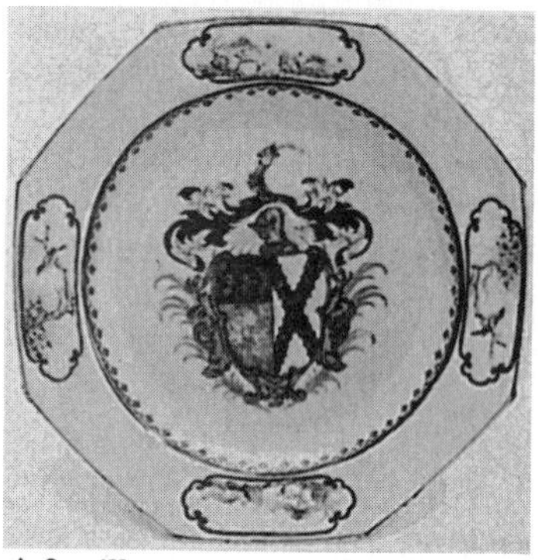

A famille rose armorial plate, within a gilt spearhead border, the rim with sepia landscape or bird vignettes, Qianlong, 8½in (21.5cm) diam.
£600–700 *L*

A pair of blue and white dishes, fritting at rims and one small chip, blue leaf mark within a double circle, Kangxi, 13½in (34.5cm) diam.
£2,000–2,500 *C*

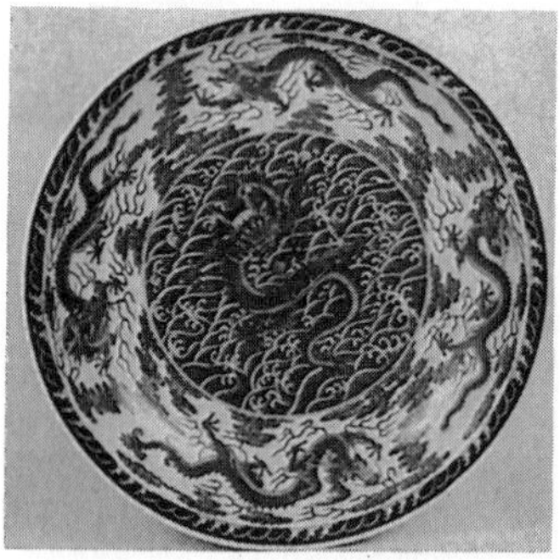

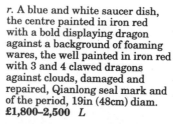

r. A blue and white saucer dish, the centre painted in iron red with a bold displaying dragon against a background of foaming wares, the well painted in iron red with 3 and 4 clawed dragons against clouds, damaged and repaired, Qianlong seal mark and of the period, 19in (48cm) diam.
£1,800–2,500 *L*

A pair of export plates, painted en grisaille and gilt within borders of scattered flowersprays and gilt spearheads, some gilt and enamel rubbing, Qianlong, 9in (23cm) diam.
£350–450 *CSK*

A set of 15 blue and white plates, painted with fishing boats before pagodas in rocky river landscapes, damaged, Qianlong, 9in (23cm) diam.
£600–900 *CSK*

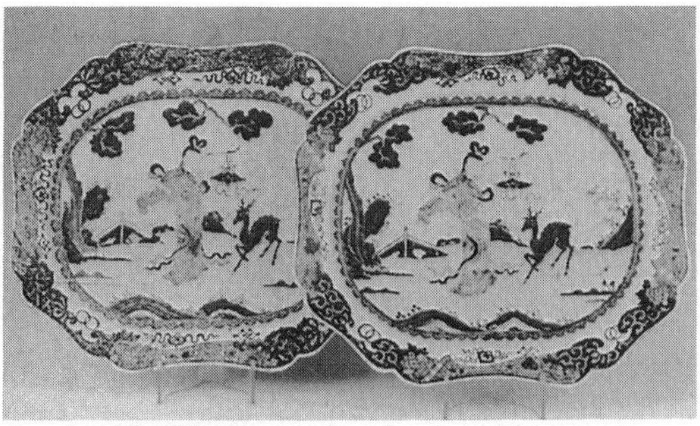

A pair of famille rose and underglaze blue meat dishes, painted and gilt, damaged, Qianlong, 16½in (42cm) wide.
£750–1,000 *CSK*

A pair of plates, each painted in famille rose enamels with cockerels in a garden and sprays of flowers, slight damage, Qianlong, 13in (33cm) diam.
£650–750 *Bea*

An Imari dish, painted and gilt, slight damage, 18thC, 15½in (39.5cm) diam.
£250–350 *CSK*

A fluted teapot stand, decorated in the Mandarin palette with a scholar and pupil, Ch'ien Lung, 5in (12.5cm) diam.
£200–240 *AnE*

An Imari dish, painted and gilt, with a central brocade ball surrounded by flowering lotus and peony stems, slight fritting to rim, 18thC, 18½in (47cm) diam.
£1,500–2,000 *CSK*

Garden Seats

A pair of famille rose pink ground barrel-shaped garden seats, with pierced cash and moulded rows of studs, painted and gilt with shaped panels of phoenix and birds among flowers, including peonies and prunus, all between yellow ground formal borders of lappets, 18½in (47cm) high.
£2,000–2,500 *CSK*

A blue and white barrel-shaped garden seat, 19in (48cm) high.
£500–700 *CSK*

A pair of blue and white garden seats, painted with peonies and scrolling foliage, 19½in (49.5cm) high.
£3,200–3,800 *CSK*

Jardinières

A pair of Cantonese jardinières, with widely flaring sides and stands, 11in (28cm) diam.
£4,000–4,500 *CSK*

A Cantonese jardinière, with flaring everted rim, painted and gilt with a continuous scene of figures in gardens among plantain, bamboo, trees and rockwork, damaged, 12½in (32cm) diam.
£350–500 *CSK*

A Cantonese jardinière and stand, painted and gilt with alternating panels of dignitaries on terraces and birds and butterflies among flowers, on a green and gold scroll ground, minor restoration, stand 11in (28cm) wide.
£850–950 *CSK*

Jars

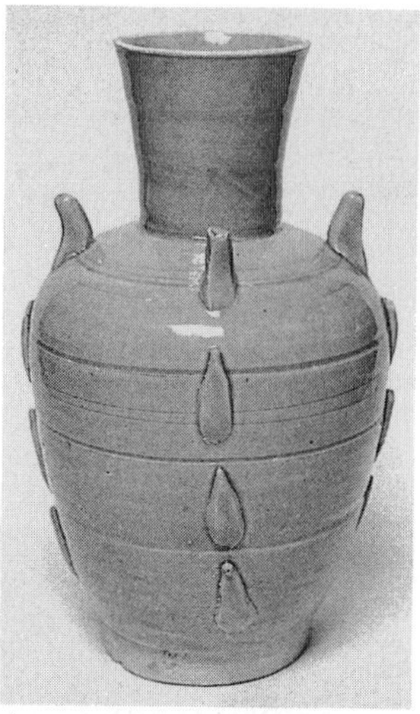

A storage jar, dark glazed, with applied flame decoration, Sung Dynasty, 9in (23cm) high.
£150–200 *AnE*

An ancestor jar, 15th/16thC, 7in (17.5cm) high.
£125–180 *GRG*

Miller's is a price GUIDE not a price LIST

A blue and white jar, painted around the sides in vivid underglaze blue, neck replaced, firing cracks from base, mark and period of Jiajing, 15½in (39.5cm) high.
£6,000–8,000 *S*

An export ware crackle glazed jar, late Sung Dynasty, 11in (28cm) high.
£75–120 *GRG*

A blue and white jar and cover, the baluster body painted with 4 oval scenes illustrating Daoist influenced stories, damaged, Ming Dynasty, Tianqi, c1625, 19in (48cm) high.
£3,800–4,200 *C*

An olive glazed storage jar, the ovoid body with broad shoulder fitted with lug handles around the waisted neck, applied with dragons chasing flaming pearls amidst clouds below lions' masks and floral motifs, all under a brownish green glaze, late Ming Dynasty, 21in (53cm) high.
£2,500–3,000 *C*

An ancestor jar, with Indian metal hook, 15th/16thC, 10in (25cm) high.
£175–210 *GRG*

A blue and white jar, decorated in vivid underglaze blue, the flat unglazed base spotted with orange and brown, neck reduced and ground, Ming Dynasty, early 16thC, 12in (30.5cm) high.
£3,000–4,000 *S*

A blue and white baluster jar, painted with a continuous garden scene below stylised cloud or lingzhi scrolls, reserved on a dense diaper ground around the slightly flaring neck, firing cracks to shoulder, Ming Dynasty, c1480, 14in (36cm) high.
£39,000–45,000 *C*

A blue and white jar, painted in underglaze blue of brilliant tone, the short neck with a diaper band reserved with barbed shou characters, the base unglazed, exterior wear, Ming Dynasty, Jiajing/Wanli period, 19in (48.5cm) high.
£18,000–22,000 *S*

A blue and white quatrefoil jar, painted overall with scrolling peonies and leaves below a band of key fret to the neck, damaged, 17thC, 7in (17.5cm) high.
£250–300 *CSK*

Tea & Chocolate Pots

A Ming pale celadon glazed flattened globular teapot, 5in (12.5cm) high.
£400–600 *CSK*

An export miniature teaset, comprising 30 pieces, all painted in rouge de fer and gilt with butterflies among peonies and lotus, 18thC, the teapot 4in (10cm) wide.
£1,600–2,000 *CSK*

A famille rose Mandarin pattern chocolate pot, with cartouches of figures on terraces on a Y-pattern ground, the domed cover with peach spray finial, painted and gilt, restored, Qianlong, 7in (17.5cm) high.
£350–450 *CSK*

A blue and white two-spouted teapot and cover, restoration to handle, Kangxi, 6in (15cm) high.
£1,400–1,700 *CSK*

r. A famille rose globular teapot and cover, chip to cover, Qianlong, 4½in (11.5cm) high.
£400–500 *CSK*

A blue and white soft paste teapot and domed cover, painted with chrysanthemums issuing from pierced rockwork between cell pattern borders, chip to spout, Qianlong, 5½in (13.5cm) high.
£310–380 *CSK*

Tureens

A porcelain blue and white tureen and cover, with branch finial, boar's head handles and decorated with a river landscape, Qianlong period, 14in (35.5cm) wide.
£750–850 *AH*

A famille rose tureen and domed cover, with Buddhistic lion finial and lions' mask handles, painted and gilt with flowersprays above a band of spearheads, damaged, 18thC, 11in (28cm) wide.
£1,200–1,700 *CSK*

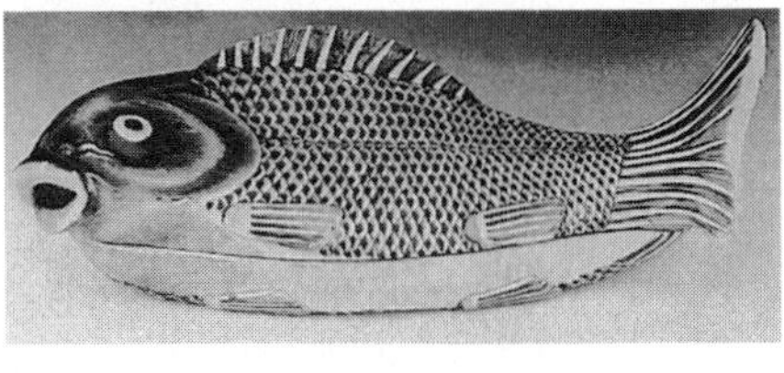

l. An export tureen and cover, modelled as an open-mouthed fish, painted in green, brown and aubergine enamels, the interior in turquoise, 15in (38cm) wide.
£1,100–1,500 *CSK*

An export tureen and cover, with animals' head handles and a pomegranate knop, painted in famille rose enamels with peonies, chrysanthemums and bamboo in a rocky garden, each piece with scrolling foliate panels, with matching dish, minor chip and some glaze rubbing, Qianlong, 15in (38cm), dish 17in (43cm) wide.
£4,500–5,500 *Bea*

Vases

An underglaze red decorated vase, painted around the sides in copper red of even warm reddish-brown colour, the underside of the base glazed white, restored, Ming Dynasty, Hongwu, 12½in (32.5cm) high.
£57,000–70,000 *S*

It is very rare to find a Hongwu pear-shaped vessel with this combination of large hatched ruyi panels above an elaborate lotus scroll. More usual is the narrow band of small trefoils in solid red or blue usually found above a peony scroll. These deep panels emphasize the strength and rhythm of the design, with a stem springing from a calyx below each panel to encircle the flowerhead.

A blue and white double-gourd vase, painted on the lower body with a scene from the Romance of the Three Kingdoms, with a messenger approaching Zhao Yun and his followers in a landscape, frits at rim, Ming Dynasty, Chongzhen, c1640, 13½in (34.5cm) high.
£3,500–4,000 *C*

Zhao Yun, famous for his expertise in using a spear, was a well-known general serving under Liu Bei, one of the uncles of the Han emperor.

A blue and white kraak style bottle vase, painted with alternating panels of precious objects and flowers issuing from rockwork, damaged and repaired, Wanli, 12in (30.5cm) high, on wood stand.
£400–450 *CSK*

A Transitional blue and white vase and a cover, damaged, 18½in (47cm) high.
£2,000–2,500 *CSK*

l. A famille verte quatrefoil vase and stand, with pierced bamboo-style handles, painted with panels of lotus flowers on a trellis pattern ground, damaged and repaired, Kangxi, 9in (23cm) high.
£500–700 *CSK*

A famille noir broad pear-shaped vase, incised Kangxi six-character mark, 18½in (47cm) high.
£550–650 *CSK*

r. A Transitional pear-shaped vase, with serpent loop handles, brightly decorated in underglaze blue and 2 taotie mask bands and yinyang symbols, damaged, 9in (23cm) high.
£300–400 *DN*

A set of 3 blue and white bottle vases, damaged, Kangxi, 9½in (24cm) high.
£2,000–2,500 *CSK*

A blue and white bottle vase, painted around the body in Ming style, Daoguang seal mark and of the period, 14½in (37cm) high.
£10,000–12,000 *C*

A pair of double-gourd reticulated vases, the alternate pierced panels in turquoise and red enamel with sprays of flowers between, damaged, a ceramic ring applied under each base, Qianlong, 5½in (14cm) high.
£300–500 *Bea*

A blue and white vase, the underglaze blue of slightly blurred brilliant blue colour, seal mark and period of Qianlong, 20½in (52cm) high.
£62,000–68,000 *S*

This vase is believed to have been presented to Sir Ralph Harwood, KCB, KCVO, by Queen Mary and to have come from the Royal collection at Windsor Castle.

A pair of famille rose Mandarin pattern vases, with dragon handles and domed covers, painted and gilt, with panels of figures on terraces overlooking river landscapes, damaged, 14in (36cm) high, and a matching beaker, 18thC.
£1,500–2,000 *CSK*

r. A famille verte porcelain vase, decorated with continuous battle scenes, within brown borders, 24in (61.5cm) high.
£320–400 *MJB*

Miscellaneous

A blue and white supper set, frits, Qing Dynasty, Qianlong, 15½in (39.5cm) diam.
£2,000–2,500 *S*

A pair of rose Mandarin bough pots, repaired, 19thC, 8½in (21.5cm) high.
£3,000–4,000 *SK(B)*

l. A pair of Cantonese joss stick holders, modelled as Buddhistic lions supporting vases on their backs, their coats painted and gilt with scrolling lotus flowers and leaves, damaged, 5½in (14cm) long.
£1,700–2,200 *CSK*

A blue and white sprinkler, painted with floral roundels and scattered flowerheads, restored, Kangxi, 7in (17.5cm) high.
£170–220 *CSK*

A pair of Ming joss stick holders, modelled as caparisoned elephants, decorated in green, ochre and cream glazes, damaged, 5in (12.5cm) high.
£360–420 *CSK*

A large celadon storage pot and lid, with lion headed lugs on the main body, 18thC, 15in (38cm) diam.
£300–350 *GRG*

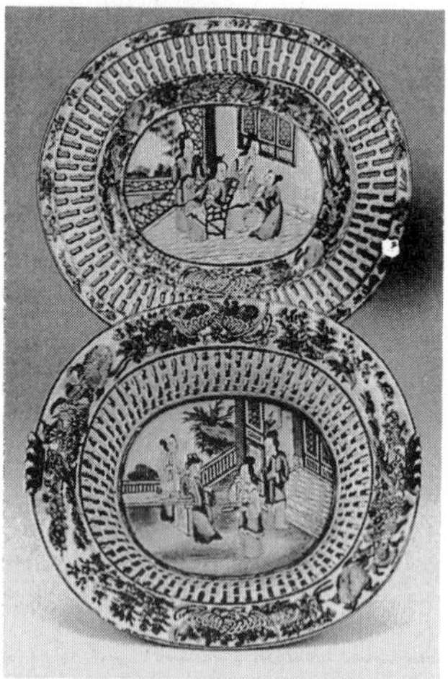

A Cantonese two-handled basket and stand, painted and gilt with oval panels of figures at leisure on terraces, within borders of birds, butterflies and bats among scattered fruit and flowersprays, 9in (23cm) wide.
£1,100–1,400 *CSK*

An export tankard, painted in sepia and gilt, Qianlong, 4½in (11.5cm) high.
£350–450 *CSK*

l. A famille verte wall cistern, cover and basin, decorated between flower-strewn seeded green ground borders, set at the base with an applied lion mask with the spout issuing from the mouth, the high back of the cistern with two fish-tailed dragons pursuing a flaming pearl, their tails flanking a scallop shell and framing the cover, repaired, Qing Dynasty, Kangxi, c1720, 16in (41cm) high.
£14,000–18,000 *S*

A blue and white cider jug and cover, with Buddhistic lion finial and entwined branch handle, painted with the Trench Mortar pattern, with a continuous scene of a thatched farmhouse on the banks of a river below a band of Fitzhugh pattern to the neck, restored, 18thC, 11in (28cm) high.
£600–800 *CSK*

The Trench Mortar pattern was also used by various English Factories including Spode and Newhall.

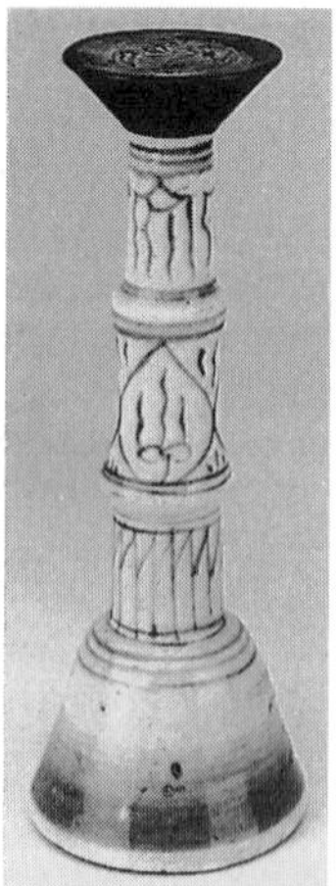

A blue and white candlestick, made for the Middle Eastern market, with tapering ribbed neck rising from a spreading foot, painted overall with bands of stylised calligraphy, early 18thC, 6½in (16.5cm) high.
£500–600 *CSK*

A cylindrical pot, the handle of the lid decorated in the form of a twisted fruit or flower, part glazed in brown, Tang dynasty, 4in (10cm) diam.
£800–850 *GRG*

A blue and white brush pot, painted with a mythical beast seated among censers, vases of lotus, precious objects, ruyi sceptres, scrolls and bowls of fruit, fritting, Kangxi, 6in (15cm) high.
£650–750 *CSK*

A pottery model of a Cantonese house, Eastern Han Dynasty, 8in (20cm) high.
£1,500–2,000 *MA*

JAPANESE CERAMICS

Beakers

A blue and white beaker, painted with bands of flowers on a ground of lappet borders and tama, 7½in (19cm) high.
£200–250 *CSK*

A pair of Artia blue and white beakers, painted with peonies and chrysanthemums issuing from pierced rockwork, damaged, late 17thC, 4½in (11.5cm) high.
£700–900 *CSK*

Bowls

An Arita bowl, painted with panels of flowers and fruit, running Fuko masks to sides, 5½in (14cm) diam.
£150–185 *AnE*

A Satsuma bowl, the interior and exterior painted with pheasants and other birds beneath wisteria and bamboo, Mount Fuji beyond, character marks, 9½in (24cm) diam.
£250–300 *L*

Figures

An Hirado model of a goat, horns restuck, 7½in (19cm) long.
£550–650 *CSK*

A pair of white porcelain models of pekinese dogs, the details well delineated, impressed marks, 5½in (14cm) high.
£600–700 *CSK*

A Kutani model of Kannon, wearing flowing robes and a high cowl, the figure holding a scroll in her right hand, her clothes painted and gilt with lotus flowers and scattered leaves, a hole in base, 24½in (62.5cm) high.
£1,200–1,700 *CSK*

Japanese Periods

c7000 B.C.: Jomon culture; first recorded pottery with very simple designs.
c300 B.C.: Yayoi culture; bronzes and more sophisticated pottery.
1st to 4th Century A.D.: Haniwa culture bronzes and distinctive red pottery.
220 A.D.: first influence from Korea.
Asuka: 552–645.
Hahuko: 672–685.
Nara: 710–794.
Heian: 794–1185.
Kamakura: 1185–1333.
Muromachi (Ahikaga): 1338–1573.
Momoyama: 1573–1615.
1598: Immigrant Korean potters built kilns at Kyushu, producing the first glazed pottery to be seen in Japan.
Edo (Tokugawa): 1615–1867.
1616: First porcelain made by Ninsei (1596–1666).
1661–1673: Great age of porcelain; Arita, Nabeshima, Kutani and Kakiemon.
1716–1736: Popularity of lacquering and netsuke as art forms.
Meiji: (1868–1912). Strong influence of Western cultures developing and growing. Japanese art appears to decline in many respects. Much trading with the West.

An Hirado white glazed model of a rabbit, the eyes in red, damaged, 6in (15cm) long.
£700–800 *CSK*

A porcelain model of a cat, 6½in (16.5 cm) high.
£200–300 *Bea*

Flatware

An Imari charger, painted and gilt, within a border of ho-o roundels and pavilions in fenced gardens, on a scattered kiku head ground, damaged and restored, c1700, 21in (53cm) diam.
£2,300–3,000 *CSK*

A pair of Arita blue and white dishes, painted with coiled dragons within broad bands of shishi lions and foliage, Chenghua six-character marks, 18thC, 6½in (16.5cm) diam.
£340–400 *CSK*

An Imari shallow basin, with flattened rim, painted and gilt with alternating panels of boats below pine and stylised peony flowers, surrounding a central basket of flowers, damaged, c1700, 18½in (47.5cm) diam.
£500–700 *CSK*

An Arita dish, with foliate chocolate rim, painted in underglaze blue, Kakiemon enamels and gilt, damaged, 18thC, 11in (28cm) diam.
£750–850 *CSK*

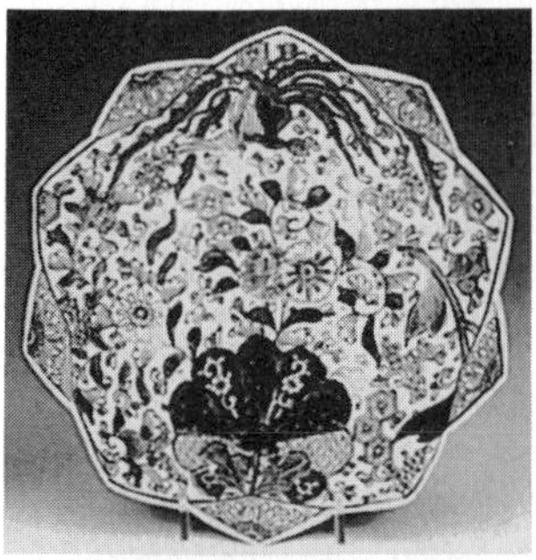

A set of 10 Imari petal-shaped dishes, painted and gilt with ho-o and brocade balls among scattered flowersprays and foliage, chipped and rubbed, 8in (20cm) diam.
£850–950 *CSK*

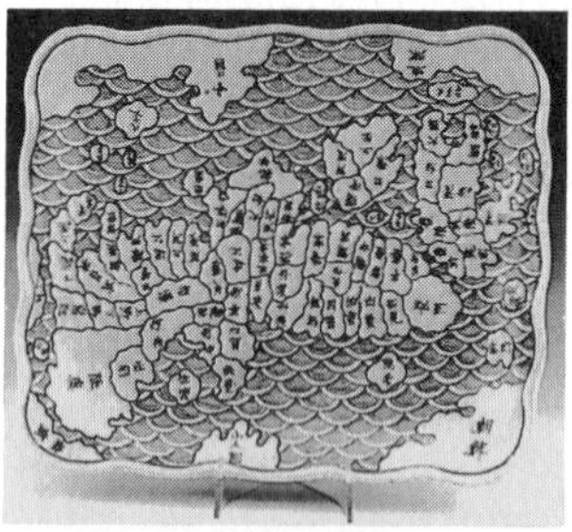

A blue and white dish, with shaped rim painted and moulded with a map of Japan and surrounding lands, divided into separate cantons, all on a ground of stylised waves, the reverse painted with mountains, restored, four-character mark, 11½in (29.5cm) wide.
£1,200–1,700 *CSK*

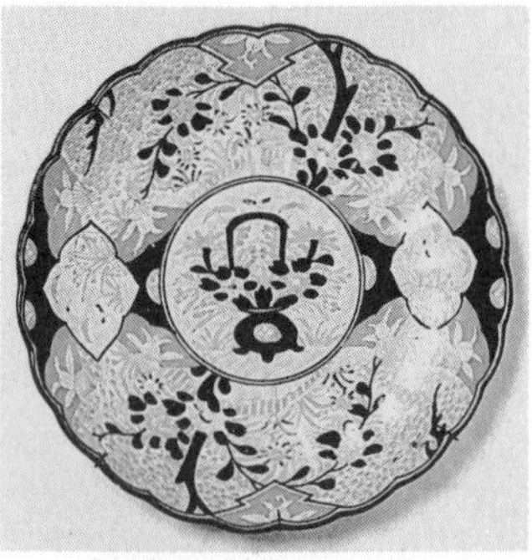

An Imari plate, c1890, 14in (35.5cm) diam.
£300–400 *AnE*

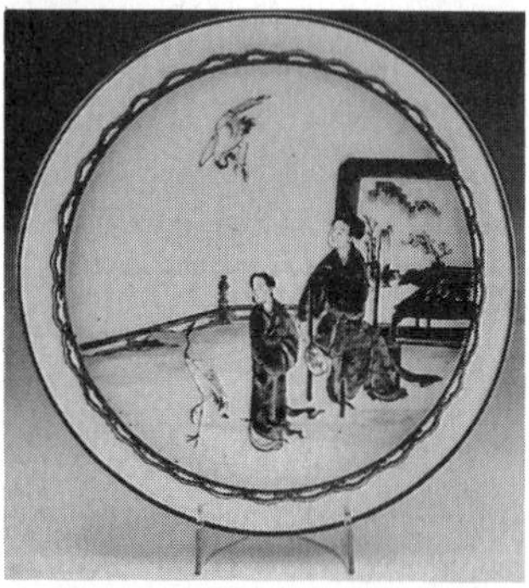

A Kutani dish, painted and gilt with a lady, attendant, screen and 2 cranes on a terrace, 9½in (24cm) diam.
£350–450 *CSK*

An Imari dish, the rim painted with birds and geometric patterns, 14½in (37cm) diam.
£350–400 *Bea*

An Arita dish, painted in colours on an iron red ground, with a turquoise and blue cracked ice border, reserved with gilt foliate motifs, 18in (46cm) diam.
£250–300 *L*

Did you know?
MILLER'S **Antiques Price Guide** ***builds up year-by-year to form the most comprehensive antiques photo-reference library available.***

Vases

A Kutani vase, painted with shishi lions among flowers and foliage between bands of lappets, damaged, 17½in (44.5cm) high.
£300–350 *CSK*

A pair of Kutani vases and covers, of double-gourd form, each painted with a panel of figures, the reverse with a pheasant beneath a flowering peony, reserved on an iron red ground, with gilt decoration, damaged, 18in (46cm) high.
£1,300–1,600 *L*

An Imari bottle vase, with lobed body, painted and gilt with trailing peony and chrysanthemum sprays, the neck with bands of geometric design and scrolling foliage, gilt rubbed, c1700, 9in (23cm) high.
£1,300–1,700 *CSK*

A Kutani double-gourd vase, painted with broad bands of scrolling peony and chrysanthemum flowers between floral and geometric lappets, signed, 13½in (34cm) high.
£700–900 *CSK*

A pair of Imari baluster vases and covers, each typically painted, reserved on a blue foliate ground, the shoulders with lappet panels of plants, the domed covers each with a bijin figure finial, covers matched, damaged, early 18thC, 20in (51cm) high.
£2,000–2,500 *L*

A Satsuma vase, painted with opposing panels depicting a furious battle and a tranquil garden scene, on a gilt and black brocade ground, impressed and painted signatures, 5½in (14cm) high.
£2,500–3,500 *P(EA)*

A pair of Imari vases and covers, decorated in bright green, orange, blue and burnished gilt, the domed covers similarly decorated, Meiji period, 24in (61cm) high.
£4,500–5,000 *N*

Miscellaneous

A Satsuma mug, early 20thC, 4in (10cm) high.
£90–120 *JHW*

An Imari lozenge-shaped box and wood cover, painted and gilt with shaped panels of Europeans aboard three-masted ships, alternating with vases of flowers, all on a floral trellis pattern ground, 6in (15cm) high.
£1,000–1,200 *CSK*

HOW TO START A GLASS COLLECTION

Customers frequently ask how they should begin collecting glass. The first step to is to choose, from the many categories, an area of glass which interests you and that you would like to collect. The list is enormous and runs from Ancient glass through to modern decorative glass. Some collectors concentrate on a particular maker, town, or country of origin. Others may favour only a particular colour of glass or items which carry a specific decorative motif. The price of glass or even display space may be inhibiting factors, but in narrowing the parameters you are establishing an area in which to begin.

Once you have selected a category, the next stage is to make use of relevant reference books and to find dealers who specialise in your field. Establishing a rapport with knowledgeable dealers is very important. If they belong to a reputable association, such as LAPADA (London and Provincial Antique Dealers' Association), they have an accepted established code of practice which assures professional and fair dealings. It is worth noting that most dealers are more than willing to share your enthusiasm and to discuss all aspects of collecting.

Handling fakes and later copies is a valuable exercise, as the feel of an item can reveal many inconsistencies. Check for reduced rims and feet, old feet from one glass stuck imperceptibly onto another of the same age, old glass with much later engraving, or copied signatures, which are all very difficult to detect. Rims and feet that have been reduced will have wheel cut marks and not the slightly bulbous rounded fire finish of English glass. Faked signatures and later engraving are more difficult to identify. Experts use ultra-violet light and also a magnifying glass to detect inconsistencies. If you are doubtful about a piece, the wisest course of action is to consult an expert.

For insurance purposes and to avoid duplication, photograph your collection as it grows, making notes of cost, measurements, and any reference book page number where a similar item in shown.

Finally, the most important criterion is to buy the things you like. It is you who will have to live with them. In the final analysis, your own feelings must be your guiding rule.

Christine Bridge

Bowls

An amethyst sugar basin, with diamond moulded ogee body and everted rim, on small foot ring, c1800, 2½in (6.5cm) high.
£200–240 *Som*

A cup-shaped fruit bowl, with cross cut diamonds and circular bands of prisms, fan cut rim, on plain foot star cut underneath, c1825, 6in (15cm) high.
£380–420 *Som*

A blue threaded vaseline bowl, with a pincer work rim, c1860, 3½in (8.5cm) diam.
£70–75 *CB*

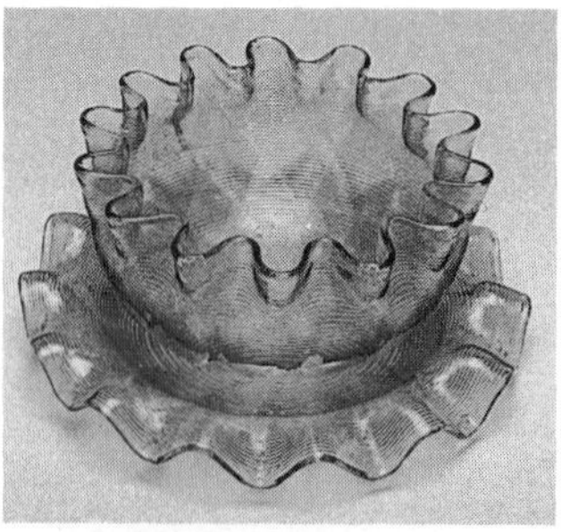

A threaded glass bowl and stand, with wavy edges, c1880, 3in (7.5cm) diam.
£50–70 *CB*

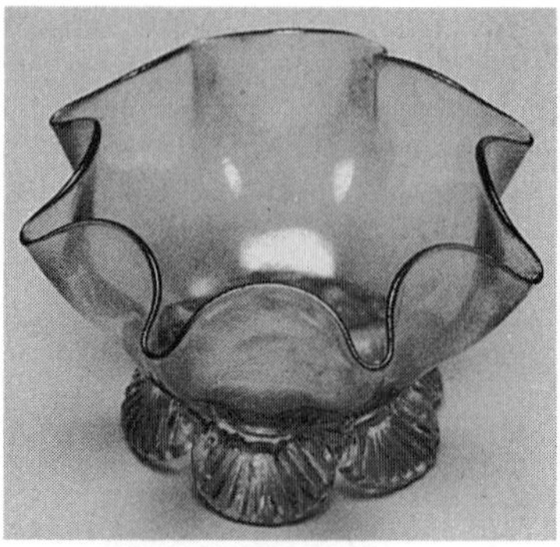

A Victorian amber bowl, 3½in (8.5cm) diam.
£60–75 *CB*

A 'rock crystal' bowl and stand, probably by Thomas Webb, cut with vertical bands and 4 panels engraved with shipping scenes, between swags and pendant ovals hung from ribbons, the silvered metal stand with 5 feet in the form of diving dolphins, c1900, 9in (23cm) diam.
£1,300–1,700 *S*

l. A Venetian enamelled deep bowl, the centre painted in yellow ochre, green and blue, within a white and iron red line, with granular gilding and iron red, blue and green enamel dots between borders of blue, white and iron red dot ornament, with everted folded rim, c1500, 13in (33cm) diam.
£22,000–24,000 *C*

A Stevens & Williams swirl satin bowl, lime green with brown spiral stripes, applied with Mat-su-Noke flowers and branches, with crimped rim, 8in (20.5cm) diam.
£420–500 *P*

Centrepieces

A Stourbridge cut glass centrepiece, possibly W.H., B., and J. Richardson, the wide shallow bowl with shaped rim, cut with stylised leaves and hobnail diamonds, above a similarly cut detachable collar and flared pedestal, c1850, 17in (43cm) high.
£2,600–3,200 *S*

A Bohemian ruby tinted centrepiece, in 2 sections, comprising a shallow footed bowl, overlaid in opaque white and cut with circular panels painted with flowers, and tall stand with 2 large oval opaque white panels painted with flowers, on a flared foot with gilt leaf scroll reserve, late 19thC, 13in (33cm) high.
£2,000–2,500 *S*

Make the most of Miller's

Condition is absolutely vital when assessing the value of an antique. Items in good condition are more likely to appreciate than less perfect examples. Rare, desirable items may command higher prices even when in need of restoration.

Decanters

An electioneering decanter, inscribed 'Lowther and Upton Huzza', c1761, 10in (25cm) high.
£1,500–2,000 *C*

The toast celebrates the Westmorland Parliamentary division of 1761 when Sir James Lowther and John Upton were elected against a third candidate.

A pair of tapered decanters, with monogram 'WMW' below a rose garland, c1780, 9½in (24cm) high.
£1,550–1,650 *Som*

A cut glass armorial mallet form decanter and stopper, engraved 'White Wine', slight wear, late 18thC, 12in (30.5cm) high.
£500–550 *CSK*

A tapered decanter, engraved with a band of hatched decoration, above monogram 'RAM' within a floral cartouche, with a plain lozenge stopper, c1780, 9½in (24cm) high.
£280–320 *Som*

A pair of plain decanters, with mallet-shaped bodies, 3 neck rings and target stoppers, c1800, 8in (20cm) high.
£580–620 *Som*

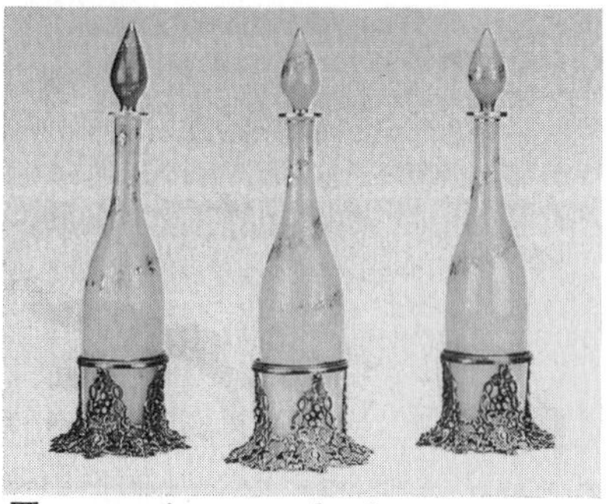

Three semi-opaque slender decanters, stoppers and pierced metal stands, in pale green, blue and pink, painted and gilt with trailing fruit and vines, slight damage, 19thC, 16½in (42cm) high.
£700–800 *CSK*

Three blue club-shaped decanters and lozenge stoppers, inscribed in gilt for 'Rum', 'Brandy' and 'Gin' within shaped panels with scrolling foliage suspended by chains from gilt bands, the stoppers initialled in gilt, slight damage, 19thC, 11in (28cm) high.
£600–700 *CSK*

A mallet-shaped ice decanter, with notched lens stopper, the base with a metal mounted cork stopper, slight chips to stopper, early 19thC, 13in (33cm) high.
£1,000–1,500 *C*

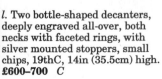

l. Two bottle-shaped decanters, deeply engraved all-over, both necks with faceted rings, with silver mounted stoppers, small chips, 19thC, 14in (35.5cm) high.
£600–700 *C*

Locate the source

The source of each illustration in* Miller's Antiques Price Guide *can easily be found by checking the code letters at the end of each caption with the Key to Illustrations located at the front of the book.

An Irish Rodney decanter, the shaped body engraved with vesica decoration, with 3 milled neck rings, moulded target stopper, marked 'Cork Glass Co.', c1810, 8½in (21.5cm) high.
£760–800 *Som*

Neck Rings

On 18th and early 19thC decanters, neck rings were applied separately and then moulded with a tool. The join in the neck ring was often carelessly made and, often appeared to look like a crack.

The neck rings on many middle to late 19thC decanters are an integral part of the decanter. If a damaged neck has been replaced, it may be possible to feel a join inside the neck.

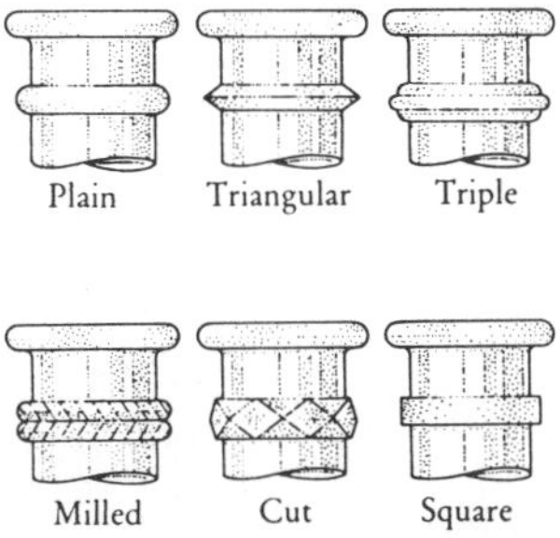

A pair of cut glass club-shaped decanters and stoppers, each fluted neck applied with 3 rings above prism cut bands, the lower sections cut with a checked pattern, on star cut bases, slight wear, 19thC, 9½in (24cm) high.
£360–420 *CSK*

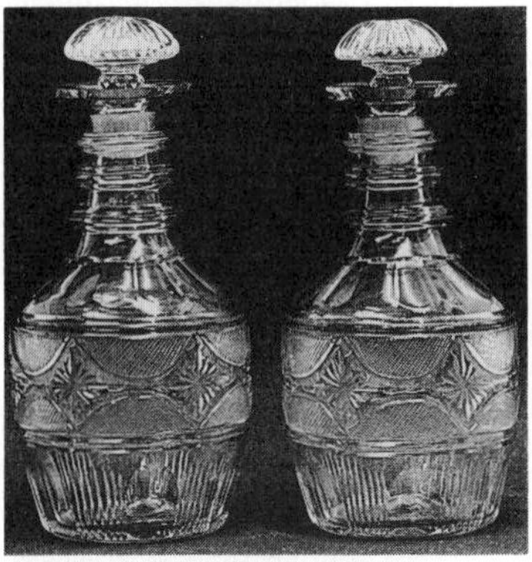

A pair of Waterford decanters, c1800, 10½in (26.5cm) high.
£450–550 *FD*

A pair of Irish cut heavy decanters, the ovoid bodies with flutes, prisms and panels of small diamond cutting, with 3 annulated neck rings and cut mushroom stoppers, c1820, 9½in (24cm) high.
£640–670 *Som*

l. An Irish decanter, with deep flute moulded base, engraved with hatched rose sprays and a 'bird in flight', the reverse with an empty star cartouche, 2-bladed neck rings, probably Belfast, c1810, 9in (23cm) high.
£480–520

r. A Cork decanter, with flute moulded base and engraved vesica decoration, 3 annulated neck rings, marked 'Cork Glass Co.', c1810, 9in (23cm) high.
£930–970 *Som*

A cut and engraved mallet form decanter and target stopper, cut with broad and narrow flutes, the neck with 3 rings, engraved with the monogram 'JB', damaged, wear, early 19thC, 12in (30.5cm) high.
£370–450 *CSK*

A set of 3 green spirit decanters, the club-shaped bodies with simulated gilt wine labels for 'Hollands', 'Rum' and 'Brandy', gilt lozenge stoppers, c1800, 7½in (19cm) high.
£1,450–1,600 *Som*

r. An Irish Rodney type decanter, engraved with vesica and star decoration, moulded fluted base, with radially moulded target stopper, the base indistinctly marked 'Cork Glass Co.', c1810, 8½in (21.5cm) high.
£650–670 *Som*

A pair of decanters, with cut spire stoppers, the pear-shaped bodies flute cut at bases, with scale cut necks, a band of engraving and solid square domed feet, c1850, 14in (35.5cm) high.
£780–820 *Som*

Cut Glass Patterns

Below are some of the most common cut glass patterns used during the 18th and 19thC. However, because they have been repeated in the 20thC, the pattern alone is not a reliable guarantee of authenticity. The earliest lead glass has a greenish tinge; it became more transparent and colourless through the next 150 years.

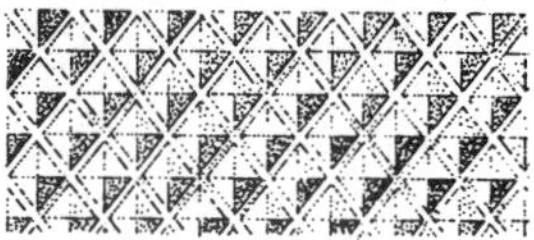

Plain sharp diamonds

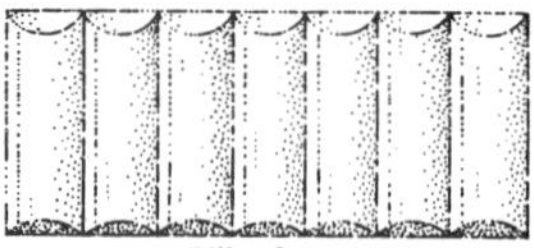

Pillar flutes

Star cutting

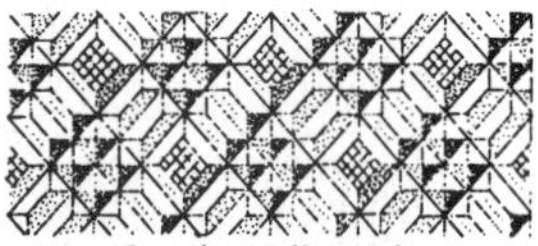

Strawberry diamonds

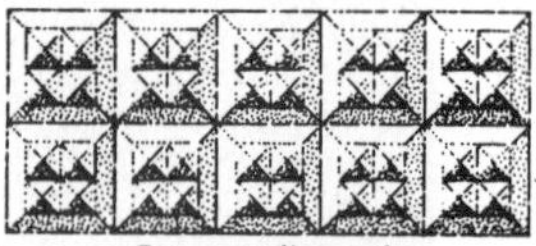

Cross-cut diamonds

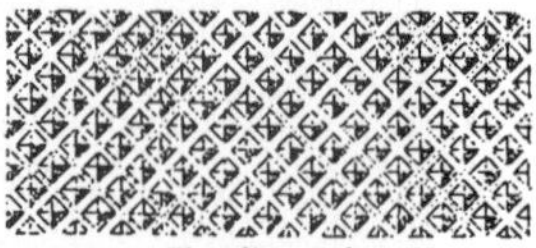

Fine diamonds

A pair of Bristol green glass mallet-shaped decanters and stoppers, each with 3 rings to the neck, mushroom stoppers, one stopper chipped.
£500–600 *L*

A two-piece cut glass dish and stand, both with alternate panels of oval and arched diamond, fluting and prism cutting, the central boss with grid pattern diamond cutting, scalloped and pointed rim, c1820, 8½in (21.5cm) high.
£780–820 *Som*

Drinking Glasses

An ale glass, with deep round funnel bowl, engraved with the hops and barley motif, on a diamond faceted stem with plain conical foot, c1770, 7½in (17.5cm) high.
£170–190 *Som*

Dishes

An oval cut glass dish, the body with fluted and diamond cutting, crenellated rim and star cut base, c1810, 6½in (16.5cm) wide.
£170–190 *Som*

A cut glass butter dish and cover, c1820, 7in (17.5cm) diam.
£400–500 *CB*

A cut glass butter dish and cover, c1820, 7in (17.5cm) diam.
£400–500 *CB*

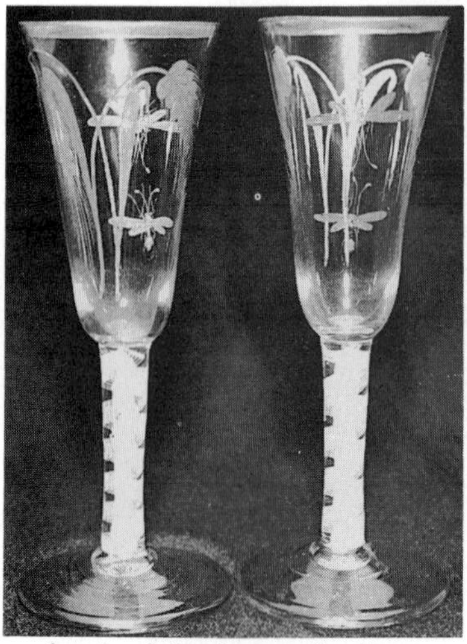

A pair of ale glasses, the deep conical bowls finely gilt with the hops and barley motif, the reverse sides showing 2 dragonflies, on stems with double series opaque twists, on plain conical feet, c1760, 7in (17.5cm) high.
£1,400–1,600 each *Som*

A Bohemian engraved flared beaker, decorated with figures of ladies and groups emblematic of Faith, Hope, Love and Charity below inscriptions, divided by flowerheads, blooms and foliage, the rim with loose sprays of fruit between scrolling leaves, slight wear, early 18thC, 4½in (11.5cm) high.
£1,000–1,500 *CSK*

An engraved portrait beaker, with a half length bust of 'Caroline Auguste Kaiserin von Oesterreich' on a matt ground, damaged, 19thC, 5½in (14cm) high.
£700–800 *C*

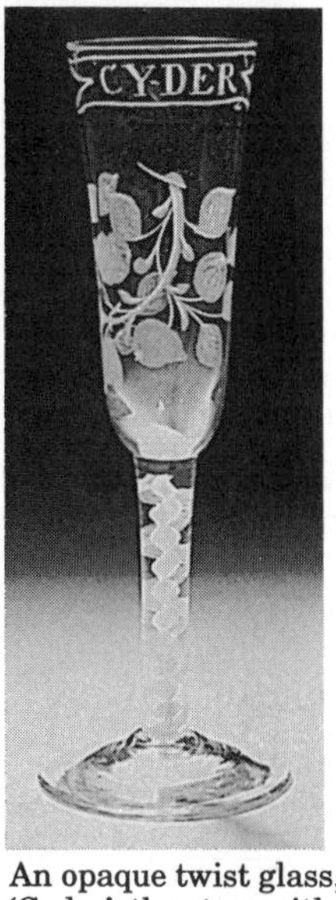

An opaque twist glass, engraved 'Cyder', the stem with an opaque corkscrew core within a multi-ply spiral, on a conical foot, c1765, 8in (20cm) high.
£4,000–4,500 *C*

Types of Drinking Glasses

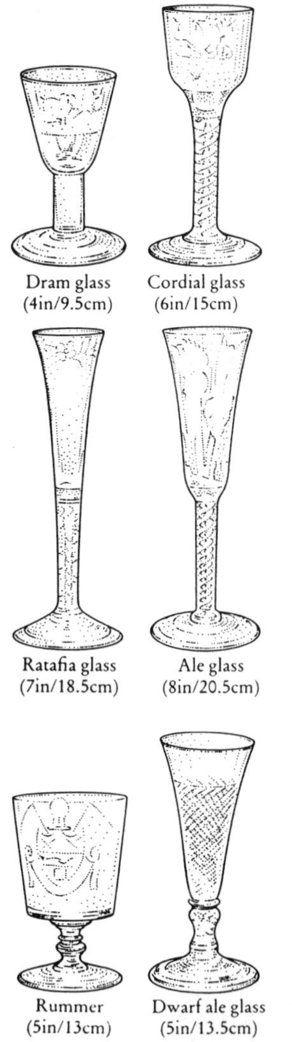

A dram firing glass, with ogee bowl, on a stem with a double series opaque twist and heavy disc firing foot, c1760, 4in (10cm) high.
£400–450 *Som*

A blue-flash waisted beaker, engraved with a topographical view entitled 'Ludwigs Kirche' within a rectangular panel, the reverse cut with lenses between cut bands of arches, late 19thC, 5½in (14cm) high.
£200–300 *CSK*

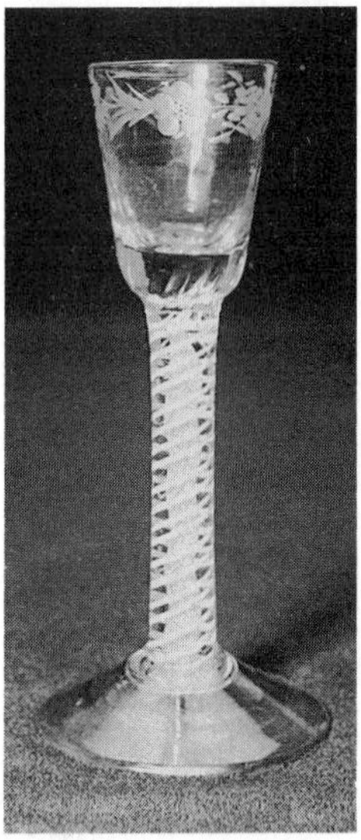

A cordial glass, the fluted round funnel bowl engraved with a band of roses, on a double series opaque twist stem and plain conical foot, c1760, 6in (15cm) high.
£550–570 *Som*

A firing glass, with deep conical bowl and flanged firing foot, c1780, 4½in (11.5cm) high.
£100–120 *Som*

A dram firing glass, with a conical bowl on a short stem with air tear, and a heavy flanged firing foot, c1780, 4½in (11.5cm) high.
£80–110 *Som*

A double dram glass, mid-18thC, 5in (12.5cm) high.
£300–350 *FD*

An early goblet, the bowl with gadrooned lower part supported on an almost hollow stem with a cushion knop, above an inverted baluster section terminating in a basal knop, on a folded conical foot, late 17thC, 12in (30.5cm) high.
£4,000–5,000 *C*

A double-coin goblet, with a hollow baluster stem, enclosing 2 silver threepenny pieces, flanked by mereses above a folded conical foot, c1689, 8in (20cm) high.
£7,000–9,000 *S*

The inclusion of 2 coins, dated 1689, in this glass might suggest that it was made to commemorate the accession of William and Mary to the English throne.

A Jacobite goblet and cover, on an eight-pointed pedestal stem terminating in a domed and folded foot, also with eight-moulded panels, the cover similarly engraved and with an octagonal spire finial, early 18thC, 12in (30.5cm) high.
£2,000–3,000 *P*

r. A large goblet, the bucket-shaped body engraved with various Masonic symbols and monogram 'TB', the stem with a bladed knop and plain conical foot, c1820, 7¼in (18.5cm) high.
£560–600 *Som*

l. A Dutch engraved Royal armorial light baluster goblet, with the crowned arms of Willem V of Orange and Nassau within the Garter, flanked by crowned lion supporters above the motto 'Je Maintiendrai', on a ribbon cartouche, supported on a slender multi-knopped stem above a conical foot, c1760, 9in (23cm) high.
£4,000–6,000 *C*

A Dutch engraved light baluster goblet, with engraved funnel bowl, inscribed 'T. Groeÿen en Bloeÿen van Oranie Meer', the multi-knopped stem including a central beaded knop above a conical foot, chipped, c1740, 8½in (21.5cm) high.
£2,800–3,500 *C*

A Dutch engraved light baluster goblet, attributed to Jacob Sang, the solid base above a bladed knop, a slender inverted baluster and basal knop, on a conical foot, c1755, 7in (17.5cm) high.
£9,500–11,000 *S*

l. A Dutch engraved friendship light baluster goblet, the funnel bowl supported on a beaded knopped and inverted baluster stem with basal knop above a conical foot, restored, chipped, signed and dated on the foot 'Jacob Sang, inv=et Fec: Amsterdam, 1759', 7½in (19cm) high.
£1,700–2,200 *C*

A Dutch facet stemmed goblet, attributed to Jacob Sang, engraved with monogram 'MAH' flanked by a boy and a girl above the date '1769', within an elaborate scrolling cartouche, the reverse inscribed 'Welvaar 'T Huys. Daar't Arme Kind Met Noot Druft. Hulp En Bystand Vindt', 8in (20cm) high.
£3,000–3,500 *S*

Cutting

Cutting decorative facets into glass was developed in England, Ireland and northern Europe in late 18th and early 19thC.
Designs were created to reflect the light making the glass object appear even more brilliant.

A Bohemian engraved goblet, the funnel bowl finely engraved, the multi-knopped stem incorporating a faceted baluster inset with spiralling gold and cobalt blue threads, the wide folded foot engraved with scroll, c1720, 8in (20cm) high.
£1,400–1,700 *S*

A coin goblet, the round funnel bowl with central band of chain trailing, the base with 'nipt diamond waies', set on a teared ball knop above a hollow knop, enclosing a silver shilling dated '1686' and applied with raspberry prunts, basal knop and folded conical foot, 10in (25.5cm) high.
£7,800–8,200 *Som*

This goblet is probably from the Savoy Glasshouse.

A Bohemian spa goblet, engraved with a topographical view, supported on a square section star cut base, chipped, 19thC, 6in (15cm) high.
£300–350 *C*

l. A Lauenstein armorial goblet, the bowl with solid base, engraved with a coat-of-arms and inscribed 'J'aime, qui m'aime', on a blue tinted inverted baluster stem encasing silver foil, on a folded domed foot, c1750, 8½in (21.5cm) high.
£2,000–2,500 *S*

A 'Façon de Venise' grey tinted goblet, the deep funnel bowl set on a hollow shoulder knopped tapering stem above a folded conical foot, Low Countries, 17thC, 7in (17.5cm) high.
£1,200–1,500 *C*

l. A Lauenstein engraved and gilt armorial goblet and a cover, inscribed 'CEC.G.U H.Z.L.' highlighted in gilding, knopped stem above a domed foot, engraved with a band of stiff leaves, the later domed cover with bud finial, late 18thC, 14in (36cm) high.
£9,000–11,000 *S*

The arms and initials are those of Carl Ernst Casimir Graf und Edler Herr zu Lippe, Lt. Col. and Adjutant-General in the service of Württemberg.

Three pressed glass goblets, with Nova Scotia Gothic, Kenlee, raspberry and shield patterns, c1890, 6in (15cm) high.
£200–300 *RIT*

A flute moulded rummer, engraved 'The Queen Forever', c1780, 5in (12.5cm) high.
£75–85 *FD*

A square based rummer, the ovoid bowl engraved with a plough and 'Speed the Plough', the reverse with initials 'IEB' between barley ears, c1800, 5½in (13.5cm) high.
£380–420 *Som*

A Sunderland Bridge rummer, the bowl engraved with sailing ships passing beneath the Iron Bridge, with a commemorative inscription, the reverse with a crest below the motto 'I Mean Well', on a ribbon cartouche within a circular sunburst and a floral swag with flowering thistle terminals pendant from pateræ, on a short spreading stem and square lemon squeezer base, chipped, c1800, 8½in (21.5cm) high.
£2,000–2,500 *C*

A set of engraved rummers, c1790, 4½in (11.5cm) high.
£380–420 *FD*

A set of 6 diamond and panel cut rummers, on blade knop stems, c1805, 5in (12.5cm) high.
£350–450 *FD*

An ovoid bowl rummer, engraved with a floral spray and the initials 'F.C.P.' in between, the reverse with a bird in flight, hatched rim, on a square domed lemon squeezer base, c1810, 5½in (14cm) high.
£250–290 *Som*

A rummer, the petal-moulded body engraved with 'God Speed the Farmer' and a band of stars, with rudimentary stem and plain conical foot, c1810, 5in (12.5cm) high.
£300–340 *Som*

l. A pair of Sunderland Bridge rummers, the bucket bowls engraved with the Bridge motif, the reverse sides with a rectangular cartouche and the initials 'R.A.', surrounded by a basket of flowers and floral sprays, with knopped stems and plain feet, c1820, 5½in (13.5cm) high.
£500–540 each *Som*

A toastmaster's glass, the thick deceptive conical bowl on a short stem with an inverted baluster knop, and folded conical foot, c1700, 4½in (11.5cm) high.
£900–1,100 *Som*

A toastmaster's baluster glass, the deceptive straight sided funnel bowl set on a teared ball knop, above a short plain section, on a folded conical foot, c1710, 4½in (11.5cm) high.
£950–1,100 *C*

Two wine glasses with kit-kat type stems, c1720:
l. the trumpet bowl solid section with inverted baluster knop and plain domed foot, 7in (17.5cm) high.
£480–520
r. with folded conical foot, 7¼in (18.5cm) high.
£1,400–1,600 *Som*

A French or Bohemian sulphide tumbler, in clear glass, with scalloped fringe to foot, dated '1840', 4½in (11.5cm) high.
£350–450 *P*

A pair of commemorative naval tumblers, each engraved with 4 anchors and inscribed 'Howe 1st June 1794, St. Vincent 14th February 1797, Duncan 11th October 1797' and 'Nelson 1st August 1798', the lower section cut with flutes, slight wear, c1800, 4½in (11.5cm) high.
£700–900 *C*

A baluster wine glass, the bell bowl on a plain stem with large base annulated knop, on a domed folded foot, c1710, 6in (15cm) high.
£1,300–1,500 *Som*

l. A part lead wine glass, with a large funnel bowl, hollow short double knop stem and a wide folded conical foot, c1680, 6in (15cm) high.
£1,800–2,000 *S(S)*

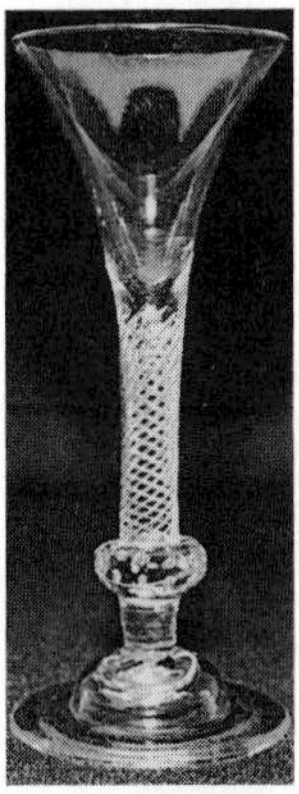

A composite stem wine glass, the trumpet bowl on a long drawn stem with short air-beaded inverted baluster section, on a domed plain foot, c1720, 7in (17.5cm) high.
£610–640 *Som*

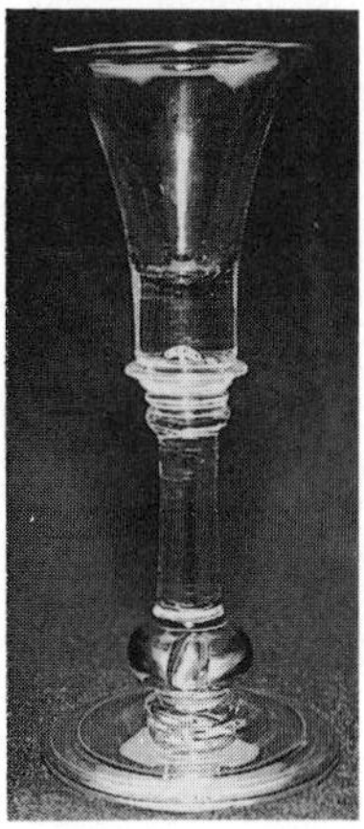

A baluster wine glass, the trumpet bowl with solid base and air tear, the stem with a double collar, above a true baluster knop with tear and folded conical foot, c1720, 7in (17.5cm) high.
£750–775 *Som*

A baluster wine glass, the bell bowl with a tear to the solid lower part, the stem with a triple annulated waist knop and basal knop, enclosing a tear above a domed and folded foot, c1715, 6in (15cm) high.
£350–550 *C*

A moulded balustroid wine glass, the bowl with all-over honeycomb moulding, the stem with 2 cushion knops above a plain section, on a conical foot, c1745, 6½in (16.5cm) high.
£420–480 *C*

Two wine glasses, with plain conical feet, c1745, 7½in (18.5cm) high:
l. with bell bowl and cable air-twist stem,
r. with pan top bowl and double air-twist stem.
£360–400 each *Som*

A wine glass, with a round funnel bowl on a six-sided Silesian stem and domed folded foot, c1720, 6in (15cm) high.
£780–820 *Som*

A round funnel bowl goblet, the lower half reticulated and flute moulded, a band of fruiting vine engraved above, on a stem with multiple series air-twist column, on a plain conical foot, c1745, 7in (17.5cm) high.
£650–680 *Som*

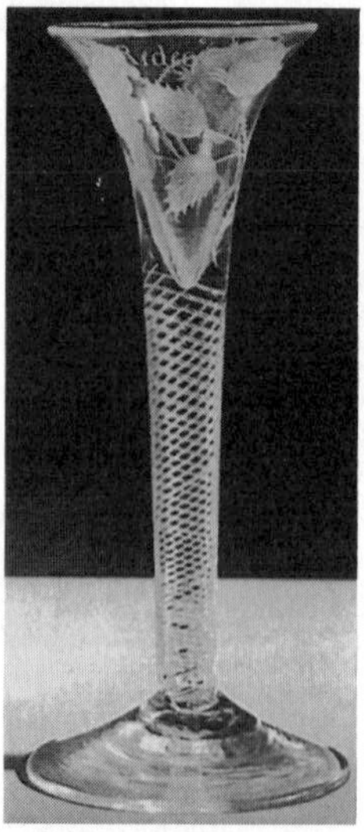

A Jacobite wine glass, engraved with 'Redeat' beneath the rim, with an air-twist stem raised on a domed foot, c1745, 6in (15cm) high.
£1,400–1,800 *WW*

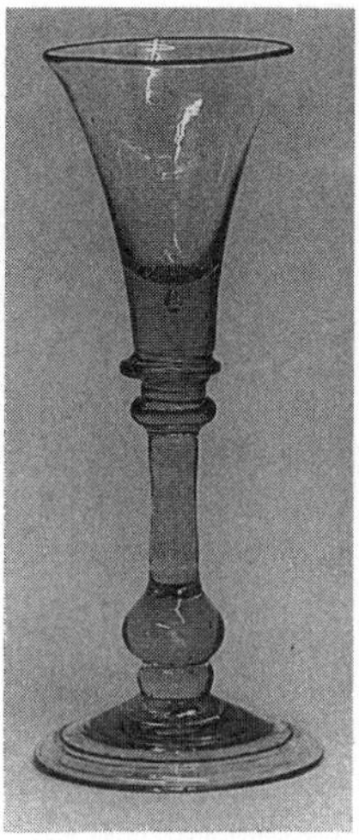

A light baluster wine glass, with teardrop in base of bowl, folded foot, c1720, 6in (15cm) high.
£650–750 *FD*

Two wine glasses, with air-twist stems, c1745, 6in (15cm) high:
l. **£370–390**
r. **£470–490** *Som*

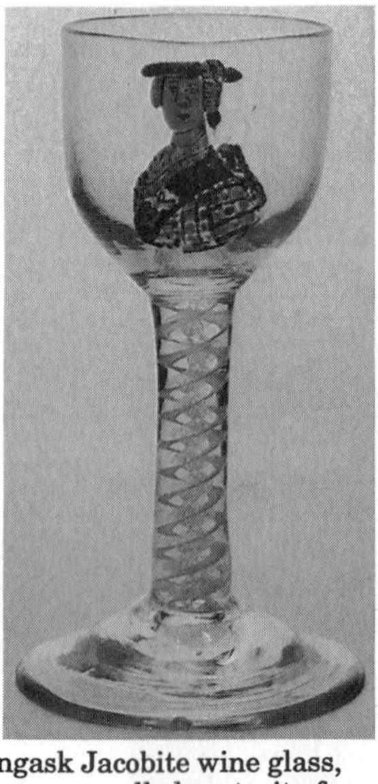

A Fingask Jacobite wine glass, with an enamelled portrait of Prince Charles Edward, wearing a blue tam-o'-shanter, yellow, red and turquoise tartan and blue sash, on an opaque twist stem composed of a gauze corkscrew encircled by 2 spiral tapes, on a conical foot, 5in (12.5cm) high.
£11,000–13,000 *P*

A Jacobite wine glass, the funnel bowl engraved with a six-petalled rose and bud, multiple spiral air-twist stem, on a plain conical foot, c1750, 6in (15cm) high.
£1,300–1,500 *Som*

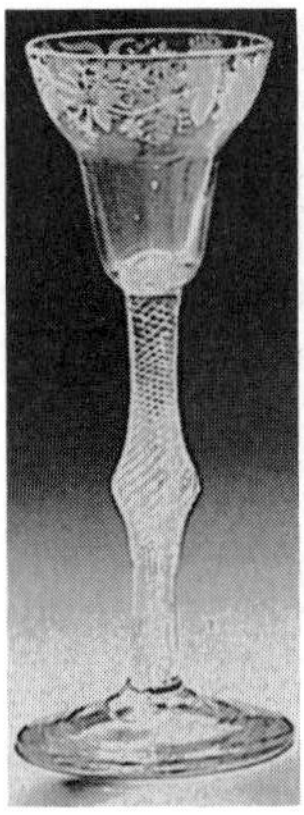

l. An engraved air-twist pan-topped wine glass, the stem with swelling waist knop and filled with spiral threads, on a conical foot, c1750, 6in (15cm) high.
£300–400 *C*

A wine glass, with funnel bowl, on a mercury air-twist stem with spiralling threads, on a plain conical foot, c1750, 6in (15cm) high.
£370–390 *Som*

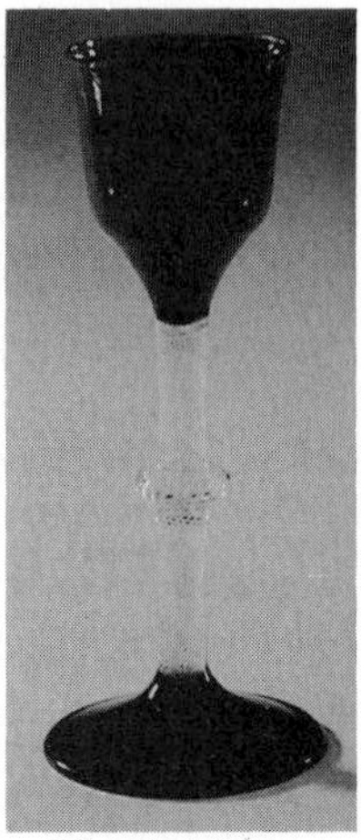

A wine glass, with cobalt blue ogee bowl, on a clear stem with swelling waist knop, filled with spiral opaque threads, terminating on a cobalt blue foot, c1765, 6½in (16cm) high.
£12,000–15,000 *C*

Although wine glasses of this type which combine green and clear glass are known, this one appears to be the only recorded example in blue and clear glass.

A wine glass, with trumpet bowl and a double knopped air-twist stem, c1755, 6in (15cm) high.
£320–350 *FD*

l. An engraved colour-twist wine glass, the stem with an opaque laminated corkscrew core edged with chocolate brown and translucent green threads, on a conical foot, c1765, 6½in (16cm) high.
£2,000–2,500 *C*

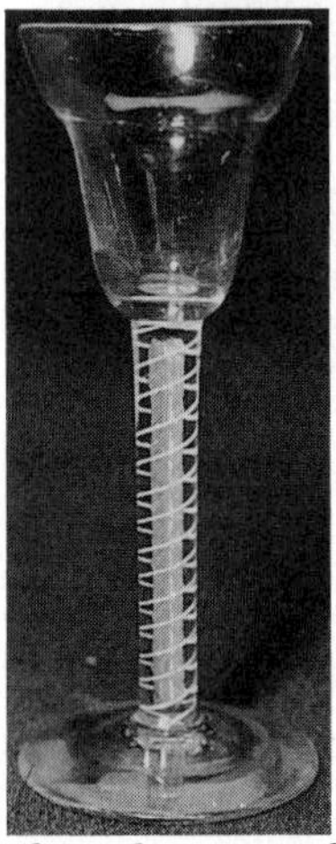

A wine glass, the pan-top bowl on a stem with a central air-twist gauze and outer pair of opaque spiralling threads, c1770, 7½in (18.5cm) high.
£680–720 *Som*

An enamelled opaque-twist wine glass of drawn trumpet shape, decorated in white, the stem filled with spiral threads above a conical foot, c1770, 7in (17.5cm) high.
£900–1,200 *C*

A set of 4 facet stem wine glasses, with round funnel bowls engraved with looped stars and printies, on hexagon faceted stems, on plain conical feet, c1770, 5½in (13.5cm) high.
£950–970 *Som*

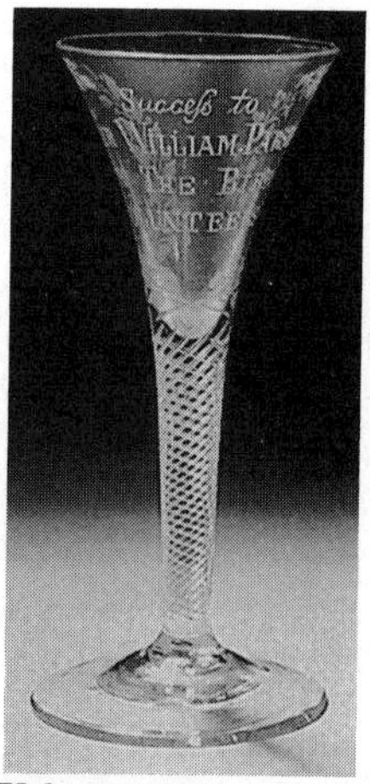

A 'Volunteer' air-twist wine glass, of drawn trumpet shape, the bowl inscribed 'Succefs to Sir William Parsons and the Birr Volunteers', *(sic),* the stem filled with spiral threads above a conical foot, small chips, late 18thC, 7in (17.5cm) high.
£1,200–1,500 *C*

A set of 6 matching wine flutes, with flute cut flared trumpet bowls, bladed knop stems and plain feet, c1830, largest 7in (17.5cm) high.
£410–430 *Som*

A set of 7 wine flutes, the trumpet bowls bridge flute cut, on stems with bladed knops and plain conical feet, c1830, 6in (15cm) high.
£400–430 *Som*

A Dutch engraved light baluster wine glass, on a multi-knopped stem comprising an angular knop, a teared ball knop above a teared inverted baluster and basal knop, on a conical foot, c1750, 8in (20cm) high.
£1,000–1,200 *S*

l. A ratafia glass, the deep round funnel bowl with a band of engraved stars and printies, diamond facet cut stem, on a plain conical foot, c1770, 7in (17.5cm) high.
£680–720 *Som*

An Anglo-Venetian wine glass, the flared funnel bowl with spiked gadrooning to the lower part, supported on a merese, four-bladed propeller stem and base knop, on a folded conical foot, c1685, 5½in (14cm) high.
£2,700–2,900 *Som*

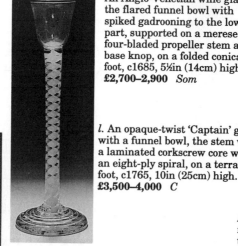

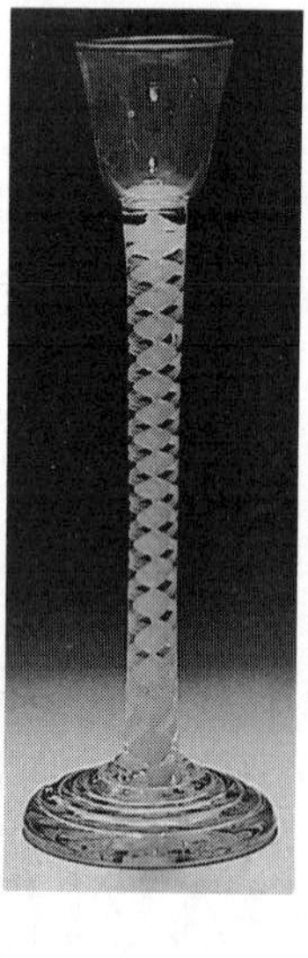

l. An opaque-twist 'Captain' glass, with a funnel bowl, the stem with a laminated corkscrew core within an eight-ply spiral, on a terraced foot, c1765, 10in (25cm) high.
£3,500–4,000 *C*

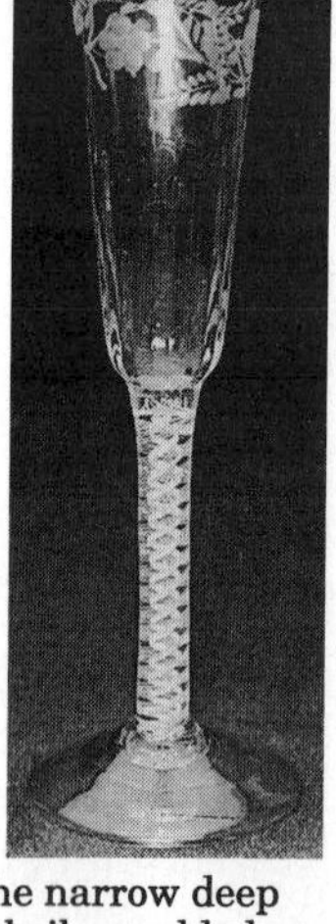

A ratafia glass, the narrow deep round funnel bowl rib-moulded on the lower half, with a band of wild roses under the rim, on a stem with double series opaque twist, on a plain conical foot, c1760, 7in (17.5cm) high.
£840–860 *Som*

l. A soda glass wine glass, on a six-sided pedestal stem with teardrop and folded foot, early 18thC, 4in (10.5cm) high.
£90–100 *FD*

Miller's is a price GUIDE not a price LIST

Jugs

A ewer or claret jug, the ovoid body cut with prism bands and vertical fluting, with notched rim, knopped stem and terraced foot, star cut underneath, applied strap handle, c1810, 11in (28cm) high.
£1,700–1,900 *Som*

A comb, panel and diamond cut claret jug, with a faceted three-ring neck and mushroom stopper, c1810, 8½in (21.5cm) high.
£300–350 *FD*

A cut water jug, the bulbous body with panels of small cut diamonds, prism and blaze cutting, notched rim, heavy strap handle and plain foot rim, c1820, 6in (15cm) high.
£280–320 *Som*

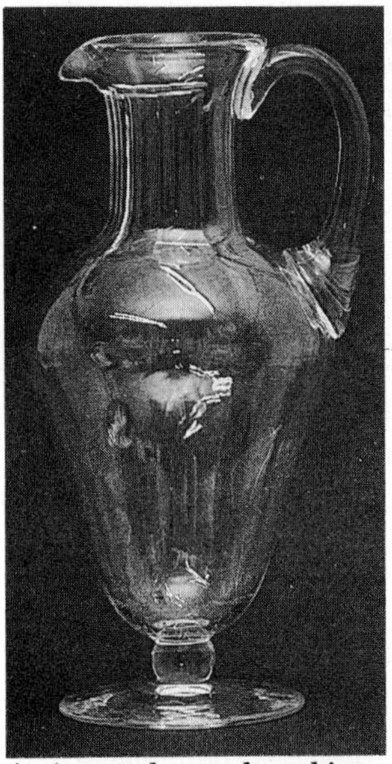

An inverted pear-shaped jug, with a panel cut neck, on a ball knop stem, 19thC, 8in (20cm) high.
£60–70 *FD*

A pillar-moulded glass claret jug, with French silver rococo mounts, c1880, 9in (23cm) high.
£1,200–1,400 *CB*

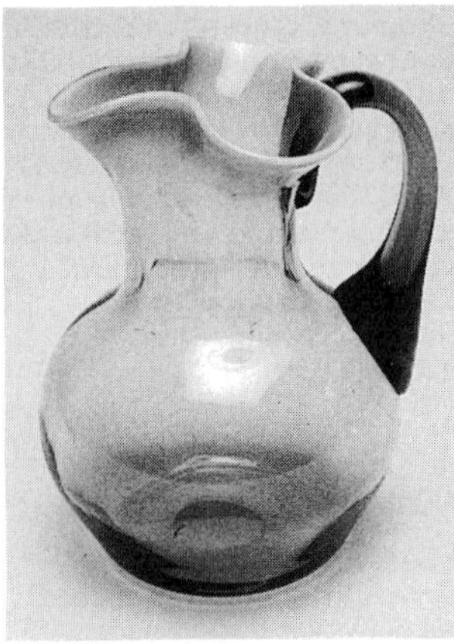

A blue opalescent jug, c1860, 6in (15cm) high.
£70–80 *CB*

A claret jug, the body flute cut with prism cut neck, notched and prism cut lip, heavy strap handle and star cut base, c1830, 9½in (24cm) high.
£360–400 *Som*

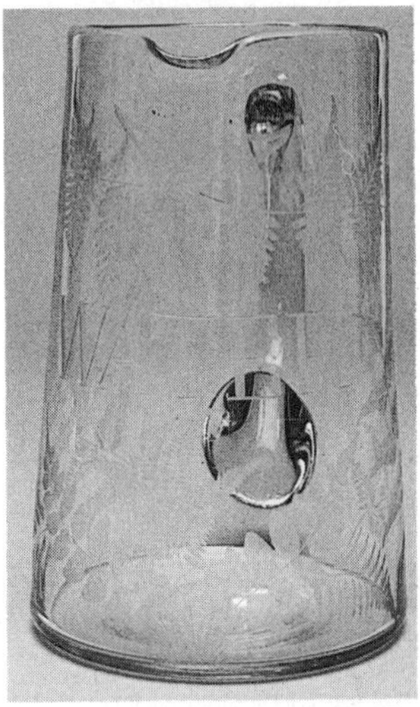

A clear jug, engraved with ferns and inscribed 'Water' c1880, 7in (17.5cm) high.
£50–80 *CB*

A pale turquoise claret jug, with faceted stopper, amber barley-sugar twist handle and star cut base, c1860, 8in (20.5cm) high.
£100–150 *CB*

Lustres

A pair of pink satin glass lustre vases, with gold decoration, each baluster body hung with clear prism drops, 11in (28cm) high.
£250–300 *Bea*

A pair of cut glass lustre vases, the shaped supports with fan cut rims, star cut feet and pillar cut drops, c1810, 8in (20cm) high.
£480–520 *Som*

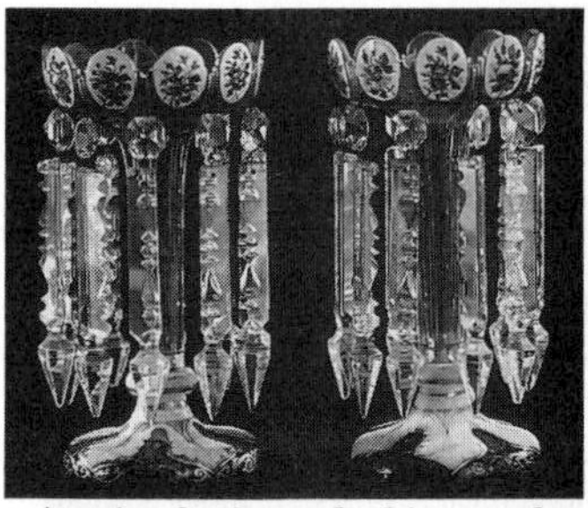

A pair of ruby and white overlay lustres, enriched in gilt, slight damage, late 19thC, 10in (25cm) high.
£620–700 *C*

A pair of Victorian glass lustres.
£1,600–2,000 *LT*

Paperweights

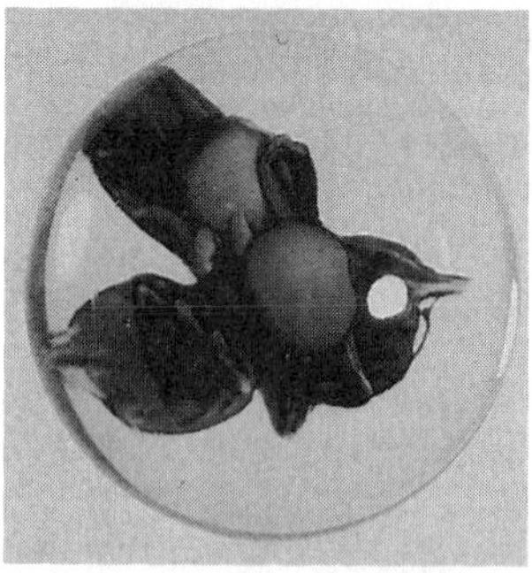

A fruit paperweight, shaded in yellow and orange on short pink stems hung from a slender russet branch, on a bed of characteristic textured leaves, 3in (7.5cm) diam.
£1,400–1,800 *P*

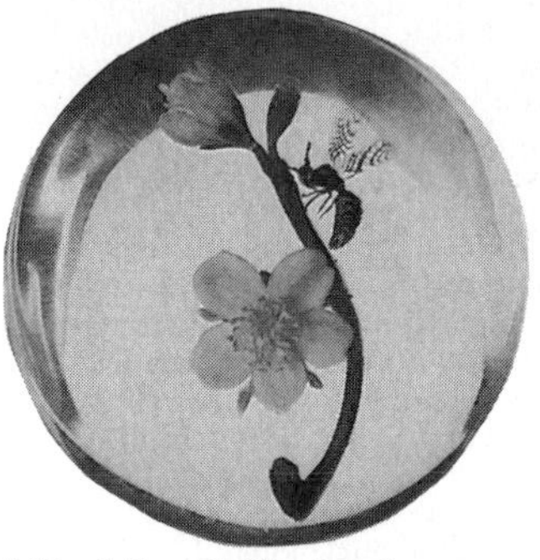

A Paul Joseph Stankard paperweight, with a bee on a branch of pink apple blossom, signed with 'S' cane, inscribed 'Experimental A317 1980', 3in (7.5cm) diam.
£600–700 *P*

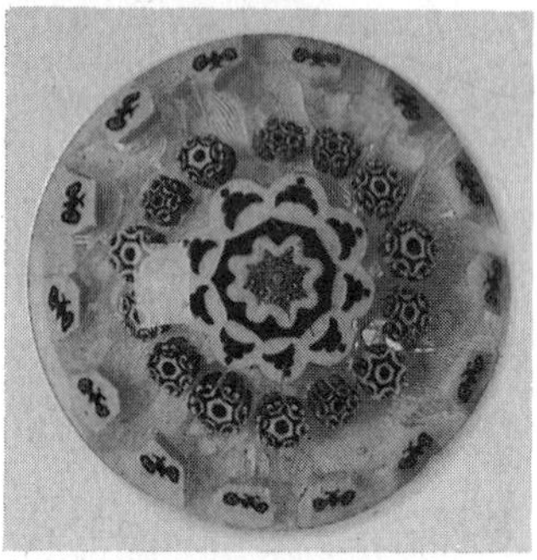

A Baccarat special patterned paperweight, 3in (7.5cm) diam.
£4,400–5,000 *P*

A Baccarat concentric mushroom paperweight, the well-formed tuft with 2 rows of white stardust canes and a row of rare shamrock silhouette canes in yellow and green, the central arrowhead cane within 6 red and green patterned canes, blue and white spiral torsade and star cut base, 3in (7.5cm) diam.
£1,500–2,000 *P*

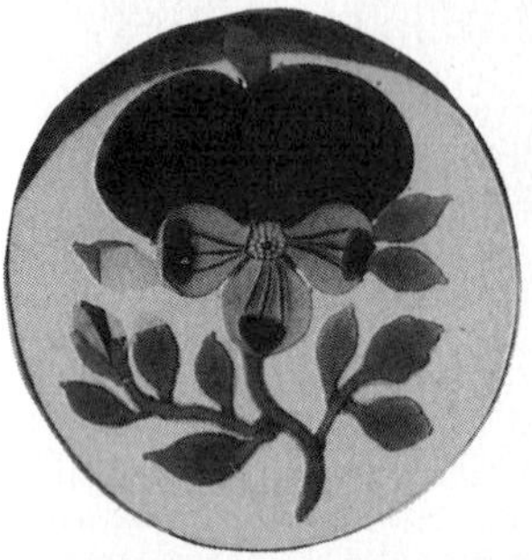

A Baccarat pansy paperweight, with 2 large purple petals and 3 smaller yellow petals with red tips and blue stamens, around a white stardust centre, the stem with 2 leaf sprigs and a bud, 3in (7.5cm) diam.
£1,000–1,200 *P*

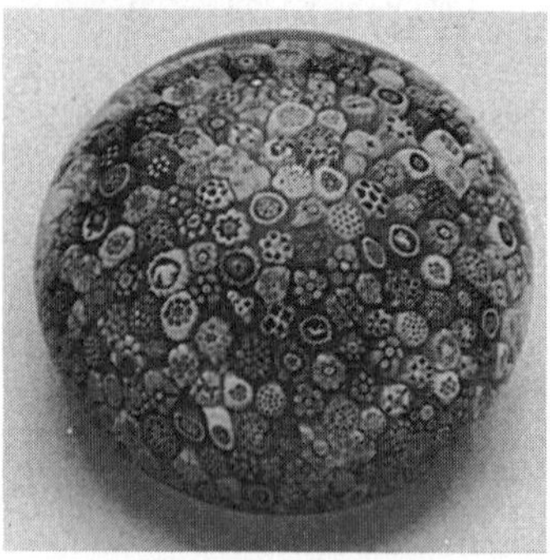

l. A Baccarat millefiori glass paperweight, the closely packed canes depicting flowerheads, birds and animals, slight damage, with initial 'B', dated '1847'.
£900–1,200 *Bea*

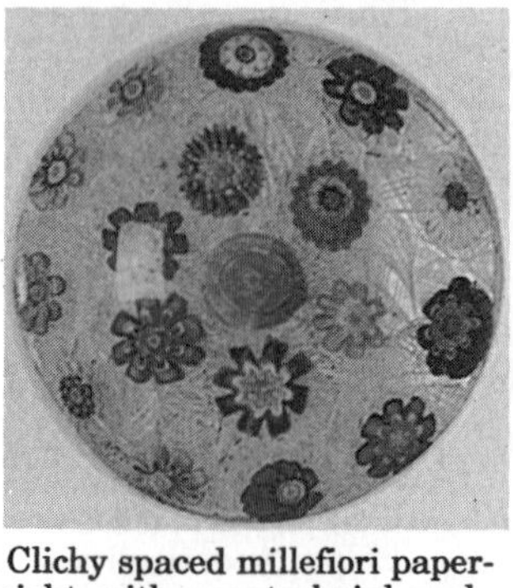

A Clichy spaced millefiori paperweight, with a central pink and green rose and 2 rows of colourful pastry mould canes on an upset muslin ground, 2in (5.5cm) diam.
£650–750 *P*

A Clichy garlanded flat bouquet paperweight, with 2 pink pastry mould canes and a red and green rose on a bed of 5 leaves, the garland with 6 large red pastry mould canes separated by groups of 3 turquoise canes, on an upset muslin ground, 3in (7.5cm) diam.
£1,500–1,800 *P*

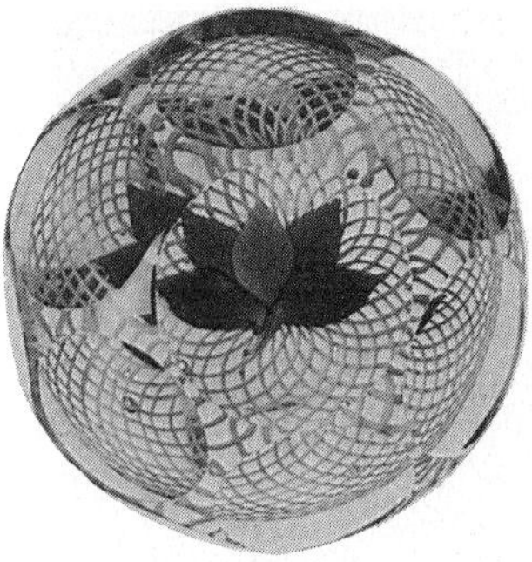

An American faceted leaf spray paperweight, set with a cluster of one pink, 2 green and 2 blue leaves above a white latticinio ground, cut with top and 2 rows of 6 side windows, 2½in (6.5cm) diam.
£500–700 *P*

A St. Louis faceted sulphide paperweight, with Napoleon III in profile, titled on the truncation 'L 'n bonaparte', within a torsade of fine red and white spirals, cut with 3 rows of circular printies around a top window, 3½in (8.5cm) diam.
£500–600 *P*

Scent Bottles

A red flattened pear-shaped scent bottle, with 2 compartments, twin silver gilt caps marked with diamond registration mark, the base with a silver gilt vinaigrette marked 'S. Mordan & Co.', c1870, 4in (10cm) high.
£970–1,000 *Som*

l. A St. Louis scent bottle, the waisted body with blue and white cane decoration, with embossed white metal mount, c1860, 4in (10cm) high.
£500–540 *Som*

A diamond cut, double-ended scent bottle, with gilt metal caps, c1790, 5½in (14cm) long.
£600–630 *Som*

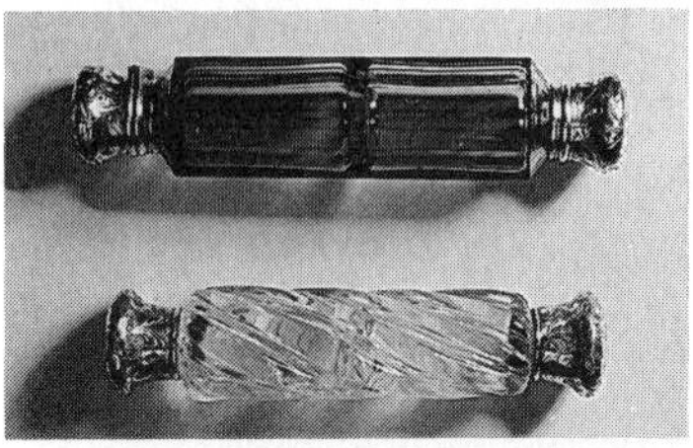

top. An amethyst tinted double-ended scent bottle, with chased gilt ends, marked 'Samson and Mordan', c1880, 5½in (14cm) long.
bottom. A vaseline double-ended scent bottle, with wrythen moulded body and chased white metal mounts, c1880, 5½in (14cm) long.
£430–470 each *Som*

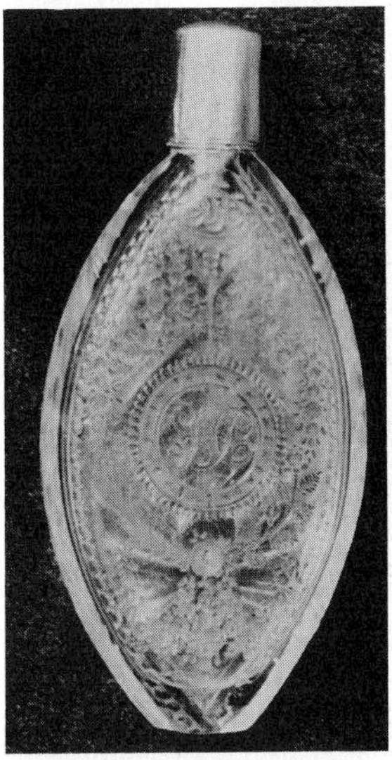

A single-ended scent bottle, with floral engraving, monogram on one side, diamond cutting on the reverse, silver metal mount, c1780, 4½in (11.5cm) high.
£480–520 *Som*

Sweetmeats

A moulded light baluster sweetmeat glass, the double ogee bowl and everted rim with all-over honey-comb moulding, the stem with a beaded knop between 2 plain sections above a honeycomb moulded domed and folded foot, c1745, 5½in (14cm) high.
£900–1,200 *C*

A baluster goblet or sweetmeat glass, the double ogee bowl supported on a collar above a ball knop and true baluster section enclosing an elongated tear, on a domed and folded foot, c1720, 6in (15cm) high.
£750–850 *C*

A Canadian green pressed glass sweetmeat dish, with a rayed heart pattern, by Dominion Glass Co., Montreal, c1915, 5½in (14cm) high.
£220–250 *RIT*

A baluster sweetmeat glass, the vertically ribbed ogee bowl with everted rim supported on an inverted baluster stem enclosing an elongated tear, terminating on a basal knop, on a radially ribbed domed and folded foot, c1740, 6in (15cm) high.
£500–600 *C*

Use the Index!
Because certain items might fit easily into any number of categories, the quickest and surest method of locating any entry is by reference to the index at the back of the book.
This index has been fully cross-referenced for absolute simplicity.

Vases

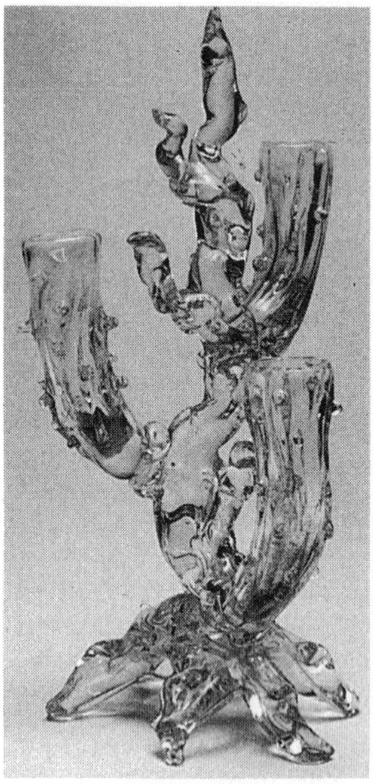

A Victorian vaseline opalescent wrythen bulb vase, 7½in (19cm) high.
£75–95 *CB*

A pair of Bohemian green tinted glass vases, each overlaid in white with 2 panels, one finely decorated in coloured enamels with a young girl, the other with flowers and leaves, on a gilt leaf scroll ground, on white overlaid base, mid-19thC, 13in (33cm) high.
£800–1,000 *DN*

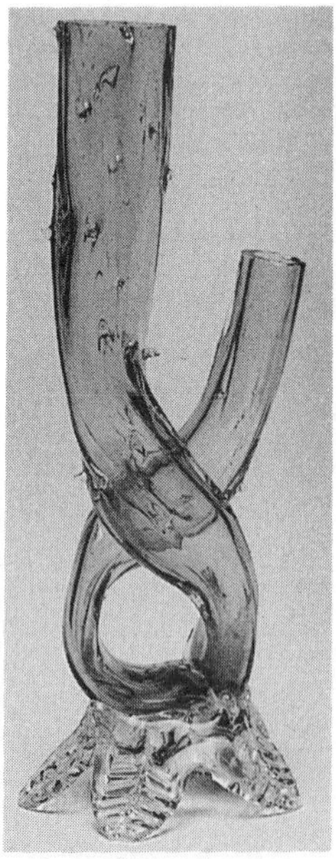

A rustic opalescent vase, c1880, 9in (23cm) high.
£60–75 *CB*

The term 'rustic' in this case means twig-like, with spurs.

A garniture of 3 engraved vases, with applied label 'Harrach. Novy Svet. Czechoslovakia', 20thC, vases 16in (40.5cm) high.
£5,000–6,000 *S*

A garniture of 4 Bohemian gilt and overlay vases, each ovoid faceted form overlaid in white and cut with stiff leaves, with tall waisted neck and overturned rim cased in blue and cut with printies, overall gilt with stars and scrolls, c1870, largest 14½in (37cm) high.
£1,500–2,500 *S*

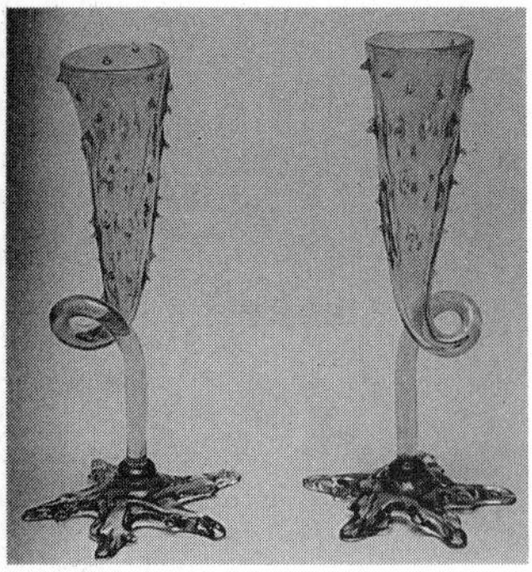

A pair of late Victorian rustic opalescent vases, with twist stems and five-leaf feet, 8½in (21.5cm) high.
£150–180 *CB*

Miscellaneous

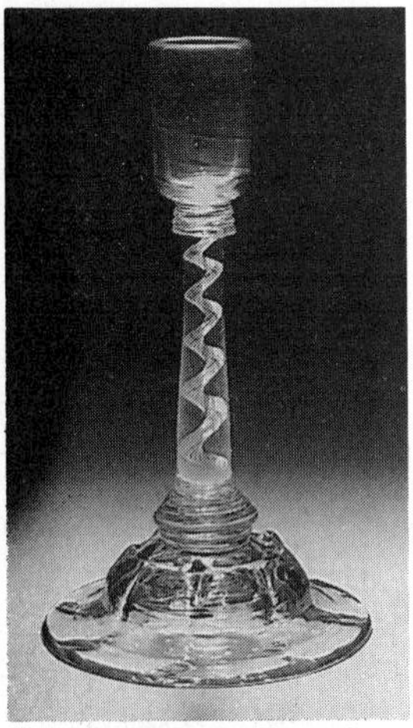

An air-twist candlestick, the cylindrical nozzle supported on a triple collar above a columnar stem, enclosing an air-twist gauze spiral and terminating on an annulated knop, the domed foot moulded with radiating ribs, c1750, 8½in (21.5cm) high.
£900–1,500 *C*

A Venetian filigree tazza, the wide shallow bowl inset with swirling bands of lacework alternating with opaque threads, set above a latticinio inverted baluster stem flanked by clear glass mereses and knops, the folded conical foot with filigree decoration, c1600, 4½in (11cm) high.
£9,500–12,000 *S*

A Bohemian white overlay baluster vase, with a ruby-flash shaped panel engraved with a recumbent stag in a wooded landscape, cut with lenses and arcaded sections, slight wear, 19thC, 13in (33cm) high.
£350–450 *C*

A pair of engraved caddies and stoppers, with star cut bases, slight damage, 19thC, 5in (12.5cm) high.
£200–300 *CSK*

A French moulded glass lace maker's lamp, 1890, 11in (28cm) high.
£100–120 *CB*

r. A Bohemian blue ground white overlay vase, painted in colours, gilt with scrolling foliage, damaged and repaired, 19thC, 18½in (47.5cm) high.
£300–400 *CSK*

An Edwardian iridescent green glass flower holder, in the form of a pig, 4½in (11.5cm) high.
£85–110 *DA*

An Irish single lipped wine glass cooler, the plain body faintly marked under the base with 'Penrose Waterford', c1800, 3½in (8.5cm) high.
£480–520 *Som*

Two pairs of glass candlesticks, with spiral cut columns, one pair with opaque twist knops, the other with spiral cut knops, all on circular bases cut with flutes to the edges, all with brass sconces, together with 4 glass drip pans, 13½in (34.5cm) high.
£500–600 *WW*

A cut glass cock fighting trophy, of goblet shape, with engraved etched panels in the Regency manner, surrounding panels of fighting cocks in the 4 stages of cock fighting, raised on a heavy pedestal base, early 19thC, 10in (25cm) high.
£600–700 *B*

A semi-opaque pale blue part dessert service, each piece silvered to the centre, with concentric lines below turnover castellated rims, comprising: a shallow bowl, 2 comports supported on baluster stems, and 6 plates, slight wear, 19thC, and a similar fluted baluster vase silvered with scrolling foliage.
£1,100–1,500 *CSK*

l. An onion-shaped blue carafe, c1840, 9in (23cm) high.
£220–240
r. An amethyst carafe, engraved with a band of thistles, c1840, 8in (20cm) high.
£250–270 *Som*

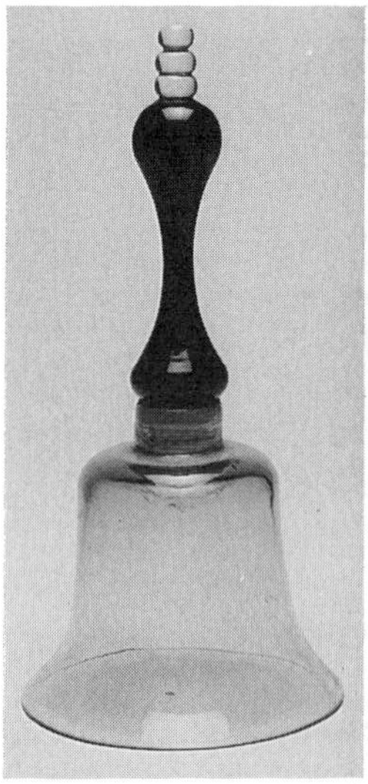

A pale green bell, with dark and clear glass handle, c1860, 9in (23cm) high.
£100–200 *CB*

A Victorian épergne, with a silver plated stand, 16in (40.5cm) high.
£200–275 *SUL*

l. Two baluster glass lamps, each on a wide folded tray base, with handles, cracked, 9½in (24cm) high.
£300–350 *P*

Five Continental hand bells, with spirally moulded bodies, below clear handles with multi-knopped terminals, damaged, late 19th/early 20thC, largest 14in (35.5cm) high.
£850–950 *C*

A green bowl, with clear pincer work frill, in a silver plated stand, c1880, 7in (17.5cm) high.
£50–80 *CB*

CLOCKS
Bracket Clocks

A mantel clock, with 8-day fusee movement by Baird of London, white enamel dial, classical case richly mounted with ormolu designs, and surmount of Cupid in a chariot drawn by 2 doves, early 19thC, 16in (40.5cm) high, beneath glass dome with satinwood plinth.
£1,400–1,800 *RBB*

A Victorian oak Gothic bracket clock, the silvered dial with black Roman numerals for the hours and subsidiary dials for regulation and 8 bells or Cambridge chimes, engraved floral decoration, the triple fusee quarter striking movement striking on a gong and chiming on a bell, top mount and finial missing, inscribed 'John Bennett, 65 & 64 Cheapside, London', 12¾in (32.5cm) high.
£1,100–1,400 *Bea*

An ebonised and gilt brass mounted quarter chiming bracket clock, the case with bell top and flame finials, the arched brass dial with silvered chapter ring signed 'J. W. Benson, Ludgate Hill', and with subsidiaries for regulation and chime/silent above, the triple fusee movement with anchor escapement striking on gongs, together with matching wall bracket, late 19thC, 43in (109cm) high.
£1,800–2,200 *P*

l. A Regency mahogany bracket clock, with white enamelled dial and Roman numerals, 8-day striking movement, the dial inscribed 'John Bentley, London', with ring handles, raised on brass ball feet, 21in (53cm) high.
£1,500–2,000 *AG*

l. A George III ebonised bracket clock, the brass dial with silvered chapter ring and date aperture signed on a recessed plaque 'Thos Clements London', with subsidiary strike/silent in the arch, the twin fusee movement with verge escapement, the case with bell top and carrying handle, on bracket feet, 19in (48cm) high.
£2,000–3,000 *P*

Bracket Clocks

Bracket clocks were developed from c1660, roughly the same time as longcase clocks. Many makers of longcases probably also made bracket clocks, and developments in the style, shape and size of both cases and dials largely follow the longcase pattern. Woods used include ebony, walnut, mahogany and rosewood. Some cases also feature lacquer decoration or complex applied metalwork.

Early bracket clocks have a square brass dial, typically with an applied chapter ring (the ring on the dial, on which the hours and minutes are engraved, attached or painted). The arched dial became increasingly common from c1715.

Silvered brass dials were used from c1760 and painted dials from c1780. The round dial – sometimes enamelled – is a feature of brackets from the late 18thC and the Regency period.

In the 1840s, the advent of the American bracket, or shelf, clock, with its mass produced stamped components, led to the gradual decline of the English bracket clock. Mass production meant that American clocks were considerably less expensive than English ones.

Both American and European bracket clocks are popular today, and French bracket clocks in particular represent good value for money.

Walnut c.1675
ht 19in/48cm

Ebony c.1685
ht 11¼in/29cm

Ebony c.1685
ht 13½in/34cm

Ebonized c.1780
ht 17in/43cm

Mahogany c.1780
ht 20½in/52cm

Mahogany c.1795
ht 15¾in/40cm

Walnut c.1685
ht 14in/35.5cm

Ebony c.1695
ht 16in/41cm

Ebony c.1690
ht 15in/38.5cm

Ebonized c.1800
ht 15in/38cm

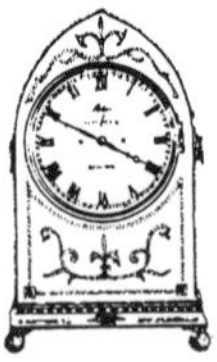
Ebonized c.1810
ht 19in/48cm

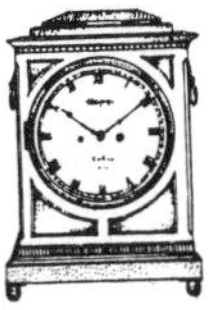
Mahogany c.1810
ht 16in/40.5cm

Ebony c.1760
ht 19½in/49.5cm

Walnut c.1760
ht 17½in/44cm

Mahogany c.1765
ht 18in/46cm

Gilt bronze c.1840
ht 18¾in/47.5cm

Mahogany c.1827
ht 26in/66cm

Mahogany c.1840
ht 13in/33.5cm

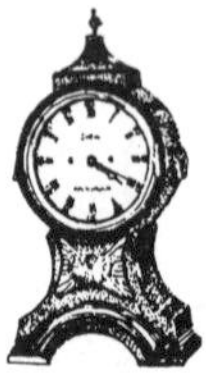
Ebonized c.1760
ht 21in/53cm

Lacquer c.1770
ht 25in/63.5cm

Mahogany c.1780
ht 19½in/49.5cm

Mahogany c.1840
ht 19in/48cm

Mahogany c.1850
ht 18in/46cm

Ormolu c.1875
ht 18¾in/46.5cm

r. A bracket clock, with brass dial inscribed 'John Drury, London', date aperture, double fusee striking movement, scroll engraved backplate, in a walnut case with bell top, on 4 brass ball feet, 18thC, 20in (50.5cm) high.
£1,600–2,000 *RBB*

l. A George III bracket clock, the 8-day repeater movement with silvered dial and ormolu spandrels, inscribed 'De Lasalle, London', in a mahogany case with brass loop handle on arched moulded top, grilled sides, glazed back revealing chased backplate, moulded base and bracket feet, 18½in (47.5cm) high.
£2,200–2,700 *AH*

A George III mahogany and gilt brass mounted musical bracket clock, the arched engraved silvered dial with subsidiaries for strike/silent and for 4 tunes, signed 'Easton, Petworth', the triple fusee movement with verge escapement playing on 12 bells, 19½in (49.5cm) high.
£3,200–4,200 *P*

A George III mahogany striking bracket clock, the case with handle to bell top, gilt metal quarter frets to front door, the dial signed 'Sam.l Denton OXFORD' on a silvered sector in the matted centre with calendar aperture, silvered chapter ring with pierced blued hands, foliate spandrels, strike/silent ring in the arch, the four-pillar twin fusee movement now with anchor escapement, strike on bell, on brass bracket feet, securing brackets to the case, 20½in (52cm) high.
£3,100–3,600 *CSK*

A William and Mary kingwood bracket clock, by Christopher Gould, London, the 6½in (16.5cm) square dial signed 'C: Gould Londini fecit' on the silvered chapter ring with finely sculpted blued steel hands, the matted centre with central rosette, ringed winding hole and decorated calendar aperture, the 6 ringed pillar movement with single gut fusee, knife edge verge escapement with Webster style backcock, pull quarter repeat on 2 bells, the backplate similarly signed within a foliate engraved rosette among further profuse tulip and foliate engraving, secured to the case with dial turn screws, 13½in (34.5cm) high.
£15,000–18,000 *C*

Miller's is a price GUIDE not a price LIST

l. A mahogany bracket clock, the painted dial signed 'Jas Henfrey, Leicester', the twin fusee movement with anchor escapement, signed on the backplate, 19thC, 21in (53cm) high.
£1,500–2,000 *P*

l. An ebonised bracket clock, the brass dial with silvered chapter ring, and mock pendulum aperture signed on a plate 'John Ellicot London', and with subsidiary strike/silent in the arch, the 5 pillared movement with verge escapement and pull quarter repeat on 6 bells, with signed and scroll engraved backplate, 18thC, 16½in (42cm) high.
£6,000–7,000 *P*

A Charles II ebonised striking bracket clock, the phase III case with handle and gilt metal foliate mount to the cushion moulded top, glazed sides, later foliate pierced sound fret to the front door, the 6in (15cm) dial signed 'Joseph Knibb, London', beneath the silvered Roman and Arabic chapter ring with finely pierced and sculpted blued steel hands, the matted centre with calendar aperture below XII, foliate spandrels, the movement with latches to the 5 pillars of tapering baluster form, rebuilt knife edge verge escapement, twin fusees, wire lines, numbered countwheel strike on bell via Knibb's pulley system, the movement secured with turn screws at back of dial, 12in (30.5cm) high.
£25,000–30,000 *C*

An ebonised fruitwood bracket clock, the brass dial with silvered Roman and Arabic chapter ring enclosing a matted centre within foliate spandrels, the fusee movement with pull repeat, anchor escapement striking a bell, the foliate engraved backplate signed 'Jacobus Markwick, Londini', with pendulum and key, mid-18thC, 11in (28cm) high.
£3,000–3,500 *C*

An ebonised fruitwood bracket clock, with white enamel Arabic dial, brass fish scale sound frets to the sides, the fusee with verge escapement striking a bell, the foliate incised backplate signed 'Holliwell & Son, Derby', 18thC, 7in (17.5cm) high.
£1,300–1,800 *C*

Did you know?
MILLER'S* Antiques Price Guide *builds up year-by-year to form the most comprehensive antiques photo-reference library available.

A George III mahogany musical bracket clock, the dial with original cream painted Roman and Arabic chapter disc signed 'Marriott Fleet Street', the upper spandrels with subsidiary dials for chime/silent and 6 tune selection, the arch with a later painted cut-out of Chronos automated to the escapement, the 6 pillar triple fusee, chain lines, movement now with anchor escapement, the music playing on a nest of 9 bells with hour strike on a further bell, 26in (66cm) high.
£4,000–5,500 *C*

A George III mahogany striking bracket clock, the painted dial signed 'Thos. Logan Maybole', Roman and Arabic chapters with pierced blued hands, calendar aperture, the spandrels painted with wild roses and strawberries, the 4 pillar twin fusee movement with knife edge verge escapement and strike on bell, the similarly signed backplate with centrally engraved Prince of Wales feathers, 20in (50.5cm) high.
£1,500–2,000 *C*

A mahogany quarter striking bracket clock, the repainted dial signed 'Jas. McCabe, London', the signed twin fusee movement with shaped plates and anchor escapement chiming on 8 bells, the movement with some alterations, together with a brass mounted mahogany wall bracket with sliding base, 19thC, 32in (71cm) high.
£850–1,200 *P*

A Regency mahogany bracket clock, by Nickisson, Newcastle-under-Lyme, 16in (40.5cm) high.
£3,000–3,500 *LT*

A late Victorian oak quarter chiming bracket clock, the dial signed 'Joseph Penlington, Liverpool' within the Arabic chapter ring, with blued hands, subsidiary rings above for chime/silent, regulation and chime on 8 bells/Westminster chimes, the 5 pillar triple chain fusee movement with anchor escapement and chime on 8 bells or 4 gongs with hour strike on further gong, pendulum securing piece to the plain backplate with securing brackets to the case, with bracket, 33½in (85cm) high.
£1,300–1,700 *C*

l. A fruitwood and gilt brass mounted bracket clock, the brass dial with date and mock pendulum apertures, with strike/silent above 12, signed in the arch 'Stepn. Rimbault London', the twin fusee movement with verge escapement and engraved backplate, 18thC, 16½in (42cm) high.
£3,000–4,000 *P*

A Continental ebonised striking bracket clock, the 6½in (16.5cm) dial with Roman and Arabic chapter ring now signed 'E. Norton London', plain steel hands, the pounced centre with mock pendulum aperture engraved 'I.G.E.' on the background, lacking alarm disc in the centre, the 4 pillar single going barrel movement with strike on bell above, verge escapement with crown wheel extended above the plates, pull wind alarm (partially lacking), early 18thC, 14in (36cm) high.
£700–900 *C*

An Edwardian bracket clock, with 8-day chiming movement having chased and brass dial, with silvered chapter ring inscribed 'Pearce & Sons Leeds', in tortoiseshell and gilt metal mounted case, 18in (46cm) high.
£1,700–2,000 *AH*

A late Victorian oak quarter chiming bracket clock, the dial signed 'Parkinson & Frodsham Exchange Alley, London' on the Gothic chapter ring with blued fleur-de-lys hands, subsidiary rings above for chime/silent, regulation, and chime on 8 bells/Westminster chimes, the 5 pillar twin chain fusee movement with anchor escapement, pendulum securing piece to plain backplate with securing brackets to the case, with oak bracket, 39in (99cm) high.
£1,300–1,700 *C*

A George III ebonised and gilt metal mounted musical turntable bracket clock, the dial signed 'Stepn: Rimbault London' on a silvered sector within the arch flanked by subsidiary dials for chime/silent and strike/silent, silvered arch above engraved with the 6 tune selections, the white enamel Roman and Arabic dial with pierced blued hands, foliate spandrels, the 5 pillar triple fusee, wire lines, movement with verge escapement, the music playing on 12 bells via 25 hammers and 6½in (16.5cm) long transverse mounted pin barrel, hour strike on further bell, pendulum holdfast to the foliate engraved backplate, restored, 27in (68.5cm) high.
£4,000–6,000 *C*

A George II green lacquer striking bracket clock, the dial signed 'Ralph Tolson London' on a silvered plaque in the matted centre having mock pendulum and calendar apertures, silvered chapter ring with pierced blued steel hands, Indian-head foliate spandrels, the arch with strike/silent ring flanked by foliate spandrels, the 5 pillar movement with twin fusees, wire lines, knife edge verge escapement, pull quarter repeat on 6 bells with hour strike on further bell, later quarter frets to the front end rear doors, the moulded base on block feet, 18½in (47cm) high.
£6,700–7,200 *C*

A Regency table/bracket clock, with 8-day duration double fusee movement striking the hours on a bell and repeating, the 6in (15cm) diam. white dial with matching steel hands, the rosewood veneered chamfer top case with brass bordered blind frets to the front, and brass fish scale sound frets to each side, together with 2 brass carrying handles, by Thomas Woolfield, Liverpool, c1820, 14in (35.5cm) high.
£3,000–3,500 *PAO*

An early Victorian brass inlaid mahogany striking bracket clock, with glazed brass bezel to the cream painted Roman dial signed 'Smith, St. Peters', blued spade hands, the 5 pillar twin fusee movement with anchor escapement and strike/trip repeat on bell on plain backplate, lacking feet, 20½in (52cm) high.
£700–900 *C*

A mahogany bracket clock, with silvered arched dial date indicator in the arch and strike/silent to the base, the 8-day striking movement with verge escapement by John Tucker, Exeter, with bracket, 19thC, 20in (50.5cm) high.
£1,400–1,800 *E*

A Regency brass inlaid mahogany and ebonised striking bracket clock, with painted Roman dial signed 'Trendell, Reading', blued spade hands, the 5 pillar twin fusee, wire lines, movement with anchor escapement and strike on bell on similarly signed border engraved backplate, 17in (43.5cm) high.
£750–850 *C*

A Regency mahogany bracket clock, with white painted Roman dial, brass fish scale sound frets to the sides, the twin fusee with anchor escapement striking a bell, the backplate signed 'Viner, London', 10in (25cm) high.
£1,000–1,500 *C*

r. A walnut bracket clock, the silvered Roman and Arabic dial with date aperture, the twin fusee movement with anchor escapement striking a bell, with foliate incised backplate, 18thC, 12½in (32cm) high.
£2,000–2,500 *C*

A rosewood bracket clock, the 7½in (19cm) silvered dial signed '75 Old Broad St, Royal Exchange, London', with fast/slow and strike/silent subsidiary dials in the arch, the fusee movement with anchor escapement and shaped brass plates, striking on a bell, early 19thC, 16in (40.5cm) high.
£2,000–2,500 *DN*

A Regency style bracket clock, the 8-day striking and chiming movement having a brass face, with decorative cast spandrels, provision for chime/silent and chime on 8 bells/Westminster chimes, supported on gadrooned brass half cut feet, late 19thC, 29in (73.5cm) high.
£2,200–2,700 *L&E*

A late Victorian chiming bracket clock, with silvered dial, the movement chiming on 8 bells and a gong, in brass mounted mahogany case with pineapple finial, a plaque inscribed 'Presented to the Revd. Edward Page, M.A. by the Workers and parishioners of St. John's with St. Paul's, Battersea, Advent 1888', 28in (72.5cm) high.
£1,300–1,800 *Bea*

l. A Louis XV tortoiseshell boulle striking bracket clock, the 4 pillar twin going barrel movement with silk suspended verge escapement and count wheel strike on bell, with conforming bracket, restored, 36½in (93cm) high.
£2,600–3,000 *C*

r. A Napoleon III faux tortoiseshell boulle striking bracket clock, the cast dial with individual blue enamel Roman chapters and pierced blued hands, the twin going barrel movement with anchor escapement and strike on bell, with conforming bracket, restored, 20in (50.5cm) high.
£1,400–1,800 *C*

Carriage Clocks

A French carriage clock, with repeater chiming movement, pierced brass and blue enamel dial, in glass and brass case with loop handle and bracket feet, 19thC, 7in (17.5cm) high.
£500–600 *AH*

A French brass carriage clock, the movement with lever platform escapement with push repeat striking on a gong, the backplate numbered '9697', with enamel circular dial signed for 'Mackay, Cunningham & Co., Edinburgh', set in a gilt mask within an engraved corniche case, 19thC, 9in (22.5cm) high.
£2,500–3,000 *P*

An architectural carriage clock, the enamelled dial above a small alarm to an 8-day striking repeat alarm movement, 19thC, 8½in (21.5cm) high, in original leather case.
£900–1,200 *B*

A carriage timepiece, the 8-day movement with single fusee and under platform lever escapement, the engine turned gilt brass case with columns at the corners and scroll handle, 19thC, 5in (12.5cm) high.
£1,300–1,700 *DN*

A French carriage clock, with quarter striking and repeater, 3in (9.5cm) diam. white enamelled annular chapter ring and blued steel moon hands, the movement with bimetallic compensated balance wheel, lever escapement and blued steel spring, striking the quarters and repeating the hours and the quarters on 2 bells, the backplate signed 'C^les^ Frodsham Paris', in gilt brass corniche case, with key, 10in (25cm) high.
£1,700–2,000 *L*

A French carriage clock made for James Grohe of London, the 8-day movement striking the hours and half hours on a bell, the brass mask dial surround engraved and silvered, with round enamel chapter ring signed by Grohe, c1865, 6in (15cm) high, including handle.
£2,800–3,000 *PAO*

r. A French brass grande sonnerie striking carriage clock, with later trefoil hands and alarm ring, plain gorge case with engine-turned gilt mask for the top viewing glass, 6in (15cm) high.
£950–1,200 *C*

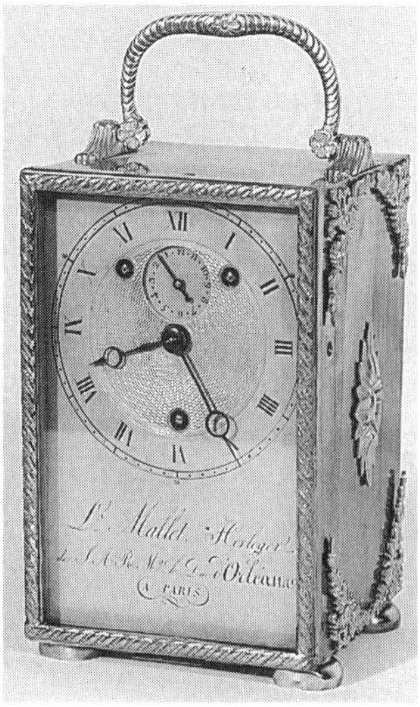

A carriage clock, by Louis Mallet, with 8-day escapement, grande sonnerie movement striking on 2 bells, pull-wound alarm and a pull repeat cord, in brass case with applied mounts, silvered dial and bun feet, 8in (20cm) high.
£3,000–3,500 *AH*

A Continental early striking carriage clock, the movement with simple balance to the cylinder platform, strike/repeat/alarm on bell housed in the base, the rack and snail strike work planted on the backplate, white enamel Roman dial with blued moon hands and subsidiary alarm ring below, case possibly composite, 7½in (19cm) high.
£600–800 *C*

A French carriage clock, the 8-day duration repeating movement with lever escapement striking the hours and half hours on a gong, together with alarm, the dial showing the retailer's name, 'Dent, Strand, London', c1860, 6½in (16.5cm) high.
£1,800–2,000 *PAO*

Cartel Clocks

l. A Louis XV gilt bronze cartel clock, the dial and movement signed 'Ferdinand Berthoud', the case formed of flower and leaf-cast scrollwork with a cherub above the dial, mid-18thC, 24½in (62.5cm) high.
£13,000–15,000 *S*

r. A French ormolu cartel clock, with a convex glazed enamel dial signed 'Bryson & Sons/Paris', with blue Roman chapters and black Arabic 5-minute divisions, with pierced gilt hands, the twin train movement with bell strike, above a pierced trellis grille and female mask, late 19thC, 20in (51cm) high.
£1,100–1,500 *C*

A Louis XV gilt bronze cartel clock, the movement signed 'Jean Fol à Paris', the case signed 'St. Germain' and formed of bold scrollwork cast with flowers and leaves, 22in (56cm) high.
£10,000–12,000 *S*

Jean-Joseph de St. Germain, 1719-91, was the son of cabinet maker Joseph de St. Germain.

MILLER'S COMPARES . . .

I. A Louis XV gilt bronze cartel clock, the case stamped 'St. Germain', with circular white enamel dial, the movement signed 'Jean Fol à Paris', mid-18thC, 24½in (62cm) high.
£9,500–12,000 *S*

II. A Louis XV gilt bronze cartel clock, the dial and movement signed 'Etienne Lenoir à Paris', mid-18thC, 14½in (37cm) high.
£4,500–6,500 *S*

These cartel clocks are described in very similar terms, however *Item I* sold for much more at auction than *Item II*. This is due to the superior quality of both the gilding and casting of *Item I*. The fully rococo style of *Item I* – demonstrated by the asymmetrical design and the elaborate scrollwork and shell motif ornamentation – adds to its desirability and value. The casting of *Item II* is symmetrical and so not as sought after. *S*

Cuckoo Clocks

A Black Forest cuckoo clock, the case of typical form with a cuckoo for the quarters and a trumpeter below for the hours, the movement stamped 'G.H.S.', with anchor escapement, 19thC, 27in (69cm) high.
£800–1,000 *P*

A Black Forest cuckoo clock, the 5½in (14cm) dial with carved bone hands, 2 train weight driven brass plated movement skeletonised in the form of a lyre, the leaf carved chalet case surmounted by a stag's head, c1890, 27½in (70cm) high.
£750–950 *S*

Garnitures

A French gilt metal clock garniture, decorated with Paris porcelain urns and panels, the dial with Roman numerals, fitted 8-day striking movement by Japy Frères, retailed by A. Carlhian and Beaumetz à Paris, stamped 'P.H. Mourey', raised on a gilt painted stand, 26in (66cm) high, together with a pair of candelabra, 27in (69cm) high.
£1,500–1,800 *AG*

l. A French ormolu and champlevé enamel clock garniture, the whole case with all-over polychrome geometric and floral designs, with decorated circular dial, the twin train movement striking on a bell, 19thC, 21½in (54.5cm) high, together with a matching pair of side ornaments.
£2,500–3,000 *P*

A Louis XVI ormolu and salmon marble clock garniture, the enamel dial with zodiac signs, time and strike movement, key missing, 19thC, clock 22½in (57cm) high, with a pair of candelabra, 23in (59cm) high.
£4,500–6,500 *SK(B)*

Lantern Clocks

A silver plated lantern clock, the 6½in (16.5cm) silvered chapter ring with engraved Roman numerals, engraved centre signed 'Andrew Allan in Grabb St Londini fecit', the movement stamped 'W & H sch', striking on a bell mounted above, English/ German, c1890, 15½in (39cm) high.
£400–600 *Bon*

A brass lantern clock, with a 6¾in (17cm) brass chapter ring, twin fusee movement striking the hours and quarters on 2 bells, in a case with turned corner columns and finials, pierced frets, on ball feet, c1870, 16in (40.5cm) high.
£750–1,000 *Bon*

A brass 30 hour lantern clock, by Robert Watts, with a 6in (15cm) brass Roman numeral chapter ring, signed in the foliage engraved centre 'Robt Watts, Stamford', with a single hand, post weight driven movement and verge and short bob pendulum, outside locking, plate striking on a bell mounted above the case with slender columns and turned finials, c1760, 14in (36cm) high.
£1,500–2,000 *Bon*

Longcase Clocks

A mid-Georgian mahogany longcase clock, the long pendulum door with shaped ogee moulded edge, 2 quartered reeded pilasters, moulded shoulder, plinth base, the 8-day movement with a phases of the moon dial, second hand and date aperture, with raised brass chapter ring and rococo scrolled spandrels, the centre decorated with Masonic emblems, inscribed 'Benjamin Barlow Oldham.'
£1,200–1,500 *L&E*

A Charles II longcase clock, the 8-day striking movement converted from verge to anchor escapement, the brass dial with a skeleton chapter ring with minute numbering, inscribed 'Edmond Appley Londini', black japanned pine case, with remains of twist pilasters to hood, oval glazed aperture and raised panels to trunk door, plinth base, incomplete, 70in (177.5cm) high.
£6,500–7,500 *WW*

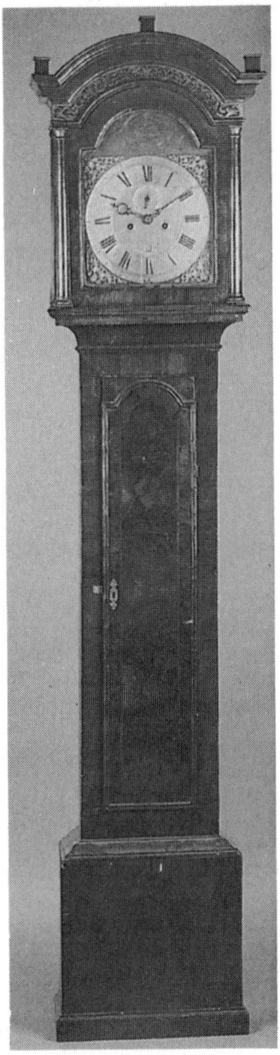

r. A walnut longcase clock, the 12in (30.5cm) dial with silvered chapter ring, signed in the engraved arch 'Tho. Baker, Portsmouth', the matted centre with subsidiary seconds, date, double cherub and crown spandrels, the 5 ringed pillar movement striking on a bell, c1740, 91in (231cm) high.
£2,500–3,500 *Bon*

l. A mahogany longcase clock, the 8-day striking movement with arched silvered dial, the lunette with strike/silent regulation above seconds and calendar subsidiary dials, inscribed 'Walder Arundell,' mahogany veneered oak trunk with moulded edge arcaded waist door, the base with outline panel and stepped scrolling plinth, early 19thC, 93in (237cm) high.
£4,000–4,500 *WW*

An oak longcase clock, by John Chapple, Littlehampton, the 12in (30.5cm) painted dial with Roman numerals and calendar aperture, pull wind, bell striking movement in a flat top case with plain corner columns, c1780, 72in (182.5cm) high.
£500–600 *Bon*

A longcase clock, by John Bennett, London, the brass and silvered dial with subsidiary seconds dial and calendar aperture, the 8-day movement striking on a bell, in red, black and gilt chinoiserie lacquer case, mid-18thC, 86½in (220cm) high.
£2,500–3,000 *Bea*

An oak longcase clock, the 12in (30.5cm) dial with silvered Roman and Arabic chapter ring, signed 'Willm Cockey, Yeovil', matted centre, subsidiary and calendar aperture, the 5 pillar movement racking striking on a bell in the flat top case, with flanking plain columns, long trunk door, 74in (188cm) high.
£1,400–1,800 *Bon*

An oak and mahogany longcase clock, by Rich Bridgewater, the 12in (30.5cm) painted dial with Roman numerals, subsidiary seconds and calendar sector, bell striking movement, c1790, 84in (213cm) high.
£650–850 *Bon*

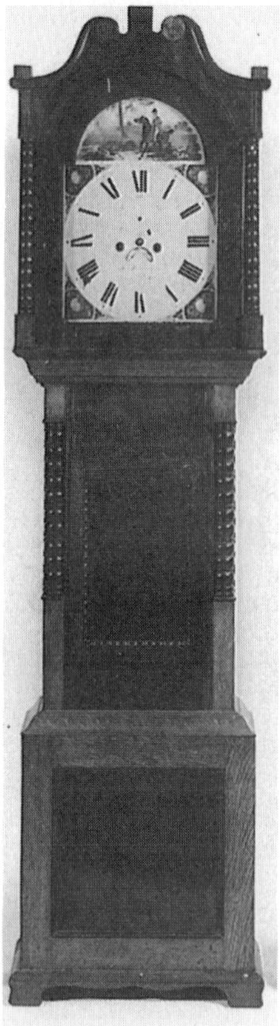

An oak and mahogany longcase clock, by Jas. Burroughs, Iron Bridge, the 13¼in (34cm) painted arch dial with Roman numerals, subsidiary seconds and calendar sector, four-pillar bell striking movement in a case, scroll cresting, break arch door flanked by ribbed columns with short trunk door flanked by similar columns, 84½in (215cm) high.
£550–750 *Bon*

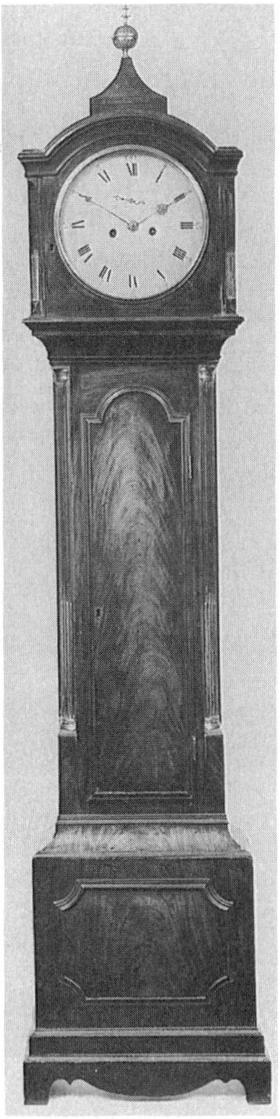

A Regency mahogany longcase clock, the arched hood with swept spire and 3 ball finials and canted brass mounted reeded angles, the 12in (30.5cm) painted dial with subsidiary seconds, signed 'R. Cole, Ipswich', the twin train movement with anchor escapement, 88in (223.5cm) high.
£2,000–2,500 *P*

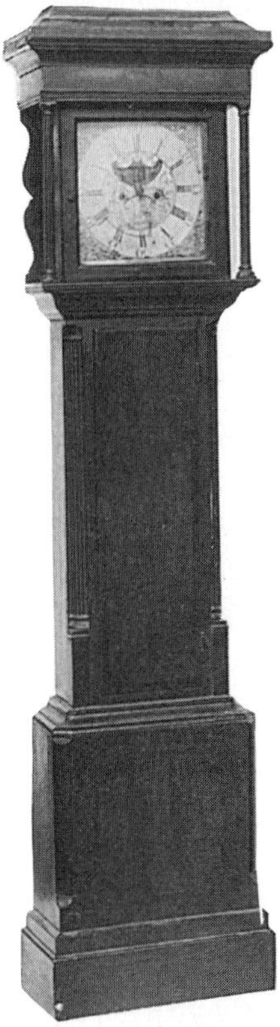

A George III oak and mahogany banded longcase clock, by D. Collier, Gately, the dial with moon phase having calendar subsidiary dial between pierced spandrels supported by a twin train striking movement.
£1,400–1,800 *P(EA)*

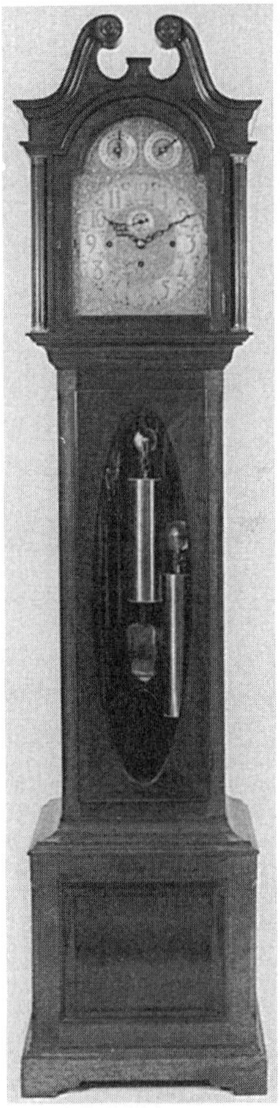

l. An Edwardian chiming longcase clock, by C. S. Davies, Haverfordwest, the brass and silvered dial with scrolling foliate mounts, subsidiary chime/silent, Whittington/Westminster and seconds dials, the movement chiming and striking on 9 tubes, brass cased weights, in a mahogany case with bevelled glass trunk door, 93in (236cm) high.
£1,500–2,000 *Bea*

A George III style mahogany and inlaid longcase clock, the painted dial marked 'William Dobbie Falkirk', lunar and subsidiary dials, 19thC, 90½in (230cm) high.
£1,500–2,000 *SK(B)*

r. A mahogany longcase clock, the 12in (30.5cm) brass dial signed 'A. M. Cressener, London', with moon phase and subsidiary date dial in the arch, with further date aperture and subsidiary seconds dial, the movement with anchor escapement rack striking on a bell, in a later case with swan neck pediment and fluted columns, above a satinwood crossbanded and marquetry waist door flanked by further fluted columns, on bracket feet, 96in (243.5cm) high.
£1,700–2,000 *DN*

An early George III mahogany longcase clock, by Dudds of London, the 12in (30.5cm) arched brass dial with wide silvered chapter ring, curved date aperture, seconds dial and strike/silent dial to arch, 8-day striking movement, 94in (238cm) high.
£3,500–4,000 *CAG*

Parts of a Clock

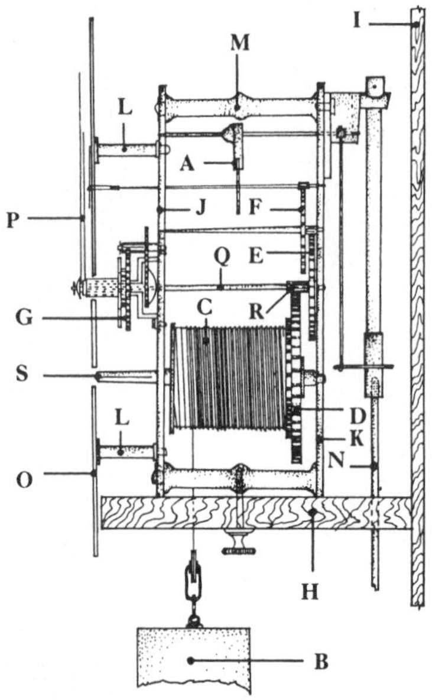

The main components of a simple weight-driven clock, include:

A anchor escapement	**J** front plate
B weight	**K** backplate
C barrel	**L** dial feet
D main wheel	**M** pillars
E centre wheel	**N** pendulum
F third wheel	**O** dial plate
G dial wheels	**P** hands
H seatboard	**Q** centre arbor
I backboard	**R** pinions
	S winding arbor

A 19thC mahogany and chequer strung longcase clock, the 13in (33cm) arched brass dial with silvered chapter ring, subsidiary seconds and date aperture, signed 'Thos. Evans, Bont Uchel', with moon phase in the arch, the twin train movement with anchor escapement, 19thC, 88in (223.5cm) high.
£1,200–1,700 *P*

A mahogany longcase clock, the 13in (33cm) brass dial signed 'John Galbraith, Falkirk', in the arch, with date aperture and seconds subsidiary dial, the movement with anchor escapement rack striking on a bell, 87in (221cm) high.
£900–1,500 *DN*

John Galbraith is recorded working c1770.

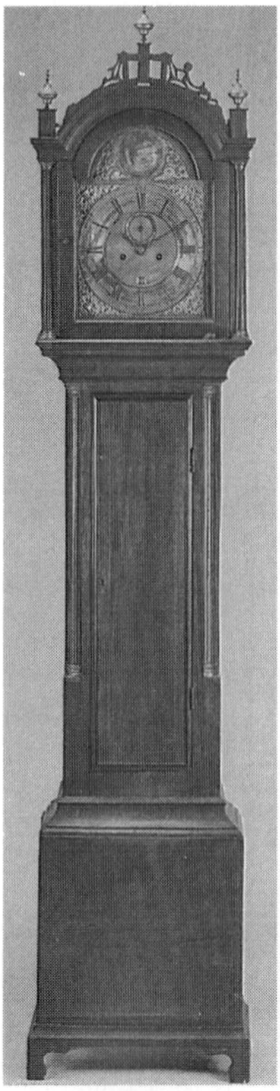

r. A Regency inlaid mahogany and satinwood longcase clock, by W. Helliwell, Leeds, with brass dial, the maker's name in the arch, a silvered metal chapter ring below, enclosing a two-train movement with seconds hand and date register, repaired, associated, early 19thC, 93in (236cm) high.
£1,500–2,000 *S(NY)*

l. A Federal inlaid mahogany longcase clock, the hood with pierced fretwork surmounted by brass finials above an arched glazed door opening to a brass dial with Roman and Arabic chapter ring, enclosing a sweep second hand surmounted by a disk inscribed 'Thomas Gardner London', on bracket feet, damaged and restored, 90in (228.5cm) high.
£2,000–2,500 *CNY*

An oak and mahogany banded longcase clock, the brass dial with silvered chapter ring, 30-hour striking movement, by Hindley, York, c1750.
£800–900 *M*

A George III mahogany longcase clock, the painted dial indistinctly signed 'Husband, Hull', with Roman and Arabic chapters, pierced steel hands, subsidiary seconds and calendar rings, the arch with rolling moon phase with blued hand, the motto above reading 'sic est vita Hominis', the four-pillar rack striking movement with anchor escapement, 90in (228.5cm) high.
£3,500–4,000 *C*

A 30-hour oak longcase clock, by John Hocker, Reading, with 10in (25cm) dial, a Roman numeral chapter ring, bird-cage movement striking on a bell, in a case with flat pediment and door flanked by plain columns, long trunk door, standing on a plinth, c1750, 84½in (215cm) high.
£600–800 *Bon*

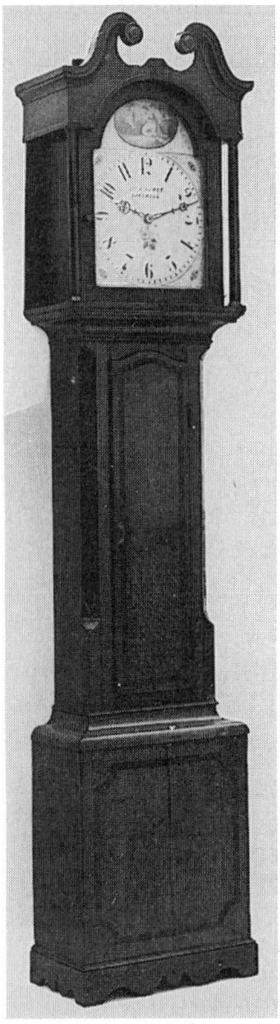

A 30-hour oak longcase clock, with white dial, by G. A. Hurst, Bakewell.
£650–700 *DaD*

A walnut longcase clock, by James Jenkins, the 12in (30.5cm) dial with a silvered Roman and Arabic chapter ring, matted centre with subsidiary seconds and calendar aperture, double cherub and crown spandrels in the corner, 5 ringed pillar movement with inside locking plate and striking on a bell, the later purpose-made case with a flat top and plain columns and gilt capitals in the corners, on a trunk with a long door, veneered in burr walnut, 19thC, 85in (216cm) high.
£800–900 *Bon*

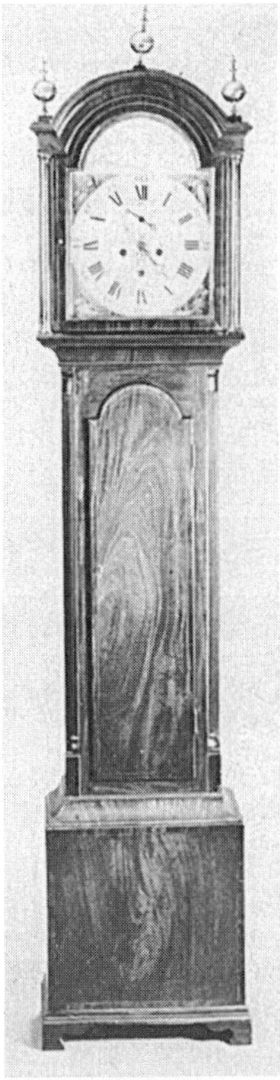

l. A mahogany longcase clock, the 12in (30.5cm) painted dial signed 'Thos Ivory, Dundee' in the arch, with seconds subsidiary dial and date aperture, the spandrels painted with allegorical representations of the seasons, the movement with anchor escapement, rack striking on a bell, 88in (223.5cm) high.
£4,000–5,000 *DN*

Thomas Ivory is recorded working 1795–1825.

Parts of the Dial

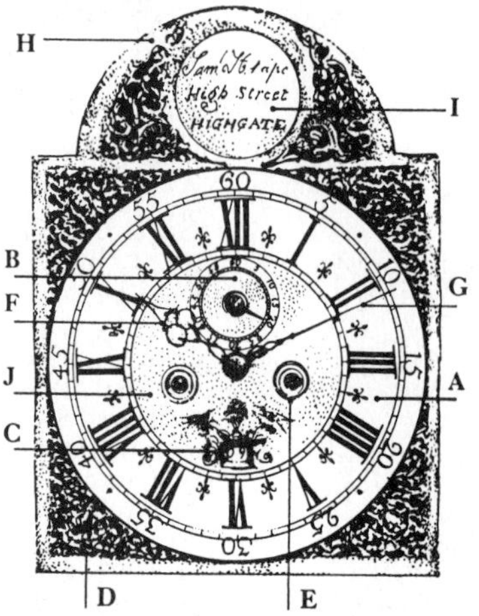

The basic parts of the dial, as on the 18thC arched example above, include:

- **A** chapter ring
- **B** subsidiary dial
- **C** calendar aperture
- **D** applied corner spandrels, usually of brass
- **E** winding holes
- **F** hour hand
- **G** minute hand
- **H** dial arch
- **I** engraved boss (may also be a strike/silent lever)
- **J** matted centre

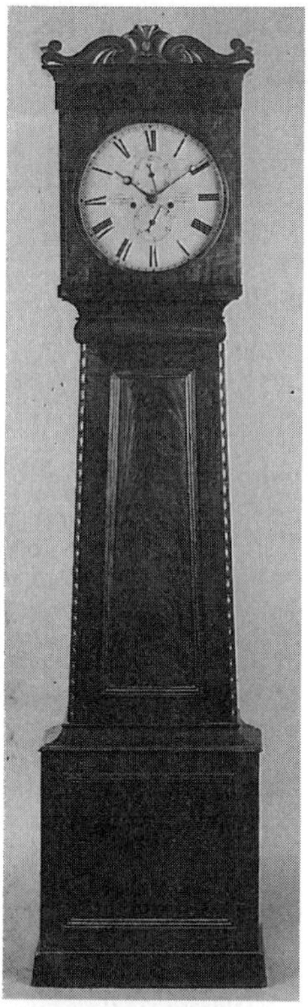

A mahogany longcase clock, the 13in (33cm) round dial with Roman numerals, signed 'Ja^{s} and W. Kelley, Glasgow', rack and bell striking movement, the case with a carved pediment, c1830, 81in (205.5cm) high.
£1,500–2,000 *Bon*

A George III longcase clock, the movement with a chime of 8 bells, the arched brass and silvered dial with subsidiary seconds dial and calendar, strike/silent regulator to the lunette, the name plate inscribed 'John Mansfield, London', 90in (228.5cm) high.
£4,500–5,000 *WW*

An oak 8-day longcase clock, by Lawson, Newton.
£1,600–2,000 *DaD*

l. **An 8-day mahogany longcase clock, by Lister, Bolton, with 14½in (37cm) painted dial.**
£3,000–3,500 *DaD*

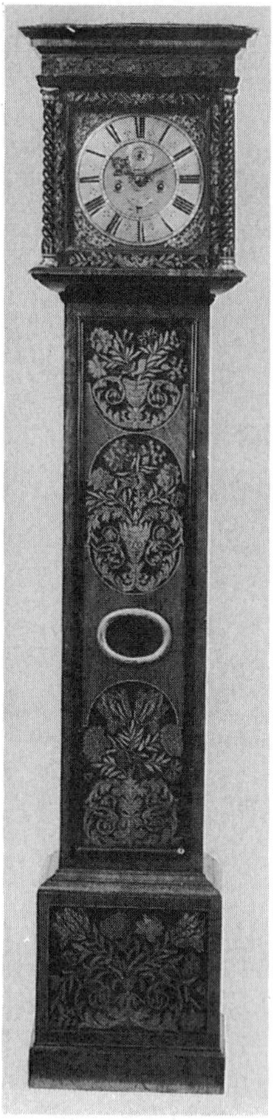

l. A walnut and floral marquetry month going longcase clock, the 11in (28cm) brass dial with winged cherub head spandrels and silvered chapter ring, signed 'Daniel Le Count, London', with subsidiary seconds, date aperture and ringed winding holes, 5 ring turned pillar movement, one replaced, with outside countwheel strike and anchor escapement, restored, late 17thC, 82in (208cm) high.
£5,000–7,000 *P*

r. A late Georgian oak and mahogany banded longcase clock, the 11in (28cm) brass dial with 'Benjamin Ratcliffe of Welshpool' plaque, rococo spandrels, 30-hour movement, bell strike, 83in (210cm) high.
£1,000–1,500 *WL*

An oak longcase clock, the 12in (30.5cm) painted dial with Roman numerals, bell striking movement, by S. & J. Porter, Oakingham, c1800, 78in (198cm) high.
£500–700 *Bon*

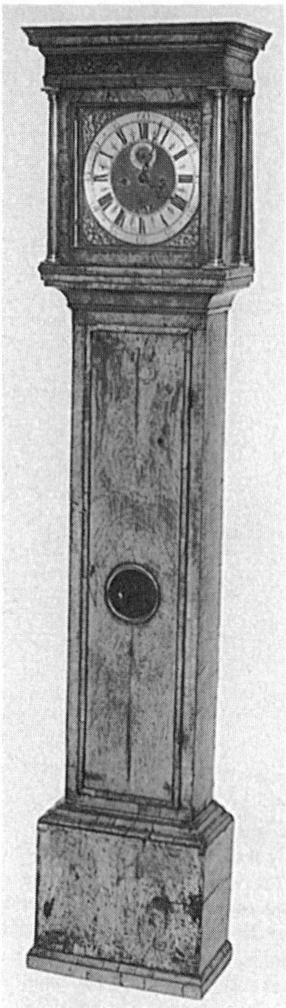

A walnut longcase clock, with silvered chapter ring, engraved with Roman numerals, seconds dial and date aperture, engraved 'John Miller, London', 8-day striking movement, early 18thC, 84in (213cm) high.
£2,000–3,000 *AG*

l. A mahogany longcase clock, the 13in (33cm) round painted dial with Roman numerals, signed 'Recorden, Greek Street, London', subsidiary seconds, bell and rack striking movement, c1790, 92in (234cm) high.
£3,000–3,500 *Bon*

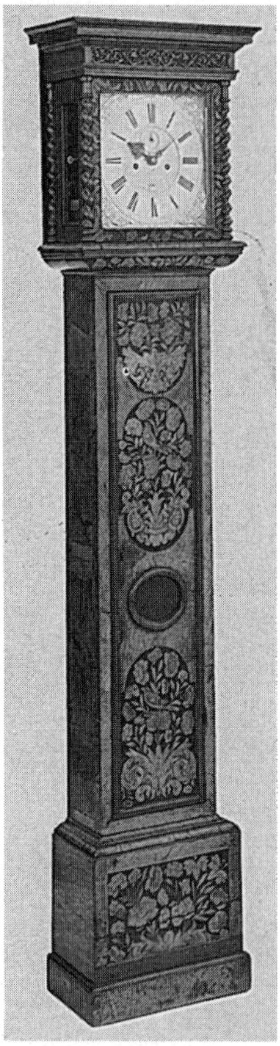

r. A longcase clock, with brass dial, date aperture, seconds hand dial, silvered chapter ring, inscribed 'W. Tomlinson, London', 8-day movement in walnut case, early 18thC.
£3,200–4,000 *RBB*

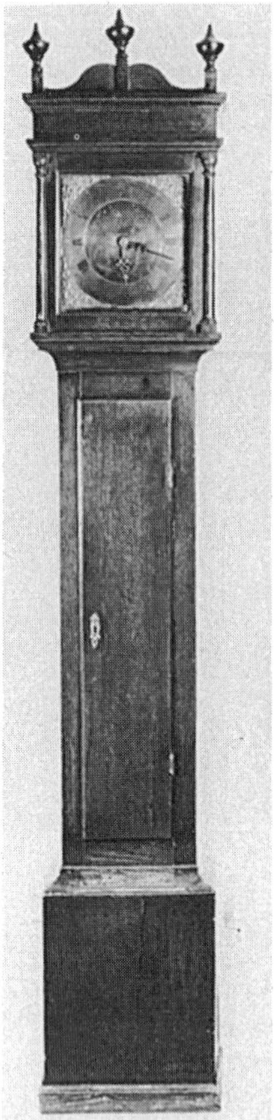

An oak longcase clock, the 9½in (24cm) brass dial signed 'Paul Thackwell, Ross', with brass scroll spandrels, with a 30-hour posted movement with outside countwheel striking on a bell, the case with 3 urn finials and waist door, 83in (210.5cm) high.
£1,500–2,000 *DN*

A William and Mary walnut and mahogany longcase clock, the 11in (28cm) brass dial with silvered chapter ring, Roman numerals, Arabic 5 minute intervals, half-hour markers, the matt centre with subsidiary seconds dial, calendar aperture and ringed winding holes and with pierced gilt foliate winged cherub spandrels, separated by engraved foliage, signed on the chapter ring, 'Sam Stevens Londini fecit', the pinned 5 pillar movement now with anchor escapement, rack striking on a bell, in walnut veneered and crossbanded case, with pendulum, brass cased weights and keys, 81in (205.5cm) high.
£5,000–6,000 *L*

A Dutch style walnut veneered longcase clock, with chevron inlay, the movement striking on a bell with a later arched brass dial with moon phase aperture, the engraved centre with a calendar aperture, the chapter ring inscribed 'J. Schofield Rochdale', 18thC, 88in (223.5cm) high.
£2,000–2,500 *WW*

r. An oak and mahogany longcase clock, the 13in (33cm) dark blue painted dial with gilt Arabic numerals, subsidiary seconds and calendar sector, signed 'W. Toleman, Caernarvon, 1797', a painted sundial in the arch, and 4 pillar bell striking movement, c1780, 86in (218.5cm) high.
£800–900 *Bon*

An oak musical longcase clock, the 12in (30.5cm) brass dial with silvered chapter ring, subsidiary seconds and date aperture with engraved centre and ringed winding holes, signed 'Josiah Stringer, Stockport', the three-train movement with inside countwheel strike and anchor escapement playing on 6 bells, 18thC, 85in (216cm) high.
£1,600–2,000 *P*

A George II inlaid oak 30-hour longcase clock, the bird-cage movement behind engraved brass dial inscribed 'John Tickle, Crediton', with single hand, date aperture, striking on a bell, the case door and plinth base with star inlay, c1730, 79in (200.5cm) high.
£800–900 *MJB*

r. An ebonised longcase clock, the 12in (30.5cm) dial signed 'W. Tomlinson London', on the silvered chapter ring, with pierced blued hands, the matted centre with subsidiary seconds ring, ringed winding holes and calendar aperture, cherub-and-crown spandrels, the 5 ringed pillar movement with anchor escapement and inside countwheel strike on bell, in later case, the movement c1700, 87in (221cm) high.
£2,000–2,500 *C*

l. A mahogany longcase clock, by James Walker, Montrose, with 8-day movement striking the hours on a bell, the painted dial showing both seconds and date and painted fisherman to the arch, the case with excellent flame veneers, rosewood crossbanding and boxwood stringing, c1810, 91in (231cm) high.
£4,800–5,200 *PAO*

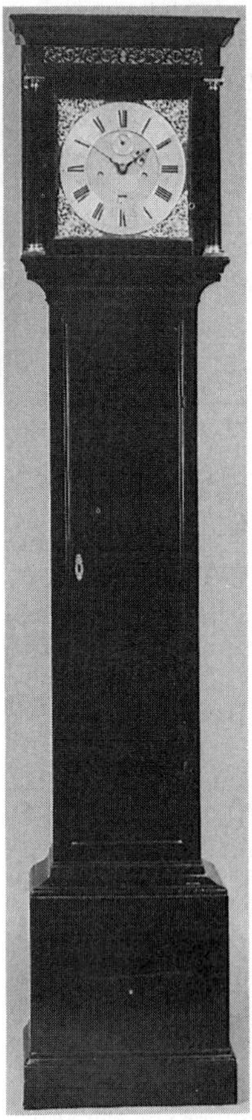

An ebonised longcase clock, the 11in (28cm) brass dial with floral engraved border between double screwed spandrels with silvered chapter ring, subsidiary seconds and date aperture, with applied oval plaque signed 'Tho. Tompion London', over original signature 'Thos. Tompion, Edw. Banger, London', with bolt and shutter maintaining power and latched dial feet, the movement with 5 ringed and latched pillars and anchor escapement numbered on the backplate '500', with restraining bracket, early 18thC, 82in (208cm) high.
£20,000–24,000 *P*

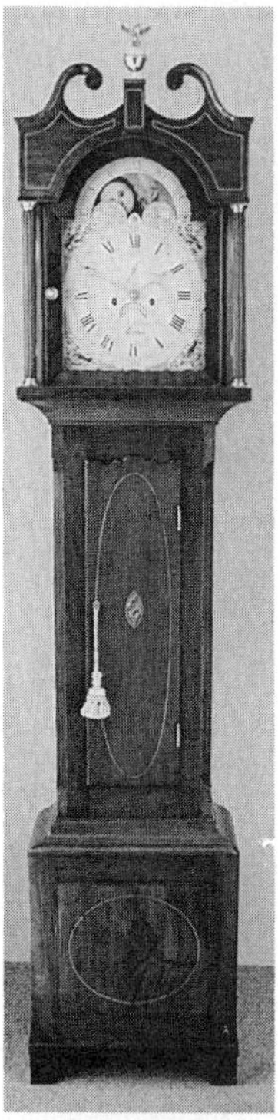

An 8-day mahogany longcase clock, by Webb & Sons, Frome, c1810, 87½in (222cm) high.
£4,500–4,700 *ALS*

A Cuban mahogany 'Manchester' longcase clock, with brass dial and moon phases, by Samuel Whalley, c1770.
£6,500–7,000 *ALS*

An 8-day oak and mahogany longcase clock, by Witheridge, Bridgewater, c1830, 80in (203cm) high.
£1,750–2,000 *ALS*

A Victorian mahogany longcase clock, with rocking ship in arch, 8-day movement, by Hugh Williams, Caernarvon.
£1,000–1,200 *DaD*

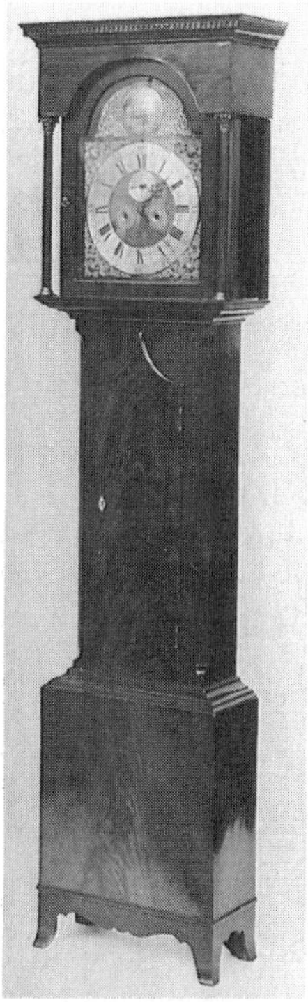

A mahogany longcase clock, by John Watts, Chesterfield, the arched brass dial with silvered chapter ring headed by name plate, dolphin ornament and pierced cherub spandrels having seconds subsidiary dial supported by a twin-train striking movement, early 19thC.
£2,200–2,500 *P(EA)*

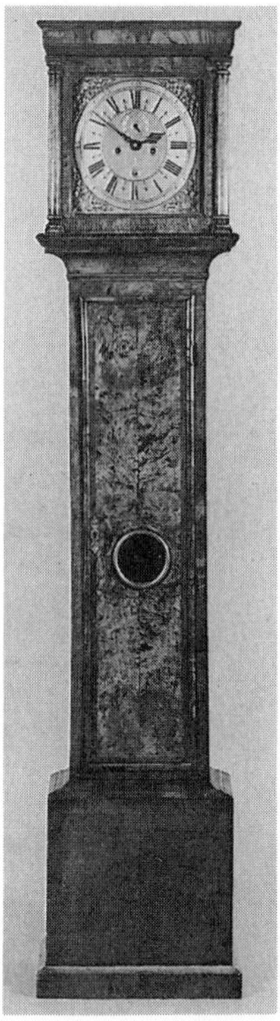

A walnut veneered longcase clock, the 12in (30.5cm) dial with Roman and Arabic numbers, signed 'Jams Walker, London', matted centre containing subsidiary seconds and calendar aperture, gilt double cherub and crown spandrels in the corners, the 5 ring pillar movement with inside countwheel striking on a bell, c1700, 84in (213cm) high.
£2,800–3,200 *Bon*

r. A George III mahogany longcase clock, the pagoda top surmounted by associated carved giltwood figures of heralds flanking Atlas, the engraved giltwood dial signed 'Jas. Wilson Loop', with Roman and Arabic chapter ring, pierced blued hands, subsidiary florally-engraved spandrels, the added arch inscribed 'Tempus Fugit', the 5 pillar rack striking movement with anchor escapement, restored and composite, 72in (182.5cm) high.
£2,200–2,700 *C*

A George III mahogany longcase clock, with arched brass dial inscribed 'Vale, Birmingham', 8-day striking movement and phases of the moon to the arch, with blind and fret carved panel and fluted pilasters to the trunk, on bracket feet, 86in (218.5cm) high.
£1,000–1,500 *AG*

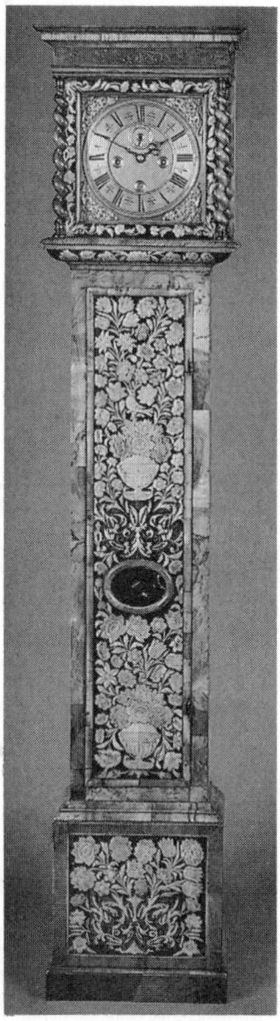

l. A William and Mary walnut and floral marquetry longcase clock, the 11in (28cm) dial signed 'Ben Wright Londini Fecit' on the silvered chapter ring, with blued steel hands, the matted centre with subsidiary seconds, ringed winding holes and calendar aperture, winged cherub-and-foliate spandrels, the movement with latches to the 4 ringed pillars, anchor escapement, inside countwheel strike on bell above, 82in (208cm) high.
£9,500–11,500 *C*

Benjamin Wright, c1664–1709, was apprentice to Abraham Prime until 1685 and believed to have been working in Bell Alley and Coleman Street, London.

An oak and mahogany longcase clock, the 14in (35.5cm) dial with subsidiary seconds and date dials, the spandrels painted with the Evangelists and with moon phase in the arch, the movement with false plate and anchor escapement rack striking on a bell, 90in (228.5cm) high.
£700–900 *DN*

A mahogany longcase clock, the brass dial with Roman and Arabic numerals, mid/late 18thC.
£1,800–2,200 *BWe*

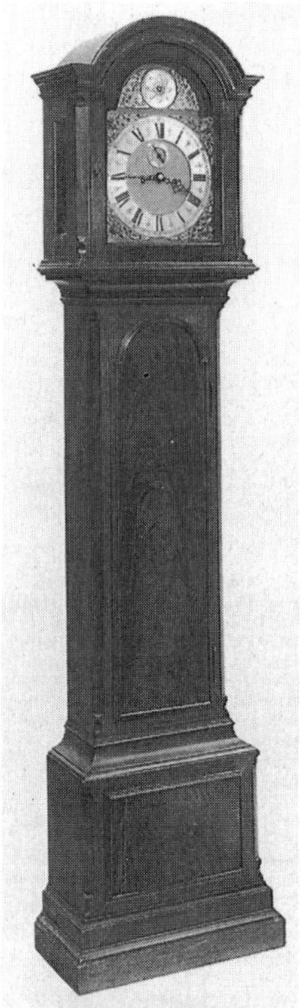

A mahogany longcase clock, the 8-day movement striking on a gong, the brass and silvered dial with subsidiary seconds dial and cast gilt mask scroll corner spandrels, late 19thC, 88in (223.5cm) high.
£500–800 *WW*

A figured mahogany Yorkshire longcase clock, the arched dial hand painted with a reaper to the arch and peaceful rural buildings to the corners, with 8-day movement and seconds, 95in (241cm) high.
£500–600 *DA*

l. A George III miniature mahogany longcase clock, the hood with swan necked pediment and reeded columns, the trunk enclosed by an arched panel door between reeded quarter columns, the door and base inlaid with fan corner motifs, with 9in arched painted dial, the weight driven movement with anchor escapement, hood door missing, 65in (165cm) high.
£1,200–1,700 *P*

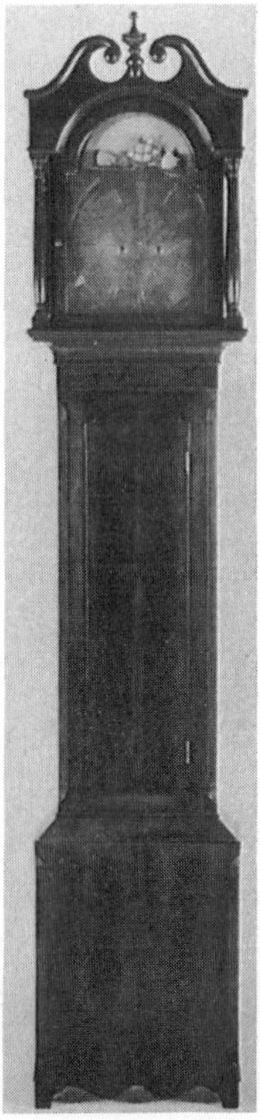

r. A Federal mahogany longcase clock, the brass dial marked 'Benjamin Morris, New Britain', painted arch with a rocking ship, subsidiary dial and calendar aperture, 106in (269cm) high.
£2,500–3,000 *SK(B)*

l. A George III style oak miniature longcase clock, the brass dial with Roman chapter ring, the centre incised with foliage within mask spandrels, the arch painted with a coastal scene and automaton ship in the foreground, the 4 pillar rack striking movement with anchor escapement, 2 lead weights and a pendulum, late 19thC, 66in (167.5cm) high.
£2,500–3,000 *CSK*

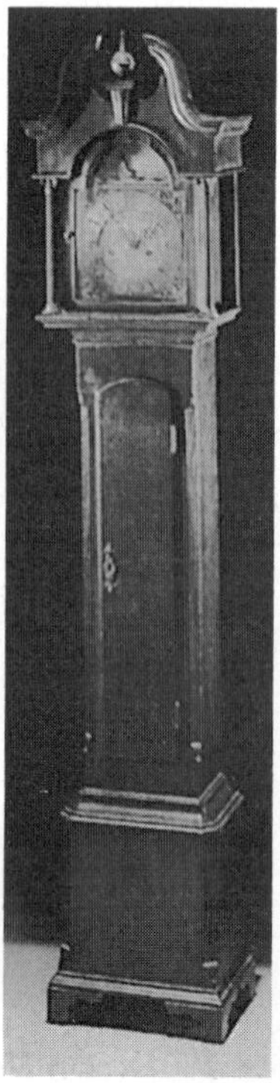

Mantel Clocks

A Classical revival black and white marble mantel clock, 19thC, 22in (55.5cm) high.
£1,250–1,500 *SK(B)*

A gilt metal and marble mantel clock, by R. Ganthony, Cheapside, London, the drum movement with scroll and swag frieze on spool feet, the enamelled dial supporting a single train movement, 19thC, 8½in (21.5cm) high.
£550–650 *P(EA)*

An Austrian ormolu grande sonnerie mantel clock, the 4in (10cm) silvered dial signed 'Brändl in Wien', with central calendar, 3 train movement with silk suspension and striking on 2 bells, drum case surmounted by an eagle and raised on bird feet, and a later white onyx plinth, c1820, 10in (25cm) high.
£1,300–1,700 *S*

r. A French Empire ormolu mantel clock, the case depicting Minerva urging on the horses of Diomedes, signed 'Alibert a Paris', with later glazed bezel, the later twin train movement striking on a bell, slight damage, 17½in (44.5cm) high.
£4,000–4,500 *P*

l. An Empire gilt metal mantel clock, with a bronze figure of Brutus, 21in (53cm) high.
£1,300–1,700 *LRG*

r. A French gilt-spelter mantel clock, with white enamel Roman dial, the twin going barrel movement with count wheel strike on bell, late 19thC, 12in (30.5cm) high.
£200–300 *CSK*

l. A French Louis XV style mantel clock, with gilt dial with enamel numerals, 8-day striking movement in red tortoiseshell and brass boulle case with leafage scroll ormolu mounts, 19thC, 17in (43cm) high.
£700–900 *RBB*

l. A French Empire ormolu and marble mantel clock, with a 3⅜in (8.5cm) dial, the movement with outside count wheel striking on a bell, in a gilt brass case in the form of a cloth-covered table, with a figure of a woman reading a book by the light of an oil lamp, on an antico verde marble base and turned feet, damaged, c1805, 12½in (32cm) high.
£2,500–3,500 *L*

A mantel clock, with brass and bevelled glass case, the 8-day movement by Marti et Cie, striking to bell, the enamel dial with exposed deadbeat escapement having a compensating mercury pendulum, late 19thC, 13½in (34.5cm) high.
£300–400 *DA*

A French oak cased mantel clock, the 5in (13cm) enamel dial with Roman numerals, signed for 'Goldsmiths Co. 112 Regent St.', gong striking movement, in a case with broken arch pediment, late 19thC, 14in (36cm) high.
£150–200 *Bon*

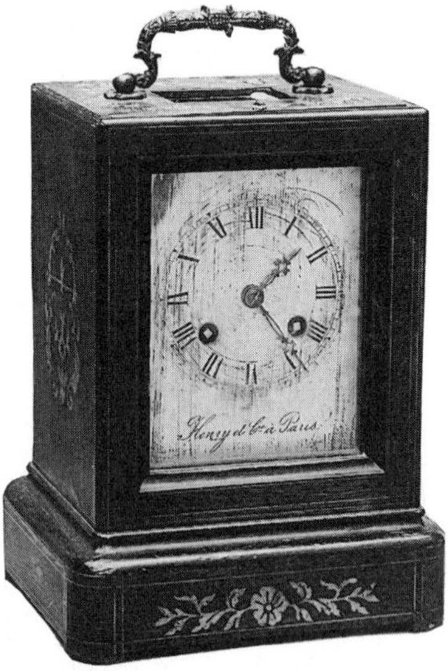

l. A rosewood mantel clock, with drum movement.
£350–400 *DaD*

r. A French mantel clock, the 3¾in (9.5cm) dial textured and painted in tones of grey, cerise and olive green, black Roman numerals and blued steel hands, the movement with outside count wheel striking on a bell, in rococo bronzed spelter case, 27in (68.5cm) high.
£400–500 *L*

r. A Directoire ormolu and bronze striking mantel clock, the white enamel Roman dial signed 'Cronier Ainé, rue St. Honoré Mo. 165 à Paris', foliate ormolu hands, the twin going barrel movement with anchor escapement with silk suspended pendulum, count wheel strike on bell on plain backplate, 14in (35.5cm) high.
£1,800–2,200 *CSK*

Table Clocks

An ebony veneered quarter repeating table clock, by Joseph Knibb, with 5¾in (14.5cm) latched dial, silvered Roman numeral chapter ring with Arabic 5 minute numerals, strike/ silent lever at 12 o'clock, finely matted centre and crisply cast winged cherub head spandrels, signed on the bottom edge, 5 finely turned ringed pillar movement, latched plates, inside rack striking and repeating on a second bell, backplate engraved with tulips and leaves, signed, c1685, 12in (30.5cm) high.
£16,000–18,000 *Bon*

Joseph Knibb, born in 1640, became one of the finest clock makers. He started his career in Oxford, then moved to London in 1670 where he was made freeman of the Clockmaker's Company. In 1700 he moved to Hanslop, and died in 1711.

An Irish table clock, the single fusee movement with an anchor escapement and rise and fall to the pendulum with an engraved backplate, the arched brass and silvered dial inscribed 'Chas. Hull, Dublin', late 18thC.
£1,700–2,000 *WW*

Urn Clocks

An ormolu mounted bluejohn urn clock, with pineapple finial on a domed lid, swan neck handles, revolving enamel dial, fluted socle and square plinth, 19thC, 14½in (37cm) high.
£6,500–7,500 *AH*

l. A Continental silver gilt and enamel miniature urn clock, with revolving chapter ring, the guilloche blue enamel ground decorated with fleur-de-lys and floral sprays, probably Austrian, the Swiss movement by Schild & Co., 3in (8cm) diam.
£520–600 *Bea*

Wall Clocks

l. A George III mahogany cased dial wall clock, by F. Berguer of London, the 12in (30.5cm) silvered dial to the 8-day movement with heavy brass plates and shaped tops, in a mahogany case with turned front bezel, 15in (38cm) high.
£800–900 *CAG*

r. An oak Gothic wall clock, the 10in (25cm) painted dial with Gothic Roman numerals, signed 'Short & Mason, Hatton Garden, London', the single fusee movement in a honey oak case, spire pediment with applied carved cresting, Gothic foil and carved foliage, decorated and carved front panel and base, 29in (73.5cm) high.
£500–600 *Bon*

A French bronze lobster wall clock, the 3in (7.5cm) annular enamel dial with gilt centre, bell striking Japy Frères movement No. 105, with cylinder escapement, mid-brown patination with gilt highlights, dial cracked, c1890, 29in (73.5cm) high.
£2,200–2,700 *S*

A mahogany cased dial wall clock, the 12in (30.5cm) painted domed metal dial to the 8-day movement with heavy brass plates, early 19thC, 25in (63.5cm) high.
£600–700 *CAG*

r. A French gaming wall clock, the chequerboard dial with counter numeral plaques, playing card spandrels and billiard motifs, square Japy Frères gong striking movement with Brocot escapement, in a moulded square case with chess piece finials, c1890, 24in (61cm) square.
£1,300–1,700 *S*

Miscellaneous Clocks

A Napoleon III parcel gilt bronze souvenir Eiffel Tower clock, the going barrel movement with anchor escapement, crutch piece, bell and hammer missing, the backplate with stamp for 'Japy Frères No. 10005', 43½in (110cm) high.
£1,700–2,000 *C*

l. A Federal giltwood mahogany and églomisé banjo clock, attributed to Simon Willard, Roxbury, Massachusetts, throat panel below decorated with an American eagle and shield, inscribed 'Willards Patent', an églomisé door below, above a shaped pendant ending in an acorn terminal, finial support and finial missing, slight damage, c1820, 37in (94cm) high.
£4,000–5,000 *S(NY)*

This banjo clock is fitted with a T-Bridge movement.

r. A George III mahogany balloon clock, the case with swept spire and cone finial, flanked by carrying handles, on bracket feet, the painted dial signed 'Chas. Goodall London', the twin fusee movement with shaped plates and anchor escapement, signed on backplate, 19in (48cm) high.
£1,500–2,000 *P*

A French chinoiserie salon clock, inscribed 'Janvier a Paris', the 8-day movement striking on a bell, the ormolu drum case surmounted by a Chinaman beating a drum and suspended between tiered pagodas with milled galleries and spirals hung with bells and chains, sunburst pendulum, the shaped white marble base with ormolu balustrade and chains, on milled feet, late 18thC, 23½in (60cm) high.
£4,500–5,500 *N*

A French equestrian clock, with 8-day striking silk suspension movement, mounted with bronze anthemion and leaf decorated corners, a floral border and scrolled classical bronze feet, mid-19thC, 23in (58.5cm) high.
£2,000–2,500 *B*

r. A gilt metal and wood strut timepiece, by Baudin Frères, Geneva, with cylinder escapement, gilt metal signed cuvette, 19thC, 8in (20cm) high, in original velvet lined shaped tortoiseshell box, velvet replaced.
£600–700 *S*

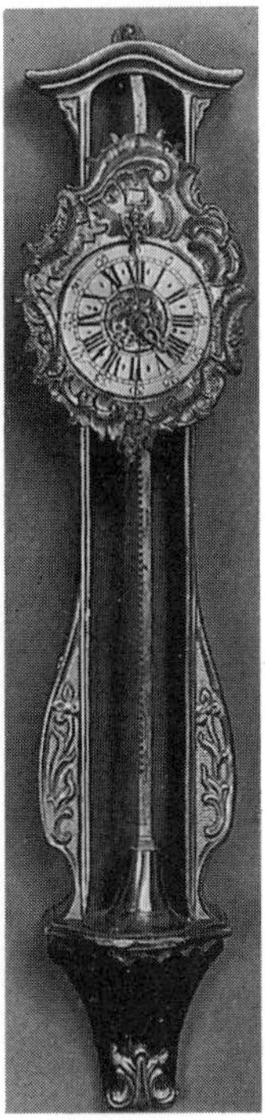

An Austrian ebonised and parcel gilt rack clock, the silvered rococo dial with Roman and Arabic chapter ring with pierced brass hands, calendar aperture above, front swinging pendulum to the verge escapement of the 5-wheel movement, with glazed sides having lead weights top and bottom, with steel rack, c1780, 30in (77cm) high.
£3,300–3,900 *C*

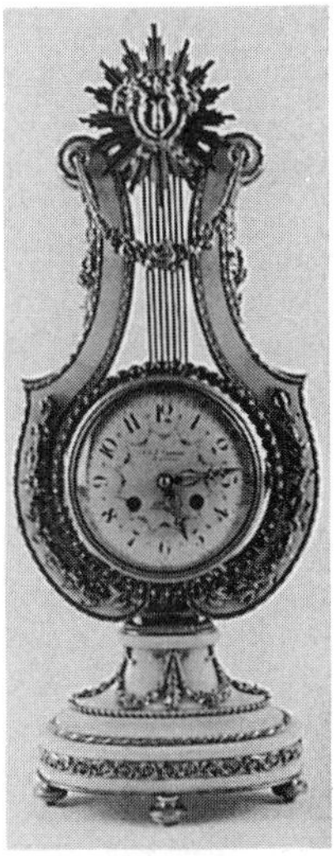

A French ormolu and white marble lyre clock, the enamel dial marked 'Camus, Paris', 19thC, 22in (55.5cm) high.
£2,500–3,000 *SK(B)*

Regulators

l. A Victorian mahogany regulator, the 12in (30.5cm) silvered dial with subsidiary hour and seconds dials, inscribed 'O. Axmann, London', the movement with deadbeat escapement, agate palettes and adjustable mercury pendulum, the shallow arched case with foliate carved cresting, glazed trunk and panelled plinth, c1850, 74½in (190cm) high.
£7,500–8,000 *S(S)*

A Regency mahogany and crossbanded regulator, by Benjamin Russell, Norwich, the arched hood and convex glazed door flanked by canted angles, the trunk enclosed by a full length glazed door, on plinth base, the silvered dial with second subsidiary supporting a timepiece movement.
£3,300–3,800 *P(EA)*

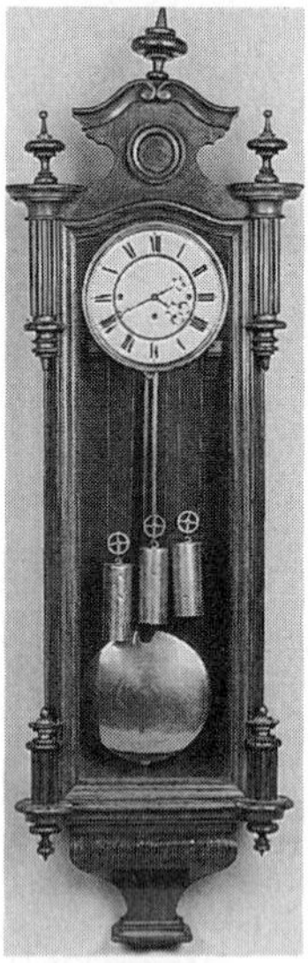

An Austrian walnut veneered petite sonnerie wall regulator, the 6½in (16.5cm) two-piece enamel dial with Roman numerals, the triple-train weight driven movement with a deadbeat escapement, wooden rod pendulum and striking on 2 gongs, in a fully glazed case with shaped pediment, the door flanked by fluted columns and turned finials, with an under carved base with finials, c1870, 45in (114cm) high.
£1,700–2,000 *Bon*

A walnut spring driven wall regulator, by Chapman, Oxford, the 10in (25cm) silvered dial with engraved Arabic numerals, subsidiary seconds and 24 hour dial, sweep minute hand, the 5-pillar angle force movement with a deadbeat escapement and steel/mercury compensated pendulum, the case with giltwood dial around diamond shaped decoration around the pediment, side pegged and wedged joints, glazed trunk door with Gothic detail, c1860, 62in (157cm) high.
£1,500–2,000 *Bon*

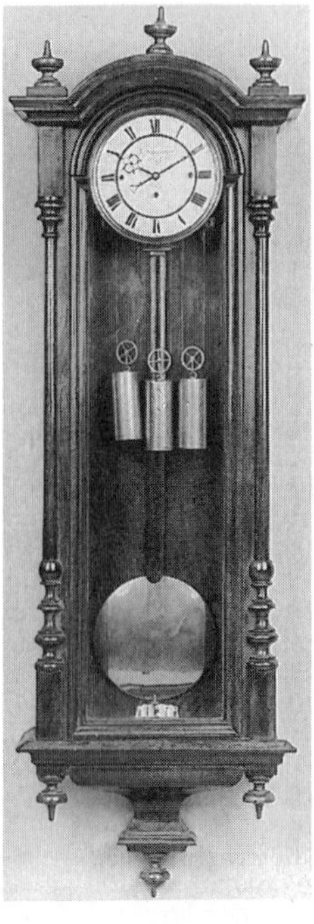

r. An Austrian walnut veneered petite sonnerie wall regulator, the 6½in (16.5cm) 2-piece enamel dial with Roman numerals, signed 'A. Schlesinger in Wien', the triple-train weight driven movement with a deadbeat escapement, wooden rod pendulum and striking on 2 gongs, in a fully glazed case with a swallow break arch pediment and turned finial, the shaped door flanked by half columns and under curved base with finials, c1875, 46in (116.5cm) high.
£1,200–1,700 *Bon*

Watches

A silver pair cased calendar verge pocket watch, signed on escutcheon 'D. Decharmes, London', blued steel beetle and poker hands, in plain silver inner and outer case, the inner case with split bezel with casemaker's mark 'PR', early 18thC, 55mm diam.
£1,100–1,400 *C*

A Georgian silver pair cased watch, by Harry Arnold of Eccleston, with verge escapement movement and white enamel dial, Chester 1820.
£200–250 *AH*

A 9ct gold open face pocket watch, by Dent, 28 Cockspur Street, and 84 Royal Exchange, London, No. 62787, white dial with Roman numerals and subsidiary seconds, three-quarter plate keyless lever movement, the case Birmingham 1932.
£200–300 *DN*

A French silver quarter repeating automaton open face watch, signed 'Ch^{s} Oudin Fils', decorated with gilt and painted figures of American Indians, c1820, 54mm diam.
£2,500–3,000 *PT*

A silver pair cased watch, the verge movement signed 'Turner, London', the dial with central painted roundel depicting a riverside scene, London 1806.
£400–500 *CSK*

An 18ct gold full hunter watch, signed 'Dent 61 Strand & 55 Royal Exchange, London 40647', the enamel dial with Roman numerals and subsidiary seconds, key wound three-quarter plate movement similarly signed, in a crisp engine turned case with enamel initials stamped, London hallmark for 1882, 50mm diam.
£400–500 *Bon*

An 18ct gold keyless lever watch, by Nicole Nielsen, the movement signed 'Dent, London, No. 40904', the signed and numbered enamel dial with centre seconds, the case marked 'London 1880', 50mm diam., together with a heavy gold guard chain, in a presentation case.
£1,600–2,200 *P*

Miller's is a price GUIDE not a price LIST

A George III gilt metal verge watch and pedometer, the movement with pierced cock signed 'Ralph Gout, London 68, By the Kings letters Patent', the signed enamel dial with offset chapter, centre and subsidiary recorders for tens, hundreds and thousands, the case with recording button in the pendant, dial with hair crack, hands missing, 54mm diam.
£400–600 *P*

A silver hunter cased keyless lever watch, the movement with freesprung compensated balance, jewelled to the centre signed 'Chas Frodsham, 84 Strand London, No. 06467, ADfmsz', the signed and numbered enamel dial with Arabic numerals, the numbered case applied with a gold monogram, joints and bow, marked 'London 1881', 54mm diam.
£400–600 *P*

An 18ct gold watch, by William Lockwood, Huddersfield, with white enamel dial and lever movement.
£200–300 *AH*

An 18ct gold pair cased cylinder pocket watch, signed 'Willm Story, London, Number 371', with plain outer and inner case, hallmarked 'London 1781', movement and dust cover signed, 55mm diam.
£2,000–2,500 *C*

William Story, of Red Lion Street, London, was first mentioned in 1737 and died in 1784.

A silver open faced keyless lever free sprung deck watch, the half-plate movement signed 'P. & A. Guye Ltd., 77 Farringdon Rd., London, No. 12643', the plain case hallmarked '1899', in a mahogany deck box with named and numbered roundel, 57mm diam.
£1,700–2,000 *S*

An 18ct gold duplex hunter pocket watch, signed 'James McCabe, Royal Exchange, London number 12971', the engine turned case with hallmark for London 1829, with casemaker's stamp 'TW' and engraved 'IMC', case, dial and movement signed and numbered, 51mm diam.
£820–920 *C*

A silver full hunter watch, signed 'Rob[t] Roskell Liverpool', the enamel dial with Roman numerals and subsidiary seconds, the lever movement with a pierced and engraved top plate, in a case with decorated band, c1820, 50mm diam.
£150–200 *Bon*

A pair cased watch, by Higgs & Evans, London, with a white enamel dial, verge escapement movement, the case with embossed mythological scene.
£320–370 *AH*

A silver pair cased watch, signed 'David Morice, Fenchurch Street, London 3335', the enamel dial with Roman numerals and subsidiary seconds, gilt movement with a cylinder escapement and pierced balance cock, diamond endstone, in a plain polished case with outer pair, London hallmark for 1808, 58mm diam.
£300–400 *Bon*

A gold pair cased verge watch, signed 'Willm Story, London, No. 5180', the enamel dial with steel beetle and poker hands and arcaded chapter, the inner case marked 'London 1776', the outer of fine repoussé work, 18thC, 47mm diam.
£1,500–2,000 *P*

A triple calendar and moon phase sports watch, by Movado, the silvered dial with Arabic numerals, concentric calendar chapter and aperture for day/date and moon phase, 15 jewel movement, in a polished case with sliding lizard skin covered outer, c1940, 50mm wide.
£700–900 *Bon*

A Georgian silver pair cased watch, by Richard Thame, London, with white enamel dial, lever movement, and enamelled outer case.
£200–250 *AH*

A gold and gilt metal pair cased verge watch, with enamel Roman and Arabic numeral dial, the movement signed 'T. D. Thornhill, London', pierced balance cock, in a plain gold case with outer gilt metal and painted shell pair case, c1760, 45mm diam.
£300–400 *Bon*

An 8-day keyless lever deck watch, the damascened nickel movement signed 'Waltham Watch Co.', with 15 jewels, adjusted, bimetallic compensation balance, micrometer regulator, silvered dial, Arabic numerals, subsidiary dials for seconds and up-and-down, 75mm diam., the brass bowl gimballed in a brass bound mahogany box with named plaque, together with a rating certificate, c1908.
£700–900 *S*

l. An 18ct gold open faced watch, the enamel dial with Roman numerals, marked centre seconds, chronograph, and outer quarter second scale, three-quarter plate fusee lever movement in a polished case with a ribbed band, London hallmark for 1879, 56mm diam.
£350–450 *Bon*

l. A French/English nickel case masonic pocket watch, the enamel dial with Roman and Arabic numerals, key wound cylinder movement, in a case with red stone set in the pendant and engraved with masonic symbols and scenes, mid-19thC, 85mm high.
£1,800–2,200 *Bon*

r. A Georgian silver pair cased watch, by Jn. Wilbot, London, with white enamel dial, and verge escapement movement.
£200–300 *AH*

A Georgian gold pair cased watch, with white enamel dial, and verge escapement.
£500–600 *AH*

A French gold verge watch, the movement in the form of a twin-handled vase, the visible balance with diamond endstone set on pierced floral scrolls, with enamel dial, in a gold case stamped 'FLP', late 18thC, 55mm diam.
£2,000–3,000 *P*

A French open faced verge watch, the offset enamel dial with Arabic numerals, with 2 painted enamel plaques, gilt movement with a pierced balance cock in a case with a ribbed band and turned back, c1820, 56mm diam.
£450–550 *Bon*

A lady's gold and enamelled fob watch and brooch, with an unsigned gilt cylinder movement, the case front enamelled with Leda and the Swan in a red enamelled scrollwork border set with a row of rose diamonds, the case back enamelled with violets, the top with a floral decorated gold bar brooch, with the original case, c1910.
£900–1,200 *S(S)*

A French silver quarter repeating verge watch, the movement with pierced bridge cock, the silver dial with floral border decoration, 19thC, 56mm diam.
£300–500 *P*

l. A German keyless lever watch, the movement with micrometer regulation, signed 'Deutsche Uhren-Fabrikation Glashütte 55954', the signed enamel dial inscribed 'A Lange & Sohne', with subsidiary seconds, 49mm diam.
£800–1,200 *P*

A gold keywind 5 time zones hunter pocket watch, signed 'Hahne Frères, number 1044', indicating times at Moscow, London, Madrid and New York, in engine turned gold hunter case with gold cuvette, movement and case numbered, 50mm diam, with a presentation box.
£1,000–1,500 *C*

A French First Consulate sedan clock, the movement with a pull repeat ting tang having a convex white enamel dial, inscribed 'Courvoisier Frères', the chased framed glazed cover to a gilt case with ring fixing, 1801–04.
£1,000–1,500 *WW*

A silver open face 8-day two-train pocket watch, the dial signed 'Ate. Krause', mid-19thC, 50mm diam.
£1,000–1,500 *C*

A 14ct pink gold hunting cased keyless lever watch, the matt gilded movement signed 'Deutsche Uhren-Fabrikation, Glasshütte', gold escape wheel and pallets, compensation balance, blued steel spiral spring and regulator with micrometer adjustment, white enamel double sunk dials, Arabic numerals, subsidiary seconds, all 3 covers with Glashütte/Lange stamp, Louis XVI type case with engraved monogram on front cover, 53mm diam., in original named box with guarantee and spare glass.
£3,000–3,500 *S*

A Continental niello and gilt highlighted keyless lever watch, the enamel dial with subsidiary seconds, signed 'Extrafino', hair crack and hands missing, 45mm diam.
£200–300 *P*

A Third Reich keyless lever deck watch, the movement with micrometer regulation signed 'Vacheron & Constantin, Genève, 444889', the signed silvered dial with subsidiaries for seconds and for state of winding, 60mm diam.
£1,200–1,700 *P*

A Swiss blued steel open faced watch with barometer, the enamel dial with Roman numerals, marked 'Allitudo Déposé' and subsidiary seconds below, engraved silvered outer barometer scale, gilt lever movement, in a plain steel case, c1900, 55mm diam.
£300–400 *Bon*

A Swiss 18ct gold hunting cased minute repeating keyless lever chronograph, blued steel hands, three-quarter plate movement with bimetallic compensated balance wheel, jewelled lever escapement, overcoil blued steel spring, plain cuvette, plain outer case, chronograph button and repeating slide in the band, plain suspension ring, c1900, 55m diam.
£1,700–2,000 *L*

l. A Swiss silver keyless lever watch and barometer, the enamel dial within an engraved silvered barometer scale calibrated from 21 to 31, with centre recording hand, 55mm diam.
£550–650 *P*

A gold keyless demi-chronometre hunter pocket watch, signed 'Henry Capt., Genève, number 28426', the frosted gilt bar movement jewelled to the third with bimetallic balance, blued steel hairspring and lever escapement, wolf-tooth winding, blued steel spade hands, the plain heavy case with gold cuvette and engraved monogram to the front cover, case, dial and movement signed, 52mm diam., with original presentation box.
£700–900 *C*

This watch bears an inscription on the inside of the front cover, 'To Captain Horatio McKay from the cabin passengers of the RMSS "Servia" carried to safety and comfort through the four days Atlantic hurricane on January 1885 by his seamanship, tact and courage'. The watch is accompanied by a photocopied extract from Cunard Magazine *with an article on the life and times of Captain Horatio McKay, and whilst not mentioning the hurricane for which this watch was presented, it describes some of the dangerous situations from which Captain McKay managed to extricate his ships and passengers, for which he was awarded no less than 46 testimonials and a score of medals and watches by grateful passengers or representatives of foreign governments.*

A gold, enamel and diamond set notelet box, incorporating a watch, the frosted gilt movement with cylinder escapement, initialled 'HG 1211', under translucent blue enamel on guilloche background with a diamond set spray of flowers, the rectangular shaped engine turned gold box with scalloped edges decorated to the front and back with floral sprays and scrollwork to the edges, opening to reveal a gold note and pencil holder, 19thC, 93mm wide.
£2,700–3,200 *C*

A Swiss gold open faced chronograph watch, enamel dial with Arabic numerals, subsidiary for running second and 30-minute recording, the gilt movement in a polished case with engraved cuvette 'Winner of most events Rhine Army sports 1919, 100yds, 220yds, High Jump, Long Jump', c1915, 55mm diam.
£270–370 *Bon*

A Continental niello and gilt highlighted keyless lever watch, the movement of 8-day duration with enamel dial and visible balance, 47mm diam.
£200–300 *P*

r. An 18ct heavy gold hunter cased one-minute triple gold bridge tourbillion watch, with chronometer escapement, the damascened nickel movement signed on barrel 'Girard Perregaux No. 6, Mars 1984', typical triple gold bridges, fully jewelled in screwed-in gold chatons, gold train, case similarly numbered, case, cuvette and dial signed, 61mm diam., and a fitted leather box.
£32,000–35,000 *S(NY)*

An ebonised and gilt brass mechanical display piece, comprising a beam supporting a watch at either end raised on dolphin supports from a pillared and stepped base, under a glass shade, the whole rotating by clockwork on a plinth, the 2 gold watches each with gilt bar movements and English lever escapement, the smaller with gilt dial, the larger enamel, both signed on the cuvette 'Edwd Funnell, Brighton', in engraved cases with gold chains and keys, smallest 12.5mm diam.
£14,000–16,000 *P*

Wristwatches

A pink gold automatic water resistant wristwatch, signed 'Baume & Mercier Genève', with automatic movement, the matt gilt dial with raised dagger quarter hour marks and baton 5 minute divisions, subsidiary seconds, pink gold hands, case with unusual straight down turned lugs and screwed back, 1950s, 33mm diam.
£700–800 *C*

A wristwatch, the square engine turned dial with dot markers and reeded bezel, the case signed 'Boucheron, Paris BT 908247', to a leather strap and slide clasp.
£800–1,200 *CSK*

An early steel chronograph wristwatch, signed 'Breitling Watch Corp', the nickel plated bar movement jewelled to the centre, outer tacheometric scale, sweep centre seconds operated by 2 square buttons in the band, the circular steel case with shaped lugs, snap-on back, No. '712197 181', case, dial and movement signed, 32mm diam.
£650–750 *C*

A steel self-winding chronograph calendar wristwatch, signed 'Breitling, Genève', model Navitimer Chrono-matic', the steel case with water resistant screwed back inscribed 'Breitling automatic, number 11525/67 1806 1255824', with maker's original black leather strap and steel buckle, case and dial signed, 48mm diam., in a presentation box.
£700–900 *C*

A pink gold wristwatch, signed 'International Watch Co., Schaffhausen', the nickel plated bar movement jewelled to the centre with gold alloy balance, the matt silvered dial with raised pink Arabic quarter hour marks and baton 5 minute divisions, sweep centre seconds, case, dial and movement signed, 1950s, 35mm diam.
£700–800 *C*

r. A Cartier Continental automatic wristwatch, with signed 17 jewel movement, the signed dial with Roman numerals and sweep centre seconds, with enclosed winding button, the rear cover secured by 4 screws signed 'Cartier, Paris', and numbered, fitted with maker's burgundy leather strap and deployant clasp.
£1,700–2,000 *CSK*

l. A gentleman's gold rectangular wristwatch, signed 'Jaeger-LeCoultre', the nickel plated movement jewelled to the third, the brushed silvered dial with Arabic numerals and gold hands, the case with D-shaped lugs, the back secured by 4 screws in the band, case, dial and movement signed, 1930s, 28mm wide.
£500–600 *C*

l. A gold automatic water resistant wristwatch, signed 'Gubelin', with automatic movement, the cream coloured dial with raised gilt baton numerals and sweep centre seconds, case, dial and movement signed, 1950s, 26mm square.
£500–700 *C*

A Jaeger-LeCoultre gold day/date calendar wristwatch, signed 'LeCoultre Co', the lozenge shaped nickel plated movement jewelled to the third numbered 56531, the outer date ring with central date hand, aperture below 12 for the day in German, the case with snap-on back numbered '29708', case, dial and movement signed, 1950s, 30mm diam.
£600–700 *C*

A Jaeger-LeCoultre steel chronograph wristwatch, signed 'Jaeger', the gilt movement jewelled to the centre, the matt black dial with outer tacheometric and inner telemetric scales, elapsed minutes and hours, sweep centre seconds operated by 2 buttons in the band, the case with water resistant back, case, dial and movement signed, 1950s, 40mm diam.
£800–900 *C*

A Jaeger-LeCoultre gold triple calendar chronograph wristwatch, signed 'Jaeger', the nickel plated movement jewelled to the centre, subsidiary dials for running seconds, elapsed minutes and hours, apertures for day and month, the case with snap-on back, dial and movement signed, 1950s, 37mm diam.
£1,800–2,200 *C*

A Jaeger-LeCoultre gold Memovox alarm wristwatch, signed 'Jaeger-LeCoultre', with automatic movement, luminous gold hands, alarm disc to the centre set by second button in the band, case with water resistant back, case, dial and movement signed, 47mm diam.
£1,800–2,200 *C*

A steel chronograph wristwatch, signed 'Longines', the nickel plated movement jewelled to the centre with gold alloy balance numbered '330' and '72' followed by an 'R' in a shield, the white dial with outer tacheometric scale, inner telemetric scale, case, dial and movement signed, 36mm diam.
£650–750 *C*

A gold triple calendar wristwatch, signed 'Movado', the nickel finished lever movement with 15 jewels, mono-metallic balance, apertures for day and month, outer date ring with central date hand, subsidiary seconds dial, circular case with down turned lugs, case, dial and movement signed, c1940s, 32mm diam.
£650–800 *C*

r. A gold wristwatch, signed 'Longines Watch Co.', the nickel plated movement jewelled to the third, the gold alloy balance with micrometer regulation, the silvered dial with raised Roman quarter hour marks and dot and dagger 5 minute divisions, subsidiary seconds, the gold case with domed crystal and snap-on back, case, dial and movement signed, 25mm wide.
£700–900 *C*

l. A WWII German airman's wrist-watch, the snap-on back inscribed 'Lange & Sohne', with movement No. '212752' and case No. 'F1 23883', the movement also signed and numbered, on a leather strap.
£600–800 *Bea*

An 18ct gold automatic chronometer constellation wristwatch, signed 'Omega Watch Co.', the pink gilt movement jewelled to the centre, the brushed silvered dial with raised gilt baton numerals, date aperture at 3, sweep centre seconds, the circular case with scalloped lugs and screwed back with import mark for 'Birmingham 1989', 34mm diam.
£700–900 *C*

A silver wristwatch, signed 'Rolex' and 'W & D', the cushion case with hinged lugs and snap-on back numbered '721606', import mark for London 1917, case and movement signed, 32mm square.
£800–1,200 *C*

A pink gold automatic wristwatch, made for the XVI Olympiad, signed 'Omega Watch Co.', model 'Seamaster', the matt silvered dial with raised pink 5 minute marks, sweep centre seconds, with raised Roman numerals XVI for the Olympiad, snap-on back, centred by the crest for the Olympic Games, case, dial and movement signed, 34mm diam.
£1,000–1,200 *C*

A 9ct gold tonneau wristwatch, signed 'Rolex, R.W.C. Ltd.', the nickel plated ultra prima precision movement jewelled to the third, the plain case with stepped shoulders, the snap-on back numbered '15968 2387' with engraved presentation, import mark Glasgow 1934, case, dial and movement signed, 21mm wide.
£700–900 *C*

A lady's 18ct gold quartz wristwatch, signed 'Omega', with quartz movement, 5 minute divisions and outer 13 to 24 hour ring, the gold tortue case with integral flexible gold bracelet and clasp, case, dial and movement signed, 22mm diam.
£800–900 *C*

An 18ct gold wristwatch, signed 'Omega Seamaster', with subsidiary seconds, the pink movement in a case with a snap-on back, c1965, 34mm diam.
£300–350 *Bon*

r. A 9ct gold wristwatch, signed 'Rolex, R.W.C. Limited', the matt silvered engine turned dial with Arabic numerals and subsidiary seconds square, the gold case with hinged back and domed glass numbered '556 63221', import mark for Glasgow 1928, case, dial and movement signed, 25mm wide.
£750–1,000 *C*

A gentleman's wristwatch, by Patek Philippe, with 18ct gold case and strap.
£3,000–3,500 *RBB*

r. A steel wristwatch, signed 'Rolex, R.W.C. Limited', the nickel plated ultra prima movement timed to 6 positions and jewelled to the third, with separate signed dust cover, the snap-on back numbered '012157 1879', case, dial and movement signed, 1930s, 20mm wide.
£1,100–1,500 *C*

A steel self-winding waterproof bubbleback wristwatch, signed 'Rolex, Oyster Perpetual', tonneau water resistant type case with milled bezel, screw down crown, case, dial and movement signed, c1940, 32mm diam.
£1,200–1,700 *C*

A gold wristwatch, signed 'Universal, Genève, the nickel finished jewelled lever movement with monometallic balance, silvered matt dial with applied dot and Arabic numerals, subsidiary seconds dial, case, dial and movement signed, c1940, 35mm diam.
£400–550 *C*

A steel precision wristwatch, signed 'Rolex', the nickel plated bar movement jewelled to the third, the matt black dial with raised gilt dagger numerals, subsidiary seconds and gilt hands, the steel case with snap-on back numbered '4658', case, dial and movement signed, 1950s, 32mm diam.
£400–500 *C*

A gold/steel Oyster Perpetual Datejust chronometer wristwatch, signed 'Rolex', self-winding movement, screw back and maker's gold steel bracelet with deployant clasp, case, dial and movement signed, 35mm diam., with maker's presentation box and spare link.
£1,300–1,700 *C*

l. A gentleman's 9ct gold tonneau wristwatch, signed 'Rolex' and 'R.W.C. Limited', the nickel plated prima movement jewelled to the third, timed to 6 positions and for all climates, the gold case with down turned lugs and stepped bezel, domed glass, snap-on back numbered '710226 870', import mark for Glasgow 1930, case and movement signed, 1950s, 28mm wide.
£1,100–1,500 *C*

A steel and white gold waterproof date quartz wristwatch, signed 'Rolex, Oysterquartz, Datejust', with quartz movement, blue brushed dial with applied baton numerals, date aperture under magnifying glass, sweep centre seconds, tonneau shaped water resistant type case with ribbed white gold bezel, with steel flexible Rolex bracelet and deployant clasp, case, dial and movement signed, 36mm diam., in a presentation box.
£900–1,200 *C*

A steel chronograph wristwatch, signed 'Universal, Genève, Uni-Compax', case, dial and movement signed, 1940s, 35mm diam.
£500–700 *C*

r. A steel Oyster Perpetual Explorer chronometer wristwatch, signed 'Rolex', with automatic movement, luminous Mercedes hands, sweep centre seconds, the screwed back with maker's hologram and steel bracelet with deployant clasp, case, dial and movement signed, 36mm diam.
£1,100–1,700 *C*

A steel triple calendar and moon phase wristwatch, signed 'Universal', with mechanical movement, case, dial and movement signed, 32mm diam.
£900–1,200 *C*

A steel chronograph wristwatch, signed 'Universal Genève', the frosted gilt movement jewelled to the centre numbered '256370', the matt black dial with Arabic numerals, subsidiary dials for running seconds, elapsed minutes and hours, sweep centre seconds operated by 2 round buttons in the band, case, dial and movement signed, 33mm diam.
£500–700 *C*

A Swiss gold single button chronograph wristwatch, the nickel finished jewelled lever movement with bimetallic balance, subsidiary dials for running seconds and 30 minute register, sweep centre seconds, the case with hinged bar lugs, hinged back, the chronograph operated through a single button via the crown, c1920, 32mm diam.
£900–1,200 *C*

A Swiss gold masonic wristwatch, the nickel finished lever movement with 15 jewels, mono-metallic balance, masonic symbols for the numerals, blued steel hands, engraved masonic symbols to the reverse, c1940, 30mm long.
£400–600 *C*

A lady's French wristwatch, the dial with Roman numerals, the broad bezel set with 8 diamonds, the cuvette signed 'Le Roy & Fils', with integral tapering twin row curb link bracelet.
£1,100–1,700 *CSK*

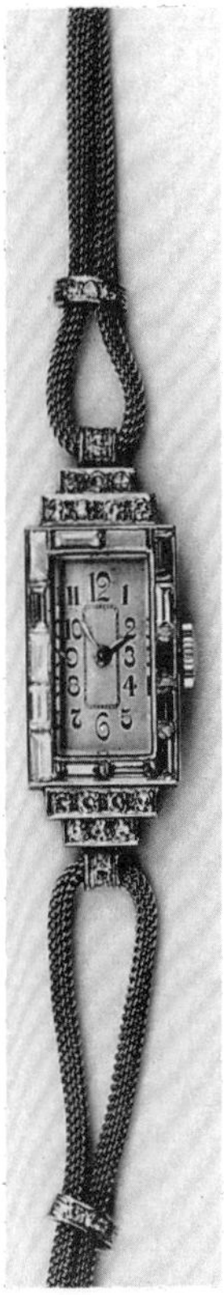

r. A lady's wristwatch, with baguette diamond bezel, diamond twin row shoulders, and mesh design bracelet with diamond set collars.
£800–1,200 *CSK*

A lady's platinum and diamond bracelet watch, the dial with diamond bezel and graduated diamond panel bracelet, to a mesh cordette back strap, movement and case signed 'M.P.G.'.
£800–1,000 *CSK*

A lady's 18ct gold wristwatch with alternately set diamond and ruby bezel, the case with import marks for London, 1930, with expanding bracelet.
£450–550 *CSK*

BAROMETERS

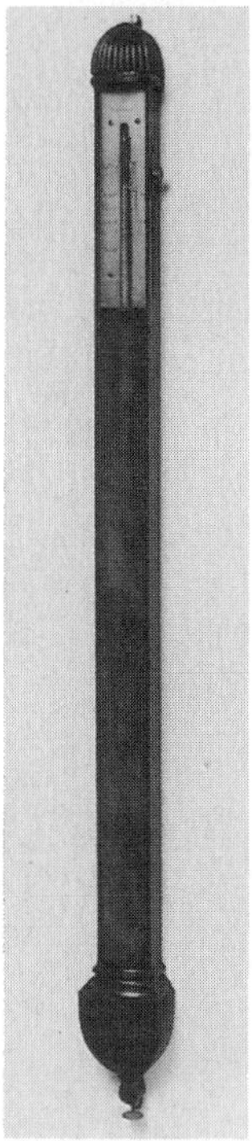

l. A bowfronted stick barometer, by Adie, Edinburgh, with silvered scale, the mahogany case with reeded pediment and reserve cover, early 19thC, 41in (104cm) high.
£5,000–6,000 *Bea*

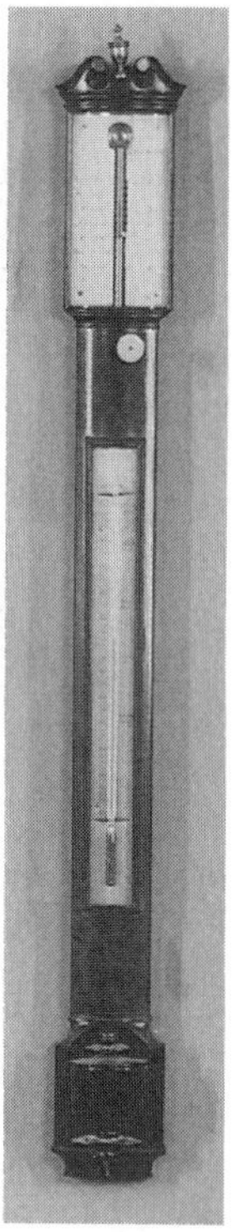

l. A mahogany bowfront stick barometer, concealed tube with silvered plates and vernier signed 'Cary London', inset at the front with a thermometer, bordered with ebony stringing and with urn cistern cover flanked by ebony inlaid angled corners, c1820, 40in (101.5cm) high.
£5,000–6,000 *S*

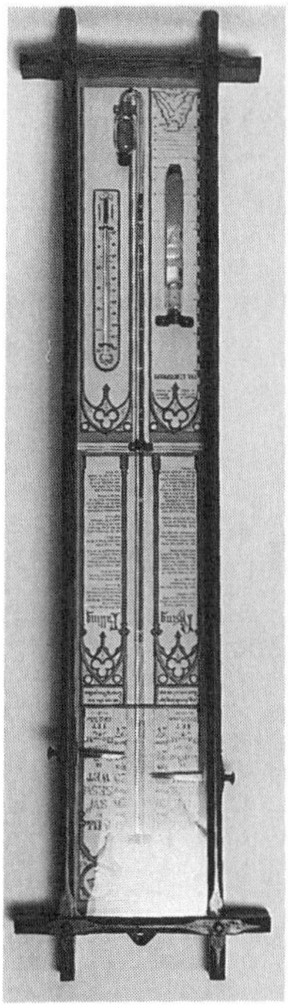

A Fitzroy barometer, with an oak frame, c1890, 40in (101.5cm) high.
£260–320 *JHW*

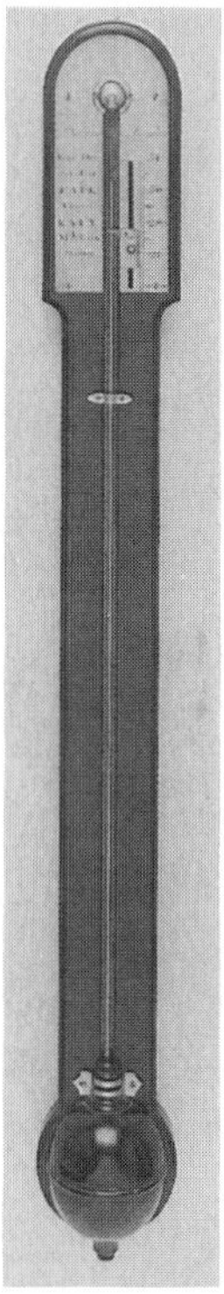

A mahogany stick barometer, the exposed tube with silvered plates and vernier signed 'Nairne, London', the case veneered with well figured wood and with moulded edge and hemispherical cistern cover, c1780, 38½in (98cm) high.
£1,300–1,700 *S*

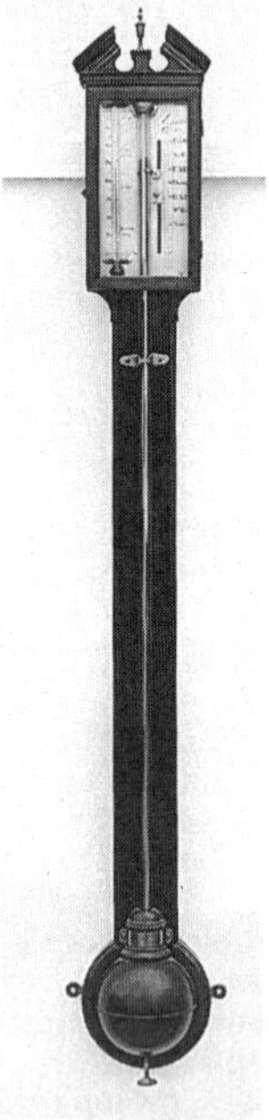

A feathered mahogany stick barometer, with engraved silvered plate, incorporating a thermometer, turned 'beetle cap' cistern cover, arched pediment top, signed 'Ezekiel Exeter', late 18thC, 39½in (100cm) high.
£1,800–2,000 *WL*

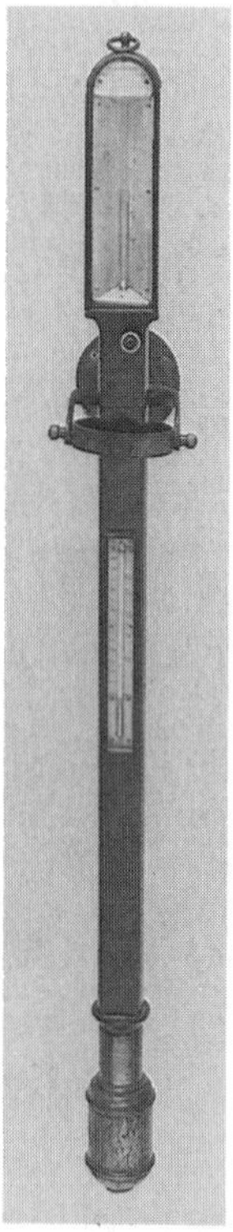

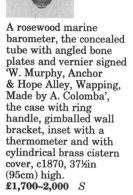

A rosewood marine barometer, the concealed tube with angled bone plates and vernier signed 'W. Murphy, Anchor & Hope Alley, Wapping, Made by A. Colomba', the case with ring handle, gimballed wall bracket, inset with a thermometer and with cylindrical brass cistern cover, c1870, 37½in (95cm) high.
£1,700–2,000 *S*

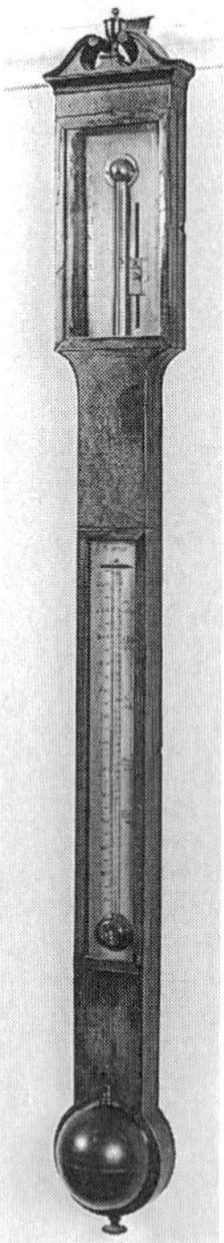

A stick barometer, by Nairne & Son, Cornhill, London, with engraved brass dial, and silvered thermometer in walnut case, late 18thC.
£1,300–1,700 *RBB*

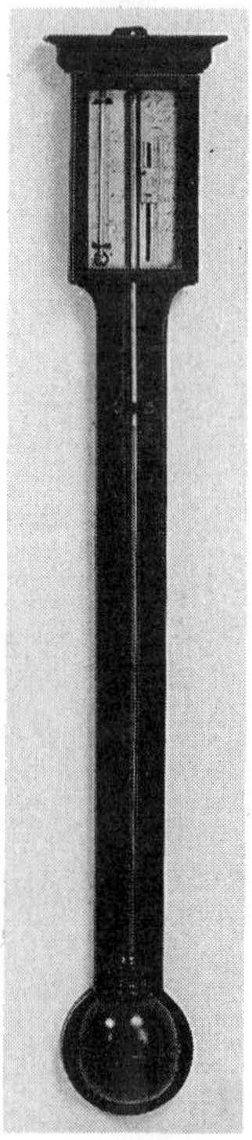

r. A mahogany stick barometer, with visible tube and turned cistern cover, the engraved silvered dial with thermometer, signed 'D. Ortelly & Co., Bath', 19thC, 37in (94cm) high.
£800–1,200 *P*

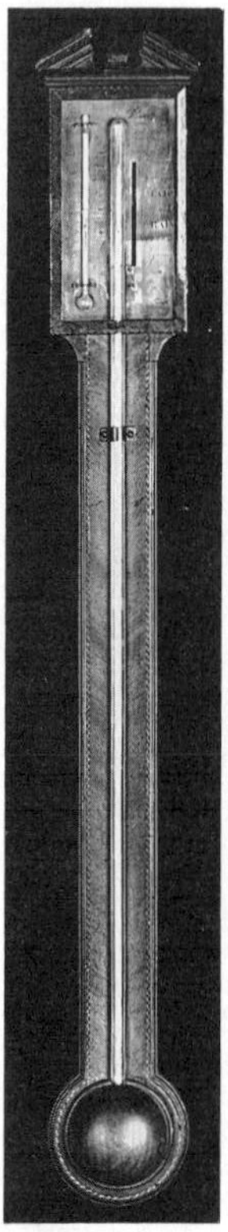

A George III mahogany barometer, the broken triangular pediment above a chequer banded shaft with brass dial signed 'Josh. Pastorele & Co./London', above a domed reservoir, 37½in (95cm) high.
£550–750 *C*

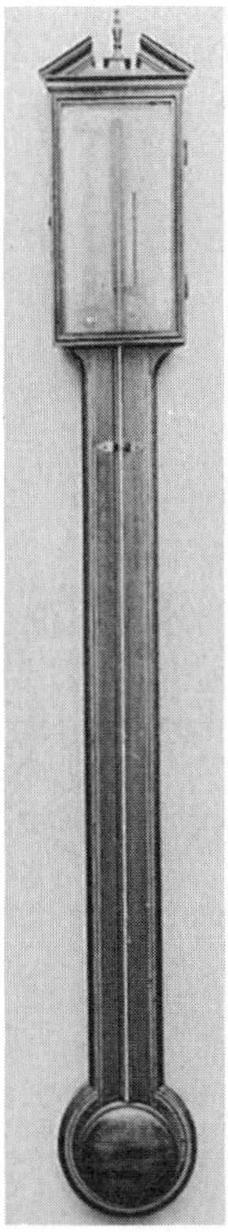

l. A mahogany stick barometer, the brass register signed 'Fra Pinni and Co., Holborn, No. 81 London', with vernier gauge and thermometer, the case with a broken pediment and turned boss, 38½in (98cm) high.
£400–500 *DN*

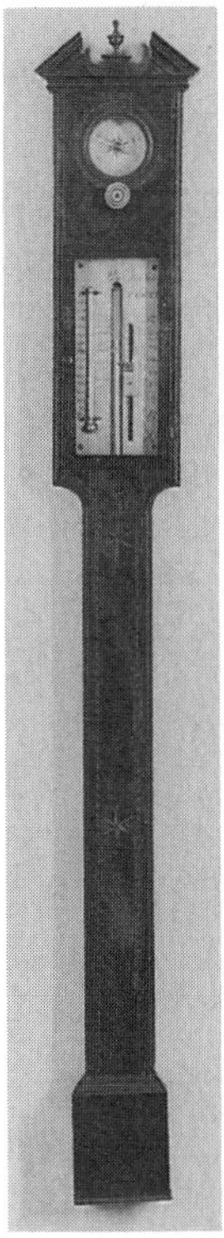

r. An inlaid mahogany stick barometer, the concealed tube with silvered plate signed 'Bapst. Ronchetti Fecit' with vernier and thermometer, adjustable hygrometer above, the case with broken architectural pediment and urn finial, inlaid at the front with stars and bordered with rope-twist stringing, cistern cover, c1800, 46in (116.5cm) high.
£2,000–2,500 *S*

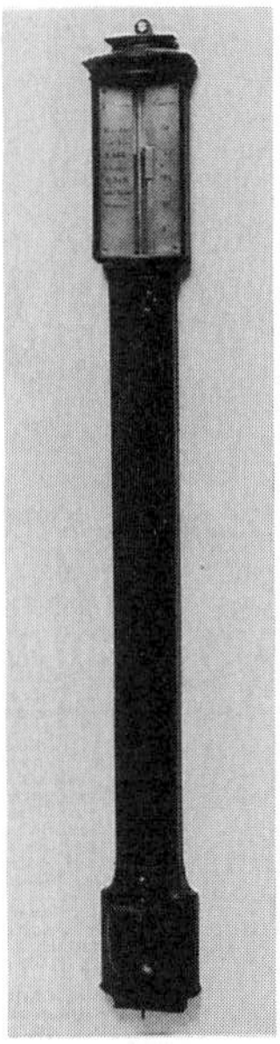

A George III stick barometer, by J. Ramsden, London, with engraved silvered dial, the bowfronted mahogany case with ebony stringing and reservoir cover, 38in (96.5cm) high.
£3,500–4,000 *Bea*

An Admiral Fitzroy improved barometer, with a paper register, hygrometer and thermometer, in an oak case carved with foliage, 47½in (121cm) high.
£550–650 *DN*

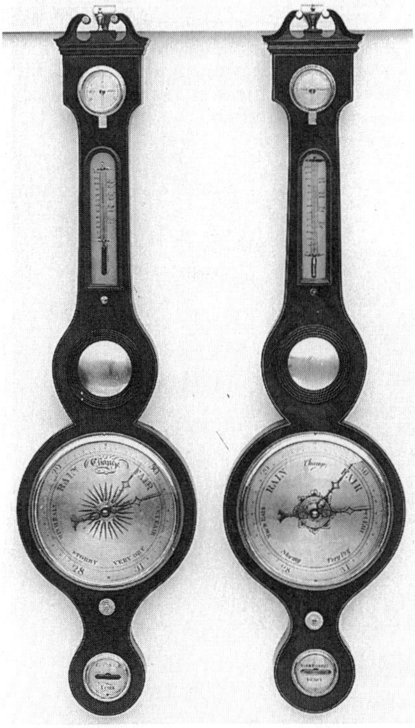

l. A late Georgian mahogany cased and strung wheel barometer, with 8in (20cm) silvered dial, including thermometer, hygrometer, level and convex mirror, signed 'G. Croce, York', 40in (101.5cm) high.
£350–450
r. A Georgian mahogany cased wheel barometer, with 8in (20cm) silvered dial, including thermometer level and convex mirror, signed 'G. Bregazzi Derby'.
£375–475 *WL*

A mahogany angle barometer, by E. Scarlet, London, the frame with broken pediment centred by a ball and spire finial, the visible angled tube with engraved silvered scale from 28 to 31in above a silvered hygrometer and with a signed alcohol thermometer to the side with spirally turned knopped cistern covers and mirror, the glazed centre with an engraving titled 'A Perpetual Regulation of Time' with apertures for high water at London Bridge, equation of time, fixed feasts, sunrise/sunset, length and break of day, declination of the sun and day of the month, with further tables for the year of the Lord with dominical letter from 1753-1852, 18thC, 40in (101.5cm) high.
£24,000–26,000 *P*

A Regency mahogany banjo barometer, inlaid with boxwood and ebony lines, paterae and oval shell motifs, with thermometer and barometer, signed 'L. Biaggini, Uckfield Warranted'.
£550–650 *CSK*

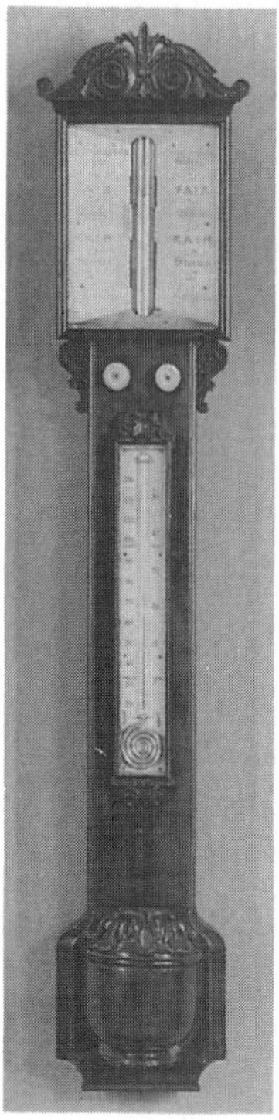

A rosewood stick barometer, with 2-day bone plates and verniers signed 'Josh. Somalvico & Co. 2 Hatton Garden London', the case with leaf carved cresting, applied at the front with a spiral reservoir thermometer, carved corbels to the side and urn cistern cover with carved lid, c1850, 44in (111.5cm) high.
£3,000–3,500 *S*

A rosewood wheel barometer/thermometer by R. Mears, Boston, with silvered register plate, dry/damp dial, spirit level inscribed with maker's name, and bone turner, in a banjo case with broken swan neck pediment inlaid with bands of leaves in mother-of-pearl, 19thC, 42½in (108cm) high.
£400–600 *HSS*

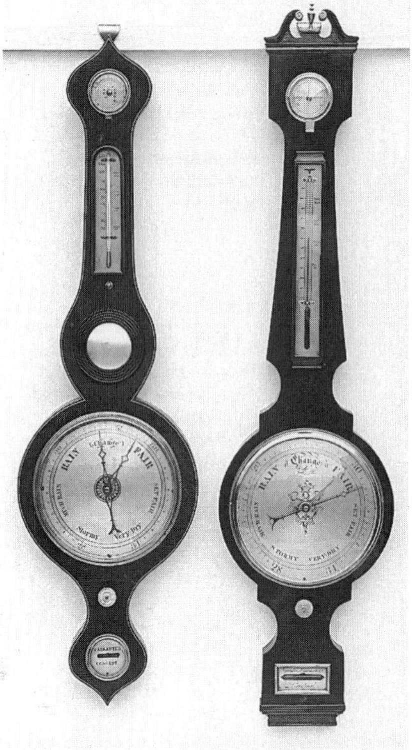

l. A Georgian mahogany wheel barometer, with 8in (20cm) dial, with thermometer, hygrometer, level and convex mirror, 37in (94cm) high.
£200–250
r. A late Georgian mahogany wheel barometer, with 8in (20cm) silvered dial incorporating thermometer, hygrometer and level signed 'Bywater and Dawson', 40in (101.5cm) high.
£400–450 *WL*

A Victorian oak aneroid barometer.
£200–250 *DaD*

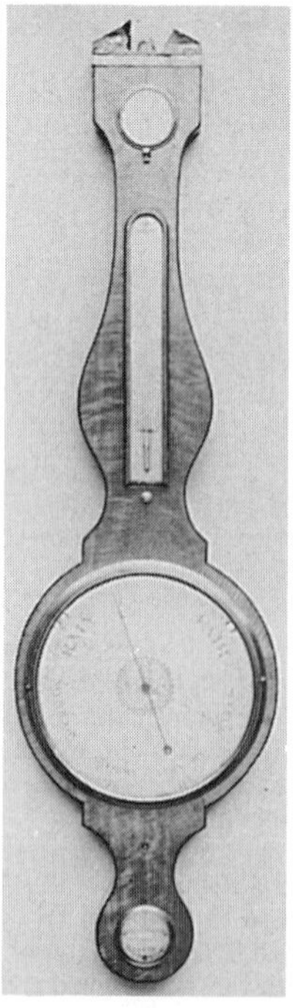

A George III satinwood wheel barometer, signed 'D. Poncia' on the silvered level, with 10in (25cm) silvered register, thermometer and hygrometer in a shaped case, the pediment lacking, in need of restoration, 42in (106.5cm) high.
£700–800 *DN*

A mahogany wheel barometer, silvered 11in (28cm) dial, humidity dial, mercury thermometer and convex mirror, the bubble level signed 'L. Martinelli, Brighton', the case with swan neck pediment and rounded base, c1840, 42½in (108cm) high.
£500–700 *S(S)*

A Victorian inlaid rosewood wheel barometer, with 10in (25cm) silvered dial, shaped case set with a thermometer and inlaid mother-of-pearl bird and leaf motifs, c1860, 42in (106.5cm) high.
£400–500 *S*

Barographs

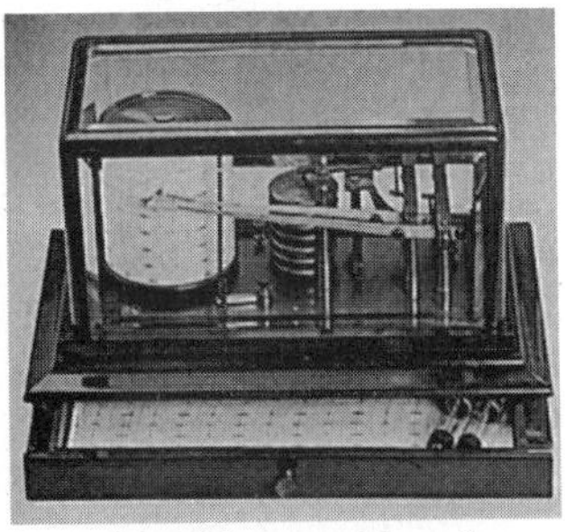

A combined barograph and thermograph, with revolving clockwork barrel, one inking arm attached to vacuum chamber and the other to the bimetallic strip, on glazed mahogany case with graph drawer in the base, early 20thC.
£700–800 *S*

A barograph, with an aneroid barometer, in a glazed oak case with a chart drawer to the base, on pad feet, 14in (36cm) wide.
£650–750 *WW*

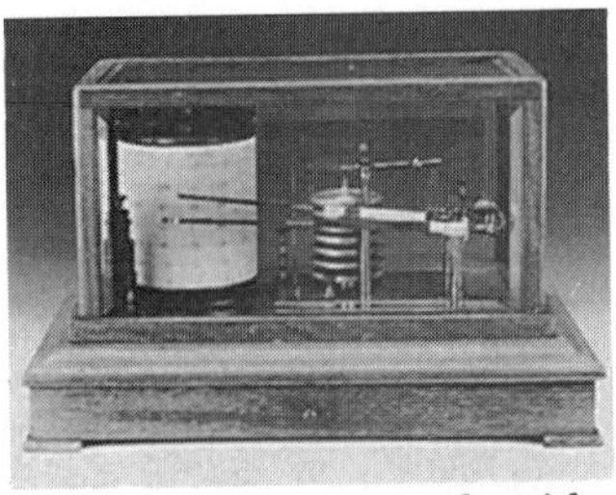

A barograph/thermograph, with drum, vacuum chamber, twin recording styli and ink bottle, in bevel-glazed oak case with drawer in base containing charts, 14½in (37cm) wide.
£500–600 *CSK*

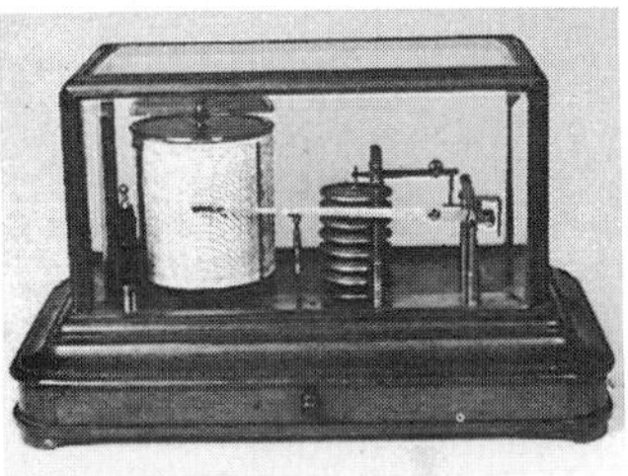

A lacquered brass barograph, with 7 tier vacuum, in a glazed mahogany case with fitted drawer below, 15in (38.5cm) wide.
£500–600 *P*

A French ballooning or aviation barograph, by J. Richard, No. 81682, with revolving barrel, contained in a glazed mahogany case with brass carrying handle, c1910, 7in (17.5cm) wide.
£400–600 *S*

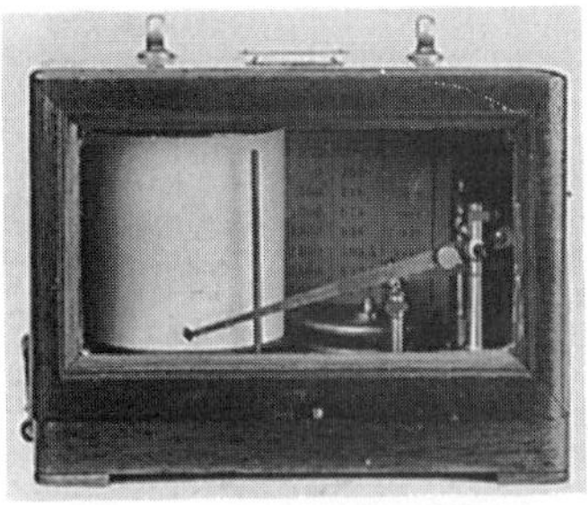

A barograph, by Richard Frères, Paris, No. 83859, with drum, vacuum chamber and recording pen, in a hinged mahogany case with glazed front, conversion chart and 'Jules Ricard' retailer's label, 7in (17.5cm) wide.
£350–400 *CSK*

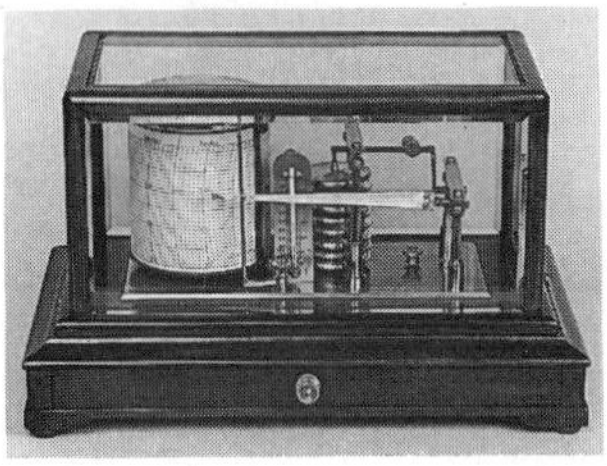

l. A barograph, with a thermometer, by Negretti and Zambra, in a mahogany case with a drawer to base, c1910.
£1,000–1,100 *W&W*

r. A barograph, by Negretti and Zambra, with aneroid dial and thermometer, in an oak case, c1900.
£1,200–1,400 *W&W*

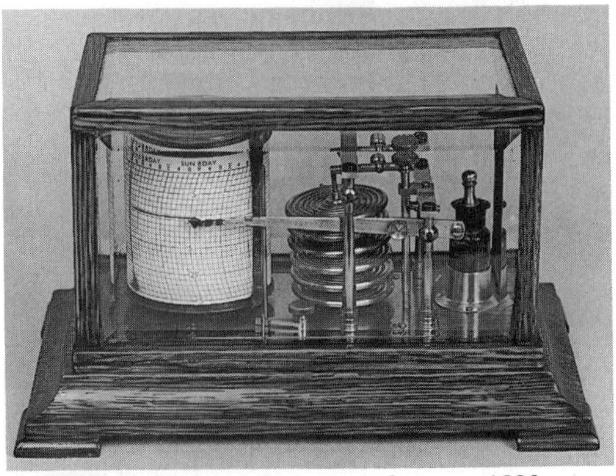

A miniature barograph, in an oak case, c1890.
£900–1,000 *W&W*

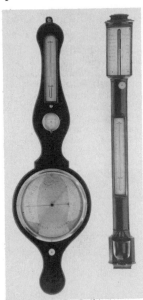

SCIENTIFIC INSTRUMENTS

Dials

A brass universal equinoctial dial, by Elliott Brothers, the base plate mounted with 2 spirit levels, 2 bubble levels, hour ring, latitude arc and gnomon, on 3 levelling screws, 3in (7.5cm) wide, in a shaped red morocco case.
£650–750 *S*

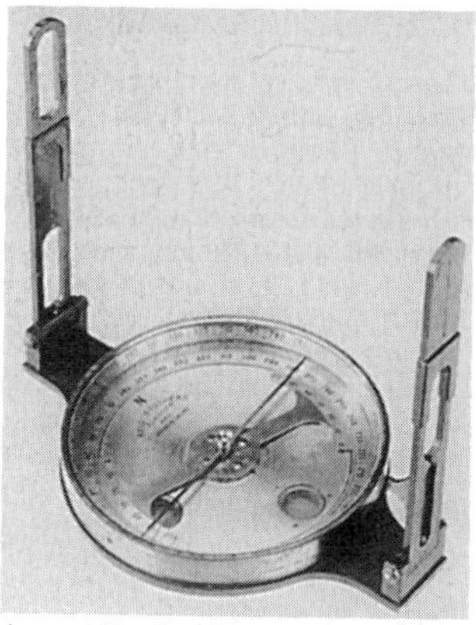

An oxidised and lacquered brass mining dial, by Reid Brothers, Glasgow and Johannesburg, the twin folding sights with extensions and silvered dial with edge bar needle, spirit level and cross level, scales and twin verniers, on staff mount, 10in (25cm) long, in a fitted mahogany case, dated '1915'.
£200–300 *CSK*

A French noon cannon sundial, for latitude 48°50"13', Paris, the circular white marble base with engraved sundial, brass gnomon, mounted with burning lens on adjustable arc, and a miniature brass cannon, late 19thC, 10in (25cm) wide.
£1,500–2,000 *S*

A French brass Butterfield dial, signed 'Meurand à Paris', the dial engraved with 4 hour scales for latitudes 43, 45, 49 and 52, inset compass well and mounted with shaped gnomon with bird indicator, the base engraved with French towns and latitudes, late 18thC, 3in (7cm) long.
£500–600 *S*

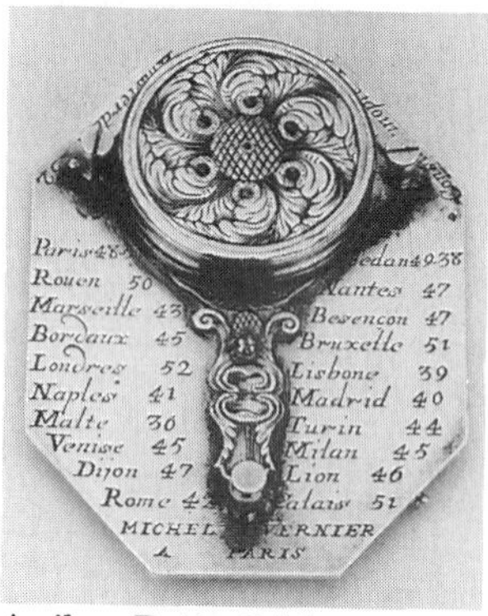

A silver Butterfield pattern sundial, the plate with compass box, engraved hour scales and folding bird gnomon, the underside engraved with the latitudes of 22 Continental cities and signed 'Michael Vernier a Paris', 2½in (6cm) long, in a shaped, velvet lined leather case.
£1,500–2,000 *CSK*

Globes

An 8½in (21cm) table celestial globe, by John and William Cary, mounted on a mahogany stand, with 4 baluster turned legs and cross stretcher, brass centre post, 1816.
£1,000–1,500 *CSK*

An oxidised and lacquered brass circumferentor, the compass box with cap, silvered dial, blued/silvered needle and clamp, bubble level and cross bubble, the circle divided 0°–350°, and with twin detachable sights, the alidade with twin verniers and detachable sights, on three-screw tripod stand, with tripod mounting bush, 9½in (24cm) diam., in a fitted wooden case with label 'Technical, Industry and Factory Engineer R. A. Dombrovskavo, Kiev, Kreshatuk No. 8'.
£500–700 *CSK*

A lacquered brass mining dial, by Troughton & Simms, London, with twin folding sights, bubble level, engraved silvered dial with edge bar needle, clamp and lid, 12in (30.5cm) long, with staff mount, in a fitted mahogany case with maker's label.
£250–300 *CSK*

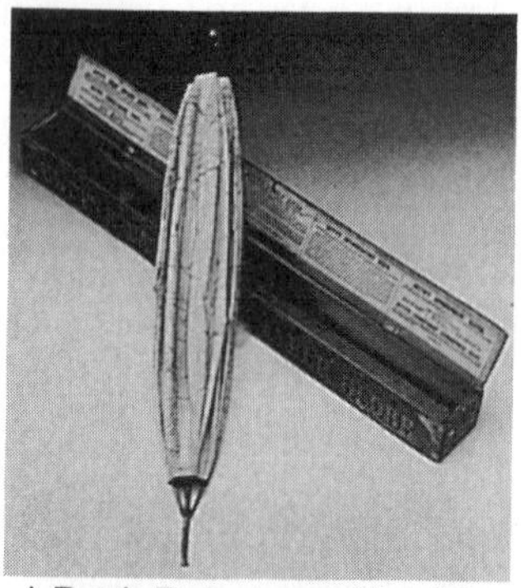

A Bett's Patent portable globe, the expanding printed fabric globe contained in original pine box with printed labels, c1890, 28in (71cm) long.
£600–650 *S*

An 11in (28cm) 'Cary's New Terrestrial Globe Delineated From the best Authorities extant; Exhibiting the different Tracks of Captain Cook, and the New Discoveries made by him and other Circumnavigators', with brass hour and meridian circles and paper horizon circle, on a mahogany stand with turned legs and cross stretchers, the cartouche with 'A. Mackenzie' retailer's label, damaged, c1810, 18in (45.5cm) high, and an 11in (28cm) 'Cary's New Celestial Globe', with brass hour and meridian circles, damaged, dated '1816'.
£2,700–3,200 *CSK*

An 8in (20cm) terrestrial table globe, by Cary's, London, the circumference encased with brass slide, on turned baluster legs, dated '1813', and a similar celestial globe, by Cary's, dated '1803'.
£2,000–3,000 *P(EA)*

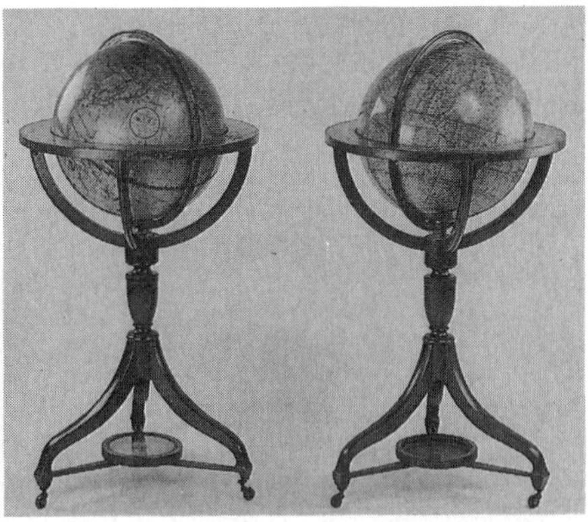

A pair of 15in (38cm) Cary's terrestrial and celestial library globes, the terrestrial inscribed 'Drawn from the most recent geographical works showing the whole of the new discoveries with tracks of the Principal Navigators and every improvement in Geography to the present time, London, published by J. & W. Cary, 181 Strand, November 24th 1820', the celestial inscribed 'on which are carefully laid down the whole of the Stars and Nebule contained in the catalogues of Wollast, Herschel, Bode, Piazzi, Zach XC, calculated to the year 1820, made and sold by J. & W. Cary, 181 Strand, London 1818', with calibrated brass horizons and papers, 40in (101cm) high.
£18,000–22,000 *P(NE)*

An 18in (45.5cm) terrestrial globe, with hand drawn and coloured paper gores in antique style, the continents in a variety of colours, labelled and with mountain ranges shown, and domestic animals suitably placed, various cartouches show historical information relating to voyages of discovery and dedications in Italian and Latin, the oceans labelled and illustrated with marine monsters, vessels and compass roses, the meridian circle with 360° scale, divided in 4 quadrants, the horizon ring with zodiac and calendar scale, on a fruitwood stand, 46in (116.5cm) high.
£3,600–4,200 *CSK*

A 12in (30.5cm) terrestrial table globe, by C. Smith & Son of London, with hand coloured paper gores, the panel inscribed 'Smiths 12in Terrestrial Globe', showing all the most recent discoveries, with curved brass support, on a walnut baluster, damaged, 19thC, 20in (50.5cm) high.
£400–600 *HSS*

r. A Malby's 12in (30.5cm) celestial globe, the sphere mounted in brass meridian, on a mahogany tripod base, mid-19thC, 17in (43cm) high.
£900–1,200 *S*

A pair of 12in (30.5cm) library globes, the terrestrial signed 'C. Smith & Son, 172 Strand, London 1842', each set within brass meridians, on turned mahogany stands with tripod supports, each set with a presentation plaque, both damaged, 34in (86cm) high.
£6,000–7,000 *P*

A 3in (7.5cm) pocket globe, the sphere applied with hand coloured gores and printed within cartouche 'Cary's Pocket Globe agreeable to the latest Discoveries, London, by J. & W. Cary, Strand', and tracks of 'Cook and Clerke, Resolution and Discovery 1780' and 'Gore and King, 1780', in sharkskin case
£2,200–2,700 *N*

A 3in (7.5cm) terrestrial pocket globe, with 12 hand coloured gores, the maker's label inscribed 'Jacob and Halse London 1809', in a fishskin covered case with a print of the castellations applied to inner surfaces.
£2,000–2,500 *AH*

Microscopes

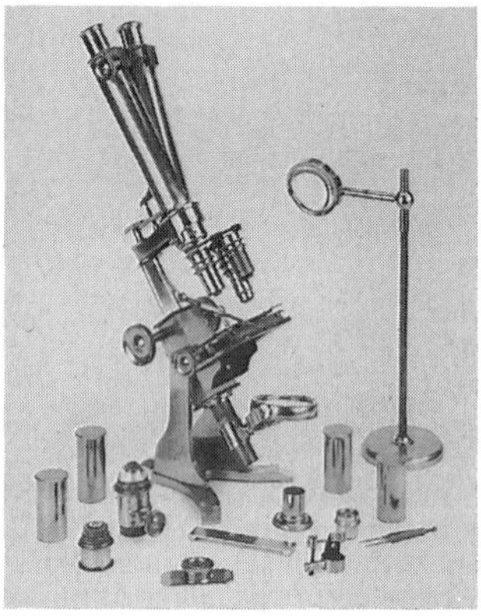

A lacquered brass binocular microscope, by Baker, London, with dividing eyepieces, coarse and fine focusing, prism, triple nosepiece, square stage, sub-stage condenser and mirror, on Y-shaped stand, 16in (40.5cm) high, with accessories, in a damaged case.
£600–700 *CSK*

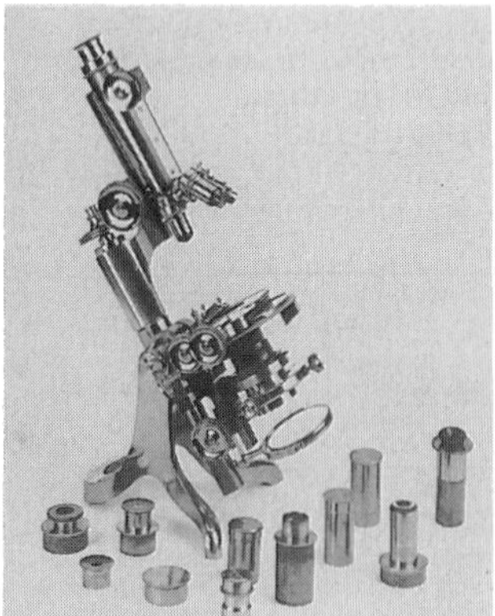

A lacquered brass petrological microscope, by Henry Crouch, London, No. 1218, with coarse and fine focusing, triple nosepiece, mechanical circular stage, sub-stage condenser with iris diaphragm and plano/concave mirror on a sliding collar, on a raised horseshoe base, 12in (30.5cm) high, with accessories, in a fitted mahogany case, with a quantity of slides.
£850–1,000 *CSK*

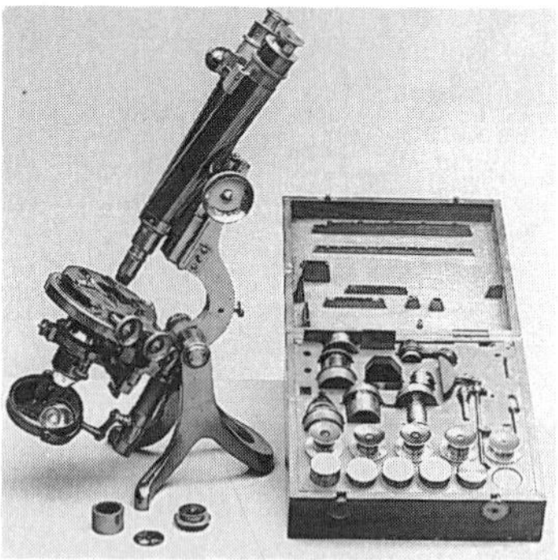

A Victorian brass binocular microscope, by Henry Crouch, London.
£2,000–2,500 *DaD*

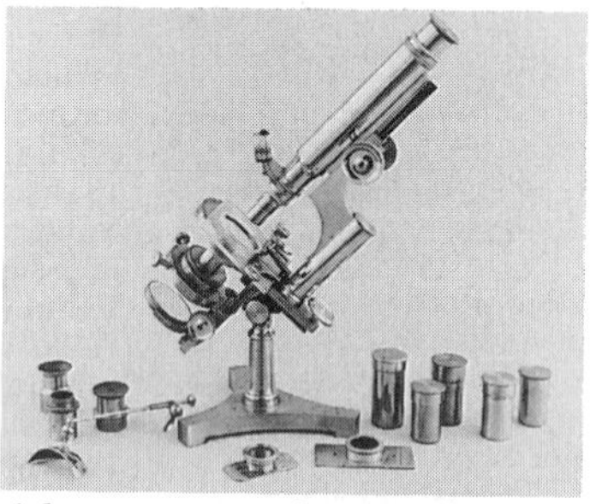

A brass compound monocular microscope, by R. & J. Beck, London, No. 12239, with rack-and-pinion and fine focusing, sub-stage condenser, plano/concave mirror, with objectives, eyepieces and accessories, in a mahogany case, together with an oil lamp by Swift and Son, London, late 19thC.
£400–450 *DN*

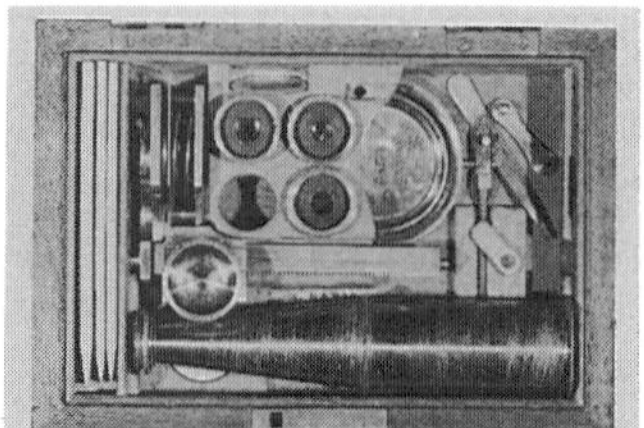

A lacquered brass botanical microscope, by Davis, Worcester, with tapered body tube, sprung stage with rack-and-pinion focusing and accessories, in a fitted mahogany box, 19thC, 11½in (29.5cm) high.
£200–300 *P*

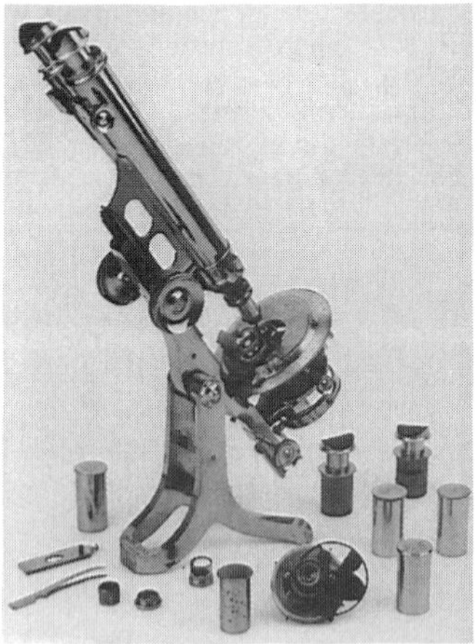

A lacquered brass binocular petrological microscope, with dividing eyepieces, twin prisms in carrier, rack-and-pinion and fine focusing, circular stage with silvered scale divided 0°–360°, signed 'Watson & Son, Patent No. 41', sub-stage condenser and plano/concave mirror, on a raised horseshoe foot signed 'C. Collins, London, 157 Gt. Portland Street', 18in (45.5cm) high, with a Webster Condenser, objectives and other accessories, in a fitted mahogany case.
£900–1,200 *CSK*

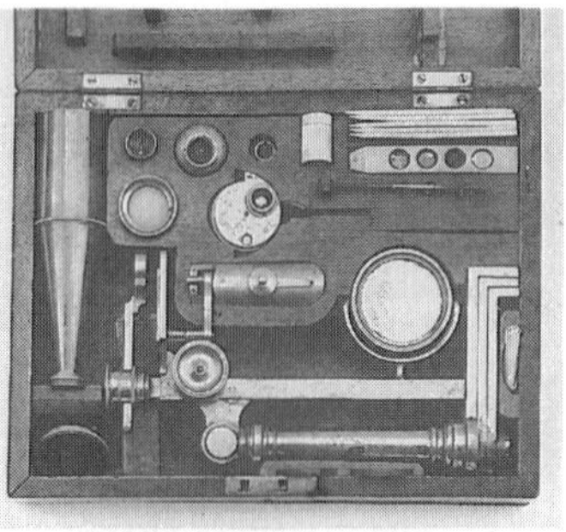

A brass compound/simple microscope, by Dollond, London, with folding tripod feet, 12½in (32cm) high, with six-objective rotating disc, lieberkuhn, live-box, fish plate, stage forceps with black/white dot, talc box, and 6 ivory sliders, early 19thC, all in a fitted mahogany case.
£900–1,200 *CSK*

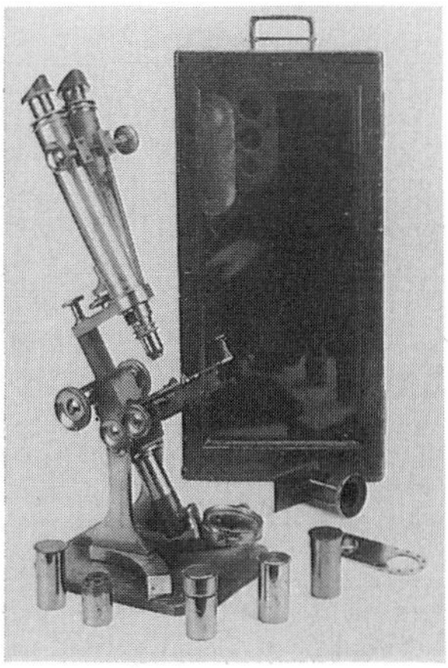

A lacquered brass binocular microscope, by R. M. Hatch, Bristol, with dividing eyepieces, coarse and fine focusing, square stage, sub-stage and mirror, on a Y-shaped foot, prism missing, 15in (38cm) high, with accessories, in a glazed case.
£350–500 *CSK*

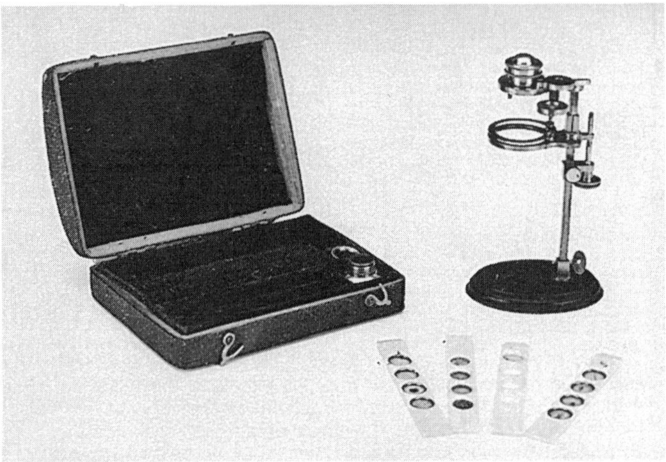

A botanical microscope, by W. & S. Jones, Holborn, London, with elliptical ebony base stamped with maker's name, mounted with square brass column fitted with a stage and 2 simple lenses, with a reflector, and a black shagreen covered dome topped case, together with 4 ivory slides, early 19thC, 4½in (11.5cm) high.
£400–450 *HSS*

Miller's is a price GUIDE not a price LIST

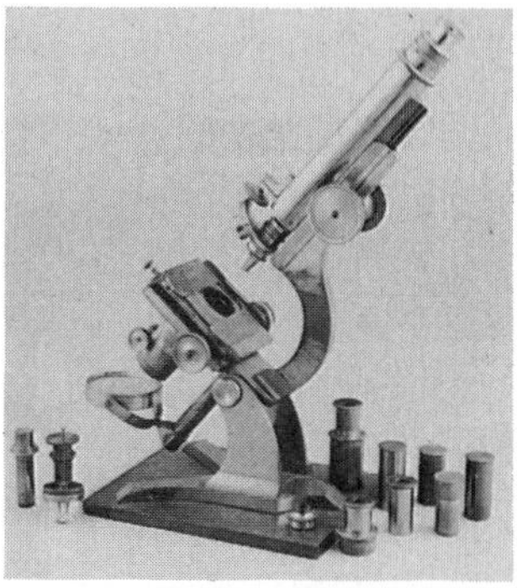

A brass compound microscope, by M. Pillischer, 398 Oxford Street, London, No. 117, with rack-and-pinion and fine focusing, triple lens turret, mechanical stage with sub-stage condenser, and plano/concave mirror, in a mahogany case, together with a mahogany case containing objectives, eyepieces and other accessories, 19thC.
£200–300 *DN*

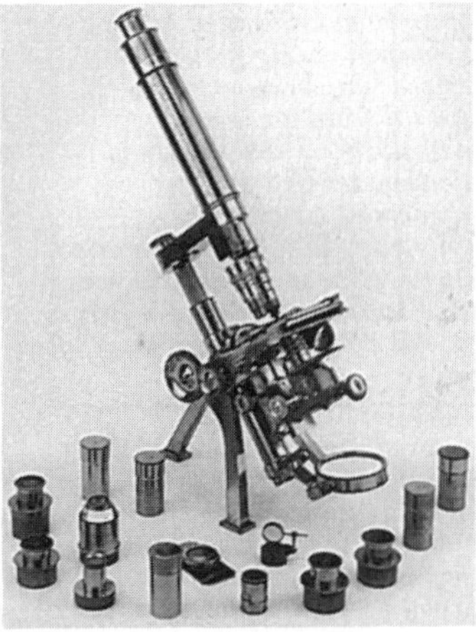

A lacquered brass No. 2 microscope, with draw tube graduated 1–4, limb signed 'Powell & Lealand, 170 Euston Road, London', and dated '1863', rack-and-pinion and micrometer focusing, mechanical square stage, mechanical sub-stage with wheel-stops and jointed plano/concave mirror on sliding collar, on a tripod stand, 15in (38cm) high, with 5 objectives, 5 eyepieces, stage forceps and other accessories, in a fitted mahogany case.
£4,200–4,800 *CSK*

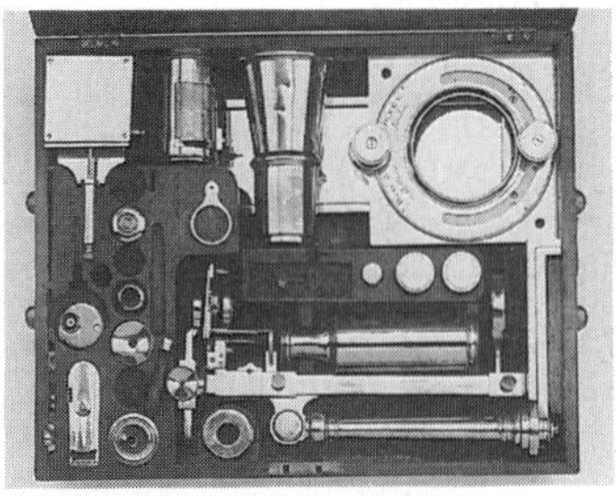

A microscopist's compendium, by W. & S. Jones, London, comprising a lacquered brass solar microscope, condenser body tube and barrel, opaque box and objective slider, a Most Improved Model simple/compound microscope, with body tube, swivelling arm, square stage with rack-and-pinion focusing, sub-stage bull's eye condenser and plano/concave mirror, mounted on universal joint to turned pillar support on folding tripod legs, one signed 'W. & S. Jones, 30 Holborn, London', with revolving objective disc, 2 lieberkuhn, spring stage, fish plate, cone, slide carriers and other items, the base with drawer containing various ivory and wood sliders, glass phials, cleaner and manuscript list of slides inscribed 'A list of the objects to the improved Microscopical Magazine of Instruments', all in a fitted mahogany case with brass carrying handles, re-lacquered, c1800, 16in (40.5cm) wide.
£7,000–8,000 *CSK*

l. A lacquered brass No. 3 microscope, with eyepiece clamp, body tube struts, single nosepiece, limb signed 'Powell & Lealand, Makers, London', square mechanical stage with sub-stage wheel-stops and plano/concave mirror on sliding collar, on a raised tripod stand, 14½in (37cm) high, with 7 objectives, eyepiece, and various condensers, all in a fitted mahogany case with maker's label, c1845.
£1,500–2,000 *CSK*

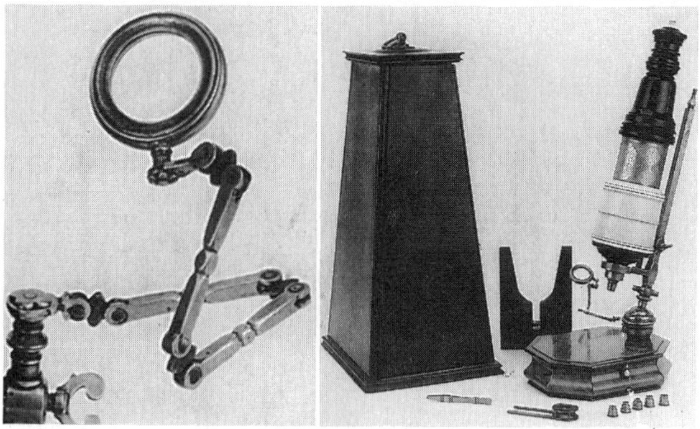

A Marshall pattern compound monocular microscope, attributed to John Marshall, London, the ebony upper body tube with threaded lens cover and turned ivory finial, on ball-and-socket joint and lead filled walnut base, the condenser on articulated arm held in bracket by wing nut, the drawer with spring catch, the bottom lined in multi-coloured paper and containing 6 objectives numbered '1–6', and a pair of shaped tweezers, early 18thC, 18in (45.5cm) high, in a stained wood, fitted pyramid shaped case with retaining slide, remnants of a paper label and ring carrying handle, restored.
£31,000–37,000 *CSK*

John Marshall, 1663–1725, originally worked at The Sign of the Gun in Ludgate, London. In 1689 the name was changed to The Archimedes and Two Pairs of Golden Spectacles. He pioneered the method of grinding a number of lenses simultaneously on blocks of the same size, having developed it from an idea in Hooke's publication Micrographia. *He appears to have invented his Double Microscope or Great Double-Constructed Microscope around 1693. Marshall's microscope incorporated many important features, including having the body tube on a limb and pillar, the stage being on the same axis as the main body, the use of a condenser on a movable arm, coarse and fine focusing, a fish plate and a graduated set of objectives. All these characteristics were incorporated into later microscopes.*

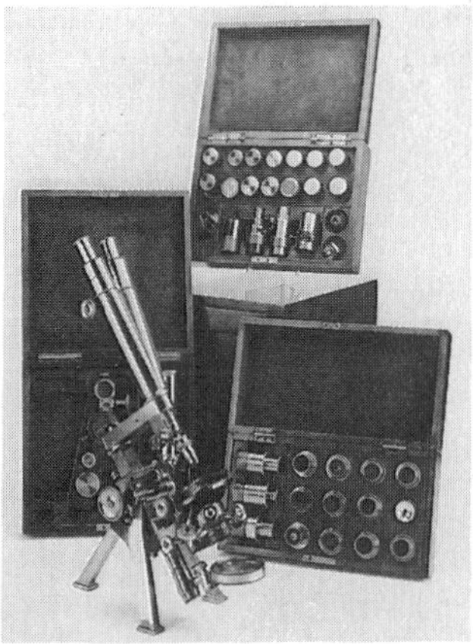

A lacquered brass No. 1 binocular microscope, with dividing eyepieces, prism, limb, signed 'Powell & Lealand, 170 Euston Road, London', dated '1895', with rack-and-pinion and micrometer focusing, double nosepiece, square mechanical stage with concentric movement and silvered scales divided 0°–180°–0°, mechanical sub-stage with concentric movement and plano/concave mirror on double jointed arm on sliding collar, on tripod stand, 17½in (44.5cm) high, in a fitted mahogany case, with 3 cases of accessories.
£7,000–8,000 *CSK*

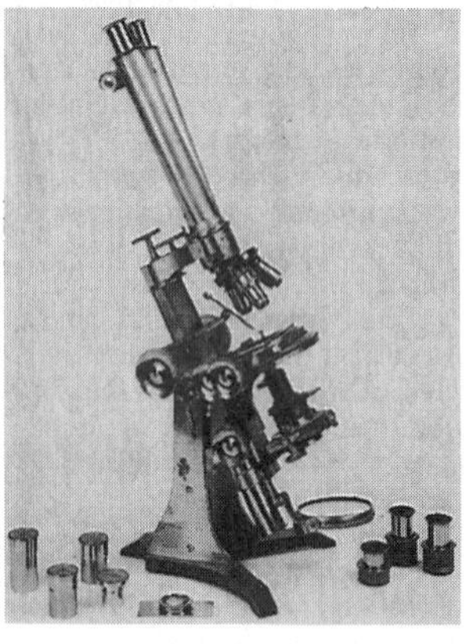

l. A lacquered and oxidised brass compound binocular microscope, by Ross, London, numbered 3506, with Wenham's body tube, coarse and fine rack-and-pinion focusing, prism and casing, later triple nosepiece, a circular mechanical stage above a rack-and-pinion sub-stage condenser with aperture wheel and plano/concave mirror on a sliding collar, raised on twin trunnions on a flat tripod base, 19in (48cm) high, within a fitted double-doored mahogany box with 5 eyepieces, 3 signed objectives and other accessories, 19thC.
£700–800 *P*

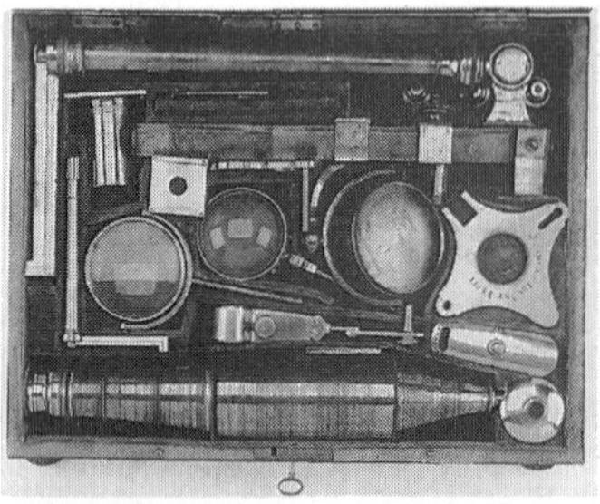

A lacquered brass compound microscope, the shaped body tube with a bioconvex lens, 2 plano/convex lenses and a bio/convex field lens, connected to limb by bracket, the limb with cruciform stage signed 'J. Simons Invt. et Fecit', late 18thC, 23in (59cm) high, with accessories, and a quantity of later slides, all in a later mahogany case with twin drawers and inset handle, on bun feet, the case c1830.
£4,000–5,000 *CSK*

James Simons, active between 1774 and 1793, described himself as a mathematical, philosophical and optical instrument maker. His shop was at the sign of Sir Isaac Newton's Head, Marylebone Street, London. This massive instrument is idiosyncratic in design, showing elements of standard 18thC microscopes and the early 19thC attempts to improve the optical tube. There are many novel features, including the high powered objective which is unusual for this date, the candle-holder and the extra stages.

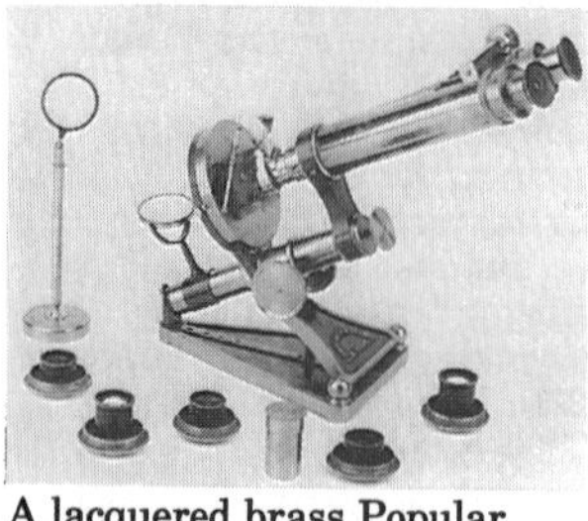

A lacquered brass Popular binocular microscope, No. 4133, by Smith, Beck & Beck, London, with dividing eyepieces, prism, rack-and-pinion and fine focusing, circular stage and concave mirror, on a folding stand, 15in (38cm) high, with accessories in a fitted mahogany case.
£500–600 *CSK*

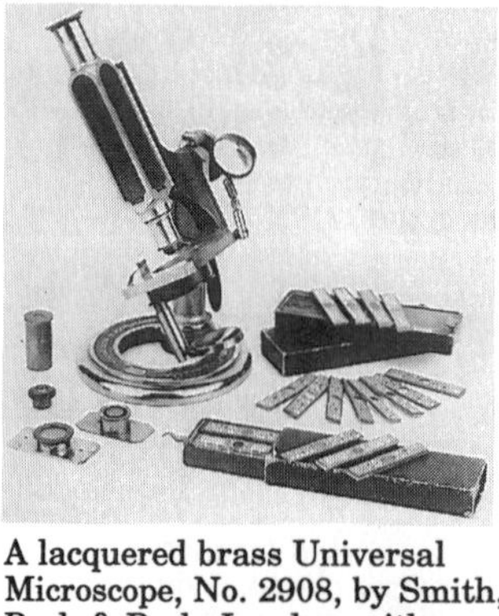

A lacquered brass Universal Microscope, No. 2908, by Smith, Beck & Beck, London, with a square body tube, fusee chain focusing, square stage with condenser and mirror, on a circular stand, c1860, 11in (28cm) high, with accessories in a fitted mahogany case.
£400–600 *CSK*

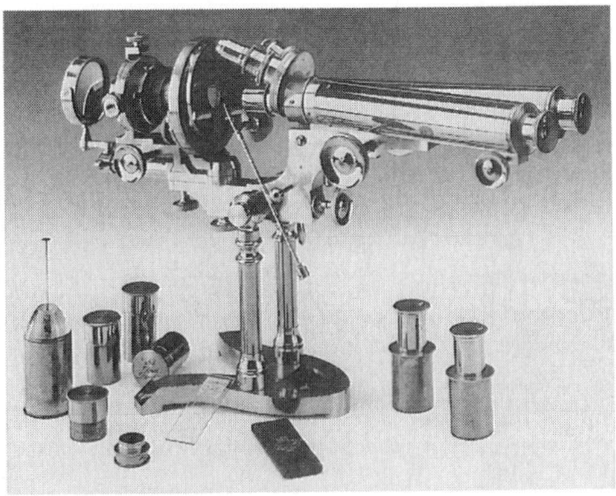

A lacquered brass binocular microscope, by Ross, London, No. 5311, 16in (40.5cm) high, with accessories, in a fitted mahogany case with metal bindings.
£2,500–3,000 *CSK*

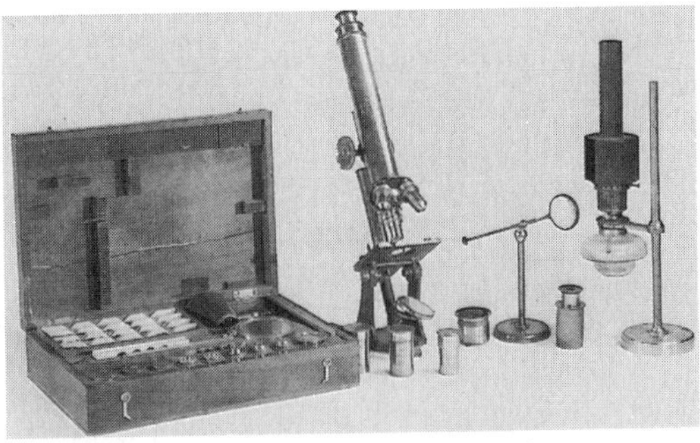

A lacquered brass compound monocular microscope, by Smith, Beck & Beck, London, No. 3750, with rack-and-pinion focusing, 19thC, 14in (35.5cm) high, in a fitted mahogany box with bull's eye condenser, and other accessories, together with another fitted box of accessories, a cased microscopist's oil lamp marked 'Deitz & Co., London', and a monocular microscrope by Beck.
£750–800 *P*

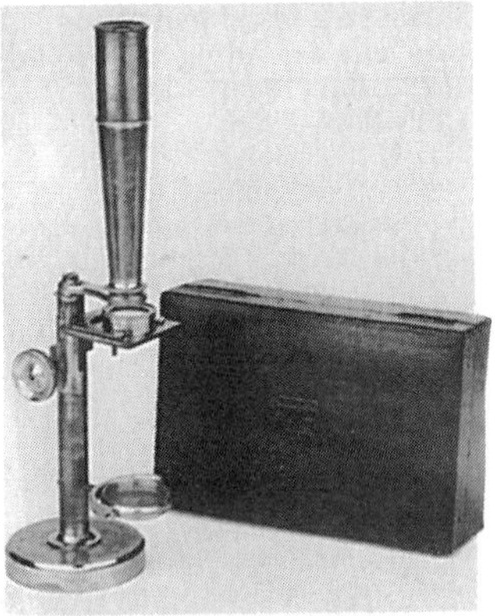

A lacquered brass Gould pattern microscope, by Watkins & Hill, London, with tapered body tube, rack-and-pinion focusing, square stage and circular base, 9½in (24cm) high, in a fitted leather covered case.
£300-400 *CSK*

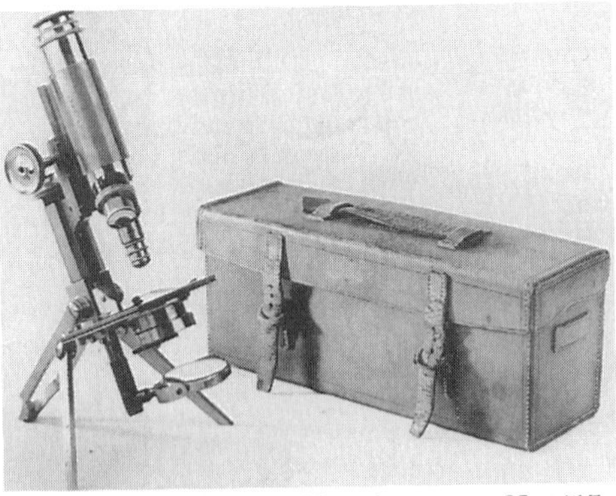

A lacquered brass portable microscope, No. 415, by J. Swift & Son, London, with graduated draw tube, rack-and-pinion and fine focusing, double nosepiece, square sprung stage, sub-stage condenser and plano/concave mirror, cracked, on a folding tripod stand, 9in (22.5cm) high, in a fitted leather case.
£400–500 *CSK*

A black enamel Vickers/Cooke M4000 series Universal Microscope, No. M40541, with micrometer focusing, triple nosepiece, micrometer stage and adjustable Abbe condenser, with built-in illumination system and reflex camera attachment, with accessories and manufacturer's instructions, in a fitted box, 34in (86cm) high.
£250–350 *P*

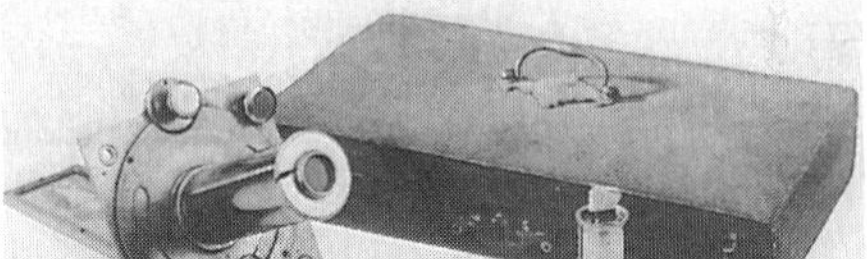

A lacquered brass solar microscope, with coarse-screw mirror adjustment and body tube, with brass illuminant, in plush lined, fitted fishskin covered wood case with brass carrying handle, mid-18thC, 13in (33cm) wide.
£400–500 *CSK*

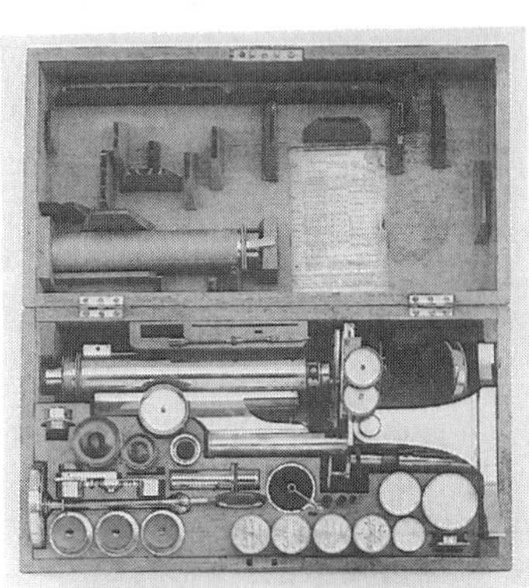

A brass binocular microscope, No. 3383, by Smith & Beck, London, with dividing eyepieces, prism, rack-and-pinion focusing, square mechanical stage, Reynolds & Branson sub-stage condenser and plano/concave mirror, on 'reversed' Y-shaped stand, 15in (38cm) high, with monocular body tube, bench condenser, sub-stage condenser and other accessories, in a fitted mahogany case with applied objective list in lid, c1862.
£1,200–1,700 *CSK*

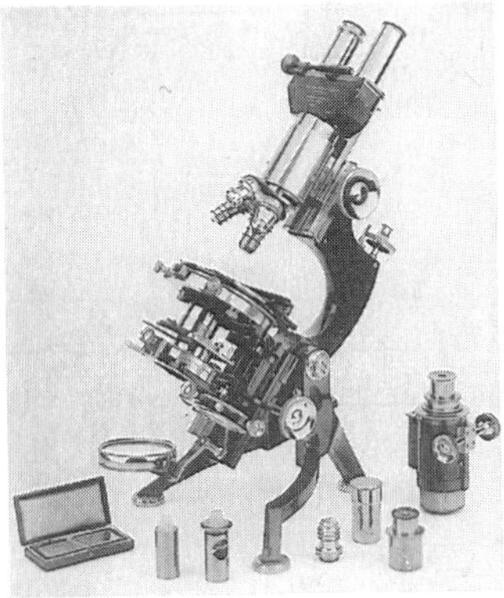

l. A black enamelled and lacquered brass Van Heurk pattern binocular microscope, by W. Watson & Sons Ltd., London, No. 42573, with high powered binocular eyepiece with dividing eyepieces, triple nosepiece, rack-and-pinion and micrometer focusing, circular mechanical stage with silvered scales, sub-stage condenser and plano/concave mirror, trunnion mounted to raised tripod stand, 16in (40.5cm) high, with monocular body tube and other accessories.
£3,000–3,500 *CSK*

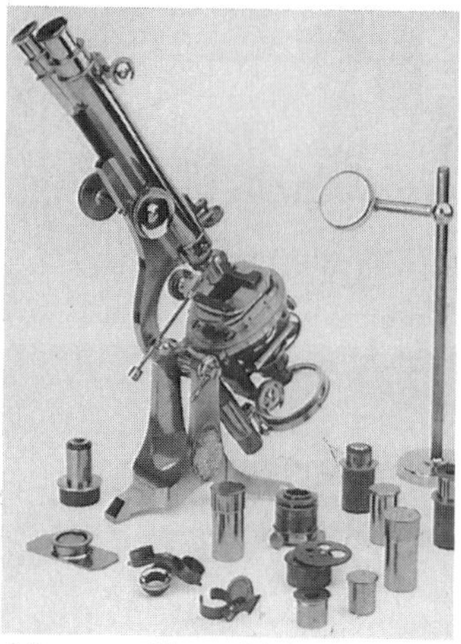

A lacquered brass binocular petrological microscope, No. 1200, by Watson & Son, London, with silver presentation plaque engraved 'Presented to William Hobkirk as a token of esteem and in recognition of valuable service rendered to the United Methodist Free Church Cramlington October 9th 1880', 15½in (39cm) high, with a bench condenser, sub-stage condenser, objectives and other items, all in a fitted mahogany case.
£1,300–1,700 *CSK*

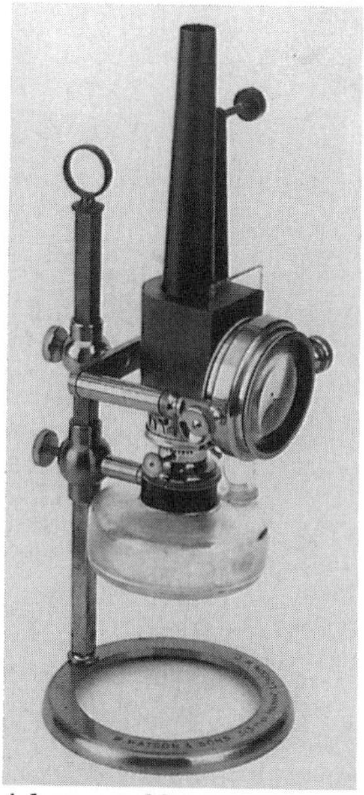

A lacquered brass microscopist's lamp, by W. Watson & Sons, London, with burner, shade and condensing lens, 11in (28cm) high, in a fitted mahogany case.
£1,000–1,500 *CSK*

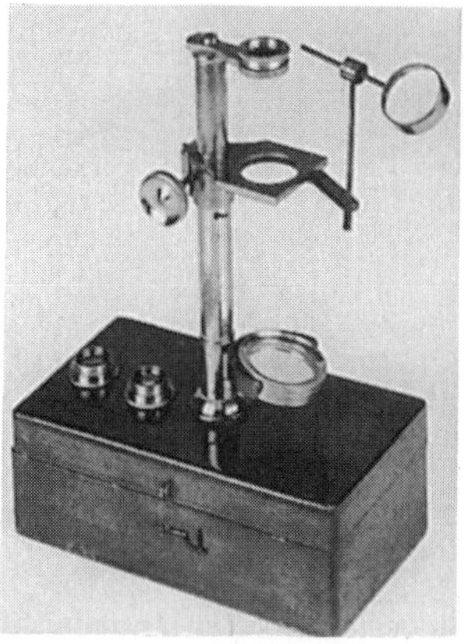

A lacquered brass simple microscope, with swivelling limb, rack-and-pinion focusing, square stage with condenser, plano mirror and one ivory slider, in a fitted mahogany case with mounting bush in lid, c1850, 6in (15cm) wide.
£200–300 *CSK*

A lacquered brass microscope, with draw tube focusing, body tube with bull's-eye condenser, signed 'Vincent Chevalier, Ingenieur Opticien, Quai del horloge 69, Paris', rack-and-pinion stage focusing and plano/bevelled mirror, in a mahogany case with storage drawer and mounting bush in the top, 8in (20cm) wide.
£420–500 *CSK*

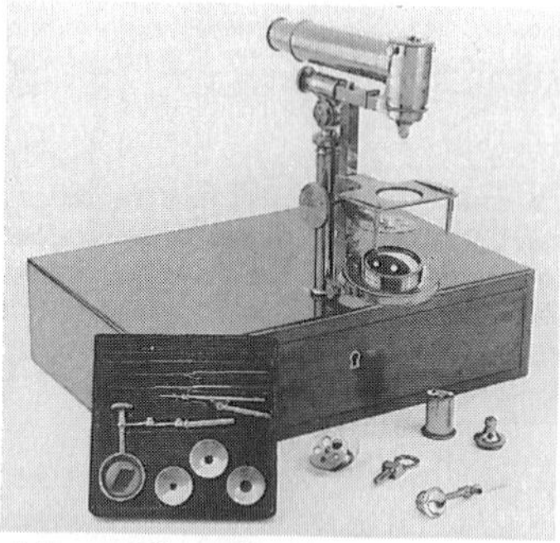

A brass Chevalier pattern horizontal compound microscope, with swivelling body tube, prism housing and location bracket, connecting to limb with vertical bar, rectangular stage, rack-and-pinion focusing and sub-stage wheel-stops, plano/concave mirror below, mounted by universal joint to turned pillar support with mounting bracket, in a fitted mahogany case with drawer containing eyepiece, 2 objectives, stage condenser and forceps, sub-stage wheel-stops and simple lens bracket, the top with mounting bush, 15in (38.5cm) wide.
£1,700–2,200 *CSK*

A black painted toolmaker's microscope, Werkzeugmikroskop, No. 3190, by Carl Zeiss, Jena, with rack-and-pinion and eyepiece focusing, adjustable limb, clockwork moving stage, micrometer stage adjustment and electric light source, with various accessories, c1925, 16in (40.5cm) high.
£550–700 *CSK*

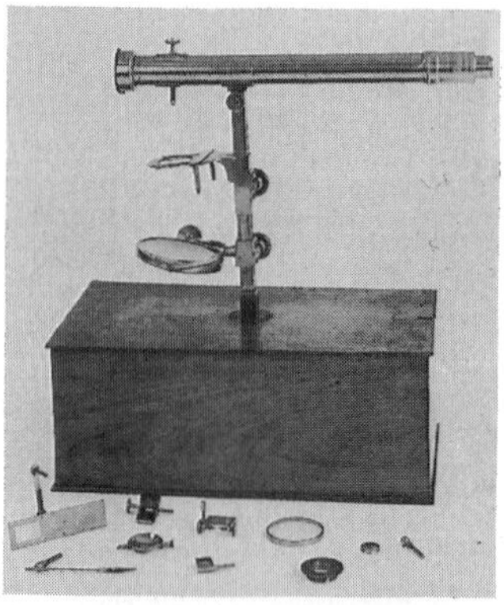

An Italian lacquered brass reflecting microscope, the tube with eyepiece, mirror and bracket, signed at the end 'Amici, Modena', tube 14½in (37cm) long, in a fitted mahogany case with a single drawer containing some accessories, 19thC.
£6,500–7,500 *P*

r. A lacquered brass microscope with graduated draw tube and rack-and-pinion focusing, triple nosepiece, mechanical stage and sub-stage and plano/concave mirror, on Y-shaped stand, 12½in (32cm) high, with accessories, in a fitted mahogany case.
£1,200–1,700 *CSK*

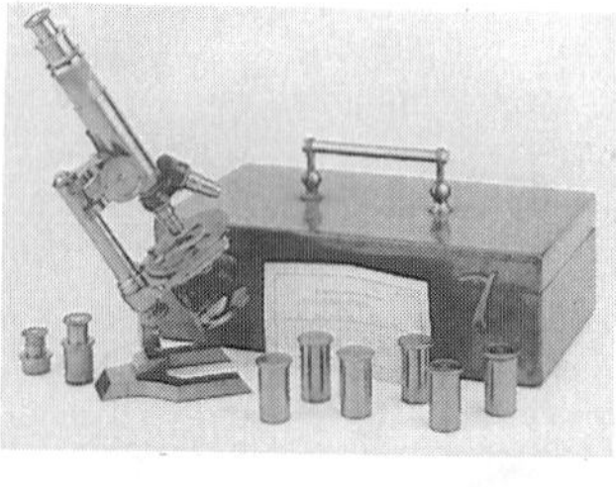

Telescopes

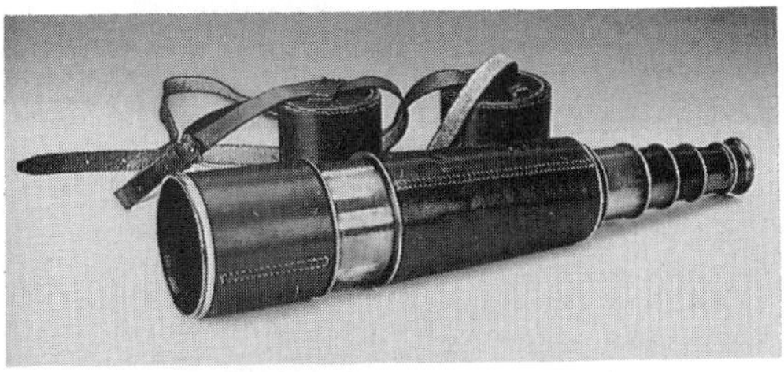

A 3in (7.5cm) brass 5-draw refracting telescope, the ocular tube with graduated range finder numbered 30–60 yards, with leather sleeve and slide hood, engraved with maker's name 'Broadhurst Clarkson & Co. Ltd., 63 Farringdon Road, London EC', with stitched leather carrying case, 42½in (108cm) long.
£200–250 *HSS*

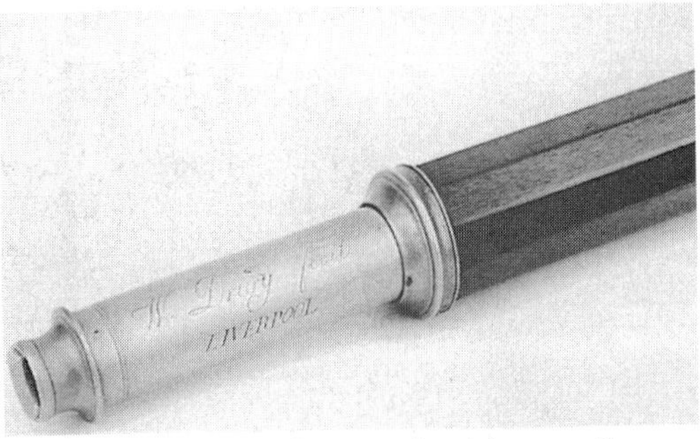

A ½in (1.5cm) single draw marine telescope, the brass tube in 3 sections, one signed 'W. Drury, fecit, Liverpool', with dust slides and ten-sided mahogany body tube, objective missing, late 18thC, 13in (33cm) long.
£250–300 *CSK*

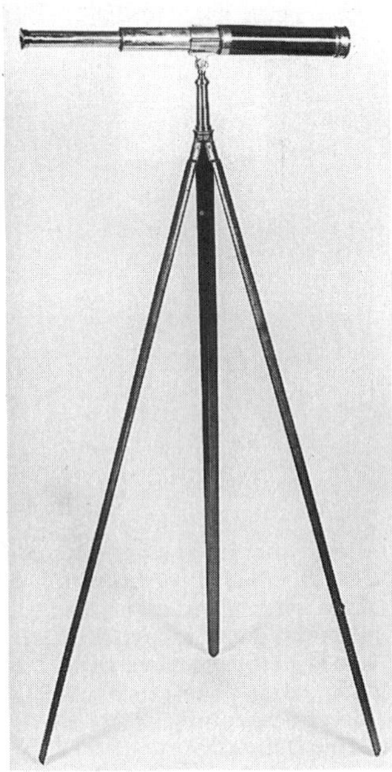

A 2in (5cm) 4-draw mahogany and brass telescope, on tripod stand, the inner tube engraved 'G. & W. Proctor, London', 43in (109cm) extended, the tripod with brass clamp and bracket above a tapering column, mahogany legs, 19thC, 64in (162.5cm) high.
£650–700 *N*

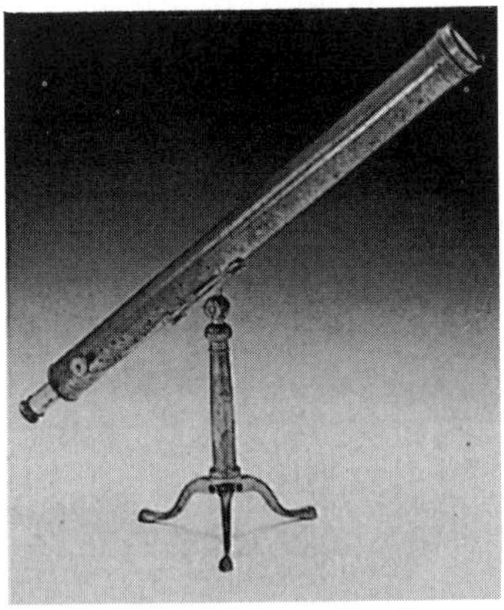

A 2½in (6.5cm) brass refracting telescope, the tube with rack-and-pinion focusing, mounted on tapering column above folding tripod base, mid-19thC, tube 37in (94cm) long.
£600–700 *S*

Make the most of Miller's

Condition is absolutely vital when assessing the value of an antique. Items in good condition are more likely to appreciate than less perfect examples. Rare, desirable items may command higher prices even when in need of restoration.

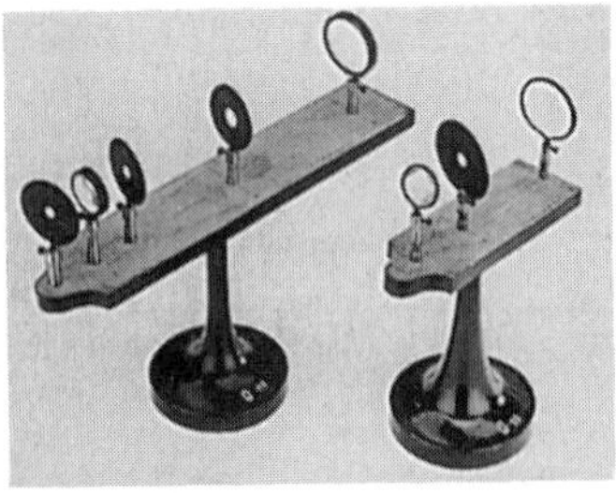

r. A pair of demonstration telescopes, by F. Steflitschek, Vienna, on turned ebonised bases, longest 10½in (26.5cm) long.
£200–250 *CSK*

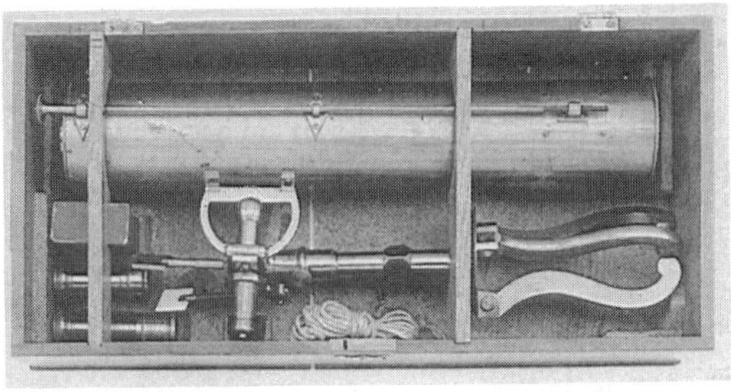

A 3¼in (8cm) lacquered brass reflecting telescope, by James Short, London, No. 220/1250=12, the 17½in (44.5cm) body tube with eyepiece, screw-rod focusing, sight and lens cap, mounted on racked semi-circle to turned pillar support with folding inswept tripod legs, alternative eyepiece, speculum and sight, in a fitted mahogany case, c1760.
£3,000–3,500 *CSK*

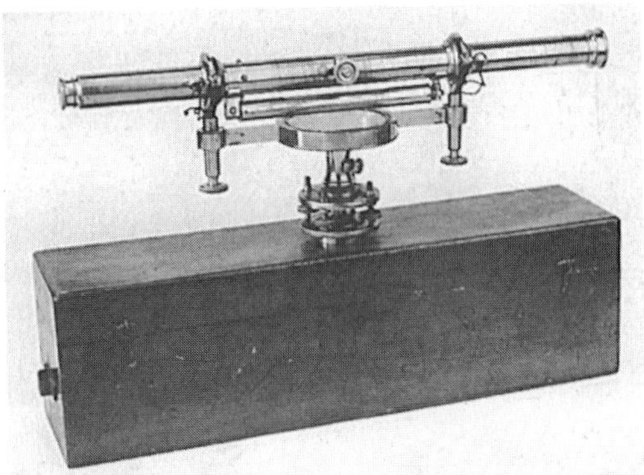

A lacquered brass Y-level, by Harris, London, the telescope with rack-and-pinion focusing, lens cap, dust slide and bubble level below, mounted in Y-shaped brackets over compass box with engraved silvered dial signed 'Harris, 17 Holborn, London', with edge bar needle and clamp, on four-screw tripod mount, early 19thC, 22in (55.5cm) long, in a fitted mahogany case.
£300–350 *CSK*

Thermometers

An 18ct gold cased pocket thermometer, No. 3, with blued steel and brass expansion spring, blued steel needle, white enamel dial divided 0°-200° and labelled for 'Freezing, Temp., Sum., Blood and Fever', with suspension ring, by Henry Kessels, marked 'London', c1821, in part wood case, 2in (5cm) diam.
£3,500–4,000 *CSK*

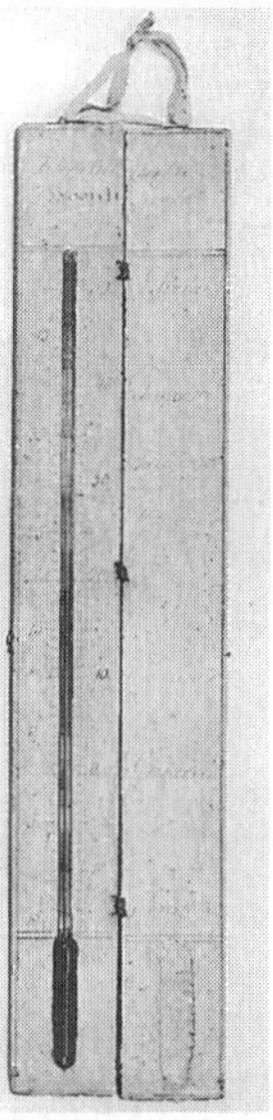

A wood cased thermometer, graduated 15°-0°-50°, the hinged cover indistinctly signed in ink and dated 'Torino 1702', 13½in (34cm) high.
£1,400–1,700 *CSK*

An Ashford marble thermometer, marked 'J. Turner of Buxton', c1880, 7½in (19cm) high.
£300–325 *WN*

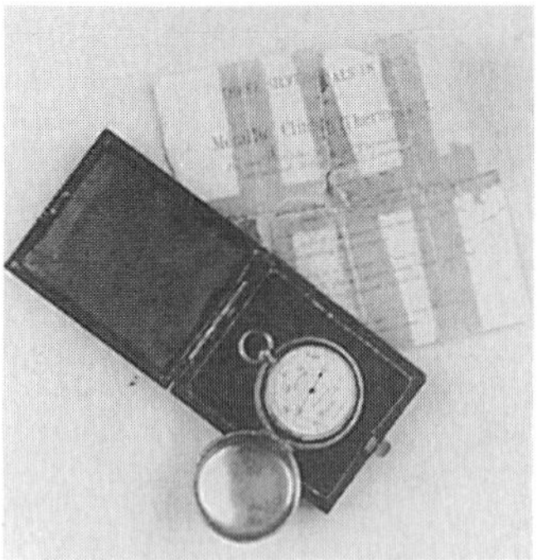

A gilt metallic clinical thermometer, by Eggington, Manchester, of pocket watch form, with blued steel needle, in metal outer case and fitted leather covered case, with instruction sheet, torn, c1885, 1in (2.5cm) diam.
£250–300 *CSK*

Surveying & Drawing Instruments

l. A surveyor's compass, by J. & W. Watkins, London, with silvered dial, needle, clamp and bubble level, in mahogany frame with hinged lid, lacks cross bubble, 7in (17.5cm) diam.
£130–170 *CSK*

A Lerebours surveying compass, the printed paper compass rose with engraved brass circle of degrees, in a fruitwood case with sliding lid and adjacent sight, French, c1800, 8in (20cm) diam.
£500–600 *S*

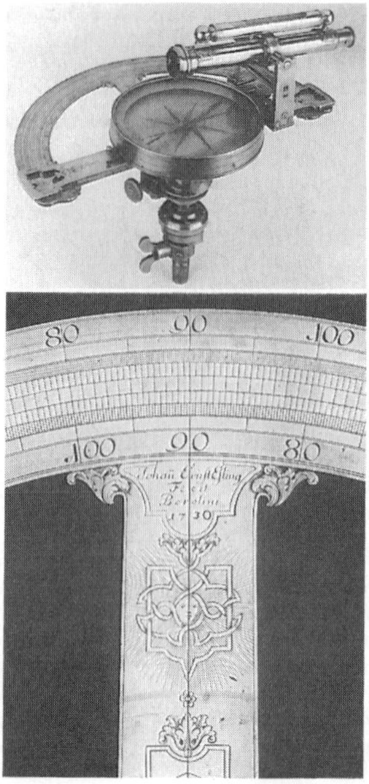

l. A lacquered brass graphometer, by Johan Ernst Esling, Berlin, the outer scale divided 180°–10°–180°, the inner scale divided 180°–10°, now with compass box with silvered dial, blued/silvered needle and clamp, the telescope with bubble level and cross bubble, on adjustable staff mount, signed and dated on the main frame '1730', 13½in (34.5cm) diam.
£5,000–6,000 *CSK*

The signature on this piece is engraved, as well as the '17' of the date. However, the figure '30' is stamped, suggesting that the final year was inserted when the graphometer was sold. This piece illustrates how scientific instruments were upgraded over the years, being enhanced c1800 by the addition of the compass, and again c1875 by the addition of the telescope.

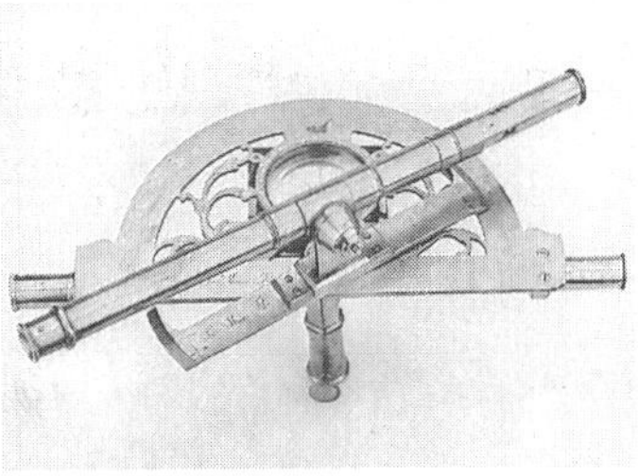

A brass graphometer, with telescope on pivot, twin vernier scales on rotating limb, on pierced and engraved hemispherical arc with similar signature, divided 0°–180° 180°–0°, the compass box with engraved dial and steel needle, the underside with fixed telescope and tripod mount with ball socket and butterfly wing nut, signed 'Le Maire Fils, Paris', c1775, 15in (38.5cm) wide.
£800–1,200 *CSK*

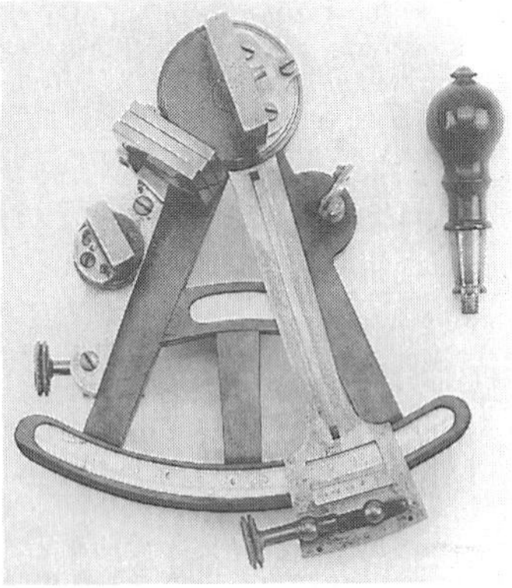

A Ramsden pattern ebony and brass miniature surveying octant, with ivory scale divided 100°-0°, pinhole sights, twin mirrors, and 3 shades, the index arm with ivory vernier scale, tangent screw and clamp, and screw mounted handle, c1900, 4½in (11.5cm) wide.
£2,500–3,500 *CSK*

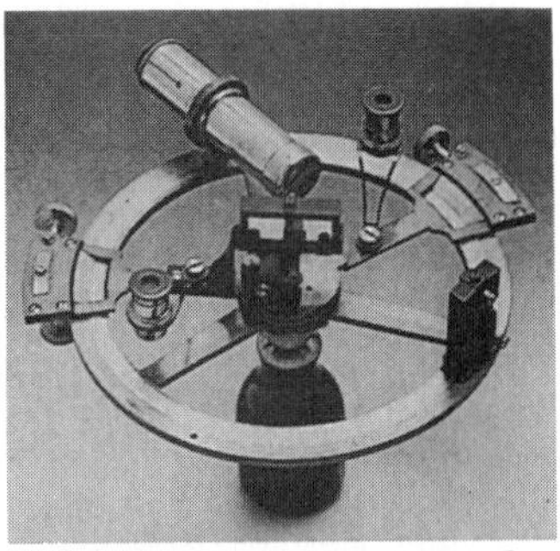

A reflecting circle or improved double sextant, with double index arm, tangent screws, verniers and magnifiers and silver circular scale, on turned lignum vitae handle, signed 'Henry Hughes & Sons Improved Double Sextant, 59 Fenchurch St. London Nº 2776', late 19thC, 5in (12.5cm) diam., in a mahogany case with 2 telescopes and one filter.
£2,000–2,500 *S*

A boxwood and lacquered brass Francis patent universal surveying level, with compass box with silvered dial, no needle and glass, 3 pairs of folding sights, 2 pairs of bubble levels, stamped and engraved with various scales, the base signed 'Inventer *(sic)* & Patentee George Francis, C.E. Chester', c1890, 8in (20cm) long.
£500–700 *CSK*

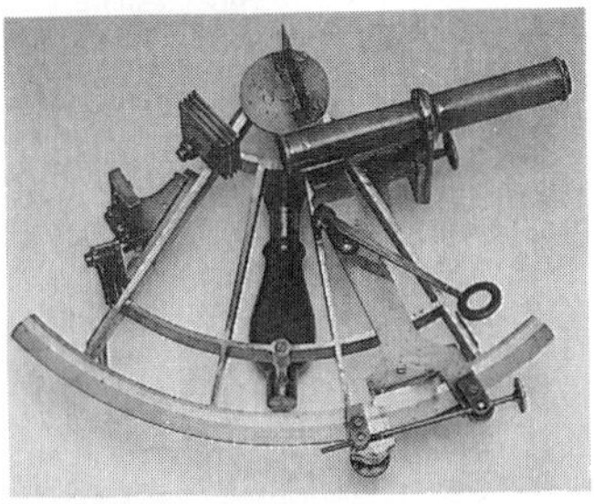

A French Gambey brass sextant, the lattice frame with silver scale and vernier, tangent screw adjustment, 2 sets of coloured filters, shaped mahogany handle, signed 'Gambey à Paris', 7½in (19cm) radius, in original mahogany case.
£1,200–1,700 *S*

The son of a clockmaker at Troyes, Henry-Prudence Gambey (1787–1847), worked with Ferrar and Lenoir and became 'chef d'Atelier' at the Ecole des Arts & Metiers before setting up his business in Paris in 1809. A specialist in the dividing of circles, he was the most noted precision instrument maker of the time, receiving the Légion d'Honneur in 1827 and became a member of the Académie des Sciences in 1837.

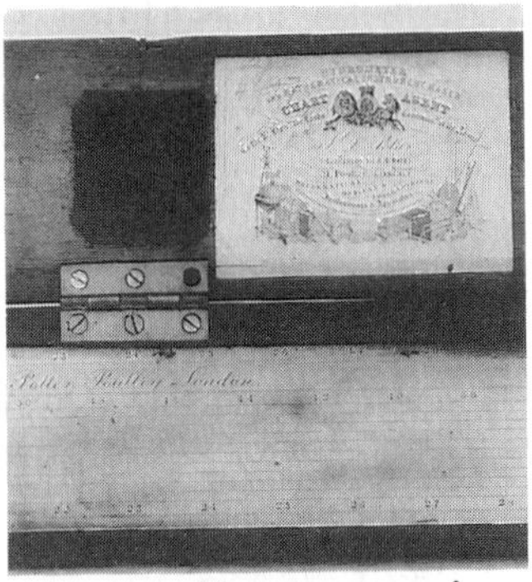

A lacquered brass surveyor's scale, signed 'Potter, Poultry, London' and engraved with various inch scales, in a fitted mahogany case with maker's label, c1850, 52in (132cm) long.
£300–400 *CSK*

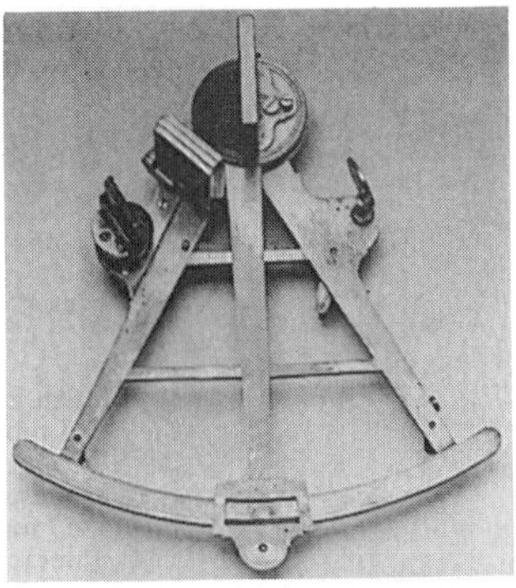

An all brass sextant, by Richard Lekeux, signed 'Lekeux, 138 Wapping', the brass scale engraved '2 to 0 to 125 degrees', peephole eyepiece, set of coloured filters, early 19thC, 7in (18cm) radius, in a light mahogany case.
£1,500–2,000 *S*

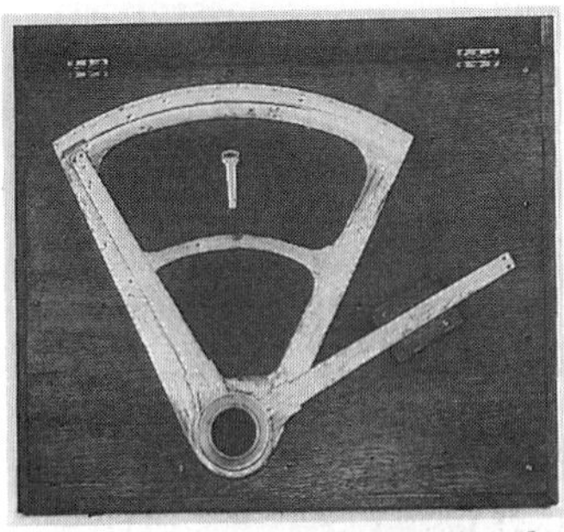

A lacquered brass protractor, the arc divided 0°-60°, with vernier on L-shaped arm, in a mahogany fitted case, 12in (30.5cm) long.
£250–350 *CSK*

An accompanying printed description describes this protractor as being for 'transposing and anticipating azimuth bearings during chart work'.

A brass transit theodolite, by W. Chapman, with silver scales and verniers, magnifiers, 2 bubble levels and 4 levelling screws, late 19thC, 12in (30.5cm) high, in a mahogany case, with trade label, accessories and leather carrying case, a separate case containing a cross staff and a mahogany tripod.
£900–1,200 *S*

An oxidised lacquered brass transit theodolite, signed on the silvered compass dial 'Negretti and Zambra London' number '1542', the telescope with rack and pinion focusing and graduating level, in a fitted mahogany case.
£500–600 *DA*

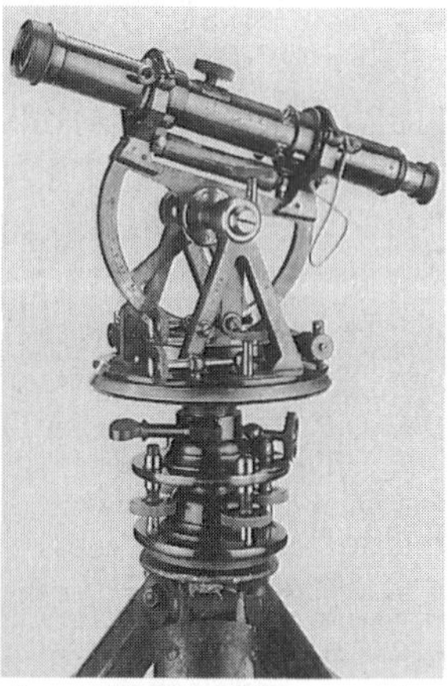

An oxidised and lacquered brass theodolite, by Troughton & Simms, London, 10in (25cm) high, in a fitted mahogany case, with maker's paper label and adjustment label, and a tripod.
£650–750 *CSK*

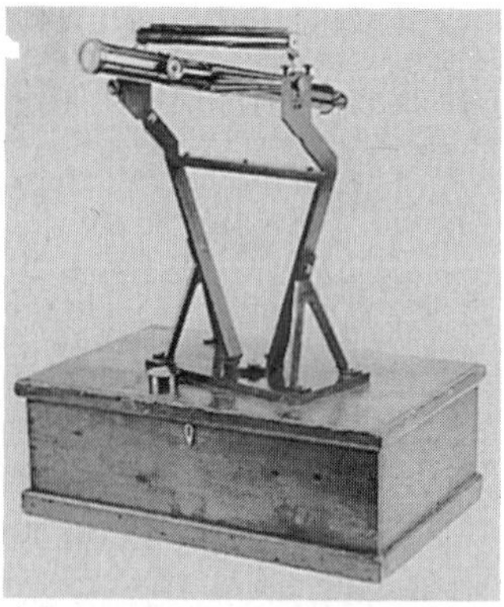

A lacquered and oxidised brass transit instrument with bubble level, 1¾in (4cm) lens, rack-and-pinion focusing and base, one clamp and focusing knob missing, 10in (25cm) wide, in a fitted wood case.
£350–550 *CSK*

A brass theodolite, signed 'Pyefinch London', mounted on a racked arc above a magnetic compass and horizontal circle of degrees, late 19thC, the telescope of later date, 9in (23cm) high.
£800–900 *S*

An oxidised and lacquered brass combination theodolite/mining dial, by Stanley, London, No. 10963, the 1in (2.5cm) telescope with rack and pinion focusing, cross wire adjustment and spirit level, on detachable brackets on shaped supports, with vertical circle with brass scale divided 90°–0°–90° and vernier, over compass box with silvered scale, edge bar needle, spirit level and cross level and brass horizontal scale divided 0°–360° with vernier, on a tripod mount, 8½in (21cm) high, with twin detachable alternative folding sights, in a fitted mahogany case, and a tripod.
£450–550 *CSK*

This instrument appears to be an attempt by Stanley to produce an economical surveying instrument.

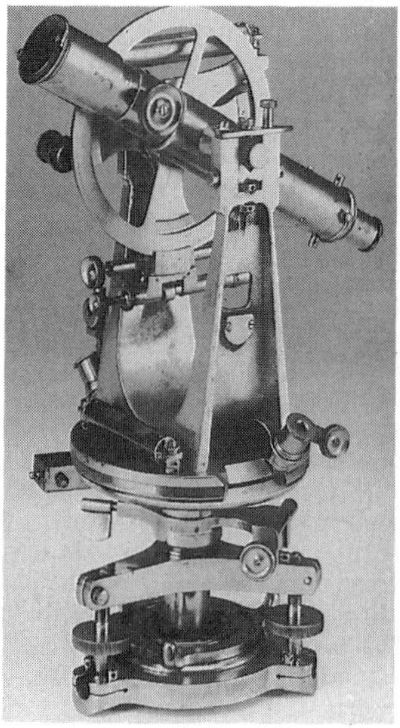

A brass and aluminium transit theodolite, by Reynolds & Co. Ltd., Leeds, the telescope with rack-and-pinion focusing and ray-shade, with vertical and horizontal scales with verniers, on 3 screw tripod mount, in a mahogany case, 20in (51cm) wide.
£350–550 *CSK*

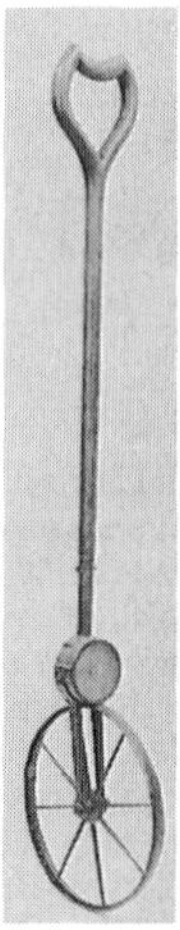

r. A mahogany and brass single wheel Waywiser, the shield shaped handle to a 3½in (9cm) silvered dial signed 'Addisn. Smith, London', with scales calibrated in yards, poles and furlongs, the 12in (30.5cm) wheel with 8 spokes, late 18thC, 50½in (128cm) high.
£500–600 *P*

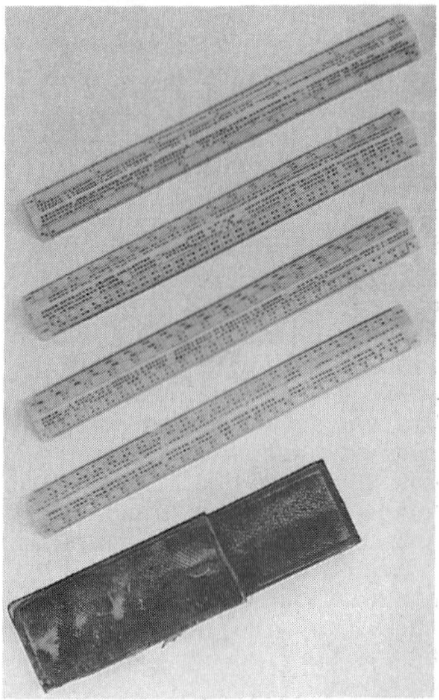

r. A set of 4 triangular ivory rules, one signed 'Pastorelli & Co., London', another signed 'Arranged by W. E. Metford, C.E.', each stamped with scales and conversions, including expansion, force of gravity and many others, in a part fitted leather covered card case, each rule 6½in (16.5cm) long.
£1,000–1,500 *CSK*

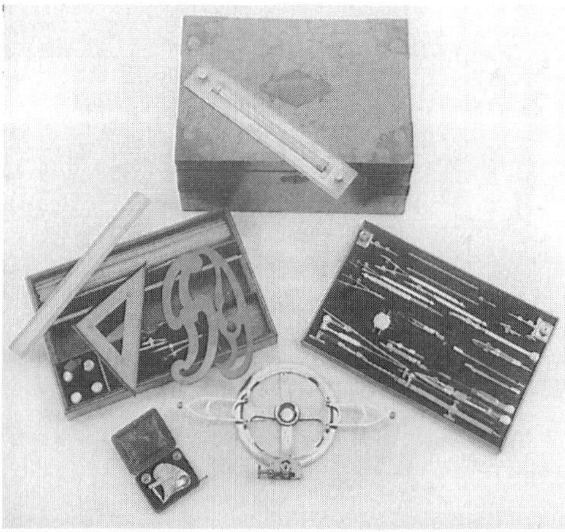

A part set of drawing instruments, by Troughton & Simms, London, including a swinging arm protractor, various electrum compasses, a proportional divider, rules and other items, in a brass mounted oak case with twin trays and drawer in the base, dated '1910', 14½in (37cm) wide.
£400–500 *CSK*

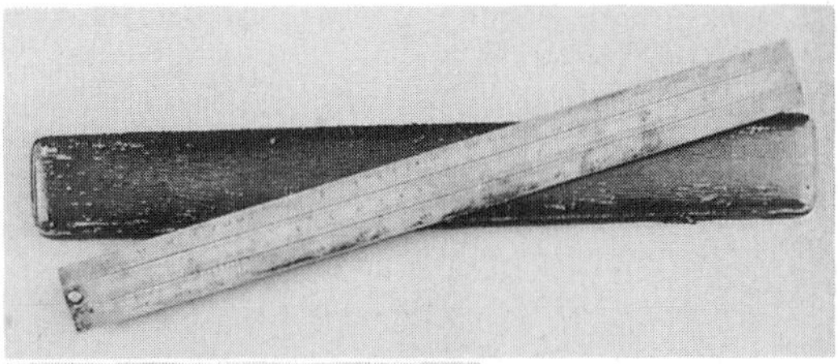

A lacquered brass Roget pattern slide rule, by J. A. Rooker, London, with single slide and engraved scales, the back signed 'Dr. Roget Sec: R.S. Inv:, Rooker London', 10½in (26.5cm) long, in a red leather covered case.
£600–700 *CSK*

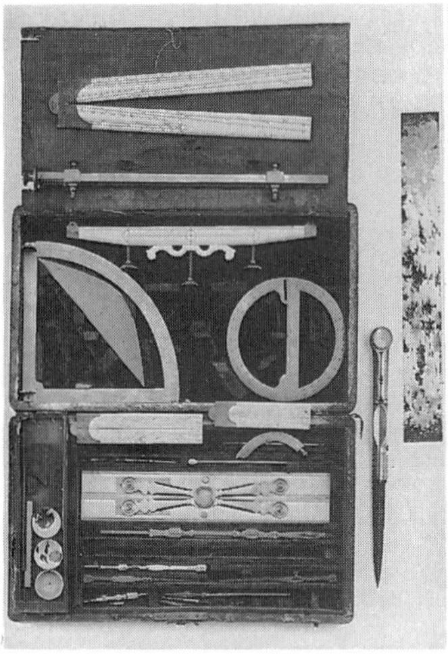

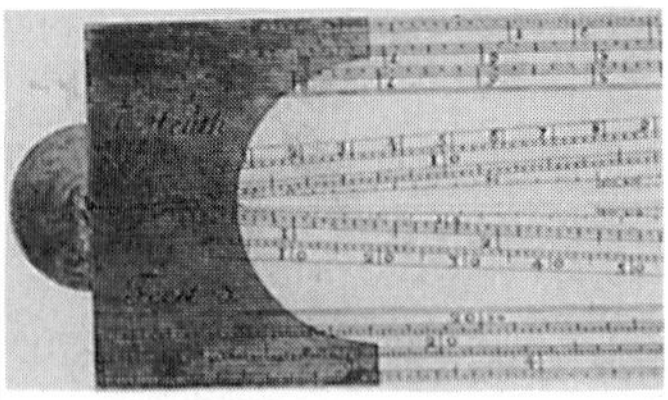

A part set of drawing instruments, with ivory sector, signed 'T. Heath Fecit' on the brass hinge, engraved with various scales, beam compass graduated 0–11 with micrometer, hyperbola curve, drawing quadrant, ivory parallel rule, ivory curve, large dividers, wing dividers, protractor and other items in a plush and silk lined, fishskin covered wood case with ink drawer, c1735, 16½in (42.5cm) wide.
£4,000–4,500 *CSK*

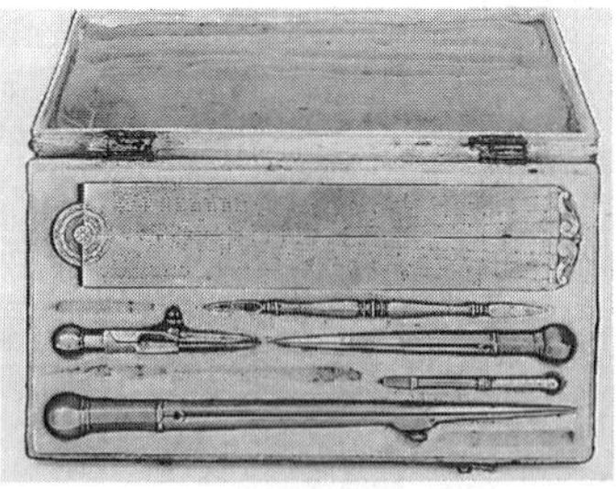

A part set of brass drawing instruments, by Jacob Lusuerg/Joseph Maccarius, Rome, comprising a sector signed and dated 'Joseph Maccarius Romanus Fecit Par ma 1708', engraved with various scales, a divider signed and dated 'Iacobus Lusuerg Fa Roma A 1676', 2 further dividers, a wheel pen, and a double-headed ruling pen, in a chamois and silk lined brown leather covered case with gilt tooling, including dividers, 10½in (27cm) wide.
£4,000–4,500 *CSK*

Joseph Maccarius may have been the son of Joannes Maccarius who worked in Modena at the same time as Lusuerg. Lusuerg appears to have been working in Rome from at least 1673. This set may have been made by Lusuerg and the sector replaced with one by Maccarius.

Miscellaneous

A Young's revolving measure, with nickel frame and wheel measuring 4in (10cm) per revolution, fretted ivorine front and back to mechanism with aperture for readings, signed 'Louis Young's Revolving Measure patent Nov 20th 1855', 4in (10cm) long, in a case.
£300–400 *CSK*

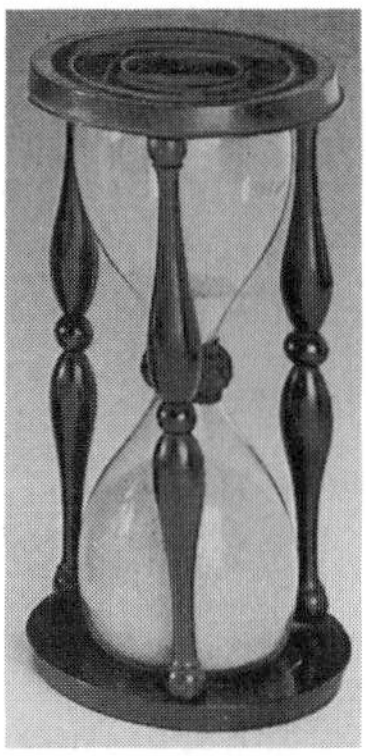

An ebony sand glass, the 2 glass ampoules joined by wax and thread, in an ebony frame with 3 turned wood struts, mid-18thC, 8in (20cm) high.
£800–900 *S*

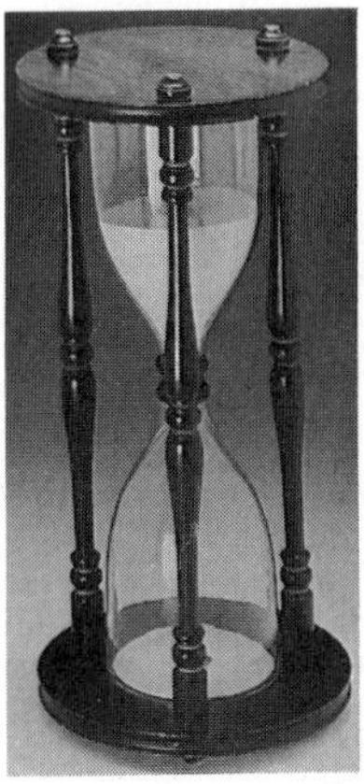

r. An hour glass, the 2 glass ampoules mounted in an ebonised and gilded wood frame, late 19thC, 22½in (57.5cm) high.
£1,500–2,000 *S*

A lacquered brass precision balance, by L. Oertling, London, with ivory fittings and accessories, in a glazed mahogany case with silver presentation plaque, dated '1912', 16½in (42.5cm) wide.
£270–320 *CSK*

A steel beam balance with brass pans, by George Senell, in a fitted mahogany case, with a set of cup weights and maker's paper label in the lid, late 18thC, 18in (46cm) wide.
£600–700 *CSK*

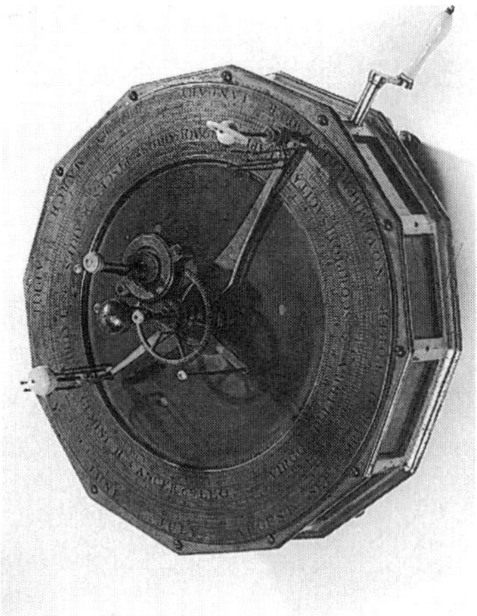

A miniature planetarium, or orrery, in a twelve-sided brass casing engraved with a calendar of zodiac signs, glazed side panels revealing the lower section of the hybrid gearing, the planets with their satellites being connected to the upper geared cone, on brass arms, the lunar ivory fitted with a cam to show the moon's diurnal rotation, c1860, 9in (22.5cm) diam., with a mahogany travelling case, the hinged lid with a brass clasp and carrying handle.
£15,000–18,000 *WW*

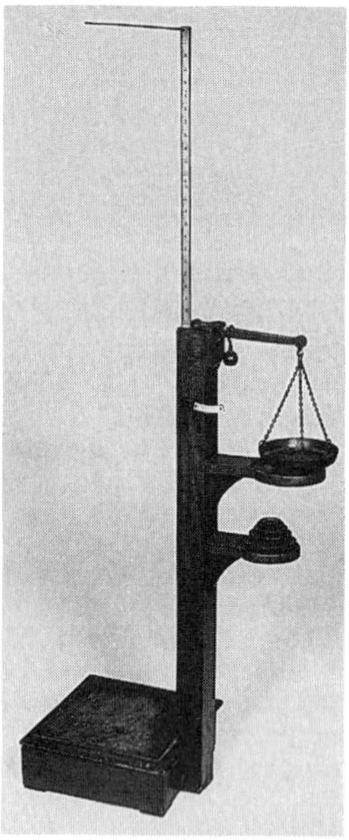

l. A set of mahogany personal scales, by Young & Son, London, the square section pillar with brass beam, pan and weights, with 2 round trays to hold the weights and incorporating a boxwood height measure, the pointer damaged, 19thC.
£500–600 *DN*

r. A collection of approximately 200 preserved crustaceans, of various species, some dissected, most in glazed cases with paper identification labels, some labelled 'Collection de S.A.S. Le Prince de Monaco'.
£2,000–2,500 *CSK*

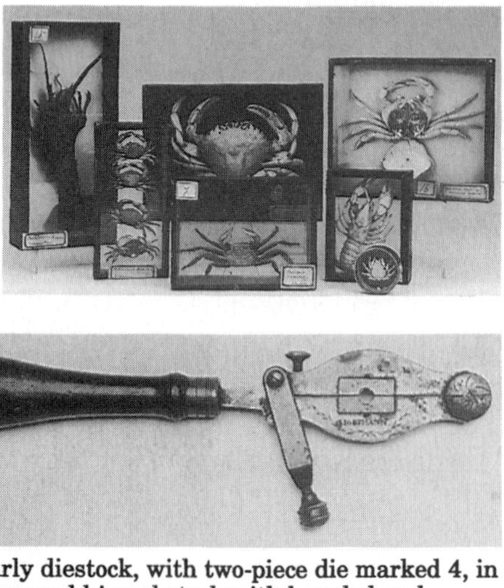

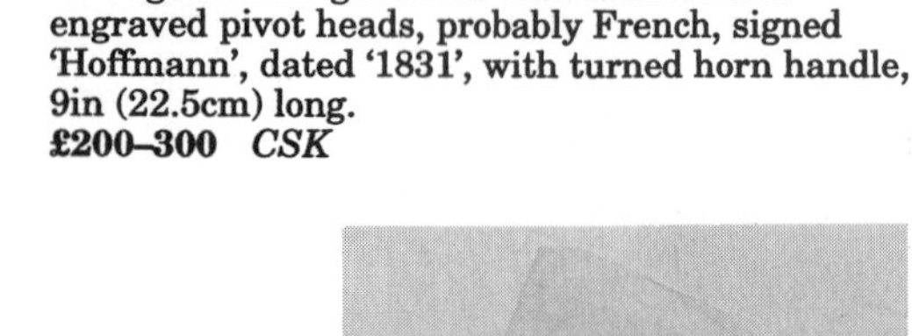

An early diestock, with two-piece die marked 4, in an engraved hinged stock with knurled and engraved pivot heads, probably French, signed 'Hoffmann', dated '1831', with turned horn handle, 9in (22.5cm) long.
£200–300 *CSK*

A papier mâché anatomical model of a cockroach, with well detailed and painted internal organs, with paper labels, French, 19thC, 18in (45.5cm) long.
£1,000–1,500 *CSK*

r. A calculator, with printed spiral scale, in a graduated brass sleeve with wood knobs at ends, instruction sheet and leatherette covered tube case, labelled 'Prof. R. H. Smith's Cylindrical Logarithm Slide', late 19thC, 7½in (19cm) long.
£370–420 *CSK*

Dental

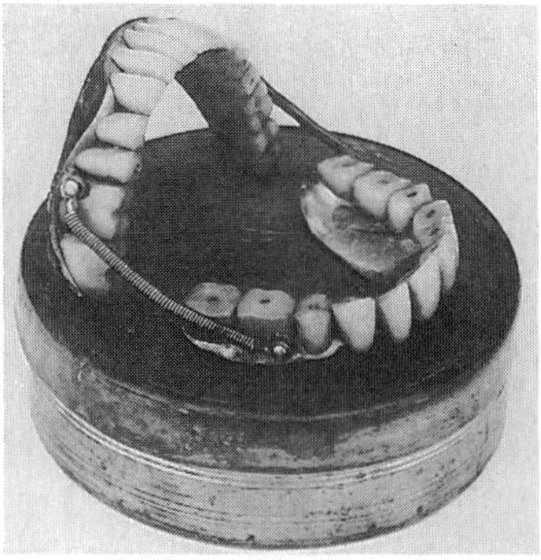

A set of false teeth, the carved agate teeth set in dental gold mounts, with wax infill, joined by twin spiral springs, in a pewter case, c1820.
£900–1,200 *CSK*

A similar set was discovered during the excavation of Smithfield Vaults in London. The coffin from which they came did not bear a coffin plate, so it was not possible to precisely date the skeleton. However, judging from the known period of the vault, the position of the coffin and other factors, the set was dated as no later than 1830.

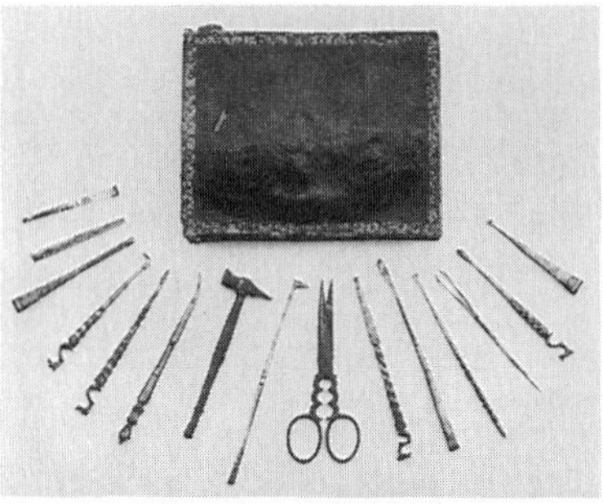

A case of dental and related instruments, 4 with dragon heads on tapered spiral-twist stems, with remains of gilding, and other instruments including scissors, hammer and tweezers, in a gilt tooled, red leather covered wood case of book form, 17thC, 6in (15cm) wide.
£1,600–2,000 *CSK*

A mahogany dental cabinet, with a tambour cover over a drawer above 6 further drawers, 13in (33cm) wide, and a quantity of dental instruments.
£300–350 *CSK*

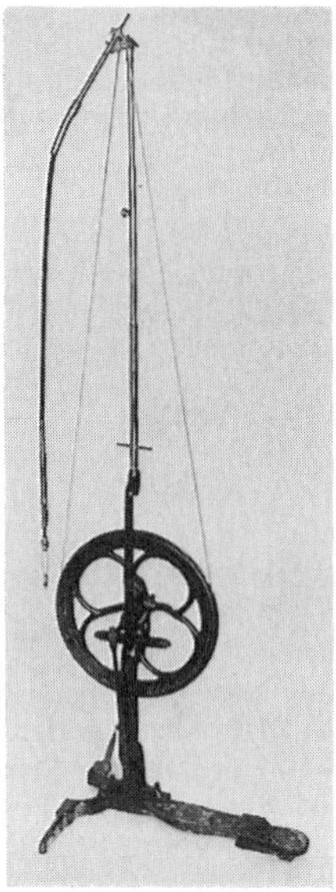

A dentist's early pedal driven drill, 56in (142cm) high, and accessories.
£120–200 *AG*

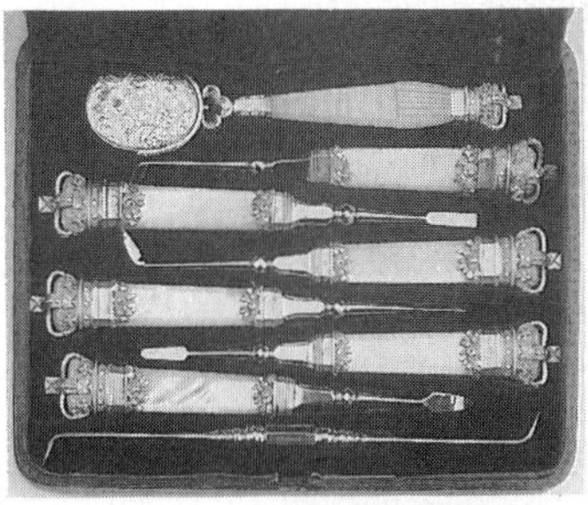

A set of dental instruments, made for Sir Edwin Saunders, and used exclusively when treating Her Majesty Queen Victoria, the first compartment containing 6 scalers with mother-of-pearl handles, and silver gilt mounts in the form of the Queen's crown, roses, thistles and shamrocks, examination mirror with agate handle, crown mount and chased yoke and back plate, the mounts hallmarked 'Charles Rawlings and William Summers, London 1846', and a steel double headed plugger with turned central grip stamped 'London', the second compartment with mercury phial with boxwood stopper, ivory amalgam bottle and 12 replacement instruments, including a mother-of-pearl handled mirror, 2 scalers and a silver plated toothpick, in a fitted, velvet lined, leather covered case, the lid with gilt tooled crown, in a leather pouch with similar gilt tooled crown.
£15,000–20,000 *CSK*

Sir Edwin Saunders, FRCS, James Snell and W. A. Harrison opened in 1840 the first dental dispensary for the poor. He took over Alexander Naysmith's practice and later became dentist to Queen Victoria and other members of the Royal Family. He was author of Advice on the Care of the Teeth *and* Teeth the Test of Age. *He was twice President of the Odontological Society and of the Metropolitan Branch of the BMA. In 1883, he became the first dentist to receive a knighthood.*

Medical

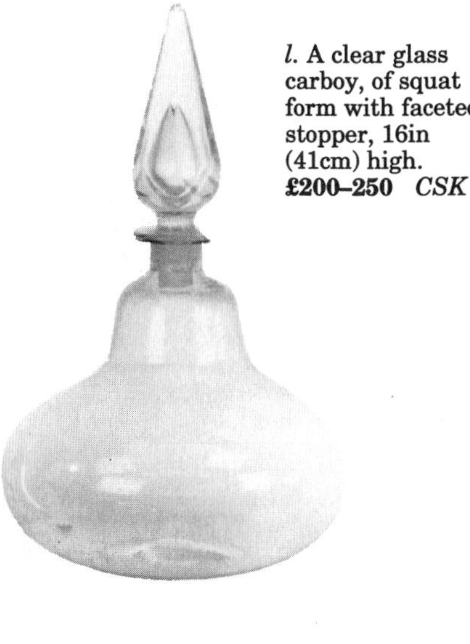

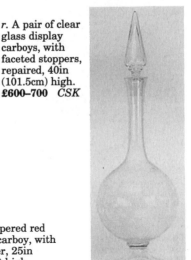

l. A clear glass carboy, of squat form with faceted stopper, 16in (41cm) high.
£200–250 *CSK*

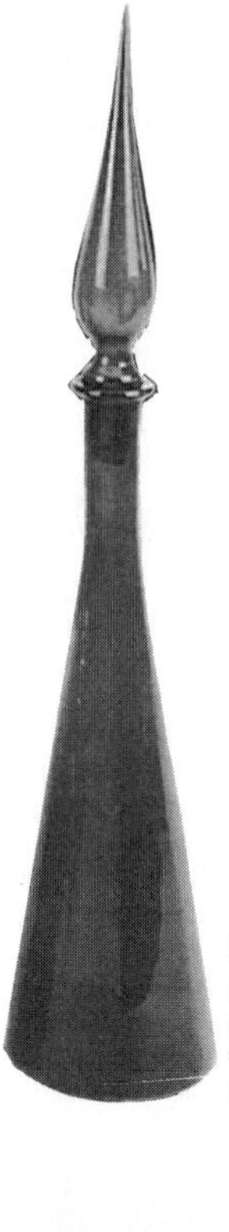

l. A tapered red glass carboy, with stopper, 25in (64cm) high.
£100–150 *CSK*

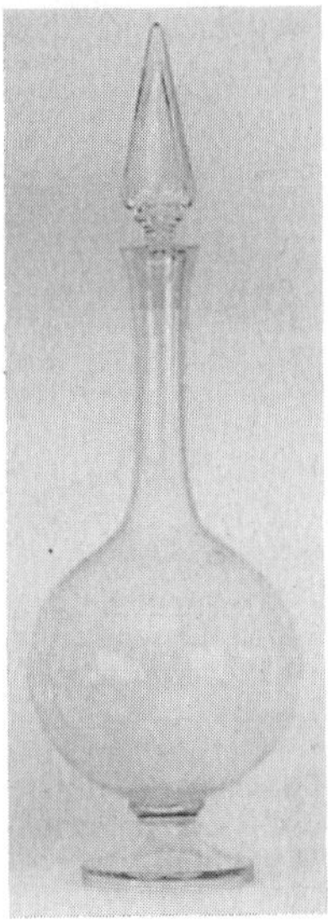

r. A pair of clear glass display carboys, with faceted stoppers, repaired, 40in (101.5cm) high.
£600–700 *CSK*

A glass specie jar, painted with the Prince of Wales' coat-of-arms, by Evans, Sons & Co., Liverpool, labelled 'Jalapae', on mustard ground, with gilded lid, 27in (69cm) high.
£250–350 *CSK*

A glass specie jar, decorated with a painted shield, and labelled 'Irish Moss', with gilt cover, 12½in (32cm) high.
£250–300 *CSK*

An oak grained domestic medicine chest, the upper compartment containing 28 various bottles, most with 'Savory & Moore/John Savory' labels, the drawer containing 35 similar bottles, 14½in (37cm) wide.
£500–650 *CSK*

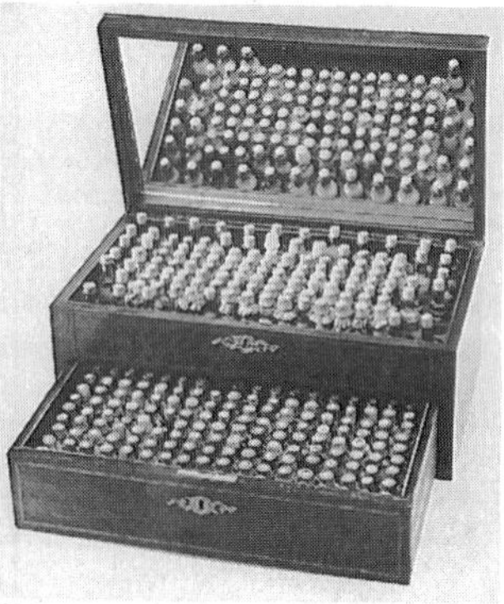

A large mahogany homeopathic medicine chest, the top section containing 128 (of 140) bottles with numbered lids, the drawer containing 161 (of 172) similar bottles, the lid with boxwood stringing and inlay decoration of an eight-pointed star, the interior with mirror, 22in (55.5cm) wide.
£750–850 *CSK*

A mahogany travelling medicine chest, late 18thC, 21in (53cm) wide.
£600–900 *S*

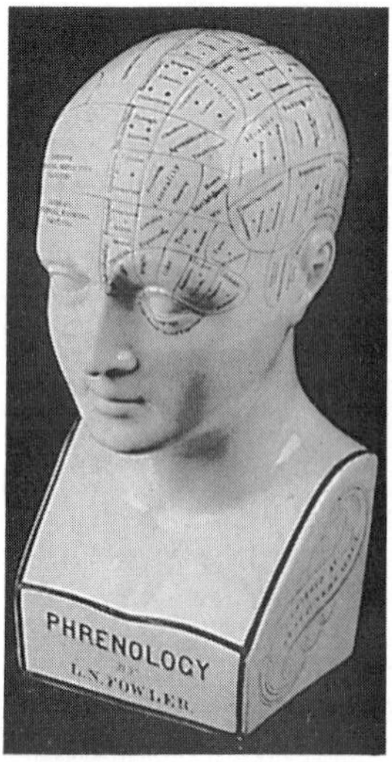

A porcelain phrenology head, by L.N. Fowler, London, the cranium divided into various characteristics, 11½in (29cm) high.
£500–700 *CSK*

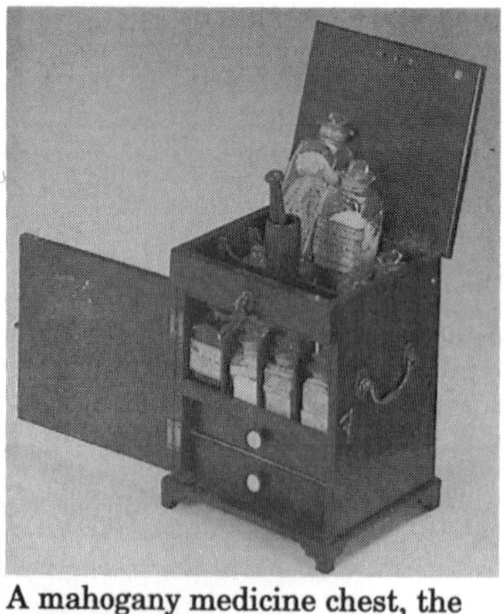

A mahogany medicine chest, the hinged lid opening to 6 compound bottles, wood pestle and mortar, hinged door at the front opening to 4 further bottles and 2 drawers of accessories, brass carrying handles at the sides, c1820, 10in (25cm) high.
£900–1,200 *S*

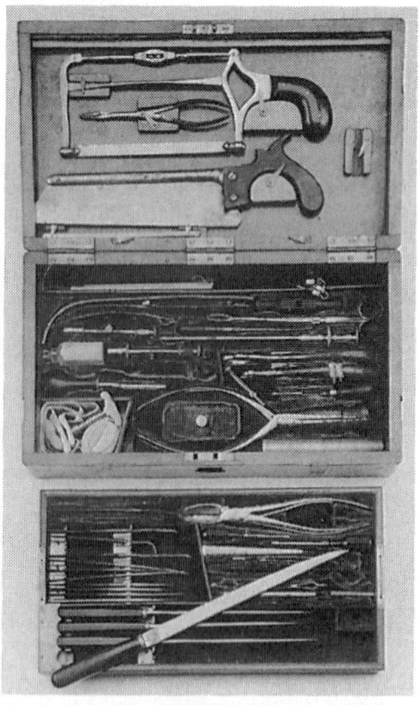

A surgeon's set, by Evans & Co., London, with Butcher's pattern saw, bone saw, 4 Liston knives, trephine with 2 crowns, elevator, obstetric forceps, 2 trocars, 2 bone scoops and 11 scalpels and tenactulum, all with smooth ebony handles, bullet extractor, lithotomy/bullet forceps, catheters, various forceps and other items, all in a velvet lined, fitted, brass bound mahogany case with lift-out tray, some instruments missing, and some rusty, 18in (46cm) wide.
£3,700–4,200 *CSK*

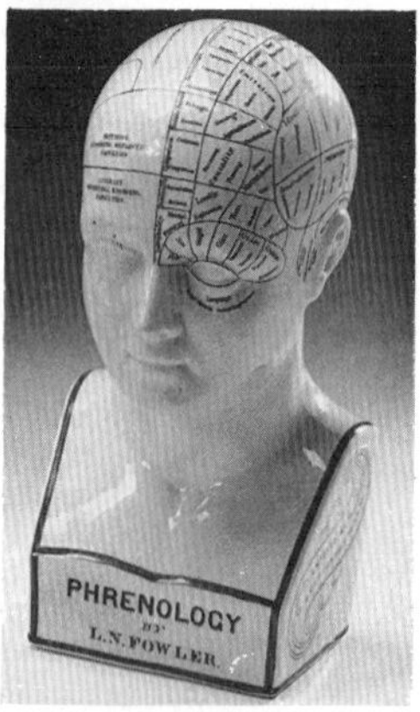

A ceramic phrenology head, by L. N. Fowler, London, with painted blue lining, c1870, 11½in (29cm) high, with a copy of Donovan (C). *A Handbook of Phrenology.*
£800–900 *S*

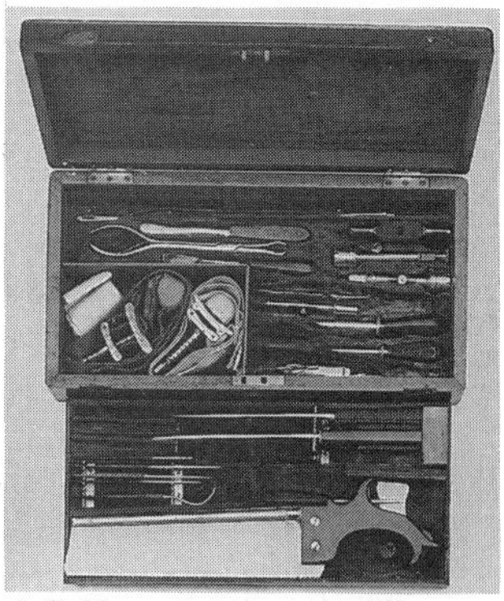

A field surgeon's set, with bone saw with smooth ebony handle, 2 Liston knives, one with smooth handle, the other signed '(Pl)um, Bristol', Hey's skull saw, bullet forceps by Savingay, trephine with 3 crowns, lenticular and elevator and other items, in a brass bound mahogany case, c1830, 16in (40.5cm) wide.
£900–1,200 *CSK*

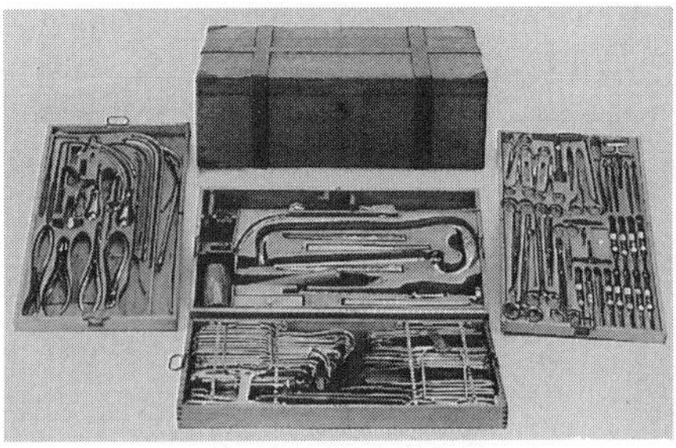

A surgeon's set, by Knole & Dresler, Dresden, including Rust pattern bone saw, chain saw handles, various Liston and other knives, osteopathic drill, trocar and canulae, forceps, retractors, probes, catheters and many other instruments, all in brass bound oak case with metal inner cover and 4 lift-out trays, c1925, 20in (50.5cm) wide.
£850–1,200 *CSK*

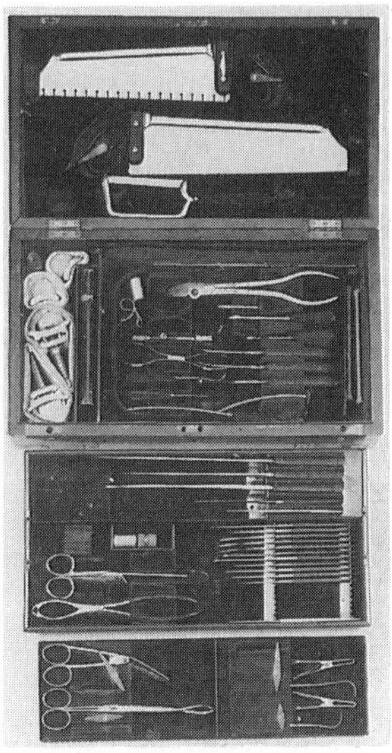

A field surgeon's set, some instruments with pressed horn handles, Royal Coat-of-Arms and signed 'J. Weiss, Razor Maker to His Majesty', in a brass bound mahogany Weiss's Improved Air-Tight case, with central plaque engraved 'P. W. Bussett-Smith', some instruments replaced or lacking, 17in (43.5cm) wide.
£2,000–3,000 *CSK*

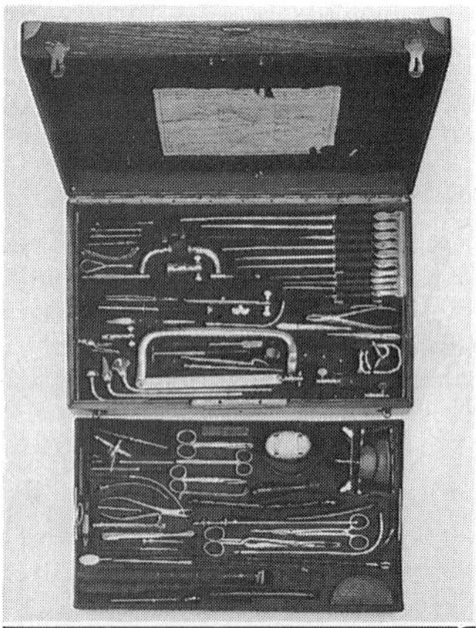

l. A naval surgeon's set, by Mon. Charriere, Collin & Co., Paris, comprising primarily silver plated, ebony handled instruments, in a fitted, brass bound mahogany case, with lift-out tray, the lid interior with original paper contents list, inscribed 'Composition de la Caisse complet d'Instruments de (Chirugue) pour les Batimenta de l'Etat ...', the lid exterior with brass plaque engraved 'Mr. J. M. Corot, Médecin de la Marine', the front with inset carrying handle, 23in (58.5cm) wide.
£8,000–10,000 *CSK*

Although a few of the instruments in this case are signed by other makers, for instance the tooth key is signed 'I. Elcros', owing to the fact that they are all silver plate and fit into the case properly it can be assumed that these items were bought-in by Charriere Collin.

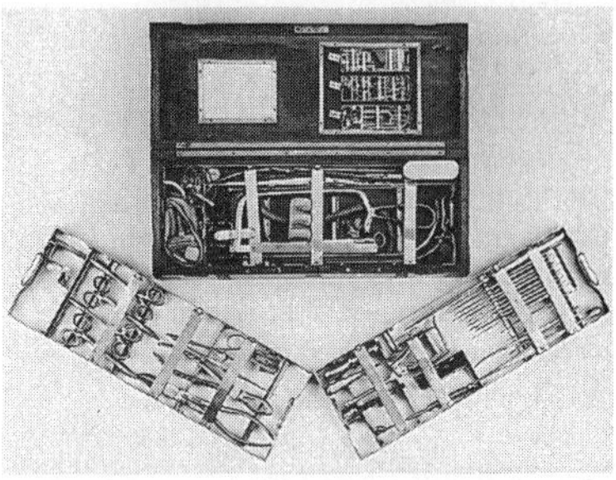

A field surgeon's set, by John Weiss & Son, London, with bone saw, trephine, Liston knife, various bone and other forceps, scalpels and other items, all with metal handles, in a brass bound mahogany case with 3 lift-out trays, contents list and illustration in lid, the top with brass plaque with War Ministry marking, dated '1911', 18in (45.5cm) wide.
£500–700 *CSK*

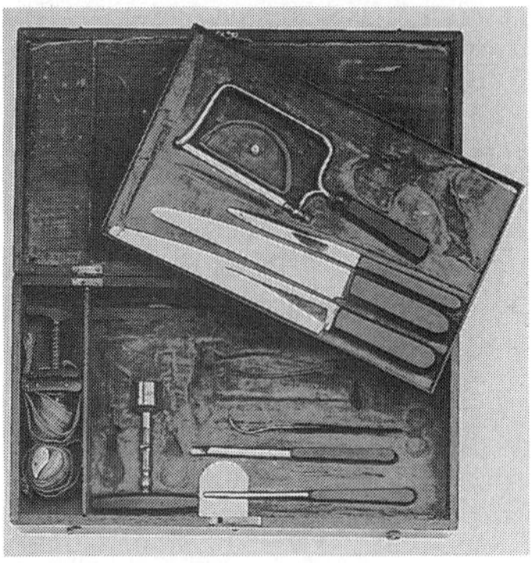

A field surgeon's set, with 3 Liston knives, metacarpal saw, trephine, Hey's saw, tenactlium and elevator all with smooth ebony handles, in mahogany case with lift-out tray, the lid stamped 'U.S.M.H.', c1840, 15in (38cm) wide.
£600–800 *CSK*

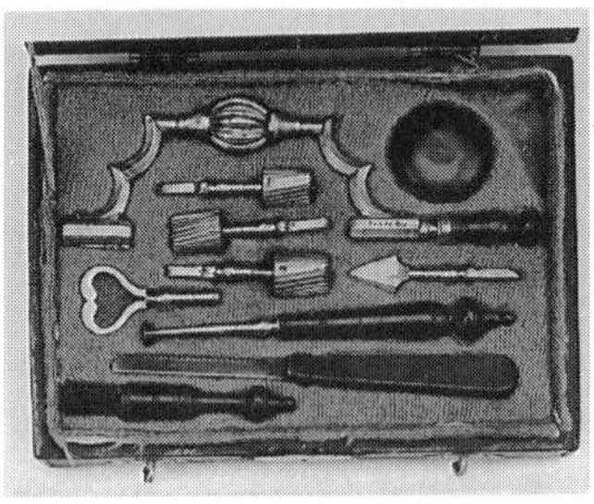

A trepanning set, possibly by Grangeret, comprising: drill, 3 crowns, arrowhead perforator, centre pin key, lenticular, skull saw and bone brush, in a canvas lined, fitted, leather covered case with brass carrying handle, late 18thC, 10in (25cm) wide.
£2,500–3,500 *CSK*

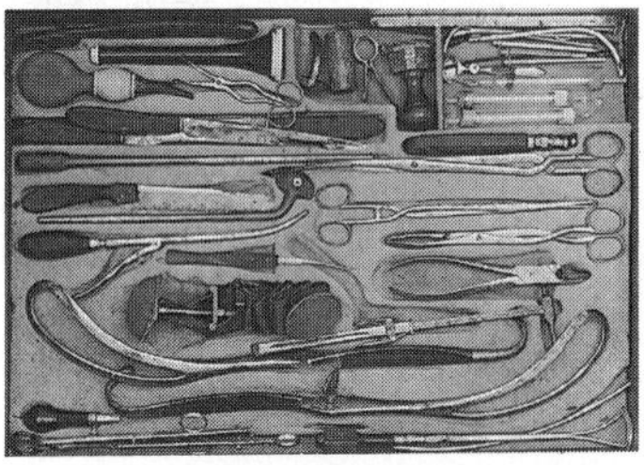

A French set of surgeon's instruments, including a large pair of Levret forceps, an ebony and ivory monaural stethoscope, a set of Liston knives, a bone saw with ebony handle and chain saw, a tonsillectomy instrument and various other medical instruments, mid-19thC, in a mahogany fitted case, 23in (58.5cm) wide.
£4,500–5,000 *S*

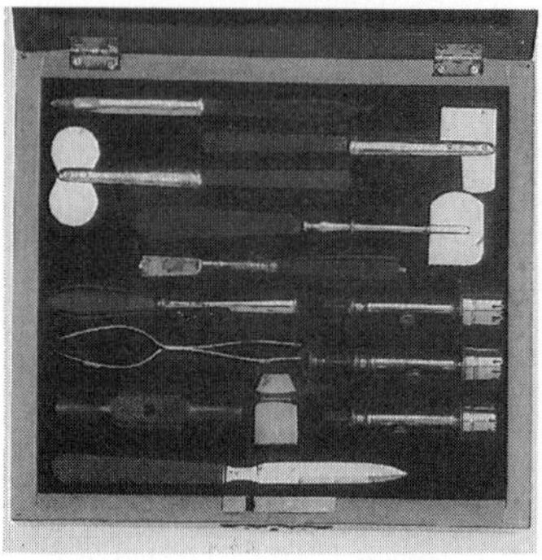

A set of trepanning instruments, by Stodart, London, comprising 3 trephines with interchangeable handle, 3 Hey's pattern saws, 2 lenticulars, elevator, scalpel signed 'Evan', forceps and bone brush (lacking bristles), in a velvet lined fitted mahogany case with brass carrying handle, c1810, 11½in (29.5cm) wide.
£2,000–2,500 *CSK*

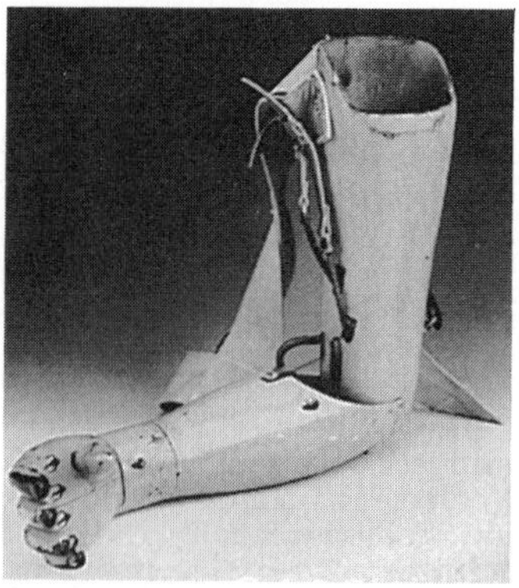

A painted steel and wood, artificial right arm, with finger, hand, wrist and elbow motion, cord control and straps, by The Carnes Artificial Limb Co., Kansas City, 27in (69cm) long.
£400–550 *CSK*

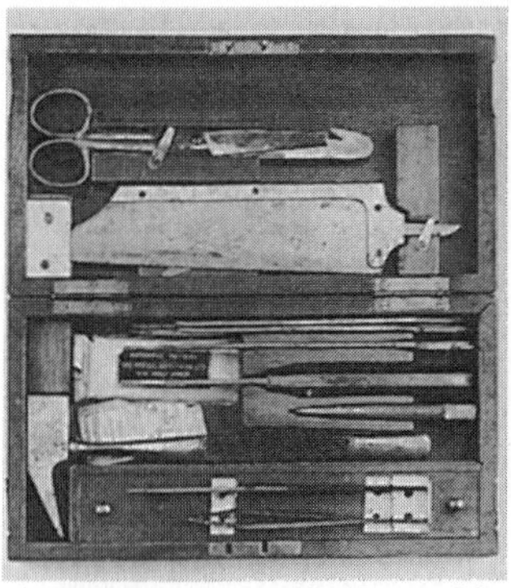

A post mortem set, by Reynolds & Branson, Leeds, with saw, brain knife and catlin on interchangeable ebony handle, hammer, chisel, head rest, tweezers and two scalpels, all in a fitted, brass bound mahogany case, 10in (25cm) wide.
£230–270 *CSK*

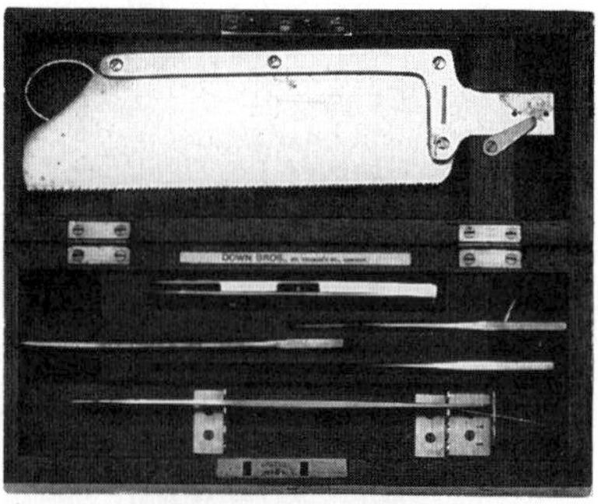

A post-mortem set, by Down Bros., London, with saw, catlin and brain knife on interchangeable metal handle, one scalpel, scissors, tweezers, blowpipe and chain hooks, 2 scalpels missing, in fitted mahogany case, 9in (23cm) wide.
£90–120 *CSK*

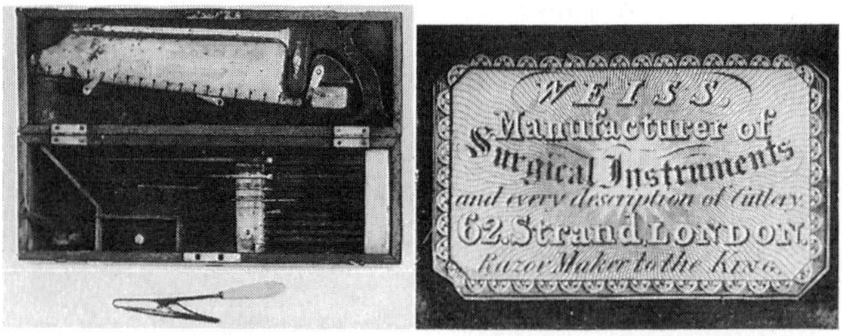

A part amputation set, by Weiss, London, the bone saw with serrated blade and pressed horn handle with coat-of-arms, a finger saw, 2 Liston knives and 2 tenactlii, one with ivory handle, in a brass bound mahogany case with maker's label, c1835, 13½in (34.5cm) wide.
£400–450 *CSK*

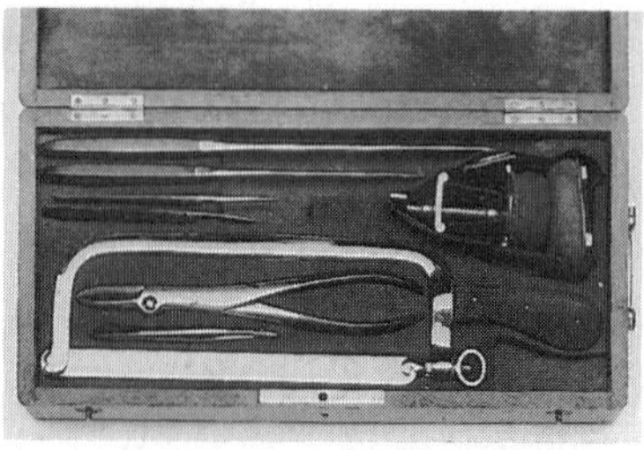

An amputation set, by Mon. Charriere, Collin & Cie., Paris, with bow saw and spare blade, 2 Liston knives all with chequer gripped ebony handles, bone forceps, tourniquet, scalpel by Maw, and a bistourie by Young, in a fitted mahogany case with carrying handle, 16in (40.5cm) wide.
£1,500–2,000 *CSK*

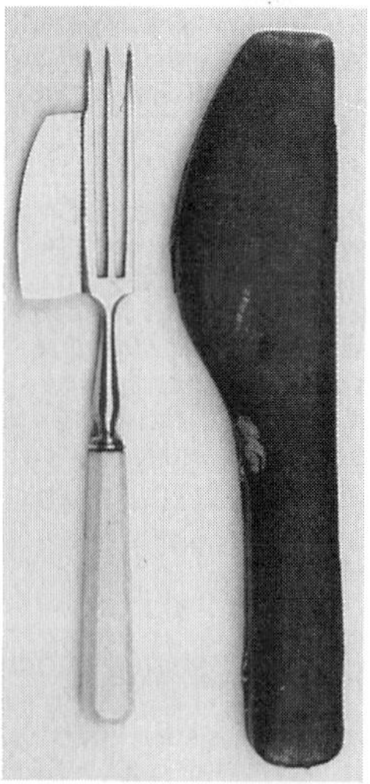

An amputee's combination fork and knife, with silver fork, steel blade and bone handle, hallmarked Sheffield, dated '1805', in a shaped red leather case, 10in (25cm) long.
£500–550 *CSK*

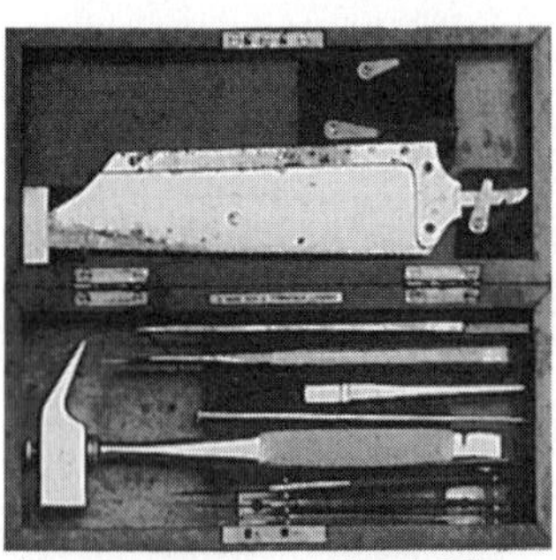

A post mortem set, by S. Maw, Son & Thompson, London, with saw, catlin, knife and chisel on interchangeable handle, mallet, blowpipe and two scalpels, lacks scissors and one scalpel, 9in (23cm) wide.
£300–350 *CSK*

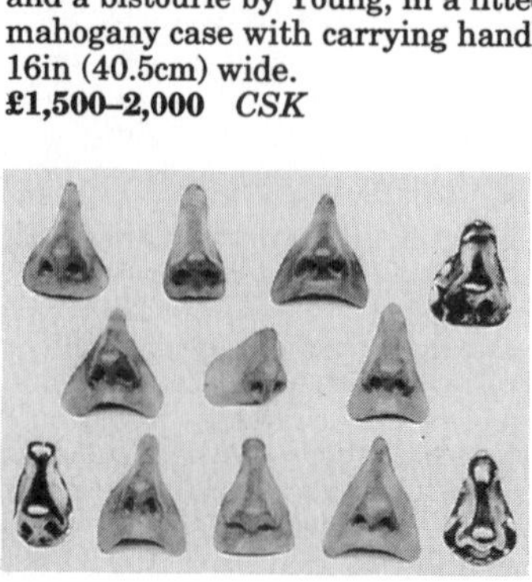

l. Nine painted brass artificial noses, of various styles, and three others, unpainted.
£550–650 *CSK*

r. A black painted wood peg leg, 42in (106.5cm) high.
£80–100 *CSK*

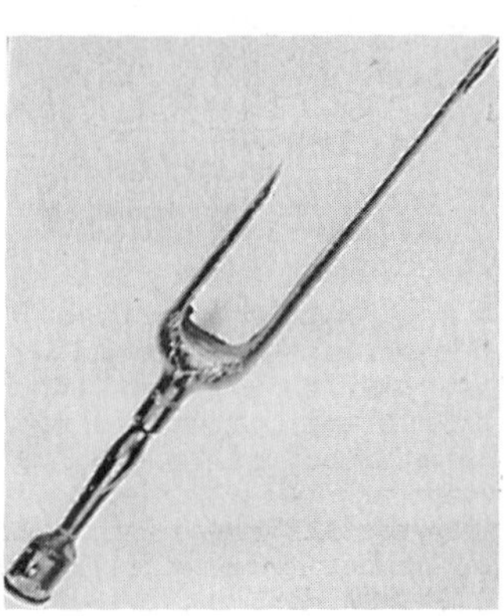

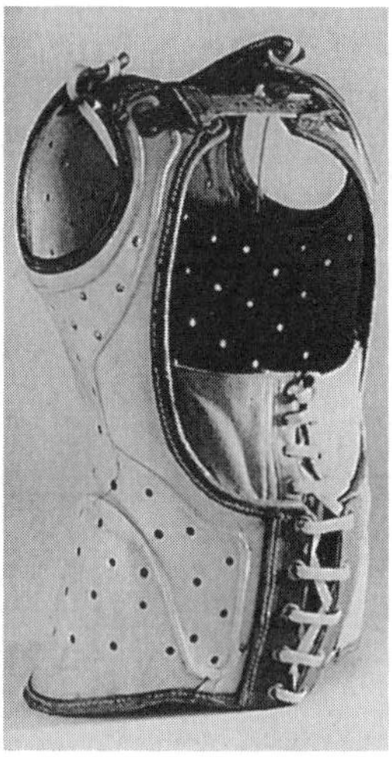

A child's back and hip brace, with cord strapwork and steel clasp, 14½in (37cm) high, and a spring loaded crutch.
£200–250 *CSK*

A dissected human skull, mounted on metal supports and divided to show the divisions of the various bones, some with swivelling movement, on a black ceramic base, 16½in (42cm) high.
£1,000–1,200 *CSK*

A Codman & Shurtleff steam atomiser, complete with brass boiler, burner, glass face mask and jets, in original pine box with set of instructions on the sliding lid, 1870s, 8½in (21cm) high.
£300–400 *S*

An Otophone composition hearing aid, by E. B. Meyrowitz, New York, with curved bell and diaphragm cover, in maker's carton.
£130–170 *CSK*

An electro-medical machine, by Breton Frères, Paris, with large internal magneto, in a mahogany case with winding handle, adjusting knob, carrying handle and maker's ivory label, the base with drawer containing electrodes, c1855, 10½in (26.5cm) wide.
£350–450 *CSK*

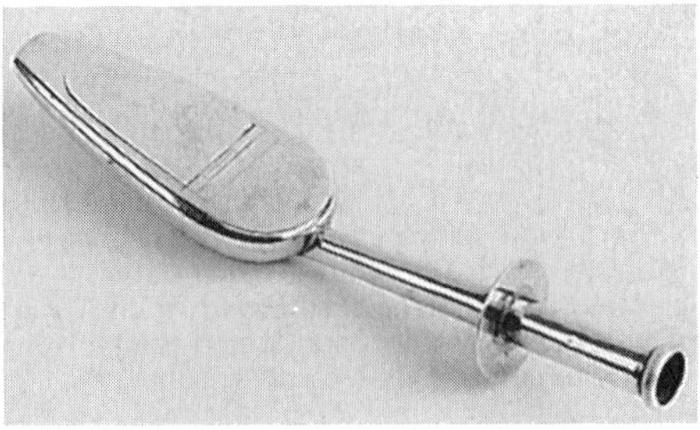

A silver Gibson spoon, hallmarked with maker's initials 'WK', London, dated 1829, 6in (15cm) long.
£500–600 *CSK*

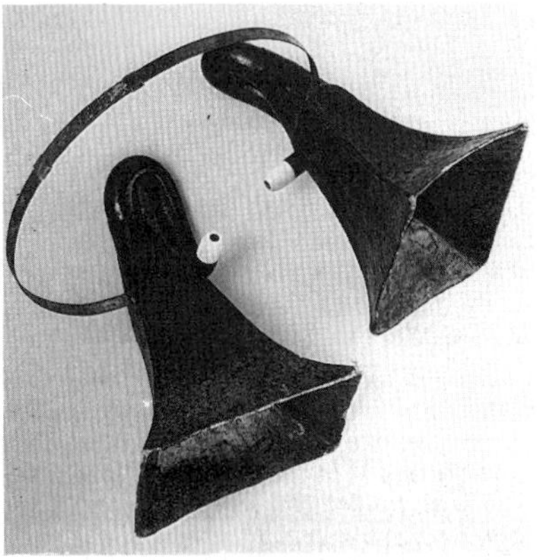

A pair of ear trumpets, with adjustable head band, ivorine ear pieces and papier mâché shaped trumpets, c1900, 4in (10cm) high.
£350–450 *S*

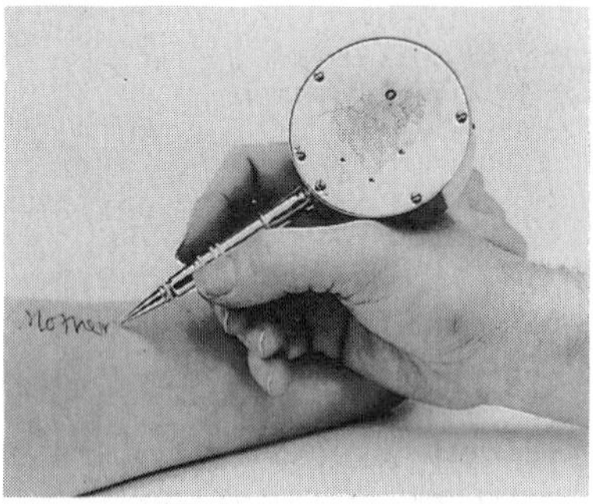

A hand held clockwork tatooist's needle, No. 471, the nickel-plated circular casing with fixed key wind mechanism, the needle carrier with pressure bar and screw mounted needle cover, signed 'Newton Wilson & Co., Patentees, 144 High Holborn, London', in a shaped leather covered case, 6in (15cm) long.
£300–350 *CSK*

Newton Wilson & Co. are best known as sewing machine makers, c1860–70. Their experience in that field led them to manufacture tatooing devices, which were produced in small numbers.

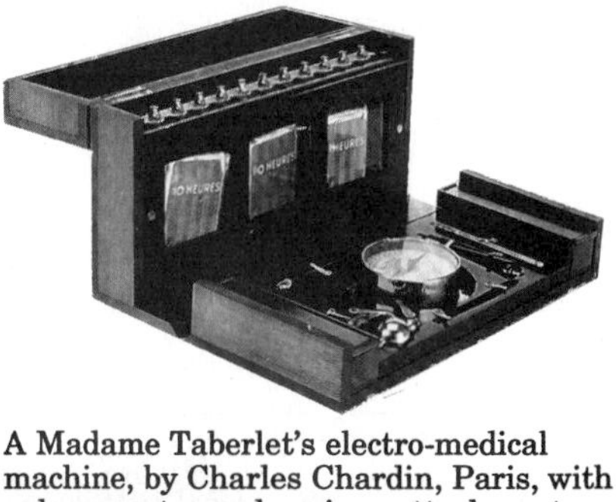

A Madame Taberlet's electro-medical machine, by Charles Chardin, Paris, with galvanometer and various attachments, in a mahogany case, 11in (28cm) high.
£250–300 *CSK*

r. A set of 12 comical figures of various types of medical men, in carved and painted wood, 10 in original boxes, tallest 6in (15cm) high.
£400–450 *CSK*

A Baumscheidt's Lebenswecker counter-irritation/inflamation instrument, the spring loaded needles in a turned ebony case with screw mounted cover, 10in (25cm) long.
£250–300 *CSK*

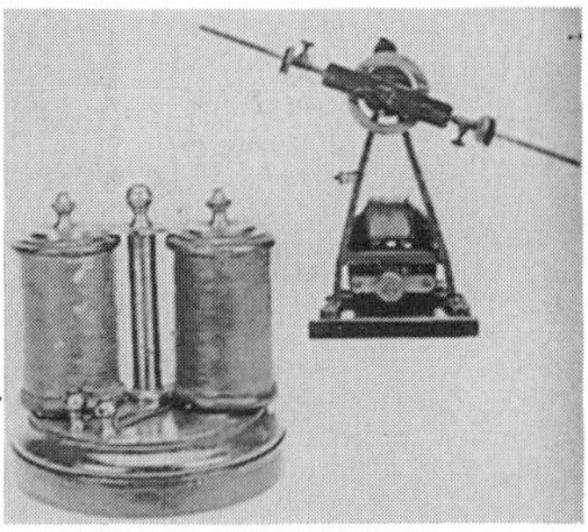

r. An electro-induction instrument, with twin coils mounted on a central pillar on a circular mahogany base, with scale divided 1–8, signed 'Invented by G. Davis, Leeds', 7in (17.5cm) diam., and a Geissler tube demonstration instrument.
£130–170 *CSK*

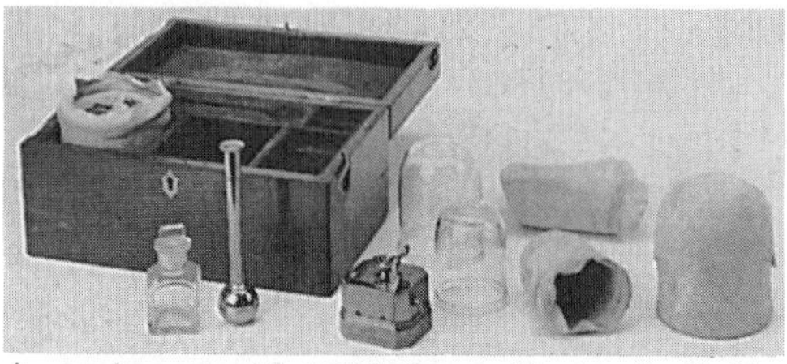

A cupping set with 12 blade scarificator, by S. Maw, Son & Thompson, London, with lamp, spirit bottle and 6 glasses, in chamois covers, in velvet lined, fitted mahogany case, 9in (23cm) wide.
£900–1,200 CSK

There is a redundent compartment in the upper right hand corner of the case, yet the set is complete when compared to the list and the woodcut illustration. It is possible that the same case was also used for the dry cupping set and that the compartment would hold a valve.

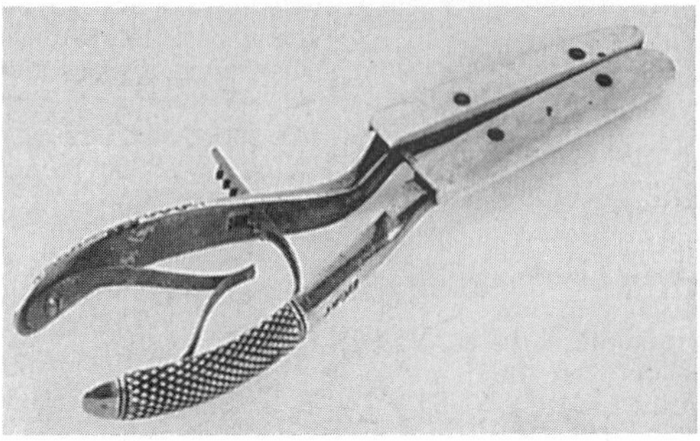

A steel Gowland's pattern haemorrhoid clamp, by Coxeter, London, with ivory plates, spring and notched clasp, late 19thC, 5in (12.5cm) long.
£300–350 *CSK*

The ivory plates were used as a non-conductor when cauterising was employed.

l. A card bodied bodyscope, by Bodyscope, New York, the 4 sections with twin rotating discs illustrating the various parts of the human anatomy, in original envelope, 20in (51cm) high.
£200–250 *CSK*

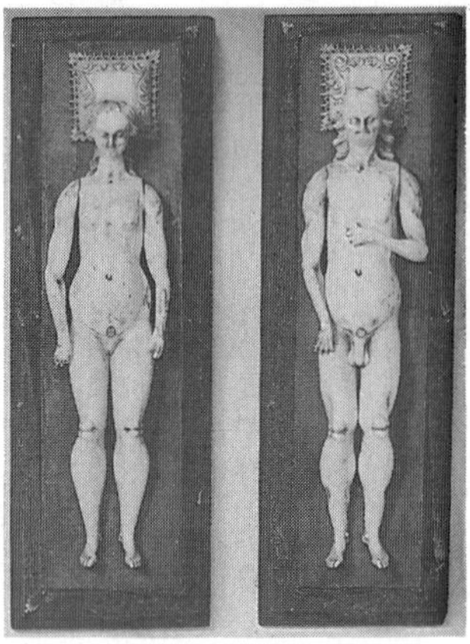

r. A pair of ivory anatomical male and female models, attributed to Stephen Zick, each reclining figure with head resting on a cushion and front torso removeable to show some inner organs, on ebonised wood plinths, Nuremberg, late 17thC, 8in (20cm) long.
£1,400–1,700 *S*

Veterinary

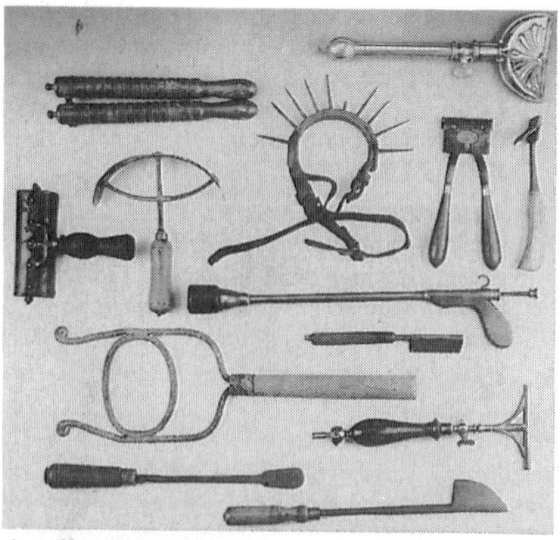

A collection of veterinary instruments, including a pill carrier by Arnold & Sons, hair clippers, twitch, sweat scraper, weaning collar, docking instrument and others.
£250–300 *CSK*

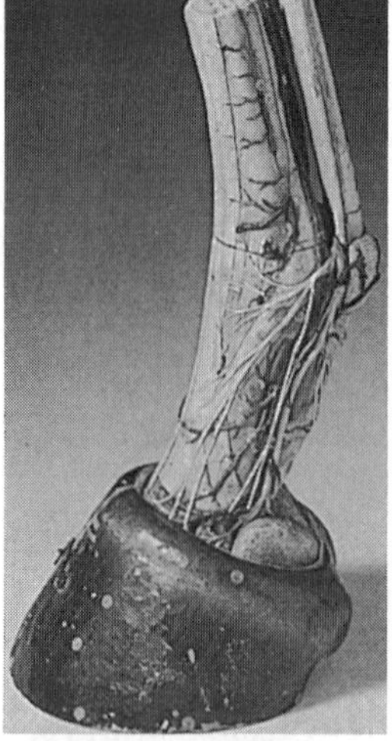

A French anatomical model of a horse's foot, the well detailed painted plaster model, Dr. Auzoux design, opening to many constituent parts showing the internal structure, early 20thC, 11½in (29.5cm) high.
£900–1,200 *S*

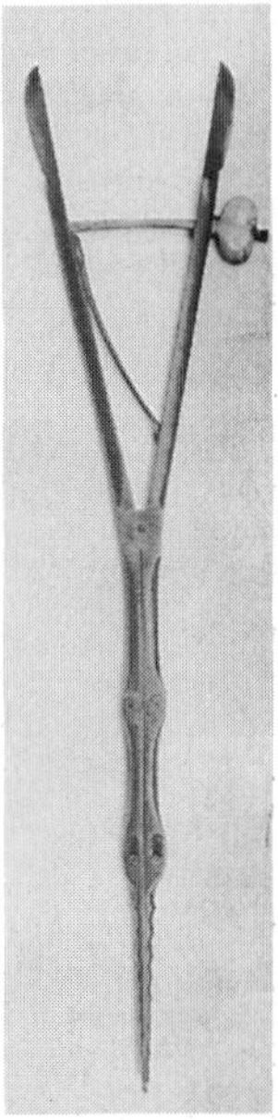

r. A veterinary uterine dilator, by Arnold & Sons, London, with ribbed ends, parallel hinge, spring and adjustable clamp, 26in (66cm) long.
£130–170 *CSK*

A George III style mahogany bracket clock, the 4 pillar single wire fusee movement with anchor escapement, 20thC, 14in (36cm) high.
£500–700 *CSK*

A George III ebonised striking bracket clock, dial signed 'Robt. Best, London', 16in (40.5cm) high.
£6,000–8,000 *C*

A mid-Victorian painted mahogany striking bracket clock, signed 'D. Bagshaw, 28 Poland St, Oxford Street', 26in (66cm) high.
£900–1,200 *CSK*

An 8-day mahogany bracket clock, by Benjamin Ward, London, the brass dial with chapter ring and spandrels, strike/silent to the arch, brass handle, feet and mounts, c1770, 20in (51cm) high.
£5,000–6,000 *PAO*

An 8-day mahogany bracket clock, by John Saunders, London, striking and repeating the hours on a bell, the backplate engraved with maker's name, c1810, 16in (40.5cm) high.
£2,500–3,000 *PAO*

A George II ebonised bracket clock, signed on brass chapter ring, 'Jon. Crampton Dublin 396', damaged, 16½in (41.5cm) high.
£3,000–4,000 *CSK*

An Italian tortoiseshell quarter striking bracket clock, the dial signed 'Giovanni Hisla, Napoli', the top with a figure of Chronos, early 18thC, 26in (66cm) high.
£9,500–10,500 *C*

A Louis XVI tortoiseshell boulle striking bracket clock, signed 'Roi à Paris', the top with later cherub, restored, 32in (81cm) high.
£2,000–2,500 *C*

A Louis XV tortoiseshell boulle month-going bracket clock, the enamel dial signed 'Julien Le Roy, de la Société des Arts', 21in (53.5cm) high.
£2,500–3,500 *C*

An 8-day burr walnut longcase clock, by Philip Abbot, London, c1725, 85in (216cm) high.
£7,500–7,800 *ALS*

An 8-day striking longcase clock, by William Avenell, Farnham, the brass silvered dial with seconds and date, c1790, 86in (218.5cm) high.
£3,400–3,600 *PAO*

An oak and mahogany crossbanded longcase clock, with painted dail, by Barton, Whitehaven, c1785, 85in (216cm) high.
£2,200–2,400 *ALS*

An 8-day mahogany longcase clock, by Abraham, Frome, c1830, 86in (218.5cm) high.
£4,300–4,600 *ALS*

An 8-day oak longcase clock, by Barlow, Ashton, with a Halifax moon, c1770, 84in (213cm) high.
£4,450–4,650 *ALS*

An 8-day walnut marquetry longcase clock, the brass and silvered dial signed 'Jno. Bennett, Plymouth', 82in (208cm) high.
£3,000–4,000 *Bea*

An 8-day oak longcase clock, by Batt, Petersfield, with lunar arch and strike/silent, c1770, 81½in (207cm) high.
£4,500–4,750 *ALS*

A flame mahogany longcase clock, by Wm. Beavington, Stourbridge, with rocking ship automata, c1800.
£4,500–4,750 *ALS*

A Scottish mahogany domestic regulator longcase clock, by James Bell, Edinburgh, with 13in (33cm) silvered brass dial showing seconds and Roman chapters, c1840.
£4,000–4,400 *PAO*

An 8-day oak longcase clock, by Thomas Bodle, Reigate, the brass dial with silvered brass chapter ring, seconds and date, c1760, 86in (218.5cm) high.
£3,500–4,000 *PAO*

An 8-day oak longcase clock, by William Bothamley, Kirton, striking the hours on a bell, c1765, 74½in (189cm) high.
£4,000–4,250 *PAO*

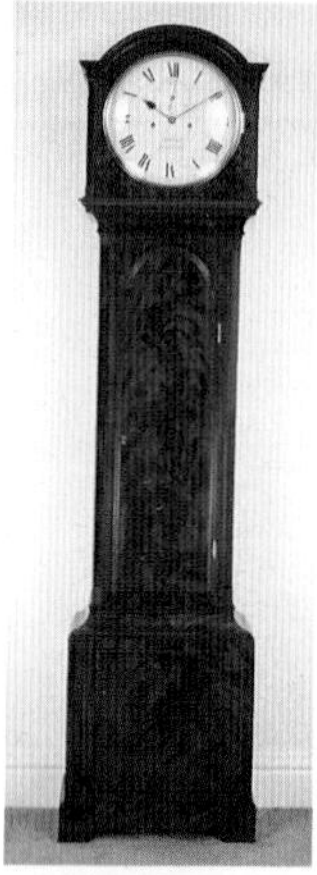

An 8-day mahogany veneered longcase clock, by Braund, Dartford, with 12in (30.5cm) dial, c1825, 76in (193cm) high.
£4,400–4,700 *PAO*

An 8-day mahogany veneered longcase clock, by Thomas Bullock, Corsham, striking the hours on a bell, the painted dial with seconds and date, c1840, 85in (216cm) high.
£2,500–3,000 *PAO*

An 8-day walnut longcase clock, by Thomas Cartwright, London, with brass dial and silvered chapter ring, c1710, 85in (216cm) high.
£12,000–12,750 *PAO*

An 8-day oak longcase clock, by Campbell, Bo'ness, c1790, 89in (226cm) high.
£2,450–2,650 *ALS*

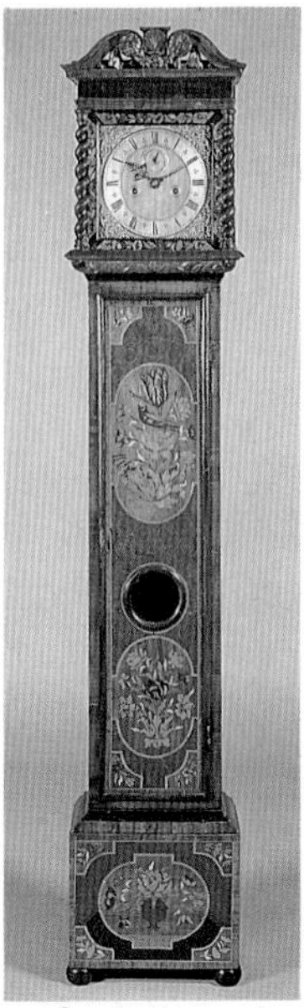

A walnut marquetry longcase clock, by William Cattel, c1685, restored, 79in (200.5cm) high.
£6,000–7,000 *Bon*

r. A boxwood and inlaid mahogany longcase clock, by Claridge, Chepstow, c1840, 90in (228.5cm) high.
£2,750–3,000 *ALS*

l. An oak and mahogany longcase clock, by Chapman, Lincoln, c1830, 80in (203cm) high.
£2,150–2,250 *ALS*

An 8-day mahogany longcase clock, by Edwd. Jones, Bristol, c1830, 86in (218.5cm) high.
£4,450–4,650 *ALS*

An 8-day oak and mahogany crossbanded longcase clock, by William Kemp, Lewes, the 5 pillar movement with latched centre pillar, c1770, 85in (216cm) high.
£4,000–4,250 *PAO*

An 8-day mahogany longcase clock, by Thomas Ogden, Ripponden, with dat aperture, 18thC, 84i (213cm) high.
£2,000–2,350 *MAT*

An 8-day longcase clock by Thomas Kefford, Royston, with green lacquered chinoiserie decoration, c1750, 84in (213cm) high.
£5,250–5,750 *PAO*

An 8-day oak longcase clock, by Thomas Rayment, Stamford, with a brass dial, and silvered chapter ring, c1770, 78½in (199cm) high.
£3,000–3,600 *PAO*

An 8-day mahogany veneered longcase clock, with ebony line inlay, by William Latch, Newport, c1830, 87in (221cm) high.
£2,500–3,000 *PAO*

An 8-day mahogany regulator style longcase clock, by Laurence, Southampton, with glazed trunk door, c1850, 81in (205.5cm) high.
£5,000–5,250 *PAO*

A Scottish 8-day mahogany longcase clock, the 13in (33cm) dial signed 'J. Paterson', c1810, 85½in (217cm) high.
£2,200–2,700 *S(S)*

An 8-day walnut marquetry longcase clock, by Francis Reynolds, Kensington, late 17thC, 85½in (217cm) high.
£3,500–4,000 *S(S)*

An 8-day oak longcase clock, by William Mayhew, Woodbridge, the 5 pillar movement striking the hours on a bell, with silvered chapter ring and brass spandrels, c1775, 78in (198cm) high.
£3,500–4,000 *PAO*

An 8-day mahogany longcase clock, by Morse, Stratton, c183 82in (208cm) high.
£2,200–2,400 *ALS*

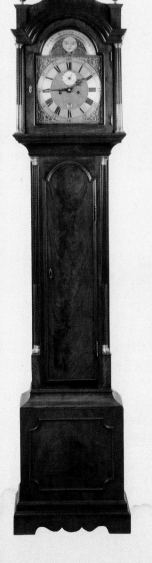

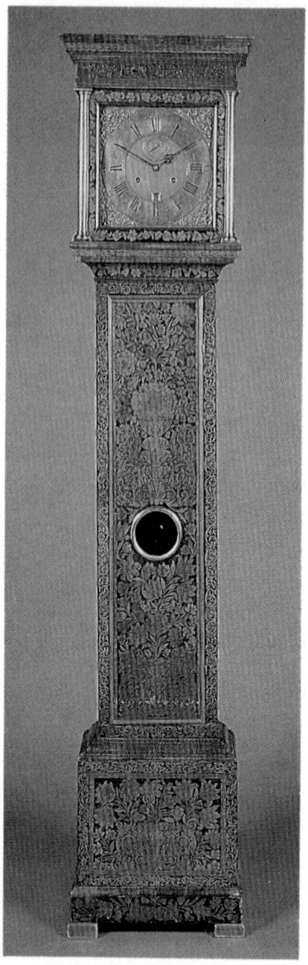

A William and Mary month-going walnut and marquetry longcase clock, by Daniel Quare, London, on later block feet, restored, 87in (221cm) high.
£7,000–8,000 *C*

An 8-day mahogany and shell inlaid longcase clock, by Thristle, Stogursey, c1790, 80in (203cm) high.
£4,500–4,750 *ALS*

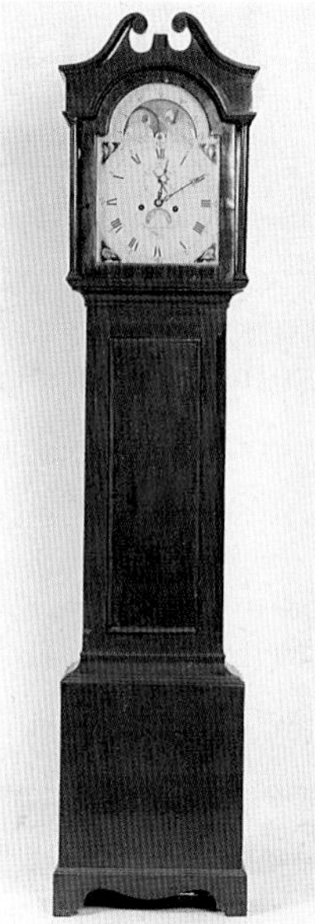

An 8-day mahogany longcase clock, by Shepherd & Potter, Wotton, the 12in (30.5cm) dial with moon-phase to arch, 19thC, 84in (213cm) high.
£1,500–2,000 *Bri*

An 8-day walnut longcase clock, by William Underwood, London, 18thC, 100in (254cm) high.
£11,000–11,500 *PAO*

An 8-day mahogany longcase clock, by E. Siedle, Merthyr, mid-19thC, 89in (226cm) high.
£3,000–3,250 *ALS*

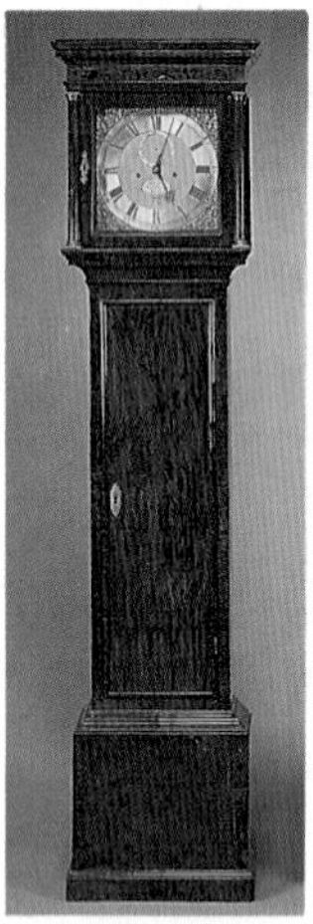

A George II walnut longcase clock, by Benjamin Gray & Justin Vuilliamy, London, c1750, 82in (208cm) high.
£3,000–3,500 *S(NY)*

An 8-day pale mahogany longcase clock, by Suggate, Halesworth, c1810, 85in (216cm) high.
£4,500–4,750 *ALS*

A Dutch mahogany and marquetry longcase clock, by Phy. Mensenbour, Groningen, c1780, 100in (254cm) high.
£3,800–4,400 *C*

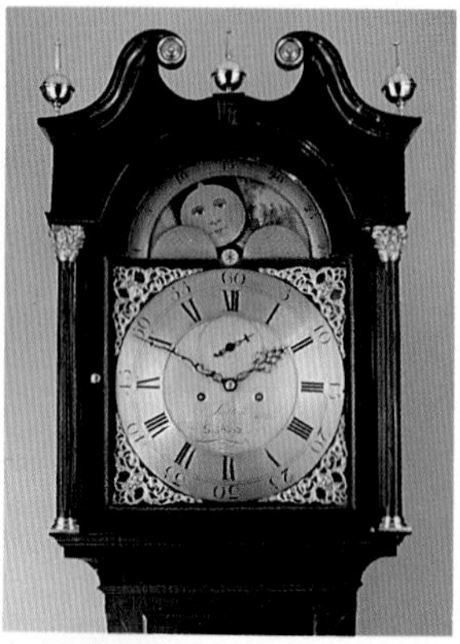

An 8-day Cuban mahogany longcase clock, by Sutton, Stafford, c1785, 89½in (227cm) high.
£5,750–6,000 *ALS*

An 8-day oak longcase clock, with lunar arch, and high water at Bristol Key *(sic)*, c1765, 82in (208cm) high.
£4,500–4,750 *ALS*

A mahogany longcase clock by S. Wilkes, Birmingham, c1830, 93in (236cm) high.
£1,400–1,600 *S(S)*

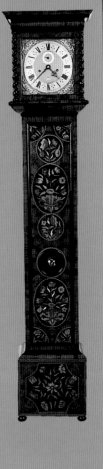

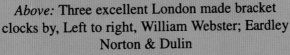

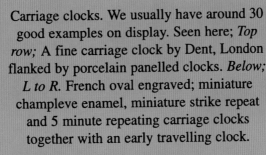

A Regency month-going mahogany longcase regulator, signed 'Barwise, St Martin's Lane, London', early 19thC, 76½in (194cm) high.
£7,500–9,000 *C*

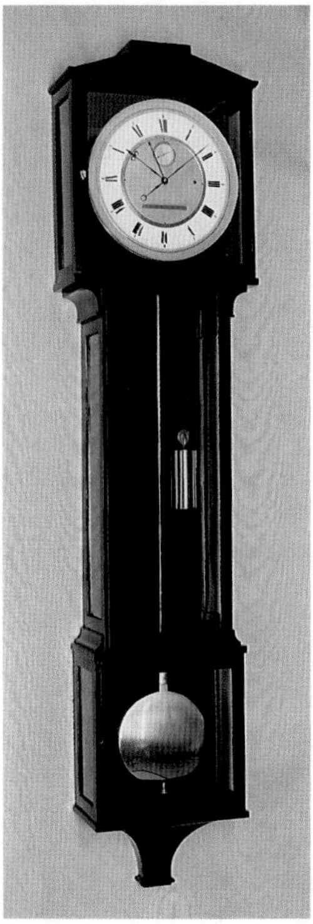

A month-going regulator, by Pfeiffer, with subsidiary seconds dial, and fully perpetual calendar hands, c1810, 45in (114cm) high.
£30,000–35,000 *GeC*

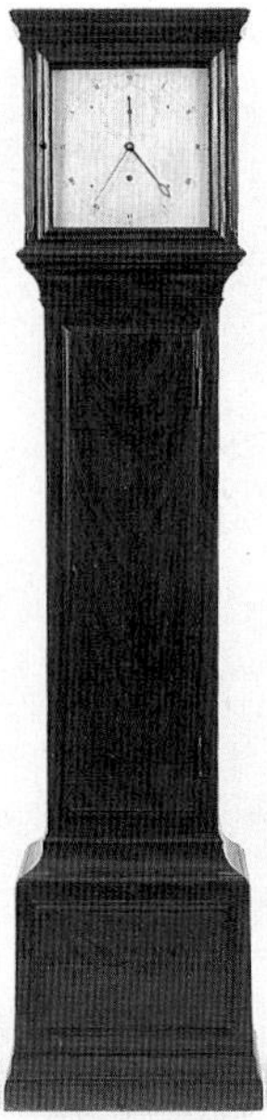

A George III mahogany regulator longcase clock,by Jas. Bullock, London, with silvered dial, subsidiary seconds dial, 69in (175cm) high.
£14,000–16,000 *Bea*

A Viennese year-going floor standing mahogany seconds beating regulator, by Binder, c1825, 76in (193cm) high.
£28,000–32,000 *GeC*

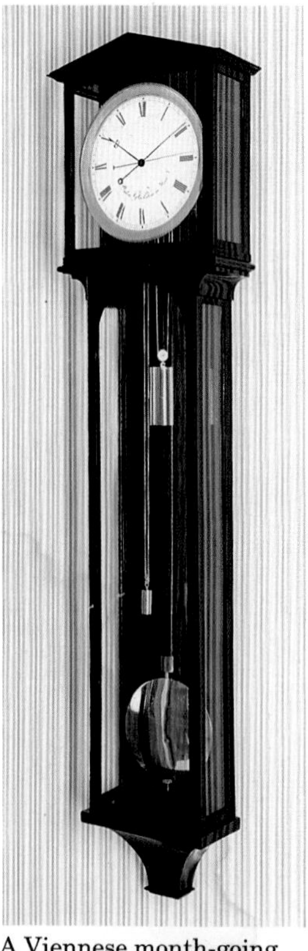

A Viennese month-going lantern style regulator, by Glückstein, with centre sweep seconds, and Huyghens method of winding, c1810, 45in (114cm) high.
£25,000–30,000 *GeC*

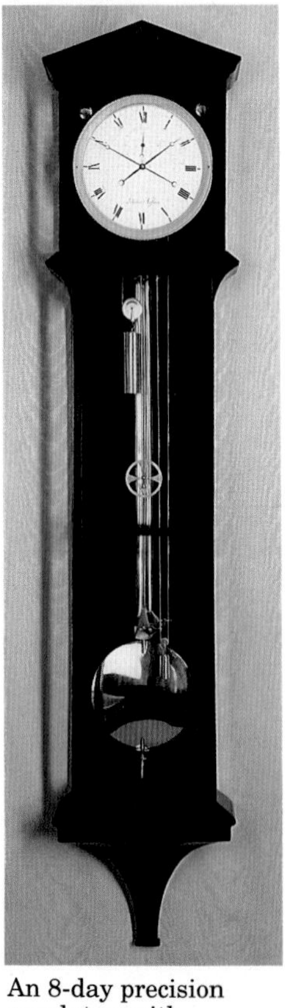

An 8-day precision regulator, with compensated pendulum and Huyghens method of winding, c1830.
£20,000–25,000 *GeC*

A Viennese 8-day 'roof-top' regulator, with an enamel dial, in a mahogany case with maple stringing, c1825, 37in (94cm) high.
£5,000–7,000 *GeC*

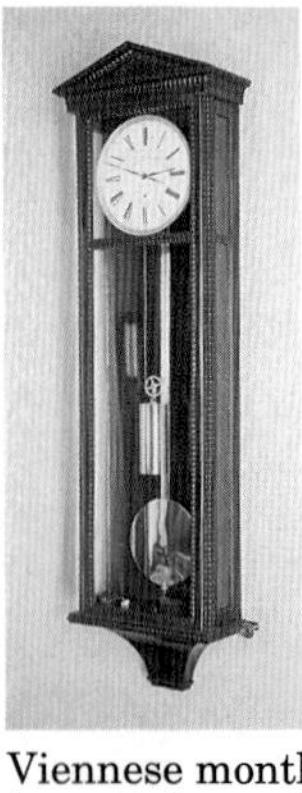

A Viennese month-going regulator, the enamel dial signed 'Joseph Jessner', c1830, 41in (104cm) high.
£6,500–7,500 *GeC*

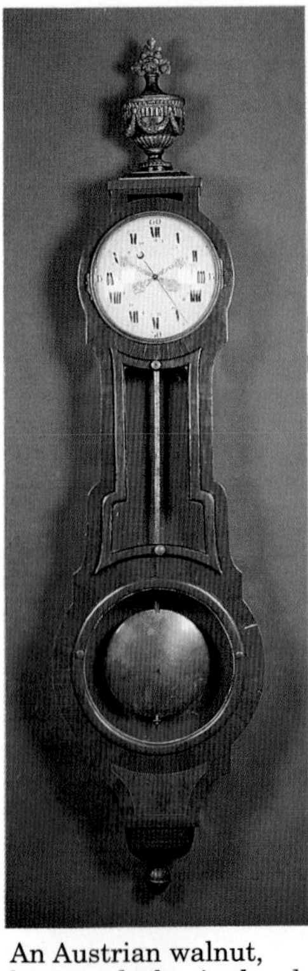

An Austrian walnut, kingwood, ebonised and parcel gilt wall regulator, c1780, 79in (200.5cm) high.
£11,000–12,000 *C*

A dome-topped mahogany shop regulator, by S. Bloomfield & Co., London, with deadbeat escapement, c1860, 71½in (181cm) high.
£4,500–4,750 *PAO*

A mahogany month-going wall regulator, signed 'Gebhard Bosch Lübeck', the bob as a terrestrial globe, 1877, 54in (137cm) high.
£10,000–12,000 *C*

A French week-duration four-glass regulator, the enamel dial signed 'Tiffany & Co.', c1890, 15in (38cm) high.
£1,550–1,650 *PAO*

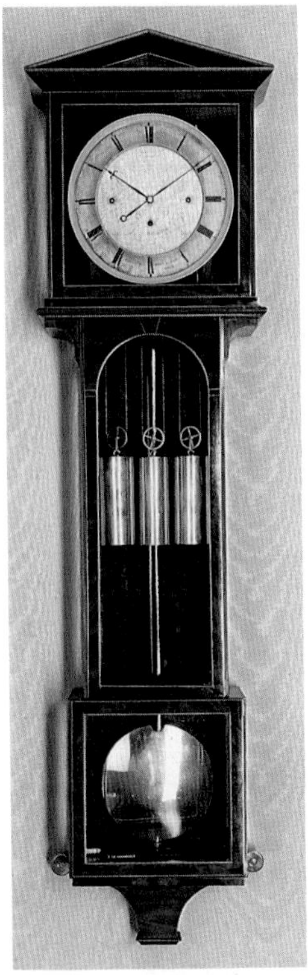

A Viennese lantern style regulator, by Phillip Happacher, the mahogany case with maple stringing, grande sonnerie striking with engraved dial centre, c1825, 44in (111.5cm) high.
£22,000–26,000 *GeC*

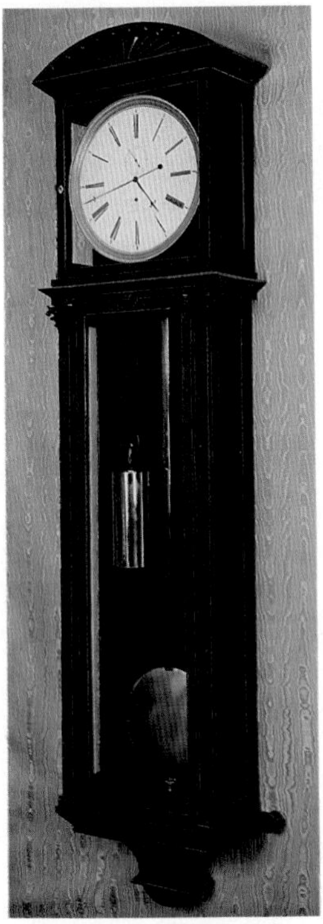

A Viennese year-going wall regulator, with precision movement, in mahogany case with maple stringing, c1835, 60in (152cm) high.
£25,000–30,000 *GeC*

A George IV mahogany mantel clock, with white painted Roman dial, the twin wire fusee movement, striking on a bell, 18½in (47cm) high.
£1,400–2,000 *CSK*

A Directoire mahogany mantel clock, the twin going barrel movement with count wheel strike on a bell, later Brocot escapement, 20in (51cm) high.
£600–700 *CSK*

A Napoleon III Egyptian style mantel clock, in marmo rosso antico, nero Belgio and parcel gilt bronze, signed 'HRY MARC, PARIS', 18½in (47cm) high.
£550–650 *CSK*

An Empire ormolu urn clock, signed 'Rodier à Paris', the twin going barrel movement with anchor escapement, 16in (40.5cm) high.
£1,500–2,000 *C*

An Empire ormolu striking urn clock, by Le Roy, Paris, with twin going barrel movement, 15in (38cm) high.
£2,000–2,500 *C*

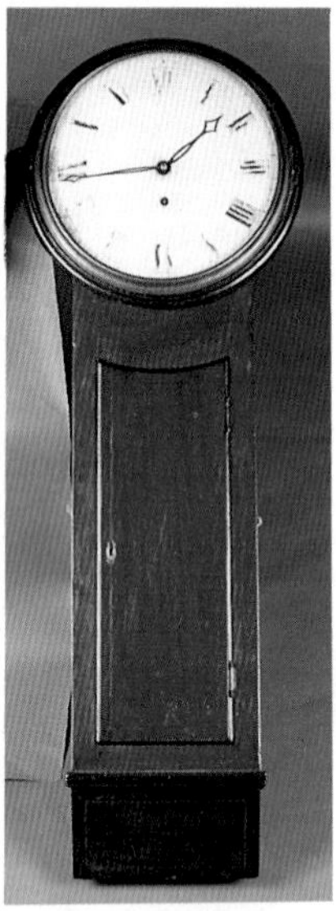

A George III mahogany tavern clock, with a painted wooden dial, single train movement.
£2,000–2,500 *SWO*

A French carriage clock, the 8-day movement with quarter and hour striking on 2 gongs, the enamel dial with chapter ring and decoration, the English brass case with carrying handle, c1880.
£1,450–1,650 *PAO*

A Swiss ormolu grande sonnerie pendule d'officier, by Robert & Courvoisier, No. 8863, c1795, 8in (20cm) high.
£7,200–8,000 *C*

A Louis XVI style ormolu mounted pink marble three-piece garniture de cheminée, the lyre form clock with Arabic chapters and glazed dial, with a pair of five-light candelabra, each with an urn form standard flanked by classical masks and floral garlands, late 19thC, clock 20in (51cm) high.
£5,000–5,500 *CNY*

A fruitwood cuckoo clock, the case with arched top and moulded base, white enamel dial with Roman numerals and pierced hands, Black Forest, late 19thC, 15½in (39.5cm) high.
£400–500 *CSK*

An early George II alarm clock, the foliate engraved gilt dial signed 'Danl. Catlin, Godmanchester', 7in (17.5cm) high.
£1,100–1,400 *C*

An automaton clock, the case surmounted by a painted wood figure of a knife grinder at a treadle wheel, Black Forest, c1875, 23in (58.5cm) high.
£5,000–6,000 *S*

A world time petite sonnerie and alarm carriage clock, by Le Roy & Fils, Paris, c1870, 5½in (14cm) high, with original signed travelling case.
£15,000–20,000 *S*

A Napoleon III gilt bronze and porcelain encrier clock, the case modelled as a rug draped over rods supported on the shoulders of 2 amorini, with urn surmount, the shaped base with 2 floral painted pots, the tray with a portrait of a lady held in a garland by cherubs, on stiff leaf cast toupie feet, 14½in (37cm) wide.
£1,100–1,500 *CSK*

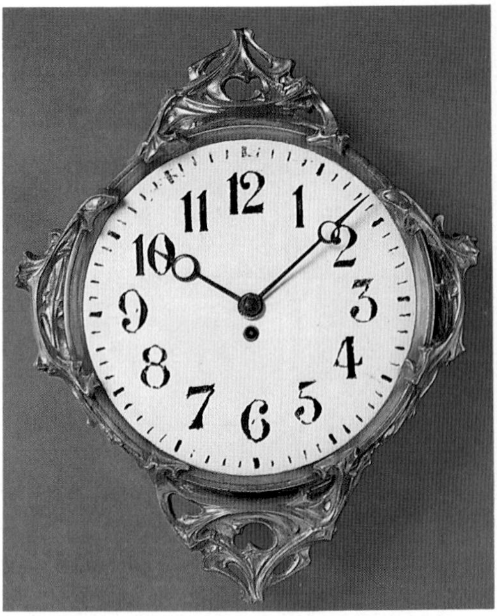

A French bronze hanging wall clock, designed by Hector Guimard, the white face with Arabic numerals, mounted on the sides with openwork plant forms, 18in (46cm) long, suspended by chains.
£1,800–2,200 *P*

A fruitwood cuckoo clock, inlaid with enamel and boulle scrolls, with painted white enamel dial, Black Forest, late 19thC, 19in (48cm) high.
£1,000–1,400 *CSK*

A silver timepiece, the movement with platform lever escapement, signed 'Asprey, 166 Bond Street, London, 1905', 3in (8cm) high.
£600–800 *CSK*

A French ormolu mounted white marble lyre mantel clock garniture, the 5½in (14cm) enamel chapter ring signed 'Le Roux A Paris', the case decorated with garlands of flowers, on an oval base, 22in (56cm) high, with a pair of paste set candelabra.
£5,200–6,000 *S*

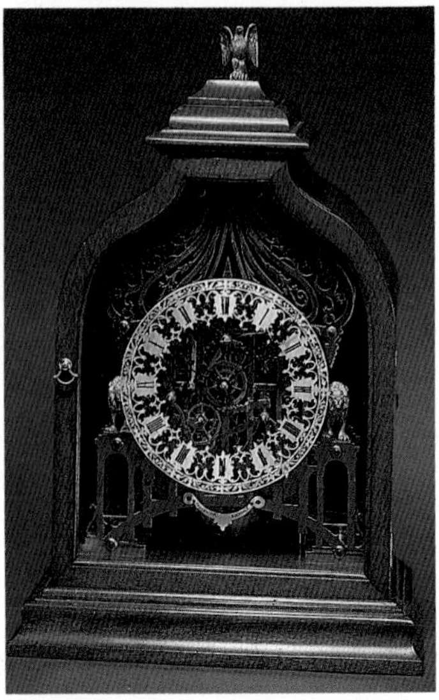

A skeleton clock, by Smiths, London, in the form of the central dome of the Royal Pavilion, Brighton, with twin fusee and chain movement, c1860, 23½in (60cm) high.
£5,000–5,500 *S(NY)*

A George III mahogany clock, the painted dial signed 'Massey, Strand, London', with brass bezel, 4 pillar single gut fusee movement, 14in (36cm) diam.
£1,100–1,400 *C*

An early Victorian mother-of-pearl inlaid ebony and rosewood striking wall clock, by James McCabe, London, No. 2438.
£1,000–1,200 *C*

An 8-day mahogany striking table clock, by Barwise, London, inlaid with brass and ebony, c1795, 21in (53.5cm) high.
£3,000–3,500 *PAO*

A 6-month duration skeleton clock, by Lepaute de Belle Fontaine, Paris, 22in (56cm) high.
£6,500–7,000 *S(NY)*

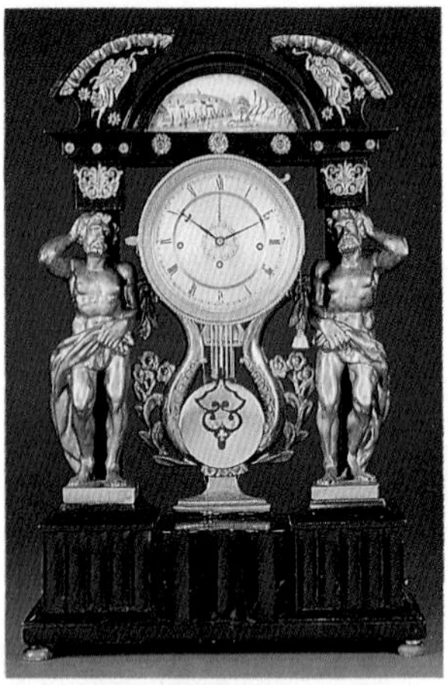

A Viennese ebonised and parcel gilt grande sonnerie musical table clock, signed 'Weillbourg', 23in (59cm) high.
£2,200–2,700 *C*

A Louis XV style parcel gilt bronze table clock, resting on the back of a bull, on a naturalistic base, late 19thC, 23in (59cm) high.
£2,000–2,500 *CSK*

A French ormolu, bronze and patinated wall clock, the case in the form of billowing clouds, with putti around the dial, c1900, 28in (71cm) high.
£3,500–4,000 *S(NY)*

A Louis Philippe ormolu musical automaton striking table clock, the twin going barrel movement with anchor escapement, 29½in (75cm) high over glass dome.
£5,500–6,500 *C*

An enamelled clock, the domed top with a peacock and fish finial, the white enamel dial signed on face 'Child & Child, London, S.W.', and with sunflower mark, the French movement No. '4639', damage to enamels, 4½in (11cm) high.
£3,000–4,000 *P*

A Louis XV/XVI Transitional gilt bronze wall clock and barometer, the clock dial signed 'Hana à Paris', in guilloche cast cases mounted with leaves and husks and surmounted by a vase, barometer movement replaced, c1775.
£29,000–33,000 *S*

A Louis XVI gilt bronze clock, signed 'Frédéric Duval à Paris', c1775, 14in (35.5cm) high.
£13,000–14,000 *S*

A gilt bronze mounted white marble and nero Belgio portico clock, signed 'Faisant à Paris', on a plinth inset with a foliate cast frieze below a stiff leaf gallery on toupie feet, mid-19thC, 20½in (52cm) high.
£2,000–3,000 *CSK*

An 8-day mahogany and laminated wood acorn clock, by Forestville Manufacturing. Co., Connecticut, c1847, 24½in (62.5cm) high.
£13,500–14,500 *CNY*

An ormolu mounted japanned table clock, by Weeks, London, c1800, 76in (193cm) high.
£2,250–3,000 *S*

A George IV gilt bronze mounted and brass inlaid ebony pedestal clock, the movement signed 'George Wilkins, London', 76in (193cm) high.
£10,000–12,000 *C*

A Viennese mahogany and parcel gilt grande sonnerie table clock, dial signed 'Johan Sachs', late 18thC, 16in (40.5cm) high.
£2,500–3,000 *C*

A Louis XIV boulle clock, surmounted with a figure of Time, decorated with Phoebus in his chariot below the dial, the movement signed 'Jacques Cogniet à Paris', c1700, 46½in (118cm) high.
£13,000–15,000 *S*

A Continental pocket watch, with inset Art Deco design dial and keyless jewelled lever movement.
£250–300 *CSK*

A 14ct gold calendar quarter repeating chronograph keyless lever hunter cased watch, with moonphase, signed 'Le Phare', c1900, 57mm diam.
£2,300–2,800 *C(G)*

Two silver pocket watches, one movement signed 'William Eves', the other 'G & R Cathro London'.
£350–450 *CSK*

A gold and enamel quarter repeating musical watch, signed 'Pierre Schneeberger La Chaux de Fonds', c1820, 59mm diam.
£5,000–5,250 *PT*

A gold calendar alarm pocket watch, engraved 'Patek & Cie., Genève, Chronomètre à Reveil', late 19thC.
£700–800 *CSK*

A silver pair cased verge watch, the movement signed 'Forbes & Son, London', c1796.
£300–400 *CSK*

A 14ct gold keyless lever hunter watch, dial and movement signed 'Uhrenfabrik-Union, Glasshutte, Dresden', c1880, 52mm diam.
£1,500–2,000 *C(G)*

A Swiss gold and enamel verge watch, with full plate fusee movement, c1780, 47mm diam.
£2,000–2,300 *PT*

A gilt open face watch, the gilt tourbillon mounted on the front plate, decorated with polychrome enamel festoons.
£1,200–1,500 *CSK*

A 18ct gold hunter cased watch, by Patek Philippe & Co., Genève, No. 162608, the case with monogram, c1920, 47mm diam.
£1,200–1,500 *S(NY)*

A Swiss 3 colour gold quarter repeating cylinder pocket watch, signed 'Godemar Frères', c1825, 43mm diam.
£2,000–2,200 *PT*

An 18ct gold chronometer keyless lever hunter cased watch, with helical hair spring, signed 'Lucien DuBois, Locle', c1890, 52mm diam., with original rosewood presentation box.
£1,400–1,600 *C(G)*

A silver calendar moonphase watch, with 4 subsidiary dials, with engine turned case.
£300–400 *CSK*

A Swiss 18ct gold quarter repeating automaton Jacquemart keywound open face cylinder watch, inscribed 'Fridel à Strasbourg', c1830, 56mm diam.
£1,800–2,200 *C(G)*

A gold and enamel open face duplex watch, made for the Chinese market, enamel by J. L. Richter, signed 'Ilbery, London, No. 5988', c1810, 60mm diam.
£33,000–35,000 *C(G)*

A gold and enamel duplex watch, enamel by J. L. Richter, signed 'Willm. Ilbery, London, No. 6536', c1810, 58mm diam.
£34,000–36,000 *C(G)*

A silver and tortoiseshell pair cased watch, the pierced silvered cock depicting the Crucifixion, the dial painted with a priest, damaged.
£400–500 *CSK*

A gold and enamel centre-seconds open face duplex watch, made for the Chinese market, signed 'Edouard Juvet, Fleurier, No. 41980', enamel by J. L. Richter, c1830, 60mm diam.
£14,000–16,000 *C(G)*

A platinum, diamond and enamel open face dress watch, signed 'Vacheron & Constantin', c1920, 41mm diam., with a platinum chain.
£2,400–2,800 *S(NY)*

l. A platinum, sapphire and diamond dress watch, with 18 jewels, by Patek Philippe & Co., No. 806417, retailed by Spaulding Gorham, c1925, 45mm diam.
£2,500–3,000 *S(NY)*

l. A platinum and enamel open face watch, with gold movement, signed 'Gruen', with 21 jewels and 2 diamonds, c1924, 45mm wide, and Gruen 50th Anniversary box.
£2,800–3,200 *S(NY)*

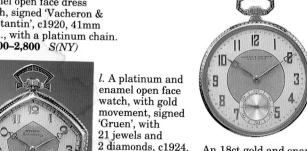

An 18ct gold and enamel open face watch, by Vacheron & Constantin, with two-toned silvered dial, c1930, 43mm diam.
£1,200–1,500 *S(NY)*

An 18ct gold rack lever pair cased watch, the frosted gilt movement signed 'Jno. Shaw, Manchester', maker's stamp 'RBGM, London 1809.
£650–750 *CSK*

A gentleman's gold wristwatch, the case, dial and movement signed 'Audemars Piguet', 33mm diam.
£900–1,200 *C*

A Rolex gentleman's gold wristwatch, signed 'Rolex SA', the nickel plated movement with 18 jewels, c1945, 35mm diam.
£1,200–1,400 *C*

A gold wristwatch, signed 'Vacheron & Constantin, Genève, No. 386873', c1920, 30mm square.
£3,000–4,000 *C*

An 18ct two colour gold wristwatch, signed 'Vacheron & Constantin', No. 415972, import mark for London 1933, 31 by 26mm.
£1,200–1,700 *C*

A gold Oyster Perpetual Chronometer bubble-backed wristwatch, signed 'Rolex', model 5050, movement numbered 'N43759'.
£3,000–4,000 *C*

A pink gold chronograph wristwatch, signed 'Ulysse Nardin', the movement with gold alloy balance jewelled to the centre, c1950, 35mm diam.
£1,500–2,000 *C*

An 18ct pink gold limited edition chronograph wristwatch, the case, dial and movement signed 'Breitling Série Limitée 102 175', 36mm diam.
£2,500–3,000 *C*

A gold and diamond set lady's wristwatch, signed 'Piaget', with integral gold bracelet, c1980, 27mm diam.
£3,000–3,500 *C*

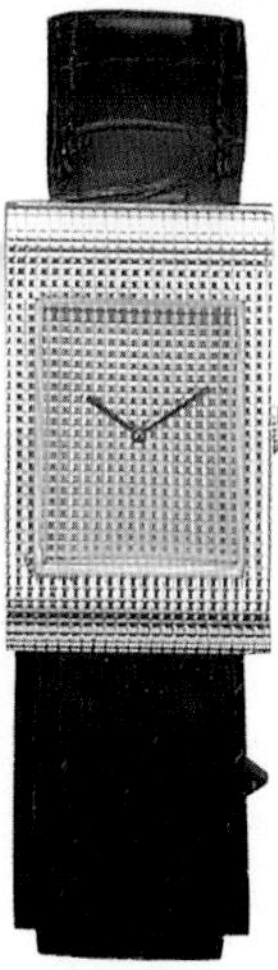

An 18ct gold wristwatch, signed 'Boucheron', London import mark for 1977, 36mm long.
£2,000–2,500 *C*

A pink gold chronograph wristwatch, signed 'Omega Watch Co.', the gilt movement jewelled to the centre with gold alloy balance, c1950, 37mm diam.
£1,200–1,700 *C*

A gold chronograph wristwatch, signed 'Zenith', No. 572302, the movement jewelled to the centre, c1940, 34mm diam.
£2,000–2,700 *C*

A gold single button chronograph wristwatch, inscribed 'Chronomètre Le Roy', the movement jewelled to the centre, c1930, 37mm diam.
£2,000–2,500 *C*

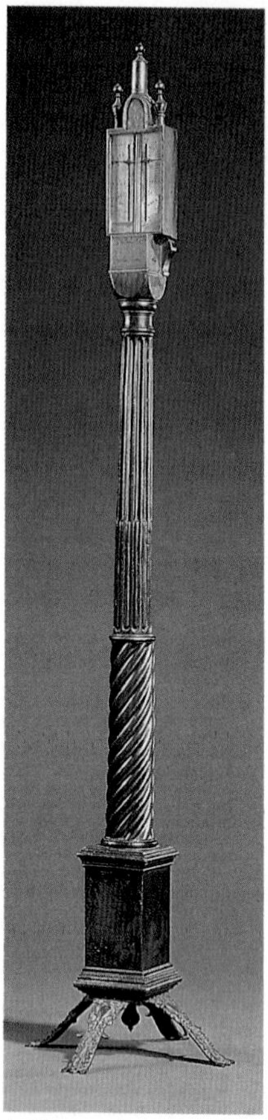

A Queen Anne walnut barometer, the silvered register plates calibrated in Quare's format, signed 'Invented & made by Danl. Quare London', No. '24' on side plate, 39in (99cm) high.
£44,000–47,000 *C*

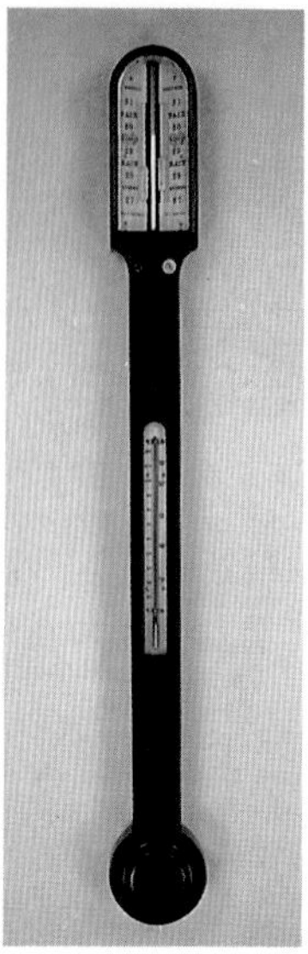

A rosewood stick barometer, by Dobell, Hastings, the ivory aslant scales with weather notations, c1840.
£1,000–1,300 *PAO*

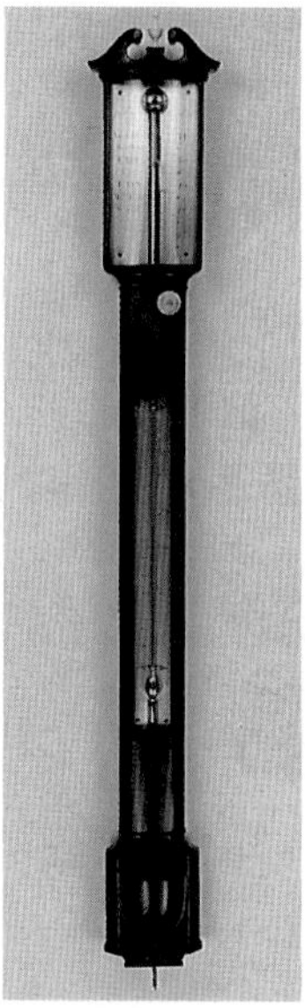

A mahogany bowfront stick barometer, by John Ewen, Aberdeen, c1810.
£4,200–4,400 *PAO*

l. A George III mahogany stick barometer, by Watkins, Charing Cross, with brass vernier scale, 39½in (100cm) high.
£1,500–2,000
c. A George III mahogany wheel barometer, by P. Aggio, Colchester, with swan neck pediment, 39½in (100cm) high.
£4,500–5,500
r. A George III mahogany stick barometer, by Troughton, London, 38in (96.5cm) high.
£1,500–2,000 *C*

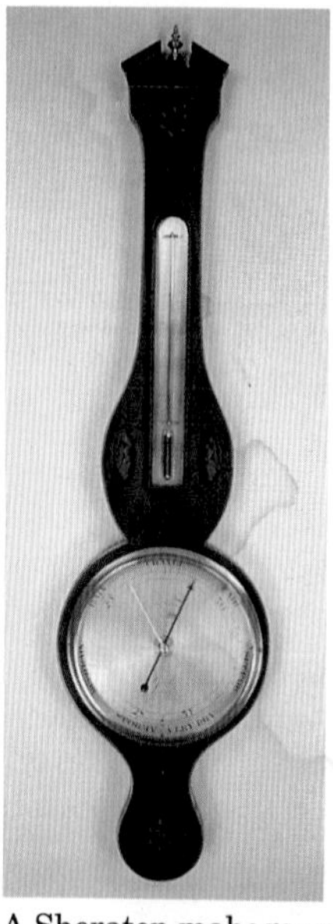

A Sheraton mahogany and boxwood inlaid wheel barometer, by G. Martinoia, York, with an 8in (20cm) diam. silvered brass scale, c1810.
£1,000–1,300 *PAO*

A George III mahogany and chequer-strung barometer, with central fluted Corinthian column, signed 'Jno. Russell Falkirk' beneath the vernier scale, c1745, 43½in (110cm) high.
£20,000–23,000 *C*

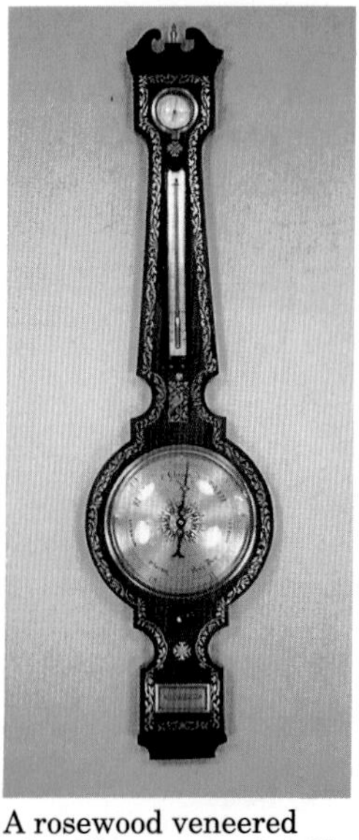

A rosewood veneered wheel barometer, inlaid with pewter leaves and central bird, with silvered brass scale, by B. Pedroncini, Southampton, c1840.
£1,000–1,300 *PAO*

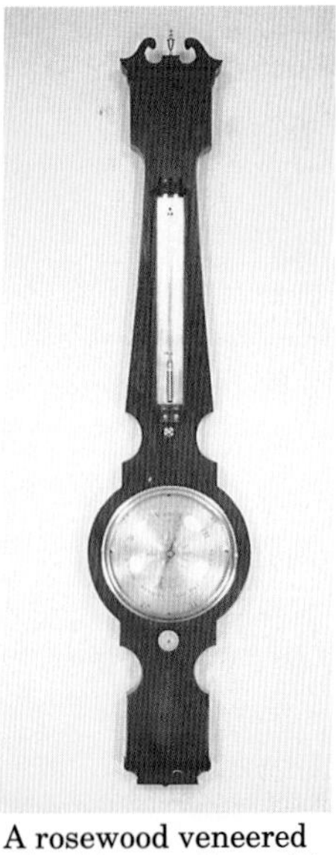

A rosewood veneered wheel barometer, with silvered brass scale, swan neck top and brass finial, by Carughi, London, c1840.
£1,000–1,400 *PAO*

A terrestrial and celestial globe, by G. Woodward, c1820, 3in (7.5cm) diam.
£3,500–4,000 *CSK*

A pair of mahogany globes, by J. & W. Cary, the celestial globe dated '1799', 21in (53cm) diam.
£12,500–13,000 *S(NY)*

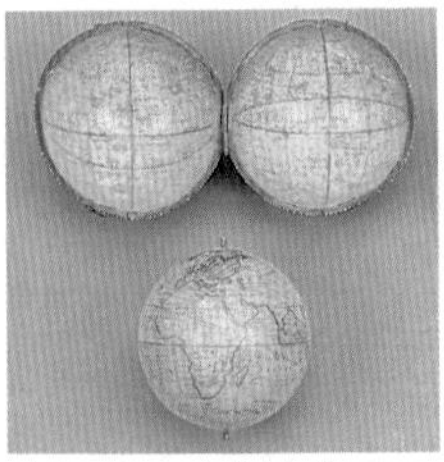

A terrestrial pocket globe, by Newton, Son & Berry, c1832, 3in (7.5cm) diam.
£3,000–3,500 *CSK*

A 'Cary's New Terrestrial Globe', damaged, c1826, 12in (30.5cm) diam. **£1,500–2,000** *Bri*

A terrestrial library globe, by R.C.A., from a design by Matthaus Greuter, c1744, 19in (48cm) diam.
£9,500–10,000 *CSK*

A Georgian oak and brass terrestrial globe, by L. Cushee, mid-18thC, 15in (38cm) diam.
£11,000–13,000 *SNY*

A pair of globes, by J. & W. Newton, dated '1818', 15in (38cm) diam, in original brass mounted hardwood cases.
£17,000–18,000 *SNY*

A pair of library globes, by G. & J. Cary, each with turned stem, down-curved legs and compass stretcher, the terrestrial globe dated '1844', 24in (61cm) diam.
£24,000–25,000 *S*

A pair of mahogany library globes, the terrestrial globe signed 'D. Adams, 1798', each on a slender stem on 3 sabre legs joined by a compass stretcher, 23½in (60cm) diam.
£38,000–42,000 *S*

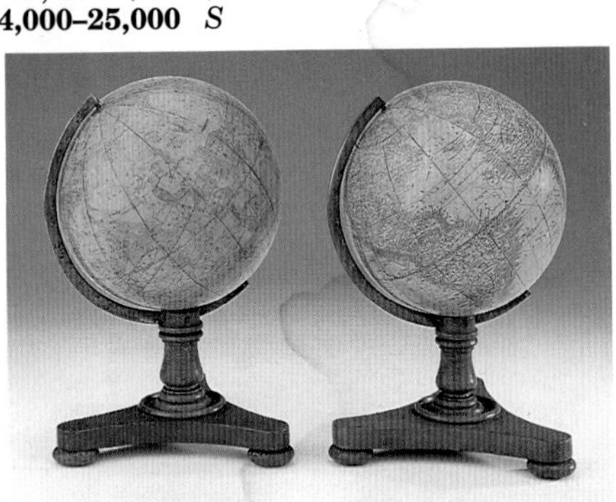

A pair of terrestrial and celestrial table globes, by Bale and Woodward, each with 12 hand coloured engraved gores, 1845, 7in (17.5cm) diam.
£7,000–8,000 *CSK*

Working Model

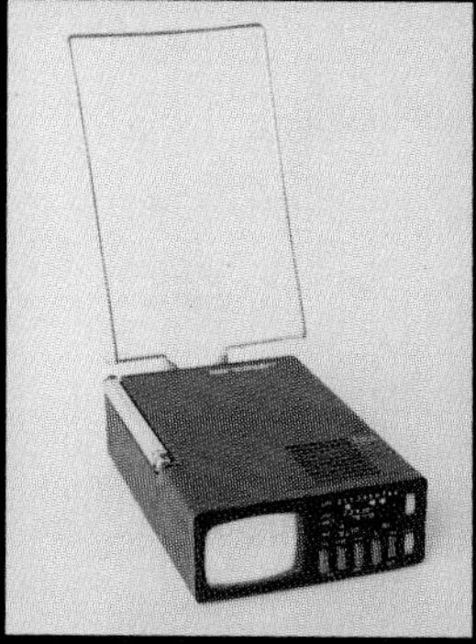

* Sinclair Microvision TV
model MTV1 1977.

Marconi 707 TV\Radio 1939

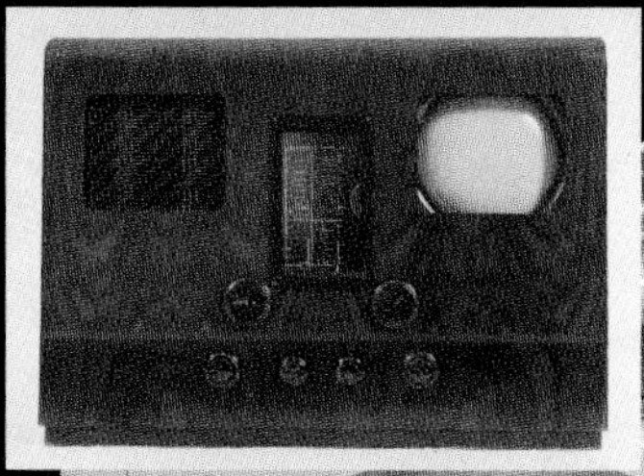

Baird "Lyric" TV\Radio 1946
specially finished in bird's-eye maple

Cossor Model 1210 TV\Radio 1939

Pye bakelite TV model VT2 1951

Pye Mark III television camera 1954

JVC Videosphere "Sputnick"
model 3240 UK
with radio stand TV\Radio 1966

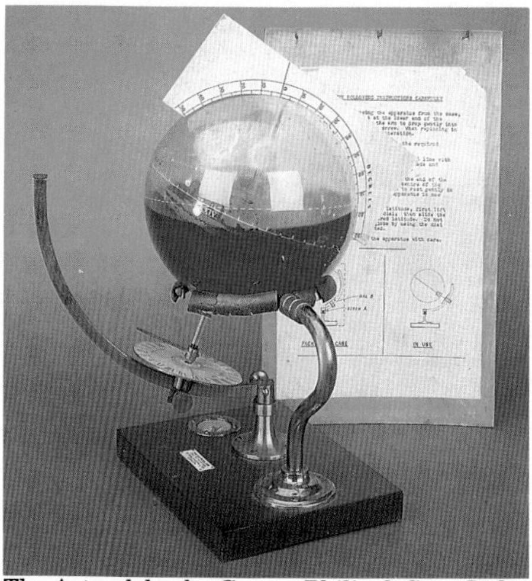

The Astroglobe, by George Philip & Sons Ltd., the glass sphere engraved, half filled with blue liquid, c1934, 6in (15cm) diam.
£1,500–2,000 *CSK*

A brass armillary sphere, after the antique, 9½in (24cm) diam.
£4,000–5,000 *CSK*

A French brass armillary sphere, on a turned brass base with fruitwood column stand, 8½in (21cm) diam.
£5,000–6,000 *CSK*

A 'Mechanical Paradox' orrery, by James Ferguson, late 18thC, 13½in (34.5cm) diam.
£2,500–3,000 *CSK*

A brass armillary sphere, by Professor J. M. Egloff, mounted on a baluster turned pillar and stand, 19thC, 14in (35.5cm) diam.
£6,000–7,000 *CSK*

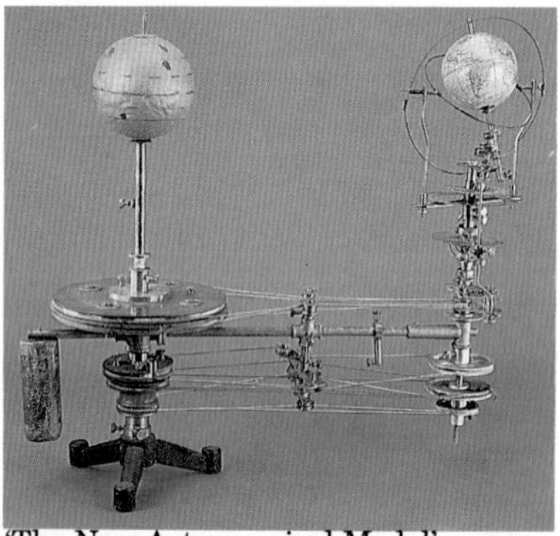

'The New Astronomical Model' orrery, by William Wilson, c1915, globe 4in (10cm) diam. **£3,500–4,000** *CSK*

An Indo-Persian metal celestial globe, signed 'Nasir al-Din al-Tusi', mounted on a stand with engraved base, c1789, 9in (22.5cm) diam.
£1,500–2,000 *CSK*

A metal and brass planetarium-orrery, late 18thC, base plate 17½in (44.5cm) diam.
£8,500–9,000 *CSK*

A brass planetarium with tellurium and lunarium facepiece, by John and William Cary, London, signed and dated '1791', in original mahogany case, 22in (55.5cm) high.
£36,000–40,000 *CSK*

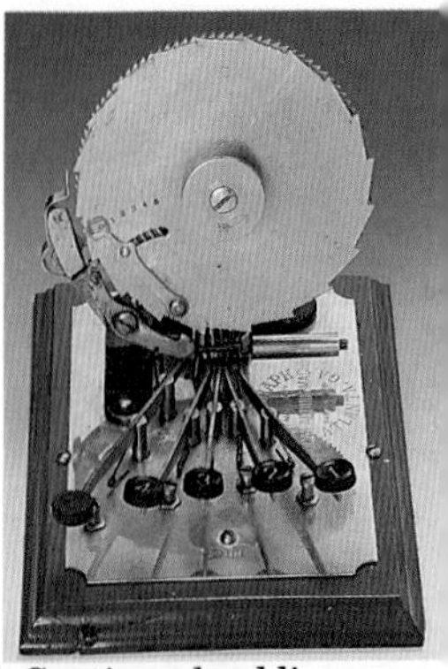

A Centigraph adding machine, by Atlanta Adding Machine Company, c1891, 8in (20cm) wide, in original fruitwood case.
£2,000–3,000 *S*

Opthalmic Antiques

SPECTACLES

Surprisingly the lens pre-dates the invention of spectacles by as much as 4000 years! The British Museum has in its collection 'lenses' from excavations to Knossos. They are made from natural occurring quartz and are only an inch or so in diameter. Incidentally, quartz was still being used for spectacle lenses in the late 19thC. People were still refering to spectacle lenses as 'pebbles' in the 1950s, this is a throw back to the time when quartz pebbles found in rivers were often the source of the raw material. It was not until the late 1930s when plastic lenses first became available.

All the early lenses were of the magnifying type, used to correct long sight. It was not until the 13thC that the first reference to spectacles appear in surviving documents, and certainly by the 14thC spectacles were established. However, very few examples from this time survive presumably because they had been constructed from wood or leather and had not worn well! However, the Museum of London does have the remains of a wooden spectacle dating from before 1440.

There was little change in design of spectacle frames over the next 200 years. By the 17thC both leather and copper rimmed 'Nuremberg' spectacles had become widely available and from the early 16thC were fitted with lenses to correct short sight. A small number of spectacles from this era come up for auction at the major salerooms every year attracting prices in the region of £2,000.

From 1700 many other materials began to be used in the construction of spectacle frames, these included silver, steel, brass, tortoiseshell and horn. Steel frames often had horn inserts to hold the lenses and although the side pieces had temple grip ends the fronts looked much like a modern frame. During the mid-18thC the first bifocal lenses were invented, consisting of no more than 2 lenses of different powers cut in half and fitted into the same rim!

The early 19thC saw the use of beautifully crafted silver spectacles in many variations of design. The lorgnette also became very fashionable for ladies, often crafted in tortoiseshell or in combination with silver or gold. By the middle of the century with the industrial revolution at its height the first protective spectacles became available. From the 1890s bifocals were no longer limited to just the split type. It was also possible to cement, with Canada balsam two lenses together to produce a bifocal as we know ittoday. The solid and fused bifocal designs in use today date from around that time! It should be noted that up until the 1950s almost all spectacle lenses were of a flat form and not curved as they are now.

At the turn of the century many types of pince-nez became popular. But like many items they were not suitable for the battlefields of 1914–18, and the well known oval or round eye rolled gold front with curl sides became widely used. These frames continued with little change into the NHS range in 1947 where they were still available at its demise in 1988.

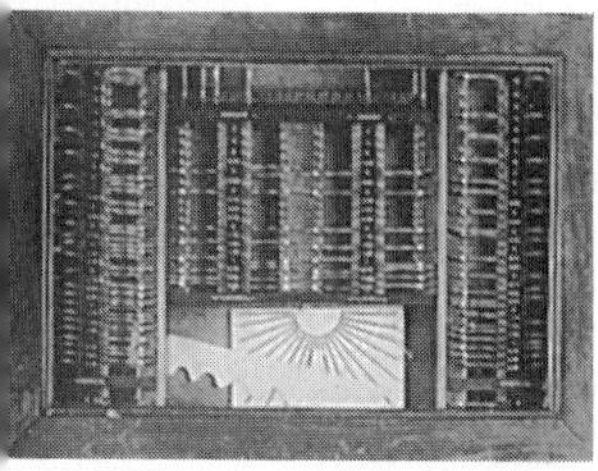

An optician's trial set, with frames and lenses, in fitted mahogany case with bevelled glazed lid, 21in (53.5cm) wide.
£200–250 *CSK*

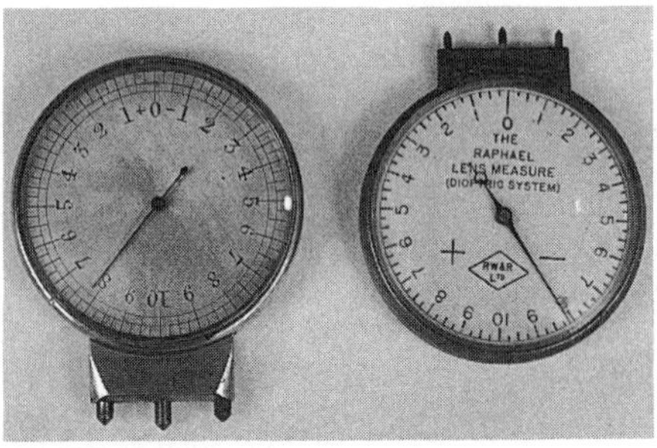

Two lens measures:
l. 19thC, 2½in (6.5cm) high.
£40–50
r. 20thC, 2in (5cm) high.
£15–20 *PC*

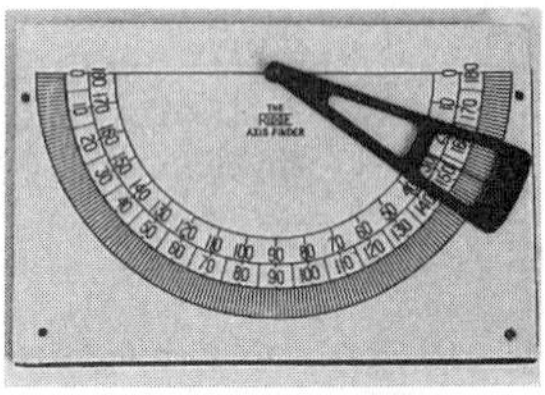

A 'The Ridge' axis finder, for measuring toric lenses, c1920, 4½in (11.5cm) wide.
£7–10 *PC*

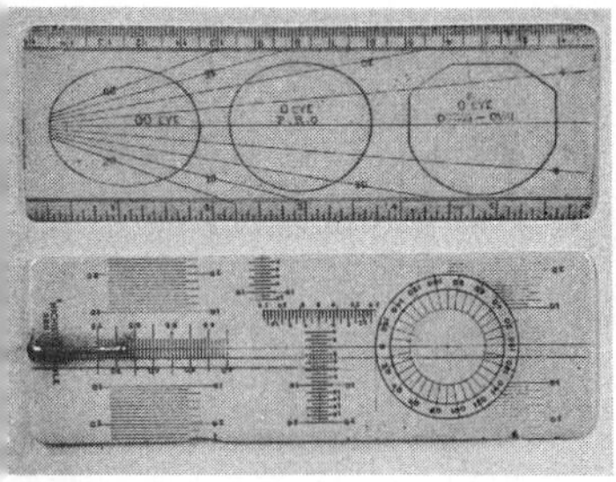

Two ivorene dispensing rulers, for measuring lenses and frames, early 20thC, 6in (15cm) long.
£8–10 each *PC*

A George III plain eye bath, the base with reeded border, probably by Joseph Taconet 1802.
£450–500 *MSW*

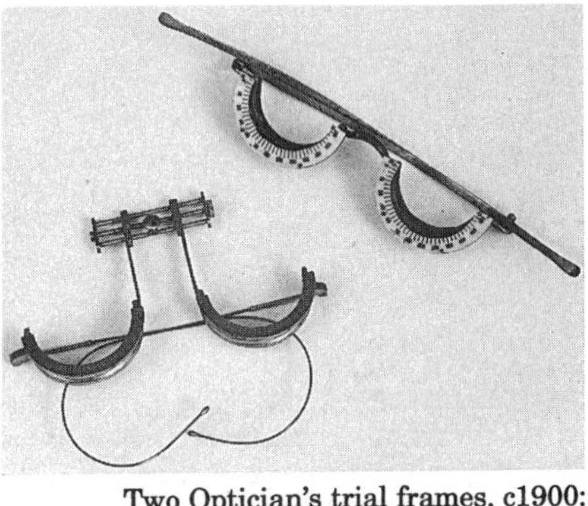

Two Optician's trial frames, c1900:
top. 7in (17.5cm) wide.
£8–10
bottom. 4½in (11.5cm) wide.
£20–25 *PC*

One blue and 2 green glass eye baths, 20thC, largest 1½in (4cm) high.
£15–20 each *PC*

One blue and two clear glass eye baths, c1920, largest 2½in (6.5cm) high.
£10–15 each *PC*

Two blue glass eye baths, c1900, 2½in (6.5cm) high.
£15–20 each *PC*

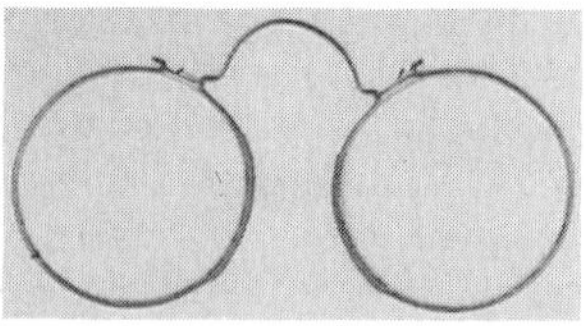

A pair of Nuremberg nose spectacles, with grooved wire frame, round lenses and nose pads, c1700.
£1,100–1,500 *CSK*

A pair of leather framed Nuremberg nose spectacles, with 1¼in (3.5cm) diam., slightly convex lenses and undecorated bridge, early 17thC.
£4,500–5,000 *CSK*

These spectacles were recently discovered in Massachusetts, USA.

A pair of silver framed nose spectacles, with round, bevelled lenses, pointed and arched bridge, in shaped wood case, possibly 17thC.
£3,000–4,000 *CSK*

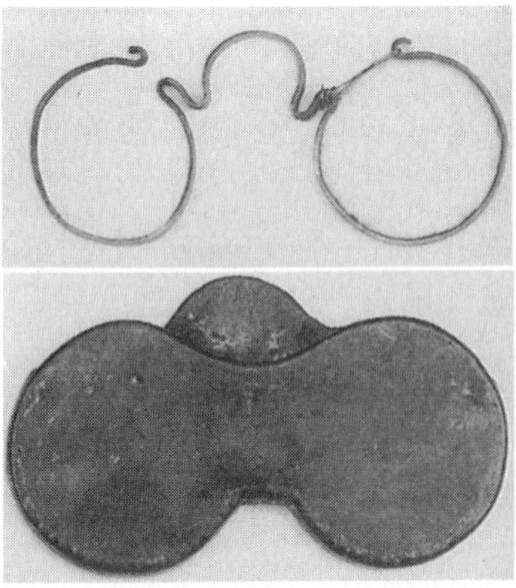

A pair of Nuremberg single wire nose spectacles, with grooved wire frame and one round lens, in leather case, c1700.
£700–1,000 *CSK*

A pair of Chinese horn and brass spectacles, with quartz lenses, 19thC, 7in (17.5cm) long, with case.
£275–350 *PC*

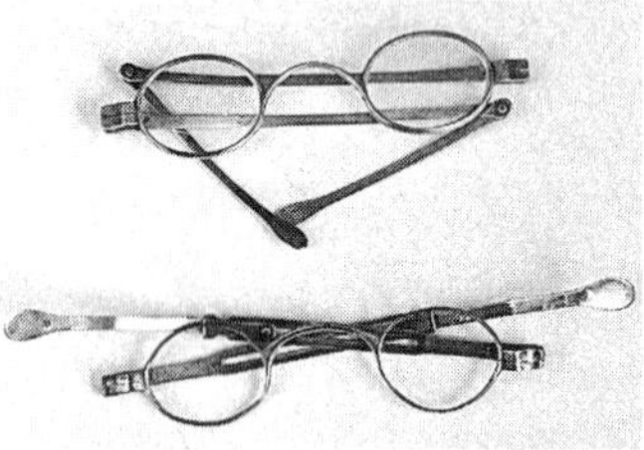

Two pairs of Georgian silver spectacles:
top. with turn pin sides, c1826.
bottom. with sliding sides, c1827, 4½in (11.5cm) wide.
£85–125 each *PC*

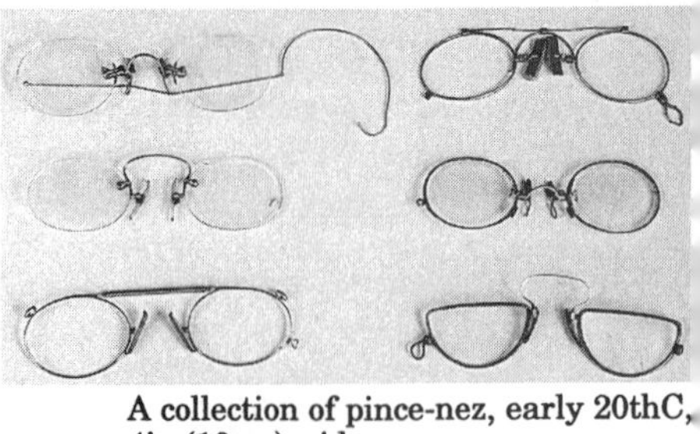

A collection of pince-nez, early 20thC, 4in (10cm) wide.
£18–20 each *PC*

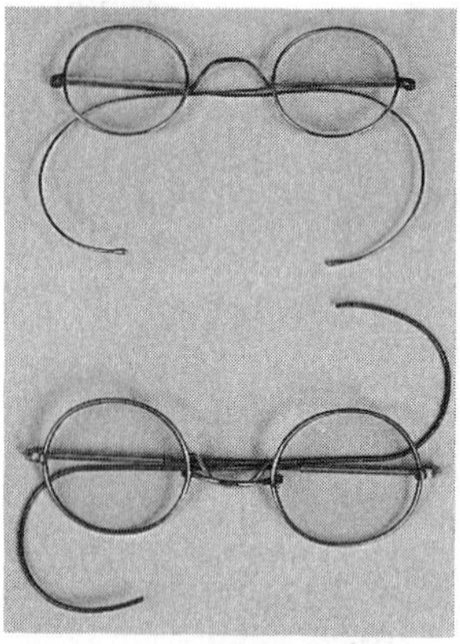

Two pairs of spectacles, with rolled gold frames, c1900:
top: Franklin bifocals, with oval lenses.
bottom. reversible spectacles.
£20–25 each *PC*

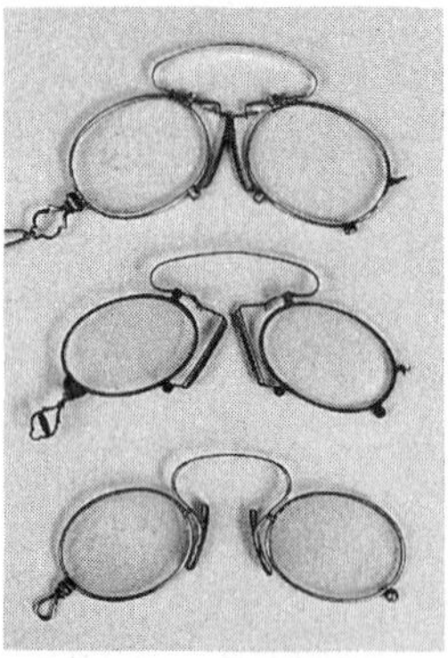

Three pince-nez, with rolled gold frames, c1860, 4in (10cm) wide.
£25–30 each *PC*

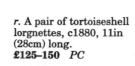

r. A pair of tortoiseshell lorgnettes, c1880, 11in (28cm) long.
£125–150 *PC*

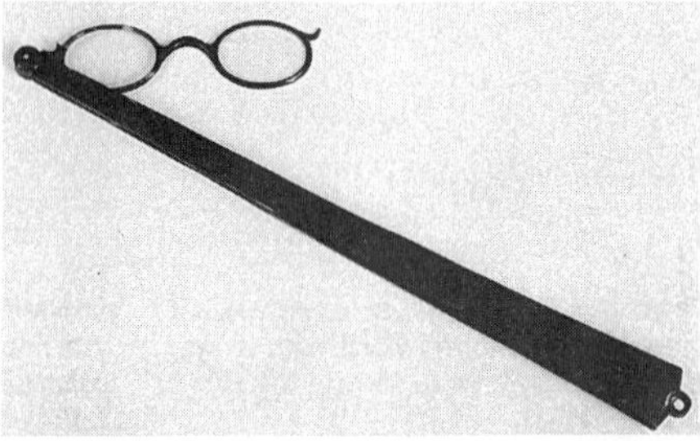

A tortoiseshell monocle, c1880, 1½in (4cm) diam.
£25–35 *PC*

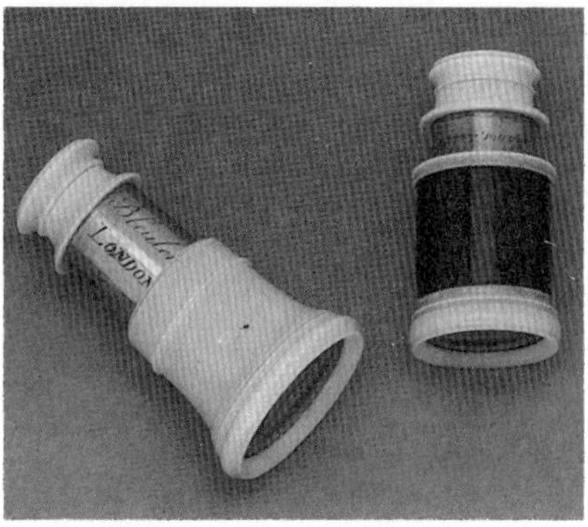

A spy glass, signed 'G Adams London', with single brass draw and turned ivory and mahogany tube, together with a Bleuler ivory spy glass.
£520–600 *S*

A pair of binoculars, with eyepiece and centre focusing, by Walter Locke & Co., Calcutta, 6in (15cm) high, with case.
£125–150 *PC*

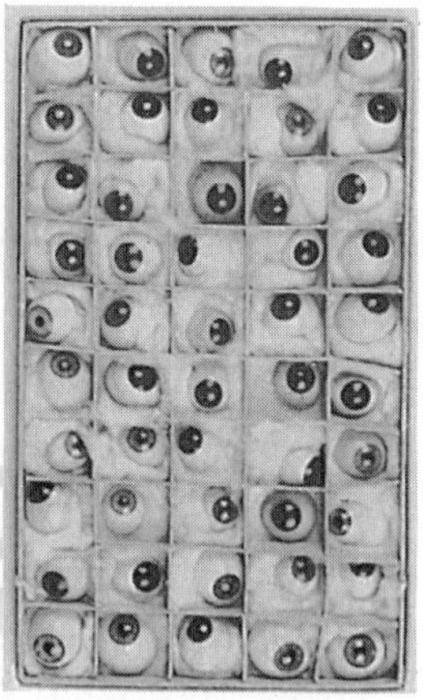

A set of 50 glass eyes of various colours, in maker's box.
£300–400 *CSK*

A trial eye, used by students, with an enamelled brass and bone scale, c1880, 2½in (6.5cm) high.
£25–35 *PC*

Use the Index!

Because certain items might fit easily into any number of categories, the quickest and surest method of locating any entry is by reference to the index at the back of the book.

This index has been fully cross-referenced for absolute simplicity.

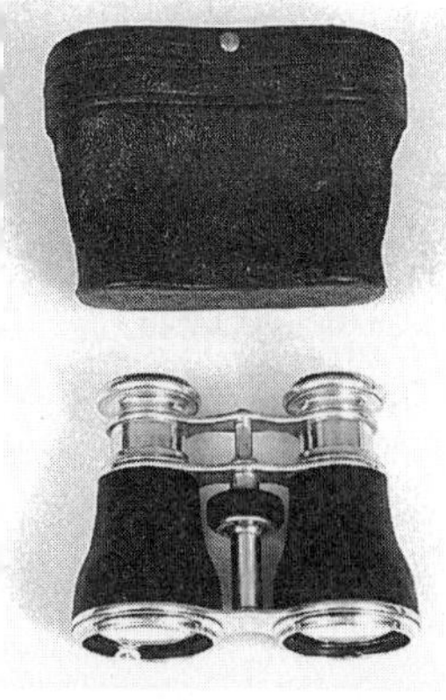

A pair of aluminium and leather covered opera glasses, by Dollond of London, c1900, 3in (7.5cm) high, with case.
£25–30 *PC*

A collection of 15 pairs of 'kitsch' spectacle frames, mostly French, 1950s.
£350–450 *CSK*

A pair of anodised aluminium opera glasses, c1920, 2½in (6.5cm) high.
£20–25 *PC*

A pair of grooved iron framed Nuremberg pattern Martin's Margins nose spectacles, with round lenses and horn visuals, damaged, early 18thC.
£600–700 *CSK*

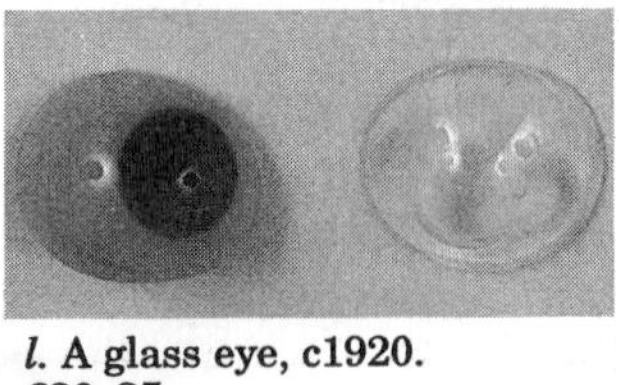

l. A glass eye, c1920.
£20–25
r. A haptic contact lens, c1950.
£1–2 *PC*

A pair of ivory and gilt brass opera glasses, c1860, 4½in (11.5cm) high, with case.
£100–125 *PC*

A pair of opera glasses, by Negretti & Zambra, c1910, with case.
£35–40 *PC*

A pair of opera glasses, by Gallo of Frankfurt, c1900, 5½in (14cm) high.
£20–25 *PC*

Two horn magnifying glasses, late 18thC, largest 3in (7.5cm) long.
£35–55 each *PC*

A plated brass magnifying glass, with a compass, c1900, 2in (5cm) long.
£20–25 *PC*

Three tortoiseshell magnifying glasses, late 19thC, 1½ to 2½in (4 to 6.5cm) long.
l. multiple. **£50–55**
r. & bottom. **£35–45** *PC*

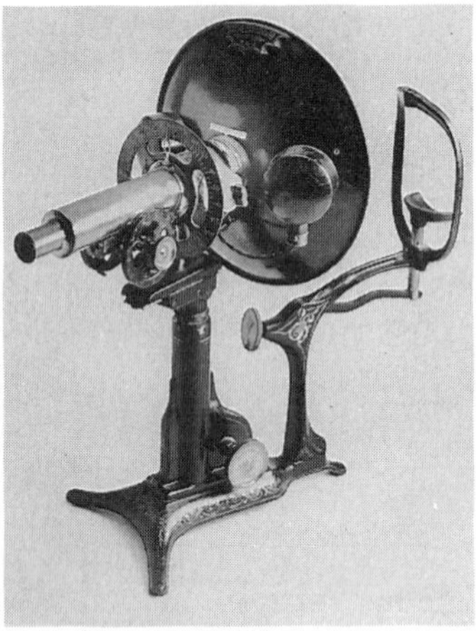

l. A Hardy's ophthalmometer with telescope, rack-and-pinion adjustment, dial graduated 0-165, electric illuminant and adjustable chin rest, on japanned base with gilt decoration, 23in (59cm) long.
£400–600 *CSK*

A brass magnifying glass, c1880, 1in (2.5cm) diam.
£10–15 *PC*

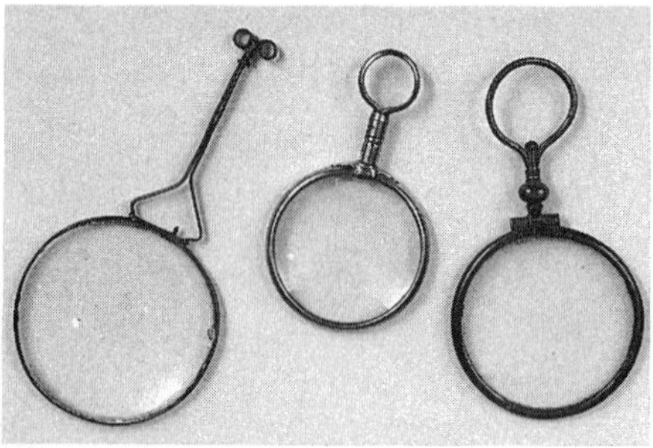

Three magnifying glasses:
l. copper 'Nuremberg' style, late 17thC, 4in (10cm) long.
£120–140
c. & r. metal, 19thC, largest 3½in (9cm) long.
£15–35 each *PC*

An ophthalmoscope, by May, for looking at the back of the eye, in original case, c1920, 6in (15cm) wide.
£45–55 *PC*

CAMERAS

A Kodak Brownie No. 2. Model A folding camera, with wooden lens board and red bellows, c1903, 7in (17.5cm) wide.
£35–40 *HEG*

A Kodak Brownie No. 2 camera, with blue box, cased, 4in (10.5cm) long.
£15–20 *HEG*

A wood and brass half plate camera, with red bellows, maker unknown, c1900, 12in (30.5cm) high.
£120–150 *HEG*

A Kodak Brownie Six-20 Model F camera, with brown and gold case, 4½in (11.5cm) long.
£10–15 *HEG*

A Kodak No. 2 Hawkette brown Bakelite Premium camera, 1930s, 7in (17.5cm) high.
£20–25 *HEG*

A Coronet Midget camera, with green body, boxed, c1930, 1½in (4cm) high.
£70–80 *HEG*

An Ansco Memo camera, No. 26738, with a Wollensak Velostigmat f/3.5 lens, in maker's leather case, condition 4F.
£250–300 *CSK*

A Pentax ES camera, No. 6530414, with an Asahi Optical Co. SMC Takumar f/1.4 50mm lens No. 5739160, condition 3F.
£160–200 *CSK*

A Robot Royal Model III camera, by Berning & Co., Germany, No. G118017, with a Schneider Xenar f/2.8 38mm lens No. 3585546, in maker's ever ready case, condition 4G.
£360–400 *CSK*

A Canon camera, No. 67693, with a Canon 50mm f/2 lens, No. 11107, condition 4F.
£270–300 *CSK*

A Canon 7 camera, No. 931275, with a Canon 50mm f/0.95 lens, No. 19994, in maker's ever ready case, condition 4F.
£550–600 *CSK*

l. A Canon Camera, No. 104510, with a Canon Serenar f/1.9 50mm lens, No. 23738, condition 5F.
£200–250 *CSK*

Camera Condition

Some of the cameras in this section have a condition code which relates to the table below. The first digit refers to cosmetic condition and the second to mechanical condition. A good/average camera will score 5F. The condition class given is only a guide to the AVERAGE condition of a piece. Specific defects may not be noted.

Cosmetic	Mechanical
0 - New, never used, sold with warranties.	**A** - As new, functioning perfectly, with factory and/or dealer warranty.
1 - As new. No warranty but with box or original packaging.	**B** - As new, functioning perfectly, but not warranted.
2 - No signs of wear. No packaging.	**C** - Everything functioning, recently cleaned or overhauled, and guaranteed.
3 - Very minimal signs of wear.	**D** - Everything functioning, major functions professionally tested.
4 - Signs of light use, but not misuse. No other cosmetic damage.	**E** - Everything functioning, major functions professionally tested.
5 - Complete, but showing signs of normal use or age.	**F** - Not recently cleaned, lubricated or overhauled. Accuracy of shutter or meter not guaranteed.
6 - Complete, but showing signs of heavy use. Well used.	**G** - Fully functioning. Shutter speeds and/or meter probably not accurate. Needs adjusting or cleaning only.
7 - Restorable. Some refinishing necessary. Minor parts may be broken or missing.	**H** - Usable, but not fully. Shutter may stick on slow speeds. Meter may not work.
8 - Restorable. Refinishing required. May be missing some parts.	**J** - Not usable without repair or cleaning. Shutter meter, film advance may be stuck, jammed or broken.
9 - For parts only or major restoration.	**K** - Probably not repairable.

A Canon camera, No. 41273, with a Canon Serenar f/1.9 50mm lens, No. 30650, condition 3F.
£320–370 *CSK*

A Canon P camera, No. 756677, with a Canon light meter, and a Canon 50mm f/1.2 lens, No. 25490, condition 4F.
£350–400 *CSK*

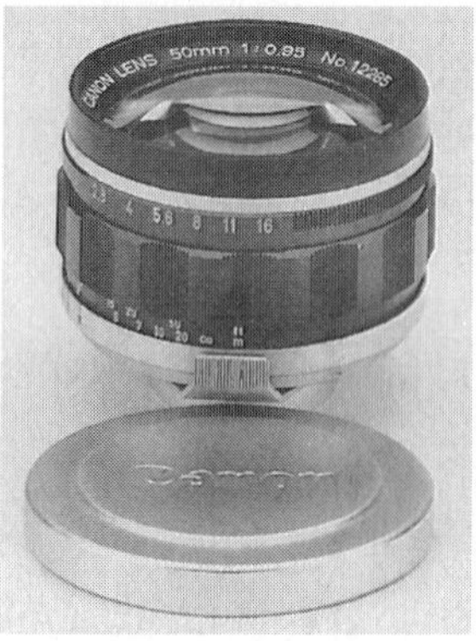

A Canon 50mm f/0.95 lens, No. 12285, with caps, in maker's case, condition 4F.
£420–500 *CSK*

A Le Coultre Compass II camera No. 2414, with a CCL3B anastigmat 35mm f/3.5 lens, a Le Coultre rollfilm back, Le Coultre tripod and film holders, in a maker's plush lined, fitted, pigskin case with outer canvas cover, condition 3F.
£4,500–5,000 *CSK*

An 18 by 24mm Ducati camera, No. 4005, with a Ducati Vitor f/3.5 35mm lens, No. 8610, condition 4F.
£1,000–1,200 *CSK*

A 120 rollfilm No. 1 Kodak camera, by Eastman Kodak Co., Rochester, NY, model D, No. 19517, with a swinging lens, condition 4F.
£250–300 *CSK*

r. A mahogany 5in square wet plate sliding box portrait camera, a Derogy lens No. 19431, the plate holder with a detachable quarter plate insert, a lens attachment and Waterhouse stops, in a black leather cloth covered case, mid-19thC.
£1,000–1,500 *HSS*

A rollfilm No. 2 Kodak camera, No. 18478, by Eastman Co., Rochester, NY, with lens in shutter and lens plug, in maker's case, condition 5F.
£500–600 *CSK*

A Fisheye-Nikkor Auto f/2.8 8mm lens, No. 241150, F-fit, built in filters and caps, in maker's case, instruction booklet, in maker's box, condition 1F.
£1,200–1,700 *CSK*

A Hasselblad outfit, with assorted lenses and equipment, each in maker's original boxes, condition 1F.
£6,000–7,000 *CSK*

A Leica I Model A camera, No. 797, with Elmax f/3.5 50mm lens, in an ever ready case, with rangefinder, damaged, c1925.
£2,700–3,000 *S*

An 828 rollfilm Kodak Bantam Special camera, No. 14320, with a Kodak Ektar anastigmat f/2 45mm lens, No. 13151, in a Compur Rapid shutter, condition 4F.
£300–350 *CSK*

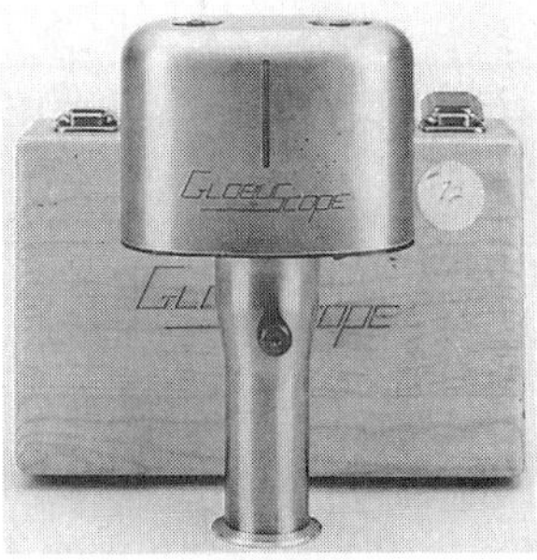

A 35mm Globuscope panoramic camera, No. 70, by Globus Brothers, New York, the baseplate engraved 'Pat. 4241985' and 'First 100 Cameras', and a Globuscope 25mm f/3.5 lens, spare film, gate masks and instruction booklet, in maker's fitted wood box, condition 3F.
£2,700–3,000 *CSK*

A mahogany and brass Sanderson Technical field camera, by Houghton Ltd., London, 11.5 by 9cm plates and a simple F. Cooke lens, by Taylor, Taylor and Hobson, London, a 7in f/6.8 lens, 3 mahogany slides, and a Cook extension lens, c1906.
£200–250 *N*

r. A 120 rollfilm Pilot 6 SLR camera, No. 13895, by K.W., Germany, with a K.W. anastigmat f/6.3 7.5cm lens, No. 289573, in maker's ever ready case, condition 4F.
£80–100 *CSK*

An 828 rollfilm Kodak Bantam Special camera, No. 8615, by Eastman Kodak Co., Rochester, NY, with a Kodak anastigmat Ektar f/2 45mm lens, No. 8034, in a Compur Rapid shutter, in maker's ever ready case, condition 3F.
£450–500 *CSK*

A 5 by 4in Crown Graphic Special camera, No. 991068, by Graflex Inc., Rochester, NY, with a Schneider Xenar f/4.7 135mm lens, No. 11354808, in a Copal No. 0 shutter, with instruction booklet, in maker's box printed 'Singer Graflex Division', and a Graflex 45 rollfilm holder RH/8, in maker's box, condition 1F.
£550–650 *CSK*

A Leica I Model A camara, No. 281, with anastigmat f3.5/50mm lens, shutter speeds 1/20 to 1/500, in a leather ever ready case, c1925.
£4,400–6,400 *S*

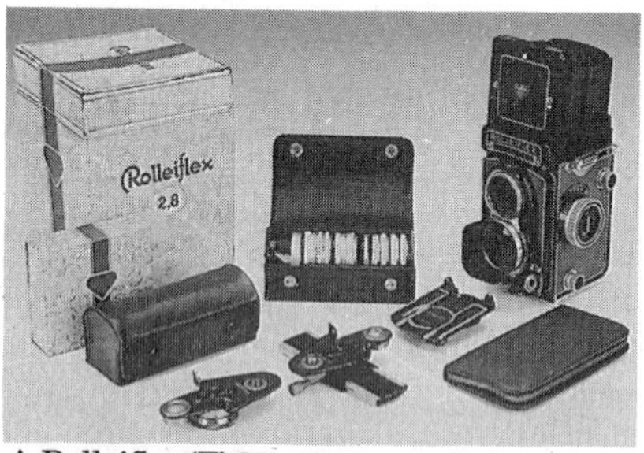

A Rolleiflex 'T' 6cm square twin lens reflex camera, in original box, and accessories comprising brown leather ever ready case, instruction book, pistol grip, quick release tripod head, panorama head, stereo slide bar, Rolleinar 3 cased set, Rolleinar 2 cased set, 2 Rollei 16 cased adaptor sets, with carrying case, and a 4 branch movie light.
£250–350 *HSS*

A screw-fit Leica II camera, No. 93826, with a Leitz Elmar 5cm f/3.5 lens No. 583842, condition 5F.
£420–500 *CSK*

An S. Lubin 35mm hand-cranked film projector, the oak case with feed and take-up arms and reels, carbon arc lamp, lantern lens, hand crank, the oak platform raised on a pair of iron legs, c1906.
£2,000–2,500 *S*

A Moy & Bastie 35mm motion picture camera, No. 174, with a Tessar f/3.5 lens, mahogany body with brass mounts and leather carrying handle, viewfinder mounted at the rear, c1910.
£1,000–1,200 *S*

A black enamelled tinplate 'Wheel of Life' zoetrope, the cylindrical drum sitting in a wrythen fluted cylindrical pillar, on a melon fluted circular pedestal foot, with red line borders, the interior painted cream, together with a hand coloured wood block print 'Wheel of Life' strip depicting a boy holding a parasol, balancing on a ball, early 19thC, 11½in (29.5cm) diam.
£280–320 *HSS*

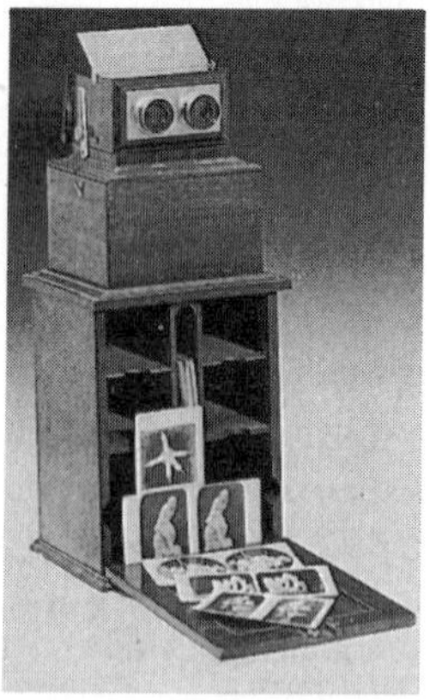

A Smith, Beck & Beck achromatic stereoscope, No. 1800, with brass eyepieces, and a mahogany case and stand for storage of stereoscope and cards, c1880, 23in (59cm) high.
£400–500 *S*

A screw-fit Leica I (a) camera, No. 44891, with hockey stick, metal retailer's label 'Messter-Berlin', and a Leitz Elmar f/3.5 50mm lens, condition 5F.
£850–1,000 *CSK*

A black screw-fit Leica camera, Standard No. 171872, with a Leitz Elmar 5cm f/3.5 lens, No. 242505, condition 5F.
£500–600 *CSK*

A wet plate Bellows camera, by Meagher of London, with mahogany body, maroon leather cloth bellows, fitted with a Newton & Co. of Liverpool lens, with 3 double plate holders.
£400–600 *HSS*

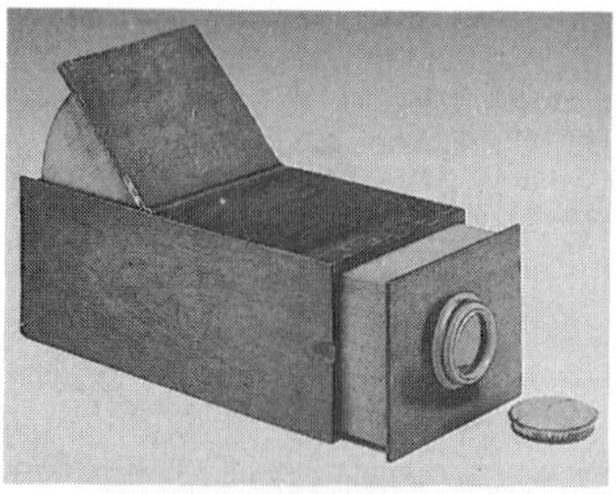

A mahogany sliding box camera obscura, the simple lens with screw cap, sliding box focusing, angled mirror and glass screen under hinged cover, early 19thC, 14in (35.5cm) long.
£1,200–1,500 *S*

Miller's is a price GUIDE not a price LIST

SILVER

THE STATE OF THE MARKET

The market for silver remains buoyant despite the fact that the effects of the recession are still with us. There are too many people chasing too few objects of the best quality and, therefore, prices remain high for certain articles. The run-of-the-mill pieces in average condition seem to be holding their own, and it is probable that good turn of the century and post-war secondhand silver will see a marked increase in price in the coming years. The amount of good everyday commercial antique silver coming onto the market is still inexplicably limited, and the best examples have seen a definite rise in price.

Small collectables in all areas, such as boxes, early spoons, medical silver, wine related silver, mote and caddy spoons, have seen an increase in value over the last twelve months. Among the articles which seem not to have moved much recently are candlesticks, which remain in the doldrums, except for the unusual – especially if allied to a worthwhile provenance. Mid-18thC coffee pots have also remained static for the past year or two. Both of these will eventually creep up in price, and there are probably bargains available in what were, after all, the mainstays of the commercial silver market.

EARLY SPOONS

The study of early English silver spoons, focuses on a period of some 400 years, from the beginning of hallmarking in the early 14thC until the introduction of the flatware service in the early 18thC. Spoons are unique in that examples of hallmarks can be found without a break in continuity for that whole period, whereas other domestic silver was consigned to the melting pot when funds were required. The reason for this is that spoons were traditionally given as christening gifts (as they still are today) and the sentimental attachment was further reinforced when they were passed from generation to generation as heirlooms. Spoons were often made for local sale, and the provincial marks they bear often add to the charm and interest of the piece. Learning how to assess an early spoon can take many years of experience. As with all antique silver, condition is extremely important; it should be as near mint condition as possible, and yet should show signs of use consistent with its age. This can be broken down into the following:

- The patina on silver is a combination of all the little nicks and scratches on the surface of the metal, and the results of acclimatisation of the metal to the atmosphere. The net result is that the metal acquires a 'skin' which looks silky and at the same time resists tarnishing, unlike new silver which will immediately show fingermarks if handled and which will tarnish overnight.
- Any hallmarks, whether in the bowl or on the stem (handle) of the spoon, should be clearly legible.
- Spoons with cast finials (such as seal tops, apostles, etc.), would originally have been gilt. This was done not only for its decorative effect, but also to disguise the fact that the castings were often well below standard and were consequently greyer in colour. This gilding should remain over most of the surface of the finial except the most vulnerable prominent points.
- There is often die-struck decoration to the bowl back and stem on trefid spoons (known as laceback trefids). Occasionally, engraved decoration will be found on the stems and bowls of West Country seal top and apostle spoons (notably Barnstaple), and of a different type on the handles of some later London trefids. Any contemporary decoration should be crisp and clear.

In an ideal world, these points would suffice. However, there are many pitfalls, some of which are a result of fair wear and tear, and others which are the result of attempts at improvements or restoration:

- The bowls of spoons will often have become extremely worn by years of use. This not only makes the spoon unpleasant to use, but also drastically affects the value. Reworking of bowls to draw the metal back to the worn areas can destroy the shape of the bowl, ruin the patination and distort any hallmark in the bowl. It will also reduce the gauge of metal in the bowl, so weakening it. Sometimes minor wear will be dealt with by filing across the bowl tip, so shortening the bowl and again spoiling the shape.
- English spoons were always wrought in one piece, so there should be no soldered joints except where a cast finial has been applied to the stem. The joints used for finials are quite distinctive: on London spoons a V-shaped joint will be seen below the finial, and on provincial spoons a 'lap' or stepped joint was used. Any other visible solder joint is a repair, and this will considerably affect the desirability of the spoon.
- Over the years spoons may have changed hands many times and often owners would engrave their crest or

initials on their heirloom. This engraving, despite being a genuine part of the spoon's history, unfortunately reduces the appeal for the purist collector and, therefore, the value on the market. Worse, though, is the practice of erasing this engraving. This will destroy any patination and probably leave the metal thin and bright.
- Another horror occasionally encountered is the Victorian practice of 'improving' their silver by embossing fruit and flowers all over the plain surfaces of earlier silver, and then gilding the lot. Spoons did not escape this practice, and should you be offered a rare 17thC 'berry' spoon, be very cautious.

There are, of course, instances where condition is not everything. In recent years there has been a massive rise in interest in provincial marks on early spoons. Should a spoon come up at auction with a very rare mark (say Dublin 1680 or Lewes c1640) the fact that it has slight bowl wear or a later crest will have a less detrimental effect on the price than it might on a London example.

Fakes and Alterations

Thankfully there are very few fake spoons around that would fool someone with knowledge, but it is worth bearing in mind what to look for:

- They can be cast from an original. This can be easily spotted in most cases as the surface has a sandy look to it and the hallmarks look 'fuzzy.' Cast spoons generally do not have the sharp edges associated with good originals, and often feel 'greasy' to the touch.
- Fake marks have occasionally been encountered on conventionally wrought, often newly made spoons. The punches for the marks usually lack the correct detailing, and are often 'soft' – that is they have been struck using punches or stamps made of soft metal – which quickly lose their sharpness.
- Over the years fashions among collectors have changed. In the late 19thC most collectors wanted examples of London apostle spoons and nothing else. This led to the practice of removing the finials from quite genuine seal top spoons and replacing them with fake apostles. The new finials were frequently not gilt, and usually the finial looks disproportionately large for the spoon as seal top spoons generally had less substantial stems than apostle spoons. Because it was not fully understood how finials were joined to the stems, these altered pieces often show no sign of jointing at all.

Things to Look Out for:

Remember that the early spoon makers were not as fussy as we might be today. They might set themselves a daily production target and set to work. The quality of finish on spoons varies enormously, and you will often find signs of original filing and hammering. Die-struck rat-tails (the rib which runs down the back of the bowl) and laceback decoration can be mis-struck, giving a double impression. Worn dies can be a cause of poorly defined decoration as much as subsequent wear to the spoon. Some spoons are quite noticeably asymmetrical and always have been.

Once a spoon left the maker's workshop and was put to use, it began to build its patination and show signs of how it was used. Concentrate on this aspect as it is where most fakers let themselves down. The greatest wear will probably be to the bowl. When used for stirring or eating, the tip of the bowl will take the brunt of the abrasion and often a series of parallel scratches can be seen on the underside of the bowl at the point of wear. As the spoon is repeatedly put down on flat surfaces, the points of contact will acquire a slightly different patina from the surrounding areas. This can often be seen on the rat-tails of trefids as a slight flattening, and less obviously, where the handle touches the surface. One may occasionally notice a slight flat-spot at the point of contact on the rim of the finial in the same way.

Another sign to look for is some quite noticeable 'nicking' to the side of the stem where it joins the bowl. This feature is found more on trefids than on earlier types and is a result of the spoon having been knocked on the side of a plate or bowl to remove some tenacious morsel of food. It will generally be found on both sides of the stem, but slightly more heavily on the same side as the bowl wear (reflecting the right or left-handedness of the user).

Finally, familiarise yourself as much as possible with the feel of a 'right' spoon. Take the opportunity to handle early spoons whenever there is a collection for sale at auction, and get to know dealers who stock early spoons. They are generally enthusiasts themselves and will take great pleasure in pointing out the pros and cons of particular specimens and will help you build a worthwhile collection.

Henry Willis

SILVER
Baskets

A George III swing-handled pedestal sugar basket, with thread edging, pierced and bright cut sides, on a pedestal base, with blue glass liner, by Peter and Anne Bateman, London 1891, 5½in (14cm) wide, silver 4.8oz.
£350–550 *Bea*

A George II silver bread basket, the detachable swing handle applied with a rococo cartouche engraved with a crest, the basket engraved with a coat-of-arms, and later inscription beneath the base, marked on reverse, maker's mark of Samuel Herbert & Company, London 1754, 14½in (37cm) long, 44oz.
£5,000–6,000 *C*

The inscription reads 'E. Dono B. Cust Baronetti Augst 31 1775'.

An early George III cake basket, with gadroon and shell cast rim, pierced sides, the centre engraved with the arms of Sir William Middleton 5th Baronet, by William Penstone, London 1770, 15½in (39.5cm) long, 45oz.
£4,000–4,500 *AG*

A Victorian swing-handled basket, decorated with foliate and strap engraving within a floral border spaced with 6 oval embossed floral medallions, stylised rope handle, by Thomas Bradbury & Sons, Sheffield 1882, 11in (28cm) diam, 15oz.
£400–500 *L*

A George II silver bread basket, on 4 shell and wheatear feet, later engraved with a coat-of-arms, maker's mark of Frederick Kandler, marked under base, London 1750, 15in (38cm) long, 67oz.
£20,000–25,000 *C*

A George III boat-shaped silver fruit basket, with beaded rim, the sides with chased swags on pierced wave patterned ground, loop handles, on pierced bracket feet with claw-and-ball supports, by George Smith, London 1817, 11in (28cm) wide, 14.35oz.
£850–1,000 *AH*

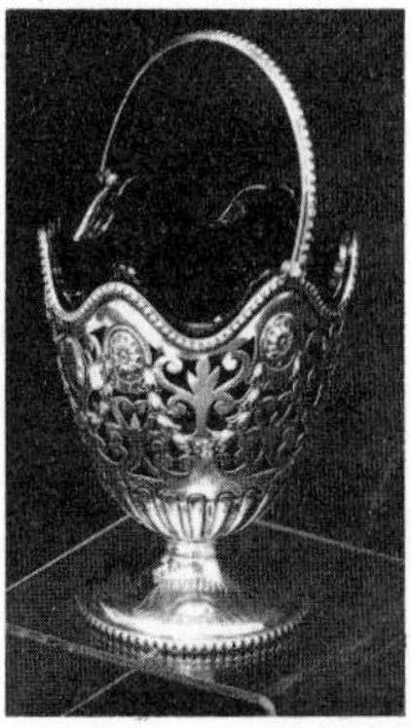

l. A Victorian sugar basket, with deeply waved beaded rim, beaded plain foot and swing handle, the body pierced with scrolling foliates, stamped with petalled medallions joined by festoons of flowerheads, with fluted lower section, with blue glass liner, by George Unite of Birmingham, Chester 1900.
£300–400 *DA*

A George III silver cake basket, by Burrage Davenport, London 1772, engraved with 2 later crests, 13in (33.5cm) wide, 25oz.
£1,700–2,000 *S(NY)*

A William IV swing-handled basket, heavily chased overall, the centre engraved with a full coat-of-arms, by Howard and Hawksworth, Sheffield 1835, 5in (12.5cm) diam, 34.75oz.
£1,000–1,500 *L*

Baskets

Silver baskets became fashionable from c1730, and were used in the centre of a table to hold fruit, bread, cakes or sweetmeats. Styles and shapes vary, but up to the end of the 18thC most had some form of pierced decoration. Chased decoration featuring flowers, shells, foliage and S-scrolls was popular during the reign of George IV. This type of basket with an unpierced body remained popular until the end of the 19thC.

The intricate pierced decoration on early baskets needs careful checking for damage or signs of previous repairs. On many baskets the rim has been folded over by having excess weight placed on top. Any basket which stands on 4 feet should be checked, as the feet are easily pushed up through the body and are also prone to cracking.

A Victorian silver cake basket, with openwork foot, maker's mark obscure, Birmingham 1897, 14in (35.5cm) long, 26.6oz.
£1,000–1,200 *SLN*

An Edward VII cake basket, pierced and bright cut with festoons and foliate motifs, with thread edging in 18thC style, by Lambert and Co., London 1901, 10in (25cm) long, 11.6oz.
£300–400 *Bea*

A George III Irish sugar basket, with fluted swing handle, by George West, Dublin 1799, 7in (17.5cm) long, 7.75oz.
£350–450 *L*

Bowls

An Edwardian bowl, the undulating border applied with flowers, the sides pierced with exotic birds and flowers and with a central cartouche, on 4 cast pierced shell and scroll feet, by Sydney Bellamy Harman, 1902, 9in (22.5cm) long, 18oz.
£450–500 *P(EA)*

An Edwardian silver monteith, with lions' heads ring handles, by Charles Stuart Harris, London c1902, 11in (28cm) diam, 68oz.
£2,250–3,000 *SK(B)*

A Victorian punchbowl, in the style of a late 17thC monteith, with ornate cartouche and cherubs' heads to the shaped rim, gilt lined, by Charles Stuart Harris, London 1881, 8½in (21cm) diam, 29oz.
£800–1,000 *L*

A late Victorian round punchbowl, with C-scroll borders, blank scroll cartouche, on embossed round base, by C. S. Harris, London 1898, 11in (28cm) diam, 44oz.
£1,300–1,700 *DN*

A silver fruit bowl, with foliate handles, the centre engraved with a crest, some wear, maker's mark of S. Kirk & Son, Baltimore, marked under base, c1885, 12½in (32cm) long, 40oz.
£1,200–1,700 *CNY*

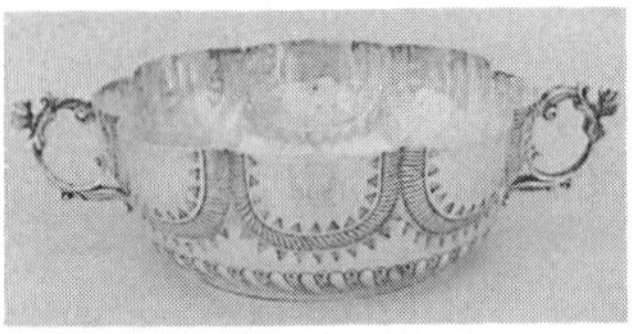

A bowl, by H. C. Lambert, Coventry St, London 1905, stamped, 10in (25cm) long, 19oz.
£400–500 *DN*

A George III punchbowl, with an elaborate coat-of-arms and the motto 'Aquila Non Capit Muscas', the foot with similar gadrooning, the interior gilded, by Charles Price, London 1813, 12in (30.5cm) diam, 63.2oz.
£6,800–7,200 *HSS*

A Victorian Britannia standard silver gilt punch bowl, with nulled border, on a fluted foot, by George Lambert, London 1882, 12½in (32cm) diam, 66oz.
£1,700–2,000 *DN*

A late Victorian punchbowl, the border embossed with a frieze of chrysanthemums and leaves, by Walker & Hall, Sheffield 1898, 9in (22.5cm) wide, 33oz.
£500–600 *DN*

Boxes

A rococo silver, silver gilt, 'Girl in a Swing' porcelain and polished steel mounted dressing table casket, surmounted by an arched triple looking glass with folding doors, opening to reveal the crimson velvet lined fitted interior, perhaps from the St. James's factory of Charles Gouyn, some slight damage, c1755, casket 10½in (27cm) wide, contained in a padded pale blue cotton lined wood box covered in black cotton.
£365,000–375,000 *C*

The recent discovery of this magnificent casket adds significantly to the knowledge of the productions currently attributed to the 'Girl in a Swing' factory. It was undoubtedly a special commission, and a tour de force of the jeweller's craft. The presence of the hitherto unrecorded 'Girl in a Swing' rococo plaques made specifically for it, and the contents including 'Girl in a Swing' scent bottles and étui, strongly point to Charles Gouyn of Bennet Street, St. James's, London, as the assembler.

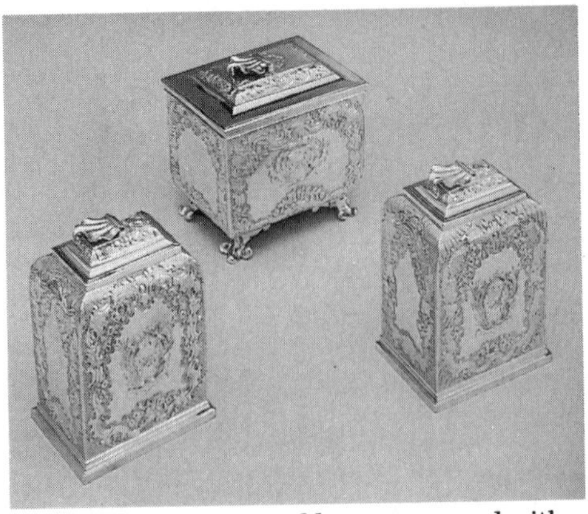

A George II silver tea caddy set, engraved with contemporary arms and crests, by Elizabeth Godfrey, London, c1744, the bases with scratch weights, 5½in (14cm) high, 46oz.
£23,000–25,000 *S(NY)*

The arms are those of Hoblyn of Bodrane and Nansahyden, Cornwall, with another in pretence.

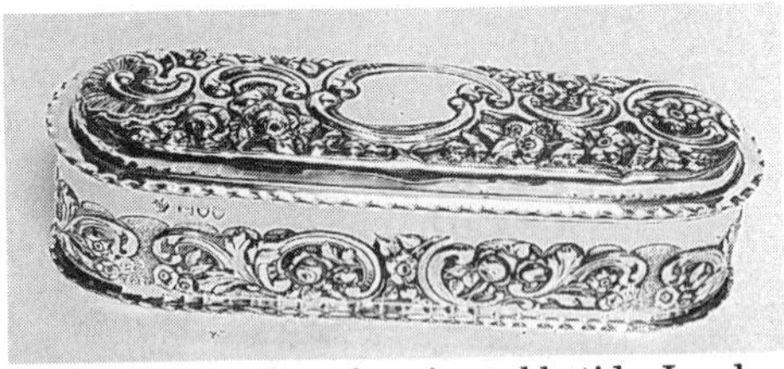

A silver dressing table tidy, London 1895, 7½in (19cm) long.
£350–375 *WN*

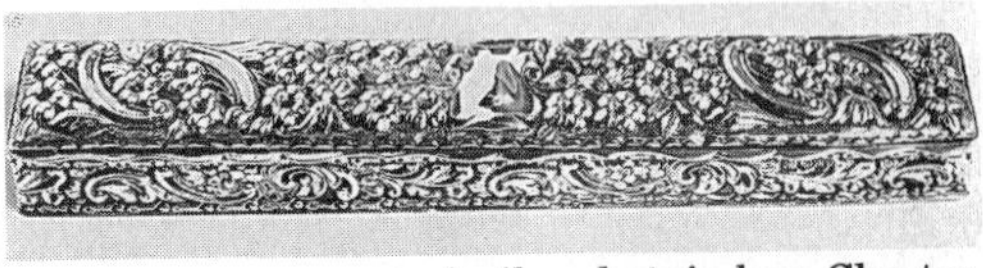

A silver hatpin box, Chester 1902, 9in (22.5cm) long.
£300–325 *WN*

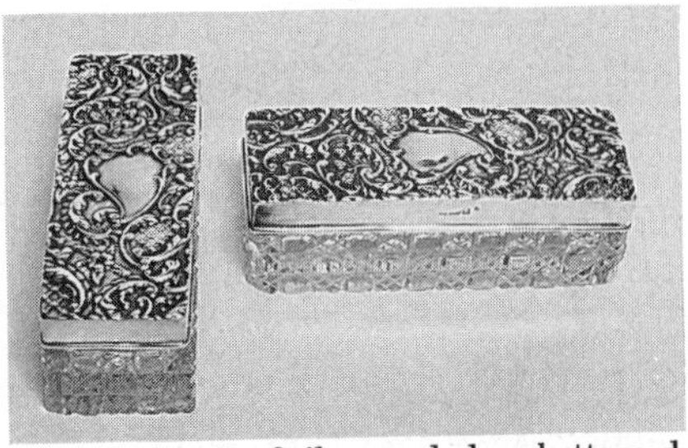

A pair of silver and glass bottomed dressing table boxes, Birmingham 1903, 4in (10cm) long.
£80–90 *WN*

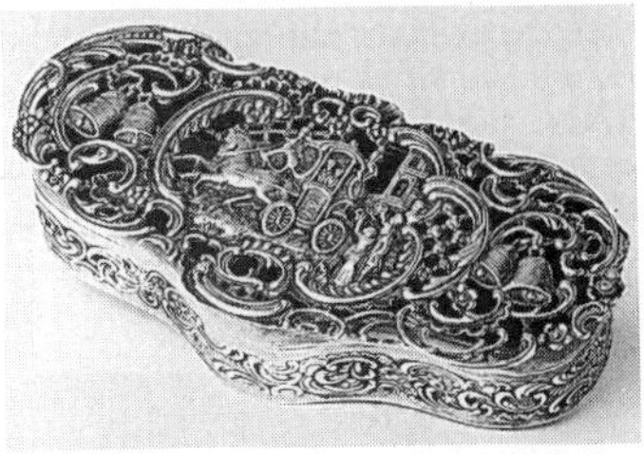

A silver pierced box, early 20thC, 6in (15cm) long.
£250–300 *DaD*

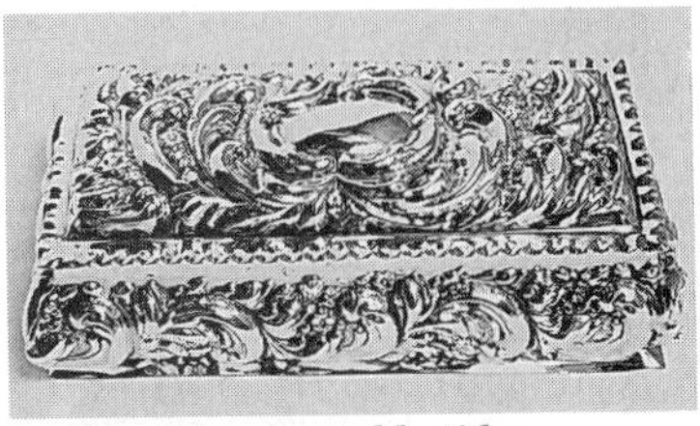

A silver dressing table tidy, Birmingham 1902, 5½in (14cm) long.
£250–300 *WN*

A George III tea caddy, by Thomas Hemming, London 1772, 7in (18cm) high, 9.25oz, with original red velvet and braid lined shaped and fitted shagreen box.
£2,500–3,000 *L*

A silver and glass bottomed dressing table tidy, c1903, 3in (7.5cm) long.
£40–50 *WN*

A silver and mother-of-pearl mounted tortoiseshell snuff box, the shell with plain silver and mother-of-pearl hinged cover, c1780, 3in (7.5cm) long.
£400–500 *Bea*

A Queen Anne tobacco box and cover, with rope-twist edging, the detachable cover embossed with beaded rope work, maker's mark 'B.E.', probably for Benjamin Bentley, London 1702, 4in (10cm) long, 4oz.
£900–1,200 *Bea*

A George IV gilt seal box, the lidded box embossed with the Royal coat-of-arms, within a chased oak leaf border, the interior of the lid stamped '8', by John Bridge, London 1825, marks rubbed, 7in (17.5cm) diam, 17.5oz.
£1,700–2,000 *L*

Candlesticks & Candelabra

l. A William IV chamber stick, 6in (15cm) diam, 3.25oz.
£200–250 *DaD*

A pair of George III chamber candlesticks, the detachable nozzles and bases with gadroon edging and plain conical extinguishers, by John and Thomas Settle, Sheffield 1818, 5½in (14.5cm) diam, 18.3oz.
£800–900 *Bea*

A set of 4 George II candlesticks, each with crested and numbered detachable nozzles, engraved with a coat-of-arms to the base, by John Cafe, 1748 and 1756, 10in (25cm) high, 90oz.
£6,000–7,000 *L*

A set of 4 German silver table candlesticks, the shaped domed bases richly chased with rococo decoration, the twisted baluster stems cast to match, engraved with the cypher 'CG' on drapery mantle below a crown, the base rims engraved 'HF' and dated '1759', 2 by Emanuel Abraham Drentwett, one by Caspar Kornmann, one by Johann Philipp Heckenauer, Augsburg, c1758, 8in (20cm) high, 60.5oz.
£35,000–37,000 *S(NY)*

The cypher is that of Carl Georg, Duke of Anhalt-Köthen, 1730–89, who married, in 1763, Princess Louise of Schleswig-Holstein-Sonderburg (1749–1812).

Candlesticks

The earliest English silver candlesticks date from the reign of Charles I (1625–49), but these are very rare.

Throughout the 17th and early 18thC candlesticks were functional rather than decorative, and were made in vast numbers in simple practical shapes for daily use. By the end of the 18thC they had almost doubled in size, to about 12in (30.5cm), and had detachable nozzles to prevent the molten wax from dripping down the sides of the stick.

In the early 19thC manufacturers were copying designs from the past, and by the end of the century surface decoration of candlesticks became highly elaborate to satisfy the Victorian taste for excessive decoration.

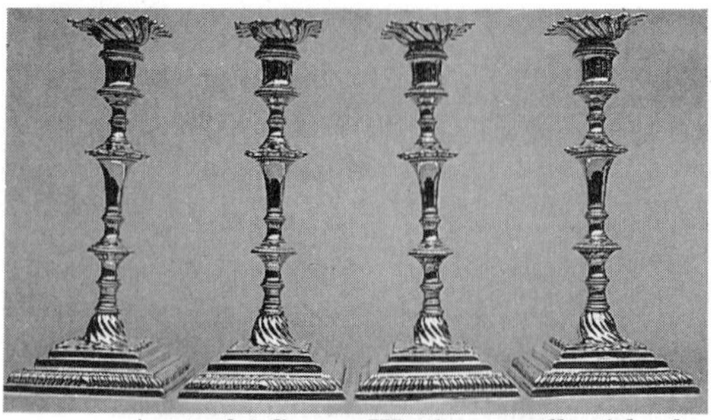

A set of 4 George III silver candlesticks, by Ebenezer Coker, London 1770, 10in (25cm) high, 20oz each.
£6,000–7,000 *AAV*

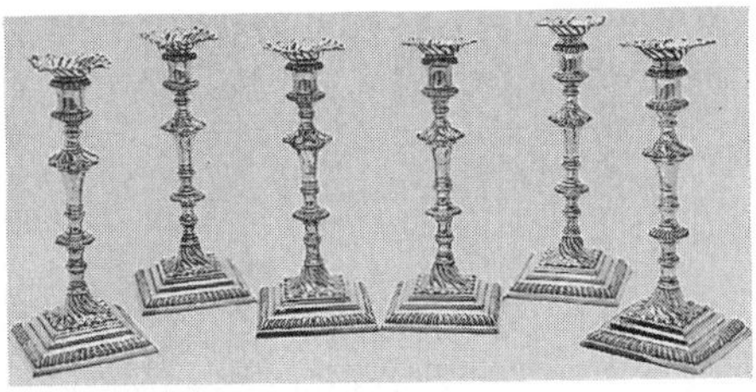

A set of 6 George III table candlesticks, with detachable nozzles, 2 engraved with the crest of a falcon, 4 with a leopard holding a branch, by William Cafe, London 1764, 10½in (27cm) high, 82oz.
£7,500–8,500 *L*

A set of 4 Edwardian Adam style candlesticks, the faceted stems with urn-shaped candleholders, detachable nozzles, on loaded bases, by Fordham and Faulkner, Sheffield, c1908, 12in (30.5cm) high.
£1,500–2,000 *WW*

A set of 4 George II cast table candlesticks, the shaped square bases, knopped stems and detachable nozzles with shell corners, by John Priest, London 1755, nozzles and bases numbered '1' to '4', 9in (22.5cm) high, 74.4oz.
£5,000–6,000 *Bea*

r. A pair of Victorian silver gilt four-light candelabra, the central urn finials topped by a bud, guilloche borders, detachable nozzles, by R. & S. Garrard & Co., in the manner of Paul de Lamerie, London, c1847, fully marked except one nozzle, 27in (69cm) high, 417.5oz.
£30,000–35,000 *S(NY)*

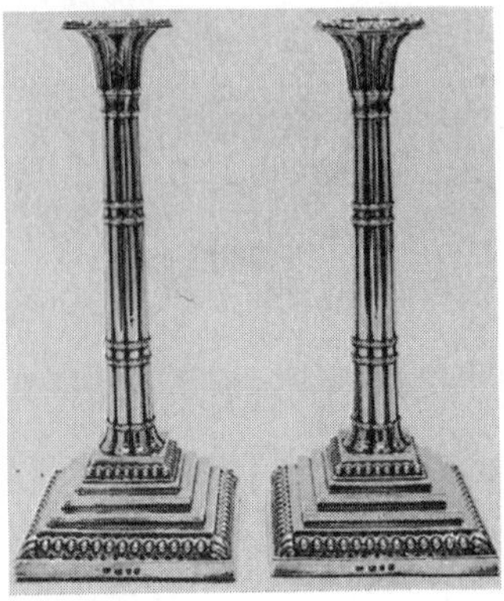

l. A pair of George III column candlesticks, with upper and lower beaded borders to the stepped square foot, classical column stems with palm capitals, by William Turton, London 1771, later removable sconces by Pairpoint, London 1925, 12½in (32cm) high, loaded, scratch weight for 24.5oz.
£1,300–1,700 *L*

Casters

A George II inverted pear-shaped caster, on a rope-twist decorated rising foot, with a conforming body band, the body engraved with a crest, maker's mark indistinct, London 1745, 6in (15cm) high.
£300–350 *CSK*

A pair of George III Adam style casters, on square bases with pierced campana-shaped lids, maker's mark rubbed, London 1805, 7in (17.5cm) high, 6.75oz.
£350–400 *L*

A set of 3 Queen Anne silver gilt casters, the finely pierced domed covers each with bayonet fittings and baluster finial, applied with bands of foliate and plain strapwork on a matted ground and with a band of shells, matted strapwork and foliate motifs, the bases with leaf-capped waved decoration, each engraved with crowned Royal cypher, attributed to Philip Rollos, c1705, largest 10½in (26.5cm) high, 56oz.
£140,000–150,000 *C*
The cypher is that of Queen Anne.

Centrepieces

A George II silver épergne, fitted with 4 detachable grape laden scroll branches each terminating in a detachable fluted dish with fruit and foliage border, the frame supporting a shaped oval bowl cast and applied with foliage scrolls, flowers and fluting, with upcurved handles formed as the head of Mercury and with goats' heads to the border, engraved with panels of scalework and twice with a coat-of-arms each within a rococo cartouche, the dishes each engraved with a crest, maker's mark of William Cripps, London 1754, marked on frame, bowl, dishes and 2 branches, 11in (28cm) high, 188oz.
£28,000–32,000 *C*

The arms are those of Sackville with Sambrooke.

A George II silver épergne, with 8 detachable leaf capped branches, 4 terminating in a detachable dish and 4 with a detachable basket, each on 4 scroll feet and with swing handle, the frame also supporting 4 detachable leaf entwined columns with detachable pierced canopy of pagoda form and detachable pineapple finial, the baskets and dishes each engraved with crest and motto, maker's mark of Thomas Pitts, London 1759, with later French control marks, 23in (58.5cm) high, 194oz.
£40,000–50,000 *C*

l. A George V table épergne, the central trumpet shaped vase with pierced border, supporting 2 sweetmeat dishes and 2 tapering vases, resting on a base with compressed sphere feet, Chester 1912, 29oz.
£600–700 *HSS*

A George III silver canopied épergne, with 9 baskets, engraved with contemporary arms and matching crests, by Thomas Hemming, London 1765, fully marked, 25in (63.5cm) high, 266.5oz.
£65,000–70,000 *S(NY)*

The arms are those of Montagu impaling Bulmer for Charles Greville, second son of Robert, 3rd Duke of Manchester, born in 1741, and married on September 20th, 1765, Elizabeth, daughter of James Bulmer.

A George III silver two-branch épergne, maker's mark of William Holmes, London 1790, the baskets each with a cut glass liner, 16in (40.5cm) high, 147oz.
£5,000–6,000 *L*

The arms are those of Porter, Lincoln and Kent, impaling Carr or Carre.

A George III silver basket épergne, engraved with contemporary arms and matching crest in rococo cartouches, by Thomas Pitts, London 1765, fully marked on stand and central basket, maker's mark on all pieces and lion passant on 4 branches, 26½in (67.5cm) wide, 166oz.
£20,000–24,000 *S(NY)*

A sterling silver épergne, with reticulated and engraved floral and scroll design, with monogram and dated '1900', 14½in (37cm) high, 85oz.
£3,500–4,000 *SK(B)*

A George III silver gilt basket épergne, the stand on 4 scroll supports linked by cast aprons of flowering foliage, detachable central basket and 4 circular baskets on detachable branches, later gilt, by Thomas Pitts, London 1767, fully marked, 15in (38cm) high, 91oz.
£7,000–8,000 *S(NY)*

A French silver centrepiece, with a figure of Plenty holding a cornucopia and laurel wreath, on a drum-shaped plinth applied with the Imperial eagle, the border of the bowl and the base of the plinth with inscriptions, engraved with maker's mark 'Christofle, Paris, 1866', 26in (66cm) high, 295oz.
£15,000–18,000 *C*

Cups

A George IV campana-shaped standing cup, with lower lobing and fruiting vine chasing to the upper rim, foliate decoration to the matted rim of the circular spreading foot, by C. B., Edinburgh 1821, presentation inscription dated '1921', 8in (20cm) high, 20.5oz.
£260–320 *L*

A Victorian chalice, the bowl half decorated with floral designs, on pricked ground, the six-sided stem with Gothic style knop, on spreading shaped foot, maker J.H., London 1891, 9in (22.5cm) high, 27.5oz.
£450–500 *L*

An American silver caudle cup, probably by John Coney, Boston, maker's mark 'IC' above fleur-de-lys on the base, dated '1676', 2in (5cm) high.
£3,000–3,750 *RIT*

An American silver can, modelled after a pottery example derived from China, engraved with contemporary crest of an arm holding a bleeding heart, by John Allen and John Edwards, Boston, c1695, engraved c1800 with initials 'AS to MC', marked 'IE' and 'IA', 4in (10cm) high, 6.2oz.
£43,000–48,000 *S(NY)*

John Allen, c1671–1760, and John Edwards, 1671–1746, had a brief partnership just before 1700.

A Victorian two-handled campana-shaped trophy cup, decorated in high relief with flowers and foliage, with scrolling acanthus handles and knopped stem, by Robert Harper, London 1862, 83.4oz.
£800–1,200 *Bea*

A Canadian silver chalice and paten, by Peter Nordbeck, Halifax, Novia Scotia, early 19thC, chalice 9in (22.5cm) high.
£3,800–4,200 *RIT*

A silver mounted ostrich egg cup, indistinct maker's mark on rim, probably early 17thC, 11½in (29.5cm) high.
£11,000–13,000 *C*

A set of 12 Victorian tumbler cups, engraved with the arms of Wakeham of Coton Hall, Co. Salop, by Arthur Sibley, London 1853, retailed by Gilliam, Serle St., London, 58oz, in a fitted baize lined oak case.
£8,700–9,500 *WW*

Cutlery

A set of 12 silver gilt fish knives and forks, with agate pistol grips, with engraved crests, maker 'M.B.', knives London 1813, forks Sheffield 1907, in a mahogany case.
£700–900 *RBB*

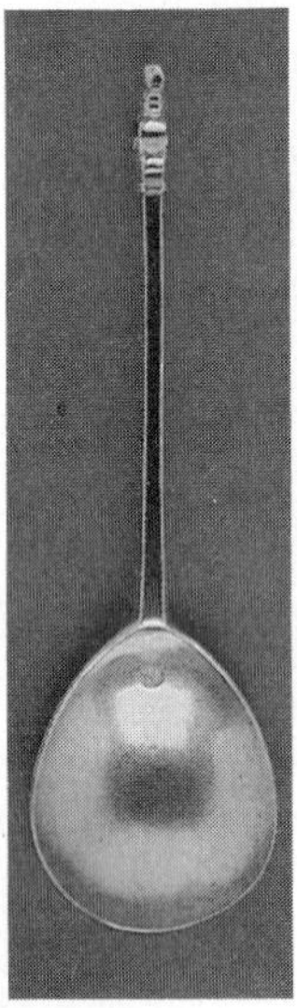

l. An Elizabeth I lion sejant silver spoon, with deep fig-shaped bowl and tapering stem, the finial parcel gilt, the reverse of the bowl engraved with initials 'WB', marked in bowl and on reverse of stem, London, 1592, 6½in (16.5cm) long.
£2,600–3,000 *C*

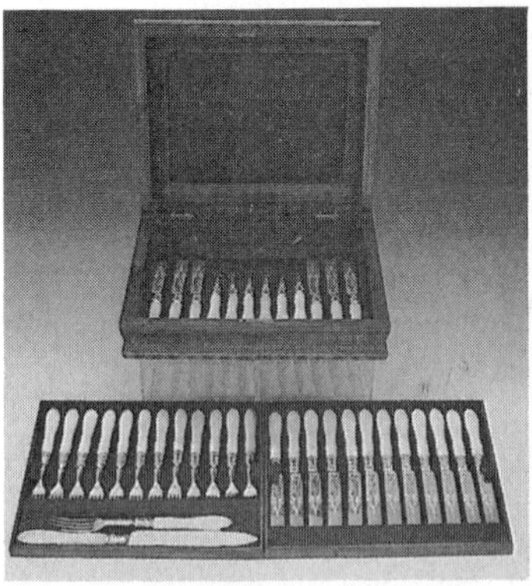

A set of 18 pairs of Victorian dessert knives and forks, with matching servers, with strapwork engraved blades and tines, acanthus leaf stamped ferrules and leaf capped carved mother-of-pearl handles, by Martin Hall & Co., Sheffield 1865, in a walnut case with blue baize fitted interior and 2 lift-out compartments.
£650–750 *HSS*

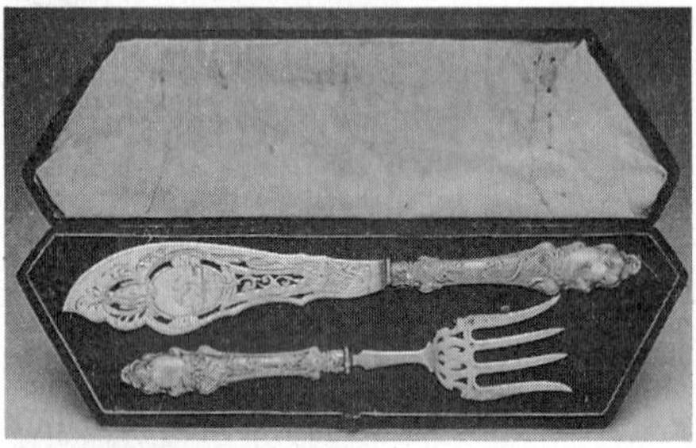

A pair of Victorian fish servers, the blade pierced and engraved with foliage enclosing a roundel bright-cut engraved with a swan and a smaller roundel above with 3 fish, the tine similarly decorated, both with stamped vine and pendant husk decorated handles, by Martin Hall & Co., Sheffield 1855, cased.
£350–450 *HSS*

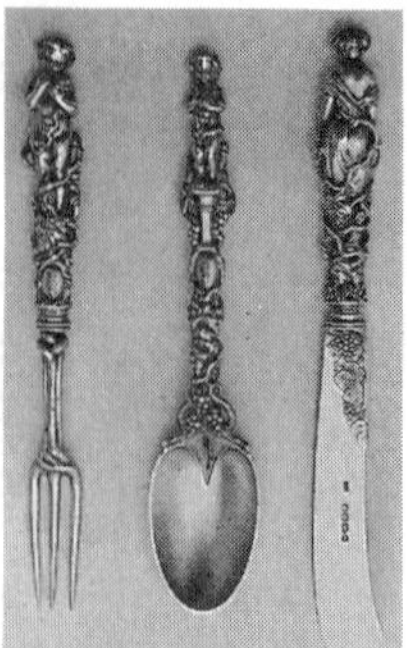

A set of Victorian figure utensils, probably by Francis Higgins, spoon 1815, knife and fork handles 1856, blade 1857, tines 1849, knife 8in (20cm) long, 6.5oz.
£350–450 *L*

A set of 12 George I silver Hanoverian pattern table forks, 10 engraved with contemporary arms, by Jane Lambe, 1723, 2 engraved with later crests and coronets, one engraved 'Nursery', by different makers, London 1719 and 1723, 26oz.
£1,500–1,800 *S(NY)*

l. A set of George III Irish silver cutlery, comprising 101 pieces, various makers, c1760–1812.
£5,000–6,000 *S(NY)*

An American silver and silver gilt Francis I pattern cutlery set, comprising 251 pieces, the silver mostly engraved with initial 'S', by Reed & Barton, Massachusetts, 20thC, 283oz.
£5,000–7,000 *S(NY)*

A pair of Victorian fish servers, with pierced and engraved blades, the knife with a vignette of a man fishing, the ivory handles each carved with a mermaid, Sheffield 1855.
£650–750 *L*

Figures

A figure of Morse Code, by The Goldsmiths and Silversmiths Company, London 1938, on a textured base, set on a wooden plinth with an inscribed silver plate, 12½in (32cm) high overall, 98oz.
£2,500–3,000 *L*

A canteen of George III and later cutlery, for 12 persons, Hanoverian and Old English patterns, engraved with initial 'M', London.
£1,200–1,700 *RBB*

Ewers

A pair of French silver ewers, by Charles Odiot, Paris, marked 'Odiot à Paris', and with an 'O' and a fluid lamp in a diamond shape cartouche, mid-19thC, 16in (40.5cm) high, 120oz.
£11,000–13,000 *SK(B)*

A silver figure of Mercury, holding the remains of a caduceus in his right hand, Italian/Flemish in 16thC style, on a marble pedestal base, 6½in (16cm) high.
£400–500 *S(NY)*

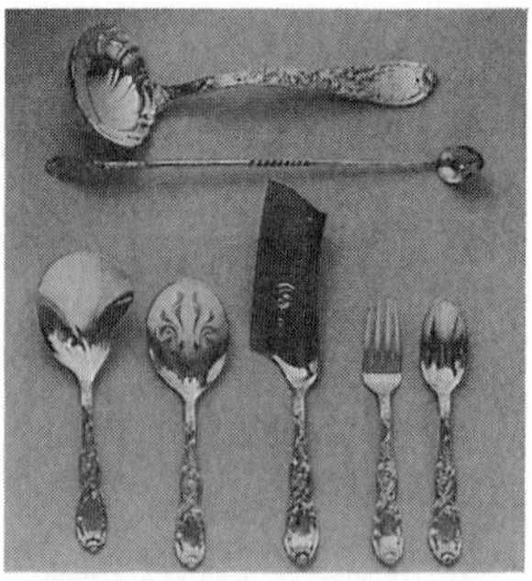

Nine American silver Chrysanthemum pattern serving items, some engraved with monograms, by Tiffany & Co., New York, c1885, 41oz.
£2,500–3,000 *S(NY)*

A French silver ewer and basin, both engraved with foliate cartouches on an engine turned ground, the ewer with a forked rustic handle capped by a spray of buds and leaves, ewer 15½in (39.5cm) high, basin 18in (45.5cm) diam., 133oz 10dwts.
£2,000–3,000 *S(NY)*

A French silver group of the Virgin and Child, on an ebony veneered and silver mounted base, damaged and repaired, stamped with 6 hallmarks, early 19thC, 13½in (34.5cm) high.
£1,900–2,200 *L*

The hallmarks indicate that the figure was made in Paris by Jean-Ange-Joseph Loque before 1809.

Flatware

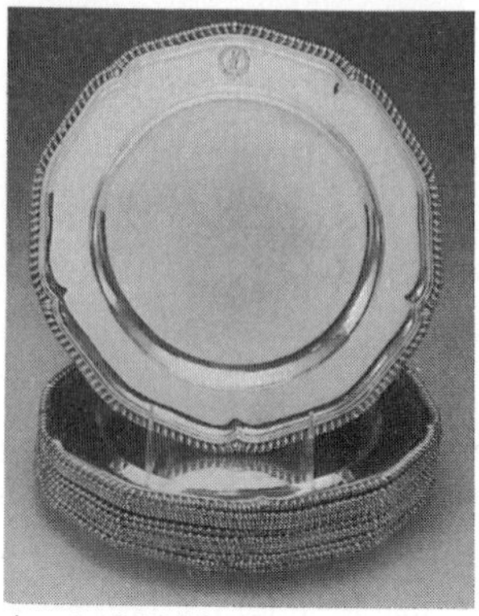

A set of 12 Victorian silver dinner plates, with shaped gadrooned rims, the borders engraved with contemporary crest within a motto, by R. & S. Garrard, London 1838, stamped, 9½in (24cm) diam., 183oz.
£3,800–4,200 *S(NY)*

The crest and motto is that of Marton, Capernwray Hall, in the county of Lancaster.

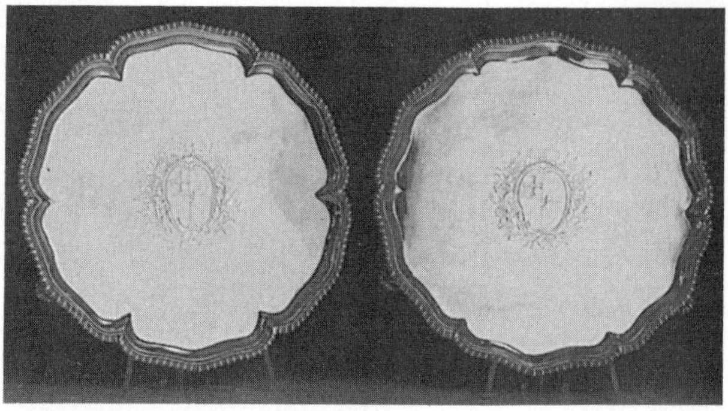

A pair of early George III salvers, engraved with the arms of Sir John Lambert in each centre, moulded and gadrooned borders, on fluted pad feet, by Ebenezer Coker, marks for London 1767 and 1769, 15in (38.5cm) diam.
£1,000–1,500 *AG*

A set of 6 Queen Anne silver soup plates, of plain form with broad rims, each engraved with a coat-of-arms, maker's mark of Philip Rollos, London 1706, 10in (25cm) diam., 109oz.
£28,000–33,000 *C*

These plates formed part of a large service made in 1706 and 1707 by Thomas Parr and Philip Rollos.

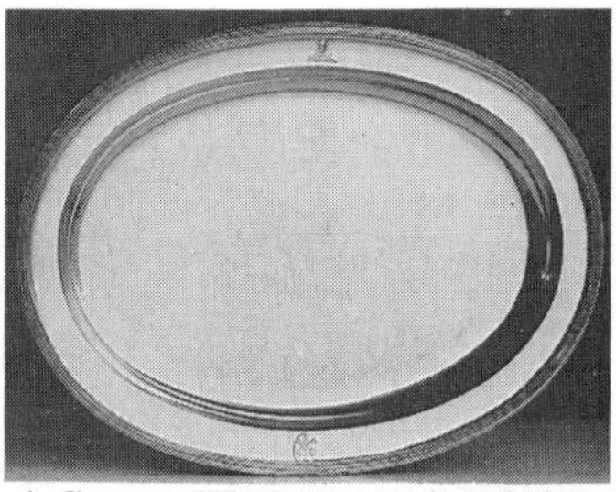

A George III plain serving dish, engraved with the arms and crest of Lawrence Monck of Caenby, Lincs, with reeded border, by W. Fountain, London mark 1798, 24in (61cm) wide.
£1,800–2,200 *AG*

A Elizabeth II plain salver, with concave corners, 4 volute feet, centred by the letter 'P', by Emile Viner, Sheffield 1963, 16½in (42cm) square, 63oz.
£600–700 *DA*

A Victorian silver gallery tray, by Mappin & Webb, Sheffield 1896, 115oz.
£1,200–1,700 *AAV*

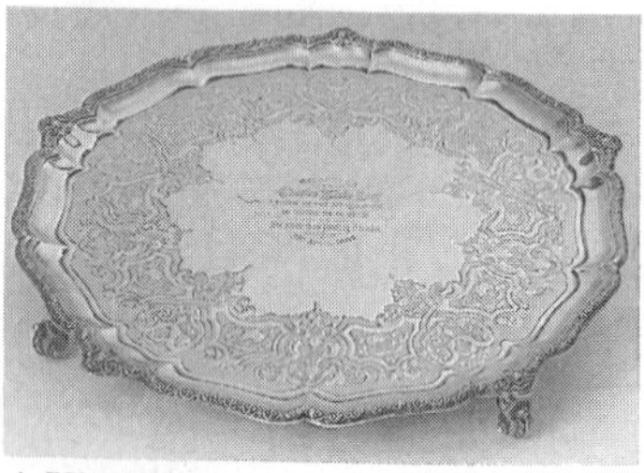

A Victorian tray, the centre with a presentation inscription, by Robert Garrard II, London 1882, 23in (59cm) long, 136oz.
£2,600–3,600 *WW*

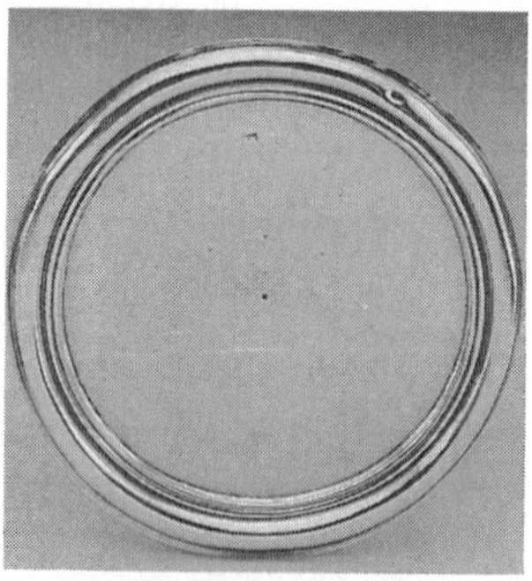

An American silver salver, plain with embossed rim of multiple mouldings, on a matching capstan foot, engraved underneath with contemporary initials 'S*P', marked on top 'EW', by Edward Webb, Boston, c1700–10, 6in (15cm) diam., 5oz.
£6,500–7,500 *S(NY)*

A two-handled tray, with shaped reeded border and dated cypher, by Mappin & Webb, Birmingham 1935, 22in (55.5cm) long, 81.5oz.
£1,000–1,500 *L*

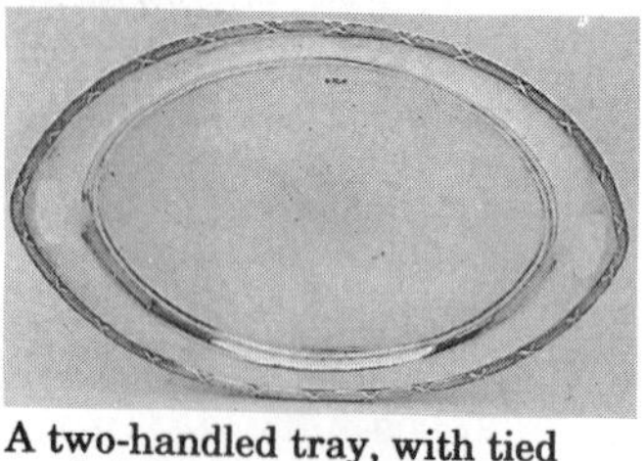

A two-handled tray, with tied reeded border, on 4 bun feet, Sheffield 1910, 23in (59cm) long, 83oz.
£800–1,000 *L*

r. A Victorian two-handled tray, with pellet border, engraved with fruiting vine decoration, within a scroll border, on 4 squat foliate feet, by Henry Wilkinson & Co., London 1891, engraved with cypher dated '1894', 28in (71cm) long, 116oz.
£2,000–2,500 *L*

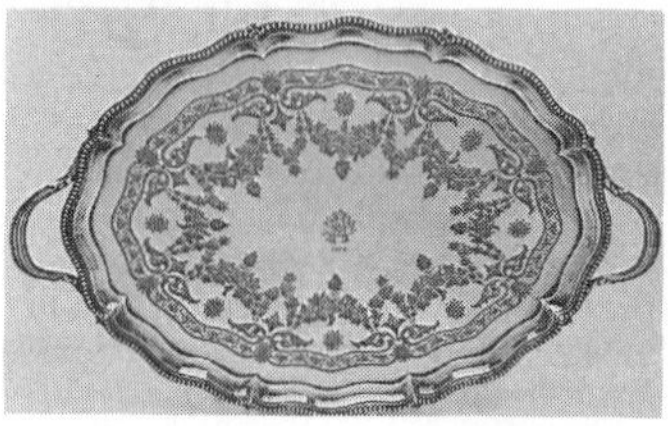

Inkwells

A Victorian silver mounted tortoiseshell inkstand, with foliate pierced gallery, 2 silver mounted glass inkwells with central box, engraved with monogram, the stand engraved 'Asprey & Sons, 166 New Bond Street', 1885, 9in (22.5cm) wide, and a silver mounted tortoiseshell paper knife.
£1,300–1,700 *C*

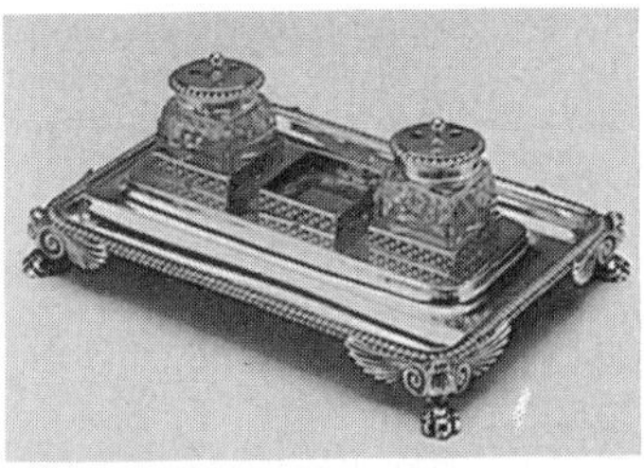

A George III three-division inkstand, with gadroon edging, on 4 winged paw feet, supporting 3 basketwork frames and 2 silver topped cut glass wells, by Thomas and Joseph Guest and Joseph Cradock, date letter removed, London, c1809, 10in (25cm) long, 26.5oz.
£550–750 *Bea*

A partners' inkstand, by Charles Stuart Harris, with gadrooned borders, pierced foliage scroll border motifs, a central sealing wax box, the cover as a taper stick with extinguisher, flanked by 2 glass ink bottles with hinged silver covers, on ball feet, London 1898, 9½in (24cm) wide, 26oz.
£900–1,200 *WW*

l. A Victorian inkwell and sunk centred tray, all on 3 scrolling bracket feet, by Francis Boone Thomas, marked London 1886, 9½in (24cm) diam., 14oz.
£460–600 *DA*

A George IV partners' inkstand, the base on winged foliate paw feet, by Samuel Roberts and George Cadman & Co., Sheffield 1822, 11½in (29cm) wide, 30oz.
£1,200–1,500 *WW*

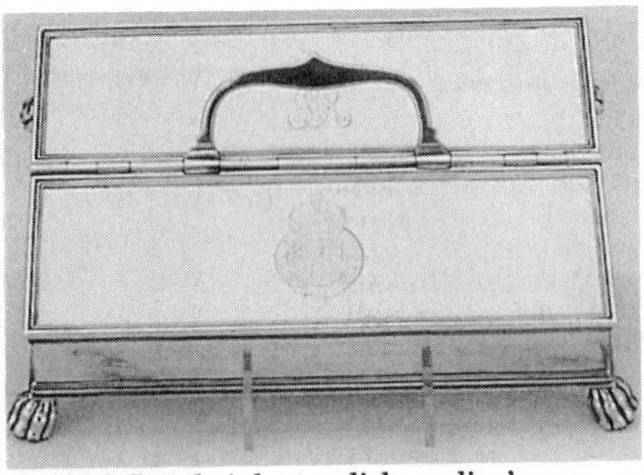

An 18thC style ink standish, on lion's paw feet, with central swing handle, one hinged cover engraved with the monogram of King George V with a crown above, the other with the Royal Armorial and motto within a garter cartouche with crown surmount, fitted with a cut glass inkwell, and a pierced pounce box, by Goldsmiths & Silversmiths Co. Ltd., London 1931, 11in (28cm) wide, 71oz.
£1,600–2,000 *CSK*

A contemporary newspaper clipping suggests that this inkstand was presented to Lord Rothschild, chairman of the Royal Commission on Gambling. The other members of the Commission were given scarlet or black leather covered despatch boxes, each bearing the Royal Cypher.

A Victorian parcel gilt inkstand, the base with foliate and scroll border, on 4 pierced scroll feet, raised centre section for the shaped square silver mounted bottles flanking the central melon shaped wafer box, supporting a taper stick with double scroll handle and extinguisher and detachable nozzle, by Henry Wilkinson, Sheffield 1846, 13½in (34cm) wide, 36.5oz without ink bottles.
£1,800–2,500 *L*

Miller's is a price GUIDE not a price LIST

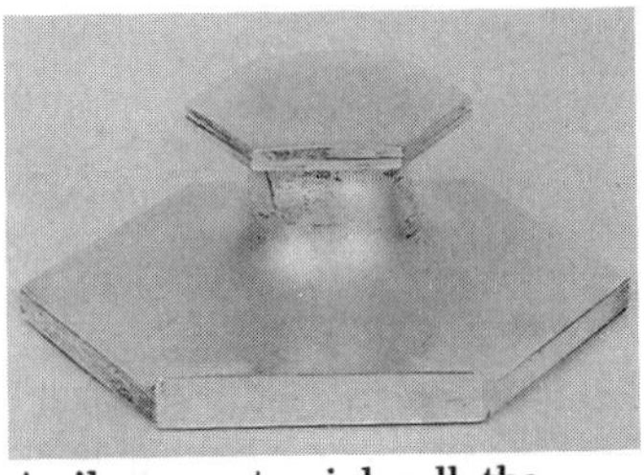

A silver capstan inkwell, the front curved for a pen rest, with a hinged cover, by Walker & Hall, Sheffield 1926, 10½in (26.5cm) wide.
£250–300 *P(EA)*

A Victorian silver inkwell, with gadrooned borders, embossed with birds, foliate scrolls, flowers and 2 moustached masks, the hinged lid engraved with a monogram, marked with a lion and date letter only on the bar restraining the cut glass jar, 4½in (11cm) diam., 4.5oz.
£150–200 *P(EA)*

Jugs

A George IV silver gilt jug, the scroll handle formed as a vine tendril with hinged slightly domed cover with detachable running fox finial, chased with bands of foliage on a matted ground and engraved with inscription, maker's mark of John Bridge, London 1829, marked on body, cover and finial, the base stamped 'Rundell Bridge et Rundell Aurifices Regis Londini', 11in (28cm) high, 92oz.
£8,500–10,000 *C*

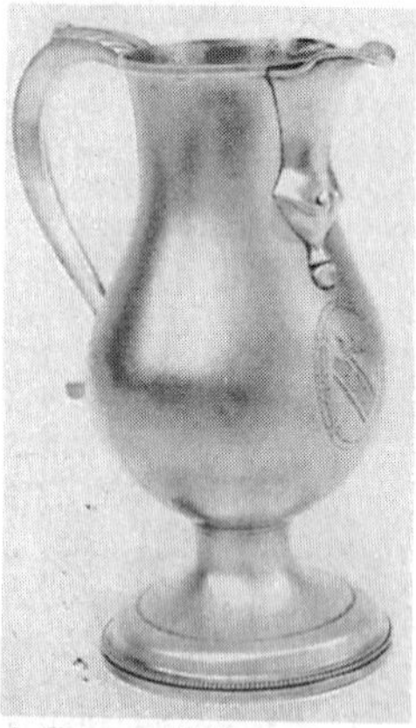

A George III beer jug, the leaf capped scroll handle with a heart shaped terminal, on a spreading beaded edge foot, by John Kidder, London 1786, 10½in (26.5cm) high, 31oz.
£4,000–5,000 *WW*

Mugs & Tankards

A George I mug, with scroll handle, initialled on thumbpiece, by John Farnell, London 1717, 4in (10cm) high, 7.3oz.
£500–700 *Bea*

A Victorian silver punch jug, with embossed rope and gadroon friezes and presentation inscription, by HH, Harrison Bros & Hawson, Sheffield 1893, 9½in (24cm) high, 42oz.
£900–1,000 *RBB*

Kettles

A George III silver tea kettle, with urn shaped double lamp with detachable cover, the partly fluted kettle with reeded spigot terminating in a lion's mask, with a carved ivory anthemion tap, a gadrooned shell and scroll rim, ivory and silver double serpent scroll handle and domed cover with wrythen bud finial, engraved twice with a coat-of-arms and with crests, maker's mark of Paul Storr, London 1808, 14in (36cm) high, 182oz.
£9,500–12,000 *C*

The arms are those of O'Callaghan impaling Ormonde for Cornelius, 1st Viscount Lismore of Shanbally, Co. Tipperary, 1775–1857.

A George III plain baluster mug, with leaf capped double scroll handle, on spreading base, maker's mark 'I.K.', possibly for John King, London 1775, 5in (12.5cm) high, 10.1oz.
£350–450 *Bea*

An American silver water pitcher, flat chased in low relief with a band of griffins, urns and foliage, classical mask at the base of the handle, engraved with contemporary monogram, by Tiffany & Co., 550 Broadway, New York, c1865, 9in (22.5cm) high, 40oz.
£2,500–3,500 *S(NY)*

A Dutch kettle, with fixed wood scroll handle, on a stand with 3 leaf scroll supports, on paw and bun feet, with burner, by HNH, Amsterdam, c1735, re-assayed in 1822, 14½in (37cm) high overall, 66oz.
£3,000–3,500 *DN*

A William IV christening mug, the campana shaped mug on a spreading circular foot with foliate decoration, gilt interior, maker's mark rubbed, London 1832, 3½in (8.5cm) high.
£200–250 *L*

A George III mug, with moulded rim and leaf capped double scroll handle, later chased, engraved with a monogram within a C-scroll cartouche, by Hester Bateman, London 1783, the underside later engraved with a retailers name and address, 5in (12.5cm) high, 11oz.
£420–480 *CSK*

A George I tankard, of slightly tapering form, with a moulded girdle, domed lid with a chair back thumbpiece and lappet pendant to the hinge, with scrolled handle terminating in a shield, stepped base, by Jonathan Newton, London 1722, 8in (20cm) high, 29oz.
£1,600–2,000 *HCC*

A George III silver lidded tankard, maker's initials 'I.S.', London 1760, 26oz.
£850–950 *JH*

r. A George II tankard, with engraved armorial, by Richard Gurney & Co., London 1741, 8½in (21.5cm) high, 42oz.
£3,200–3,700 *DN*

A Charles II parcel gilt silver tankard, with detachable cast scroll handle and leaf capped bearded mask thumbpiece, the body with detachable sleeve finely pierced and chased, the hinged cover with detachable mount similarly pierced and chased and with central flowerhead, the rim later engraved with a crest, the interior of the cover later engraved with the Royal crest, probably by Jacob Bodendick, c1670, 8in (20cm) high, 54oz.
£42,000–45,000 *C*

The crest on the rim is that of Savory for Thomas Field Savory, 1779–1847, the Royal crest is for HRH the Duke of Sussex, 1773–1843.

A William III tankard, with an applied girdle and moulded spreading foot rim, the flat stepped cover with a cast duck thumbpiece, scroll handle, engraved with an armorial within foliate mantling, maker's mark 'SM' beneath a coronet, not traced, London 1697, 7in (17.5cm) high, 33oz.
£4,000–6,000 *DN*

A George III baluster tankard, with a double scroll handle, on spreading base, with a later spout, the base and hinged cover by Samuel Godbeher and Edward Wigan, London 1787, spout London 1845, 27.3oz.
£800–1,000 *Bea*

A George III silver tankard, engraved with a monogram on the handle, probably Jacob Marsh, London 1766–67, 7in (17.5cm) high, 22oz.
£800–1,200 *SK(B)*

An Elizabeth I silver gilt tankard, with scroll handle, hinged domed cover, winged demi-figure thumbpiece and fluted baluster finial, engraved with a coat-of-arms within a shaped cartouche, maker's mark of a rose slipped, London 1578, 7in (17.5cm) high, 14oz.
£33,000–40,000 *C*

The chased decoration of strapwork panels, fruits and foliage on this tankard is typical of Elizabethan ornament.

Pots

A George II chocolate pot, with wood scroll handle, the detachable domed hinged cover secured by a pin, with detachable finial, on spreading base, maker's mark worn, London 1759, 11in (28cm) high, 23.4oz.
£1,300–1,700 *Bea*

A George II coffee pot, the hinged cover with turned finial, wood scroll handle, on a spreading base, by Robert and Albin Cox, London 1759, 10in (25cm) high, 23.4oz.
£1,500–2,000 *Bea*

A George III coffee pot, monogrammed below a bright-cut band with flowers, foliage and acorns, the hinged cover with urn shaped finial, wood scroll handle, on a spreading pedestal base, maker's mark 'I.M.' possibly for John Mince, London 1799, 10½in (26.5cm) high, 26oz.
£1,200–1,700 *Bea*

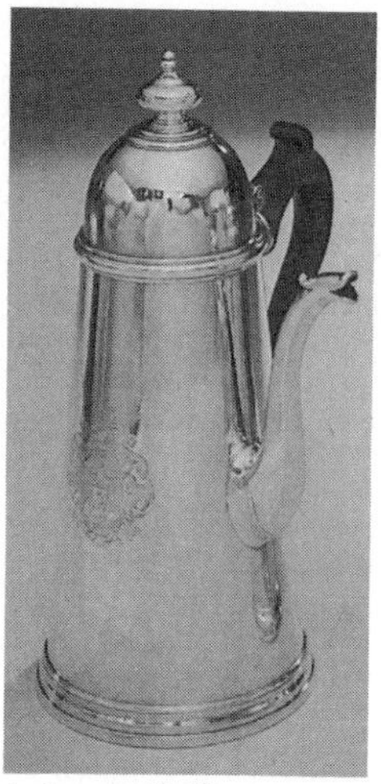

A George I silver chocolate pot, with partly faceted swan neck spout, engraved with arms in baroque cartouche, sliding baluster finial, by Pentecost Symonds, Exeter 1718, maker's mark, the base with scratch weight '32 13', 11in (28cm) high, 34.5oz.
£13,000–15,000 *S(NY)*

The arms are possibly those of Sanford.

A George III coffee pot, with panelled straight spout, domed hinged cover with turned finial and serpent carved wood scroll handle, by Thomas Farren, London 1725, 10in (25cm) high, 25.1oz.
£3,000–4,000 *Bea*

l. A George II coffee pot, with scroll spout and wood handle, domed cover with spire finial, crested, 1735, 8½in (21.5cm) high, 23oz.
£2,000–2,500 *N*

A George II coffee pot, with thread edging, wood scroll handle and finial, on a spreading pedestal base, by Peter, Anne and William Bateman, London 1800, 10½in (26.5cm) high, 23.3oz.
£1,000–1,500 *Bea*

A George II coffee pot, with a domed lid, octagonal spout, engraved crest, stepped base, replaced wooden handle, by Richard Beal, London 1733, 9in (22.5cm) high, 24oz.
£2,500–3,000 *HCC*

A George II coffee pot, of cylindrical form, crested with motto above monogram, the flat domed hinged cover with turned finial, with leaf capped panelled spout and wood scroll handle, by Edward Pocock, London 1735, 9in (22.5cm) high, 24.6oz.
£1,500–2,000 *Bea*

A George III silver coffee pot and matching teapot, of quadrangular urn form with incurved angles, bright-cut collars of grapes, acorns and fruit, reel shaped cover with ball finial, both monogrammed 'JMY', by Robert Sharp, London 1796, teapot lacks finial, coffee pot 13½in (34.5cm) high, 63oz.
£1,000–1,500 *S(NY)*

An American silver teapot, in 18thC style, the apple shaped body chased at the shoulders with rococo decoration, bud finial, inscribed underneath, by Newell Harding & Co., Boston, mid-19thC, 5½in (13.5cm) high, 16.5oz.
£1,000–1,500 *S(NY)*

A George III silver three-piece tea set, of compressed vase shape, vertically lobed, crested, comprising: teapot, by Burwash & Sibley, creamer and sugar bowl, by Emes & Barnard, London 1808–09, teapot 4in (10cm) high, 39oz.
£700–900 *S(NY)*

A Victorian melon-shaped teapot, on a foliate foot with similar spout and handle, floral finial, by the Barnards, London 1840, 6½in (16cm) high, 26oz.
£900–1,200 *L*

A George III silver teapot, with hinged domed cover and matching finial, loop handle and ivory insulators, 6in (15cm) high, on a matching stand, handle repaired, engraved with initials 'W.A.W.' within a surround, on 4 feet, maker's mark 'C.A.' for Charles Aldridge, London 1788, 7in (17.5cm) wide, 19.5oz.
£600–700 *MCA*

Services

A William IV teapot, cream jug and sugar basin, chased with flowers, scrolls and foliage, engraved with a crest, by Edward Farrell, 1833, teapot 6in (15.5cm) high, 46oz.
£800–1,200 *C*

A William IV Irish three-piece tea service, each on 4 foliate and scroll feet, by Edward Power, Dublin 1831, teapot 7in (17.5cm) high, 54.5oz.
£1,200–1,600 *L*

A George II coffee pot, with scroll chased cut-card borders to spout and handle, the domed cover with spire finial, on spreading base, Newcastle 1740, 9in (22.5cm) high, 30oz.
£1,500–2,000 *N*

A Victorian four-piece circular tapered half fluted tea and coffee service, the covers with ivory insets, on rim feet, engraved monograms, by Elkington and Company, Birmingham marks 1884–86, pattern No. 10699, 69oz., with an oak baize lined travelling case, 12½in (32cm) wide.
£1,000–1,500 *AG*

An American silver four-piece tea and coffee set, by Thomas Fletcher, Philadelphia, c1825, teapot 9in (22.5cm) high, 114oz.
£1,500–2,000 *S(NY)*

A Victorian three-piece tea service, by Edward, John and William Barnard, London 1847, and a pair of bright-cut sugar tongs, 48.6oz.
£800–1,000 *Bea*

A George III three-piece tea service, initialled above reeded lower bodies, by George Hunter, London 1817, 49.7oz.
£700–900 *Bea*

An American silver five-piece tea and coffee set, with monograms 'EHB' above applied girdles of flowers and scrolls, gadroon rims, by Tiffany & Co., New York, c1885, coffee pot 8½in (21.5cm) high, 95oz.
£2,500–3,000 *S(NY)*

A Victorian four-piece tea service, the 2 pots with fruitwood handles and wooden finials to the oval flush hinged lids, straight spout to teapot, foliate and bright-cut engraving overall, all crested, maker's mark rubbed, Sheffield 1864, teapot 5in (13cm) high, 48oz.
£1,200–1,700 *L*

Tureens

A set of 4 George III entrée dishes, with detachable handles to the similar lids, engraved with a crest to both sides of the lid, all parts numbered, by Thomas Robins, London 1809, base 11½in (29.5cm) wide, 295oz.
£5,000–6,000 *L*

A set of 4 Victorian entrée dishes, with shaped reeded and foliate borders, the covers with detachable handles, by Harrison Bros. and Hawson, Sheffield 1895, 11in (28cm) wide, 208oz.
£2,500–3,500 *AG*

A George III silver entrée dish, with domed cover, reeded cross-over handle, engraved coat-of-arms with motto 'Habere et Dispertire', and a crest, maker's mark 'P.S.' for Paul Storr, London 1800, 66.5oz, on a Sheffield plate two-handled covered warming base, with bun feet.
£4,000–4,500 *MCA*

The arms are those of Heathcote.

An American silver soup tureen and cover, by Vanderslice & Co., San Francisco, c1870, retailed by George C. Shreve & Co., one side engraved with name and date '1912', 15in (38cm) wide, 88.5oz.
£3,000–3,500 *S(NY)*

A George III sauce tureen, with part fluted sides, the cover with crescent finial, bull's head drop ring handles, nulled borders, on 4 cloven hoof feet, by Solomon Hougham, London 1805, 6½in (16cm) high, 18oz.
£500–600 *DN*

l. A set of 4 George III entrée dishes and covers, with detachable handles with foliate decoration, on two-handled warming stands, raised on scroll and acanthus leaf bracket feet, terminating in pairs, by William Burwash and Richard Sibley I, London 1810, 15in (38cm) wide, 688oz.
£27,000–32,000 *Bon*

A pair of William IV silver soup tureens, covers and stands, maker's mark of Benjamin Smith, London 1830, stands 23in (58.5cm) wide, 629oz.
£60,000–65,000 *C*

Vases

A pair of Continental baluster vases, on tripod supports with hoof feet, by William Moering, import marks for London 1901, early 20thC, 11in (28cm) high, 33.8oz.
£550–800 *Bea*

A George III silver tea urn and matching coffee urn, engraved twice with a coat-of-arms and crest, maker's mark of John Romer, London 1777, largest 22in (56cm) high, 141oz.
£6,500–7,000 *C*

The arms are those of Willis.

l. A set of 4 William and Mary shell dishes, damaged, marks rubbed, London 1699, 5in (12.5cm) long, 7.5oz.
£2,500–3,000 *S(NY)*

A pair of early George III plain gravy boats, with gadrooned borders, double C-scroll handles with acanthus leaf heads, on shell cast scroll legs with leaf feet, by William Sampel, London marks for 1761, 6½in (16cm) wide, 26oz.
£1,300–1,700 *AG*

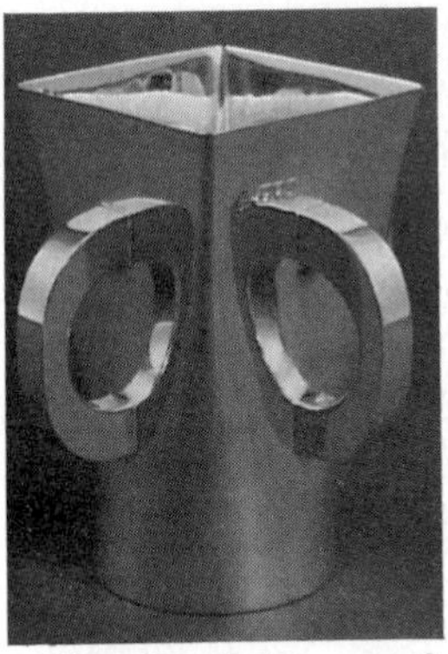

A Victorian plain vase, of square form tapering to circular and with 4 C-shaped handles, by J. Wakely & F. C. Wheeler, 1899, 5in (13cm) high, 11oz.
£200–250 *MSW*

An Italian silver holy water bucket, the scalloped swing handle rising from satyrs' masks, repaired, engraved with date '1662', 17thC, 7½in (18.5cm) diam., 19.5oz.
£1,600–2,000 *S(NY)*

Miscellaneous

A silver cow creamer, late 19thC, 3.75oz.
£680–720 *DaD*

A pair of George III silver ice pails, applied with reeded hoops and engraved with vertical pales, gadrooned rims, partly openwork swing handles, engraved on both sides with a monogram below a Duke's coronet, by George Heming & William Chawner, London 1781, the bases engraved with scratch weights 86=2 and 87=12, 9in (22.5cm) diam., 165oz.
£45,000–50,000 *S(NY)*

A pair of Edwardian gilt shell shaped sauceboats, with bird handles and moulded spreading feet, 8½in (21.5cm) wide, and a pair of matching ladles with trailing vine moulded handles, London 1906, 69.8oz.
£1,700–2,000 *AH*

A pair of silver mustards, with blue glass liners and original spoons, hallmarked London 1896, 2in (5cm) high.
£125–150 *WN*

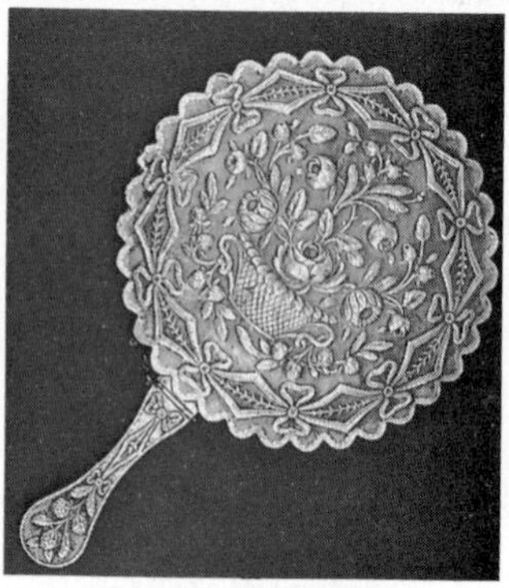

A Dutch or German hand mirror, with lobed border, embossed with a wicker basket filled with peonies and strawberries within a ribbon tie and laurel wreath border, the hinged handle with strawberries and ribbon ties, slight damage, with Turkish turgha import mark, 9½in (24cm) diam.
£550–650 *DN*

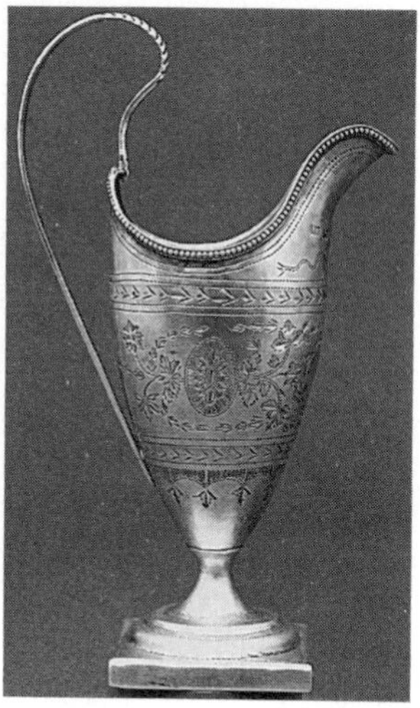

A helmet-shaped cream pitcher, bright-cut with paterae and festoons, with a beaded edge, by John Bassingwhite, London 1790, 7½in (19cm) high, 3oz.
£300–400 *WL*

A plain porringer, the pierced keyhole handle engraved, the reverse stamped 'Capt. Robert Wormsted, Æt 28, was lost at sea in Oct. 1782, R.W.A.', by Paul Revere II, 8in (20cm) long, 9oz.
£10,500–11,500 *Bon*

A composite set of 6 boat-shaped salts, the wirework sides with swags of drapery, reeded borders, and a matching mustard pot, Birmingham 1924, Chester 1905, London 1905, with blue glass liners, 16.5oz.
£400–500 *DN*

A late William IV butter dish, cover and liner, the frosted glass bowl cut to simulate staved wood, the panelled lift-off cover with cow knop, on a panelled circular base, by the Barnards, London 1836, 7in (17.5cm) diam., 11.5oz.
£550–650 *HSS*

SILVER PLATE

A pair of four-light candelabra, the bases with 2 dolphin supports to the sphere and foliate column stems, with fine chain decoration, 21½in (54.5cm) high.
£800–850 *L*

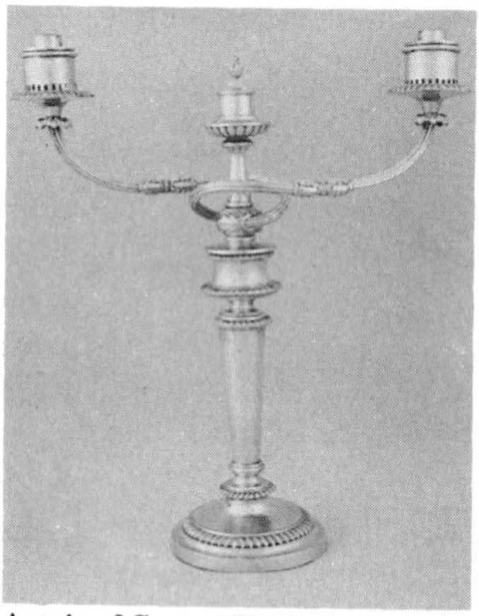

A pair of George III Sheffield plated candelabra, by Matthew Boulton & Co., 19in (48cm) high.
£1,500–2,000 *DN*

A set of 4 glass dishes on stands, with Greek key pattern border, the stands with central ball supported on 3 dolphins, each stand with registary mark for 1864, 17in (43cm) high.
£750–850 *L*

A pair of Sheffield plated three-light candelabra, 17in (43cm) high.
£500–600 *Bea*

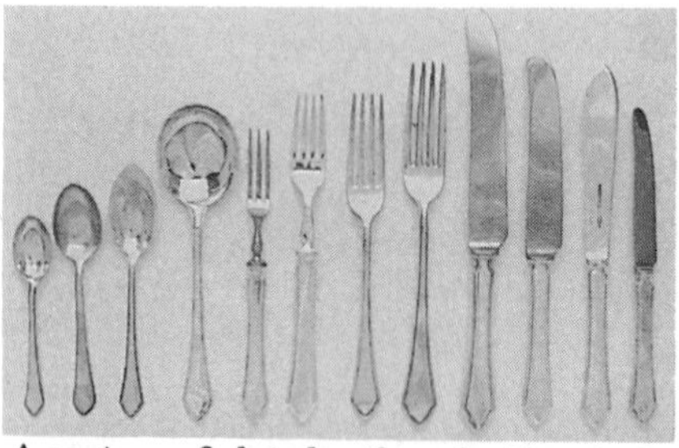

A canteen of plated cutlery, by Mappin & Webb, comprising 123 pieces, contained in 2 fitted drawers of a bow front walnut cabinet, with claw-and-ball feet.
£1,200–1,700 *L*

A Sheffield plated salver, 19thC, 10½in (26.5cm) diam.
£100–120 *STA*

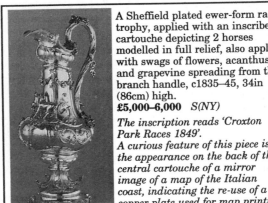

A Sheffield plated ewer-form race trophy, applied with an inscribed cartouche depicting 2 horses modelled in full relief, also applied with swags of flowers, acanthus and grapevine spreading from the branch handle, c1835–45, 34in (86cm) high.
£5,000–6,000 *S(NY)*

The inscription reads 'Croxton Park Races 1849'.
A curious feature of this piece is the appearance on the back of the central cartouche of a mirror image of a map of the Italian coast, indicating the re-use of a copper plate used for map printing.

A silver plated centrepiece, the pierced rococo style frame containing glass dish, 23½in (60cm) wide.
£1,600–2,000 *L*

A silver plated spirit kettle, on a stand, by the Goldsmiths & Silversmiths Co., c1890, 13in (33cm) high.
£270–300 *JHW*

A Sheffield plated vase-shaped coffee pot, with bead edging and scrolling acanthus spout and wood handle, on a spreading circular base, 12in (30.5cm) high.
£400–450 *Bea*

A late Victorian silver plated teapot, 6½in (16cm) high.
£30–40 *WN*

A late Victorian teapot for China tea, the sides engraved with the Willow pattern, the flat hinged cover with a seated Chinaman finial, scroll wood handle, by Hukin and Heath.
£180–200 *WW*

A silver plated soup tureen, with gadrooned rim, 2 reeded acanthus scroll handles, the domed cover surmounted by a floral acanthus scroll handle, on 4 acanthus and paw feet, 16½in (42cm) wide.
£650–700 *SLN*

A Victorian silver plated covered turkey platter, having leaf and bead motif on the border, on scroll feet, 18in (46cm) high.
£600–650 *LHA*

A silver plated four-piece tea service, c1920, teapot 6in (15cm) high.
£250–300 *JHW*

A pair of lidded sauce tureens, with gadrooned borders, on 4 scroll feet, 5½in (14cm) high.
£400–450 *L*

WINE ANTIQUES

A steel pocket corkscrew, with finger ring, set with a seal at the top, c1750.
£400–450 *CS*

A Thomason 1802 patent type corkscrew, the barrel embossed with Gothic Window design, c1820.
£300–400 *CS*

A Sir Edward Thomason's Varient corkscrew, c1815.
£250–350 *CS*

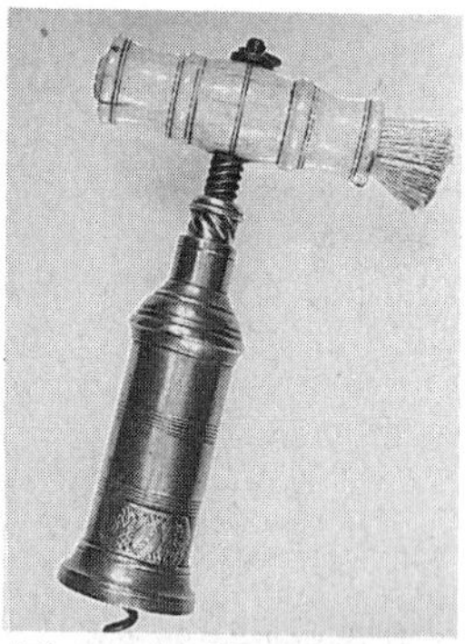

A brass double-action corkscrew, with turned barrel-shaped handle and applied Royal coat-of-arms to the brass barrel, c1820.
£100–140 *CS*

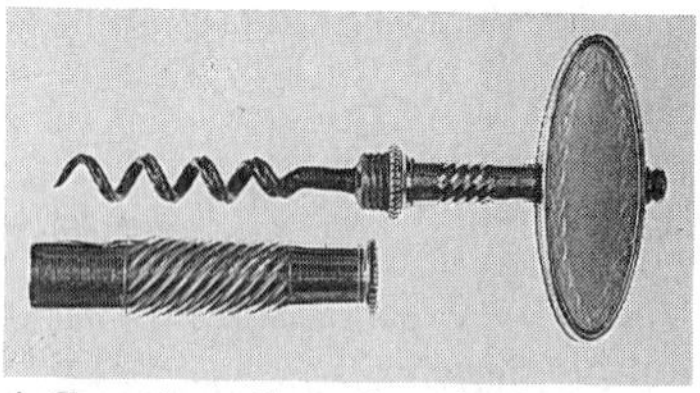

A Georgian silver sheathed pocket corkscrew, with an oval shaped mother-of-pearl handle, c1810.
£120–150 *CS*

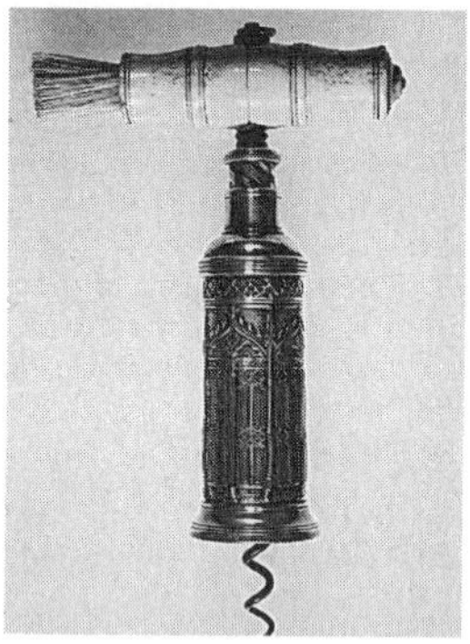

A Thomason 1802 patent type corkscrew, the barrel embossed with grapes, pears, barley flowers and foliage, with a bone handle, c1820.
£300–400 *CS*

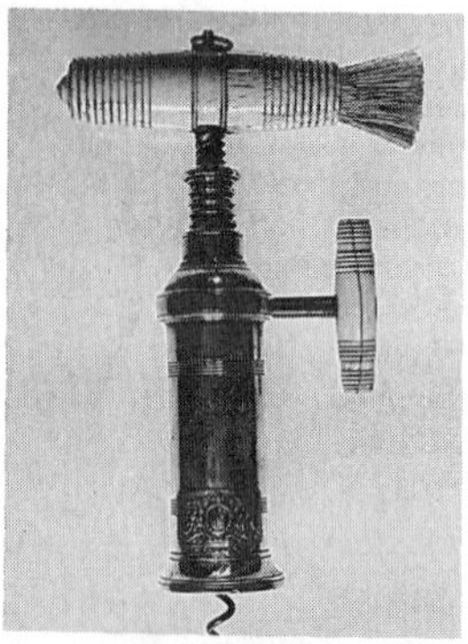

A wide rack King's Screw corkscrew, with turned bone top and side handles, applied brass Royal coat-of-arms to bronze barrel, c1820.
£200–250 *CS*

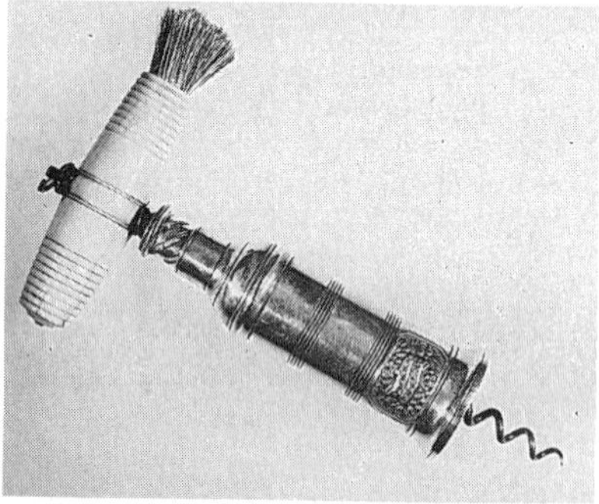

A Thomason type double-action brass barrel corkscrew, with bone handle and applied brass plaque showing maker's name and Royal coat-of-arms, c1830.
£100–140 *CS*

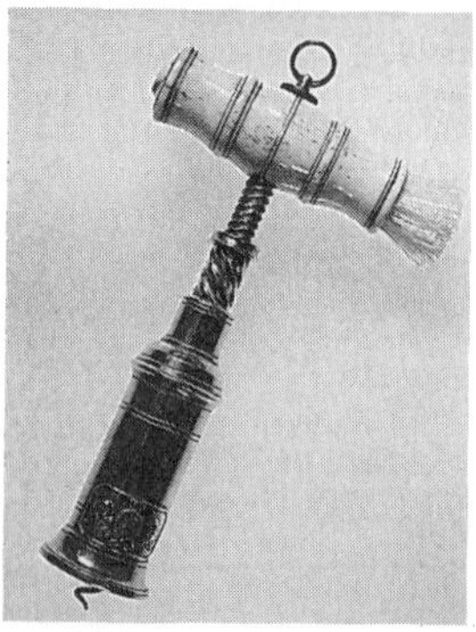

A Thomason type double-action corkscrew, with bone handle and brass barrel, c1830.
£100–140 *CS*

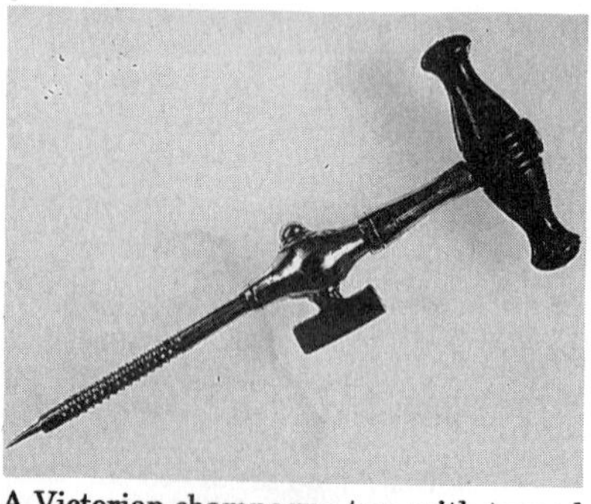

A Victorian champagne tap, with turned ebonised wood T-handle, c1880.
£18–20 *CS*

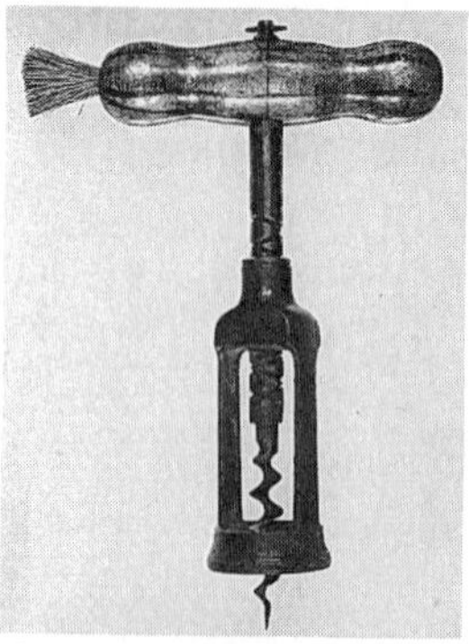

A reverse thread corkscrew, known as 'The Perpetual', c1880.
£55–65 *CS*

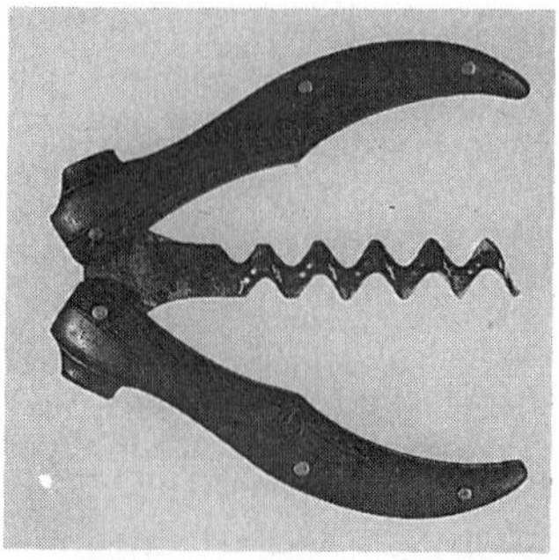

A German pocket corkscrew, in the form of a pair of shoes, c1890.
£140–160 *CS*

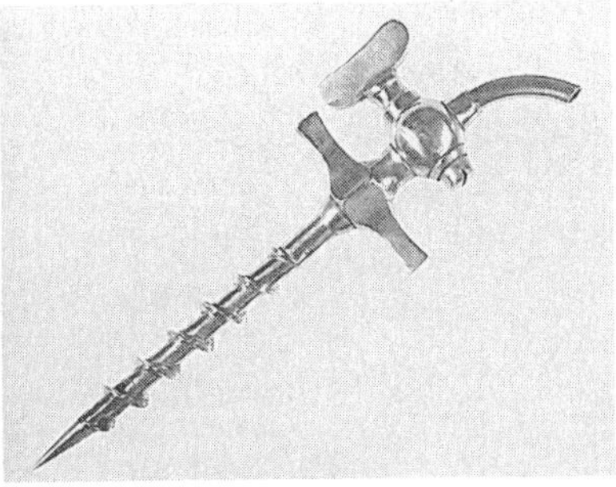

A Victorian plated champagne tap, c1880.
£20–25 *CS*

A silver topped cork, the top cast as a fawn or doe, with a tree support, hallmarked London 1827.
£100–125 *CS*

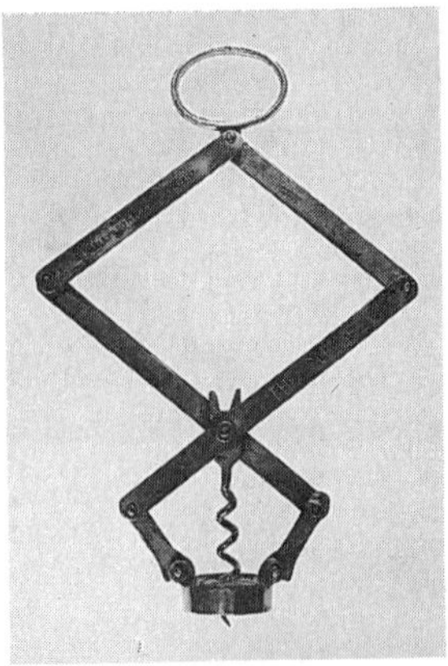

An all steel concertina-type corkscrew, with a bladed worm, of the type patented by H.D. Armstrong in 1902.
£25–40 *CS*

An amusing brass figural corkscrew, depicting a Scotsman, c1930.
£20–25 *CS*

A German spring stem corkscrew, with bladed worm and painted handle, c1890.
£25–35 *CS*

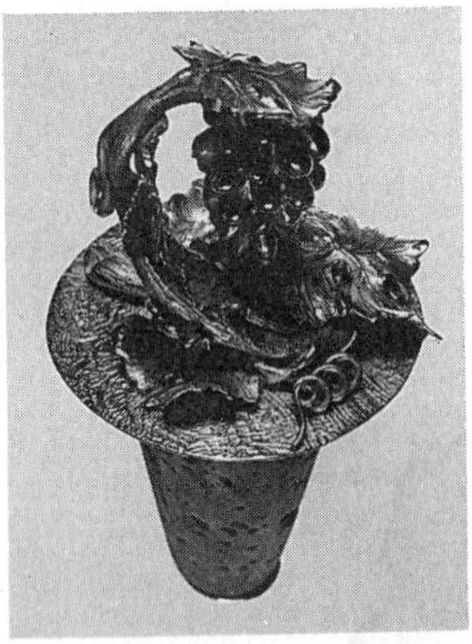

r. A magnum sized cast silver topped cork, with a bunch of grapes forming the handle, maker's initials for George Ivory, hallmarked London 1856.
£135–150 *CS*

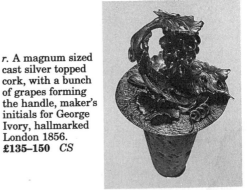

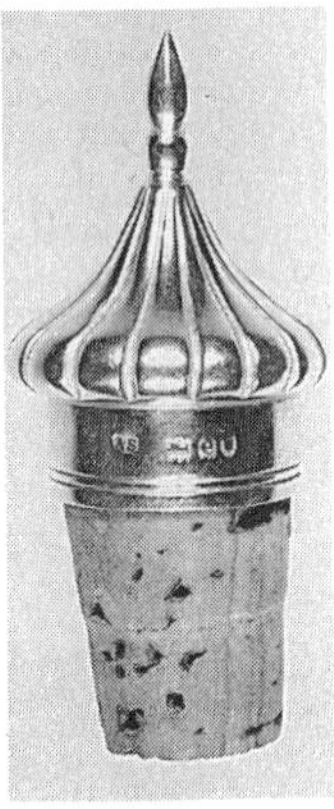

A tent or pagoda-shaped silver top bottle cork, hallmarked London 1900.
£20–25 *CS*

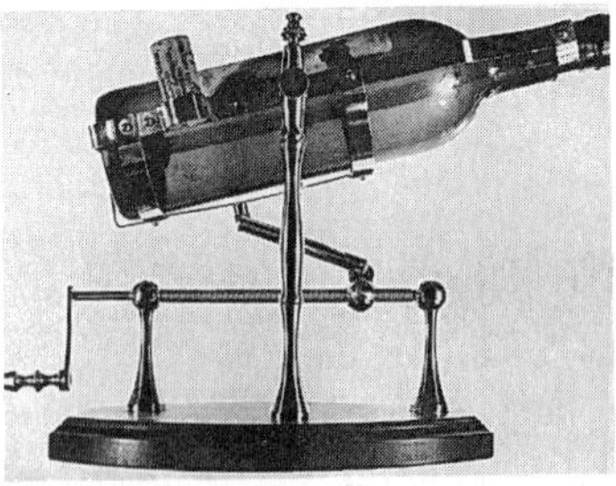

A Victorian brass wine or port decanting cradle, on mahogany base.
£100–150 *CS*

A set of 4 William IV triple vine leaf wine labels, by Charles Reily and George Storer, pierced for 'Port', 'Madeira', 'Claret' and 'Sherry', London c1835.
£350–450 *WW*

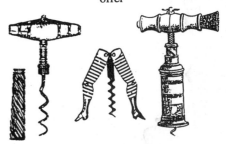

A Bilston enamel 'Red-Port' bottle ticket or decanter label, c1770.
£120–140 *CS*

A silver decanter label, depicting a man at dinner, with a salmon, boar's head, chicken, chops and bottles of wine, and a space to insert a paper title/name to denote the type of wine, early 19thC.
£100–125 *CS*

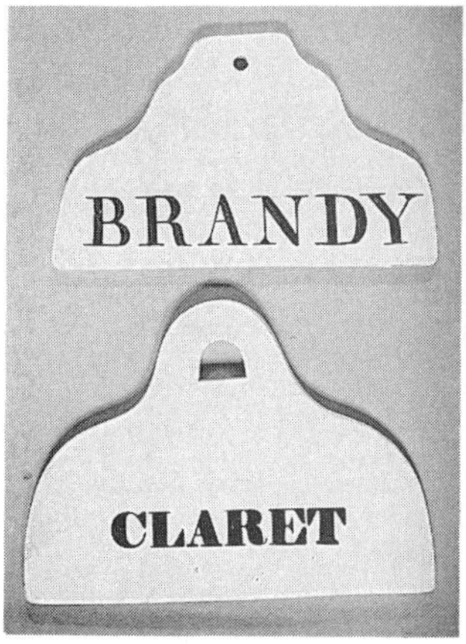

Two white pottery wine cellar bin labels, with black enamel lettering, 'Brandy' and 'Claret', c1850.
£20–40 each *CS*

Three white pottery wine cellar bin labels, with black enamel names, c1850.
£20–40 each *CS*

A pair of Victorian silver decanter labels, for 'Sherry' and 'Port', by Yapp & Woodward, hallmarked Birmingham 1852.
£80–90 *CS*

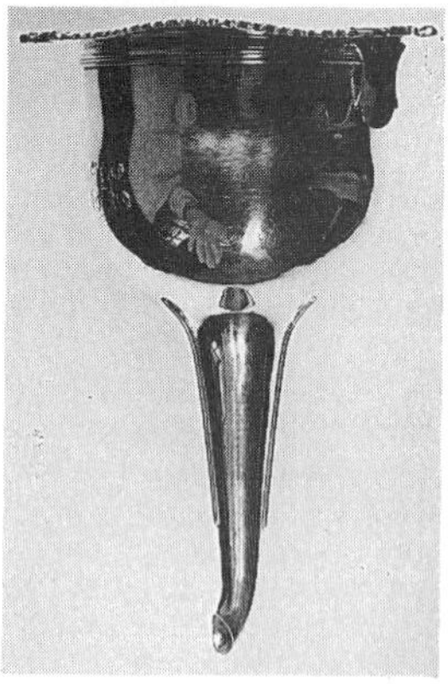

A three-piece silver wine funnel, by Rebecca Emes and Edward Barnard, London 1819.
£250–350 *CS*

A pair of ebonised and silver plated double decanter coasters, possibly Irish, with silver plated scroll handles, baluster supports and wheels, late 19thC, 12½in (32cm) wide.
£1,400–1,800 *S*

Did you know?
MILLER'S* Antiques Price Guide *builds up year-by-year to form the most comprehensive antiques photo-reference library available.

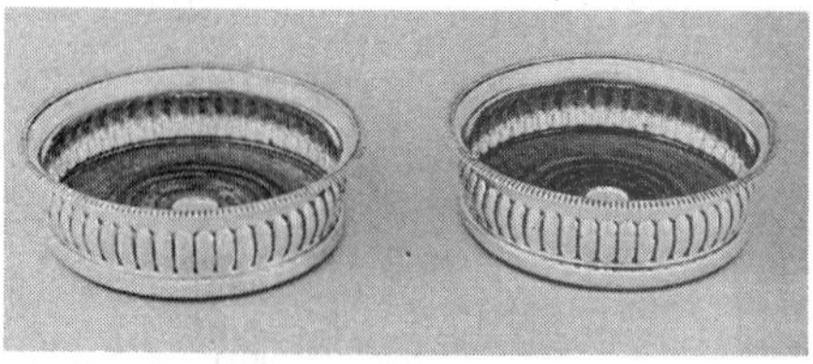

A pair of George III coasters, with fluted sides, nulled borders, wood bases, by John Roberts & Co, Sheffield 1805, 6in (15cm) diam.
£800–900 *DN*

A set of 3 silver spirit decanter labels, with cornucopia, sheaves of corn, a scythe, rake and wool sack, stamped 'Free' celebrating Free Trade, c1846.
£225–250 *CS*

A pair of George IV Scottish decanter stands, with serpentine edges, pierced fret sides, engraved paterae, crested with motto, turned mahogany bases with baize, by J. McKay, Edinburgh 1823.
£900–1,200 *WW*

Wine Funnels

Wine related antiques are very much in vogue at the moment, and wine funnels are no exception. As with all antique silver, condition is very important and some of the points to look for are given below.

When examining a wine funnel, you should ensure the patination is 'silky'. Look also for thin spots caused by the erasure of crests or initials, and check for splits and cracks.

Hallmarks should be clear. On two-part funnels, the strainer portion should have a full set of marks (the town mark, the sterling, the date and the maker's mark) and the spout end should have a lion passant, a maker's mark and a monarch's head (if made after 1784). On the full funnel type, with an internal lift-out strainer, the strainer should have partial marks and the outer funnel should have the full set.

As with all antiques, wine funnels should always be carefully examined for damage and repairs. The most frequently damaged area is the spout, which often suffers dents and splits. The usual remedy for this is to cut back the spout, but this reduces the curve which is so important in stopping the aeration of the wine during the decanting process.

The holes in the strainers were not small enough to filter the sediment from wine, so muslin was used, and this was sewn onto an internal ring. However, these rings were often lost and the muslin was, instead, jammed between the two halves of the funnel. On two-part funnels this often caused the seam to split.

The three applied ribs sometimes found on the spouts of full funnels are designed to stop the funnel jamming in the decanter neck and also to let the air out during decanting. Curiously, these are usually applied with lead solder, and therefore can easily break off, so look carefully for signs of distress.

Another area to examine carefully is the funnel rim. This is particularly prone to damage, especially behind the hook where splits usually start. The hook may sometimes be missing altogether.

Finally, it is always worth checking to make sure that the hallmarks on both parts of the funnel are the same. Occasionally funnels will be found to have been made up from two completely unrelated parts so decreasing the value.

Henry Willis

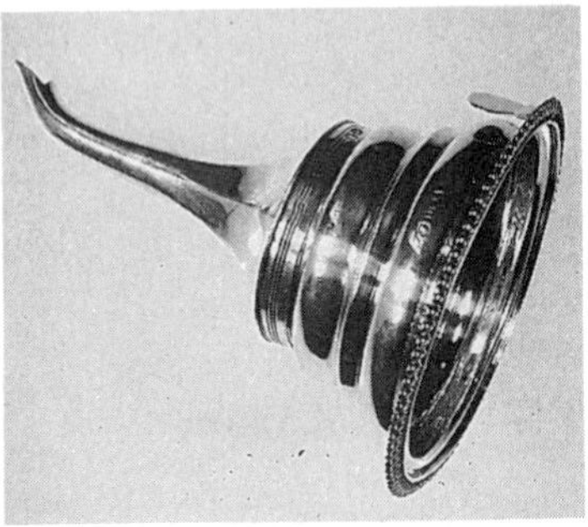

A George III two-part silver wine funnel, the bowl of double ogee shape with gadrooned rim, London 1815.
£200–300 *CS*

r. A pair of hobnail cut crystal glass and silver wine ewers, with silver handles and tops, one chipped, by FE, Birmingham 1889, 12in (30.5cm) high.
£1,800–2,000 *FFAP*

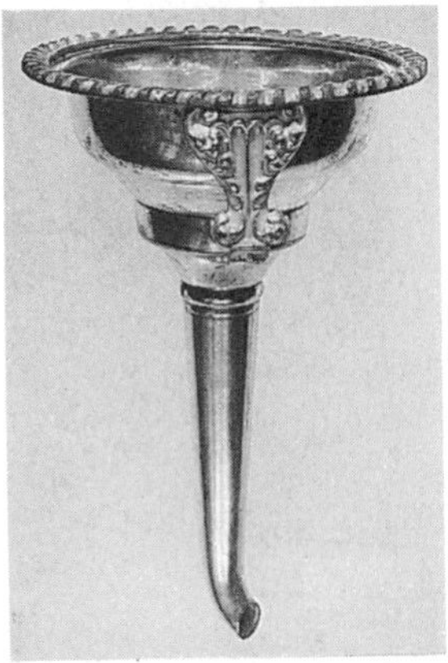

A Victorian silver plated wine funnel, with a large tab for suspending the funnel from the edge of a glass or bowl.
£40–45 *CS*

A Victorian claret jug, the bulbous glass body etched with fruiting vine and grape decoration to the handle and fittings, shaped hinged lid, by Edward Charles Brown, London 1871, 5in (12.5cm) high.
£750–850 *L*

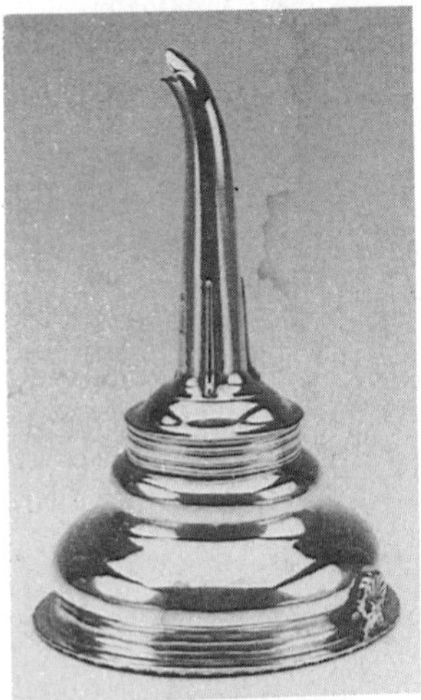

A George III Scottish wine funnel, monogrammed, with gadrooned edging and shell clip, by W. & P. Cunningham, Edinburgh 1825, 5½in (14cm) high, 3.76oz.
£400–500 *Bea*

A mahogany decanter tray, with a pierced central handle and shaped sides, together with 4 cut glass decanters and stoppers each with triple ring necks, slice and hobnail cut shoulders and wrythen strawberry cutting, headed by printies, with similar mushroom stoppers, one cracked, stand 12in (30.5cm) wide.
£750–850 *L*

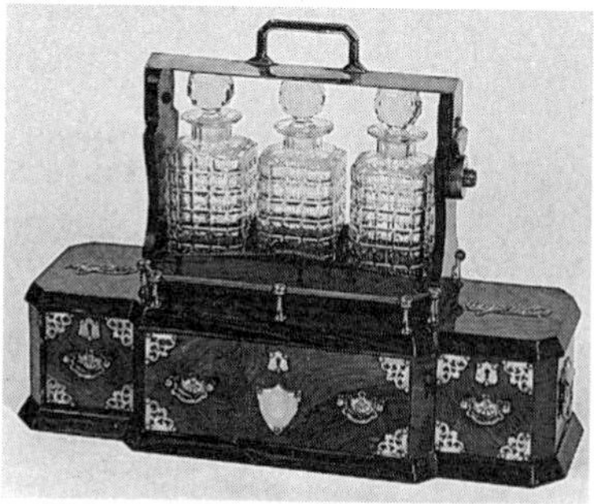

A Victorian figured walnut and brass mounted 3 bottle tantalus, inset with 3 hobnail cut square spirit decanters, brass gallery below, the base fitted with a central drawer fitted for cards and games flanked by cigar and cigarette drawers, 23½in (60cm) wide.
£900–1,200 *CAG*

An oak decanter case, with brass handles, fitted with 4 square glass decanters.
£200–250 *JH*

FURTHER READING

For further information on antique silver, please refer to *Miller's Antiques Checklist: Silver & Plate,* published by Miller's Publications, 1994.

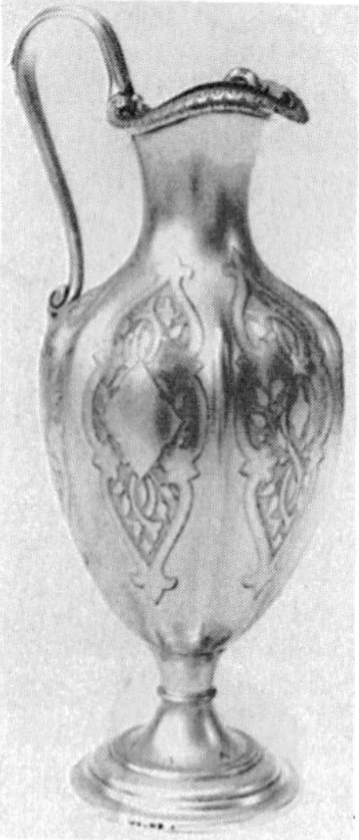

A Victorian wine jug, the panelled body with engraving, by Elkington & Co, dent to front, 14in (35.5cm) high.
£200–250 *WW*

A pair of George III silver wine coolers, each with plain detachable liner and collar with ovolo border, applied twice with a coat-of-arms, maker's mark of Paul Storr, London 1812, 8½in (21.5cm) high, 321oz.
£50,000–55,000 *C*

The arms are those of Butler quartering others for Richard, 11th Baron Caher of Caher, Co. Tipperary.

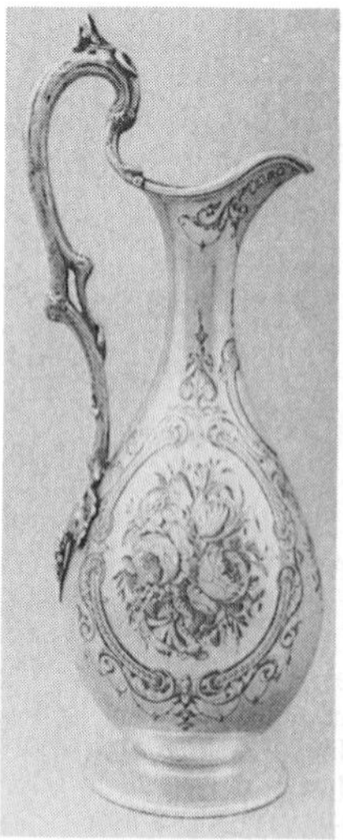

A Victorian wine ewer, engraved with vignettes of flowers and blank cartouche, cast vine branch handle, on a plain round foot, London 1857, 13in (33cm) high, 22oz.
£800–900 *DN*

A pair of silver mounted claret jugs, maker's mark of Tiffany & Co., New York, engraved 'A.R.L.', marked on interior covers '5295/300', c1885, 9½in (24cm) high.
£3,000–3,500 *CNY*

A mid-Victorian silver wine ewer, with repoussé scrolled foliate body, knop finial to cover, acanthus moulded handle, and a pair of matching goblets, by Martin Hall & Co, Sheffield 1868, 41.5oz.
£1,000–1,500 *HOLL*

r. A Victorian wine ewer, engraved with bands of anthemion and Celtic strapwork, the trefoil mouth with everted rim, with a scaly mythical beast forming the handle, on a stepped pedestal base, by Samuel Smily, 1867, 14in (35.5cm) high, 33oz.
£800–900 *P(EA)*

A pair of Sheffield plated wine coolers, the campana form with shellwork rims and bases, bodies crested and applied with grapevine spreading from forked branch handles, detachable liners, c1830, 12½in (32cm) high.
£2,500–3,000 *S(NY)*

A pair of Sheffield plated wine coolers, the partly fluted campana form decoration with applied shells, engraved with arms, crest and motto, detachable rims and liners, c1820, 9½in (24cm) high.
£2,500–3,000 *S(NY)*

A pair of silver wine coolers, each with pedestal base and detachable rim and liner, engraved with the Royal cyphers of William IV and Adelaide on both sides, stamped 'Rundell Bridge et Co., Aurifices Regis Londini', by William Bateman II, London 1835, 10in (25cm) high, 228.5oz.
£28,000–30,000 *S(NY)*

The monograms 'WR' within garter motto and 'AR' within oak and reed wreath below the Royal Crowns are those of William IV and Adelaide, who were married in 1818.

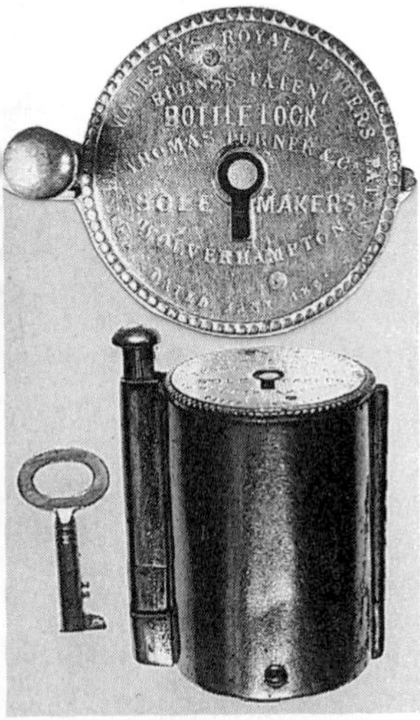

A nickel plated cylindrical bottle lock, known as the 'Butler's Enemy', engraved around the top 'By Her Majesty's Royal Letters Patent, Burns's Patent Bottle Lock, Thomas Turner & Co, Sole Makers, Wolverhampton, Dated Jany 1881', with key, 2in (5cm) high.
£85–100 *CS*

A Victorian urn-shaped wine ewer, by Edward John Barnard, 1866, 14in (35.5cm) high, 31.5oz.
£800–900 *P(EA)*

Two pairs of George III matching silver gilt wine coolers, the base rims engraved with contemporary crest below coronet, detachable rims and liners, one pair with maker's mark 'IP', engraved with the Latin signature of 'Rundell Bridge & Rundell', c1803, and a pair by William Pitts, engraved with numbers underneath, 1810, 11in (28cm) high, 570oz.
£80,000–85,000 *S(NY)*

The engraved scratch weights suggest that these coolers originally had stands.

A pair of Belgian silver gilt wine coolers, the foot rims inscribed, by Joseph-Germain Dutalis, Brussels, c1820, 13½in (35cm) high, 228oz, including original iron rods and braces.
£52,000–55,000 *S(NY)*

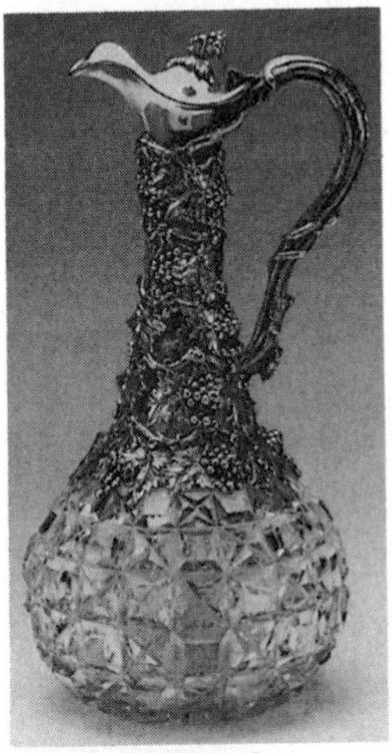

An electroplated mounted cut glass claret jug, with rustic handle, 11½in (29cm) high.
£300–400 *Bea*

A George II brandy saucepan, with turned wood handle, the moulded circular lipped bowl engraved with an armorial and with a moulded rim, maker's mark indistinct, London 1725, 6in (15cm) wide, 5.5oz.
£600–700 *CSK*

r. A George IV lidded brandy saucepan, the baluster pan on a short circular foot, with hinged lid and lip, turned wood handle, by Barber, Cuttle and North, York 1824, 4½in (11.5cm) high.
£900–1,200 *L*

METALWARE
Brass

A pierced brass candle holder, 19thC, 3in (7.5cm) diam.
£45–55 *AnE*

l. A Flemish brass relief of the Annunciation, with 2 holes drilled at the top for suspension and another under the Virgin's feet, 17thC, 5½in (14cm) high.
£900–1,000 *C*

r. A heavy cast brass letter rack, c1870.
£100–150 *CB*

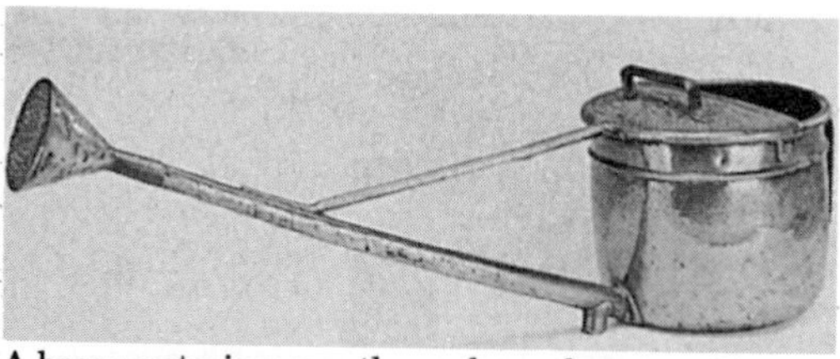

A brass watering can, the embossed cover with a stylised flowerhead, punched decoration to body, one handle damaged, c1900, 36in (91.5cm) long.
£950–1,000 *S(S)*

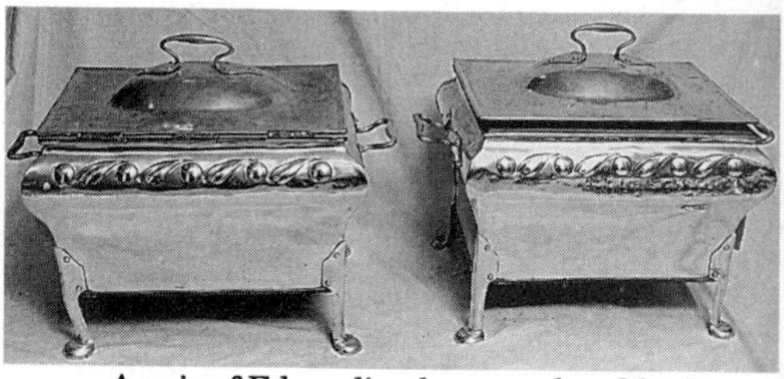

A pair of Edwardian brass coal and log boxes, 17in (43cm) wide.
£750–850 *ASH*

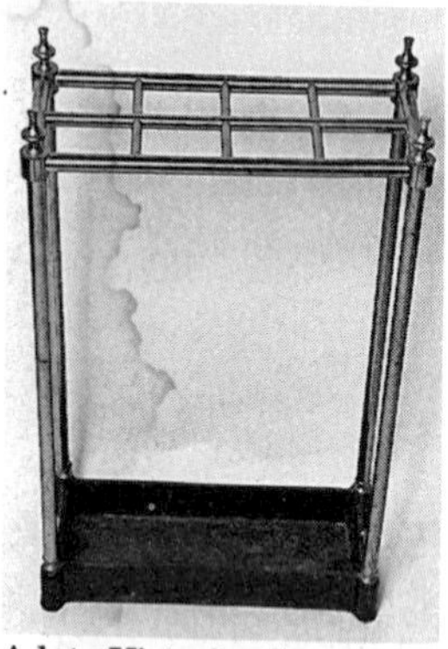

A late Victorian brass umbrella stand, 23in (58.5cm) high.
£90–120 *JHW*

An Edwardian brass coal box, with shovel, 14½in (37cm) high.
£150–200 *ASH*

A brass coal box, c1920, 16in (40.5cm) high.
£75–100 *ASH*

A brass, copper and bronze samovar, early 19thC, 19in (48cm) high.
£220–240 *McC*

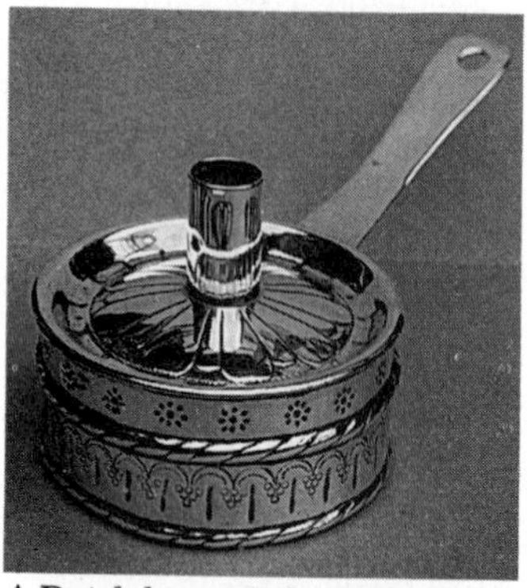

A Dutch brass tinder box, with punched decoration, c1830.
£200–250 *KEY*

A brass dog collar, engraved with a verse, early 19thC.
£250–350 *KEY*

r. A brass footman, early 19thC, 17½in (44.5cm) wide.
£200–275 *STA*

Bronze

A French bronze bust of a lady, cast from a model by Emile André Boisseau, signed, late 19thC, 21½in (54.5cm) high.
£2,000–2,500 *C*

A French silvered bronze bust, entitled 'Cheik Arabe de Caire', cast from a model by Charles Henri Joseph Cordier, signed on reverse, late 19thC, 18½in (47cm) high.
£18,000–22,000 *C*

A French silvered bronze and enamelled bust of an Egyptian harem girl, entitled 'Jeune Femme Fellah en Costume de Harem', from a model by Charles Henri Joseph Cordier, inscribed and dated '1866', on a circular spreading socle, 17in (43.5cm) high.
£15,000–20,000 *C*

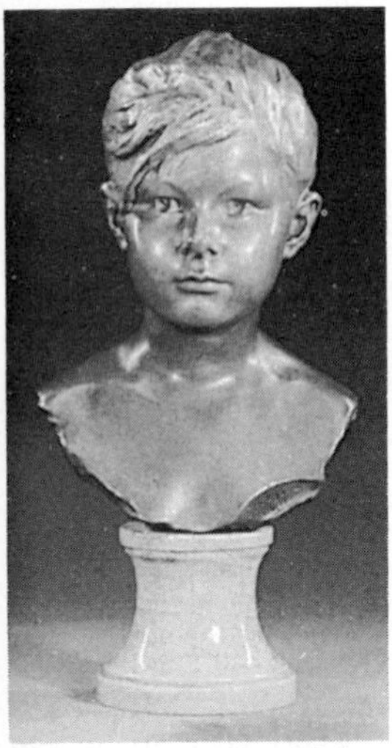

A bronze bust of a girl, by Edward Charles Marie Houssin (1847–1917), green-brown patination, signed, with foundry stamp 'F. Goldscheide Sculpture', on turned green marble socle with pink striations, 18½in (47cm) high.
£1,500–2,000 *S*

A pair of bronze busts of Juno and a Turk, from the workshop of Giovanni Battista Foggini, brown patina with traces of golden lacquer, each on a later grey marble plinth, minor chips to plinths, c1700, 6½in (16.5cm) high.
£3,700–4,200 *C*

A bronze portrait bust of a lady, by Luca Madrassi (1869–1914), light brown patination, signed, on a bronze mounted, red mottled marble plinth, 31½in (80cm) high.
£2,800–3,200 *S*

l. A set of 3 French or Italian bronze busts of Roman Emperors, the dark reddish brown patina worn to reveal greenish brown areas, each on an ebonised wooden socle and a marble plinth, one socle cracked, slight damage, 18thC, 5½in (14.5cm) high.
£2,200–3,000 *C*

A bronze bust of a lady, by William Reid Dick, signed and dated '1919', 16½in (42cm) high, on a square verde antico base.
£1,000–1,500 *C*

A bronze group of 4 young fledglings, by H. Schinger, signed, on a step domed serpentine marble plinth, 12in (30.5cm) high.
£350–400 *C*

A bronze model of a pacing bull, cast after a model by Giambologna, dark brown patina, on a green marble plinth, tail repaired, 17thC, 8½in (22cm) high.
£6,000–7,000 *C*

Giambologna produced 2 variations on the theme of the pacing bull, the major difference being that this model is less thickset than the other and has a less pronounced dewlap. It has been suggested that the bull was originally designed as a pendant for Giambologna's Walking Lion, but it was very popular paired with a horse or on its own.

A bronze model of a dragon, brown patina with brassy highlights, formerly part of a larger composition, the underside unfinished, probably German, 19thC, 10in (25cm) long.
£900–1,000 *C*

A bronze model of a cat, by John D. Edwards, black patina, stamped and numbered twice at the base 'A/A/ 9/9', 19in (48cm) high.
£2,000–2,500 *C*

A Paduan bronze crab, the pincers opening, the legs prepared to move forward, the central section with hinged top, reddish brown patina beneath black lacquer, damaged, early 16thC, 6in (15cm) wide.
£3,000–5,000 *S(NY)*

l. A bronze group depicting a setter, pointer and partridge, by Pierre Jules Mêne, signed and dated '1847', brown patination, No. 25 in Mêne catalogue, 16in (40.5cm) wide.
£1,700–2,200 *CAG*

A Paduan bronze frog, olive brown patina beneath black lacquer, early 16thC, 3½in (9cm) long.
£5,500–6,000 *S(NY)*

A bronze group depicting a kitten and sparrow, signed 'Emmanuel Fremiet', foundry mark 'Barbedienne', c1880, 16in (40.5cm) wide.
£2,500–3,000 *GAS*

A French bronze model of a double-headed eagle, with outstretched wings, on a later stained wood stand, late 19thC, 26in (66cm) wide.
£2,000–2,500 *CSK*

A German bronze model of an elephant, brown patina worn to reveal lighter brown areas, on a slate base, chipped, 16thC, 5in (12.5cm) high.
£12,000–14,000 *C*

A German bronze monkey, with an apple in each hand, the head and back with drill holes for attachment, 16thC, 2½in (6.5cm) high.
£1,000–1,500 *S(NY)*

A bronze group of a horse and dog, by Henri Alfred Marie Jacquemart, with a water bucket and tack between the horse's legs, slight damage, late 19thC, 14½in (37cm) wide.
£2,000–2,500 *Bea*

Miller's is a price GUIDE not a price LIST

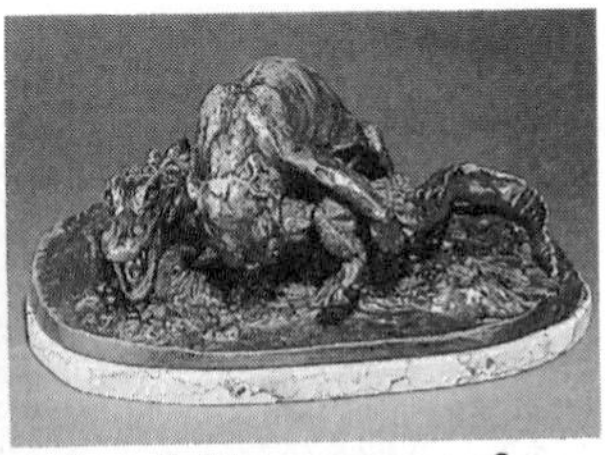

A French bronze group of a lion attacking an alligator, cast from a model by Pierre Jules Mêne, on a naturalistic base, signed, on a griotte marble plinth, late 19thC, 15in (38cm) wide.
£1,500–2,000 *C*

A pair of cold painted bronze studies, entitled 'Eastern Girls', one playing a mandolin, after Emile Guillemin, signed in the moulds, on shaped bases, 22in (55.5cm) high.
£7,000–8,000 *Wad*

A bronze group of a lion attacking a horse, by Barthélémy Prieur, c1600, 8in (20cm) long.
£30,000–35,000 *S(NY)*

r. A bronze turtle, by Antoine-Louis Barye, with mid-brown patination, 1in (2.5cm) wide.
£1,000–1,200 *S*

A north Italian bronze horse, after the antique, the dark brown patina with traces of black lacquer, c1500, 6½in (17cm) high, on a wood plinth.
£32,000–37,000 *S(NY)*

A bronze figure, entitled 'Comedy and Tragedy: Sic Vita', by Sir Alfred Gilbert, with rich modulated brown green patination, on a green marble base with an octagonal foot, with a small hole in the leg for a bee, on a green marble base with a foot, 26in (66cm) high.
£66,000–70,000 *S*

Gilbert regarded 'Comedy and Tragedy' as the climax to his series of autobiographical bronzes. The message is direct: while the world sees the façade of a successful and contented sculptor, his inner life is fraught with professional, financial and domestic difficulties. The metaphor used by Gilbert is that of a prop boy from a classical theatre who is stung by a bee as he carries the mask of Comedy. The boy holds up a mask with a grotesquely large grin while he, standing on the toes of his right foot, grimaces as he is stung on his left calf. His leg has a hole where a bee could have been affixed, but it is unlikely to have ever been there. The title alone was inspired by W. S. Gilbert's play of the same name, then in a revival at the Lyceum.

A bronze figure of an athlete wrestling with a python, by Frederick, Lord Leighton, dark brown patination, signed and dated '1877', inscribed 'Pubd. by Ernest Brown & Phillips at the Leicester Galleries, Leicester Square, London', numbered 'XXIX', 20½in (52cm) high.
£22,000–27,000 *S*

l. A bronze figure of a nude girl, entitled 'Needless Alarms', cast from a model by Frederick, Lord Leighton, with green patination, the figure 20in (50.5cm) high, on a plinth.
£5,500–6,500 *C*

First exhibited at the Royal Academy in 1886, Leighton's model of 'Needless Alarms' was one of the first examples of New Sculpture which handled the naked form in strong contraposto. The stretched muscles of the young girl's body in its twisted pose are successfully displayed as she turns in fright to find a frog at her feet. Leighton presented the original to the painter Millais, who had shown a great liking for it. In thanks, Millais painted 'Shelling Peas' for Leighton.

A pair of French bronze models of the menacing Cupid and a nymph hiding Cupid's bow, after Etienne-Maurice Falconet, each on an ormolu base, the nymph's attribute lacking, mid-19thC, largest 10½in (27cm) high.
£3,500–4,500 *C*

A French bronze group of naked lovers, entitled 'L'Age d'Or', cast from a model by Pierre Emile Leysalle, signed, on a griotte marble plinth, c1900, 22in (55.5cm) high.
£2,000–2,500 *C*

Born in 1847, Leysalle studied under Mathurin Moreau and Carpeaux. He later became professor of sculpture at the School of Industrial Arts, Geneva, and exhibited at the Salon from 1873. He was chiefly known for allegorical and genre subjects.

A bronze group of a putti and a sea monster, 32in (81cm) high.
£600–650 *AG*

A French bronze figure of an Arabian falconer, cast from a model by Pierre Jules Mêne, signed, on a stepped base cast with a captured hare, late 19thC, 26in (66cm) high.
£1,500–2,000 *C*

A French bronze figure, entitled 'Chant de l'Alouette', cast from a model by Hippolyte Moreau, on a naturalistic base, signed, and a stepped plinth with inscribed plaque, stamped '25932', late 19thC, 23in (58.5cm) high.
£2,300–2,800 *C*

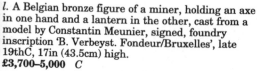

l. A Belgian bronze figure of a miner, holding an axe in one hand and a lantern in the other, cast from a model by Constantin Meunier, signed, foundry inscription 'B. Verbeyst. Fondeur/Bruxelles', late 19thC, 17in (43.5cm) high.
£3,700–5,000 *C*

This figure can be recognised as a miner by his headwear, a traditional leather cap, as opposed to the round hats of the puddlers and metal workers who also formed part of Meunier's oeuvre.

A bronze model of Diana the Huntress with a hound, by Luca Madrassi, two-colour mid-brown patinations, signed, on a shaped red marble base, 28in (71cm) high.
£1,500–2,000 *S*

A French silvered bronze figure of Atalante, stooping to pick up the golden apples, cast from the model by Jean Jacques Pradier, one apple signed and dated '1850', on an oval base, 9¼in (23.5cm) high.
£6,000–8,000 *C*

A French bronze figure of a huntress, cast from a model by Mathurin Moreau, signed 'Math. Moreau/Hors Concours', on a revolving base and stepped plinth, late 19thC, 21in (53.5cm) high.
£1,400–1,900 *C*

A French bronze statue of Narcissus, c1860, 27in (69cm) high.
£900–1,200 *CB*

r. A bronze figure of Mercury, after Giambologna, inscribed 'B Boschetti Roma', 43in (109cm) high, on a marble plinth.
£2,000–2,500 *CNY*

Boschetti worked in Rome during the first half of the 19thC, and examples of his bronzes can be found in the Villa Albani and Villa Adriana in this city.

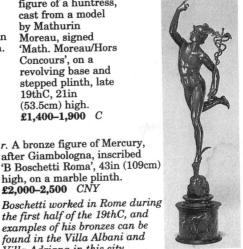

A bronze figure of Diana the Huntress, from the workshop of Barthélémy Prieur, on an integrally cast plinth and a square, ebony veneered and boulle base, damaged, early 17thC, 8¼in (21cm) high.
£22,000–24,000 *C*

A bronze figure of a clown, with voluminous pantaloons, standing on a half barrel, by Caccia, signed and dated '1895', on a turned marble base, 28in (71cm) high.
£900–1,200 *DN*

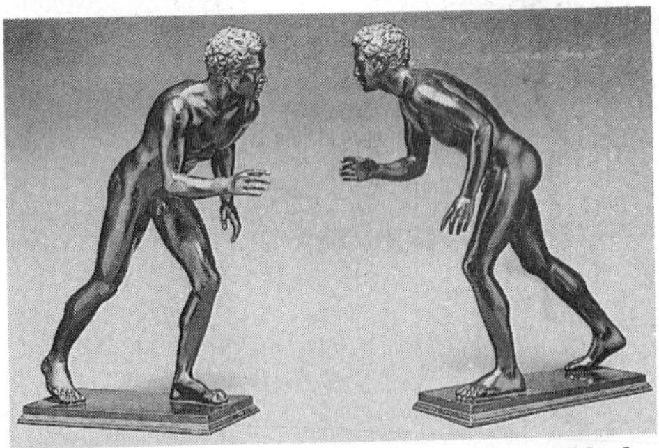

A pair of Italian bronze Spartan athletes, black patination, with inset cold painted eyes, one eye missing, founder's mark 'Sab. De Angelis & Fils, Naples 1908', 17in (43cm) high.
£2,400–3,000 *S*

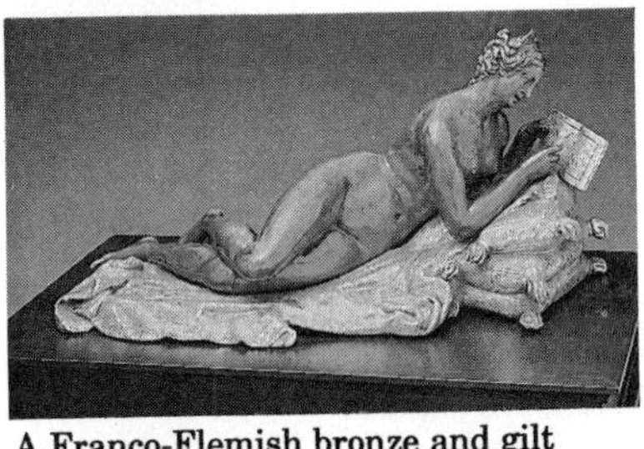

A Franco-Flemish bronze and gilt bronze allegorical group representing literature, showing a figure of Venus reclining on a gilt mattress writing in an open book, 17thC, 11in (28cm) long, on an ebonised wood base.
£35,000–37,000 *S(NY)*

r. A bronze group of Ariadne and the Panther, after the model by Johan von Dannecker, on a Siena marble spreading base and black marble plinth, 19thC, 19in (48cm) high.
£2,200–2,700 *C*

l. An Italo-Flemish bronze figure of a peasant leaning on a staff, after Giambologna, dark patina rubbed in parts, early 17thC, 5in (12.5cm) high, on square base.
£13,500–14,500 *S(NY)*

An Italian bronze figure of Venus, dark brown patina, minor casting flaws, repaired, 16thC, 8in (20cm) high, on a marble pedestal.
£3,300–4,000 *C*

A Venetian bronze putto, by the workshop of Niccolo Roccatagliata, holding the veil of St. Veronica, dark brown lacquer, late 16thC, 6in (15cm) high.
£18,500–19,500 *S(NY)*

A Venetian bronze figure of a Roman Emperor, by Niccolo Roccatagliata, his left foot resting on a helmet, c1590, 11in (28cm) high, on an ebonised wood marble base.
£43,000–45,000 *S(NY)*

A Florentine bronze group of Menelaus and Petroclus, attributed to Pietro Tacca, the hero wearing a helmet decorated with fish scales and a dolphin mask, a dagger at his side, translucent red gold lacquer over dark brown patina, c1630, 22in (56cm) high.
£31,000–33,000 *S(NY)*

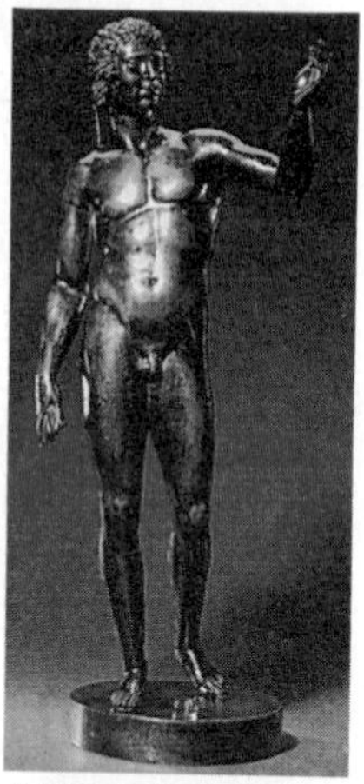

A Florentine style bronze figure of Bacchus, on a bronze base, dark brown patina worn, 16thC, 24½in (62cm) high.
£4,000–5,000 *C*

A Florentine table fountain, in the form of a putto, with drilled eyes, dark brown patina, c1500, 11½in (29cm) high, on an ebonised wood socle.
£9,500–10,500 *S(NY)*

A gilt and bronze group of Leda and the Swan, cast from a model by Edouard Drouot, signed, on a gilt bronze square stepped plinth, late 19thC, 27½in (70cm) high.
£2,000–2,500 *C*

A Venetian bronze figure of Flora, with a bow in her hair, on an integrally cast bronze base, mid-16thC, 6in (15cm) high, on a mottled marble base.
£17,000–18,000 *S(NY)*

r. A bronze figure of Abraham Lincoln, by Daniel Chester French, inscribed and dated '1911', and 'Gorham Co. Founders QZG' on the base, 38in (96.5cm) high.
£45,500–48,000 *LHA*

This bronze figure is a reduction of the original scaled down version of Abraham Lincoln executed for Lincoln, Nebraska. Daniel Chester French was also the sculptor for the Lincoln Memorial in Washington, DC. This bronze illustrates French's ability to suggest abstract qualities and achieve sculptural effects without sacrificing the individuality of the subject.

An Anglo-Italian bronze group of St. George and the Dragon, by Francesco Fanelli, St. George in classical attire, his horse rearing over the dragon, on a naturalistic bronze base, early 17thC, 8½in (21cm) high, on an ebonised socle.
£50,000–52,000 *S(NY)*

A French bronze group, 'Theseus Slaying the Centaur', cast from the model by Antoine-Louis Barye, on a naturalistic rocky base, signed, foundry inscription 'F. Barbedienne Fondeur', ink inscription '8312/ule 550', late 19thC, 16in (41cm) high.
£2,200–3,200 *C*

A French bronze group of a bacchante riding a goat, cast after the model by Philippe Laurent Roland, on a naturalistic base cast with foliage, early 19thC, 16in (41cm) high.
£2,000–2,500 *C*

An Italian bronze group of an Arab swordsman on horseback, cast from a model by Attilio Prendoni, on a shaped naturalistic base, signed 'A. Prendoni', on a modern black painted wooden pedestal, 21½in (54cm) high.
£1,500–2,000 *C*

A Russian bronze group, after Ievgueni Alexandrevich Lanceray, depicting a cossack on horseback lifting and embracing a young woman, signed in cyrillic, founded by C. F. Woerffel, St. Petersburg, late 19thC, 8in (20cm) high.
£1,000–1,500 *Bea*

The Visconti-Annoni marriage bowl, with 2 small diametrically opposed handles in the form of female figures curving from the rim to the body of the bowl, a grotesque mask below, a coat-of-arms on either side, Milanese, c1580, 13in (33cm) diam.
£68,000–70,000 *S(NY)*

This bowl celebrates the marriage of Sylvia Visconti to Giambattista Annoni shortly after the death of her first husband, Alfonso Cicogna.

A bronze mortar, with a crowned Tudor Rose, c1680.
£250–300 *KEY*

A bronze mortar, decorated with a band of flowers and shells, c1700.
£300–400 *KEY*

l. A bronze mortar, with moulded decoration and owner's initials, 17thC.
£300–350 *KEY*

A Florentine bronze mortar, mid-16thC, 12in (30.5cm) high.
£12,000–14,000 *S(NY)*

A bronze candlestick with inkwell, from the workshop of Severo da Ravenna, with brown patina, damaged and restored, early 16thC, 10½in (26cm) high.
£5,000–6,000 *C*

A north Italian bronze inkstand of a man opening a monster's jaws, with an armorial cartouche at the base of the monster's jaw, late 16thC, 4½in (11.5cm) high.
£14,000–16,000 *S(NY)*

A bronze and ormolu inkstand, the hinged cover set with a sleeping winged putto, enclosing 2 small inkpots, engraved sides, on a marble and ormolu mounted plinth, early 19thC, 6in (15cm) wide.
£650–750 *DN*

A pair of 17thC style Italian bronze candlesticks, with brown patina, later nozzles, 28½in (72cm) high.
£2,500–3,000 *C*

A pair of Second Empire gilt bronze candelabra, on candlestick bases, 17in (43cm) high.
£1,200–1,800 *CSK*

A pair of bronze candlesticks, after Gasparo de Lucca, brassy surface, each candlestick in 3 separate pieces, minor damage, c1800, 9in (22.5cm) high.
£1,200–1,500 *C*

A bronze uniface medal of Louis XIV, wearing classical armour, signed 'Bertinet sculpteur priuilegio', late 17thC, 6in (15cm) diam.
£2,000–2,500 *S(NY)*

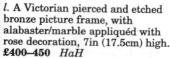

A Roman bronze relief of the Annunciation, the Virgin seated looking at the approaching figure of the Angel, the Holy Dove and winged cherubs' heads above, mid-17thC, 10 by 13in (25 by 33cm).
£12,500–14,000 *S(NY)*

A bronze bell, by Johan van den Eynde, signed and dated in a band around the bottom '1556', 4in (10cm) high.
£2,000–2,500 *C*

l. A Victorian pierced and etched bronze picture frame, with alabaster/marble appliquéd with rose decoration, 7in (17.5cm) high.
£400–450 *HaH*

Copper

A Flemish gilt copper plaque of the Annunciation, signed 'Paul Ponce Fecit', hole at the top for suspension, some wear to gilding, mid-17thC, 16½in (42cm) high.
£10,000–12,000 *S(NY)*

A copper firemark of the Licensed Victuallers & General Fire & Life Insurance, c1850, 11½in (29.5cm) high.
£200–300 *KEY*

A Victorian copper coal helmet, c1890.
£150–175 *ASH*

A copper watering can, with embossed scrolls and gadrooning to cover, with rose, c1900, 35in (89.5cm) long.
£1,100-1,300 *S(S)*

A Victorian copper coal scuttle, 19in (48cm) high.
£125–150 *ASH*

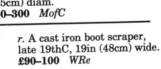

A copper tray, c1880, 36in (91.5cm) diam.
£250–300 *MofC*

A collection of 4 French keys, late 17thC, largest 4½in (11.5cm) long.
£20–80 each *KEY*

Iron

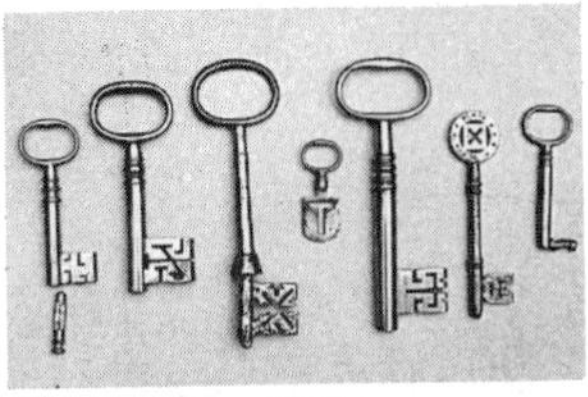

A collection of 7 keys, early 19thC, largest 7in (17.5cm) long.
£10–40 each *KEY*

A collection of 3 keys:
top: English, 18thC, 5in (12.5cm) long.
centre: Venetian, 17thC.
bottom: German, 17thC, 8½in long.
£150–250 each *KEY*

r. A cast iron boot scraper, late 19thC, 19in (48cm) wide.
£90–100 *WRe*

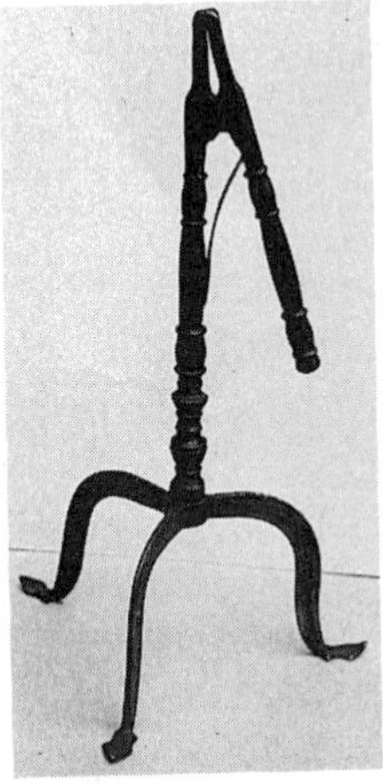

A wrought iron rushnip, c1780, 9in (22.5cm) high.
£250–300 *KEY*

A wrought iron candle or rushlight holder, with original ash base, English or Welsh, 18thC, 8in (20cm) high.
£200–250 *KEY*

A wrought iron rushnip, on original pine base, 18thC, 8in (20cm) high.
£200–250 *KEY*

Three cast iron boot scrapers, late 19thC, 6in (15cm) high.
£35–55 *WRe*

An American painted cast iron figural tethering post, in the form of a jockey, standing wearing silks, inscribed 'McWiytwick Foundry Co., Union Beach, N.J.', early 20thC, 48in (122cm) high.
£1,500–2,000 *S(S)*

r. A cast iron figural tethering post, in the form of a black jockey wearing a green waistcoat and green and white quartered cap, leaning forward holding a tethering ring in his right hand, on a square panelled base, 38in (96.5cm) high.
£500–700 *S(S)*

A German painted iron 'Armada' chest, the interior of the lid with pierced cover over intricate lock mechanism, heavy carrying handles to the sides, 17thC, 30in (76cm) long.
£950–1,200 *CAG*

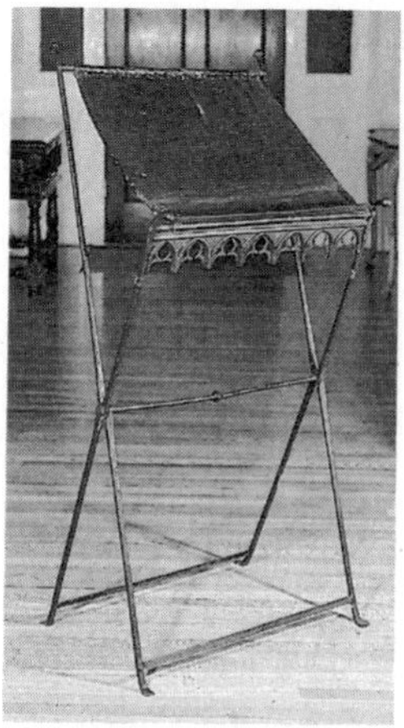

A wrought iron floor standing folding lectern or bookstand, the X-frame with stump end finials, a later leather slope above a frieze pierced with arches and tracery, the stretcher with central knop above a plain stretcher, on pad feet, French or Spanish, 16thC, 56½in (143.5cm) high.
£7,500–8,000 *C*

Make the most of Miller's

Condition is absolutely vital when assessing the value of an antique. Items in good condition are more likely to appreciate than less perfect examples. Rare, desirable items may command higher prices even when in need of restoration.

Lead

A pair of Flemish lead roundels, with scenes from the Spanish Netherlandish war, both pierced with holes for suspension, damaged, c1580, 7in (17.5cm) diam.
£4,000–5,000 *S(NY)*

A lead firemark of the Shropshire fire office, c1810, 7½in (19cm) high.
£200–300 *KEY*

A pair of tapered lead two-handled garden urns, with raised fluted and cherub's head decoration, 19thC, 15in (38cm) high.
£800–1,000 *AG*

A lead plaquette of Charity, early cast after a model by Peter Flötner, Nuremberg, inscribed 'Charatis' on the base, c1540, 3½in (9cm) high.
£120–150 *S(NY)*

Pewter

A pewter teapot, by James Duke & Sons, Sheffield, 8½in (21.5cm) high.
£200–225 *SUL*

A William and Mary flat lidded and wriggle decorated tankard, the body and cover with tulip motifs and foliage, the thumbpiece modelled with doves, on a domed foot, the interior base with touch mark 'GF', probably Garard Ford of Wigan, c1690, 5½in (14.5cm) high.
£4,500–5,500 *CSK*

A James I pewter lidded flagon, the hinged bun cover with a turned finial, the thumbpiece pierced with a heart, the cylindrical body on a skirt foot, maker's mark to the scroll handle, repaired, 13in (33cm) high.
£2,600–3,000 *WW*

MARBLE

An Anglo-Florentine white marble bust of Oliver Cromwell, by Francis Harwood, signed and dated '1759', inscribed on plinth 'Or. Cromwell', 24in (61cm) high, on a black and yellow marble socle.
£40,000–45,000 *S(NY)*

A white marble bust of Cleopatra on an octagonal fluted socle, and a conforming octagonal brocatelle marble pedestal with a spreading foot, late 19thC, bust 36in (91.5cm) high.
£18,000–20,000 *C*

A marble bust of the Duke of Wellington, by Francis Chantrey, signed and dated on reverse 'Chantrey.SC./1823', on a white marble socle and a cylindrical red scagliola column with white marble foot, column chipped, 1823, bust 25½in (65cm) high.
£48,000–50,000 *C*

A white marble bust of Hermes, after the antique, on an associated square tapering socle, early 19thC, 24½in (62cm) high.
£6,500–8,000 *C*

A marble bust of Queen Anne, wearing the Royal Crown of England, and the Collar and Order of the Garter, by Michael Rysbrack, c1738, 22½in (57cm) high.
£32,000–42,000 *S(NY)*

A white marble bust of a young woman as Diana, by Frederick William Pomeroy, signed and dated '1905', 21in (53.5cm) high.
£3,500–4,500 *S(NY)*

A white marble bust of a lady, in 18thC costume, on a square tapering socle, socle repaired, 19thC, 30in (76cm) high.
£3,500–4,000 *C*

A marble bust of a lawyer, probably French, late 16thC, 22in (55.5cm) high, on a gilt bronze socle.
£24,000–30,000 *S(NY)*

A French white marble bust of a young woman, by Albert Ernest Carrier-Belleuse, signed 'A. CARRIER', on a circular stepped socle, 19thC, 29in (73.5cm) high.
£9,000–11,000 *C*

This bust can be reliably dated to the period before 1868, when he signed his work 'A. CARRIER', rather than in full.

A French white marble bust of Diana, late 19thC, 22in (55.5cm) high.
£1,000–1,200 *S*

A French white marble bust of a young girl, wearing a shawl tied across her chest, by Georges Morin, on a base signed 'Morin', late 19thC, 25in (63.5cm) high.
£4,500–5,500 *C*

A German white marble bust of Bacchus, by Carl Voss, signed 'C. VOSS F. ROMA 1883', on a spreading socle, 21in (53cm) high.
£3,500–5,000 *C*

A French white marble bust of the Comtesse de Sabran, after Jean-Antoine Houdon, on a circular socle, late 19thC, 25in (64cm) high.
£1,500–2,000 *C*

l. A Flemish white marble bust of a girl, with a portrait relief of a male faun on a locket around her neck, surface slightly weathered, chips, restored, on a marble socle, 17½in (45cm) high.
£4,500–5,000 *C*

A Florentine white marble bust of a young nobleman, late 16thC, 23in (58.5cm) high, on a contemporary marble socle.
£23,500–24,500 *S(NY)*

An Italian fragmentary white marble head of a woman, c1800, on a modern square wooden base, head 6½in (16.5cm) high.
£2,500–3,000 *C*

An Italian white marble bust of a girl, playing a game with a cup and handkerchief, by Galerie Pietro Bazzanti, signed 'E. Giolli, Galerie P. Bazzanti Firenze', late 19thC, 18in (46cm) high.
£2,000–2,500 *S*

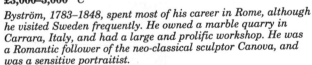

A pair of Swedish white marble busts of King Oscar I and Queen Josephina of Sweden, attributed to Johan Niklas Byström, the King wearing the Order of Serafim with band, the Queen wearing coronation robes and a cameo with a portrait of her father, Prince Eugen von Leuchtenberg, the Queen repaired, 19thC, 31in (78.5cm) high.
£3,000–5,000 *C*

Byström, 1783–1848, spent most of his career in Rome, although he visited Sweden frequently. He owned a marble quarry in Carrara, Italy, and had a large and prolific workshop. He was a Romantic follower of the neo-classical sculptor Canova, and was a sensitive portraitist.

An Italian white marble bust of Cleopatra, by Professor A. Petrilli, wearing ornate jewellery and with the asp at her breast, signed at the back 'Gall. prof. A. Petrilli. Firenze', on a shaped socle, inscribed, restored, c1900, 25½in (65.5cm) high.
£3,500–4,500 *C*

An Italian white marble three-quarter relief bust of a girl, signed 'G. Verona', late 19thC, 19½in (49.5cm) high.
£1,800–2,200 *S*

A white marble group of wrestlers, after the antique, on a plinth, early 19thC, 20in (50.5cm) high overall.
£3,000–4,000 *C*

A white marble figure of the callipygian Venus, after the antique, late 18thC, 46½in (118cm) high.
£20,000–25,000 *S(NY)*

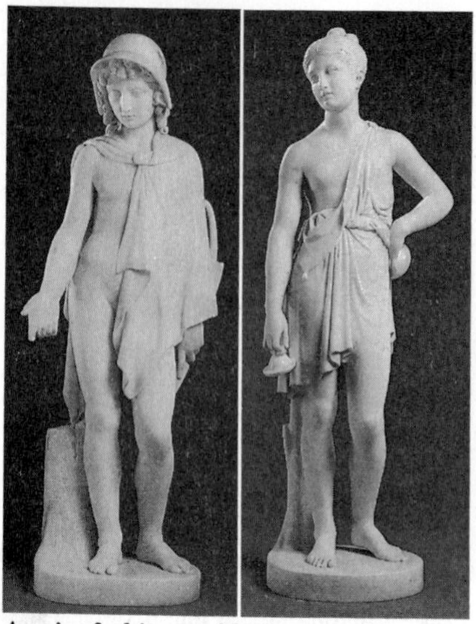

A pair of white marble figures, of Cupid disguised as a shepherd and a dancing girl, by John Gibson, each on a naturalistic base inscribed 'OPVS. IOANNIS GIBSON. ROMAE', on a white painted wooden fluted pedestal, Cupid restored, early 19thC, figures 35in (89.5cm) high.
£23,000–28,000 *C*

l. A white marble figure of a huntress, holding a leveret, with a greyhound at her side, by Richard James Wyatt, the base signed 'R. J. WYATT Fecit/ROMAE', mid-19thC, 60½in (153.5cm) high.
£68,000–80,000 *C*

This figure is the original marble sent by Richard Wyatt from his Rome studio to the Royal Academy and exhibited there in 1850, the year of his premature death.

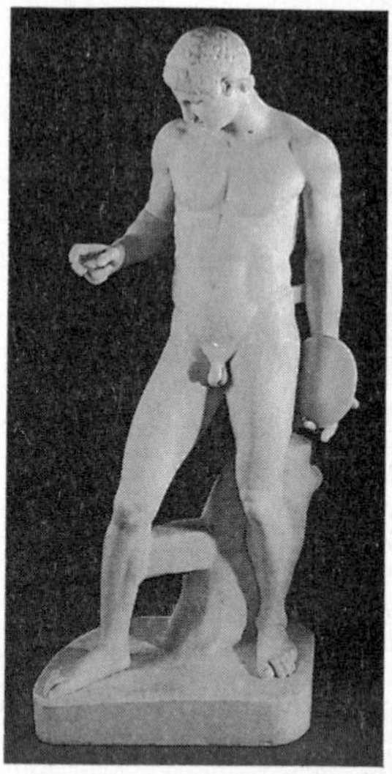

A white marble figure of a discus thrower, the naked youth standing by a tree stump, holding the discus in his left hand, damaged, 19thC, 69in (175cm) high.
£12,000–14,000 *C*

r. A white marble group of 2 putti fighting over a heart, after Pierre-Philippe Thomire, c1880, 24in (61cm) high.
£1,800–2,200 *S*

A white marble Bacchanalian group of a woman and a young faun, 19thC, 30½in (77.5cm) high.
£2,500–4,000 *C*

MILLER'S COMPARES

I An Italian white marble group of Ariadne and the Panther, after the model by Johann Heinrich von Dannecker, inscribed 'GALLERIA LAPINI FIRENZE', on a verde antico marble pedestal late 19thC, the group 31in (79cm) high.
£16,500–17,500 *C*

II An Italian white marble group of Ariadne and the Panther, after Johann Heinrich von Dannecker, signed 'P. Barzanti–Florence', late 19thC, 24in (61cm) high.
£7,000–8,000 *C*

***Item I* and *Item II* are both by prolific sculptors and are of similar quality. Bidding was fierce at the auction which offered *Item I* for sale, and was the main reason that it reached a higher price.** *C*

A white marble figure of Cupid, seated on a fountain with lion mask spout, his quiver at its foot, signed 'Steiner', restored, late 19thC, 35½in (90.5cm) high.
£3,500–4,500 *C*

A pair of white marble figures of Ceres and Bacchus, emblematic of Summer and Autumn, each figure weathered, on square bases, chipped, late 19thC, woman 99½in (253cm) high overall.
£43,000–48,000 *C*

A Venetian marble relief of the Virgin and Child, c1460, 25in (63.5cm) high.
£50,000–55,000 *S(NY)*

A French white marble figure, entitled 'La Muse d'André Chenier', by Denys Puech, holding the guillotined head of the poet and embracing it on the forehead, seated on drapery, on a naturalistic base, signed 'D. Puech 1902', 21in (53.5cm) high.
£6,500–8,000 *C*

A pair of white marble Atlantes, from the workshop of Giovanni Angelo Montorsoli, roughly finished on reverse, weathered, damaged and repaired, mid-16thC, 44in (111.5cm) high, on modern bases.
£35,000–40,000 *C*

A French white marble figure of a dancing maiden, by Henri Allouard, wearing flowing robes and supporting a basket of flowers in one hand and a rose in the other, the base signed 'H. Allouard/1914', the figure 69in (175cm) high, on a fluted stone pedestal.
£29,000–33,000 *C*

r. A carved marble group of Bacchus and a young satyr, by Francesco Bertos, slight damage, early 18thC, 23½in (60cm) high.
£68,000–70,000 *C*

An Italian white marble figure of two Cupids struggling over a heart, on an oval base carved with flowerheads, 19thC, 27in (70cm) high.
£3,000–3,500 *DN*

An Italian white marble figure of Bacchus, the youth leaning against a tree stump, with a vine garland to his hair and holding a bunch of grapes in his right hand, slight damage, late 19thC, 60in (152cm) high.
£8,000–9,000 *C*

An Italian white marble figure of Cleopatra seated on a lion, by Girolamo Masini, signed and dated 'G. Masini Fect. 1875, Roma', inscribed, 48½in (123cm) high.
£92,000–95,000 *S*

Miller's is a price GUIDE not a price LIST

l. An Italian white marble figure of a young woman, wearing peasant's costume, by Professor Antonio Bortona, signed, on a verde antico marble pedestal with an octagonal foot, late 19thC, figure 56in (142cm) high.
£8,000–10,000 *C*

An Italian white marble figure of Rebecca, signed and dated 'G. M. Benzoni F Roma A 1871', the signature infilled in red, on a grey striated marble column, with rotating top and octogonal foot, figure 61in (155cm) high.
£42,000–50,000 *S*

Benzoni came from a humble background in Bergamo, and moved to Rome in 1828 to establish a successful studio. There aristocratic families from St. Petersburg to Brazil gave him commissions. He was a favoured sculptor of Pope Pius IX.

An Italian white marble figure of a lady drying herself, after Allegrain, signed 'CANOVA', on an integral socle, late 19thC, 31½in (80cm) high.
£3,000–3,500 *C*

An Italian white marble figure of a maiden, wearing classical robes, after Antonio Canova, restored, late 19thC, 52½in (133cm) high.
£10,500–12,500 *C*

An Italian white marble figure of a girl in medieval dress, by F. Vichi, signed, on a black marble column, late 19thC, figure 43in (109cm) high.
£9,000–10,000 *S*

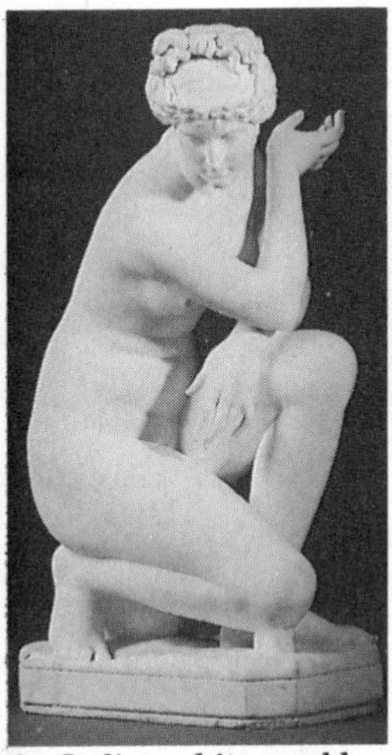

An Italian white marble figure of the crouching Venus, after the antique, restored, late 19thC, 34½in (87.5cm) high.
£5,000–6,000 *C*

An Italian white marble figure of a bather stepping into water, by E. Fiaschi, restored, late 19thC, 33in (83.5cm) high.
£5,000–7,000 *C*

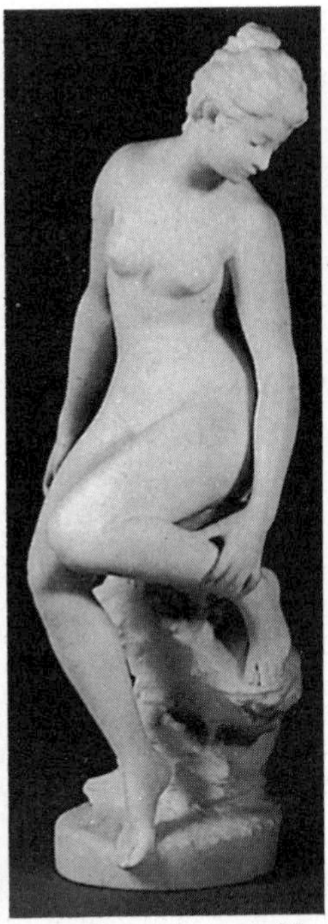

An Italian white marble figure of a woman seated on a rock, by A. Piazza Crarara, signed, restored, late 19thC, 31in (78.5cm) high.
£4,000–4,500 *C*

An Italian white marble group of Cupid and Psyche, by A. Batacchi, signed, on a liver coloured variegated marble pedestal, restored, late 19thC, group 47in (119cm) high.
£12,000–14,000 *C*

An American white marble figure of a young boy seated on a grassy mound, with flowers, by Horatio Greenough, signed and dated '1840', inscribed 'Cava di Seravezza', 27in (69cm) high.
£3,000–4,000 *S*

Horatio Greenough, born in Boston, was the first American sculptor to go to Rome to pursue neo-classical ideals. There he met Thorwaldsen, and in Florence became a pupil of Bartolini's. He is most well known for a massive statue of George Washington, and for his work on the Capitol entitled 'The Rescue' (1838–51), a marble group of white settlers defending themselves against an Indian.

An Italian white marble figure of Venus emerging from the bath, after the antique, early 20thC, 31½in (80cm) high.
£2,500–3,500 *S*

A Swedish white marble figure of Bacchus, by Eric Gustav Gothe, signed, restored, c1822, 37½in (95cm) high.
£30,000–40,000 *C*

l. A white marble profile medallion of Thomas Farmer, by John Adams Acton, signed, inscribed and dated '1864', 23in (58.5cm) diam.
£1,200–1,600 *S*

John Adams Acton first studied at the Royal Academy and then became a pupil of John Gibson's in Rome. He began exhibiting from the age of 20 at the Academy where he specialised in portrait sculpture.

r. Two Italian white marble figures of dancing nymphs, after Antonio Canova, each on circular bases with wooden pedestals, damaged, late 19thC, figures 53in (134.5cm) high.
£21,000–25,000 *C*

STONE

A French carved stone group of St. James and a royal donor, damaged, c1400, 19½in (49.5cm) high.
£13,000–15,000 *C*

A carved stone relief of the Virgin and Child, by Giovanni Bastianini, in an oak frame, repaired, late 19thC, 23in (58.5cm) high.
£2,000–3,000 *C*

TERRACOTTA

A portrait bust of Jacques Nonotte, by Clement Jayet, inscribed and signed 'Natvs. Anno 1708/Clemens. Jayet. Fecit. 1773', on a carved wooden socle, 27in (68.5cm) high.
£28,000–32,000 *S(NY)*

A terracotta group of a faun and an infant faun, by the circle of Pierre Surugue, slight damage, c1900, 14½in (36.5cm) high.
£1,800–2,200 *C*

An Italo-Netherlandish terracotta bozzetto figure of Neptune, his left arm resting on the intertwined tails of 2 dolphins at his feet, early 17thC, 8in (20cm) high.
£10,000–12,000 *S(NY)*

A Flemish terracotta model of an apostle, damaged, c1700, on an integral square plinth, 25½in (65cm) high.
£4,500–5,500 *C*

A terracotta figure of an angel, by the circle of Angelo Pio, inscribed 'G. Sammartino', repaired, on an integral plinth, early 18thC, 15in (38cm) high, and a modern ebonised wooden base.
£7,000–9,000 *C*

An Italian terracotta bozzetto for an entombment, attributed to Antonio Canova, the limp body of Christ being lifted by Joseph of Arimathea and Nicodemus, late 18thC, 9½in (24cm) high.
£24,000–28,000 *S(NY)*

l. A terracotta group, entitled 'Le Mal du Pays', by Joseph Edgar Boehm, signed and dated 'I. E. Boehm fct 1865', inscribed 'ITALIA', perhaps representing the Risorgimento, the figure seated on a bench with carved decoration, covered with cloth, 12in (30.5cm) high.
£9,000–10,000 *S(NY)*

A terracotta group of 2 nymphs and a satyr, in the manner of Clodion, signed and date on reverse 'Clodion/1783', damaged and repaired, 19thC, 21in (53.5cm) high.
£4,500–5,000 *C*

A French terracotta group of a satyr and bacchante, on a rocky naturalistic base, signed 'A. CARRIER. BELLEUSE', restored, late 19thC, 26in (66cm) high.
£1,500–2,000 *C*

A terracotta relief of Mercury, by or from the workshop of Artus Quellinus the Elder, damaged, 17thC, in a later giltwood frame, 25½in (65cm) high.
£35,000–40,000 *C*

PLASTER

A pair of 'Brighton Pavilion' nodding head plasterwork figures of an emperor and empress, their hands concealed beneath an Imperial yellow ground robe, the male wearing a gilded official cap, his Imperial consort with her hair pinned in a topknot, some repainting, minor restoration, Qianlong, c1770, 11in (28cm) high.
£40,000–45,000 *C*

r. A plaster head of Oliver Cromwell, attributed to Thomas and Abraham Simon, probably from a funerary effigy, c1598, 18in (45.5cm) high, on a later wood stand.
£22,000–25,000 *S(NY)*

Funeral effigies were an ancient tradition which carried on in England until the early 19thC with the funeral of Lord Nelson. At the funeral of a great man, a life-like model of the deceased was carried before the coffin to the grave, and was later set up in the church over the tomb. The early effigies were made of wood and some heads, hands and feet were made of plaster. Later the heads were often made of wax, with facial colouring painted on, and hair added.

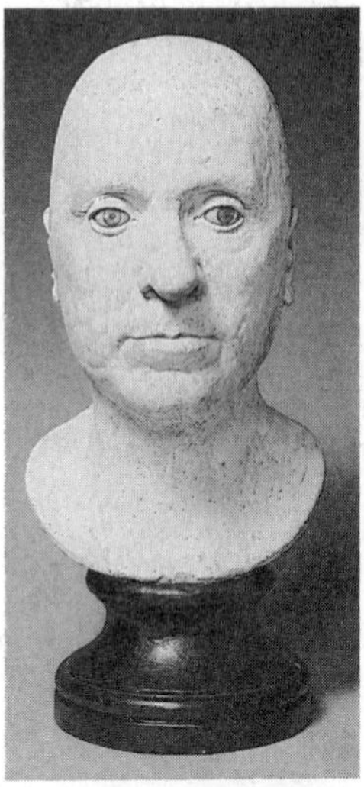

WOOD

A carved oak figure of a dog, lying with his paws outstretched, early 19thC.
£3,000–3,500 *DN*

l. A carved wooden bust of a bearded male saint, damaged, minor restoration, probably German, 17thC, 22½in (57.5cm) high.
£1,300–1,500 *C*

An oak figure of a recumbent dog, lying with his legs crossed, 19thC.
£2,200–3,000 *DN*

A pair of carved limewood heads, probably formerly from figureheads, 19thC, 15in (38cm) high.
£400–600 *DN*

A pair of carved wooden busts of 2 apostles, on integrally carved octagonal socles, damaged and restored, probably Spanish, 17thC, 19in (48cm) high.
£1,400–2,000 *C*

l. A polychrome carved oak relief figure of a bearded man, dated '1635', 15in (38cm) high, on an ebonised mahogany plinth inscribed 'Painted Wooden Figure dated 1635, from the roof of Totness Church, Devon, presented by Mrs Forbes Shillingstone 1899'.
£1,200–1,400 *CSK*

A northern European carved oak relief figure of the Virgin, within an arched niche below a scallop shell, holding a Gospel and crown, 30½in (77.5cm) high.
£1,000–1,500 *CSK*

A south German carved fruitwood figure of St Sebastian, early 17thC, 21in (53.5cm) high, on a black marble stand.
£3,200–3,800 *S(NY)*

A tobacconist's pine figure of Sir Walter Raleigh, wearing a cape, c1800, 53in (134.5cm) high.
£3,000–4,000 *CSK*

A polychrome carved tobacconist's figure of a native of Guinea, wearing a feather skirt and headdress, holding a plug of tobacco under his arm, damaged, c1700, on a circular base, 21in (53.5cm) high.
£1,400–1,500 *CSK*

A pair of carved oak figures of angels, probably north German, damaged and restored, late 17thC, 29½in (75cm) high.
£2,300–2,700 *C*

r. A Spanish carved fruitwood Corpus figure, the eyes inset with glass, 17thC, 13½in (34cm) high.
£1,700–2,000 *C*

A German pair of polychrome carved wooden figures of a shepherd and shepherdess, damaged and repaired, each on a moulded carved wooden socle, early 18thC, 9½in (24cm) high.
£2,300–2,700 *C*

A Spanish parcel gilt and polychrome carved wooden relief of the The Last Supper, damaged, c1600, 55½in (141cm) wide.
£24,000–28,000 *C*

A German carved wooden figure of a bishop saint, the reverse hollowed out, traces of polychrome, damaged and restored, 17thC, 25½in (65cm) high.
£700–1,000 *C*

An Italian carved wooden figure of Hercules, damaged and repaired, probably 19thC, 27½in (70cm) high.
£4,500–5,000 *C*

A carved wooden relief of a dead bird and a mouse, signed and dated 'Aubert Parent fecit 1794', cracked, 10½in (27cm) high, in a giltwood frame.
£15,000–17,000 *C*

Aubert-Henri-Joseph Parent, 1753–1835, was born in Cambrai, and first gained public recognition in 1777 when a panel he had carved was presented to the young Louis XVI.

A polychrome carved wooden Corpus figure, damaged and repaired, probably Austrian, 18thC, 15in (38cm) high, now mounted on a modern wooden backboard.
£2,000–2,500 *C*

A pair of German carved wooden candlesticks, in the form of standing angels, the lower section of each pedestal associated, damaged and repaired, early 18thC, 27in (68.5cm) high.
£4,000–5,000 *C*

Use the Index!
Because certain items might fit easily into any number of categories, the quickest and surest method of locating any entry is by reference to the index at the back of the book.
This index has been fully cross-referenced for absolute simplicity.

r. A German polychrome carved wooden group of The Trinity, with a recess carved out of the reverse, damaged, 15thC, 17½in (45cm) high.
£5,600–6,000 *C*

A Spanish fragmentary polychrome and giltwood relief of St. Joseph, damaged, c1700, 50in (127cm) high.
£1,800–2,200 *C*

A Spanish polychrome carved wooden group of the Madonna and Child, the reverse hollowed out, damaged and repaired, c1600, 41½in (105.5cm) high.
£3,500–4,000 *C*

A Netherlandish polychrome carved oak figure of St. Catherine, damaged, on a later oak plinth, early 16thC, 32½in (82.5cm) high.
£4,700–5,200 *C*

A pair of Spanish or Italian polychrome carved wooden cherubs' heads, damaged and repaired, early 17thC, 14½in (36.5cm) high.
£1,400–1,700 *C*

A polychrome wooden group of Hercules and the Nemean lion, probably Nuremberg, on an integrally carved wooden plinth inscribed on the underside '19(?)13', worn and repaired, c1600, 23in (58.5cm) high.
£4,000–6,000 *C*

A set of 12 parcel gilt and polychrome reliquary figures of the apostles, probably Castilian, the eyes inset with glass, damaged, one eye missing, each on an associated wooden plinth, 18thC, largest 14in (35.5cm) high.
£3,000–3,500 *C*

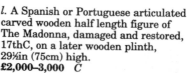

A carved wooden group of 2 cherubs' heads, from the circle of Grinling Gibbons, with 2 suspension loops on the reverse, damaged and restored, late 17thC, 29in (74cm) high.
£1,200–1,500 *C*

l. A Spanish or Portuguese articulated carved wooden half length figure of The Madonna, damaged and restored, 17thC, on a later wooden plinth, 29½in (75cm) high.
£2,000–3,000 *C*

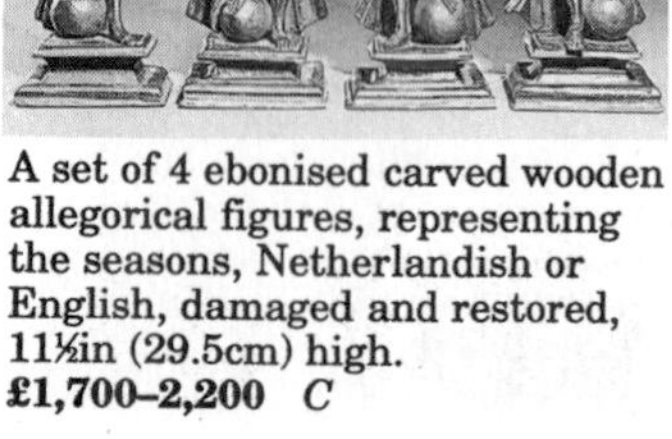

A set of 4 ebonised carved wooden allegorical figures, representing the seasons, Netherlandish or English, damaged and restored, 11½in (29.5cm) high.
£1,700–2,200 *C*

A Spanish polychrome carved wooden group of the Madonna and Child, the reverse hollowed out, damaged and restored, 40½in (103cm) high.
£32,000–40,000 *C*

A south Italian polychrome carved wooden horse, the eyes inset with glass, with a metal mounted leather bridle, reins and saddle, 18thC, on a modern black plinth, damaged, 13in (33cm) high.
£2,000–2,400 *C*

r. A pair of wooden painted candlesticks, c1900, 53in (134.5cm) high.
£450–500 *MofC*

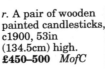

An Italian giltwood thirteen-light floor standing pricket candelabra, on tripod scroll feet, 18thC, 82in (208cm) high.
£3,000–4,000 *C*

A set of 6 boxwood carvings, each of a Caesar carved in relief with various headdresses, within an oval, 18thC, 5in (12.5cm) high.
£1,300–1,700 *DN*

An oak panel, carved with Gothic tracery, early 16thC, 13in (33cm) high.
£150–250 *KEY*

An oak panel, carved with a Roman head, 16thC, 15½in (39.5cm) high.
£400–500 *KEY*

l. A carved oak panel, depicting a Tudor gentleman, 16thC, 8in (20cm) wide.
£200–300 *KEY*

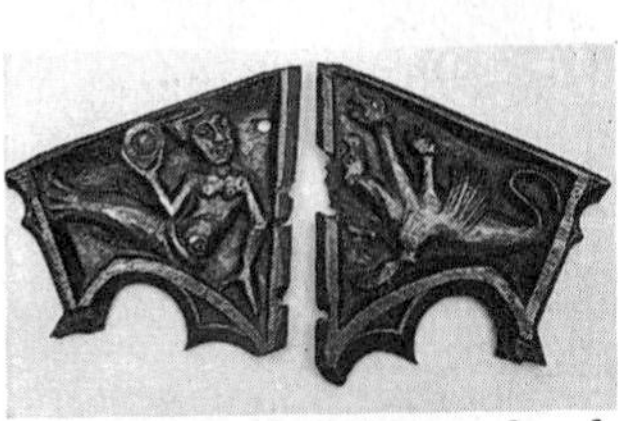

Two oak carvings from a church rood screen, depicting a mermaid and a hydra, 16thC, 8in (20cm) wide.
£180–200 each *KEY*

A pair of carved oak female figures, early 17thC, 45in (114cm) long.
£900–1,000 *KEY*

A French carved oak panel, c1580, 22in (55.5cm) high.
£150–200 *KEY*

An associated pair of dummy boards, painted on canvas and applied on oak, on ebonised spreading plinths, adapted c1800 from 17thC Flemish paintings, largest 44in (111.5cm) high.
£5,500–6,500 *CSK*

ALABASTER

An alabaster relief of the Deposition, damaged, early 15thC, on a later velvet covered mount, 17in (43cm) high.
£5,800–7,000 *C*

AGATE

A silver mounted moss agate cup, probably from the Prague Imperial Court Workshop, the gilded mounts edged with stylised acorns, the stem mount with a flowerhead, the base of the foot engraved with the French Royal Inventory No. '345', 3½in (9cm) diam.
£24,000–28,000 *S(NY)*

A silver gilt and agate goblet, with broad silver gilt rim and silver gilt mounts pierced and engraved with acanthus, 17thC, 3in (7.5cm) high.
£4,500–5,500 *S(NY)*

l. An alabaster bust of a girl in Renaissance style, by Pietro Bazzanti, signed, late 19thC, 19in (48cm) high.
£1,700–2,200 *S*

r. An alabaster relief of the Entombment, damaged and repaired, Nottingham, 15thC, on a modern black marble base, 16½in (42cm) high.
£5,200–7,000 *C*

An alabaster figure of a kneeling woman, damaged, early 17thC, 37½in (95cm) high.
£1,700–2,200 *C*

An Italian alabaster figure of a lady, by A. Cipriani, in Empire dress, reclining on a cushioned chair, on a signed base, later marble plinth, late 19thC, 24in (61.5cm) high.
£4,500–5,000 *C*

LEATHER

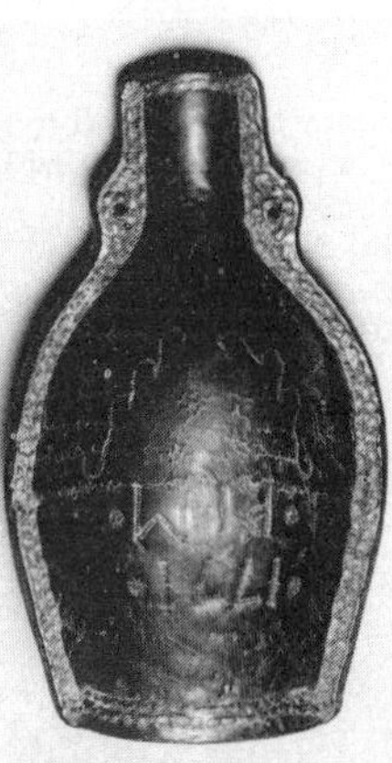

A George III leather bottle, of bulbous form, dated '1771', and inscribed 'P I M', 8½in (21cm) high.
£400–450 *DN*

A pair of alabaster figures of a man and woman, one side of each figure unfinished, hands missing, damaged, early 17thC, largest 17½in (44.5cm) high.
£800–1,200 *C*

A south Netherlandish alabaster group of The Pieta, attributed to the Master of Rimini, c1430, 10in (25cm) high.
£180,000–190,000 *S(NY)*

A leather screen, c1900, 29in (73.5cm) high.
£55–65 *Ber*

An Italian alabaster bust of a girl, on a later black marble socle, late 19thC, 23½in (60cm) high.
£2,200–2,700 *C*

An alabaster relief of Adam and Eve, extensive traces of gilding, in a giltwood frame inscribed 'Genes:3:Capit', Malines, damaged and repaired, c1600, 7in (17.5cm) high.
£2,000–3,000 *C*

A set of 4 graduated leather jacks, the baluster bodies each painted in polychrome with traces of armorial bearings, the loop handles with ring terminals, early 18thC, largest 15in (38cm) high.
£4,200–4,800 *CSK*

l. A pair of painted leather fire buckets, probably New England, all on a pale olive green ground, each with a leather covered rope swing handle, inscribed and dated 'S. Frothingham Ex. Flammis Resurgo 1794', some paint loss, 11in (28cm) high.
£1,500–2,000 *S(NY)*

BOXES

A Georgian mahogany and string inlaid serpentine fronted knife box, stamped 'Gillows, Lancaster', with a hinged lid and moulded base, 15in (38cm) high.
£300–500 *AH*

A mahogany knife box, with serpentine front, parquetry inlaid edges and star inlaid lid, flower painted wreaths and ribbons, and a moulded base, 19thC, 15in (38cm) high.
£400–500 *AH*

A George III burr yew wood and inlaid tea caddy, the hinged lid inlaid with shell, the panel below decorated with a vase of flowers flanked by serpent decorated canted angles, 4½in (11.5cm) high.
£650–700 *P(EA)*

A George II mahogany and brass inlaid tea caddy, in the manner of Landall and Gordon, with a hinged top enclosing a later fitted interior, the front with an engraved escutcheon and with a concealed drawer, on gilt brass ogee bracket feet, 8½in (21.5cm) wide.
£700–800 *DN*

A George III ivory tea caddy, of chamfered octagonal form, the vertically ribbed body set with blue jasper plaques, applied with classical motifs.
£2,500–3,500 *L*

A turned fruitwood tea caddy, in the form of an apple, with steel hinge and escutcheon, stalk missing, early 19thC, 4½in (11.5cm) high.
£1,400–1,800 *Bea*

A George III kingwood tea caddy, with a crossbanded domed hinged top, banded and crossbanded throughout, 9½in (24cm) wide.
£700–900 *DN*

A George III mahogany and ebony tea caddy, with a hinged top enclosing an interior with a tin canister and another division, inlaid with rosewood and ivory starbursts and chequer strung lines, on ebony bracket feet, 10in (25cm) wide.
£500–700 *DN*

A Regency tortoiseshell tea caddy, with geometric pewter strung decoration, the stepped cavetto hinged lid concealing twin lidded canisters, on gilt ball feet, 6in (15cm) wide.
£550–700 *P(EA)*

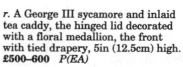

r. A George III sycamore and inlaid tea caddy, the hinged lid decorated with a floral medallion, the front with tied drapery, 5in (12.5cm) high.
£500–600 *P(EA)*

A German enamel snuff box, the exterior with a blue ground inlaid in silver with a portrait of Frederick the Great in a crowned badge, surrounded by the names and dates of his battles from 1741 to 1760, the sides with his crowned monogram and military trophies, the interior painted with a figure of Mars, Frederick's initials and inscription 'Victoria der Sieg ist da', 3⅜in (8.5cm) wide.
£2,000–2,500 *P*

This snuff box is said to have been given by Frederick the Great to an ancestor of the Scarisbrick family of Southport who fought with Frederick. The box was purchased from a sale of the contents of Scarisbrick Hall.

A Regency paper scroll tea caddy, of elliptical outline with chequer strung edge and hinged lid, the front inset with circular bosses depicting figures in various scenes, 7½in (19cm) wide.
£400–600 *P(EA)*

A Victorian tortoiseshell tea caddy, the hinged top inlaid with silver lines.
£1,300–1,500 *DN*

A German enamel snuff box, painted in colours on the inside and exterior of the cover, the sides and base with battle scenes in the style of Rugendas, with gilt scrollwork spandrels, gilt metal mount, 3in (7.5cm) wide.
£1,000–1,400 *P*

A Fromery Berlin double snuff box, the white ground gilt with diamond trellis with blue enamel gems at the junctions, and with blue and gilt ribbon bound line border, 2½in (6.5cm) wide.
£550–650 *P*

l. A tortoiseshell box and cover, inlaid with silver piqué star and initials 'VF7', between guilloche bands, slight damage and fading, 18thC, 4½in (11.5cm) high.
£240–260 *DN*

A Fromery Berlin snuff box, modelled as a pair of lady's bloomers, with a flat top and 2 'legs' painted with buildings and trees, between borders of pink and blue stripes and stars, with raised gilt scrolls and details, 3in (7.5cm) wide.
£750–1,000 *P*

A four-colour gold snuff box, probably Swiss, chased and engraved on 4 sides with oval medallions, with a plain band around the base, indistinct marks, 18thC, 3in (7.5cm) long.
£2,400–3,000 *C*

A William IV mahogany brass bound, military writing box, the fitted interior with a baize flap and writing compartment, the glass ink bottles with Sheffield plate covers, the sides with sunken brass handles and a drawer with fittings for printing dispatches, 9in (22.5cm) wide.
£700–800 *WW*

A Swiss gold and enamel bonbonnière, the detachable cover with a central painted medallion in a split pearl border, on a mauve guilloche enamel ground, with chased gold and enamel foliage border, the engine turned sides with similar borders, indistinct maker's mark, c1790, 2½in (6cm) diam.
£4,500–5,500 *C*

A note with this box states that it was the gift of the Duke and Duchess of Gloucester.

An Italian gold mounted black bonbonnière, set with a micro-mosaic plaque depicting 2 hounds in a landscape, within a gilt metal mount, the box with plain gold mounts, c1800, 3½in (9cm) diam.
£2,000–2,500 *C(G)*

A silver gilt filigree, enamel and gem set singing bird box, probably Austro-Hungarian, the mechanism probably Swiss, set with pearls and green stones at intervals, on repoussé convex base, probably later, incorporating a drawer for the key, unmarked, 4in (10cm) long.
£1,700–2,200 *C*

A China trade tortoiseshell box, with richly carved decoration, c1820, 3½in (9cm) diam.
£1,500–2,000 *RIT*

A Victorian papier mâché table cabinet, with a coved rising lid, the interior fitted with 4 drawers, the bottom drawer with a satinwood writing slope, enclosed by a pair of doors set with mirror shaped cartouches, 12in (30.5cm) wide.
£400–500 *L*

A red tortoiseshell boulle casket, with gilt brass and pewter inlay, with rising hinged top and ormolu feet and mounts, mid-19thC.
£900–1,200 *LRG*

A late Victorian mahogany and marquetry inlaid stationery box, with brass carrying handles and hinged lid, the fall front revealing a fitted interior with red morocco writing slope, letter racks, 3 small drawers, and leather bound books and accessories, 13in (33cm) high.
£800–1,200 *AH*

A bronze figure of Marie Antoinette, by Lord Ronald Sutherland Gower, signed, late 19thC, 11½in (29cm) high.
£3,000–3,500 *S*

A bronze bust of Matthew Prior, after Antoine Coysevox, circle of John Cheere, stamped, 18thC, 2½in (7cm) high.
£2,200–2,500 *S(NY)*

A Roman style bronze bust of Christ, early 17thC, 7½in (19.5cm) high.
£10,000–11,000 *S(NY)*

A bronze model of a racehorse, being led by a groom, in the manner of John Willis Good, 19thC, 11½in (29cm) high.
£1,200–1,500 *S*

A bronze portrait medallion of William Fanning, by Thomas Woolner, signed and dated '1854', 8½in (21.5cm) diam.
£8,000–9,000 *S(NY)*

A Florentine bronze figure of Morgante as Bacchus, attributed to Valerio Cioli, late 16thC, 5in (13cm) high.
£6,000–7,000 *S(NY)*

A Roman style bronze bust of Cupid, after François Duquesnoy, c1700, 14½in (37cm) high.
£3,500–4,000 *S(NY)*

A French bronze head of a satyr, inscribed, with Susse Frères foundry stamp, 5in (13cm) high, on a marble plinth.
£5,000–6,000 *S(NY)*

A pair of French bronze studies of a boy and girl, signed 'E. Villanis', foundry stamp, late 19thC, 8in (20cm) high, on marble plinths.
£1,500–2,000 *C*

A German bronze group of a maiden and deer, signed 'M. Berhtold', early 20thC, 24in (61.5cm) high.
£2,600–3,000 *C*

A French bronze figure of Diana, from the workshop of Francavilla, early 17thC, 5in (12.5cm) high.
£6,500–7,000 *S(NY)*

A French bronze figure of Cleopatra, from the school of Fontainebleau, with a rich copper brown patina and traces of black lacquer, mid-16thC, 10½in (27cm) wide, on a wooden stand.
£70,000–80,000 *S(NY)*

A French bronze group of a greyhound and hare, by Antoine-Louis Barye, black and green patina splashed with red, signed, stamped 'H', early 19thC, 8in (20cm) high.
£11,000–12,000 *S(NY)*

A bronze figure of the Porcellino, after the antique, 8¼in (21cm) wide.
£700–1,200 *S(NY)*

A French bronze figure, entitled 'Reclining Bear', signed 'Barye' with foundry mark 'F. Barbedienne Fondeur', gold seal 'FB', incised and stamped, early 19thC, 5½in (14cm) wide.
£5,500–6,000 *S*

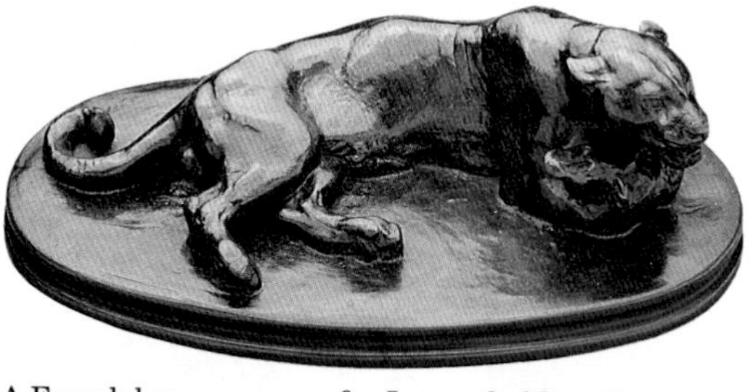

A French bronze group of a Jaguar holding the head of a horse, by Antoine-Louis Barye, signed, 3in (7.5cm) high.
£4,800–6,000 *S(NY)*

A French bronze figure of a pheasant strutting across a rockwork base, by Antoine-Louis Barye, signed, stamped and numbered '19', 4½in (11cm) high.
£5,500–6,000 *S(NY)*

An Italian bronze figure of a pacing lion, from the workshop of Tiziano Aspetti, with a label on the base inscribed 'E.G.R.', late 16thC, on a later marble base, 6½in (16.5cm) wide.
£14,000–16,000 *C*

A French bronze figure of a partridge, cast from a model by François Pompon, with foundry stamp 'Cire Perdue/C. Valsuani', early 20thC, 9½in (24cm) high.
£7,500–8,500 *C*

A bronze ecorché horse, cast from the 'Torrie Horse', by the Pastori foundry, Geneva, after the bronze by Giambologna, 1983, 34in (86cm) high, on a mahogany pedestal.
£31,000– £33,000 *S(NY)*

A French bronze equestrian group, depicting 2 jockeys hurdling a fence, cast from a model by Comte G de Ruille, on a naturalistic base, signed, late 19thC, 29in (73.5cm) wide.
£9,500–11,000 *C*

A French bronze tiger devouring a gavial of the Ganges, by Antoine-Louis Barye, stamped 'Barye' 3 times and numbered '3', lying on a naturalistic base, early 19thC, 4in (10cm) high.
£12,500–14,000 *S(NY)*

A wrought iron adjustable lectern, with candlestand, c1800, 47in (119cm) high.
£700–800 *RYA*

An Art Nouveau copper coal bucket, with brass handle, 15in (38cm) wide.
£100–115 *AnE*

A moulded copper and zinc weather vane, in the form of a running horse, with flowing mane and tail, labelled 'Cushing & White, Pat'd Aug-18 1868, Waltham, Mass.', late 19thC, 30in (76cm) long.
£2,500–3,500 *CNY*

A lead firemark of the Sun Fire Office, c1795.
£100–150 *KEY*

A pewter beefeater flagon, with stepped flat lid and twin bud thumbpiece, domed foot, 17thC, 9in (23cm) high.
£3,000–3,500 *CSK*

A French brass candlestick, with shaped base, 18thC, 8½in (21.5cm) high.
£140–160 *KEY*

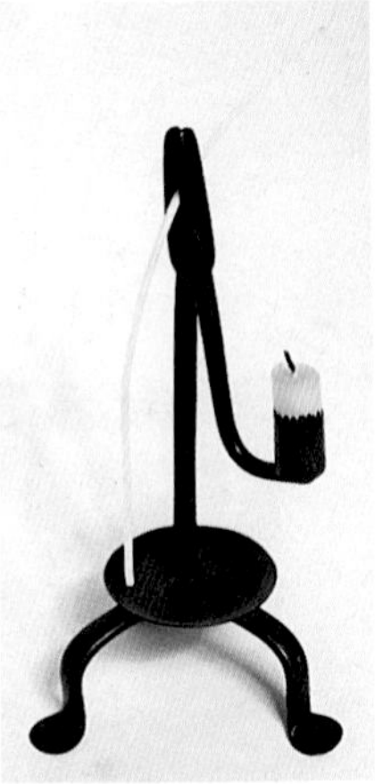

A wrought iron rush light, with a low drip pan, c1760, 11in (28cm) high.
£500–550 *RYA*

An Italian black painted wrought iron door knocker, with a mythical beast and an eagle, 19thC, 22in (56cm).
£650–750 *CSK*

A North American 14ct gold chalice and platen, late 19thC, 32.7oz.
£7,500–8,000 *RIT*

A pewter spire flagon, inscribed and dated 'John Fryer 1717', touch mark, mid-18thC, 13in (33cm) high.
£3,700–4,200 *CSK*

A pair of French blue john and ormolu mounted candlelabra, c1880, 9in (23cm) high.
£3,000–3,250 *GJC*

A pewter cider jug, c1860, 8in (20cm) high.
£140–160 *KEY*

A Victorian Britannia standard silver gilt punchbowl, by George Lambert, London 1882, 12½in (32cm) diam, 66oz.
£1,600–2,200 *DN*

A Regency ormolu mounted lacquered brass and fruitwood inkstand, stamped with 2 coats-of-arms, with a mahogany lined frieze drawer, 12½in (32cm) wide.
£9,500–10,500 *C*

A George I silver tea kettle, stand and lamp, maker's mark 'ED', c1718, 14in (36cm) high
£9,500–10,500 *C*

A George III silver épergne, by Thomas Pitts, the central basket engraved with a coat-of-arms, London 1773, 16in (41cm) high.
£27,000–30,000 *C*

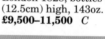

A George IV silver gilt toilet service, by Mary Ann & Charles Reily, London 1828, bottles 5in (12.5cm) high, 143oz.
£9,500–11,500 *C*

A set of 12 Victorian silver dinner plates, by John Hunt and Robert Roskell, London 1873, 9½in (24cm) diam, 222oz.
£6,500–7,500 *C*

A silver-topped box, Birmingham 1906, 8½in (21.5cm) long.
£90–100 *WN*

A pair of George IV silver gilt wine coolers, by Benjamin Smith, applied twice with a coat-of-arms, London 1826, 10½in (27cm) high, 302oz.
£63,000–65,000 *C*

A George III silver bread basket, by Paul Storr, engraved with a coat-of-arms, London 1817, 10½in (27cm) wide, 65oz.
£35,000–40,000 *C*

A pair of table candlesticks, by Ebenezer Coker, London 1764, 10in (25cm) high, 34oz.
£1,700–2,000 *HCC*

A Victorian silver stirrup cup, formed as a stag's head, by John S. Hunt, gilt lined, London 1864, 7in (18cm) long, 20oz.
£4,000–5,000 *C*

Two pairs of George III cluster column candlesticks, one pair by William Cripps, the other by Fenton Creswick & Co., London 1771, 12½in (32cm) high.
£6,000–7,000 *Bon*

A pair of electroplated parcel gilt five-light candelabra, on 4 fluted pad feet, by Elkington & Co., 1888, 26½in (67.5cm) high.
£3,500–4,500 *Bon*

A five-piece silver tea and coffee service, maker's mark of Fletcher & Gardiner, Philadelphia, c1813, coffee pot 11½in (29cm) high, 194oz.
£5,000–6,000 *CNY*

A pair of George IV silver wine coolers, with detachable collars and liners, engraved with a crest, maker's mark of Phillip Rundell, London 1821, 11in (28cm) high, 221oz.
£23,000–25,000 *C*

A set of 9 silver meat dishes, each engraved with the crest of Egerton and coronet, maker's mark of Robert Garrard, London 1857, one 1828, largest 23½in (65cm) wide, 674oz.
£14,000–18,000 *C*

A German silver nine-piece tea and coffee service, maker's marks of Anton Georg Eberhard Bahlsen and Carl Becker, c1840 and 1905, kettle and stand 16in (40½in) high, 293oz.
£5,200–6,000 *C*

A silver tankard, the side engraved with 'A*Z*S', maker's mark of Joseph Clark, Danbury, Connecticut, c1780, 8½in (21cm) high, 30oz.
£4,800–5,000 *CNY*

A Victorian silver part dinner service, maker's mark of Martin Hall and Co., London 1882, the largest dish 25in (63.5cm) wide, 834oz.
£19,000–21,000 *C*

A George III silver tea urn, engraved with 2 coats-of-arms, maker's mark of Paul Storr, London 1809 and 1810, 15in (38cm) high, 211oz.
£18,000–20,000 *C*

A pair of Victorian five-light silver candelabra, engraved with 2 crests and mottos, maker's mark of Robert Garrard, London 1866, 32in (81cm) high, 600oz.
£42,000–45,000 *C*

A German silver gilt tankard, marked on base rim 'IS' and also with later Austrian control marks, c1565, 5½in (14cm) high, 18oz.
£8,000–10,000 *S(NY)*

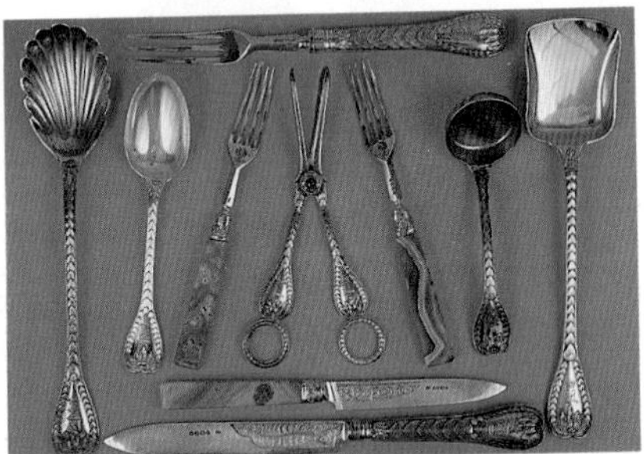

A wooden canteen of silver gilt dessert cutlery, engraved with the crest of the Duke of St. Albans, by John Samuel Hunt, London 1862, with contents list on Hunt & Roskell notepaper.
£8,500–10,000 *C*

An Italian alabaster version of the Borghese Vase, after the antique, damaged and restored, 19thC, 36in (91.5cm) high.
£3,500–4,000 *C*

A white marble bust of a girl, on a marble socle, chipped, mid-19thC, 15in (38cm) high.
£4,000–5,000 *C*

A white marble bust of a lady, carved with the monogram 'CAI' and a rearing horse, c1900, 25½in (64.5cm) high.
£1,500–2,000 *C*

An Italian alabaster group, entitled 'Primo Bacio', signed 'C. Lapini/Firenze 1889', on apedestal, 72in (182.5cm) high overall.
£5,000–6,000 *C*

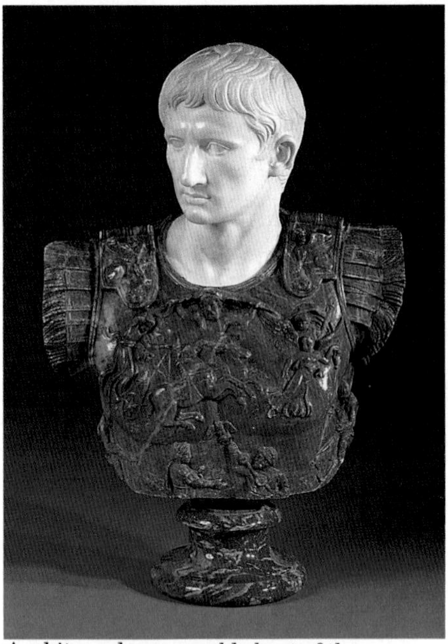

A white and grey marble bust of the Emperor Augustus, wearing a cuirass carved with a horse-drawn chariot and mythological characters, late 19thC, 35½in (90.5cm), on a marble socle.
£9,000–10,500 *C*

A white marble figure of Napoleon, on a square plinth, 19thC, 36in (91.5cm) high.
£2,500–3,000 *C*

A pair of variegated scagliola urns and pedestals, 84½in (214cm) high overall.
£2,500–3,500 *C*

A French white marble bust of a gentleman, by Henri Marius Ding, signed, late 19thC, 25in (63.5cm) high.
£1,000–1,500 *C*

An Italian white marble bust of a young lady, by A. Cipriani, signed, late 19thC, 23⅓in (59.5cm) high.
£2,000–2,500 *C*

An Italian white marble figure of Cleopatra, by F. Saul, signed, late 19thC, 42in (106cm) high.
£13,000–15,000 *C*

An Irish marble statuette of Sarah Siddons as Cassandra, by John Hickey, inscribed, late 18thC, 28½in (73cm) high.
£21,500–23,000 *S(NY)*

A French white marble group of 2 putti, on a naturalistic base, by Alfred Boucher, signed and dated '1893', 21in (53.5cm) wide.
£5,000–6,000 *C*

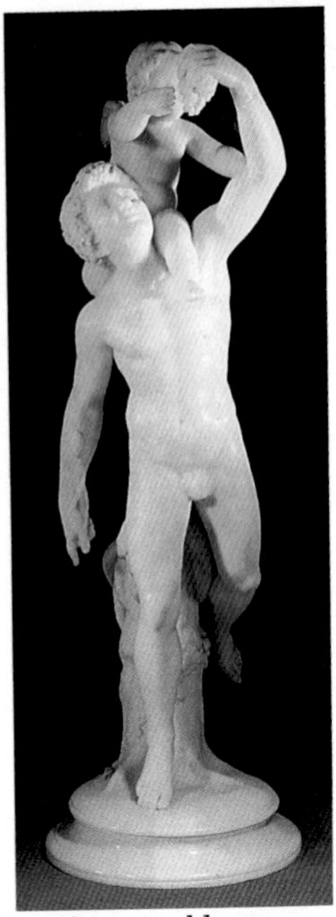

A white marble group of Bacchus supporting Cupid, on a spreading socle, probably Italian, late 19thC, 36in (91.5cm) high.
£6,000–7,000 *CSK*

An Italian white marble figure of a young girl, entitled 'Blind Man's Buff', by Francesca Barzaghi, signed and inscribed, c1874, 46½in (118cm) high.
£4,500–6,000 *C*

A rouge languedoc marble tazza, restored, probably French, late 19thC, 10½in (26.5cm) high.
£1,000–1,500 *CSK*

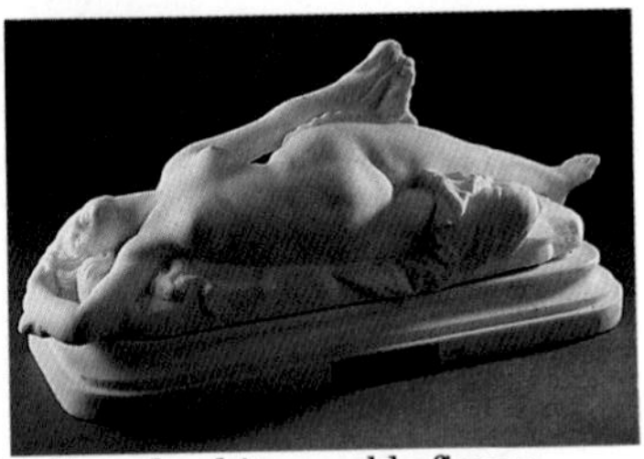

A French white marble figure, entitled 'La Venus de Pradier', by Lenhoir, inscribed and dated '7 Fevrier 1911', 24in (61.5cm) wide.
£1,200–1,700 *C*

A white marble bust of a lady, late 19thC, 29in (74cm) high, on an ebonised pedestal.
£3,500–4,000 *C*

A pair of Verona and variegated marble pedestals, mid-19thC, 47in (119cm) high.
£15,000–17,000 *C*

A pair of white marble and porphyry coloured scagiola columns, 41in (104cm) high.
£1,200–1,800 *C*

Two white marble busts of Alexander I of Russia and the Empress Elisabeth, probably French, damaged, early 19thC, 21 and 25in (53.5 and 63.5cm) high.
£5,000–6,000 *C*

A pair of patinated terracotta groups of putti, by Giuseppe Maria Mazza, one group signed, chips and repairs, early 18thC, 14 and 15in (36 and 38cm) high.
£16,500–18,000 *C*

A French terracotta group of a mother and child, signed 'A Carrier Belleuse', restored, late 19thC, 36in (91.5cm) high.
£2,000–2,500 *C*

A fragmentary terracotta group of Hercules crowned by Victory, attributed to Corneille van Cleve, the reverse unfinished, damaged, c1700, 24in (61cm) high.
£3,000–4,000 *C*

A terracotta group of Venus and Cupid, in the manner of Joseph Gott, early 19thC, on an integral base, 19in (48cm) high.
£4,000–4,500 *S(NY)*

An Austrian terracotta figure of a young girl, carrying a posy of flowers, c1880, 33in (84cm) high.
£1,000–1,250 *GJC*

A set of 4 Franco-Flemish terracotta groups of putti, representing the arts, numerous repairs and minor losses, mid-18thC, 14 to 15in (36 to 38cm) high.
£12,000–14,000 *C*

A terracotta relief of Diogenes, flanked by 2 female attendants, Alexander standing to the left, signed and dated 'W. Tyler Excu 1765', 25in (64cm) wide.
£10,000–12,000 *S(NY)*

A French terracotta bust of a lady, after Joseph Chinard, signed 'Chinard de Lyon', 24½in (62cm) high.
£1,300–1,700 *C*

A French terracotta portrait bust of Princesse de Lamballe, inscribed, 19thC, 26½in (67cm) high.
£2,000–2,500 *C*

A pair of polychrome wood candlesticks, in the form of angels, on integrally carved shaped green bases, paint restored, Tyrol, late 15thC, 23in (58.5cm) high.
£37,000–40,000 *S(NY)*

A pair of 18thC style painted dummy boards, 19thC, 39in (99cm) high.
£1,750–1,850 *S*

A Norwegian birch peg tankard, on twist fluted ball feet, c1700, 7in (17.5cm) high.
£18,000–20,000 *WW*

A pair of polychrome carved wooden angels, restored, probably south German, 18thC, largest 30½in (76.5cm) high.
£8,000–9,000 *C*

A carved wooden head, possibly Austrian, c1880, 24in (61cm) high.
£300–350 *SIG*

A pair of Italian polychrome and parcel gilt walnut relief panels, c1600, largest 54½in (138cm) high.
£5,000–7,000 *C*

A Spanish polychrome carved wooden figure of the Virgin, restored, c1800, on a later plinth 43in (109cm) high.
£3,000–4,000 *C*

A pair of Flemish carved wooden putti, each on an integrally carved plinth, cracks, c1800, 28¾in (73cm) high.
£3,500–4,500 *C*

A terracotta and wooden figure of the Virgin and Child, 18thC, 23in (58.5cm) high.
£1,200–1,500 *CSK*

A carved wooden dog, possibly Austrian, c1880, 9in (22.5cm) long.
£500–550 *GJC*

A pair of giltwood and gesso sphinxes, each with elaborate headdress and lambrequin saddlecloth, on later marblised bases, early 18thC, 11in (28cm) high.
£6,500–7,500 *S*

A pair of carved walnut models of unicorns, formed as corner supports for a centre table, applied with inscribed brass plaques, largest 17in (43cm) long.
£6,000–7,000 *C*

A miniature of a gentleman, James Green (c1771–1834), 2⅜in (6cm) high, in a gold frame, with plaited hair on the reverse.
£400–600 *C*

A miniature of a young lady, by Augustin-Christian Ritt, signed, c1790, 2⅜in (6cm) diam, in a silver gilt frame with split pearl border.
£16,800–18,000 *C(G)*

A miniature of Emperor Napoleon I of France, by Jean Parent, signed and dated '1815', 2½in (6.5cm) high, in a gilt bronze frame.
£2,000–2,500 *C(G)*

A miniature of Cornelius O'Callaghan, Viscount Lismore, by Charles Robertson, (c1760–1821), in an ormolu frame, 2½in (6.5cm) high.
£1,000–1,500 *C*

A miniature of a young lady, by Charles Noisot, signed and dated '1828', 3in (7.5cm) high.
£3,000–4,000 *C(G)*

A miniature depicting the Duchess of Berry, by Jean-Baptiste-Joseph Duchesne de Gisors, signed, c1820, 3in (7.5cm) high.
£25,000–30,000 *C(G)*

Nine miniatures set in silver buttons, French School, c1770, 1in (2.5cm) diam.
£3,500–4,500 *C*

l. A miniature of young gentleman, by Isaac Adam, signed, c1795, 2½in (6.5cm) high.
£2,000–2,500 *C(G)*

A miniature of 2 young boys and a young girl, German School, c1800, 3⅜in (8.5cm) diam., in a gilt metal mount.
£2,000–£3,000 *C(G)*

A miniature of Andrew Thomas, 11th Baron Blaney, by Horace Hone, ARA (c1754–1825), signed and dated '1806', 3in (7.5cm) high.
£2,500–3,500 *C*

A miniature of Madame de Montespan, French School, on vellum, in a gilt metal frame, c1700, 6in (15cm) high.
£26,000–30,000 *C*

A French marriage casket, with original polychromed decoration on a chalk ground, c1820, 17in (43cm) long.
£300–400 *RYA*

A George III tôle-peinte hexagonal tea caddy, painted on gilt spotted ground, with a brass handle, c1790, 5in (13cm) high.
£450–500 *S*

A Victorian tortoiseshell veneered and pewter strung two-division tea caddy, on vegetable ivory bun feet, 8in (20cm) wide.
£550–850 *CSK*

A Scandinavian dome-topped casket, with original painted decoration, c1860, 10in (25cm) long.
£200–220 *RYA*

A Norwegian rose-painted storage box, with polychrome stylised floral decoration on a blue ground, c1840, 15in (38cm) long.
£200–250 *RYA*

A George III mahogany tea caddy, the crossbanded top with brass ring handle, 8in (20cm) wide.
£500–600 *S*

A George III mahogany, kingwood and marquetry writing box, attributed to Mayhew & Ince, 15½in (39cm) wide.
£3,300–3,800 *C*

A burr yew wood tea caddy, c1850, 8in (20cm) wide.
£350–400 *RYA*

A George III sycamore casket, the cover and sides painted with rustic and classical views within oval panels, c1790, 11in (28cm) wide.
£1,700–2,200 *CSK*

A serpentine marquetry tea caddy, the interior fitted with 2 Imari lidded bowls, possibly Portuguese, c1700, 12in (30.5cm) wide.
£11,000–13,000 *S*

A North Country ditty box, with traces of original hand blocked paper to the interior, c1810, 13in (33cm) wide.
£400–425 *RYA*

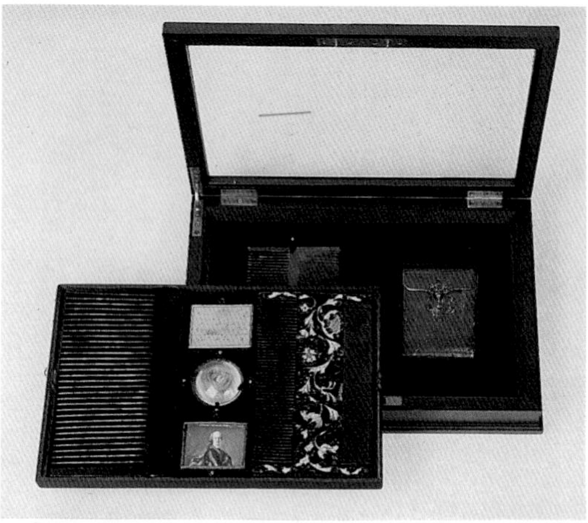

A glazed commemorative case, containing relics of Bonnie Prince Charlie, 17thC and later, largest comb 10in (25cm) long.
£4,200–5,200 *C*

A Swiss four-colour gold and enamel snuff box, set with a cameo, maker's mark 'CCS', c1830, 3½in (9cm) wide.
£3,500–4,000 *C*

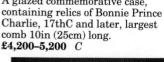

A French silver and enamel singing bird box, maker's mark illegible, 19thC, 3½in (9cm) wide.
£2,500–3,500 *C*

A travelling dressing table service, London, c1875, 12¾in (32.5cm) wide.
£4,500–5,500 *C*

A wooden hexagonal tea caddy, applied with curled paper, c1800, 5in (12.5cm) wide.
£450–550 *CB*

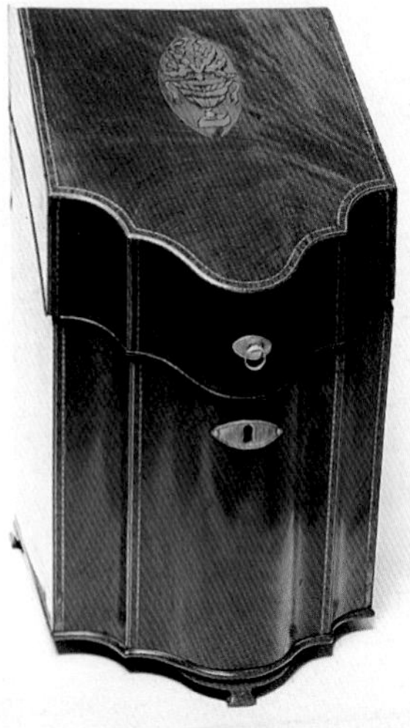

l. A Sheraton style mahogany knife box, with hardwood inlays and silver mounts, converted to a stationery box, c1780, 15½in (39.5cm) high.
£550–575 *AnE*

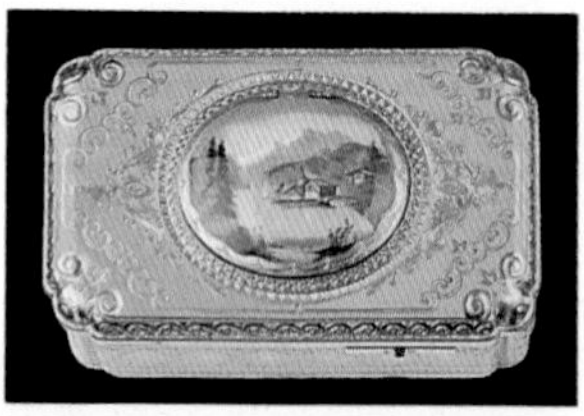

A Bruguier gold, silver gilt and enamel singing bird box, late 19thC, 3½in (9cm) wide.
£12,000–14,000 *C*

A gold mounted bloodstone two-handled box, decorated with chinoiserie scenes, the base with a fluted and rocaille border, the cover with a border of trelliswork, mounts c1750, 5½in (14cm) wide.
£9,000–10,000 *C*

An Ashford marble jewel box, inlaid with Russian and Italian coloured marbles, with French bamboo style ormolu mounts, c1900, 15in (38cm) wide.
£3,750–4,000 *GJC*

A tortoiseshell and mother-of-pearl tea caddy, adapted for stationery, early 19thC, 7in (17.5cm) high.
£700–900 *DN*

A German 4 colour gold box, the lid inset with a carved bloodstone panel, the base with a plain bloodstone panel, 3in (8cm) wide.
£15,000–17,000 *WW*

A Swiss gold and enamel snuff box, decorated with a border of opalescent and green enamel beads, maker 'LFT', Geneva, c1785, 3½in (9cm) wide.
£7,500–8,500 *C(G)*

A German jewelled, gold and mother-of-pearl snuff box, the thumbpiece also applied with precious stones, c1750, 3in (7cm) wide.
£57,000–59,000 *C(G)*

A French burr walnut work box, the interior with 2 trays of sewing accessories and glass bottles with silver metal mounts, by Herbert, Palais Royal, Galerie de Bois, 19thC, 14½in (37cm) wide.
£1,500–2,000 *S(S)*

l. A Swiss enamelled gold bonbonnière, by François Joanin, Geneva, c1800, 3½in (8cm) diam.
£6,000–7,000 *C(G)*

An oak writing box or slope, with a key, c1880, 18in (46cm) long.
£150–170 *MofC*

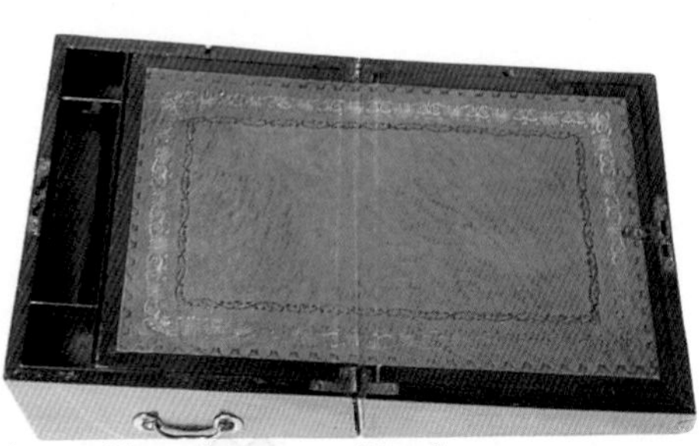

A portable mahogany writing box, c1880, 12in (30.5cm) wide.
£150–200 *MofC*

A George III harewood tea caddy, the lid and front inlaid with oval panels of flowers, 6in (15cm) wide.
£500–600 *CAG*

A Louis XVI vari-colour gold mounted rock crystal snuff box, by Claude Bourdillat, Paris, the cover and base bordered with raised beads on sablé bands, the sides of the base chased and engraved with two-colour gold, 1781, 2½in (6.5cm) wide.
£3,000–3,500 *C(G)*

A Swiss enamelled gold snuff box, set with an enamel miniature depicting Adonis and Venus, maker's mark crowned 'M&P', c1780, 3½in (9cm) wide.
£6,000–7,000 *C(G)*

A Russian gold mounted aventurine snuff box, with a miniature depicting Grand-Duke Michael Pavlovich, attributed to Henri Benner, c1820, 3in (7.5cm) wide.
£3,500–4,000 *C(G)*

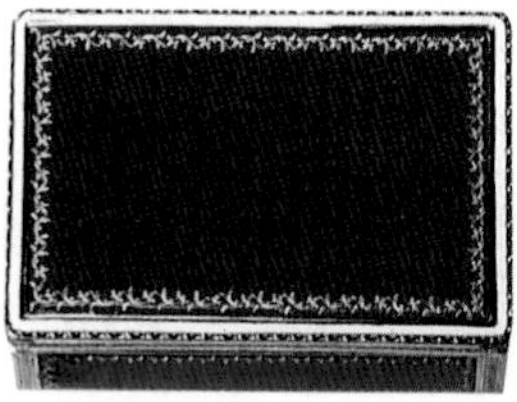

A Swiss enamelled engine turned gold boîte à mouches, by François Joanin, c1800, 2½in (6cm) wide.
£3,000–4,000 *C(G)*

A French Restauration gold and enamel snuff box, by Gabriel-Raoul Morel, Paris, decorated with scrolling foliage on a matted gold ground, with shell-shaped engraved thumbpiece, c1825, 3½in (9cm) wide.
£2,500–3,000 *C(G)*

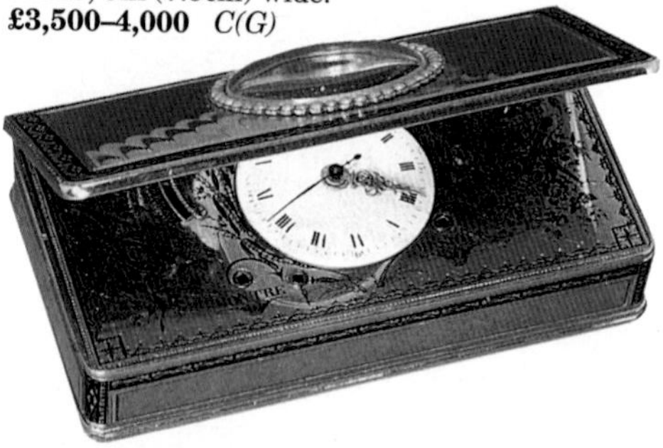

A Swiss enamelled gold musical snuff box, with a watch, interior decorated with foliage and musical trophies, probably Geneva, c1800, 3¼in (8cm) wide.
£13,000–15,000 *C(G)*

A French gold and enamel boîte à portrait, by Adrien-Jean-Maximilien Vachette, Paris, signed and engraved, c1798, 3in (7.5cm) wide.
£11,000–13,000 *C(G)*

A Louis XVI gold and enamel boîte à miniature, by Adrien-Jean-Maximilien Vachette, Paris, the miniature signed and dated 'J. J. DeGault in 1788', 3in (7.5cm) diam.
£18,000–20,000 *C(G)*

A Swiss gold snuff box, the cover with a picture of Hercules and Omphale, the front and rear decorated with Greek key pattern, marked with crowned initials 'SC', c1800, 3½in (9cm) wide, 3oz.
£3,500–4,500 *C(G)*

An Athapaskan woman's fringed and quilled hide summer costume, probably Kutchin, tunic 44½in (113cm) long.
£25,000–28,000 *S(NY)*

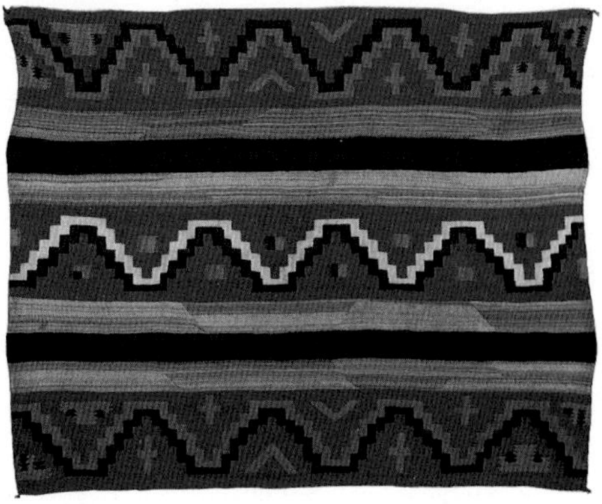

A piece of Navajo weaving, of natural and aniline dyed handspun wool, in 'second phase chief's pattern', 56 by 68½in (142 by 174cm).
£4,500–6,000 *SK(B)*

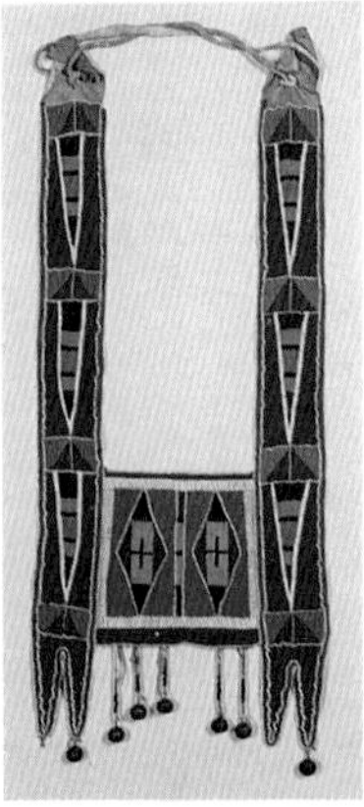

A Crow beaded hide martingale, 36in (92cm) long.
£6,000–7,000 *S(NY)*

A Blackfeet pictorial painted hide, depicting the Battle of Little Big Horn, 49in (124.5cm) wide.
£12,500–14,000 *S(NY)*

A Pomo twined utility basket, in tightly woven willow, sedge root and redbud, 12in (30.5cm) diam.
£2,000–3,000 *S(NY)*

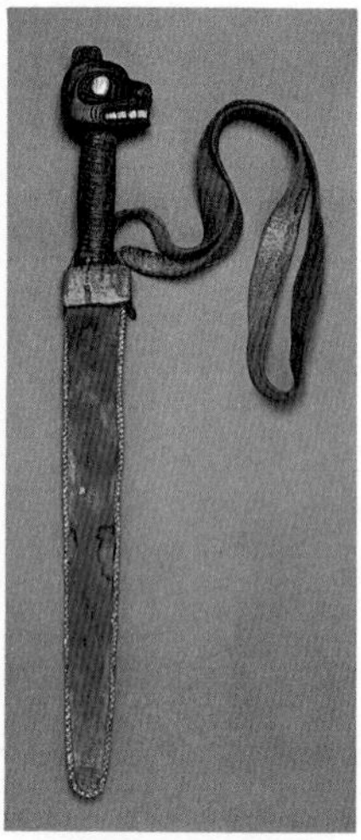

l. A Tlingit steel fighting knife and hide sheath, the pommel in the form of an animal's head, 20in (51cm) long.
£4,000–5,000 *S(NY)*

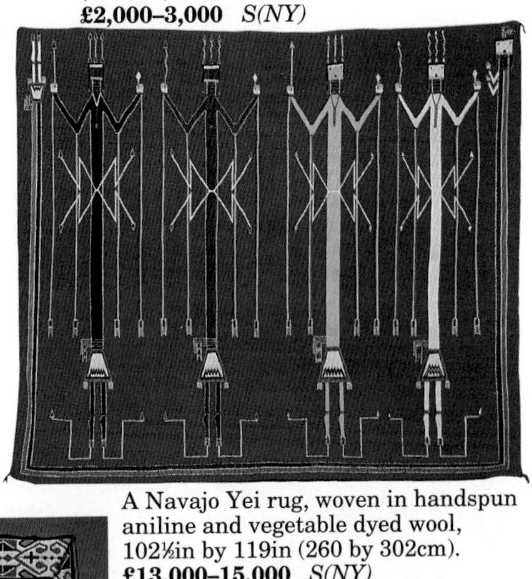

A Navajo Yei rug, woven in handspun aniline and vegetable dyed wool, 102½in by 119in (260 by 302cm).
£13,000–15,000 *S(NY)*

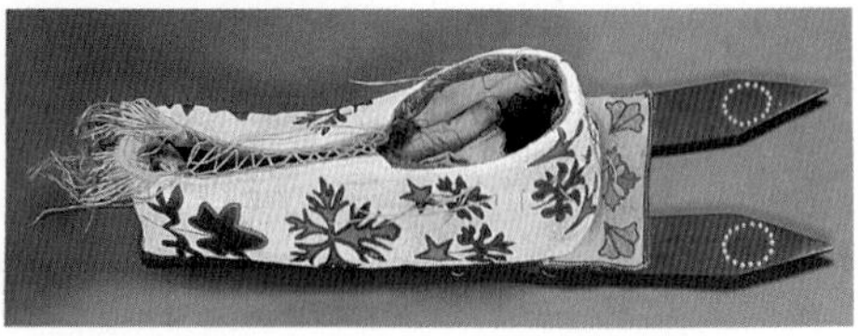

A Kiowa beaded hide cradle, mounted on a pair of pointed wooden boards, 42in (107cm) long.
£10,000–11,000 *S(NY)*

A Pueblo olla, probably Tesuque, with red band, native rawhide binding, 20½in (52cm) high.
£18,000–20,000 *S(NY)*

A Winnebago beaded cloth bandoleer bag, 36½in (93cm) long.
£5,000–6,000 *S(NY)*

A Pond Inlet dog sled whip, by Samuel Arnakallak, 1968, and a pair of Woodlands Indian beaded buckskin mukluks, 13in (33cm) high.
£150–200 each *RIT*

A gilt metal and moulded glass 24-light chandelier, the branches hung with faceted beads and lustres, 46in (116.5cm) high.
£600–700 *CSK*

A pair of French ormolu five-light candelabra, modelled as a satyr and a herm, late 19thC, 26½in (67.5cm) high.
£3,000–4,000 *C*

A pair of ormolu, rock crystal and lapis lazuli mounted three-light candelabra, hung with faceted pendants, on stepped feet with 8 lapis lazuli cabochons, 19thC, 19½in (49.5cm) high.
£4,500–5,500 *C*

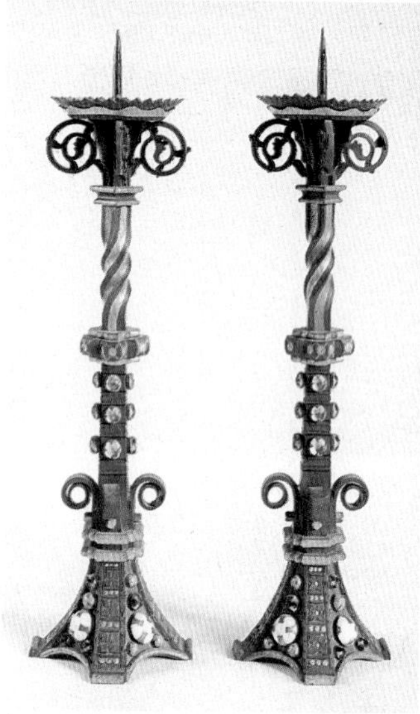

A pair of wrought iron pricket candlesticks, with parcel gilt and painted decoration, the bases set with clear and coloured glass 'jewels', 27in (68.5cm) high.
£7,000–8,000 *Bea*

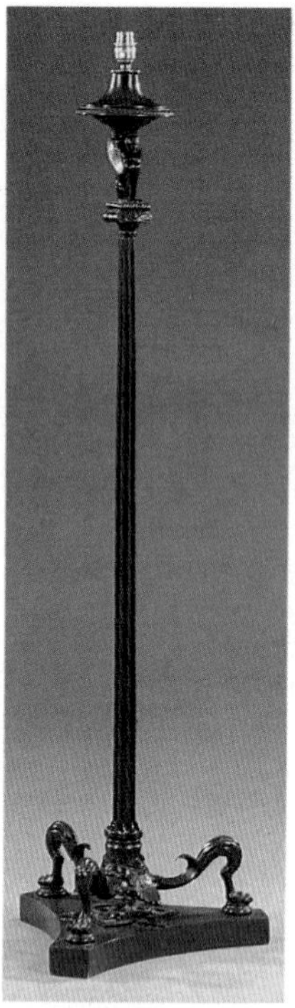

A Continental bronze torchère, after the antique, the top with a sphinx, the fluted slender column on a tricorn base, fitted for electricity, c1880, 49in (124.5cm) high.
£2,000–3,000 *S*

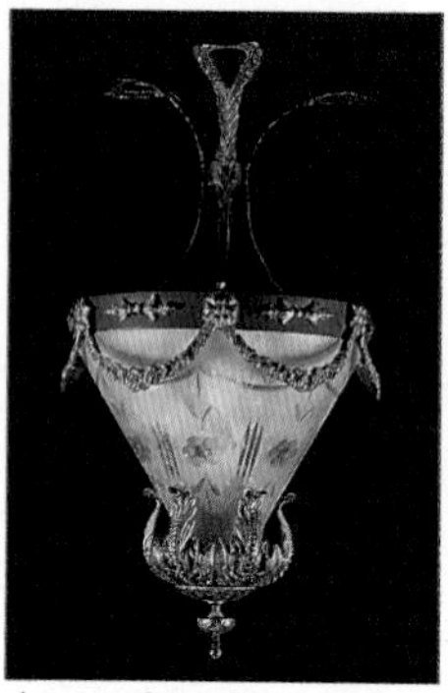

A set of 8 gilt metal lanterns, with conical frosted and cut glass shades, 20thC, 18in (45.5cm) high.
£5,000–6,000 *CSK*

A cut glass and gilt bronze hall lantern, probably French, late 19thC, 17½in (44.5cm) high.
£2,500–3,500 *CSK*

A French ormolu lantern, with fluted drip pans and turned nozzles, late 19thC, 57in (144.5cm) high.
£12,750–13,250 *C*

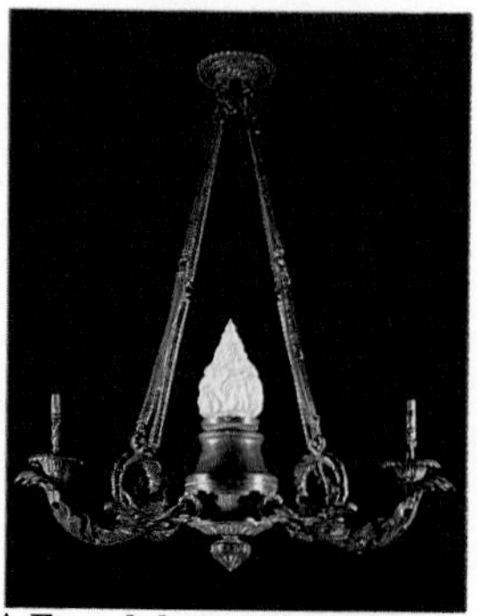

A French bronze hanging lamp, with a frosted glass flambeau shade, late 19thC, 29in (73.5cm) high.
£1,800–2,200 *CSK*

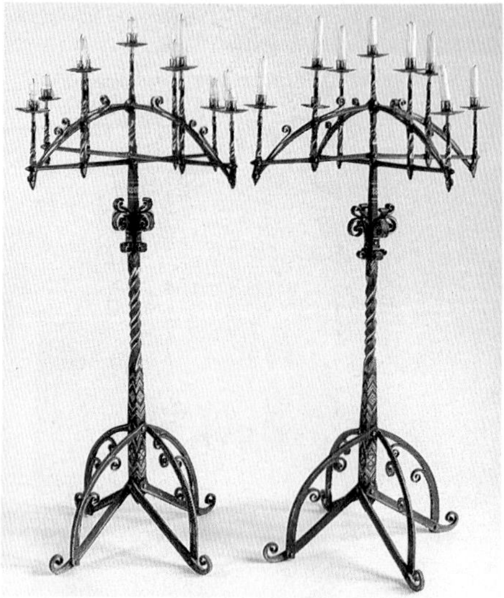

A pair of nine-light wrought iron standard candle holders, with parcel gilt and painted decoration, the columns part twisted, on quadruple bases, 55in (139.5cm) high.
£8,000–9,000 *Bea*

A pair of early Georgian padouk wood and parcel gilt wall lanterns, with mirrored backs, restored, 27in (69cm) high.
£8,000–9,000 *C*

A pair of Louis XV gilt bronze candlesticks, on spiral cast supports held by 2 cherubs, marked with crowned 'C' poinçons, c1745, 13in (33cm) high.
£9,000–10,000 *S*

An early Victorian gilt metal hall lantern, with etched panes, 45in (114cm) high.
£10,000–11,000 *C*

A gilt bronze and tôle bouillotte lamp, with 3 candle branches, c1800, 30in (76cm) high.
£5,000–6,000 *S*

A pair of Louis XVI gilt bronze candlesticks, c1780, 11in (28in) high.
£5,000–6,000 *S*

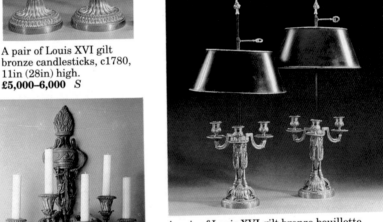

A pair of Louis XVI gilt bronze bouillotte lamps, each with 3 candle branches, the tripod stems with goats' masks, c1780, 28½in (72cm) high.
£24,000–26,000 *S*

A pair of polychrome and parcel gilt tôle peinte five-light pricket wall appliques, 19thC, 44in (111.5cm) high.
£4,500–5,500 *C*

A pair of Empire gilt bronze wall lights, with winged mask back plates, early 19thC, 9in (23cm) wide.
£5,000–6,000 *S*

A Russian gilt bronze chandelier, early 19thC, 40in (101.5cm) high.
£15,000–17,000 *S*

A pair of gilt bronze vase candlesticks, each with 4 candle branches shaped as cornucopia of fruit, the handles in the form of infant mermen, c1800, 15in (38cm) high.
£9,500–11,000 *S*

A pair of Napoleon III ormolu and patinated bronze figural ten-light candelabra, mid-19thC, 48½in (123cm) high, on later pedestals.
£25,000–27,000 *CNY*

A pair of Louis XV bronze and gilt bronze candelabra, each in the form of a triton holding lilies, on scrollwork bases, mid-18thC, 11in (28cm) high.
£12,000–14,000 *S*

A pair of Louis XVI silvered brass bouillotte lamps, c1785, 22in (55.5cm) high.
£9,500–11,000 *S*

A pair of Louis XVI style ormolu, bronze and granite candelabra, late 19thC, 45in (114cm) high.
£10,000–12,000 *CNY*

A Louis XV gilt bronze lantern, c1770, 26½in (67.5cm) high.
£13,000–15,000 *S*

A French gilt metal rococo style chandelier, c1900, 37in (94cm) high.
£1,200–1,500 *CSK*

A pair of Louis XVI gilt bronze wall lights, the backplates surmounted by a laurel swagged urn, faced by lions' masks, supporting 3 leaf cast scroll candle branches with fluted nozzles and drip pans, c1780, 21½in (54cm) high.
£23,000–25,000 *S*

A pair of Louis XVI style ormolu and griotte marble candelabra, 19thC, 29in (73.5cm) high.
£9,500–10,500
CNY

A Danish brass and cut glass chandelier, c1800, 42½in (108cm) high.
£6,500–7,500 *S*

A pair of Louis XV gilt bronze and glass photophores, the drapery mounts to the top of the shades, fluted nozzles and leaf cast socles, c1780, 17in (43cm) high.
£30,000–32,000 *S*

A brass and frosted glass hall lantern, the top ring stamped 'Prov. Pat. 4', 27in (68.5cm) high.
£2,200–2,700 *C*

A pair of brass two-tier chandeliers, with bulbous baluster columns, early 20thC, 30½in (77.5cm) high.
£1,800–2,200 *CSK*

A Chinese export red and gilt lacquer armoire, with 2 shelves and 2 drawers 19thC, 46in (116.5cm) wide.
£3,000–4,000 *C*

A Chinese coromandel lacquer ten-leaf screen, with an extensive scene of court life, the reverse with Chinese characters, restored, early 18thC, each leaf 108½ by 19in (275 by 48.5cm).
£8,000–10,000 *C*

A Chinese padouk wood chair, with a marble panel, 20thC, 24in (61cm) wide.
£350–400 *SIG*

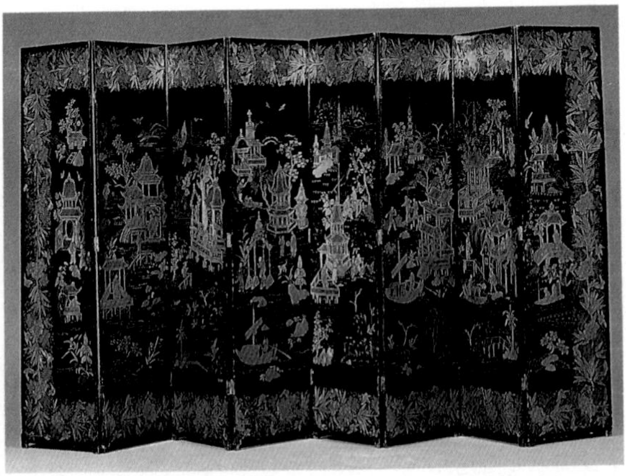

A Chinese export black and gilt lacquer eight-leaf screen, with a scene of buildings and boats, the reverse with trees and birds, 19thC, each leaf 40½ by 81in (101.5 by 205.5cm).
£8,500–10,000 *C*

A Chinese coromandel lacquer eight-leaf screen, with a scene of court life, 19thC, 97½ by 136in (247 by 345.5cm).
£6,500–7,000 *C*

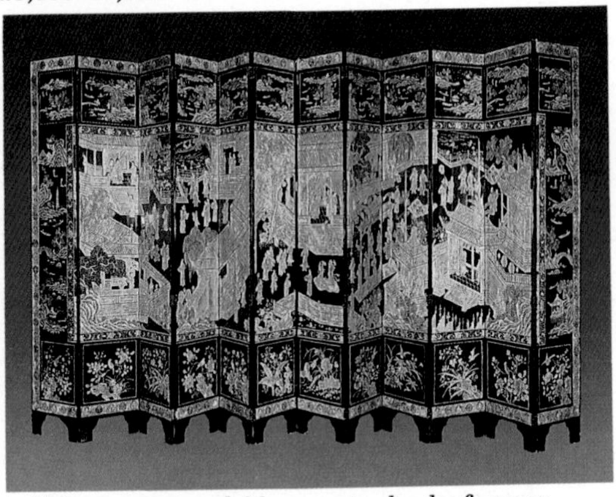

A Chinese coromandel lacquer twelve-leaf screen, with a scene of palace life, the reverse with birds and animals, 18thC, 113½ by 228in (288 by 680cm).
£15,000–16,000 *C*

A Japanese carved polychrome table cabinet and stand, 19thC, 17½in (44.5cm) wide.
£300–400 *C*

A Chinese export red and gilt lacquer armoire, 18thC, 62½in (158cm) wide.
£2,500–3,500 *C*

A Korean mother-of-pearl inlaid lacquer table, some damage, 16th–17thC, 18½in (47cm) wide, in a Japanese fitted wooden box.
£6,000–8,000 *C*

A late Ming incised red lacquer altar table, cracks, damaged, Wanli, 73½in (186cm) long.
£34,000–38,000 *C*

A Shan bronze rain drum, pale green patination overall, with azurite blue, circa lst century A.D., 28in (71cm) high, on a carved wood stand.
£35,000–40,000 *S*

A mottled grey jade figure of a horse, 17thC, 10in (25cm) long.
£5,000–5,500 *S*

A carved spinach jade dragon, Qing Dynasty, 3in (7.5cm) wide.
£2,000–2,500 *S*

A bronze vase, with a twelve-character inscription in the neck, 9th–8th Century B.C., 12in (30.5cm) high.
£15,000–16,000 *S*

A bronze tripod food vessel, with malachite, azurite and earth encrustation, 9th–8th Century B.C., 21½in (54.5cm) wide.
£8,500–9,500 *S*

A gold decorated bronze hu and cover, slight damage, 3rd–2nd Century B.C., 11½in (29.cm) high.
£12,500–13,500 *S*

A bronze mirror, with green patination, impressed with traces of fabric wrapping, 770–476 B.C., 3¾in (9.5cm) diam.
£7,200–8,200 *S*

A celadon jade plaque, mounted as a table screen, jade Qianlong, 9½in (24cm) wide.
£10,000–12,000 *C*

A carved stone pouring bowl and handle, 12th–14th Century, 10½in (26.5cm) high.
£3,000–4,000 *S*

A black inlaid bronze tripod food vessel, with three-character inscription, 9th–8th Century B.C., 15½in (39.5cm) wide.
£8,500–10,000 *S*

A white jade incense burner and cover, 5½in (14cm) wide, and a spinach jade bowl, Qianlong/Jiaqing.
£3,500–4,500 *C*

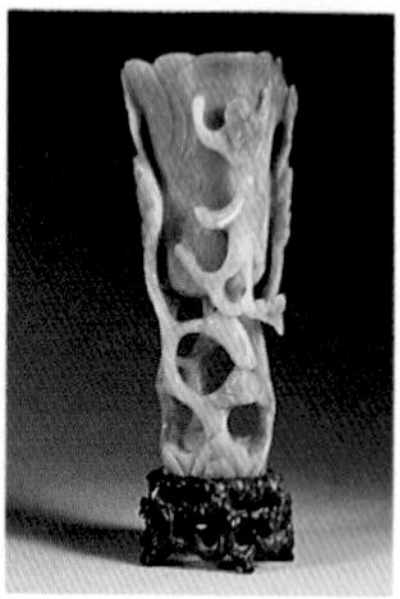

A pierced celadon green jade magnolia cup, 17thC, 10in (25cm) high, on a wood stand.
£1,000–1,500 *S*

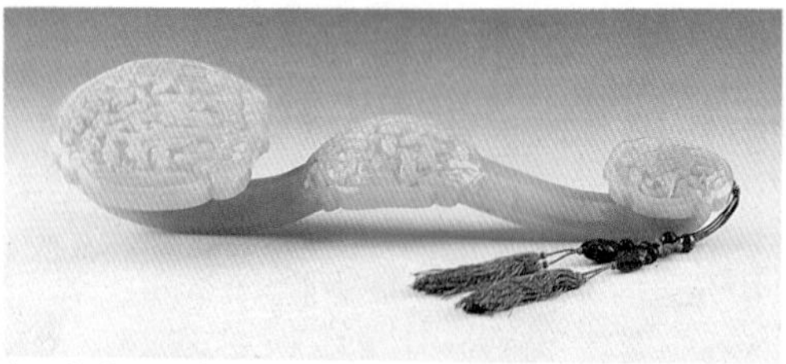

A celadon jade ruyi sceptre, carved with figures, cranes, a deer and a figure on an elephant, late Qing Dynasty, 15½in (39.5cm) long.
£4,500–5,000 *C*

A cast gilt bronze feline seal, with an eight-seal character inscription, slight damage, Eastern Han/Six Dynasties Period, 3½in (9cm) long.
£11,000–12,000 *S*

A cloisonné enamel incense burner, damaged, Qianlong mark and of the period, 13½in (34cm) high.
£7,000–8,000 *S*

A Canton enamel clock, the French twin going barrel movement with anchor escapement and strike on bell, restored, mid-Qing Dynasty, 22in (56cm) high.
£8,500–11,000 *C*

A cloisonné enamel and gilt bronze moon flask, with elaborate dragon handles, Qianlong, 21in (53cm) high.
£4,700–5,200 *C*

A cloisonné enamel jardinière, with a copper liner and stand, Qing Dynasty, 20in (51cm) high.
£4,000–4,500 *S*

A gilt bronze Buddha, wearing an open dohti and an openwork tiara, the hair with traces of blue pigment, 16thC, 9in (23cm) high.
£4,700–6,000 *C*

A tripod cloisonné koro and cover, with everted handles, gilt metal interior, late 19thC, 10½in (27cm) high.
£6,500–7,000 *C*

A cloisonné tripod incense burner, on cabriole legs, 18thC, 15in (38cm) high.
£2,500–3,000 *C*

A cloisonné enamel five-piece altar garniture, comprising: a tripod incense burner, 2 pricket candlesticks and 2 gu vases, Qianlong/Jiaqing, 22½in (57cm) high.
£5,000–5,500 *C*

A pair of gilt bronze and cloisonné enamel incense burners and covers, 18thC, 18in (46cm) high.
£8,500–10,000 *C*

A late Ming lacquered and gilt bronze Bodhisattva, 18½in (47cm) high.
£3,500–4,000 *CSK*

A silver bowl, the base stamped 'Shanghai Luenwo', 19thC, 12in (30.5cm) wide.
£2,000–2,500 *C*

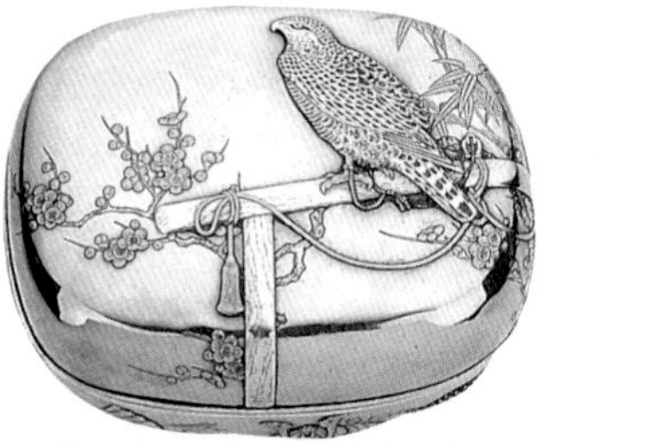

A silver box, decorated in silver and iroe hirazogan, takazogan and kebori, signed 'Ishikawaken Kanazawa, Yamakawa Takatsugu zo', 19thC, 5½in (14cm) wide.
£5,000–6,000 *C*

A pair of gold lacquer shibayama vases, each body decorated in gold hirame and hiramakie, with inset silver rimmed panels of birds and flowers on a kinji ground, restored, signed 'Shigenori', late 19thC, 12½in (32cm) high.
£11,000–13,000 *C*

A gold lacquer picnic set, the frame with a silver handle, 19thC, 8in (20cm) wide.
£7,000–8,000 *C*

A silver filigree vase, decorated in coloured shippo, signed on a metal tablet 'Asada sei', late 19thC, 10½in (26.5cm) high.
£7,000–9,000 *C*

A Japanese wood sculpture of a seated Buddha, damaged, 12thC, 23in (58.5cm) high.
£1,200–1,700 *CSK*

A Japanese wood sculpture of a standing warrior, damaged, 14thC, 24in (61cm) high.
£2,500–3,000 *CSK*

A pair of double gourd-shaped lacquer vases, decorated in gold, inlaid with mother-of-pearl, with ivory necks, 19thC, 4in (10cm) high.
£1,700–2,000 *C*

A wooden box, with inlaid and applied lacquer, metal, mother-of-pearl and horn decoration, early 19thC, 27in (68.5cm) wide.
£5,200–6,000 *C*

A cloisonné enamel and gilt bronze censer, supported on 4 gilt bronze three-talonned legs, Ming Dynasty, 17in (43cm) wide.
£14,000–15,000 *S*

A woven belt, Han Dynasty, 2½in (6cm) wide.
£3,000–4,000 *MA*

A pair of lacquered wood tigers, Han Dynasty, 9½in (24cm) long.
£7,000–8,000 *MA*

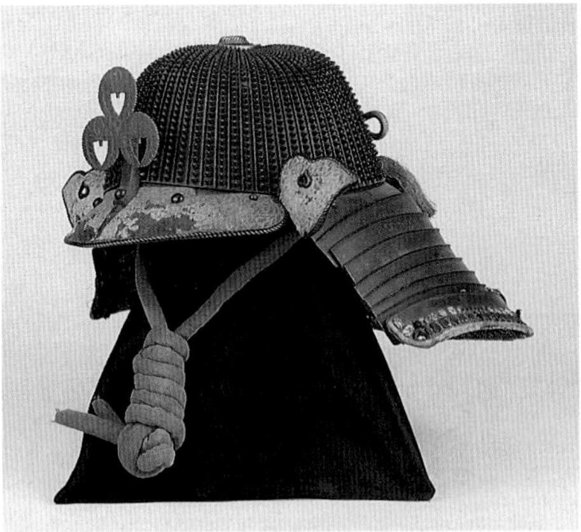

A hoshi bachi kabuto, with raised rivets, covered with printed leather, signed 'Nagamichi', early Edo period.
£8,500–9,000 *C*

A Chinese velvet carpet, with gilt metal threads and eau-de-nil silk floral design, 18thC, 117 by 72in (297 by 182.5cm).
£3,500–4,500 *CSK*

A stone figure of a judge, Ming Dynasty, 19in (48cm) high.
£1,200–1,500 *MA*

A Japanese red silk damask resist dyed furisode, 19thC.
£600–700 *CSK*

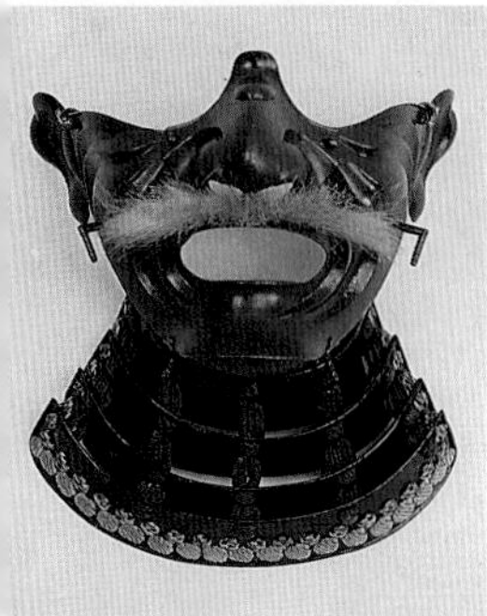

A russet iron mempo, with detachable nose, 18thC, 8in (20cm) wide.
£2,200–2,700 *C*

A Japanese bronze elephant, with ivory tusks, 19thC, 9½in (24cm) high.
£650–700 *SWO*

A Japanese embroidered blue silk furisode, lined in red silk, with padded hem, mid-19thC.
£1,000–1,400 *CSK*

A porcelain famille rose snuff bottle, Qianlong Nianzhi mark, 19thC, 2⅜in (6cm) high.
£1,400–1,600 *RHa*

Three Chinese snuff bottles:
l. A gourd grown into a mould, c1780–1850, 2⅜in (6cm) high.
c. Yixing enamelled pottery, 19thC, 2in (5cm) high.
r. Imperial yellow glass, c1780–1850, 2⅜in (6cm) high.
£2,000–3,500 each *RHa*

A quartz Jasper snuff bottle, c1750–1830, 2⅜in (6cm) high.
£10,000–12,000 *RHa*

A Chinese glass snuff bottle, c1730–1800, 2in (5cm) high.
£1,000–1,100 *RHa*

Three jade snuff bottles, c1720–1850, 2⅜in (6cm) high.
l. **£3,500–4,500** *c.* **£7,000–8,000** *r.* **£5,000–6,000** *RHa*

A Chinese porcelain snuff bottle, the base inscribed with four-character mark, c1796–1850, 2in (5cm) high.
£1,000–1,200 *RHa*

A Chinese snuff bottle, the glass imitating tortoiseshell, c1730–1800, 2in (5cm) high.
£500–600 *RHa*

A Chinese snuff bottle, with overlay of bats, c1780–1850, 2⅜in (6cm) high.
£1,500–1,600 *RHa*

A Chinese wooden snuff bottle, c1780–1850, 2in (5cm) high.
£2,000–2,800 *RHa*

A Chinese pudding stone snuff bottle, c1780–1850, 2in (5cm) high.
£2,000–2,800 *RHa*

A Chinese peach stone snuff bottle, carved with horses, 19thC, 1⅜in (3.5cm) high.
£2,000–2,400 *RHa*

A Chinese porcelain snuff bottle, moulded and enamelled with dragons, 19thC, 2⅜in (6cm) high.
£2,000–3,000 *RHa*

MUSIC
Musical Boxes

The Alexandra upright disc musical box, playing 9in (23cm) discs, in an inlaid walnut case enclosed by panelled doors, with a gallery top, 17in (43cm) wide.
£1,000–1,200 *Bea*

A forte piano oratoria box, by Nicole Frères, No. 36358, playing 4 airs, with silvered 'Savoy & Sons' tune list, ratchet crank wind, and grained case with brass and enamel inlay to the rosewood veneered lid, c1860, case 21½in (55cm) wide, the cylinder 13in (33cm) long.
£5,300–6,000 *CSK*

An interchangeable cylinder musical box with organ, by Nicole Frères, No. 46626, with seven 15½in (39cm) cylinders, each playing 6 airs, two-piece comb with central 24 note organ, in a burr maple ebonised and Rosen case with crossbanding and fruitwood inlay, brass carrying handles, 40in (101.5cm) wide, on a mahogany stand with 2 drawers, fluted square columns at each corner, gilded carved legs and caster base, c1880, 44in (111.5cm) square overall.
£3,500–4,500 *Bon*

A sublime harmony musical box, by D. Allard & Co., No. 6063, playing 8 mainly operatic airs, with zither attachments, tune selector, nickel-plated double spring motor, tune sheet and burr walnut case, c1890, case 27in (68.5cm) wide, cylinder 13in (33cm) long.
£3,600–4,000 *CSK*

A Britannia musical box, with nine 11¾in (30cm) discs, in a walnut smoker's case with bevelled mirror glass door panels, 25in (64cm) high.
£1,500–2,000 *CSK*

An organ box, by Conchon, playing 8 airs, with 20 note organ, tune indicator, tune selector, tune sheet, speed control, double-spring motor and burr-walnut case with stringing, 26½in (67cm) wide, the cylinder 13in (33cm) long.
£2,000–2,500 *CSK*

A Britannia musical box, with fifteen 9in (22.5cm) discs, twin-comb movement, in an upright walnut smoker's cabinet, 21½in (54.5cm) high.
£1,400–1,700 *CSK*

A sublime harmony musical box, by F. Conchon, No. 9464, playing 6 airs, with a full length zither attachment, tune sheet and case with crossbanded front and inlaid lid, c1890, the case 21in (53.5cm) wide.
£1,700–2,000 *CSK*

A key wind musical box, by Nicole Frères, No. 38162, playing 4 operatic airs, Gamme No. 1065, in plain fruitwood case with inner glass lid, 'Savoy & Sons' tune sheet, end flap and ratchet crank winding key, 14½in (37cm) wide, cylinder 8in (20cm) long.
£850–950 *CSK*

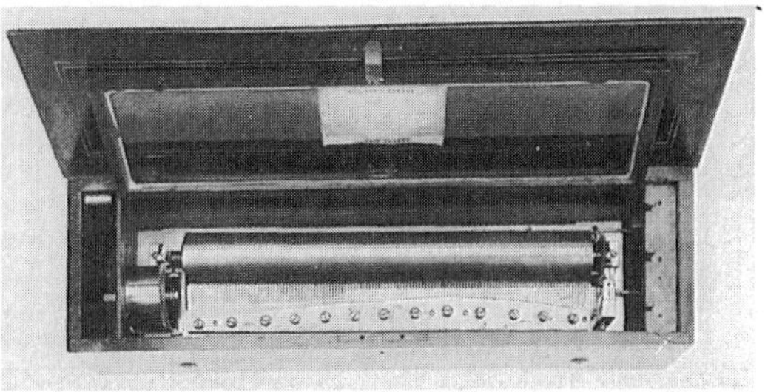

A forte piano musical box, by Nicole Frères, No. 41091, playing 8 airs, in grained case with inlaid lid, 26in (66cm) wide, cylinder 17½in (44.5cm) long.
£2,500–3,000 *CSK*

l. A musical workbox, with 5-tooth sectional comb movement playing 4 airs, signed on the comb base 'H. Rochat' and numbered '2032', in mahogany case of sarcophagus form, with fitted interior, ormolu handles and mirror in lid, 12½in (32cm) wide, cylinder 7½in (19cm) long.
£4,000–4,500 *CSK*

A Harpe Harmonique musical box, No. 11272, playing 12 airs, with zither attachment and tune sheet, with crossbanded front and crossbanded inlaid lid, 27in (68cm) wide, cylinder 16in (41cm) long.
£1,700–2,200 *CSK*

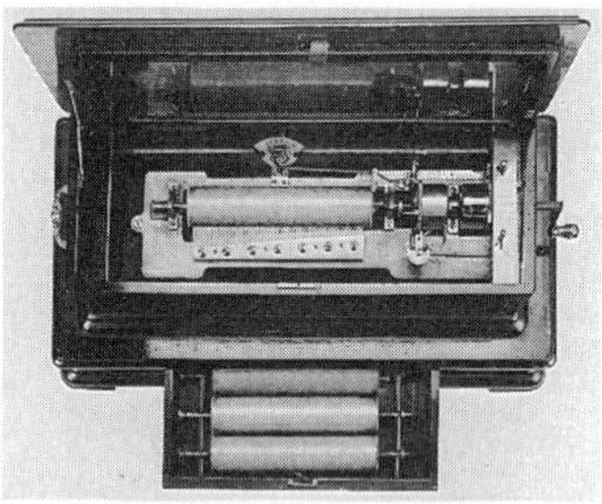

An interchangeable musical box, by E. Paillard, with 4 cylinders playing 6 airs each, nickel plated movement, double spring motor, instant check, tune indicator, selector and speed control, in crossbanded case with inlaid front and lid, on base with cylinder storage drawer, 35½in (90cm) wide, cylinders 11in (29cm) long.
£3,500–4,000 *CSK*

A musical box on table, by Nicole Frères, No. 47428, with 8 air cylinders, double spring motor, crossbanded and inlaid rosewood case, with bird's-eye maple lid lining, on matching table with 2 cylinder drawers with slides, flanking central drawer with writing slide and pen tray, on crossbanded cabriole legs with casters, 50in (127cm) wide, cylinders, damaged, 20in (50.5cm) long.
£8,000–9,000 *CSK*

A Swiss interchangeable orchestral musical box-on-stand, by E. Paillard, the 17in (43.5cm) cylinder plays 10 tunes accompanied by 7 bells, drum, organ reeds, with double motor, ratchet wound to side, stop/start and repeat/change levers, contained in a bird's-eye maple veneered case with ebonized trim, mounted on an elaborate stand with 2 drawers containing 5 additional pinned cylinders, late 19thC, 60½in (153.5cm) long.
£8,500–9,500 *S(NY)*

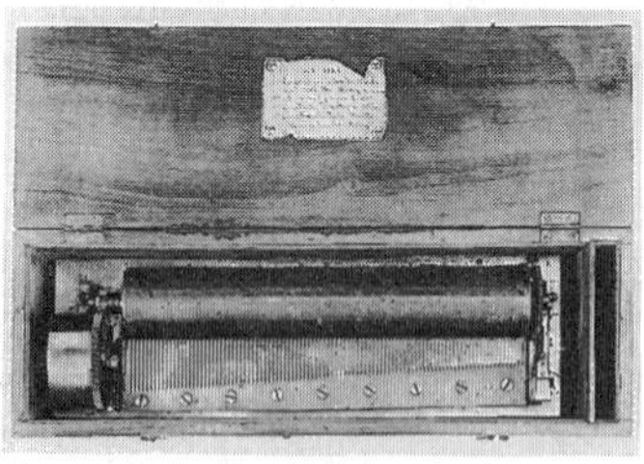

An early key wind musical box, No. 7247, playing 6 airs, in plain walnut case with exposed controls, division panel inscribed in pencil 'G.A. Noakes, Sandwich, 1836', the lid with inscribed brass plaque, 15in (38cm) wide, cylinder 10in (25cm) long.
£800–1,200 *CSK*

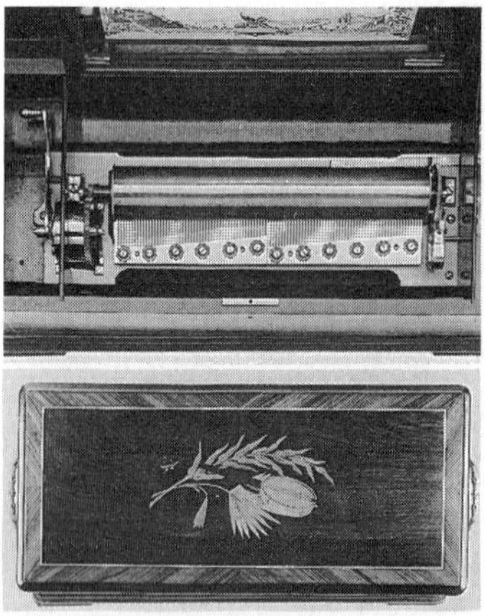

r. A sublime harmony musical box, by Ami Rivenc, No. 39897, playing 8 airs on two 54-tooth combs, with replacement tune sheet, crossbanded case with inlaid domed lid, ormolu carrying handles and later Royal Arms transfer on front, 27½in (70cm) wide, cylinder 15in (38.5cm) long.
£3,000–3,500 *CSK*

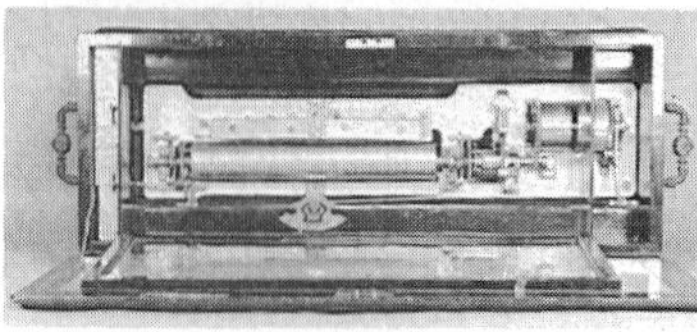

An interchangeable cylinder musical box, by E. Paillard & Co., with five 17½in (44cm) cylinders, each playing 6 airs, double spring motor, speed regulator and tune indicator, in a maple case with fruitwood stringing and banding, carrying handles, c1900, 41½in (105cm) wide, on an oak base with 2 cylinder drawers, overall 47in (119cm) wide.
£4,000–6,000 *Bon*

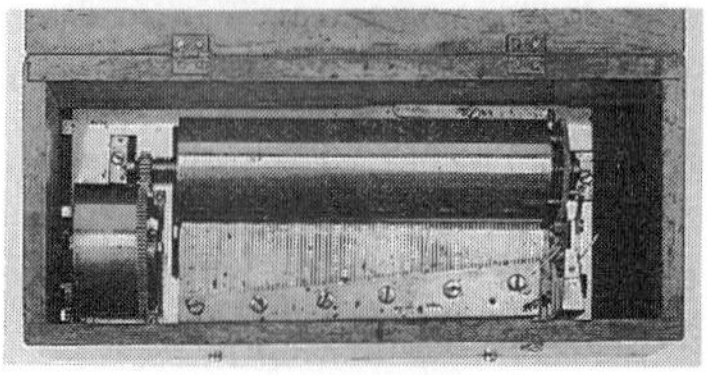

An early key wind musical box, by Martinet & Benoit, No. 3830, playing 4 operatic airs, listed on base, in plain fruitwood case with exposed controls, 10½in (26.5cm) wide, cylinder 6in (15cm) long.
£1,700–2,200 *CSK*

A Symphonion 11¾in (30cm) disc upright musical box, with twin diametric combs and coin mechanism, in walnut case with glazed door, labelled 'Geo. Salter & Co., West Bromwich' with 8 discs, 25½in (64.5cm) high.
£3,000–3,500 *CSK*

A Jerome Thibouville Lamy Bells-in-Sight cylinder musical box, serial No. 17703, 17¼in (43cm) cylinder playing 12 popular airs, two-per-turn, as listed on original green paper tune sheet, with importer's name 'Gautschi & Sons Philadelphia', case with walnut veneered lid, front and sides, with banding and boxwood stringing, late 19thC, 28in (71cm) wide.
£3,500–4,000 *S(NY)*

A Swiss bells-in-sight musical box, No. 1359, the 13in (34cm) cylinder, with 9 bells playing 10 airs as listed on the tune sheet, the marquetry rosewood and simulated rosewood case decorated with musical trophies, flowers and ribbons, 23½in (60cm) wide.
£1,300–1,700 *Bea*

A Symphonion 11¾in (30cm) table disc musical box, with twin combs, in simulated carved wood case, with plush mounted silk print in lid, and approximately 122 discs.
£4,500–5,000 *CSK*

A musical box, by Weill & Harburg, playing 12 airs, with patent tune title indicator, tune selector, drum, castanet and 6 engine turned bells with bee strikers, zither attachment, tune sheet and crossbanded inlaid front and lid, 30in (76cm) wide, cylinder 18in (46cm) long.
£5,000–5,500 *CSK*

A Swiss 6 air cylinder musical box, No. 6662, with 9in (23cm) cylinder, accompanied by 3 hidden saucer shaped bells and drum, in a stained and inlaid case, c1880, 17in (43cm) wide.
£750–1,000 *Bon*

r. A mandarin musical box, No. 39671, playing 6 airs (Gamme 971) accompanied by 6 saucer-shaped, vertically mounted bells struck by 3 seated mandarins with nodding heads, the case with tune sheet, veneered and crossbanded front and lid, inlaid with mandarin masks, 21in (53.5) wide, cylinder 11in (28cm) long.
£2,000–2,200 *CSK*

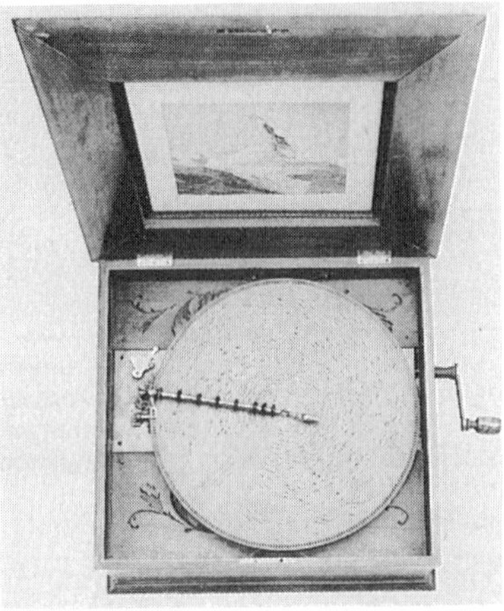

A Gloria 18½in (47cm) disc musical box, with 2 unequal length combs mounted at an angle, fretted soundboards and walnut case, 23½in (60cm) wide, with 11 discs.
£2,000–2,500 *CSK*

The Gloria was made by the Société Anonomye Fabriques Revnies, a combination of Ami Rivenc, Langdorff and Billon. The discs carry the Billon butterfly trademark.

A royal presentation musical box, with 6-air programme, accompanied by 6 engine turned bells with bee strikers, in crossbanded and inlaid case, with brass plaque 'Presented by T.R.H.'s The Prince and Princess of Wales to E. W. Wallington Esq. C.M.G. Xmas 1908', 23in (58.5cm) wide, cylinder, 2 teeth missing, 13in (33cm) long.
£900–1,200 *CSK*

A 6 bell and drum musical box, playing 8 airs with automaton Indian drummer and optional bells, tune sheet and inlaid lid, 26½in (67cm) wide, cylinder, 4 teeth missing, 16in (41cm) long.
£2,500–3,000 *CSK*

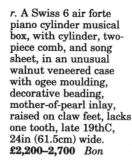

r. A Swiss 6 air forte piano cylinder musical box, with cylinder, two-piece comb, and song sheet, in an unusual walnut veneered case with ogee moulding, decorative beading, mother-of-pearl inlay, raised on claw feet, lacks one tooth, late 19thC, 24in (61.5cm) wide.
£2,200–2,700 *Bon*

A Swiss 8 air concertino cylinder musical box, No. 12305, with 17in (43cm) cylinder, double spring, zither, tune indicator and tune sheet, in an ebonised and amboyna case with fruitwood stringing and mother-of-pearl inlay, lacks one tooth, 19thC, 29½in (75cm) wide.
£1,000–1,500 *Bon*

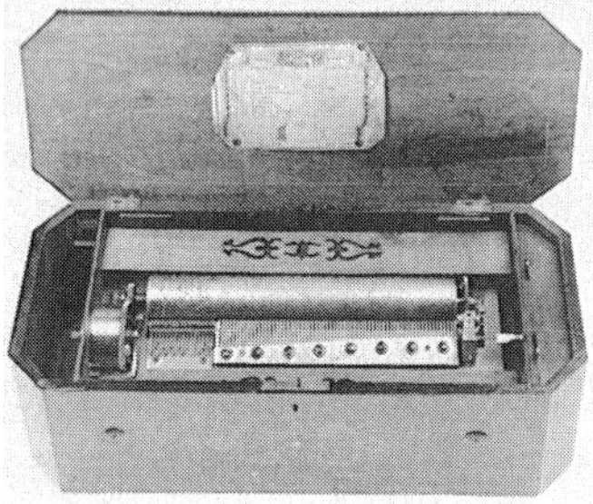

A Swiss 8 air 'Jeu de Flûtes' musical box, with 13in (34cm) cylinder accompanied by 16 note organ, with tune sheet, in a rosewood veneered case with fruitwood stringing and fruitwood and mother-of-pearl inlay, late 19thC, 25in (64cm) wide.
£700–900 *Bon*

A pair of singing birds in cage, on giltwood base, repainted, 20in (51cm) high.
£1,200–1,500 *CSK*

A Swiss chalet musical box, playing 8 airs with sublime harmony movement, hinged roof and front concealing removable fitted carrier for glasses, and plinth with pierced and carved apron, 27in (69cm) wide, cylinder 13in (33cm) long.
£1,300–1,700 *CSK*

r. A Symphonion table model disc musical box, playing 8¼in (21cm) discs, in walnut case, 14in (35.5cm) wide, with 31 discs in box.
£850–1,000 *Bea*

A coin-slot musical box, playing 8 airs with 2 dancing dolls, 3 bells with bird strikers, tune indicator, key wind and grained case with glass panel in lid and coin drawer, 20in (51cm) wide, cylinder 6in (15cm) long.
£1,200–1,500 *CSK*

r. A Swiss mandolin piccolo musical box, No. 78079, the 13½in (34cm) cylinder with indicator dial and playing 12 airs as listed on the tune sheet, in marquetry and stencilled rosewood and simulated rosewood case, late 19thC, 26in (66cm) wide.
£1,300–1,500 *Bea*

Gramophones

A portable gramophone, with Alba soundbox, on turned wood pivoted horn, in oak case stamped 700, c1925, 11in (28cm) square.
£80–100 *CSK*

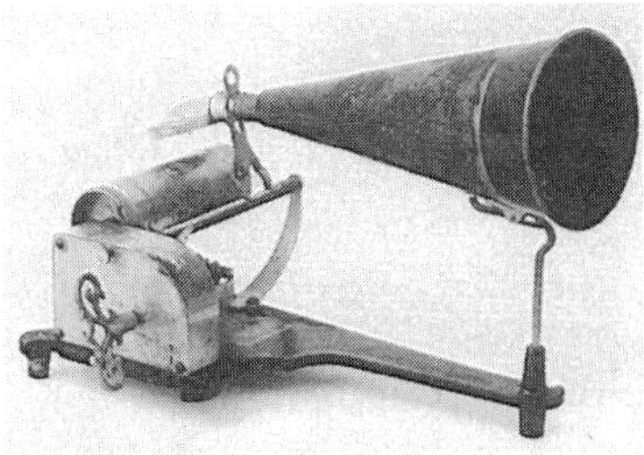

A Columbia type AQ Graphophone, with floating reproducer, coarse feedscrew and conical horn, on gilt lined, shaped black base.
£175–200 *CSK*

A Columbia type AT Graphophone, No. 267058, with floating reproducer and nickelled bedplate, in moulded oak case with 17in (43cm) red flower horn and table stand.
£350–400 *CSK*

An Edison Bell Electron cabinet gramophone, Model EB248, in black chinoiserie lacquered cabinet with gilt internal fittings, Electrotone soundbox and internal horn, enclosed by fret and doors, c1928, 28½in (72cm) wide, with a small quantity of records.
£1,000–1,200 *CSK*

Miller's is a price GUIDE not a price LIST

An EMG gramophone, with mark IX case adapted for mark X sound conduit, mark Xb horn, 4 spring soundbox, spring motor and papier mâché horn, c1935, 29½in (75cm) diam.
£1,800–2,200 *CSK*

A New Style No. 3 gramophone, by the Gramophone & Typewriter Ltd., with bevelled 7in (17.5cm) turntable, top wind motor with combined brake and speed controls, concert soundbox, zinc horn and oak case, c1904.
£1,000–1,200 *CSK*

This early example of the 'New Style No. 3' includes a blanked-off speed-control hole and altered cut-out in the top of the case for the governor bearing indication that this is an adapted No. 5 case, fitted to a No. 3 base.

An HMV gramophone, Model No. 194A with exponential re-entrant tone chamber, in mahogany case, on cabriole supports with carved paw feet, 24in (61.5cm) wide.
£3,700–4,000 *RBB*

l. A Klingsor gramophone, with Klingsor soundbox and single spring motor in dark oak Arts and Crafts style case, with internal horn covered by tuned strings and double doors, 41in (104cm) high.
£950–1,200 *CSK*

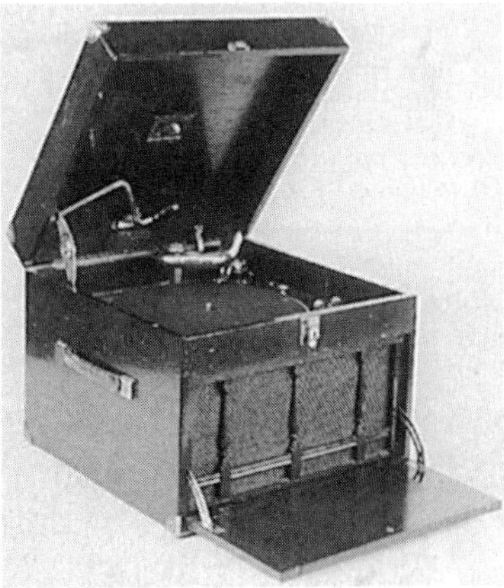

An HMV Model 113 portable gramophone, with double spring motor, 5a soundbox, internal horn enclosed by hinged flap and cloth backed grille with baluster turned columns, in teak case with corner reinforcements, carrying handle and trade plaque of 'The Haydn Coy., Karachi', c1929, 16½in (42cm) wide.
£350–400 *CSK*

A HMV gramophone, Model No. 202, in oak case, 27½in (70cm) wide.
£9,500–10,000 *RBB*

This gramophone was purchased secondhand after repossession in 1930.

A Zonophone Champion horn gramophone, with 10in (25cm) turntable, G & T Exhibition soundbox, on goose neck tone arm and small green Morning Glory horn, c1908.
£800–900 *CSK*

The Champion was identical in all but name to the Gramophone Company's Victor Monarch of October 1908. It was the first Zonophone to have a goose neck tone arm, 'Under licence from the Gramophone Co. Ltd'.

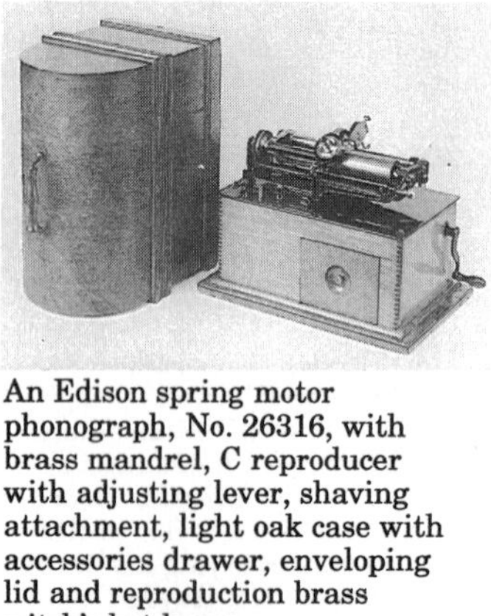

An Edison spring motor phonograph, No. 26316, with brass mandrel, C reproducer with adjusting lever, shaving attachment, light oak case with accessories drawer, enveloping lid and reproduction brass witch's hat horn.
£1,500–2,000 *CSK*

A Peresphone gramophone, in a well figured case, with 2 tone green enamelled tin fluted horn, paper label to the underside.
£450–550 *HSS*

A Zonophone Champion gramophone, with turntable, HMV No. 4 soundbox and green painted horn, c1910.
£350–450 *Bon*

Phonographs

An Edison Opera phonograph, Model A, No. 2932, with diamond A and Sapphire L reproducers, mahogany case and grained fibreglass horn, on mahogany stand with fielded panels and door enclosing shelves, restored, 27in (69cm) high.
£2,700–3,000 *CSK*

An HMV Automatic 1 gramophone, with 5a, bronzed, and 5b soundboxes, re-entrant tone chamber enclosed by fret, electric motor for turntable and record changing mechanism, walnut case, c1930, 42½in (107cm) wide, with turned pedestal for remote control.
£2,200–2,700 *CSK*

An Edison Opera phonograph, Model A, No. 2851, with brown bedplate, transversing mandrel, Model L reproducer and mahogany Music Master horn, in mahogany case, with oxidized handles.
£4,000–4,500 *CSK*

An Edison Home phonograph, Model D, No. 355846, with combination gearing and H reproducer, in oak case with instructions in lid, c1909.
£350–450 *CSK*

An Edison Red Gem phonograph, Model D, 340946D, with combination gearing, K reproducer and 2-piece Fireside horn, mainspring defective, lacks crane.
£600–800 *CSK*

A Pathé Gaulois phonograph, in black metal case with gilt lining, with composition reproducer and recorder in cartons.
£400–450 *CSK*

Polyphons

A Polyphon table model disc musical box, playing 15½in (40cms) discs, having picture panel under the lid and floral marquetry decorated case, 21in (53.5cm) wide, with 65 discs.
£1,200–1,700 *Bea*

An Edison Standard phonograph, No. S58081, with aluminium turned horn and approximately 24 cylinders, in an oak case.
£300–400 *HSS*

A small mahogany cased phonograph, with sound horn and various wax cylinders.
£250–270 *MST*

Did you know?
MILLER'S* Antiques Price Guide *builds up year-by-year to form the most comprehensive antiques photo-reference library available.

A Polyphon upright automatic, penny-in-the-slot disc musical box, playing 16in (40.5cm) discs, side winding handle, in walnut case with glazed door, 33in (84cm) high.
£2,000–2,500 *Bea*

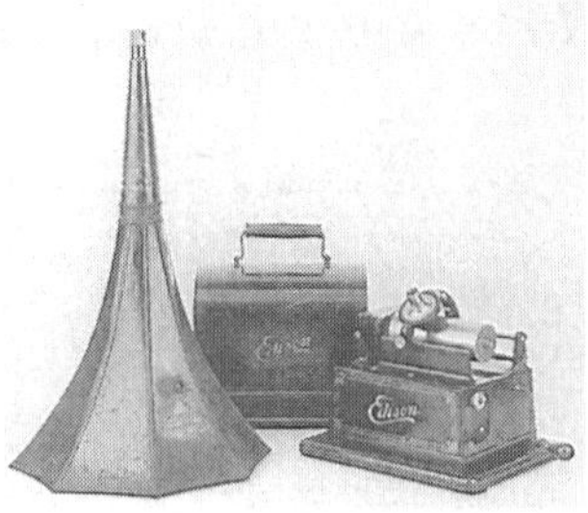

An Edison Red Gem phonograph, Model D, No. 319799D, with combination gearing, K reproducer and 2-piece maroon Fireside horn with part crane.
£850–950 *CSK*

An American Reginaphone phonograph, Style 171, the 16in (41cm) disc with a double comb, start/stop lever and a large horn with arm, mechanism contained in a mahogany case with approximately 20 discs, c1907, 10in (25cm) high.
£3,300–4,000 *S(NY)*

A 24⅝in (62cm) upright Polyphon, with twin combs, side wind motor, coin mechanism and drawer, with provision for manual override, typical walnut case with arched glass panel in door and 'New Polyphon Supply Co. Ltd.' coin slot plaque, lacks pediment and door spandrels, open joints in backboard, 45½in (115cm) high, with 15 discs.
£4,000–6,000 *CSK*

Musical Instruments

A Tanzbaer accordion, with 28 note trigger-operated action, walnut veneered case with coloured geometric inlay banding, and 32 rolls, in carrying case.
£1,200–1,700 *CSK*

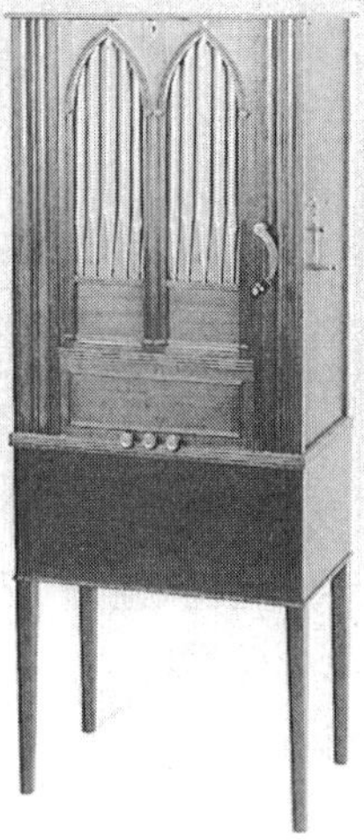

l. A small chamber barrel organ, with 16-key action playing one rank of wood and one of metal pipes with 2 striker triangle, one 10 air barrel and mahogany case with front crank, 3 stops and Gothic lancets with gilt simulated pipes, c1820, 29½in (75cm) high, on later mahogany stand.
£1,000–1,500 *CSK*

A Hicks pattern barrel piano, with 27 note action playing 8 airs, in rosewood veneered case, with pleated silk front panel, c1830, 38in (96.5cm) high.
£850–1,100 *CSK*

A portable barrel piano, the keyboard later converted to 10 automaton figures in national costume, mahogany case with turned feet, pleated silk panel front, maker's label 'Joseph Hicks Junr. Manufacturer of barrel organs, cylinder pianos etc. ...Bristol', front panel and case stamped '71', mid-19thC, 37½in (95cm) high.
£800–900 *WW*

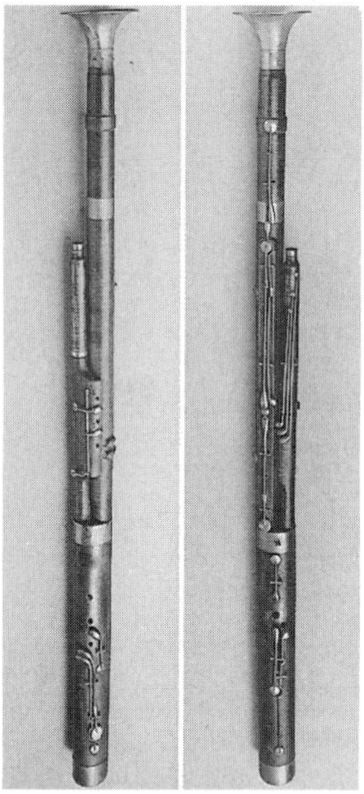

A 16-keyed stained maple bassoon, by Johann Wenzel Horák, (1817–1903) brass mounts and keys with circular covers, the a^1, c^2 and d^2 keys with extendable touchpieces, the bell joint terminating in a flared brass bell, crook absent, c1860, 50in (127cm) long.
£2,000–3,000 *S*

l. A silver mounted cello bow, by A. Lamy, stamped on the shaft 'A Lamy à Paris', the round stick of chestnut colour, the ebony frog, the pearl eye, the ebony button with 2 silver bands, 61g, no hair, no lapping.
£2,000–2,500 *Bon*

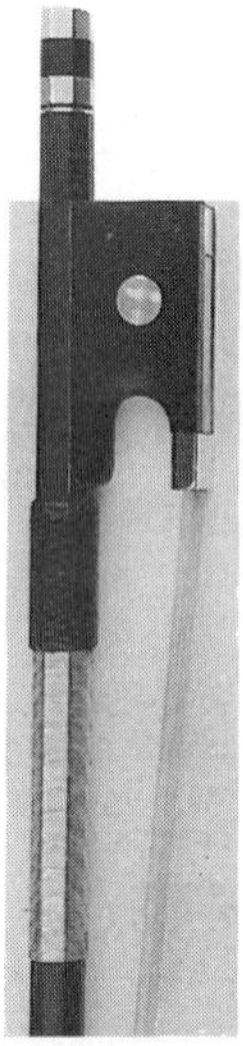

A silver mounted viola bow, by Alfred Lamy, Paris, stamped 'A Lamy à Paris' on the shaft, the round stick of a chestnut colour, the ebony frog, the pearl eye, the ebony button with 2 silver bands, 71g.
£14,500–16,000 *Bon*

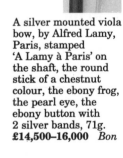

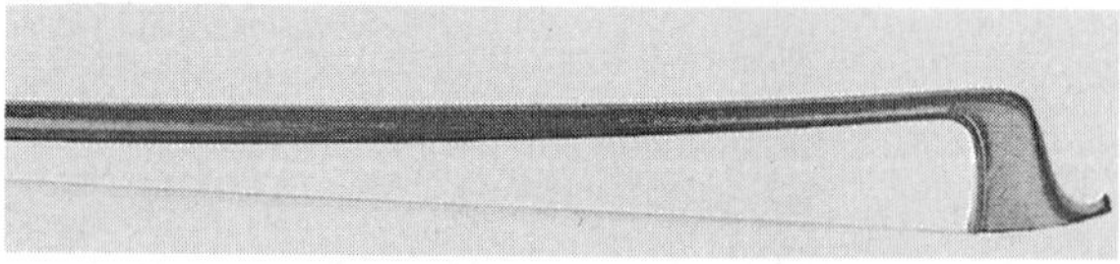

A silver mounted violin bow, stamped on the shaft 'V. Fetique à Paris', the round stick of a chestnut colour, the ebony frog, the Paris eye, the ebony button with 2 silver bands, 59g.
£900–1,200 *Bon*

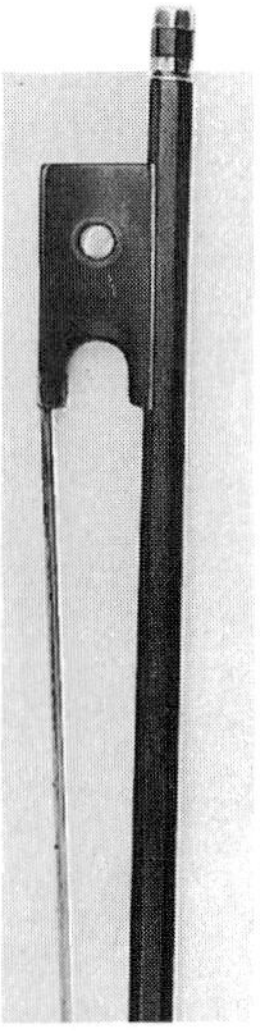

l. A silver mounted violin bow, stamped 'Dodd' on the shaft, the round stick of a chestnut colour, the ebony frog, the pearl eye, the ebony button with 2 silver bands, one missing, 54g.
£300–400 *Bon*

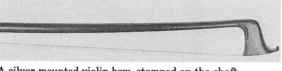

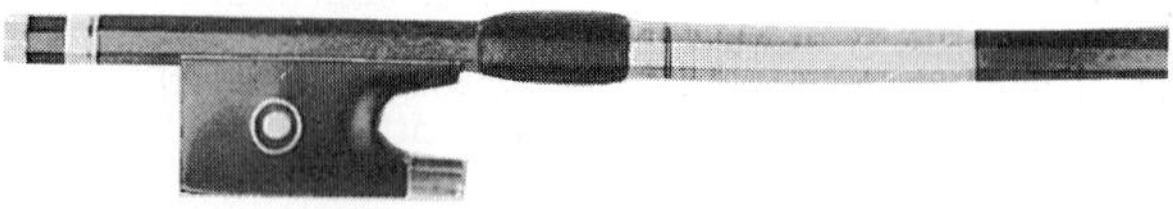

l. A silver mounted violin bow, by J. Thibouville-Lamy, stamped 'Jerome Thibouville-Lamy' on the stick, the round shaft of a chestnut colour, ebony frog, the silver covered ebony button, with silver bands, 60g.
£900–1,200 *Bon*

A cello, by David Collins, labelled 'David Collins Abingdon 1986 DC', the 2-piece back of narrow curl, the ribs and scroll of irregular curl, the top of medium grain, the varnish an orange colour, length of back 30in (76.5cm).
£1,500–2,500 *SK(B)*

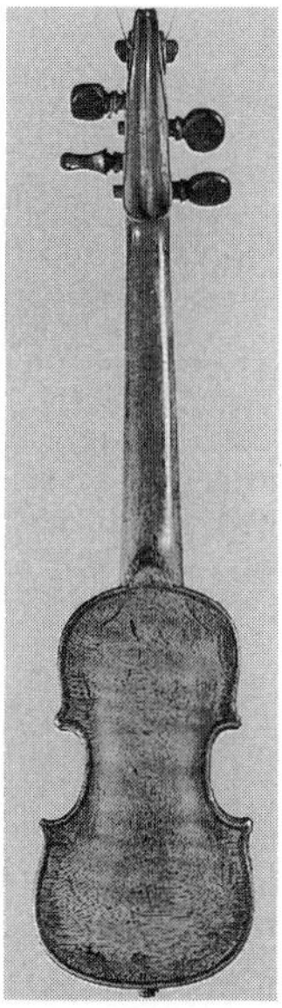

A dancing master's kit, the one-piece back of broad curl, the ribs and scroll similar, the table of medium grain, the varnish a golden brown colour, probably English, c1770.
£600–800 *Bon*

An American clavichord, by John Challis, Detroit, Michigan, fruitwood case having square tapering legs, signed 'John Challis, Detroit, MI', 57in (144.5cm) long.
£1,300–1,600 *LHA*

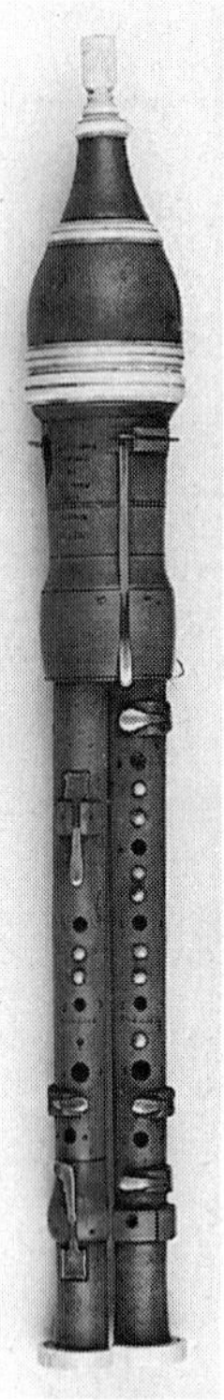

r. A boxwood double flageolet, stamped 'Bainbridge & Wood inventor, 35 Holborn Hill, London', with silver keys, ivory mounts and case.
£400–600 *Bon*

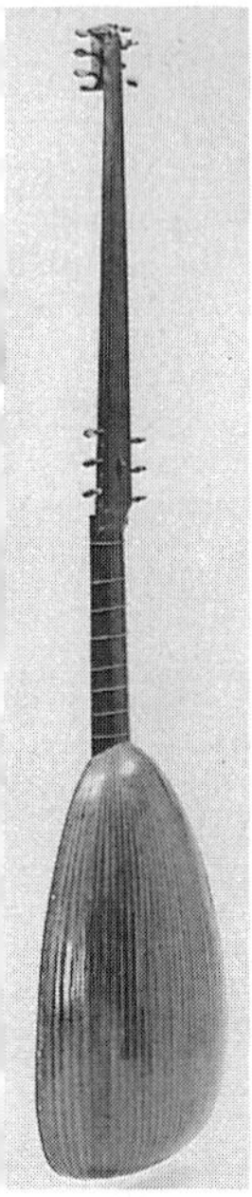

l. A chitaronne, the body by Matthäus Buchenberg, the remainder of the instrument by Ian Harwood, labelled 'Matheus Buchenberg Roma 1608 and Restored by Ian Harwood, Henfield 1975', c1608, body 27½in (69.5cm) long, in case.
£3,000–5,000 *S*

Buchenberg's reputation rests primarily on his chitaronne. Nine instruments ascribed to him are believed to exist, of which a few have survived intact but most have suffered varying degrees of alteration. At least 7 of these instruments are now in public collections.

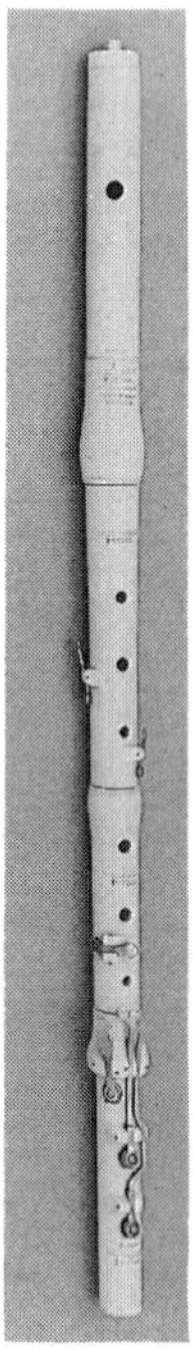

l. A six-keyed ivory flute, with silver keys, the C & C# keys with pewter plugs, graduated tuning slide and stopper, stamped 'Patent, Willm. Hen^y. Potter, Johnson's Court, Fleet Street, London', early 19thC, sounding length 23in (58.5cm), in wallet.
£1,000–1,500 *S*

r. A rosewood flute, stamped 'Buffet Crampon & Co. à Paris' on the joints and 'Brevetes SGDG' on the middle joint, with nickel keys, and fitted case.
£150–200 *Bon*

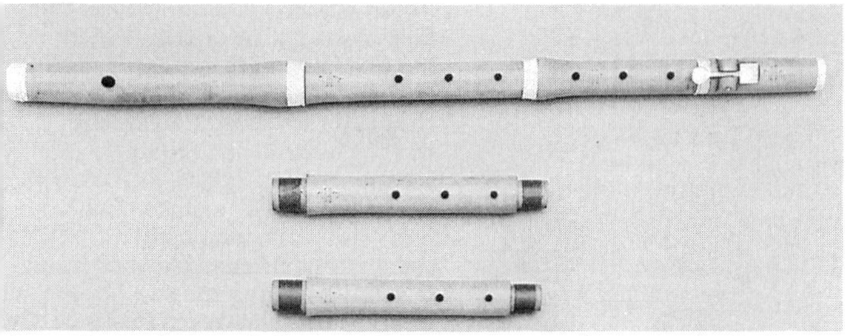

A one-keyed boxwood flute, with ivory mounts, the later single key of silver with square cover, three corps de rechange, stamped 'Bühner & Keller' on each joint, Strasbourg, c1810, sounding lengths 21in (53.5cm).
£1,800–2,500 *S*

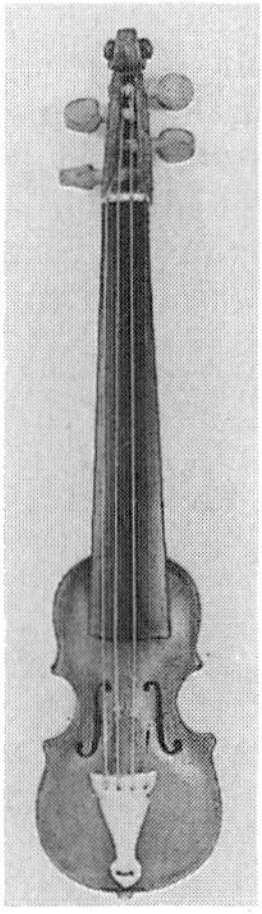

r. A dancing master's kit, the back, ribs, neck and head carved from a single piece of maple of irregular curl, the table of fine grain in the centre opening out towards the flanks, bone tailpiece, labelled 'Marco Obbo Napoli 17*0', probably Italian, 18thC, 15in (38cm) long.
£700–1,000 *S*

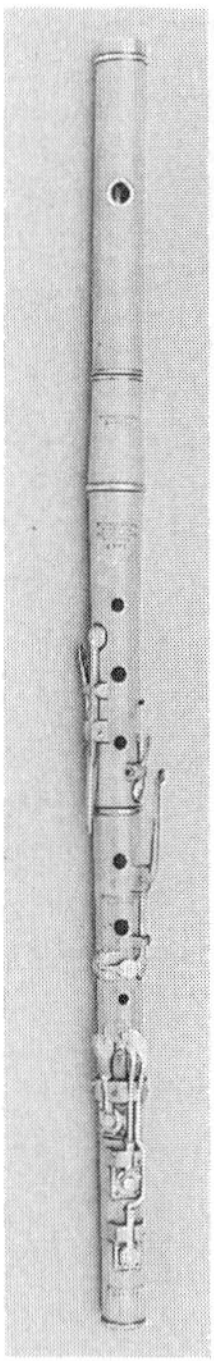

l. An eight-keyed boxwood flute, with silver mounts, silver salt spoon cup keys, patent head joint and further tuning slide between the lower middle and foot joints, stamped 'Rudall & Rose, No. 15, Piazza, Covent Garden, London, 2976', c1830, sounding length 22½in (57.5cm), in wallet.
£1,000–1,500 *S*

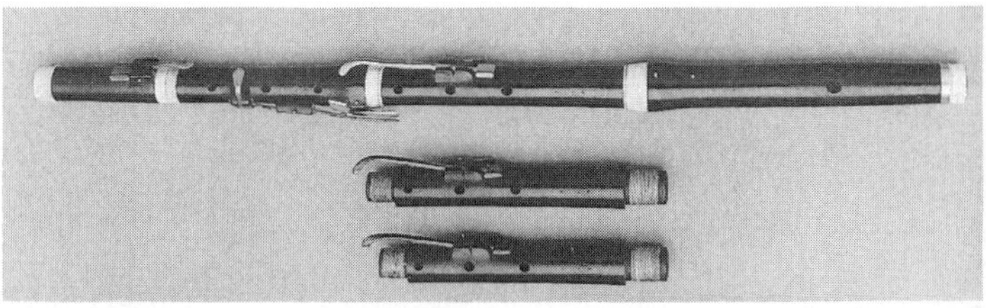

A six-keyed ebony flute, by Johann Wendelinus Weisse (fl. Berlin, 1814–c1840), with ivory mounts, the keys of silver with bevelled square covers, adjustable stopper, 3 corps de rechange, stamped 'Weisse in Berlin' with the device of an eagle, c1820, sounding lengths 21in (53.5cm), in case.
£1,000–1,500 *S*

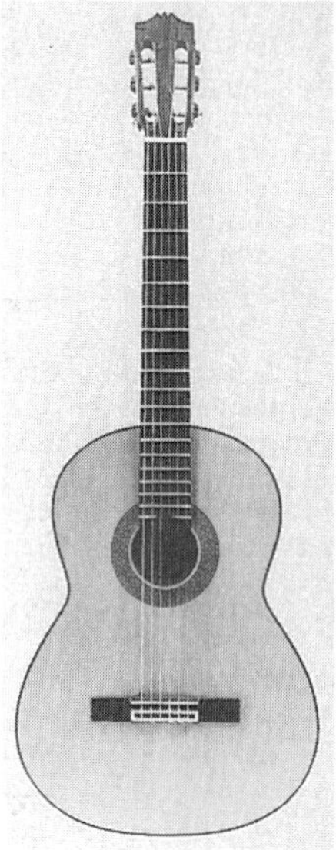

l. A concert guitar, by Arcángel Fernández (Madrid b. 1931), the two-piece table of pine, with traditional rosewood bridge, the two-piece back and ribs of rosewood with rosewood edgebindings and stained wood stringing, 4 transverse bars internally, ebony fingerboard with nickel-silver frets, nickel-silver machine heads with carved ivory buttons, cedar head and neck with rosewood facing to the headstock, variously labelled and stamped, in fitted case labelled 'Constructor de Guitarras, Arcángel Fernández, Jesòs y Maria 26, Madrid', c1965, length of back 19½in (49cm).
£10,000–12,000 *S*

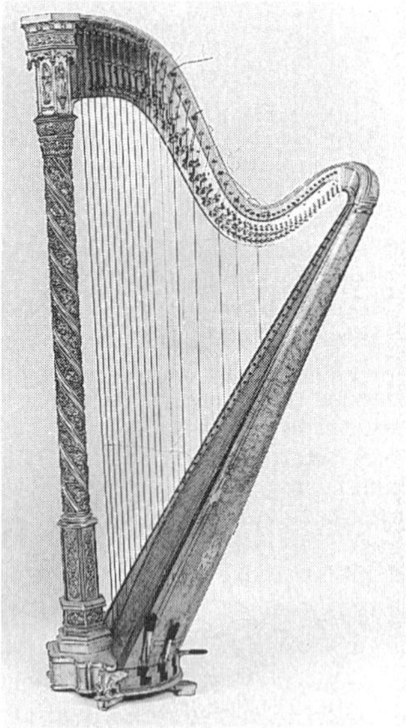

A Gothic double-action harp by Sebastian & Pierre Erard, 18 Great Marlborough St. London, Patent No. 6784.
£1,800–2,200 *LT*

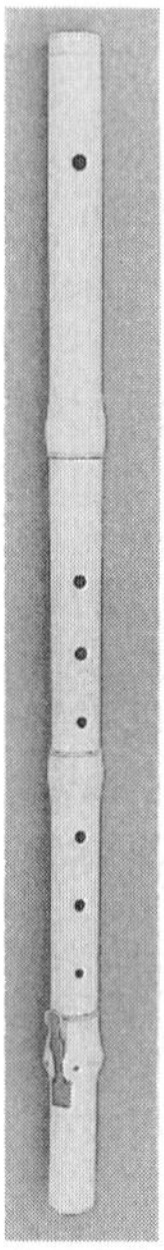

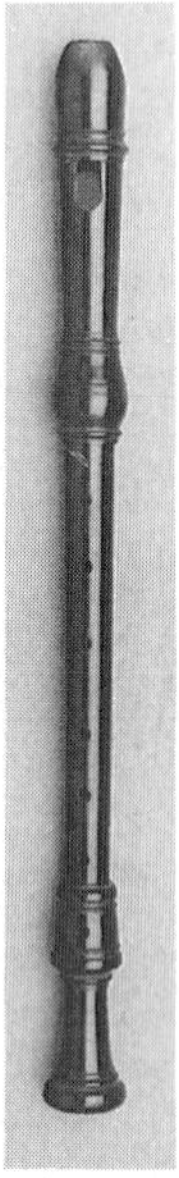

l. A two-keyed boxwood oboe, by Thomas Cahusac, The Elder (London b. c1755, d. 1798), with onion and cotton reel finial, the keys of brass with circular covers, the C key with fishtailed touchpiece, stamped 'Cahusac, London' on all joints, late 18thC, 22½in (57.5cm) long.
£1,100–1,500 *S*

A one-keyed ivory flute, by Henry Waylett (fl. London, c1743-1765) the single key of silver with square cover, stamped 'Waylett', mid-18thC, sounding length 21in (53.5cm), in wallet.
£3,000–3,500 *S*

An American harpsichord, by John Challis, Detroit, Michigan, in fruitwood case, 96in (243.5cm) long.
£2,000–2,600 *LHA*

A single manual harpsichord, by Jacob Kirckman (1710–1792), the fasciaboard of root walnut with boxwood stringing and kingwood crossbanding, the walnut case with shaped brass strap hinges, the walnut jackrail with holly stringing, the 5 octave keyboard, FF to f^3 with FF# omitted, with ivory naturals and ebony accidentals, 2 brass knobbed hand levers controlling the two 8ft. stops, the machine stop mechanism partly absent, on trestle stand, with later walnut music desk, inscribed 'Jacobus Kirckman Londini fecit 1770', 87in (221cm) long.
£32,000–40,000 *S*

r. A rosewood veneered grand piano, by John Broadwood & Co., Serial No. 1631, 86½in (219cm) long.
£1,200–2,000 *SLN*

l. A Dutch composite giraffe piano, possibly by Corneille Charles Emanuel van der Does (1769–1827), in mahogany, the keyboard supported by gilded rams' heads, the fasciaboard of rosewood with double brass stringing, the later action by J. J. Nissen, Amsterdam, the six and half octave keyboard, CC to g^4, with ivory naturals and ebonised accidentals, 2 pedals controlling forte and una corda stops, inscribed on the wrest plank 'J. J. Nissen, Amsterdam' and labelled internally with the dealer's label 'J. A. Buschen', c1820 and c1900, 46½in (118cm) wide.
£3,300–3,800 *S*

An American rococo revival rosewood Steinway grand piano, c1879, 86in (218.5cm) long.
£11,500–13,000 *C(NY)*

This Steinway grand piano, dating from 1880, was owned by Mme Margaret Stedman Chaloff, pianist and teacher, who taught in America at The New England Conservatory of Music, Brandeis University and The Berklee School of Music. As a pianist and accomplished teacher, Mme Chaloff attracted the attention of many great artists including Leonard Bernstein, George Shearing, Arthur Fiedler, Toshiko, Dr Nicholas Zervas, Serge Chaloff, Herbie Hancock, Steve Kuhn, Allan Hovaness, Miklos Schwalb, Dick Twortzig, Dave McKenna, George Wein and Lee Berk. All of these musicians are reputed to have enjoyed playing on this grand piano.

An aquamarine, parcel gilt and chinoiserie lacquered grand piano, by C. Bechstein, Berlin, decorated all-over in heightened gilt, the metal frame No. 38619, with wooden sound board signed 'C Bechstein', with hinged music rest, 59in (149.5cm) wide.
£7,000–10,000 *C*

The celebrated firm of piano makers was established in 1853 by Friedrich Wilhelm Carl Bechstein in Berlin. The action of this instrument was produced c1896.

r. An early Victorian boudoir grand piano, No. 2594/36981, by Collard & Collard, the carved rosewood case on octagonal tapering legs with brass casters, 88in (223.5cm) long.
£700–900 *Bea*

l. A Blüthner baby grand piano, with ebonised case, maker 'Julius Bluthner, Leipzig 104824', c1920, 67in (170cm) long.
£2,000–2,500 *MJB*

r. A boudoir grand piano, No. 48364, by John Broadwood and Sons, with barless iron frame, Schwander roller action and rosewood case, 66in (167.5cm) long.
£2,000–2,500 *Bea*

A George III square pianoforte, by John Broadwood & Son, London, with 68-note action and Sheraton mahogany case, the satinwood fascia panel having dated maker's inscription flanked by fretted scrollwork, the detachable base fitted with pedal undershelf, squared tapering legs and casters, restored, c1803, 66in (167.5cm) long.
£1,500–2,000 *RBB*

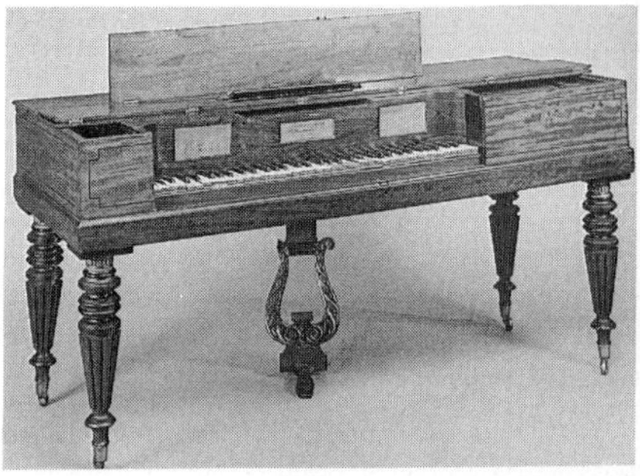

r. A Federal inlaid mahogany and satinwood pianoforte, by Dubois and Stodart, 6 old ivory keys missing, New York, c1820, 69½in (176cm) long.
£800–1,000 *S(NY)*

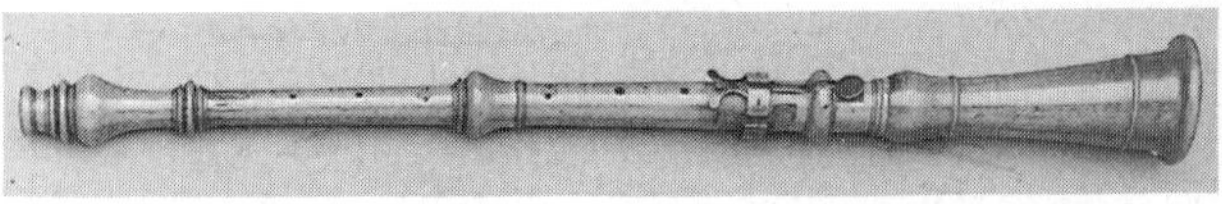

A rosewood treble, alto, recorder, by Arnold Dolmetsch (1858–1940), the tube unmounted, with ornamental turnery around the tenon sockets, below the beak and around the bell, stamped 'Arnold Dolmetsch' and bearing the serial No. '1', c1919, 19½in (50cm) long.
£2,000–3,000 *S*

A Victorian walnut piano, by Henry Ward, fully restored with new musical components, c1880.
£6,500–7,500 *CPi*

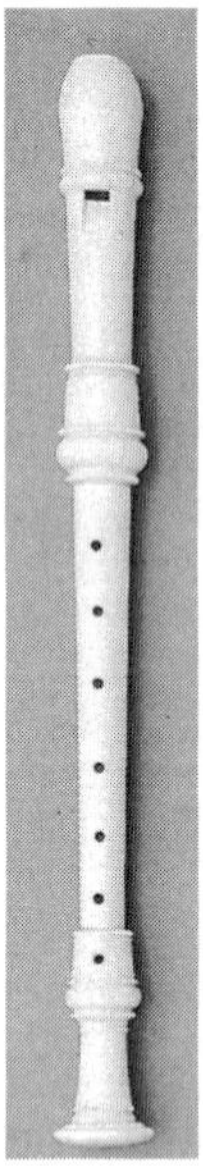

r. An ivory treble recorder, by Johann Benedikt Gahn (fl. Nuremberg, 1698–1711), stamped 'I. B. Gahn' on the head joint, c1700, 19½in (50cm) long.
£10,500–15,000 *S*

A French violin, by Paul Serdet, Paris, the two-piece back of strong broad curl, the ribs similar, the scroll of medium curl, the top of medium grain, the varnish a red colour, labelled, c1909, 14in (35.5cm) long, with case.
£4,500–5,500 *SK(B)*

A grand pianoforte, by John Broadwood & Son (fl.1795–1808), the satinwood nameboard with holly and stained fruitwood stringing and maple crossbanding, the five and a half octave keyboard, FF to C^4, with ivory naturals and ebony accidentals, English grand action, two pedals controlling forte and una corda stops, mahogany music desk, inscribed on the nameboard within an oval boxwood plaque '1802, John Broadwood and Son, Makers to his Majesty and the Princesses, Great Pulteney Street, Golden Square, London', 92in (233.5cm) long.
£10,500–12,000 *S*

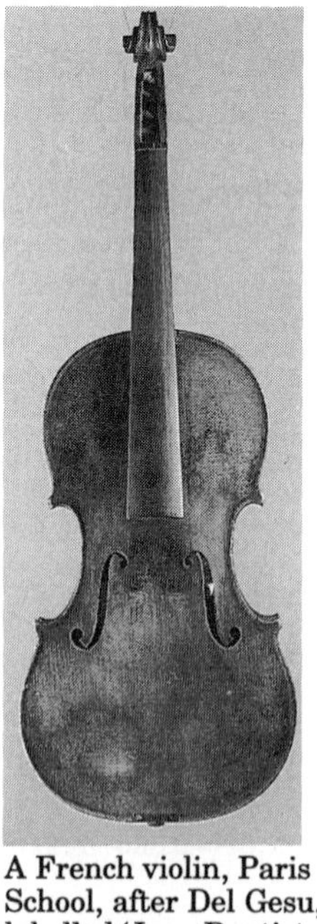

A French violin, Paris School, after Del Gesu, labelled 'Jean Baptiste Vuillaume' the 2-piece back of medium broad curl, the ribs and scroll similar, the table of medium curl, the varnish a golden-red colour, c1870, 14in (35.5cm) long.
£1,700–2,200 *Bon*

A drawing room grand pianoforte, by J. Blüthner, Leipzig, No. 43334 'Aliquot' patent, 88 notes, overstrung, in rosewood finished case, on fluted turned tapering legs, c1895, 76in (193cm) long.
£2,000–2,500 *RBB*

An Italian violin, the two-piece back of strong irregular curl, the ribs and scroll similar, the top of fine to medium grain, with orange-red varnish, labelled 'Joannes Antonius Marchi, Fecit Bononia Anno 1768', 14in (35.5cm) long.
£26,000–28,000 *SK(B)*

This instrument retains its original neck.

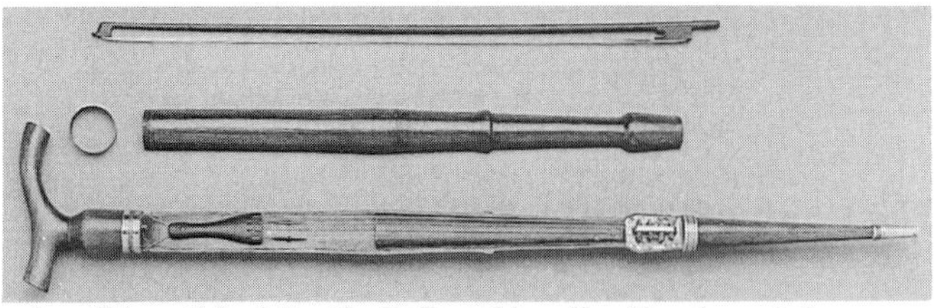

A walking stick violin, the body and handle of beechwood, the upper section of the stick in 2 parts opening to reveal the pine table, brass tuning pins operated by a metal key, the shaped handle forming a chinrest and unscrewing to give access to the bow, nickel mounts, Markneukirchen, mid-19thC, 34½in (88cm) long.
£3,500–4,000 *S*

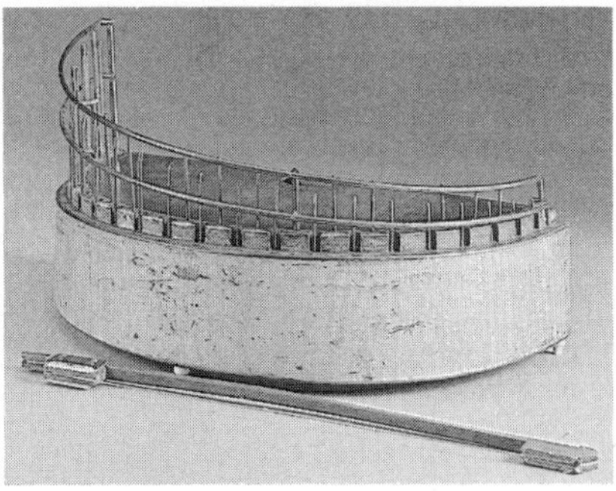

A nail violin, by John Joseph Merlin (1735–1803), the body of maple cut on the slab, pine table pierced by a D-shaped soundhole, with 37 iron nails arranged in a semi-circle giving a chromatic compass of 3 octaves c^1 to c^4, with two iron bow guide rails, one for the naturals, the other for the accidentals, on 3 ivory feet, labelled, 13½in (34.5cm) wide, in a box with brass handles.
£6,500–7,000 *S*

An American violin, by Isaiah H. Arey, Boscawen, stamped internally 'Made by I. M. Arey, Boscawen N.H., 1858', and stamped below the button 'I.M.A.', the two-piece back of narrow curl, the ribs and scroll of medium curl, the top of medium grain, the varnish of a yellow-brown colour, 14in (35.5cm) long.
£1,200–1,800 *SK(B)*

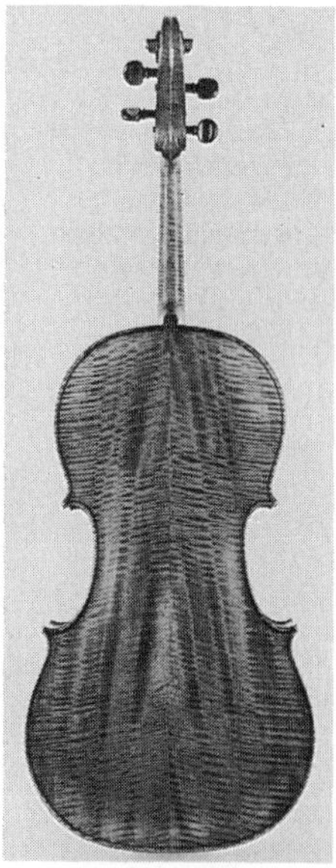

A child's violoncello, by Mirecourt, the two-piece back of medium curl, the ribs and scroll similar, the top of fine grain, the varnish of an orange-yellow colour, labelled 'Paul Jombar Luthier, 20 Rue Rochechouart, Paris, No. 12 AN 1898', c1885, length of back 24½in (62.5cm).
£1,800–2,000 *SK(B)*

A Bohemian violin, of dark brown colouring, labelled 'Joannes Udalricus Eberll, recit. Prague 1760', with one bow signed 'P. Baltzerson', the other unsigned, both with silver and mother-of-pearl mounts, purfling needs some restoration, with case, 23½in (60cm) long.
£500–600 *EL*

RECEIVERS

A small receiver, with 4 valves, in a Bakelite case with Gothic fretted front, 8½in (21.5cm) wide.
£170–200 *CSK*

A Marconi Type 23 two-valve receiver, with sloping control panel and mahogany case, c1928.
£250–270 *CSK*

BOOKS & BOOK ILLUSTRATIONS

The Art of
ANGLING.
WHEREIN
Are discovered many rare Secrets, very necessary to be knowne by all that delight in that Recreation.
LONDON,
Printed in the Yeare 1653.

Thomas Barker, *The Art of Angling,* published London 1653, second issue, 18thC diced Russia, covers with gilt dogtooth roll border and central fishtool, each corner containing an aquatic bird, fish motif repeated in spine compartments, damaged.
£2,000–2,400 *CSK*

Edward Ardizzone, (1900–79), 'Ridley shows us his picture of Clive', pen and black ink, 8 by 5in (20 by 12.5cm).
£720–800 *CSK*

Grimm Brothers, *Little Brother & Little Sister and other tales,* published by Constable, London 1917, limited to 525 copies signed by the artist, 13 mounted coloured plates by Arthur Rackham, original cloth gilt, slight damage.
£350–450 *CSK*

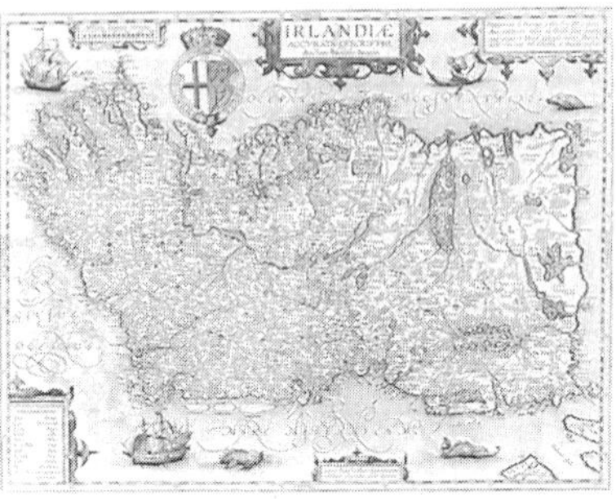

Baptista Boazio, 'Irlandiæ Accurata Descriptio', a hand coloured engraved map, published by Joannes Baptista Vrints, Antwerp, Italian text verso, damaged, c1600, 17 by 22½in (44 by 57cm).
£1,500–2,000 *CSK*

Molly Benatar, (active 1919–29), complete set of illustrations to *Margaret and the Currant Bunny,* by Edith L. Elias, all signed and inscribed, pen and black ink, one in watercolour, 14½in by 10½in and smaller.
£300–500 *CSK*

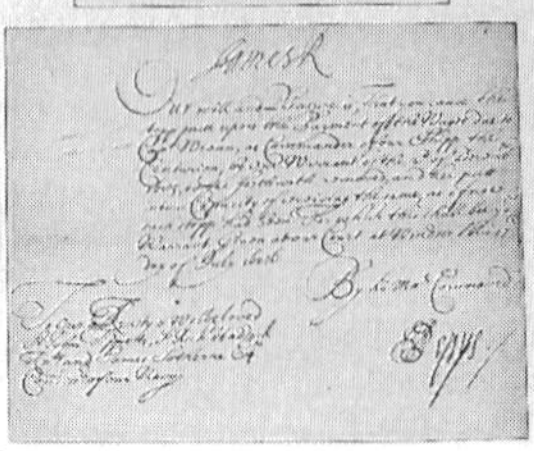

l. Peter Cunningham (ed.), *The Story of Nell Gwyn . . . extended by the insertion of illustrative portraits etc.* by James A. Garland, published by J. F. Sabin 1887, New York, one volume bound in 2, limited to 500 copies, this is No. 3 of 6 paper copies signed by the publisher, with approx. 230 engraved portraits and views, 2 hand coloured, including a signed letter from Samuel Pepys to James II, contemporary red morocco gilt by Bradstreet's, spines gilt in compartments.
£3,000–4,000 *CSK*

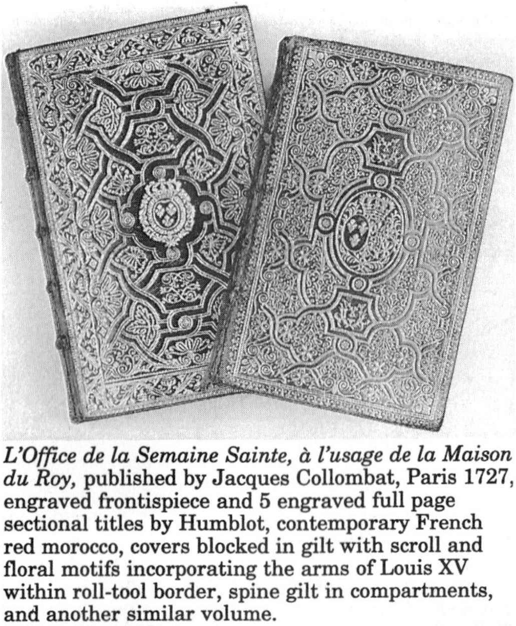

L'Office de la Semaine Sainte, à l'usage de la Maison du Roy, published by Jacques Collombat, Paris 1727, engraved frontispiece and 5 engraved full page sectional titles by Humblot, contemporary French red morocco, covers blocked in gilt with scroll and floral motifs incorporating the arms of Louis XV within roll-tool border, spine gilt in compartments, and another similar volume.
£700–900 *CSK*

l. Denis Diderot, and Jean le Rond d'Alembert, *Recueil de Planches, sur les sciences, les arts libéraux, et les arts méchaniques, avec leur explication,* published by Briasson, David & Le Breton, Paris 1768, 271 engraved plates, 2 folding and 25 double page, contemporary vellum, slight damage.
£1,400–1,700 *CSK*

The subjects of the plates include mammals, birds, butterflies, a folding view of the Giant's Causeway and a sequence showing the eruption of Vesuvius in 1757.

John Hancock (1896–1918), 'A Lady in a Garden at Dusk, upon beholding her re-incarnate affinity', inscribed, pen and black ink, 7½ by 13in (19 by 33cm) one framed drawing entitled 'The Little Dust-Makers', 2 unframed drawings entitled 'Life is Devotion . . .' and 'Aeolus flies invisible across the Sky . . .'.
£600–700 *CSK*

John Hancock was a poet, artist and mystic who committed suicide at the age of 22, after suffering from Bright's disease for two years. He was taken to Canada as a small child, returning to the Midlands with his parents when in his early teens. He studied at the St. John's Wood Art School, London, from the age of 15, and from then until his death worked at home, living with his parents, drawing and painting in the mornings, then reading and writing at night.
His work bears similarities to that of Aubrey Beardsley (with whom he shared the publisher, John Lane). He was often compared to William Blake and many of his pictures indicate the soul shown as a serpent, after a vision which he had at the age of 17. He read widely and worked out his own meaning of life, many of his theories being expounded in his writings and poetry as well as in his art.
His short life came to a sad end when, having kept his disease secret from his parents and friends, he drowned himself in the Regent's Park Canal.

l. Kay Nixon, (1895–1988), 'A Koala with Green Shoes', pencil and watercolour, unframed, 7½ by 6in (19 by 15cm), and a large quantity of unframed watercolours and drawings.
£900–1,000 *CSK*

Faith Jaques (b.1923), 5 illustrations to *Tilly's Day Out,* pen and black ink and watercolour heightened with white, 8¾ by 10¼in (22 by 26cm) and smaller.
£1,000–1,200 *CSK*

Kay Nixon, (1895–1988), 'Two White Doves', signed, pencil, watercolour and bodycolour, unframed, 6½ by 7in (16 by 17.5cm), and an unframed watercolour of a squirrel with insects.
£300–400 *CSK*

Beatrix Potter, (1866–1943), *The Tale of Mrs Tittlemouse,* published by Frederick Warne, London and New York 1910, first edition, presentation copy, inscribed on front free endpaper, 'For Victoria with love from Cousin B. Aug 15th 10', coloured frontispiece and 26 coloured plates, original 'de-luxe' decorated cloth gilt with mounted pictorial label on upper cover, coloured pictorial endpapers.
£2,000–2,200 *CSK*

Andrea Palladio, *The Four Books of Andrea Palladio's Architecture,* published by Isaac Ware, London 1738, 4 engraved titles, 212 engraved plates and text illustrations, slightly damaged and repaired.
£600–700 *CSK*

Ernest Howard Shepard, (1879–1976), 'Boccherini's minuet and the Caliph of Baghdad', and 'You've got to wash them all', both signed with initials and inscribed as titles, pencil and pen and black ink, 4 by 6½in (10 by 16cm) and 6 by 10¾in (15 by 27cm).
£600–700 *CSK*

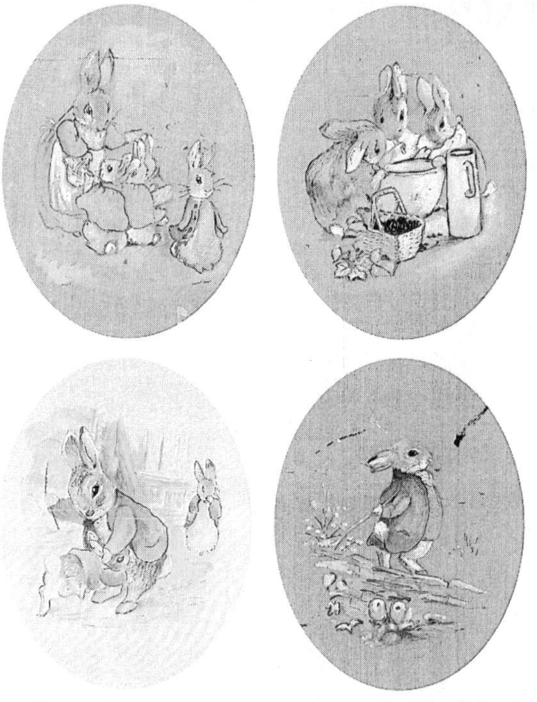

Beatrix Potter, (1866–1943), 5 illustrations for *The Tale of Peter Rabbit,* and *The Tale of Benjamin Bunny,* pen and ink and watercolour, on silk with lace trim, 6½in (16cm) wide.
£22,000–27,000 *CSK*

Mary Evans Price, 'Pixies to the Rescue', signed, pen and black ink and watercolour heightened with white, 12½in by 9in (32 by 23cm), and a quantity of unframed illustrations by the same artist.
£1,800–2,200 *CSK*

Louis Wain's *Annual,* 1921, illustrated, slight damage.
£90–110 *MCA*

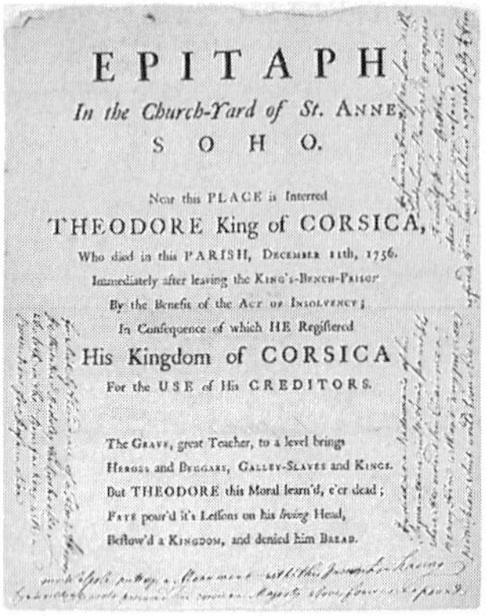

EPITAPH
In the Church-Yard of St. ANNE, SOHO.
Near this PLACE is Interred
THEODORE King of CORSICA,
Who died in this PARISH, December 11th, 1756.
Immediately after leaving the KING'S-BENCH-PRISON
By the Benefit of the ACT OF INSOLVENCY;
In Consequence of which HE Registered
His Kingdom of CORSICA
For the USE of His CREDITORS.

The GRAVE, great Teacher, to a level brings
HEROES and BEGGARS, GALLEY-SLAVES and KINGS.
But THEODORE this Moral learn'd, e'er dead;
FATE pour'd it's Lessons on his living Head,
Bestow'd a KINGDOM, and denied him BREAD.

Horace Walpole, *Epitaph in the Church-Yard of St. Anne, Soho,* published by Strawberry Hill Press, London 1757, broadsheet, limited to 24 copies, 9½ by 7½in (23.5 by 20cm), with contemporary inscriptions in margins and on verso, modern cloth portfolio.
£700–750 *CSK*

Ellen Willmott, *The Genus Rosa,* published by John Murray, London 1910–14, 25 original parts bound in 2 volumes, 132 chromolithographed plates by Alfred Parsons, original wrappers to parts bound in at end of each volume, contemporary roan-backed boards, slight damage.
£1,700–2,200 *CSK*

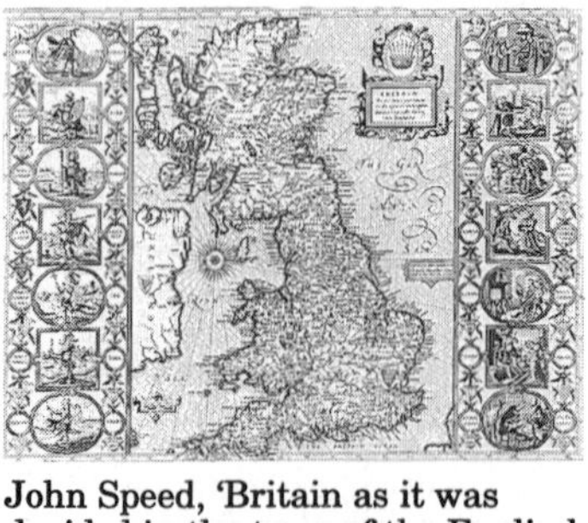

John Speed, 'Britain as it was devided in the tyme of the Englische Saxons especially during their heptarchy', published by John Sudbury & George Humble, London c1614, hand coloured engraved map with vignettes of Anglo-Saxon kings along borders, English text on verso, 15 by 20in (38 by 51cm) framed and glazed.
£720–800 *CSK*

Louis Wain, *Cat's Cradle,* illustrated, slight damage.
£110–140 *MCA*

ARTISTS' MATERIALS

An artist's oak studio easel, with adjustable winding and tilt mechanism above a materials shelf, on an H-frame, 19thC, 66in (167.5cm) high, unextended.
£420–470 *CSK*

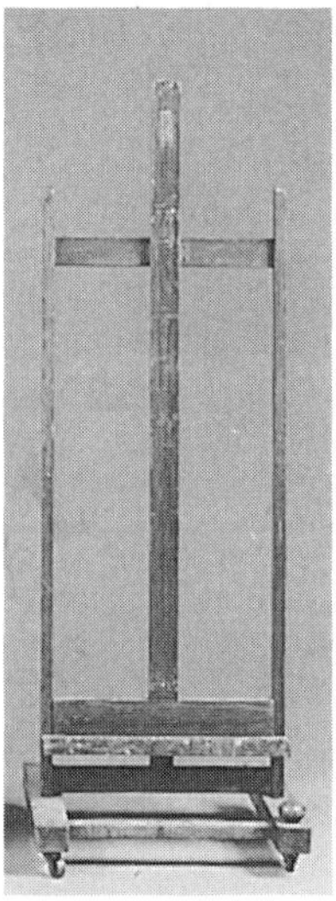

An artist's oak studio easel, with sliding adjustable height mechanism, on an H-frame, with label for Reeves & Sons, 60in (152cm) high, unextended.
£150–250 *CSK*

An artist's oak studio easel, with adjustable winding mechanism, on an H-frame, 19thC, 94in (238cm) high, unextended.
£400–600 *CSK*

An artist's oak studio easel, with adjustable winding and tilt mechanism, on an H-frame, with label for Winsor and Newton Ltd., 94in (238cm) high, unextended.
£1,400–1,700 *CSK*

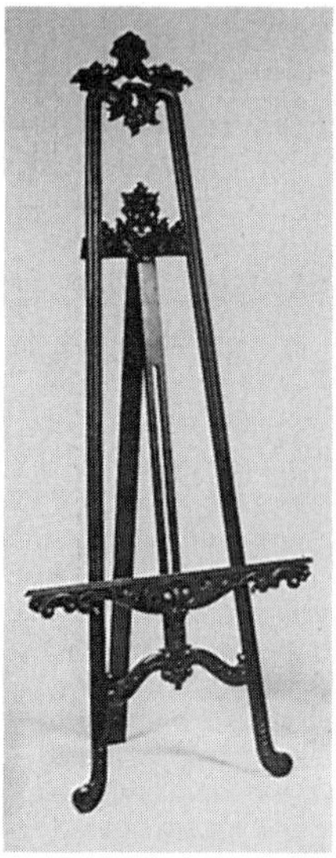

A mahogany A-frame gallery easel, with carved foliate decoration, with adjustable shelf, 85in (216cm) high.
£2,500–3,000 *CSK*

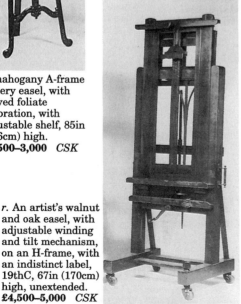

r. An artist's oak studio easel, with adjustable winding and tilt mechanism, ratchet drawing slope to the reverse, on an H-frame, with label for J. Newman, 24 Soho Square, London, late 19thC, 87in (221cm) high.
£800–1,000 *CSK*

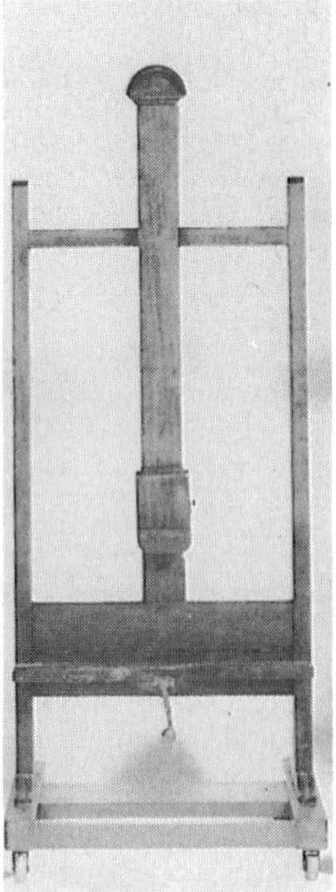

An artist's mahogany studio easel, with adjustable winding and tilt mechanism, on an H-frame, with label, 19thC, 68½in (174cm) high, unextended.
£900–1,200 *CSK*

r. An artist's walnut and oak easel, with adjustable winding and tilt mechanism, on an H-frame, with an indistinct label, 19thC, 67in (170cm) high, unextended.
£4,500–5,000 *CSK*

l. A walnut A-frame gallery easel, with fixed shelf and carved foliate decoration, 78in (198cm) high.
£1,700–2,000 *CSK*

ORIENTAL
Cloisonné

A cloisonné bowl, decorated with a band of stylised scrolling lotus and foliage above a band of lappets, on a turquoise ground, Ming Dynasty, 5in (12.5cm) diam.
£700–900 *CSK*

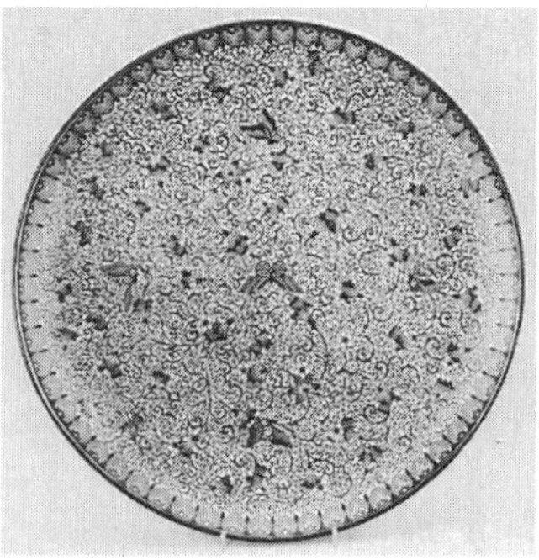

A Chinese cloisonné dish, decorated within a lappet border, the underside with lotus flowers, on a pale blue ground, 20in (50.5cm) diam., on a wood stand.
£450–500 *CSK*

A pair of Japanese cloisonné chargers, decorated with flowering prunus, peonies and daisies within stylised borders on turquoise grounds, small cracks, 18in (45.5cm) wide.
£470–520 *CSK*

A pair of Chinese cloisonné censers and covers, modelled as standing quails with their heads turned to one side, Qianlong, 5½in (13.5cm) high, on wood stands.
£1,800–2,200 *CSK*

A pair of Chinese cloisonné flaring gu-shaped vases, decorated with stylised scrolling lotus above and below lappet-shaped bands and flanges, on turquoise grounds, Qianlong, 9in (23cm) high.
£780–850 *CSK*

A cloisonné waisted baluster vase, with flaring neck, decorated with a bird among flowering chrysanthemums and peonies issuing from rockwork, on a turquoise ground reserved with key-frets, 10in (25cm) high.
£100–150 *CSK*

A pair of Chinese cloisonné censers, modelled as standing stylised ducks, decorated with floral bands, on turquoise grounds, 7½in (19cm) high.
£300–400 *CSK*

A pair of Chinese cloisonné vases, with garlic necks, decorated with stylised bats and shou characters among hanging tassels and scrolling foliage between ruyi heads and lappet borders, on turquoise grounds, slight damage, Jiaqing, 9in (23cm) high.
£350–450 *CSK*

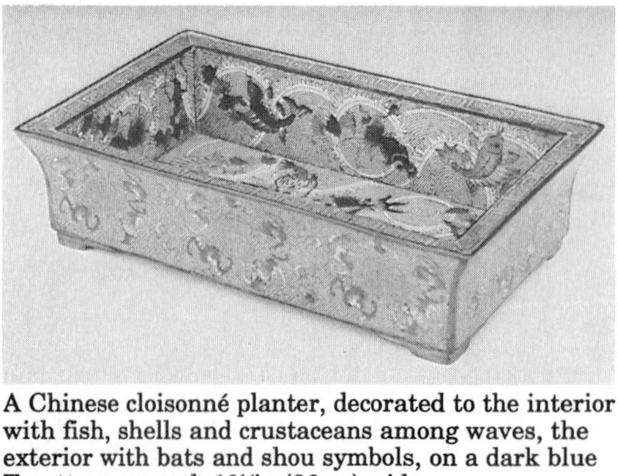

A Chinese cloisonné planter, decorated to the interior with fish, shells and crustaceans among waves, the exterior with bats and shou symbols, on a dark blue T-pattern ground, 10¼in (26cm) wide.
£600–700 *CSK*

A pair of Chinese cloisonné and gilt filigree censers, the details inlaid in coral and turquoise beads, 14½in (37cm) long.
£300–400 *CSK*

A Japanese cloisonné tapering oviform vase, with shakudo rims, decorated in silver wire with trailing flowers and leaves on a grey ground, 13½in (34.5cm) high.
£1,100–1,300 *CSK*

A Chinese cloisonné censer and domed cover, with knop finial and elephant head handles, on three mask feet, decorated with stylised taotie and scrolling lotus between ruyi head borders, on a turquoise ground, damaged, Jiaqing, 12in (30.5cm) high.
£1,200–1,500 *CSK*

A pair of Chinese cloisonné censers and covers, modelled as ducks, decorated with bands of scrolling and geometric motifs, on turquoise grounds, 9in (23cm) high.
£250–350 *CSK*

A pair of Chinese cloisonné models of walking deer, on pierced stands, decorated with scrolling flowers, on turquoise grounds, 16½in (42cm) high.
£550–650 *CSK*

A pair of Chinese cloisonné wig stands, on domed bases, the bodies with gourd-shaped flasks below issuing clouds and lotus pods, decorated with scrolling lotus and breaking waves, two finials added, chipped, 13in (33.5cm) high.
£600–700 *CSK*

A Japanese cloisonné slender tapering vase, decorated in gold and silver wire with two birds among a variety of flowers on a midnight blue ground, signed 'Inaba Nanaho', 7in (17.5cm) high.
£1,200–1,500 *CSK*

A cloisonné flattened quatrefoil vase, with flaring neck, decorated with buildings and pagodas among trees and rockwork between borders of scrolling lotus, ruyi-heads, leaves and roundels, all on a turquoise ground, Jiaqing, 13in (33cm) high.
£800–900 *CSK*

Glass

A Peking red overlay glass flaring bowl, decorated to the exterior with flowering branches on a milky-white ground, 6in (15cm) diam.
£70–90 *CSK*

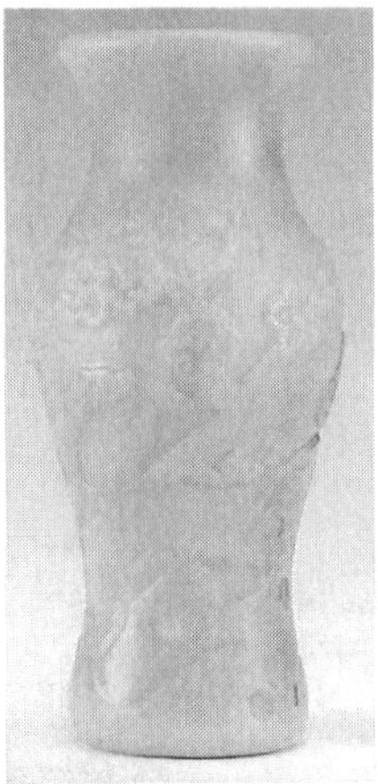

l. A Peking yellow glass baluster vase, with flaring neck, carved with prunus, pine and bamboo issuing from rockwork, 6in (15cm) high, in a fitted box.
£470–520 *CSK*

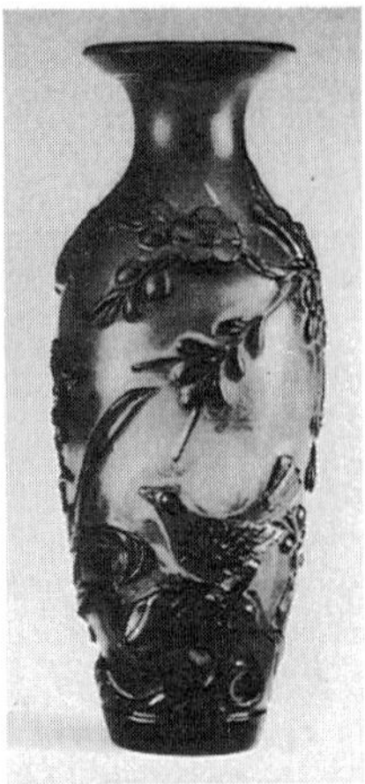

A Peking blue and green overlay glass tapering oviform vase, carved in relief with birds among flowering prunus issuing from rockwork, 5in (12.5cm) high.
£500–550 *CSK*

Inros

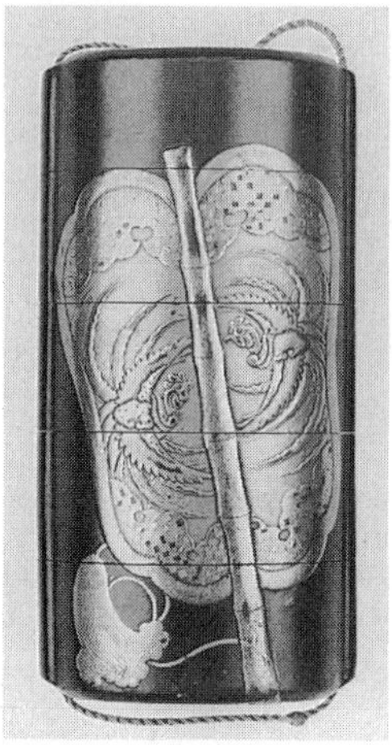

A roironuri ground lacquer four-case inro, decorated to each side in iroe hiramakie, takamakie and kirigane with fans depicting a coiled dragon, a tiger and confronting ho-o, the interior in nashiji, worn, 3½in (9cm) long.
£450–550 *CSK*

Inro

An inro is a small Japanese partitioned medicine box worn on the belt (obi).
It is usually attached by the netsuke, or toggle.

A gold lacquer four-case inro, decorated in hiramakie, takamakie and kirigane with huts among pine and wisteria in a rocky landscape, the reverse with a waterfall and further rockwork, restored, 3in (7.5cm) long.
£600–700 *CSK*

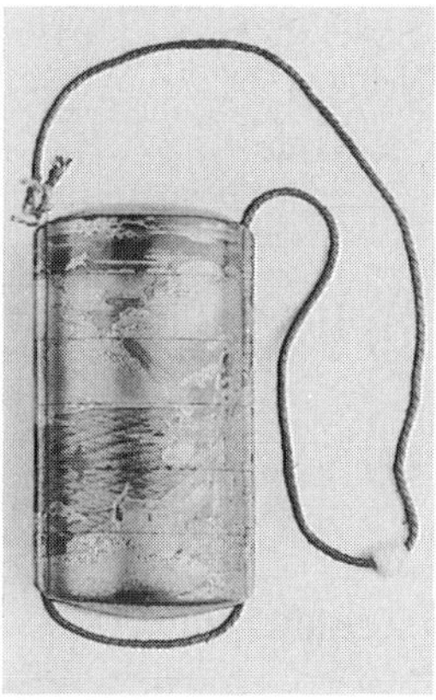

A gold lacquer five-case inro, decorated in hiramakie, kirigane and togidashi with huts and buildings on river banks before a bridge among mountainous landscapes, the interior in nashiji, rubbed, 3½in (9cm) long.
£600–700 *CSK*

A Japanese gold and black lacquer four-case inro decorated in relief with a Hannya mask, the reverse with a sword, necklace and hat, the details in aogai, with brass pomegranate ojime and wood mask netsuke.
£400–500 *CSK*

A gold lacquer two-case inro, decorated in iroe hiramakie and scattered nashiji with numerous horses, on a nashiji ground, restored, 2½in (6.5cm) long.
£470–520 *CSK*

Jade

A Chinese dark grey jade bowl, with paler grey inclusions, probably Ming Dynasty, 5in (12.5cm) diam., in a plush box.
£800–900 *CSK*

A carved jade bowl, the sides decorated in light relief, the interior with a begonia spray in high relief, the stone of pale celadon colour with darker markings and chalky inclusions, rim lightly ground, Qing Dynasty, Kangxi, 6½in (16.5cm) diam.
£4,400–5,000 *S*

A pierced jade bowl and cover, the sides carved in high relief below the rim with 4 winged beasts, the domed cover pierced with a lotus and bat scroll below the crouching dragon knop, the stone of even pale brown colour, Qing Dynasty, Jiaqing, 6in (15cm) diam.
£5,800–6,200 *S*

A celadon jade bowl and cover, the inner rim with a narrow channel to receive the low domed cover, set on the top with a flared knop, the stone of even pale greenish white colour, Qing Dynasty, Qianlong, 5in (12.5cm) diam.
£3,700–4,200 *S*

A white jade marriage bowl, the rim carved on top with a border of ruyi heads interrupted at 2 sides with bats flying amid lotus forming a loop below, supporting a ring handle, the stone of fine even white colour with one chalky inclusion, Qing Dynasty, Qianlong, 9½in (24cm) diam.
£51,000–55,000 *S*

A jade brush pot, of cylindrical form, carved on the sides in varying relief with a continuous mountainous scene depicting the Three Star Gods, a crane and a deer, the stone of greenish-white colour with some darker areas, Qing Dynasty, Qianlong, slight damage, 8½in (21cm) diam.
£55,000–60,000 *S*

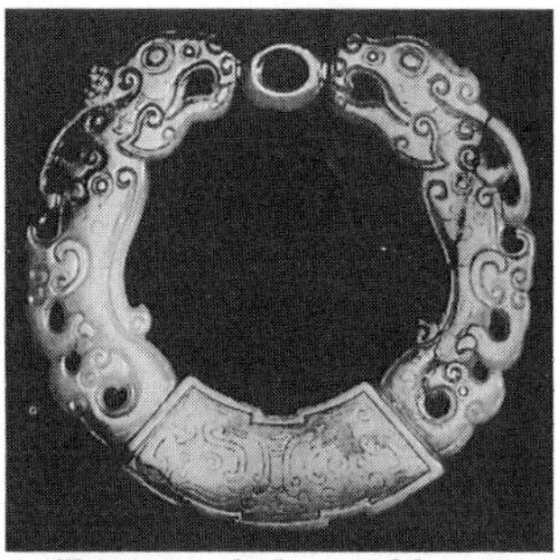

A Chinese celadon and brown jade bangle, in the form of confronting dragons above bands of stylised taotie, Ming Dynasty, 3½in (9cm) wide.
£300–400 *CSK*

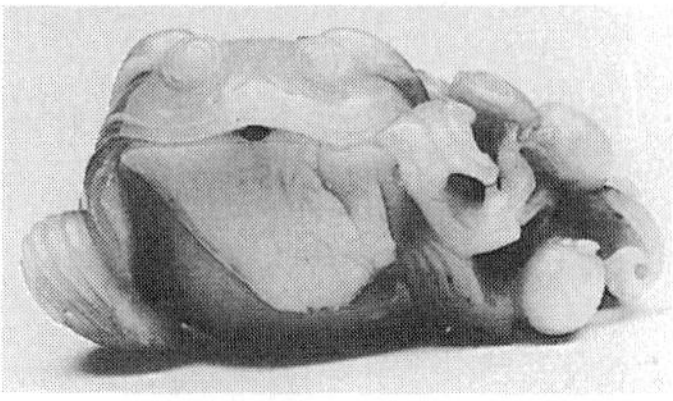

A Chinese pale celadon jade carving of a toad, among fruiting pomegranates, 4½in (11cm) long.
£1,200–1,700 *CSK*

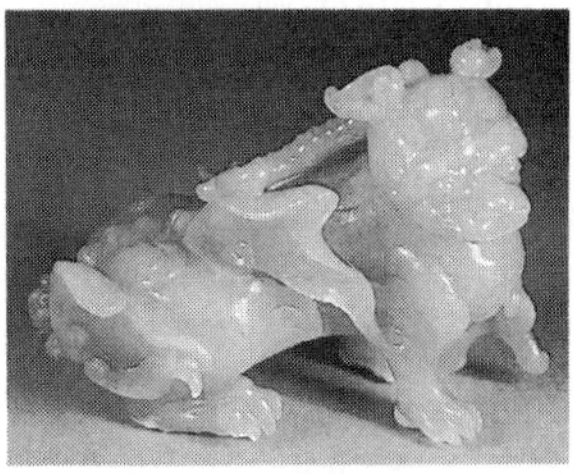

A carved jade figure of a mythical beast, the underside with the clawed feet picked out using the opaque white colour in the brownish-grey stone, Qing Dynasty, Qianlong, 6in (15cm) long.
£6,000–7,000 *S*

A Chinese calcified jade seal, surmounted by a crouching lion, the sides incised with further animals and archaic calligraphy, Ming Dynasty, 4½in (11cm) square.
£400–450 *CSK*

A Chinese spinach-green jade box and cover, carved with butterflies surrounding a flowerspray, 4½in (11.5cm) wide.
£200–300 *CSK*

A Chinese mottled grey jade carving of a mythical lion, turning to look behind, with bifurcated tail, russet inclusions, 2½in (6cm) long.
£300–400 *CSK*

A Chinese dark green jade flattened vase and cover, with mask ring handles, carved in deep relief with confronting guei dragons, 10½in (26.5cm) high.
£420–500 *CSK*

A celadon jade plaque, with slightly rounded top, both sides carved in high relief with a monastery and pavilions in a rocky landscape with knotty pines and bamboo and a waterfall, the stone of brownish celadon colour with pale brown and darker inclusions, Qing Dynasty, 18thC, 11in (28cm) high, on a wood stand.
£3,500–4,500 *S*

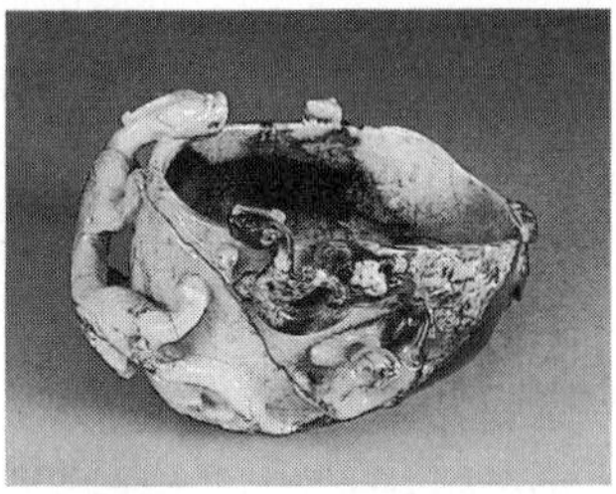

A carved jade libation vessel, the deep cup shape boldly carved, the stone of mottled pale grey colour with extensive areas of darker grey and brown tending to a 'chicken bone' effect on the interior, Song/Ming Dynasty, 12th–15thC, 6½in (16.5cm) long.
£9,300–10,000 *S*

l. A yellow jade vase, carved in high relief with 3 chilong around the sides and one on the shoulder, the stone of rich greenish-yellow colour with areas of pale brown and silky polish, Qing Dynasty, Kangxi, 5½in (14cm) high.
£13,000–15,000 *S*

A white jade double-gourd vase and cover, carved in low relief with a ji character on each side of the lower bulb, and da character on the upper bulb, the neck flanked by strapwork double handles and the low domed cover set with a double loop and ring handle, the stone of even white colour, Qing Dynasty, Qianlong, 8in (20cm) high.
£24,000–28,000 *S*

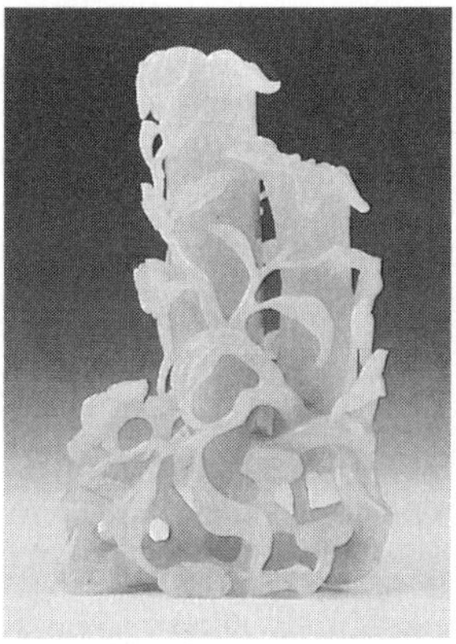

An elaborate celadon jade double vase, carved as 2 deep magnolia flowers issuing from openwork leafy branches with lingzhi stems, the jade of even pale grey-green tone, chipped, 18thC, 8¼in (21cm) high, on a wood stand.
£8,000–10,000 *C*

A white jade flattened baluster vase, with 2 openwork dragon handles, the polished stone of an even pale tone, one loose-ring missing, Qianlong, 5½in (14cm) high.
£800–1,200 *C*

Lacquer

A Chinese guri-lacquer box and cover, carved with a central roundel of stylised scrolling motifs within a band of ruyi heads, 3in (7.5cm) diam.
£300–350 *CSK*

A Chinese guri-lacquer box and slightly domed cover, carved with stylised ruyi heads and scrolling motifs surrounding a central roundel, 3in (7.5cm) diam.
£400–450 *CSK*

A Chinese guri-lacquer carved box and cover, 3in (7.5cm) diam.
£300–350 *CSK*

A Chinese guri-lacquer flattened box and cover, carved with stylised ruyi heads and scrolls surrounding a central star-shaped cartouche, 3in (7.5cm) diam.
£450–500 *CSK*

A Chinese red lacquer box and domed cover, slight damage, 18thC, 6½in (16cm) wide.
£780–820 *CSK*

A Japanese red, black and gold lacquer box and cover, with pewter rims, decorated in hiramakie with fan-shaped panels of bamboo, pine and mountainous landscapes, on a nashiji ground, 17thC, 3¼in (8.5cm) long.
£720–780 *CSK*

l. A Chinese red lacquer foliate rimmed dish, carved with an Immortal and an attendant in a building among pine and bamboo issuing from rockwork, within a border of floral bands, damaged, 18thC, 8¼in (21cm) wide.
£1,000–1,200 *CSK*

A Japanese black lacquer zushi with brass mounts, the 2 doors opening to reveal a gilt interior fitted with a wooden standing Buddha on a lotus petal and rockwork base, slight damage, 10in (25cm) high.
£250–300 *CSK*

Miller's is a price GUIDE not a price LIST

r. A black and gold lacquer four-sided kodansu, with silver handles modelled as butterflies, each side fitted with sliding drawers decorated in hiramakie and scattered nashiji with insects among flowering chrysanthemums issuing from rockwork, one small door missing, some wear, 4½in (11.5cm) square.
£250–400 *CSK*

Metalware

A pair of Chinese inlaid bronze censers, modelled as Immortals, 26in (66cm) high.
£2,000–2,500 *CSK*

A Chinese bronze bombé censer, with mythical head handles, decorated with bands of stylised taotie on a key pattern ground, large areas of malachite remaining to the surface, worn, Ming Dynasty, 7½in (19cm) diam.
£450–500 *CSK*

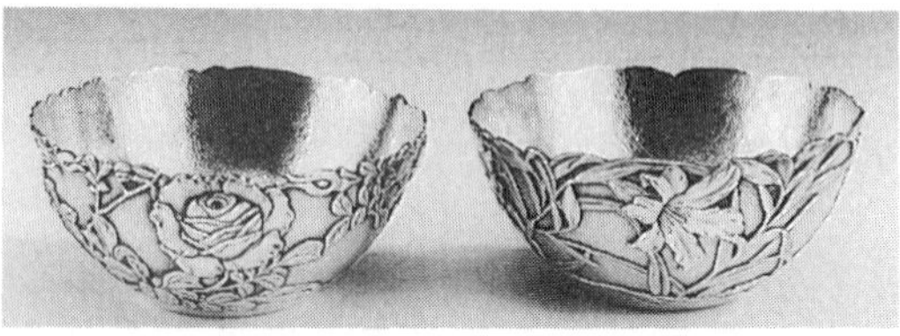

Two similar Japanese white metal bowls, decorated with flowering peonies and irises issuing from rockwork on stippled grounds, the interiors gilt, one rubbed, stamped 'Arthur & Bone, Yokohama, sterling', 5in (12.5cm) diam.
£950–1,100 *CSK*

A Chinese bronze bombé censer, with pierced handles and flattened rim, Xuande six character mark, 12in (30.5cm) diam.
£420–470 *CSK*

A Japanese bronze group of 2 tigers attacking an elephant, the latter with flared ears, raised trunk and inset ivory tusks, 11in (28cm) long.
£450–650 *CSK*

A Chinese bronze cylindrical censer, on 3 lions' head feet, decorated with a central band of trigrams between borders of precious objects, seal mark, 3½in (9cm) high.
£350–400 *CSK*

A Japanese bronze model of a striding elephant, with its trunk raised, signed, 17½in (44.5cm) long.
£550–650 *CSK*

l. A Japanese bronze model of a lion, the details naturalistically rendered, the eyes inlaid in mother-of-pearl and horn, worn, seal mark, 17½in (44.5cm) long, on a wood stand.
£450–550 *CSK*

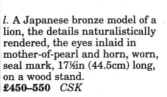

A Japanese bronze model of a standing elephant, with inset ivory tusks, signed, 11½in (29.5cm) long, on a wood stand.
£600–800 *CSK*

A Japanese bronze model of a hawk, perched on a tree stump base, 13½in (34.5cm) high.
£800–900 *CSK*

A late Ming gilt bronze model of a seated Buddha, old wear, early 17thC, 7in (17.5cm) high.
£200–300 *CSK*

A Japanese bronze model of a figure holding a scroll, seated on the back of a recumbent caparisoned elephant, 10in (25cm) high.
£500–600 *CSK*

A bronze inkwell, modelled as a miniature kabuto, the kuwagata depicting a karashishi and hoshi, the hinged cover with a knop, the interior with lining and a glass inkwell, 19thC, 3in (7.5cm) wide.
£1,000–1,200 *C*

A Japanese bronze jardinière, on 4 feet, with mythical head handles, decorated with birds and hares above breaking waves, seal mark, 16in (40.5cm) wide.
£400–500 *CSK*

A Japanese bronze two-handled koro and domed cover, seal mark, 36in (91.5cm) high.
£2,400–2,700 *CSK*

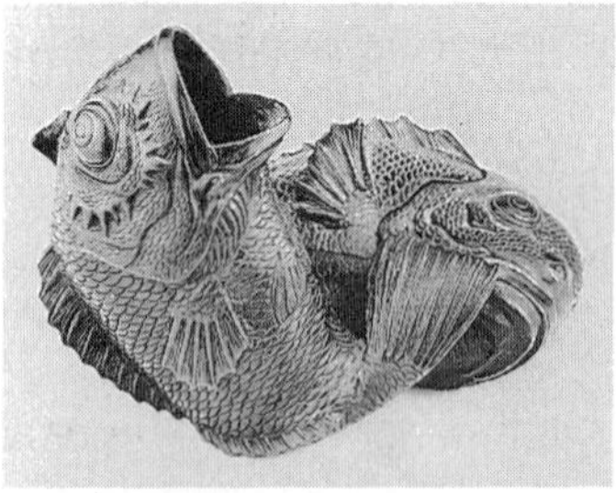

A Japanese bronze koro and cover, modelled as two carp, one leaping up and the other lying flat with its tail flicked up, 6½in (16.5cm) long.
£600–700 *CSK*

A Japanese pierced bronze spherical lantern, decorated with bamboo, lilies and flowers, chipped, 12in (30.5cm) diam.
£500–550 *CSK*

A Japanese bronze foliate rimmed tazza, the everted rim with a band of swastikas, above a coiled dragon among clouds, the base modelled as another coiled dragon, seal mark, 8½in (21.5cm) high.
£700–800 *CSK*

A Chinese bronze weight, modelled as a reclining horned mythical beast looking to one side, the tail flicked over its back, 17thC, 3½in (9cm) long, on a carved wood stand.
£720–800 *CSK*

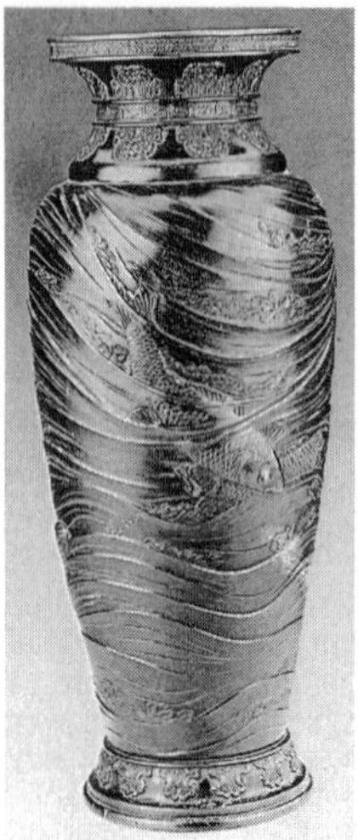

l. A Japanese bronze vase, with flaring neck, decorated in relief with carp and a crayfish among simulated waves and aquatic plants between foliate and geometric borders, old wear, signed, 24½in (62cm) high.
£1,200–1,500 *CSK*

A Japanese red and green patinated bronze baluster vase, inlaid in gilt and silver, damaged, 14½in (37cm) high.
£350–400 *CSK*

A pair of Chinese bronze pear-shaped vases with garlic necks, decorated in relief with coiled dragons to the neck and 2 bands of flowering branches, old wear, early 17thC, 10in (25cm) high.
£400–600 *CSK*

r. A Japanese bronze well bucket, decorated in relief with 2 coiled dragons, one to the body and another to the handle, 20in (50.5cm) high, on a wood stand.
£600–650 *CSK*

A Ming bronze brush rest, modelled as a figure with a horse below a monkey and a bird beside a large jar among rockwork, 16thC, 8¼in (21cm) wide.
£400–500 *CSK*

A Chinese silver stem cup, above a coiled dragon among cloud scrolls, decorated with a continuous band of numerous figures in boats and among buildings, trees and rockwork, surrounding a monogram 'The Banker's Cup, Hong Kong Nov 1866, Victoria Regatta Club', 8½in (21.5cm) high.
£650–700 *CSK*

A pair of iron tetsubin, with loop handles and Arita blue and white covers painted with flowers and rockwork, the covers 18thC, 11½in (29.5cm) long.
£600–700 *CSK*

An iron tetsubin and bronze cover, with loop handle, inlaid in silver and gilt with a flowerspray, the body decorated with Kinko on the back of a carp above waves, and another panel of calligraphy, the cover signed, 8in (20cm) wide.
£300–400 *CSK*

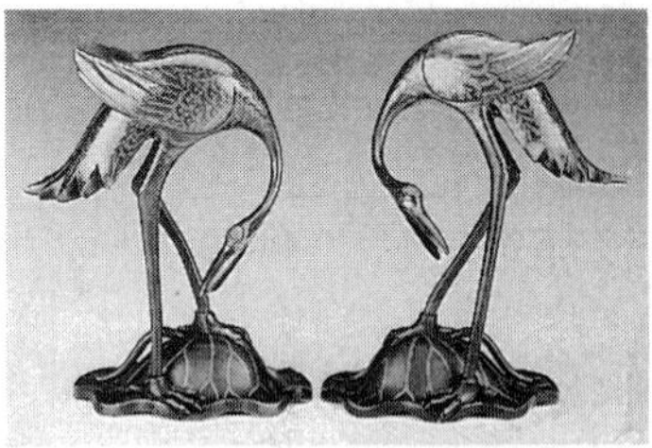

A pair of Chinese silver inlaid joss stick holders, modelled as cranes perched on lotus pods, the heads lowered to look to the side, 11½in (29.5cm) high.
£420–500 *CSK*

Did you know?
MILLER'S* Antiques Price Guide *builds up year-by-year to form the most comprehensive antiques photo-reference library available.

Netsuke

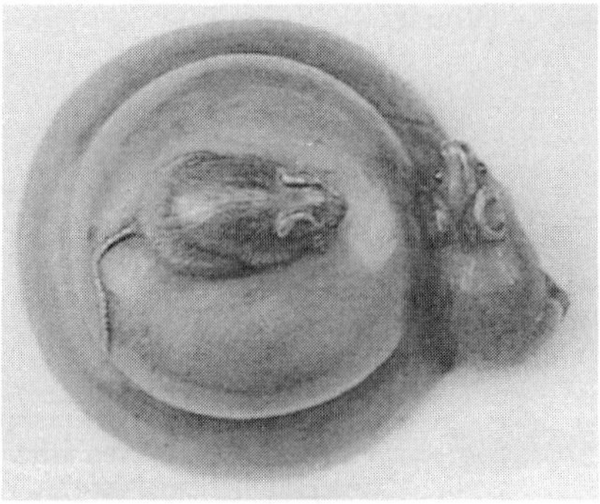

A wood netsuke, modelled as 2 rats on a mushroom, the eyes inlaid in dark horn, signed, 1¾in (4.5cm) signed.
£300–350 *CSK*

A wood netsuke, modelled as 2 nuts, one enclosed with a coral nut, 1½in (4cm) long.
£300-350 *CSK*

A wood mask netsuke, carved with a smiling expression, signed, and another mask netsuke with grimacing expression and protruding teeth, both 1½in (4cm) high.
£200–300 *CSK*

Snuff Bottles

A Peking red overlay glass snuff bottle, decorated to each side with a coiled chilong between mask ring handles, on a snowstorm ground, jadeite stopper, 3in (7.5cm) high.
£550–650 *CSK*

A Peking yellow glass flattened snuff bottle, carved with a bearded Immortal holding a staff with attached gourd flask beside a bat in flight, the reverse with a crane in flight holding a lingzhi spray in its mouth above a deer, with a stopper, 2¼in (5.5cm) high.
£370–450 *CSK*

Netsuke

Netsuke are Japanese carved toggles, originally made to secure a portable medicine box (inro), or similar item, which hangs from the waist on a cord.
They date from the 16thC, and are most commonly made from ivory but were also made from wood.

A Peking six-colour overlay glass snuff bottle, carved with bats in flight among clouds, on a snowstorm ground, stopper missing, 2in (5cm) high.
£250–350 *CSK*

A Peking dark amber glass flattened table snuff bottle, with gilt metal filigree stopper, spoon missing, 5½in (14cm) high.
£250–350 *CSK*

Wood

A Japanese boxwood koro and pierced domed cover, on 3 feet, carved with a group of rats clambering over the whole among a string of beads and on a fly whisk, the eyes inlaid in horn, 9¼in (23.5cm) long.
£1,500–2,000 *CSK*

A wood netsuke, modelled as a tortoise, its head and limbs hidden under its shell, old wear, 2¼in (5.5cm) long.
£300–350 *CSK*

A famille rose snuff bottle, painted with an Immortal crossing a bridge before a rocky river landscape, stopper missing, 2¼in (5.5cm) high.
£470–520 *CSK*

A pair of Chinese wood ducks, with slightly stretched wings and raised heads, the birds with some polychrome and paint remaining, damaged, 11½in (29cm) high.
£250–300 *CSK*

A pair of Chinese bamboo carvings of Buddhistic lions, playing with numerous cubs beside brocade balls and pierced rockwork, chipped, 11in (28cm) high.
£500–550 *CSK*

A Chinese bamboo carving of a seated, bearded Immortal, on a pierced rockwork base, carrying a ruyi sceptre, 3in (7.5cm) wide.
£350–400 *CSK*

A Japanese boxwood carving, of a ferocious oni holding a mortar between his feet, into which he grinds his club, signed 'Gyominchi', Meiji, 3in (7.5cm) high.
£650–700 *WW*

A Chinese wood carving of a standing figure, wearing long flowing robes, 18thC, 9½in (24cm) high, on a wood stand.
£200–300 *CSK*

A pair of late Ming wood figures of standing Immortals, damaged, 16th–17thC, 12in (30.5cm) high.
£400–600 *CSK*

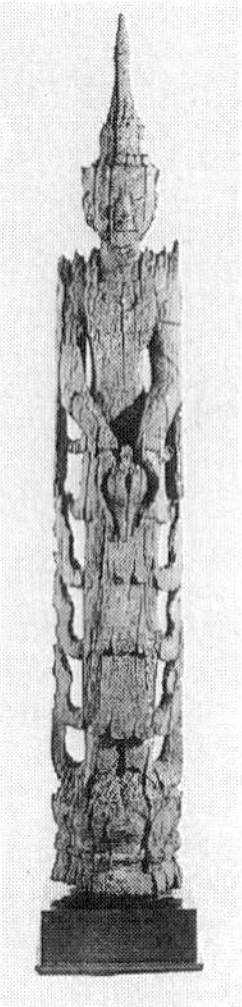

l. A Burmese wood model of a standing Buddha, with a flamiform usnisa, wearing long robes, and holding a bird in both hands, on a raised base, traces of paint, damaged, 85in (216cm) high, on a metal stand.
£700–1,000 *CSK*

Tsuba

Tsuba is the name of the guard on a Japanese sword, usually consisting of an ornamental plate.

Tsuba

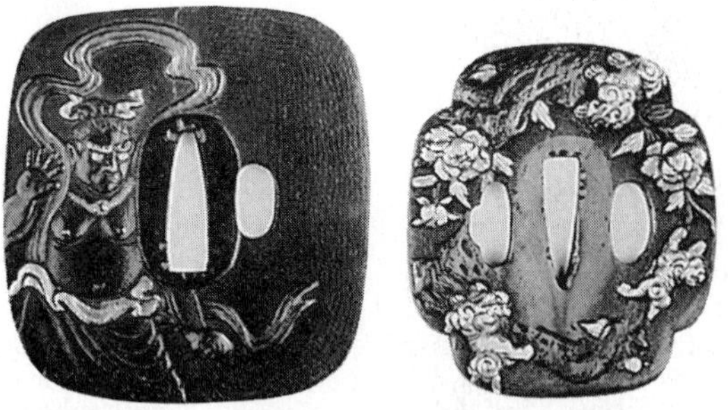

An iron tsuba, decorated with a standing figure wearing a celestial robe, the reverse with panels of calligraphy, signed, 3½in (9cm) long, and a gilt bronze tsuba, decorated in silver and gilt hirazogan and takazogan with karashishi among peonies and rockwork, 3in (7.5cm) long.
£360–400 *CSK*

A Japanese bronze tsuba, of quadruple shaped outline, decorated in gold with leaf pattern and trailing ornament with textured border, unsigned, 3in (7.5cm) high.
£300–350 *CAG*

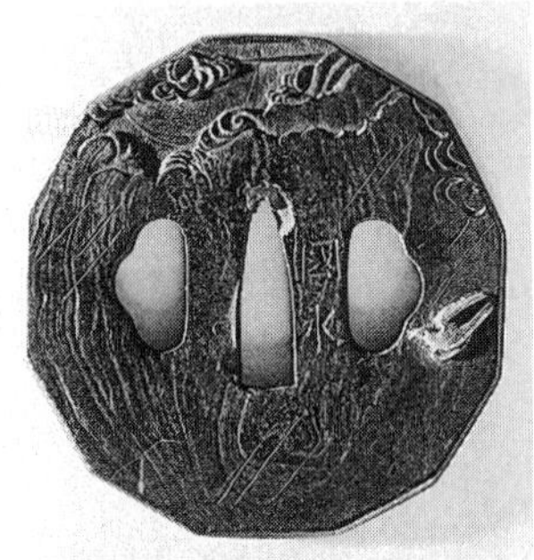

A Japanese iron tsuba, of polygonal outline, decorated with a silver crescent moon and gold bird in flight throughout a rainstorm, signed 'Noritsura', 2¾in (7cm) high.
£150–200 *CAG*

A Japanese iron tsuba, decorated and gilt with leafy bamboo sections, the reverse with prunus trees issuing from rockwork, signed, 3in (7.5cm) wide.
£400–450 *CSK*

Arms & Armour

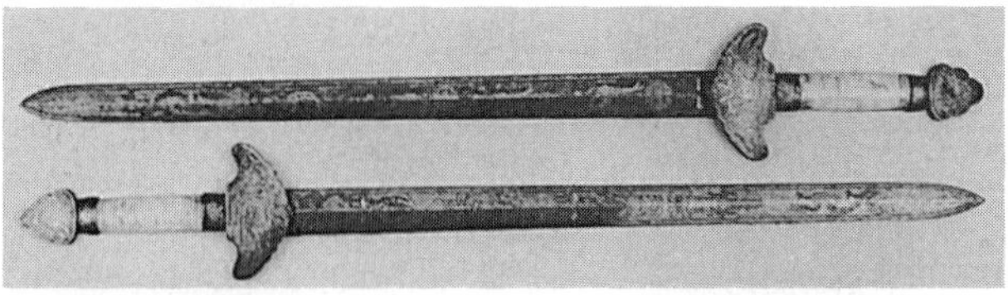

A Chinese double sword, the blades inlaid in silver and brass with deities interspersed with coiled dragons and shou characters, the brass guards decorated with further stylised dragons and the bone hilts incised with standing Immortals among rockwork, old wear, Qianlong seal marks, 29½in (75.5cm) long.
£700–1,000 *CSK*

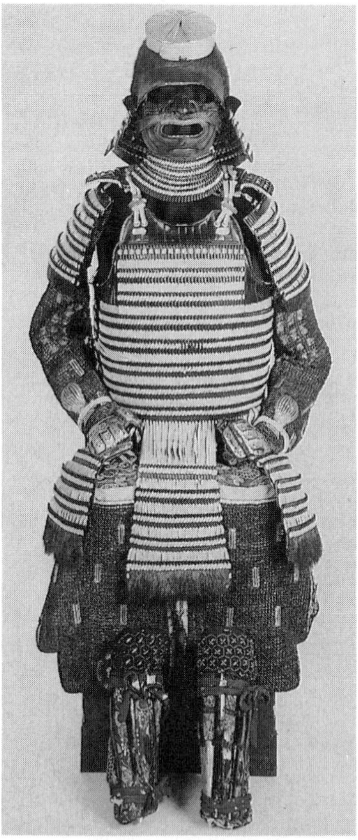

A composite armour, late Edo period, c1800, with a wood storage box.
£10,500–12,500 *C*

This style of armour, Tosei Gusoku, was developed during the Momoyama period. Its development drew heavily from experience derived from prolonged periods of warfare. It is characterised by its simplicity and flexibility. The small iron gold lacquered plates are laced together with white lacing (kebiki odoshi). On the reverse is the gattari, a means for supporting a banner on the upper part and machiuke for the lower part. The Momoyama period was the golden age of flags and crests. Every soldier carried a small flag (sashimono) mounted in these brackets. The kote (armoured sleeves) are Bishamon gote type with shoulder guards (sode) attached to the upper part of the sleeves.
The armour is entirely in the style of the Momoyama period, and although mainly dating from the late Edo period, certain portions could well be earlier pieces remounted.

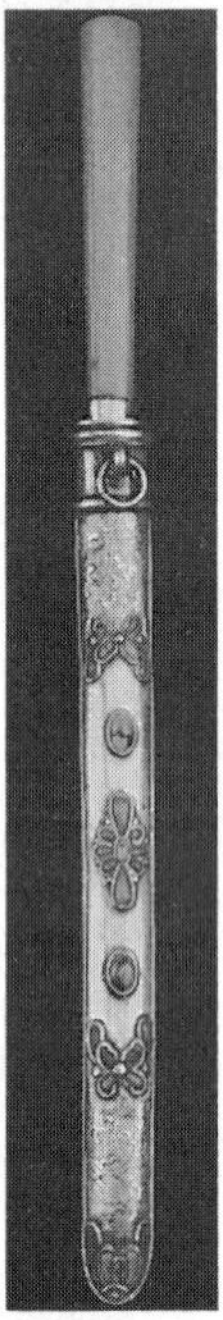

A Mongolian dagger, with narrow double-edged blade and pale celadon jade hilt, the silver sheath inlaid in coral and turquoise and engraved with foliage, damaged, 13¾in (35cm) long.
£600–700 *CSK*

An iron gunsen, or general's war fan, constructed of 2 plates with repoussé designs of the sun, the moon and a constellation, Meiji Period, 23in (59cm) high.
£2,000–2,500 *C*

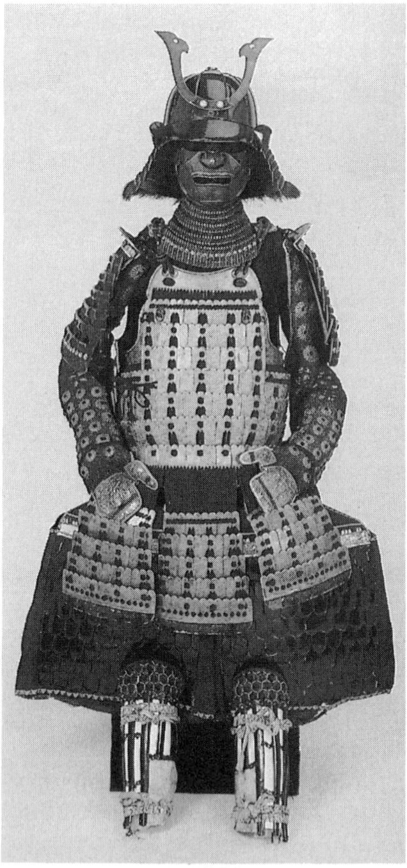

A composite armour, Edo period, helmet probably late Muromachi period.
£5,000–6,000 *C*

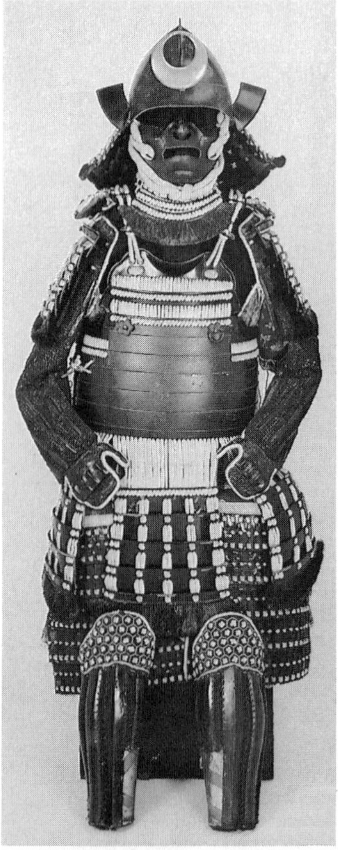

A composite armour, mid-Edo period, mostly associated, late 17thC.
£16,000–18,000 *C*

A composite armour, mid-Edo period, 18thC.
£17,500–20,000 *C*

The half mask (mempo) and cuirass (do) match each other, as do the armoured sleeves (kote), the thigh guards (haidate), and the shin guards (suneate).

A composite armour, late Edo period, c1800.
£7,500–9,000 *C*

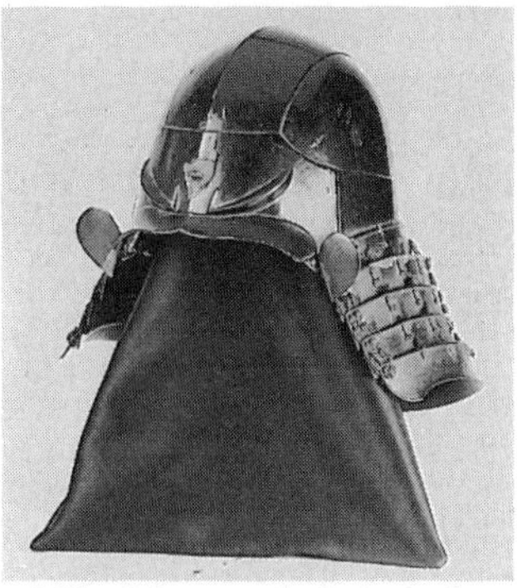

A black lacquer kabuto and a do (cuirass), the black lacquered iron helmet of basic three-plate construction with medial ridge and embossed eyebrows, black lacquered neck guard (itamono Hineno jokoro) with fukigaeshi and the do of okegawa hishinui ryo takahimo (opening on both sides), matching seven-piece hip guards (kusazuri) and thigh protectors (karuta haidate), old wear, with a black wooden box, 19thC.
£2,000–2,500 *C*

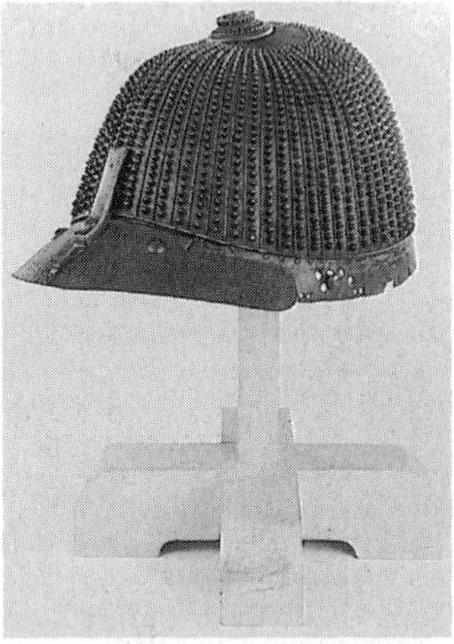

r. A 62 plate hoshi bachi, the russet iron helmet bowl with raised rivets, a five-stage tehen kanamono, russet iron peak, indistinctly signed, c1650.
£3,500–4,500 *C*

Textiles & Costume

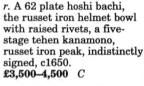

A Chinese formal blue silk satin robe, c1800.
£1,500–2,000 *CSK*

A Chinese informal coat, of dark blue silk satin embroidered in brightly coloured silks, worked in Peking knot stitch with the peony and cicada design on centre front and back, with embroidered ivory satin borders, 19thC.
£900–1,200 *CSK*

A Chinese winter formal robe, of dark blue padded silk satin embroidered in coloured silks and gilt threads, with a later sea wave border, lined in blue silk, c1800.
£1,000–1,500 *CSK*

A Chinese dragon robe, of brown summer weave gauze embroidered in coloured silks and gilt threads, the border of charcoal grey embroidered gauze, the pair of horseshoe cuffs loose, 19thC.
£1,000–1,500 *CSK*

l. A Chinese dragon robe, of blue silk worked with couched gilt threads with 9 dragons among clouds and emblems, over a sea wave border, with horseshoe cuffs, 19thC.
£700–800 *CSK*

A Chinese lady's stole, of black silk satin with couched silver and gilt metal threads with dragons over a sea wave border and with the 7th civil rank badges of the Mandarin Duck, with coral beaded sun, fringed, lined with salmon pink silk damask, late 19thC.
£600–700 *CSK*

A Chinese bridal robe, of crimson silk satin embroidered in brightly coloured silks and couched metal threads with 10 dragons among clouds and flowers, over a peony filled sea wave border, the wide sleeves with a narrow brocade border, lined in green silk damask, 19thC.
£1,400–1,700 *CSK*

A Chinese informal robe, of dark blue silk satin embroidered in white and shades of blue, the pale blue damask sleeve bands worked in coloured silks with blossom, lined in blue silk, 19thC.
£350–400 *CSK*

A Chinese semi-formal robe, of red/orange silk satin embroidered with flower sprigs and a sea wave border in white and shades of blue silks, and flying birds in coloured silks, the front and back worked with the 7th civil rank Mandarin Duck, lined in emerald green silk, 19thC.
£400–500 *CSK*

A Chinese robe, of red/orange silk satin embroidered in coloured silks and couched gilt threads with 8 dragons among cloud scrolls, bats, blossom and phoenix, over a sea wave border with lions, with blue satin borders, lined in pale olive silk damask, 19thC.
£600–700 *CSK*

This robe was traditionally part of a Chinese lady's bridal dress.

> **Locate the source**
> ***The source of each illustration in* Miller's Antiques Price Guide *can easily be found by checking the code letters at the end of each caption with the Key to Illustrations located at the front of the book.***

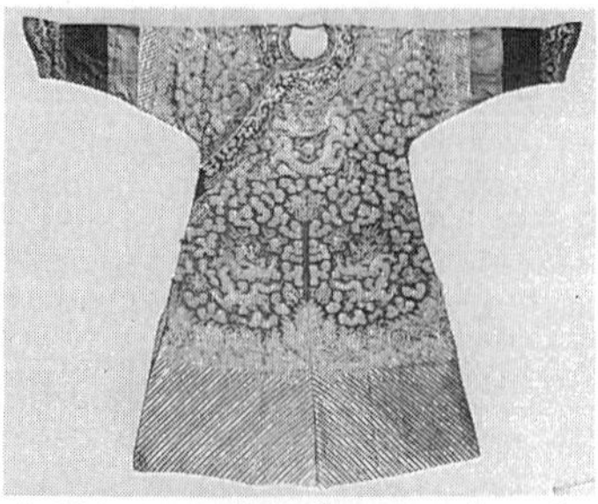

A Chinese lady's dragon robe, of blue silk satin with couched gilt thread, black embroidered horseshoe cuffs and trimming, lined with blue silk damask, late 19thC.
£1,200–1,500 *CSK*

A Chinese informal coat, of dark blue silk satin embroidered in white and shades of blue, the ivory satin sleeve bands worked with a wading bird, and black satin embroidered borders, lined in pale blue silk damask, 19thC.
£470–550 *CSK*

A Chinese semi-formal coat, of black silk satin embroidered with dragon roundels, over a sea wave border, lined in blue silk, late 19thC.
£600–700 *CSK*

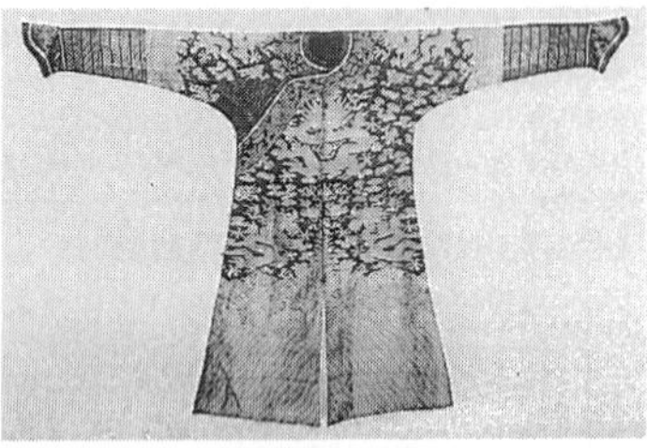

A Chinese summer dragon robe, of blue gauze woven with ivory silk, the horseshoe cuffs with silk brocade trimming, 19thC.
£800–900 *CSK*

A Chinese winter semi-formal robe, of red silk satin embroidered in coloured silks with flower filled roundels with cicada, over a sea wave border, the wide horseshoe cuffs of dark blue satin with similar embroidery and borders of the same, re-lined in yellow silk, interlined, early 19thC.
£770–820 *CSK*

A Chinese informal robe, of crimson silk satin embroidered in coloured silks, lined in salmon pink silk, 19thC.
£950–1,200 *CSK*

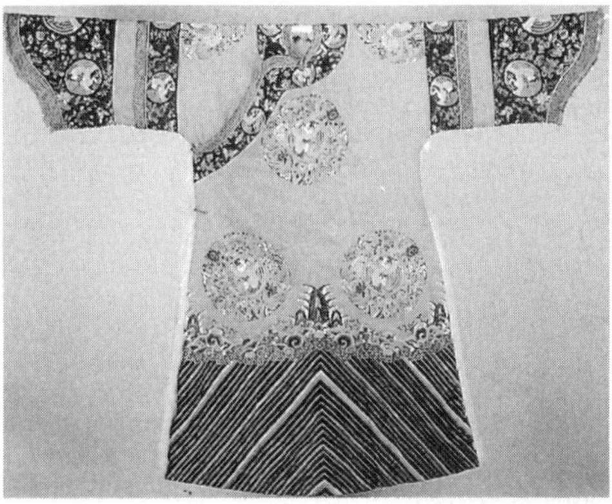

A Chinese winter semi-formal robe, of red silk embroidered in coloured silks, the cuffs and borders of black silk with similar embroidery, fully lined with fur, 19thC.
£1,200–1,700 *CSK*

A Japanese embroidered hanging, elaborately worked in coloured silks with 2 dragons, one holding a dagger in its tail, and a phoenix, among cloud scrolls, the ground composed of coils of couched thread, within a brocaded border, 19thC, 84 by 55in (213 by 139.5cm).
£1,200–1,700 *CSK*

A Chinese informal robe, of blue silk satin decorated with 8 densely embroidered roundels in coloured silks and gilt threads, the golden yellow satin sleeve bands worked in Peking knot stitch and gilt threads, the borders of ivory satin with cartouches against a ground of couched gilt threads, lined in blue silk, late 19thC.
£800–900 *CSK*

A Chinese semi-formal coat, of dark blue silk satin embroidered in coloured silks with roundels, the centre with a vase of flowers enclosed within a border of cranes and blossom, over a sea wave border, the cuffs with roundels and narrow sea wave border, lined in blue silk damask, buttons replaced, 19thC.
£1,200–1,500 *CSK*

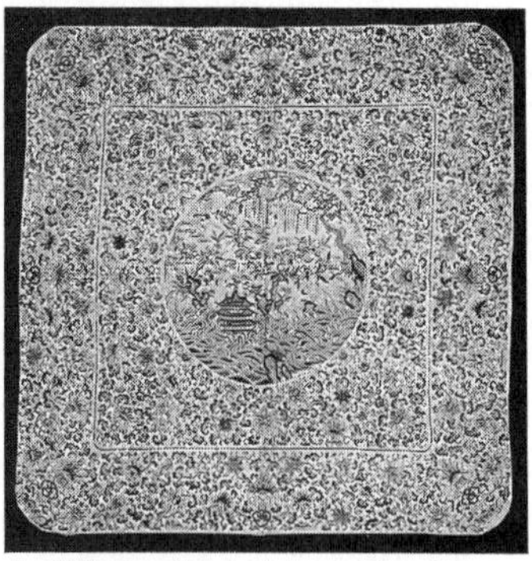

A Chinese Imperial cover, of golden yellow silk satin densely embroidered in coloured silks, the central roundel with cranes flying over turbulent sea waves, fruit trees and a pagoda in the distance, set in a field of lotus flowers and scrolling stems, and an outer border of the same, backed with silk damask, c1800, 58in (147cm) square.
£2,700–3,200 *CSK*

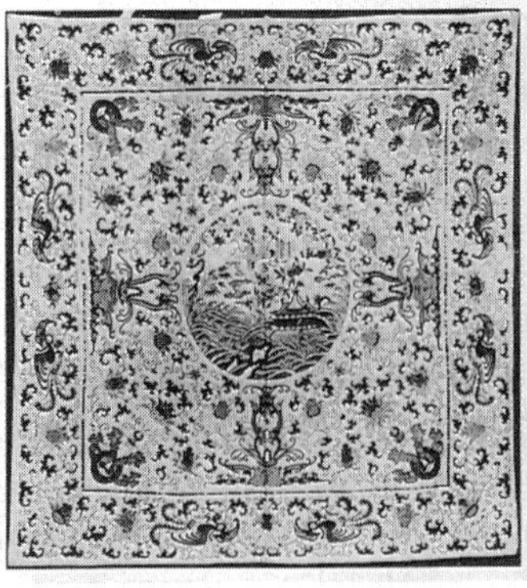

A Chinese Imperial cover, of golden yellow silk satin couched with coloured twisted silks and metal threads, the central roundel with a crane flying over turbulent seas and a pagoda behind, the field with lotus flowers and scrolling tendrils, within a border of the same with phoenix, backed with silk damask, 19thC, 44 by 41in (111.5 by 104cm).
£2,500–3,000 *CSK*

A Japanese embroidered hanging, worked in coloured floss silks with a dragon confronting a tiger, among cloud scrolls, against a coiled ground, 19thC, 58 by 36in (147 by 91.5cm).
£600–1,000 *CSK*

SPORT

Baseball

An official American League baseball, signed by 17 members of the 1929 New York Yankees.
£1,800–2,200 *CNY*

An official American League Reach baseball, signed by 20 members of the 1932 New York Yankees team, worn, signatures still legible.
£3,500–4,000 *CNY*

An official American League baseball, signed by 22 members of the legendary 1927 New York Yankees, covered with clear shellac.
£4,000–4,500 *CNY*

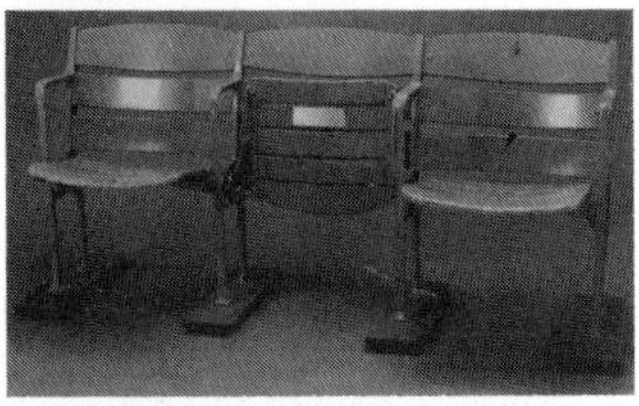

Three Yankee Stadium seats from Mantle's restaurant, with original blue paint.
£1,200–1,500 *CNY*

These seats have been on display at the restaurant in New York City since the day it opened. On the middle seat is a brass plaque reading 'To Mickey Mantle – Good Luck – 2/5/88 [the opening day of the restaurant] Bill Wade'.

Don Larsen's 'Perfect Game' ball, inscribed 'To Johnny, my best wishes Don Larsen', and printed 'The Perfect Game – 1956 World Series', shows game use, and 2 letters of authenticity.
£9,500–11,500 *CNY*

Mr Lewin attended the 1956 World Series as a reporter for the New York Mirror and witnessed the perfect game pitched by Don Larsen in the the 5th game. It was the most outstanding post-season performance in the history of baseball. Lewin obtained a game ball from Frank Crosetti and had it autographed by Don Larsen and the opposing pitcher, Sal Maglie. It is the only known ball from that game signed by both pitchers.

Cricket

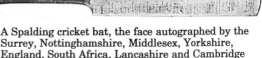

A Spalding cricket bat, the face autographed by the Surrey, Nottinghamshire, Middlesex, Yorkshire, England, South Africa, Lancashire and Cambridge sides, the reverse by Sussex, Hampshire, Worcestershire, Gloucestershire, Essex, Somerset, Warwickshire and Kent, 189 signatures in all, c1921–24.
£500–600 *CSK*

l. A Sandhams special cricket bat, with the signatures of the Australian touring team and several English counties on reverse, 96 signatures in all, c1930.
£1,700–2,000 *S*

A cricketing trophy in the form of a presentation inkstand within a glass dome, with presentation plaque inscribed 'Presented to Harry Luff by H. Carter, of the 1902 Australian XI Aug. 14th 1903'.
£1,800–2,000 *CSK*

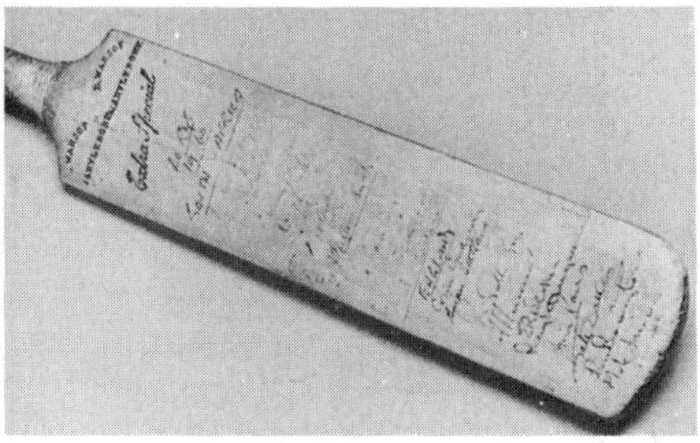

l. A miniature cricket bat, signed by the South African and England teams for the 1960 Lord's test, many signatures indistinct.
£50–70 *DN*

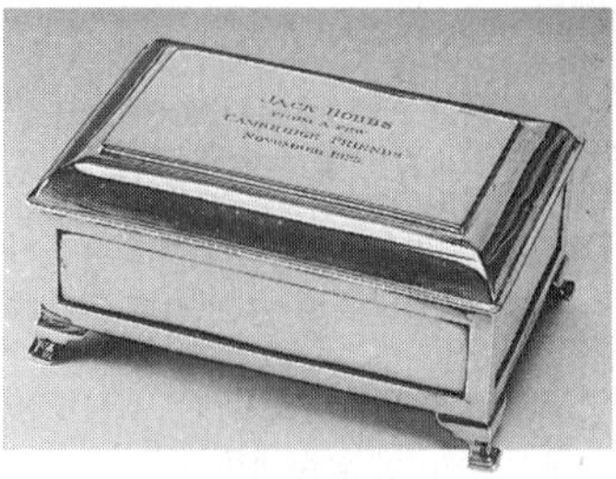

A silver cigarette box, inscribed 'Jack Hobbs from a few Cambridge friends, November 1925', Birmingham 1924, 7½in (19cm) long.
£1,300–1,700 *S*

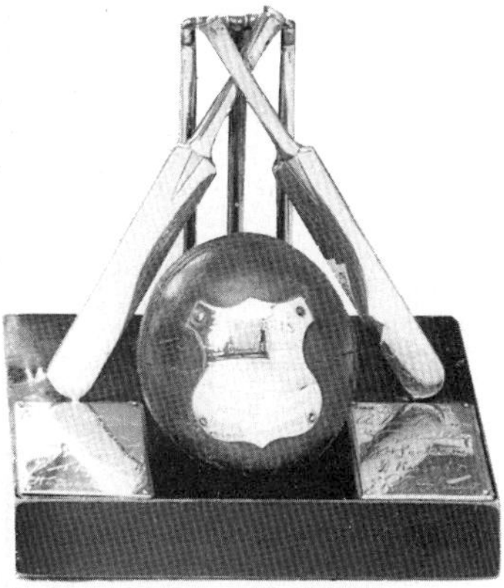

A presentation cricket ball, presented to Jack Hobbs by the Surrey team to commemorate his 14th century of the 1925 season, and 127th century of his career, the trophy comprising a wicket and 2 bats, and 2 panels signed by the rest of the team.
£1,800–2,200 *S*

A charcoal and watercolour picture, by Coller, depicting Hobbs and presumably Sutcliffe going out to bat, with the artist's inscription 'To Jack Hobbs, December 1938', 17½ by 13½in (44.5 by 34.5cm), and a photograph of Jack Hobbs wearing his Surrey CC cap.
£1,200–1,500 *S*

An illuminated MCC tribute of the Australian Tour, 1928–29, in a gilded cricket frame, damaged.
£1,000–1,200 *S*

Fishing

l. A brass winch, marked 'Chas. Farlow, Makers, 191 Strand, London', with bone handle, 19thC, 2½in (6.5cm) diam.
£100–120 *GHA*

r. A brass clamp foot multiplied winch base, and a Hardy reel, 19thC, 2¼in (5.5cm) diam.
£200–220 *GHA*

l. A brass 3¼in Mallochs Patent side caster reel, 19thC.
£100–110 *GHA*

A 2½in Mallochs side caster reel, 19thC.
£70–80 *GHA*

A 3in Hardy Perfect all brass fly reel, unperforated drum, 'Rod in Hand' trade mark, c1896.
£1,800–2,000 *GHA*

A 4in Nottingham wooden reel, 19thC.
£30–35 *GHA*

A 2¾in Hardy Perfect all brass fly reel, 'Rod in Hand' trade mark, ivory handle, c1896.
£1,000–1,200 *GHA*

l. A brass face 3¼in Perfect reel, narrow drum, 'Rod in Hand' trade mark, with an ivory handle, 19thC.
£550–650 *GHA*

r. A 2½in Hardy Perfect reel, Duplicated Mark II, 19thC.
£80–90 *GHA*

l. A 3½in brass plate wind reel, horn handle, 19thC.
£30–40 *GHA*

r. A 2¾in Hardy Hercules brass reel, 'Rod in Hand' trade mark, ivory handle, 19thC.
£325–380 *GHA*

A 2¾in Hardy wide drum alloy trout fly reel, the handle plate inscribed 'Hardy's Pat.', 'The Field', and 'Hardy's, Alnwick', with ivorine handle, brass pillars and foot.
£500–550 *EP*

This is the smallest size of 'Field' reel.

A 3¾in early Hardy St. Geroge trout fly reel, with knurled drum locking nut, strapped rim regulator screw, agate line guide, ivorine handle and brass foot, c1911.
£2,400–2,700 *EP*

A 4¼in Hardy 'Perfect' brass faced salmon fly reel, with 'Rod and Hand' trademark, open oval and straightline logos, strapped tension screw with turks head locking nut, early check, ivorine handle and brass foot.
£280–320 *EP*

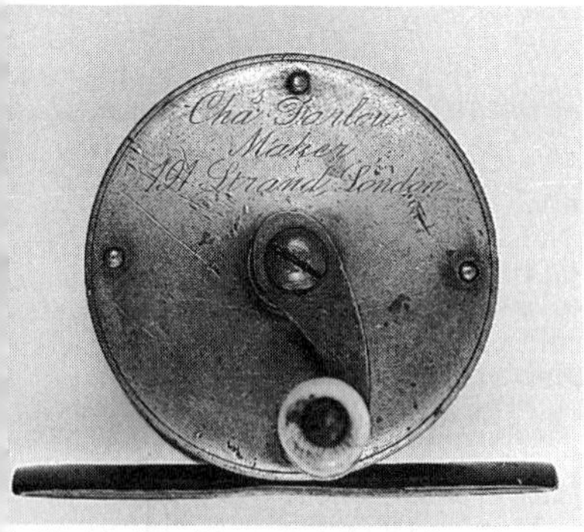

A 2in Farlow brass crankwind reel, the curved crank with ivory handle, fixed check, inscribed 'Chas Farlow, Maker, 191 Strand, London'.
£200–250 *EP*

r. A 3in alloy side caster reel, with brass release lever, stamped 'Malloch's Patent', optional check with rim button, horn handle on plate, inscribed.
£200–240 *EP*

l. A 4in Hardy 'Silex No. 2' casting reel, with auxiliary brass rim brake, twin handles, ivorine brake handle, knurled turn button regulator and alloy foot.
£70–120 *EP*

l. A 3¾in Hardy 'Uniqua' wide drum salmon fly reel, with oval nickel silver drum latch stamped 'Oil', fixed check, ivorine handle and brass foot.
£75–120 *EP*

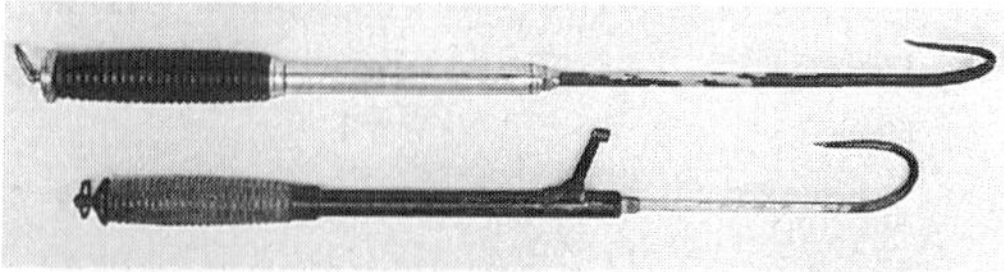

Two telescopic salmon gaffs, 19thC, largest 23in (58.5cm) long.
£60–80 *GHA*

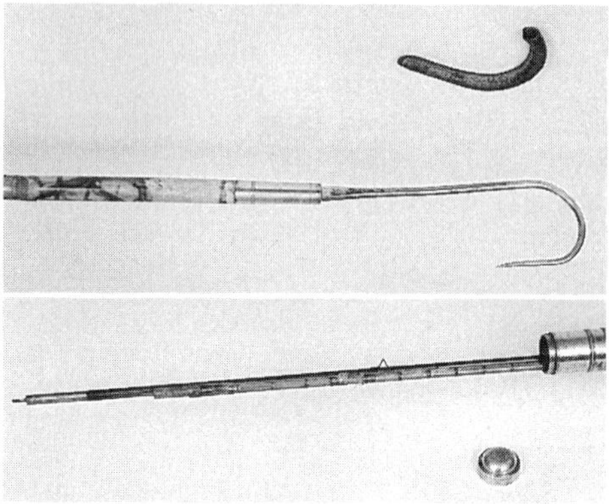

A salmon gaff, with a leather cover and bamboo handle, enclosing 2 rod tips in the handle, 19thC, 70in (177.5cm) long.
£80–90 *GHA*

l. A stuffed and mounted pike, by J. Cooper & Sons, displayed among reeds, in a bow-fronted case inscribed 'Pike 5lb. 14oz. caught spinning the plug, Ramsdales Flash, 1st Dec. 1946', 14 by 33in (35.5 by 83.5cm).
£650–800 *S(S)*

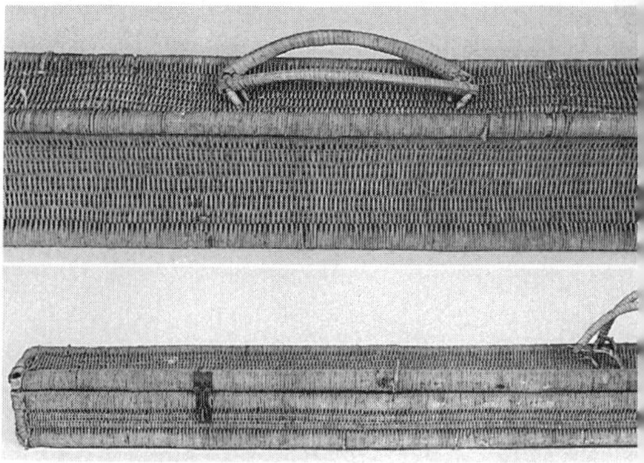

Two wickerwork rod cases, 19thC, 66in (167.5cm) long.
£80–85 each *GHA*

r. A sterling silver model of a trout fisherman, inscribed 'R. Chadwick', c1970, 9in (22.5cm) high.
£600–650 *GHA*

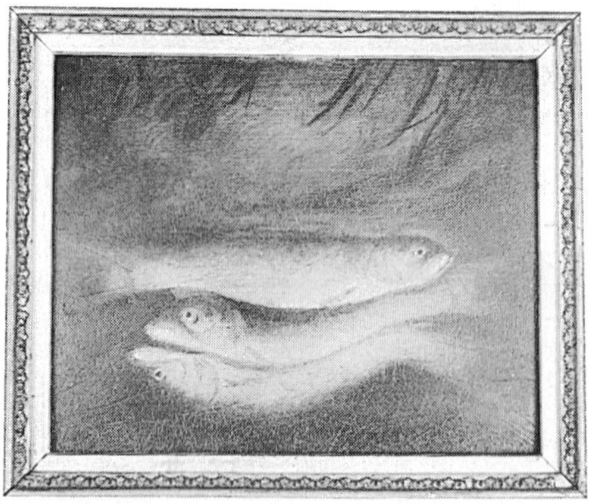

A painting of trout, oil on board, 19thC, 7 by 8in (17.5 by 20cm).
£200–220 *GHA*

A stuffed and mounted chub, in a bow fronted case inscribed 'Chub caught by Chas. P. Phillips, at Goring September 8th 1907', 14½ by 28in (37 by 71cm).
£300–350 *S(S)*

American Football

A 14ct gold bracelet, once belonging to Vince Lombardi, containing 9 gold charms commemorating the highlights of his coaching career.
£2,800–3,200 *CNY*

An official Riddell NFL New York Giants football helmet, signed by 28 members of the 1993 team.
£500–600 *CNY*

A Reach football, signed by Hall of Fame quarterback Sid Luckman, excellent condition, in a plexiglass display case.
£350–400 *CNY*

Golf

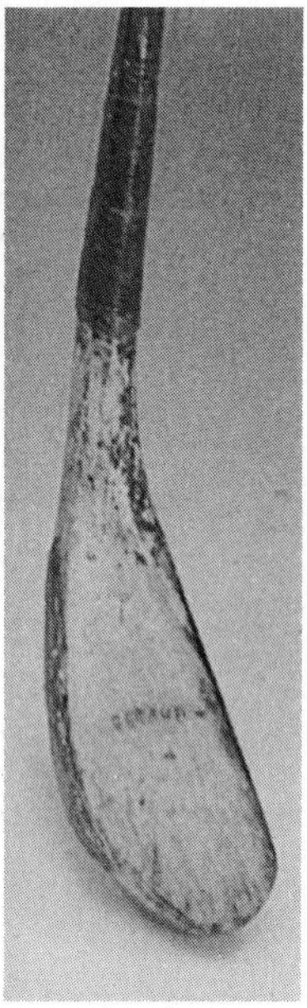

A Tom Morris St. Andrew's long nosed driver, with golden beech head and hickory shaft, engraved with initials 'R.B.B.', c1875.
£1,500–2,000 *S*

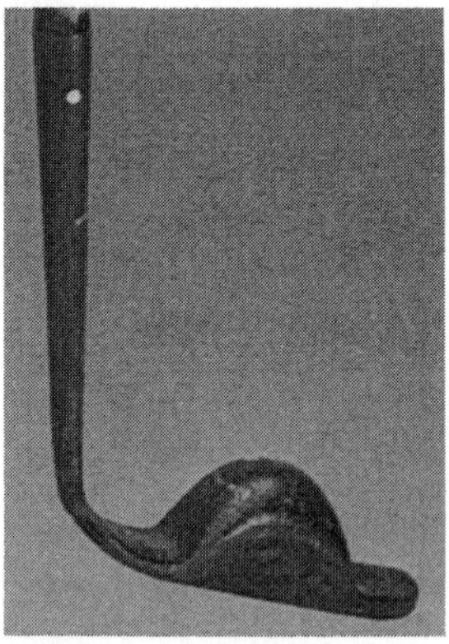

A Gibson of Kinghorn Jonco type putter, with snail-like profile, hickory shaft, and replacement grip, c1912.
£1,100–1,800 *S*

A long nosed driver, by J. Allan of Prestwick, with thorn head and hickory shaft, in original condition, late 1880s.
£1,100–1,300 *S*

r. A general iron, with deeply dished face, replacement but early hickory shaft, sheepskin grip, 5¾in (14.5cm) hosel, late 18thC, 39½in (100cm) long.
£17,500–19,000 *S*

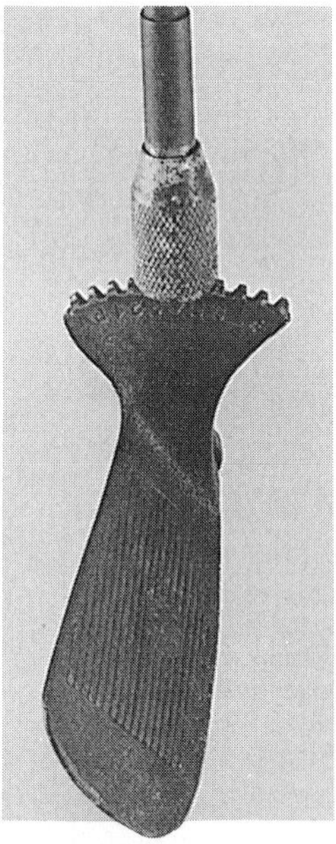

A steel shafted adjustable iron, with a rare adjusting mechanism, c1930.
£350–450 *S*

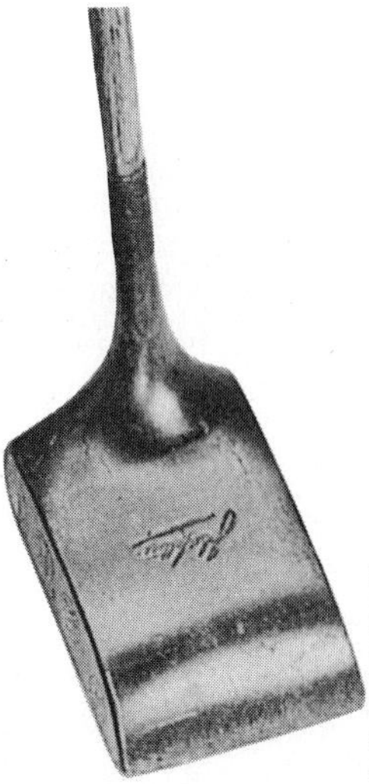

l. A Gassiat-type putter, by John Letters, Glasgow, with persimmon socket head and 4 lead weights with shaped hickory shaft and grip, c1938.
£520–600 *S*

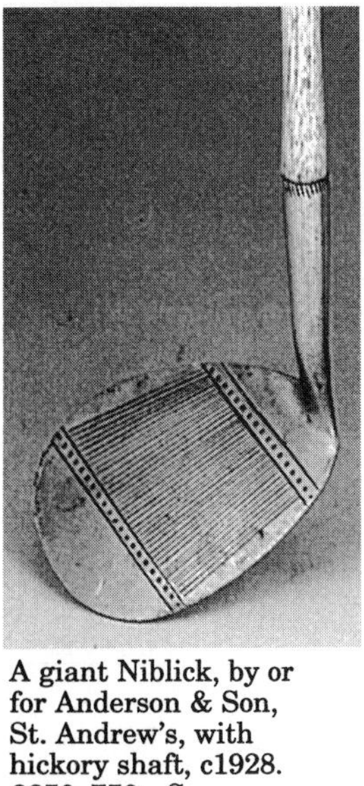

A giant Niblick, by or for Anderson & Son, St. Andrew's, with hickory shaft, c1928.
£650–750 *S*

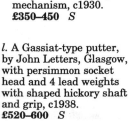

A Jean Gassiatt LCL model putter, registered No. 627752, with beech head, hickory shaft and pistol grip, c1920.
£300–400 *S*

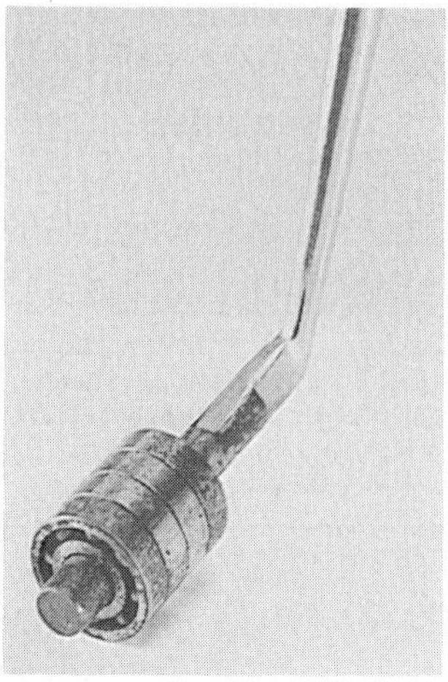

A roller putter, with hickory shaft, roller added to a rustless putter at a later date.
£250–350 *S*

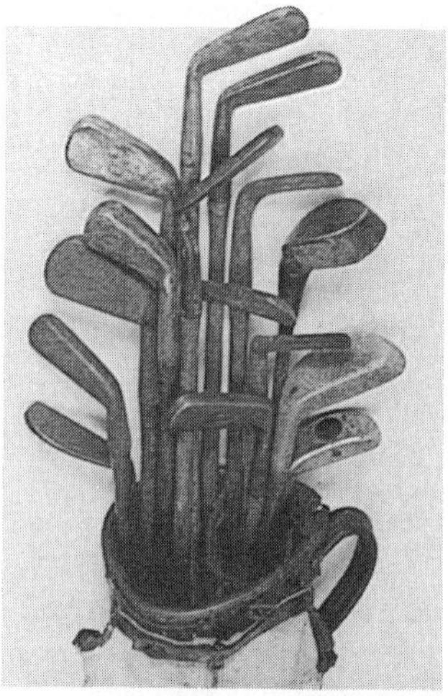

A collection of 15 wood shafted golf clubs, including a Scott patent Brassie, a Bunny putter, 3 antishank irons and 10 other clubs, various dates and conditions.
£550–750 *S*

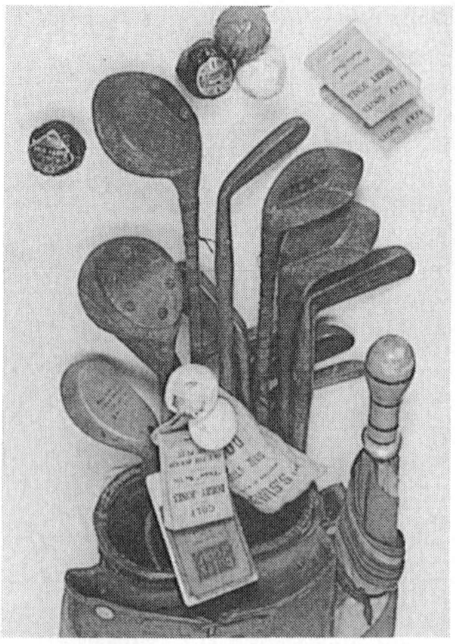

A collection of 12 hickory shaft golf clubs, in a leather bag with umbrella, 3 Bobby Jones Flicker books, some wrapped balls, tees, etc.
£520–600 *S*

A feather-filled golf ball, by W. & J. Gourlay of Musselburgh, stamped 'Gourlay', inscribed '26', mint condition, c1840.
£11,000–14,000 *C(S)*

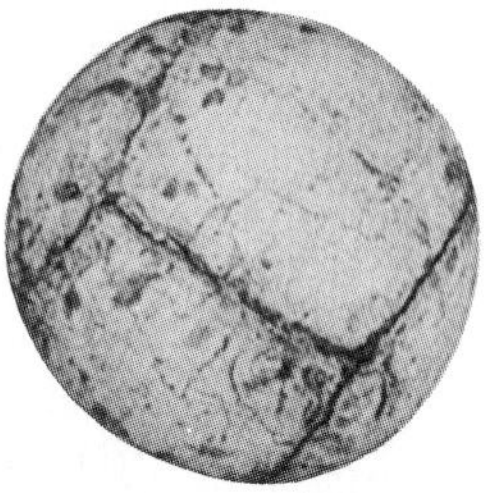

A 1¾in feathered golf ball, indistinctly stamped 'J. Gourlay', c1840.
£4,000–4,500 *S*

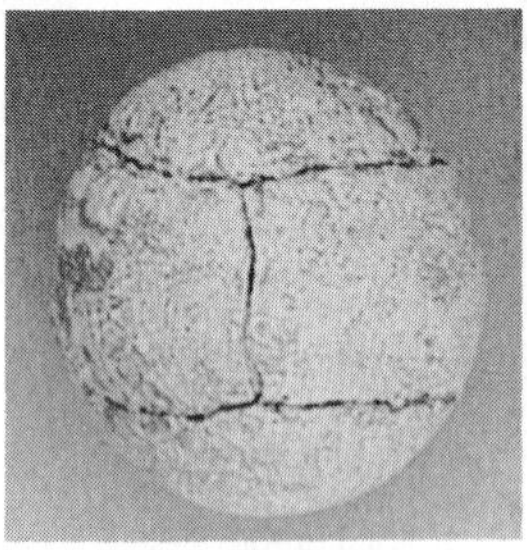

A 1½in feather golf ball, original paint, slightly out of shape, c1840.
£4,000–4,500 *S*

A collection of 8 rubber core golf balls, including Joyces Indented, Star Pattern Challenger, and Challenger King, various dates and conditions.
£1,800–2,200 *S*

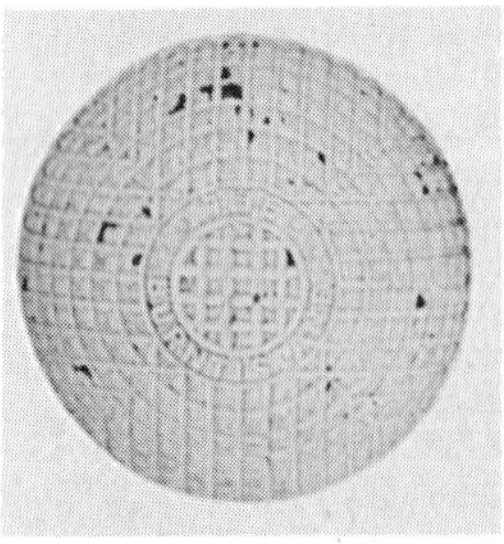

An unused Burntisland Gutty, c1890.
£700–750 *S*

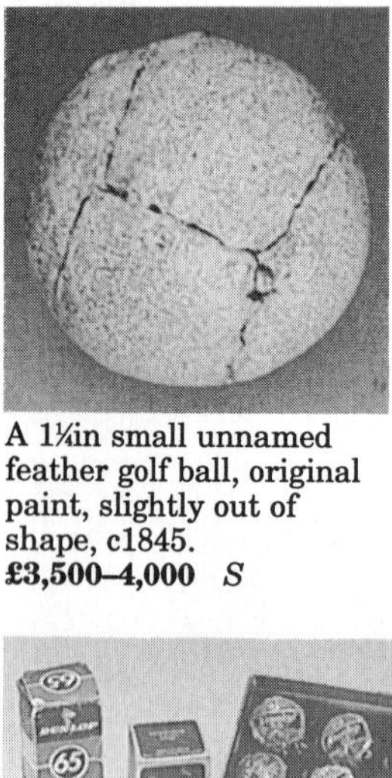

A 1¼in small unnamed feather golf ball, original paint, slightly out of shape, c1845.
£3,500–4,000 *S*

r. Two boxes of wrapped Dunlop Warwick golf balls, c1955.
£500–600 *S*

l. A collection of wrapped and unwrapped golf balls, including a wrapped Penfold, several Bromfords, a silver King, 2 boxes of 6 Dunlop '65', c1965, and various ball cleaners, tees, etc.
£300–400 *S*

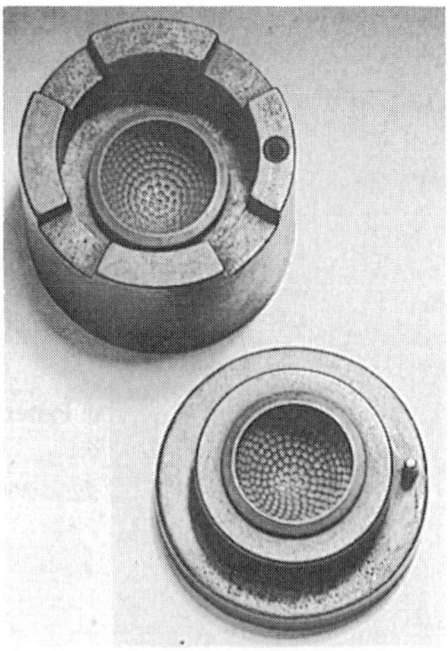

A dimple ball mould, stamped 27½ penny weights, c1905.
£750–900 *S*

A pair of Copeland dark blue and white jugs, slight damage, 6in (15cm) high.
£350–400 *S*

A Copeland late Spode teapot, registered No. 345322, c1905, 6in (15cm) high.
£350–450 *S*

l. A bachelor's novelty golfing tea set, the bodies in the form of golf balls, the teapot with a swan neck spout, scroll handle, the hinged cover with a golf ball finial, on golf ball feet, maker's mark Mappin & Webb, c1897.
£550–650 *WW*

An Edwardian golfing paperweight timepiece, with Swiss 'Doxa' movement, in working condition.
£450–600 *S*

A silver plate golfing desk set, decorated with 2 crossed golf clubs, c1920, 7in (17.5cm) wide.
£270–350 *S*

A silver coloured Royal Blackheath medal, inscribed with the name of the winner 'A. T. Hawkins, 1922, 1924, 1926', 1½in (4cm) high.
£550–650 *S*

A Cambridge University Golf Club red jacket, with label for 'A. W. Smith, Hosier, Shirtmaker and Athletic Outfitter, 20 King's Parade, Cambridge', 2 buttons missing, c1890, and a wry-necked putter for Hodges of Cambridge, c1905.
£300–400 *S*

A bronze figure of Harry Vardon, by Henry Pegram, the naturalistic base inscribed, '1908', 13in (33cm) high.
£4,500–5,500 *C(S)*

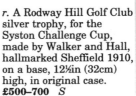

r. A Rodway Hill Golf Club silver trophy, for the Syston Challenge Cup, made by Walker and Hall, hallmarked Sheffield 1910, on a base, 12½in (32cm) high, in original case.
£500–700 *S*

A pressed fibreboard Silver King Golf Ball counter display, 14½in (37cm) high.
£1,800–2,000 *S*

Two framed and glazed prints, 'The man who plays because . . .', and 'The man who plays for exercise', initialled 'JB', both framed and glazed, c1900, 16½ by 12in (42 by 30.5cm).
£300–400 *S*

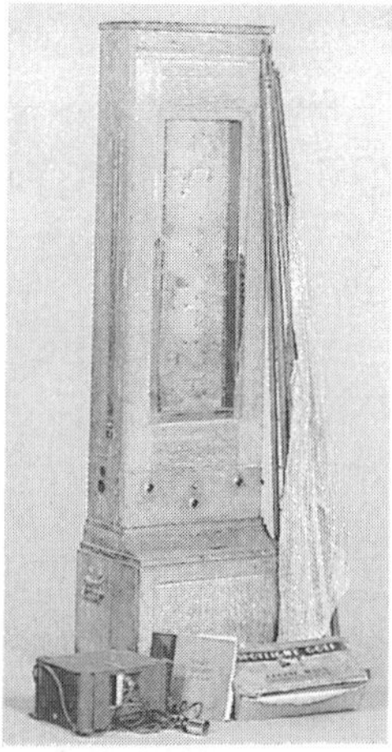

A Spotlight Golf machine, in an oak cabinet, with course maps, nets and an electrical box of tricks, holes, balls etc., with instruction booklet with foreword by Bernard Darwin, 71½in (181cm) high.
£400–600 *S*

Two club stamps, an autographed card by J. H. Taylor, and various other items.
£450–500 *S*

Wm. C. Maughan, *Picturesque Musselburgh and its Golf Links,* published in London by Simkin Marshall Hamilton Kent & Co. Ltd., contents loose.
£400–500 *S*

Hilton Garden Smith, *The Royal & Ancient Game of Golf,* subscriber edition No. 193/900.
£600–1,000 *S*

Four colour lithographs for January, February, March/April and May, from a golf calendar, by Edward Penfield, monogrammed, 14 by 8½in (35.5 by 21.5cm).
£900–1,000 *S*

Snooker & Billiards

r. A full size oak billiard table, by George Wright, with fluted legs, in excellent original condition, c1880.
£1,500–1,700 *BRA*

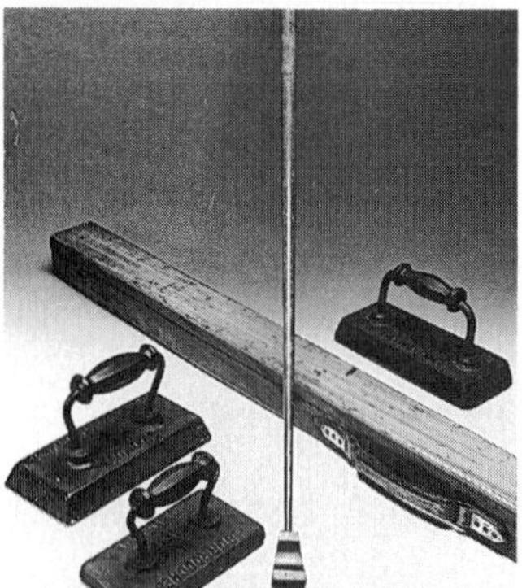

A selection of billiard room ephemera, comprising:
Irons, 1880–1920. **£20–40 each**
A double mahogany cue case, c1910. **£125–150**
Mace. **£200–250** *BRA*

l. A full size mahogany billiard table, by Burroughes & Watts, with 30in (76cm) circumference bold fluted legs, ornately carved cushion, frieze and knee plates with decorative acanthus leaf scrolls and moulded and reeded side frame, c1900.
£8,000–10,000 *BRA*

l. A billiard/life pool marker board, by Burroughes & Watts, c1860.
£1,800–2,200 *HAB*

A full size mahogany billiard table, by Thurstons & Co., with hexagonal legs and carved scrolls, c1884.
£1,800–2,000 *BRA*

A walnut scoreboard, by Orme & Son, c1865.
£6,500–7,500 *WBB*

A free standing mahogany life pool/billiard scoreboard, by G. Wright, c1890.
£3,000–3,500 *HAB*

A Victorian mahogany framed slate marking board, by Burroughes & Watts, 14in (35.5cm) wide.
£150–200 *BRA*

A life pool marker, by Burroughes & Watts, with reversible slate/mirror, 1870–1910.
£2,000–3,000 *WBB*

An Art Deco billiard table, by Burroughes & Watts, with steel vacuum cushion, 54in (137cm) wide.
£4,500–6,000 *WBB*

l. A quarter size billiard/dining table, with cabriole legs, c1920.
£1,500–1,800 *HAB*

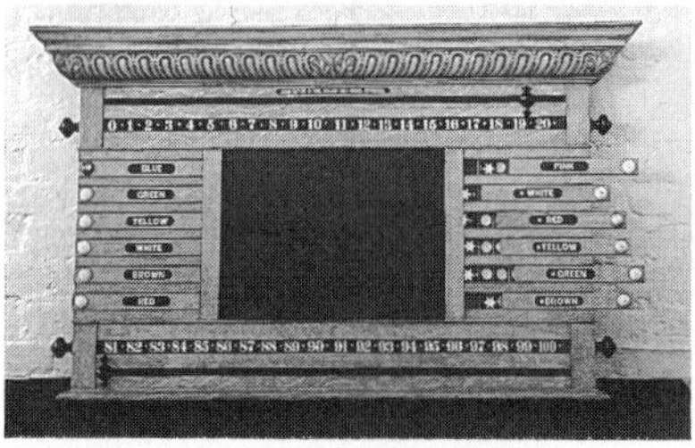

An oak billiard/life pool marker board, by J. Taylor, c1890, 50in (127cm) wide.
£500–750 *HAB*

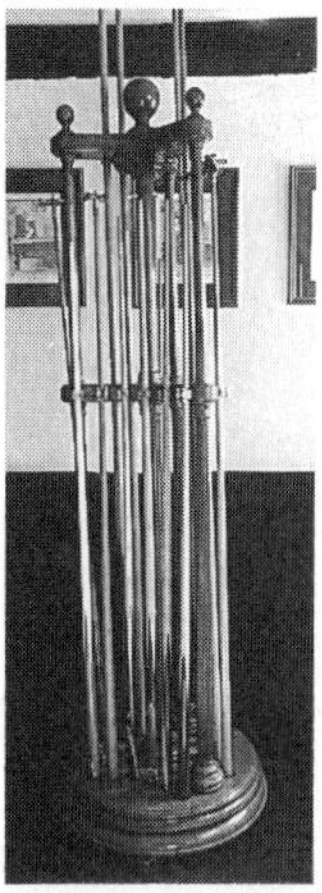

A Victorian Cuban mahogany revolving cue rack, 84in (213cm) high.
£2,000–2,500 *HAB*

A Victorian billiard room sofa, by J. Taylor of Edinburgh, oak with decorative carving, 96in (243.5cm) long.
£2,000–2,500 *HAB*

A free standing billiard scorer, by George Wright & Sons, c1890, 16in (40.5cm) long.
£150–200 *BRA*

An oak billiard marker board, by Orme & Son, with revolving mirror and ball box, on an oak carved shelf, c1865, 48in (122cm) wide.
£900–1,500 *HAB*

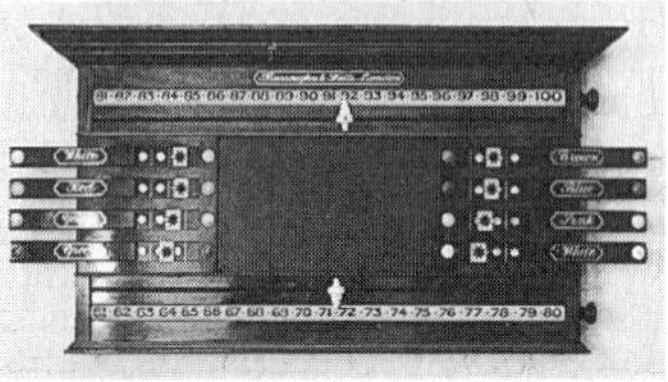

A mahogany life pool board, by Burroughes & Watts, c1880.
£450–600 *HAB*

A Victorian marker board, with life pool and ball box/till, c1890.
£2,000–2,500 *HAB*

An oak billiard room accessories cabinet, c1910, 72in (182.5cm) high.
£3,000–4,000 *HAB*

An oak and walnut full size billiard table, by Burroughes & Watts, with 6 gothic style legs, 1860.
£8,000–10,000 *HAB*

A full size oak billiard table, by George Wright & Co., c1890.
£4,500–5,500 *HAB*

A mahogany billiard table, by Gillow's, with rosewood veneer, c1810.
£14,000–16,000 *HAB*

Before restoration, this table had an oak bed.

A full size burr walnut and ebony billiard table, by Ashcroft, inlaid with bone, c1870.
£20,000–24,000 *HAB*

A full size billiard table, by Burroughes & Watts, with heavily carved tulip legs, c1885.
£3,500–4,000 *HAB*

A half size mahogany billiard table, by Ashcroft, c1890, 96in (243.5cm) long.
£2,500–3,000 *HAB*

A Victorian mahogany convertible billiard/dining table, with 6 carved legs, c1894.
£6,000–7,500 *HAB*

A Dutch oak carom table, with ivory and ebony inlay, c1930.
£2,500–3,000 *HAB*

A Victorian half size oak billiard/dining table, with carved tulip legs and winding mechanism.
£2,800–3,200 *HAB*

A full size billiard table, by Burroughes & Watts, the figured mahogany framework supported on 8 hand carved fluted tulip style legs, with carved scroll brackets, c1880.
£5,500–6,000 *ABC*

A full size billiard table, by Thurston, finished in pale English oak, the hand carved cushion and framework supported on 8 square fluted and carved legs, c1890, with matching scoreboard and cue stand.
£23,000–25,000 *ABC*

A Victorian mahogany bagatelle table, with turned legs, 120in (304.5cm) long.
£2,000–3,000 *HAB*

A half size swivel top oak billiard/dining table, by George Edwards of London.
£3,000–3,500 *HAB*

Tennis

An electroplated cruet set, in the form of 2 tennis balls and a half tennis ball, the base formed as a tennis racket, engraved with the diamond registration mark, c1880, 7½in (18.5cm) long.
£200–300 *CSK*

r. An early laminated racket, possibly a child's racket or for indoor tennis played on a miniature court, with convex wedge, flat head and square handle, c1880, 19in (48cm) long.
£150–250 *CSK*

TRIBAL ART

Three slipware pottery plates, made in Gujerat, north west India, mid-18thC, 10in (25cm) diam.
£60–70 each *GRG*

A Fang white face mask, Nlo Ngo Ntang, of naturalistic style, scarifications around the mouth, the nose, the cheeks and the forehead, pierced around the edges for attachment, overall white pigment, 15in (38cm) high.
£14,000–16,000 *S*

A Kota reliquary figure, the face overlaid with red copper, the back with a rectangular strip, old label inscribed '2' in black ink, 23½in (60cm) high.
£6,000–8,000 *S*

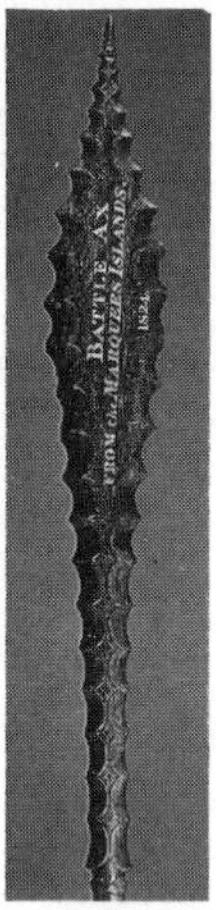

l. A Raratonga pole club, 'akatara, carved from toa wood, the broad leaf-shaped blade with scalloped border, one side inscribed in gilt 'For T. N. Mitchell', the other 'Battle Ax from the Marquees Islands, 1824', old varnish over glossy brown patina, chips to blade, 96in (243.5cm) high.
£13,000–15,000 *Bon*

This pole club was found in Scotland.

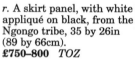

r. A skirt panel, with white appliqué on black, from the Ngongo tribe, 35 by 26in (89 by 66cm).
£750–800 *TOZ*

An open weave embroidered raffia skirt panel, from the Bushoong tribe, 50 by 22in (127 by 55.5cm).
£550–600 *TOZ*

Part of a skirt panel with raffia appliqué, from the Ngongo tribe, central Africa, 36 by 32in (91.5 by 81cm).
£550–600 *TOZ*

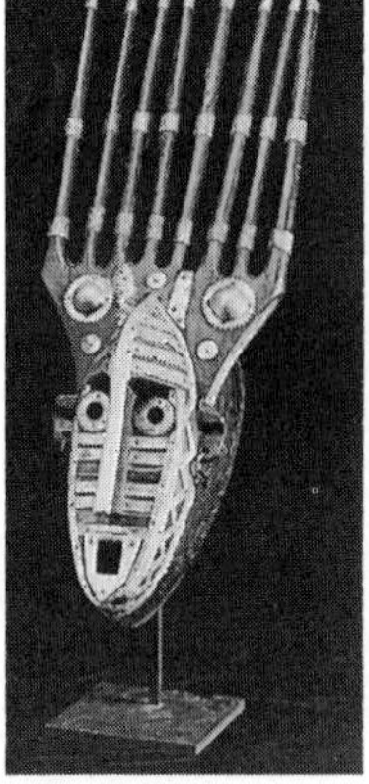

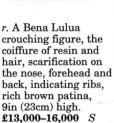

l. A Marka mask, covered with metal plaques, pierced around the edges for attachment, brown patina, 24½in (62cm) high.
£2,400–2,800 *S*

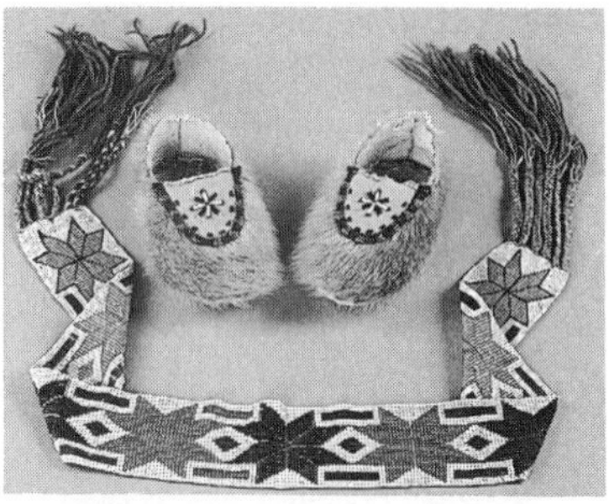

An African beaded sash, decorated with stars between geometric patterns, 40in (101.5cm) long, and a pair of Canadian Indian sealskin beaded child's moccasins.
£100–200 each *RIT*

r. A Bena Lulua crouching figure, the coiffure of resin and hair, scarification on the nose, forehead and back, indicating ribs, rich brown patina, 9in (23cm) high.
£13,000–16,000 *S*

A tent band, late 19thC.
£100–120 *GRG*

An Afghanistan Turkoman Turbah, or Saryk tent bag, late 19thC.
£700–800 *GRG*

Although smaller than a Jauar, this is of superb quality in both aesthetic and weaver's skill, and is used for the same purpose. The Göi in the centre was woven by members of the Saryk tribe, and is different to the usual geometric Göi.

A tent hanging, late 19thC, 68in (172.5cm) long.
£300–350 *GRG*

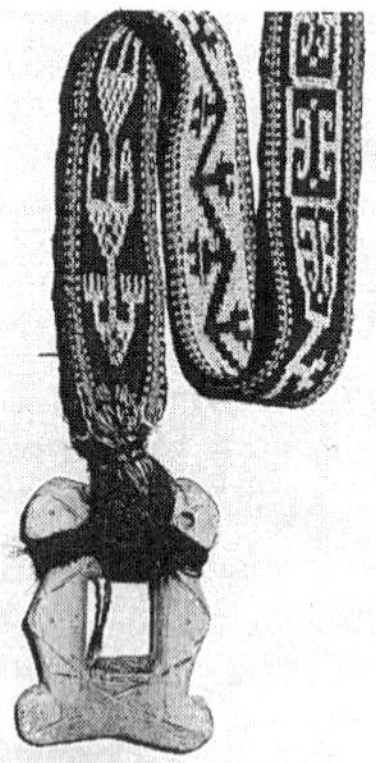

A Qashqai tent band, late 19thC, 17in (43cm) long.
£150–185 *GRG*

A Cree Indian pouch, the front embroidered with a floral quillwork motif, surrounded by a green and white quillwork band, c1860, 8in (20cm) high.
£1,200–1,500 *S*

A ceremonial skirt, with raffia appliqué, usually worn at funerals, from the Ngongo tribe of the Kuba Kingdom, c1920, 25 by 14in (63.5 by 35.5cm).
£900–1,000 *TOZ*

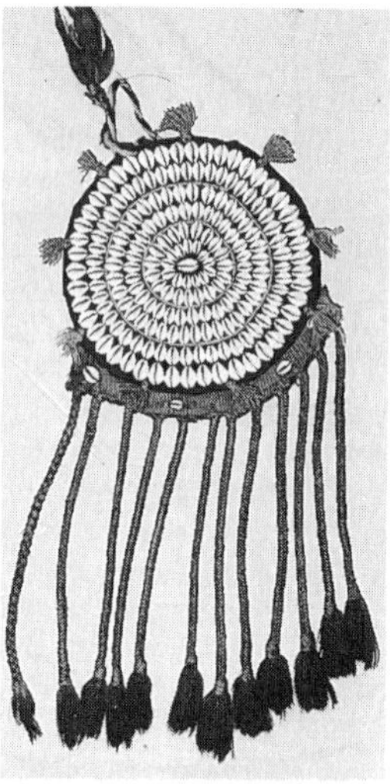

A decorative tent hanging, from the Caucasian border region, eastern Turkey, early 20thC, 11in (28cm) diam.
£125–160 *GRG*

A Balouch bag, late 19thC, 19 by 14in (48 by 35.5cm).
£35–40 *GRG*

A Balouch pillow bag, from southern Iran, late 19thC.
£90–100 *GRG*

Two Balouch bags, late 19thC, largest 19 by 14in (48 by 35.5cm).
£35–40 *GRG*

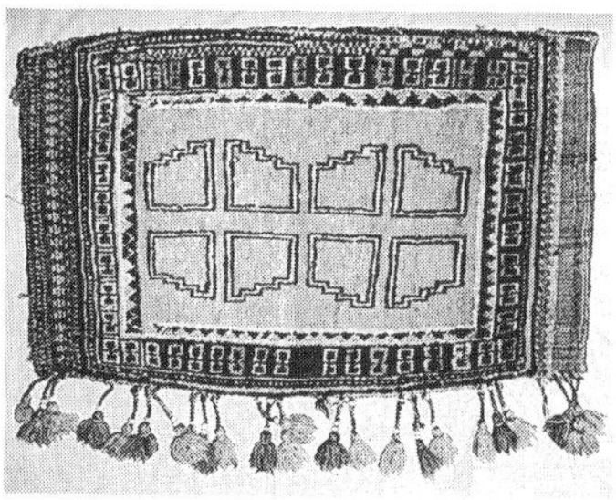

A Balouch pillow bag, late 19thC.
£100–120 *GRG*

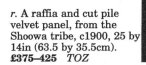

A finely woven Turkoman Soumak bag, late 19thC, 26 by 16in (66 by 40.5cm).
£75–85 *GRG*

A Balouch salt bag, late 19thC, 25 by 16½in (63.5 by 42cm).
£60–70 *GRG*

A Cisim woven bag, from the Shuh Suvun weavers, decorated with small figures, late 19thC, 20 by 15in (50.5 by 38cm).
£90–110 *GRG*

A Balouch salt bag, late 19thC, 19 by 15in (48 by 38cm).
£80–95 *GRG*

A raffia and cut pile velvet panel, from the Shoowa Tribe, Kuba Kingdom, central Africa, c1900, 20 by 17in (50.5 by 43cm).
£350–400 *TOZ*

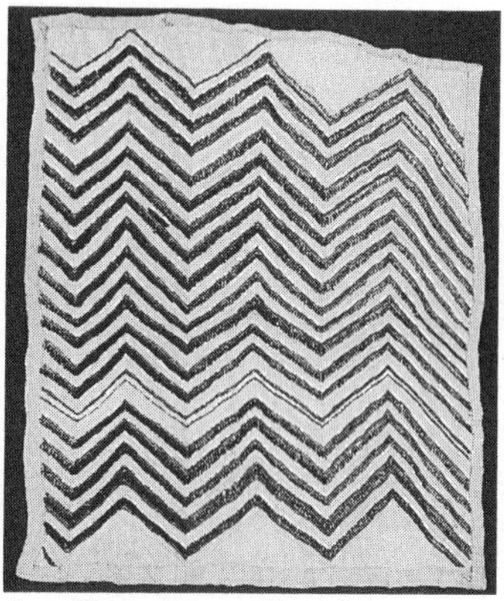

A raffia and cut pile velvet chevron design panel, from the Shoowa tribe, Kuba Kingdom, central Africa, 22 by 19in (55.5 by 48cm).
£550–600 *TOZ*

A raffia and cut pile velvet panel, from the Shoowa tribe, Kuba Kingdom, central Africa, 20in (50.5cm) square.
£400–450 *TOZ*

r. An open weave embroidered raffia skirt panel, from the Bushoong tribe, c1900, 63 by 20in (160 by 50.5cm).
£700–800 *TOZ*

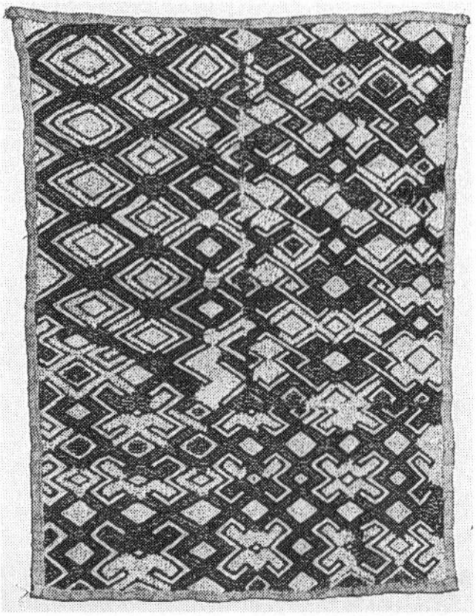

l. A raffia and cut pile velvet panel, from the Shoowa tribe, c1920, 26 by 19in (66 by 48cm).
£125–150 *TOZ*

r. A raffia and cut pile velvet panel, from the Shoowa tribe, c1900, 25 by 14in (63.5 by 35.5cm).
£375–425 *TOZ*

A raffia and cut pile velvet panel, from the Shoowa tribe, c1920, 25 by 22in (63.5 by 55.5cm).
£125–150 *TOZ*

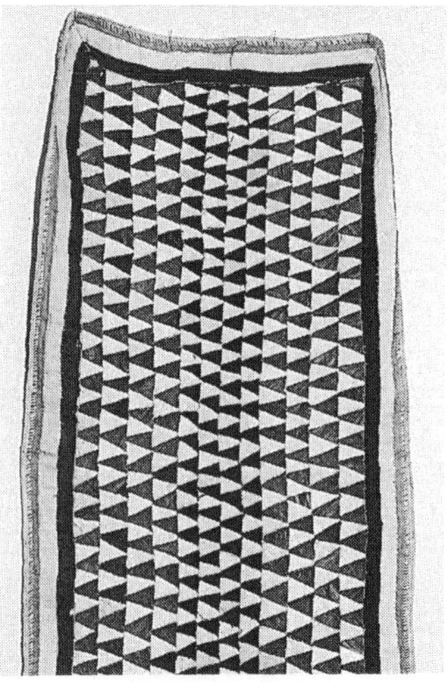

A bark cotton raffia skirt panel, from the Bushoong tribe, Kuba Kingdom, 76 by 18in (193 by 45.5cm).
£300–400 *TOZ*

A raffia and cut pile velvet panel, from the Shoowa tribe, 24 by 14in (61 by 35.5cm).
£200–250 *TOZ*

A raffia embroidered panel, from the Kuba Kingdom, central Africa, c1900, 40 by 27in (101.5 by 68.5cm).
£550–600 *TOZ*

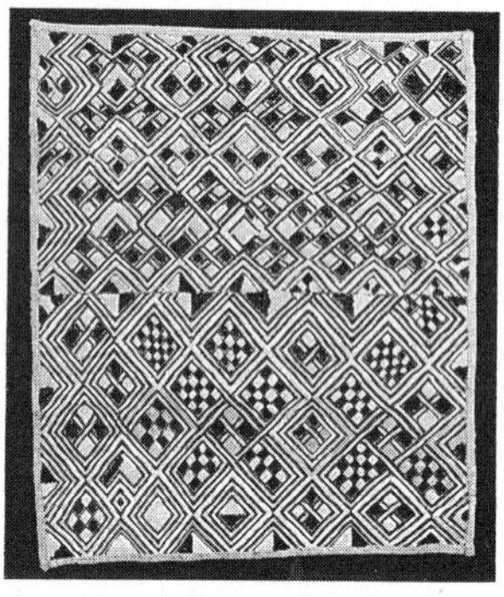

A raffia and cut pile velvet embroidered textile panel, from the Shoowa tribe, Kuba Kingdom, Zaire, central Africa, c1900, 24 by 20½in (61 by 52cm), mounted.
£250–300 *TOZ*

A raffia and cut pile velvet panel, from the Shoowa tribe, Kuba Kingdom, central Africa, c1900, 24 by 22in (61 by 55.5cm).
£350–400 *TOZ*

AMERICAN INDIAN ART

A south western figural pottery vessel, the pinkish buff clay body decorated in dark brown over a creamy-white slip, pierced at crown of head, slight damage, 10in (25cm) high.
£2,500–3,000 *SK(B)*

l. A south western polychrome pottery jar, with indented base, darkened orange slip over a red clay body, black and orange paint decoration, slip enhancement, restored, Zia, 9in (23cm) high.
£350–450 *SK(B)*

r. A south western polychrome pottery jar, with indented base, rag polished greyish-white slip over pink micaceous clay body, black painted decoration, painted red base and lip, interior base weighted with plaster fill, slight damage, Cochiti, 10½in (26.5cm) high.
£1,000–1,500 *SK(B)*

A south western polychrome pottery jar, with indented base, painted in white and brown heart-line deer, geometric and foliate devices on an orange clay body, minor abrasions, possibly Hopi, 8in (20cm) high.
£400–500 *SK(B)*

A south western polychrome pottery olla, with a white clay body, painted with black and brick red decoration over creamy white slip, design elements include broken linear banding at neck and above puki line, red painted base, 11in (28cm) high.
£5,000–6,000 *SK(B)*

Two south western polychrome cottonwood Kachina dolls, ram and ewe figures, black, red and shades of grey, each with applied lamb's wool, natural pigments over a kaolin surface, slight damage, largest 8½in (21.5cm) high.
£1,000–1,500 *SK(B)*

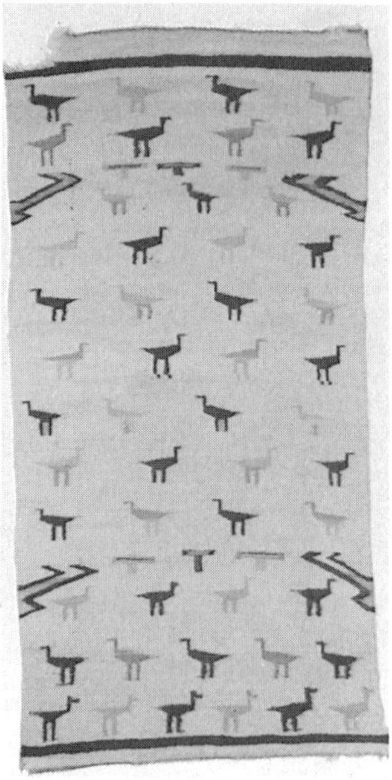

A Navajo pictorial weaving, of natural and aniline dyed homespun wool, woven in red, brown, shaded brown and pale orange with bird motifs against an ivory ground, damaged, 98½ by 48½in (250 by 123cm).
£1,000–1,500 *SK(B)*

A Navajo pictorial weaving, of natural and aniline dyed homespun wool, woven on a yellow ivory ground with violet blue, black, orange, rose and shaded greyish-brown geometric and arrow devices, damaged, 74 by 44in (188 by 111.5cm).
£500–600 *SK(B)*

A Navajo weaving, of natural and aniline dyed homespun wool, woven on a white ground with a chief's blanket pattern in red, dark brown, yellow and purple, 75 by 54in (190.5 by 137cm).
£5,000–6,000 *SK(B)*

A Navajo carpet, of natural and aniline dyed homespun wool, woven in black, white and shaded grey concentric geometric devices against a dark red field, 144 by 120in (365.5 by 304.5cm).
£3,500–4,000 *SK(B)*

A south western polychrome pottery jar, red clay body, rag polished creamy-white slip paint decorated in brick red and black, red painted base band, lip interior rim, slight damage, San Ildefonso Pueblo, 11½in (29.5cm) high.
£5,500–6,500 *SK(B)*

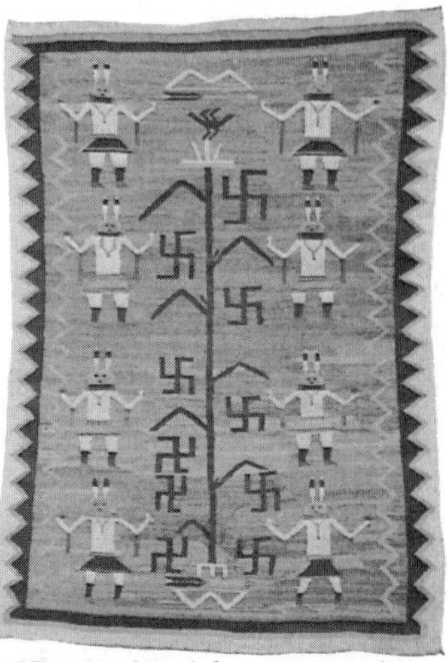

A Navajo pictorial rug, woven in sand, cranberry, dark brown, white, grey and black against a shaded brownish-grey ground, damaged, 89 by 66in (226 by 167.5cm).
£1,500–2,000 *SK(B)*

A late classic Navajo weaving, brown and indigo stripes detailed with white ticking, white wool warp, damaged, 69 by 47in (175 by 119cm).
£2,000–3,000 *SK(B)*

A Navajo Germantown weaving, with vibrant multi-coloured field woven with a pattern of concentric serrated diamonds, linear banded and wool fringed ends, black, royal blue, red, burgundy, green, lavender, salmon, white and violet wools, damaged, 83 by 55in (210.5 by139.5cm), excluding fringe.
£2,000–2,500 *SK(B)*

l. A north west coast Argillite totem model, with flat back, finely carved, incised and pierced detailing, minor stone loss, Haida, 8½in (21.5cm) high.
£550–650 *SK(B)*

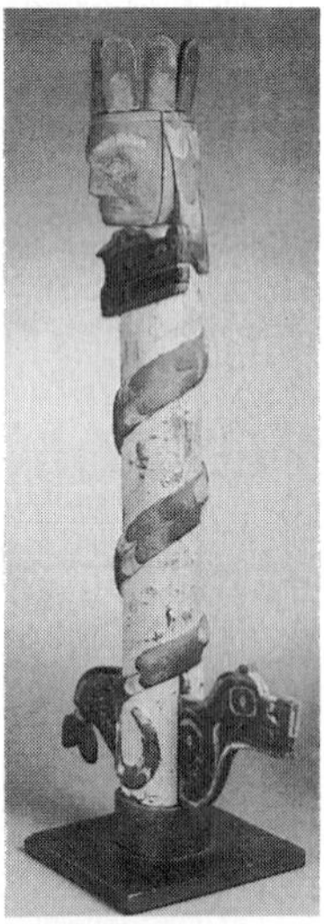

A Navajo rug, Transitional period, woven on a shaded red ground with a pattern of black, white and grey banded stripes and concentric crosses, damaged, 84 by 61in (213 by 155cm).
£1,200–1,700 *SK(B)*

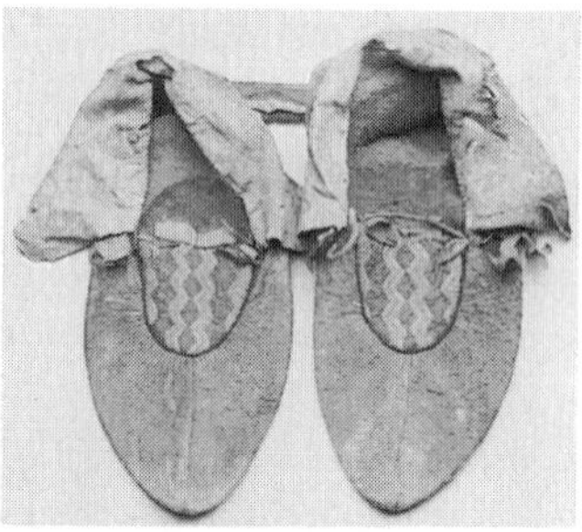

A pair of Great Lakes ribbon appliquéd hide moccasins, smoke tanned hide, with pink, yellow, azure, blue and violet ribbonwork, backed with coarse red stroud cloth, silk thread and sinew sewn, remnant of heel fringe, damaged, 10in (25cm) long.
£3,000–3,500 *SK(B)*

l. A north west coast polychrome red cedarwood model totem pole, with mineral paint decoration, in turquoise, navy blue, vermillion, forest green and white, slight damage, 38in (96.5cm) high, excluding mount.
£5,500–6,500 *SK(B)*

A Great Lakes loom beaded cloth bandoleer bag, composed of blue wool stroud trade cloth, with black, mustard yellow, clear green and wine decoration, with applied loom beaded panels, glass tube beads and three-ply wool tassels, red and mustard worsted tape binding, golden yellow, turquoise and navy blue beads, some wear, 34 by 12in (86 by 30.5cm).
£1,500–2,000 *SK(B)*

A pair of beaded hide moccasins, with soft soles, each stitched on dark turquoise ground, remnant of hide heel fringe, white, yellow, white-heart red and navy beads, slight wear, 10in (25cm) long.
£1,300–1,800 *SK(B)*

A Great Lakes birchbark canoe, split-root stitched, wood sheathing, ribs and crossbars, the seams sealed with spruce gum, 132in (335cm) long.
£1,800–2,200 *SK(B)*

This canoe has an accompanying note, 'Circa 1914, crafted by the Indians in Clock, Ontario as a wedding present for my mother who was their teacher'.

A north east woodlands birchbark carrying box, or handled double-lidded basket, with bentwood handle, peeled decorated birchbark depictions of the Shaman Rabbit and the Wild Cat, peeled signature on base 'Tomah Joseph', minor watermarks, 11in (28cm) long.
£1,400–1,800 *SK(B)*

DECORATIVE ARTS

It is undoubtedly getting harder to find a consistent supply of good quality Art Nouveau and Art Deco artefacts. The highly decorative nature of those items which typify the style has ensured an avid and sustained interest from a growing body of collectors. Whilst some people are happy to amass anything that denotes the period, others choose to confine their collecting in a variety of ways, concentrating on the work of a particular artist, or group of artists, by gathering many examples of the same object or even by restricting their purchases to work executed in specific materials.

Collecting antiques, particularly the work of the major artists of the Art Nouveau and Art Deco periods, can be very expensive. At the same time, it is possible for those without unlimited wealth to form worthy collections and derive just as much pleasure in the pursuit. However, whether you wish to furnish your home in the Art Deco style, collect those wonderfully evocative bronze dancing figures, indulge in a passion for French cameo glass, or to seek out Arts and Crafts furniture to augment a collection of Studio pottery, you should always endeavour to acquire the best quality work you can afford.

Fakes and forgeries have appeared on the market due to the increase in demand and the rising price of original works. These invariably lack the skill and craftsmanship of the pieces they emulate. They do attempt to dupe, so it is necessary to examine objects very closely.

Copies of bronze and ivory Art Deco figures, often by the more famous sculptors, such as Ferdinand Preiss and D. H. Chiparus, exist in abundance. Because casting in bronze is expensive, fakes are usually made from inferior materials and are crudely cast. The fakes display none of the fine detailing and hand finishing techniques employed by the original artists and founders. Where the head and hands of an original piece would often have been individually carved from ivory, these are replaced with limbs cast from a synthetic material with properties more akin to plastic. Brown staining is sometimes introduced around the eyes and between the fingers of such figures in an attempt to disguise the material and to suggest ageing. The Art Deco sculptors experimented extensively with their finishes. Electroplating, cold painting, gilding and enamelling were used in various combinations. A poor quality finish or 'patina' could be another indicator that all is not well.

Attempts have been made to copy Art Nouveau cameo glass and iridescent glass. Examples of the latter have appeared on the market bearing an engraved signature for the Austrian company of Loetz. In fact, very little of this company's work was signed. Loetz produced some of the finest iridescent Art Glass at the turn of the century and the more desirable pieces now command sums in excess of £1,000. Both Loetz and the American glass designer, Louis Comfort Tiffany, managed to produce glass vessels which, though thin bodied, displayed high levels of iridescence, particularly when light is glanced off their surfaces. Bright light directed through the objects disperses these properties and only the core colour is visible.

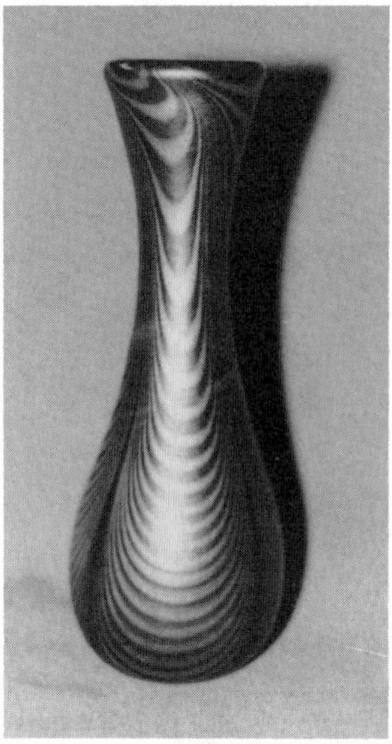

The vase pictured above may resemble a piece of Loetz glass but is, in fact, a modern vase emulating the work of the masters. The art of producing true iridescent glass seems to have thwarted modern imitators as close examination shows that the glass is much thicker than the original and that its iridescence is not contained within, but is actually a lustrous finish applied to the outer surface. Glancing light onto the surface or directing light through the vessel causes no material change to its appearance.

Even items which are genuine lose value if flawed. Where possible, avoid building a collection of damaged goods. Always carefully examine the condition of any item you may wish to purchase. On some items, such as furniture, minor damage is tolerable and will not greatly impair the value because it can usually be rectified by a skilful restorer. A chip on the base of a Lalique vase though can reduce its value by more than fifty per cent. Moreover, while the passage of time has proven that items of quality, in good condition, appreciate markedly in value, those with defects may only ever retain a decorative value. As ever the message remains the same. Buy less if you must, but always buy better.

Audrey Sternshine

ARTS & CRAFTS AND ART NOUVEAU

Furniture

An Aesthetic Movement elbow chair, after a design by Holman Hunt.
£350–400 *P*

An Arts & Crafts oak firescreen, by Stanley Davies of Windermere, framing a silk embroidery in the manner of Louise Powell, on block supports with chamfered edges, 'AP' and 'SDW' monograms, dated '1929', 32½in (83cm) high.
£350–500 *P*

A wardrobe, inlaid with pewter and various woods, with panels depicting a formalised tree, bun feet, with retailer's labels 'Thomas Justice & Sons Ltd., Dundee', c1900, 77in (195.5cm) wide.
£3,300–3,700 *C*

A pair of oak side chairs, designed by Charles Bevan for Gillow's, the leather backrests and seats with tasselled ends.
£1,200–1,500 *P*

A mahogany and inlaid upright piano, by John Brinsmead & Sons, decorated in the manner of Walter Crane, the front and sides inlaid with figures, maidens, masks, foliage and scrolls and heightened with penwork, 60½in (153cm) wide.
£1,000–1,200 *P*

An oak dresser, the open plate rack with arched frieze above 2 frieze drawers, on carved legs joined by a stretcher, 57½in (146cm) wide.
£800–1,200 *CSK*

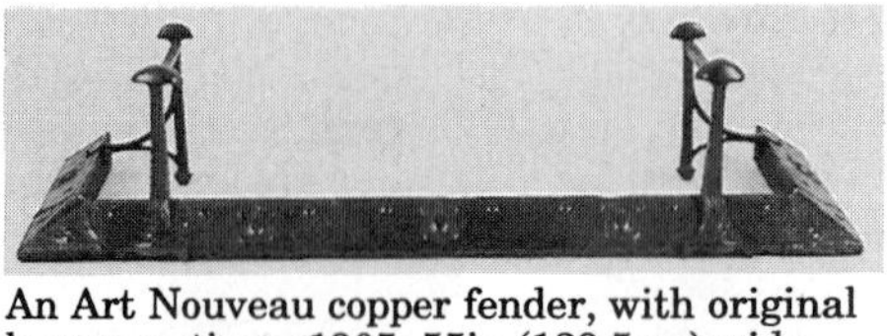

An Art Nouveau copper fender, with original bronze patina, c1905, 55in (139.5cm) wide.
£600–700 *SK(B)*

A Gothic revival oak armchair, with upholstered panel back between turned and carved uprights, carved arms, on turned and square supports united with a turned stretcher.
£750–900 *P*

An Art Nouveau mahogany coffer, 39½in (100cm) wide.
£600–800 *P*

An Art Nouveau mahogany secrétaire, the upper part with a deep reverse breakfront, the triple panelled fall inlaid with boxwood flowering plants, enclosing an arrangement of satinwood faced pigeonholes and drawers surrounding a central cupboard, the lower part with a long drawer above a pair of panelled doors, each inlaid with a foliate cartouche, 50½in (128cm) high.
£800–900 *L*

A mahogany corner settle, with padded back above trellis lower frieze, curved arms with a central pierced foliate motif, stamped 'Lamb of Manchester', c1875.
£950–1,200 *C*

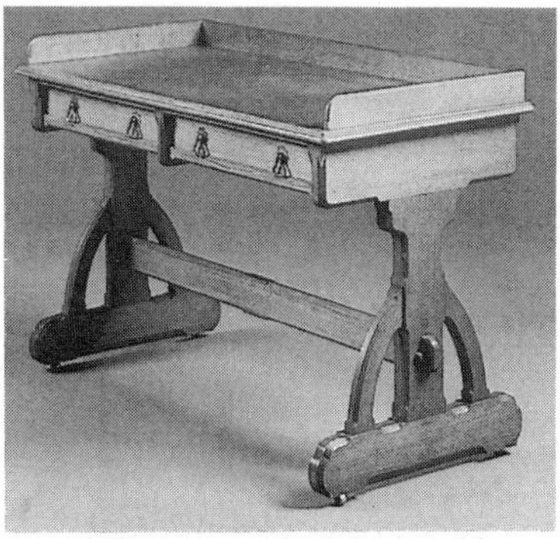

A mid-Victorian oak writing table, the design attributed to A. W. N. Pugin, 48in (122cm) wide.
£1,000–1,200 *CSK*

An ebonised wood 'Old English' or 'Jacobean' armchair, designed by E. W. Godwin, with an upholstered seat above a cross stretcher, c1877, 34in (86cm) wide.
£450–650 *S*

An oak 'Abingdon' chair, by George Walton, with tapering back splat, curved arms and rush seat, c1895, 34in (86cm) high.
£800–1,000 *S*

A late Victorian inlaid oak library cabinet, inset with panels of various burr veneers and 'AD1901', opening to reveal 6 drawers opposed by 2 glazed cupboard doors, on bun feet, 42in (106.5cm) wide.
£1,000–1,200 *CSK*

An Art Nouveau brass, marquetry and copper inlaid mahogany display cabinet, 36in (91.5cm) wide.
£1,400–1,800 *CSK*

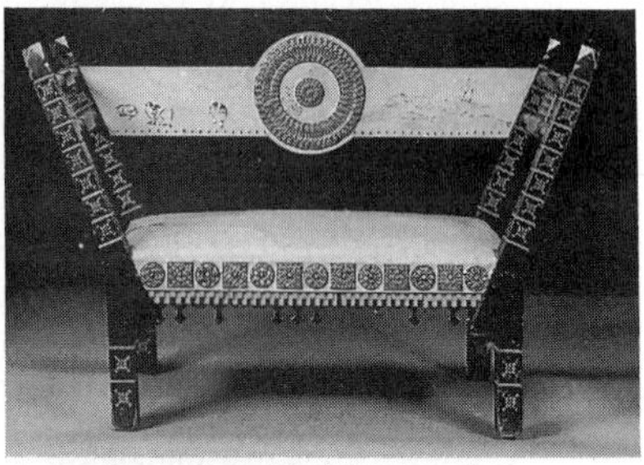

A parchment and inlaid bench, by Carlo Bugatti, with splayed arms, parchment covered back with copper roundel, the frame inlaid with a geometric pewter design, c1900, 46½in (118cm) wide.
£3,500–4,500 *CNY*

l. An Aesthetic Movement oak cabinet, the centre with an inlaid panel of bronze and pewter, brass handles, 2 keys, c1880, 66½in (169cm) high.
£1,400–1,700 *S*

A dressing table, chest-on-legs, towel rail and 2 side chairs, the majority with retailer's labels for 'Thomas Justice & Sons Ltd., Dundee', c1900, dressing table 47½in (121.5cm) wide.
£2,000–2,500 *C*

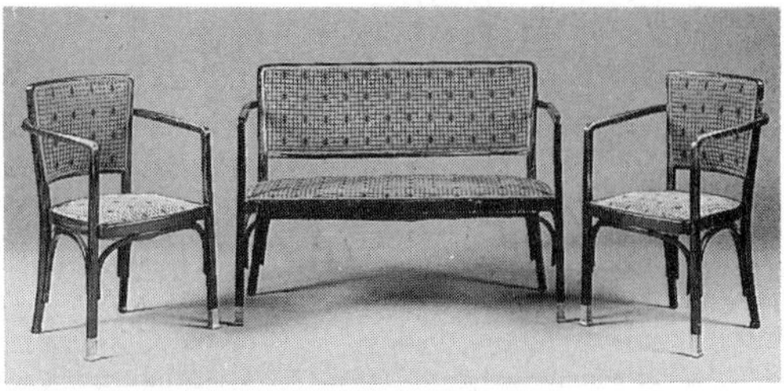

A three-piece dark stained beech and brass mounted suite, by Koloman Moser, 1901, the settee 47in (119cm) long.
£1,600–1,800 *CSK*

A bentwood side table, by J. & J. Kohn, after a design by Josef Hoffmann, c1910, 29½in (75cm) diam.
£1,200–1,700 *C*

A Viennese mahogany cabinet-on-chest, 41½in (105cm) wide.
£720–800 *CSK*

Three stained mahogany and beech 'Fledermaus' side chairs, by Josef Hoffmann, with close-studded padded back and seats, on turned legs joined by stretchers, c1906.
£600–700 *CSK*

A glazed cabinet, the upper section with 3 bevelled glass doors, the lower section with 2 doors enclosing shelves, inlaid with geometric motifs and plaque inscribed 'Möbelfabrik L. Ernst, Düsseldorf, Benratherstra. 28-29, Fabrik Martin Str. 97', c1910, 70½in (179cm) high.
£1,700–2,200 *S*

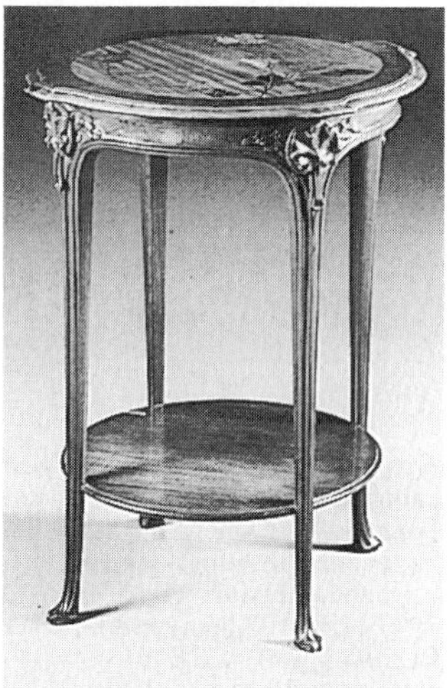

A carved and inlaid two-tier mahogany occasional table, the design attributed to Louis Majorelle, the top inlaid with various fruitwoods, on pad feet, c1905, 24½in (63cm) diam.
£1,400–1,600 *C*

A pair of armchairs, by Koloman Moser for Prag Rudniker, with oak frames, plaited rush seats and 'chequerboard' backs, worn, c1903, 49in (124.5cm) high.
£2,500–3,500 *S*

An oak sideboard, by Gustav Stickley, designed by Harvey Ellis, No. 804, original medium finish and hammered iron hardware, red label and remnants of craftsman's paper label, c1907, 54in (137cm) wide.
£5,000–6,000 *SK(B)*

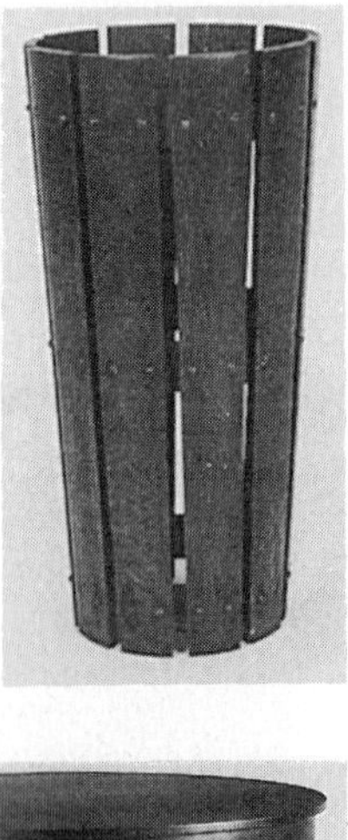

r. An oak slat umbrella stand, by Gustav Stickley, No. 100, with original medium finish, 10 slats riveted to 3 hammered iron hoops, red label, pan missing, c1907, 24in (61cm) high.
£850–1,000 *SK(B)*

A European Arts and Crafts ebonised and carved table, with intaglio design highlighted in green, incised 'Werderman', 27in (69cm) high.
£220–280 *SK(B)*

r. An oak pedestal dining table, No. 9057, with original medium finish, with extending top, on squared pedestal with 4 radiating legs, 3 leaves, with 'Paine Furniture' retail tag, c1907, 48in (122cm) diam.
£700–1,000 *SK(B)*

l. A set of 6 Limbert Furniture oak dining chairs, No. 1851, original light-medium finish, upholstered seat, branded mark, c1907.
£1,500–2,000 *SK(B)*

An oak sideboard, by Gustav Stickley, No. 814, original medium finish and hammered iron hardware, red label and partial paper label, some veneer loss, c1910, 66in (167.5cm) wide.
£2,200–2,500 *SK(B)*

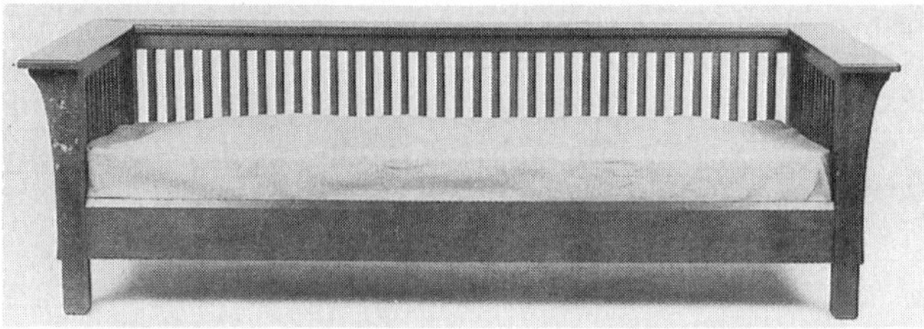

An oak spindle 'Prairie' settle, by L. & J. G. Stickley, No. 234, original medium finish and box spring cushion, c1912, 86in (218.5cm) long.
£25,000–30,000 *SK(B)*

An oak two-door bookcase, by Gustav Stickley, No. 510, original medium finish, overhanging top above 2 twelve-pane doors with mitred mullions, the interior with 6 adjustable shelves, the platform base with reverse corbels at each corner, top reinforced, escutcheons missing, c1901, 58½in (151cm) wide.
£10,000–12,000 *SK(B)*

An oak chest, by Gustav Stickley, with cedar lining, original dark finish and black iron hardware, unsigned, later paint decoration, c1901, 41in (104cm) wide.
£5,000–6,000 *SK(B)*

A Limbert oak Morris chair, No. 818, original medium finish, fixed back, branded mark, worn and re-upholstered, c1910.
£1,200–1,600 *SK(B)*

A Roycrofters oak two-drawer library table, No. 75, with original medium finish and copper hardware, carved orb mark, c1906, 52in (132cm) long.
£1,500–2,000 *SK(B)*

An oak sideboard, by Gustav Stickley, medium finish and hammered iron hardware, red label, restored, c1904, 54in (137cm) wide.
£1,500–2,000 *SK(B)*

A Lifetime oak mirrored sideboard, original medium finish and hammered copper hardware, 'Paine Furniture' retail tag, c1907, 48in (122cm) wide.
£400–500 *SK(B)*

An oak smoker's cabinet, by Gustav Stickley, No. 522, original finish, interior drawer and compartments, red label, top stained, c1902, 27in (69cm) high.
£2,500–3,000 *SK(B)*

An oak bow arm Morris chair, by Gustav Stickley, No. 336, original medium finish, adjustable back with pyramidal pegs, rope seat, slight damage, c1904.
£5,500–6,000 *SK(B)*

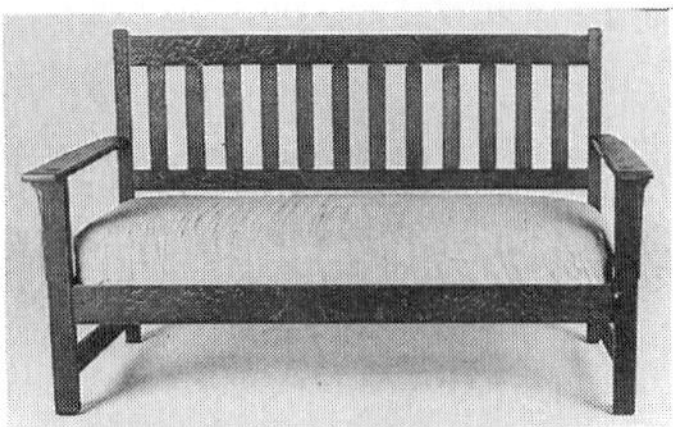

An oak settle, by J. M. Young, No. 3701, medium finish, original spring cushion, stencilled model number, slight damage and restoration, 68in (172.5cm) long.
£400–600 *SK(B)*

ART NOUVEAU
Ceramics & Studio Pottery

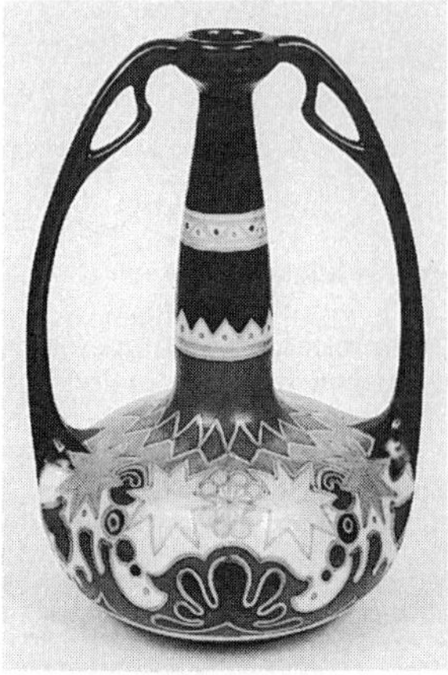

An Arnhem Astra vase, c1930, 13½in (34cm) high.
£250–300 *OO*

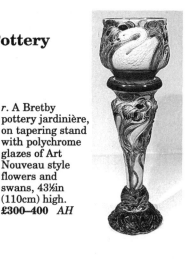

r. A Bretby pottery jardinière, on tapering stand with polychrome glazes of Art Nouveau style flowers and swans, 43½in (110cm) high.
£300–400 *AH*

An Ault Creke Ware four-handled vase, designed by Christopher Dresser, with brown, purple and white streaked glaze, the underside impressed 'Chr Dresser', numbered '247', factory mark in relief, c1900, 19½in (50cm) high.
£750–1,000 *S*

A pair of Gouda pottery Crocus design candlesticks, c1927, 10½in (26cm) high.
£250–300 *OO*

A tin glazed pottery model of a seated cat, decorated with yellow and white hearts and circles on a dark mottled blue ground, with inset blue glass eyes, signed 'E. Gallé, Nancy', 13in (33cm) high.
£950–1,200 *Bea*

r. A Gouda pottery vase, painted by P. Woerlee, signed, c1906, 8½in (21cm) high.
£600–700 *OO*

A Gouda pottery vase, made for Liberty's, c1903, 20in (51cm) high.
£300–400 *OO*

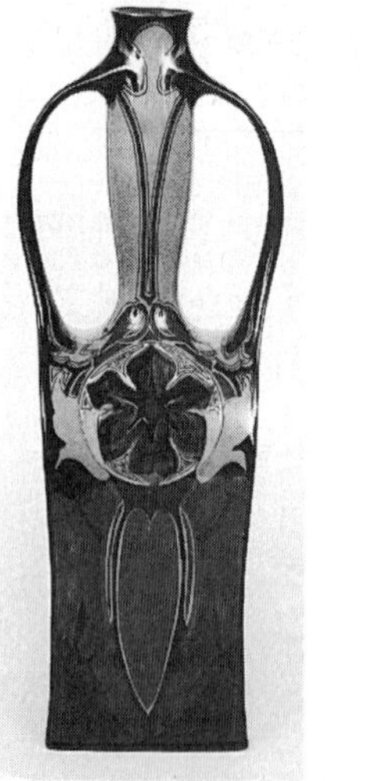

A Gouda pottery vase, decorated by Van der Heydt, c1905, 18in (46cm) high.
£1,000–1,400 *OO*

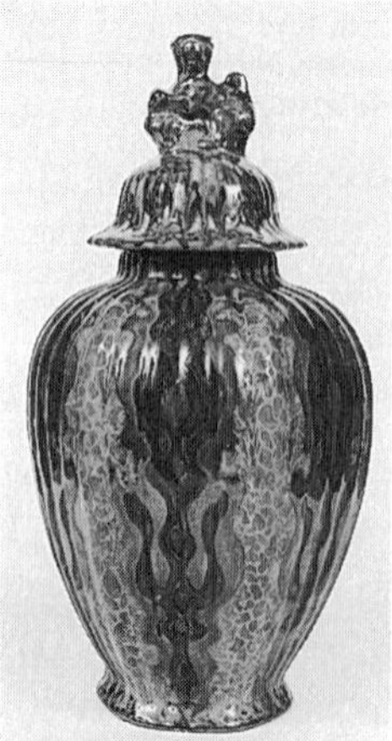

A Gouda pottery Unique design lustre vase with cover, c1928, 12in (30.5cm) high.
£250–350 *OO*

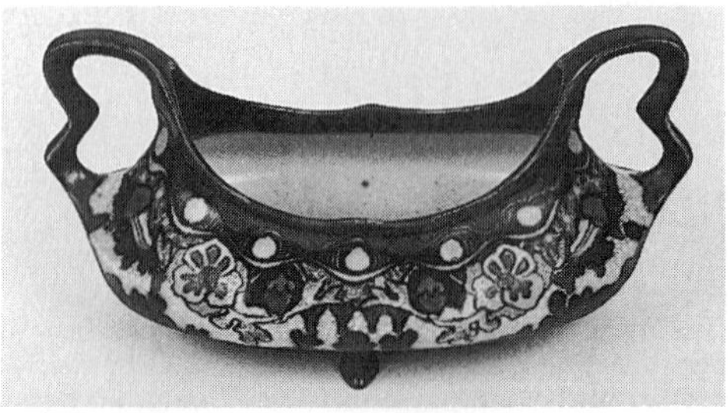

A Gouda pottery Corona design vase, on 3 feet, c1919, 12½in (32cm) wide.
£200–250 *OO*

A Gouda pottery Egyptian design vase, c1924, 8½in (21cm) high.
£150–250 *OO*

A Liberty stoneware jardinière, designed by Archibald Knox, applied with 2 lug handles below a band with incised Celtic knot motifs, impressed Liberty mark, minor restoration, 19½in (49cm) high.
£1,200–1,500 *CSK*

A pottery vase, by Haga von Purmerend, designed by C. J. Lanouy, with metallic lustre, c1905, 10in (25cm) high.
£2,000–2,500 *OO*

A Martin ware two-handled vase, decorated with fish and seaweed, in brown, blue and green glaze, incised signature 'Martin Bros, London and Southall, 6-1888', 9in (23cm) high.
£900–1,200 *RBB*

A William Moorcroft bowl and cover, decorated with fish and plants under saltglaze, c1930, 6½in (16cm) diam.
£450–550 *HEA*

A pair of Art Nouveau stoneware jardinières and stands, possibly for Liberty, covered in an oatmeal glaze, minor damage, 26in (66cm) high.
£1,100–1,300 *CSK*

l. A Grueby Pottery, vase, designed by George P. Kendrick, modelled by Wilhelmina Post, with matt cucumber green glaze, on low relief foliate decoration, impressed mark and incised artist's initials, drilled, minor traces of blue paint, c1902, 16½in (42cm) high.
£14,000–15,000 *SK(B)*

A James MacIntyre pottery salad bowl, with plated rim, the exterior decorated with the brown chrysanthemum design, on a mottled green ground, the interior with a band of cornflowers, 9½in (24cm) diam., and a pair of plated salad servers.
£550–650 *Bea*

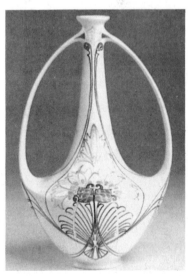

A Martin Brothers stoneware mug, by Ernest Marsh, incised with spiny fish and an octopus, in shades of brown on a pale blue ground, incised 'Marsh 2–1908 Martin Bros London & Southall EBM', 4½in (12cm) high.
£200–250 *CSK*

A Moorcroft MacIntyre Peacock Feather pattern vase, c1900, 5in (12.5cm) high.
£450–600 *HEA*

A Minton stoneware encaustic bread plate, designed by A. W. N. Pugin, with moulded decoration of stylised foliage and ears of wheat, the rim with the text 'Waste Not Want Not', covered in rust and blue encaustic glazes, c1849, 13in (33cm) diam.
£1,000–1,200 *C*

A Moorcroft MacIntyre Poppy pattern jug, c1904, 6½in (16cm) high.
£350–450 *HEA*

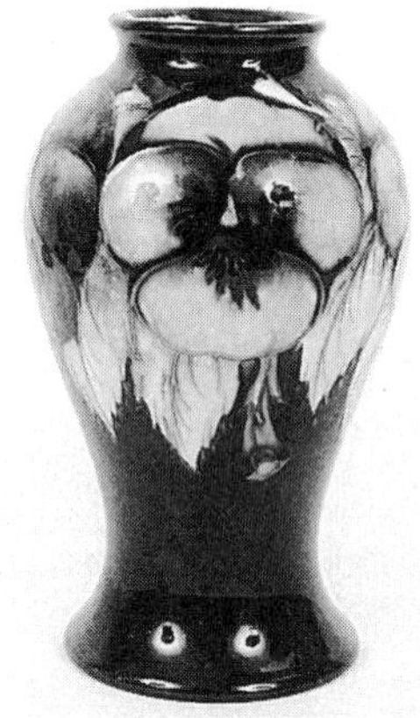

l. A William Moorcroft Pansy pattern vase, c1925, 6in (15cm) high.
£260–320 *HEA*

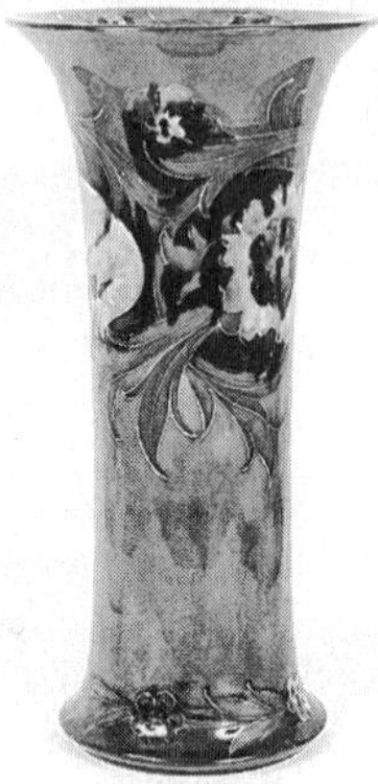

r. A William Moorcroft late Florian Ware vase, c1918, 12in (30.5cm) high.
£650–900 *HEA*

A Bernard Moore flambé vase, decorated with a Viking longship in turquoise and lustrous red against a dawn background, detailed with gilding, printed mark, numbered '1068', c1906, 7½in (19cm) high.
£300–350 *C*

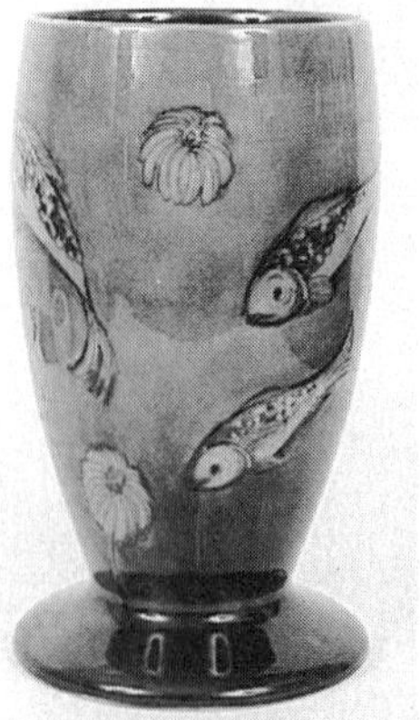

A William Moorcroft Fish and Waterweed pattern vase, under a flambé glaze, 1930s, 9½in (24cm) high.
£1,100–1,300 *HEA*

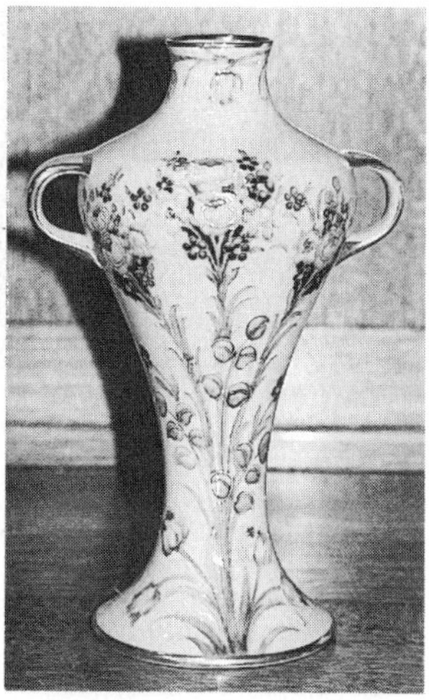

A William Moorcroft Florian Ware vase, with Roses, Tulips and Forget-me-Nots design, c1906, 9in (23cm) high.
£800–950 *RUM*

A William Moorcroft revived Poppy design vase, c1930, 7in (17.5cm) high.
£600–700 *RUM*

A William Moorcroft Landscape design vase, with chevron bands in shades of ochre, red and purple, c1926, 10in (25cm) high.
£3,000–3,500 *RUM*

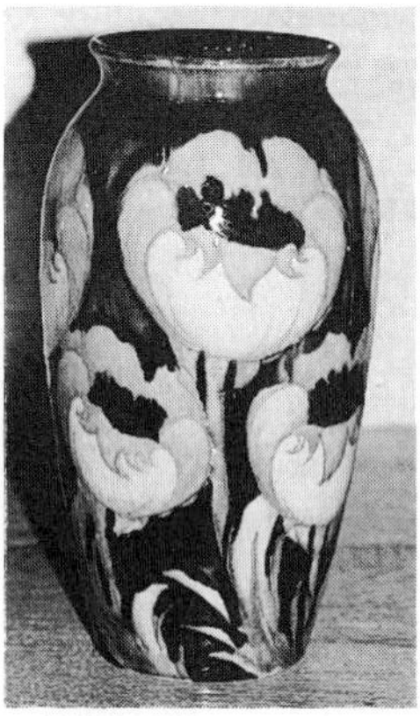

r. A William Moorcroft ochre Big Poppy design vase, c1925, 8in (20.5cm) high.
£700–800 *RUM*

A Rozenberg eggshell porcelain cup and saucer, with design by Roelof Sterken, c1902, saucer 5in (12.5cm) diam.
£700–800 *OO*

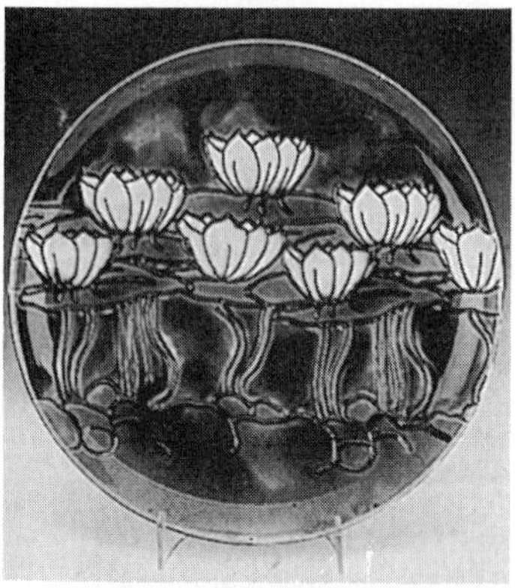

A Minton Secessionist charger, painted with water lillies in shades of purple and blue, printed factory marks, 15in (38cm) diam.
£450–500 *CSK*

A William Moorcroft Spanish design vase, c1915, 9in (23cm) high.
£1,200–1,400 *RUM*

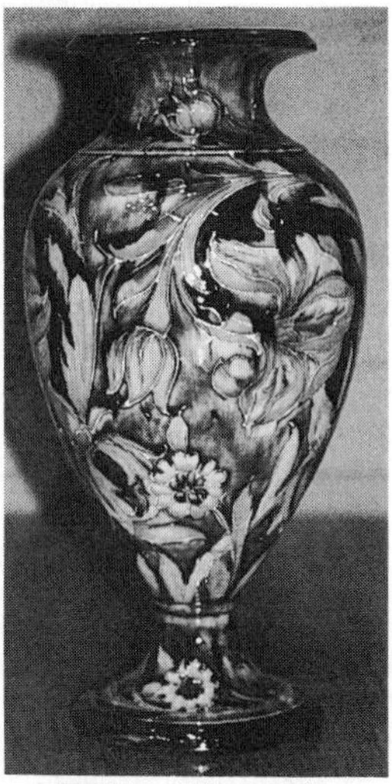

A William Moorcroft Spanish design vase, c1915, 12in (30.5cm) high.
£1,900–2,000 *RUM*

A Rozenburg vase, with design by J. Van Rossum, c1896, 7in (17.5cm) high.
£500–600 *OO*

A Sèvres Art Nouveau pottery vase, with green ground, and gold drips from rim, minor glaze frits, printed factory marks, 10½in (26cm) high.
£500–700 *CSK*

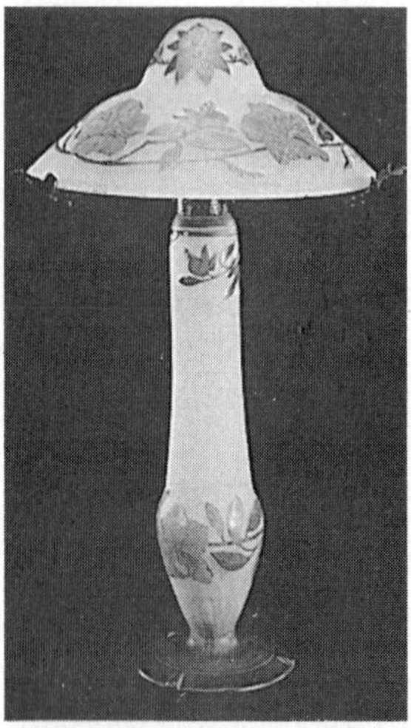

A colourless glass lamp and shade, by André Delatte, internally decorated with white streaks, overlaid with pink and etched with flowering branches, the base and shade marked 'A Delatte Nancy', the shade with 2 cameo marks, 1920s, 22in (56cm) high.
£1,800–2,000 *S*

A Rozenberg eggshell porcelain vase, with design by Sam Schellink, c1904, 8¼in (21cm) high.
£1,800–2,000 *OO*

A Van Briggle stoneware vase, moulded in low relief with peacock feather motifs, covered in a puce and green mottled matt glaze, incised monogram 'Colo Sprgs 761', 6in (15cm) high.
£350–550 *CSK*

Cameo Glass

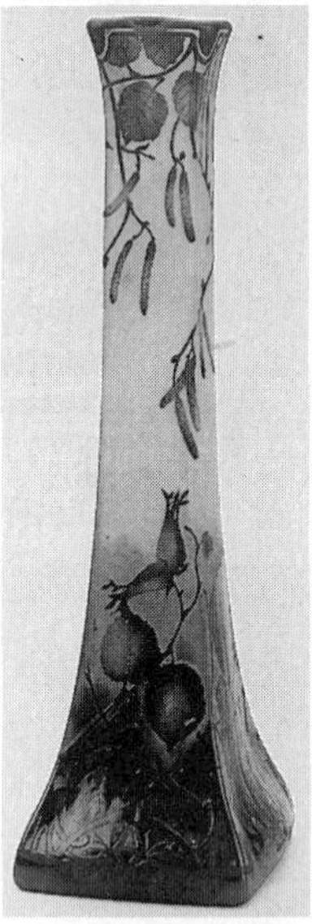

A Daum cameo grey glass vase, overlaid in orange and brown, acid-etched and carved with pendant sprays of catkins, cameo factory mark, 19¼in (49cm) high.
£1,500–1,800 *CSK*

A Daum etched and enamelled painted square glass vase, depicting sailing boats in orange, yellow, blue and green, engraved mark 'Daum Nancy', 4½in (11cm) high.
£500–600 *AH*

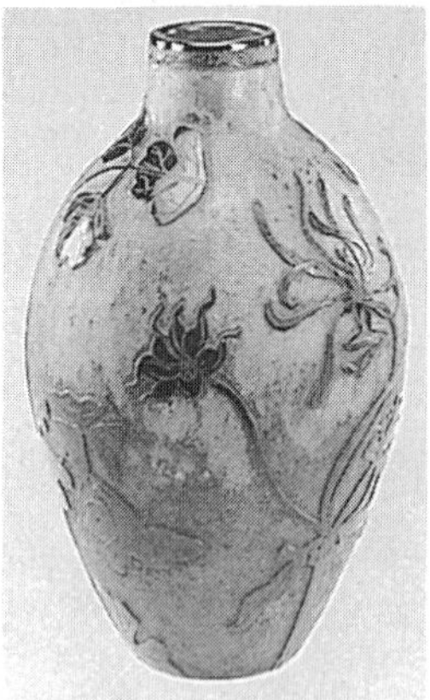

A Nerine vase, in colourless glass overlaid with pink and green, etched with flowering sprays against a textured ground, the underside with gilded inscription 'Daum Nancy fecit d'après E. Lachenal 1896', 10in (25cm) high.
£1,700–2,000 *S*

A ribbed vase, in pale yellow glass, horizontally ribbed with acid textured ground, etched mark 'Daum Nancy France' with a Cross of Lorraine, 1920s, 8in (20cm) high.
£800–1,000 *S*

A Daum enamelled cameo 'Summer' glass vase, the mottled yellow-green and blue frosted glass body etched and enamel painted in sunny waterfront riverscape with trees and purple mountains beyond, inscribed in black on base 'Daum Nancy' and 'HF', 9½in (24cm) high.
£5,000–6,000 *SK(B)*

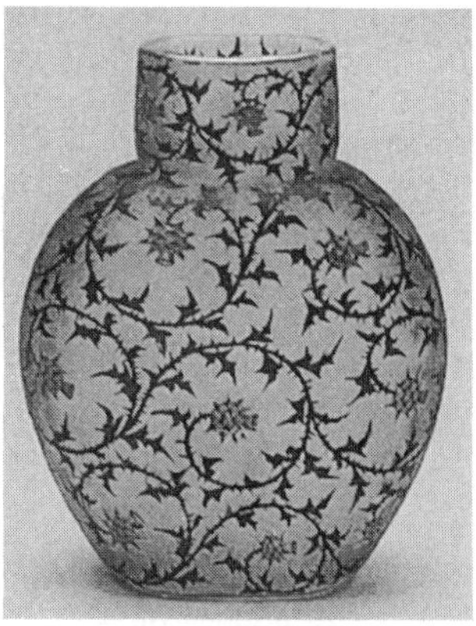

A Daum enamelled cameo glass thistle vase, etched overall with scrolling thorny branches and gold and red enamel painted thistle burrs, gold borders and 'Daum Nancy' on base, 7in (17.5cm) high.
£1,700–2,000 *SK(B)*

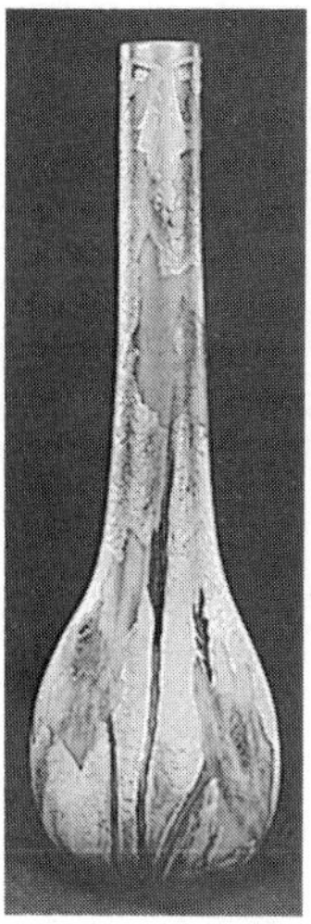

l. A Legras Indiana vase, in flame red glass with green foil inclusions, overlaid with clear glass with large poppy heads in low relief, on an acid finished ground of verdigris colour, the neck with gilt collar of geometric design, chipped, the underside with gilded maker's monogram and 'Indiana', chip to base, c1900, 24in (61cm) high.
£2,200–2,700 *S*

A Gallé cameo glass lamp base, the yellow glass overlaid with deep blue and etched with flowering chrysanthemums, light wheel finishing, the rim with metal mount, cameo marks 'Gallé', c1900, 21½in (55cm) high.
£4,000–6,000 *C*

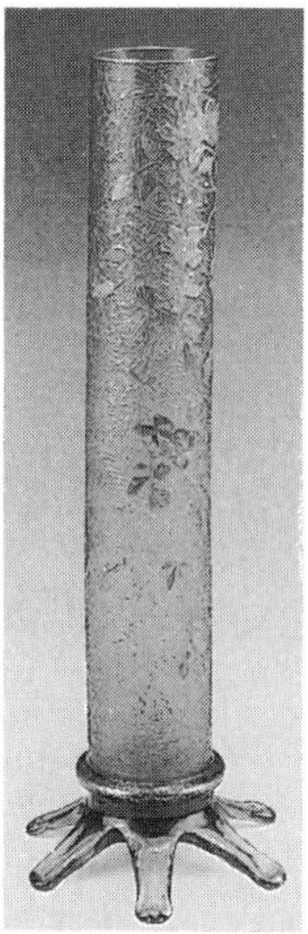

l. A Gallé smoked glass vase, decorated in raised gilt with pendant sprays of apple blossom, carved 'Gallé 1884', 16in (40.5cm) high.
£800–900 *CSK*

A Le Verre Français vase, with narrow neck and everted rim, mottled pink and yellow glass overlaid in mottled brown, fading to orange, with pendant sprays of columbine, on domed foot, incised factory mark, 18½in (47cm) high.
£1,000–1,500 *CSK*

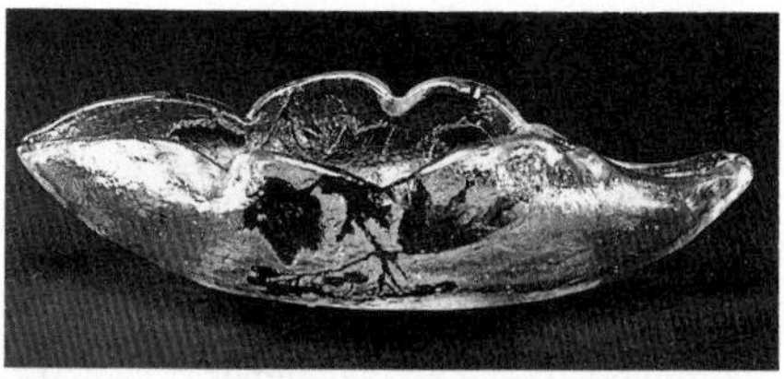

A redcurrant coupe in clear glass, overlaid with pink and etched with flowering redcurrants, the ground textured and fire polished, cameo mark 'Gallé', c1900, 11½in (29cm) wide.
£1,500–2,000 *S*

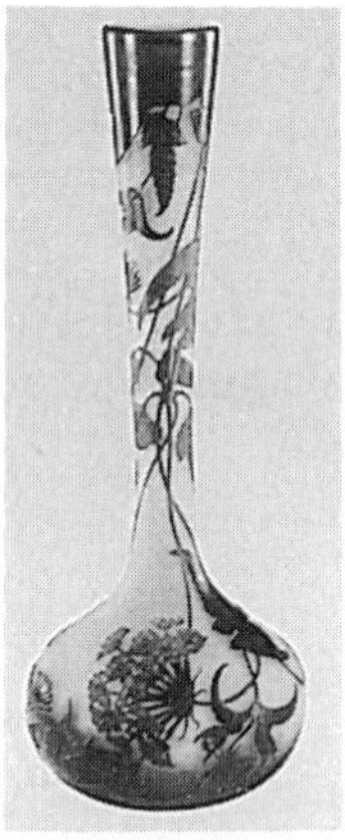

A grey glass vase, by Emile Gallé, internally decorated with pink at the neck and base, overlaid with purple and brown and etched with flowering branches, cameo mark 'Gallé' with star, after 1904, 23in (58cm) high.
£2,000–2,500 *S*

l. A Gallé cameo vase, the yellow glass overlaid in brown, acid-etched and carved with trees overlooking a river, cameo signature 'Gallé', 6½in (16.5cm) high.
£950–1,100 *CSK*

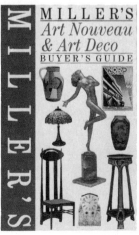

A French smoked glass dish, in the manner of Gallé, trefoil with inverted rim, the exterior textured with fine foliage, the interior enamelled in colours and gilt with sprays of thistles, 9½in (24cm) wide, and 2 other enamelled glass bowls.
£500–600 *CSK*

A Gallé acid-etched and carved cameo glass shade, of bell form, the frosted glass overlaid in orange with pendant trails of fruit and flowering squash, cameo signature 'Gallé', 13½in (34cm) diam.
£1,000–1,200 *CSK*

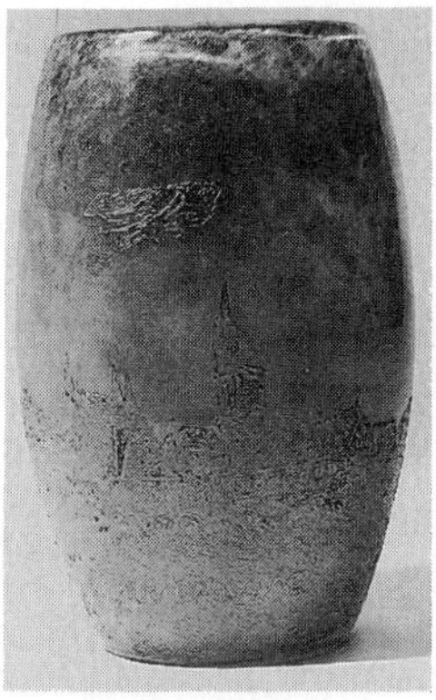

A Müller Frères commemorative vase, the yellow cased glass flecked with pink and blue around the rim, intaglio etched with a bi-plane flying over Strasbourg, with indistinct inscription '5 May 1928', etched factory mark, 6½in (16.5cm) high.
£550–750 *CSK*

Glass

A Quezal iridescent glass thistle shade, amber glass decorated with green and yellow feathers, beneath applied fine random trails, etched factory mark, 5½in (14cm) high, and a Quezal iridescent amber glass ribbed bell shade.
£200–300 *CSK*

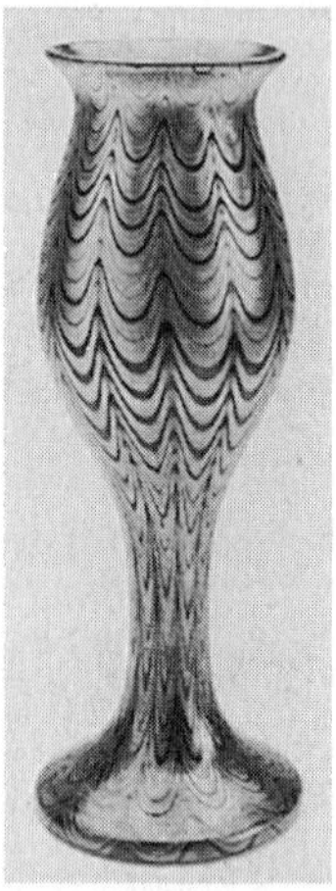

A Loetz Art glass vase, the amber cased to luminescent crimson red glass, with lustrous golden combed iridescent surface, recessed pontil marked 'Loetz Austria', 12½in (32cm) high.
£2,000–2,500 *SK(B)*

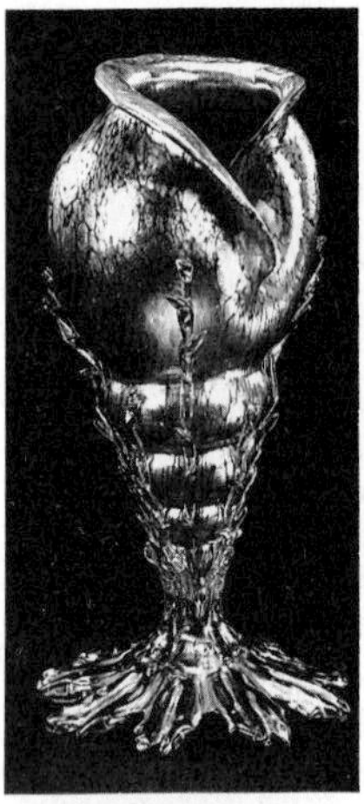

A Loetz shell form candleholder, in yellow pink glass, with blue iridescence, set in clear, slightly iridescent glass with applications, the interior with moulded mark 'Regsns 787802 FGC', c1900, 12in (30cm) high.
£1,300–1,800 *S*

An Austrian Secession mounted glass vase, with clear body, the flat flange mounts pierced with typically formalised geometric design, remains of manufacturer's paper label, mounts stamped 'Austria 925', c1905, 5in (13cm) high.
£1,100–1,300 *C*

A Loetz tapered brown tinted and blue iridescent decorated vase, with crimped rim, signed 'Loetz, Austria' on base, 10in (25cm) high.
£1,400–1,700 *AG*

A Frederick Carder Steuben intarsia vase, stemmed bowl form of colourless crystal, internally decorated with true blue repeating leaf and vine design, blue lip wrap and unusual six-sided blue base below colourless stem, inscribed 'Fredek Carder' at base, 7in (17.5cm) diam.
£6,000–7,000 *SK(B)*

r. A Steuben gold aurene on alabaster bowl, shape 6283, of cream white crystal, lightly overlaid with lustrous gold aurene, acid-etched in floral Chinese pattern, 7in (17.5cm) diam.
£1,800–2,200 *SK(B)*

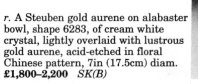

Metalware

An Erhardt & Sohne biscuit barrel, of wood inlaid in brass with floral cartouches, the handles cast in the form of stylised birds, with brass liner, 9in (23cm) high.
£200–400 *CSK*

A W.M.F. silvered pewter centrepiece, with supporting glass dish and solifleur, each etched with flowers, stamped marks, 29½in (75cm) high.
£1,000–1,200 *CSK*

An 'Ornery Cuss', by Bob Parks, in bronze, copper and brown patina, inscribed, set on a wood base, 19in (48cm) high.
£800–1,000 *LHA*

A set of 6 Art Nouveau silver and enamel liqueur glasses, gilt lines, the base with blue enamel tudor rose, in original fitted case stamped 'JP', Birmingham, 1919, 3in (8cm) high.
£450–550 *CSK*

An electroplated tea service, designed by Paul Follot, comprising: teapot, sugar bowl and cover, cream jug and 2 cups with saucers, cast with deeply fluted details, each piece with stamped manufacturer's marks, all but the saucers signed 'P. Follot', c1900, teapot 7½in (19cm) high.
£2,600–3,200 *C*

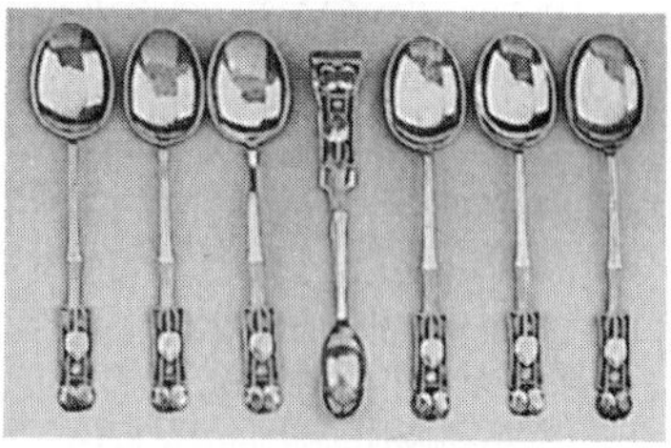

A set of 6 silver Liberty teaspoons and sugar tongs, the design attributed to Archibald Knox, the handles cast in relief with stylised honesty, in original fitted case, Birmingham 1923.
£360–450 *CSK*

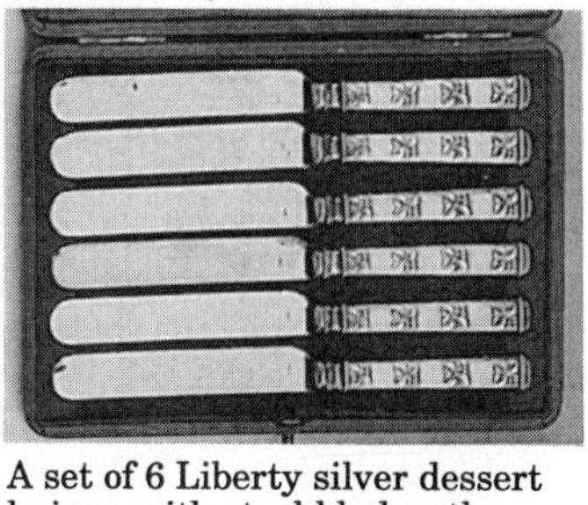

A set of 6 Liberty silver dessert knives, with steel blades, the square section handles cast in relief with stylised berries and leaf design, in original fitted case, London 1908.
£200–300 *CSK*

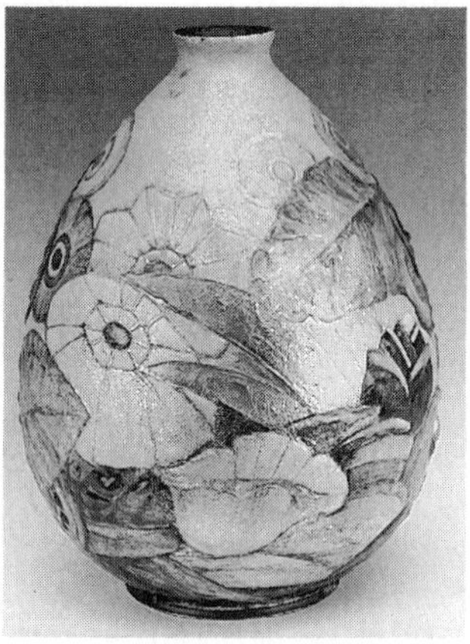

A Limoges enamelled metal vase, by Camille Fauré, with narrow neck and everted rim, geometric flowers and foliage in shades of green and white, enamelled factory mark, 12in (31cm) high.
£1,500–1,700 *CSK*

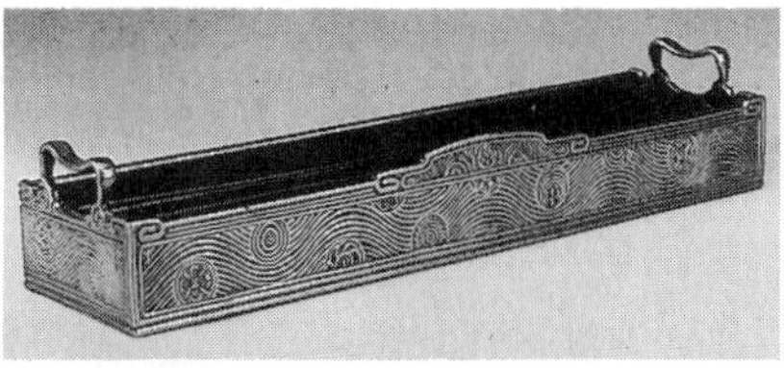

A silver vase, by Eugène Feuillatre, the front stamped in relief with a cartouche with an Art Nouveau maiden, above a frieze of waves, stamped monogram and French poinçons, 4½in (11.5cm) high, in original fitted box.
£420–520 *CSK*

l. An Arts & Crafts brass and metal heater tray, designed by Thomas Jeckyll, stamped registration mark, 18in (46cm) long.
£600–700 *CSK*

A Tiffany bronze fern planter, dark patina with green and red highlights, on a deeply sculpted marsh marigold interwoven motif, impressed 'Tiffany Studios New York 834', 10½in (27cm) diam.
£6,500–7,500 *SK(B)*

Six electroplated cake forks, designed by Charles Rennie Mackintosh for Miss Cranston's Tearooms, Glasgow, each with trefoil end, stamped 'Miss Cranston's', 3 also stamped 'B', and 3 teaspoons of variant trefoil design, each stamped in plain lettering 'Miss Cranston's', with imitation hallmark, c1905.
£2,000–2,500 *C*

A Liberty Tudric pewter clock, designed by Archibald Knox, with a copper dial and blue enamel centre, stamped 'Tudric 0371', c1905, 9in (22.5cm) high.
£1,200–1,700 *C*

A W.M.F. figural mirror, cast with a young woman gazing at her reflection, the wooden back with easel support, in Britannia metal, c1900, 14½in (37cm) high.
£1,000–1,500 *S*

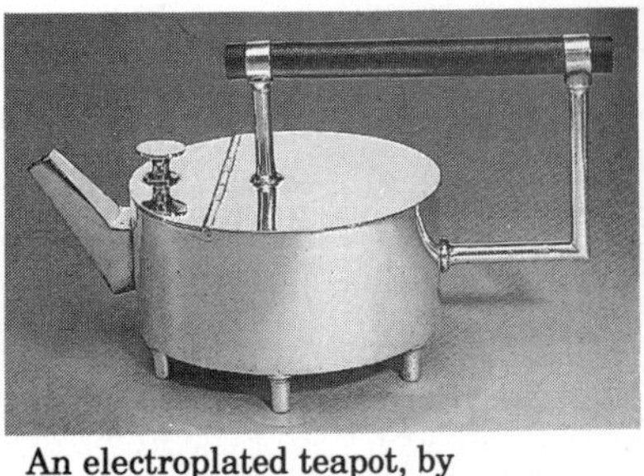

An electroplated teapot, by Christopher Dresser for James Dixon & Sons, the shallow drum-shaped body with hinged lid and angular ebonised handle, on 6 small cylindrical feet, the underside with designer's facsimile signature 'Ch. Dresser', maker's mark and numbered '2275', the 2 small end sections on the handle replaced, 1879, 4½in (11.5cm) diam.
£66,000–72,000 *S*

This teapot is only the second version known of this particular form. It is one of a series of teapots conceived in dramatic geometric forms which are known through the very few surviving examples, and which are documented in a costing book of 1879 for the manufacturers, James Dixon & Sons.

A pair of Arts and Crafts copper and brass wall lights, with brass shades, and an adjustable ceiling light.
£550–650 *CSK*

Lighting

A reverse painted scenic lamp, inscribed on lower edge '2360 Jefferson M.G.', mounted on a two-socket bronzed metal urn form base with foliate devices, 21in (53.5cm) high.
£700–900 *SK(B)*

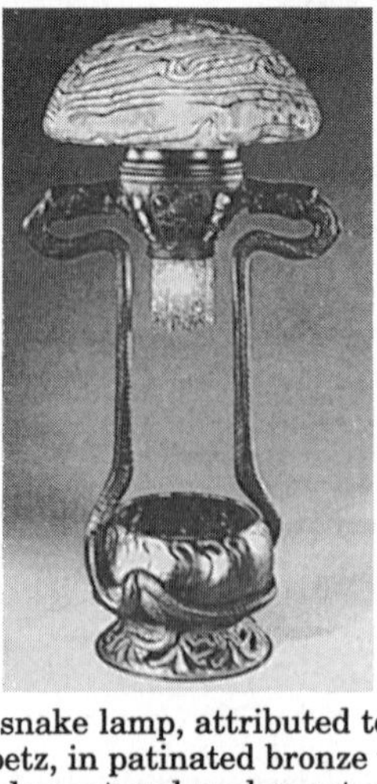

A snake lamp, attributed to Loetz, in patinated bronze with iridescent and opalescent glass shade, with lustrous glazed earthenware bowl, lamp numbered '780', bowl stamped 'Heliosine Ware Austria', and incised 'N. 21074', c1900, 28½in (72.5cm) high.
£4,600–5,000 *S*

A table lamp, with iridescent yellow/green glass shade, supported on a green patinated bronze base cast with pine cones and leaves, c1900, 18in (45.5cm) high.
£900–1,200 *S*

A Handel Peacock lamp, by George Palme, the peacocks cameo etched and enamel painted in metallic gold against a burgundy red background with orange and blue blossoms, green leaves and amber highlights, inscribed at rim 'Handel 7126 Pal', mounted on tripartite gilt metal shaft and simulated onyx platform base, 24in (61cm) high.
£13,500–15,000 *SK(B)*

A reverse painted table lamp, the flared dome Copley shade with a green, purple and white canopy top bordered by a colourful leafy urn and scroll motif on a yellow background, stamped 'Pairpoint Corp.', mounted on a copper coloured urn form metal base stamped with 'Pairpoint' logo, 22in (55.5cm) high.
£1,100–1,300 *SK(B)*

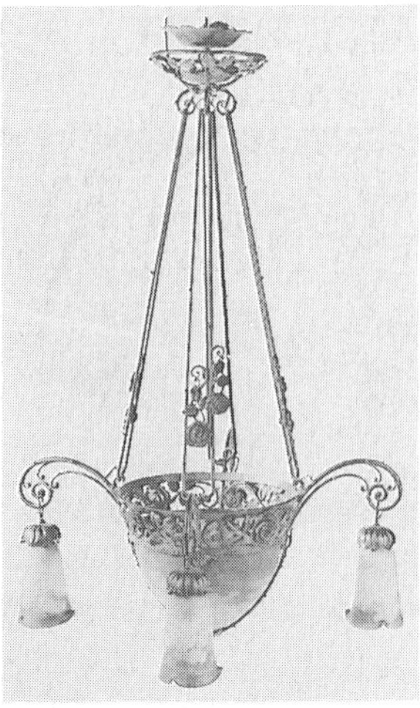

A frosted glass and wrought iron hanging light, the foliate cast ceiling mount with 4 rods supporting a circular frame fitted with a graduated purple to orange shade and 4 bell shades, the frame decorated with leafy flowers, acid stamped 'Muller Frères, Luneville', 40in (101.5cm) high.
£1,200–1,400 *Bon*

An Art Deco glass lamp, decorated with stylised lipstick red over black amethyst, the back deeply cut with angular stripes and geometric devices, a matching cone shade and internally lit shaft mounted on a wrought iron base with applied flowers, the shade signed 'Degue' in cameo, 16½in (42cm) high.
£1,650–1,850 *SK(B)*

A globe lamp, by Handel, the orange/amber sphere with a painted parrot on branches at front and back, the original metal hardware tassel and cap painted green, shade 10in (25cm) diam.
£350–550 *SK(B)*

A Treasure Island lamp, painted in shades of blue, green, grey and brown, signed 'Handel 6891', and marked on ring, mounted on a metal base with grey patina to match the shade, 24¼in (61.5cm) high.
£5,500–6,500 *SK(B)*

l. A reverse painted scenic lamp, painted with white, green, blue, yellow, and orange, signed 'Handel 6939', and 'Handel Lamps' on ring, mounted on a three-socket bronzed metal base with threaded label, 23in (58.5cm) high.
£3,000–4,000 *SK(B)*

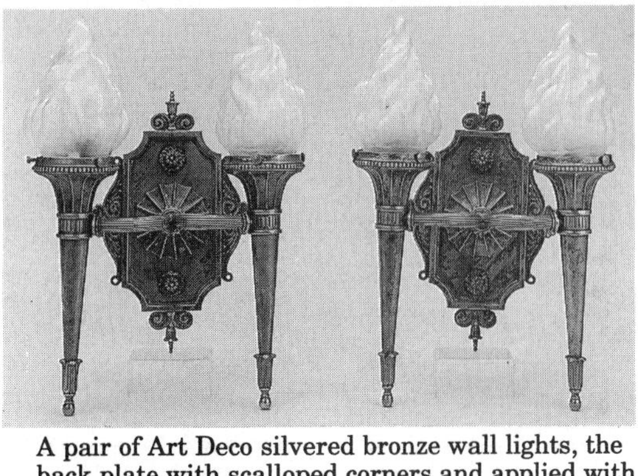

A pair of Art Deco silvered bronze wall lights, the back plate with scalloped corners and applied with rosettes, supporting 2 torchère style fittings with flamiform shades, 16½in (42cm) high.
£500–600 *CSK*

ART DECO
Furniture

A panelled oak wardrobe, by Robert Thompson, the 'Mouseman', with wrought iron door furniture, carved with mouse cypher, 54in (137cm) wide.
£3,500–4,000 *C*

An oak armchair, by Robert Thompson, the 'Mouseman', with a leather back and seat, the mouse carved on the front leg.
£550–650 *AAV*

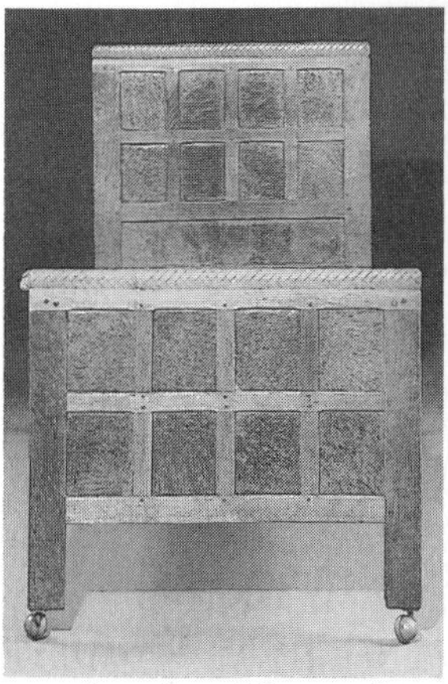

An oak and burr oak panelled single bed, by Robert Thompson, the 'Mouseman', with hand carved decoration and carved mouse signature, 79in (200.5cm) wide.
£550–650 *CSK*

A panelled oak dressing table and stool, by Robert Thompson, the 'Mouseman', the tapered upright mirror support carved with the mouse cypher, the stool with brown hide strapping, 54½in (138cm) wide.
£2,000–2,500 *C*

An oak stool, by Robert Thompson, the 'Mouseman', the adzed seat raised on square and octagonal supports united by stretchers, carved with a mouse, 32½in (82.5cm) long.
£350–550 *P*

A limed oak stool, by Jean Michel Frank, stamped on the underside, re-upholstered, c1920, 15in (38.5cm) wide.
£4,000–4,500 *S*

A plywood table, designed by Marcel Breuer for Isokon, formed from a single piece of cut and bent laminated plywood, the underside stamped 'Made in Estonia', 1936, 23¾in (60.5cm) wide.
£520–650 *C*

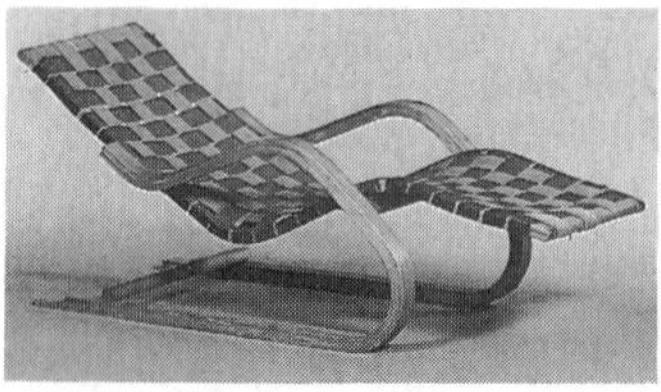

A chaise longue 'Armchair 39', by Alvar Aalto, made by Artek, on laminated beechwood with cotton webbing seat, 1936–37, 65½in (166cm) long.
£3,000–4,000 *S*

A gentleman's limed oak wardrobe, by Heal's, with mirror and tie-rack, and an inset circular label, 36in (91.5cm) wide.
£400–500 *P*

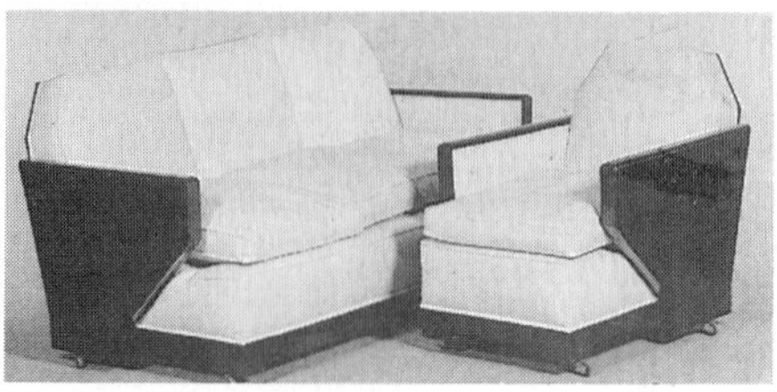

A salon suite, comprising a three-seater sofa and 2 armchairs, in stained mahogany upholstered in white leather, on casters, c1930, sofa 73in (185cm) long.
£2,000–2,500 *S*

A set of 6 chairs, by Louis Sognot, the chromium plated tubular steel frame upholstered in leather, c1928, 28½in (72.5cm) wide.
£3,000–4,000 *S*

Nine dining chairs, designed by Ambrose Heal for Heal's, one in chestnut, one oak and 7 walnut, with hair seating, number 'D1020', designed in 1925, 38½in (97cm) high.
£1,500–2,000 *S*

An Art Deco table mirror, the black glass base surmounted by a circular stepped silvered bronze base supporting a disc fitted with a mirror, 20½in (52cm) high.
£420–500 *CSK*

An Art Deco kingwood and ash secrétaire side cabinet, with 2 open shelves above a fall front enclosing a fitted interior and 2 cupboard doors flanked by 2 large bowed doors, on a plinth base, 80in (203cm) wide.
£500–700 *CSK*

A bent and laminated plywood table, designed by Marcel Breuer for the Isobar at the Isokon Lawn Road flats, the top bent to overhang on 2 sides, tapering angled plywood legs, the open ends with cut plywood bracing panels below the top, c1936, 27in (68.5cm) square.
£4,000–5,000 *C*

An Art Deco ebonised and gilt stool, the padded seat upholstered in contemporary black and gold floral brocade, c1920.
£650–950 *C*

An Art Deco style wall mirror, the frame of simulated shagreen with chrome stringing, 32½in (82.5cm) high.
£250–350 *CSK*

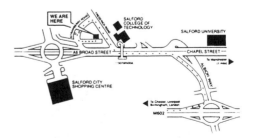

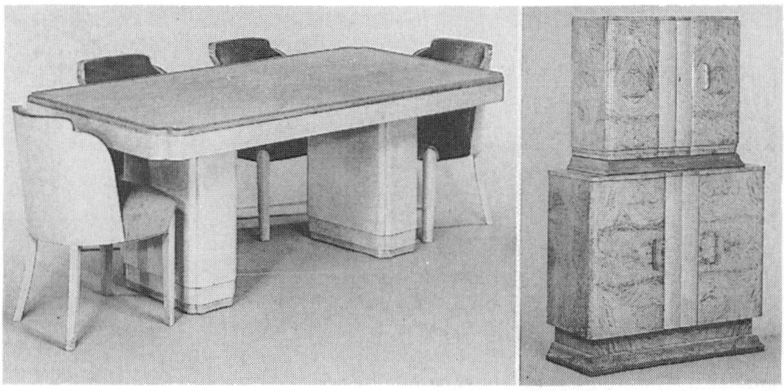

A dining room suite, comprising: a table, 6 side chairs, cocktail cabinet and standard lamp, in light wood veneer, the chairs with cloud-shaped backs, c1930, table 39in (99cm) wide.
£2,000–2,500 *S*

A Templeton's Axminster tufted wool carpet, designed by Frank Brangwyn, decorated with a polychrome abstract floral design incorporating a central quatrefoil cartouche, with a mushroom border and woven monogram 'FB', c1930, 180 by 140in (458 by 358cm).
£3,000–4,000 *C*

A maple veneered dining room suite, by N. Norman, c1930, 39in (99cm) wide.
£2,000–2,500 *S*

A bentwood trolley, by Alvar Aalto, of bent and laminated wood with painted wheels, c1936, 13in (33cm) wide.
£2,200–2,800 *S*

A limed oak desk, possibly by Maples, the top with damaged leathered inset, 42in (106.5cm) wide, and a limed oak rush-seated chair.
£350–450 *P*

Miller's is a price GUIDE not a price LIST

An oak sideboard, possibly made by the Bath Cabinet Makers, with simulated ebony/ivory octagonal pulls, c1930, 50½in (128.5cm) wide.
£500–700 *P*

A Modernist desk, by Gilbert Rohde for the Herman Miller Furniture Co., No. 3427, the shaped glass top supported on a chromium plated metal frame with circular drawers on one side, c1934, 44in (111.5cm) wide.
£900–1,200 *S*

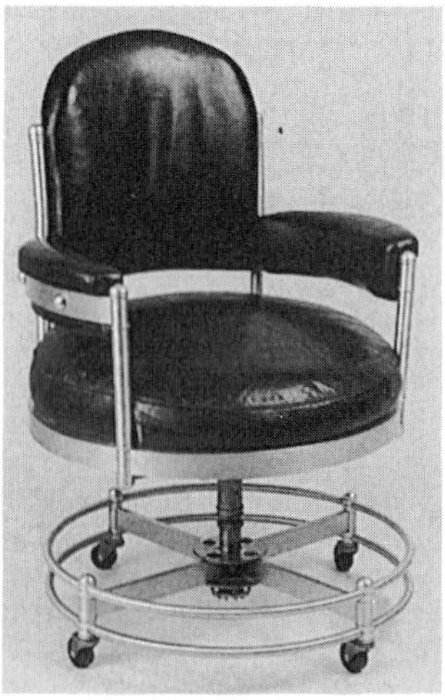

An upholstered aluminium tilting swivel armchair, by Warren McArthur, with original blue leather upholstery on spun aluminium frame with 4 casters, c1935, 38in (96.5cm) high.
£4,300–5,000 *SK(B)*

A palissandre sideboard, by J. & M. Leleu, the mirrored superstructure with 3 glazed cupboard doors above a marble top and 2 short drawers and 3 doors, 66½in (169cm) wide, and a matching buffet with a marble top.
£1,000–1,500 *CSK*

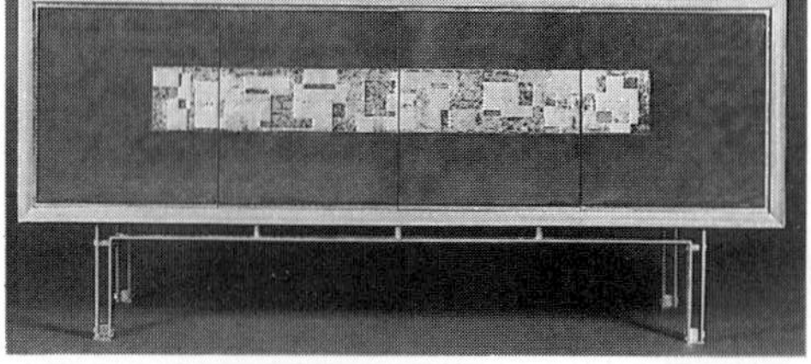

l. A gilt decorated, lacquered and mahogany sideboard, by J. Leleu, with 4 geometrically decorated doors, on wrought iron supports, 78½in (199.5cm) wide.
£850–1,000 *CSK*

Lalique Glass

A Lalique 'Ondines' pattern opalescent glass fruit bowl, moulded with 6 mermaids within swirling water and with blue stained finish, engraved 'R. Lalique, France', numbered '381', 8in (20cm) diam.
£500–600 *CAG*

A 'Filix' clear and frosted glass bowl, No. 389, the exterior moulded in relief with spear-shaped foliage, wheelcut 'R. Lalique, France', 13in (33cm) diam.
£600–700 *CSK*

A 'Degas' frosted glass box and cover, No. 66, the top with a finial moulded in the form of a ballerina, the tutu forming the cover, engraved 'R. Lalique', and numbered, slight damage, 3in (7.5cm) diam.
£450–550 *CSK*

l. A cire perdue box and cover, the oviform box moulded with spiralling berried branches, the conical cover with a meandering lizard stalking an insect, the cover and base inscribed 'R. Lalique', numbered on base '323-2, 4½in (11.5cm) high.
£17,000–20,000 *CNY*

Lalique's cire perdue pieces were not mass produced and, as a result, are very rare today.

A 'Primavères' opalescent glass bowl, No. 86, the exterior moulded in relief with a band of spring flowers, with traces of blue staining, stencil-etched 'R. Lalique', slight damage, 8in (20cm) diam.
£350–450 *CSK*

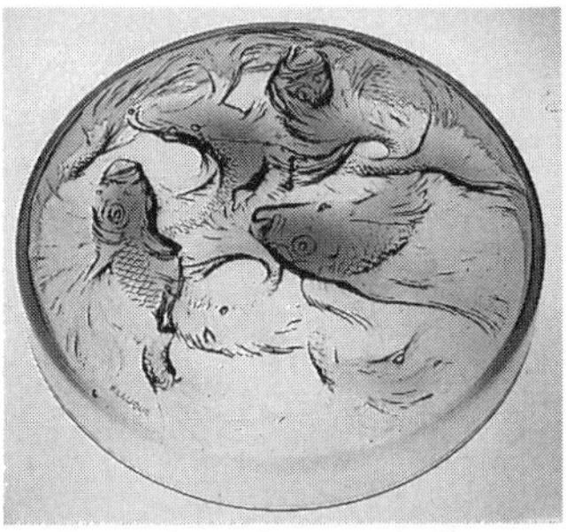

A 'Cyprins' opalescent amber glass box cover, No. 42, the underside moulded in relief with fan-tailed goldfish, moulded 'R. Lalique', slight damage, 10in (25cm) diam.
£600–800 *CSK*

An 'Amour Assis' frosted glass powder box and cover, the cover surmounted by a seated cherub, the sides with flowers and foliage, moulded 'R. Lalique', 4½in (11.5cm) diam.
£1,600–2,000 *CSK*

A 'Perruches' opalescent glass bowl, No. 419, moulded in relief with a band of budgerigars perched on foliage, stencil-etched 'R. Lalique', slight damage, 9½in (24cm) diam.
£2,000–3,000 *CSK*

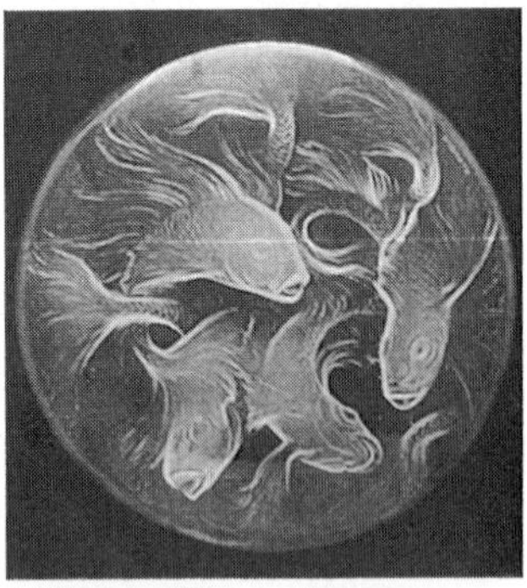

A 'Cyprins' box and cover, Marcilhac, No. 42, in opalescent glass, the cover moulded with swimming fish, moulded mark 'R. Lalique', 10½in (26cm) diam.
£1,100–1,500 *S*

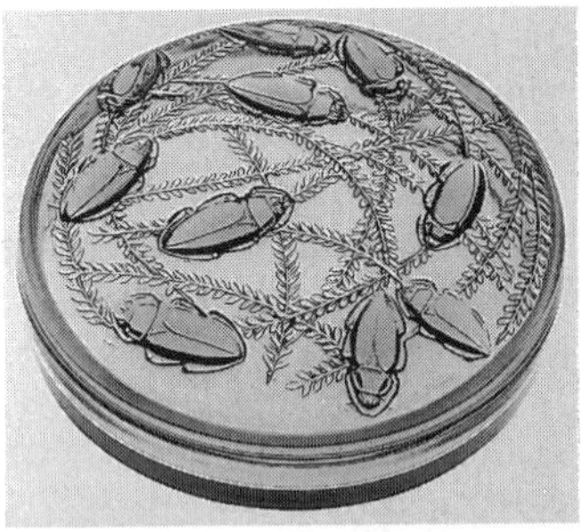

A 'Cleones' amber glass box and cover, No. 49, the cover moulded in relief on the underside with beetles, moulded 'R. Lalique', 6½in (16.5cm) diam.
£600–800 *CSK*

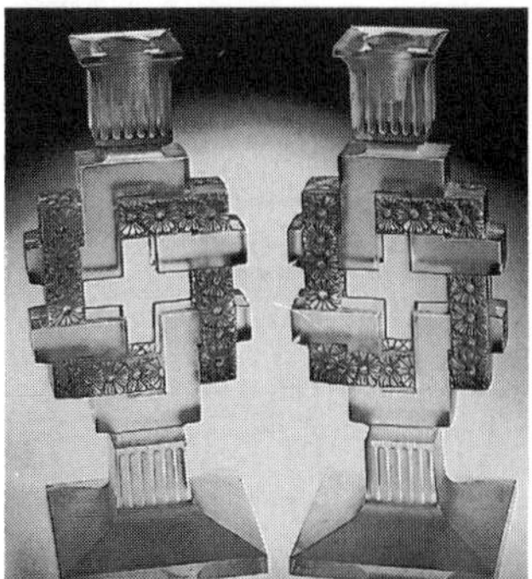

A pair of 'Pâquerettes' clear and frosted glass candlesticks, No. 2123, the reserve stained blue, stencil-etched 'R. Lalique', slight damage, 9½in (24cm) high.
£1,000–1,200 *CSK*

A 'Marienthal' amber glass carafe and stopper, No. 5126, the stopper moulded with fruit and foliage, etched 'R. Lalique', and numbered, 8½in (21.5cm) high.
£300–400 *CSK*

A 'Gaillon' colourless frosted glass ceiling light, Marcilhac, No. 2474, moulded with concentric acanthus leaves, wheelcut mark 'R. Lalique, France', 17½in (44.5cm) diam.
£1,000–1,300 *S*

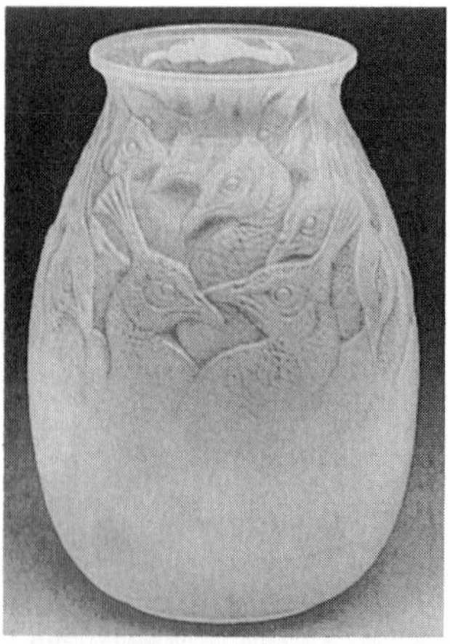

A 'Borromee' opalescent vase, Marcilhac No. 1017, with moulded peacock heads highlighted in grey, engraved 'R. Lalique, France' on base, 9in (22.5cm) high.
£1,200–1,500 *SK(B)*

A 'Oiseau de Feu' surtout de table, Marcilhac, No. 1111, in frosted and clear glass, intaglio moulded with an exotic firebird and 'R. Lalique', after 1922, 12½in (32cm) high.
£11,000–13,000 *S*

A 'Formose' vase, the opaque glass moulded with swimming fish, heightened with blue staining, the underside with engraved mark 'R. Lalique, France, No. 934', after 1924, 6½in (17cm) high.
£900–1,200 *S*

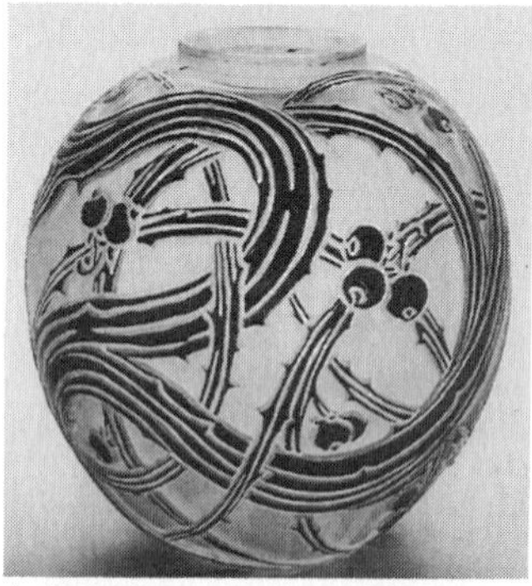

A 'Baies' vase or lamp base, Marcilhac No. 894, decorated with black enamelled berries on thorny brambles, engraved on base rim 'R. Lalique, France' in script, slight damage, 10½in (26.5cm) high.
£700–900 *SK(B)*

l. A 'Fougères' opalescent glass vase, moulded overall with formalised ferns, signed 'R. Lalique, France' and 'No. 996', 7in (17.5cm) high.
£600–800 *P*

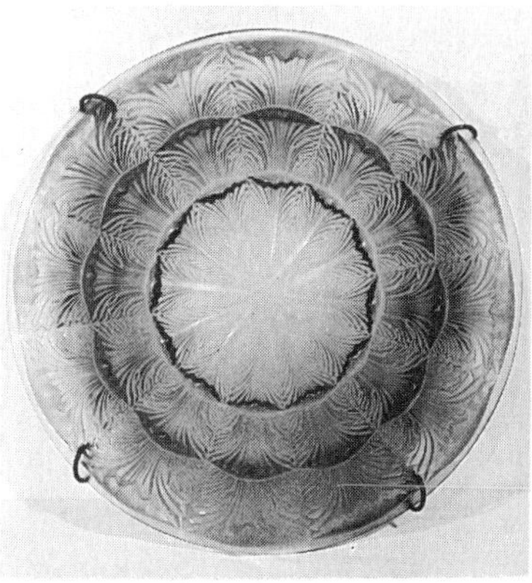

An 'Acanthus' white glass ceiling light, with satin finish and polished relief, signed 'R. Lalique, France' in relief, 18in (45.5cm) wide.
£700–800 *AH*

A glass vase, with frosted curved horn-shaped handles, etched script signature 'Lalique, France', 7½in (18.5cm) high.
£1,300–1,700 *JL*

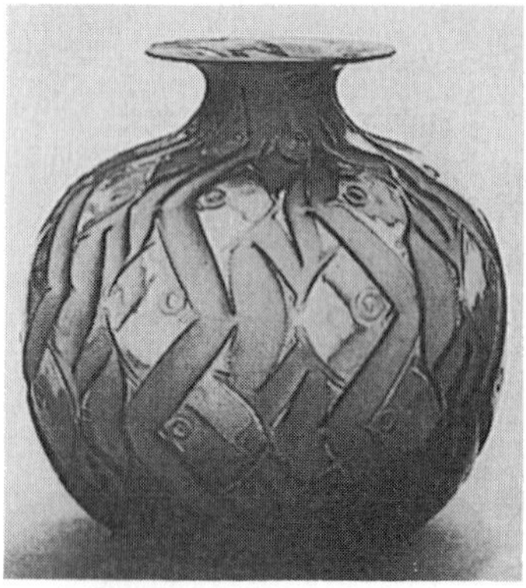

A 'Penthiève' blue glass vase, with everted neck rim, moulded in polished relief with stylised tropical fish swimming in alternate directions, the neck applied with white metal fish, signed 'R. Lalique' on base, 10in (25.5cm) high.
£2,500–3,000 *P*

A Lalique plaque, moulded and part frosted as Christ on the cross on a sunburst ground, etched mark, 12½in (31.5cm) high, on an ebonised stand with light.
£500–600 *Bri*

Seventeen 'Phalsburg' drinking glasses, stencil etched 'R. Lalique'.
£750–900 *CSK*

A 'Pouilly' part service, each piece moulded with leaping fish stained blue, comprising: a carafe and stopper, 6 water, 5 Bordeaux, 5 Burgundy and 5 liqueur glasses, slight damage, stencil-etched 'R. Lalique', carafe 11½in (29.5cm) high.
£2,500–3,000 *CSK*

Glass

An Orrefors 'Ariel' glass bowl, designed by Edvin Ohrstrom, internally decorated with narrow vertical bubbles and muted strawberry pink bands, supported on a solid foot, signed and numbered 'Ariel 1001E', 4½in (11cm) diam.
£200–250 *P*

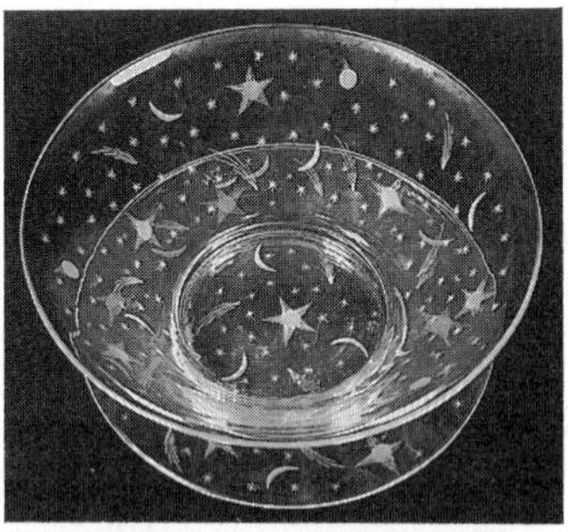

An Orrefors engraved glass flared bowl on stand, by Edward Hald, decorated with shooting stars, crescent moons and planets, engraved factory mark, numbered 'H 584.29 HC', 11in (28cm) diam.
£400–450 *CSK*

A Sabino frosted glass ceiling light, moulded with graduated roundels and cloud-like scrollwork, moulded 'Sabino Paris Déposé', 10in (25cm) diam.
£200–300 *P*

l. An Art Deco clear glass drinks set, comprising: a faceted decanter with black painted and frosted glass radial patterned sides, 8in (20cm) high, and 6 matching glasses.
£200–300 *AH*

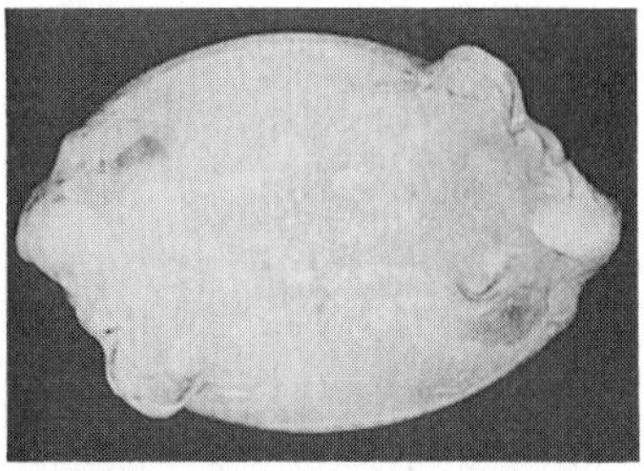

A shallow pâte de verre dish, by Almeric Walter, modelled by Alfred Finot, decorated with maidens' heads, marked, c1920, 9in (22.5cm) wide.
£1,000–1,500 *S*

A pair of clear glass wall lights, with alternating textured and satin glass bands, each with engraved mark 'Daum Nancy France' with a Cross of Lorraine, c1920, 11½in (29.5cm) wide.
£1,000–1,200 *S*

A set of 4 Lobmeyr blown and facet cut drinking glasses and a decanter, designed by Otto Prutscher, c1920, decanter 12in (30.5cm) high.
£1,700–2,200 *C*

This design was manufactured and sold by Lobmeyr until c1935.

A French clear and opalescent glass vase, the exterior of the body moulded in relief with 5 mermaids and dolphins, footrim chipped, 9in (22.5cm) high.
£100–130 *CAG*

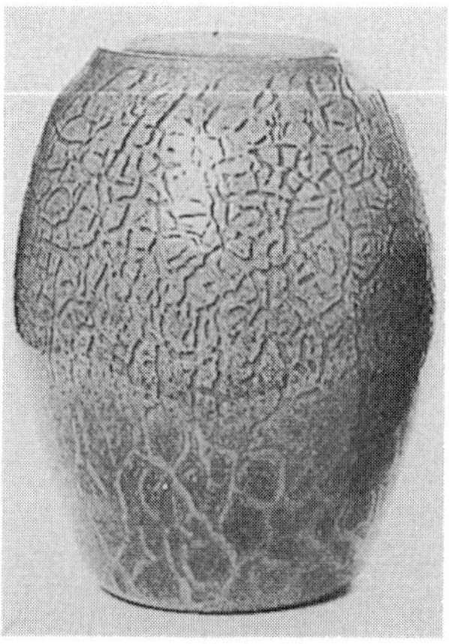

A Monart glass oviform vase, the bright orange interior cased in clear glass and overlaid with a textured 'cracked skin' of mottled grey, 10½in (27cm) high.
£750–950 *P*

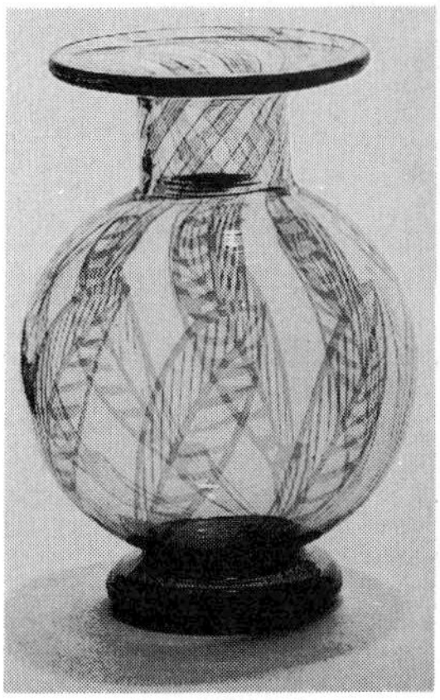

An Orrefors 'Graal' glass vase, designed by Eva Englund, with flared everted rim, the clear body of pink tint, internally decorated with blue foliage and supported on a solid black foot, signed and numbered '3099-80', 4in (10cm) high.
£300–400 *P*

Silver & Metalware

A sterling silver bowl, by Georg Jensen, Denmark, No. 445, the hammered bowl with flaring rim, supported by dramatic foliate and bead openwork on stepped cup base, impressed marks, c1930, 8in (20cm) diam., 558g.
£1,000–1,500 *SK(B)*

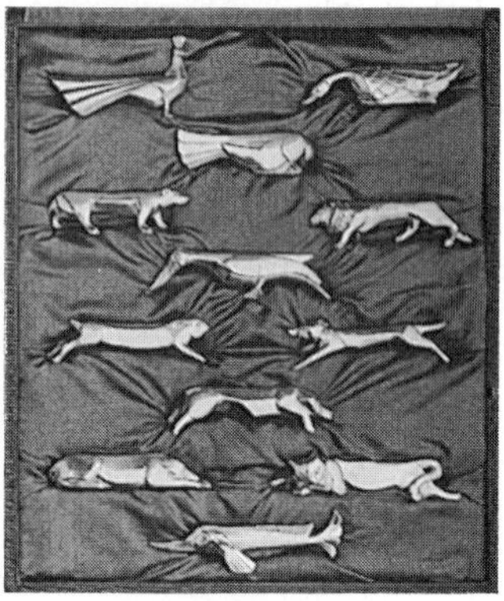

A set of 12 silver coloured metal figural knife rests, each cast as a stylised member of the animal kingdom, each with impressed mark 'Gallia', c1925, 4½in (11cm) long.
£2,000–3,000 *S*

A tazza, by Charles Boyton, in lightly hammered silver, the bowl with a broad rim raised on 6 spheres above a spreading foot, the underside with designer's facsimile signature, maker's mark, London, 1938, 5in (12.5cm) high.
£700–800 *S*

A pair of 5-branch candelabra, with circular sconces, by Georg Jensen, with leaf decorated stems and domed oval bases, 9in (22.5cm) high, 2108g.
£7,500–8,000 *AH*

A 238 piece canteen of table silver, by Georg Jensen, c1930.
£15,000–18,000 *S*

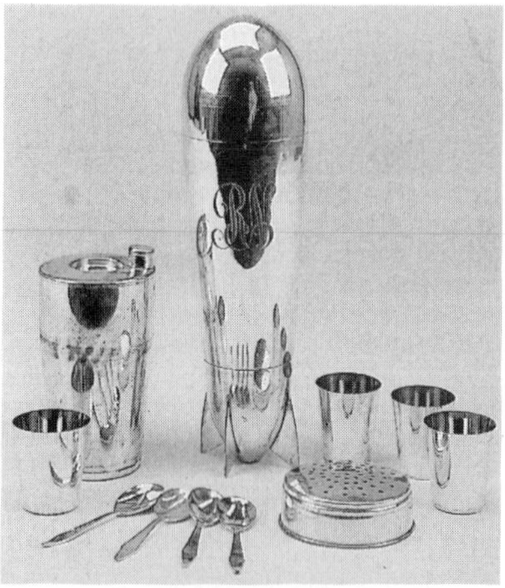

An Art Deco cocktail shaker, in the form of a zeppelin, the electroplate body fitted with 4 spoons and beakers, combination lemon squeezer and strainer, and spirit flask, the front engraved with monogram 'RN', 12in (30.5cm) high.
£800–1,000 *CSK*

A 68 piece canteen of silver coloured metal cutlery, 'Acanthus', designed in 1915 by Johan Rohde for Georg Jensen, the majority with Jensen marks for after 1945.
£3,000–3,500 *S*

An Art Deco silvered metal purse, the mount and the belt hook cast in the form of a bat with outstretched wings, set with green diamanté, 4in (10cm) wide.
£300–400 *CSK*

A pair of pewter doors, for Georg Jensen Inc., New York, the centre raised with an oval wreath of stylised blossoms and berries enclosing inscription, surmounted by a royal crown, with moulded frame and 4 raised flowers, and 2 mounted cylindrical handles.
£5,000–6,000 *CNY*

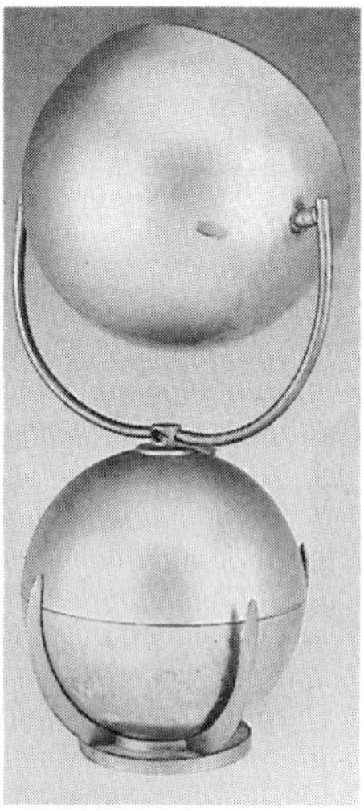

A Modernist chromed metal table lamp, the spherical swivel base resting on stepped circular foot and 3 curved arms, surmounted by swivel dome shade 16in (40.5cm) high.
£1,000–1,200 *CSK*

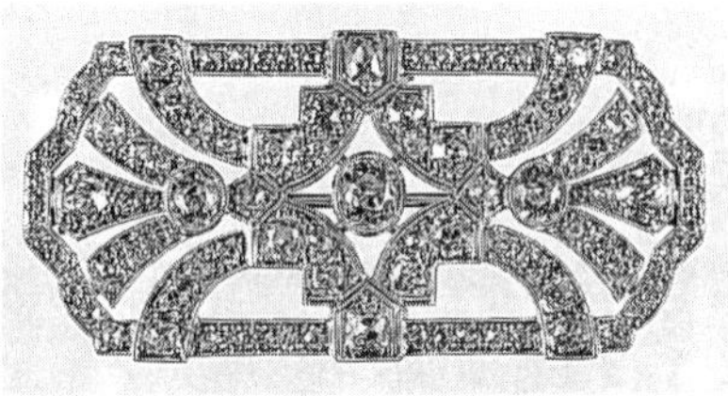

An Art Deco platinum panel brooch, set with brilliant and 8 cut diamonds, 3.50ct total.
£1,700–2,000 *WL*

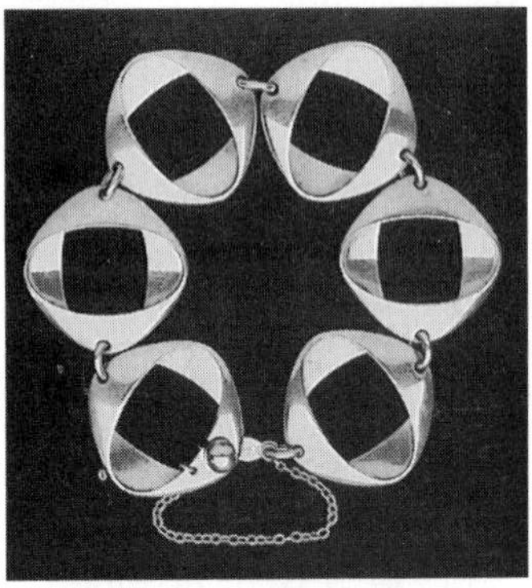

A bracelet, by Georg Jensen, designed by Henning Koppel, with 6 bowed open lozenge-shaped links, stamped with designer's monogram 'HK', and post-1945 manufacturer's mark, c1950.
£1,000–1,200 *C*

A white metal cocktail shaker, by Asprey, modelled in the form of a lantern, with a glass liner, stamped factory marks, '3883', 10½in (26.5cm) high.
£250–300 *CSK*

Sculpture

A German cold painted bronze and ivory figure of Radha, a dancer, cast and carved from a model by Paul Philippe, on a brown onyx base signed 'P. Philippe', early 20thC, 22½in (57.5cm) high.
£5,500–6,500 *CNY*

A French cold painted bronze and ivory figure, 'Adieu', cast and carved from a model by Demêtre Chiparus, inscribed 'Chiparus', stamped '5795', on a stone base, early 20thC, 14½in (37cm) high.
£2,500–3,500 *CNY*

A French parcel silvered bronze and ivory equestrian group of a knight and his lady, cast from a model by Pierre le Faguays, on a brown onyx base, signed, early 20thC, 23in (58.5cm) high.
£14,000–15,000 *CNY*

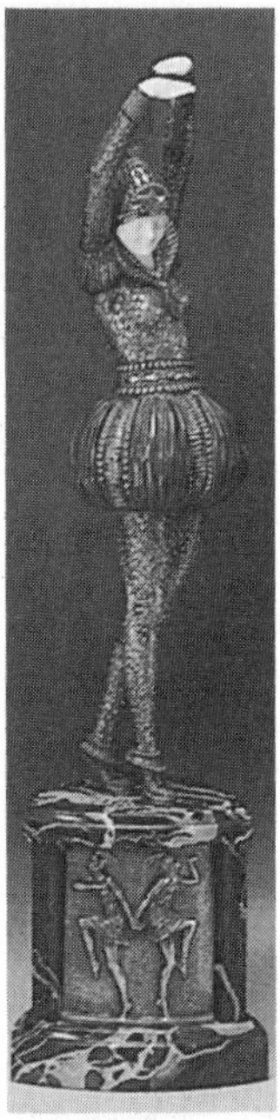

A carved ivory and polychromed bronze figure, 'Bayadère', by Demêtre Chiparus, inscribed, 21in (53cm) high.
£10,000–12,000 *S(NY)*

A German carved and stained ivory, gilt and polychromed bronze figure, 'Autumn Dancer', by Johann Philipp Ferdinand (Fritz) Preiss, inscribed, 14½in (37cm) high.
£5,000–6,000 *S(NY)*

A carved ivory, gilt and polychromed bronze figure, 'Vested Dancer', by Demêtre Chiparus, inscribed, 19½in (49.5cm) high.
£12,000–14,000 *S(NY)*

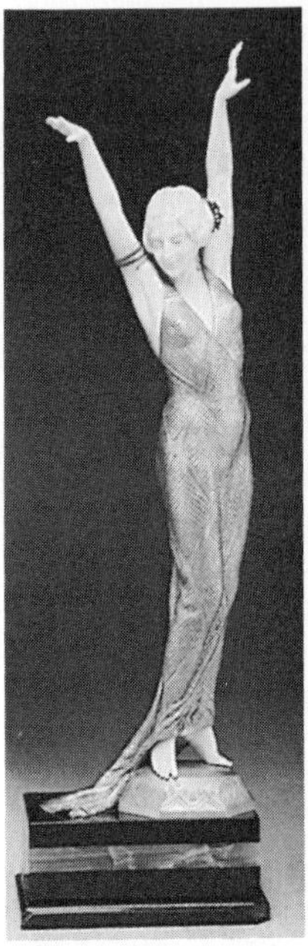

A carved ivory and polychromed bronze figure, 'Serpentina', by Professor Otto Poertzel, inscribed, 24in (61cm) high.
£9,000–11,000 *S(NY)*

A carved ivory and polychromed bronze figure, 'Ayouta', by Demêtre Chiparus, inscribed, 18½in (47cm) high.
£10,000–12,000 *S(NY)*

A French carved ivory, silvered, gilt and polychromed bronze figure, 'Testris', by Demêtre Chiparus, inscribed, 26½in (67.5cm) high.
£32,000–35,000 *S(NY)*

A carved ivory and polychromed bronze figure, entitled 'Civa', by Demêtre Chiparus, 21½in (54.5cm) high.
£27,000–35,000 *S(NY)*

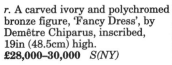

r. A carved ivory and polychromed bronze figure, 'Fancy Dress', by Demêtre Chiparus, inscribed, 19in (48.5cm) high.
£28,000–30,000 *S(NY)*

l. An ivory and polychromed bronze figure group, 'Maiden and Suitor', by Professor Otto Poertzel, inscribed, 21½in (54.5cm) high.
£19,000–22,000 *S(NY)*

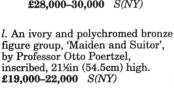

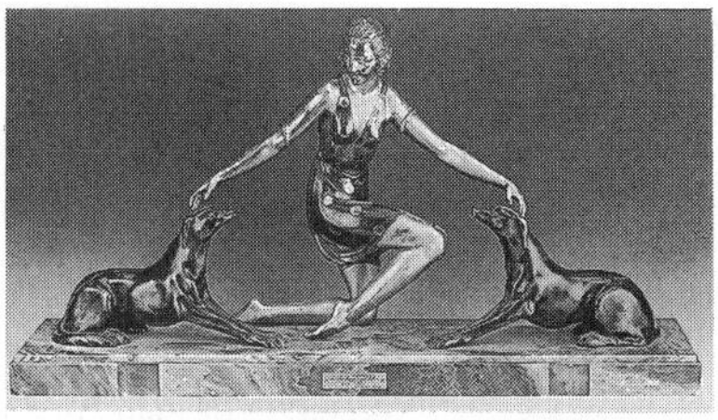

An Art Deco spelter group, cast from a model by Arisse, of a young woman with 2 hounds, in shades of black, silver and gold, on a brown onyx base, base engraved, 33in (83.5cm) long.
£300–400 *CSK*

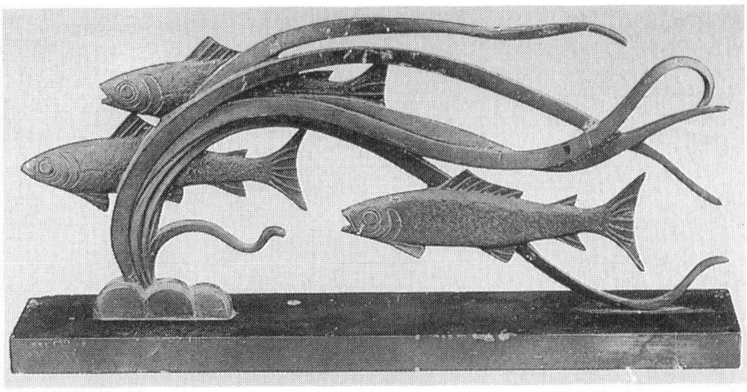

A patinated bronze group, cast from a model by Becquerel, of two-dimensional form depicting fish swimming among waterweeds, on a black basalt base, base inscribed with signature, 15in (38cm) long.
£350–450 *CSK*

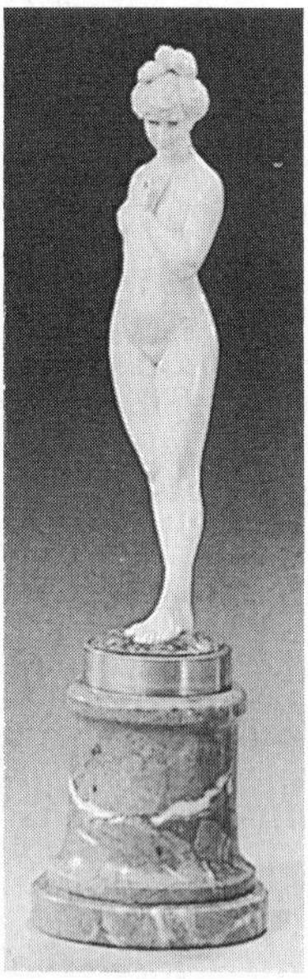

A carved ivory female figure, from a model by Ferdinand Preiss, inscribed and stamped with the Preiss-Kassler foundry seal, early 20thC, on a marble socle, 10in (25cm) high.
£3,000–4,000 *CNY*

A female mask, cast in bronze with stylised features, stamped 'Hagenauer', 8½in (21cm) high.
£500–700 *S*

An Art Deco bronze group, depicting a tiger crouching down observing a monkey swinging from a palm tree, on a black onyx base, 17in (43.5cm) high.
£400–500 *CSK*

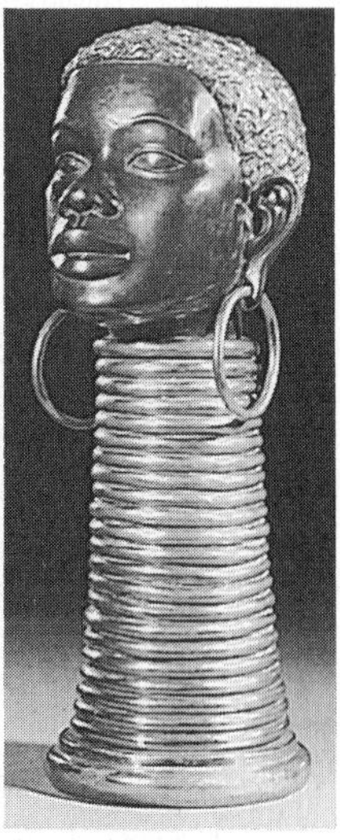

A polished and patinated bronze head of a Burmese woman, her neck elongated by ritual metal rings, c1930, 16in (40.5cm) high.
£900–1,200 *C*

A bronze study of a male eagle, cast from a model by L. Schulz, macassar ebony veneered pedestal, signed in the maquette, the mount with a plaque inscribed 'Souvenir de l'Attachement et de la Reconnaissance de vos collaborateurs, 1er Janvier 1941', 23½in (60.5cm) high.
£1,800–2,000 *C*

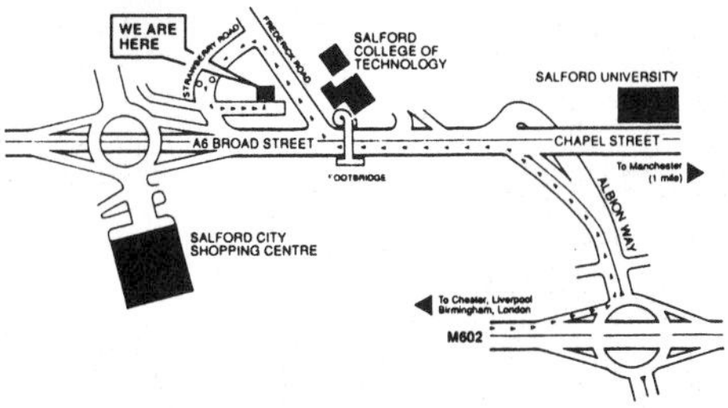

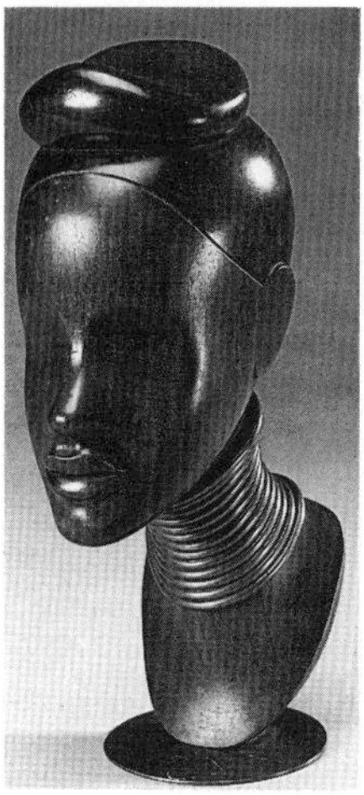

A stylised female head with necklaces, in wood, stained wood, bronze and copper, the underside stamped with monogram 'WHW', 'Hagenauer Wien', 'Made in Austria', and 'Handmade', c1930, 12in (30.5cm) high.
£900–1,200 *S*

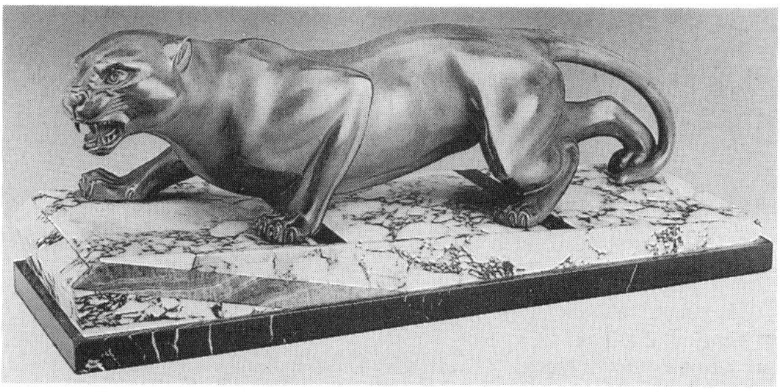

An Art Deco bronze figure of a jaguar, on a sloping onyx base, base inscribed 'D H Chiparus', 21½in (54.5cm) long.
£500–700 *CSK*

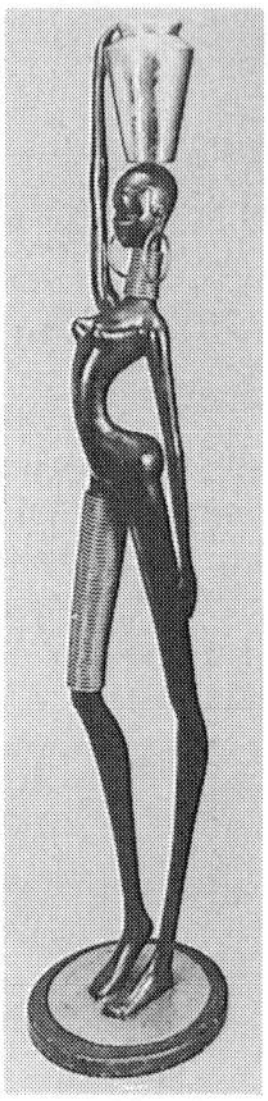

A bronze and dark patinated bronze figure of a standing female, in the style of Hagenauer, the bronze base with a wooden surround, 66in (167.5cm) high.
£2,500–3,000 *S*

A dark patinated bronze figure, 'Cleopatra', cast from a model by Chiparus, the queen reclining on a day bed, signed, on a black marble base, 16in (40.5cm) long.
£3,000–3,500 *CSK*

A bronze equestrian group, 'Amazon', cast from a model by Bruno Zach, medium brown patina, inscribed, on a Belgian marble base, early 20thC, 14in (35.5cm) high.
£1,600–1,800 *CNY*

An Art Deco figural clock, the onyx case surmounted by a gilt spelter figure of a young woman in a short dress, reclining on a lion skin, reading a book, 18½in (47cm) wide.
£400–500 *CSK*

A silvered bronze figure, 'Girl with Hind', by M. Guiraud Rivière, on a marble base, base marked, c1930, 19½in (49.5cm) high.
£2,000–3,000 *S*

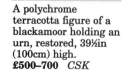

A polychrome terracotta figure of a blackamoor holding an urn, restored, 39½in (100cm) high.
£500–700 *CSK*

An Art Deco carved gilt wood plaque, carved in relief with an owl on stylised foliage, 18in (46cm) high.
£500–600 *CSK*

A terracotta bust of a Spanish soldier, by Goldscheider, painted in shades of brown and green, impressed factory marks, 24½in (62cm) high.
£300–400 *CSK*

Ceramics

An Adderley ware bone china coffee set for 6, printed and painted in silver lustre, yellow and blue, with abstract triangular foliage hanging from thin sinuous stems, comprising: coffee pot and cover, milk jug and sugar bowl, 6 cups and saucers, printed factory marks, painted '08177', coffee pot 8in (20cm) high.
£250–350 *CSK*

A Clews Tunstall hand painted Chameleon ware charger, c1930, 12in (30.5cm) diam.
£95–125 *YY*

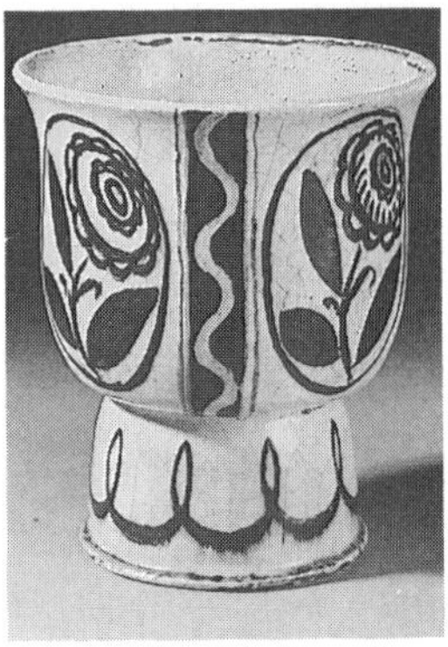

A René Buthaud earthenware bell-shaped vase, on a raised foot, decorated with floral reserves and bands in turquoise, black and brown on grey/white crackled ground, marked 'R. Buthaud', 1920s, 8in (20cm) high.
£750–850 *C*

A Clarice Cliff Fantasque Bizarre conical part tea set, Double V pattern, comprising: teapot and cover, 2 cups and saucers and a side plate, painted in colours, printed factory marks, damaged.
£450–550 *CSK*

A Clarice Cliff Fantasque oval meat platter, Umbrellas pattern, painted in colours, printed factory marks, 21in (53cm) wide.
£700–900 *CSK*

A Clarice Cliff Bizarre bowl, in Delecia Citrus pattern, 9in (22.5cm) diam.
£200–250 *WTA*

r. A Clarice Cliff Bizarre table lamp base, in the form of an Isis vase, boldly painted with the Apples pattern, rim chipped, 11in (29.5cm) high.
£500–600 *Bea*

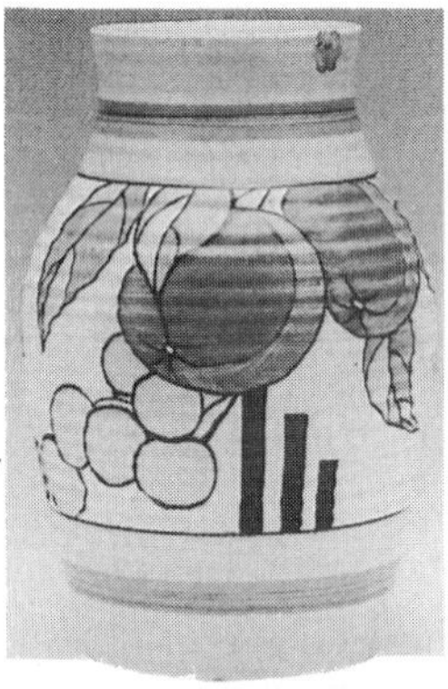

A Clarice Cliff Biarritz pottery dinner and dessert service, comprising: 2 tureens and covers, a gravy boat, a graduated set of 3 large rectangular plates, 6 dinner plates, 6 dessert plates and 6 smaller plates, each piece painted with a tree, a yellow trunk and pink and blue blossom, c1934, one tureen cover damaged.
£800–1,200 *Bea*

A Clarice Cliff three-handled cup, with Delecia script mark, c1930, 9in (22.5cm) high.
£400–500 *WTA*

A Hancock Rubens ware bowl, hand painted in Pomegranate pattern, by F. X. Abraham, c1923, 9½in (24cm) diam.
£50–60 *CSA*

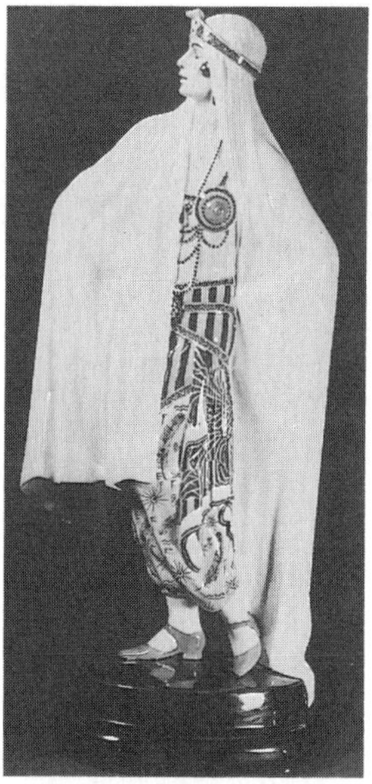

A Goldscheider pottery figure, from a model by Lorenzl, of an Arabian beauty wearing a long white headdress, over a beaded bodice and colourful pantaloons, on an oval black base, impressed facsimile signature, '5281/329/8', printed factory marks, chipped, 18½in (47cm) high.
£1,300–1,700 *Bon*

A Clarice Cliff Clouvre vase, brightly painted with orange, purple, blue and yellow flowers against a mottled purple ground, the interior turquoise, printed marks and script pattern name, 6in (15cm) high.
£450–550 *N*

A Sèvres porcelain vase, designed by Camille Roche, incised with leaping deer, covered in a shaded buff glaze, printed and painted marks, numbered '9/10', firing flaw, 12½in (32cm) high.
£200–300 *CSK*

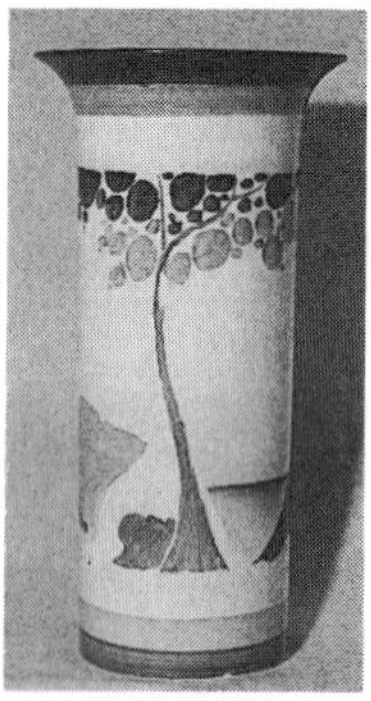

A Clarice Cliff Secrets pattern spill jar, shape 196, 9in (22.5cm) high.
£460–480 *WTA*

r. A Robj porcelain covered vase, the cover moulded in relief with fruit and leaves, the fruit with painted faces, in purple and green, printed retailer's marks, 7in (17.5cm) high.
£550–650 *CSK*

A Hancock Rubens ware jug, hand painted in Pomegranate pattern, by F. X. Abraham, c1923, 6in (15cm) high.
£80–90 *CSA*

A Wedgwood 22 piece part tea set for 6, in the Garden pattern, designed by Eric Ravilious, printed in shades of yellow, black and blue, printed factory marks, damaged, teapot 5½in (14cm) high.
£450–500 *CSK*

A set of 3 Guinness toucan wall decorations, painted in colours, printed factory marks, and two others, damaged.
£200–250 *CSK*

l. An Art Deco Anzac pattern part tea set, comprising: a tapered teapot, milk jug, cream jug, a plate and a saucer, c1931, teapot 7½in (19cm) high.
£1,000–1,200 *AG*

r. A Villeroy & Boch tea set for 2, in the Bauhaus manner, the oviform teapot with arched angled handle, and half moon lid, glazed shell pink with bands of turquoise and orange, printed factory marks, teapot 7½in (19cm) high.
£250–350 *CSK*

Charlotte Rhead

l. A Charlotte Rhead Persian Rose charger, c1935, 12in (30.5cm) diam.
£100–130 *HEA*

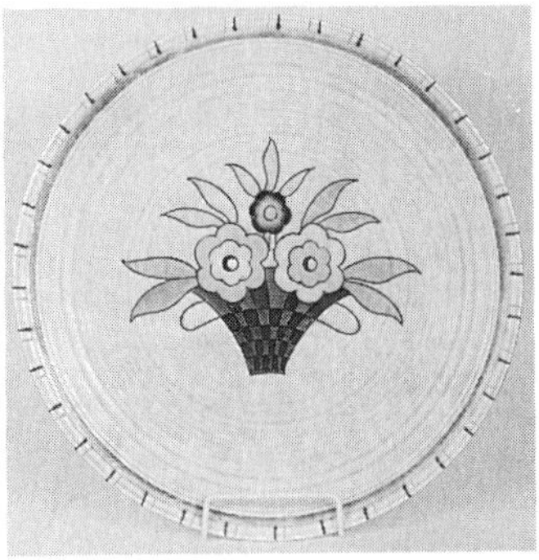

l. A Crown Ducal charger, pattern No. 6198, by Charlotte Rhead, c1940, 14in (35.5cm) diam.
£110–150 *HEA*

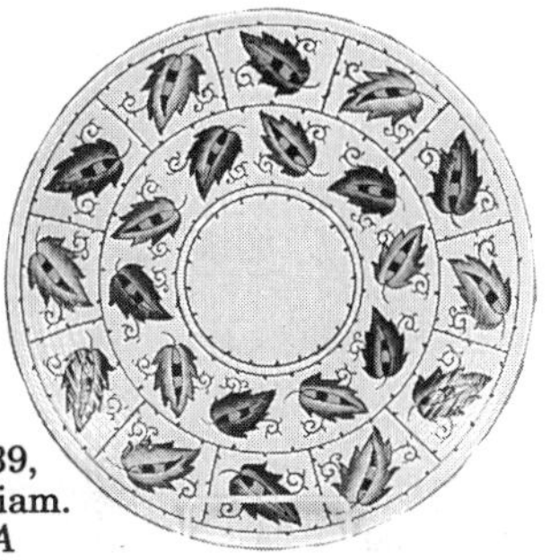

r. A Charlotte Rhead charger, unmarked, c1939, 12in (30.5cm) diam.
£100–130 *HEA*

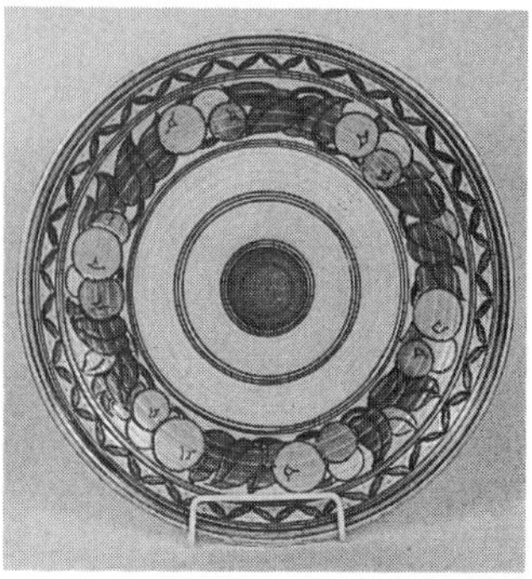

A Charlotte Rhead charger, Apples pattern, c1938, 12in (30.5cm) diam.
£120–150 *HEA*

A Crown Ducal tankard, pattern No. 6189, by Charlotte Rhead, c1939, 8in (20cm) high.
£140–180 *HEA*

A Bursley ware jug, pattern No.TL14, by Charlotte Rhead, c1940, 11in (28cm) high.
£160–200 *HEA*

A Burgess & Leigh Florentine pattern tankard, c1931, 9½in (24cm) high.
£100–130 *HEA*

A Crown Ducal jug, pattern No. 6822, by Charlotte Rhead, c1940, 9in (22.5cm) high.
£100–130 *HEA*

A Crown Ducal jug, pattern No. 4298, by Charlotte Rhead, c1935, 6½in (16.5cm) high.
£40–60 *HEA*

A Crown Ducal vase, Persian Rose design, by Charlotte Rhead, c1930, 8½in (21cm) high.
£200–280 *YY*

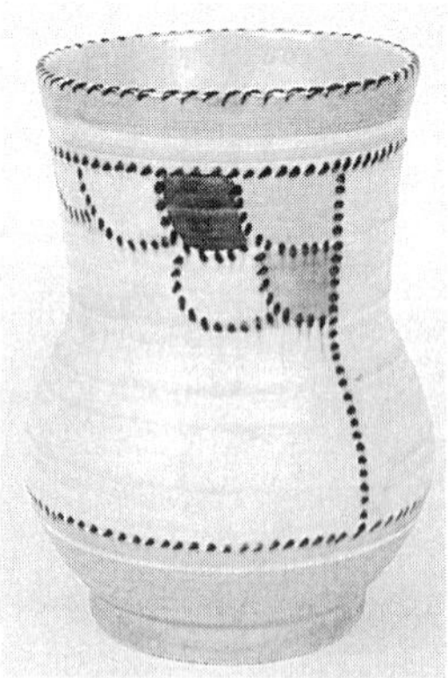

l. A Crown Ducal vase, Patch pattern, by Charlotte Rhead, c1935, 7in (17.5cm) high.
£30–40 *HEA*

r. A Manchu design vase, by Charlotte Rhead, c1935, 9½in (24cm) high.
£120–140 *HEA*

A Byzantine design vase, by Charlotte Rhead, c1935, 6in (15cm) high.
£110–130 *HEA*

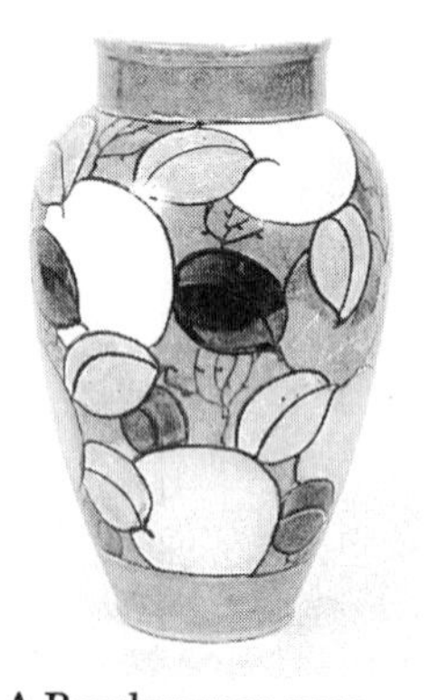

A Bursley ware vase, pattern No. 735, by Charlotte Rhead, c1926, 7in (17.5cm) high.
£140–170 *HEA*

A Primula design vase, by Charlotte Rhead, c1931, 8in (20cm) high.
£90–110 *HEA*

A Crown Ducal vase, pattern No. 5391, by Charlotte Rhead, c1938, 8in (20cm) high.
£180–220 *HEA*

A Crown Ducal three-handled jug, Hydrangea pattern, c1935, 8in (20cm) high.
£180–220 *HEA*

A Crown Ducal vase, pattern No. 5411, by Charlotte Rhead, c1938, 5¼in (13.5cm) high.
£80–100 *HEA*

A Crown Ducal vase, Green Patch pattern, c1935, 6½in (16cm) high.
£35–45 *HEA*

A Crown Ducal vase, pattern No. 4521, c1936, 8¼in (21cm) high.
£70–90 *HEA*

A Manchu design double-handled vase, c1935, 5¼in (13.5cm) high.
£80–100 *HEA*

A Crown Ducal vase, pattern No. 5623, by Charlotte Rhead, c1935, 7½in (19cm) high.
£120–150 *HEA*

A blue Manchu ginger jar, by Charlotte Rhead, c1940, 7in (17.5cm) high.
£250–350 *HEA*

A Crown Ducal vase, pattern No. 6016, by Charlotte Rhead, c1939, 7in (17.5cm) high.
£100–130 *HEA*

l. A Crown Ducal vase, pattern No. 5983, c1938, 7in (17.5cm) high.
£80–100 *HEA*

Royal Doulton

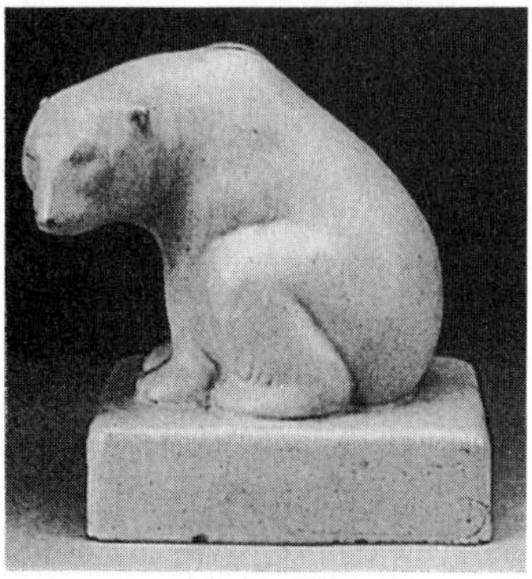

A Doulton Carrara Ware figure of a polar bear, designed by Leslie Harradine, on rectangular base, covered in a matt white glaze, with raised inscription 'Doulton Carrara', 6½in (16.5cm) high.
£160–200 *CSK*

A pair of Royal Doulton figures, entitled 'The Flower Sellers Children', HN 1342, 7½in (19cm) high.
£300–400 *AG*

A Royal Doulton figure, entitled 'Prized Possessions', HN 2942, Collectors Club, 6½in (16.5cm) high.
£200–250 *AG*

A Royal Doulton figure, entitled 'Sabbath Morn', 7in (17.5cm) high.
£150–200 *AG*

r. A Royal Doulton character jug, in the form of a white haired clown, entitled 'Clown', No. D6322, withdrawn 1955.
£300–400 *Bea*

A Royal Doulton figure, of 'The Bather', from a model by John Broad, the naked female with a garland of flowers in her hair, seated on a blue globe applied with a lizard on a base in the form of 4 frogs, 13in (33cm) high.
£600–800 *P(EA)*

A Royal Doulton character jug, entitled 'Friar Tuck', withdrawn 1960.
£150–200 *Bea*

A Royal Doulton figure, 'Captain MacHeath', from the Beggar's Opera, designed by Leslie Harradine, HN 464, printed and painted marks, 7in (17.5cm) high.
£300–500 *DN*

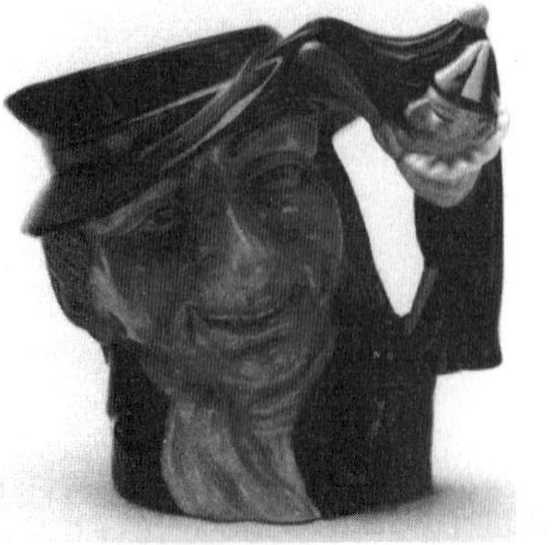

A Royal Doulton character jug, entitled 'Punch & Judy Man', withdrawn 1969.
£220–260 *Bea*

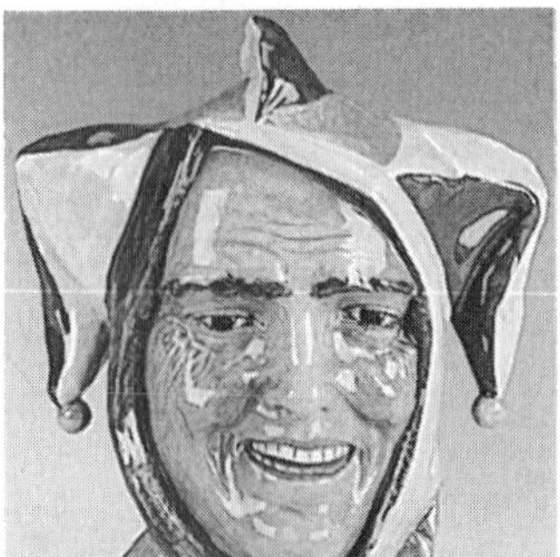

A Royal Doulton wall mask, entitled 'Jester', painted in colours, printed factory marks, 10½in (26.5cm) high.
£300–400 *CSK*

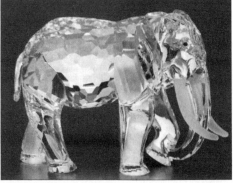

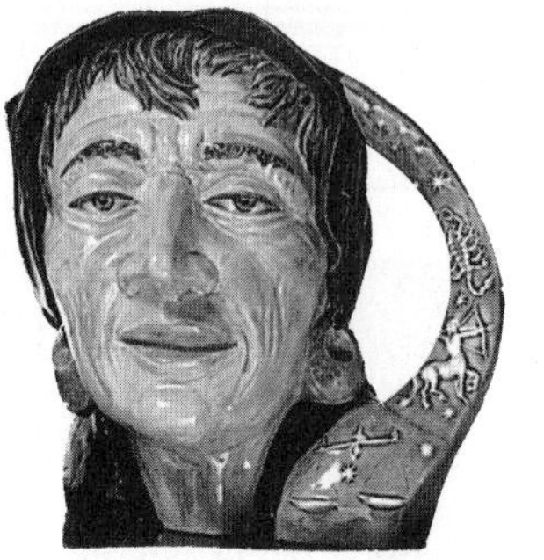

A Royal Doulton character jug, entitled 'Fortune Teller', No. D6497, 7in (17.5cm) high.
£200–300 *AG*

A Royal Doulton character jug, entitled 'Toby Weller', 6½in (16.5cm) high.
£120–150 *AG*

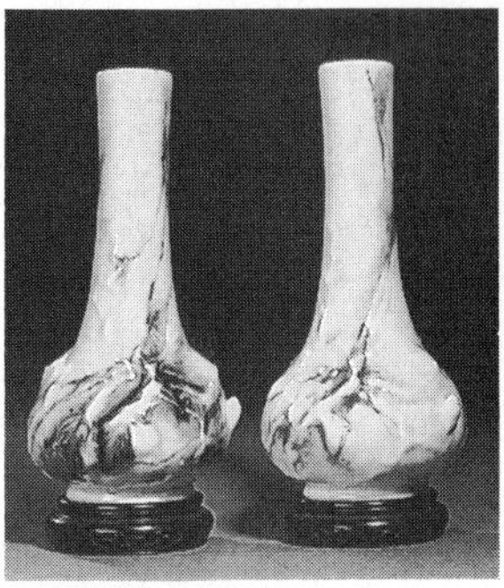

A pair of Royal Doulton porcelain vases, by Charles Noke and Harry Nixon, covered in a streaked white and green glaze to simulate jade, glaze chips to one, printed Royal Doulton marks, painted marks and signature 'Chinese Jade, Noke', HN, impressed '3.12.30', with ebonised stands, 10in (25cm) high.
£1,000–1,500 *C*

A pair of Royal Doulton stoneware vases, by Florence Roberts and Hannah Barlow, the mottled green shoulder and foot moulded with scrolling foliage, impressed and incised marks, chipped, 13½in (34.5cm) high.
£600–700 *Bea*

Miller's is a price GUIDE not a price LIST

l. A pair of Royal Doulton baluster vases, by Hannah Barlow, with streaked green glazed necks and bases, incised ponies and goats on a grassy background, incised monogram to the base, 9½in (24cm) high.
£750–850 *WL*

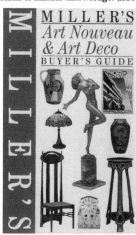

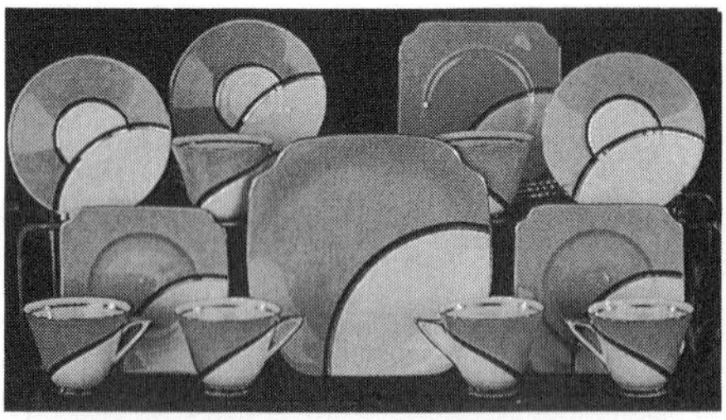

A Royal Doulton porcelain 15-piece tea service, each piece decorated in pale green, black and silver lustre with geometric devices, printed and impressed marks and pattern name 'De Luxe', c1934.
£330–370 *S(S)*

A Royal Doulton 16-piece part dinner service, designed by Frank Brangwyn, with an organic design in shades of green, yellow and blue, printed factory marks, painted 'D5033'.
£1,000–1,200 *CSK*

POST WAR DESIGN

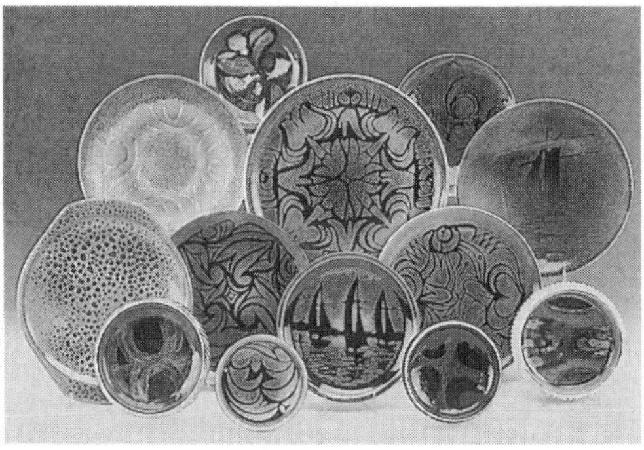

A collection of Poole Pottery Delphis and Aegean plates, printed factory marks, mixed condition.
£200–250 *CSK*

An Italian hand painted pottery 14-piece dressing table set, by Diritti d'Autore, for a teenage girl, painted in pastel colours, painted marks, c1960.
£200–250 *CSK*

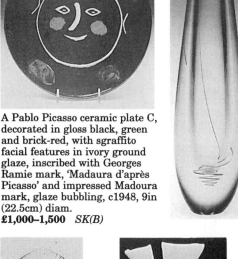

A Pablo Picasso ceramic plate C, decorated in gloss black, green and brick-red, with sgraffito facial features in ivory ground glaze, inscribed with Georges Ramie mark, 'Madaura d'après Picasso' and impressed Madoura mark, glaze bubbling, c1948, 9in (22.5cm) diam.
£1,000–1,500 *SK(B)*

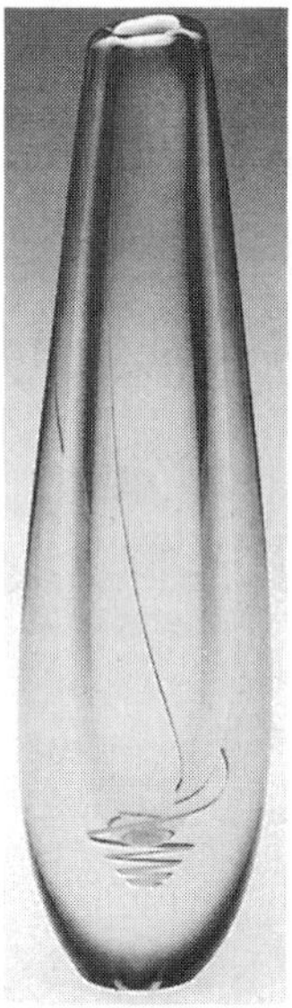

l. A Gunnel Nyman clear glass vase, designed by Nuutajärvi Notsjö, internally decorated with a single spiral, the underside marked 'G. Nyman Nuutajärvi Notsjö', c1950, 15in (38cm) high.
£1,300–1600 *S*

A Dale Chihuly basket set, the blown glass bowl with 11 'squashed' bowl shapes, in shades of pink and green, with markings, engraved signature to large bowl, 12½in (30.5cm) wide.
£750–850 *CSK*

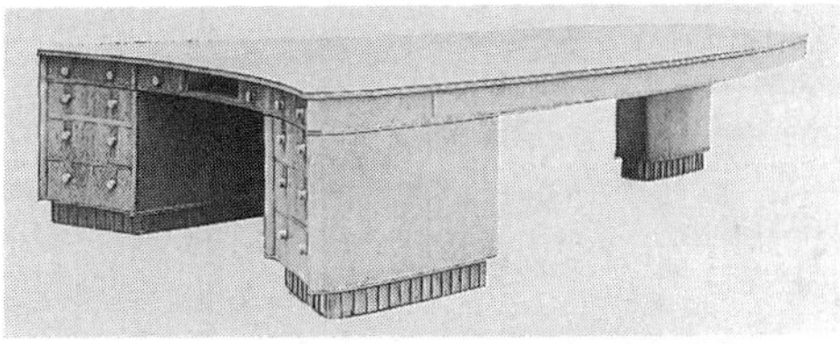

A mahogany boardroom table, designed by Lazlo Hoenig, the top veneered with shaped panels separated by narrow bands, supported on a tail pedestal with fluted base, the front made as a pedestal desk with centre space possibly for a radio, flanked on either side by 2 curved drawers, each pedestal with 3 drawers, with orange plastic handles with brass backs, on fluted bases, 79in (200.5cm) wide.
£1,200–1,700 *P*

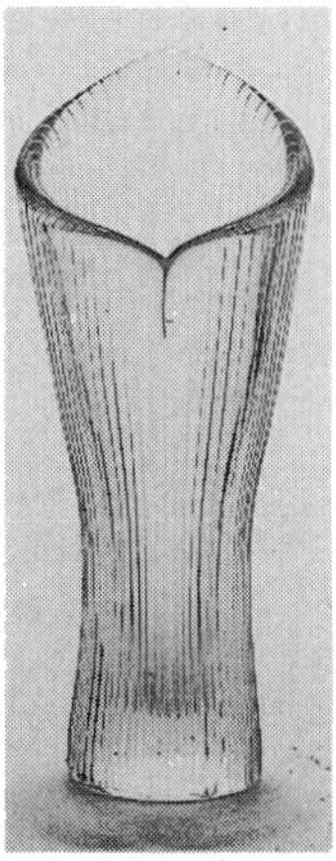

An Iittala clear glass vase, designed by Tapio Wirkkala, in the shape of a small lily, with engraved linear decoration, signed on base, 4½in (11.5cm) high.
£250–350 *P*

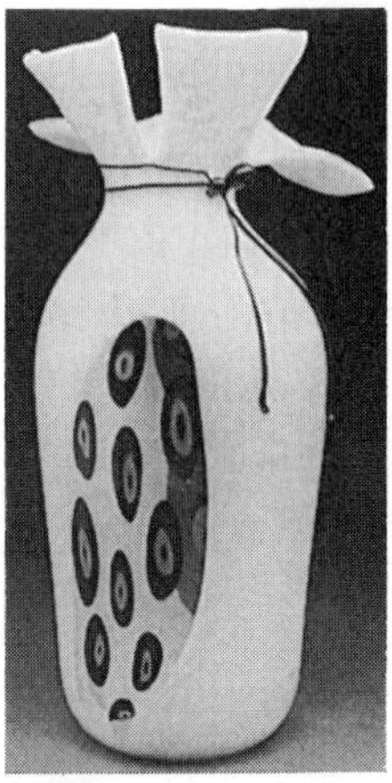

A Murano Studio glass vase, decorated with windows incorporating turquoise centred dark amethyst murrhine, applied black bow tie and snipped collar, surface scratches, 16½in (41.5cm) high.
£450–600 *SK(B)*

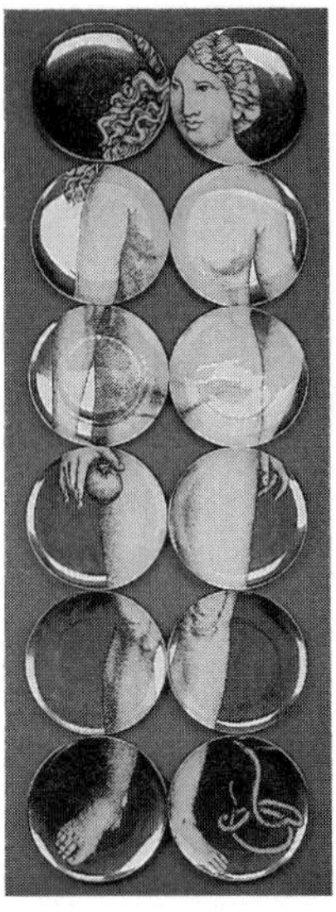

r. A set of 12 Fornasetti porcelain plates, each printed in black on a textured gilt ground, forming a composite picture of Eve, printed factory marks, 10½in (26cm) diam.
£700–900 *CSK*

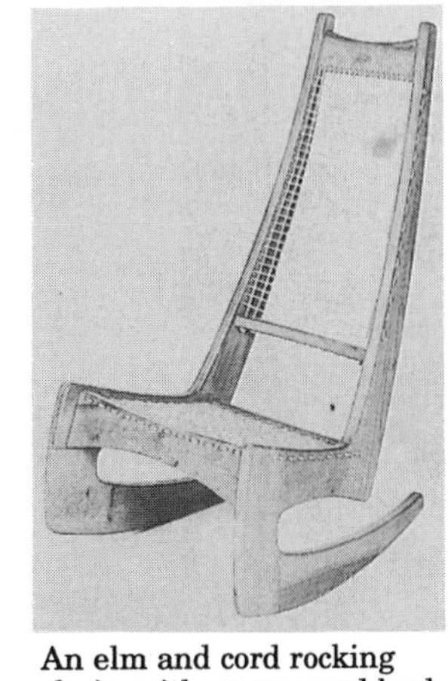

An elm and cord rocking chair, with woven cord back and seat, stamped 'Jeremy K. Brolin, Designer Craftsman in Wood'.
£200–300 *P*

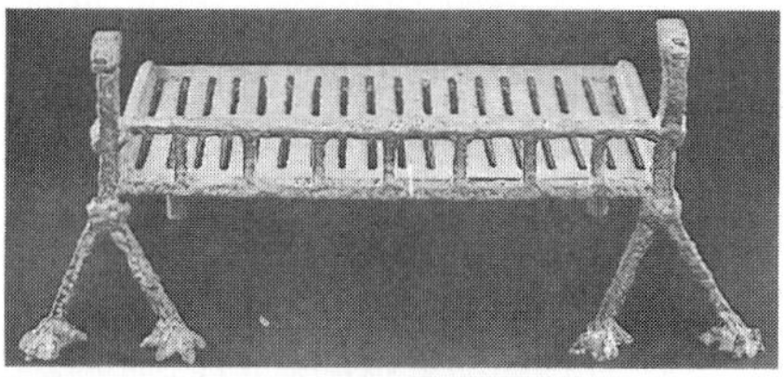

Two wrought iron fire grates, by Diego Giacometti, the supports modelled as mythical beasts with splayed claw-like feet, 10½in (26cm) wide.
£18,000–20,000 *S*

Two prototype blue painted metal chairs, and a blue-green painted metal occasional table, by Philip Starck, France, c1982, the table 31½in (80cm) wide.
£400–450 *CSK*

A black American walnut drop-leaf dining table, designed by Martin Grierson, the top inlaid with square panels of curl mahogany supported on 4 hinged lattice trestles, signed 'Martin Grierson, 16.1.1976', 59½in (151cm) wide.
£2,000–2,500 *CSK*

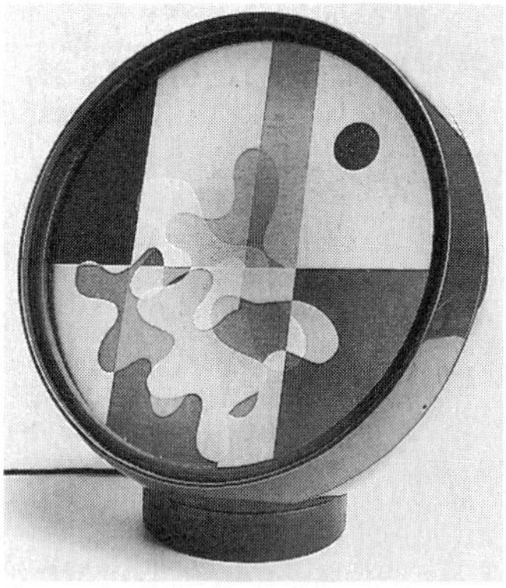

A pyschedelic 'television', the semi-spherical case with circular screen which, when activated, displays a continuously changing image in various colours, c1960, 22½in (57cm) high.
£300–400 *CSK*

A Philco Predicta television, on original stand, c1960, television 24½in (62.5cm) wide.
£280–350 *SK(B)*

A chandelier, for Georg Jensen, New York, with matt black finished steel arms, with blue, green, amethyst and red glass candle cups, unsigned, c1960, 24in (61.5cm) diam.
£480–550 *SK(B)*

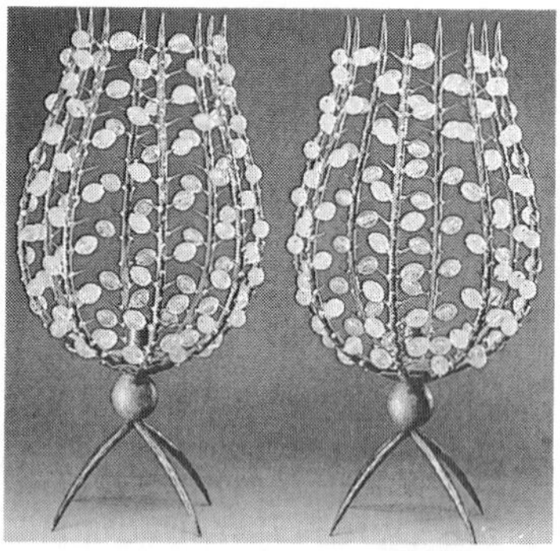

A pair of wrought iron and glass candleholders, by André Dubreuil, each on 4 spindley legs, with a gilt spherical knop, with 8 thorny branches, surrounding the central candleholders, with glass beads, 24in (61.5cm) high.
£5,000–6,000 *CNY*

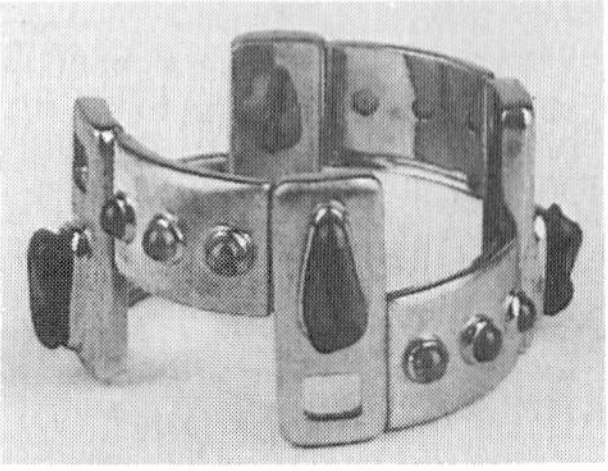

An 18ct yellow gold gem-set bracelet, designed as a semi-flexible sculptural bracelet, set with carved green tourmalines and cabochon citrines in a satin finish, signed 'Burle Marx', Brazil, c1970.
£1,700–2,000 *SK(B)*

A ceramic bust of the artist Francis Bacon, entitled 'Francis B', by Robert Arneson, on a pedestal in polychrome glazes, c1980, 9½in (24cm) high.
£2,000–2,500 *CNY*

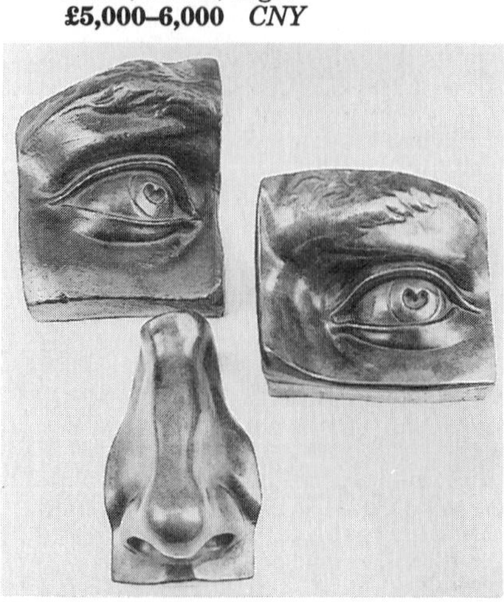

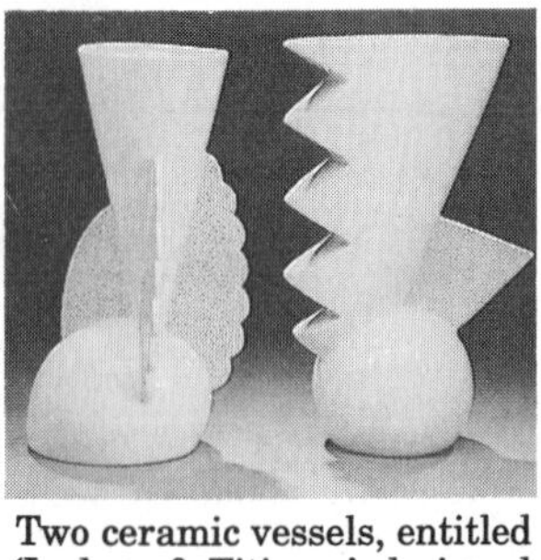

Two ceramic vessels, entitled 'Ladoga & Titicaca', designed by Matteo Thun, with glazed white silvery-grey stippling, each labelled 'M. Thun per Memphis', Memphis, c1982, 10½in (25cm) high.
£480–550 *CNY*

l. Three bronze casts of a left eye, a right eye, and a nose, each 8in (20cm) high.
£200–250 *CSK*

TUNBRIDGE WARE

A Tunbridge ware coromandel box, containing 3 perfume bottles, c1850, 4in (10cm) long.
£440–475 *AMH*

A Tunbridge ware games box, by Edmund Nye, c1855, 10½in (26cm) wide.
£1,100–1,200 *AMH*

A Tunbridge ware coromandel inkstand, c1850, 12½in (31.5cm) wide.
£675–725 *AMH*

A Tunbridge ware cabinet and work box, the lid with a view of Bayham Abbey Ruins, c1870, 9½in (22.5cm) wide.
£1,350–1,450 *AMH*

top. A Tunbridge ware silk skein holder, c1870, 9½in (24cm) long.
£310–330
bottom. A Tunbridge ware box, with pincushions, c1860, 8in (20cm) wide.
£275–300 *AMH*

A Tunbridge ware work box, with fitted interior, by Edmund Nye, c1855, 10½in (26cm) wide.
£1,350–1,450 *AMH*

LEATHER & LUGGAGE

A brass studded leather bound coffer, the domed top decorated in studs with stylised flowers, and to the front forming the date '1642', old replacement hinges and lock, 17thC, on a 19thC wooden plinth, 47in (119cm) wide.
£1,200–1,700 *MJB*

A tin travelling trunk, c1880, 21½in (54cm) wide.
£30–40 *Cou*

An American leather and canvas coaching trunk, with brass, copper and wood bands, 19thC, 30in (76.5cm) wide.
£220–250 *Cou*

TRANSPORT

A Victorian Humber safety cycle, with one inch pitch chain, fixed gear, and spoon break, together with a bell and 2 lamps.
£5,600–7,000 *AH*

A Victorian baby carriage, with spindle detail to side panels, black leather cloth upholstery with decorative braid trimming and child restraining straps, fold-down hood with brass plated fittings, C-sprung suspension and rubber tyred spoked wheels.
£500–600 *S*

A child's perambulator, by Simpson & Fawcett, the wooden body painted brown with red and yellow lining, button leatherette interior, centre well and folding hood, 4 leather suspension straps above a large spring, 4 radially spoked wheels and turned wood handles at each end, with trade stamp on base, leather straps renewed, hood damaged, patented 1887, 45½in (115cm) long.
£700–800 *S(S)*

FANS

A fan, painted with pilgrims, the ivory sticks carved and pierced with figures, c1750, 12in (30.5cm) wide.
£3,600–4,200 *CSK*

A fan, with ivory sticks, the guard with piqué and clouté work, having a vellum leaf painted with 'Moses drawing water from the rock', probably Dutch, c1720, 11in (28cm) wide.
£300–350 *P*

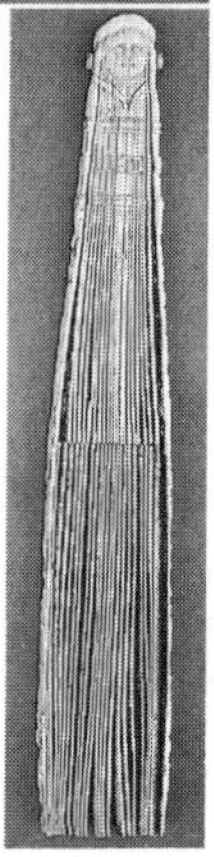

A fan, the leaf painted with an allegory of marriage, the ivory sticks carved and pierced with figures, the handle carved to form a man's head wearing a hat when closed, one stick broken, sticks c1740, leaf c1860, 11in (28cm) wide.
£550–800 *CSK*

l. A fan, the chicken skin leaf with a pen and ink drawing after Rubens, entitled 'The Rape of the Sabine Women', the verso with Romulus and Remus, the ivory sticks pierced and carved with chinoiserie figures in gazebos, repairs to leaf, c1720, 11in (29cm) wide.
£2,000–2,500 *CSK*

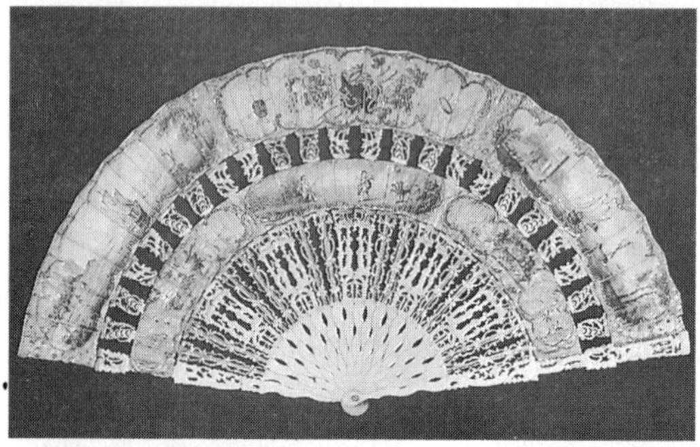

A cabriolet fan, the leaves painted with shipping in an estuary by a church and putti fishing by Cerberus, the ivory sticks carved and pierced with Chinese figures, painted and gilt, c1750, 10in (25cm) wide, in a 19thC box.
£950–1,200 *CSK*

A fan, the leaf painted with a banquet, the verso with 2 figures in a landscape, the tortoiseshell sticks carved, pierced and gilt, c1760, 10in (25cm) wide.
£700–1,000 *CSK*

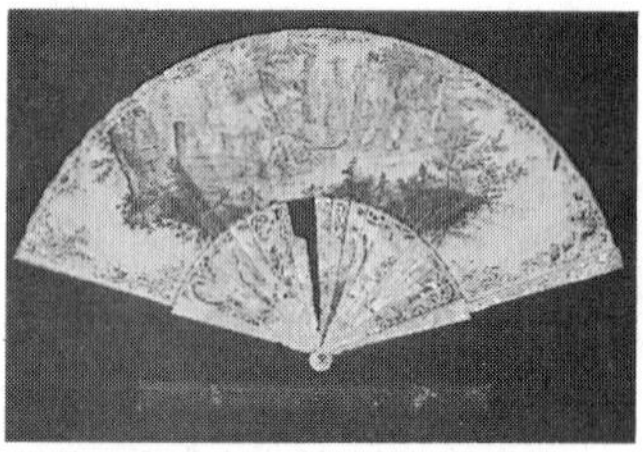

A fan, the paper leaf painted with lovers and attendants among classical ruins, with carved mother-of-pearl sticks, probably French, c1760, 11½in (29cm) long, in a hinged box.
£150–200 *P*

A triple cabriolet fan, the verso with a small house, the ivory sticks painted, damage to leaves, c1770, 10in (25cm) wide.
£500–600 *CSK*

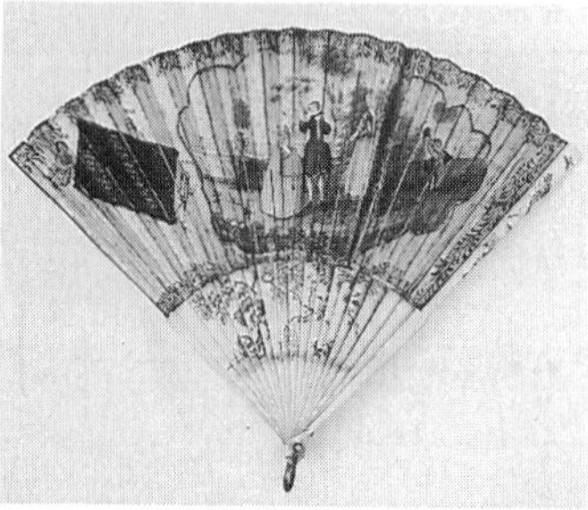

A fan, entitled 'Le (sic) Eventail Necromantique', leaf painted with lovers and a lady by a mirror beside a black pageboy in a park, 3 men inscribed 'Eo', 'Meo', and 'Areo', a slide concealed in the mirror with 2 portraits of 2 pairs of kissing couples operated by a lever concealed at the back of the painted ivory sticks, leaf worn, c1750, 10in (25cm) wide.
£1,600–2,000 *CSK*

A fan, painted with a classical marriage, the mother-of-pearl sticks carved and pierced with lovers and putti, silvered and gilt, Dutch, c1770, 11in (28cm) wide.
£720–800 *CSK*

A paper fan, with large shaped insertions of catgut, applied with muslin spot motifs of flowers, the paper leaf also painted to resemble lace against a brown ground painted with flowers, the bone sticks pierced and painted with a trompe l'oeil of lace, possibly German, c1750, 10in (25cm) wide.
£950–1,200 *CSK*

A Grand Tour fan, the chicken skin leaf painted with the Pantheon, Rome, the reserves with brightly coloured etruscan decoration, the verso the Tempio del Sole, the ivory sticks pierced, tips of guardsticks missing, c1780, 10in (25cm) wide.
£600–1,000 *CSK*

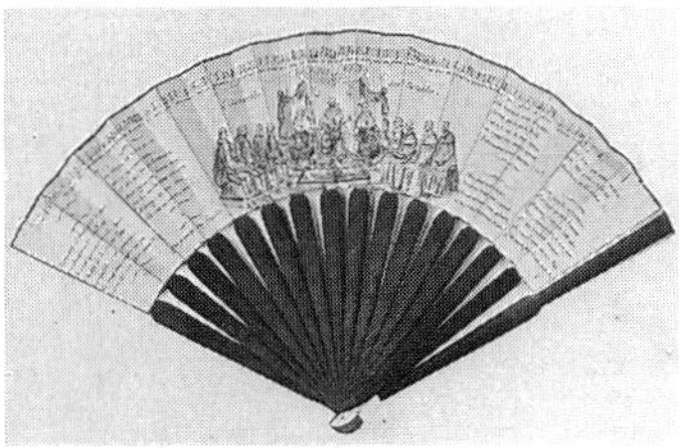

A printed fan, entitled 'L'Assemblée de Notables', the leaf a hand coloured etching printed in brown with Louis XVI, his 2 brothers, 4 gentlemen and 4 clergymen, and a satirical verse set to the music of Air de Figaro, with wooden sticks and bone filets, 10in (25cm) wide.
£200–400 *CSK*

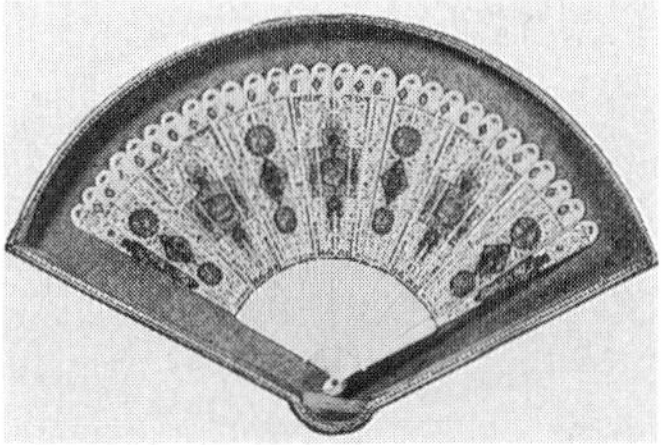

A ivory brisé fan, carved, pierced and painted with doves, musical instruments and flowers, probably French, c1790, 10½in (26cm) long, in a glazed gilt case.
£270–320 *P*

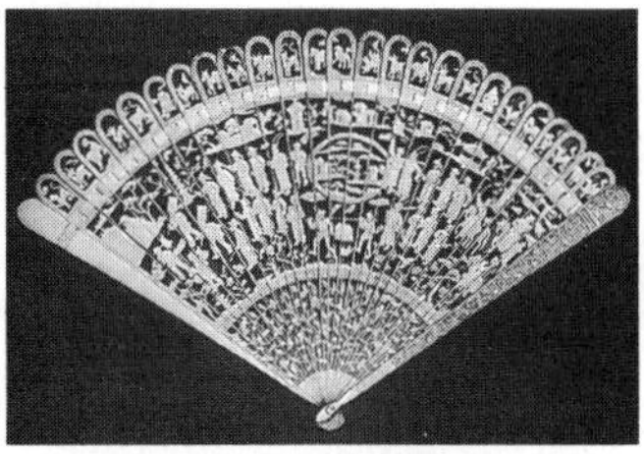

A Canton ivory brisé fan, damaged, c1790, 10in (25cm) wide, in a lacquer box.
£1,500–2,000 *CSK*

A pierced ivory brisé fan, carved and scrolling flowers, and monogram 'I. R.', c1790, 10½in (26cm) wide.
£1,500–2,000 *CSK*

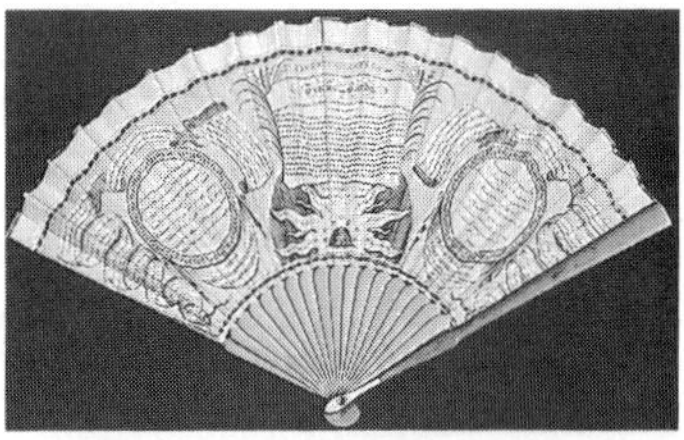

A fan, printed with Tricks on Cards, the leaf etched with conundrums, partly tinted in yellow, published by Robt. Hixon, 13 Bridges St., Covent Garden, Dec. 1794, with wooden sticks, slightly split at folds, 10in (25cm) wide.
£1,200–1,500 *CSK*

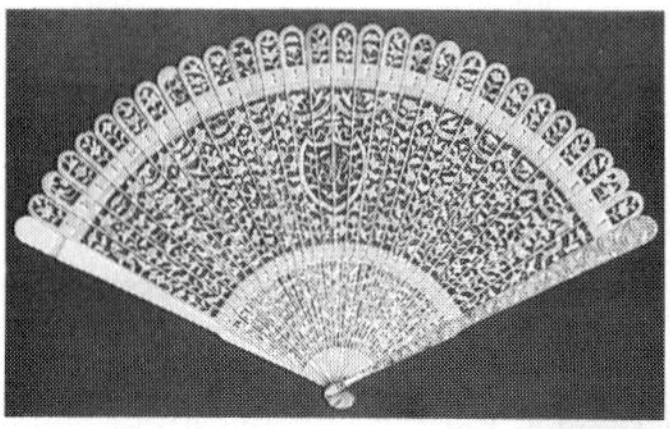

l. A Canton ivory brisé fan, carved and pierced with birds and flowers, and monogram 'I. P.', c1800, 10in (25cm) wide.
£1,400–1,700 *CSK*

r. A Canton fan, the leaf painted with the Hongs of Canton flying flags, the bone sticks pierced, guardstick repaired, c1820, 10in (25cm) wide.
£1,100–1,500 *CSK*

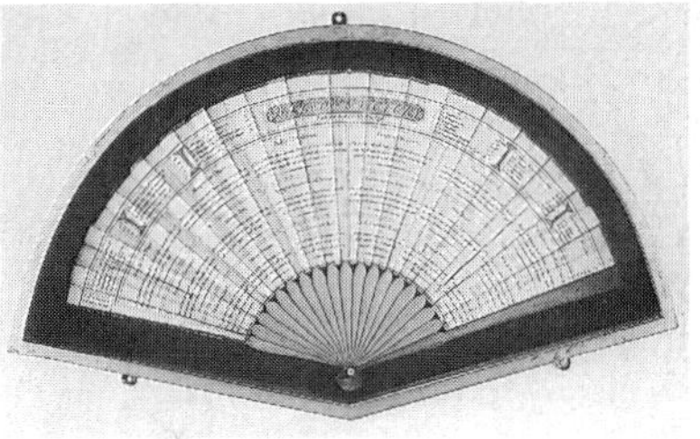

A printed fan, of Nelson & Victory, the leaf line engraved with names and comic choreography of 18thC fictional country dances, together with a list of ships and captains who 'fought off the Mouth of the Nile, 1st Aug. 1798', with wooden sticks, one guardstick inscribed 'E. B. 1799', 10in (25cm) wide, in a glazed fan shaped case.
£850–1,000 *CSK*

A Canton ivory brisé cockade fan, carved and pierced with a pagoda and a border of animals and vines, damage to one stick, c1820, 4in (10cm) diam., in a fitted box.
£800–900 *CSK*

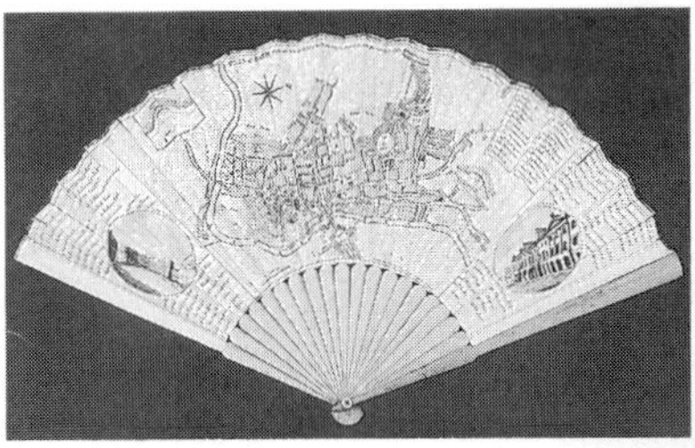

l. A printed fan, the leaf engraved with a plan of Bath, a detail of Lansdown Place, and 2 views after Malton, with gazeteer including Inns, published 1793 by Cock and Crowder, Wood Street, London, with wooden sticks, 9in (22.5cm) wide.
£800–1,200 *CSK*

r. A Canton ivory brisé fan, carved with pavilions, boats and figures, with monogram 'E. I.', damaged, re-ribboned, c1820, 7in (17.5cm) wide.
£300–500 *CSK*

A silk fan, the blonde tortoiseshell sticks carved, pierced and gilt with figures at the altar of love, c1820, 10in (25cm) wide, in a glazed fan-shaped case.
£700–800 *CSK*

A lace fan, the leaf worked with a vignette of the sale of putti, the ivory sticks finely carved and pierced to match the leaf, slight damage to sticks, mid-19thC, 10in (25cm) wide.
£4,000–5,000 *CSK*

A Canton ivory brisé fan, carved and pierced with inscription 'Madame F. D. J. Card née Hte Boulanger Souvenir de S.V.C. Canton 1 Janvier 1825', the reserves carved with figures, pavilions and birds, 7in (17.5cm) wide.
£1,200–1,500 *CSK*

r. A Canton gilt filigree brisé fan, enamelled in blue and green with the pagoda of Whampoa, repaired, damaged, c1830, 8in (20cm) wide.
£900–1,100 *CSK*

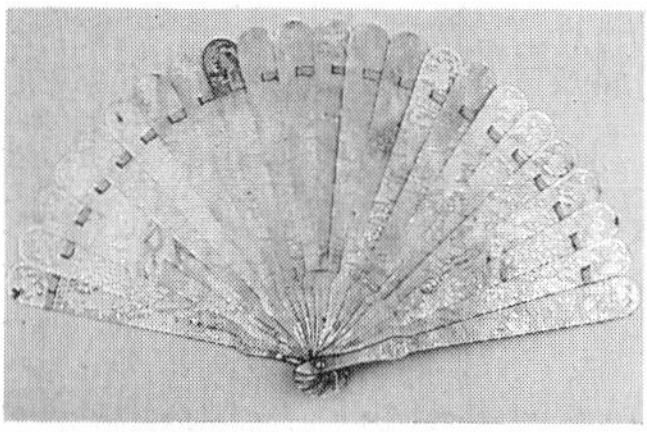

A Canton mother-of-pearl brisé fan, etched recto and verso with figures and animals, repaired, c1820, 7in (17.5cm) wide.
£1,000–1,500 *CSK*

A Canton fan, the chicken skin leaf brightly decorated on both sides, with shaped ivory sticks and carved guard sticks, slight damage, mid-19thC, 11in (28cm) wide, in a lacquered box.
£400–500 *DN*

A fan, with chinoiserie sticks and needlelace leaf designed with classical ladies, satyrs and masks, with scrolling foliage and fruit, within a narrow border of small animals and birds, mid-19thC, 11in (28cm) long, in a glazed display case.
£1,000–1,500 *P*

l. A Macao fan, the sticks lacquered in black and gold, mid-19thC, 11in (28cm) wide.
£550–650 *CSK*

A sequinned fan, with painted figures in a classical scene, pierced guards and sticks, in a fan-shaped glazed case.
£300–400 *RBB*

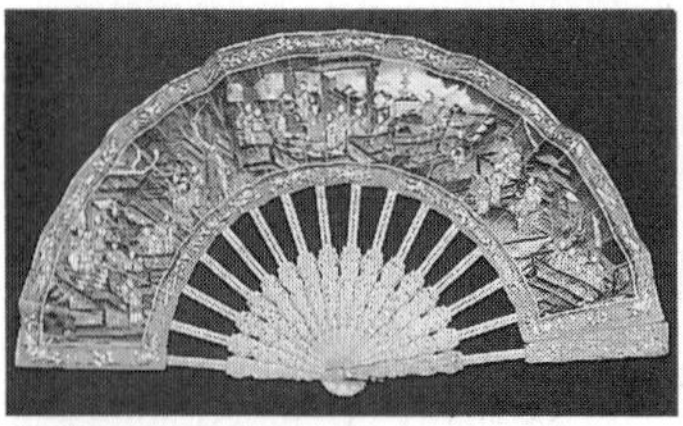

A Canton telescopic fan, the leaf painted with figures on terraces, their faces of ivory, their clothes of silk, the verso similarly decorated, with carved sandalwood sticks, c1870, 11in (28cm) wide.
£400–500 *CSK*

A fan, signed 'Lievre', the mother-of-pearl sticks carved with 4 figures and a child in a walking frame, pierced, gilt and backed with mother-of-pearl, c1870, 11in (28cm) wide.
£400–500 *CSK*

A hand coloured lithographic fan, depicting Queen Isabella of Spain attending a bull fight, the mother-of-pearl sticks carved, pierced and gilt, c1860, 11in (28cm) wide.
£350–400 *CSK*

A fan, signed 'A. Ledoux', the silk leaf painted with gipsy dancers, the verso with a gipsy, the mother-of-pearl sticks carved, pierced and gilt with figures and trophies of love, damaged, c1875, 11in (28cm) wide, in a Duvelleroy box.
£500–600 *CSK*

A black Chantilly lace fan, worked with a peacock in a formal garden, the blonde sticks pierced, the upper guardstick with monogram 'R. M.' in rose diamonds, leaf torn, c1890, 12in (30.5cm) wide.
£1,200–1,500 *CSK*

A French fan, with pierced and gilt decorated horn sticks, the green silk and white net leaf designed with medallions and swags of ribbon, the whole with gilt sequins and appliqué, c1900, 8½in (21cm) long, with a box labelled 'Mlle M. Boyer, 5 Galerie de la Madeleine, Paris'.
£130–200 *P*

r. A Japanese fan, with silk leaf, ivory sticks gilded and each guard designed with slender trailing blossom and small birds in shibyama, Japanese, 19thC, 16½in (41.5cm) wide.
£600–800 *P*

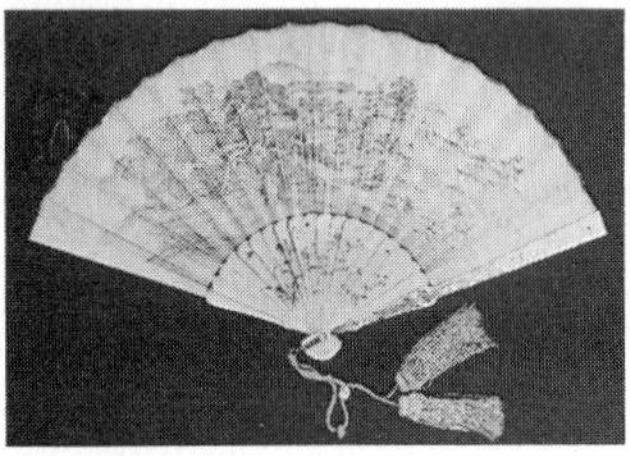

r. A chromolithographic fan, by Barbier, of the Exposition Universelle, Paris 1889, depicting a crowded scene outside the Opéra and Siraudin's shop with celebrities including Victor Hugo, with wooden sticks, one broken, 13in (33cm) wide.
£1,100–1,400 *CSK*

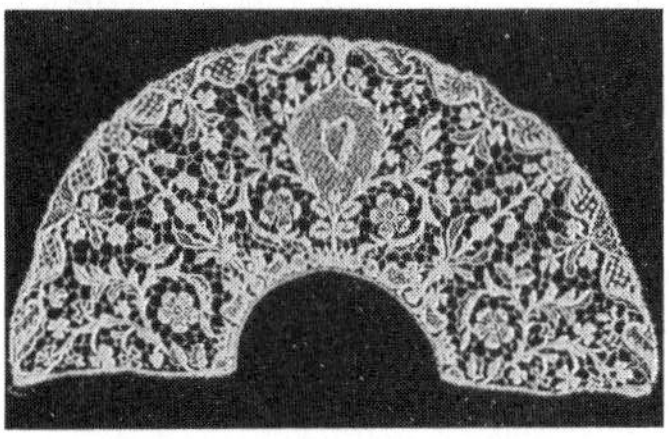

An Irish fan, the leaf of Youghal needlelace, designed with a harp to the central cartouche, flanked by roses, thistles, a shamrock and 3 coronets, c1890, 6½in (16cm) wide.
£350–400 *P*

This fan was possibly made to celebrate the marriage of the Duke of York, later King George V, to Princess Mary of Teck in 1893.

A ballooning fan, signed 'Van Garden', the silk leaf painted with figures in 18thC dress, the reserves painted in shades of blue, the blonde sticks carved, the upper guardstick with a balloon, 2 centre folds split, c1890, 10in (25cm) wide.
£750–850 *CSK*

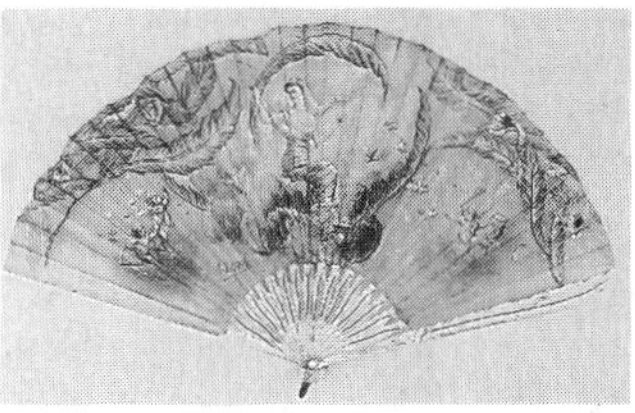

A fan, signed 'A. Lefève', painted with a lady sitting in the clouds amongst blue feathers, with shaped gauze reserves painted with putti, the mother-of-pearl sticks carved to resemble feathers, damaged, c1890, 9½in (22.5cm) wide.
£500–800 *CSK*

A Russian fan, with piqué decorated mother-of-pearl sticks, the initial guard of gold standard 56, decorated in salmon pink moiré design enamel with latticework and trailing flower spray in rose-cut diamonds, repaired, with the 'St. Petersburg' mark with Kokoshnik 'Fabergé' in Cyrillic, maker's mark, c1896, 8in (20cm) long.
£10,000–13,000 *P*

The marks are those of Michael Perchin (1860–1903) who succeeded Erik Kollin, the head workmaster, in 1886. He produced all types of objets de fantaisie to a very high aesthetic and technical standard.

A lithographic advertising fan, by Louis Vuitton, brown, published by J. Ganne, overstamped 'The Cunard Steam Ship Company Limited', the verso with a chromolithograph of couples fishing, with wooden sticks, tear to leaf, c1900, 9in (22.5cm) wide.
£200–300 *CSK*

A chomolithographic fan, depicting the 'Souvenir du Village Suisse, Exposition de Genève 1896', with wooden sticks, 13in (33cm) wide.
£200–250 *CSK*

A fan, attached to a pair of opera glasses, the leaf of maroon gauze embroidered with sequins, the sticks of tortoiseshell, the opera glasses inscribed 'Asprey & Co., London', c1900, 6in (15cm) long.
£700–800 *CSK*

A fan leaf, 'Spring', by Charles Conder, heightened with gold on silk, signed 'Conder', c1902, 16½in (42cm) wide, in a contemporary French fan-shaped glazed frame.
£2,500–3,000 *CSK*

A fan, the black net leaf applied with lace vines, embroidered with purple, gold and green sequins, signed 'Van Santen, Berlin' on verso, the simulated horn and tortoiseshell sticks carved and pierced with vines, silvered and gilt, one guardstick repaired, damage to net, c1905, 11in (28cm) wide, in a box.
£550–600 *CSK*

SEWING

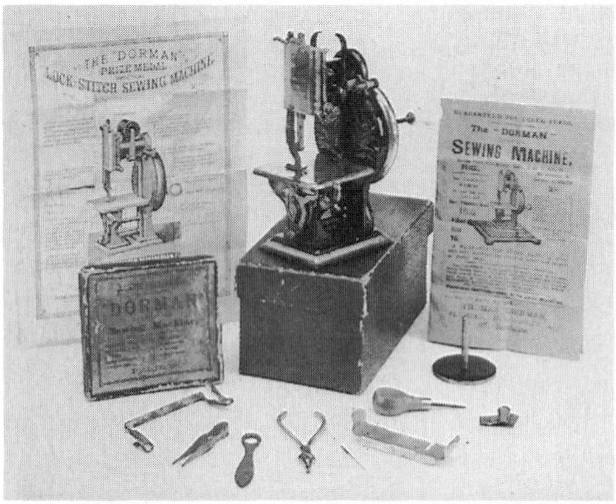

A Dorman lockstitch sewing machine, with spare cotton reel stand, accessories box, instructions and guarantee.
£420–500 *CSK*

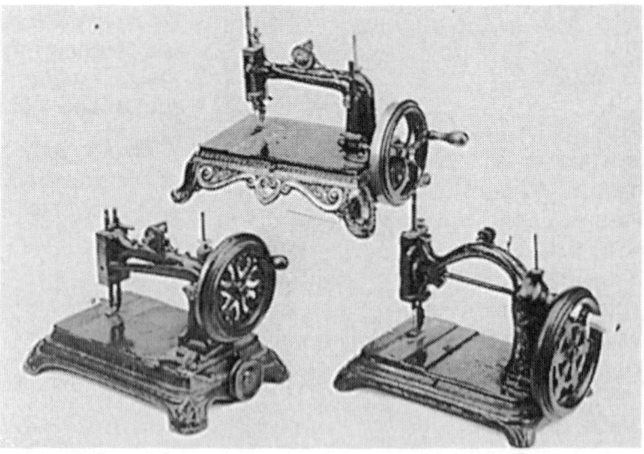

An 'Atlas A' sewing machine, with gilt decoration and tools, and 2 others.
£200–250 *CSK*

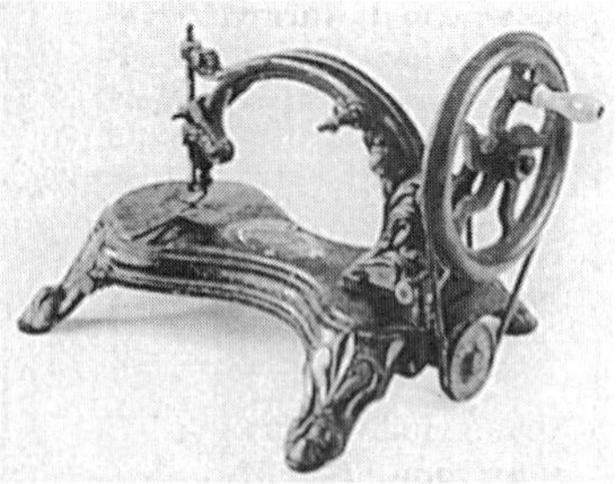

A Starley Swiftsure sewing machine, with belt drive to camshaft, fiddle pattern base with scroll feet and traces of gilt and simulated malachite ornament, lacking shuttle and shuttle cover.
£700–1,000 *CSK*

A Cookson's sewing machine, No. 923, with nickel plated finish on japanned iron base, stained wood cover with plaque 'Cookson's Patent Lock Stitch Sewing Machine'.
£1,100–1,300 *CSK*

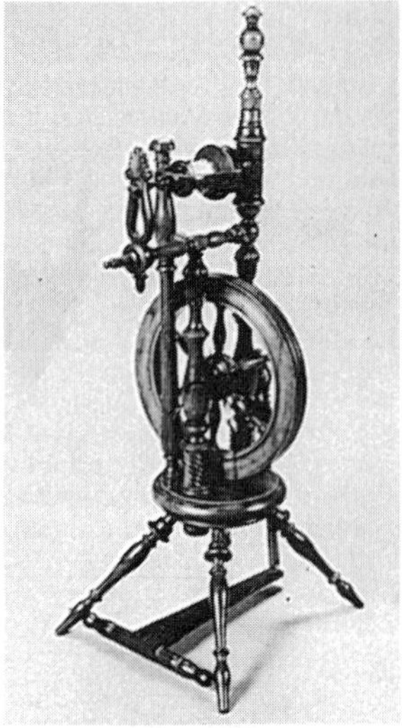

A fruitwood spinning wheel, the spool holder carved with an anthemium and gothic motifs, on turned legs, 19thC, 30½in (77.5cm) high.
£350–500 *DN*

An Arm & Platform sewing machine, with partial gilt transfers and instruction leaflet, lacking shuttle.
£400–500 *CSK*

l. A treadle sewing machine, by Whight & Mann Excelsior, No. 5730, with double-thread chainstitch mechanism, in gilt and japanned frame with fluted column end standard, side-to-side cloth movement, with swinging needle feed and tapered wood cover, damaged.
£3,000–3,500 *CSK*

A Taylor's Patent sewing machine, with belt drive, shuttle, and gilt, red and green decoration, in wood case, worn.
£600–700 *CSK*

A treadle sewing machine, by Weed Sewing Machine Co., Hartford, Conn., U.S.A., with exposed bell-crank lever, flywheel on underbed camshaft and patent dates to 1866.
£250–400 *CSK*

A vertical fruitwood treadle spinning wheel, with a tripod heart-shaped horizontal table, the turned uprights and wheel decorated with inlay and painted leaves, early 19thC, 39½in (100cm) high.
£2,000–2,500 *P*

A Celanese coromandel wood work casket, with 2 fitted lift-out trays with covers, a rising section to the back containing small drawers and reels of silk, 19thC, 16in (41cm) wide.
£450–550 *HSS*

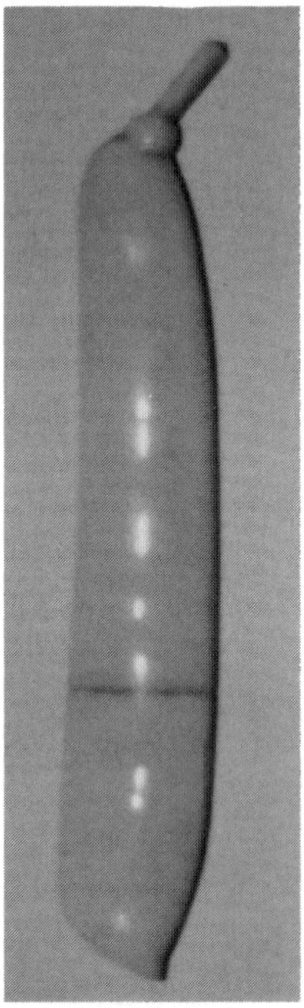

A Georgian ivory needlecase, in the form of a pea pod, 4in (10cm) long.
£125–150 *RA*

A needlework casket, of ivory silk embroidered in coloured silks, with scenes of Jacob's dream, the lid with the return of Jephtah, bound in silver braid, with fitted interior, the whole lined with pink silk, velvet, and silver and gilt stencilled paper, c1660, 11in (28cm) wide, with later pad feet.
£5,000–6,000 *P*

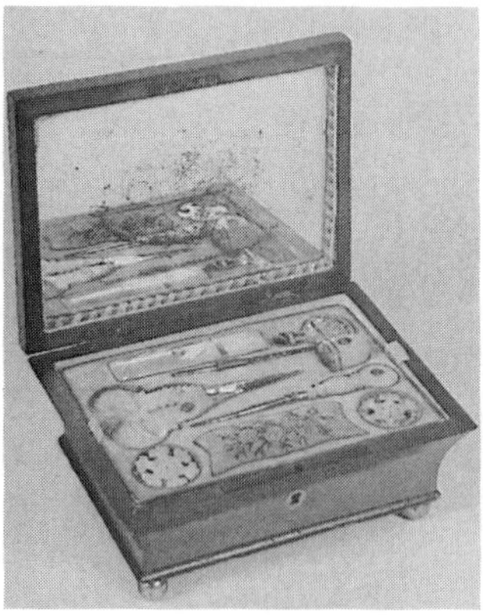

A Palais Royale satinwood needlework box, with beaded decoration, ivory plush and pink silk interior, a mirror to the lid, and a loose tray fitted with mother-of-pearl accessories, French, c1800, 6½in (16cm) wide, standing on 4 gilt ball feet.
£600–800 *CSK*

A Charles II needlework covered casket, with a domed top, covered in needlework with exotic flowers, leaves and animals, the interior lined in salmon coloured fabric, c1700.
£1,000–2,000 *S(NY)*

TEXTILES
Covers & Quilts

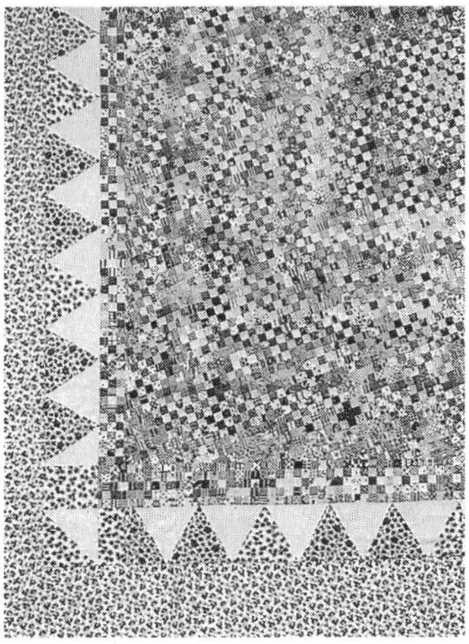

A patchwork coverlet, with blue, red, green and sand cotton print diamonds, on a cream ground, the cottons dating from 1790s, 96in (243.5cm) square.
£500–700 *CSK*

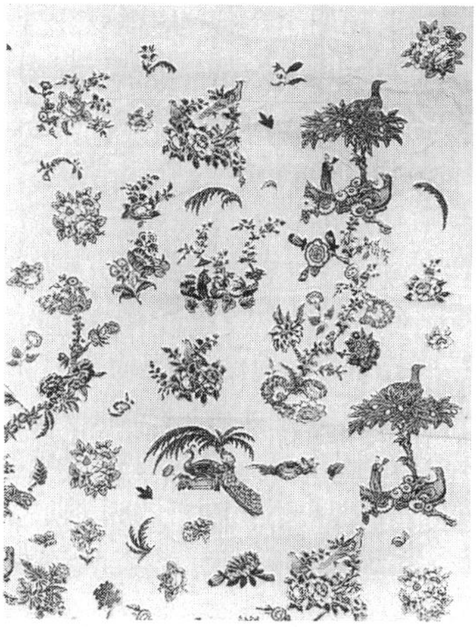

A Broderie Perse quilt, the ivory linen ground applied with chintz cut-outs of peacocks, pheasants and other birds among flowers, each piece finely outlined in buttonhole stitch, with all-over diamond quilting, c1815, 114 by 104in (289.5 by 264cm).
£800–900 *CSK*

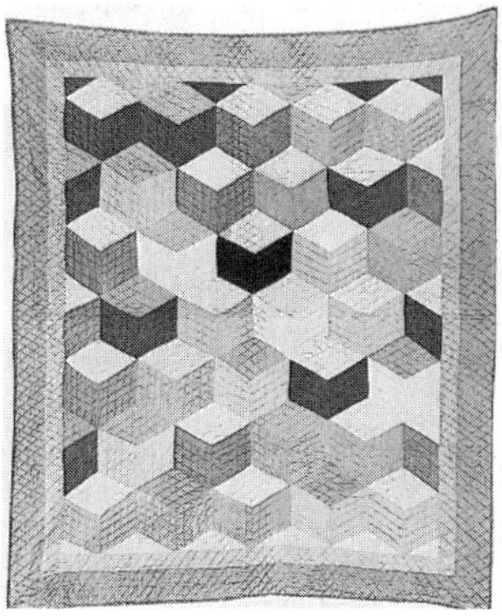

A pieced and appliquéd cotton quilted coverlet, the central field worked in a Tumbling Blocks pattern, in pink, teal, navy, plum, beige, salmon, green, mint and taupe, with light green inner border, green outer border, all enclosed by a grey surround, the whole with diamond quilting, Pennsylvania or Ohio, 19thC, 71 by 59in (180 by 149.5cm).
£700–800 *CNY*

A patchwork quilt, of Grandmother's Flower Garden design, worked by Mary Ann Freeman, Burnham, Essex, dated '1824', 62 by 48in (157 by 122cm).
£850–1,000 *RA*

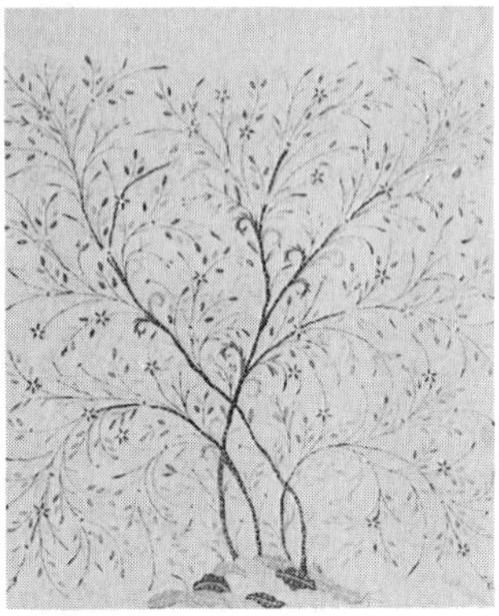

A Turkish cover of yellow silk, embroidered in mainly green, blue and brown silks with a stylised tree-of-life design worked in chain stitch, with a chenille and cotton fringe, lined, early 19thC, 53 by 42in (134.5 by 106.5cm).
£350–400 *P*

An American pieced and appliquéd quilted cotton coverlet, worked in blue, red, green and brown chintz and calico on a white ground, 3 edges hemmed by hand, mid-19thC, 98 by 88in (249 by 223.5cm).
£4,500–5,000 *CNY*

A Meadow Lily pattern quilt, of cream cotton with olive green flower stems and Turkey red flowers, with a large diamond border, reversing to a strip pattern in the same green and red, quilted in red cotton with waves, chevrons, flowerheads and diamonds, late 19thC, 98 by 79in (249 by 200.5cm).
£550–750 *CSK*

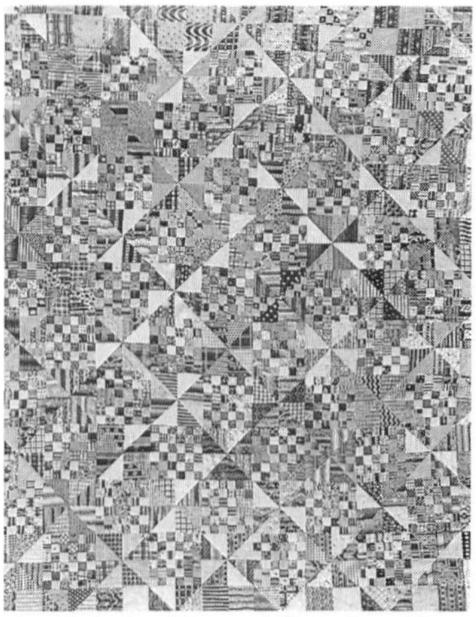

A printed cotton patchwork quilt, made up of 121 squares and triangles in a pinwheel design, quilted with a shell pattern, early 19thC, 118 by 106in (300 by 269cm).
£1,100–1,400 *CSK*

A French burgundy silk cover brocaded in bright yellow with flowers and foliate scrolls, in 5 widths, with braided borders, reversing to lavender cotton printed with leaf motifs, 19thC, each panel 24in (61cm) wide.
£300–400 *DN*

A pieced and appliquéd Royal Hawaiian flag quilt, composed of brightly coloured red, yellow, navy blue and white patches, Royal Hawaiian insignia and inscription in the centre, the borders with stylised Union Jacks, the field heightened with diamond and diagonal line stitching, slight stain, c1900, 72in (182.5cm) square.
£2,400–3,000 *S(NY)*

Royal Hawaiian quilts date from 1845 and are still being made today. The 4 flags are those of the island kingdom and the stripes represent a major island. The canton contains a representaion of the British Union Jack. The Hawaiian flag reflects an early association between Great Britain and Hawaii.

r. A coverlet arranged as a set table, made up of plain and printed cottons, mainly Laura Ashley, c1978.
£60–70 *CSK*

Embroidery

A Bruges millefleur medallion tapestry panel, all on a millefleur ground, a fruiting grapevine and guilloche chain above, mid-16thC, 61½ by 63in (156 by 160cm).
£25,000–30,000 *S(NY)*

A tent stitch embroidery, portraying Solomon seated beneath a canopy receiving gifts from the Queen of Sheba, c1660, 22 by 23½in (55.5 by 60cm), mounted.
£1,500–1,800 *P*

r. A needlework picture, worked in tent and cross stitch in coloured silks and wools, depicting Elijah ascending in a chariot of fire and his falling mantle being retrieved by Elisha, early 18thC, 24 by 18in (61 by 45.5cm), framed and glazed.
£900–1,100 *CSK*

An embroidery worked in long and short stitch and couched silk on an ivory satin ground, probably from a casket, c1670, 5 by 8in (13 by 20.5cm), glazed, in a later maple frame.
£1,500–2,000 *P*

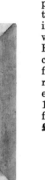

A needlework picture, in coloured wools in petit point, 17thC, 13 by 15½in (33 by 39.5cm), framed and glazed.
£1,000–1,400 *CSK*

A needlework picture, worked in buttonhole and tent stitch with coloured silks with spot motifs against a ground of ivory silk satin, 17thC, 18 by 20in (45.5 by 50.5cm).
£1,200–1,400 *CSK*

A needlework picture, of coloured wools and silks finely worked in tent stitch, with a gentleman addressing a seated lady in a rural landscape with birds and animals, a red brick house with a smoking chimney in the distance, early 18thC, 20 by 15in (50.5 by 38cm), framed and glazed.
£1,000–1,200 *CSK*

A pair of needlework pictures, worked in coloured wools and silks, early 18thC, 8½ by 10in (21 by 25cm), framed and glazed.
£1,700–2,200 *CSK*

l. A pair of needlework panels, early 18thC, 54 by 21in (137 by 53cm), each within partially gilt wood and glazed frames.
£6,000–7,000 *S(NY)*

An embroidered picture by J. Adams, worked in brightly coloured silks, with a soldier and his love, underneath a verse from him with a reply from her, 1836, 12 by 15in (30.5 by 38cm).
£1,200–1,500 *CSK*

An embroidered portrait of a small girl with long curly hair feeding a rabbit, worked in fine wool on a painted silk ground, late 18thC, 10½ by 14in (26 by 35.5cm), glazed in a contemporary gilded frame.
£600–800 *P*

A pair of embroidered pictures, finely worked in coloured silks, one with chenille threads, both with painted details, one depicting a lady seated under a tree with a dog, the other with a peasant woman with a rake, 8½ by 7in (21 by 17.5cm), framed and glazed.
£550–650 *CSK*

These pictures are inscribed on the reverse, ' "The Reaper", a Satin Piece worked by Margaret Colville aged 14 in 1789. She married Capt. Carruthers. Died 1847'.
'Sterne's "Poor Maria", a Satin Piece worked by Agnes Colville aged 13 in 1789. She died unmarried 1844.'

A French needlework panel for a stool, worked in silk and wool, ivory silk background to sprays of roses within a bead and trailing rose border, inscribed 'M . . Riffard, 10 rue de Mt Thador, Paris. 8h 10.' 19thC, 43 by 20in (109 by 50.5cm) wide, and 2 seperate bands with trailing roses, 32 by 3½in (81 by 9cm) wide.
£350–550 *WW*

An embroidered and plush picture, worked in coloured wools in gros point, mid-19thC, 34 by 26in (86 by 66cm).
£200–400 *CSK*

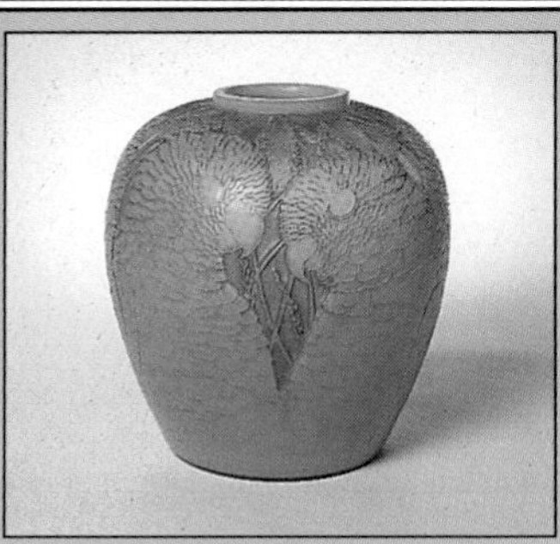

"Alicante", a Lalique cased glass vase, 25cm high, signed, "R. Lalique, France". Sold for £13,500

Two rare Villeroy & Boch "Mettlach", wall plates by Heinrich Schlitt, 44.2cm diam. nos 2697 & 2698. Sold for £3,760 and £4,000

An early Martin Brothers stoneware bird, 30.5cm high, signed and dated 5-12-82 Sold for £5,880

A rare Moorcroft pottery vase 32.5cm high, signed and dated 1916. Sold for £6,120

A Guild of Handicrafts Ltd silver cup & cover by C.R. Ashbee, 1902, 36.5cm high. Sold for £14,115

An Almeric Walter Pâte-de-Verre covered bowl, 17.5cm diameter, signed "A.Walter Nancy" and "H.Berge Sc.". Sold for £2,580

"Crimean Dancer", a fine painted bronze and ivory figure from a model by Claire Colinet, 44.5cm high. Sold for £7,645

19TH & 20TH CENTURY DECORATIVE ARTS

The pieces shown here illustrate the wide range of items that we have sold successfully in recent auctions. We are happy to value your items either in person or by means of an adequate photograph. Entries are always being accepted for inclusion in one of our specialised Decorative Arts sales, held eight times a year in London.

For further information on buying or selling at auction please contact the Art Nouveau Department on (0171) 629 6602

LONDON

Phillips

INTERNATIONAL AUCTIONEERS & VALUERS

101 New Bond Street, London W1Y 0AS

A giltwood display cabinet, by William Burges, with glazed doors and side panels, decorated with quatrefoil motifs, grotesque beasts and heraldic device, c1875, 38in (96.5cm) wide.
£10,500–11,500 *S*

A sideboard, by Wylie & Lockhead, inlaid with chequer stringing, 78in (198cm) wide.
£3,500–4,500 *C*

An Arts & Crafts oak desk, the top with green leather lining above 6 frieze drawers, with 4 further drawers to each pedestal and 4 chanelled cupboard doors with wrought iron strapwork, 72in (182.5cm) wide.
£3,000–4,000 *CSK*

A mahogany and satinwood cabinet-on-stand, by Charles Spooner, c1910, 37in (94cm) wide.
£3,500–4,500 *C*

An Aesthetic Movement stained and painted glass screen, attributed to J. Moyr Smith, the panels depicting birds in a landscape, in an ebonised wood frame, the lower panels painted and stencilled, c1875, 80½in (204cm) high.
£21,000–23,000 *C*

A cast iron tiled fireplace, with Art Nouveau tiles, c1890, 38in (96.5cm) square.
£400–500 *ASH*

An Art Furnishers' Alliance gilt, ebonised and carved side chair, designed by Christopher Dresser, c1870.
£21,000–25,000 *C*

An oak desk, attributed to Charles Rennie Mackintosh, the wooden handles inlaid with mother-of-pearl, c1905, 48in (122cm) wide.
£1,800–2,200 *S*

An oak washstand, by Charles Rennie Mackintosh, the work surface and back panel inlaid with ceramic tiles and leaded glass, c1904, 51in (129.5cm) wide.
£250,000–300,000 *S*

An Art Nouveau mahogany three-legged chair, inlaid with satinwood, 21in (53cm) wide.
£600–700 *ASA*

An ebonised wood table, by Carlo Bugatti, inlaid with pewter and bone, c1900, 23in (59cm) diam.
£3,500–4,500 *S*

A corner chair, by Carlo Bugatti, c1885, 27in (68.5cm) wide.
£1,800–2,800 *ASA*

A carved mahogany and marquetry three-tiered sideboard, by Louis Majorelle, 65in (165cm) wide.
£8,500–9,500 *CNY*

A curvelinear bed, by Louis Majorelle, the wooden frame carved with stylised flowerheads, c1900, 77in (195.5cm) long.
£8,750–10,000 *S*

An oak cabinet, designed by Peter Waals, c1920, 42in (106.5cm) wide.
£3,500–4,500 *C*

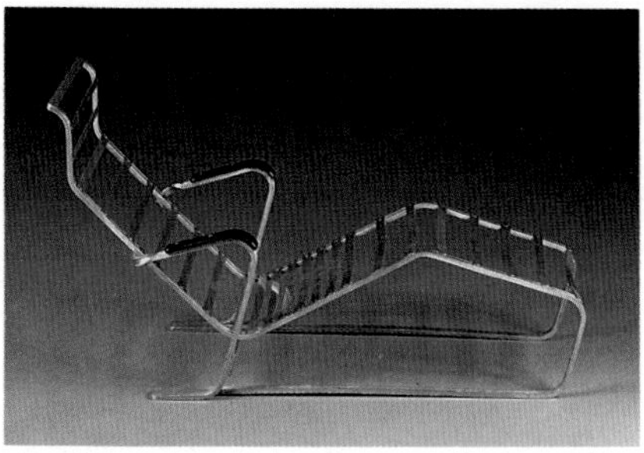

An aluminium chaise longue, designed by Marcel Breuer, with black painted wooden arm rests, c1935.
£20,000–22,000 *C*

A display cabinet, by Carlo Bugatti, covered in vellum, inlaid with pewter, applied with bone and wood strips, 41in (104cm) wide.
£9,500–10,500 *C*

A beechwood and laminated wood side chair, designed by Gerrit T. Rietveld, made by G. A. van de Groenekan, 34in (86cm) high.
£8,500–9,500 *CNY*

An ebène de Macassar 'lit soleil', by Jacques-Emile Ruhlmann, the headboard veneered with a sunburst pattern, 71in (180cm) wide.
£112,000–115,000 *CNY*

A limed oak special edition writing table and chair, by Ambrose Heal, c1931, table 51in (129.5cm) wide.
£4,500–6,000 *S*

A four-leaf screen, with glazed panels of striped silk, each panel 15½in (39.5cm) wide.
£1,500–2,000 *CSK*

A wrought iron table, by Paul Kiss, the base formed of stylised fern leaves, with a marble top and base, 24½in (62cm) diam.
£8,000–9,000 *CNY*

A steel and marble console table, attributed to Walter van Alen for the Chrysler Building, New York, c1930, 41½in (105.5cm) wide.
£8,500–9,500 *CNY*

A Clarice Cliff Bizarre Nasturtium jam pot, 4½in (11.5cm) high.
£200–250 *WTA*

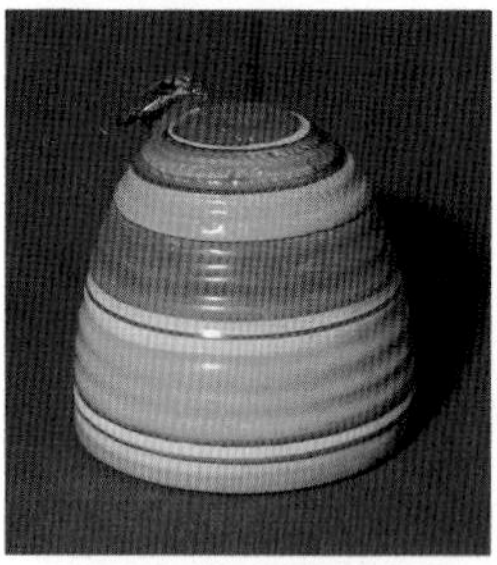

A Clarice Cliff Bizarre bee-hive honey pot, in early banded pattern, 5in (12.5cm).
£160–180 *WTA*

A Clarice Cliff Fantasque cup and saucer, in Umbrellas and Rain pattern, c1929, cup 2in (5cm) high.
£200–220 *BKK*

A Clarice Cliff Chester fern pot, in Umbrellas and Rain pattern, c1929, 3½in (9cm) high.
£450–550 *BKK*

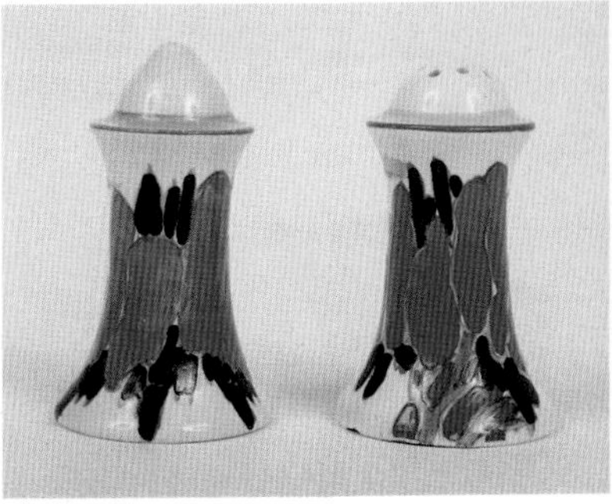

A Clarice Cliff Solitude pattern salt and pepper pot, damaged, 3in (7.5cm) high.
£140–160 *BKK*

A Clarice Cliff Blue Autumn pattern plate, c1931, 9in (22.5cm) diam.
£180–220 *BKK*

A Clarice Cliff single handled Lotus jug, in Gardenia pattern, c1931, 11in (28cm) high.
£1,200–1,500 *BKK*

A Clarice Cliff Geometric pattern stick stand, slight crack, c1920s, 18½in (47cm) high.
£600–1,000 *YY*

A Clarice Cliff Conical jug, in Oranges pattern, c1931, 6in (15cm) high.
£450–550 *BKK*

A Clarice Cliff Crocus pattern sandwich set, c1928, plates 5½in (14cm) wide.
£400–500 *BKK*

A set of Clarice Cliff Crocus pattern egg cups and saucer, c1932, 6½in (16.5cm) diam.
£200–250 *BKK*

A Clarice Cliff sugar sifter, in Capri pattern, c1936, 5in (12.5cm) high.
£120–150 *BKK*

A Clarice Cliff Newport pattern hot water jug, Bon Jour shape, 1935, 7in (17cm) high.
£200–250 *BKK*

A Clarice Cliff Crocus pattern coffee set, in Tankard shape, 16 pieces, c1931, pot 7¼in (18.5cm) high.
£1,300–1,500 *BKK*

A Clarice Cliff Oasis pattern bowl, shape 55, c1932, 8½in (21cm) diam.
£400–500 *BKK*

A Clarice Cliff plate, in Orange Trees and House pattern, c1931, 7in (17.5cm) diam.
£100–120 *BKK*

A Clarice Cliff Bridgewater pattern jam pot and lid, Bon Jour shape, c1934, 4½in (11cm) high.
£250–300 *BKK*

A Gray's Pottery plaque, c1930, 13in (33cm) diam.
£200–250 *HEW*

A ceramic wall mask, unmarked, 10½in (27cm) high.
£90–100 *WTA*

A Bursley Ware charger, by Charlotte Rhead, pattern No. 1714, 1920s, 14in (35.5cm) diam.
£650–750 *HEA*

A Royal Copenhagen owl, marked, c1950, 15½in (39.5cm) high.
£400–600 *ASA*

A Crown Ducal Link design three-handled vase, by Charlotte Rhead, c1930, 8in (20cm) high.
£140–180 *YY*

A Burgess & Leigh 4 person sandwich set, by Charlotte Rhead, in New Jazz pattern, c1920.
£80–120 *HEA*

A Charlotte Rhead bowl, signed, and with Burleigh mark, c1925, 9½in (24cm) diam.
£450–500 *WN*

A Charlotte Rhead Rhodian pattern vase, c1933, 9½in (24cm) high.
£120–140 *HEA*

A Hancock Rubens Ware footed bowl, Pomegranate pattern, hand painted by F. X. Abrahams, c1923, 12in (30.5cm) wide.
£80–90 *CSA*

A Royal Doulton Night Watchman pattern jug and basin set, with a chamber pot and 2 soap dishes, jug 9in (22.5cm) high.
£400–430 *AnE*

A Rozenburg pottery vase, designed by W. P. Hartgring, c1896, 19in (48cm) high.
£1,500–2,500 *OO*

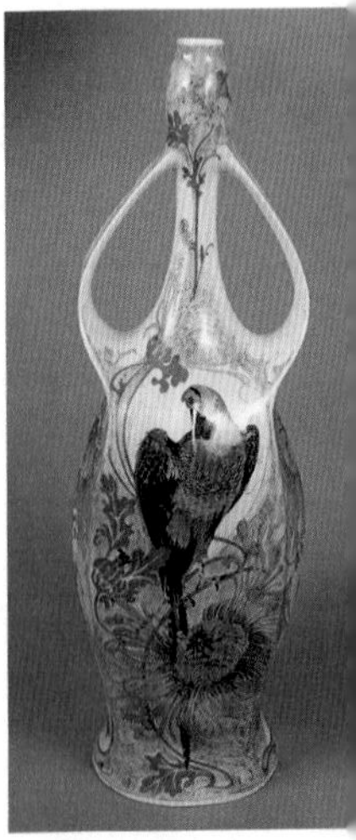

A Rozenburg vase, designed by L. Hakker, c1914, 16in (40.5cm) high.
£2,500–3,500 *OO*

An earthenware vase, by George Ohr, 11in (28.5cm) high.
£8,500–9,500 *CNY*

A Burmantofts jardinière, marked on base, late 19thC, 8½in (21.5cm) high.
£150–250 *ASA*

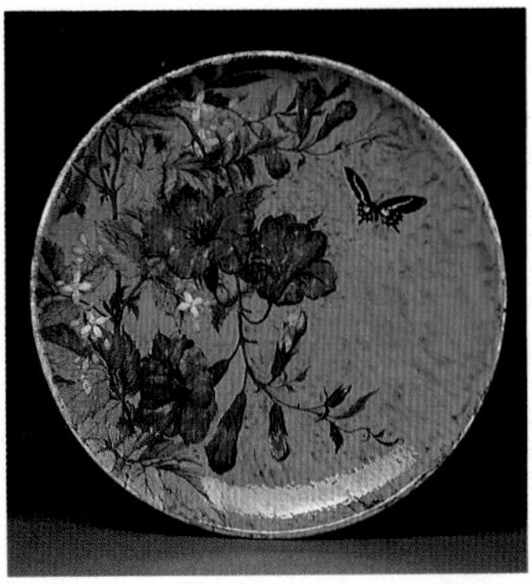

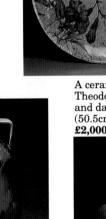

A ceramic charger, by Theodore Deck, signed and dated '1884', 20in (50.5cm) diam.
£2,000–2,500 *CNY*

An Art Nouveau Lancastrian lustre bowl, 9½in (24cm) diam.
£400–600 *ASA*

A Rookwood ceramic vase, marked, stamped '04xxx' and 'W', 1893, 30in (76cm) high.
£4,000–4,500 *CNY*

A high-fired vase-on-stand, marked 'Ruskin, England', 1920s, 17in (43cm) high overall.
£3,000–3,500 *C*

Two seated cats, by Emile Gallé, with faience decorated bodies and glass eyes, c1880, largest 13½in (34cm) high.
£4,400–4,800 each *S*

A Lancastrian lustre vase, 7½in (19cm) high.
£200–300 *ASA*

A pair of Minton cloisonné vases, designed by Christopher Dresser, each impressed and numbered '1592', c1871, 11in (28cm) high.
£4,500–5,000 *C*

A Lancastrian lustre vase, 4½in (11.5cm) high.
£150–300 *ASA*

A ceramic jardinière, attributed to Albert Macarthur, 1928, 18½in (47cm) wide.
£6,000–6,500 *CNY*

An Amphora baluster form ceramic vase, decorated with a bat, stamped underglaze mark, 10in (25cm) high.
£2,800–3,200 *CNY*

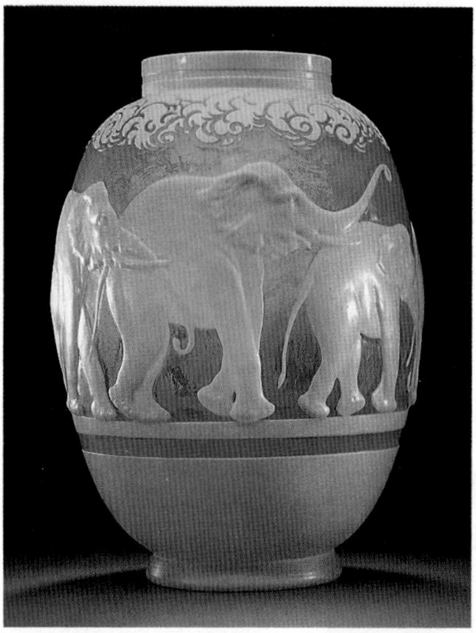

A mould blown, overlaid and etched glass vase, by Emile Gallé, overlaid and etched with elephants, 15in (38cm) high.
£27,000–30,000 *CNY*

An internally decorated acid cut vase, cameo mark 'Daum Nancy' and Cross of Lorraine, 21in (53cm) high.
£4,500–5,000 *Bon*

An internally decorated, carved and acid etched vase, engraved mark 'Daum Nancy' and Cross of Lorraine, 18in (45.5cm) high.
£10,000–13,000 *Bon*

A cameo glass vase, marked 'Misale', 4½in (11cm) high.
£500–700 *ASA*

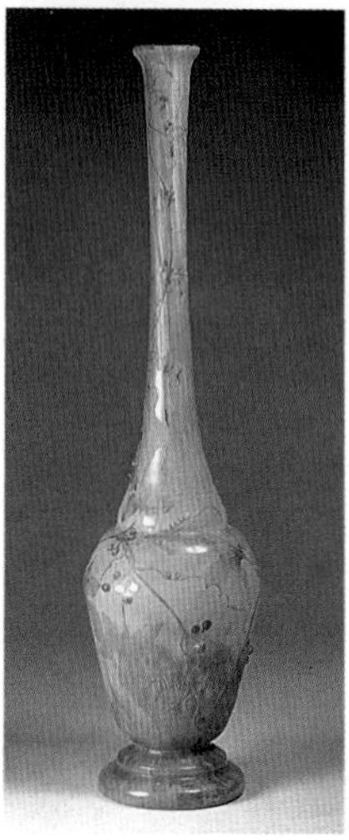

An internally decorated, acid cut enamelled and applied vase, signed in cameo 'Daum Nancy' and Cross of Lorraine, 21½in (54.5cm) high.
£4,700–5,300 *Bon*

A cameo glass vase, by Emile Gallé, 7in (17.5cm) high.
£1,000–1,500 *ASA*

A glass vase, with floral design in 3 layers, signed in cameo 'Gallé', c1900, 6½in (16.5cm) high.
£1,000–1,200 *PSG*

An internally decorated and acid cut trumpet vase, engraved 'Daum Nancy' and Cross of Lorraine, 13½in (34.5cm) high.
£11,000–13,000 *Bon*

An overlaid and etched glass vase, by Emile Gallé, with cameo signature, 22in (55.5cm) high.
£22,000–24,000 *CNY*

An enamelled and wheel carved glass bowl, with gilding, by Emile Gallé, inscribed, 3½in (9cm) high.
£19,000–21,000 *CNY*

A Chrysanthemum vase, by Emile Gallé, c1900, 23in (58.5cm) high.
£10,500–12,000 *S*

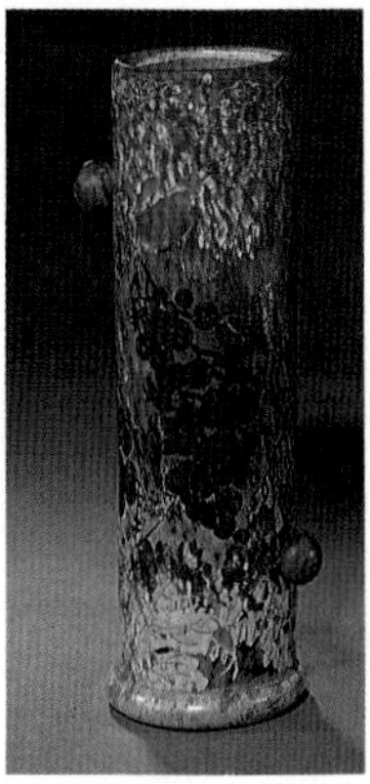

A glass vase, marked 'Daum Nancy', c1900, 13in (33cm) high.
£10,000–11,000 *C*

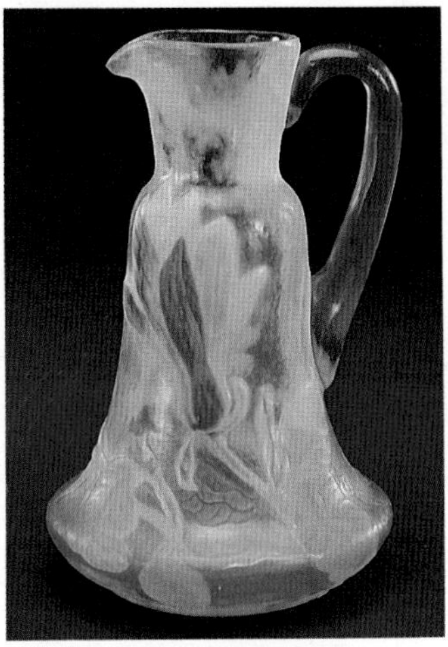

A clear glass jug, by Emile Gallé, carved with magnolias, with an applied handle, marked, 10in (25cm) high.
£19,000–22,000 *S*

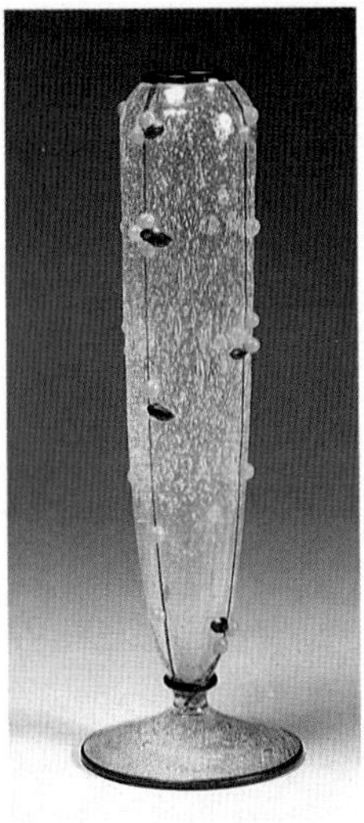

An internally decorated vase, with applied decoration, engraved mark 'Daum Nancy', 10½in (26.6cm) high.
£8,000–9,000 *Bon*

A cameo glass table lamp, by Emile Gallé, marked, c1900, 13in (33cm) high.
£25,000–27,000 *C*

A Favrile flowerform glass vase, by Tiffany Studios, engraved 'L.C.T.' and numbered, 18in (45.5cm) high.
£8,500–9,500 *CNY*

A cameo glass table lamp, the shade with quatrefoil rim, the base applied with 2 carved glass snails, marked 'Daum Nancy', c1900, 18½in (47cm) high.
£42,000–45,000 *C*

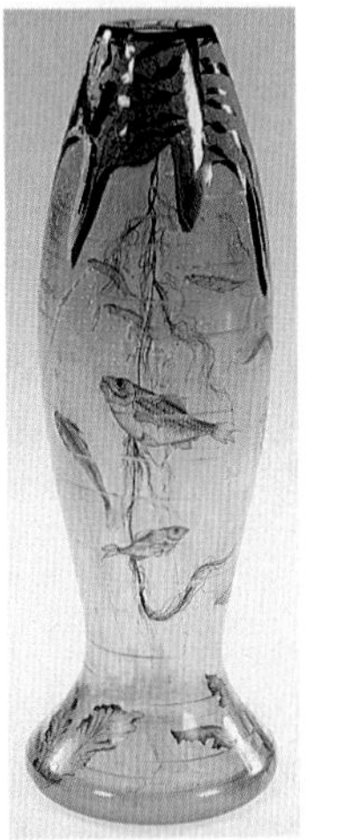

A vase, engraved and enamelled with aquatic plants and animals, marked 'Daum Nancy', c1900, 16in (40.5cm) high.
£14,000–16,000 *S*

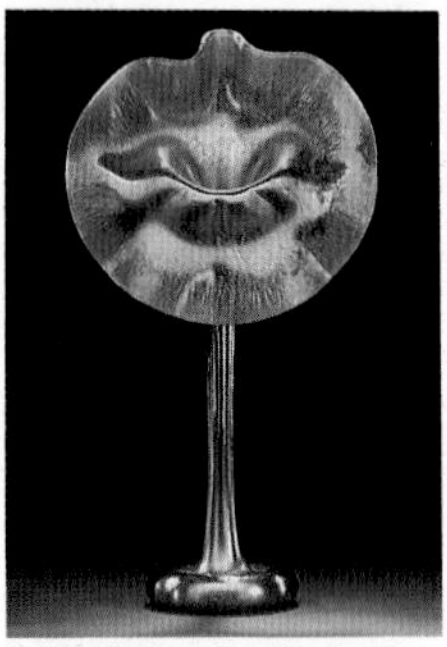

A 'Jack-in-the-Pulpit' Favrile vase, by Tiffany Studios, marked '2466H', 20in (50.5cm) high.
£7,000–8,000 *CNY*

A Lotus flower vase, by Emile Gallé, decorated with applied scarab beetles, c1900, 11in (28cm) high.
£9,500–10,500 *S*

A cameo glass Polar Bear vase, intaglio carved mark 'Gallé', c1925, 11in (28cm) high.
£30,000–35,000 *C*

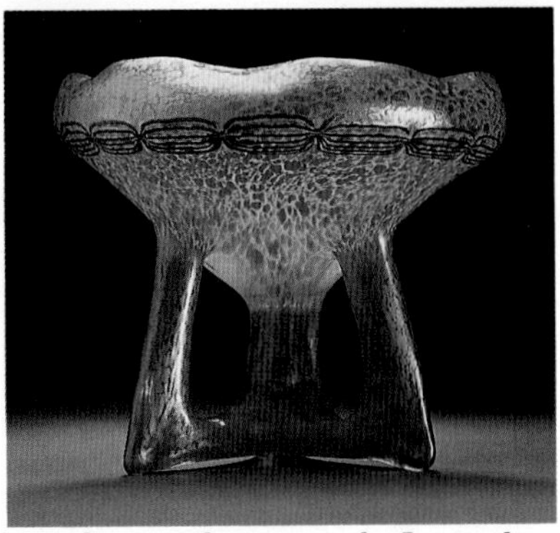

An iridescent glass coupe, by Loetz, the bowl on a tripod base with central support, decorated with gold oil spot motif and a cobalt band, 10½in (26.5cm) diam.
£16,500–17,500 *CNY*

A leaded glass and bronze Laburnum table lamp, stamped 'Tiffany Studios New York 9933', 31in (78.5cm) high.
£45,000–47,000 *CNY*

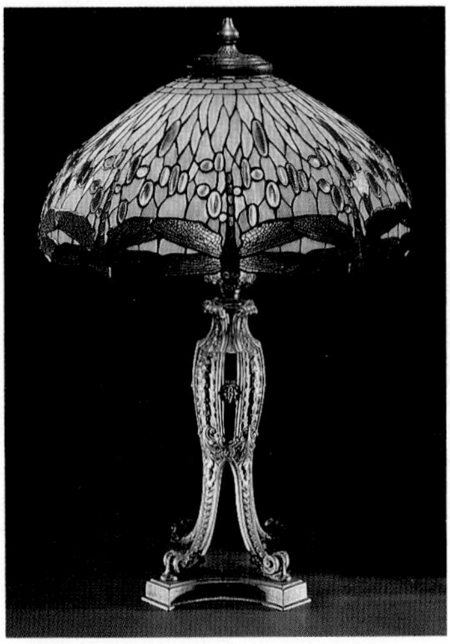

A leaded glass and gilt bronze Hanging-head Dragonfly table lamp, stamped 'Tiffany Studios New York 550', 32in (81cm) high.
£24,000–26,000 *CNY*

A ten-light Favrile glass and gilt bronze Lily table lamp, stamped 'Tiffany Studios New York 381', 21½in (55cm) high.
£12,500–14,000 *CNY*

A leaded glass and bronze Daffodil table lamp, stamped 'Tiffany Studios New York 1443', 22in (55.5cm) high.
£15,000–16,000 *CNY*

A leaded glass, turtle-back tile and bronze Acorn chandelier, by Tiffany Studios, 34in (86cm) high.
£12,500–14,000 *CNY*

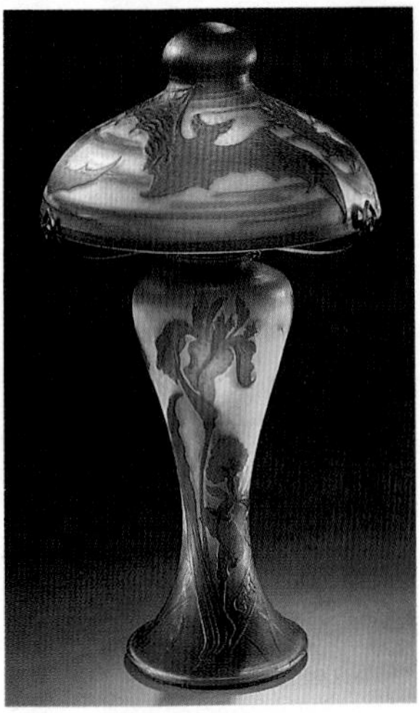

A double overlaid, wheel carved and etched glass table lamp, by Emile Gallé, c1901, 26in (66cm) high.
£32,000–35,000 *CNY*

A leaded glass and bronze Daffodil table lamp, with conical shade, stamped 'Tiffany Studios New York 1497', 24in (61.5cm) high.
£16,000–18,000 *CNY*

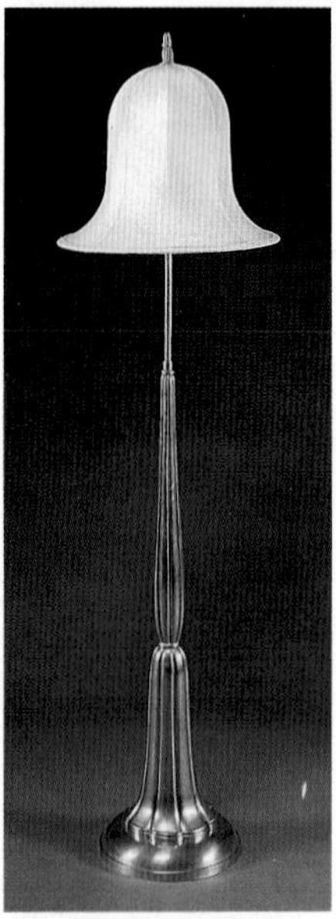

A gilt bronze floor lamp, by Süe et Mare, with a waisted domed silk shade, c1925, 64in (162.5cm) high.
£20,000–22,000 *CNY*

A leaded glass and bronze Zodiac table lamp, stamped 'Tiffany Studios New York 507a', 30in (76cm) high.
£40,000–42,000 *CNY*

A leaded glass and bronze Rose table lamp, stamped 'Tiffany Studios New York 1915', 32in (81cm) high.
£30,000–32,000 *CNY*

A pair of inlaid mahogany and leaded glass wall sconces, with square lanterns, by Greene and Greene, mounted on mahogany wall brackets, c1907, 19in (48cm) high.
£31,000–32,000 *CNY*

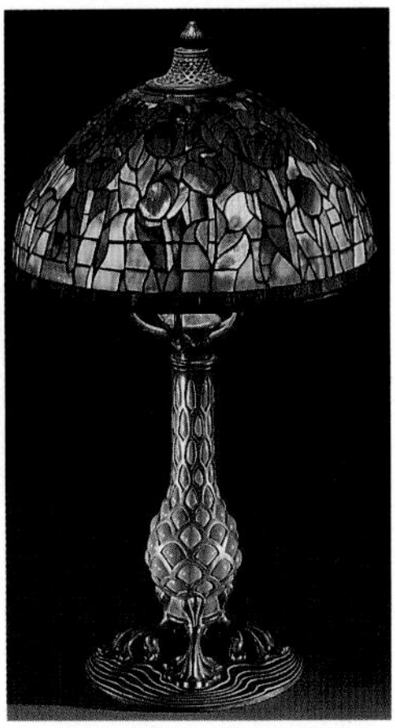

A leaded glass and bronze Tulip table lamp, stamped 'Tiffany Studios New York 29727', 23½in (60cm) high.
£88,000–90,000 *CNY*

A leaded glass and bronze Hydrangea floor lamp, stamped 'Tiffany Studios New York 21551', 80in (203cm) high.
£82,000–85,000 *CNY*

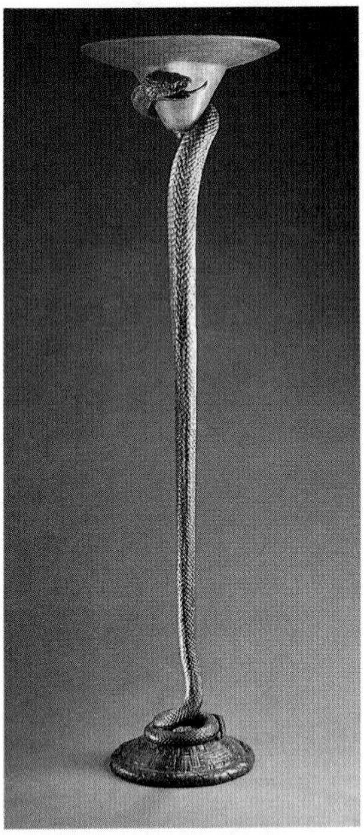

A bronze and glass floor lamp, 'La Tentation', the bronze by Edgar Brandt, the glass by Daum, c1924, 64½in (164cm) high.
£35,000–38,000 *CNY*

A leaded glass and bronze Pond Lily lamp, stamped 'Tiffany', 27in (68.5cm) high.
£54,000–56,000 *CNY*

A leaded glass and bronze Woodbine table lamp, by Tiffany Studios, 19½in (49.6cm) high.
£12,500–13,500 *CNY*

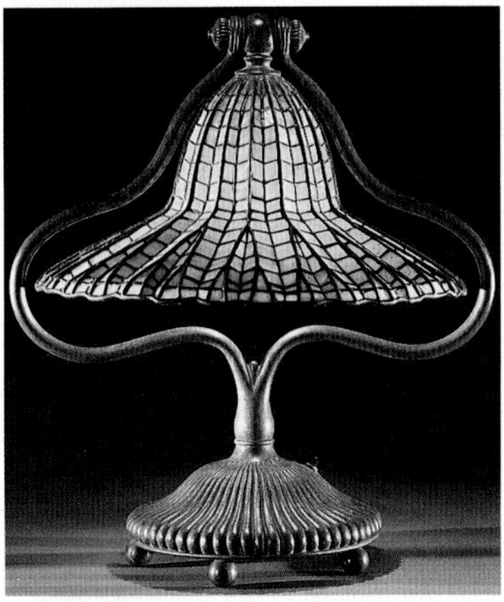

A leaded glass and bronze Lotus table lamp, stamped 'Tiffany Studios New York 1460', 20in (50.5cm) high.
£20,000–22,000 *CNY*

A leaded glass and bronze Tulip table lamp, stamped 'Tiffany Studios New York 26877', 22in (55.5cm) high.
£24,000–26,000 *CNY*

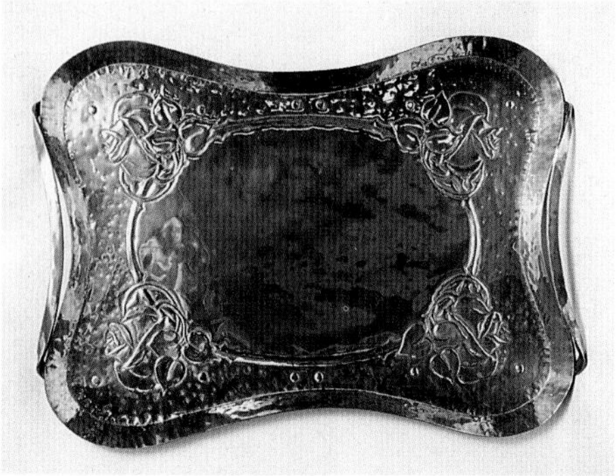

An Art Nouveau copper tray, by Hugh Wallis, 22in (55.5cm) wide.
£400–450 *BRD*

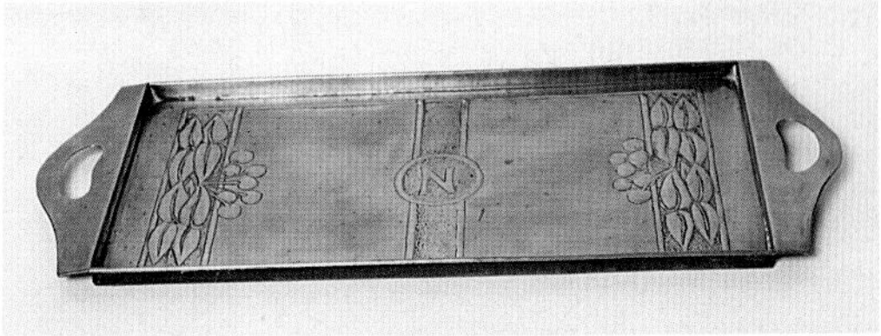

An Art Nouveau brass tray, 26in (66cm) long.
£50–90 *ASA*

An Art Nouveau copper coal scuttle, with wrought iron work, c1890, 15in (38cm) high.
£100–150 *ASH*

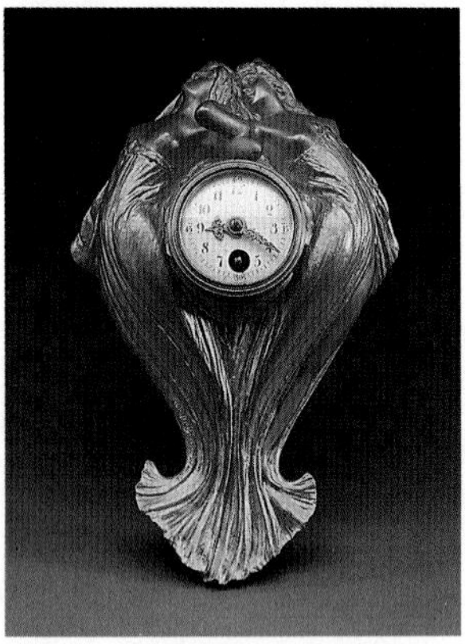

A gilt bronze clock, stamped 'P. Moreau Vauthier Daubree', 8in (20cm) high.
£2,000–2,500 *CNY*

An Art Nouveau copper and wrought iron fire screen, c1890, 24in (61cm) wide.
£175–200 *ASH*

An Art Nouveau copper coal scuttle and shovel, c1910, 14in (36cm) high.
£75–100 *ASH*

A pair of Art Nouveau pewter candelabra, 9½in (24cm) high.
£700–800 *ASA*

A pair of Art Nouveau brass fire irons, c1910, 16½in (42cm) high.
£175–200 *ASH*

An Art Nouveau silver patinated bronze clock, from models by Maurice Dufrène and Voulot, c1900, 22in (55.5cm) high.
£4,500–5,500 *C*

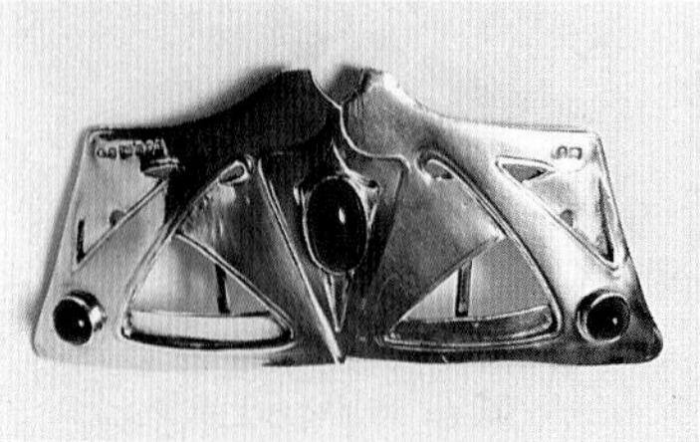

An Art Nouveau silver and cornelian buckle, 4in (10cm) wide.
£200–300 *ASA*

An Art Nouveau Liberty silver and enamel cigarette box, 6½in (16.5cm) wide.
£400–500 *ASA*

A WMF Art Nouveau inkstand, decorated with a shamrock, containing original ink bottle, 8in (20cm) wide.
£250–350 *ASA*

A pair of Danish silver five-light candelabra, by Georg Jensen Silversmithy, decorated with grapes and leaves, marked '383', post-1945, 10in (25cm) high, 186oz.
£17,000–20,000 *CNY*

An Art Deco silver tray, with a coffee and liqueur set, 15in (38cm) wide.
£500–700 *ASA*

An Art Nouveau claret jug, with a silver mount, 12½in (31.5cm) high.
£500–600 *ASA*

A Wiener Werkstätte brass vase, designed by Josef Hoffmann, c1924, 7in (17.5cm) high.
£5,250–6,000 *C*

An Art Nouveau silver cigarette box, 3½in (9cm) square.
£350–450 *ASA*

A Danish silver mantel clock, designed by Johan Rohde, by Georg Jensen Silversmithy, marked '333' on base, c1945, 12in (30.5cm) high.
£15,500–17,000 *CNY*

A patinated metal mantel clock, by Josef Maria Olbrich for Eduard Hueck, c1900, 8½in (21.5cm) high.
£4,000–5,000 *S*

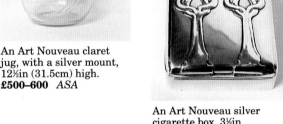

A silver coloured metal tea and coffee service, by Josef Hoffmann for the Wiener Werkstätte, stamped, c1920, coffee pot 8in (20cm) high.
£10,500–12,000 *S*

An Art Nouveau wrought iron and glass basket, 12in (30.5cm) diam.
£300–400 *ASA*

An Art Deco shagreen cigarette box, with silver inlaid panel, 6in (15cm) wide.
£300–450 *ASA*

An Art Deco enamelled cigarette case, 1930s, 3½in (9cm) wide.
£15–30 *ASA*

A cold painted bronze and ivory dancer, by Demètre H. Chiparus, restored, 1920s, 23in (58.5cm) high.
£14,000–15,000 *S*

A cold painted bronze figure, 'Kneeling Dancer', by Demètre H. Chiparus and marked, 1920s, on a marble base, 23in (58.5cm) wide.
£30,000–32,000 *S*

A bronze figure, by Bruno Zach, on a marble base, 1920s, 28in (71cm) high.
£8,000–10,000 *ASA*

A cold painted bronze and ivory figure of a dancer, inscribed 'Gerdago', early 20thC, 13½in (34.5cm) high.
£3,500–4,000 *CNY*

A cold painted bronze woman's head, marked 'Dakon', 1930s, 11in (28cm) high.
£1,500–2,000 *S*

A bronze and ivory figure, Cabaret Girl, by F. Preiss, on a marble base, 15in (38cm) high.
£8,000–10,000 *ASA*

A bronze and ivory figure, 'Con Brio', by F. Preiss, 15in (38cm) high.
£10,000–12,000 *ASA*

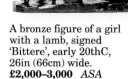

A bronze figure of a girl with a lamb, signed 'Bittere', early 20thC, 26in (66cm) wide.
£2,000–3,000 *ASA*

An Art Nouveau brass figure, holding a mirror, on a marble base, 20in (50.5cm) high.
£800–900 *ASA*

A bronze figure, by Samuel Lypsitch, c1930, on a marble base, 17in (43cm) high.
£2,500–3,500 *ASA*

A cold painted bronze and ivory group, 'Russian Dancers', from a model by Demètre H. Chiparus, early 20thC, inscribed 'Etling, Paris', 24in (61cm) high.
£22,000–25,000 *CNY*

Antique Galleries
26 Broad St., Pendleton, Salford
Manchester, M6 5BY, Tel: 0161 737 5938
AUDREY STERNSHINE
Specialist in Art Nouveau & Art Deco.

A frosted and clear glass shade, 'Oiseau de Feu', marked 'R. Lalique', wheel cut 'France', after 1922.
£12,000–14,000 *S*

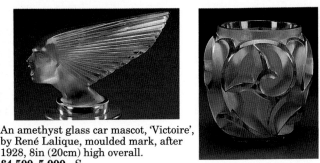

An amethyst glass car mascot, 'Victoire', by René Lalique, moulded mark, after 1928, 8in (20cm) high overall.
£4,500–5,000 *S*

An amber glass vase, 'Tourbillons', by René Lalique, after 1926, 8in (20cm) high.
£6,000–7,000 *S*

A glass vase, 'Perruches', decorated with lovebirds and prunus blossom, etched 'R. Lalique', 10in (25cm) high.
£5,500–6,000 *P*

A dark amber vase, 'Poissons', moulded mark 'R. Lalique', 9½in (24cm) high.
£6,500–7,500 *CSK*

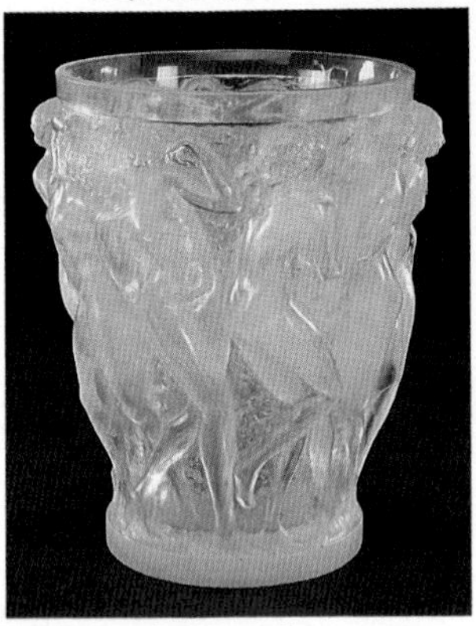

An opalescent glass vase, 'Bacchantes', by René Lalique, wheel cut mark and engraved 'No. 997', after 1927, 9½in (24cm) high.
£8,000–10,000 *S*

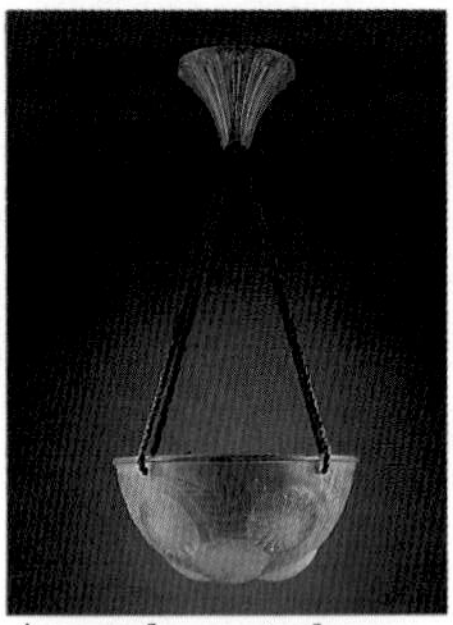

An opalescent glass chandelier, 'Dahlias', by René Lalique, 12in (30.5cm) diam.
£3,000–3,500 *CNY*

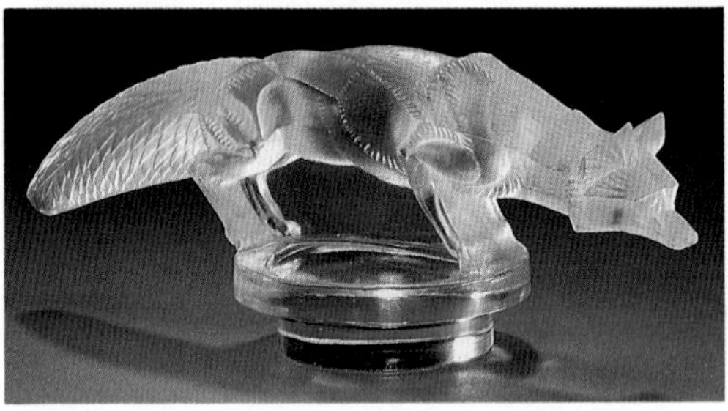

A clear and frosted glass mascot, moulded as a fox, 'Renard', acid etched 'R. Lalique', 8½in (21.5cm) long.
£80,000–85,000 *CNY*
This model is considered the rarest of Lalique's mascots.

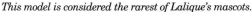

A deep amber glass vase, 'Serpent', impressed 'R. Lalique', 10in (25cm) high.
£7,500–8,500 *CSK*

A frosted glass mascot, 'Tête de Paon', moulded 'R. Lalique', c1928, 7in (17.5cm) high.
£30,000–32,000 *CNY*

An electric blue glass vase, 'Sauterelles', moulded in relief with grasshoppers, engraved 'R. Lalique', 10½in (27cm) high.
£6,500–8,000 *CSK*

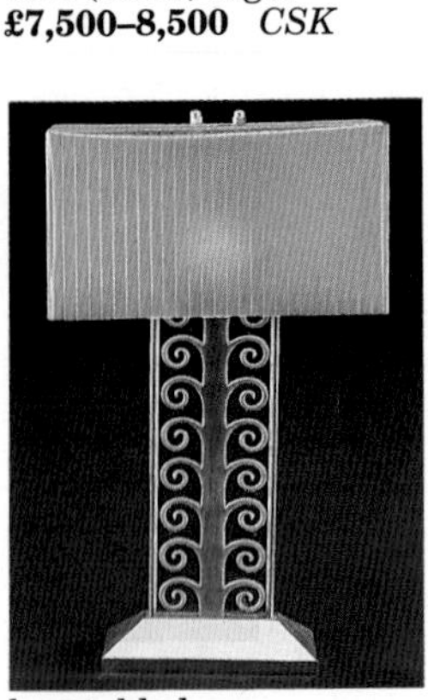

A glass table lamp, 'Cardamine', wheel cut mark 'R. Lalique France', after 1928, 18in (45.5cm) high.
£4,500–6,000 *S*

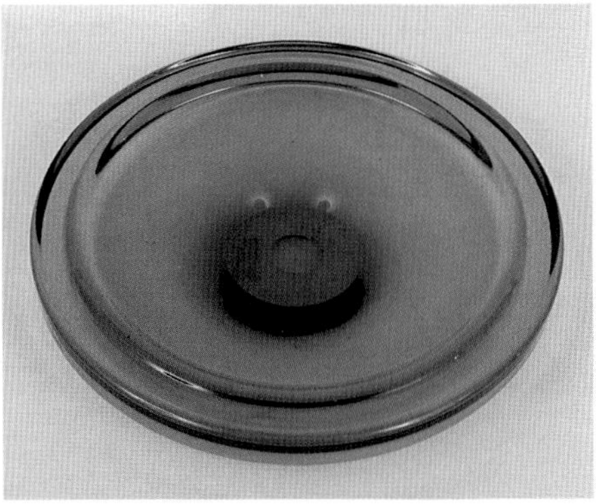

A Kosta glass platter, c1970, 13in (33cm) diam.
£45–65 *BEN*

A Poole Pottery vase, c1924, 5½in (14cm) high.
£60–70 *YY*

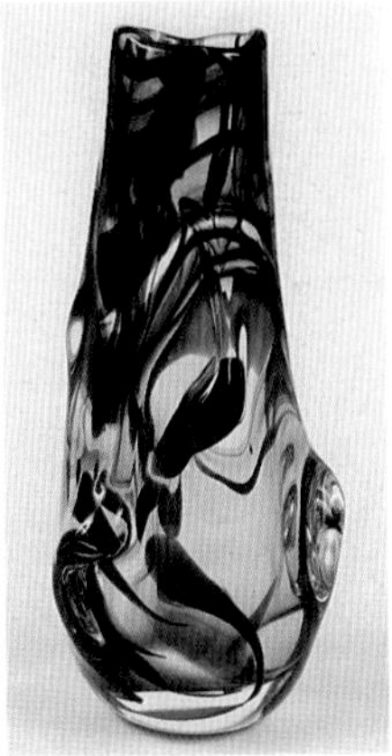

A Whitefriars 'tree trunk' vase, 1960s, 9in (23cm) high.
£20–30 *JHa*

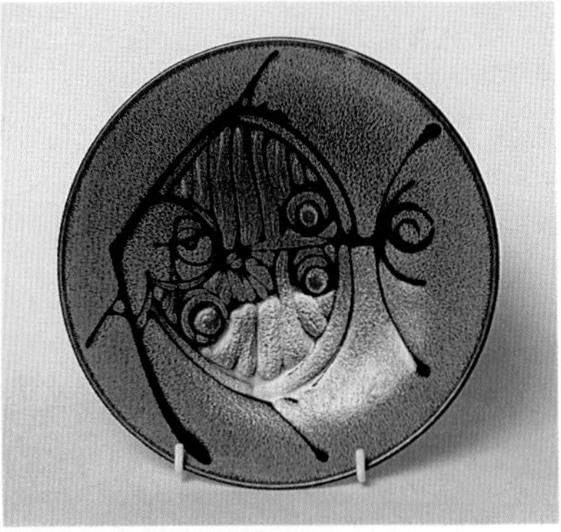

A Poole Pottery Aegean plate, c1960, 8in (20cm) diam.
£25–30 *YY*

A Sckruffs glass vase, coloured amethyst at the top, c1960, 7in (17.5cm) high.
£30–40 *BEN*

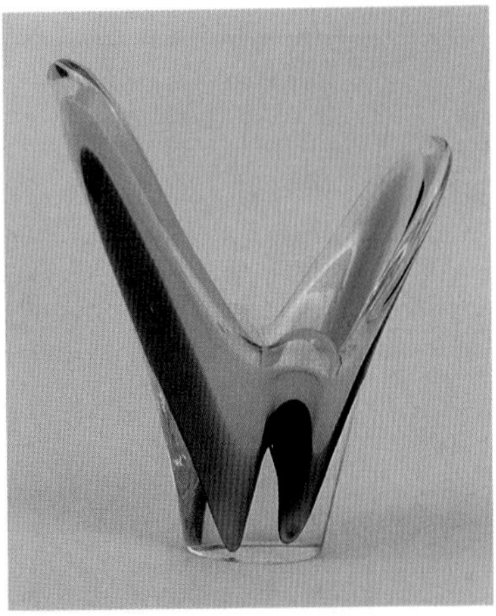

A Swedish glass vase, with 2 compartments, by Flygfors, c1959.
£30–40 *BEN*

A Whitefriars glass bowl, 1960s, 8in (20cm) diam.
£60–80 *JHa*

A Whitefriars glass ribbon vase, 1930–50, 8in (20cm) high.
£40–50 *JHa*

Two Sam Hermann Studio glass vases, 1980s, largest 10in (25cm) high.
£400–600 *JHa*
Sam Hermann was given permission to set up a glass Art Studio at the Royal College of Art, London, in 1968.

An overstrung baby grand piano, by Emile Paver, No. 29954, the frame No. 6985, in a satinwood case with painted decoration.
£3,750–4,250 *CSK*

A stained wood violin, by Guisseppe Pedrazzini, 1926.
£10,000–12,000 *HCH*

A beechwood and oak grand piano, by Blüthner, Leipzig, No. 46245, with carved decoration, on cabriole legs, 1896, 61in (155cm) long.
£6,500–7,500 *CSK*

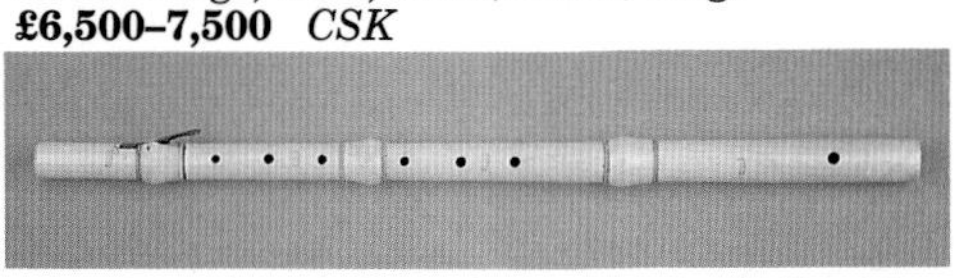

A one-keyed ivory flute, by Benjamin Hallet, the silver key with square cover, stamped on each of the 4 joints, boxed, c1740.
£2,000–2,500 *Bon*

A double bass, by Bernard Simon Fendt after Maggini, labelled, the two-piece flat back of medium curl, ribs and scroll similar, table medium grain, London, 1836.
£22,000–24,000 *Bon*

A viola, by Nathaniel Cross, labelled, the one-piece back of medium curl, ribs and scroll similar, table of medium grain, Lonson, 1732,
£19,000–24,000 *Bon*

A single-manual harpsichord, by P. Gasparro Saberino, inscribed on reverse of the fascia board and under the keyboard, 1712, 76in (193cm) long.
£16,500–18,000 *S*

A marquetry and parcel gilt semi-grand piano, by Broadwood, No. 45955, with paterae decorated panels of musical trophies, on ribbon bound reeded tapered legs, c1895, 76in (193cm) long.
£20,000–22,000 *CSK*

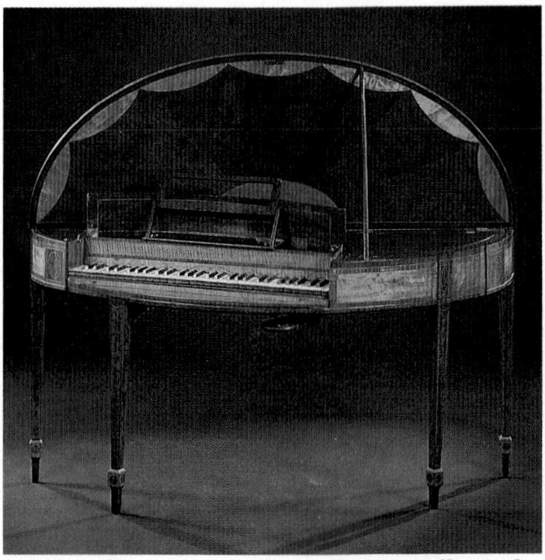

A piano, the case in the form of a semi-elliptical side table, the hinged top inlaid with satinwood and yew wood, inscribed on the nameboard 'Southwell fecit', c1785, 63in (160cm) long.
£33,000–35,000 *S*

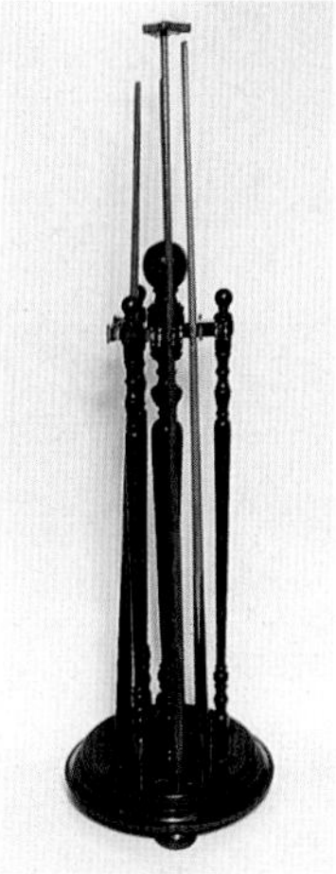

A mahogany billiard cue stand, c1870, 47in (119cm) high.
£800–850 *GJC*

A full size carved cuban mahogany billiard table, by Burroughes & Watts, fitted with steel vacuum cushions, c1895.
£18,000–22,000 *HAB*

A late Victorian oak billiard room cabinet, by George Wright & Sons, London, with a carved pediment, 48in (122cm) wide.
£4,500–5,000 *BRA*

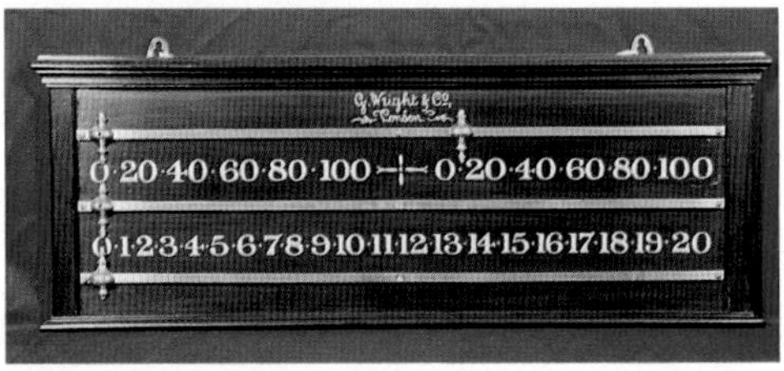

A mahogany billiard marker board, by G. Wright & Co., London, 30in (76cm) wide.
£180–200 *HAB*

The World Sculling Championship Trophy, by the Goldsmiths & Silversmiths Co., London 1912.
£2,000–3,000 *S*

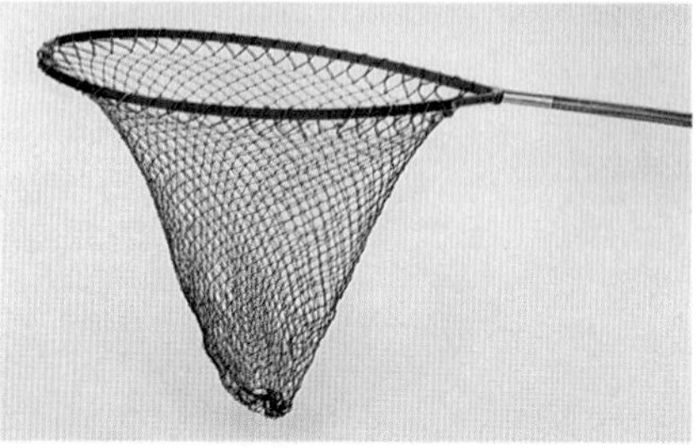

A landing net, with brass fittings and bamboo handle, 19thC, 85in (216cm) long.
£70–150 *GHA*

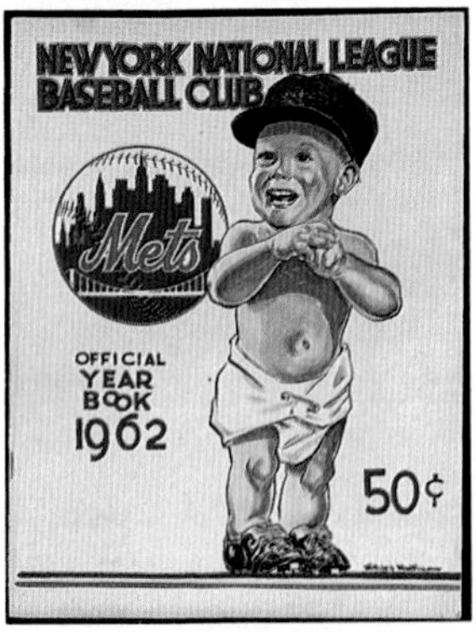

Thirty-nine New York Mets year books, 1962–92 run, and 8 others.
£800–1,000 *CNY*

A Hardy 4½in Nottingham Silex reel, with Bickerdyke line guard, c1900.
£250–300 *GHA*

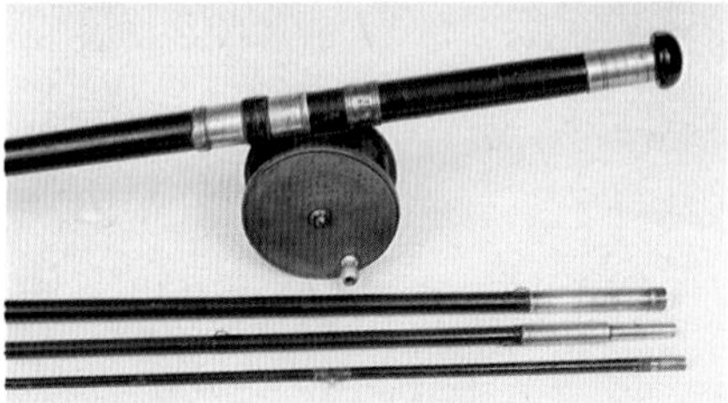

A greenheart salmon rod, in 4 parts, by Eaton & Deller, London, with a 4½in brass plate wind reel, marked, c1850, 192in (486cm) long.
£300–400 *GHA*

A wicker fishing creel, 19thC, 14in (35.5cm) wide.
£60–65 *GHA*

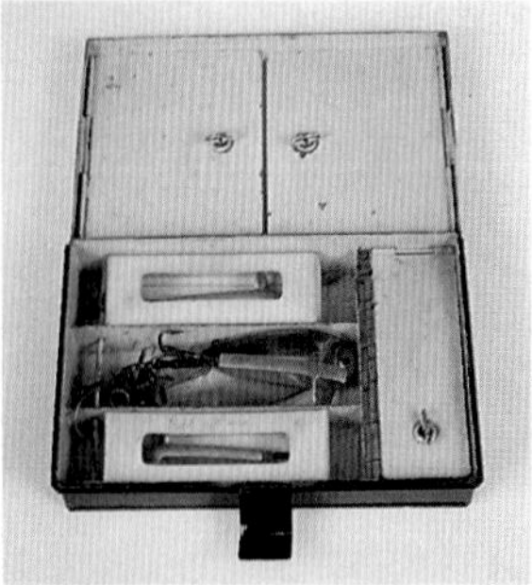

A black japanned tin box, containing lures, 19thC, 7in (17.5cm) wide.
£50–60 *GHA*

A hand carved and painted decoy wood pigeon, with original glass eyes, c1880, 10in (25cm) wide.
£150–180 *RYA*

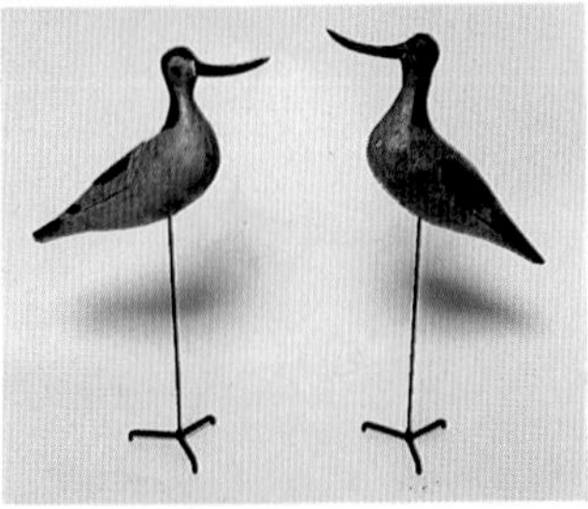

A pair of painted decoy birds, on stands, c1880, 16in (40cm) high.
£600–700 *RYA*

An oak billiard table, by George Wright, c1880.
£10,000–15,000 *WBB*

An olive wood, satinwood, kingwood, rosewood and walnut billiard table, converted to a pool table, c1796.
£10,000–15,000 *WBB*

A burr oak billiard table, by Orme & Sons, with matching burr oak ball retainers.
£15,000–20,000 *WBB*

A Burroughes & Watts sporting table, with 12 carved panels depicting 12 Medieval sports, the turrets as pockets/ball catchers.
£60,000–70,000 *WBB*

A Grenfell Mission hooked mat, 15½ by 12in (39.5 by 30.5cm).
£450–550 *RIT*

A Tabriz rug, c1920, 78 by 49½in (198 by 125.5cm).
£1,800–2,000 *RIT*

A south Caucasian kelim, 91 by 61in (231 by 155cm).
£1,000–1,200 *CSK*

A south-east Bulgarian kelim, from the Sarkoy area, representing the Thracian Tree of Life, 19thC, 155 by 107in (393.5 by 272cm).
£800–900 *GRG*

A Kazak Karatchopf rug, 77 by 64in (195.5 by 162.5cm).
£1,600–2,000 *CSK*

A Persian senna rug, woven by Kurdish weavers using slit weave and curvilinear techniques, using wool and cotton warp, late 19thC, 120 by 72in (304.5 by 182.5cm).
£225–250 *GRG*

A Maimana kelim, from north-west Afghanistan, late 19thC, 36 by 24in (91.5 by 61.5cm).
£40–45 *GRG*

A kala-i-Zuz design storage bag, from Tkkamitis on the southern banks of the Oxuf River, late 19thC, 36 by 21in (91.5 by 53cm).
£100–140 *GRG*

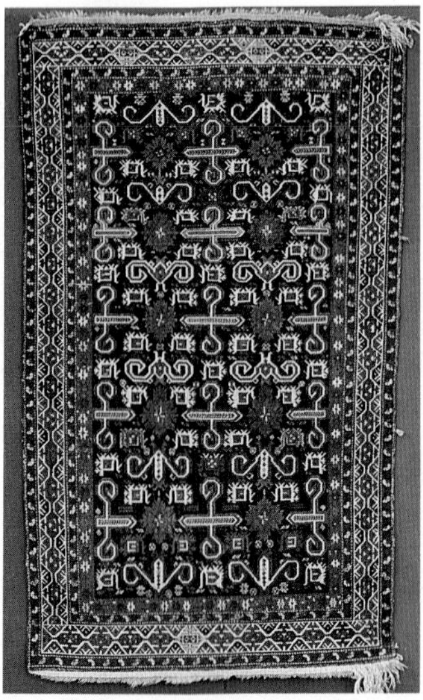

A Kuba rug, decorated with animals, rosettes and horns, 81 by 50in (205.5 by 127cm).
£1,000–1,200 *MSW*

A beaded purse, with a gilded frame, c1830, 3½in (9cm) wide.
£25–35 *JPr*

A blue cut steel beaded bag, c1850.
£100–120 *CB*

A Beauvais tapestry portière, woven in coloured wools and silks, with caryatids supporting urns of fruit, 18thC, 97in (246cm) wide overall.
£8,500–9,000 *CSK*

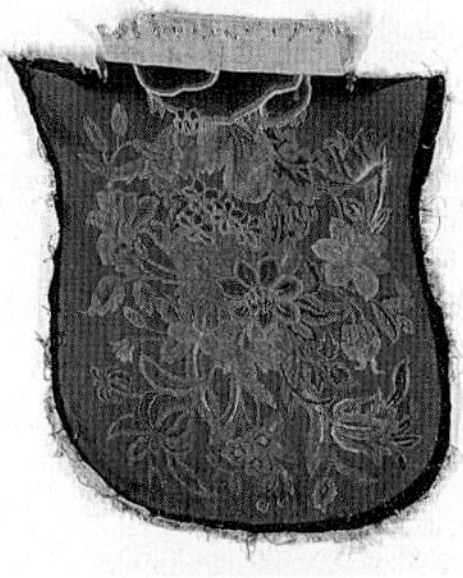

A set of 6 early 18thC style needlework chair back and seat covers, partly worked in metal thread.
£2,400–2,800 *S*

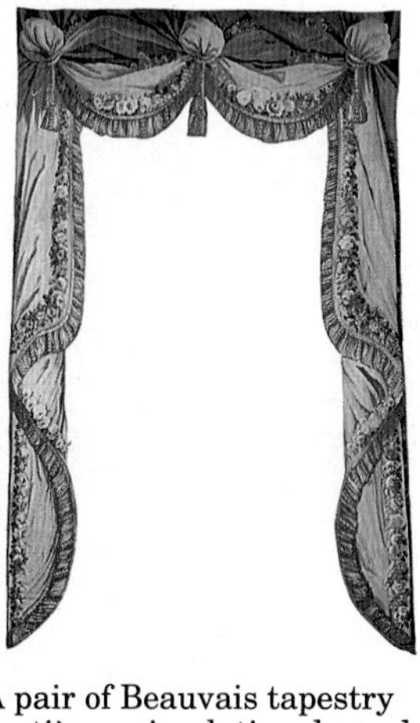

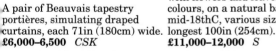

A pair of Beauvais tapestry portières, simulating draped curtains, each 71in (180cm) wide.
£6,000–6,500 *CSK*

Nine crewelwork curtains, worked with flowers and leaves in various colours, on a natural background, mid-18thC, various sizes, longest 100in (254cm).
£11,000–12,000 *S*

A pair of French mid-Victorian silk curtain ties.
£50–70 *JPr*

Three Regency pelmets, attributed to George Bullock, the turned poles with giltwood lotus leaf finials, hung with blue silk edged with gimp and silk covered wooden bobbin fringe, 56in (142cm) wide.
£3,200–3,700 *C*

A pair of Queen Anne needlework panels, probably decorated with the Duke and Duchess of Marlborough, restored, framed, 24in (61cm) high.
£14,000–15,000 *C*

Three butter stamps, 19thC, largest 3in (7.5cm) diam.
£45–50 each *AnE*

A copper banded oak wine tray, with scroll carved handles, c1740, 15½in (39.5cm) wide.
£450–550 *RYA*

Two butter stamps, 19thC, largest 3½in (9cm) diam.
£60–70 each *AnE*

A Welsh carved heart-shaped love token box, c1780, 3½in (8.5cm) wide.
£200–250 *RYA*

A drinking goblet, turned from a single piece of laburnham, c1760, 7½in (19cm) high.
£700–800 *RYA*

A Norwegian carved and rose painted casket, bearing the arms of King Frederick III, decorated with horses, hearts and scrolls, dated 1649, 21½in (54cm) wide.
£8,500–9,500 *RYA*

A Norwegian rose painted bentwood box, used for dry storage, c1884, 8in (20cm) wide.
£150–180 *RYA*

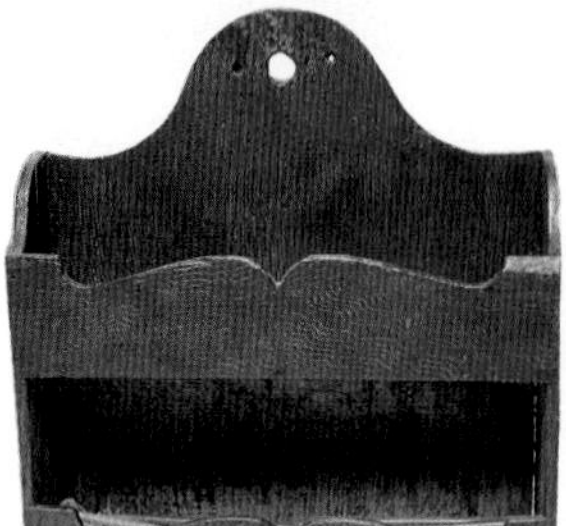

A decorated double wall-hanging candle box, 18thC, 14in (35.5cm) wide.
£300–350 *RYA*

A Norwegian hand carved food box, c1870, 8½in (21.5cm) wide.
£400–450 *RYA*

A butter stamp, 19thC, 4in (10cm) diam.
£70–80 *AnE*

A sycamore dairy bowl, c1780, 13½in (34.5cm) diam.
£400–450 *RYA*

A two-handled solid walnut mortar, north African or Spanish, c1870, 5½in (14cm) high.
£40–45 *RYA*

A Norwegian braid loom, with original painted decoration, dated '1855', 10½in (26.5cm) wide.
£300–400 *RYA*

Hangings

A 'flame stitch' tapestry wall hanging, woven in green, brown and cream wools, undyed linen and hemp, the border woven with the mirror image of the maker's name, 'Pierre Maille', c1730, altered, 94½ by 89in (239 by 226cm).
£2,000–2,500 *P*

A pair of hangings of blue velvet with applied silver gilt and gilt thread embroidery with large urns hung with floral wreaths, palms tied with ribbon, and scrolling patterns at the base, trimmed with braid, 19thC, 65 by 35in (165 by 89.5cm).
£150–250 *CSK*

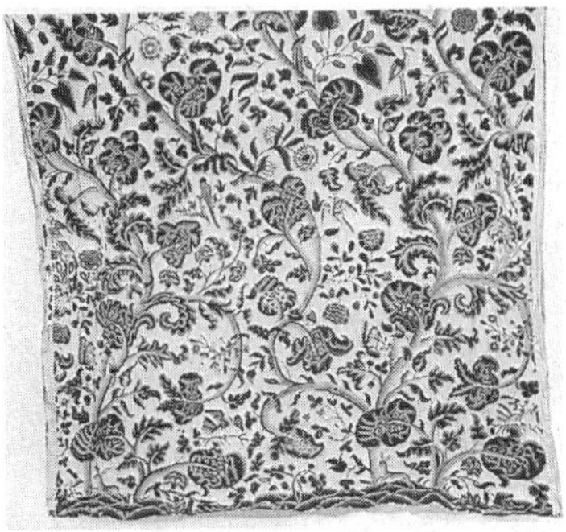

A crewelwork hanging, the exotic leafy trees filled with various flowers and birds, underneath leaping stags, 19thC, 82 by 80in (208 by 203cm).
£2,200–2,700 *CSK*

l. A pair of Aubusson hangings, the ivory field woven with roses, within a crimson border and triple slip borders of shades of brown, 19thC, 108 by 39in (274 by 99cm).
£2,000–2,200 *CSK*

A Turkish prayer arch hanging, of ivory silk satin, the centre of crimson satin, with applied coloured satins or embroidered in floss silks, c1900, 71 by 48in (180 by 122cm).
£600–700 *CSK*

l. Two pairs of Aubusson hangings, each cream cartouche within acanthus leaf frame at top and bottom, enclosing a hanging floral arrangement and flowers at the base, within a crimson border and a triple slip border of shades of brown, late 19thC, 116 by 40in (294.5 by 101.5cm).
£4,200–4,800 *CSK*

Lace

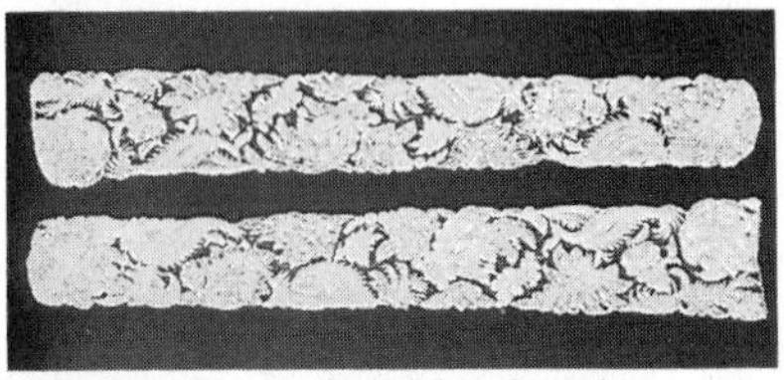

A pair of Brussels bobbin lace lappets, worked with foliage and flowers, c1730.
£250–400 *CSK*

A wedding veil of Brussels mixed lace, the borders worked with tulip-like flowers, the field sprigged with needle lace butterflies, late 1860s, 70in (177.5cm) square.
£1,400–1,600 *CSK*

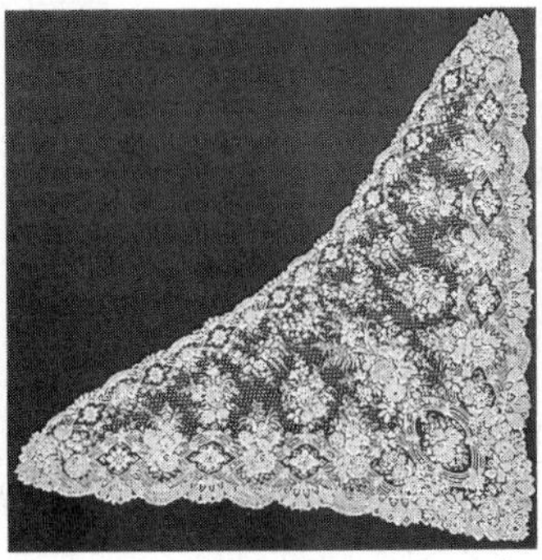

A Brussels mixed lace triangular shawl, worked with posies of flowers and a border of undulating ribbons, c1860.
£1,000–1,200 *CSK*

A wedding veil of Brussels needle and bobbin appliqué lace, worked with a border of undulating ribbons, with needle lace leaf sprays in each corner, c1860, 80in (203cm) square.
£1,200–1,500 *CSK*

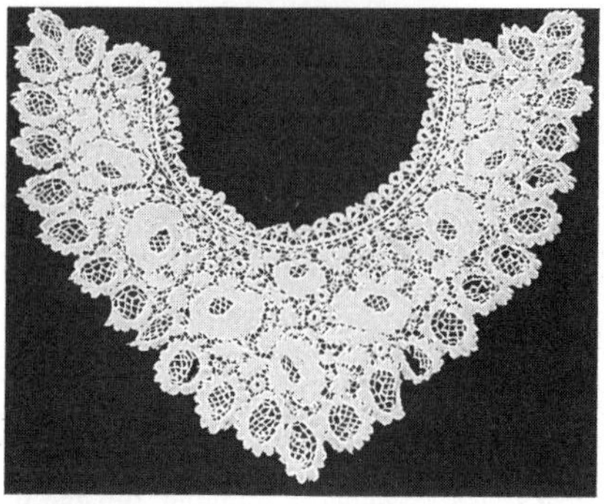

A Brussels lace collar, 19thC, 24in (61.5cm) long.
£45–55 *LB*

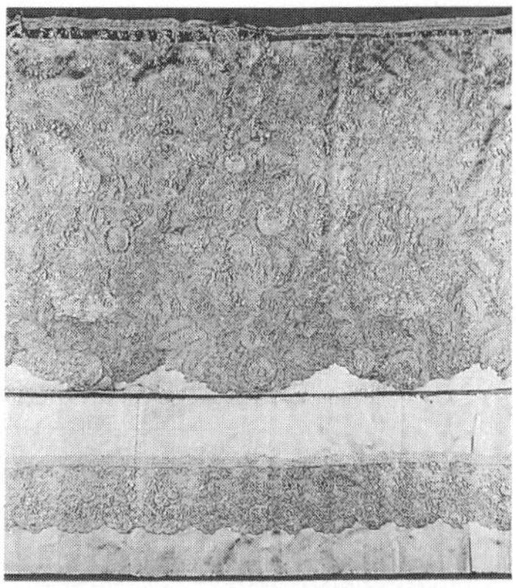

r. A deep flounce of Point de Gaze needle lace, in 2 parts, worked with a scallopped edge of ribbons and flowers, with three-dimensional roses above, c1860, mounted on silk, 67 by 19in (170 by 48cm), and 150 by 19in (381 by 48cm), and a matching narrower border, 82 by 4in (208 by 10cm).
£1,200–1,800 *CSK*

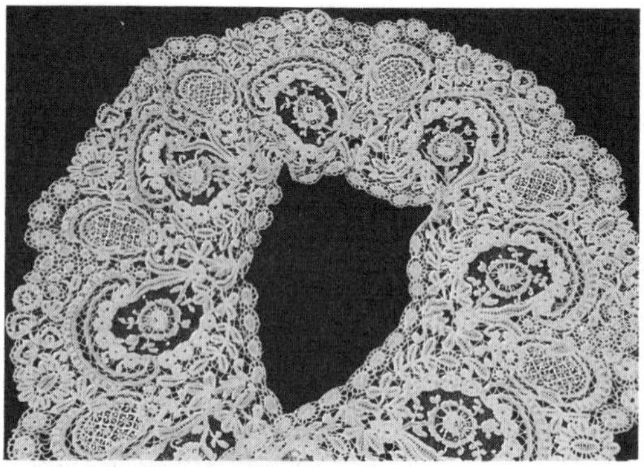

A lace 'Bertha' needlepoint collar, 19thC, 44in (111.5cm) long.
£100–150 *LB*

A tape lace shoulder collar, early 20thC, 48in (122cm) long.
£50–60 *LB*

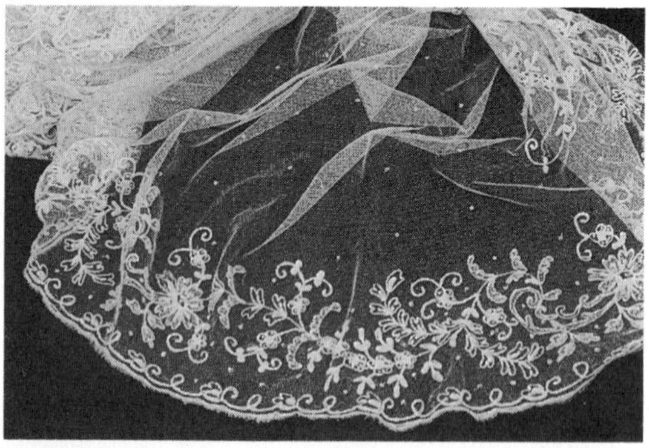

An Edwardian circular machine lace wedding veil, 60in (152cm) diam.
£120–150 *LB*

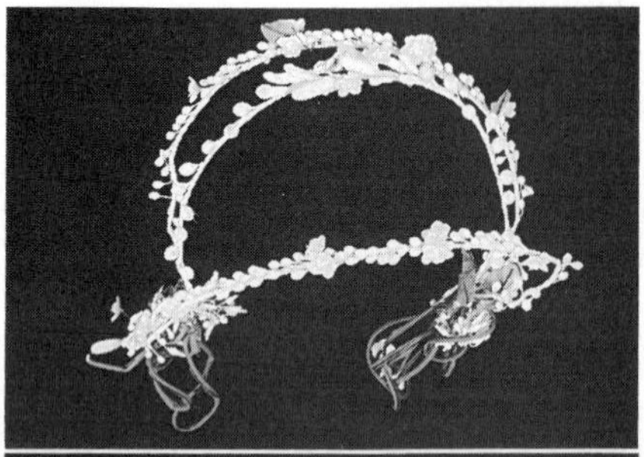

Two Edwardian bridal headdresses, with wax flowers.
£20–40 each *LB*

An Italian panel of needle lace, depicting a goddess being presented with 3 cherubs within an Italianate landscape, c1900, 27 by 30in (68.5 by 76cm).
£600–700 *CSK*

r. A Victorian handkerchief, in fine lawn with Valencia lace border, 13½in (34cm) square.
£20–30 *LB*

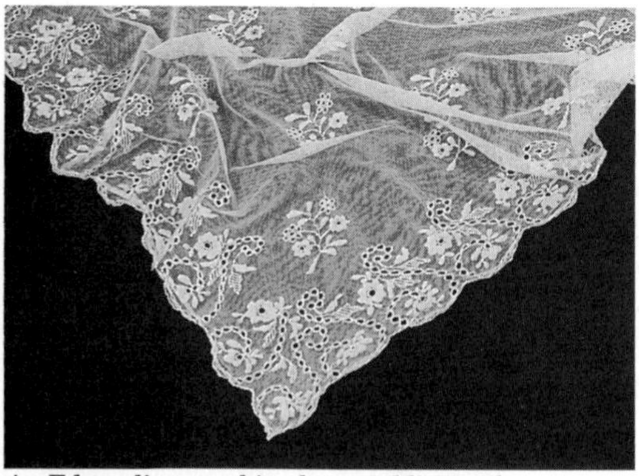

An Edwardian machine lace wedding veil, 72in (182.5cm) long.
£60–80 *LB*

A fine lawn and Valencia lace handkerchief, 11in (28cm) square.
£10–20 *LB*

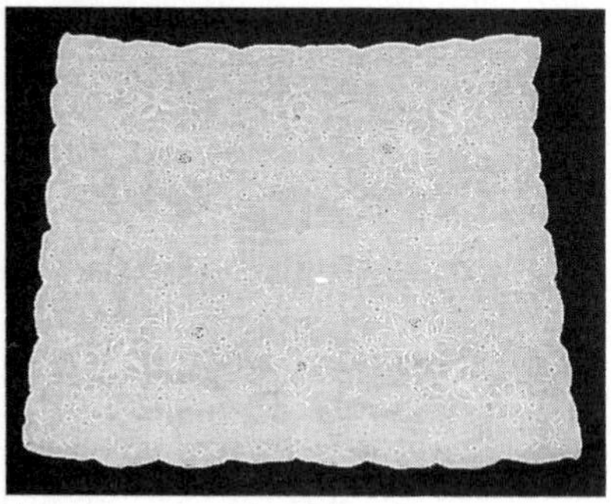

A Swiss embroidered handkerchief, c1920, 11in (28cm) square.
£12–15 *LB*

An Italian shoulder collar, in Boro lace, c1920, 40in (101.5cm) long.
£40–50 *LB*

A lace curtain, woven with a depiction of the proclamation of Kaiser Wilhelm I of Prussia as Emperor of Germany in the Hall of Mirrors, Versailles, 18 January, 1871, 140 by 67in (355.5 by 170cm).
£4,500–5,000 *CSK*

This commemorative panel was made by Enoch Shipley & Co., of Nottingham, and there is another panel at the Nottingham Museum of Costume & Textiles. No other examples are known at this time, although given the expense of producing the Jacquard cards for such a complicated design it is likely that several would have been manufactured.

Samplers

A reticella sampler, worked with 6 rows of reticella including one with a running figure, late 17thC, 16 by 6in (41 by 15cm).
£1,100–1,300 *CSK*

A sampler by Elizabeth Foxwell, dated '1724', worked in coloured silks with bands of decorative motifs, alphabets and numerals in various stitches, 18 by 8in (45.5 by 20cm).
£1,400–1,800 *CSK*

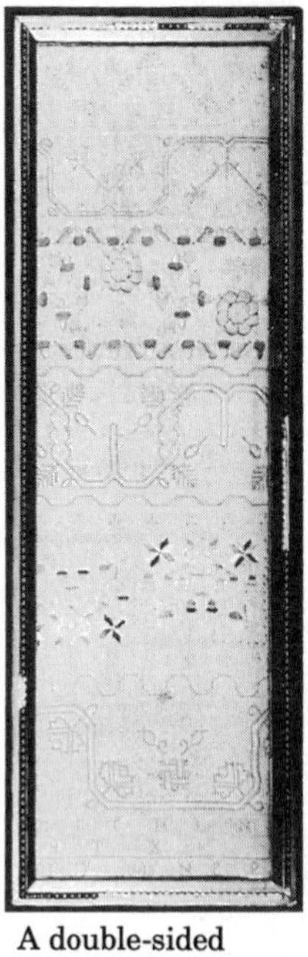

A double-sided sampler, by Mary Body, 1665, worked in coloured silks in various stitches and some applied roses, 29 by 8½in (73.5 by 21cm), framed and glazed.
£2,000–2,500 *CSK*

A sampler, by Isobella Low, dated '1760', worked in coloured silks with the Ten Commandments, 17½ by 12½in (44.5 by 32cm), framed and glazed.
£1,700–2,000 *CSK*

MILLER'S COMPARES . . .

I A sampler, by Elizabeth Goodman, dated '1796', worked in brightly coloured silks with a verse 'On Mortality', and at the base 'E. Girton. Governess. Newark', within a detailed stylised border, 16 by 13½in (41 by 34cm).
£600–800 *CSK*

II A sampler, by Rachel Hook, dated '1805', worked in coloured silks and gilt metal threads, with a verse 'Next unto God...', 14½ by 11½in (36.5 by 29cm), framed and glazed.
£2,000–2,500 *CSK*

No two samplers are ever quite the same and despite the fact these two are similar in age and size, they are quite different in price. ***Item I*** **is also finely worked but shows signs of wear and is also unframed.** ***Item II*** **is finely worked but is in good condition and has a contemporary frame of the period. The subject matter of** ***Item II*** **is particularly rare for a sampler and thus adds to its value.** *CSK*

A darning sampler, by Rachel Hook, dated '1803', worked in shades of green, yellow, blue and pink silks, 15½ by 13in (39.5 by 33cm), framed and glazed.
£900–1,200 *CSK*

r. An Adam and Eve sampler, worked by E. Wilson, dated '1811', worked in very brightly coloured silks, 19 by 14½in (48.5 by 37cm).
£3,300–3,700 *CSK*

A silkwork sampler, worked by Ann Rogers, dated '1816', with Adam, Eve and the Serpent, and a poem entitled 'Friendship', slight damage, 16 by 12in (40.5 by 30.5cm).
£600–700 *DN*

A George III silkwork and cross stitch band sampler, worked by Anna Collins, aged 9, dated '1814', 13 by 9½in (33 by 24cm).
£550–650 *DN*

A needlework sampler, signed 'Jessy Alexander', dated '1811', worked in gold, blue, green, black and white silk threads on a linen ground, slight wear, 11 by 8in (28 by 20cm).
£350–400 *S(NY)*

A sampler, by Sarah Siddall, dated '1818', worked in coloured silks, 13in (33cm) square, framed and glazed.
£550–650 *CSK*

A sampler, by Hannah Arnott, dated '1823', with flowers, birds, sailing ships, dogs, and a poem, 20½ by 20in (51.5 by 50.5cm), framed and glazed.
£400–500 *DA*

A sampler, by Margaret Moffitt, Gateshead, dated '1819', worked in coloured silks, 19½ by 13in (49.5 by 33cm), framed.
£600–700 *CSK*

A sampler, by Mary Ann Chignell, dated '1824', worked in coloured silks illustrating a scene from Luke XV 17.20, within a naturalistic floral border, 18½ by 12in (47 by 30.5cm), framed.
£1,000–1,200 *CSK*

A needlework family record, of the Joseph and Lucy Murchin Stevens family, from 1798 to 1826, by Mary A. Stevens, aged 12, c1826, in green, gold, beige and brown silks on a linen ground, 26 by 17in (66 by 43.5cm).
£2,500–3,000 *S(NY)*

A German linen sewing sampler, worked by 'H.T.IG. 1829', showing needle lace patches, decorative buttonholes and corners, 7in (17.5cm) square.
£240–300 *P*

l. A sampler, by Mary Ann Coward, dated '1828', worked in shades of green, ivory and brown silks, 12½in (32cm) square, framed and glazed.
£720–800 *CSK*

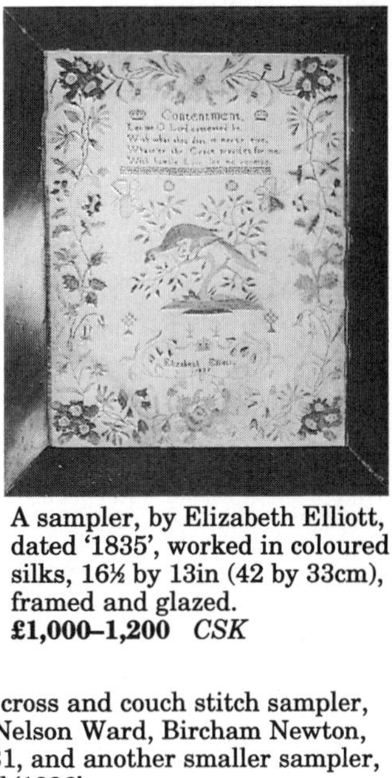

A sampler, by Elizabeth Elliott, dated '1835', worked in coloured silks, 16½ by 13in (42 by 33cm), framed and glazed.
£1,000–1,200 *CSK*

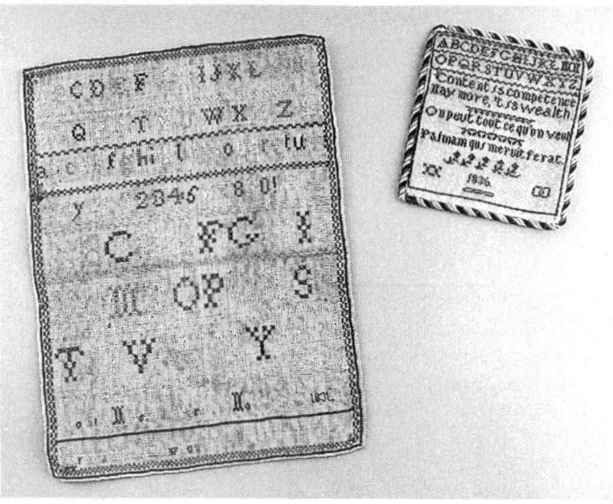

l. A William IV silk cross and couch stitch sampler, worked by Horatia Nelson Ward, Bircham Newton, November 30th, 1831, and another smaller sampler, worked in red, dated '1836'.
£700–1,000 *DN*

This is the work of Horatia Nelson, née Nekon, 1801–81, the illegitimate daughter of Lord Nelson and Lady Emma Hamilton.

A sampler, by Sarah Elizabeth Whiting, dated '1839', worked in coloured silks with a verse, alphabets and numerals, 12½in (32cm) square.
£250–350 *CSK*

A sampler, by Mary Payne, dated '1846', worked in shades of green, cream and brown silks, 12½ by 15½in (32 by 39.5cm), framed and glazed.
£500–600 *CSK*

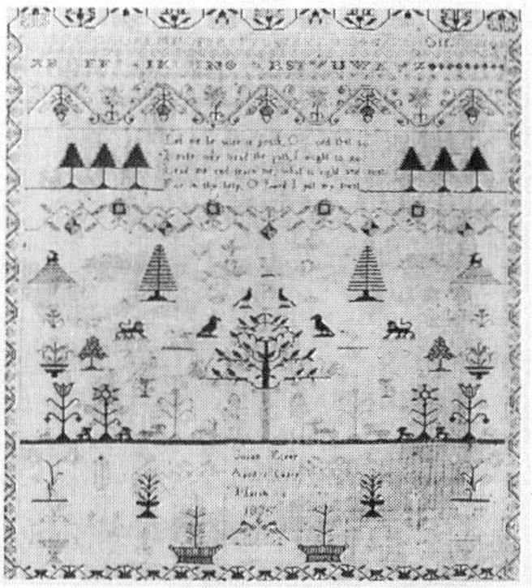

A sampler, by Susan Elsey, dated '1835', finely worked in coloured silks with a verse, alphabets and numerals, Adam and Eve, birds and animals, trees and flower urns, within a stylised floral border, 13½ by 12½in (34.5 by 32cm), framed and glazed.
£600–700 *CSK*

Suzani

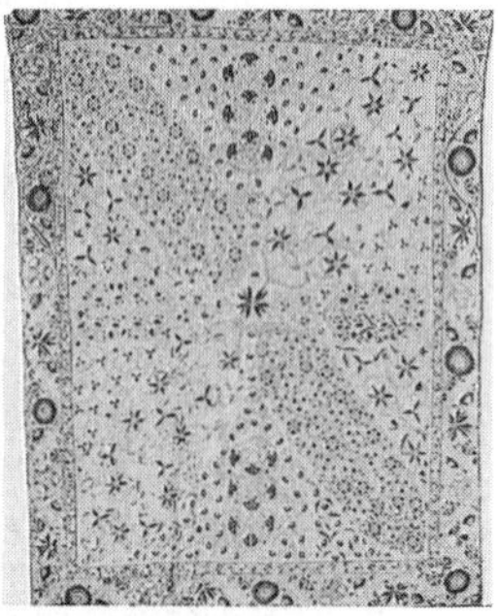

An Uzbek suzani, the cotton ground embroidered in mainly blue, green and red silks, designed with a central flower and 4 radiating flower sprays, the border with guhls, worked in laid, couched and chain stitches, lined, Nurata, 19thC, 86 by 69½in (218.5 by 176cm).
£650–750 *P*

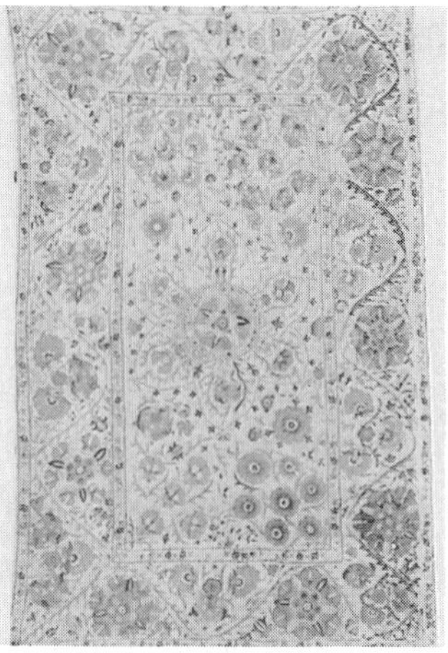

An Uzbek suzani, the cotton ground embroidered in green, orange, crimson and blue silks in chain stitch, designed with a central guhl within a shaped border of leaves and flowers, the border and corners with guhls and flower sprays, Bochara, 19thC, 67 by 46in (170 by 116.5cm).
£400–500 *P*

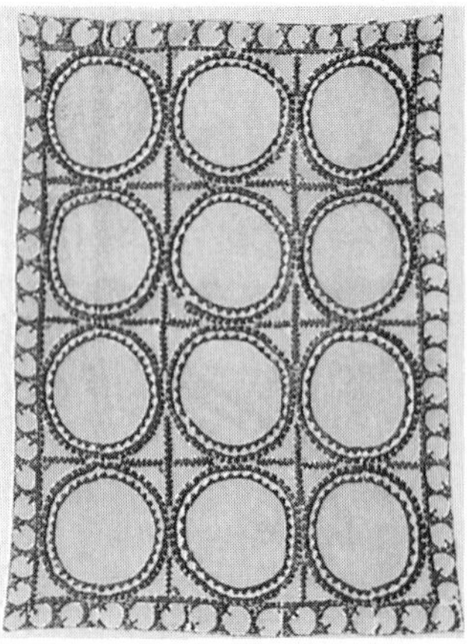

An Uzbek suzani, the cotton ground embroidered in mainly crimson, yellow and black silks, the centre designed with guhls having a border of leaves and florets worked in laid, couched and chain stitches, printed cotton lined, Pskent, 19thC, 97½ by 71in (248 by 180cm).
£300–400 *P*

Tapestry

A pair of Brussels entre fenêtre mythological tapestry panels, c1700, each 125 by 55in (317.5 by 139.5cm).
£13,000–15,000 *S(NY)*

A Flemish biblical tapestry panel, depicting a queen, perhaps Esther, kneeling before an enthroned king, perhaps Ahasuerus, mid-16th, 99 by 63in (251.5 by 160cm).
£4,700–5,300 *S(NY)*

An Aubusson armorial tapestry, late 17thC, 92½ by 90½in (234.5 by 229.5cm).
£14,000–16,000 *S(NY)*

Miller's is a price GUIDE not a price LIST

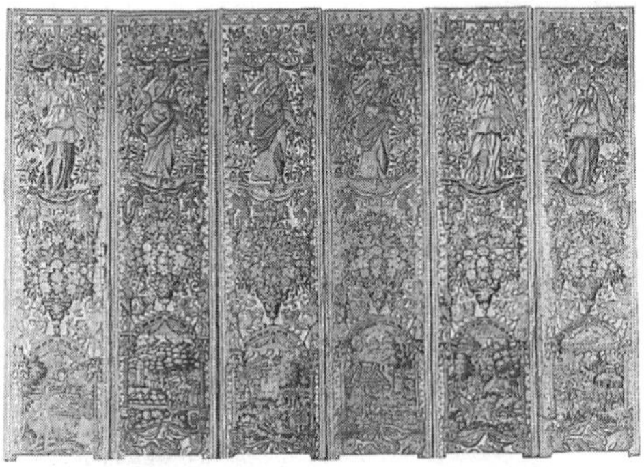

A Brussels tapestry covered six-fold screen, the tapestry c1600, each panel 84 by 20in (213 by 50.5cm).
£12,000–14,000 *S(NY)*

A Flemish verdure tapestry fragment, late 17thC, 53 by 79in (134.5 by 200.5cm).
£7,000–8,000 *S(NY)*

A tapestry, depicting Vulcan's forge and a lady, possibly Venus, woven in coloured wools and silks, Antwerp, late 17thC, 78 by 155in (198 by 393.5cm).
£5,500–6,500 *CSK*

This tapestry apparently formed a very early part of the furnishings at Fountains Hall, Ripon, Yorkshire.

A French tapestry picture, woven in coloured silks and wools, 18thC, 22 by 18in (55.5 by 45.5cm).
£1,200–1,400 *CSK*

A French verdure tapestry panel, depicting a tree with blossoming flowers, surrounded by a flower chain border interspersed with birds, flower-filled vases and tassels, 18thC, 108 by 57in (274 by 144.5cm).
£6,000–7,000 *S(NY)*

A mid-Victorian woolwork patriotic picture, inscribed 'I. Stewart' and 'J. Stewart', 16 by 20in (40.5 by 50.5cm).
£500–600 *DN*

A French or Flemish verdure tapestry, the border of interwoven floral garlands tied with ribbons, 18thC, 129½ by 171in (329 by 434cm).
£13,000–15,000 *S(NY)*

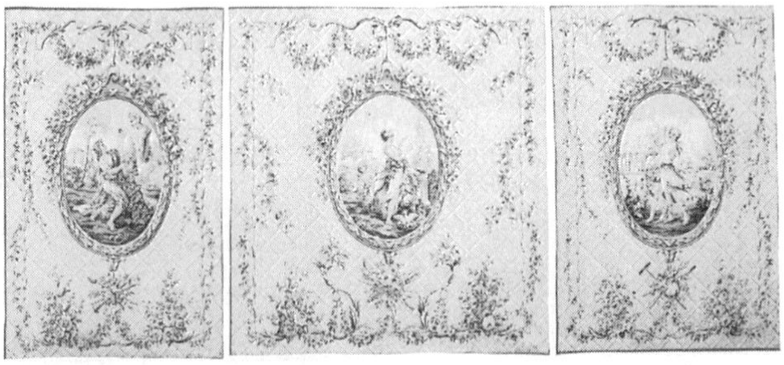

A set of 3 Aubusson medallion tapestries, early 19thC, largest 74 by 69in (188 by 175cm).
£22,000–24,000 *S(NY)*

A tapestry portrait of Gilbert Burnet, Bishop of Salisbury, dressed in robes as Chancellor of the Order of the Garter, after Sir Peter Lely, finely woven in wools and silks, probably 18thC, 26 by 20in (66 by 50.5cm), framed and glazed.
£200–400 *CSK*

COSTUME

A mauve silk dalmatic, brocaded in coloured silks, edged with metal braid, materials 17thC, possibly made in 18thC.
£300–400 *CSK*

A girl's fancy dress shepherdess costume, pink wool with blue quilted petticoat and hat, and a young boy's fancy dress costume in 18thC style, with sky blue frock coat, waistcoat and breeches and another of plum sateen, together with accessories.
£200–250 *CSK*

A Victorian day dress, in net and lace trimmed lilac silk, c1865.
£300–350 *HOLL*

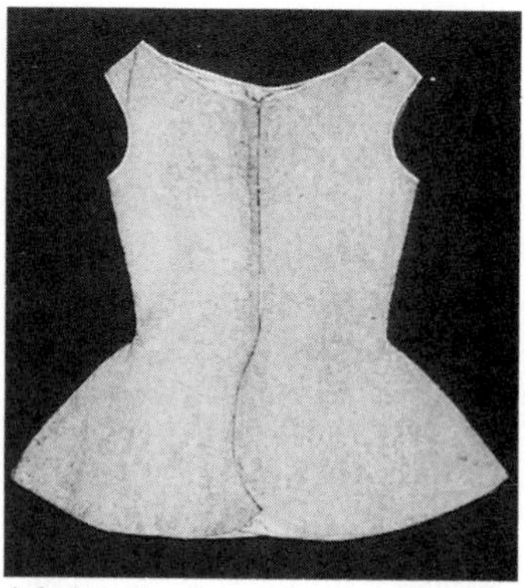

A lady's linen waistcoat, quilted in pale yellow silk with scrolling flowers, the fronts with twisted linen braid lacing loops, flaring skirts, early 18thC.
£1,500–2,000 *CSK*

r. A Spanish sleeved waistcoat, with knitted back and sleeves, quilted fronts in blue striped satin woven with chiné rosebuds, faced in pink and white striped satin, late 18thC.
£200–300 *CSK*

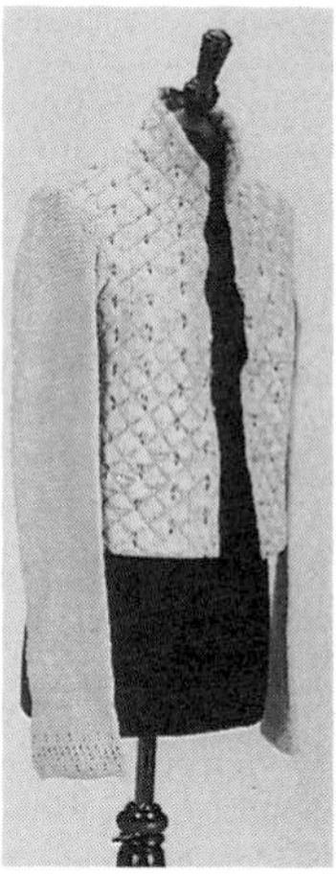

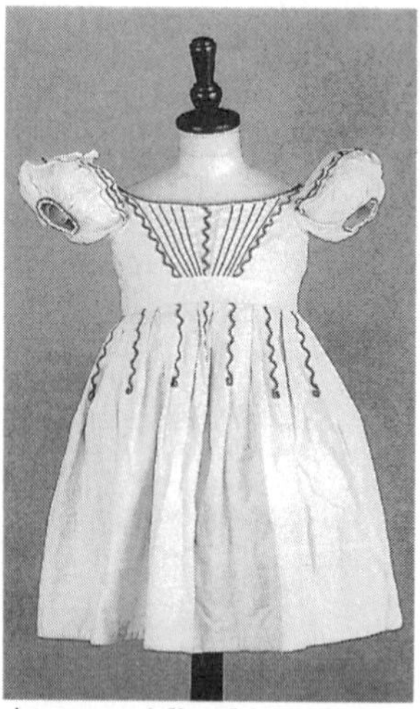

A young girl's white cotton dress, with wide puff sleeves, trimmed with olive green wool embroidery, c1825, with a paper tag inscribed 'Frock given to Augusta's Mother by her God Mother, Mrs Wm Walsh, June 1832', together with another muslin dress, trimmed with maroon wool embroidery, and a quantity of early 19thC baby clothes.
£350–400 *CSK*

A cut velvet coat, the borders embroidered with simulated lace and flowers, c1760.
£1,000–1,500 *CSK*

A fine white muslin dress, the bodice embroidered with whitework flowers, the skirt with climbing fruiting vines, early 19thC.
£150–200 *CSK*

An Edwardian machine lace wedding dress, with crochet top and border.
£200–300 *LB*

A Prussian blue silk afternoon dress, c1870s.
£300–350 *P*

A canary yellow trouser suit, the tunic top fastening with a white zip and press studs, and appliqué Courrèges logo, labelled 'Hyperbole, Courrèges, Paris', stamped '0571903', also paper tag 'No de Modèle 193 - Blazer Manches courtes, 15015/55 Jaune, ERB', the trousers with similar tag with 'Model No 171.'
£120–180 *CSK*

A pink lamé mini dress, woven with diamond patterns, and another in blue, trimmed with a large bow at the back, 1960s.
£90–100 *CSK*

A sleeveless long evening dress, by Givenchy, with alternating narrow and wide navy horizontal stripes on an off-white ground, over an underdress of jap silk printed with the same design, marked 'Printemps-ete 1966, model number 302'.
£850–950 *CSK*

A grey sheepskin maxi coat, trimmed and lined with sheepskin, labelled 'Antartex Lambskin', 1960s.
£30–40 *CSK*

A plush velvet evening dress, printed in blue and grey tones with spheres and stripes, 'Traffico', labelled 'Emilio Pucci, Florence-Italy', 1970s.
£120–180 *CSK*

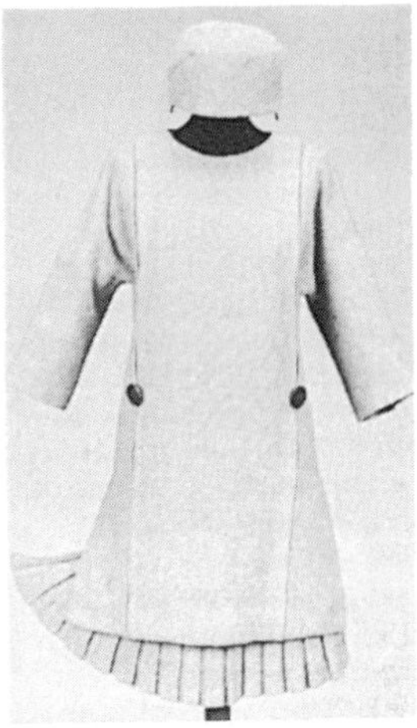

l. A mustard yellow wool dress, trimmed with large leather disc buttons, separate underskirt with pleated hem, and matching pill box hat, labelled 'Mary Quant', c1962.
£110–130 *CSK*

l. An evening ensemble by Givenchy, of black double silk crepe, the top with bateau neckline, crossed at the back, bias cut sash, the hem of the bodice and top of the skirt trimmed with 3 rows of pear-shaped strass beads laid diagonally, c1968.
£1,000–1,200 *CSK*

A black 'wet look' plastic jacket, with white press studs and cut away logo, labelled 'Courrèges, Paris, Made in France, A', and a black corduroy coat dress with 2 vertical zip breast pockets and drawstring waist, labelled 'Courrèges, Paris, Couture Future', stamped '0025423', c1978.
£150–180 *CSK*

A 'bondage shirt' of white cheesecloth, the shoulders slashed, the sleeves with clips, printed with a swastika with up-turned crucifix and the word DESTROY, Vivienne Westwood, Seditionaries collection.
£550–650 *CSK*

This model was often worn on stage by members of the Sex Pistols.

A bright orange wool tunic dress, lined with white silk, the front cut to reveal the 'C' logo of Courrèges, labelled 'Hyperbole, Courrèges', stamped '0568865'.
£90–120 *CSK*

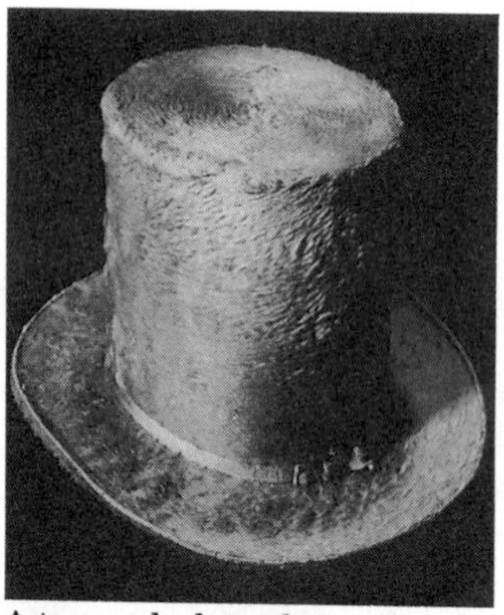

A taupe plush top hat, with narrow silk hatband fastening with blued steel buckle, stamped in crown 'T H Satchell, Hatter, London, 48 Lord Street, Liverpool, by Special Appointment to HRH Prince Albert, Best Quality', c1840.
£1,500–2,000 *CSK*

r. An evening suit, with short plush velvet jacket, printed in mauves, pinks and black with swirling bows, 'Rondo Vis', labelled 'Emilio Pucci, Florence-Italy'.
£120–180 *CSK*

A silk jersey cocktail dress, printed in bright colours with a psychedelic pattern, labelled 'Emilio Pucci'.
£220–400 *CSK*

A pair of Queen Victoria's black silk stockings, with ivory feet and tops, with a crown above the monogram 'VR', embroidered with a black arrow each side of each leg, repaired.
£200–250 *WW*

A silk jersey cocktail dress, printed in flourescent pink, blues and brown, with psychedelic pattern, labelled 'Emilio Pucci'.
£220–400 *CSK*

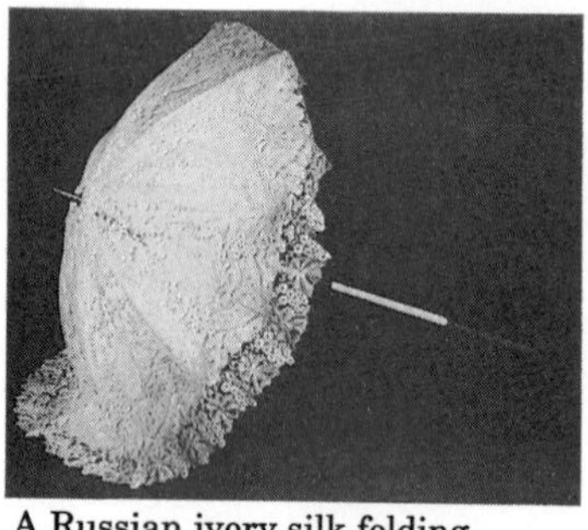

A Russian ivory silk folding carriage parasol, overlaid with applied Brussels mixed bobbin and needlelace, designed with peacocks and flowers, whalebone spokes, the plain ivory shaft with gold ferrule, slide and handle in the form of a buckled strap, assay mark 'St. Petersburg 56 (zolotniki-14 carats) S.A.', c1860.
£800–1,000 *P*

Samuel Arndt was a master goldsmith in St. Petersburg 1845–90, and is regarded as a forerunner of Carl Fabergé.

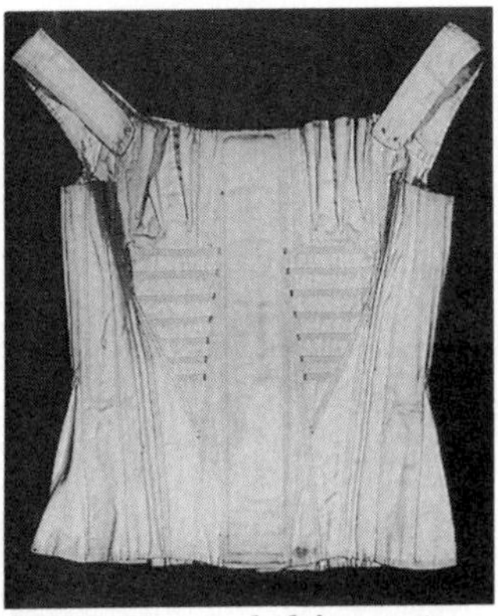

An ivory sateen lady's corset, stitched in ivory silk, the front panels worked with an embroidered spot motif, c1820.
£350–550 *CSK*

An Edwardian Cantonese silk shawl, hand embroidered in cream.
£100–150 *LB*

A child's silk and lace bonnet, c1900.
£30–50 *LB*

A Paisley pattern shawl, woven with a black centre, the ends with tapering cones reserved in ivory against dense foliage, probably French, c1855, 64 by 140in (162.5 by 356cm).
£450–550 *CSK*

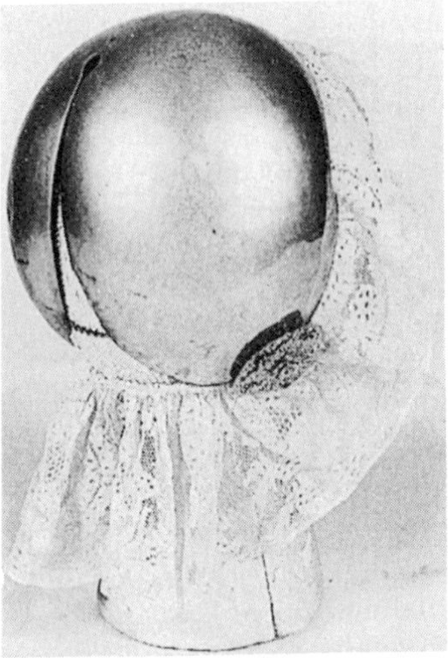

A cap, with lace undercap and 2 gilt metal pins, Dutch silver mark, c1890, in a cardboard box.
£300–350 *P*

A snood cap, crocheted with silk rosebuds, c1930.
£15–25 *LB*

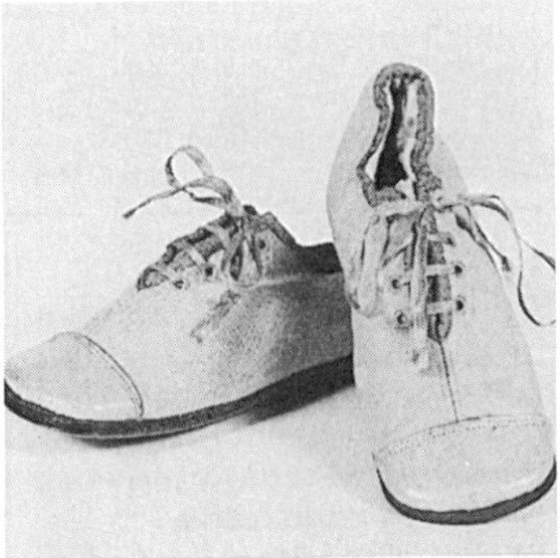

l. A pair of girl's indoor shoes, made of fawn cotton, with beige leather toe caps, and leather soles with wedge flat heels, unworn, c1860, 5in (12.5cm) long.
£200–250 *P*

A Paisley pattern shawl, woven with elaborate vegetative designs around a black residual medallion, c1855, 66in (167.5cm) wide.
£600–700 *CSK*

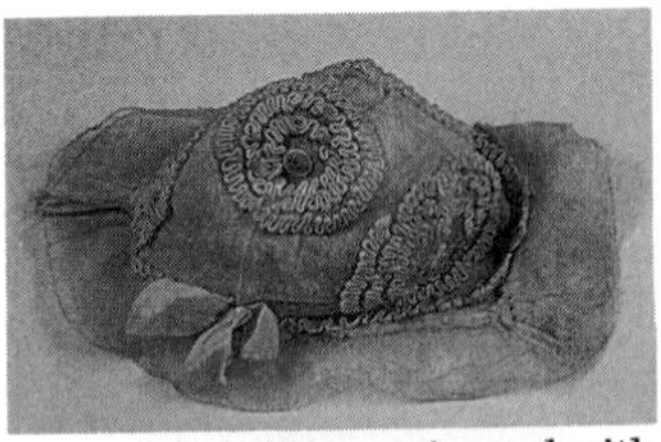

A baby's cap, trimmed with braid, c1930.
£20–30 *LB*

A child's Belgian bonnet, of stiffened whitework on lace, c1900.
£30–40 *LB*

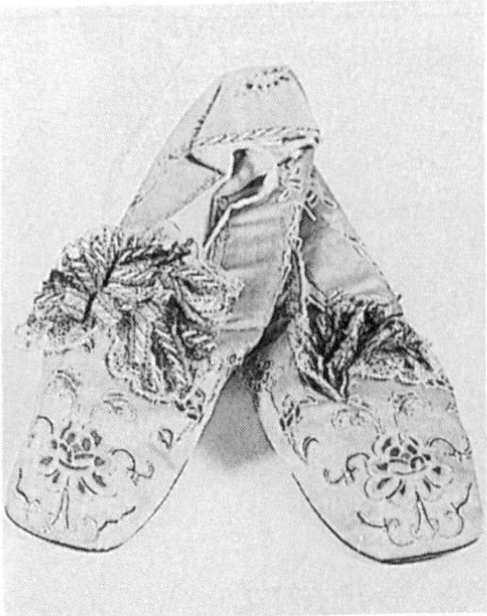

A pair of lady's salmon pink satin slippers, decorated with flower sprays worked in Pekin knot embroidery and rosettes of looped pink and green ribbons, with square toes and flat heels, lined with ivory taffeta silk, probably French, c1860.
£500–550 *P*

A Victorian silk wedding bag, applied with Brussels lace, 8½in (21.5cm) high.
£80–100 *LB*

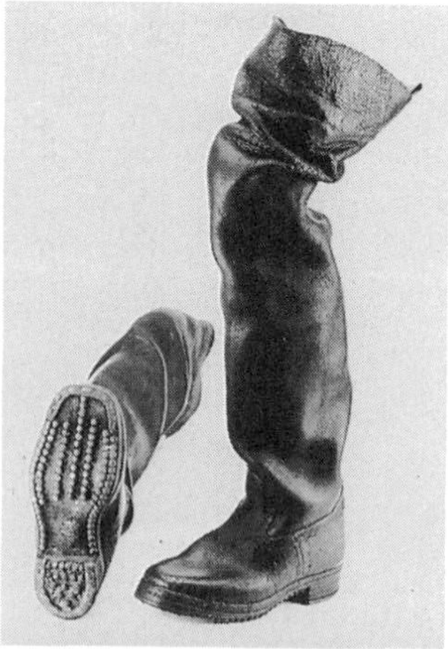

A pair of gentleman's black leather high riding boots, with rounded toes and stacked heels, the soles heavily studded and the toes and heels with iron banding, late 19thC, 31in (78.5cm) high.
£200–400 *CSK*

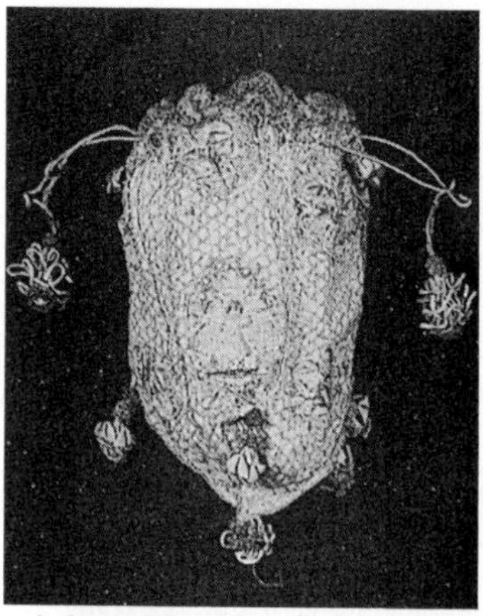

A drawstring bag, of aloe thread lace, with torchon lace to the border and embellished with tassels and wired flowers of twisted thread, lined with taffeta silk, 8in (20cm) long.
£800–900 *P*

A collection of 6 European petit point purses, c1900.
£800–900 *SK(B)*

r. A pair of bead embroidered bracelets, with gilded clasps, joined together to make a necklace, c1860.
£150–300 *CB*

RUDOLPH NUREYEV

Rudolph Nureyev was probably one of the most celebrated male dancers of his generation. Between June 1961 and the late 1970s he had danced over 100 different roles, and performed with more than 30 companies throughout the world. He choreographed 8 major productions, including *Swan Lake, The Nutcracker* and *Romeo & Juliet.* In one six-month period, from September 1975 to February 1976, he gave no less than 113 performances in 18 cities.

Following his untimely death in 1992, Christie's New York held a sale of part of his vast collection of costume and memorabilia, a selection of which can be found on the following pages. The sale also included some fine furniture and works of art.

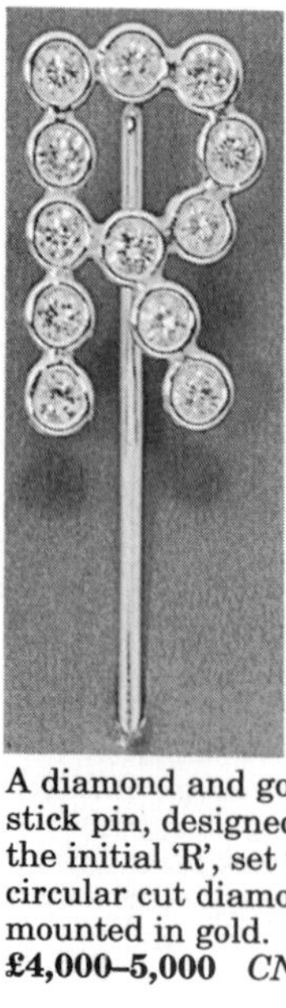

A diamond and gold stick pin, designed as the initial 'R', set with circular cut diamonds, mounted in gold.
£4,000–5,000 *CNY*

A collection of various performance and theatre posters, and lobby cards.
£800–1,000 *CNY*

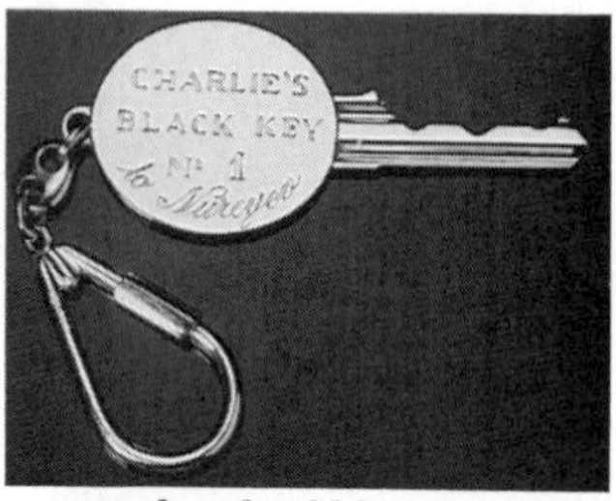

An enamel and gold key, engraved with 'Charlie's Black Key No. 1, to Nureyev', suspended from an 18ct gold key ring.
£1,700–2,200 *CNY*

Did you know?
MILLER'S* Antiques Price Guide *builds up year-by-year to form the most comprehensive antiques photo-reference library available.

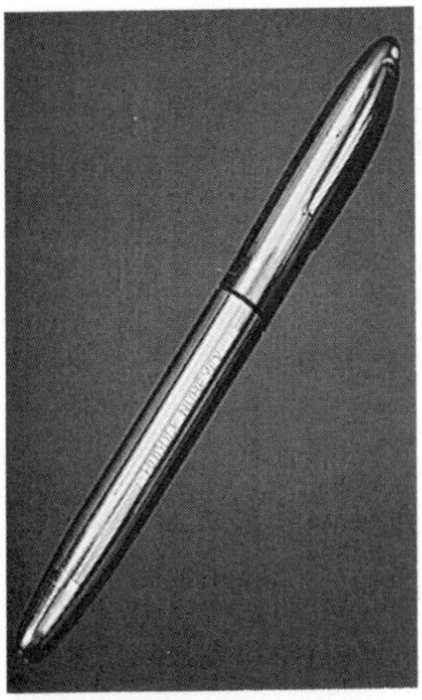

A gold fountain pen, the engine turned 14ct gold case engraved 'Rudolf Nureyev', dated '17th March 1977', with two-colour nib marked 'Shaeffer's Lifetime, Reg. U.S. Pat. Off., made in USA'.
£4,000–5,000 *CNY*

This pen was a present for Nureyev's 39th birthday.

A fawn stockinette tunic piped in brown wool, with a false shirt, for Prince Albrecht, *Giselle,* Act I, 1960 production, labelled 'Royal Opera House; Production: Giselle; Act I; Character: Prince: Name: Nureyev; Covent Garden'.
£35,000–36,000 *CNY*

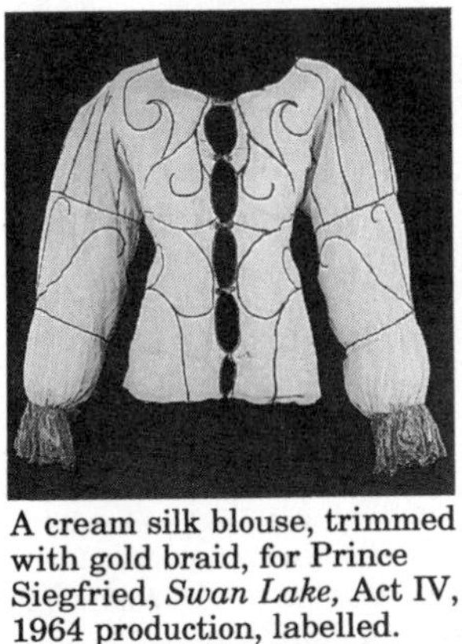

A cream silk blouse, trimmed with gold braid, for Prince Siegfried, *Swan Lake,* Act IV, 1964 production, labelled.
£4,000–5,000 *CNY*

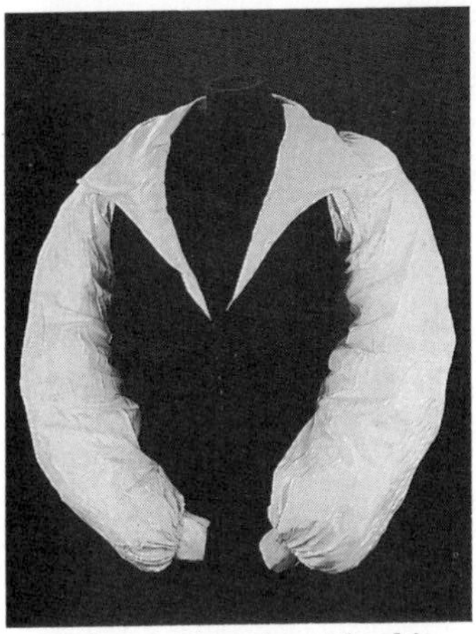

A black velvet tunic, with white silk full sleeve shirt and collar, for *Les Sylphides,* 1932 production.
£17,000–20,000 *CNY*

A black velvet tunic, decorated with gold braid, for Prince Siegfried, *Swan Lake,* Act III, 1963 production.
£20,000–22,000 *CNY*

A black ribbed silk tunic, trimmed with gold braid, paste and artificial pearls, with a false shirt, for Prince Siegfried, *Swan Lake,* Acts II and III, 1963 production, labelled.
£9,000–10,000 *CNY*

A costume for the Cavalier of the Golden Vine, for *The Sleeping Beauty,* 1946 production, the cloth of gold applied with painted leather vine leaves and perspex vines, elaborately trimmed with gold braid, with built-in hose slashed to reveal burgundy taffeta, labelled 'Royal Opera House; Sleeping Beauty; Character; Golden Vine; Name: Mason', and a burgundy mask stamped with a butterfly.
£2,500–3,000 *CNY*

A blue velvet jacket, trimmed with gold lace and gold braid, for Prince Siegfried, *Swan Lake,* Act I, based on the 1963 production.
£9,500–10,500 *CNY*

r. A dark blue velvet jacket, with brass buttons, for James, *Les Sylphides,* Acts I–II, 1964 production, labelled 'National Ballet of Canada, La Sylphide, Nureyev'.
£6,000–7,000 *CNY*

A pale green silk tunic, applied with lace flowers, with a simulated shirt of green gauze, smocked from the shoulders to the elbows, for Prince Florimond, *The Sleeping Beauty,* Act II, 1966 production.
£20,000–22,000 *CNY*

A green velvet jacket, the cuffs trimmed with painted lace, and a brown sash trimmed with a gilt fringe, for Prince Florimond, *The Sleeping Beauty,* Act II 1966 production.
£5,000–6,000 *CNY*

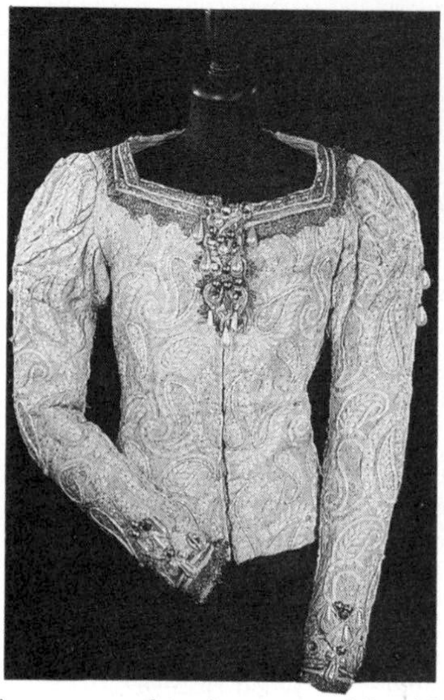

A cream wool tunic, woven with gold thread and pearlised thread, for , Jean de Brienne, *Raymonda,* Act III, 1965 production.
£13,500–14,500 *CNY*

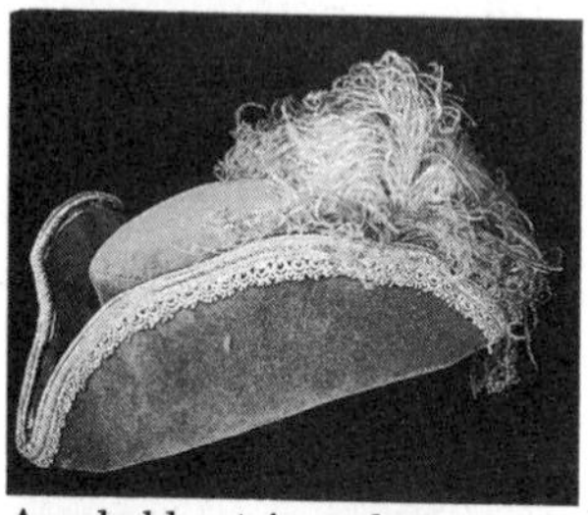

A pale blue tricorn hat, trimmed with braid and curling ostrich feathers, inscribed in the crown 'The Prince', for Prince Florimond, *The Sleeping Beauty,* Act II, 1966 production.
£2,500–3,000 *CNY*

A pink ribbed silk bolero, trimmed with bands of orange and gold brocade and black and gold braid, decorated with 2 rows of gilt coins, and with a false shirt, for Basilio, *Don Quixote* Act I, 1966 production.
£2,200–2,500 *CNY*

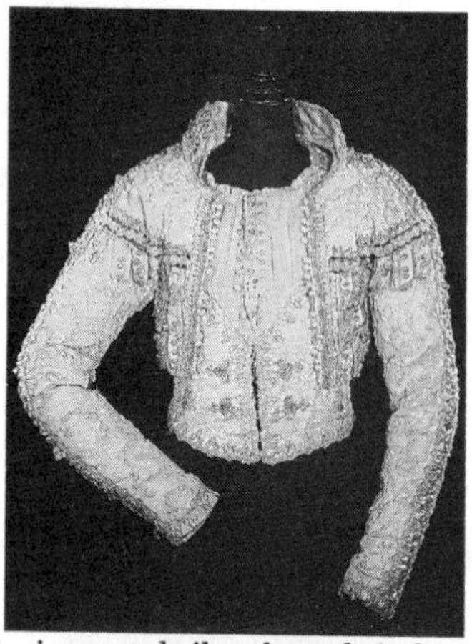

An ivory and silver brocade jacket, trimmed with gold lace, with a matching waistcoat, and false pleated muslin shirt at the front, for Basilio, *Don Quixote*, Act III, 1966 production.
£5,500–6,000 *CNY*

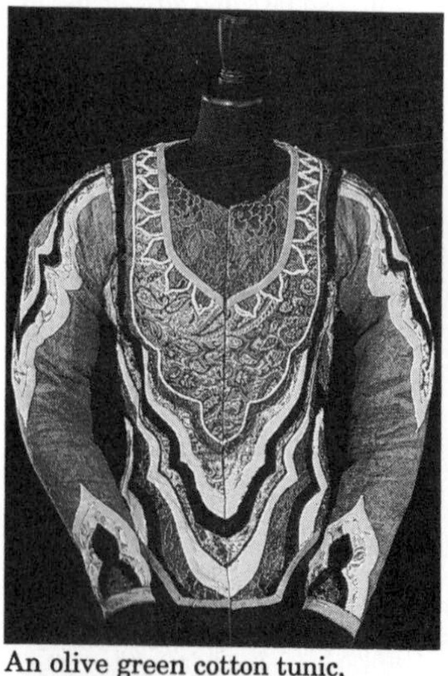

An olive green cotton tunic, woven with gold thread and applied with pale pink silk black velvet and silver cloth, for Jean de Brienne, *Raymonda*, Act II (?), 1975 production.
£8,500–9,000 *CNY*

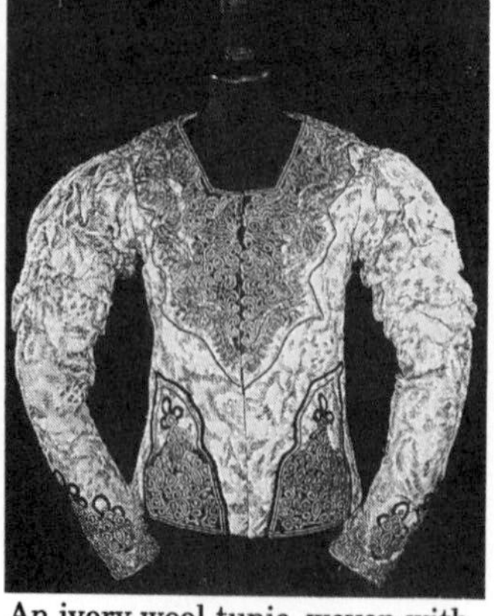

An ivory wool tunic, woven with gold lace and pearlised plastic thread, trimmed with lace and braid, for Jean de Brienne, *Raymonda*, Act I, 1972 production.
£9,500–10,000 *CNY*

A gold tunic, trimmed with black satin, edged with gold lace, embroidered with red and gold paste and simulated pearls, for Jean de Brienne, *Raymonda*, Act III, 1972 production.
£12,000–13,000 *CNY*

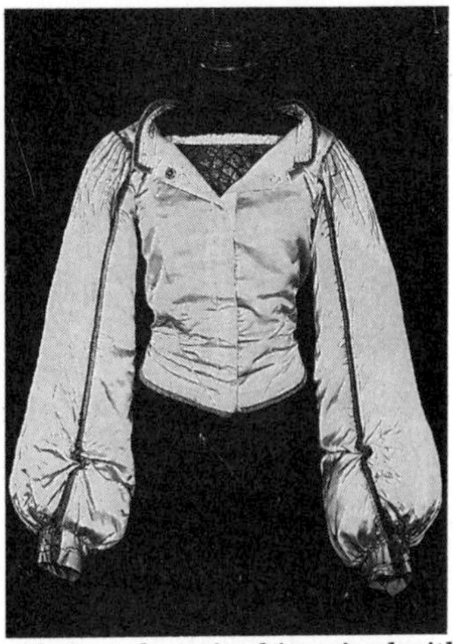

A burgundy satin shirt, piped with velvet, with green velvet insert stencilled in silver with garlands of flowers, for Romeo, *Romeo and Juliet,* Act I, 1977 production.
£8,500–9,000 *CNY*

A green velvet doublet, appliquéd with silver scrolling flowers, with a white silk shirt underneath, for Romeo, *Romeo and Juliet,* Act II, 1977 production.
£5,000–5,500 *CNY*

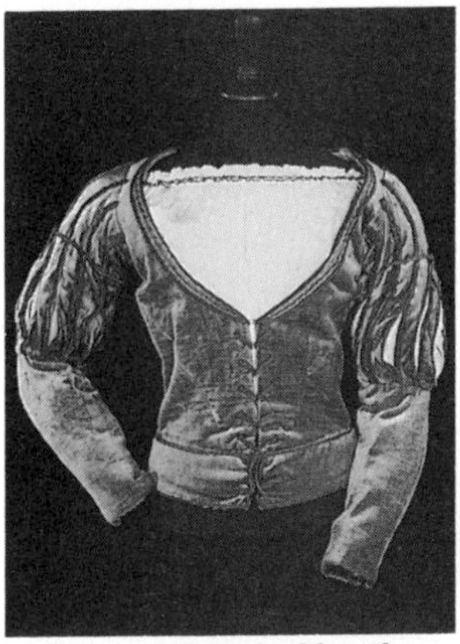

A brown velvet doublet, the slashed sleeves revealing orange silk, with a false shirt of pleated silk, elasticated and trimmed with braid.
£2,000–2,500 *CNY*

A yellow wool jacket, decorated with green and gold brocade and gold braid, filigree buttons, with a false shirt, for Basilio, *Don Quixote*, Act III, 1979 production.
£25,000–26,000 *CNY*

A mid-19thC style emerald green velvet waistcoat, bound with silk braid, with gold filigree buttons, labelled 'Nureyev', and a black silk stock, also labelled.
£3,500–4,000 *CNY*

A pink stockinette jacket, trimmed with gold braid and artificial pearls, with a black fur collar and embroidered epaulettes.
£3,000–3,500 *CNY*

l. A gold tunic, decorated with gold lace, trimmed with bands of red paste and simulated pearls, for Prince Siegfried, *Swine Lake,* 1978 production.
£12,500–13,000 *CNY*

On 23 January, 1978, Nureyev appeared as a guest on The Muppet Show. *In addition to dancing a pas de deux with an oversized Miss Piggy, Nureyev also sang 'Baby, it's cold outside', and sang and danced 'Top hat, white tie and tails' similar to Fred Astaire.*

A black velvet tunic, decorated with gold and amber coloured paste and gold sequins, with a false shirt.
£7,000–7,500 *CNY*

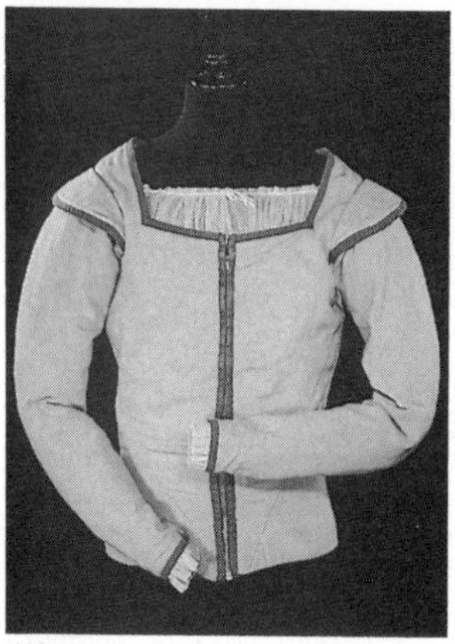

A beige woollen tunic, piped with brown braid, and a false shirt of ruched muslin, for Prince Albrecht, *Giselle,* Act I.
£1,000–1,500 *CNY*

A cotton under-tunic, with brown leather sleeves, decorated with simulated slashes at the shoulders, trimmed with gold cord, for Prince Albrecht, *Giselle,* Act I, labelled 'National Ballet of Canada, Giselle, Nureyev'.
£1,500–2,000 *CNY*

This costume was presumably used when Nureyev performed with the National Ballet of Canada in the late 1970s and 1980s.

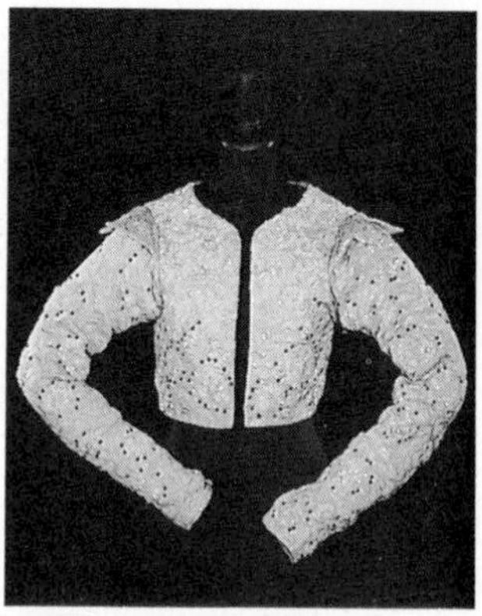

An ivory and silver silk jacket, trimmed with ribbonwork flowers painted pink and orange and embroidered with black sequins.
£2,500–3,000 *CNY*

It has not been possible to relate this jacket to any specific production of Don Quixote, *the ballet to which it obviously relates. Given the excellence of its condition, it may be a rejected design or reserved solely for gala performances.*

A ballerina's tutu, the bodice of ivory silk with an overlay of silver lace and trimmed with silver lace, the net skirt trimmed with feathers and simulated pearls, for *Swan Lake.*
£12,000–12,500 *CNY*

This costume was given by Dame Margot Fonteyn to Nureyev.

RUGS & CARPETS

A needlepoint carpet, of Aubusson design, in pale green, rose-red, beige and dusky pink, surrounded by a floral frame border between flowering vine stripes, 115 by 91in (292 by 231cm).
£750–900 *CSK*

An Afshar rug, with shaded indigo field, decorated in yellow, pistachio green, rust red, blue and brown surrounded by rust red and sky blue triple border of meandering palmette vine and linked lozenge between zig-zag and barber pole stripes, 75 by 60in (190.5 by 152cm).
£950–1,200 *CSK*

A needlepoint carpet, of Aubusson design, the cream field with meandering leafy vines and tendrils around an ivory oval medallion with flowerhead vines and stylised floral bouquet surrounded by floral garlands, in an ivory frame border of flowering vines, floral bouquets and similar cartouches in each corner between stripes, 119 by 98in (302 by 249cm).
£1,600–2,000 *CSK*

A needlepoint carpet, of Aubusson design, 77 by 74in (195.5 by 188cm).
£550–650 *CSK*

r. A needlepoint carpet, of Aubusson design, 138 by 103in (350 by 261.5cm).
£3,000–4,000 *CSK*

An Aimaq rug, decorated in midnight blue, red, rose, aubergine and blue-green on a camel field, with camel diagonal hook motif border, slight wear, north east Persia, late 19thC, 57 by 38in (144.5 by 96.5cm).
£800–1,000 *SK(B)*

An Empire carpet, of Aubusson design, the chocolate brown field with an overall light brown tracery vine, in a shaded green border with a dense floral wreath between plain orange, ivory and light brown stripes, woven to fit a fireplace, 226 by 210in (573 by 533cm).
£4,000–6,000 *C*

A Bakshaish carpet, north west Persia, 132 by 113in (335 by 287cm).
£9,000–10,000 *S*

An Ardebil carpet, the indigo field with hooked lozenges, stylised animal figures and hooked bars in brick red, yellow, blue, ivory and pistachio green around 3 brick red and light blue large gabled medallions, slight wear, 129 by 84in (327 by 213cm).
£900–1,200 *CSK*

A Bakhtiari carpet, central Persia, 164 by 77in (416 by 195.5cm).
£5,300–5,600 *S*

An Armenian Kazak rug, c1900, 90 by 62in (228.5 by 157cm).
£3,800–4,200 *RIT*

A Bakhtiari Garden carpet, the field with rust red, ivory and blue linked squares, panels in various colours, between rust red and fox brown flowering vine stripes, outer minor stripes, slight wear, 149 by 127in (378.5 by 322cm).
£1,000–1,200 *CSK*

r. A Bakhtiari Garden carpet, the field with 4 columns of linked squares in brick red, green, indigo, ivory and blue containing multi-coloured angular floral sprays, 106 by 62in (269 by 157cm).
£600–800 *CSK*

A Bakhtiari kelim rug, decorated in dovetail technique with a grid pattern of diamonds, late 19thC, 76 by 40in (193 by 101.5cm).
£300–400 *GRG*

A Baluch rug, decorated in red, navy blue, brown and ivory on a light red brown field, with a flowerhead border of similar colours, slight damage, north east Persia, late 19thC, 60 by 36in (152 by 91.5cm).
£200–300 *SK(B)*

A Baluch rug, decorated with motifs in navy blue, red, brown and light aubergine on a camel field, a red rosette border, slight wear, north east Persia, late 19thC, 57 by 31in (144.5 by 78.5cm).
£750–850 *SK(B)*

A Bidjar carpet, north Persia, 178 by 126in (451.5 by 320cm).
£20,000–25,000 *S*

A south Caucasian lesghi design rug, the charcoal brown field with hooked lozenges, 'S' motifs, and small floral motifs around a column of large lesghi medallions in shaded brick red, yellow, pistachio green, ivory, indigo and sky-blue, 125 by 59in (317.5 by 149.5cm).
£1,600–2,000 *CSK*

A Bidjar runner, the shaded indigo field with a column of multi-coloured serrated flowerhead medallions, repaired, 159 by 36in (403.5 by 91.5cm).
£400–600 *CSK*

l. A Bidjar rug, decorated with a brick red field with overall stylised multi-coloured open herati pattern surrounded by a sky-blue border, 72 by 44in (182.5 by 111.5cm).
£400–600 *CSK*

A Caucasian kelim, decorated with dramatic bands in natural dyes, Shirham region, 118 by 85in (300 by 215cm), c1900.
£1,800–2,200 *GRG*

A Caucasian silk and wool runner, late 19th, 116 by 40in (294 by 102cm).
£1,100–1,250 *GRG*

A Chichi rug, the indigo field with horizontal rows of multi-coloured hooked panels and flowerheads, slight wear, 60 by 42in (152 by 106.5cm).
£900–1,200 *CSK*

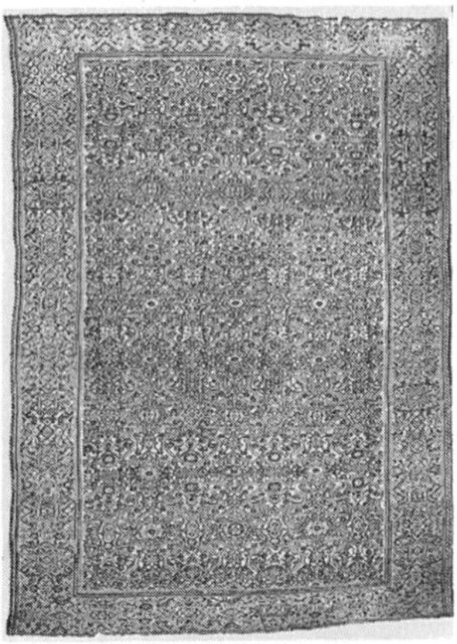

A Feraghan carpet, the ivory field with overall stylised angular and serrated open lattice, enclosing a variety of flowerheads and palmettes linked by angular floral vines in brick red, yellow, blue, green, indigo and brown, slight wear, 174 by 124in (441.5 by 315cm).
£2,500–3,500 *CSK*

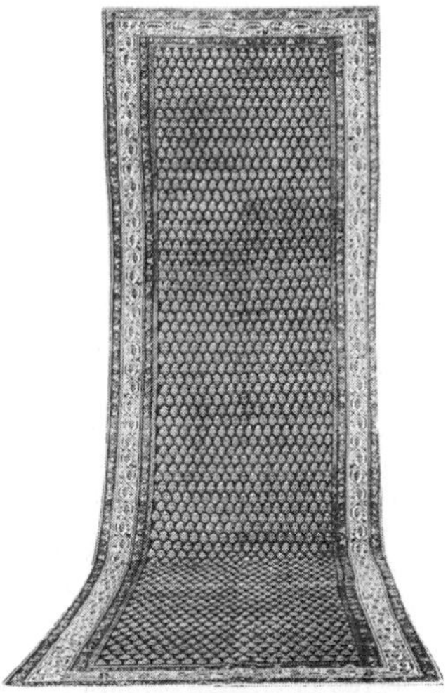

A Hamadan kelleh, of Serabend design, the shaded indigo field with overall diagonal rows of stylised floral boteh in brick red, yellow, green, ivory and blue surrounded by an ivory border of meandering boteh vine between indigo palmette vine and barber pole stripes, 228in by 72in (578.5 by 182.5cm).
£800–1,000 *CSK*

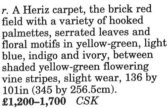

A Hamadan kelleh, the shaded indigo field with an overall stylised boteh design in brick red, ivory yellow, pistachio green and fox brown, repaired, 135 by 74in (342 by 188cm).
£500–700 *CSK*

r. A Heriz carpet, the brick red field with a variety of hooked palmettes, serrated leaves and floral motifs in yellow-green, light blue, indigo and ivory, between shaded yellow-green flowering vine stripes, slight wear, 136 by 101in (345 by 256.5cm).
£1,200–1,700 *CSK*

l. A Heriz carpet, decorated with navy blue, red-brown, ivory and blue-green on a red field, stepped ivory spandrels, navy blue turtle border, slight wear, north west Persia, early 20thC, 140in by 106in (355 by 269cm).
£1,400–2,000 *SK(B)*

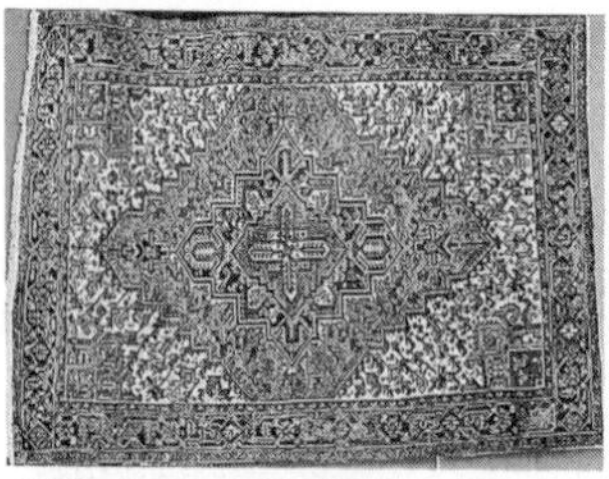

A Heriz carpet, 132 by 96in (335 by 243.5cm).
£550–650 *CSK*

A Heriz carpet, with an ivory field flanking a brick red panel around a shaded blue and powder pink central medallion with shaded blue pendants, within a narrow indigo border of turtle palmettes and angular vine between powder pink reciprocal floral stripes, slight wear, 140 by 91in (365 by 231cm).
£1,400–2,000 *C*

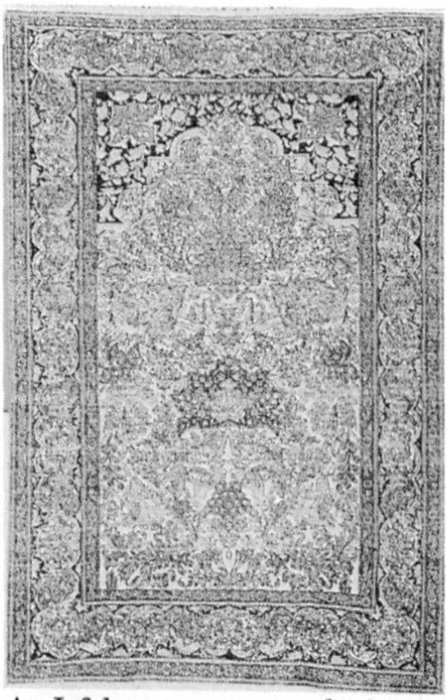

An Isfahan prayer rug, the ivory field with stylised multi-coloured flowering vines in the shape of a tree, a shaded indigo mihrab with flowering tendrils and palmettes surrounded by an indigo border of linked floral cartouches between raspberry red flowering vines and zig-zag stripes, slight wear, 80 by 56in (203 by 142cm).
£700–800 *CSK*

A Heriz carpet, the light brick red field with angular floral sprays in yellow, indigo, ivory, light blue and fox red, 130 by 92in (329.5 by 233.5cm).
£550–750 *CSK*

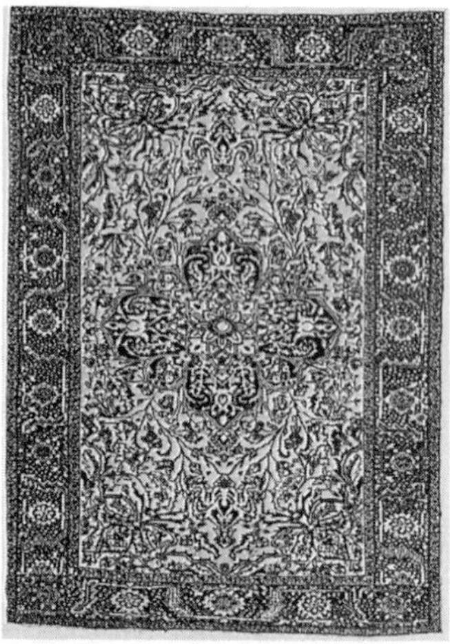

A Heriz carpet, with a shaded brick red field, stylised multi-coloured flowering vines, 135 by 98in (342.5 by 249cm).
£1,000–1,500 *CSK*

An Isfahan carpet, decorated overall with palmettes, scrolling vines, serrated leaves and rosettes in blue, burgundy, olive, gold and green on a cream field, with a burgundy palmette and vine border, central Persia, mid-20thC, 116 by 84in (294.5 by 213cm).
£3,000–3,500 *SK(B)*

A Heriz carpet, with a broad brick red rosette and meandering serrated leaf border between medium blue and sandy yellow angular floral vine and inner pink spiralling ribbon stripes, slight wear, 140 by 119in (365 by 302cm).
£2,000–2,500 *C*

A Heriz carpet, the rust field with various multi-coloured hooked palmettes, in an indigo border of serrated palmettes, flowerheads, leaves and angular vines between blue flowering vines and brick red linked floral motif stripes, 163 by 120in (413.5 by 304.5cm).
£3,500–4,000 *CSK*

An Isfahan carpet, the blue field with overall design surrounded by brick red broad border of palmettes and meandering leafy vines between ivory and indigo similar stripes, signed, 211 by 122in (536 by 310cm).
£4,000–5,000 *CSK*

A Karabagh carpet, the shaded black field with overall diagonal rows of stylised serrated cartouches, each with hooked palmette in yellow, brick red, brown, ivory and blackcurrant red, 233 by 76in (592 by 193cm).
£7,200–8,000 *CSK*

A Kashan carpet, the royal blue field with multi-coloured decoration, and outer stripes of ivory flowering vine, signature cartouche at one end, 158 by 112in (401 by 284.5cm).
£1,500–2,000 *CSK*

A Kashan rug, the shaded sky blue and ivory field with stylised rose bouquets, flowering vines and perching birds in various colours around burgundy and ivory cusped floral medallion with pendants, surrounded by pistachio green and ivory stylised floral frame border, slight damage, 84 by 56in (213 by 142cm).
£700–800 *CSK*

A Kazak rug, decorated with 3 hooked medallions in navy blue, ivory, gold and blue-green on the red field, gold serrated leaf and quatrefoil arrowhead border, slight wear, south west Caucasus, late 19thC, 86 by 62in (218.5 by 157cm).
£2,000–3,000 *SK(B)*

l. A Kazak rug, decorated with 3 hooked hexagonal medallions in red, ivory, ice blue and green, on sky blue field, with ivory wineglass border, slight wear, south west Caucasus, late 19thC, 78 by 50in (198 by 127cm).
£300–400 *SK(B)*

A Kashan carpet, the burgundy field with overall design in multi-colours, signature cartouche at one end, 165 by 117in (419 by 297cm).
£900–1,000 *CSK*

A Kazak rug, the shaded indigo field with a column of 4 brick red, ivory, sky blue, apricot and sea green serrated lozenge medallions, containing stylised flowerheads and rosettes, short kilim and braiding at each end, 117 by 56in (297 by 142cm).
£750–850 *CSK*

Locate the source

The source of each illustration in* Miller's Antiques Price Guide *can easily be found by checking the code letters at the end of each caption with the Key to Illustrations located at the front of the book.

A Kurdish carpet, the shaded indigo field with 3 columns of 7 large multi-coloured Tauk-Nuska guls, divided by hooked lozenges surrounded by ivory border of linked polychrome hooked motifs, between barber pole, lapped and hooked running dog stripes, short kilim at each end, 152 by 88in (386 by 224cm).
£1,200–1,700 *CSK*

A Kazak rug, the shaded charcoal brown field, with hooked motifs and various small flowerheads around 4 pistachio green, indigo, ivory and brick red lesghi medallions, 99 by 50in (251.5 by 127cm).
£1,600–2,000 *CSK*

A Mahal carpet, the brick red field with bold overall design in ivory, green, yellow, blue and indigo, surrounded by ivory angular flowerhead vine border, between yellow and blue flowering vine stripes, 130 by 84in (330 by 213cm).
£900–1,200 *CSK*

A Mahal rug, the shaped indigo field with central hooked lozenge medallion with stylised double pendants in ice blue, sandy yellow, brick red and ivory, surrounded by brick red stylised open pattern frame, 81 by 53in (206 by 135cm).
£450–600 *CSK*

A Maimana kilim, north west Afghanistan, late 19thC, 36 by 24in (92 by 61cm).
£40–50 *GRG*

A Malayer Kelleh, with shaded brick red field, flowerhead border between blue scrolling floral vine stripes, slight wear, 205 by 72in (520 by 183cm).
£800–1,000 *CSK*

r. A Sarouk rug, the shaded brick red field with green, yellow, ivory and blue angular flowering vines, 84 by 57in (213 by 145cm).
£850–1,000 *CSK*

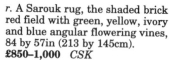

l. A south west Persian carpet, with shaded burgundy field, floral vines around green and ivory large stylised cypress tree flanked by a pair of birds, one at each side, surrounded by yellow border of radiating flowerheads and serrated leaf vine between indigo cypress tree wide stripes, outer floral, barber pole and hooked stripes, areas of wear, 180 by 144in (457 by 366cm).
£1,800–2,500 *CSK*

A north west Persian runner, the indigo field with overall stylised flowerheads, various floral sprays, chequered lozenges, human and animal figures in brick red, ivory, blue, pistachio green, yellow and brown, 108 by 47in (274 by 119cm).
£600–900 *CSK*

A Shirvan prayer rug, the hexagonal lattice with stars, in midnight and sky blue, red, gold, aubergine brown and blue green, on an ivory field, narrow sky blue rosette border, some wear and repair, east Caucasus, late 19thC, 42 by 27in (106.5 by 69cm).
£1,000–1,200 *SK(B)*

A Serapi carpet, the shaded brick red plain field with ivory serrated large panel, other decoration in brick red, blue, bottle green, dusky pink, indigo and yellow around cusped indigo medallion with yellow centrepiece issuing similar angular vines, slight wear and small cut, 177 by 114in (450 by 289.5cm).
£3,500–4,000 *CSK*

A Tabriz carpet, the ivory field with indigo centre, wide pale brick red main border of ivory cartouches, pale blue trailing floral guards and indigo floral stripes, c1920, 146 by 107in (371 by 271.5cm).
£3,000–4,000 *WW*

A Shirvan rug, the brick red field with multi-coloured hooked lozenges, various small flowerheads and S-motifs, around sky blue panel containing yellow shaped centrepiece with flowerheads and angular motifs surrounded by hooked and indented chequered shaped wide spandrels, in brick red border of multi-coloured hooked motifs between charcoal black running dog and angular S-motif stripes, 66 by 47in (167.5 by 119cm).
£450–600 *CSK*

A Shirvan Karagasjli rug, the brick red field with 3 blue, yellow, ivory, brick red and indigo stepped and gabled medallions, in ivory broad border of polychrome hooked motifs between charcoal black stepped flowerhead stripes, outer barber pole stripes, areas of corroded black, 79 by 48in (200.5 by 122cm).
£900–1,100 *CSK*

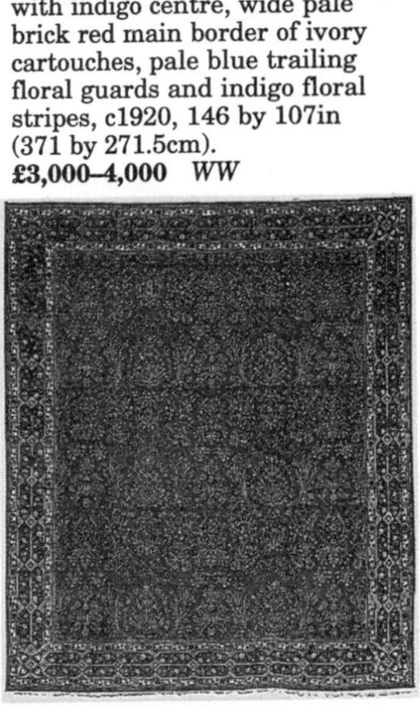

l. A Sivas carpet, the blue field with multi-coloured floral sprays and palmettes surrounded by brick red border of blue floral cartouches, between apricot meandering flowerhead vine and comb motif stripes, short kilim at each end, 134 by 117in (340 by 297cm).
£1,200–1,700 *CSK*

A Shirvan rug, patterned in brick red, ivory, yellow, blue and brown, very slight wear, small repairs, 69 by 45in (175 by 114cm).
£1,000–1,300 *CSK*

A Shirvan rug of Seychour design, the ivory field with a single column of stylised radiating sunburst medallion in brick red, indigo, yellow, blue and brown surrounded by a variety of serrated floral and S-motifs, 108 by 65in (274 by 165cm).
£400–600 *CSK*

A Tabriz carpet, the ivory field with overall meandering vines connecting various multi-coloured stylised palmettes and floral sprays within delicate flowering tendrils, surrounded by brick red border, 156 by 121in (396 by 307cm).
£800–1,000 *CSK*

A Tabriz carpet, the ivory field patterned in pale apricot and pistachio green, 153 by 114in (389 by 289.5cm).
£1,600–2,000 *CSK*

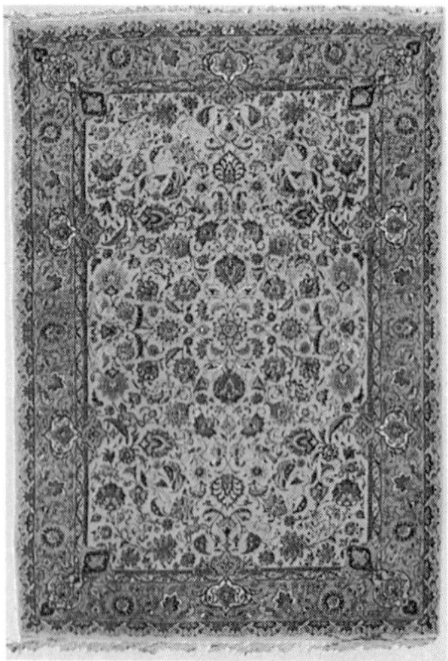

A Tabriz carpet, the light pistachio green field with overall scrolling leafy vines connecting serrated multi-coloured palmettes, signature cartouche at one end, 120 by 84in (304.5 by 213cm).
£2,000–2,500 *CSK*

A Tabriz carpet, the shaded brick red field with overall multi-coloured pattern, 150 by 114in (381 by 289.5cm).
£2,000–2,500 *CSK*

An American cotton hooked rug, worked in a variety of colours with 4 black cats, black cotton binding, later backing, 19thC, 28½ by 44in (72 by 112cm).
£1,000–1,200 *CNY*

r. A Turkoman rug, with Salukial influenced design, early 20thC, 62½ by 43½in (158 by 110cm).
£400–450 *GRG*

l. Three pictorial hooked rugs, each with dog designs, damaged, 20thC, 24 by 35in (61 by 89cm).
£160–260 *SK(B)*

PINE

A pine open bookcase, c1860, 63in (160cm) wide.
£400–600 *HOA*

A folding park chair, c1890.
£30–35 *AL*

A folding park chair, c1900.
£30–35 *AL*

r. A pine breakfront library bookcase, with serpentine front open shelves, the sides with adjustable open book shelves, panelled backs to the duck egg blue panelled interiors, the base with panelled doors with beaded and petal mouldings, on a plinth, 96in (243.5cm) wide.
£3,500–4,000 *WW*

A pine breakfront bookcase, with moulded cornice above 3 pairs of astragal glazed doors and 3 pairs of panelled cupboard doors below, 126in (320cm) wide.
£3,000–4,000 *CSK*

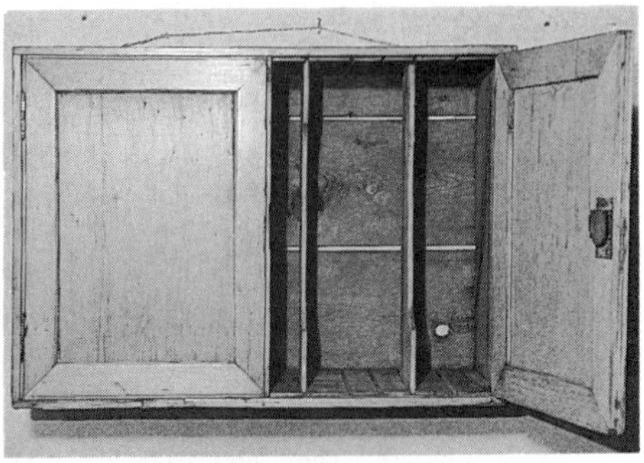

A pine fitted wall hanging cabinet, c1880, 24in (61.5cm) wide.
£100–125 *MofC*

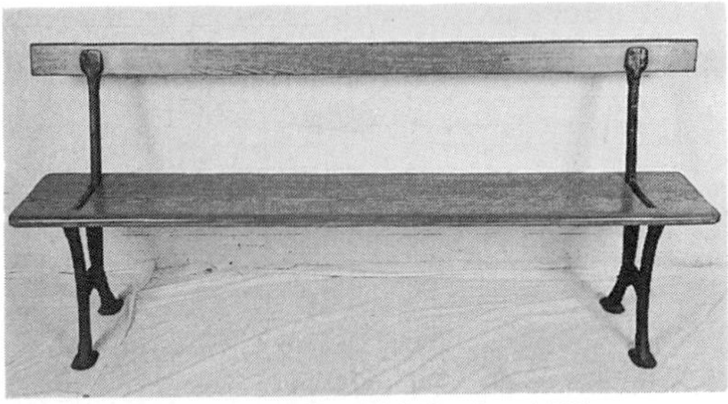

A pine bench, with adjustable back, c1880, 72½in (183.5cm) wide.
£170–220 *AL*

A milking stool, c1880, 15in (38cm) high.
£30–40 *AL*

A painted pine blanket chest, early red paint with scrubbed lift top, restored, New England, 18thC, 30in (76cm) high.
£850–1,000 *SK(B)*

A pine blanket chest, with 3 drawers, moulded feet, stripped to original finish, 19thC, 21in (53.5cm) wide.
£650–800 *EL*

An American pine blanket chest, with oval brasses, 40in (101.5cm) wide.
£250–400 *EL*

A pine blanket chest, with wrought-iron hinges, opening to a deep well with till, on trestle feet, the whole painted in red and black swirls, New England, early 19thC, 39in (99cm) wide.
£3,500–4,000 *S(NY)*

A pine chest, late 19thC, 36in (91.5cm) wide.
£150–180 *CPA*

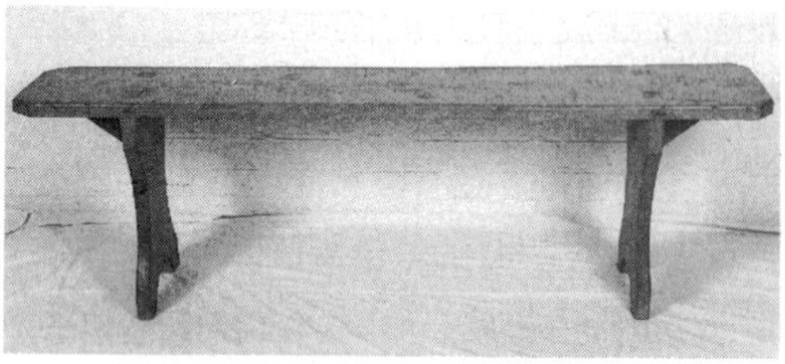

A pine bench, c1880, 57in (144.5cm) wide.
£80–100 *AL*

A pine bench, c1880, 97in (246cm) wide.
£100–120 *AL*

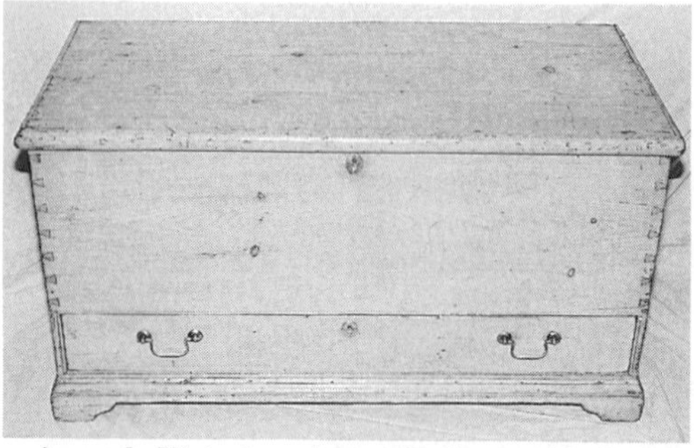

An early Victorian pine mule chest, with drawer under, 43½in (110cm) wide.
£300–400 *Cou*

A pine 3 drawer dower chest, the lid opening to a well, the moulded base on scroll carved bracket feet on pads, the whole painted all-over in red and black paint to simulate rosewood, Pennsylvania, early 19thC, 43in (109cm) wide.
£5,000–6,000 *S(NY)*

A pine chest, with single drawer, worn black paint, old brasses, New England, late 18thC, 24in (61.5cm) wide.
£4,000–4,500 *SK(B)*

A Georgian painted pine coffer, 26in (66cm) wide.
£125–200 *Cou*

A Continental pine chest of drawers, c1840, 39in (99cm) wide.
£300–400 *WAT*

A Scottish pine chest of drawers, c1850, 36in (91.5cm) wide.
£300–400 *HOA*

A pine chest of 5 drawers, New England, restored, refinished, late 18thC, 37½in (95cm) wide.
£550–700 *SK(B)*

l. A pine chest, with 3 drawers, on style feet, traces of original art work, c1850, 36in (91.5cm) wide.
£350–400 *CCP*

r. A pine chest of drawers, c1860, 35in (89.5cm) wide.
£280–300 *MIL*

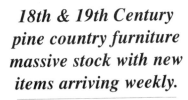

l. A pine chest of drawers, c1880, 34in (86cm) wide.
£500–535 *AL*

A pine chest of drawers, c1880, 38in (96.5cm) wide.
£800–900 *FAG*

An American pine corner cupboard, with raised panel doors and shaped bracket base, 41in (104cm) wide.
£800–1000 *EL*

A Victorian pine 5 drawer chest of drawers, with original handles, on bun feet, 40½in (103cm) wide.
£385–450 *CCP*

r. A Federal pine glazed corner cupboard, old refinish, replaced brasses, Pennsylvania, c1810, 50in (127cm) wide.
£1,700–2,200 *SK(B)*

l. A pine 5 drawer chest of drawers, with original lock and key, on bun feet, c1860, 39in (99cm) wide.
£300–450 *CCP*

l. A pine breakfront housekeeper's cupboard, on bracket feet, early 19thC, 84in (213cm) wide.
£1,000–1,200 *TPC*

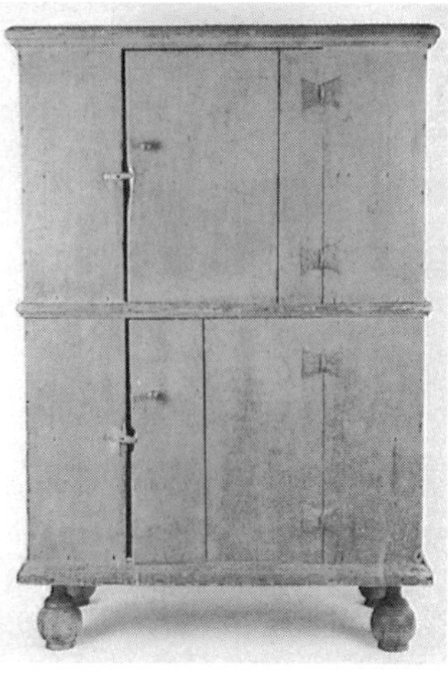

r. A painted pine cupboard, with shelved interior, red paint, restored, New England, 18thC, 41in (104cm) wide.
£5,000–6,000 *SK(B)*

A Michelangelo. Only in Florence.

A Van der Tol. Only in Almere.

We carry one of the world's finest collections of antique pine furniture. Available in unstripped, stripped and finished & painted versions. Plus pine reproductions and decorative items. We offer quality, quantity & profit and full packing service. Please visit our 65.000 sq.ft. warehouse in Almere and enjoy the personal and friendly service.

Jacques van der Tol

unique antique pine furniture

Jacques van der Tol wholesale BV. (20 min. from Schiphol Airport)
Antennestraat 34, 1322 AE Almere-Stad, Holland. Industrial Estate 'Gooise Kant'
Tel.:(0)36-5362050. Fax:(0)36-5361993

A pine hanging wall cupboard, sponge-decorated all over with ochre fans on a yellow-mustard ground, with original stamped brass mounts, New England, early 19thC, 29½in (75cm) wide.
£3,500–4,500 *S(NY)*

A pine cupboard, with moulded top, 4 interior shelves and 2 panel doors, 47in (119cm) wide.
£250–400 *EL*

A Tyrolean pine and decorated cupboard, painted brown and blue, enclosing shelves, on flattened bun feet, one loose, c1800, 54½in (138cm) wide.
£1,000–1,500 *CSK*

An Irish pine cupboard, c1880, 40in (101.5cm) wide.
£300–380 *FAG*

A pine pot cupboard, c1870, 12in (30.5cm) wide.
£175–210 *AL*

r. A pine pot cupboard, c1880, 18in (45.5cm) wide.
£85–100 *AnD*

r. A pair of Continental pine bedside pot cupboards, c1900, 18in (45.5cm) wide.
£265–325 *AnD*

A gamekeeper's pine cupboard, with 4 panel doors, on bun feet, Gloucester, 83in (210.5cm) wide.
£500–600 *CCP*

A Continental pine cupboard, c1870, 40in (101.5cm) wide.
£500–525 *AnD*

A Continental pine cupboard, c1880, 42in (106.5cm) wide.
£500–525 *AnD*

A Continental collapsible pine armoire, 48in (122cm) wide.
£550–600 *AnD*

r. A German pine wardrobe, c1880, 42in (106.5cm) wide.
£450–500 *AnD*

l. A German painted pine armoire, Saxony region, c1800, 45in (114cm) wide.
£3,500–4,000 *Cou*

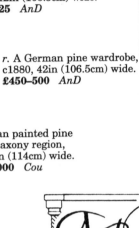

l. A Continental pine cupboard, c1880, 42in (106.5cm) wide.
£500–525 *AnD*

r. A Continental pine wardrobe, c1850, 38in (96.5cm) wide.
£400–500 *AnD*

A Continental pine wardrobe, c1890, 42in (106.5cm) wide.
£375–475 *AnD*

Locate the source
The source of each illustration in* Miller's Antiques Price Guide *can easily be found by checking the code letters at the end of each caption with the Key to Illustrations located at the front of the book.

MILLER'S COMPARES . . .

I A French collapsible pine armoire, with fitted interior and 2 drawers, c1880, 60in (152cm) wide.
£1,000–1,250 *AnD*

II A Continental collapsible pine armoire, c1880, 49in (124.5cm) wide.
£500–600 *AnD*

Although both pieces appear similar, *Item I* is made from French pine which is a more sought after wood than the German or Dutch pine from which *Item II* is made. *Item I* has several raised and fielded panels on the sides as well as on the front, whereas *Item II* only has panels on the front. *Item I* has striking rounded corners on the cornice, while *Item II* has the more usual squared corners. The interior of *Item I* has been fitted with shelves whereas the interior of *Item II* has not. *AnD*

l. A pine dresser, a moulded cornice above an inverted breakfront partitioned with an arrangement of shelves and a plate rack, above 3 frieze drawers and central open shelf, flanked by panelled cupboard doors, on bun feet, late 19thC, 60in (152cm) wide.
£800–1,200 *CSK*

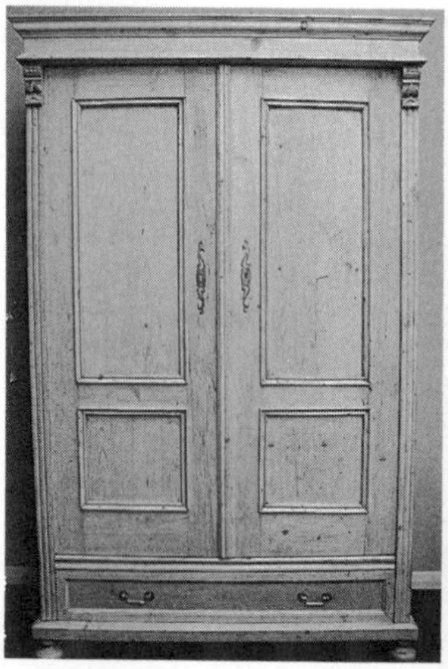

r. A pine armoire, c1890, 46in (116.5cm) wide.
£800–850 *MofC*

A pine Chippendale style raised panel hutch cupboard, 49in (124.5cm) wide.
£600–800 *SLN*

l. A pine triple wardrobe/press, c1850, 70in (177.5cm) wide.
£1,750–1,850 *AL*

A pine dresser, associated, on a plinth, late 19thC, 74in (188cm) wide.
£1,800–2,200 *CSK*

A Continental pine dresser base, c1890, 46in (116.5cm) wide.
£225–350 *AnD*

A pine dresser, c1820, 64in (162.5cm) wide.
£1,300–1,500 *FAG*

r. A Welsh pine dresser, with shelves, 18thC, 50in (127cm) wide.
£800–1,000 *TPC*

r. A pitch pine dresser, with a moulded cornice above a pair of glazed doors, the lower part with 2 panelled doors flanking 3 small drawers, on bracket feet, 19thC, 48in (122cm) wide.
£2,000–2,500 *DN*

This dresser is of an Irish form and originated from the vicinity of Bangor in Co. Antrim.

A pine console table, with a marble top and boldly carved pierced frieze, with acanthus sprays and rocaille scrolls, on cabriole legs, joined by cross stretchers and terminating in acanthus scroll feet, 45in (114cm) wide.
£2,500–3,000 *CSK*

An American pine hutch table, with storage under, top repaired, refinished, 45in (114cm) wide.
£600–800 *EL*

A pine table, cut down for a coffee table, c1880, 40in (101.5cm) wide.
£150–200 *FAG*

An American pine Empire frame, boldly painted in red, black and gold stripes, the corners with scrolling anthemia leafage, with a mirror, c1850, 50in (127cm) wide.
£3,000–3,500 *S(NY)*

An American chip-carved pine frame, painted red, dark green, black and brown, with a mirror, c1930, 14in (35.5cm) wide.
£400–500 *S(NY)*

A pine drop-leaf table, 38in (96.5cm) wide.
£180–280 *FAG*

An American Federal pine frame, painted and stencilled, with a mirror, mid-19thC, 20in (51cm) wide.
£480–680 *S(NY)*

A pine side table, with one drawer, on turned legs, c1880, 36in (91.5cm) wide.
£250–280 *AL*

A Victorian pine work table, with one drawer, 22½in (56.5cm) wide.
£100–150 *CCP*

A pine table, on turned legs, late 19thC, 28in (71cm) wide).
£200–225 *CPA*

r. A Victorian pine side table, with shaped frieze, 29in (73.5cm) wide.
£100–120 *CCP*

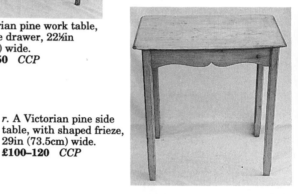

A pine table, on turned legs with casters, c1870, 48in (122cm) wide.
£450–500 *AL*

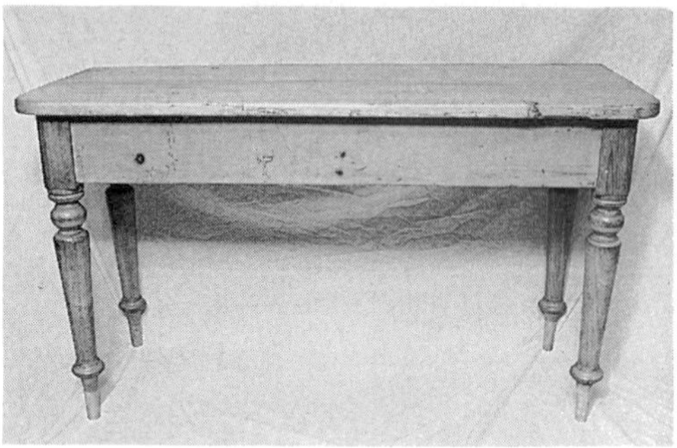

A pine table, c1880, 54in (137cm) wide.
£200–300 *FAG*

A pine serving table, with 2 drawers, c1860, 60in (152cm) wide.
£250–350 *FAG*

A pine kitchen table, c1860, 96in (243.5cm) wide.
£775–850 *AnD*

A pine tray-top washstand, c1880, 36in (91.5cm) wide.
£250–300 *AL*

A pine table, on turned legs, c1880, 34in (86.5cm) wide.
£150–200 *AL*

A George III pine corner washstand, with splayed legs, and an oak side table, damaged.
£250–300 *C*

A pine tray-top washstand, c1880, 24½in (62.5cm) wide.
£150–200 *AL*

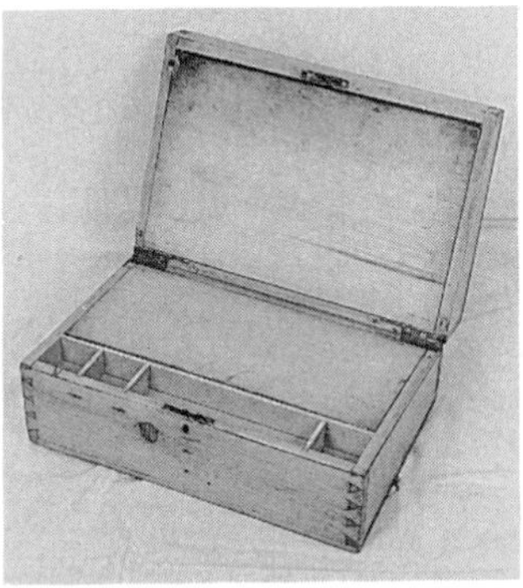

A Victorian pine writing slope, 17in (43.5cm) wide.
£80–110 *FOX*

r. A pine washstand, with a shelf, c1880, 32½in (82.5cm) wide.
£150–200 *AL*

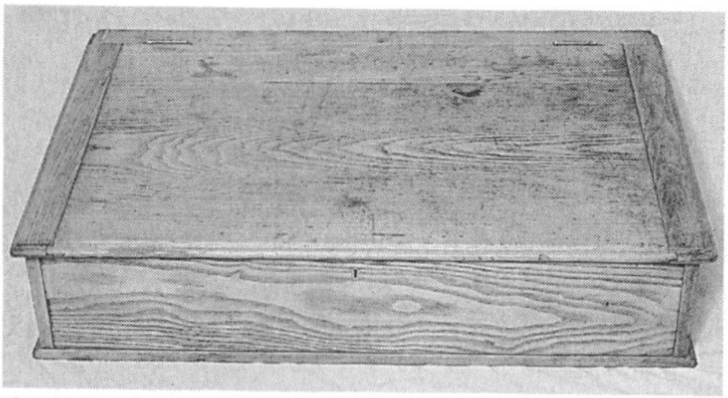

A pitch pine writing slope, c1900, 36in (91.5cm) wide.
£100–150 *FAG*

A pair of pine window pelmets, painted and stencilled, probably New York, mid-19thC, 43½in (110cm) wide.
£400–500 *S(NY)*

An Edwardian 31 drawer filing chest, by John Houlton & Son Ltd., Hull, 21in (53.5cm) wide.
£450–550 *CCP*

A set of pine steps, c1900, 24in (61.5cm) high.
£40–50 *AL*

A pine saddle horse, c1890, 49in (124.5cm) wide.
£150–180 *AL*

A pine luggage rack, c1890, 28in (71.5cm) wide.
£50–100 *AL*

A set of pine shelves, c1890, 78½in (199cm) high.
£300–350 *AL*

A George III style carved pine and composition fire surround, the breakfront swag-hung cornice above a central tablet with classical scene, with grey marble jams and hearth piece, 68in (172.5cm) wide.
£1,100–1,500 *CSK*

An Edwardian pine step ladder, patented, 31in (79cm) high.
£80–100 *CCP*

A pine chest of 2 drawers, 18thC, 12in (30.5cm) wide.
£125–150 *AnE*

A pine plant stand, c1890, 39in (99cm) wide.
£180–220 *AL*

TEDDY BEARS

A Bing golden mohair teddy bear, with black boot button eyes, pronounced clipped snout, black stitched nose, mouth and claws, clockwork operated turning head, elongated jointed shaped limbs, hump, keyhole to right side and pewter Bing button to left side, pads recovered, c1910, 21in (53cm) high.
£2,000–2,500 *CSK*

A Bing white mohair teddy bear, with black boot button eyes, pronounced snout, beige horizontally stitched nose, mouth and claws, swivel head, elongated jointed shaped limbs and hump, overall wear, pads recovered, c1910, 20in (51cm) high.
£750–850 *CSK*

Two white wool mohair bears, Elizabeth and Daughter, with pale stone coloured pigskin pads and inner ears, shaven snout, silk salmon coloured nose and claws, Canterbury Bear and Blackburn Family Collection labels, signed 'John and Maude Blackburn', large bear 24in (61cm) high.
£70–90 *CSK*

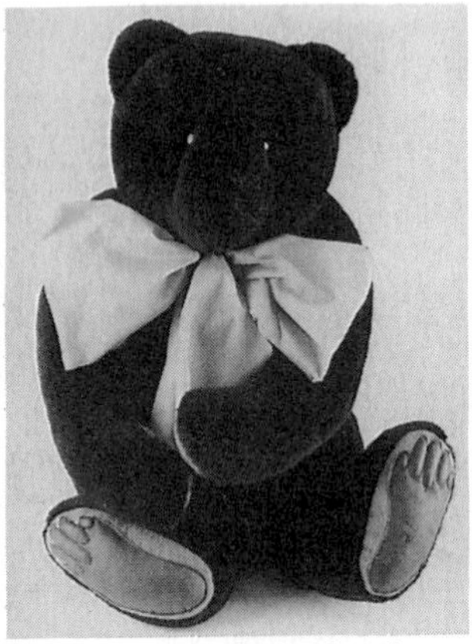

A dark brown alpaca Auction Bear, soft filled with siliconised dacron, amber glass eyes, large black wool nose, tan cashmere pads with shaped and detailed leather pads attached, Canterbury Bear and Blackburn Family Collection labels, signed 'John and Maude Blackburn', 26in (66cm) high.
£60–90 *CSK*

A group of Genie Buttitta Rail Yard Buddies bears, 2 mohair, 1 wool blend plush, another man-made fabric, the dog of soft plush, 3 to 6in (7.5 to 15cm) high, all in a hand painted wooden frame, 13in (33cm) high.
£125–200 *CSK*

A light brown Auction Bear, filled with oak shavings, amber glass eyes, black wool nose, tan cashmere pads with shaped leather detail, hump, ankles detailed with leather, Canterbury Bear and Blackburn Family Collection labels, signed 'John and Maude Blackburn', 24in (61cm) high.
£60–90 *CSK*

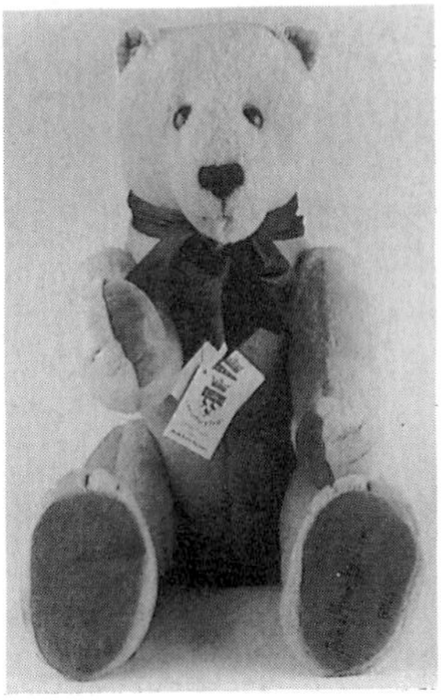

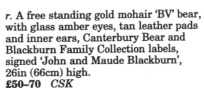

r. A free standing gold mohair 'BV' bear, with glass amber eyes, tan leather pads and inner ears, Canterbury Bear and Blackburn Family Collection labels, signed 'John and Maude Blackburn', 26in (66cm) high.
£50–70 *CSK*

l. Two hand dyed coffee mohair bears, Alexander & Son, cotton filled, leather inner ears, amber glass eyes, black wool nose, handmade leather shaped collar, camel hair pads with leather detail, Canterbury Bear and Blackburn Family Collection labels, signed 'John and Maude Blackburn', larger bear 24in (61cm) high.
£70–90 *CSK*

A Chiltern bear, Master Teddy, the stuffed cloth body with mohair hands and feet and cardboard inner soles, painted googlie glass eyes, black embroidered nose and mouth, red tongue, dressed in a jacket and trousers, with Teddy Tail League badge, worn, 1915, 9½in (24cm) high.
£2,200–2,700 *Bon*

Master Teddy was used as the Daily Mail character.

Chiltern

In 1920 Leon Rees and Harry Stone formed H. G. Stone & Co., and in 1922 they made their first baby teddy. The name 'Chiltern Toys' was registered in 1924 when the Company acquired a factory in Chesham, Buckinghamshire. Harry Stone designed and manufactured the bears and soft toys and Leon Rees was responsible for marketing and sales. Chiltern bears were renowned for their softness, created by the use of fine quality long mohair plush.

In 1945 soft toys started to be made at Amersham, with Madeleine Biggs and Pamela Williams as the main designers. In 1947 Chiltern introduced their popular line of 'Hugmee' bears. Leon Rees died in 1963, and in 1967 Chiltern became a subsidiary of Chad Valley and started using the 'Chiltern Chad Valley' label.

A Chiltern golden curly mohair bear, Edwin, with pronounced clipped snout, black stitched nose, mouth and claws, swivel head, jointed shaped limbs, velvet pads, shaped paws, cardboard lined feet and slight hump, eyes replaced, 1930s, 28in (71cm) high.
£800–900 *CSK*

A Chiltern Sooty on a Bicycle bear, orange plush with black ears, orange plastic eyes, black plastic nose, pink plush hands and feet, riding a red tricycle, with label 'Chiltern Hygienic Toys Made in England', 1950s, 11in (28cm) high.
£250–300 *Bon*

A Corla Cubillas Father bear and daughter Katie, Dancing with Daddy, both made of imported mohair and fully jointed, 27in (69cm) and 17in (43cm) high.
£400–500 *CSK*

A Chiltern golden mohair teddy bear, with amber and black glass eyes, swivel head, jointed shaped limbs, linen pads and small hump, slight wear, 1930s, 26in (66cm) high.
£350–400 *CSK*

r. A Chiltern Skater teddy bear, with golden plush head, hands and lower body, card lined felt feet, clear and black glass eyes, black stitched nose and mouth, wearing a pink and white artificial silk plush jacket with high collar and muff, pink velvet pillbox hat with squeaker, with printed label, 11in (28cm) high.
£300–350 *CSK*

A Chiltern golden mohair teddy bear, with swivel head, jointed shaped limbs, velvet pads, cardboard lined feet and hump, eyes missing, 1930s, 26in (66cm) high.
£600–700 *CSK*

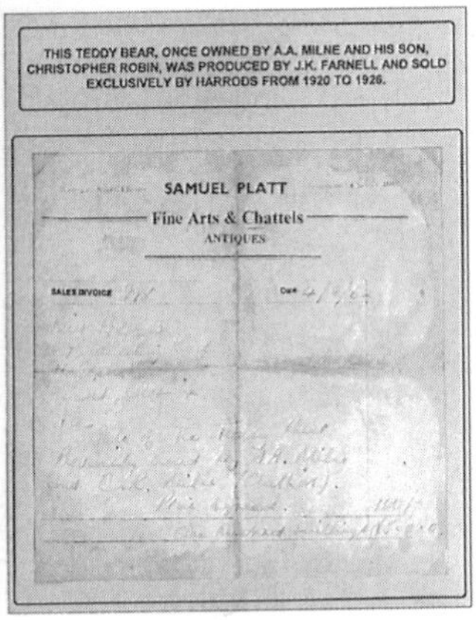

A gold mohair J. K. Farnell bear, with painted black glass eyes, black embroidered nose and mouth, fully jointed, straw filled, cream cloth pads with black webbed claws, cardboard inner soles, slight damage, c1920, 18in (46cm) high.
£5,000–5,500 *Bon*

This bear, once owned by A. A. Milne and his son Christopher Robin, was sold exclusively by Harrods from 1920–26. The bear was sold by Samuel Platt Fine Arts and Antiques on 4th August 1962 to Miss Harlow for one hundred shillings. The framed receipt comes with the bear as well as a framed print of A. A. Milne.

A Farnell bear, Fritz the P.O.W. bear, previously thought to be Steiff, with brown boot button eyes, black embroidered nose, fully jointed, cloth pads, five claws, straw filled, c1910, 10½in (26cm) high.
£1,500–2,000 *Bon*

Fritz was found hidden under the floorboards of a German prisoner of war camp in Scotland when it was being dismantled in 1949. He is wearing all his medals and badges.

A teddy bear bride and groom, Edwina and Winstone, both in original box, with certificate of authenticity and 2 letters from Franklin Mint to Col. T. R. Henderson, 1980s.
£220–270 *CSK*

A Dee Hockenberry curly mohair bear and cat, Teddy and Puss In Boots, both dressed in leather boots, hats with plumes, capes and brass swords in scabbards.
£200–400 *CSK*

l. A Hermann pale beige mohair teddy bear, with amber and glass eyes, clipped plush cut muzzle, black stitched nose, mouth and claws, swivel head, jointed shaped limbs, cream felt pads and growler, slight wear, 1930s, 23in (59cm) high.
£180–210 *CSK*

A Farnell golden curly mohair teddy bear, with painted glass eyes, swivel head, jointed shaped limbs and cream felt pads, slight wear, squeaker broken, 1930s, 15in (38cm) high.
£400–500 *CSK*

An Ideal golden mohair teddy bear, with black button eyes, black stitched nose, mouth and claws, swivel head, jointed shaped limbs and hump, worn, pads replaced, c1905, 15in (38cm) high.
£850–950 *CSK*

A selection of 5 teddy bears, including Farnell and Chad Valley bears, all fully jointed, 1920s–50s, largest 20in (51cm) high.
£420–500 *CSK*

Seven fully jointed, hand stitched miniature teddy bears, Surf's Up, by The Nostalgic Bear Company, comprising: 2 surfers, 2 hippies, 2 sunbathers and a college bear driving his car, 2½in to 4in (6 to 10cm) high.
£360–400 *CSK*

The bears and clothing are by Sue Foskey. The hand fashioned accessories are by Randall Foskey.

A Merrythought golden mohair teddy bear, with amber and black glass eyes, pronounced clipped snout, black stitched nose, mouth and claws, swivel head, jointed shaped limbs, slight hump, pads recovered, 1930s, 21in (53cm) high, together with a colour photograph of Col. T. R. Henderson and part of his collection, including this bear.
£550–650 *CSK*

Merrythought

Merrythought was part of the spinning industry affected by the advent of synthetic fibres. The firm hired C. J. Rendle from Chad Valley and H. C. Jamish from Farnell and began producing Merrythought Toys. Florence Atwood was recruited as chief designer from Chad Valley, a position she occupied from the early 1930s to 1949. Production has continued at Ironbridge, Shropshire interrupted only by the war. In 1986 the publication of *The Magic of Merrythought* inspired the company to create the first of their many replica bears available today.

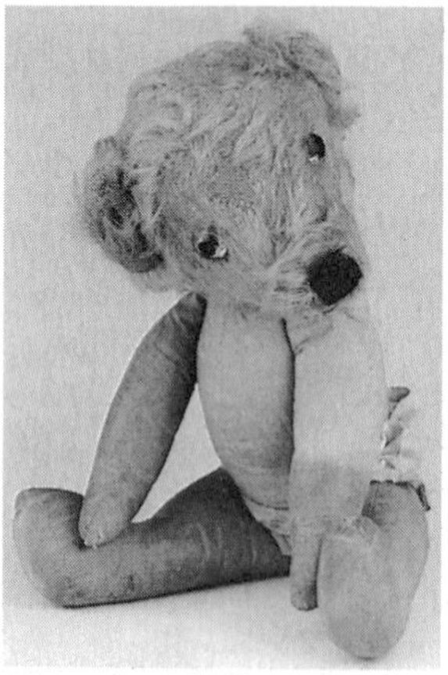

A Merrythought Bare Bingie teddy bear, with golden mohair covered face, clear and black glass eyes, black stitched nose and mouth, swivel head, jointed limbs, cotton covered body and limbs, c1931, 13in (33cm) high.
£300–350 *CSK*

A gold mohair teddy bear, by Peacock & Co., with brown glass eyes, black embroidered nose and mouth, fully jointed, kapok and straw filled, brown felt pads, claws, with label, 1920s, 27½in (70cm) high
£750–950 *Bon*

A Schuco bell hop teddy bear, with gold plush head, hands and feet, and 'Yes/No' head movement operated by its tail, with original label, 1920s, 11in (28cm) high.
£1,500–2,000 *Bea*

Five miniature teddy bears, Maypole Dancers, by Kathryn M. Riley, each hand stitched and fully jointed, dressed in cottons and silks trimmed with silk flowers, beads and bows, each bear 3in (7.5cm) high, on a musical revolving base, 10in (25cm) diam.
£600–700 *CSK*

This piece was created specially for the Walt Disney World Teddy Bear & Doll Convention, 1993.

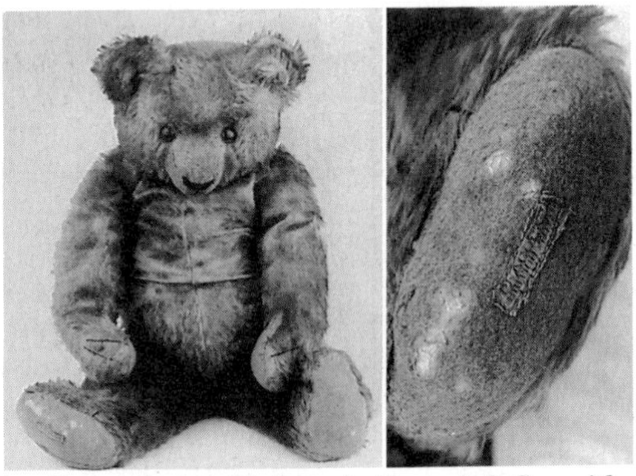

A golden mohair teddy bear, by Peacock & Co., with amber and black glass eyes, clipped snout, black stitched nose, mouth and claws, swivel head, jointed shaped limbs, felt pads, with embroidered label, slightly worn and repaired, 1930s, 27in (69cm) high.
£620–700 *CSK*

A Schuco miniature golden mohair teddy bear, with black stitched nose and mouth, swivel head, jointed padless limbs and tail operating 'Yes/No' head movement, damaged, 5in (12.5cm) high, and a Steiff golden mohair fox, with brown and black glass eyes, black stitched nose, swivel head and jointed limbs, worn, c1910, 8in (20cm) high.
£420–560 *CSK*

A pair of Schuco blonde mohair bears, one with orange and black glass eyes, stitched nose, open mouth with felt palate and red tongue, three-claw paws and velveteen pads, 11½in (29cm) high, the other with brown and black glass eyes, stitched nose and mouth, shaved mohair feet, ears and muzzle, four-claw paws and felt pads, worn, 14in (36cm) high, both 1937.
£700–900 *Bon*

These 2 bears were purchased by the original owner in Berlin in 1937 and have always been together.

A Schuco blonde mohair teddy bear, with red and black glass eyes, stitched nose and mouth, shaved muzzle and pads, dressed in a red and black guardsman's uniform, 1950s, 25in (64cm) high.
£400–500 *Bon*

A Steevans golden mohair teddy bear, Pery, with black boot button eyes, pronounced snout, black stitched nose, mouth and claws, swivel head, jointed padless limbs and metal stud in ear marked 'Steevans England PT 126846', wearing a collection of Henley Regatta badges and medals, one eye scratched, c1918, 9½in (24cm) high.
£1,800–2,200 *CSK*

The previous owner of this bear was William Pery Goodbody (1905–42), who rowed for Shrewsbury and Cambridge. Pery was the family middle Christian name.

l. A Schuco golden mohair teddy bear, with amber and black glass eyes, pronounced snout, black stitched nose, mouth and claws, swivel head, jointed shaped limbs, felt pads, cardboard lined feet, tail operating 'Yes/No' head movement, original chest ribbon, worn, 1950s, 13in (33cm) high.
£500–600 *CSK*

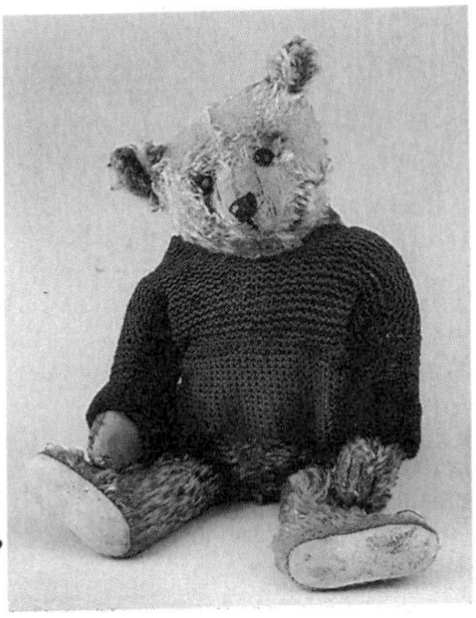

r. A Steiff centre seam teddy bear, with golden curly mohair, black boot button eyes, pronounced clipped snout, black stitched nose, mouth and claws, swivel head, elongated jointed shaped limbs, shaped paws and feet, hump and button in ear, well worn, pads recovered, c1907, 19in (48cm) high.
£1,600–2,000 *CSK*

MILLER'S COMPARES . . .

I A Steiff cinnamon teddy bear, with black boot button eyes, pronounced snout, black stitched nose, mouth and claws, swivel head, elongated jointed shaped limbs, shaped paws, feet and hump, pad recovered, growler inoperative, c1910, 20in (51cm) high.
£2,700–3,200 *CSK*

II A Steiff golden mohair teddy bear, with black boot button eyes, swivel head, elongated jointed shaped limbs, felt pads, hump and button in ear, growler inoperative, moth damage to paws, c1906, 13in (33cm) high.
£1,600–1,800 *CSK*

As a rule the bigger the size and better the condition of a teddy bear the higher the price. ***Item I*** **is 7in larger than** ***Item II.*** **The plush fur of** ***Item I*** **is in much better condition than** ***Item II*** **which is showing signs of wear. The cinnamon colour of** ***Item I*** **is unusual and will therefore ensure that it is more sought after.** *CSK*

A Steiff beige and cream mohair Zotty teddy bear, brown and black glass eyes, felt open mouth, swivel head, jointed limbs, felt pads, squeaker and button in ear with yellow label, 6½in (16cm) high, another similar, with no squeaker or button, 8½in (21cm) high, a Steiff Floppy Zotty, 6½in (16cm) high, and a beige plush teddy bear, with amber and black glass eyes, felt open mouth, red felt tongue, swivel head, unjointed flexible limbs, felt pads, cardboard reinforced feet, chain linked from nose to collar, slight damage, 13in (33cm) high.
£220–270 *CSK*

r. A Steiff cinnamon coloured centre seam teddy bear, Arthur, with black boot button eyes, swivel head, elongated jointed shaped limbs, felt pads, card reinforced feet, hump and button in ear, worn, growler inoperative, c1908, 19in (48cm), and a photograph of Arthur in his youth.
£2,500–3,000 *CSK*

A Steiff golden mohair teddy bear, with black boot button eyes, pronounced snout, black stitched nose, mouth and claws, swivel head, elongated jointed shaped limbs and hump, well worn, pads recovered, c1910, 12in (30.5cm) high, and a Breton style carved doll's armchair with hinged seat.
£600–700 *CSK*

A Steiff golden brown mohair teddy bear, with black boot button eyes, swivel head, elongated jointed shaped limbs, felt pads, hump and button in ear, worn and repaired, c1908, 15in (38cm) high.
£2,000–2,500 *CSK*

A Steiff long black plush teddy bear, with pointed snout, stitched nose, black boot button eyes, inoperative growel box, embossed button to ear, later felt pads, early 20thC, 21in (53cm) high.
£8,500–9,500 *HSS*

A Steiff honey golden mohair teddy bear, with black boot button eyes, black stitched nose, mouth and claws, swivel head, elongated jointed shaped limbs, felt pads, hump and button in ear, slight wear, c1910, 11in (28cm) high.
£1,400–1,800 *CSK*

A Steiff beige mohair teddy bear, with brown and black glass eyes, pronounced snout, stitched nose, mouth and claws, swivel head, jointed shaped limbs, felt pads and slight hump, 1950s, 17in (43cm) high.
£420–500 *CSK*

A Joan Woessner burgundy mohair teddy bear, Easter Surprise, with glass eyes, black stitched nose and mouth, fully jointed, musical movement, carrying an Easter basket, 26in (66cm) high.
£200–250 *CSK*

A Steiff white teddy bear, with black boot button eyes, beige stitched nose, mouth and claws, swivel head, elongated jointed shaped limbs, felt pads, hump, growler and button in ear with remains of white label, c1910, 13in (33cm) high.
£2,500–3,000 *CSK*

A Steiff golden mohair teddy bear, with brown and black glass eyes, remains of black stitched nose, mouth and claws, swivel head, elongated jointed shaped limbs, shaped paws and feet, felt pads, hump and button in ear, slight wear, growler inoperative, c1920, 20in (51cm) high.
£1,400–1,700 *CSK*

A pale gold plush teddy bear, straw filled, with articulated limbs, wearing a muzzle, worn, 15in (38cm) high.
£80–100 *HSS*

A Steiff pale golden curly mohair teddy bear, with brown and black glass eyes, swivel head, jointed shaped limbs, felt pads, hump and growler, slight wear, 1950s, 19in (48cm) high.
£370–420 *CSK*

A Steiff pale golden curly mohair teddy bear, with brown and black glass eyes, swivel head, jointed shaped limbs, paws and feet, felt pads, cardboard lined feet, hump, growler and button in ear with remains of yellow label, slight wear, 1950s, 30in (76cm) high.
£1,500–2,000 *CSK*

A Kathleen Wallace cream and brown tipped mohair teddy bear, Samuel, with black glass eyes, clipped snout, stitched nose, mouth and claws, fully jointed, felt pads and growler, wearing a hand knitted jumper, 23in (59cm) high.
£300–400 *CSK*

A honey golden mohair teddy bear, with amber and black glass eyes, pronounced clipped snout, black stitched nose and mouth, swivel head, jointed shaped limbs and hump, slight wear, pads recovered, c1912, 14½in (37cm) high.
£250–300 *CSK*

A golden plush covered teddy bear, with brown and black glass eyes, pronounced snout, swivel head and jointed limbs, worn, growler inoperative, 1920s, 20in (51cm) high.
£250–300 *CSK*

A golden plush covered teddy bear, with brown and black glass eyes, pronounced snout, swivel head, jointed limbs, felt pads, slight hump and growler, slight wear, 1920s, 13in (33cm) high.
£400–450 *CSK*

A blonde mohair teddy bear, Horace the Caged Bear, with stitched nose, metal disc joints, three-claw and card pads, well worn, 1930s, 9½in (24cm) high.
£150–200 *Bon*

A golden plush covered teddy bear, with black boot button eyes, pronounced cut muzzle, black stitched nose, mouth and claws, swivel head, jointed solid limbs, solid body and cloth pads, slight wear, possibly French, 17in (43cm) high.
£160–220 *CSK*

A German short clipped golden mohair teddy bear, with amber painted and black glass eyes, stitched nose, mouth and claws, swivel head, jointed limbs, cloth pads and cardboard reinforced feet, slight wear, 1920s, 22in (56cm) high.
£200–220 *CSK*

l. A German blonde mohair bear, with black button eyes, wooden and wire body, cloth and mohair hands and feet, dressed in blue outfit, 1920s, 8in (20cm) high.
£120–150 *Bon*

r. A German golden mohair teddy bear, with black boot button eyes, pronounced clipped snout, stitched nose, mouth and claws, swivel head, jointed shaped limbs, felt pads, cardboard reinforced feet, slight hump, worn, squeaker inoperative, 22in (56cm) high.
£670–720 *CSK*

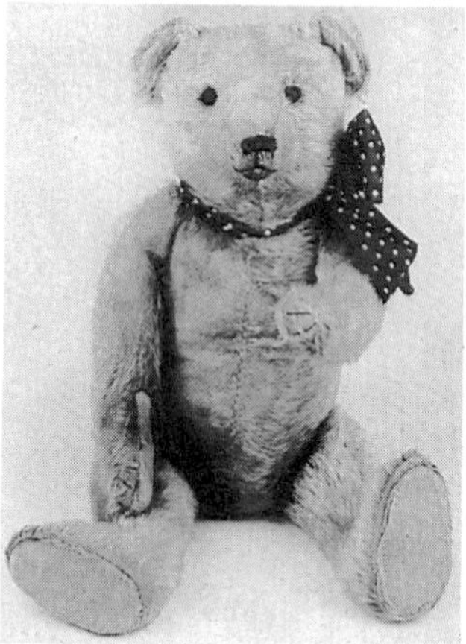

An American honey golden mohair Stick teddy bear, with black boot button eyes, slotted head, pronounced snout, stitched nose, mouth and claws, jointed limbs, wearing multi-coloured knitted cardigan, pads recovered, c1910, 10in (25cm) high.
£150–180 *CSK*

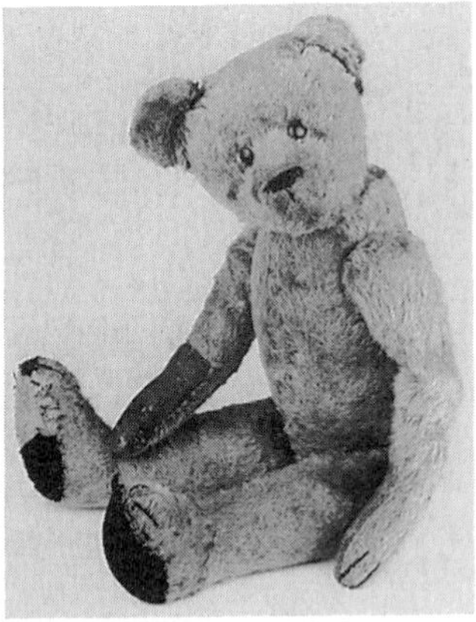

A golden mohair teddy bear, black boot button eyes, pronounced snout, stitched nose and claws, swivel head, elongated jointed limbs and growler, possibly American, slight wear, pads recovered, c1910, 18in (46cm) high.
£700–800 *CSK*

An American golden mohair teddy bear, with black boot button eyes, pronounced clipped snout, stitched nose, mouth and claws, swivel head, jointed shaped limbs, felt pads, hump and side squeaker, leather patch, possibly Ideal, c1912, 19in (48cm) high.
£900–1,000 *CSK*

A 9ct gold teddy bear brooch, textured overall to simulate fur, with sapphire nose and eyes and ruby paws, hallmarked, 1¼in (3cm) high, and a 9ct gold charm modelled as a standing bear holding an imitation pearl, suspended from a staple link neck chain, hallmarked.
£270–300 *CSK*

r. A white, black and blue wool teddy bear rug, with blue and white marching bears, 1930s, 27 by 55in (69 by 139.5cm).
£250–300 *CSK*

r. A selection of teddy bear money banks, comprising: 2 cast iron bears on hind legs, c1911, a Staffordshire Sandland Ware money bank, 3 other porcelain banks, and another with a black and white photograph of Col. T. R. Henderson.
£45–55 *CSK*

Three bear costumes for a Kellogg's commercial, the realistic head masks with movable jaws, brown plastic realistic eyes, moulded black nose and lips, Mummy, Daddy and Baby Bear sizes.
£800–1,000 *Bon*

The Kellogg's 1992 television commercial starred Goldilocks and The Three Bears.

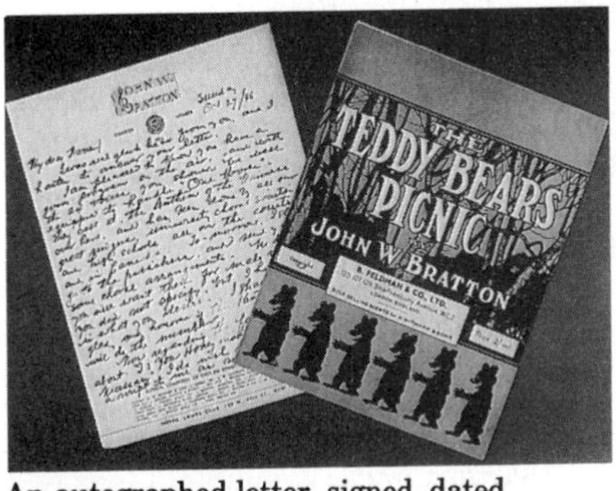

An autographed letter, signed, dated Sunday Oct 27/46, from John Bratton to Warren, commenting on 'The Teddy Bears Picnic', and a copy of the sheet music.
£420–500 *CSK*

DOLLS' HOUSES

Dolls' houses first began to be made in the late 16thC. The earliest houses were built in Germany and Holland, probably originally for adult gratification, either as a hobby, an exercise in cabinet making, or as an architectural model. Attention was paid to the construction of the house itself rather than to the contents.

By the 18thC dolls' houses began to imitate the grand and elaborate houses of the aristocracy. These were still adult toys and were not really intended to be played with. The furniture was made of a variety of materials, such as silver, wood, bone, metal filigree and glass, and served to demonstrate the skills of the craftsmen of the day. Nowadays these types of houses and furnishings are rare and require serious commitment and investment by today's collectors.

In the 19thC the dolls' house began to develop into the plaything that we know today. The new wealthier middle classes began to buy toys for their children from the increasing number of retail shops that sprang up at this time, or to have them built to order, while the poorer classes built their own. These houses were furnished with all the accoutrements of life in the home. An enormous choice of furniture became available, for example, china tea sets, dinner services with plaster food, glassware from Bohemia, pewter plates, table lamps, pictures, candlesticks, inkwells, sewing baskets, smoothing irons and cutlery, not to mention pianos, sofas, longcase clocks, library shelves and nursery furniture. Of course, a family of dolls to live in the house was also required.

The demand for dolls' houses became so great that new methods of manufacture were introduced and the emphasis turned away from craft to mass production. Inevitably the quality suffered and towards the end of the century plywood began to be used as a construction material. The detail of the furnishings gradually became inferior in quality. These were made to a variety of scales and most houses coming on to the market nowadays have accessories of many different sizes.

In the 20thC the trend towards less expensive materials and ease of manufacture, coupled with the very greatly increased demand from a newly affluent society, brought about dolls' houses made from cardboard, tinplate, plywood and cheaper woods such as pine. The dolls' houses became less grand in appearance and began to reflect the type of mass housing that sprang up with urban development. They were relatively inexpensive to buy, and a wide choice of dolls' house furniture was available. Lines and Tri-ang were two manufacturers who were popular, and they introduced electricity for lighting, which was initally battery operated.

Today, plastic and plywood are the most usual materials used to make dolls' houses, and dolls' houses have become smaller and smaller to fit in with our modern life style. Manufacturers such as Fisher-Price, one of the market leaders, make small portable houses with fairly limited accessories which appeal to ever younger children.

Collectors of dolls' houses need space. Half a dozen large dolls' houses will fill up a good sized room and this must be a serious consideration to those contemplating starting a collection. Rather than acquiring a collection of houses, most private collectors are content to concentrate on furnishing one particular house. The purists will stick rigidly to the correct period and the correct scale, and this is where the hunt begins. Finding just the right piece of furniture of the right size is becoming increasingly difficult, but it is very rewarding to watch your house interior take shape as you scour the antiques markets for tiny household items thus creating a miniature world that echoes a bygone era.

It is a hobby with endless possibilities. It is possible to buy a genuine Georgian dolls' house, perhaps from an auction, and furnish it with exquisitely crafted pieces from the 18thC. This will require more time and a higher outlay than buying a late Victorian household where the furnishings are more readily available. You could even buy a house dating from, say, the 1930s, and collect an Art Deco interior. Whatever the period, there will be rare items, and there is much competition in the auction rooms, pushing the price up to extraordinary levels.

In short, first buy your house then have years of fun collecting all the furnishings to suit it from antique shops, auction rooms, markets and boot sales, or start swapping pieces with your friends. This is a fascinating and absorbing hobby that can be operated at any level to suit your pocket. Just think how much social history you will pick up along the way!

Clare Fletcher

DOLLS' HOUSES

A Gothic style T-plan dolls' house, with 3 dormers and part-leaded windows, back opening to reveal 4 rooms and separate opening to kitchen extension containing a tinplate range, 33½ by 32½in (85 by 83cm), on a swivel table.
£180–200 *P(B)*

A Tri-ang mock Tudor plywood dolls' house, with twin gables, bay windows, a garage and 2 entrances, metal windows, 1930s, 47½in (120cm) long, together with a collection of contemporary furniture.
£150–250 *P(B)*

An American Victorian painted wood dolls' house, with hinged façade, 4 rooms, double glazed windows, the corners of the roof mounted with red finished finials, mounted on a base, finished in white with red trim and a grey roof, c1900, 56in (142cm) high.
£800–1,000 *S(NY)*

An 18thC style dolls' house with hinged façade, 2 storeys, 4 rooms and central staircase, finished in light yellow with white trim, mounted on a base, c1900, 72in (182.5cm) high.
£1,500–2,000 *S(NY)*

A Georgian style dolls' house, comprising: 3 opening sections to reveal 7 rooms, hall and landing, 2 bay windows, constructed partly from plywood with moulded beading to the mullions, stucco rendering and tinplate roof and balconies, on a plinth base, c1900, 62 by 44½in (157 by 113cm), together with a collection of contemporary fireplaces and furniture.
£1,000–1,500 *P(B)*

A double-fronted plywood dolls' house, with gabled extended porch, 4 rooms, hall and landing, opening at rear, repainted, 31½in (80cm) wide.
£20–30 *P(B)*

A 3 storey dolls' house, with brick effect finish, furniture and fitments, 30in (76cm) high.
£800–900 *RBB*

A half-timbered, hipped gable dolls' house, with overhanging upper storey, porch, 4 rooms with original fireplaces, repainted, 23in (59cm) wide.
£40–45 *P(B)*

A Tri-ang dolls' house, modelled on Princess Elizabeth's Welsh cottage, with stucco walls and painted thatched roof, double bay windows and 2 openings to the front, repainted, 30in (76cm) wide.
£100–150 *P(B)*

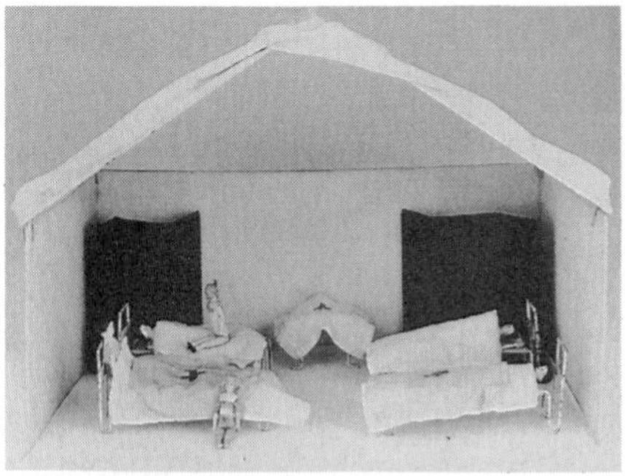

The British Dolls' Field Hospital, constructed of material supported by wire, with 6 bisque shoulder headed dolls, 4 hospital beds and 2 red screens, in original box.
£200–250 *CSK*

A pine part-stripped dolls' house, with 4 rooms and a staircase, one opening to the front, 22in (56cm) wide.
£40–60 *P(B)*

An Edwardian dolls' house, by Lines Bros., made of painted wood, with metal framed windows, sundial at side, opening to the front in 2 parts, 4 rooms with fireplaces and internal doors, hall and stairs, 2 attic rooms, original wall and floor papers, wooden dresser in kitchen, 34in (86cm) high.
£600–700 *CSK*

A Gottschalck wooden dolls' house, with hinged openings on each side, 4 rooms, original flooring, remains of original wallpapers, pitched blue painted roof with gable and chimney, re-papered brick effect exterior, on brown painted wood base, restored, stamped on base 'Gesetzlich Geschutzt', 34in (86cm) high, together with a quantity of furniture and effects.
£2,000–2,500 *S(S)*

l. Gordon House, a painted wooden dolls' house, the right section formed as a glazed conservatory with grape house above, the left side with 3 windows and kitchen door, opening in 3 sections, 5 rooms, original wallpapers, chimney breasts, Märklin fireplaces, gilt framed overmantel mirrors and hand-worked carpets, 61in (155cm) high, fully furnished, including some rare items.
£31,000–35,000 *CSK*

This house was made for Lillian Mary Gordon in 1870, for her third birthday. The carpets were worked by her mother, grandmother and aunt and are signed on the undersides.

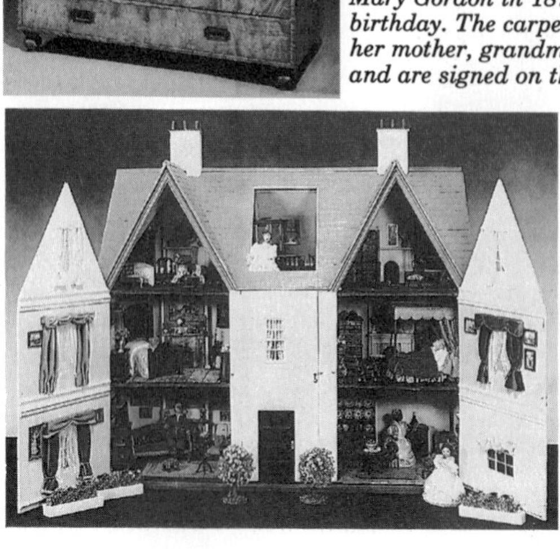

l. A modern dolls' house, painted white, with tiled roof and 2 gables, 2 floors and an attic, 1980s, 32in (81cm) high, and a collection of furnishings.
£400–600 *Bon*

A Claud Lovat Fraser painted wooden dolls' house and a quantity of painted Bavarian style furniture.
£150–200 *CSK*

The house is similar but simpler than the house illustrated in Lovat Fraser's book, Simple Toys.

DOLLS
Wax

A wax over composition shoulder head doll, with fixed eyes, composition forearms and lower legs with painted high-heeled bootees, dressed as Queen Victoria, with a crown and black lace, bead-trimmed silk two-piece, with a boned corset under, bearing the monogram 'VR', crack to neck and shoulder, 21½in (54.5cm) high.
£300–500 *P(B)*

A wax over composition shoulder head doll, with black glass eyes, red hair, wooden lower limbs, stuffed calico body, wearing original late 19thC linen dress with purple satin trim, 17in (43.5cm) high.
£175–250 *P(B)*

A poured wax shoulder head doll, with blue glass eyes and wax lower limbs, dressed in a white cotton pinch pleated and tuck pleated dress, with underwear, damaged, late 19thC, 17½in (44.5cm) high.
£50–70 *P(B)*

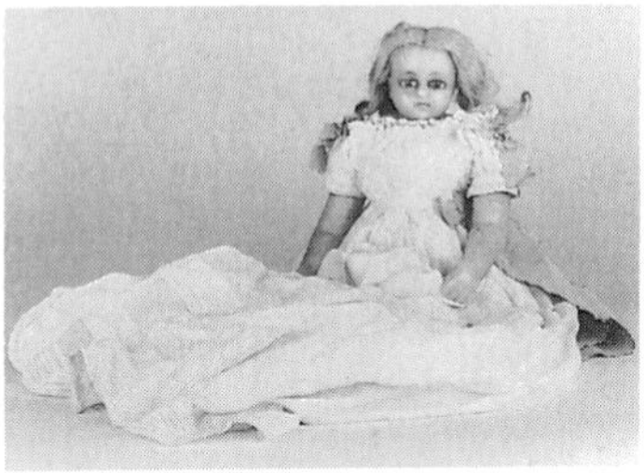

Beatrice Mabel Gordon, a poured wax child doll, with large deep blue eyes, inset ash blonde mohair, stuffed body, wax limbs with brass eyelets, robe with duck egg blue silk ribbons, and original underclothes, c1874, 19½in (49.5cm) high, in original box.
£400–600 *CSK*

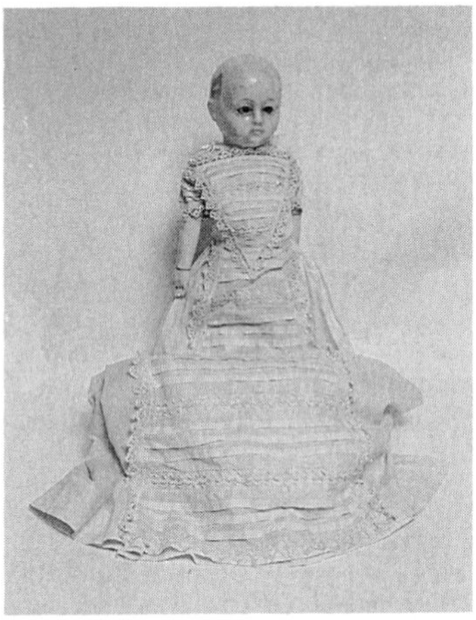

A wax over composition shoulder head doll, with jointed composition limbs, stuffed body, wearing a long white cotton gown with tuck pleats and lace trim, damaged, 20in (51.5cm) high.
£180–220 *P(B)*

A poured honey-wax shoulder head doll, with blonde curly hair, painted features, wax arms and composition legs, dressed in a late 19thC style cotton dress with braid trim, 16in (40.5cm) high.
£150–200 *P(B)*

A poured wax child doll, hazel eyes, inset long blonde mohair with fringe, stuffed body, wax limbs attached through metal eyelets, cream wool embroidered frock, cape, maribou trimmed matching bonnet, socks and red shoes, repaired, 22in (56cm) high.
£400–600 *CSK*

Use the Index!

Because certain items might fit easily into any number of categories, the quickest and surest method of locating any entry is by reference to the index at the back of the book.

This index has been fully cross-referenced for absolute simplicity.

Bisque

A bisque socket head doll, with fixed brown eyes, closed mouth, painted eyelashes and rosy cheeks, on a jointed composition body, some original clothing, marked '23', 12½in (31.5cm) high.
£525–575 *P(B)*

A Strobel & Wilken bisque head doll, with weighted brown eyes, open mouth and jointed composition body, 9½in (24cm) high, another doll by Strobel & Wilken, 8in (20cm) high.
£180–220 *P(B)*

A Schoenau and Hoffmeister bisque headed doll, with blonde mohair wig, sleeping eyes, 4 teeth, on a composition body, with original silk and machine lace dress, bonnet, cotton stockings, leather bootees, with a baby's christening gown, incised 'S', star 'P B', 'H', dated '1909', 22in (55.5cm) high.
£400–450 *WW*

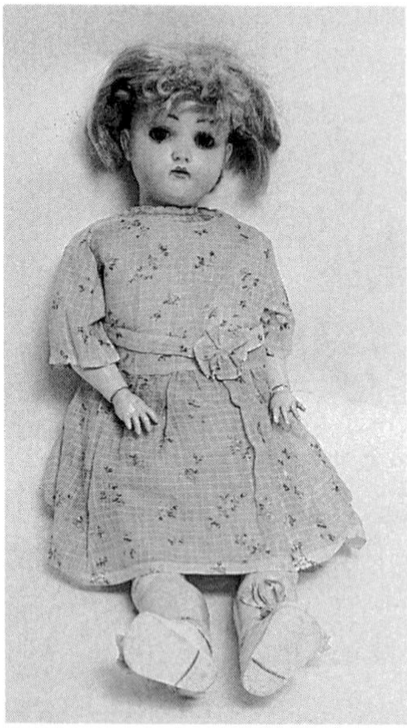

A German bisque doll, No. 139/9, with red hair, brown weighted eyes, open mouth, on a ball jointed composition body.
£180–200 *P(B)*

A French bisque shoulder head lady doll, with pale blue stationary paperweight eyes, closed mouth, pierced ears, blonde mohair wig, cloth body and limbs, composition hands, dressed in a champagne satin ball gown with train, white kid boots, wear and staining, c1880, 9½in (24cm) high.
£1,400–2,000 *SK(B)*

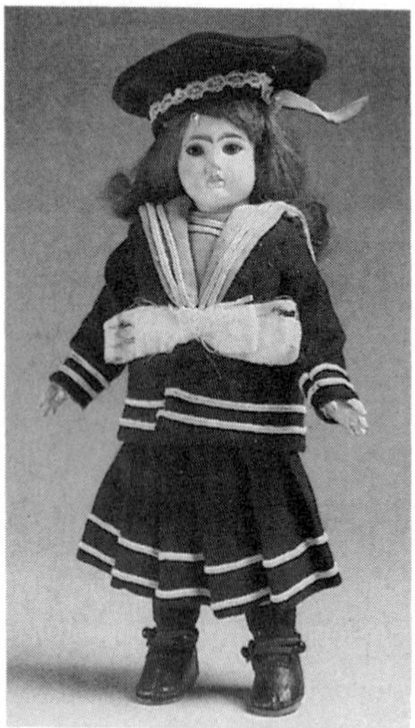

l. A Steiner bisque headed 'Bébé Le Parisienne' doll, with fixed blue glass eyes, brown mohair wig, swivel straight limb composition body with purple maker's stamp on torso, in old underwear, blue wool sailor suit, comprising pleated skirt and jacket with light blue collar, white silk cord trim, matching hat, old socks and leather shoes, chipped, incised 'A O Paris', stamped in red 'Le Parisienne', c1890, 8in (20cm) high.
£1,000–1,500 *S(NY)*

A Schoenau and Hoffmeister bisque headed doll, on a composition bent limbed body.
£380–400 *DN*

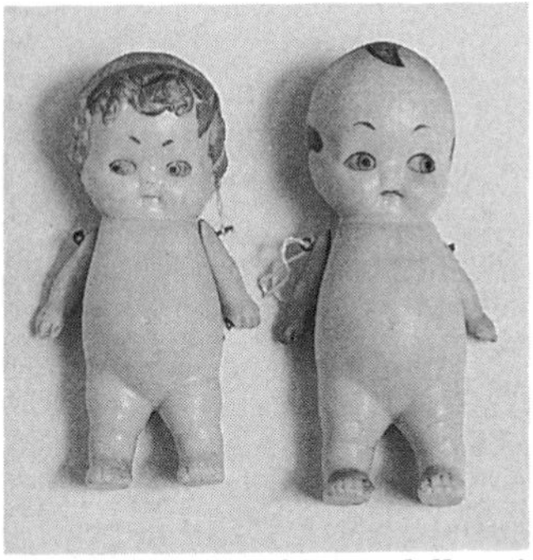

A pair of Kewpie bisque dolls, with painted features and movable arms, 5in (12.5cm) high.
£100–120 *P(B)*

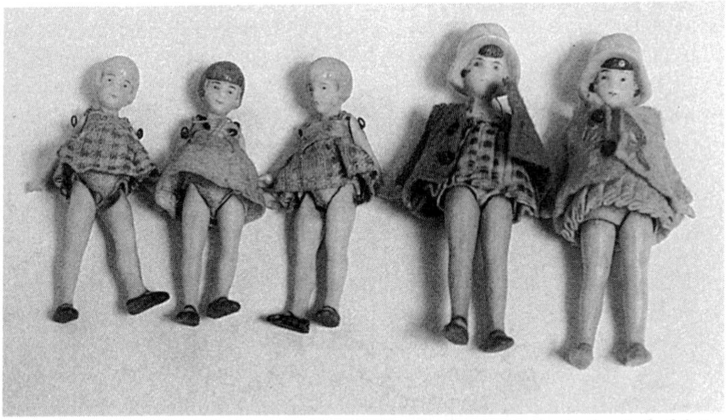

A pair of bisque dolls, with cloche hats and pleated skirts, 3in (7.5cm) high, and 3 smaller dolls, c1930.
£225–275 *P(B)*

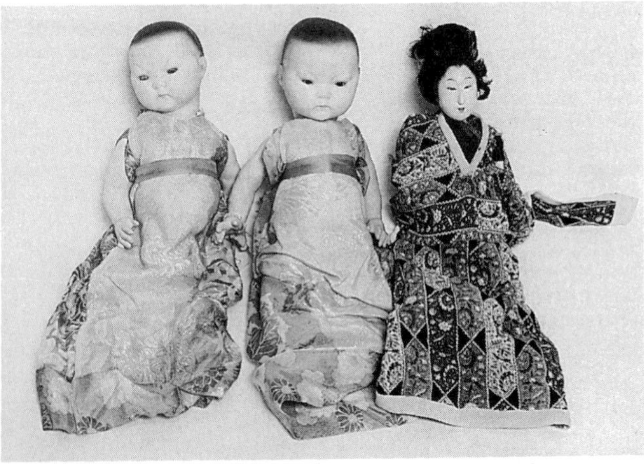

A pair of German bisque head Chinese dolls, each with weighted brown eyes, closed mouth and painted hair, on a bent limb composition body, both dressed in Oriental clothing, 10½ and 11in (26 and 28cm) high, and a Japanese style bisque doll, feet missing.
£750–800 *P(B)*

A German spray painted bisque headed doll, with weighted blue eyes, open mouth, with jointed composition body, dressed in Russian costume, 11in (28cm) high.
£60–80 *P(B)*

A bisque headed fashionable doll, with blue eyes, pierced ears, blonde mohair wig, kid body, with individually stitched fingers, dressed as a bride in original white organdie outfit, trimmed with lace and eau de nil ribbon, underwear and white kid boots, 12in (30.5cm) high.
£1,200–1,700 *CSK*

An SFBJ bisque headed doll, with brown weighted eyes, brown hair in ringlets, on a jointed composition body, wearing a silk gingham dress and a straw hat, 19½in (49.5cm) high.
£230–250 *P(B)*

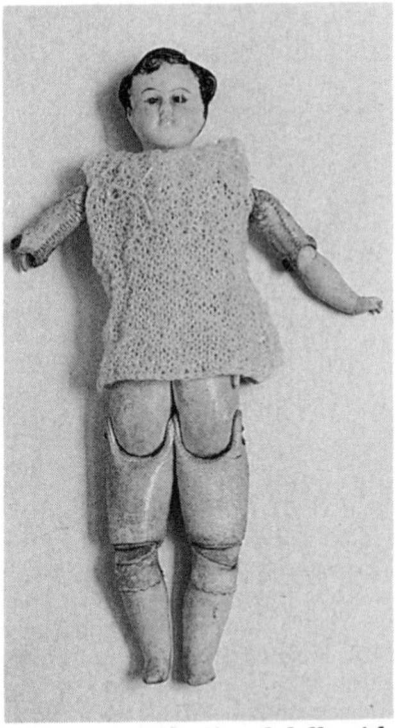

A bisque shoulder head doll, with painted moulded curly hair and features, on a hinged kid body with bisque lower limbs, 11½in (29cm) high.
£60–80 *P(B)*

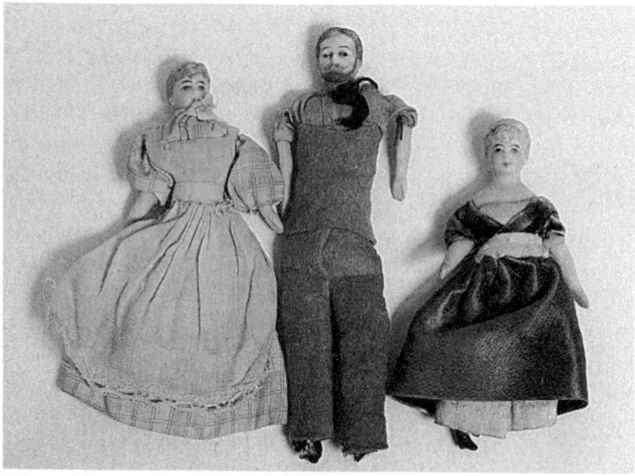

Three bisque shoulder head dolls, modelled as a father, mother and daughter, father 6in (15cm) high.
£250–270 *P(B)*

A French bisque headed doll, with pale face and fixed brown glass eyes, brown mohair wig over cork pate, jointed wood and composition body, re-dressed in pink velvet frock, matching straw hat and underwear, damaged, incised 'Eden Bébé Paris M', c1890, 22in (55.5cm) high.
£800–1,200 *S(NY)*

l. A French swivel head bisque fashion doll, with fixed blue glass eyes, black wig over cork pate, gusseted kid body, with separately stitched fingers, in original Spanish costume, impressed '1', c1880, 14in (36cm) high.
£900–1,200 *S(S)*

r. A bisque headed doll, by Heinrich Handwerck, with weighted blue eyes, heavy brows, open mouth, upper teeth, on a kid body, forearms missing, 13½in (34cm) high.
£50–60 *P(B)*

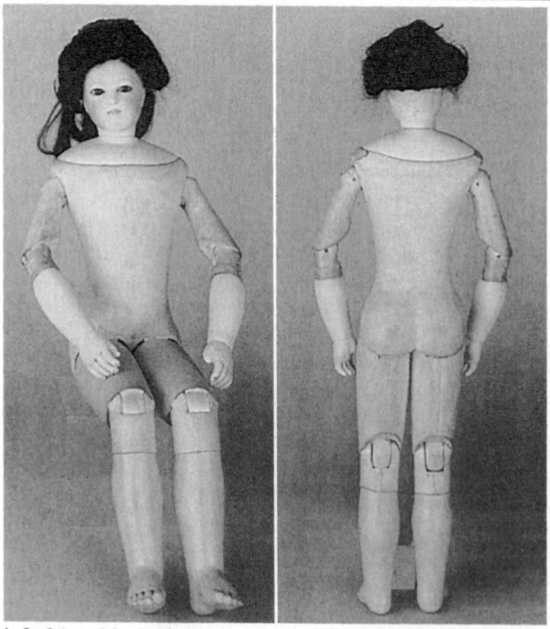

A fashionable doll with original wardrobe and accessories, with bisque swivel head, fixed deep blue eyes with white striations, ears pierced into the head and jointed kid over wood body, with lower arms of bisque and lower legs of painted gutta-percha, 17½in (44.5cm) high, in re-covered original box labelled 'a la Petite Amazone MAISON DELCRO Boul t. des Italiens Paris'.
£4,200–6,000 *CSK*

This doll was bought at the Paris Exhibition of 1867 by Charles-Joseph Pipart of Menin, near Lille, and given to Miss Ellen Richardson, who later took it back to Halifax.

A bisque shoulder head doll, by Bahr & Proschild, with blue sleeping eyes, blonde mohair wig, kid body with bisque hands, dressed in contemporary pink woollen frock and bonnet, underwear, socks and shoes, impressed '309', 12in (30.5cm) high.
£420–500 *CSK*

Armand Marseille

An Armand Marseille bisque headed doll, distributed by George Borgfeldt, No. 327 A15M, with fixed blue eyes, open mouth, upper teeth, on a jointed composition body with bent legs, 24½in (62.5cm) high.
£300–400 *P(B)*

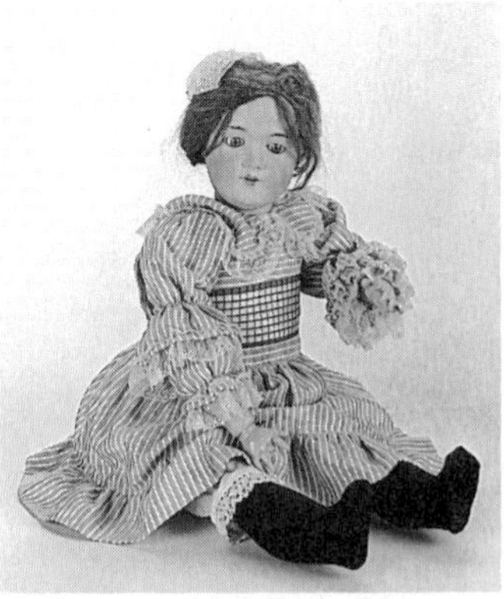

A German girl doll, the bisque head with sleeping blue eyes, open mouth, 4 teeth, brown mohair wig, jointed composition and wood body, wearing later costume, fingers missing, impressed 'Armand Marseille Germany 390 A 11 M', 27in (68.5cm) high.
£250–300 *L&E*

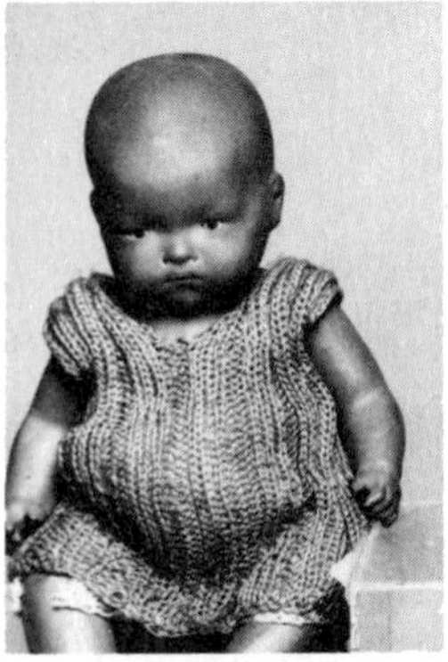

An Armand Marseille doll, with fixed brown eyes, painted mouth, on a composition bent limbed body, No. 341/2½/K, 11in (28cm) high.
£200–250 *DN*

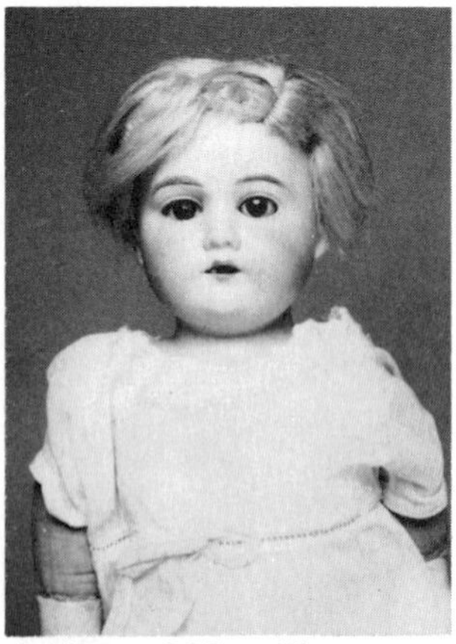

An Armand Marseille shoulder plate doll, No. 370/5, with sleeping blue eyes, open mouth, stuffed cloth body with bisque lower arms, teeth and fingers damaged, 20in (51cm) high.
£100–120 *DN*

An Armand Marseille bisque headed baby doll, with weighted blue eyes, open mouth, 2 lower teeth, on a bent limb composition body, 15in (38.5cm) high.
£140–160 *P(B)*

An Armand Marseille bisque head doll, No. 390, with weighted blue eyes, open mouth, blonde hair, on a jointed composition body, wearing a cream silk dress.
£280–300 *P(B)*

An Armand Marseille bisque headed doll, No. 1330/7, with weighted brown eyes, and a trembling tongue, on a bent limb composition body, 17½in (44.5cm) high.
£170–200 *P(B)*

An Armand Marseille bisque head doll, No. 390, with blue weighted eyes, an open mouth with upper teeth, on a composition ball jointed body, 26½in (67.5cm) high.
£250–280 *P(B)*

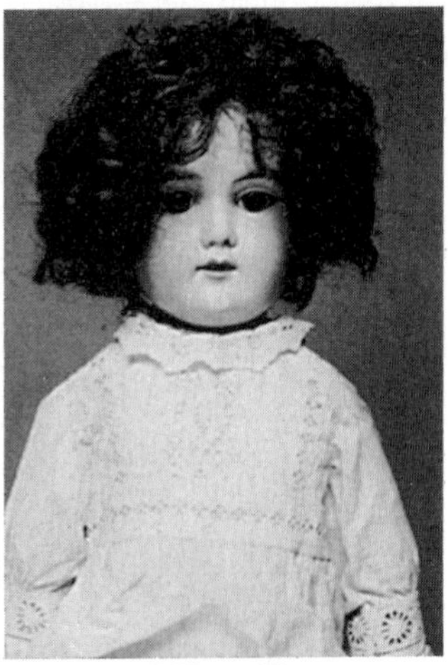

An Armand Marseille Floradora/10 bisque headed doll, with sleeping brown eyes, on a composition ball jointed body, damaged, 25½in (64.5cm) high.
£130–170 *DN*

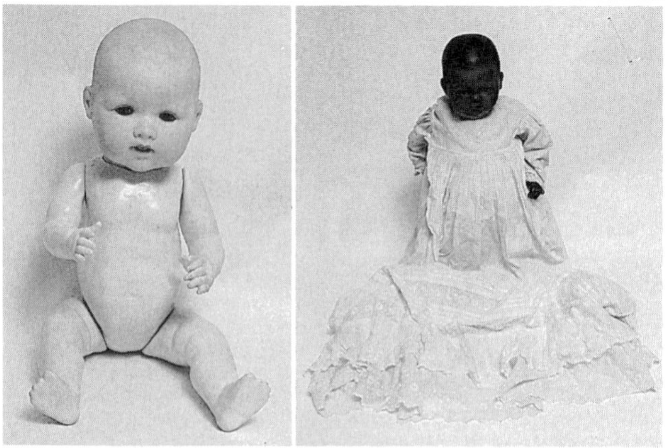

An Armand Marseille bisque headed baby doll, No. 351/8K, with open mouth, on a bent limb composition body, cracked face, 23½in (60cm) high, and another, with brown weighted eyes, on a bent limb composition body, No. 341/6K, head cracked, 22in (55.5cm) high.
£140–160 *P(B)*

An Armand Marseille bisque shoulder head doll, No. 370, with weighted brown eyes, open mouth, dimple to chin, bisque forearms, on a stuffed calico body, 19½in (49.5cm) high.
£140–160 *P(B)*

l. An Armand Marseille bisque headed doll, with large fixed brown eyes, open mouth, on a jointed composition body, c1894, 10in (25cm) high, and another, with weighted brown eyes and dressed in costume, No. 390, 8½in (21.5cm) high.
£120–140 *P(B)*

An Armand Marseille Floradora bisque headed doll, with fixed blue eyes, open mouth, on a jointed composition body, 14½in (37cm) high.
£100–120 *P(B)*

Bruno Schmidt

A Bruno Schmidt bisque headed doll, with blue weighted eyes, open mouth, upper teeth, on a jointed composition body and wearing an original lace trimmed dress, head loose, 29½in(75cm).
£350–380 *P(B)*

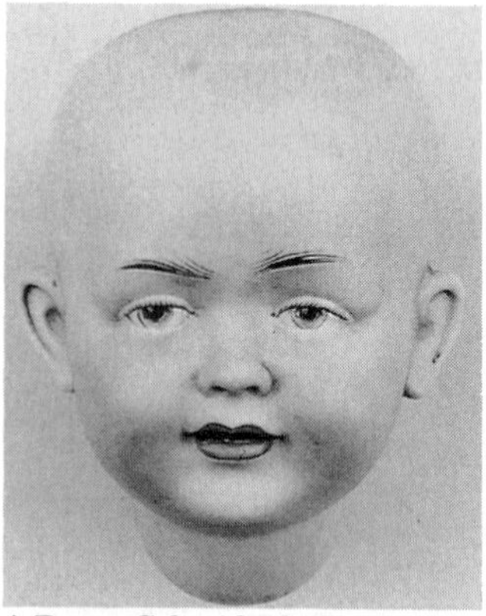

A Bruno Schmidt character doll, with bisque head, closed mouth, blue intaglio eyes, with jointed wood and composition toddler body, impressed '2025 BSW' in heart '529', the head 4in (10cm) high.
£1,100–1,300 *CSK*

r. A Bruno Schmidt bisque headed doll, the open mouth with 4 teeth, sleeping brown glass eyes, an auburn wig, on a jointed composition body, impressed with maker's heart shape trademark, 23½in (59.5cm) high.
£300–400 *Bea*

Heubach Koppelsdorf

r. A Heubach Koppelsdorf bisque headed doll, No. 302.9, with weighted blue eyes, open mouth, upper teeth, on a jointed composition body, 28in (72.5cm) high.
£220–240 *P(B)*

l. A Heubach Koppelsdorf bisque headed baby doll, No. 399, with black weighted eyes and a bent composition body, 12½in (31.5cm) high.
£220–240 *P(B)*

Jumeau

A bisque headed doll, with blue eyes, open mouth, with six teeth, cork pate, human hair wig, on fully jointed composition body, with period clothes, original shoes, incised '11' and stamped in red 'Tête Jumeau', 24in (61.5cm) high, with original box.
£1,500–3,000 *CNY*

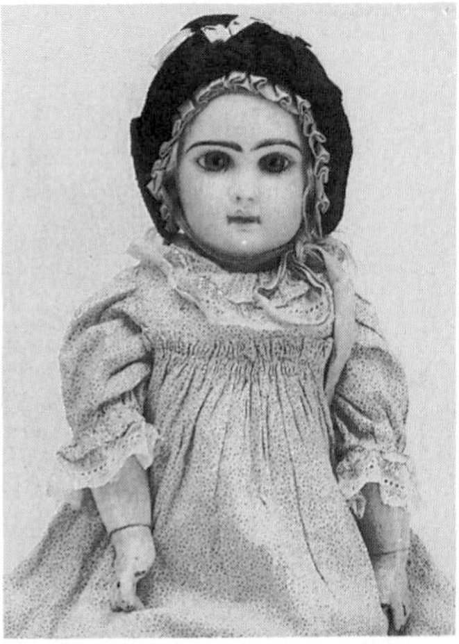

r. A Tête Jumeau doll, the cork pate with blonde hair, blue paperweight eyes, pierced ears, on jointed composition body, wearing an original blue velvet bonnet, lace trimmed printed cotton dress and contemporary underclothes, the bisque head with re-mark, late 19thC, 18½in (47cm) high.
£2,200–3,000 *Bea*

l. A Lioret phonograph doll, the Bébé Jumeau body with Merveilleux movement, one cylinder, bisque head and composition limbs, 24in (61.5cm) high.
£2,000–2,500 *CSK*

Kämmer & Reinhardt

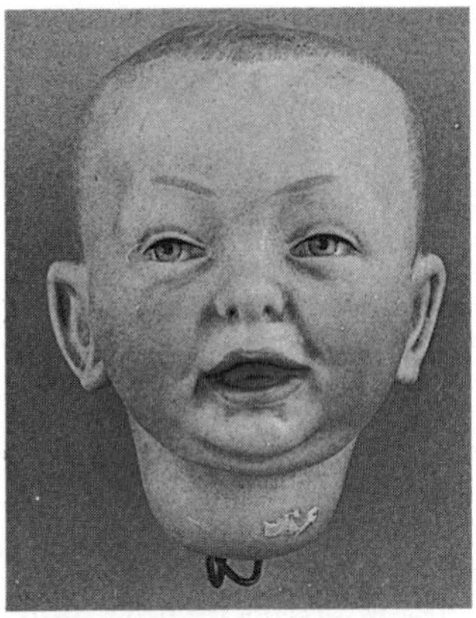

A Kämmer & Reinhardt bisque character head, with intaglio eyes and painted features, marked 'K*R 100 36', 4½in (11cm) high.
£200–220 *DN*

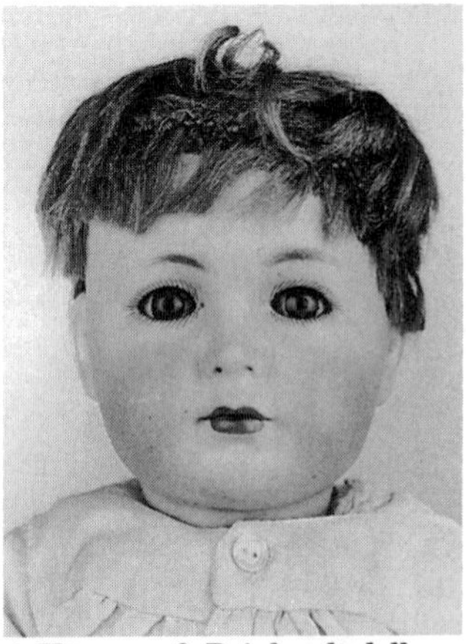

A Kämmer & Reinhardt doll, No. 117, with blue sleeping eyes, short fair mohair wig, jointed body, rayon shirt and blue velvet knee breeches, damaged, 19in (48.5cm) high.
£950–1,000 *CSK*

A German bisque headed character doll, by Kämmer & Reinhardt, with weighted brown glass eyes, two painted upper teeth, jointed wood and composition body, in possibly original pink and white cotton check short dress with lace trim, damaged, incised '112/34', c1909, 13in (33cm) high.
£4,800–5,200 *S(NY)*

Kämmer & Reinhardt/ Simon & Halbig

A Kämmer & Reinhardt/Simon & Halbig Wimpern-80 bisque headed companion doll, with weighted blue eyes, open mouth, upper teeth, on a jointed composition body, 32in (81.5cm) high.
£750–800 *P(B)*

Kestner

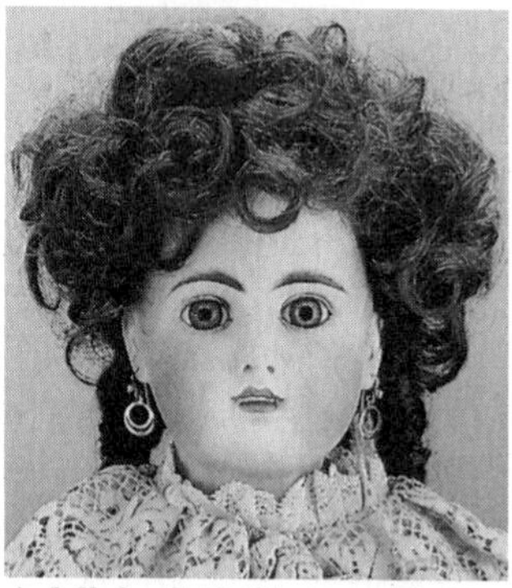

A doll, by J. D. Kestner, No.137, with solid pate, fixed blue eyes, open/closed mouth, pierced ears, fixed wrists, jointed body, impressed '14', 23in (59cm) high, and an umbrella with cane handle, 12in (30.5cm) long.
£1,500–2,000 *CSK*

Simon & Halbig

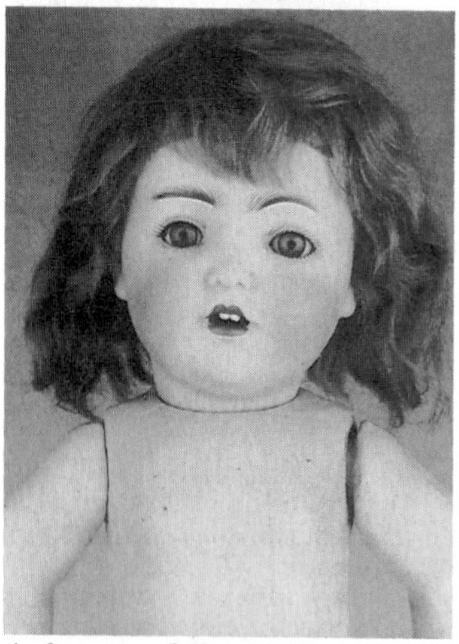

A character doll, with bisque head, blue sleeping eyes, light brown mohair wig and bent limbed composition body, impressed '1294 Simon & Halbig', 14in (35.5cm) high.
£360–400 *CSK*

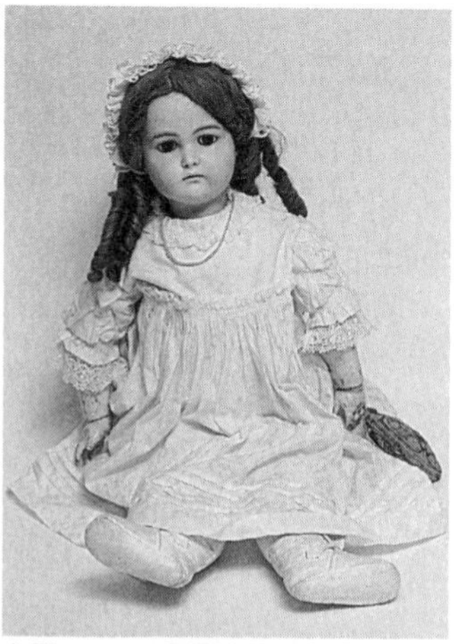

A Kämmer & Reinhardt/Simon & Halbig Wimpern bisque headed doll, with brown eyes, open mouth, upper teeth, and brown ringlets, on a composition body, wearing kid boots, chipped, 31½in (79.5cm) high.
£750–800 *P(B)*

A Kestner character bisque headed doll, with open mouth, blue weighted eyes, blonde hair, on a jointed composition body, chipped, 15½in (39.5cm) high.
£340–360 *P(B)*

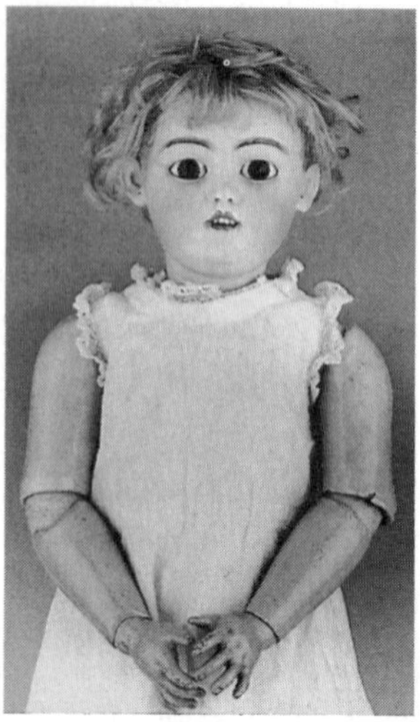

A Simon & Halbig/Kämmer & Reinhardt bisque socket head walking girl doll, with long blonde mohair wig, blue glass sleeping eyes, painted eyebrows and lower eyelashes, real hair upper eyelashes, open mouth with 4 moulded teeth, pierced ears, wood and composition ball jointed arms, body and walking legs, wearing original cream silk lace trimmed bonnet, jacket, lace decorated and pin tucked cotton muslin dress, silk underskirt and petticoats, socks and kid shoes, the head stamped 'Simon & Halbig K*R', 15in (38cm) high, in original cardboard box.
£500–600 *HSS*

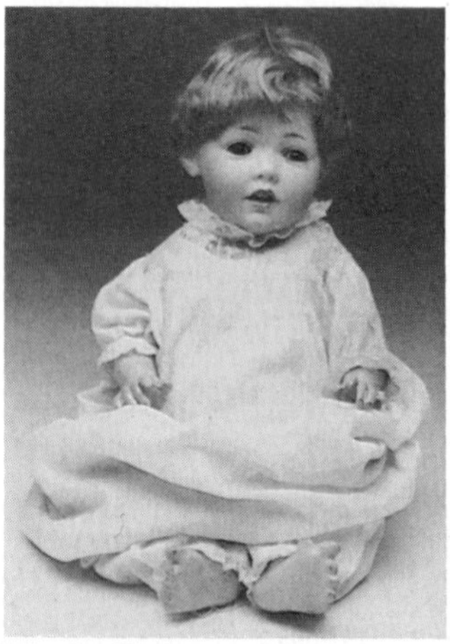

Hilda, by Kestner, with bisque head, brown glass sleeping eyes, open mouth, original blonde mohair wig, jointed bent limb composition body, impressed '245', with mark, 17in (43.5cm) high.
£2,000–2,500 *SK(B)*

l. A bisque headed doll, by Simon & Halbig, No. 1079, with brown sleeping eyes, blonde mohair wig, pierced ears, jointed wood and composition body, dressed in a white cotton petticoat, impressed 'DEP Germany', 22in (55.5cm) high.
£550–600 *CSK*

A bisque headed male doll, with black moulded hair and moustache, body with rigid limbs, and original khaki officer's uniform from the Boer war, possibly by Simon & Halbig, hat missing, damaged, c1900, 11in (28cm) high.
£700–800 *CSK*

Mould No. 1308 by Simon & Halbig was made in a male version similar to this doll, but with a wig instead of moulded hair, a less curving moustache, teeth showing and smooth brows rather than slightly frowning and no painted eyelashes. The female version of 1308, however, does have painted eyelashes and red dots at the inner eyes.

A Simon & Halbig bisque headed doll, with weighted blue eyes, open mouth and upper teeth, on a composition jointed body, with original silk and voile clothing, marked 'WSK', 20in (50.5cm) high.
£600–620 *P(B)*

A Simon & Halbig bisque headed doll, No. 1078, with blue weighted eyes, open mouth, pierced ears and blonde hair, on a jointed composition body, wearing a Viyella dress, with a broderie anglaise pinafore, 16½in (41.2cm) high.
£380–400 *P(B)*

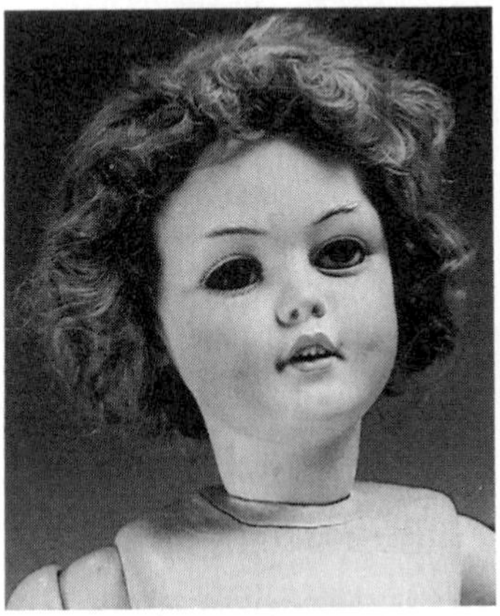

l. A German bisque headed character doll, by Simon & Halbig, with moulded eyebrows, weighted brown glass eyes, open mouth with upper teeth, dimpled chin, pierced ears, jointed wood and composition body, body probably not original, incised '1279/141/2', c1910, 32½in (82.5cm) high.
£2,500–3,500 *S(NY)*

Miscellaneous

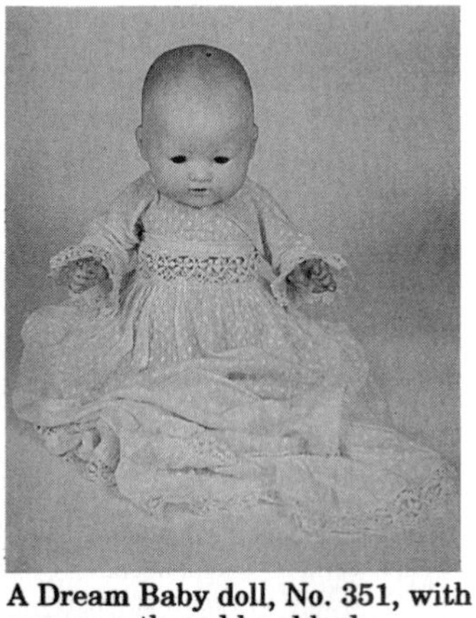

A Dream Baby doll, No. 351, with open mouth and hard body, c1920, 15in (38cm) high.
£100–150 *SP*

A late Victorian glazed porcelain shoulder head doll, with black moulded ringlets, painted features with highlighted eyes, porcelain lower limbs and stuffed body, 17½in (45cm) high.
£180–200 *P(B)*

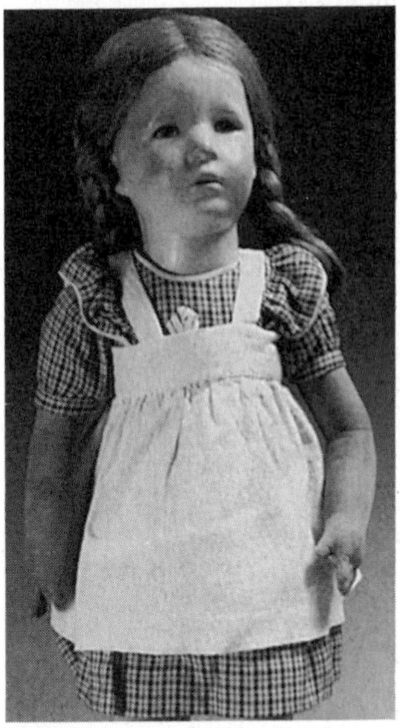

A German cloth doll, by Käthe Kruse, with an oil painted face, brown eyes, brown human hair wig, swivel jointed body, in old blue and white check cotton dress and short white pinafore, stamped in red on foot '15469', 19½in (49.5cm) high.
£800–1,200 *S(NY)*

A pair of Japanese composition dolls, with dark inset eyes, black wigs, dressed in original silk outfits with high red hats, carrying bells, on carved wooden stands, 14½in (37cm) high.
£300–400 *CSK*

Three Sasha dolls, with painted features, 2 brunette and one blonde, dressed in original outfits, one with wrist tag, 16in (40.5cm) high.
£350–400 *CSK*

A composition headed doll, modelled as Lord Kitchener, with painted hair and features, stuffed body, composition hands and feet, dressed in original uniform, c1915, 18½in (47cm) high.
£470–520 *CSK*

A boxed set of the Canadian Dionne quintuplets, dressed in pastel rompers and bonnets, each with a name pendant necklace, in a cream kiddi-car, c1936, dolls 7in (17.5cm) high, with original pamphlet and carton.
£800–1,000 *SK(B)*

Two turned and painted wooden dolls, with added arms akimbo, one with wide straw hat, each painted yellow with red, brown and black details, south German, damaged, c1750, 5in (12.5cm) high.
£400–600 *CSK*

A Kling doll, with bisque shoulder head, painted features with blonde moulded curly hair, stuffed body with bisque limbs and moulded socks and shoes, dressed as a boy in contemporary sailor suit, 18in (45.5cm) high, and a bisque headed dolls' house doll, dressed in cream silk with needlecase skirt, 5in (12.5cm) high.
£500–600 *CSK*

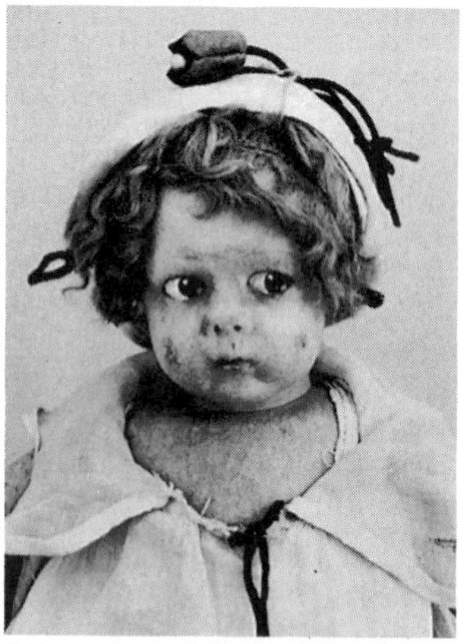

A Lenci type felt girl doll, with moulded painted features, brown eyes glancing to the side, short curly hair, wearing original muslin short dress and hat trimmed with yellow felt and felt flowers, arms damaged, 17in (43cm) high.
£150–200 *DN*

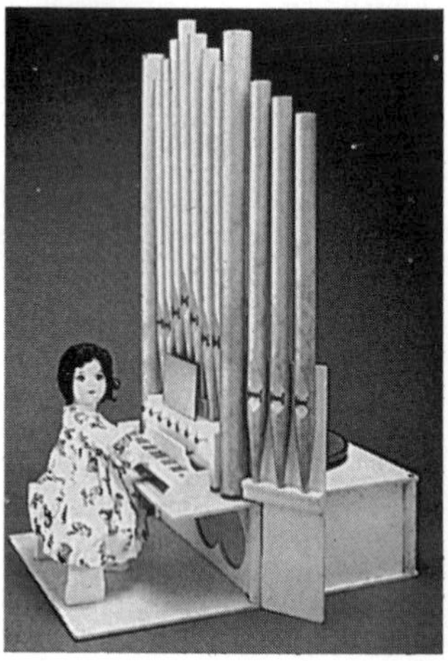

r. A mechanical Knickerbocker Store Co. display, featuring Snow White seated at a wooden pipe organ, together with original clothes and records, and packing crate, 1939.
£1,750–2,000 *CNY*

TOYS

Money Banks

A painted cast iron Paddy and the Pig mechanical bank, by J. & E. Stevens, slight chipping, minor repair, 7in (17.5cm) wide.
£2,500–3,000 *CSK*

A painted cast iron Hoop La Bank, by John Harper & Co., some wear, mounted on wooden base, 8¼in (21cm) wide.
£270–350 *CSK*

It appears that the wooden base is original to the bank and possibly was made for a shop counter as it has a larger area to contain the coins. It originally had a label on the front panel.

A painted cast iron and tin Peter Pan League charity collecting box, featuring Nana the dog carrying a towel and wearing a mobcap, inscribed, 1930s, paint chipped, 6½in (16.5cm) high.
£1,500–2,000 *CSK*

The Peter Pan League was a children's club set up in 1929, designed to encourage children to help fund-raise for Great Ormond Street Children's Hospital Fund. In the same year the author, J. M. Barrie, donated all rights to his book Peter Pan *to the hospital, which was later confirmed in his will when he died in 1937.*

l. A Jonah and the Whale cast iron mechanical bank, by Shepherd Hardware Company, inscribed 'patented July 15, 1890, Griffith #142, Davidson #282', with key, some wear, 10in (25cm) wide.
£650–1,000 *S(NY)*

Games

l. A Victorian mahogany bagatelle board, the folding top enclosing a green baize lined playing surface, with wells and arched obstacles, damaged, 36in (91.5cm) long.
£300–400 *C*

The London to Brighton Veteran Car Game, by Furnel Developments Ltd., comprising Lesney Models of Yesteryear, Rolls Royce Silver Ghost and 1904 Spyker, cards, plastic winding roadway and dice shakers, in original box, c1960.
£200–300 *CSK*

This game was only sold at Mobil Oil Company petrol stations.

Rocking Horses

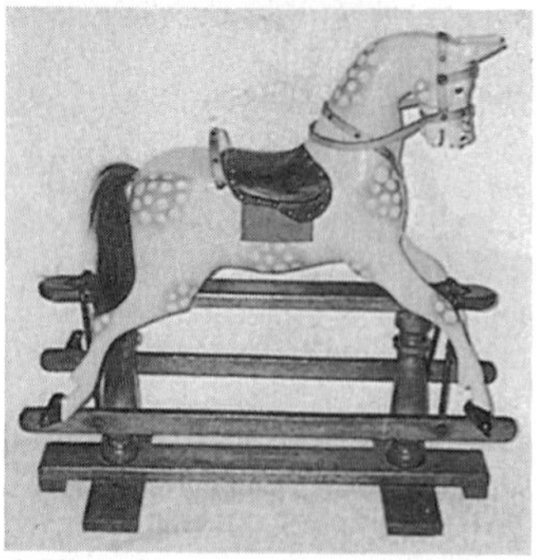

A Victorian carved wood patent rocking horse, on a trestle, c1880, 39in (99cm) long.
£200–250 *AP*

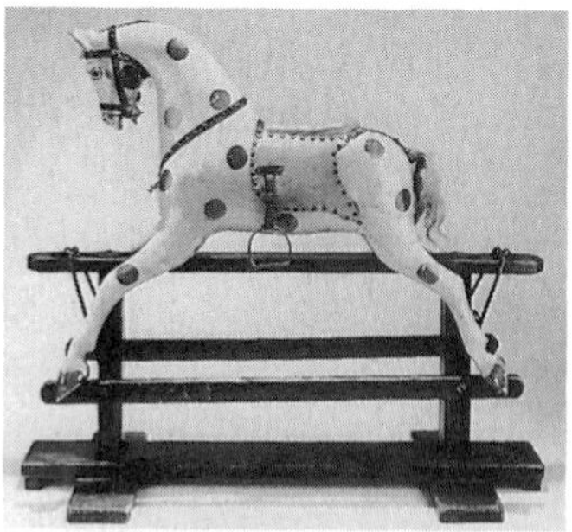

A carved wood rocking horse, with original tack, painted with red and blue spots and green hooves, on a trestle with posts, 33in (84cm) high.
£300–400 *CSK*

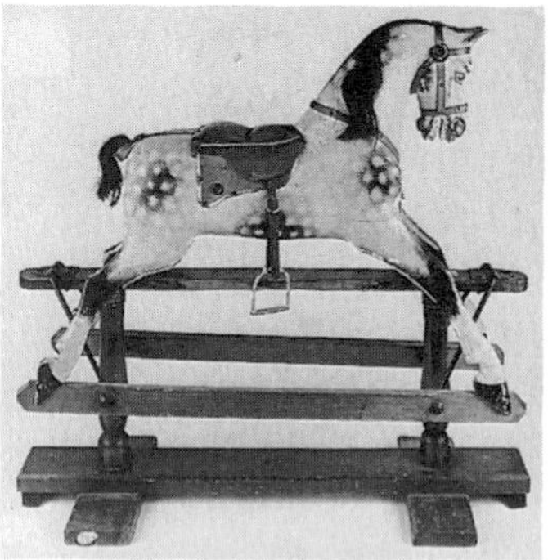

A carved and painted wooden rocking horse, by Ayres of London, with original tack, mane and tail, on a trestle with turned posts, labelled 'Supplied by Harold Wrightman, Sports Depot, Hinkley', some wear, 34in (86cm) high.
£400–600 *CSK*

l. A rocking horse, with saddle and bridle, on a trestle with posts, early 20thC.
£550–650 *DaD*

r. A hide covered rocking horse, with a well detailed head, leather bridle with tassels, leather driving harness with long red reins, mounted on a painted wooden platform with 4 small metal wheels, some wear, c1900, 35in (89cm) high, together with a red painted wooden rocker base.
£300–500 *S(S)*

Soft Toys

Three German musicians, by Steiff, the felt faces with centre seams, glass eyes, mohair wigs, wearing original regional outfits, with instruments, largest 13in (33cm) high.
£1,800–2,200 *CSK*

A collection of 12 gollies.
£250–300 *Bon*

A Chad Valley pig school, including teacher pig, with pink velvet face and ears, amber and black glass eyes, pink stitched nose, black stitched mouth, wearing original black felt mortarboard, black felt jacket, yellow felt waistcoat, white felt collar, black and white trousers and black felt shoes, with label stitched to left foot, 6 pink velvet pupil pigs, with blue bead eyes, felt jackets and books, 5 wooden chairs, one wooden table and easel, c1930, teacher 11in (28cm) high, pupils 4in (10cm) high.
£750–800 *CSK*

A lambswool rabbit wedding group, comprising bride and groom, preacher and bridesmaid, in original dress, c1930, 15in (38cm) high.
£200–300 *CSK*

l. A Schuco monkey, with brown tipped white mohair, moulded tin face, open mouth, felt ears, hands and feet, tail operating the yes/no head movement, wearing original felt cap, c1920, 9in (23cm) high.
£300–400 *CSK*

A Steiff monkey, with cinnamon mohair, black boot button eyes, felt face with centre seam, felt ears, hands and feet, swivel head, elongated jointed shaped limbs and tail, repairs to hands and feet, c1905, 13in (33cm) high.
£450–500 *CSK*

A Chad Valley Snow White and Seven Dwarfs, with Snow White dressed in white, each dwarf wearing brightly coloured clothes, with hats, c1930, Snow White 17in (43.5cm), dwarfs 10in (25cm) high.
£800–1,000 *Bon*

l. Four Chad Valley dwarfs, Doc, Grumpy, Happy and Dopey, with pressed and painted cloth faces, stuffed bodies, dressed in original outfits, 3 with swing tickets, marked with Chad Valley label, 6in (15cm) high.
£200–300 *CSK*

Clockwork

A Bing clockwork four-funnel torpedo boat, with original key, restored, good condition, c1925, 39½in (100cm) long.
£2,000–2,500 *CSK*

A Bing clockwork tinplate twin-funnel battle cruiser, named 'King Edward', painted in grey and red, missing masts, lifeboats, flags and funnel mount, c1910, 20in (50.5cm) long.
£2,500–2,800 *CSK*

A Bing clockwork lithographed tinplate open tourer, painted in grey and green, with white lining, brown seats, the driver dressed in a tan coloured suit, good condition, c1914, 10in (25cm) long.
£350–550 *CSK*

r. A Carette clockwork lithographed tinplate four-light limousine, finished in lined ivory, good condition, c1912, 16in (40.5cm) long.
£1,100–1,400 *CSK*

A Carette clockwork limousine, hand enamelled in cream, blue roof and lining, with chauffeur, luggage rack, opening doors, headlamps, sidelights, operating brake, reversing mechanism and steering, slight damage, c1910, 16in (40.5cm) long.
£1,600–2,000 *AH*

l. An Eberl clockwork lithographed tinplate six-light limousine, finished in lined lake, fair condition, c1908, 13½in (34cm) long.
£750–1,000 *CSK*

l. A German Tippco clockwork lithographed army ambulance, in camouflage finish, with red crosses and blue opaque windows, registration number WH-914, with opening rear doors and composition driver, good condition.
£300–350 *CSK*

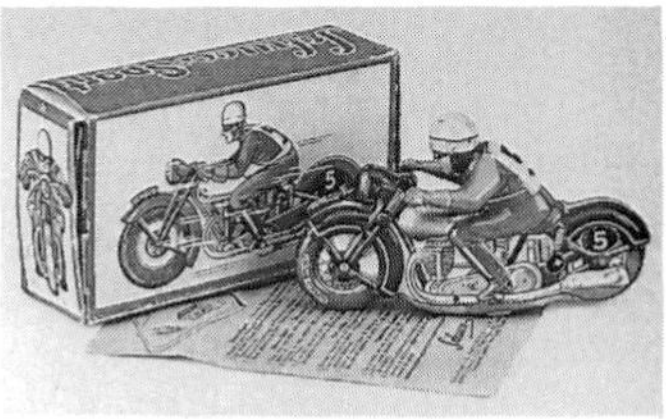

Two Schuco clockwork lithographed tinplate toys, a green and cream Sport Motorcyclist, racing number '5', and a Command Car AD 2000, with instructions, in original boxes, pre-1939.
£420–500 *CSK*

l. A German clockwork lithographed tinplate ice cream vendor, the boy printed in red and white, pushing a two-wheeled blue and white cart, with red and white sign above 3 covered storage containers, c1912, fair condition, 7¼in (18.5cm) long.
£400–500 *CSK*

A Märklin factory-constructed clockwork M1101/03/09B constructor streamline tourer, with electric headlights, finished in green with dark green lining, with a fawn roof, orange display plinth, with original box and packing.
£3,000–3,500 *CSK*

A Märklin factory-constructed clockwork M1101/07 B constructor racing car, with electric headlights, with composition R 99 driver in white overalls, with chock and key, original box and packing, on a display plinth.
£2,700–3,000 *CSK*

A Märklin factory-constructed clockwork M1101/03 constructor streamline tourer, finished in two-tone blue, electric headlights, on a display plinth, Italian market colour leaflet dated '10.33', instruction booklet, dated '8.35' with key, original box, good condition.
£2,500–3,000 *CSK*

A Märklin factory-constructed clockwork M1101/05 B constructor lorry, with electric headlights, finished in red and green, with spare tyre, display plinth and key, with original box and packing, slight damage.
£1,600–2,000 *CSK*

A Bing 0 gauge clockwork model of a tramcar, with original claret, cream and orange paintwork.
£800–1,000 *DN*

A Marx Merrymakers tinplate and clockwork mouse band, comprising: 3 musicians, a dancer, and a piano with clockwork mechanism, defective, c1950, 9½in (24cm) high.
£500–600 *S(S)*

A Hornby Series No. 0 clockwork lithographed Silver Jubilee train set, comprising: Silver Link locomotive and tender, two-car articulated set and track, in original box with instructions, c1938, good condition.
£420–480 *CSK*

A pine rocking cradle, c1820, 36in (91.5cm) long.
£350–400 *HeR*

An old tram style pine bench, c1880, 72in (182.5cm) long.
£500–525 *AnD*

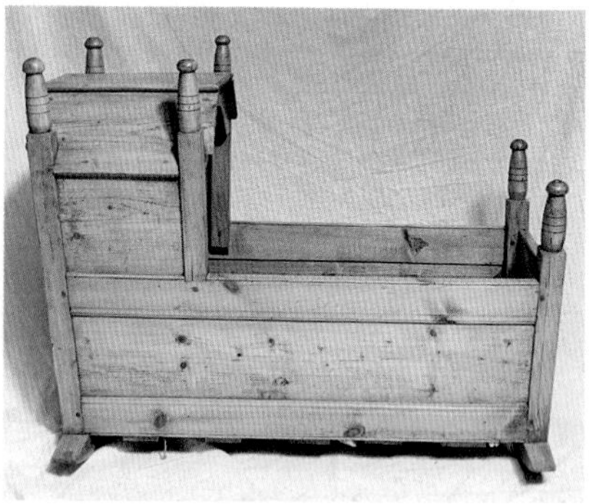

A Scandinavian pine rocking cradle, c1850, 37in (94cm) long.
£300–375 *HeR*

A pine carver chair, with turned legs and spindles.
£120–145 *CPA*

A pine bedside cabinet, c1880, 16½in (42cm) wide.
£75–125 *AnD*

A pine sewing box, c1890, 26in (66cm) wide.
£150–200 *FAG*

A pine box, c1880, 42in (106.5cm) long.
£150–200 *AnD*

A painted pine deed box, 19thC, 15in (38cm) wide.
£60–70 *Cou*

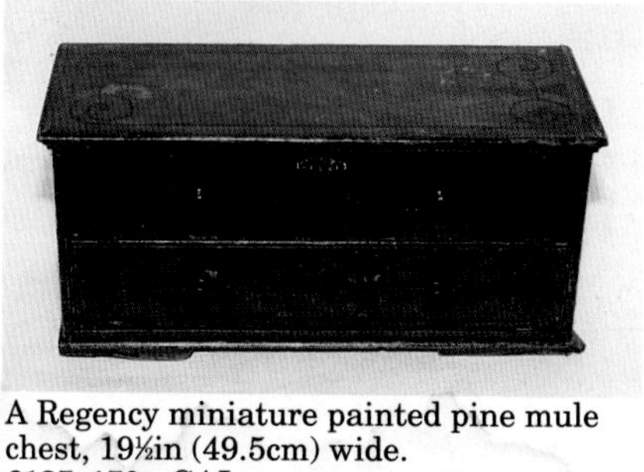

A Regency miniature painted pine mule chest, 19½in (49.5cm) wide.
£125–150 *GAL*

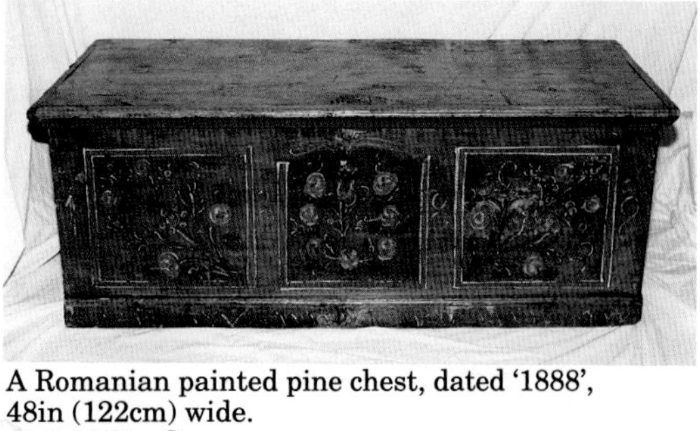

A Romanian painted pine chest, dated '1888', 48in (122cm) wide.
£275–375 *Cou*

A Victorian pine chest of drawers, the 2 short and 3 long drawers with porcelain handles, 44in (111.5cm) wide.
£350–375 *HeR*

A Continental pine chest of drawers, with 3 long drawers, c1890, 40in (101.5cm) wide.
£275–375 *AnD*

A pine chest of drawers, with bracket feet, c1880, 40in (101.5cm) wide.
£300–320 *MIL*

A Victorian chest of drawers, with 2 short and 2 long drawers, 42in (106.5cm) wide.
£300–340 *HeR*

An Estonian pine chest of drawers, with turned pillars to sides, c1850, 46in (116.5cm) wide.
£500–600 *HeR*

A Dutch pine sècretaire chest, c1880, 60in (152cm) wide.
£275–375 *AnD*

A Victorian Welsh pine chest of drawers, with 2 short and 3 long drawers, 1875, 46in (116.5cm) wide.
£340–360 *OPH*

A pine chest, c1900, 27in (69cm) wide.
£150–200 *FAG*

A Victorian pine chest of drawers, c1880, 40½in (102cm) wide.
£300–350 *MofC*

A Continental pine pot cupboard, late 19thC, 16in (40.5cm) wide.
£115–135 *CPA*

A pine cupboard, with a raised back, 2 drawers and 2 cupboard doors, early 19thC, 36in (91.5cm) wide.
£370–430 *CPA*

A Bavarian food cupboard, fitted with drawers and shelves, c1840, 72in (182.5cm) high.
£275–400 *AnD*

A Continental pine wardrobe, with 2 doors and a long drawer in the base, early 20thC, 47in (119cm) wide.
£400–500 *AnD*

A pine cupboard, with 4 doors, c1870, 50in (127cm) wide.
£800–900 *FAG*

A Regency pine pot cupboard, c1820, 13in (33cm) wide.
£130–150 *WAT*

A Hungarian painted pine coffer, mid-18thC, 33½in (85cm) wide.
£325–375 *BRD*

A pine cupboard, with 2 doors, c1900, 26½in (67.5cm) wide.
£125–135 *Ber*

A Dutch pine armoire, c1870, 50in (127cm) wide.
£600–750 *AnD*

A pine vertigo, with enclosed adjustable shelving, a narrow drawer above, and turned columns to sides, c1880, 42in (106.5cm) wide.
£400–500 *AnD*

A German vertigo, with enclosed adjustable shelving, late 19thC, 40in (101.5cm) wide.
£500–600 *AnD*

A Continental pine dresser, 19thC, 27in (68.5cm) wide.
£250–350 *FOX*

A European pine wardrobe, c1880, 50in (127cm) wide.
£425–525 *AnD*

A Dutch pitch pine desk, c1910, 49in (124.5cm) wide.
£600–700 *FAG*

A Dutch pine collapsible armoire, with a later top, c1900, 54in (137cm) wide.
£450–550 *AnD*

A Victorian pine desk, with a fitted interior, on turned legs, 30in (76cm) wide.
£200–300 *TAR*

A pine dresser, with 2 shelves, 2 cupboards and 2 drawers, c1880, 36in (91.5cm) wide.
£480–500 *MIL*

A pine dresser, with delft rack over 3 drawers and 4 cupboard doors, 19thC, 80in 203cm) wide.
£1,800–2,200 *TPC*

A Hampshire pine dresser, with a dog kennel base, 19thC, 76in (193cm) wide.
£1,400–1,800 *TPC*

A Victorian Hampshire pine dresser, with 3 drawers and doors, 72in (182.5cm) wide.
£1,500–1,800 *TPC*

A Continental pine bowfronted dresser base, c1900, 62½in (158cm) wide.
£600–700 *WAT*

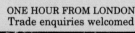

A pine dresser, with a dog kennel base, 18thC, 62in (157cm) wide.
£1,000–1,500 *TPC*

A Hampshire pine dresser, with an open plate rack, 18thC, 52in (132cm) wide.
£600–900 *TPC*

A pine open rack dresser, with 2 cupboard doors and 2 drawers, c1870, 48in (122cm) wide.
£750–850 *MIL*

A Victorian pine dresser, c1875, 48in (122cm) wide.
£450–550 *OPH*

A pitch pine dresser base, with 2 cupboard doors below 2 drawers, c1840, 39½in (100cm) wide.
£230–260 *DMA*

A pine base, with 2 cupboard doors below one drawer, c1835, 31in (78.5cm) wide.
£150–185 *DMA*

A Welsh pine dresser, constructed from old pine, 43in (109cm) wide.
£500–600 *AnD*

A Dutch pine larder cupboard, c1870, 37in (94cm) wide.
£400–480 *FAG*

A pine meat safe, c1900, 25in (63.5cm) wide.
£30–50 *FOX*

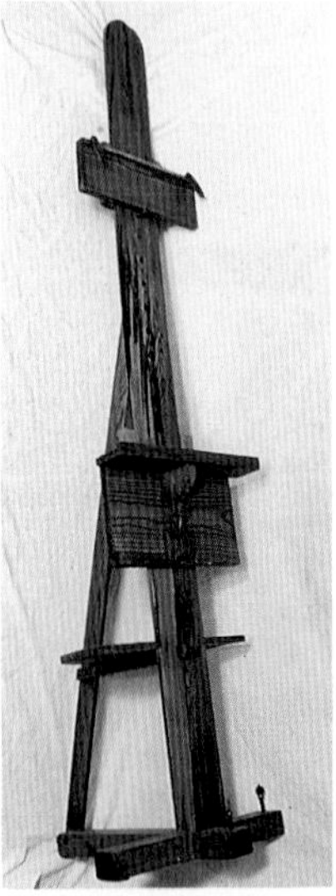

A pine easel, c1910, 75in (190.5cm) high.
£180–250 *FAG*

A carved pine horse's head, c1930, 23in (58.5cm) wide.
£350–375 *MofC*

A painted pine grape press, 19thC, 30in (76cm) wide.
£125–145 *AnE*

A pine sideboard, with a shield-shaped panel door and 3 drawers, early 20thC, 48in (122cm) wide.
£250–300 *CPA*

A pine stool, c1880, 12in (30.5cm) wide.
£18–25 *WaH*

A circular pine stool, with a painted base, 19thC, 8½in (21.5cm) diam.
£50–60 *Cou*

A pine table, on turned legs, early 18thC, 54in (137cm) wide.
£250–300 *AnD*

A pine table, with drawer, c1860, 48in (122cm) wide.
£450–500 *MIL*

A pine table, with straight legs, c1890, 35½in (90.5cm) wide.
£120–125 *AL*

A painted pine dressing table, attributed to C. & R. Light, c1881, 54in (137cm) wide.
£1,000–1,500 *S*

An octagonal pine table, c1910, 21½in (54.5cm) diam.
£80–100 *FAG*

A pine kitchen table, with one drawer, c1835, 48in (122cm) long.
£150–200 *DMA*

A Victorian pine kitchen table, c1890, 42in (106.5cm) long.
£175–225 *AnD*

A pine side table, c1890, 36in (91.5cm) wide.
£150–200 *FAG*

A Cumbrian pine serving table, c1850, 73in (185cm) long.
£400–500 *HOA*

A pine serving table, with 3 drawers, c1860, 54in (137cm) long.
£300–400 *HOA*

A Victorian pine kitchen table, with one drawer, c1835, 54in (137cm) wide.
£150–185 *DMA*

A wind-out pine table, late 19thC, 66in (167.5cm) long extended.
£540–635 *CPA*

A pine table, c1860, 28½in (73cm) wide.
£150–200 *FAG*

A painted pine washstand, with bamboo style legs, c1880, 39½in (100cm) wide.
£450–525 *MofC*

A pine serving table, c1900, 47in (119cm) wide.
£225–275 *MofC*

A pine wine rack, c1860, 36in (91.5cm) wide.
£200–250 *FAG*

A Victorian pine washstand, 28in (71cm) wide.
£200–250 *TAR*

A pine whatnot, c1890, 21in (53.5cm) wide.
£300–350 *FAG*

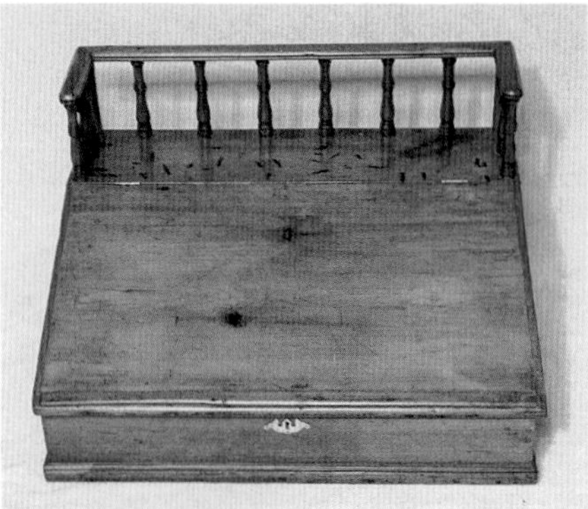

A pine writing slope, c1880, 26in (66cm) wide.
£150–200 *FAG*

A pine washtub, c1870, 32in (81cm) wide.
£60–70 *MIL*

A Chiltern Winter Skater teddy bear, 1930s, 16in (41cm) high.
£500–600 *Bon*

A Farnell Yeti bear, made without ears, 1920s, 19½in (49.5cm) high.
£450–600 *Bon*

A Farnell Alpha bear, 1930s, 28in (71cm) high.
£950–1,200 *Bon*

A black and cream mohair bear, fully jointed, brown cloth pads, 1920s, 24in (61cm) high.
£550–650 *Bon*

A pink mohair straw filled bear, with cream felt pads, 3 claws, c1920s, 24in (61cm) high.
£450–550 *Bon*

A teddy bear purse, with jointed limbs, purse lined with Rexine, c1918, 6½in (16.5cm) high, and a photograph of the original owner.
£3,600–4,200 *CSK*

A Rabery & Delphieu No. 1 bisque headed doll, shoes marked 'RS', 19½in (50cm) high.
£300–400 *P(B)*

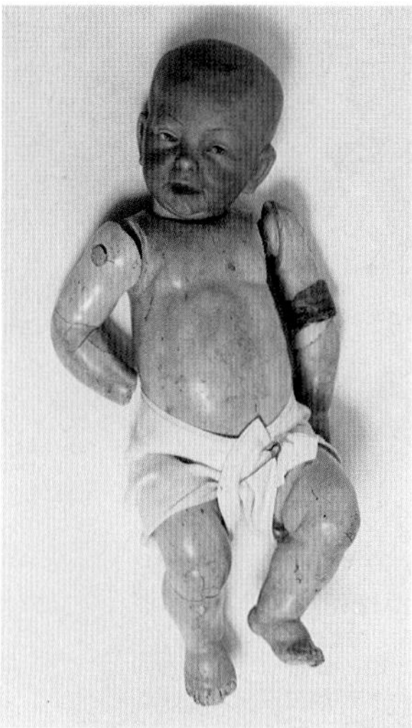

A Kämmer & Reinhardt character bisque headed baby doll, No. 36, 14in (36cm) high.
£600–800 *P(B)*

A Simon & Halbig bisque headed doll, original clothes, c1890, 18in (45.5cm) high, boxed. **£500–550** *SP*

An SFBJ No. 60 bisque headed character doll, with brown weighted eyes, 21½in (54.5cm) high.
£160–220 *P(B)*

A Simon & Halbig 949 bisque shoulder headed doll, with a leather body and swivel neck, c1890, 13in (33cm) high.
£600–700 *SP*

A Jumeau style bisque headed doll, shoes marked Jumeau, repaired, 22in (56cm) high.
£500–700 *P(B)*

An Armand Marseille bisque shoulder headed doll, No. 3200, fixed blue eyes, hands missing, 19in (48cm) high.
£80–100 *P(B)*

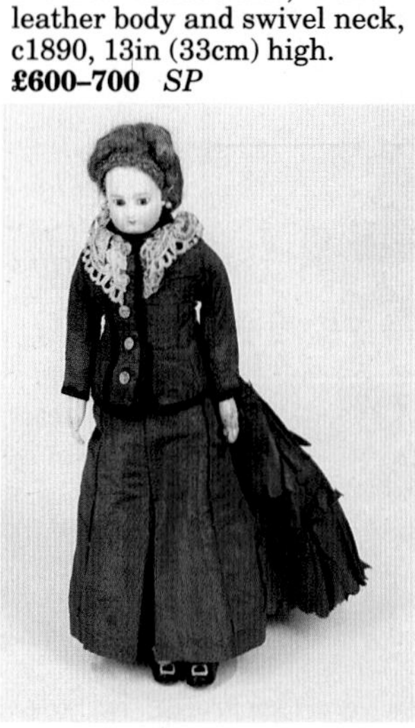

A German shoulder plate doll, with leather body, original clothes, c1880, 15½in (39.5cm) high.
£500–550 *SP*

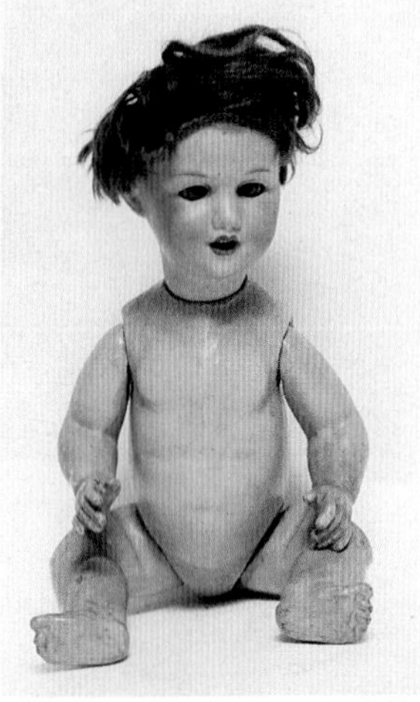

A character head bisque doll, with painted features, marked 'Germany 410/1', 13½in (34cm) high.
£400–500 *P(B)*

An SFBJ Paris bisque headed doll, with weighted black eyes, open mouth, and jointed composition body, slight chips to ears, 17½in (44cm) high.
£150–200 *P(B)*

A Heubach-Koppelsdorf 321 4/0 bisque headed doll, with bent limb composition body, 12½in (32cm) high.
£150–200 *P(B)*

An Armand Marseille porcelain headed doll, with realistic hair, sleeping eyes, open mouth and jointed body, late 19thC.
£250–300 *MR*

A Simon & Halbig No. 126 bisque headed doll, with blue flirty eyes, moving tongue, and bent limb composition body, one tooth missing, 15½in (40cm) high.
£300–350 *P(B)*

An Armand Marseille No. 996/7 bisque headed character doll, with weighted blue eyes, open mouth, dimple to chin and bent limb composition body, 17½in (45cm) high.
£150–200 *P(B)*

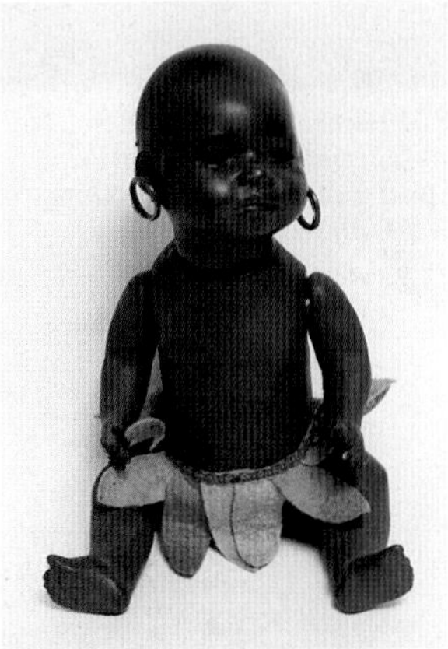

A Heubach Koppeldorf No. 399 spray painted bisque baby doll, with black weighted eyes, with jointed composition body, wearing earrings and a hula skirt, 11in (28cm) high.
£200–250 *P(B)*

A Jumeau fashion doll, with original clothes, c1880, 15½in (40cm) high.
£1,200-1,500 *SP*

An Armand Marseille No. 990/4, bisque headed doll, with weighted blue eyes, open mouth and nylon hair, 15½in (40cm) high.
£110–130 *P(B)*

A Tête Jumeau bisque headed doll, with fixed blue paperweight eyes, on a jointed composition body, 19in (48cm) high.
£800–1,000 *P(B)*

A Lines dolls' house, with fitted kitchen, c1924, 30in (76cm) high.
£250–300 *P(B)*

A dolls' house, with painted red bricks, with 2 chimneys and oval astragal window within a two-panelled hinged front, 19thC, 49½in (126cm) high.
£650–750 *C*

A bagatelle game, c1870, 46in (116.5cm) long.
£150–200 *RYA*

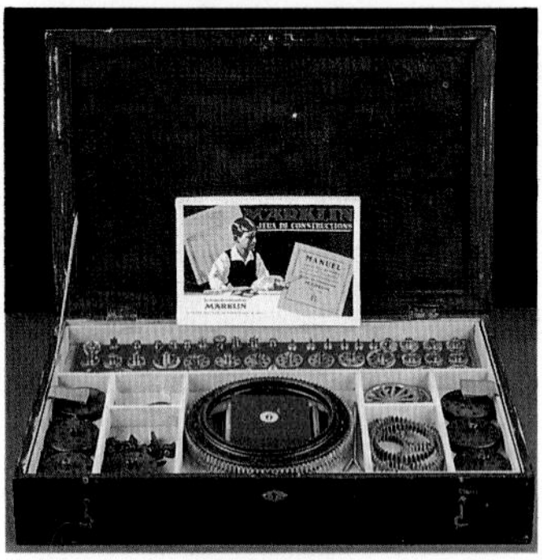

A Märklin Constructor Set No. 5, with instruction booklet Edition No. 22, in fitted oak case, 22½in (57cm) wide.
£220–300 *CSK*

A collection of 48 Steiff animals, most with buttons and labels in ears, mostly 1950s. **£1,600–2,000** *Bon*

A hand carved and painted Folk Art model of a roundabout, in working condition, c1870, 18in (45.5cm) diam.
£2,000–2,200 *RYA*

A toy horse, on a platform with wheels, original painted decoration, c1860, 13in (33cm) wide.
£150–180 *RYA*

A wooden pull-along toy, in the form of an articulated rabbit, c1890, 8in (20cm) wide.
£100–120 *RYA*

A toy mangle, with original green paint, c1880, 8in (20cm) wide.
£100–120 *RYA*

A hand carved and painted bowfronted dolls' house money box, c1800, 7in (17.5cm) high.
£700–800 *RYA*

A hand carved and painted toy tram, c1920, 11½in (29.5cm) long.
£100–140 *RYA*

A toy locomotive, with original green paint and cast iron wheels, c1880, 11⅝in (29.5cm) long.
£200–250 *RYA*

A 7¼in coal fired live steam 0-4-0 tank locomotive, by Cromar White Ltd, finished in LSWR green and black livery.
£2,000–2,500 *S(S)*

A wooden toy locomotive, with original painted decoration, c1940, 23in (58.5cm) long.
£50–80 *RYA*

A French market 20 volt electric ME Mountain 4-8-2 locomotive and bogie tender, varnish discoloured and some repainting, c1939.
£4,000–5,000 *CSK*

A Bing clockwork hand painted tinplate four-seater double phaeton, finished in green and gold, with 2 scuttle mounted bulls'-eye lamps, repaired, c1906.
£2,700–3,500 *CSK*

An American Ives china headed washer woman and ironing lady, with clockwork washtub, with original packing box and key, c1870s, 8in (20cm) wide.
£7,500–8,000 *CNY*

A Gauge I spirit fired live steam 4-6-2 LNER streamlined locomotive, Mallard No. 4468, with tender, probably constructed from a kit.
£2,500–3,000 *S(S)*

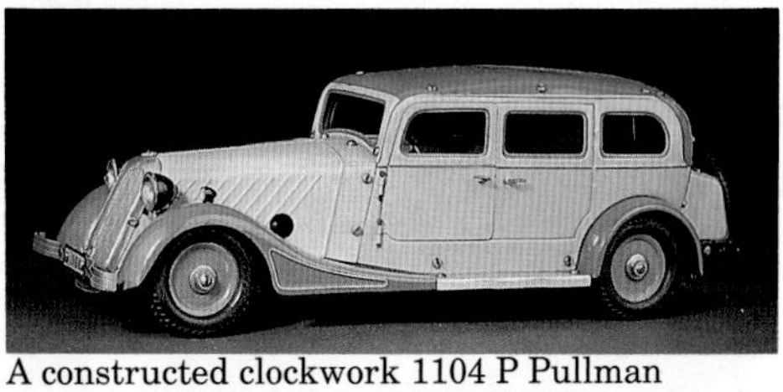

A constructed clockwork 1104 P Pullman limousine, with key, and British market *Car Construction Sets* catalogue, 1933.
£2,000–2,500 *CSK*

A clockwork single funnel 35cm river cruiser, named 'London', with an operating rudder, and removable superstructure, damaged, c1912.
£4,500–5,500 *CSK*

A clockwork 75cm river paddle steamer, named 'Rheingold', with original key, repaired, c1927.
£8,000–9,000 *CSK*

A ruby, emerald and diamond bracelet, with central ruby and diamond two-row cluster, 7½in (19cm) long.
£4,800–5,200 *C*

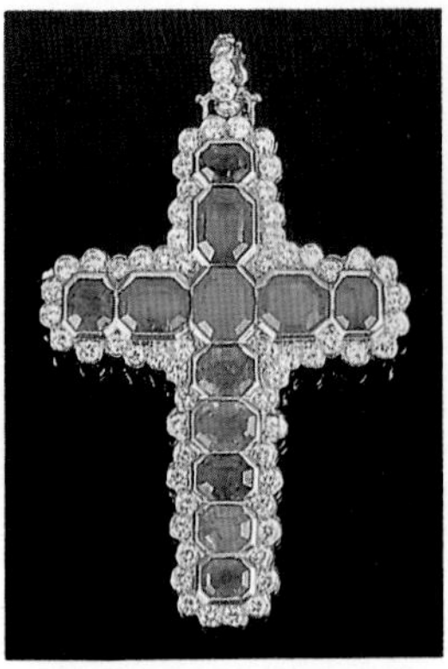

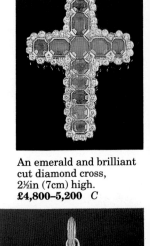

An emerald and brilliant cut diamond cross, 2¾in (7cm) high.
£4,800–5,200 *C*

A Victorian diamond, sapphire, ruby and emerald brooch, set in platinum.
£700–800 *RA*

A shell cameo, depicting the head of Jupiter, in a gold brooch mount of scroll and bead scalloped design.
£1,500–1,750 *CSK*

A neo-Renaissance pendant, with a garnet cameo of the Madonna, c1870, 2½in (6.5cm) long.
£3,000–3,500 *C*

A ribbed design gold bangle, with central shell cameo panel depicting a classical female, 19thC.
£650–800 *CSK*

An emerald, diamond and pearl brooch, with pear-shaped emerald terminals, c1920, 2in (5cm) wide.
£4,800–5,200 *C*

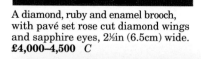

A diamond, ruby and enamel brooch, with pavé set rose cut diamond wings and sapphire eyes, 2½in (6.5cm) wide.
£4,000–4,500 *C*

A diamond flower vase brooch, signed by Bulgari, c1950, 2in (5cm) wide.
£6,000–6,500 *C*

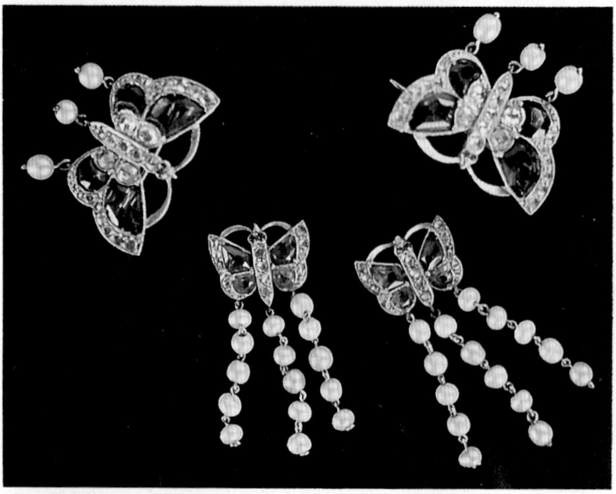

A Victorian tourmaline, diamond and pearl demi-parure, set in platinum and 18ct gold, c1890s.
£2,500–3,000 *RIT*

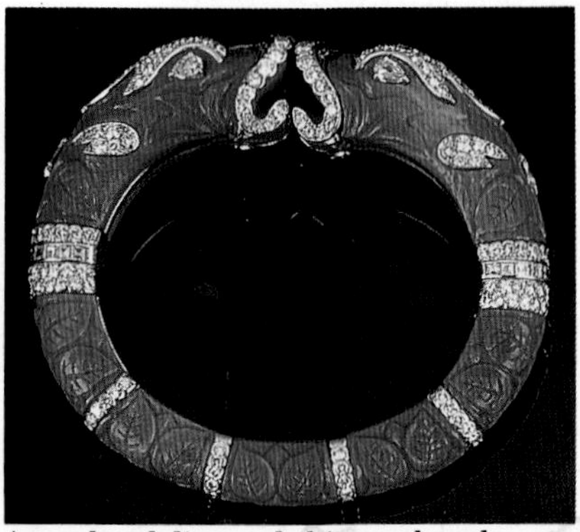

A coral and diamond chimera bangle, with marquise, pear and baguette cut diamond detail, French assay marks, c1950, 3in (7.5cm) wide.
£40,000–45,000 *C*

A Victorian Officer's helmet, cuirass, shoulder belt and pouch, of the Royal Horse Guards (The Blues), slight wear.
£3,000–3,500 *WAL*

A Georgian Officer's 1817 pattern helmet, of the Household Cavalry, with 'Peninsula' and 'Waterloo' honours, in original case.
£2,300–2,800 *WAL*

An Imperial German Officer's helmet, Garde du Corps, c1900.
£3,500–4,000 *WAL*

A military padded quilted headdress, perhaps Indian, 18thC, turban 12½in (32cm) diam.
£5,500–6,000 *S(NY)*

A Victorian Life Guards Officer's silver plated helmet, and plated cuirass with leather edging and brass studs.
£3,000–3,500 *WAL*

A Greek bronze helmet, forged in one piece, of slightly carinated domed form with out-turned flaring cheeks, slight damage, 9in (22.5cm) high.
£27,000–30,000 *S(NY)*

A fireman's 'Merriweather' type brass helmet, with helmet plate, chin strap and part liner, dented.
£380–420 *MR*

An Officer's full dress sabretache, shoulder belt and embroidered pouch of the Nepal Foot Artillery, c1895.
£2,200–2,600 *WAL*

An Augsburg silver mounted trousse, by Hans Selber, with 2 knives and a bodkin, c1570–84, 8in (20cm) long.
£11,000–13,000 *S(NY)*

A Bohemian or Austrian archer's pavise, with Imperial colours and crown, c1470–90, 43½in (110cm) high.
£28,000–30,000 *S(NY)*

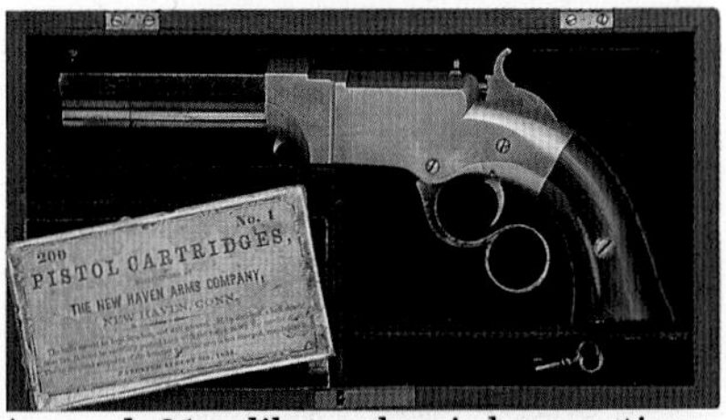

A cased .31 calibre volcanic lever action No. 1 pocket pistol, by the New Haven Arms Company, No. 1923, c1857–62, 9in (22.5cm) long.
£9,000–11,000 *S(NY)*

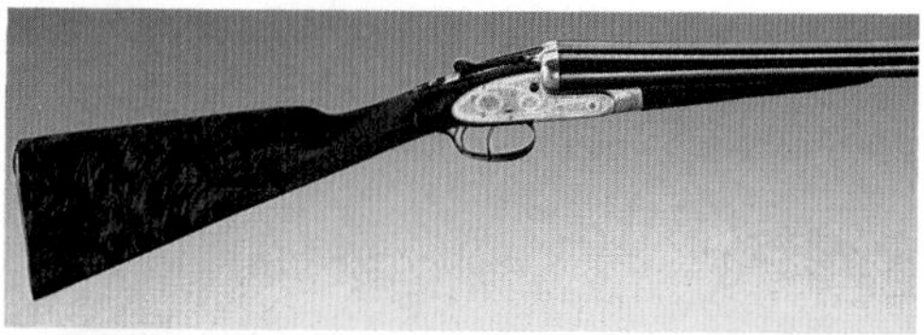

A J. Purdey & Sons 20-bore 2½in self-opening sidelock ejector gun, No. 21470, in original case.
£6,500–7,000 *S(S)*

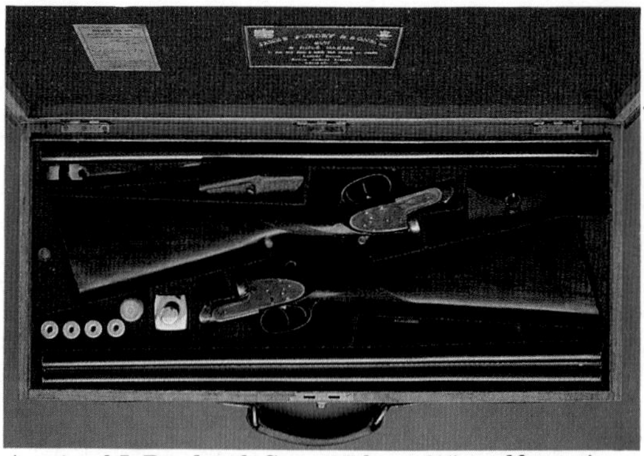

A pair of J. Purdey & Sons 12-bore 2½in self-opening sidelock ejector guns, Nos. 25523/4, with 28in chopper-lump barrels, in oak and leather case.
£30,000–32,000 *S(S)*

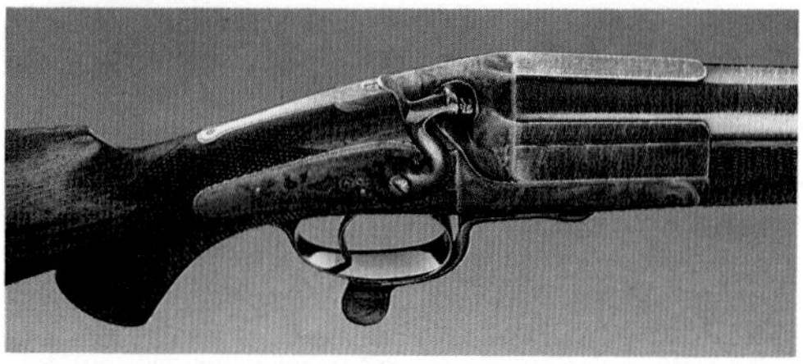

A J. Purdey & Sons 4-bore 4in hammer wildfowling gun, No. 13073, with 41¼in damascus barrel.
£7,500–8,000 *S(S)*

A Smith & Wesson .44 S&W New Model No. 3 single action revolver, No. 35477, with 7½in barrel.
£3,500–4,000 *S(S)*

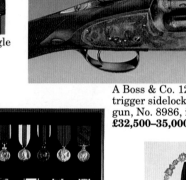

A Boss & Co. 12-bore 2¾in single trigger sidelock ejector over/under gun, No. 8986, in a leather case.
£32,500–35,000 *S(S)*

A Polish Hurricane pilot's Battle of Britain group of 12 medals, mounted.
£2,800–3,200 *S(S)*

The Orders and medals of M. Henri Cedard, Chef to HRH The Duke of Connaught until 1901, and HRH The Prince of Wales 1901–35, mounted in a frame.
£1,200–1,500 *WAL*

The Military Order of the Tower and Sword, Portugal, before 1910.
£1,000–1,500 *WAL*

A group of 11 medals, awarded to Sergeant. F. Finch ASC, valet to The Duke of Windsor from 1910.
£1,500–2,000 *WAL*

A Czechoslovakian Hurricane pilot's Battle of Britain group of 10 medals, mounted.
£2,000–2,500 *S(S)*

A Victorian Officer's full dress embroidered sabretache of the 8th The King's Royal Irish Hussars, c1856.
£1,500–2,000 *WAL*

A group of 11 medals from WWI and WWII, awarded to Vice-Admiral Marcel Harcourt Attwood Kelsey, CB, DSC, with matching set of miniatures.
£800–1,200 *WAL*

A selection of 139 *Superman's Girl Friend Lois Lane* comics, March/April 1958–September/October 1974, published by National Comics Publications, good condition.
£1,500–2,000 *S(NY)*

A selection of 194 *Superman's Pal Jimmy Olsen* comics, September/October 1954–March/April 1980, published by D.C. Comics Inc., good condition.
£1,500–2,000 *S(NY)*

Three *All-Flash Quarterly* comics, Nos. 1, 4 & 5, Summer 1941–42, published by National Periodical Publications, No. 1 restored, good condition.
£1,200–1,500 *S(NY)*

The Amazing Spider-Man comic book No.1, March 1963, published by Marvel Comics, good condition.
£4,000–4,500 *S(NY)*

A *Captain America* comic, No. 1, March 1941, published by Timely Publications, unrestored condition.
£11,000–12,000 *S(NY)*

The artists Jack Kirby and Joe Simon brought to life one of Marvel's most important and popular super-heroes when they created Captain America. The first issue is one of the 10 most sought after Golden Age comics.

An *Amazing Fantasy* comic, No. 15, first appearance of Spider-man, published by Marvel Comics Group, good condition, 1962.
£5,000–6,000 *CNY*

A selection of 176 of *Marge's Little Lulu* comics, published by The Western Files, comprising *Marge's Little Lulu, Marge's Tubby* and *Marge's Lulu Giant Animals*, good condition.
£3,200–3,500 *S(NY)*

A selection of 174 *Walt Disney's Comics,* comprising *Uncle Scrooge, The Beagle Boys and Moby Dick* comics.
£3,500–4,000 *S(NY)*

A selection of 76 comics, *The Flintstones, Cave Kids, Bigger and Boulder* and *Bam Bam Pebbles.*
£620–650 *S(NY)*

A *Marvel Comics,* No. 1, November 1939, published by Timely Publications, good restored condition.
£11,500–12,000 *S(NY)*

A poster, advertising a concert at Carnegie Hall, featuring Duke Ellington, Billie Holiday, Charlie Parker, Dizzy Gillespie and Stan Getz, for November 14, 1952, and a concert programme.
£5,000–5,500 *CSK*

A pair of Madonna's stage shorts, from the 1993 *Girlie Tour*, decorated with purple sequins.
£1,200–1,500 *CNY*

A blue denim hat, labelled 'Funky & Dom near New La Puente', signed 'John Lennon', c1980, and a photograph.
£1,200–1,500 *CSK*

A cane chair, the painted wood seat upholstered in patterned cotton, used in the Warner Bros. film *Casablanca*, 1942.
£4,000–4,500 *CNY*

A Stratocaster guitar, serial No. 86176, with 3 pick-ups, 2 controls, 3 switches, Kahler themolo unit and cream pickguard, with tweed case.
£1,000–1,500 *CNY*

A Ludwig Weather Master bass drumskin, decorated with hand painted black lettering, 21½in (54.5cm) diam, framed.
£12,000–13,500 *CSK*

A tunic, worn by Errol Flynn in the Warner Bros. production of *The Adventures of Robin Hood,* with a tag sewn in the lining 'Western Costume Co. 21739 Errol Flynn 42 1/25', 1938.
£3,300–3,600 *CNY*

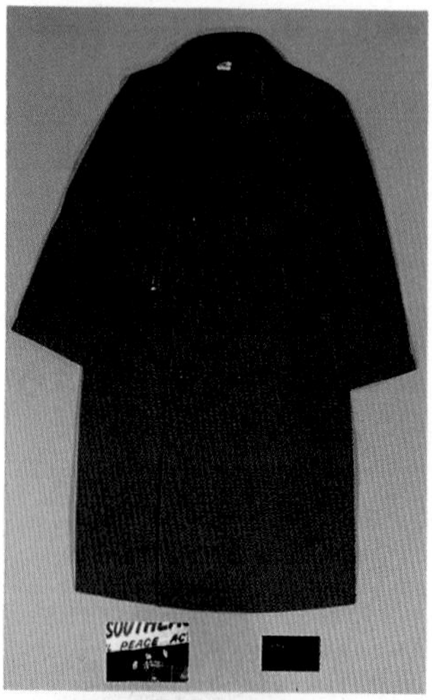

A cotton trenchcoat, worn by John Lennon, c1973, mounted with a photograph and plaque, 62 by 42½in (157 by 108cm), framed.
£1,000–1,500 *CNY*

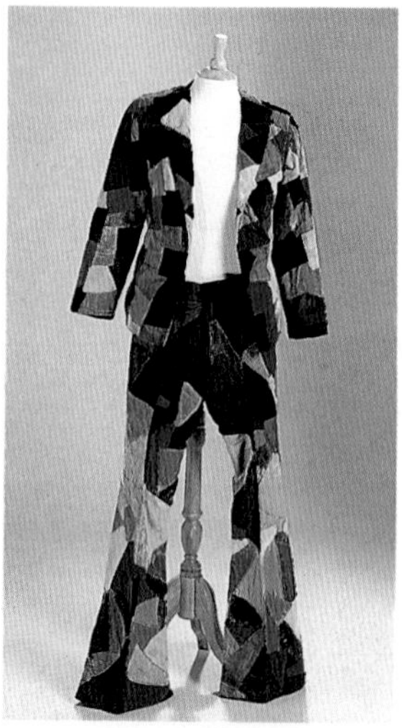

A crushed velvet two-piece stage outfit, worn by Jimi Hendrix on a flight to Sweden 1970, and various letters.
£16,500–17,500 *CNY*

A pair of green felt 'Munchkin' shoes, designed by Gilbert Adrian, for *The Wizard of Oz,* with 'Leona Parks' label, 1939.
£3,800–4,400 *CNY*

Three pairs of French brass and leather and brass field glasses, late 19thC.
£90–160 each *Tem*

A clockwork convoy clock, with a bell and alarm system to inform the helmsman when to alter course, c1940.
£210–230 *Tem*

A modern sign, with the 'Hero' sailor hand painted in relief.
£180–200 *Tem*

A pine and brass studded travelling trunk, repainted in traditional marine style, early 19thC.
£170–200 *Tem*

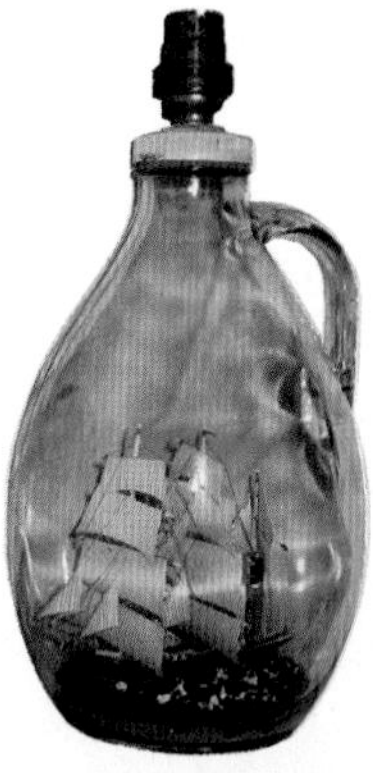

A ship in a demijohn bottle, converted to a table lamp, c1955.
£45–65 *Tem*

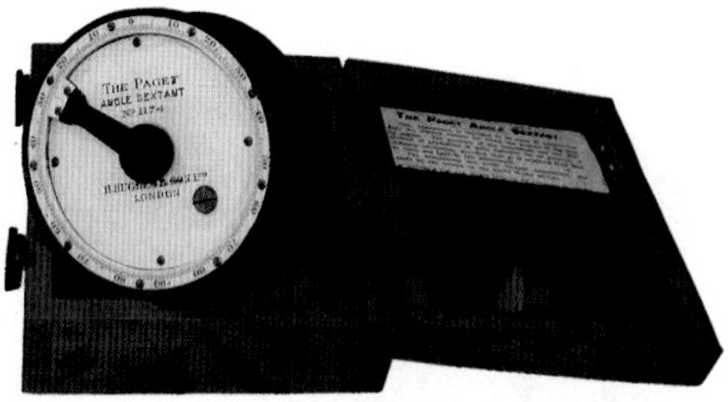

A Paget Angle Sextant, No. 1174, by H. Hughes & Son Ltd, London, c1930, 4½in (11.5cm) diam, with box.
£160–180 *Tem*

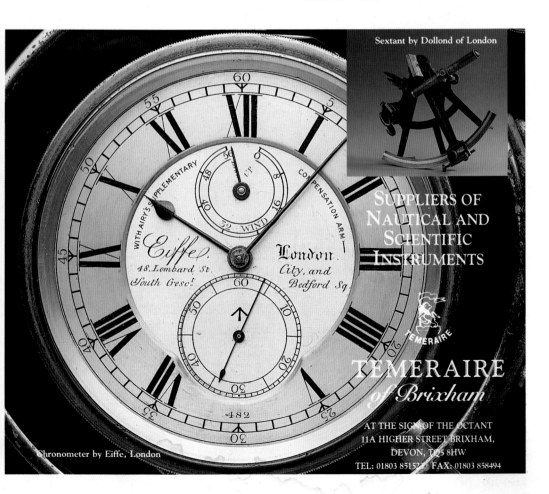

A two-day marine chronometer, by Thomas Mercer, St. Albans, with wooden box, c1953, 7in (17.5cm) square.
£800–1,200 *PWh*

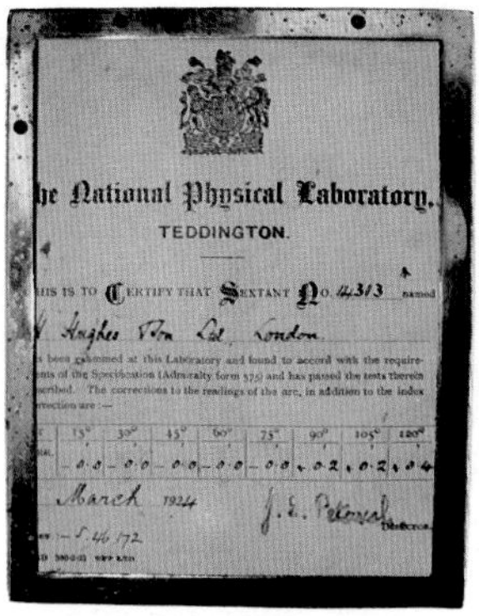

An original certificate of examination for a 1924 sextant.
£4–6 *Tem*

A 130mm radius vernier sextant, with detachable rosewood handle, in original mahogany case, early 19thC.
£1,100–1,300 *Tem*

A copy of a diver's helmet, incorporating various incorrect details from an original helmet, decorative value only.
£225–250 *Tem*

An eight-day marine chronometer, by Denham, Leeds, in a rosewood box, c1860, 6½in (16.5cm) square.
£4,500–5,500 *PWh*

A terrestrial globe, the glass sphere with interior light, on a mahogany pedestal with small compass, c1950.
£250–270 *Tem*

A Morse code signal bell, in oak case with resistors, c1940.
£140–160 *Tem*

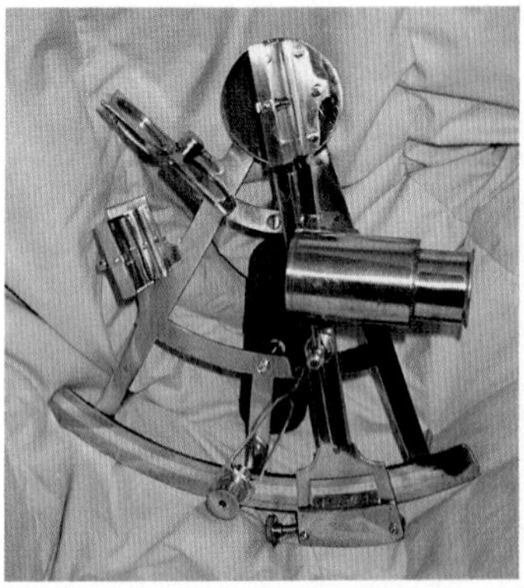

A brass and aluminium survey sextant, with original carrying case, c1920.
£350–450 *Tem*

A hand painted 1870s style chest of drawers, fitted with brass military handles and corner plates.
£425–450 *Tem*

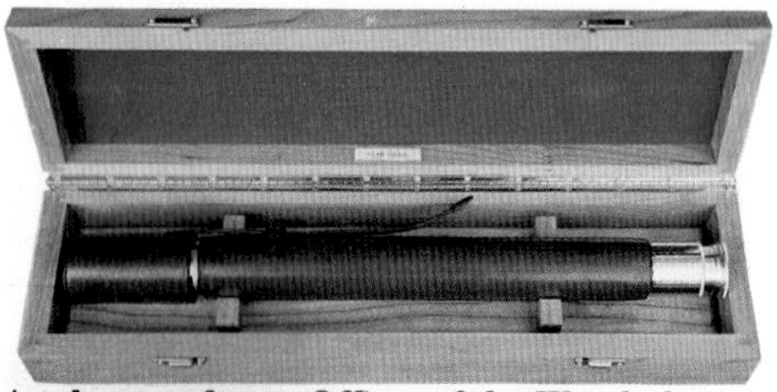

A telescope for an Officer of the Watch, by W. F. Stanley, London, 8x magnification, nickel plated, leather covered, c1900.
£150–180 *Tem*

A copy of Admiral Fitzroy's pocket barometer, made by Temeraire of Brixham.
£225–245 *Tem*

A chronometer, with twin barrels, by Breguet et fils, c1830, 7in (17.5cm) diam.
£35,000–40,000 *PWh*

A two-day chronometer, by Charles Frodsham, c1855, 7in (17.5cm) diam.
£3,000–3,500 *PWh*

An eight-day chronometer, by Brockbank Atkins, c1880, box 8in (20cm) square.
£4,500–5,500 *PWh*

A two-day chronometer, by Lange & Söhne, Glashütte, c1940, case 7in (17.5cm) square.
£1,200–1,500 *PWh*

An eight-day chronometer, by Thomas Mercer, retailed by Kelvin Hughes, c1962, box 8in (20cm) square.
£1,200–1,800 *PWh*

A two-day survey chronometer, by Thomas Mercer, St. Albans, in an aluminium case, with electrical contacts, c1955, case 11 by 8in (28 by 20cm).
£800–1,200 *PWh*

An American one-day gimballed deck watch, by Elgin National Watch Co., in mahogany box with carrying case, early 20thC.
£800–1,200 *PWh*

An Apulian red figure bell krater, repaired, circa 4th Century B.C., 14½in (36.5cm) high.
£4,500–5,500 *C*

An Etruscan black figure neck amphora, repaired, circa 550–525 B.C., 14½in (36.5cm) high.
£4,000–5,000 *CNY*

An Attic black figure amphora, repaired, early 6th Century B.C., 14in (35.5cm) high.
£6,000–7,000 *C*

An Italo-Corinthian ring aryballos, with strap handle, circa 600 B.C., 9½in (23.5cm) high.
£7,200–7,800 *C*

A British Iron Age solid gold bracelet, circa 1st Century B.C., 2½in (6cm) wide, 5oz.
£21,000–23,000 *C*

An Attic black lekythos, of Deianeira shape, circa 540 B.C., 6½in (16cm) high.
£17,500–18,500 *S*

An Egyptian cartonnage mummy mask, Ptolemaic period, circa 320–30 B.C., 22in (56cm) high.
£53,000–57,000 *S*

An Italo-Corinthian oinochoe, repaired, circa 600 B.C., 13in (33cm) high.
£4,500–5,500 *S*

An Iranian bronze figure of a stag, circa 1000–700 B.C., 4in (10cm) high.
£3,500–4,500 *CNY*

An Egyptian bronze seated figure of a cat, with pierced ears, circa 664–525 B.C., 8in (20cm) high.
£10,500–12,500 *S*

A Cambodian lime container, in the form of a sacred Bull-Nandi, circa 850–1200 A.D., 4½in (11cm) wide.
£300–400 *GRG*

An Attic black figure band cup, repaired, circa 550–530 B.C., 8½in (21.5cm) diam.
£7,000–7,500 *C*

A Roman Imperial marble bust of the Empress Sabina, circa 117–138 A.D., 28in (71cm) high.
£220,000–250,000 *S(NY)*

Tinplate

A Linemar friction powered lithographed tinplate Mickey Mouse Mouseketeers Moving Van, in original box, good condition.
£250–300 *CSK*

A Schuco tinplate and plastic 5700 Synchromatic Packard Convertible, painted green, with red lithographed tinplate interior, together with battery operated control, in original box, one wing mirror missing, good condition.
£420–500 *CSK*

A Distler free-wheeling lithographed tinplate elephant and howdah novelty toy, on 4 Dunlop Cord wheels, the front 2 enabling the trap door trunk to move, acting as a dispenser, good condition.
£420–500 *CSK*

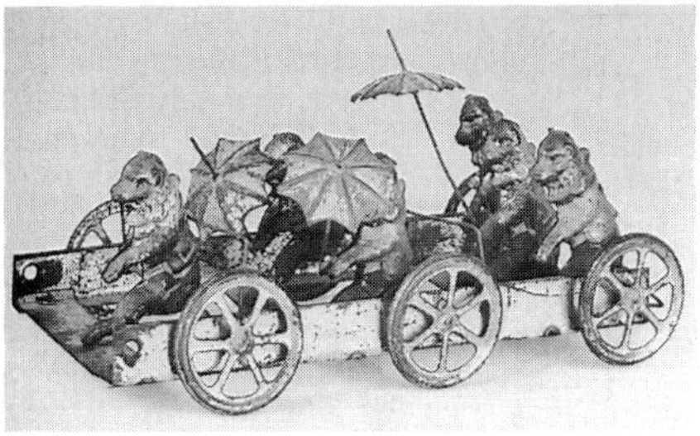

l. A lithographed and lacquered tinplate circus dog cart, with 6 dogs, dressed in red, blue and yellow suits, 3 with parasols, some parasols missing, fair condition, 7½in (19cm) long.
£300–400 *CSK*

A Bing steam tinplate single funnel torpedo boat, with externally fired boiler and spirit lamp, driving a single oscillating cylinder engine to flywheel and propeller shaft, on a trolley, Cat. Ref. 13090, c1909.
£900–1,200 *CSK*

l. A Bub electric tinplate limousine, finished in lined green and black, c1928, good condition, 10½in (26cm) long.
£450–550 *CSK*

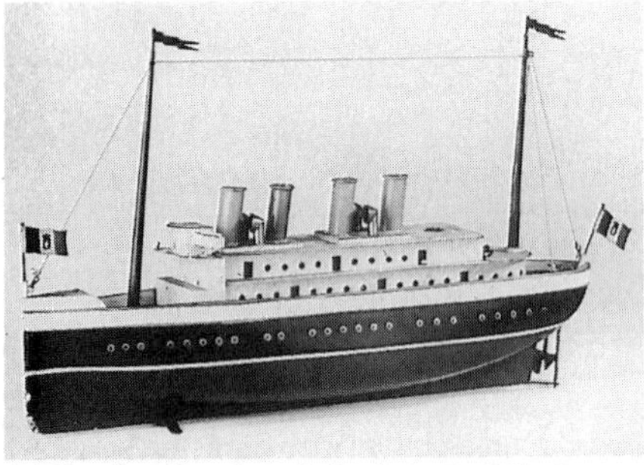

A Bing hand painted tinplate 2nd Series four-funnel liner, finished in dark blue, red and ivory with fore and aft lithographed Italian flags, good condition, 16½in (42cm) long.
£1,200–1,700 *CSK*

A Bing tinplate four-funnel steam torpedo boat, finished in 2 shades of grey, with externally fired boiler, spirit lamp, driving a single oscillating cylinder engine to flywheel and propeller shaft, some chips and repairs, good condition, Cat. Ref. 155/551, 23in (59cm) long.
£1,600–2,000 *CSK*

A Bing hand painted tinplate steam turbine river boat, finished in red and black with blue detailing, striped awning, white cabin with grey roof, a lithographed stern flag, with spirit fired boiler, the propeller shaft driven by a transverse turbine wheel, good condition, c1914, 19½in (49.5cm) long.
£1,600–2,000 *CSK*

A painted and lacquered tinplate sidewheel steam gunboat carpet toy, mounted on 4 revolving spoked wheels, with cannon, red and blue flag and 2 soldiers wearing colonial pattern pith helmets, probably French, c1880, fair condition, 12in (30.5cm) long.
£350–450 *CSK*

A penny toy painted and lithographed tin bird cage, with sliding dirt tray, bird and stand, probably German, c1920, 6in (15cm) high, and a miniature tin, in the shape of a violin case, marked 'Rowntree', probably made by Barringer, Wallis and Manners, 3in (7.5cm) long.
£270–320 *CSK*

Trains

l. Three painted metal models of steam locomotives, with cotton wool smoke, bearing a label 'John Harris at Southend Farm, Cublington, Bucks. He is supposed to have made them at the age of twelve years (in 1851)', engines 4in(10cm) and 8in (20cm) long, in a glazed display case.
£150–200 *DN*

A Louis Marx & Co. Marlines stream line steam type electric train, comprising a 2-4-2 locomotive and tender, finished in black with New York Central logo, 4 twin bogie wagons, a quantity of 3 rail track, 110 volt controller and instructions, in original box.
£100–150 *DN*

A 3½in gauge coal fired steam 4-6-0 GWR 1000 Class locomotive, named 'County of Caernarvon', with twin outside cylinders, superheated copper boiler, fully fitted cab, tender with hand feed pump, on fully sprung chassis, no boiler certificate, fitted carrying case.
£2,200–2,500 *N*

A 3½in gauge coal fired Springbok 2-6-0 locomotive and tender, finished in green with 'LNER' to tender, and Springbok name plates, with carrying boxes and display track, 35in (89.5cm) long.
£1,200–1,700 *AH*

A Twerenbold Märklin replica electric 4-6-4 Hudson Locomotive, No. 5273, with twelve-wheeled bogie tender, named 'New York Central', finished in black and silver livery, c1979, good condition.
£3,500–4,000 *CSK*

A Bing 0 gauge clockwork LMS 4-4-0 locomotive, No. 1924, with matching six-wheeled tender, finished in maroon, black and yellow lined, some wear.
£200–250 *N*

l. An LNER class O4 2-8-0 locomotive, No. 5348, and tender, with fluted connecting and coupling rods, brake and sanding gear, riveting firebox, washout plugs, scale cab and backhead fittings, the tender with brake handle, lifting eyes, steps, hand and lamp irons, finished in black, 16½in (41.5cm) long.
£550–750 *CSK*

A GWR Metro 2-4-0T No. 974 locomotive, built and painted by H. J. Dumas, with internal and external details, finished in green livery, 12in (30.5cm) long.
£850–1,200 *CSK*

An SR No. 768 live steam coal fired locomotive, by Aster for Fulgurex, named 'Sir Balin', with original fittings and paintwork, 24in (61.5cm) long, with new carrying box.
£1,400–1,700 *CSK*

Two German Märklin 0 gauge Paris cars, each unpowered first class car with hinged peacock blue roof with yellow lining, fitted interiors with 6 seats, a composition passenger, the exterior finished in rust brown with teak effect sliding double doors, gold transfer coats-of-arms, restored paintwork, each 8½in (21cm) long.
£4,200–6,000 *S*

r. An American train set, 'The Flying Colonel', with a blue wide gauge engine, 'The Ace', No. 4686, a 'Hancock' observation car No. 4382, an 'Adams' Pullman car No. 4381, and a 'Madison' club car No. 4380, good condition.
£4,000–6,000 *CNY*

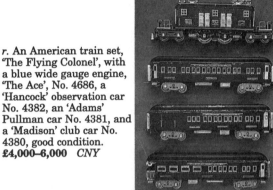

A steam spirit fired MR 4-4-0 compound style locomotive, with tender No. 999, Cat. Ref. E4021, some wear, c1922.
£1,000–1,500 *CSK*

A Bing lithographed Southern bogie 1st corridor coach, for Bassett-Lowke, good condition, c1927, and a matching 3rd luggage brake, roof repainted, good condition, one in original box.
£370–470 *CSK*

A steam spirit fired GNR 4-4-0 locomotive, and a non-matching four-wheeled GNR green tender, Cat Ref. E4021, good condition, c1904.
£1,400–2,000 *CSK*

A high voltage electric NBR 4-4-2 locomotive, with tender, Cat Ref. CE 1021, good condition, c1926.
£2,000–2,500 *CSK*

A steam spirit fired L&NWR 4-4-0 locomotive, semi-rigid six-wheeled tender, lacks wooden handrail grips, fair condition, c1902.
£2,500–3,500 *CSK*

A 20 volt electric Continental outline lithographed 4-4-0 locomotive, with tender, axle boxes missing, Cat. Ref. 3041, fair condition, c1926.
£700–800 *CSK*

A steam spirit fired Continental 0-4-0 locomotive, with twin double acting cylinders, external firing and wick burner, with a tender, fair condition, c1909.
£750–1,000 *CSK*

A steam spirit fired PLM 4-6-2 Pacific locomotive, with bogie tender, finished in black livery, cast iron bogie frames, good condition, c1919.
£3,500–4,500 *CSK*

A Carette for Bassett-Lowke 8/10 volt DC electric painted tinplate 4-4-2 'Atlantic' locomotive, with matching six-wheeled GNR tender, fair condition, c1910.
£1,500–2,000 *CSK*

l. A steam spirit fired Continental 0-4-0 locomotive, with twin double acting cylinders, with tender, good condition, c1909.
£1,400–1,800 *CSK*

A French market country station, good condition, Cat. Ref. R2151, c1927, 13½in (34cm) wide.
£1,500–2,000 *CSK*

A German market station, with internal electric lighting, good condition, Cat. Ref. 2033, c1933, 19in (48cm) wide.
£1,400–1,800 *CSK*

An Italian market Continental station, with internal electric lighting, good condition, Cat. Ref. 2029, c1930, 18⅜in (46.5cm) wide, and various figures.
£2,400–2,700 *CSK*

Soldiers

A Britains Set 11 plug-handed Highlanders of the Black Watch, 5 infantrymen with rifles, officer with sword, 2 Scots Guards pipers and piper of the Gordon Highlanders, all on oval bases, c1890, good condition.
£200–250 *CSK*

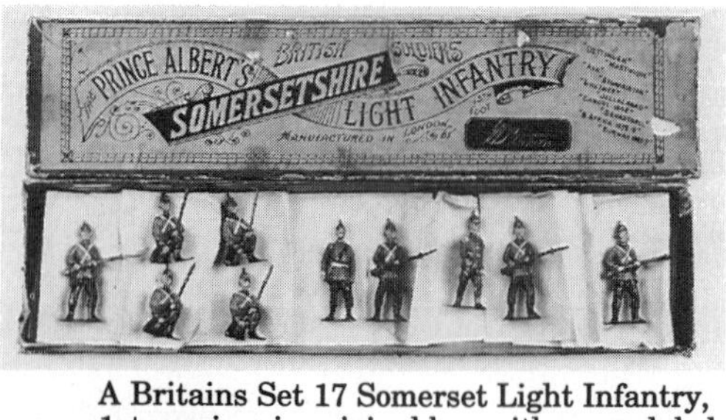

A Britains Set 17 Somerset Light Infantry, 1st version, in original box with green label, fair condition, c1894.
£200–300 *CSK*

l. Twelve German hollow cast khaki Infantrymen, similar to The York and Lancaster Regiment, 10 men running at the trail, with officer and bugler, good condition, c1898.
£150–180 *CSK*

A Britains Set 123 Bikanir Camel Corps., 1st version, with wire tails, good condition, c1901.
£400–450 *CSK*

A Britains Set 1339 Royal Horse Artillery, with gun limber team at the gallop, good condition, c1931.
£550–800 *CSK*

A Britains Set 1294 British Infantry, in tropical service dress shorts, c1934, good condition.
£200–250 *CSK*

A Britains Set 171 Greek Infantry, running at the trail, with officer, good condition.
£220–270 *CSK*

A Britains Set 94 21st Lancers, 3rd version, with steel helmets, fair condition, c1919, with reproduction box.
£450–550 *CSK*

A Britains Set 54 First Lifeguards, 2nd Dragoon Guards and 9th Lancers, in original red box with black and gold label, good condition, c1920.
£500–550 *CSK*

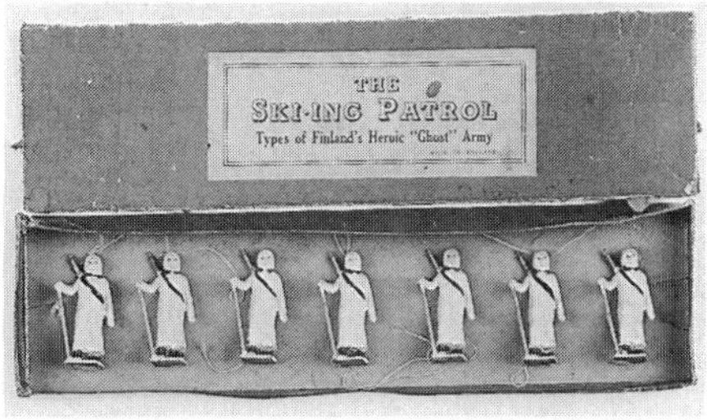

A Johillco skiing patrol, Finland's Heroic Ghost army, in original green box, good condition, c1935.
£600–650 *CSK*

Miscellaneous

A Britains Set 1413 police car, with 2 officers, in original box, fair condition, 1936–41.
£200–250 *CSK*

Two Britains Set 1334 army lorries, with drivers, in original boxes with packing tissues and packing slip, good condition, c1947.
£200–230 *CSK*

r. Two Britains army lorries, No. 1335 army lorry with driver, and No. 1877 Beetle lorry, in original boxes with packing tissue, good condition, c1947.
£180–200 *CSK*

Two Chad Valley tractors, painted blue and orange, a Fordson Major tractor, in original box, good condition, 7in (17.5cm) long, and Fordson Dexta tractor, in original box, good condition, 5¼in (13.5cm) long.
£330–370 *CSK*

A blue Dinky 205 (230) Talbot-Lago with yellow plastic hubs, and a blue Dinky 209 (234) Ferrari with triangular nose and yellow hubs, in original cellophane and card bubble front display packets, good condition.
£300–350 *CSK*

A Dinky Set No. 6 US export issue of commercial vehicles, comprising: a green and cream 29c double decker bus, a grey 29b streamline bus, a cream 30f ambulance, a grey/red 30e breakdown car, and a 25h streamline fire engine, all with black hubs, in original chequered blue box with yellow and purple label and 'H. Hudson Dobson' US wholesale label, c1946.
£3,000–3,500 *CSK*

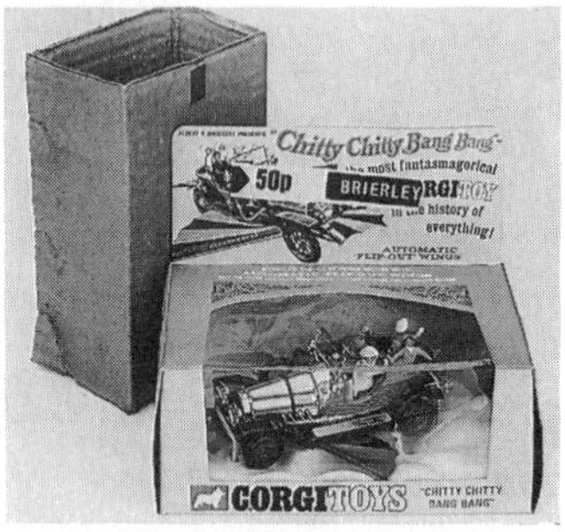

A Corgi 266, Chitty Chitty Bang Bang, with inner card and plastic clouds, in original box and corrugated brown card outer sleeve, good condition.
£190–220 *CSK*

A Dinky Toys Guy 'Warrior' flat truck, No. 432, painted in green and red, in original box, dated on inside end flap '8.58'.
£400–450 *CSK*

A Dinky Toys Triumph Spitfire 114, metallic gold, with 'I've got a Tiger in my Tank' transfer, driver in blue outfit, seat belt, in cellophane and card box, good condition, c1964.
£80–100 *CSK*

A Corgi diecast gift set No. 38, depicting the 1965 Monte Carlo Rally, good condition, boxed.
£350–400 *N*

A Dinky Austin Somerset saloon, with mid-blue hubs, in original box.
£125–150 *CSK*

A Dinky Toys Guy 'Warrior' 4 ton lorry, No. 431, painted fawn and green, with light green hubs, packing piece in original box, dated '9.54'.
£270–300 *CSK*

A Dinky Supertoys US export issue 581 'Express Horse Van Hire Service' horsebox, white and grey cast metal horses and packing pieces, in original box with special US market label, good condition.
£400–500 *CSK*

A Dinky Toys Guy flat truck with tailboard, painted grey, with black chassis and hubs.
£150–200 *CSK*

r. A Dinky Supertoys 923 Big Bedford van, advertising 'Heinz 57 Varieties', in original box, lid dated '11.55'.
£230–270 *CSK*

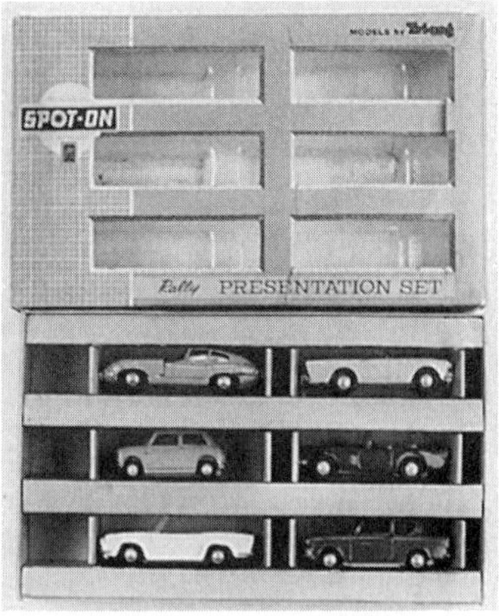

A Tri-ang Spot-On PS.7 Rally Presentation Set, comprising: a beige Austin 7, a beige Jaguar XK 'E', a white Renault Floride, a pale blue Sunbeam Alpine, a red Daimler SP250 Dart, and a red Ford Anglia, in original box with cellophane windows, good condition.
£420–500 *CSK*

r. A fibreglass model of Bluebird, and a copy photograph of Prince Philip and Donald Campbell, c1960, 55in (139cm) long.
£1,200–1,500 *N*

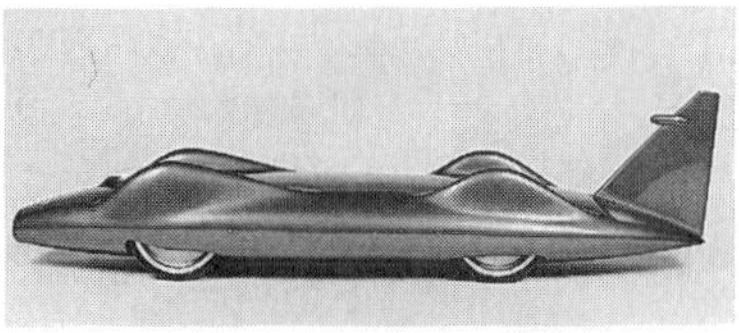

A Hubley cast iron motorcycle and sidecar, finished in red with gold decal, gold detailing, black rubber tyres, rider and sidecar passenger, c1930, 9in (23cm) long.
£500–750 *S(NY)*

A Dinky Toys Tow-Away Glider set, comprising: a Triumph 2000, a flying model glider and transporter, in original box with cellophane wrapping.
£100–150 *CSK*

A Meccano Dinky Toys No. 48 Petrol Station, with a turquoise roof and base, in original orange box, fair condition.
£500–550 *CSK*

A Dinky Supertoys 934 blue and yellow diecast Leyland Octopus Wagon, boxed.
£600–650 *N*

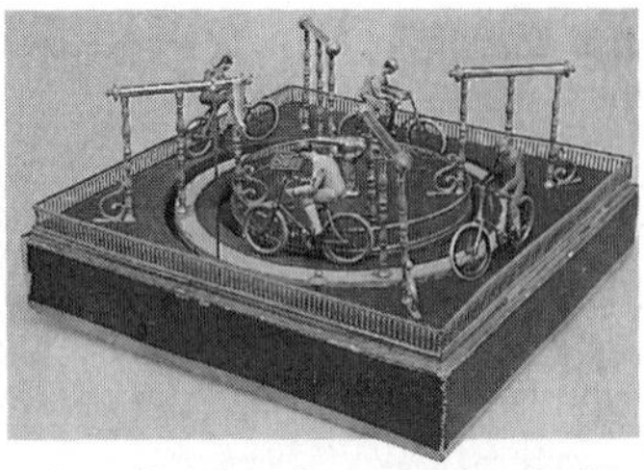

A cycling jeu de course, probably by Günthermann for the French market, mechanism operative, good condition, c1905, base 18in (46cm) wide.
£3,500–4,500 *S*

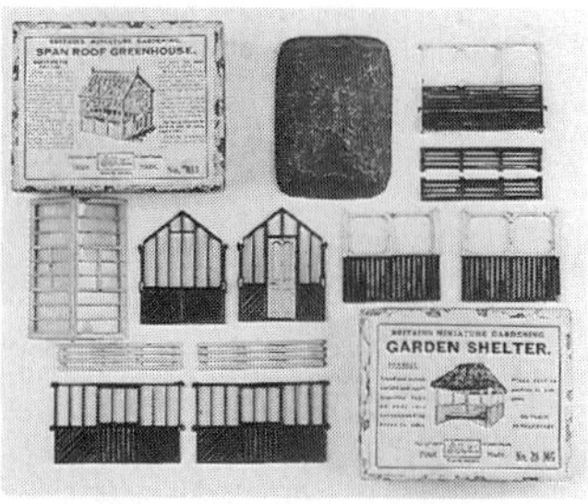

A Britains No. 053 Span Roof Greenhouse, and No. 28 MG Garden Shelter, in original white and gold patterned boxes, good condition.
£600–700 *CSK*

A Nomura battery operated Batman, in blue, pale blue and yellow, with walking movement, illuminating face and fabric cape, in original box, with Fairylight importer's mark to lid, good condition, 11½in (29cm) high.
£1,000–1,300 *CSK*

l. A Britains figure, 'Village Idiot', with green jacket, grey breeches, and carrying straw, 2½in (6cm) high.
£200–230 *S(S)*

A Britains Set 1392 Civilian Autogiro, finished in blue and white, and a pilot, c1935, good condition.
£1,000–1,500 *CSK*

A Spot-On/Rovex CS100 Captain Scarlet Escape and Capture Road Way, comprising: 2 red plastic battery operated spectrum patrol cars, card press-out Mysteron H. Q. buildings, brown plastic elastic band activated vehicle traps, original box, good condition, c1967.
£250–300 *CSK*

A Pelham Puppet Theatre, the electrically operated tableau including Rupert the Bear, the Wizard, Dick Whittington and his cat, Jolly Policeman and Andy Pandy, 1930s–60s.
£650–750 *Bon*

A Meccano No. 1 Motor Car Constructor outfit, comprising: a four-seater open tourer, with sports body, 2 doors, saloon roof, tonneau cover, spanner and instructions dated '12.35', in original box with white edging to label, good condition, c1935.
£300–350 *CSK*

A Lehmann Zig-Zag vehicle, the driving wheels supporting a gondola containing 2 figures, EPL No. 640, c1910, 5in (12.5cm) diam.
£500–700 *HSS*

A Britains model zoo, with animals, railings, etc., and a desert scene with Arabs, camels, and palm trees, approximately 100 pieces.
£150–200 *DN*

A painted wood Noah's Ark, with hinged lid opening to interior, and a collection of composition animals, late 19thC, 26in (66cm) long.
£700–800 *S*

JEWELLERY
Bracelets

A diamond, zircon, gold and enamel bracelet, signed 'C. G.', for Carlo Giuliano, c1875, 7¼in (18.5cm) long.
£4,500–5,000 *C*

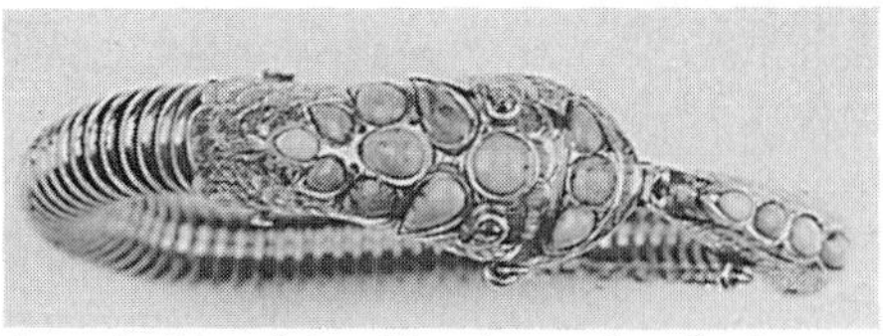

A snake bracelet, with a turquoise cluster head, diamond single stone eyes and a turquoise tail, 19thC.
£350–450 *CSK*

A diamond bracelet, with French gold marks, 1920s, 7¼in (18.5cm) long.
£8,000–9,000 *S*

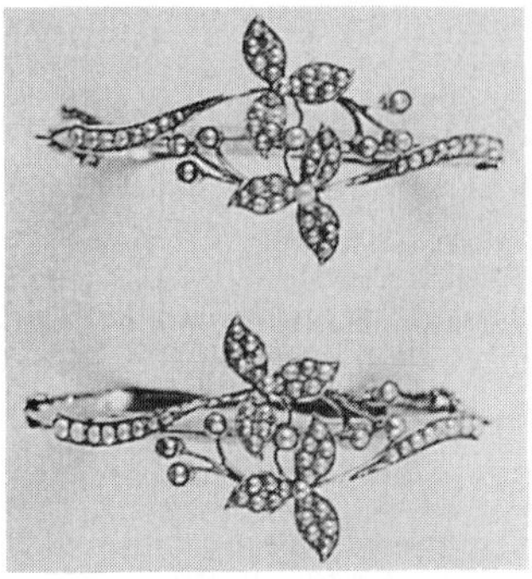

A Victorian diamond bracelet, stones c1880, with a later gate-link flexible bracelet.
£10,000–11,000 *C*

l. A pair of Edwardian hinged bangles, with applied half-pearl foliate crossover motif.
£700–900 *CSK*

A diamond bracelet, each link of swirl design set with baguette and brilliant cut diamonds, the largest brilliant cut collet-set at the centre, 1930s.
£13,000–17,000 *S*

A diamond bracelet, c1930.
£5,200–7,000 *S*

A Van Cleef & Arpels platinum fancy link bracelet, with 3 suspended charms, one stone missing.
£1,300–1,800 *CSK*

A diamond bracelet, designed as a line of foliate motifs set with brilliant cut diamonds, 1960s.
£3,300–4,000 *S*

An emerald and diamond bracelet, designed as a line of open links alternating with motifs, set with baguette and brilliant cut diamonds, decorated at intervals with calibré cut emeralds, c1930, 7½in (19cm) long.
£6,500–7,500 *S*

A Continental bracelet, with reeded links and 3 suspended charms, one pierced barrel foliate form with rectangular cut amethyst two-stone terminals, the other 2 of lantern design set with citrines and amethysts.
£1,000–1,200 *CSK*

r. A 9ct gold curb link charm bracelet, with 9ct gold charms, the fob and mask set with gems.
£550–750 *CSK*

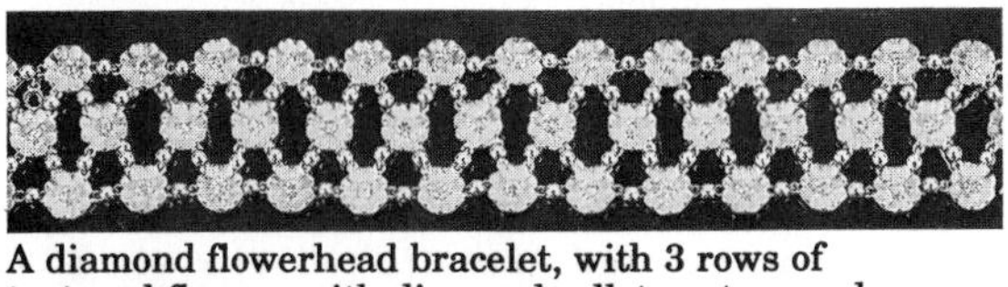

A diamond flowerhead bracelet, with 3 rows of textured flowers with diamond collet centres and beadwork spacers, 8in (20cm) long.
£2,000–2,500 *C*

A sapphire and diamond bracelet, the 5 cushion cut sapphire single stone links with rose diamond four-stone surround, connected by links, one stone missing.
£450–550 *CSK*

A coral bracelet, modelled as a mermaid, the carved figure terminal with graduated carved and wired tail.
£700–900 *CSK*

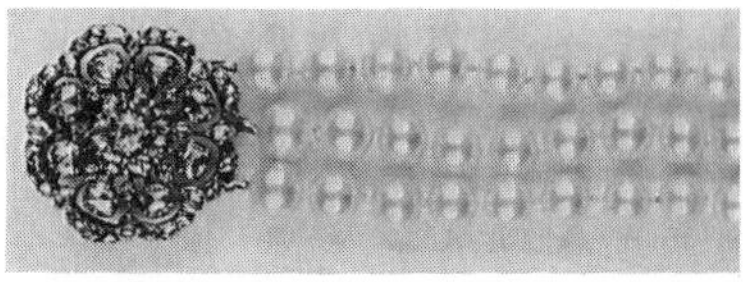

A rose diamond and cultured pearl bracelet, the pearls formed in 3 rows and attached to the diamond openwork flowerhead clasp.
£700–900 *CSK*

l. A Finnish 18ct gold bracelet, of nugget textured crystal form links, with import marks.
£600–700 *CSK*

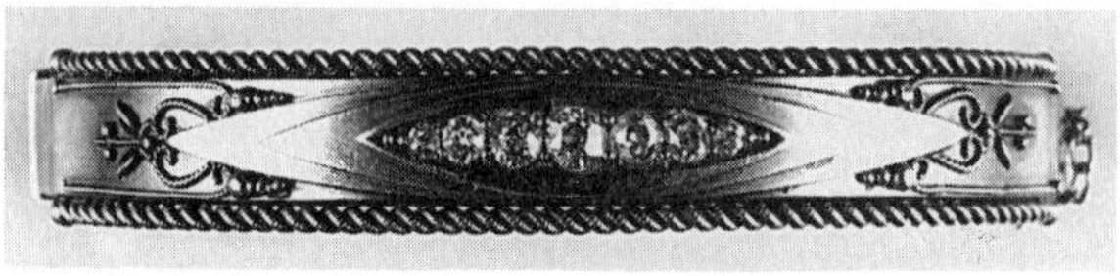

An Etruscan style hinged bangle, set with 7 brilliant cut diamonds in a boat-shaped setting, stamped '15ct'.
£650–750 *WL*

A bangle, of sculptured tubular form set with a line of diamonds.
£1,000–1,300 *CSK*

A Berlin ironwork bracelet, of pierced foliate design with central circular panel, and a composite simulated cameo bangle.
£300–400 *CSK*

A foiled gem bracelet, of two-colour engraved hinged panels, alternately set with a central foiled emerald or garnet, with engraved leaf surround forming a flowerhead motif.
£1,600–2,000 *CSK*

Brooches, Pins & Clips

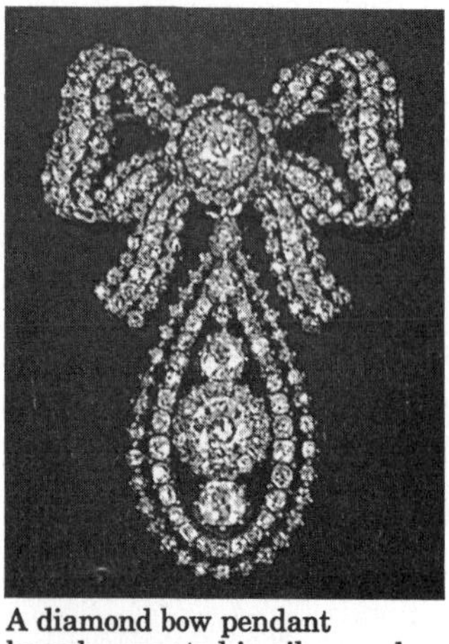

A diamond bow pendant brooch, mounted in silver and gold, c1830, 2½in (6cm) high, in later fitted leather case.
£7,000–8,000 *C*

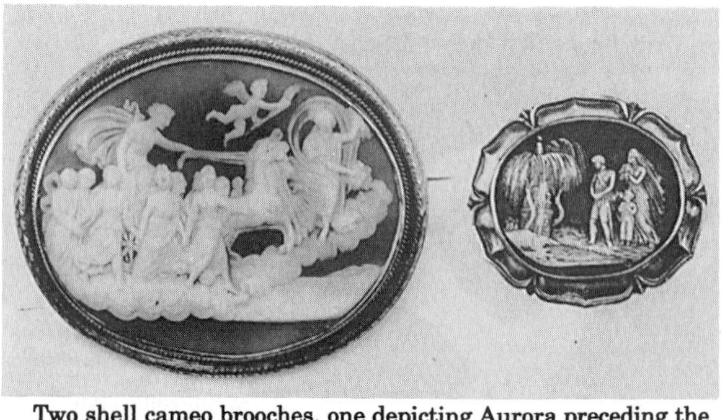

Two shell cameo brooches, one depicting Aurora preceding the chariot of Apollo, after Guido Reni, in a gold mount with engraved decoration, the other depicting mourners attending a sepulchral monument, the clasp mount converted to a brooch, with scalloped surround, 19thC.
£1,000–1,500 *CSK*

r. An emerald and diamond brooch, modelled as a floral bud, with central polished emerald, and rose diamond cluster decoration and stem, 19thC.
£1,500–2,000 *CSK*

l. A gold circular panel, with applied decoration in the form of a cherub among flowerheads, with ropework surround, mounted as a brooch, with later pendant loop, 19thC.
£350–450 *CSK*

An enamel, amethyst, ruby and diamond winged scarab brooch, late 19thC.
£1,300–1,700 *S*

A rose diamond brooch, modelled as a flying swallow, with rose diamond body, mounted on a bar with seed pearl terminal, late 19thC.
£300–400 *CSK*

A diamond and pearl pendant brooch, in a scroll pierced and floral design, the centre as a flowerhead, set with small cushion-shaped diamonds and pearls at intervals, late 19thC.
£850–1,100 *S(S)*

A Victorian gold brooch, with a single citrine in a scroll mount and suspending twin swags.
£420–500 *CSK*

A Victorian gold brooch, the locket back body with a scrollwork border and applied bird and flower centre, set with a rose diamond and gems.
£600–650 *CSK*

An Edwardian aquamarine brooch, with diamond four-stone points and diamond and rose diamond garland quatrefoil surround.
£1,000–1,200 *CSK*

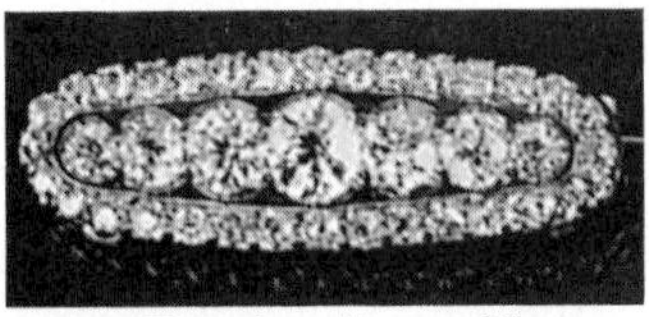

A late Victorian diamond bar brooch, c1890, 1½in (4cm) wide.
£3,000–3,500 *C*

A Victorian diamond cluster brooch, the gold and silver mounted cluster with diamond single-stone shoulders and detachable brooch mount.
£1,800–2,200 *CSK*

An Edwardian aquamarine brooch, with rose diamond and half-pearl double row surround.
£720–800 *CSK*

An opal and diamond brooch, shaped as a fuchsia, the rose cut diamond sepals and stamens to calibré cut opal and diamond petals, with opal and diamond stem and pavé set diamond leaf, mounted in silver and gold, c1890, 3in (8.5cm) wide.
£4,500–5,500 *C*

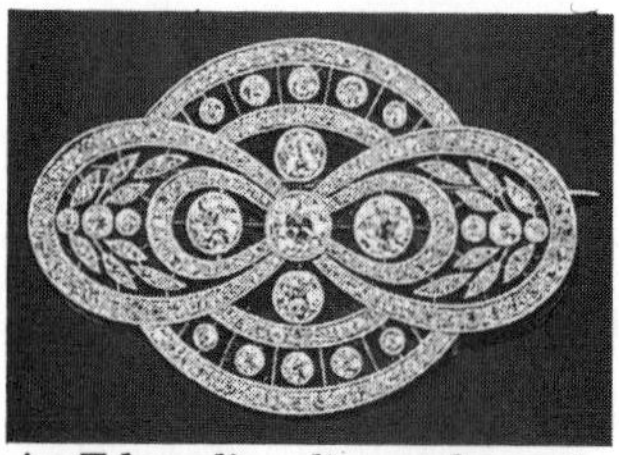

An Edwardian diamond panel brooch, c1905, 2½in (6cm) wide.
£6,000–7,000 *C*

A rose diamond bar brooch, of trelliswork design, with rose diamond surround and centre, backed with moiré ribbon, early 20thC.
£600–800 *CSK*

An Edwardian diamond and sapphire brooch, of openwork foliate cluster design, with sapphire cluster flowerheads and ribbon decoration, the mount engraved and dated '1907–1920.'
£500–600 *CSK*

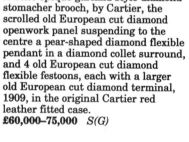

A belle époque garland style diamond stomacher brooch, by Cartier, the scrolled old European cut diamond openwork panel suspending to the centre a pear-shaped diamond flexible pendant in a diamond collet surround, and 4 old European cut diamond flexible festoons, each with a larger old European cut diamond terminal, 1909, in the original Cartier red leather fitted case.
£60,000–75,000 *S(G)*

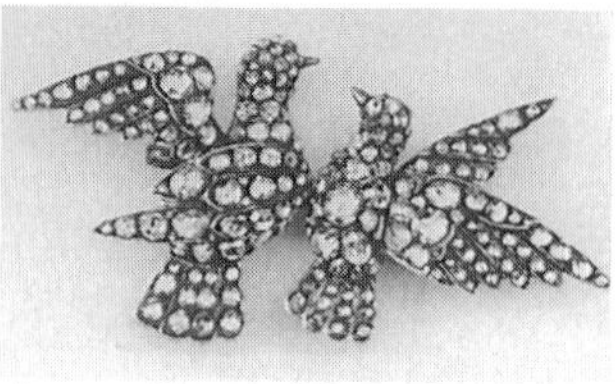

A rose diamond brooch, modelled as 2 birds in flight, with gem-set eyes.
£1,700–2,000 *CSK*

r. A ruby and diamond trefoil leaf brooch, each leaf with a cushion-shaped ruby cluster within a diamond border, c1935, 2in (5cm) wide.
£3,500–4,500 *C*

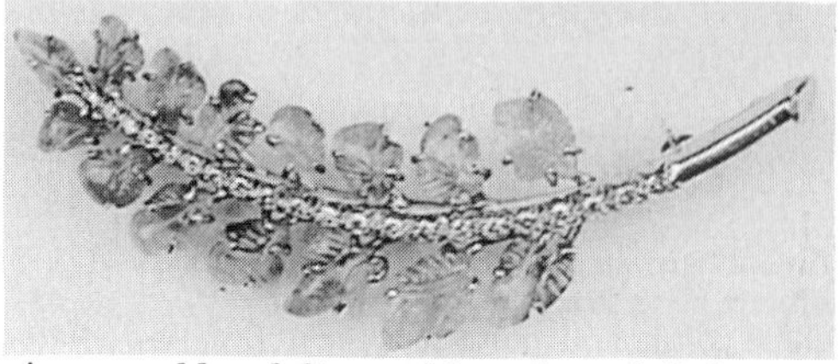

An emerald and diamond brooch, modelled as a leaf spray, the graduated diamond line stem with carved emerald leaves attached.
£500–600 *CSK*

A diamond and pearl brooch, the rose diamond triple line centre with applied half-pearl and blue enamel circle motif.
£700–800 *CSK*

A diamond cluster brooch, the oval openwork mount with central solitaire, diamond shoulders and rose diamond decoration.
£1,400–1,700 *CSK*

A diamond brooch, the centre set single stone in a textured and polished stylised star surround.
£600–700 *CSK*

A coral brooch, carved in Oriental style representing a stem of bamboo, with engraved bamboo flowerhead and butterfly border decoration.
£300–400 *CSK*

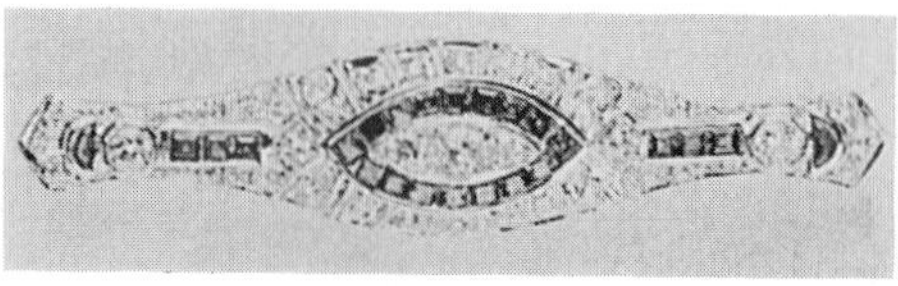

l. A diamond and calibré sapphire cluster brooch, with central diamond and calibré sapphire marquise cluster, tapering to diamond and lunette sapphire cluster terminals.
£1,400–1,900 *CSK*

A diamond cluster brooch, in a silver and gold claw-set mount.
£500–600 *CSK*

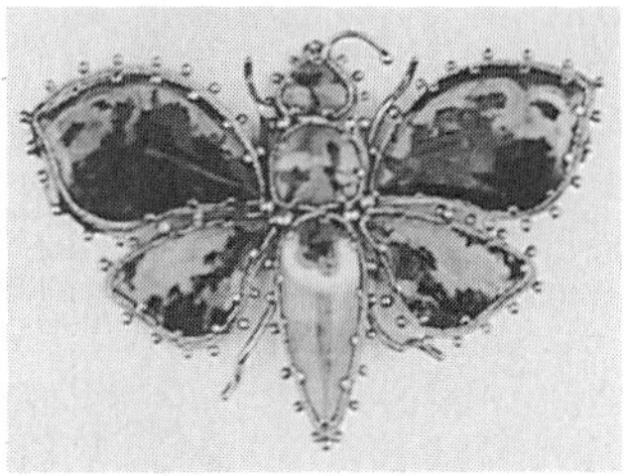

A butterfly brooch, the agate body and wings with gold beadwork mounts, pin and one antenna damaged.
£400–500 *CSK*

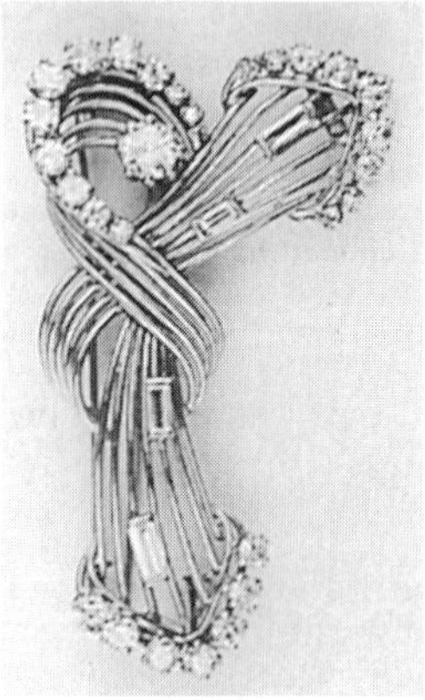

A diamond cluster brooch, of knotted wirework spray design, with diamond line terminals, baguette diamond four-stone decoration and central solitaire.
£900–1,000 *CSK*

A jewelled gold and enamel Egyptian revival brooch, with French control marks, c1870, 3in (7.5cm) wide.
£6,000–7,000 *C*

A gold locket brooch pendant, the border modelled as 3 entwined snakes, each suspending a charm representing faith, hope and charity.
£600–700 *CSK*

A ruby and diamond brooch, of cluster and circle design.
£650–750 *CSK*

A gem and diamond brooch pendant, the cut-cornered central emerald with diamond and rose diamond openwork scroll design surround, the ribbon bow surmount with untested pearl decoration.
£800–900 *CSK*

A gold and gem brooch, of quatrefoil openwork scroll and tendril design, with turquoise and rose diamond decoration, locket reverse and pendant loop, 19thC.
£350–450 *CSK*

A panel brooch, with a central green tourmaline and a diamond openwork border.
£700–800 *CSK*

A diamond and gem brooch, modelled as a vase of flowers, including a sapphire, emerald and ruby.
£720–800 *CSK*

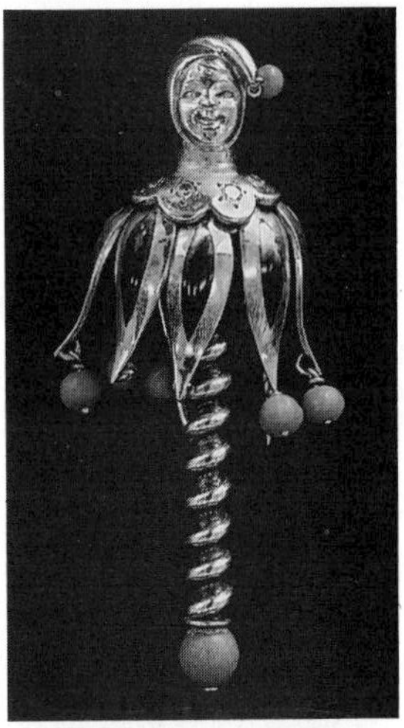

A Van Cleef & Arpels gold pin brooch, modelled as a jester's stick, decorated in coloured enamels, inset with small diamonds and hung with beads, signed and numbered '47652'.
£1,300–1,500 *HSS*

l. A diamond and pearl-mounted sard intaglio brooch, the intaglio c1800, 1½in (4cm) wide, with a fitted case.
£2,600–3,000 *C*

A tourmaline, emerald and diamond brooch, the carved pink tourmaline strawberry with pavé set emerald and diamond leaves, 2½in (6cm) wide.
£3,700–4,200 *C*

A diamond flower spray brooch, each of the 2 flowerheads with a solitaire diamond centre.
£700–800 *CSK*

A diamond double clip brooch, each of the 2 tapering clips set with 15 diamonds.
£1,300–1,700 *CSK*

A diamond brooch, of openwork foliate design, with diamond and rose diamond decoration.
£600–700 *CSK*

A three-colour diamond and cultured pearl brooch, with diamond leaf, cultured pearl flower and calibré synthetic ruby stem, maker's mark 'RHB.'
£500–600 *CSK*

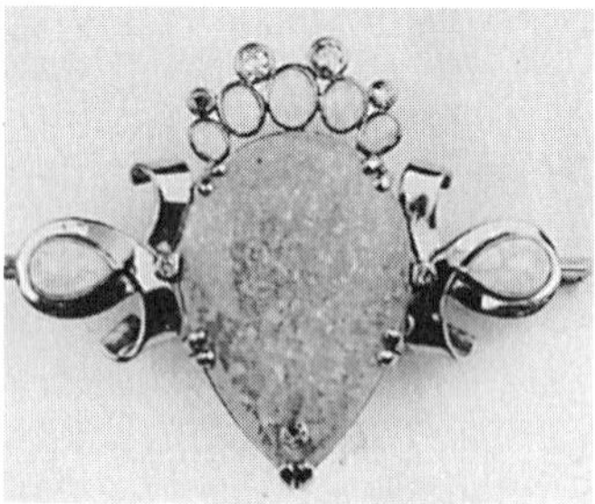

An opal and diamond cluster brooch, the central drop-shaped opal with diamond and opal cluster surmount, and drop-shaped opal and diamond two-stone shoulders.
£1,400–1,600 *CSK*

A Continental abstract loop design brooch, with randomly set diamond decoration.
£300–350 *CSK*

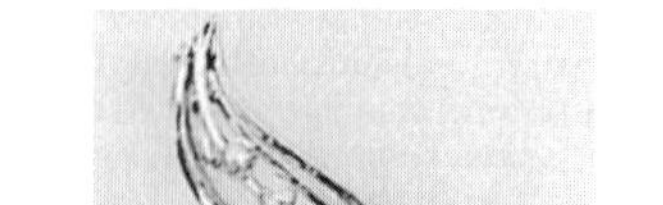

A quartz cat's-eye and diamond circular cluster knife edge bar brooch.
£420–470 *CSK*

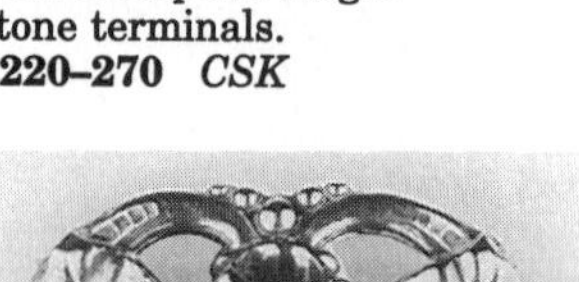

A sapphire and ruby, rose diamond cluster twin heart and ribbon bow bar brooch, with seed pearl single stone terminals.
£220–270 *CSK*

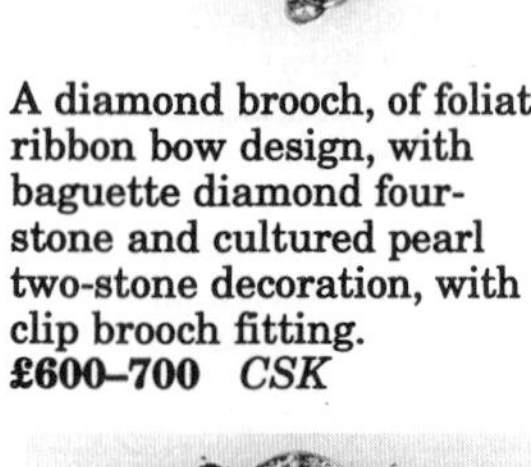

A diamond brooch, of foliate ribbon bow design, with baguette diamond four-stone and cultured pearl two-stone decoration, with clip brooch fitting.
£600–700 *CSK*

A diamond ribbon bow spray brooch.
£600–700 *CSK*

l. A panel brooch, of floral and foliate design, with green chrysoprase single-stone decoration, with matching drop.
£320–370 *CSK*

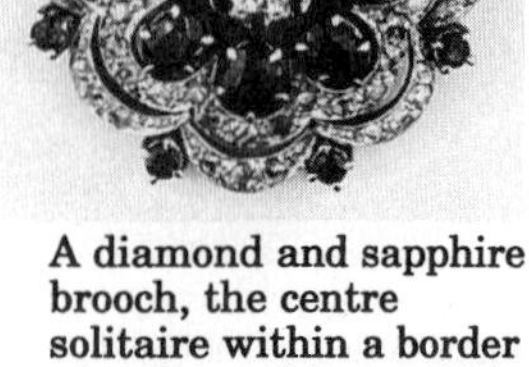

A diamond and sapphire brooch, the centre solitaire within a border of oval sapphires, with a rose diamond surround.
£1,000–1,200 *CSK*

A diamond clip brooch, modelled as a lily of the valley, the pavé set diamond leaves with bud and collet detail, 2½in (6.5cm) high.
£1,500–1,800 *C*

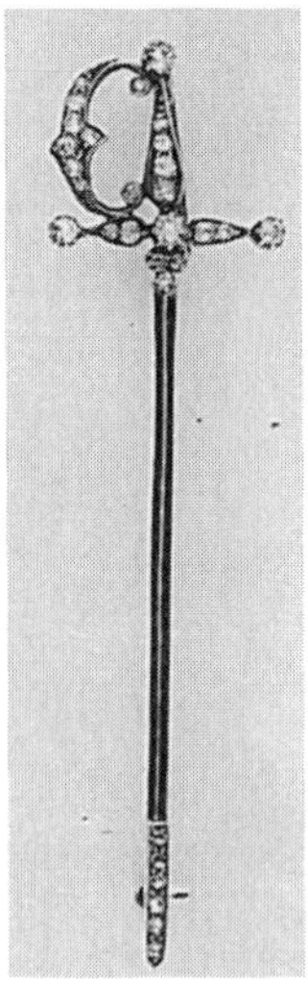

A diamond novelty brooch, modelled as a sword, with diamond hilt and rose diamond scabbard end.
£600–700 *CSK*

An emerald and diamond brooch, of textured and polished ribbon bow design, with drop cut diamond terminal.
£800–1,000 *CSK*

A diamond dress clip, set with brilliant cut, marquise, rectangular and keystone cut diamonds, one diamond missing.
£2,000–2,500 *CSK*

l. A portrait brooch, the oval porcelain plaque with the head and shoulders of a maiden in period dress, the frame with untested half-pearl surround.
£400–500 *CSK*

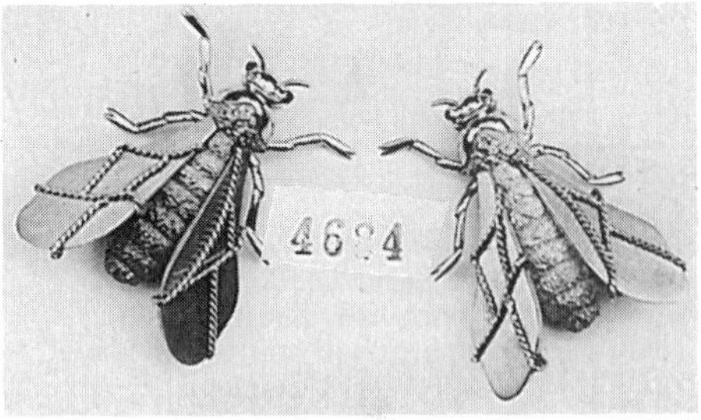

Two 18ct gold Chaumet brooches, modelled as a pair of bees, with gem-set eyes, signed on reverse.
£1,000–1,400 *CSK*

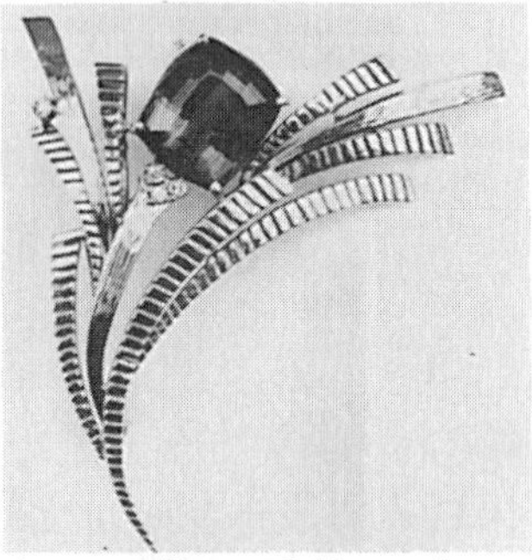

A tourmaline and diamond brooch, the mixed cut green tourmaline with four-stone diamond decoration, in a two-colour spray design mount.
£200–300 *CSK*

Cameos

A shell cameo, depicting the head and shoulders of the Greek gods Night and Day, in a gold brooch mount with engraved rope-twist surround, 19thC.
£1,200–1,700 *CSK*

A cornelian cameo, depicting a classical bearded male profile, in 19thC gold Etruscan style surround, with applied wire decoration, later pin hook.
£350–450 *CSK*

A coral cameo brooch, the coral carved as a classical female head, in a gold openwork shell and scroll mount.
£250–300 *CSK*

A shell cameo, depicting the profile of Psyche, in a gold brooch mount, with applied foliate and wire decoration, 19thC.
£900–1,000 *CSK*

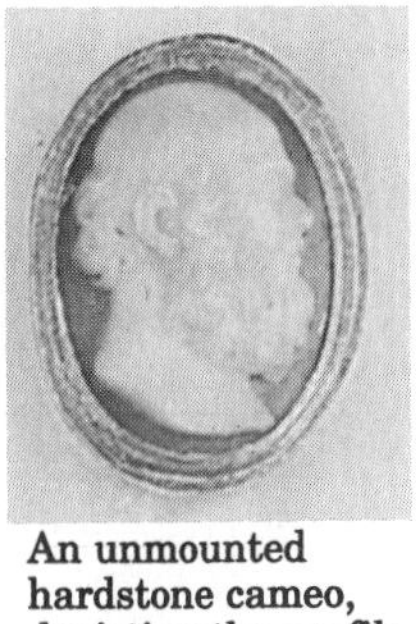

An unmounted hardstone cameo, depicting the profile of a classical bearded gentleman.
£370–400 *CSK*

An unmounted hardstone cameo, of a classical scene depicting Venus in a scallop shell carried by dolphins and surrounded by cupids.
£550–650 *CSK*

An unmounted onyx cameo, depicting a muse, possibly Euterpe with Cupid standing on a podium.
£500–600 *CSK*

A shell cameo, depicting a twin-faced male and female portrait in the classical style, with dog beneath symbolising fidelity, mounted as a clasp, with plain surround.
£450–550 *CSK*

Cuff Links

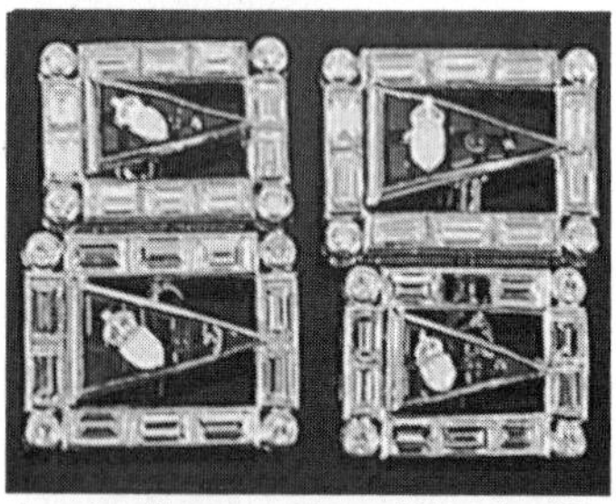

A pair of gem-set Royal London Yacht Club cuff links, each link designed as a calibré cut sapphire and enamel pennant to a baguette cut diamond, the frame with diamond collet corner detail, one diamond missing, c1930.
£4,000–5,000 *C*

A pair of Cartier cuff links, with ropework ends, the sprung bar with pyramidal sapphire terminals, signed 'Cartier Paris' and numbered.
£900–1,100 *CSK*

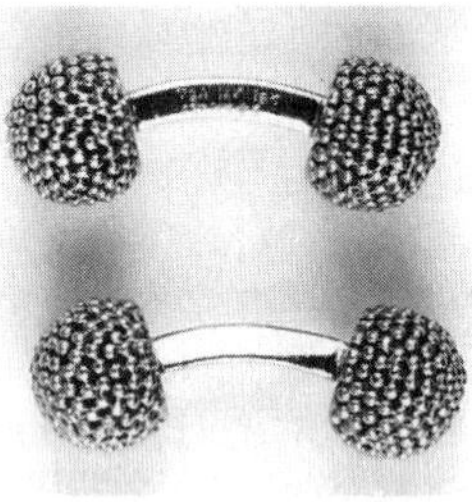

A pair of Van Cleef & Arpels cuff links, of domed beadwork curved dumbell design, signed 'VCA, NY', numbered.
£500–600 *CSK*

Earrings

A pair of ruby and diamond cluster earclips, each with 3 ruby and diamond flowerheads with diamond detail, and a three-row cultured pearl, ruby and diamond bracelet, 7in (17.5cm) long.
£2,500–3,000 *C*

A pair of Whitby jet earrings, c1860, 2in (5cm) high.
£125–175 *PHay*

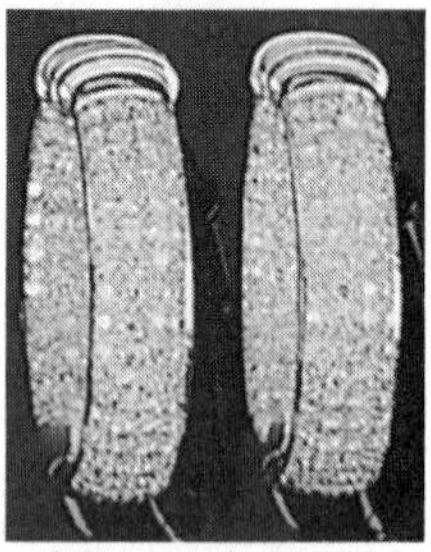

A pair of diamond earrings, one small diamond missing.
£2,200–2,700 *C*

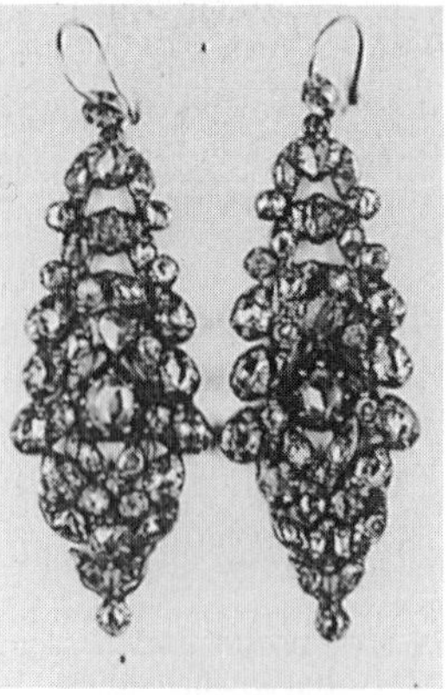

A pair of silver and foiled rose diamond openwork panel drop earrings.
£700–800 *CSK*

A pair of cut-cornered aquamarine single-stone drop earrings, to a diamond and oval aquamarine two-stone suspension.
£1,100–1,400 *CSK*

A pair of foiled rose diamond and lasque diamond panel drop earrings, in a later case.
£800–900 *CSK*

Fob Seals

A gold cased crystal seal, c1840, 1in (2.5cm) high.
£80–90 *PUR*

A gold and foiled amethyst seal, engraved with a snake, 1in (2.5cm) high.
£80–100 *PUR*

Six gold cased fob seals, suspended from a link bracelet, each fob with reeded, scroll or floral chased decoration, one with plain yellow glass matrix, the others of cornelian, each engraved with a crest, monogram or figure, one with a hinged hidden locket compartment.
£1,500–2,000 *CSK*

A fob seal, with citrine three-sided swivel and gold cased foliate scroll handle.
£400–450 *CSK*

Necklaces

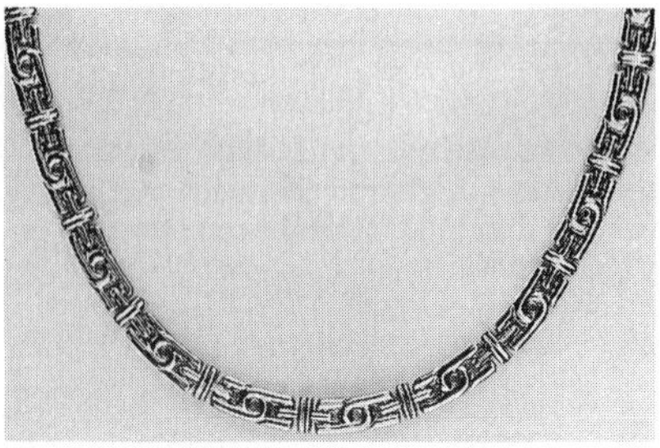

An 18ct gold necklace, the crossover design openwork links with white gold connections.
£600–700 *CSK*

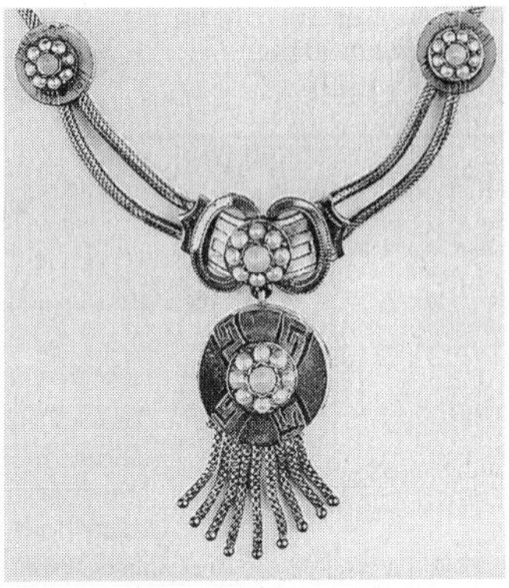

r. A gold and gem necklace, the locket drop with Greek key decoration and central turquoise and half pearl cluster, with chain and bead fringe, strapwork design suspension panel and snake link chain with circular cluster panel shoulders, 19thC.
£500–600 *CSK*

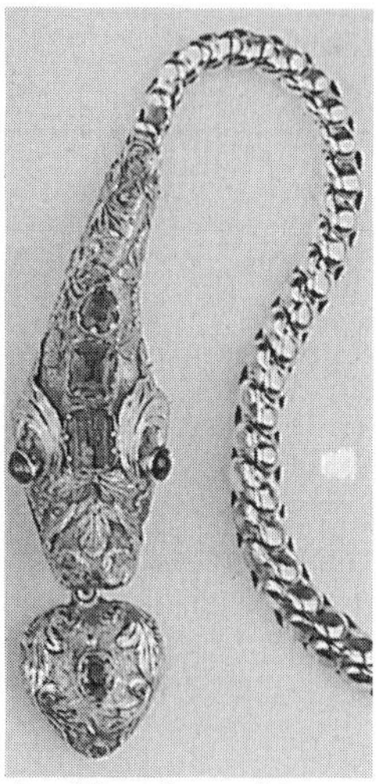

A gold snake necklace, the engraved three-colour gold head set with 3 foiled emeralds and gem-set eyes, suspending a matching heart-shaped locket drop with central foiled single emerald, in a fitted case, 19thC.
£1,700–2,000 *CSK*

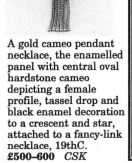

A gold cameo pendant necklace, the enamelled panel with central oval hardstone cameo depicting a female profile, tassel drop and black enamel decoration to a crescent and star, attached to a fancy-link necklace, 19thC.
£500–600 *CSK*

An Edwardian necklace, the centre peridot and half-pearl scrollwork panel, with matching drop and cluster shoulders, neck chain attached.
£1,100–1,400 *CSK*

An Edwardian necklace, the central diamond star and half-pearl crescent panel supporting a half-pearl multi-flowerhead cluster pendant, to a fringe and half-pearl line necklace, together with a half-pearl crescent brooch.
£1,000–1,500 *CSK*

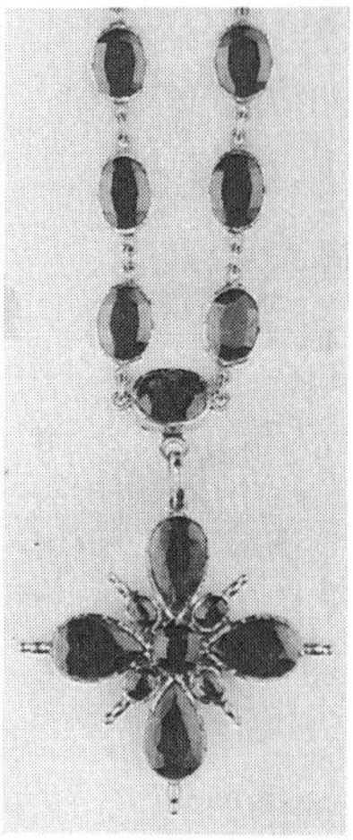

A garnet necklace, the oval foiled garnets with central quatrefoil foiled garnet pendant, together with a pair of Bohemian garnet cluster earstuds.
£600–700 *CSK*

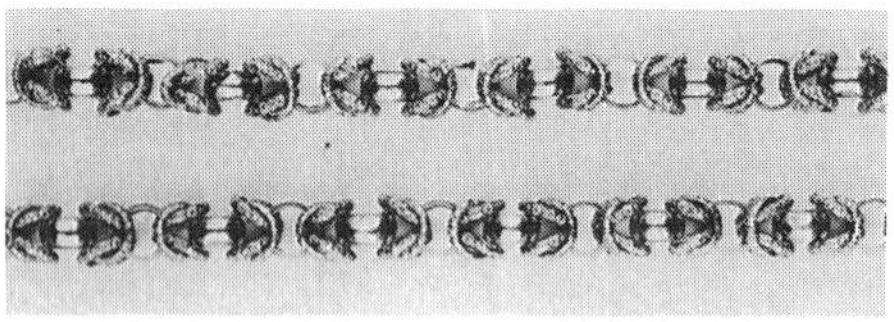

l. A gold necklace, of fancy engraved chain link design, 23½in (60cm) long.
£1,400–1,700 *CSK*

Pendants & Lockets

An emerald pendant necklace, the rectangular cut emerald with diamond articulated panel suspension to a platinum belcher-link neck chain, in a case.
£900–1,200 *CSK*

Jewellery

The value of jewellery depends on age and condition, the intrinsic value of the materials used and current fashions. Unique or hand made pieces generally fetch higher prices than mass-produced items. A famous owner can also increase the value of an item considerably.

A cultured pearl single row necklace, with ruby, sapphire and diamond flowerhead spacers, 13½in (34cm) long.
£1,300–1,600 *C*

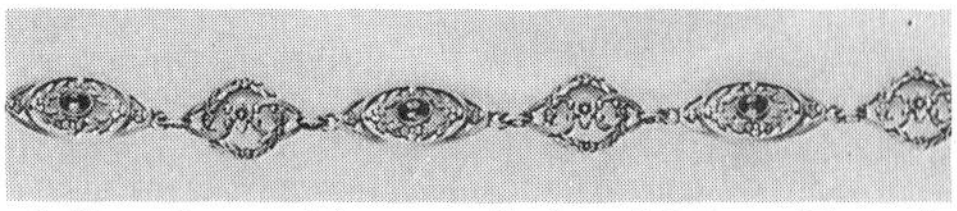

A French sapphire panelled necklace, with oval pierced foliate panels, alternately set with a single cabochon sapphire, with detachable clasp fitting for optional wear as a bracelet.
£1,700–2,000 *CSK*

An emerald and rose diamond cluster pendant, the central emerald with rose diamond foliate surround, diamond two-stone points, single diamond and untested pearl three-stone drop and diamond and ruby four-stone decoration, one stone missing, 19thC.
£900–1,100 *CSK*

A gold, diamond, untested pearl and grey pearl drop pendant, of openwork design, with green guilloche enamel leaf decoration and central untested pearl single-stone drop, late 19thC.
£1,400–1,700 *CSK*

Two cross pendants, each set in gold, the larger of bead and wirework design, with coral beadline centre, suspended from a ropework neck chain, the smaller of rubies and rose diamonds, 19thC.
£500–600 *CSK*

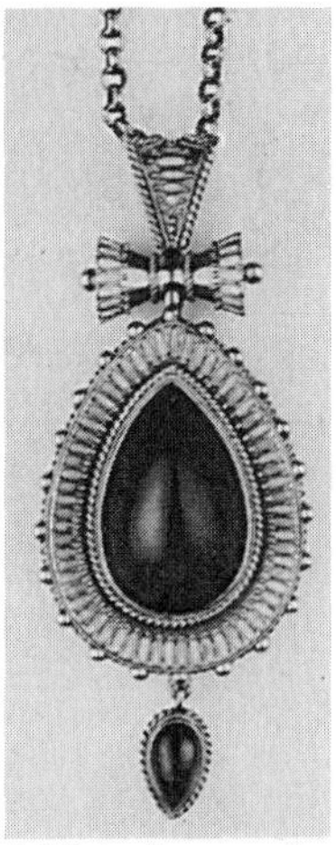

A Victorian pendant, the gold locket-back pear-shaped mount with central cabochon garnet and two-colour enamel dot surround suspending a pear-shaped foiled garnet single-stone drop to a stylised bow and loop suspension, with antique gold belcher-link neck chain attached.
£1,500–1,800 *CSK*

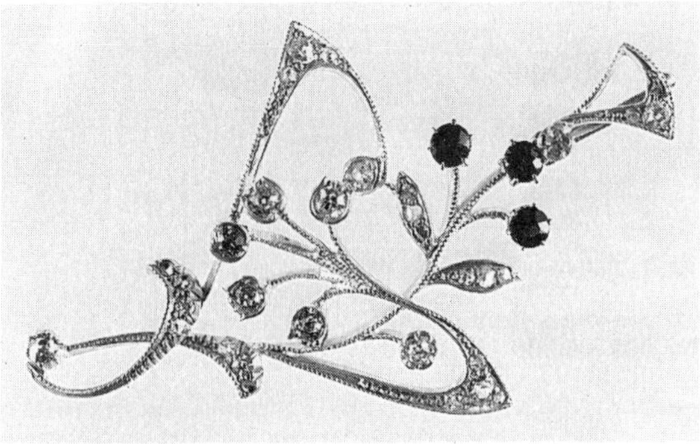

An Edwardian silver openwork pendant, set with sapphires and diamonds.
£370–400 *WL*

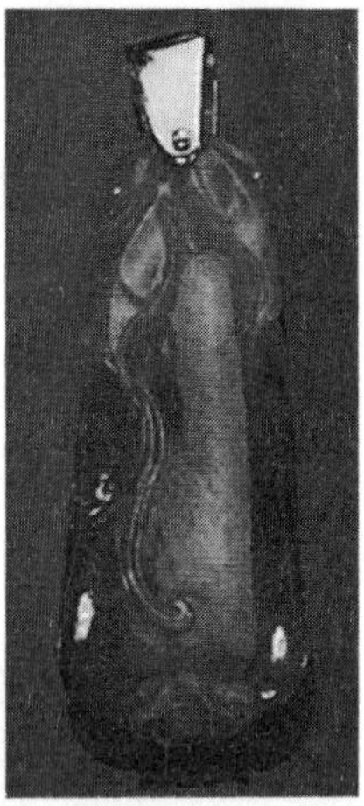

A carved jade pendant, with gold suspension loop.
£1,100–1,400 *S(S)*

An Austro-Hungarian pendant, the blister pearl centre with scroll and caryatid figures, and foiled sapphire two-stone decoration.
£300–400 *CSK*

A gold, enamel and baroque pearl pendant, in the neo-Renaissance style, the central panel comprising 2 pearls and red and white enamel flowerheads, supporting graduated foliate and pearl-set drops, surmounted by a seated cherub bearing a garland, with brooch fittings, in a case, 19thC.
£2,200–2,700 *CSK*

An Edwardian half-pearl brooch pendant, with ribbon bow top, latticework body and pearl drop.
£600–700 *CSK*

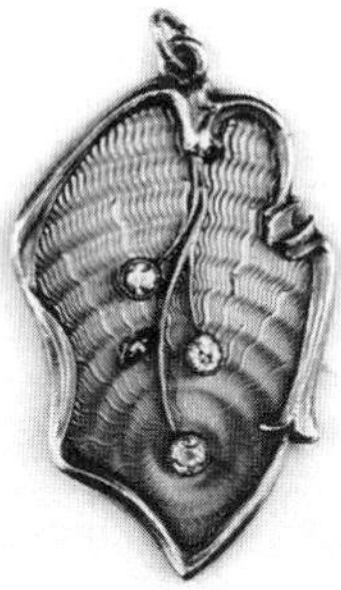

r. A Russian pendant, of free form shape, with diamond three-stone applied branch over a blue guilloche enamel ground, the reverse with maker's mark.
£550–650 *CSK*

Rings

A diamond and emerald set gold cluster ring, the central old cut brilliant diamond of .75ct, surrounded by 8 rectangular cut emeralds, 19thC.
£520–600 *MJB*

An amethyst and diamond cluster ring, the central square cut single amethyst with diamond set pierced stylised foliate shank.
£350–400 *CSK*

An 18ct gold marquise ring, set with sapphires and old cut diamonds, hallmarked '1833'.
£420–500 *WL*

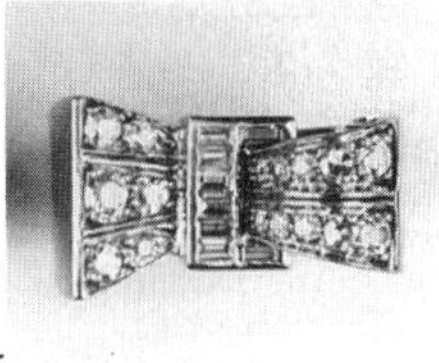

r. A diamond cluster ring, of stylised bow design, with baguette diamond crossband, 1940s.
£800–1,000 *CSK*

A diamond five-stone coiled serpent ring, the 18ct gold shank hallmarked 'London 1911'.
£720–800 *CSK*

A three-stone diamond ring, colour E, clarity V52.
£23,000–25,000 *PC*

A diamond ring, of marquise cluster design.
£420–600 *CSK*

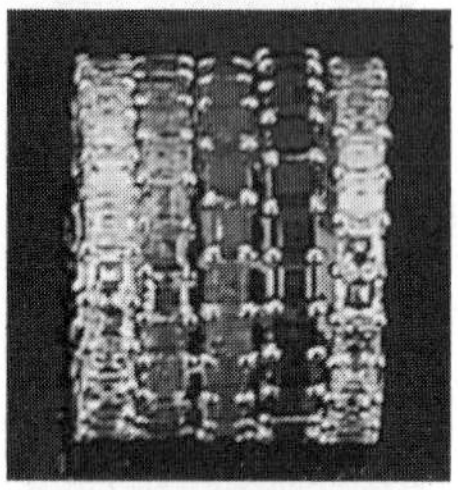

A group of 5 eternity rings, comprising 2 square cut diamond, a calibré cut sapphire, an emerald and a ruby ring, all with French assay marks.
£5,600–6,000 *C*

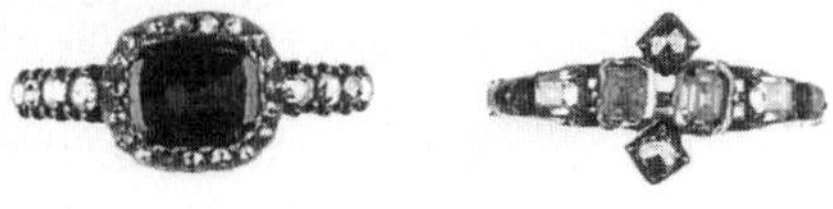

Two antique diamond and foiled gem rings, one of garnet and rose diamond cluster, with rose diamond four-stone shoulders, the other of gem, rose diamond and table cut diamond openwork cluster design.
£720–800 *CSK*

A diamond ring, the front bombé section composed of alternate rows of pink diamonds and diamonds to the graduated loop.
£3,700–4,000 *C*

r. A diamond and gem triple eternity ring, the centre ring set with calibré sapphires and rubies with twin swing-over arms.
£850–900 *CSK*

l. A ruby and diamond ring, of half-hoop design, the central oval ruby bordered by a double-row of 6 square cut diamonds, the gallery with diamond line decoration.
£900–1,200 *CSK*

A pink tourmaline single-stone ring, the cabochon tourmaline with diamond surround, with wirework decoration and shank.
£600–700 *CSK*

A diamond and green tourmaline ring, the central oval tourmaline with diamond two-row surround.
£650–700 *CSK*

A square cut and baguette diamond ring, of triple-row band design.
£1,200–1,500 *CSK*

An emerald and diamond ring, the square cut emerald within a baguette diamond ballerina setting.
£1,200–1,500 *CSK*

Miscellaneous

A suite of paste jewellery, comprising an antique gilt mounted blue foiled paste uniform panel necklace, with pear-shaped drop, together with a pair of gilt mounted foiled blue paste drop earrings.
£900–1,100 *CSK*

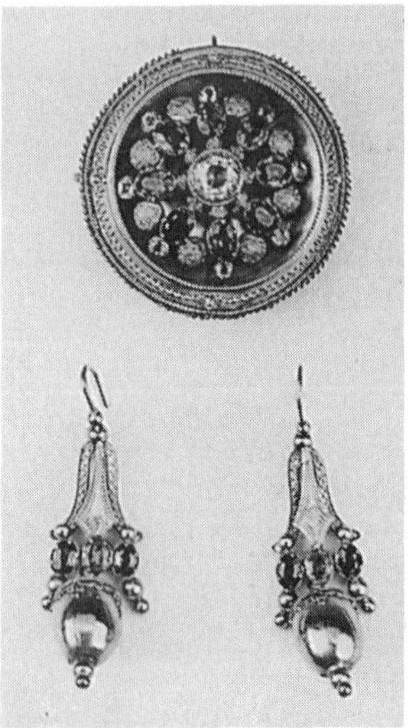

A Victorian gold and gem demi-parure, comprising a locket brooch, with foiled garnet and gem circular central cluster, together with a pair of matching stylised amphora drop earrings.
£700–800 *CSK*

ARMS, ARMOUR & MILITARIA

The state of the market for Arms and Militaria is in the main quite healthy, due primarily to the fact that it is not subject to the vagaries of fashion which affect other fields of collecting. Arms and Militaria have gone along at a steady pace over the years and even during the recession demand remained constant. Lately, however, due to the growing number of collectors, auction houses and dealers are experiencing a shortage of items.

ARMOUR

One cannot give comparisons of 16thC European Armour because very little appears on the market, and most items which have survived can be found in museums, castles or stately homes. Fortunately, from the 17thC, there is a modest supply of helmets, breast and back plates of the English Civil War period (1642–1651). The English lobster tailed helmet with single adjustable nasal bar has a single remedial ridge across the top from front to back, whereas the Dutch examples, which were imported here at the time, have crowns made with raised ribs, rather like a hot cross bun. Scarcer items are the three barred faceguard helmets, which can be lifted like a visor. Breast and back plates, if complete with shoulder straps and in good condition, usually realise the same price as helmets at auction. Breast plates often bear a musket ball test mark, some very heavily indented, which must have given the wearer some confidence, although the back plates were quite thin by comparison – one way to keep your troops facing the enemy!

Eastern Armour can still be bought at fairly reasonable prices, although I do believe it is only a question of time before we see values rise in this field of collecting as interest in Islamic Armour and Weapons is most certainly on the increase. The best representation of Indo-Persian armour a collector can buy is a garniture of khula khud (helmet), dhal (shield) and bazu band (arm guard). These sets, if matching in design, are going to be an investment bought at today's prices.

MILITARIA

Militaria items cover a large field. Some collectors embrace all facets but to do justice to any section, specialisation is necessary. The main collecting areas are headdress, uniforms, badges and printed ephemera such as postcards, diaries, photographs and documents.

Military headdress, in its grander sense, stops at 1914 for, after the WWI it was decided by the War Office not to put the army back into blue cloth helmets and scarlet although, fortunately, we can still appreciate the regimental bands in ceremonial dress. During the 19thC many obsolete helmets, busbies and shakos were ruined through being used by Victorian families in charades on festive occasions. The original tin cases in which headdress are housed have often been their saviour in keeping the headdress protected from damage while in storage. Rare and early examples are always sought after and headdress with good provenance of its original owner will have added value.

Uniform of the late 19th/early 20thC is still fairly easy to obtain through auction houses and dealers. With a modest £100 and some careful buying, one can still make the odd purchase of scarlet tunics, though Officers' patterns of regular regiments, in good condition, are now selling for £300–£400. The great enemy to preservation of uniform is the moth and a collector is fortunate indeed to acquire, for example, a mid-19thC coatee without some moth holes or traces of moth. However high your standards, you have to come to terms with the fact that if a uniform is to be included in your collection then a degree of moth damage must be accepted.

Badge collecting covers a broad field: cap, collar, shoulder belt and pouch badges. Some collectors collect by regiment and embrace all types of badges from the foundation of the regiment to the present day, others will adopt a period, say the numbered Glengarry badges (1875–1881) or Officers' blue cloth helmet badges. Officers' shoulder belt plates, worn until 1855 (with the exception of the Scottish regiments which continued until 1914) are another well collected area.

Probably the most active section is, of course, cap badge collecting. This is a strong area which, unfortunately, has been spoilt by reproductions entering the market. By virtue of the fact that they are made of brass and white metal, cap badges are easy to reproduce and when distressed can give the appearance of being old. Although there are many dealers who sell them as gap fillers at £1.50 each, beware that they are not being offered as originals. The nucleus of an original collection can average around £12–15 per badge, but some cap badges can realise £100–300 each, so remember to take advice when large sums of money are being asked. Collectors are strongly advised to buy only at specialist auction houses and from reputable dealers.

Military diaries and documents can be a good source for information, helping to increase a collector's knowledge and enthusiasm, but will command prices according to their importance so no yardstick can apply here. Military postcards, by the military artist Harry Payne, are the most sought after and fetch around £3–5 each. Showing great uniform detail, they were printed by Tuck's prior to WWI and sold in barrack shops. The messages on the reverse side are amusing at times and mostly they bear a green halfpenny Edward VII postage stamp.

FIREARMS

Antique firearms, both civil and military, fall into two categories, flintlock and percussion. Civilian weapons under their main types are: duelling, target, holster, coaching, travelling and pocket pistols. Cased duelling pistols have a fascination for most collectors and prominent makers that come to mind are Manton, Egg and Wogden, although there were many others. Many holster pistols were bought by serving officers as private purchases and were worn in a pair of leather holsters across the neck of the horse. Coaching and travelling pistols are self-explanatory. The accepted definition for the coaching type are the Queen Anne style cannon barrelled pistols with grotesque mask butts. Although this type continued well outside the reign of Queen Anne, almost to the 19thC, they were considered classics, hence their popular appeal. Pocket pistols were sold for personal protection, possibly when making a long journey carrying important or valuable items, or as bedside protectors. Pistols were, in the main, always made in pairs except for military pistols which were made to a pattern and therefore two military pistols are always referred to as a brace of pistols.

The popular collecting period for military flintlock pistols is, of course, the Napoleonic Wars. During the 18thC, military flintlock holster pistols were long and graceful, often bearing the maker's name, such as Grice or Jordan, on the tail of the lockplate. The New Land pattern flintlock holster pistol of 1796 saw service throughout the wars until 1815. The Light Cavalry also carried the Elliott flintlock carbine and later the Jacob pattern.

The longest history for any soldiers' musket must be the famous 'Brown Bess', which entered into Army Service during the reign of Queen Anne (1702–1714), and finally discontinued in 1840. This was a fairly heavy musket with a 46in length barrel which was reduced to 42in by the time of the American Revolution as the weapon had become too cumbersome for the mode of fighting. Its final length was 39in and was used throughout the Napoleonic Wars. Collectors with a Battle of Waterloo interest wanting a Brown Bess should not refuse an India pattern if offered, as this pattern was the one used at Waterloo.

Bear in mind that very fine specimens can fetch much higher prices, especially in the case of civil weapons, when value depends on quality and refinement.

EDGED WEAPONS

Edged weapons, European and Eastern, are fairly plentiful and supply and demand are pretty well balanced. Military swords have a good following for they can be collected by pattern dates. Throughout the 19thC there were a series of patterns issued: 1821, 1853, 1864, 1885 and 1896 to name a few. It is the Napoleonic period that is most sought after. The 1796 heavy and light cavalry patterns can be purchased for about £200–400, while Officers' 1796 pattern swords with mercuric gilt and blue blades reach about £1,500–2,000, if in fine condition. Presentation swords, for swordsmanship and for Officers leaving the regiment, can be purchased at auction from about £300, although Lloyds Patriotic Fund swords, presented mostly to Naval Officers for their valour during the Napoleonic Wars, can realise from £10,000–20,000 each.

Eastern swords are still quite reasonably priced. Indian tulwars from the Indian Mutiny period can be bought for as little as £30–40, although fine specimens inlaid with gold and silver workmanship are worth a great deal more. More expensive are the Turkish and Indian mameluke patterns which realise £300–600. During the Egyptian War, later in the last century, the Dervishes carried a sword called a kaskara which were brought back by serving soldiers and can be found regularly in specialised auction houses for £50–200, or more, depending on quality.

European daggers are not so frequently found as they are more a weapon used by Eastern warriors. Italian gunners in the 17thC carried a stiletto and often the blades were marked with bore measurements. The other notable use of daggers in Europe were, of course, those worn by the Third Reich from 1933–1945. There are many in England which were brought back in kit bags after the war and prices range from £150–3,000. The most common are those used by the Navy, Army and Air Force. Those which command higher prices were issued to more obscure units or departments – waterways police, diplomats, customs and technical emergency corps.

The most common Eastern dagger is the jambiya, found in various shapes and sizes and used by Arab countries throughout the Mediterranean and the Red Sea. The average price for a common type is as little as £30 but the lavish silver overlaid Arab jambiyas sell at auction for £700–1,000. Many are bought by Arabs or their agents to be returned to the Middle East. Whilst touching on this fact, it is becoming a strong trend these days for antique arms and armour to be returned to their country of origin.

Britain during the 19thC and into the 20thC had a repository of arms and armour from countries all-over the world. Regiments returning from wars in Africa, India and the Far East brought back every kind of weapon and defensive armours as trophies, but it was the soldiers themselves who brought back the vast amount of weapons that can still be found here.

It has been said that there are more Gurkha kukries in England than there are in Nepal. Despite this the budding collector should be aware of modern copies coming from India as well as modern reproductions of arms, firearms, swords and bayonets, from European firms. Buy only from specialised auction houses and reputable dealers. All prices quoted here are for guidance only – there are always exceptions to the rule.

Roy Butler

ARMS & ARMOUR
Armour

A German composite suit of armour, some repairs, restoration and patination, late 16thC.
£9,000–11,000 *S(S)*

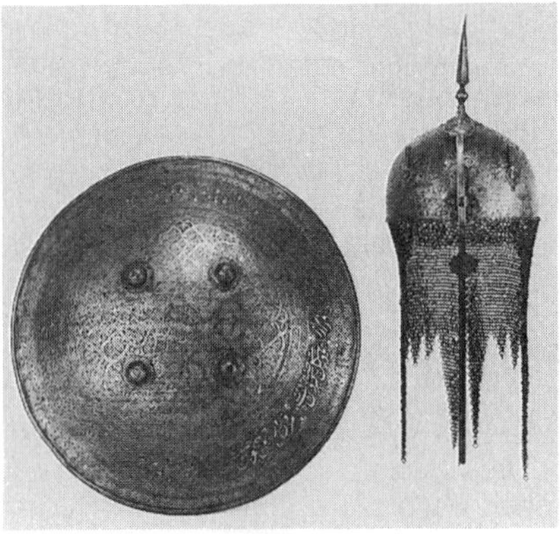

A dhal and khula khud, the helmet fitted with nasal, 2 plume holders and patterned vandyked camail of iron and brass butted rings, 19thC, 18½in (47cm) diam.
£1,500–2,000 *S(NY)*

A late 16thC style full suit of armour, on a wooden stand with base, together with a sword.
£3,500–4,000 *S(NY)*

A German composite fluted full suit of armour, restorations and replacements, 16thC, on a wooden stand, together with a 16thC style sword.
£7,000–8,000 *S(NY)*

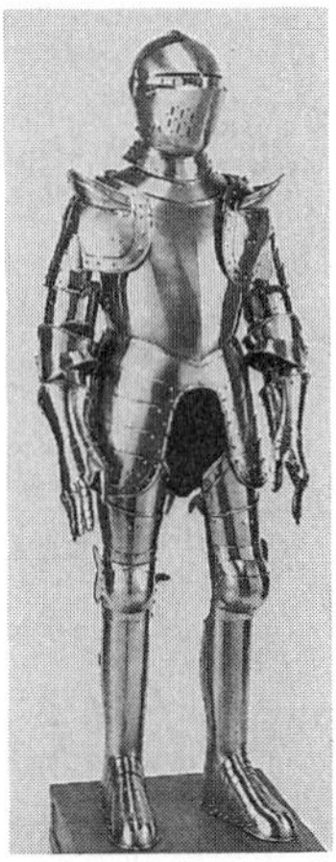

A mid-16thC style full suit of armour, of bright steel, in excellent condition throughout, on an articulated wooden stand with base.
£10,000–11,000 *S(NY)*

A burgonet, the one-piece steel skull with raised roped comb, the peak and neck guard with roped edges, the hinged ear flaps embossed with a star motif, lacquered overall, c1600.
£850–1,000 *P*

A silver painted 'monkey faced' close helmet, the one-piece, steel skull with twin roped combs, part fluted visor, and roped lower edge, 19thC.
£1,600–1,800 *P*

A cuirassier's helmet, the two-piece skull with fluted decoration, the hinged visor with a peak, the bevor pierced with vertical ventilation slots, early 17thC.
£1,200–1,700 *P*

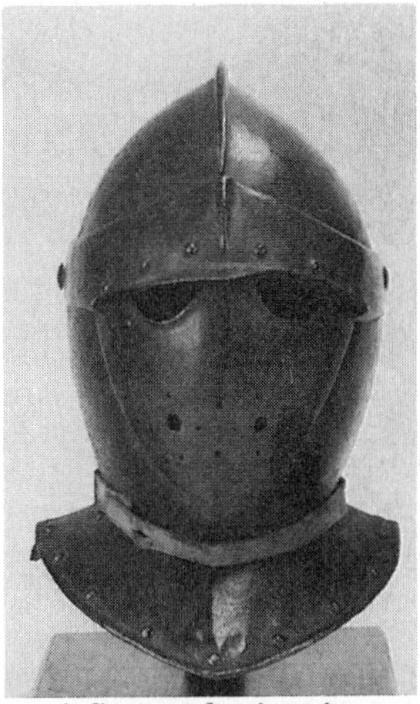

A Savoyard cuirassier blackened steel helmet, c1630, 12in (30.5cm) high.
£3,800–4,200 *S(NY)*

An etched and gilt 'Spanish' morion, north Italian, c1600, later gilding, 7½in (19cm) high.
£2,000–2,500 *S(NY)*

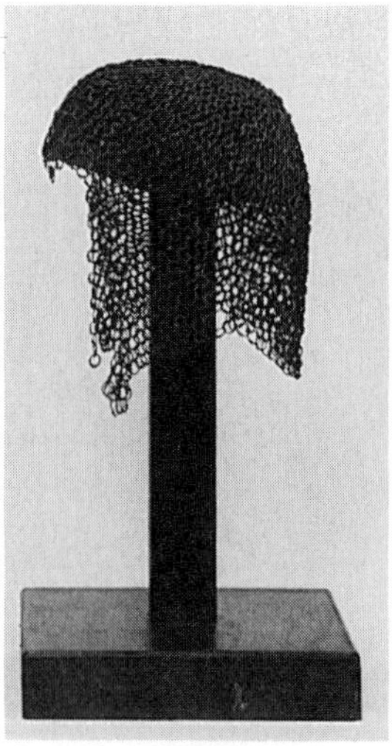

A mail coif, formed of rounded riveted iron rings, radiating from a single ring at the apex, the sides extending to long triangular points, extended at the rear as a short neck defence, some rings missing, 15thC, on a later steel pate plate of shaped profile.
£2,000–2,500 *S(NY)*

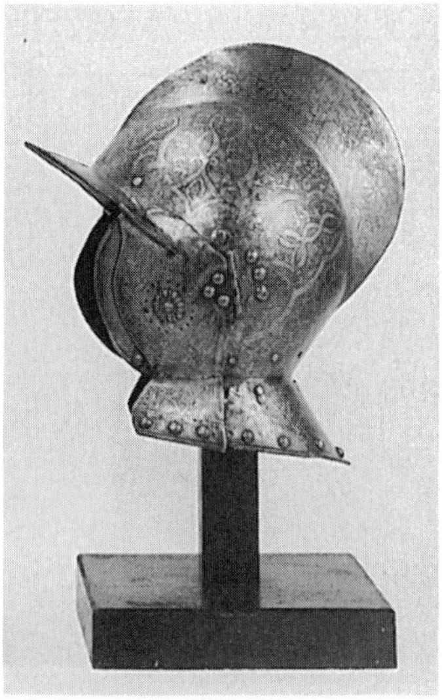

A German burgonet, restored, late 16thC, the etched decoration 19thC, 12in (30.5cm) high.
£2,500–3,000 *S(NY)*

A mail shirt, made of riveted iron rings of rounded section, hip length, with elbow length sleeves, and opening at the front of the neck, c1600, 26in (66cm) long.
£1,000–1,500 *S(NY)*

r. A Victorian cast iron shield, of dished form, with cast decorations of battle scenes, a central spike, and a cast iron gorget.
£300–350 *S(S)*

An Italian late 16thC style iron parade shield, 22in (55.5cm) diam.
£1,800–2,200 *S(NY)*

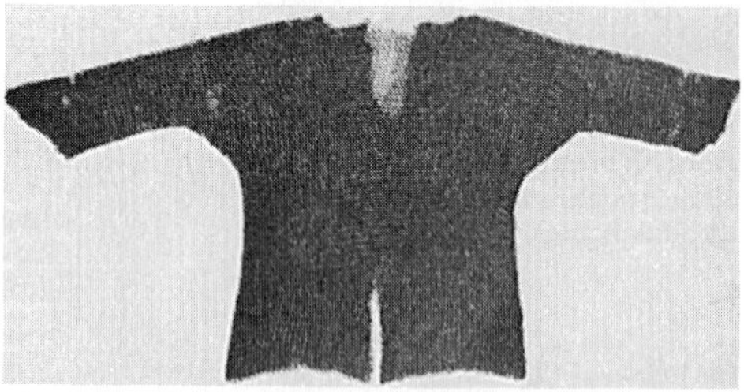

A mail shirt, formed of rows of rounded riveted oval rings alternating with rows of rounded butted circular rings, formed with elbow length sleeves, and V-shaped openings at the neck and at the front and rear vents, c1600.
£1,600–2,000 *S(NY)*

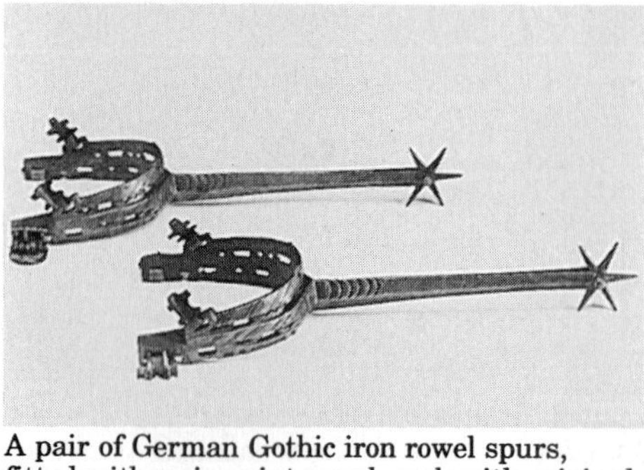

A pair of German Gothic iron rowel spurs, fitted with a six-point rowel, each with original hooks and buckles, some missing, late 15thC, 10½in (26.5cm) long.
£4,800–5,200 *S(NY)*

A pair of iron parade stirrups, Hungarian or Transylvanian, fitted with iron loops for suspension, the sides decorated with gilt copper filigree flowering vines set with shaped alloy plaques, all overlaid on a gilt metal ground, 18thC, 6in (15cm) high.
£1,000–1,500 *S(NY)*

Headdress

A Bavarian Landwehr Officer's pickelhaube, the leather skull with gilt fittings including a tall fluted spike, leather backed chin scales, a brass and white metal plate, silk and leather liner, in its original fibre storage case.
£500–700 *P*

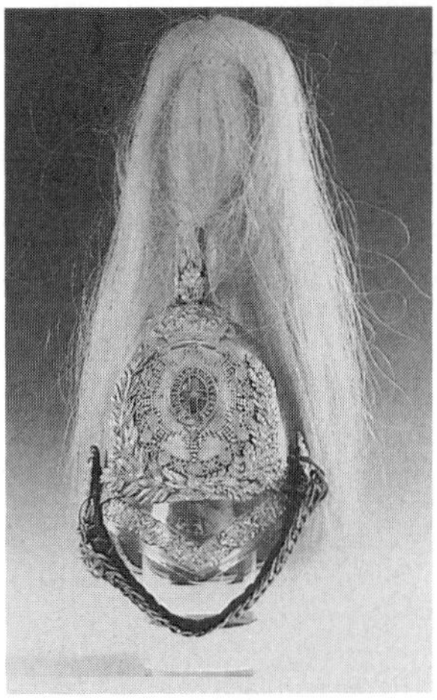

A Victorian 1842 pattern Lifeguards Officer's helmet, with a white metal skull, gilded and silvered helmet plate with enamelled centre, gilded plume holder with white horsehair plume, with chin chain and lining, slight damage.
£1,300–1,700 *S(S)*

A Georgian Officer's 1817 pattern helmet of the Household Cavalry, with a silver plated skull and high comb, copper gilt acanthus foliage, edging, leather backed ornamental chin scales and ear rosettes, rayed helmet plate bearing Royal Arms and motto on Prince of Wales' feathers, with battle honours 'Peninsula' and 'Waterloo', black bearskin crest, some wear, in original shaped case.
£2,000–2,500 *WAL*

l. A Victorian Officer's 1869 pattern shako, with a silvered and gilded badge with 'VR' in the centre surrounded by a garter bearing a motto, on a red and blue enamel ground surmounted by a crown, eight-pointed star backing, black felt skull with bullion lace bands, red and white ball gilded chin chain leather and velvet lining.
£600–700 *S(S)*

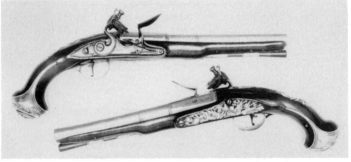

A Royal Engineers Volunteers Officer's blue cloth spiked helmet, supplied by Stemson & Son, Exeter, with silver plated mounts, rosettes and velvet backed chin strap.
£320–400 *Bea*

A fireman's brass Merryweather pattern helmet, slight damage.
£350–450 *Bea*

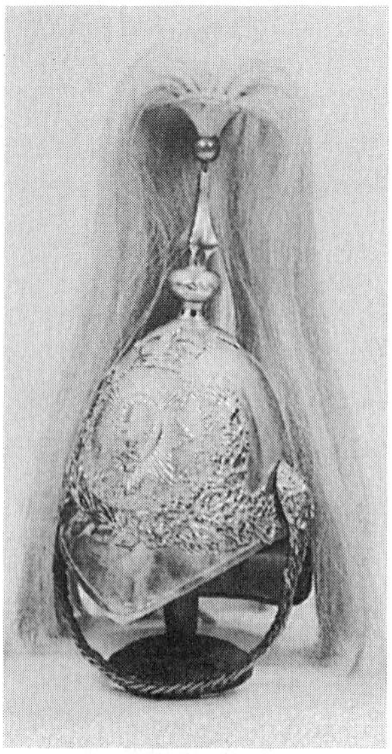

A Lifeguards Trooper's helmet, the plated skull with a brass plate applied with a garter star, brass trim including rosette bosses, a leather backed chin chain, white horsehair plume, leather liner.
£750–900 *P*

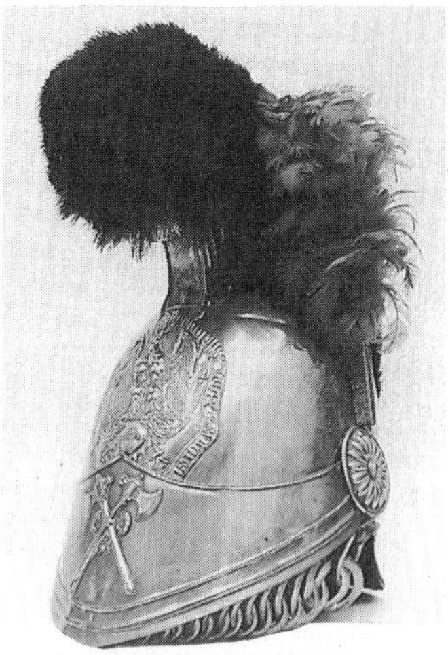

A French fire chief's brass helmet, with black horsehair plume, red feather hackle, the helmet plate with a French eagle clutching a torch, the scroll surround inscribed 'Sapeurs Pompiers Lucy Lebois', the hinged front copper visor with applied device of crossed brass axes, velvet lined large chin chains, slight damage.
£300–350 *WAL*

Uniform

r. An Other Rank's dress uniform of The Royal Wiltshire Yeomanry, comprising: a blue tunic with scarlet facings, white cord trim including 5 loops to chest, silver plated ball buttons, busby of NCO's quality, scarlet bag with braid trim and button, white triple cord and rosette, cloth backed beaded link silver plated chin chain, scarlet hair plume in plated socket, WD stamp for 1913 inside, some wear.
£230–280 *WAL*

A Hussar Captain's (Reserve) full dress blue tunic, with gilt gimp and braid trim, including 6 loops with olivets and purl buttons to chest, shoulder cords with 'R', embroidered cuff ornaments for Captain, slight wear.
£280–320 *WAL*

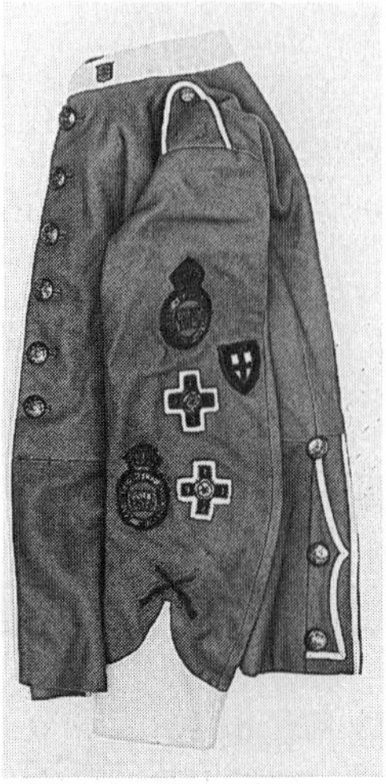

l. A Sergeant's full dress scarlet tunic of The Essex Regiment, with gilt chevrons to the right sleeve, 5 embroidered badges to the left sleeve, some damage.
£600–650 *WAL*

r. A Sergeant's full dress green tunic of The 1st Volunteer Battalion The Essex Regiment, with black facings and lace trim, shoulder straps edged with light green and embroidered '1/V/Essex', a similar green star and chevrons to the right sleeve, 11 embroidered badges to the left sleeve.
£650–700 *WAL*

Crossbows

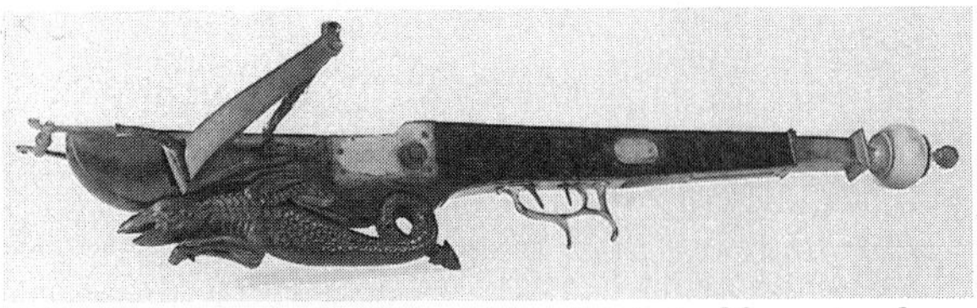

A Flemish target crossbow, with robust steel bow struck twice with the letters 'SD', retained by large iron loops each with floral finial, original string, worn, early 19thC, bow 25½in (65cm) long.
£2,500–3,000 *S(NY)*

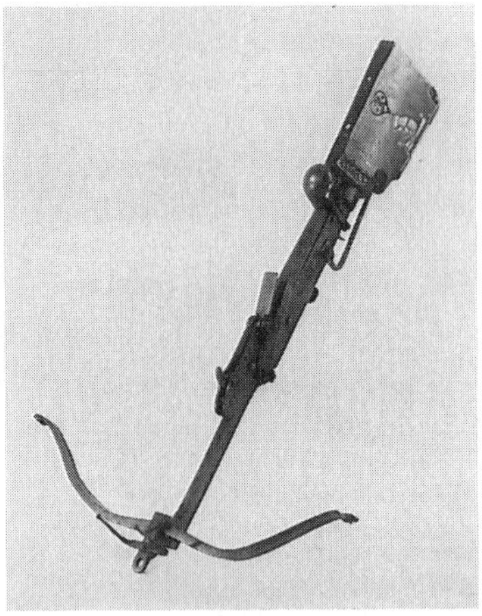

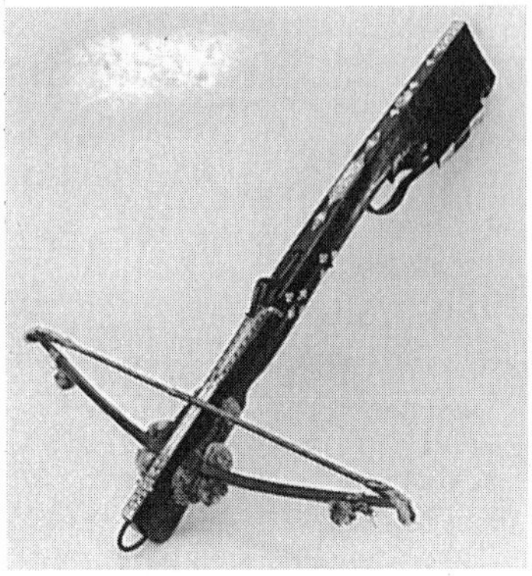

l. A Saxon sporting crossbow, with steel bow struck with maker's mark and retaining its original blued finish and horn butt plate, restored, inscribed with the armoury number '15', dated '1728', bow 22½in (57cm) long.
£2,800–3,200 *S(NY)*

A German steel sporting stonebow, the tiller with built-in gaffle struck with maker's mark and carrying the nut and backsight, retained by a spring catch, inlaid with engraved horn plaques, including a bear feeding and a wounded wolf, 2 plaques missing, stamped with owner's monogram 'EK' in a heart, early 17thC, bow 18½in (47cm) long.
£1,500–2,000 *S(NY)*

Daggers & Knives

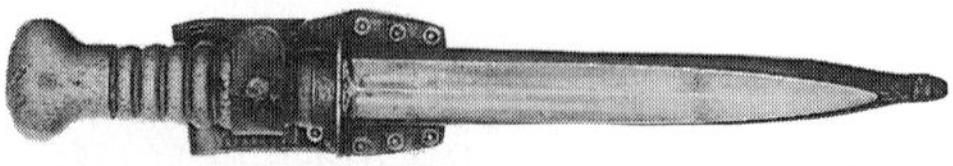

A Dutch WWII fighting knife, with a double-edged spear point 8in (20cm) blade, traces of blueing, ribbed wood hilt, in brown leather sheath with frog secured with brass rivet, good condition.
£100–120 *WAL*

A Marine Artillery 1858 pattern sword bayonet, with slightly curved 26in (66cm) blade by 'CK', steel mounts, diced black leather grips, minor marking.
£220–270 *WAL*

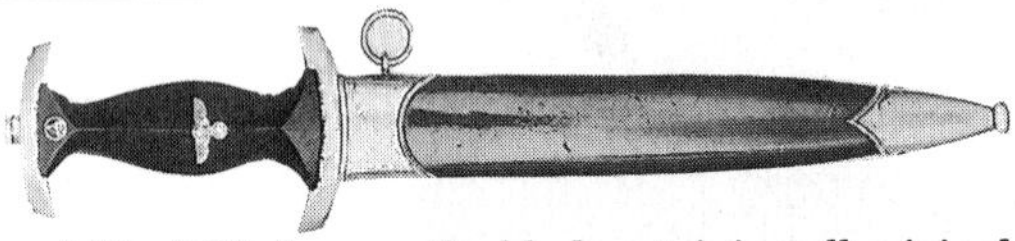

A Nazi SA dagger, the blade retaining all original polish, plated mounts, in its metal sheath with plated mounts, slight wear.
£150–200 *WAL*

A Nazi army Officer's dagger, with plated mounts, orange grip, in its plated sheath, worn and chipped, together with an East German 'Volksmarine' round hat, West German Cavalry peaked cap, both with badges and 2 others, in very good condition.
£100–150 *WAL*

Maces

r. A Russian steel mace (Bulawa), with a large hollow globular head formed with 6 low flanges each set in brass, turned brass finial and tubular haft in 2 stages, fitted with brass mouldings above and below the polygonal grip, 17thC, 24in (61cm) long.
£2,500–3,000 *S(NY)*

l. A Russian parcel gilt all steel mace (Bulawa), with a small faceted domed pommel, c1600, 22in (56cm) long.
£2,000–2,500 *S(NY)*

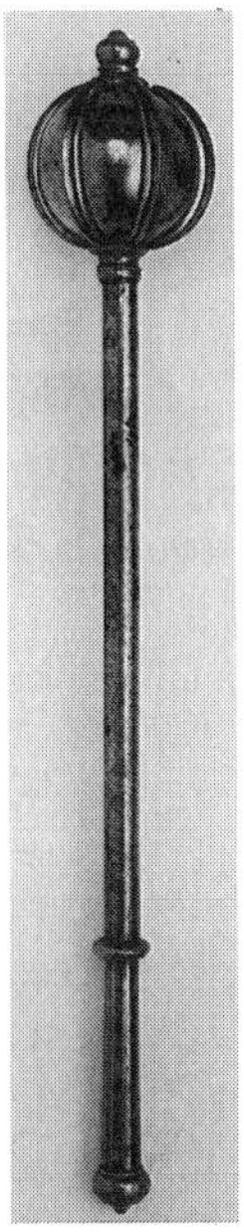

Make the most of Miller's

In* Miller's Antiques Price Guide *we do NOT just reprint saleroom estimates. Our consultants work from realised prices and then calculate a price range for similar items, avoiding uncharacteristic 'one off' high or low results.

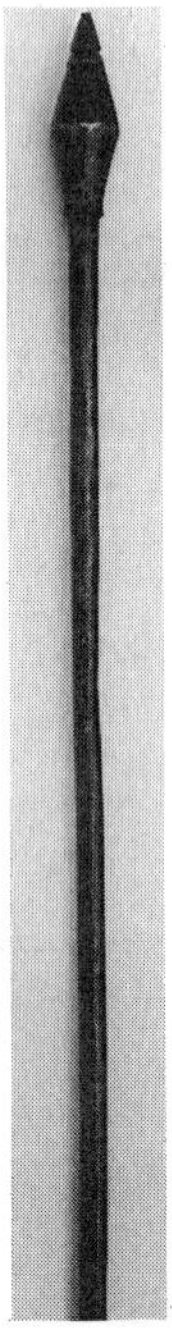

r. A Russian all steel mace, with a moulded tall conical head, solid haft, incised with crosshatch marks for damascening over its full surface, c1600, 31in (79cm) long.
£1,200–1,700 *S(NY)*

Pistols

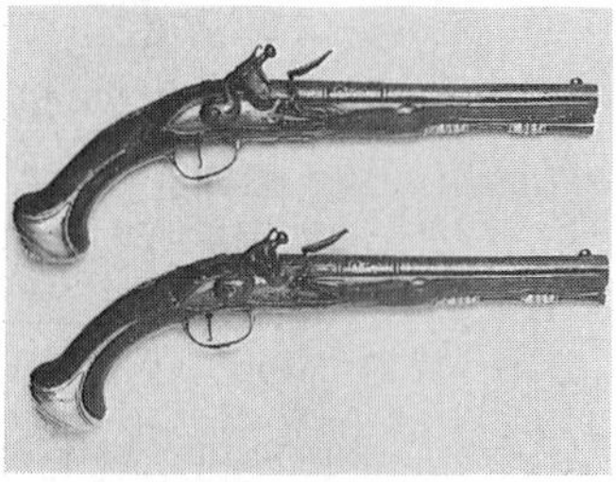

A pair of flintlock holster pistols, by Barbar, swamped three-stage barrels, with gold foliate scroll panel and crowned shield panel at breech, rounded lock with unbridled frizzen, full stocked, silver coloured metal furniture, grotesque mask butt caps, retaining their rammers, damaged.
£6,000–6,500 *S(S)*

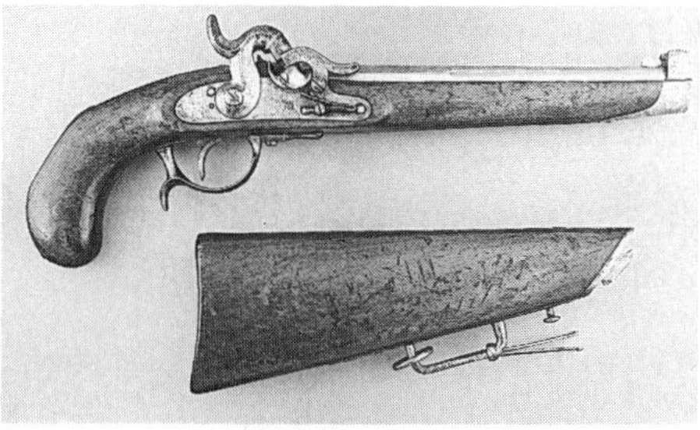

r. A military percussion pistol, with detachable butt, stamped '1855', engraved 'Schl V.C.S.'
£600–650 *DN*

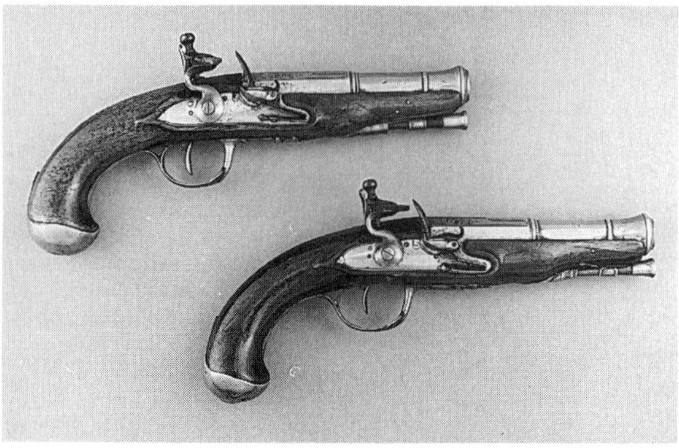

A pair of Continental brass-barrelled flintlock pistols.
£650–700 *DN*

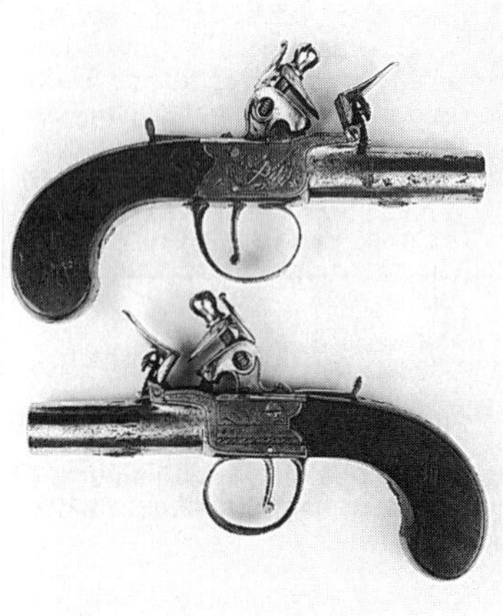

A pair of flintlock percussion combined boxlock pistols, by Gallyon, with screw-off barrels, safety catches, engraved steel trigger guards and lockplates, bag shape butts, barrels 1½in (4cm) long.
£1,000–1,400 *N*

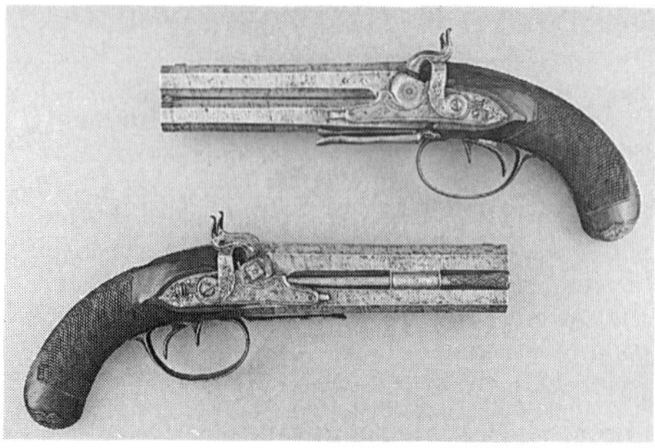

r. A pair of double-barrelled percussion pistols, converted from flintlock, signed 'D. Egg London.'
£1,400–1,600 *DN*

A pair of Continental flintlock pistols, early 19thC, 8in (20cm) long.
£500–600 *SLN*

A pair of brass-mounted flintlock pistols, with sighted barrels, signed engraved flat bolted locks with rollers, one jaw screw and steel replaced, figured walnut full stocks, chequered butts, engraved mounts including butt caps and trigger guards, with pineapple finials, horn-tipped ramrods, signed 'SPENCER, London', early 19thC.
£1,000–1,200 *CSK*

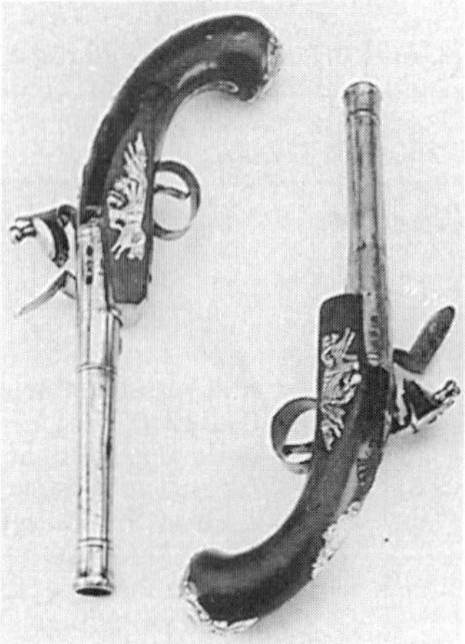

A pair of silver mounted pistols, with turn-off cannon barrels, border engraved rounded locks, signed below the pans, one cock replaced, figured walnut butts, repaired, each carved with a shell behind the barrel tang, mounts comprising Trophy of Arms side plates, escutcheons engraved with owner's crest, grotesque mask butt caps and iron trigger guards, signed 'GANDON', London proof marks, mid-18thC.
£2,000–2,500 *CSK*

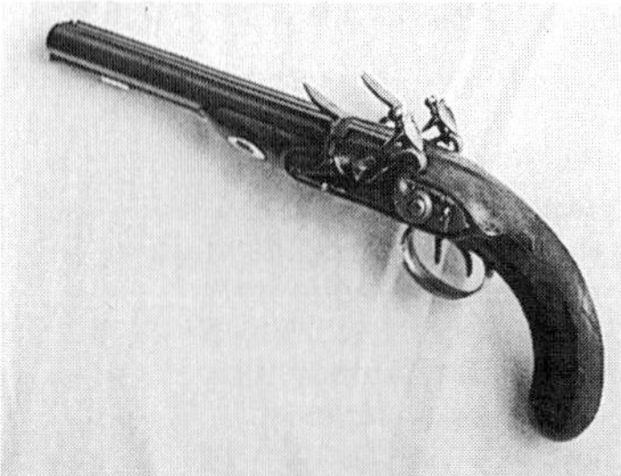

l. A double-barrelled flintlock travelling pistol, by Howe.
£600–630 *MR*

Revolvers

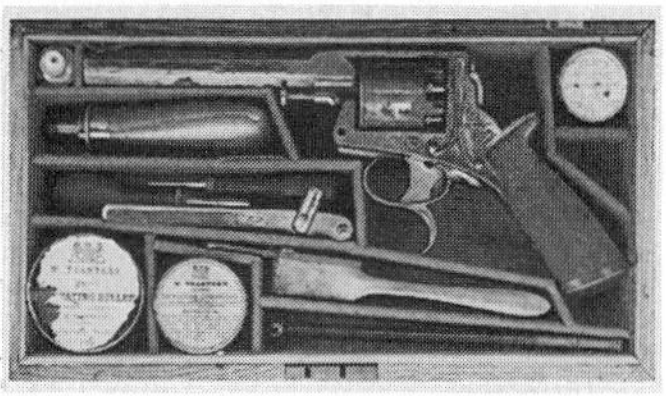

A cased 54 bore Tranter patent percussion five-shot self-cocking revolver, No. 12832T, rust and flaking, in original fitted oak case, lid and escutcheons missing, lined in worn red baize, with almost all of the original accessories, c1856, 12in (30.5cm).
£1,200–1,500 *S(NY)*

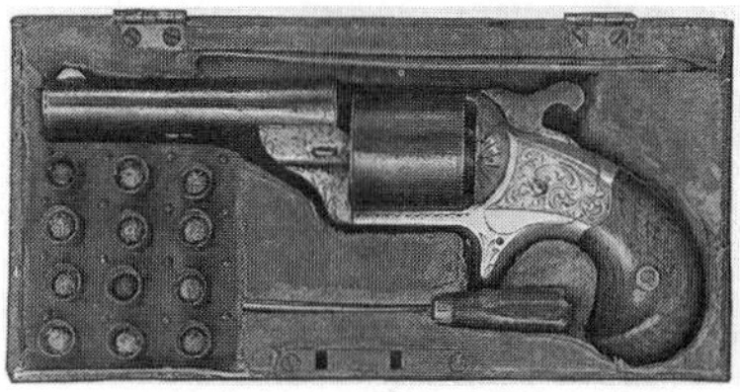

r. A cased Moore's Patent Firearms Co. six-shot front loading teatfire revolver, No. 5126, slight chips, c1865, with 12 unfired cartridges, original extractor rod and cleaning rod, 7in (17.5cm) long.
£500–600 *S(NY)*

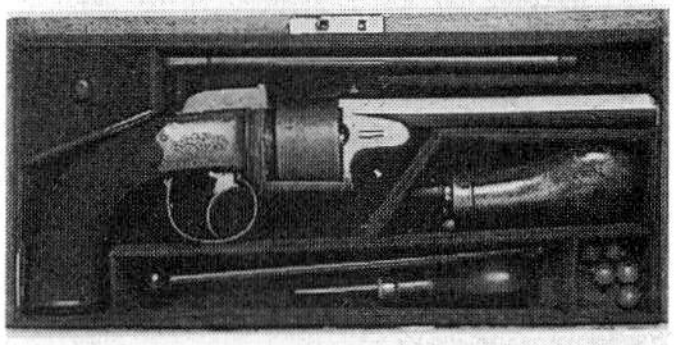

r. A 38 bore six-shot percussion transitional revolver, by Holland, London, with sighted octagonal barrel 6¼in (16cm), plain cylinder, in maroon lined fitted mahogany case with turnscrew, copper powder flask, cleaning rod, rammer and oil bottle.
£2,000–2,500 *S(S)*

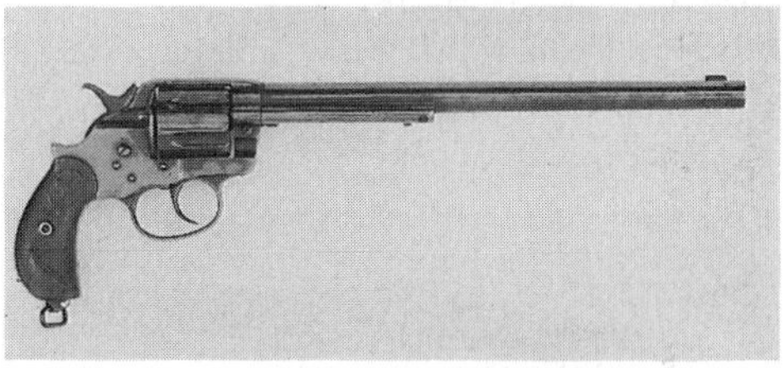

A Colt .38 model 1878 double-action army revolver, No. 23295, with a 12in (30.5cm) barrel, plain frame, ejector rod and loading gate, chequered composition grips, lanyard ring, certificate of unprovability, refinished.
£2,600–3,000 *S(S)*

Colt records show that the barrel length is as described but a most unusual length for this model of revolver. It was shipped on June 18, 1889, as the letter which accompanies it confirms.

Rifles

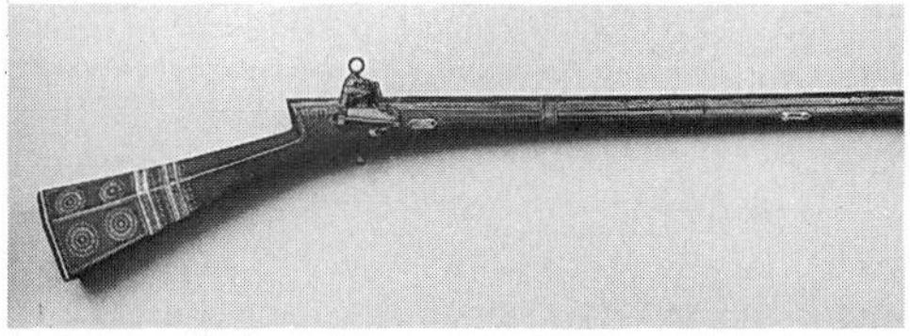

A Turkish miquelet, the octagonal barrel with integral peep rear sight, with 8 groove rifling.
£620–700 *DN*

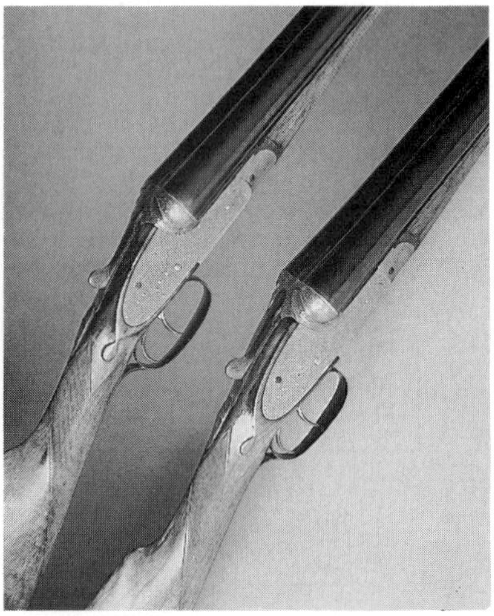

A pair of S. Grant left hand opening 12 bore sidelock ejectors, Nos. 6227/8, 28in (71cm) replacement barrels by another, engraved with maker's name, 2¾in (7cm) chambers, imp cyl. x ¼ choke, scroll engraved actions with fluted fences, 14⅝in (37cm) figured stocks, including pads, weighing 6lbs 10ozs, in oak and leather case.
£4,000–6,000 *Bon*

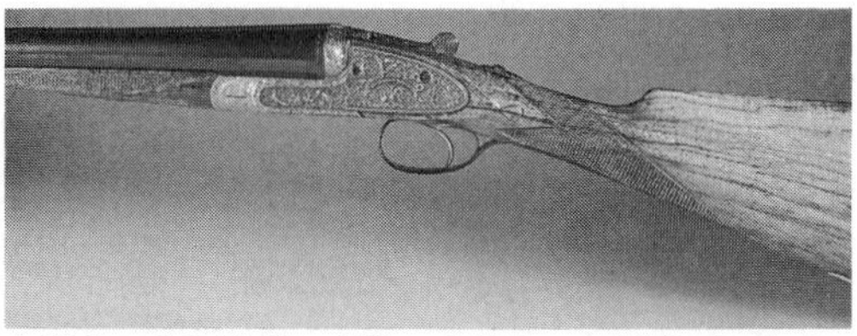

A Holland & Holland Royal 12 bore sidelock ejector, No. 23075, with semi-selective single trigger, re-sleeved 28 by 2½in (71 by 6.5cm) nitro barrels bored ½ x full choke, polished bold scroll engraved lockwork, 13¾in (35cm), well figured stock, weighing 6lbs 10ozs.
£4,000–4,500 *Bon*

A German wheel-lock sporting rifle, cheek-piece altered, cracked below the lock, pieces of inlay missing, with original iron-tipped wooden ramrod, late 17thC, barrel 26½in (67cm) long.
£3,500–4,000 *S(NY)*

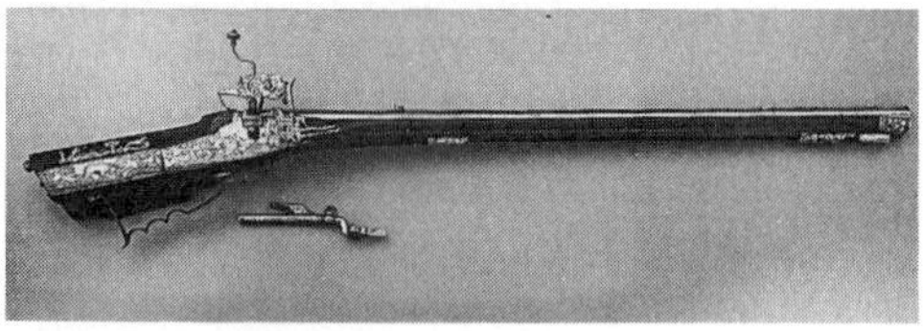

A German wheel-lock rifle, the heavy octagonal barrel with 7 groove rifling, brass front sight, signed at the breech, 17thC.
£3,200–3,700 *DN*

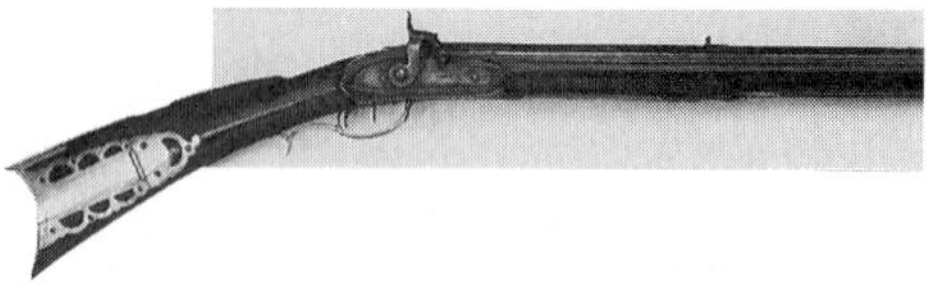

A percussion Kentucky rifle, with smooth bore heavy octagonal sighted barrel marked 'D.S.' near the breech, engraved lock signed 'RASHMORE & SON', early 19thC, barrel 41¾in (106cm) long, together with a leather pouch and a small powder horn, both 19thC.
£900–1,300 *S(NY)*

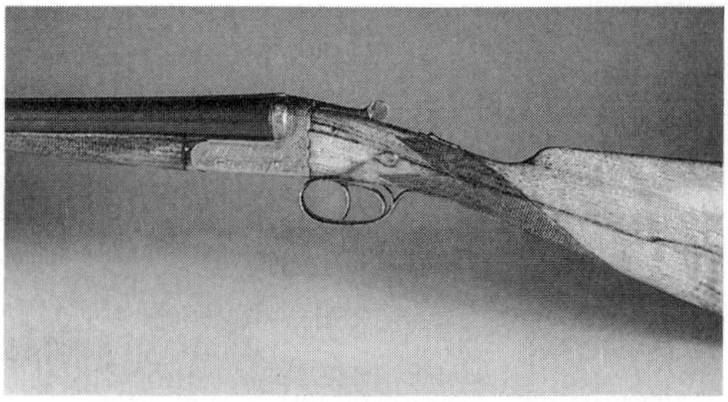

A Holland & Holland 12 bore boxlock ejector, 'Northwood' model, with 26 by 2½in (66 by 6cm) nitro barrels bored ¼ x ¾ choke, scrolled back action engraved with scrollwork retaining traces of finish, 15in (38cm) well figured stock, including a pad, in a leather case.
£1,500–2,000 *Bon*

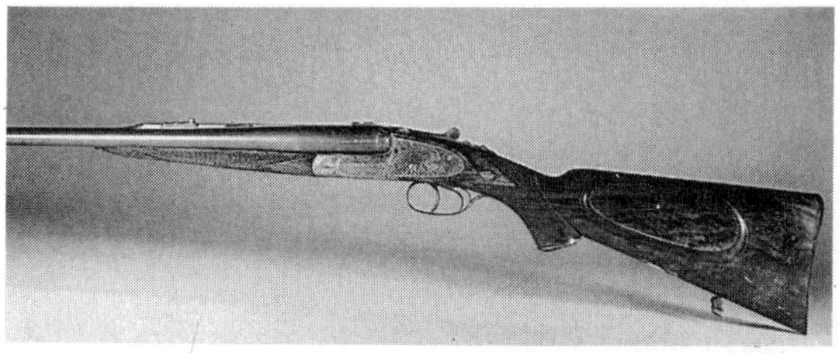

A Holland & Holland Royal sidelock non-ejector .375 (2½in) nitro express double rifle, No. 17783, 26in (66cm) barrels, fitted with folding leaf sights to 300yds, and detachable Voight Lander scope, lock-work superbly engraved with profuse bold scroll-work covered with light patina of original finish, well figured 14½in (37cm) stock with cheek piece, grip cap and trap, complete in its oak and leather case with accessories.
£9,000–11,000 *Bon*

Firearms

Each country has its own laws affecting the collecting and owning of guns. It is the responsibility of the collector to make absolutely certain that he or she is conforming to these laws.

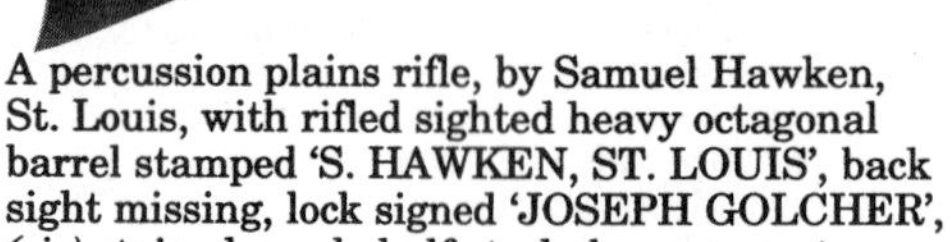

A percussion plains rifle, by Samuel Hawken, St. Louis, with rifled sighted heavy octagonal barrel stamped 'S. HAWKEN, ST. LOUIS', back sight missing, lock signed 'JOSEPH GOLCHER', *(sic)* stained maple half-stock, brass mounts comprising crescent butt plate, trigger guard and ramrod pipes, white metal fore-end cap, set trigger and later wooden ramrod, worn, mid-19thC, barrel 37¾in (96cm) long.
£2,000–2,500 *S(NY)*

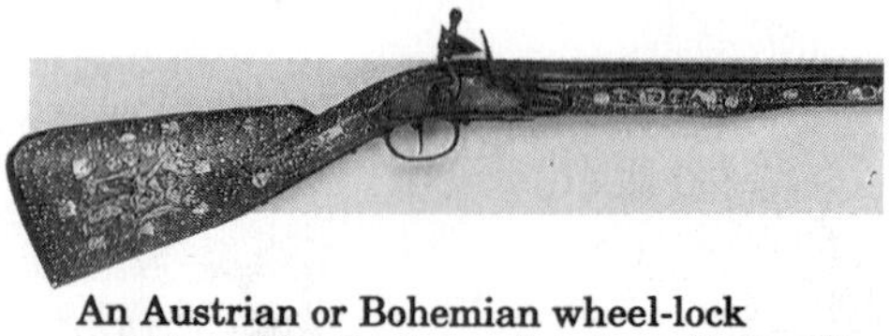

An Austrian or Bohemian wheel-lock sporting rifle, the base plate inscribed with the stockmaker's initials 'ELH', dated '1738', wooden ramrod with engraved bone tip, barrel 33in (84cm) long.
£3,500–4,000 *S(NY)*

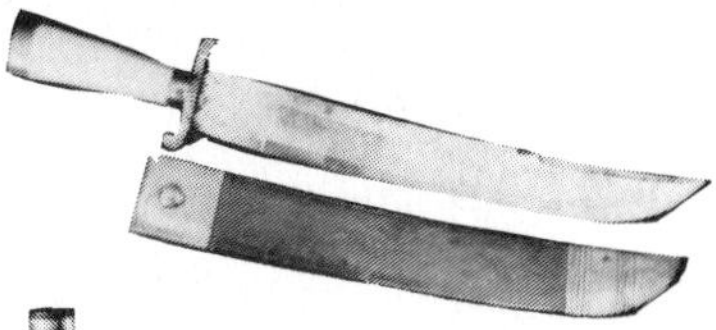

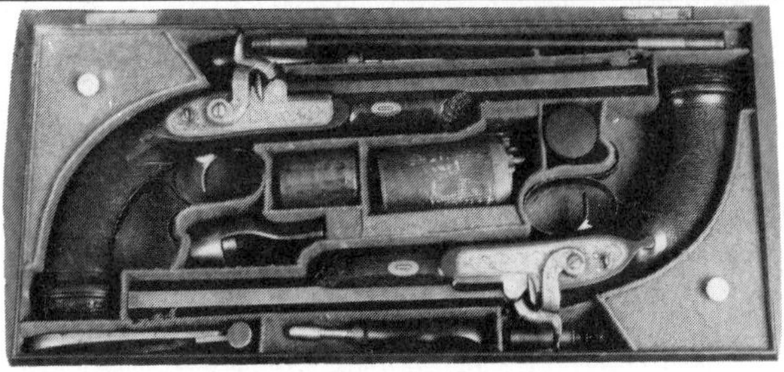

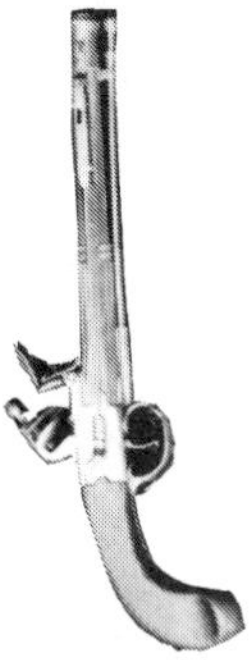

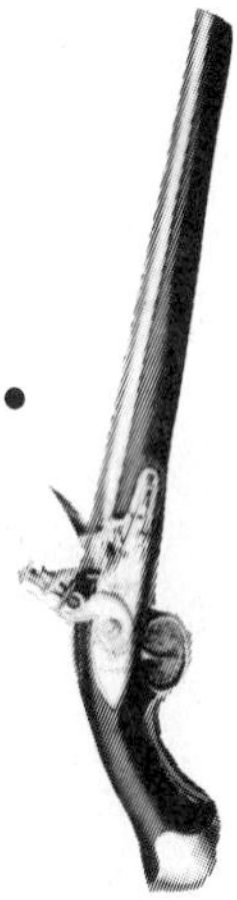

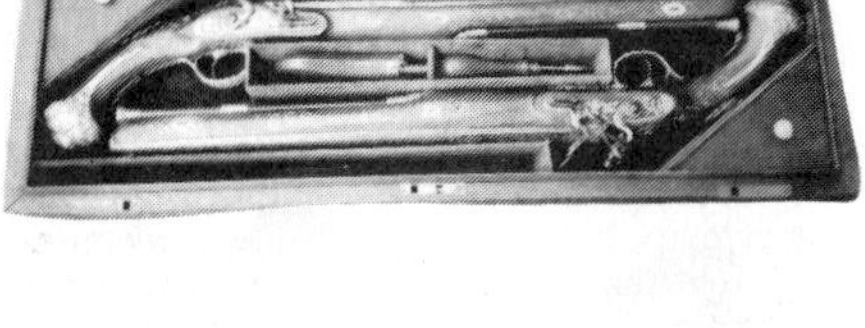

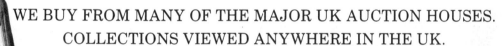

Shotguns

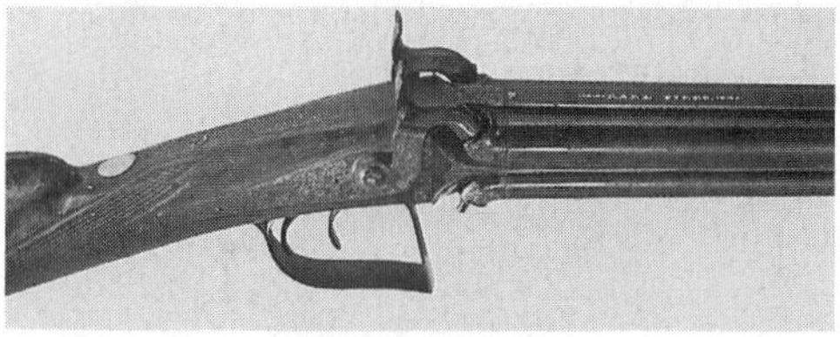

An Austrian 20 bore four-barrelled percussion turn-over shotgun, by Karl Pirko in Wien, with sighted browned twist barrels signed in gold on the top and bottom ribs, respectively designated 'R' and 'L' in gold, Liège proof, engraved case-hardened breeches and baseplate with trigger guard release, original brass-tipped blued iron ramrod, silver escutcheon, and most of its original finish, one sling eye missing, one hammer retaining screw broken but complete, mid-19thC, barrels 26in (66cm) long.
£2,500–3,000 *S(NY)*

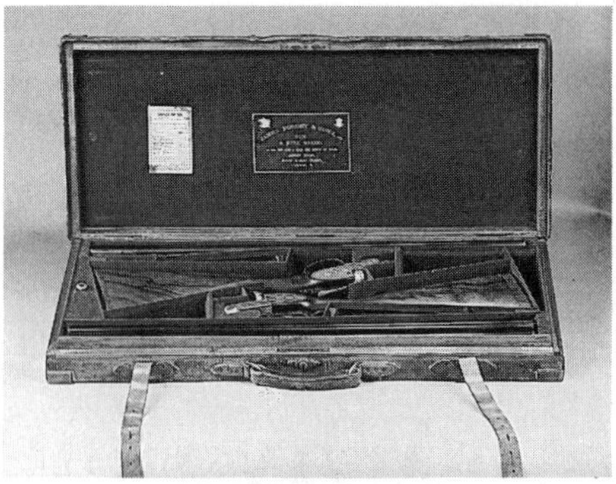

A pair of James Purdey & Sons 12 bore sidelock ejector shotguns, with self-opening action, walnut stocks, chased foliate designs to plates, in original oak and hide upholstered case bearing the original labels, No. 16919, dated '1900.'
£9,000–10,000 *HOLL*

Swords

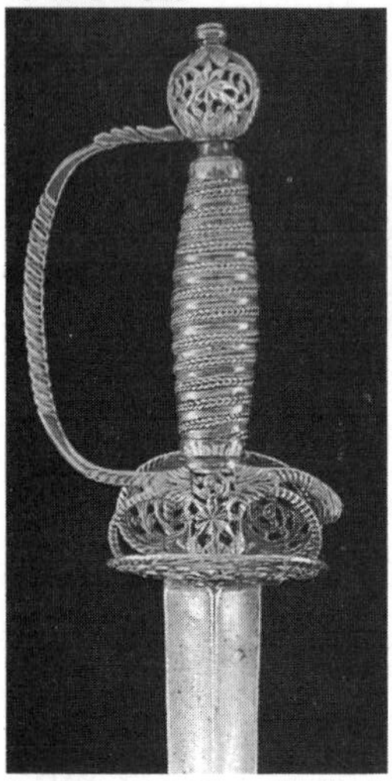

A silver-hilted smallsword, pierced globose pommel, silver grip with plaited wire binding, c1740.
£800–900 *S(S)*

A mortuary sword, the straight 33½in (85cm) double-edged blade with the forte engraved with orb and cross marks and 'STETZIVS KEVLLER, MEFECIT SOLINGEN, the solid basket finely chiselled with scrolls, winged heads and a grotesque feathered head, knuckle guard with scrolling side arms, globose chiselled pommel, wire bound sharkskin grip, c1640.
£1,100–1,500 *S*

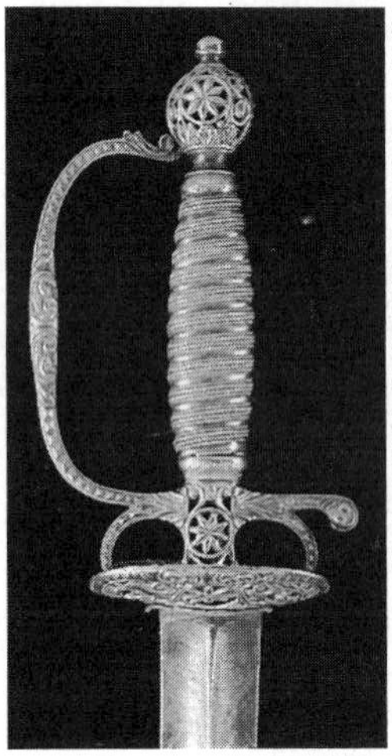

l. A silver hilted sword, the 31½in (80cm) colichemarde blade with incised scrolling decoration at the forte, the hilt with twin shell guard pierced with scrolling and star pattern, arms-of-hilt, rear quillon, knuckle guard, the pommel pierced en suite, grip with plaited silver wire binding, c1750.
£750–850 *S(S)*

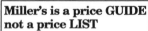

Miller's is a price GUIDE not a price LIST

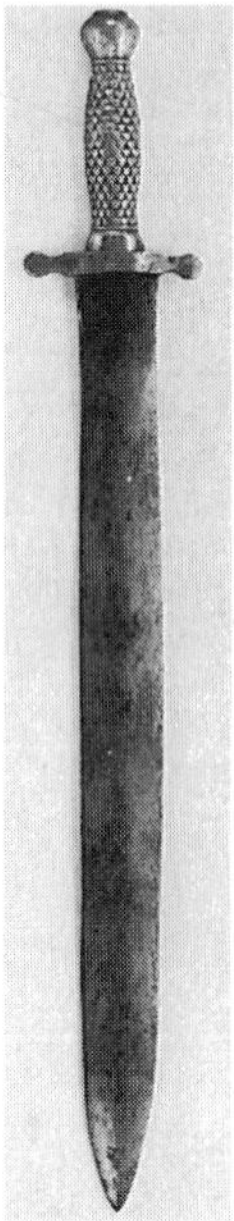

A Confederate shortsword, for either Foot Artillery or Naval issue, with crudely forged unfullered blade, the hilt of brass, in one piece, the straight cross guard with plain flat sided rounded terminals, the grip cast with scale pattern, and globular pommel with a low field for the tang, c1861, blade 18½in (47cm) long.
£700–1,000 *S(NY)*

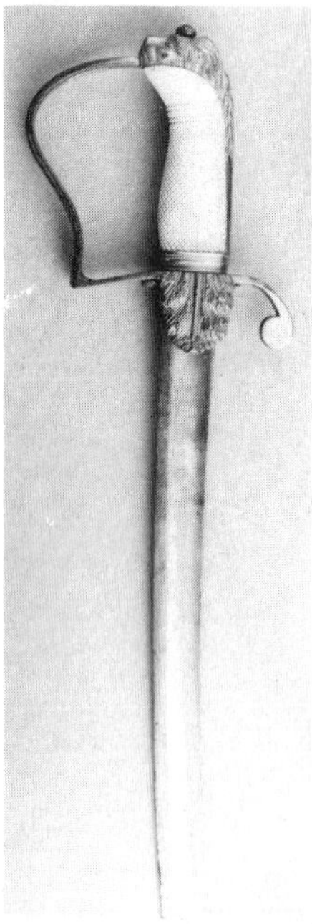

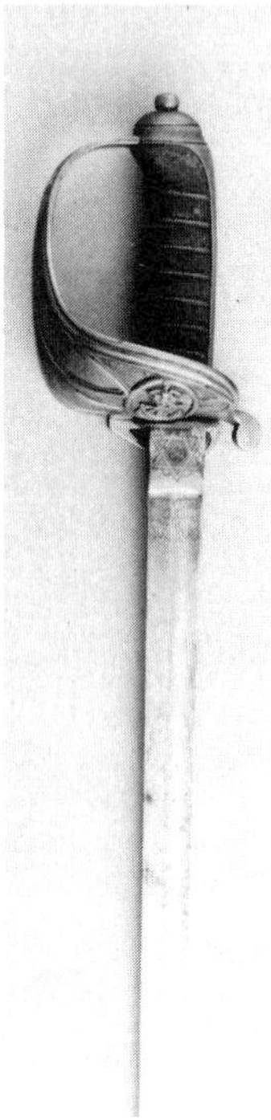

r. A George V Naval Officer's hanger sword, 31in (79cm) long steel blade by Wilkinson & Co., black fishskin and wirebound grip, plain pommel, gilt brass mounted leather scabbard, slight pitting to blade.
£140–180 *DN*

l. A George III Officer's naval hanger type sword, with curved sabre style blade, gilt stirrup hilt, with lion's head pommel, chequered ivory grip, brass mounted black leather scabbard, damaged.
£100–150 *DN*

Miscellaneous

l. A coromandel model of a cannon, with ring-turned barrel, on a carriage with associated wheels, mid-19thC, 15in (38cm) long.
£200–300 *CSK*

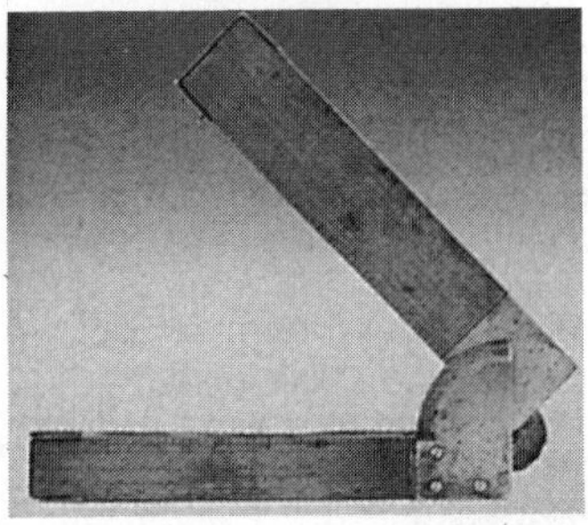

l. A gunner's wooden rule, with 2 wooden sections hinged at the centre, marked with various measures for a variety of shells and formulae, built-in spirit level and protractor, damaged, late 19thC.
£450–500 *S(S)*

A pair of miniature oak cannons, modelled after those on the frigate USS 'Constitution' and built with materials taken from the original hull, each with a four-stage moulded barrel on a four-wheel carriage, one with a plaque inscribed 'US FRIGATE CONSTITUTION', and another plaque to the side, c1927, 10in (25cm) long.
£1,800–2,200 *S(NY)*

In 1927 the Navy was overseeing the rebuilding the frigate 'The Constitution', also called 'Old Ironsides'. To raise funds the Navy sold souvenirs made from materials from 'Old Ironsides', and the cannons were amongst these items.

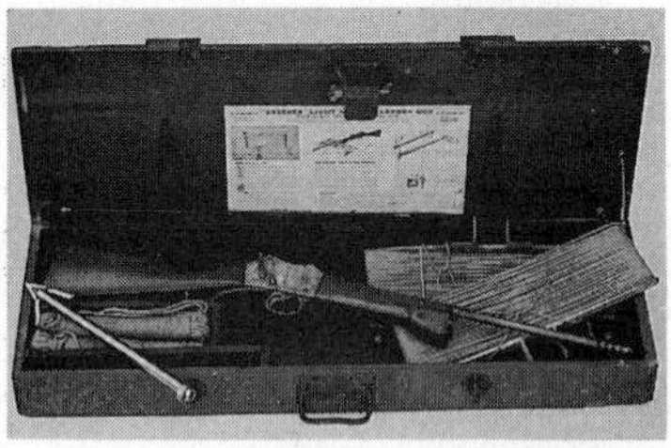

l. A W.W. Greener martini-action light harpoon gun, with a 20in (51cm) barrel, plain frame, fore-end with line winder groove, nitro proof, in its wooden box with 2 harpoons, 2 line winders and instruction label.
£700–800 *S(S)*

A model of a 17thC cannon, the brass barrel cast with arms, on oak carriage with brass mounts and wheels, 19thC, 14in (36cm) long.
£150–200 *CSK*

A bronze 4½in (11cm) bore mortar, with trunnions, the centre section of barrel with engraved monogram 'GR3' below a moulded crown, the chamber section engraved 'P. VERBRUGGE FECIT Ao 1782', vent set in raised pan with simple engraved decoration, below vent is engraved '0 3 2' spaced with broad arrows, and on underside of chamber 'No 32', dated '1782', 13in (33cm) long.
£7,200–8,000 *S(S)*

A pair of north European iron saluting cannons, with slender iron carbine barrels adapted for hand-ignition, each with raised moulded muzzle ring, on their original iron-mounted painted wooden split trail carriages, with iron shod spoked cambered wheels, in uncleaned condition, 17thC, barrels 19½in (49.5cm) long.
£1,750–2,000 *S(NY)*

Medals & Orders

A Victorian Royal Sherwood Foresters shako plate, silvered and blue enamel, excellent condition.
£700–750 *N*

A Delhi Durbar gold medal, 1911, in case of issue, excellent condition.
£720–760 *S(S)*

A Japanese Order of the Rising Sun, 2nd class breast star, in silver with gilt and enamel appliqué centre, with central cabochon, in palownia flower lacquer case of issue, complete with red tassels, excellent condition.
£2,100–2,700 *S(S)*

A Polish Hurricane pilot's Battle of Britain group of 12 medals, awarded to Lieutenant Marian Domagala, No. 238 Squadron.
£2,600–3,000 *S(S)*

A Royal Household medal group, comprising: a Royal Household Long and Faithful Service Medal, George V, with dated suspension '1894–1914', and additional scroll bar for 'Thirty Years' (Annie Clark), Jubilee Medal 1897, in silver, a bronze Coronation Medal 1902, and silver Coronation Medal 1911, all in very good condition, together with silver presentation box with enamelled Royal Crown and Cypher, slightly chipped.
£600–700 *S(S)*

An Indian Volunteer Forces Officer's decoration, George V issue, reverse engraved 'Col G C Godfrey, 1st Bn BNRY Voltr Rifle Corps', not hallmarked, with top brooch bar, very good condition.
£130–160 *WAL*

A Crimean War three-bar medal, Sebastopol, Inkermann and Balaklava, engraved 'Adols Octs Hawker Paymaster Ordce Corps', replaced rivets, very good condition.
£250–300 *WAL*

An Indian Army Meritorious Service medal, Victorian issue, engraved 'Sergt Major Joshua Burton, 34th N.I.G.O.C.C. 1853', good condition.
£150–170 *WAL*

A New Zealand Medal, inscribed '1863–1865', awarded to Corporal Wm McClunighan, 70th Regiment, very good condition.
£160–200 *WAL*

Garth Vincent
Antique Arms and Armour
LAPADA
MEMBER
THE GUN TRADE ASSOCIATION
THE GUILD OF MASTER CRAFTSMEN
I have customers worldwide
and I am interested in purchasing
single items or complete collections,
advice freely given
Dealer in antique and reproduction
arms and armour for the collector,
investor and interior decorator
Commission buying at auction
Access & Visa accepted
Brochure available
The Old Manor House,
Allington, Nr Grantham,
Lincolnshire NG32 2DH
Telephone: (01400) 281358

KITCHENALIA

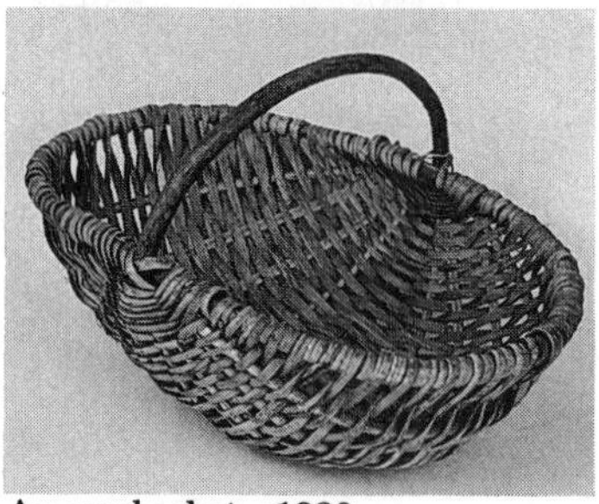

An egg basket, c1930, 19in (48cm) wide.
£25–30 *AL*

A maid's wooden box, 13in (33cm) wide.
£65–75 *AL*

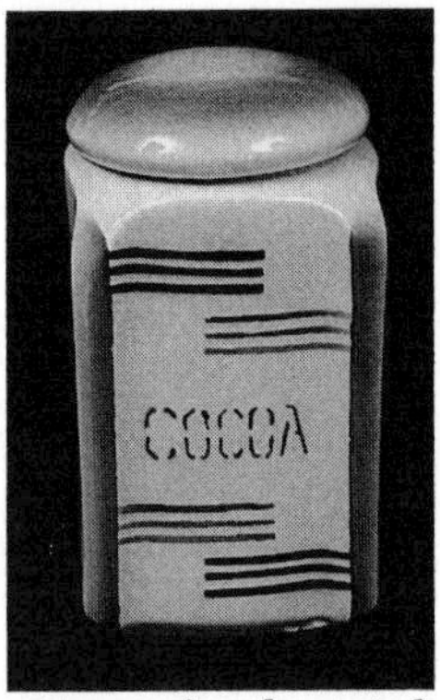

A cream cocoa jar, decorated with green and black stripes, c1920, 6½in (16cm) high.
£25–30 *AL*

Three Sussex trugs, 13in (33cm) wide.
£25–28 each *MIL*

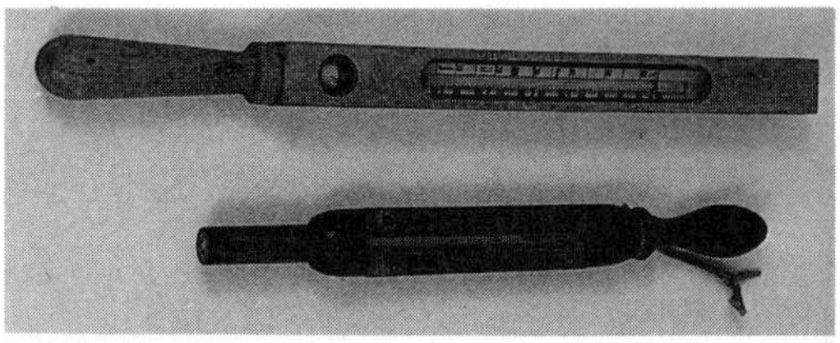

l. A wooden dairy thermometer, c1920, 15½in (39.5cm) long.
£10–12
r. A wooden thermometer, c1900, 12in (30.5cm) long.
£6–8 *AL*

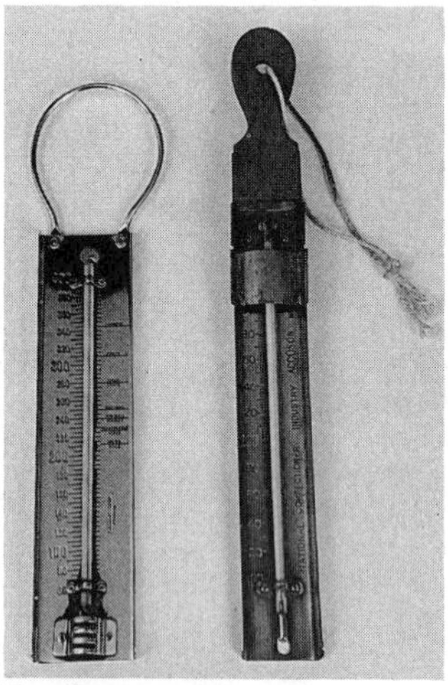

Two brass sugar thermometers, c1930, largest 12in (30.5cm) long.
£15–20 each *AL*

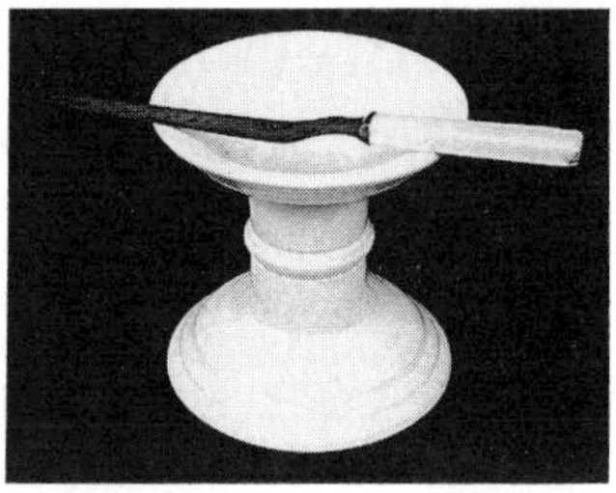

A white pottery ham stand, c1900, 7½in (18.5cm) high.
£45–50
A ham carving knife, c1890, 12½in (31.5cm) long.
£10–12 *AL*

A brown enamel kettle, c1900, 9½in (23.5cm) high.
£10–12 *AL*

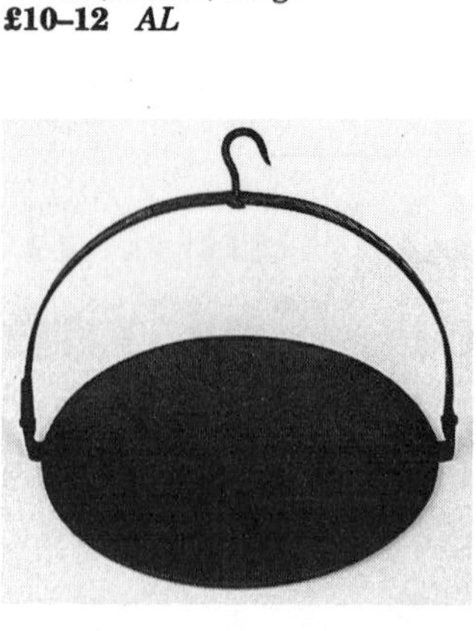

l. An iron griddle, with half hoop handle and hook, c1890, 12in (30.5cm) diam.
£25–30 *AL*

A wall mounted tea leaf tin, inscribed 'Tea from Ceylon', c1950, 7½in (18.5cm) high.
£10–12 *AL*

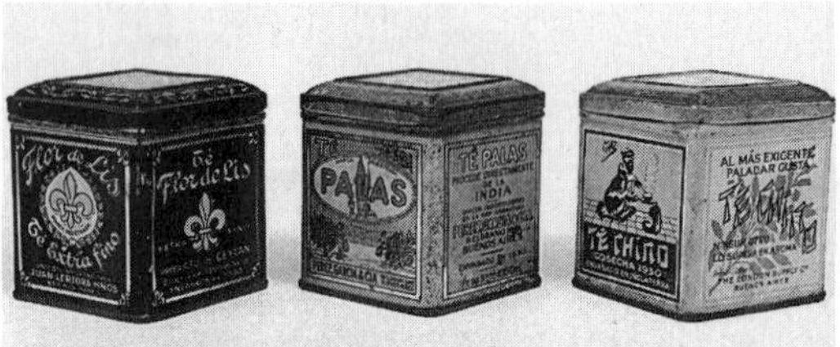

r. Three tea tins, for Ceylon, Indian, and China teas, 3½in (8.5cm) high.
£8–10 each *AL*

A blue enamel jug, c1900,
11in (28cm) high.
£25–30 *AL*

A light blue cake tin, c1930,
8½in (21cm) high.
£10–12 *AL*

A brown enamel double saucepan,
c1920, 9in (22.5cm) high.
£10–12 *AL*

Three cream enamel colanders,
11in (28cm) wide.
£8–10 each *AL*

A white enamel jelly mould,
c1900, 6in (15cm) wide.
£12–16 *AL*

A resin container,
inscribed 'R. R. SHIELDS,
MANCHESTER, Rº Nº
126381', 2in (5cm) high.
£10–12 *AL*

l. A Coleman's
Mustard display
case, in original
black paint, with
a pine finish, 26in
(66cm) high.
£150–200 *CCP*

A Colman's Mustard tin, decorated
with a scene of Parliament
Buildings, Ottawa, Canada, c1890,
5in (12.5cm).
£20–25 *AL*

An enamel washing boiler, c1920, 18in (45.5cm) diam.
£25–30 *AL*

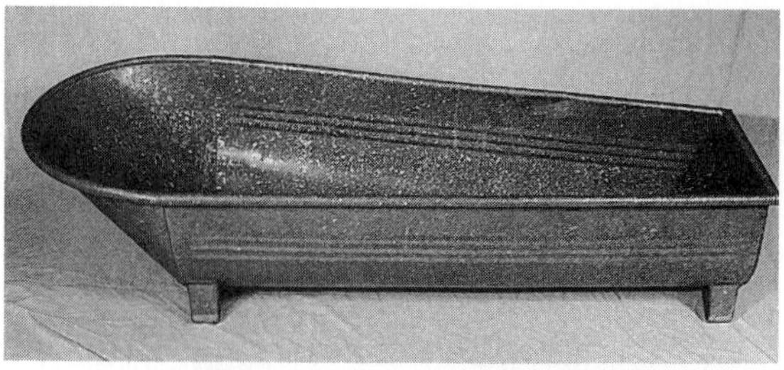
A large galvanised washing tub, c1900–20.
£20–40 *NWE*

An oval galvanised iron wash tub, with handles, drain and plug, c1900.
£20–30 *NWE*

Two pottery jugs, c1890, largest 11in (28cm) high.
£30–35 *AL*

A tongue press, early 20thC, 14in (35.5cm) high.
£30–40 *CCP*

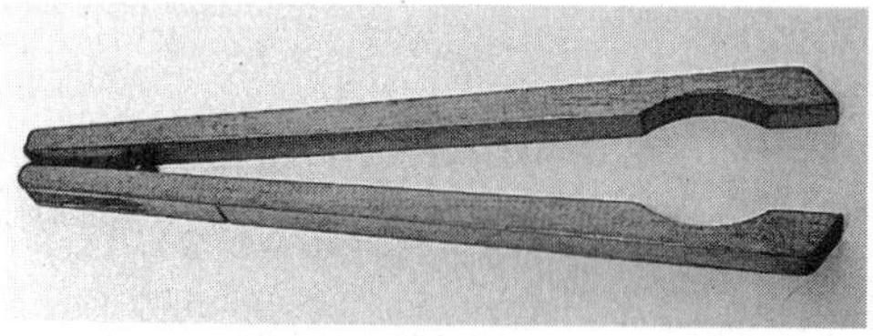
l. A pair of washing tongs, c1930, 15in (38.5cm) long.
£4–6 *TaB*

An American tin cake mixer, 9in (22.5cm) wide.
£15–20 *AL*

A steel saucepan, c1890, 4½in (11cm) high.
£18–22 *AL*

A set of Ritway kitchen scales, c1930, 11in (28cm) high.
£25–30 *AL*

A Colman's Mustard pot, c1910, 2in (5cm) high.
£10–12 *AL*

A pottery storage jar, used for sugar or rice, c1920, 6¼in (16cm) high.
£15–20 *AL*

A white glazed tapioca jar, c1890, 5¼in (13.5cm) high.
£20–22 *AL*

Two tin patty moulds, with Registration mark.
£10–15 *AL*

r. Four glazed bowls, 2 for potted meat and 2 for potted shrimps, 1½in (3.5cm) high.
£5–6 each *AL*

A white enamel flour bin, c1890, 10in (25cm) wide.
£15–18 *AL*

A white enamel flour bin, c1890, 12in (30.5cm) wide.
£20–22 *AL*

A green enamel bread bin, c1920, 13in (33cm) high.
£20–25 *AL*

A Carr's biscuit tin, c1930, 9½in (23.5cm) square.
£16–18 *AL*

A Lipton's brass souvenir tea caddy, c1920, 5½in (13.5cm) high.
£25–30 *AL*

A wooden bread board, c1870, 11½in (29cm) diam.
£40–45 *AL*

Two wooden rushlight nips, c1780.
l. retaining original paint, 8in (20cm) high.
r. 5½in (13.5cm) high.
£800–850 each *RYA*

A rectangular bread board, c1900, 29½in (75cm) long.
£10–15 *NWE*

l. Two storage jars, with wooden lids, decorated with a blue chequered design, one inscribed 'Sugar', 7in (17.5cm) high.
£15–20 each *AL*

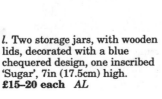

ANTIQUITIES

An Attic pottery askos, in the form of an astragal or knucklebone, the cylindrical spout with rounded lip, the double ribbed hoop handle in the form of a knot, remains of black glaze, 5th–4th Century B.C., 3½in (8.5cm) high.
£500–800 *CSK*

A Roman marble relief fragment of Apollo, wearing a cloak over his left shoulder, mounted, circa 150–200 A.D., 13½in (34cm) high.
£6,000–9,000 *C*

A Roman bronze mirror, of plain form, the interior with incised concentric bands, the later handle with lotus head terminal, ribbed shaft and ram's head finial, circa 1st Century A.D., 12in (30.5cm) high.
£650–750 *S*

A Greek pottery askos, modelled in the form of a duck, with an ivy leaf band tied around the neck and a single cylindrical spout, with arched handle, the bill open for pouring, restored, circa 3rd Century B.C., 7½in (18.5cm) long.
£8,000–10,000 *CNY*

A Roman marble head of a boy, mounted on a marble draped bust, circa 2nd Century A.D., 18in (45.5cm) high including bust.
£4,700–5,300 *S*

A Roman bronze figure of a water bird, with long neck and bill, its wings displayed horizontally, incised details of feathers, lower part of legs missing, circa 2nd Century A.D., 2in (5cm) high.
£400–500 *C*

A Roman bronze figure of a crouching hare, ears folded back, circa 1st–2nd Century A.D., 1½in (3.5cm) high.
£2,000–2,500 *C*

An Apulian red-figure fish plate, attributed to the Cuttlefish Painter, with two bream, a flatfish, a small fish and a scallop, a rosette in the central depression, and a band of laurel on the rim, circa 350–325 B.C., 11in (28cm) diam.
£3,500–4,000 *CNY*

An Etruscan terracotta antefix, in the form of a female mask, with black and red painted details, wearing circular earrings and a necklet with pendants, circa 6th Century B.C., 8in (20cm) high.
£1,500–2,000 *S*

A Greek bronze hydria, the handles with plain disc-shaped terminals, the overhanging rim decorated with tongue motifs, a short inscription on the top of the rim, circa 400 B.C., 15½in (39.5cm) high.
£12,000–15,000 *S*

MARITIME

A Captain's registration compass, by D. Napier & Son No. 113, using replaceable paper compass cards which over a 24 hour period are pierced at 3 minute intervals by a fine needle mounted over the card, with brass handled carrying box and a supply of replacement paper compass cards, 10in (25cm) wide.
£5,750–6,750 *CSK*

A miniature sextant, signed on the arc 'C. Plath–Hamburg', the black enamelled lattice frame with 7 shades, mirrors and telescope mounting socket, index arm 3in (7.5cm) radius, with ivorine micrometer, vernier and handle, in fitted mahogany case with key, 6in (15cm) wide.
£800–1,000 *CSK*

A one-day marine chronometer, by Barraud's London, with up-and-down aperture and Pennington balance, c1820, in a box, 5in (12.5cm) square.
£3,500–4,500 *PWh*

A white enamelled dial clock, with cylinder escapement, in a brass drum case within a brass representation of a Kisbie lifebuoy, supported on 3 feet, the 2 front feet part of a pair of oars extending diagonally across and above the clock, engraved with the White Star Line house-flag, the rear support representing the rudder of a lifeboat, mounted on a mahogany base, 8in (20cm) high.
£250–350 *CSK*

A lacquered brass reflecting circle, of Troughton pattern, signed 'W. & S. Jones, London', the silvered scale divided into 4 quadrants, with 6 shades, mirrors, 3 verniers with 2 clamps and tangent screw adjustment, vernier magnifiers missing, 2 telescopes, stand and extending handles, in mahogany case, 11½in (29cm) wide.
£1,200–1,500 *CSK*

A brass ship's bell, engraved 'Nethergarth 1907', ex Rea Towing Company, with replaced clapper, 9in (23cm) wide.
£300–400 *CSK*

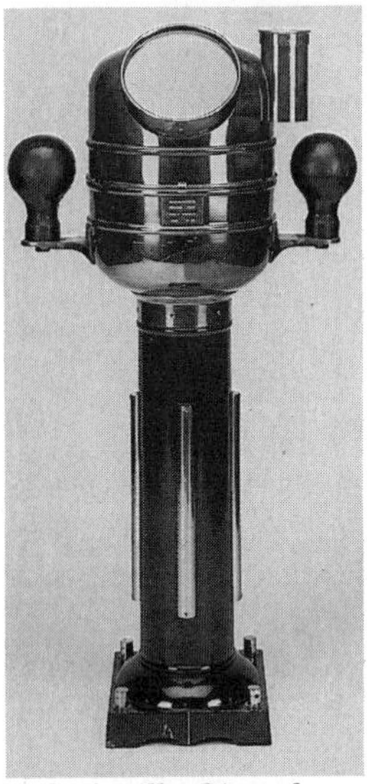

A ship's pillar binnacle, with brass bulbous shaped cover, corrector magnets, the painted column with 4 brass ribs, on a square base, compass removed, 51in (129.5cm) high.
£650–750 *CSK*

A two-day marine chronometer, by E. J. Massey, with Admiralty history, c1840, in a mahogany box, 6in (15cm) square.
£2,500–3,500 *PWh*

A copper and brass diver's helmet, with a 12 bolt clamp, 16½in (42cm) high.
£850–950 *CSK*

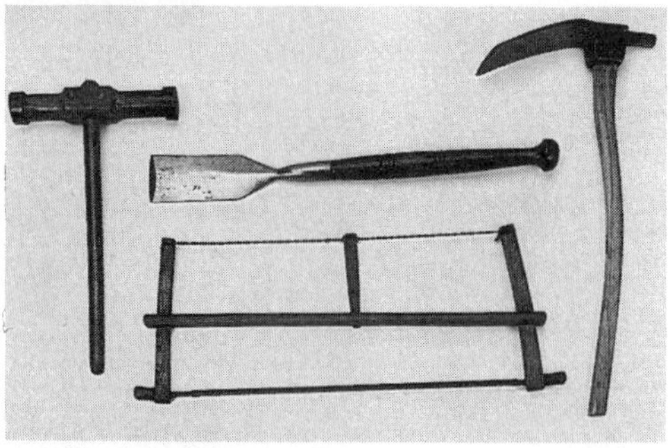

A collection of shipwright's tools, including an adze, bow saw, iron bound wooden mallet and an American hand chisel, the blade indistinctly stamped 'Hawk 1891-W10-N-'.
£350–450 *CSK*

A diorama depicting the bow and stern of a ship in distress, mounted on a carved seascape and a beach, some old damage, the base with paper label inscribed 'James Hall Surveyor of E India Shipping Sept 1851', glass fronted case for wall mounting, 45in (114cm) long.
£1,200–1,500 *CSK*

A static display model of the Spanish 104-gun first rate 'San Felipe' of 1690, by J. Greenwood, in a display case, 46½in (87cm) long.
£2,500–3,000 *CSK*

A French prisoner-of-war bone model of the 24-gun HM frigate 'Pandora', on 4 carved later legs, in a glazed case with legend, restored, early 19thC, 18½in (47cm) long.
£3,000–4,000 *CSK*

A rigged static display model of the American topsail schooner 'Eagle' of c1847, mounted on 2 turned brass columns, display base and perspex cover, 24½in (62cm) long.
£580–680 *CSK*

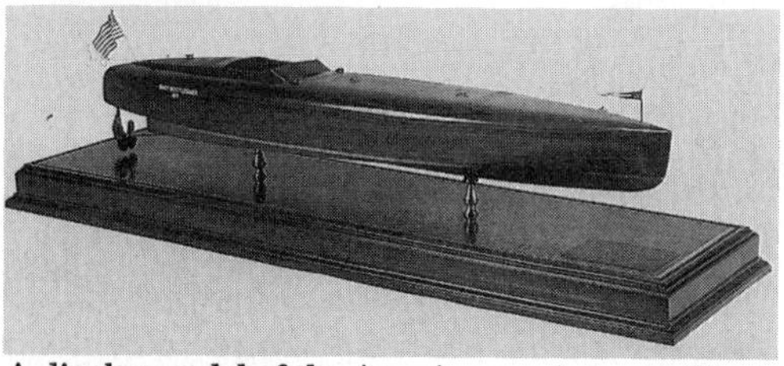

A display model of the American racing speedboat 'Baby Bootlegger' of New York, on a display base in a brass bound glazed case, 38in (96.5cm) long.
£850–1,000 *CSK*

A radio controlled model of the harbour tug 'Yarra', built by P. E. Corbett, 43in (109cm) long, together with stand, transmitter battery charger and spare propulsion unit.
£350–450 *CSK*

A model of the J Class destroyer HMS 'Kelly' of 1938, built by L. S. Griffiths, mounted on 4 turned brass columns, on a display base with a glazed cover, 66½in (169cm) long.
£2,000–3,000 *CSK*

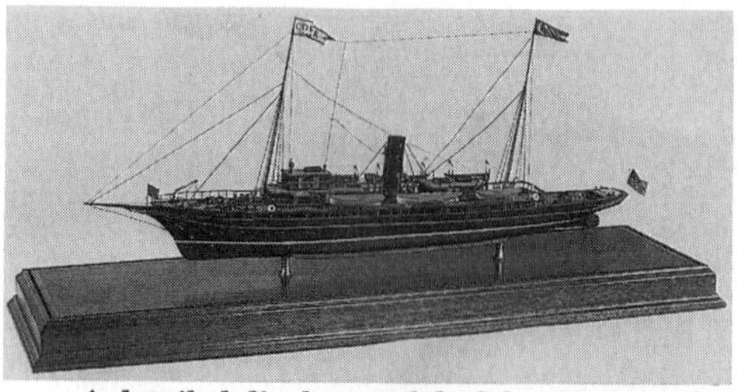

A detailed display model of the steam yacht 'Corsair II' of New York, mounted on 2 brass columns, on a display base in a brass bound glazed case, 35in (89cm) long.
£2,000–2,500 *CSK*

A clockwork powered wooden model lifeboat, built by Basset-Lowke, some old damage, 24½in (62cm) long, with a wooden carrying case.
£350–450 *CSK*

r. An electric powered model of a river launch, with planked decks, 12v motor to single shaft, three-blade propellor, 50in (127cm) long.
£275–400 *CSK*

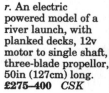

ROCK & POP

A white scarf, worn by Elvis Presley during his last performance at the Arizona State University on 23rd March, 1977, together with a ticket stub from the concert and a photograph taken during the show, scarf 45in (114cm) long, photograph 3½ by 4¼in (8.5 by 11cm).
£1,000–1,500 *CNY*

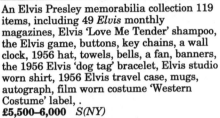

An Elvis Presley memorabilia collection 119 items, including 49 *Elvis* monthly magazines, Elvis 'Love Me Tender' shampoo, the Elvis game, buttons, key chains, a wall clock, 1956 hat, towels, bells, a fan, banners, the 1956 Elvis 'dog tag' bracelet, Elvis studio worn shirt, 1956 Elvis travel case, mugs, autograph, film worn costume 'Western Costume' label, .
£5,500–6,000 *S(NY)*

A white jumpsuit, worn by Elvis Presley, the one-piece suit with lace-up and zipper front, decorated with silver coloured grommets on the collar and along the lace-up front and cuffs, the stage suit is accompanied by an orange scarf, c1970.
£20,000–23,000 *S(NY)*

A selection of handwritten sheet music for 'Heartbreak Hotel', by Brian and Murray Wilson, for the Beach Boys, including band part arrangements for the horn section, guitar, drums, cello and violin, 1961, 13 by 9¼in (33 by 23.5cm).
£450–600 *CNY*

A studio sport's jacket, worn by Elvis Presley, the brown toned tweed jacket with rust coloured velvet accents on the collar, pockets and sleeves, worn by him in the film *Frankie and Johnny*, stamped 'Western Costume Co'. on inside sleeve, with 'Elvis Presley' label inside pocket.
£2,500–3,500 *S(NY)*

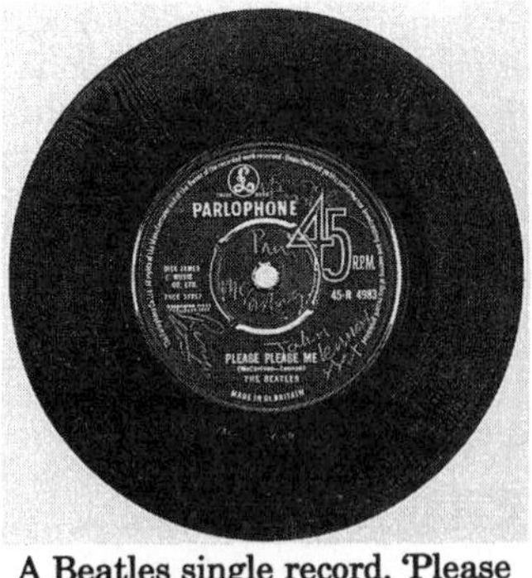

A Beatles single record, 'Please Please Me', signed on the record label by all 4 Beatles, 1963.
£1,100–1,400 *CSK*

A set of 4 Beatles drinking glasses with colour images of each of The Beatles, in original box, stamped 'Joseph Lang & Company Ltd., London for Nems Enterprises Ltd.'
£700–1,000 *S(NY)*

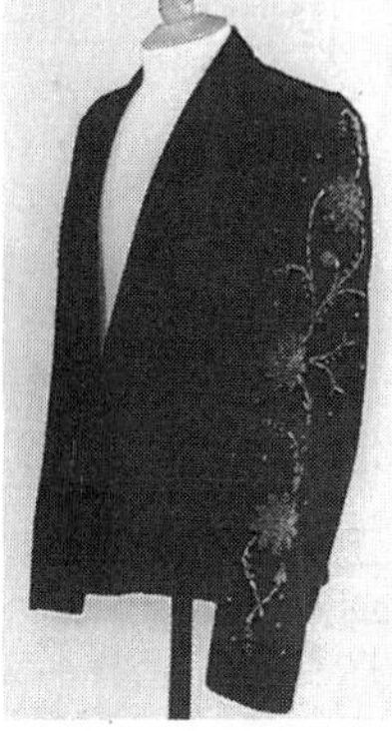

r. Marc Bolan's bolero, worn on stage by the Elfin King, in black velvet, with piped collar and cuffs, with diamanté trim on both arms, made by Granny Takes a Trip, World's End, Chelsea.
£1,500–2,500 *Bon*

A Beatles memorabilia collection, including a Shea stadium pennant, a New Sound guitar, a pillow, Ringo and George 'Yellow Submarine' hangers, loose-leaf binder, Ringo and Paul Ravell models, in original boxes, a hummer, 4 blow-up dolls, 52 items in all.
£3,000–4,000 *S(NY)*

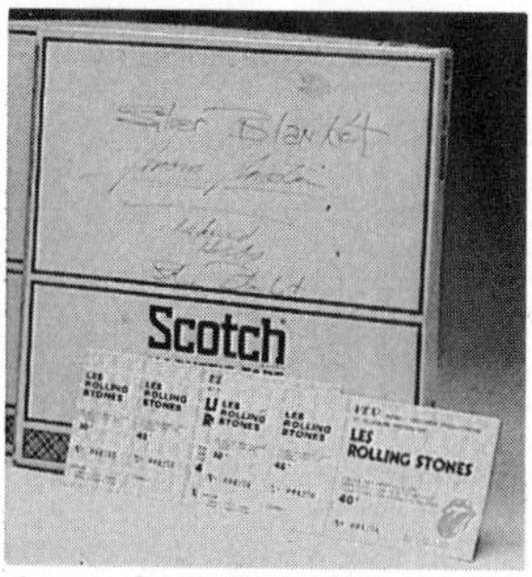

A set of 2 Rolling Stones reel-to-reel mono master tapes, for 'Silver Blanket' and 'Street Fighting Man', together with 2 unused tickets for a Rolling Stones 1976 concert at Palais Des Sports in Lyon, France.
£450–600 *CNY*

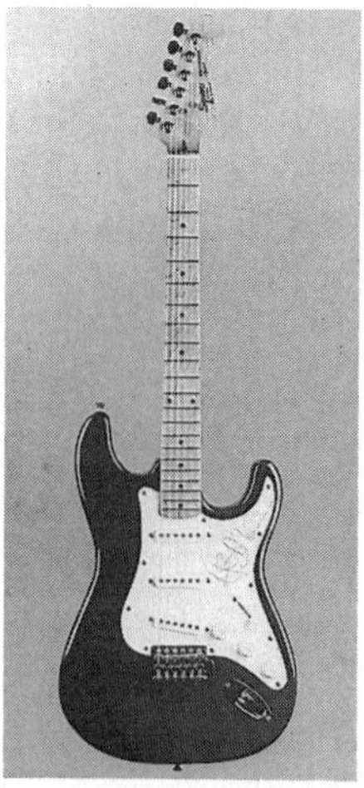

l. A red Fender Squire Stratocaster, with conventional fittings, signed 'Hank Marvin', member of The Shadows.
£400–600 *Bon*

r. A 12-string electric Dobro guitar, belonging to Jimi Hendrix, with mahogany body, 21 fret rosewood finger board with mother-of-pearl inlay, resonator, 2 sound holes, single pick-up, 2 controls, bridge and tailpiece, with a soft case.
£7,000–9,000 *Bon*

A Vincent Price/Michael Jackson presentation platinum disc, 'Thriller', R.I.A.A. certified, strip plate format 'Presented to Vincent Price', 20½ by 17in (51 by 43cm).
£350–500 *CNY*

A bronze moire underwired bikini top, embellished with gold, pink, green and orange bugle beading, belonging to Madonna and marked in black felt pen, with a letter of authenticity from Maverick Records stating that the bra was worn by Madonna on *The Girlie Show - Live Down Under*.
£2,000–3,500 *CNY*

Rock & Pop

The best prices are reserved for ephemera connected with the giants of the pop world. Elvis Presley and The Beatles are obvious examples. Good prices are also achieved for the ephemera of artists who are no longer alive, partly because of the 'legendary' status they acquire, and partly because this limits the amount of ephemera which is in circulation.

The Sex Pistols acetate, for the track 'Pretty Vacant', recorded at Pye Recording Studios, Custom Disc Cutting Service.
£400–500 *Bon*

EPHEMERA
Film & Theatre

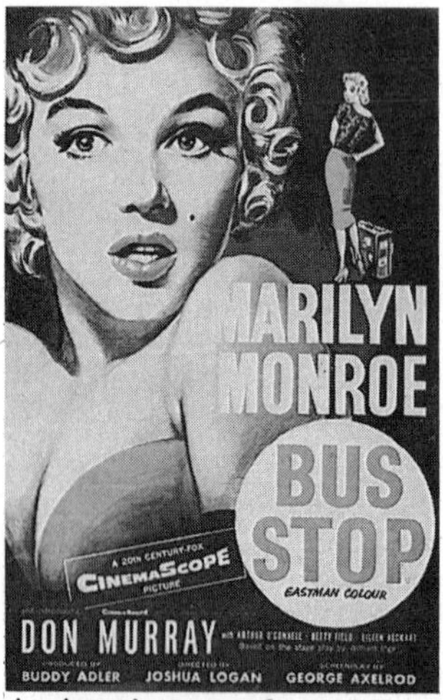

An American one sheet poster, for *Bus Stop* with Marilyn Monroe, 20th Century-Fox, 1956, good condition, 41 x 27in (104 by 69cm).
£220–270 *Bon*

A black cocktail dress, worn by Marilyn Monroe, with spaghetti straps, together with a leopard print scarf.
£1,350–1,700 *S(NY)*

An original Decca record set of *The Wizard of Oz*, comprising 4 records including Judy Garland's first recording of 'Over the Rainbow', the cover depicts scenes from the movie, good condition, 1939, 10½ by 12in (26 by 30.5cm).
£650–1,000 *S(NY)*

A vanity case, of tan leather, the maroon leather interior with holding straps for jars and bottles, inscribed on the front of the case 'MAE WEST', c1940, 14½in (36.5cm) wide.
£1,550–1,650 *CNY*

r. **Two Bette Davis pictures, including a colour picture of Bette inscribed 'For my grandson love from Grandmother', framed, with vintage photograph of Bette as a child, inscribed 'For Ashley His Grandmother at 5 years old', framed.**
£200–300 *S(NY)*

A pair of black suede platform shoes, worn by Shirley Temple, hand inscribed on the interior '4½ B S5122 2373 S. Temple', accompanied by a black and white photograph of Shirley Temple dancing in the shoes with soldiers at the Hollywood canteen, c1940s, 10 by 8in (25 by 20cm).
£500–600 *CNY*

A mask, worn by actor Jim Carey in the film *The Mask*, the latex foam rubber head mask is textured to simulate wood grain, and painted various shades of green and brown, c1994, 10in (25cm) high.
£1,700–2,000 *CNY*

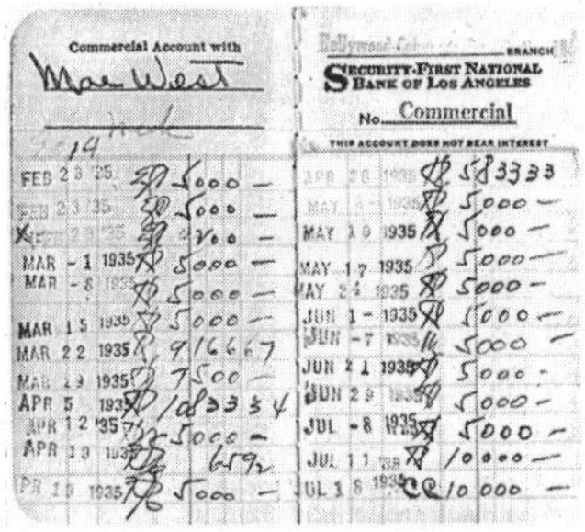

A Security First National Bank of Los Angeles bank book, belonging to Mae West, 1935–36.
£1,200–1,400 *CNY*

A book, from the film *Gone with the Wind*, featuring illustrations and theatre posters, 4 separate books describe publicity, advertising and accessories, 1939, 18½ by 17in (47 by 43cm).
£4,000–4,500 *CNY*

Twelve items of Mae West career memorabilia, one magazine features Mae West's signature on the cover.
£200–400 *CNY*

A *Superman and the Mole Men* poster, by Lippert Pictures, good condition, 1951, 41 by 27in (104 by 68.5cm).
£1,800–2,000 *S(NY)*

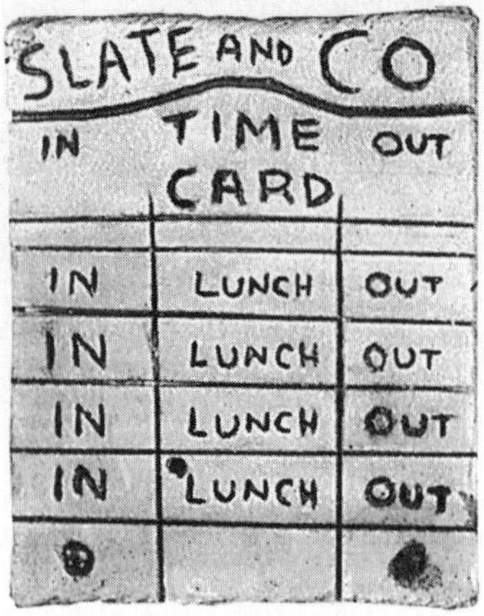

A grey styrofoam time card, from *The Flintstones*, inscribed 'Slate & Company', 1994, 8½ by 7in (21 by 17.5cm).
£500–700 *CNY*

A *Peter Pan* poster, by Disney/RKO, good condition, framed, 1953, 41 by 27in (104 by 68.5cm).
£350–500 *S(NY)*

A green foam licence plate, from Fred Flintstone's car, with yellow lettering reading 'Bedrock Yabado BC', from the film *The Flintstones*, 1994, 19½in (49cm) wide.
£1,700–2,000 *CNY*

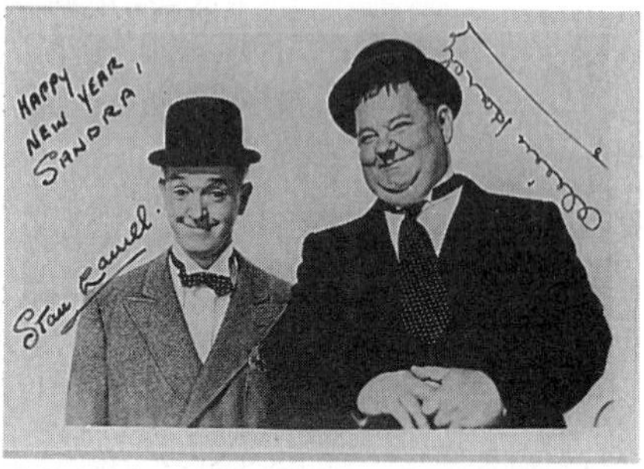

A Laurel and Hardy signed dedicated postcard, and an autographed letter from the Empire Theatre Nottingham, dated 30 December 1953 from Laurel, with envelope and a programme from that theatre.
£300–400 *N*

Cigarette Cards

r. Happy Home, Women on War Work, silks, complete, medium, good condition, set of 12.
£25–35 *VS*

Burlesque, Latin American issues, by Flora de Cuba, Las Hermanas Larrisson, showing ladies on the beach, national and other types, complete, good condition, set of 24.
£40–50 *VS*

Burlesque, by Flora de Cuba, La Hora del Descanso, lady preparing for bed, complete, good condition, set of 21.
£40–50 *VS*

l. Edwards Ringer & Bigg, Easter manoeuvres of our volunteers, 'The Battle', slight corner knocks, good condition.
£100–120 *VS*

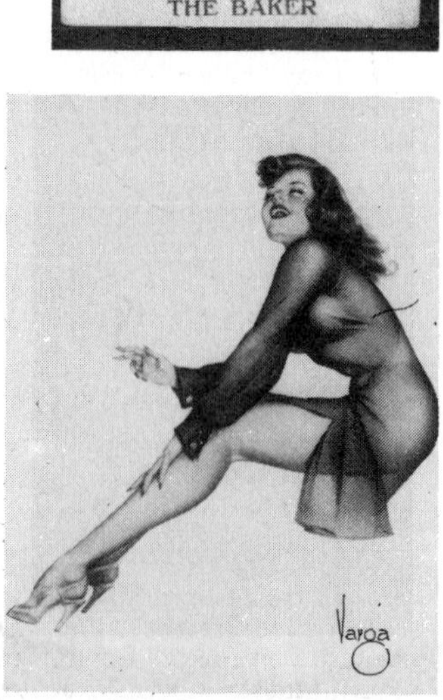

Glamour, Calendar Girls by Varga, complete, mint condition, set of 50.
£40–60 *VS*

Glamour Magazine Covers, by Kitchen Sink, 1930, complete, mint condition, set of 36.
£23–28 *VS*

British Cigarette Company, Chinese Children Games, complete, good condition, set of 50.
£40–50 *VS*

County Cricketers, Lancashire Team, excellent condition, set of 15.
£280–300 *P*

Phillips, Red Indians, complete, excellent condition, set of 25.
£30–35 *VS*

Cassells, Butterflies and Moths, complete, slight foxing, generally good condition, set of 12.
£30–40 *VS*

County Cricketers, Leicestershire Team, excellent condition, set of 14.
£260–280 *P*

County Cricketers Yorkshire team, plus Dr. W. G. Grace, excellent condition, set of 14.
£290–310 *P*

Prominent Footballers, Plymouth Argyle Team, set of 15, Queens Park Rangers, set of 15, and Sheffield Wednesday, set of 15, excellent condition.
£350–370 *P*

Miscellaneous

A lady's travel scrapbook, with embossed simulated leather cover, written on the spine 'Souvenir d'Amitié', opening to reveal 2 engravings of rural towns, tapestries, hand painted pictures of flowers, pressed flowers and poems, mid-19thC, complete with slipcase.
£250–300 *CSK*

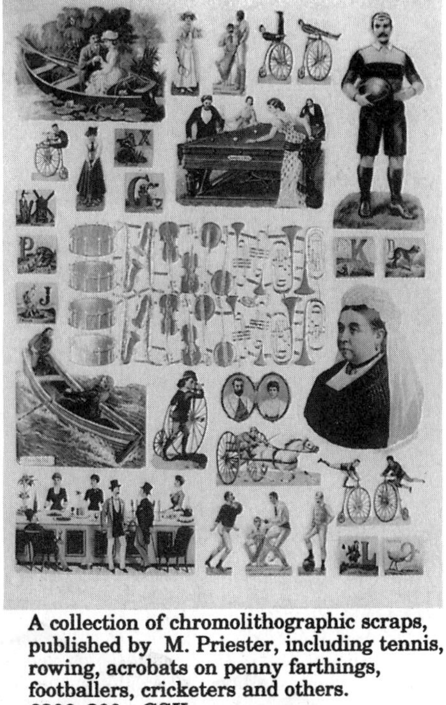

A collection of chromolithographic scraps, published by M. Priester, including tennis, rowing, acrobats on penny farthings, footballers, cricketers and others.
£200–300 *CSK*

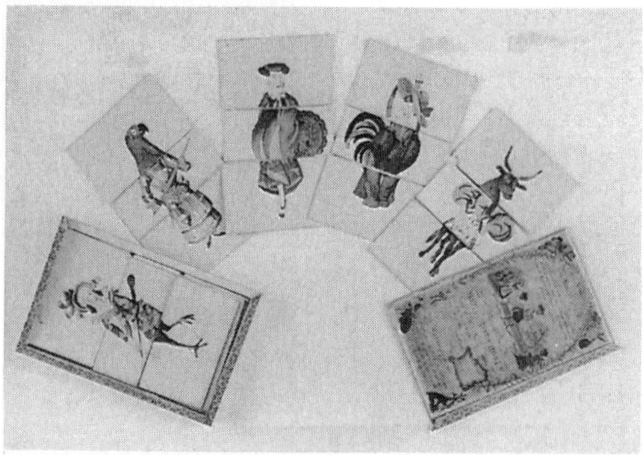

An engraved and hand coloured metamorphic game, called Nouvelles Metamorphoses, the comical figures with interchangeable heads, bodies and legs, 54 parts, original box, each part 3½ by 5in (8.5 by 12.5cm).
£250–300 *CSK*

An engraved and hand coloured game, called Huit Mille Metamorphoses, the comical figures with interchangeable heads, bodies and feet, original box, each part 3 by 4in (7.5 by 10cm).
£180–220 *CSK*

l. A collection of reliefs and miniature scraps, late 19thC.
£210–240 *CSK*

A collection of chromolithographic scraps and relief, including animals in tails, elephant sitting at a table, riding a tricycle and performing circus tricks, butterflies, dressed rabbits, and a relief of piglets at school making trouble, 11½ by 6½in (29 by 16cm).
£270–350 *CSK*

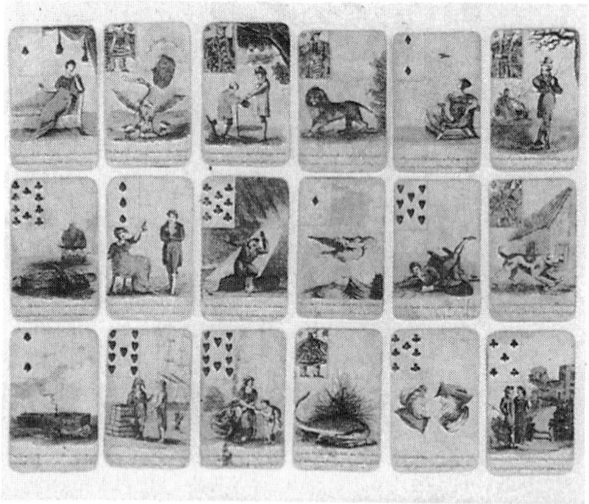

l. A deck of fortune telling playing cards, with spades and clubs engraved in black, hearts and diamonds in ochre, each card with an illustration and description below, c1750, one card missing.
£400–450 *CSK*

Comics

A collection of *Action Comics*, National Comics Publications.
£2,700–3,300 *S(NY)*

A collection of *Mickey Mouse Magazines*, volume 4, Nos. 1-12, from the Western Files.
£3,000–3,500 *S(NY)*

A *Tarzan* Sunday page, entitled 'The Fiery Flood', No. 517, dated '2-2-41', by Burne Hogarth, pen and ink on paper, 27 by 21in (68.5 by 53cm).
£2,500–3,000 *S(NY)*

A collection of the *World's Finest Comics*, approximately 185, from May 1951 to January 1986.
£2,000–2,200 *S(NY)*

A miscellaneous collection of *Marvel Comic* books, from the White Mountain Collection.
£1,000–1,500 *S(NY)*

A 4-colour Walt Disney cover, *Mickey Mouse Outwits the Phantom Blot*, No. 16, series No. 1, by Dell Publishing Company, good condition, 1939.
£1,400–1,600 *S(NY)*

A cover re-creation and interior artwork for *Yuppies from Hell*, No. 3, by Barbara Slate.
£3,000–3,500 *S(NY)*

A Jack Kirby cover re-creation to Marvel's original cover of *The Amazing Fantasy*, No. 15, pencil, on paper, signed, 18½ by 12in (46.5 by 30.5cm).
£7,500–8,500 *S(NY)*

Jack Kirby was the original artist of the original cover.

An *All-Flash Quarterly,* No.1, by DC Comics, 1941.
£2,500–3,000 *CNY*

This book is unique having a double cover.

A collection of *Archie Comics*, Nos. 1,2,3,5,6,7,9,10,73, by MLJ Publishing, 1942.
£4,500–5,000 *CNY*

This was the first comic of its kind to deal with high school adventures and is listed as scarce in The Overstreet Guide.

A Jack Kirby cover re-creation to Marvel's original cover of *Tales of Suspense,* No. 39, pencil on paper, signed, 18½ by 12in (46.5 by 30.5cm).
£5,000–5,500 *S(NY)*

Jack Kirby was the original artist of the original cover.

Captain America Comics, No.1, Timely Publications, 1941, artwork by Simon & Kirby.
£24,500–26,000 *CNY*

GLOSSARY

We have attempted here to define some of the terms that you will come across in this book. If there are any terms or technicalities you would like explained or you feel should be included in future, please let us know.

Aalto, Alvar (1898-1976): A Finnish Art Deco architect and furniture designer, noted for his bentwood chairs, made from the 1930s onwards.
acid engraving: Technique of decorating glass by coating it in resin, incising a design and exposing the revealed areas to hydrochloric acid fumes.
acid-gilding: 19thC technique for decorating pottery whereby the surface is etched with hydrofluoric acid and the low-relief pattern gilded.
acorn knop: Wine glass stem moulding in the shape of an upturned acorn - the cup uppermost.
Adam, Robert (1728-1792): A Scottish born architect who created a neo-classical architectural and decorative style of furniture.
Admiral jug: Toby jug depicting an admiral; originally to commemorate Lord Howe's victory over the French in 1794.
agate ware: 18thC pottery, veined or marbled to resemble the mineral agate.
air-beaded: Glass containing bubbles of air, like strings of beads.
air-twist: Helical decoration in the stem of wine glasses, developed 1740-70, in which an air bubble in the glass is drawn out and twisted to form complex spirals, e.g. lace twist, multiple spiral, spiral gauze, corkscrew multi-ply, cable, etc.
ale glass: Drinking glass with tall stem and tall narrow bowl, capacity 3-4 fluid ounces, used for strong beer, sometimes decorated with barley ears and hops, 18thC.
all-bisque doll: One with body and limbs as well as head of biscuit-fired ceramic.
American Victorian: The period between 1830-1900 that incorporates several styles of furniture; Victorian, Gothic, Victorian rococo, Victorian renaissance and Eastlake.
Americana: Antiques and collectables that reflect the growth, culture and character of American culture.
Amish: Followers of Jacob Amman who made up a religious sect that settled in Pennsylvania during the 1700s. They produce quilts and other primitive handcrafts that are highly prized.
Ansbach: Factory specialising in large, colourful faience ornaments from the 1730s, and porcelain tableware late 18th and 19thC.
antiquities: Generally accepted to mean objects made before AD600 in Europe, and of ancient Egyptian, Greek or Roman origin. Also used to cover the pre-Columbian era in the Americas and the products of civilisations now extinct.
architect's table: Table or desk, the top of which rises at the back to provide an angled working area.
Arita (1): Blue and white Japanese pottery imported from the mid-17thC and much imitated by European makers.
Arita (2): Japanese 18thC porcelain, typically with flower-basket pattern in blue, red and gold, also called Imari ware after the port from which it was exported.
armoire: A large French cupboard or wardrobe, usually of monumental character.
associated (1): Term used of a set of silverware in which one part is of the same design but not originally made for it - e.g. of a teapot and associated stand.
associated (2): Of weapons, any part which is not original.
Aubusson: French town producing tapestries, and tapestry-weave carpets, since 17thC although formal workshops were not established until c1743.
automata: Any moving toy or decorative object, usually powered by a clockwork mechanism.
ball-jointed doll: One with ball-jointed limbs, able to swivel in all directions, as opposed to stiff jointed.
baluster stem: Glass with a swelling stem, like an architectural baluster: 'true' if the thicker swelling is beneath, 'inverted' if above. From late 17thC.
barley-twist: Form of turning popular in late 17thC which resembles a spiral of rope.
basaltes: Black porcelain invented by Josiah Wedgwood with a polished, stone-like finish; modern reproductions are called basalt wares.
Bauhaus: Influential German artistic style which was inspired by new industrial materials, such as stainless steel, with the emphasis on cubic, unadorned shapes. The term was coined by the architect Gropius who became director of the Weimar School of Arts and Crafts in 1919, and renamed it the Bauhaus.
bébé: French dolls made by Bru and others in the latter half 19thC, modelled on actual children of 8-12 years of age.
Belleek: Very thin and iridescent parian ware, originally made at Belleek, in Ireland, late 19thC.
bisque: French term for biscuit ware, or unglazed porcelain.
Bizarre: Name of a highly-colourful range of Art Deco tableware designed by Clarice Cliff and manufactured by the Staffordshire potter, A. J. Wilkinson Ltd, in the 1930s.
bladed knop: Knop with a concave outward curve, culminating in a sharp edge.
bombé: Outswelling, curving or bulging. Term used to describe a chest with a bulging front. In fashion from Louis XV period.
bonheur du jour: Small French writing table of delicate proportions with a raised back comprising a cabinet or shelves.
Bow: Important London porcelain factory producing blue and white wares 1749-76, and polychrome wares 1754 onwards; early work shows Chinese influence (peony and chrysanthemum flower decorations), later work in Meissen style.
bowfront: An outwardly curving front.
boxwood: A closely grained yellow coloured wood.
bracket clock: Originally a 17thC clock which had to be set high up on a bracket because of the length of the weights; now generally applied to any small mantel or table clock.
bracket foot: A type of foot for case pieces which appears somewhat shaped as a right-angled bracket below the front edge.
Brameld: Family that acquired the Rockingham factory, Yorkshire, early 19thC; producers of the fine bone china noted for its rich enamelling and gilt decoration.
Breakfast table: A small table with hinged side leaves, suitable for one or two people.
Bristol: Important porcelain factory established c1749, producing delftware, and (c1770) enamelled and gilded wares decorated with flowers and swags. Also, 17th and 18thC delftwares (bowls, figure groups, jugs) produced by several factories in the area.
Bru & Cie: Leading French doll maker 1866-99; noted for dolls in elaborate contemporary costumes.
buffet: Open structures, of more than one tier.
bureau: Writing desk with either a fall, a cylinder or a tambour front.

bureau bookcase: Bureau with a glazed-fronted bookcase fitted above it.
bureau cabinet: Bureau with a solid-doored or mirrored cabinet fitted above it, often containing further fitted cupboards and drawers.
bureau de dame: Writing desk of delicate appearance and designed for use by ladies. Usually raised above slender cabriole legs and with one or two external drawers.
bureau-plat: French writing table with a flat top and drawers in the frieze.
cabriole leg: Tail curving leg subject to many designs and produced with club, pad, paw, claw-and-ball, and scroll feet.
caddy: Usually silver (but also of ceramic, wood or enamel) container for tea with a lead-lined compartment; often two compartments with a spoon and glass bowl for blending two types of leaf.
camaieu: Porcelain decoration using different tones of the one colour.
cameo glass: A sandwich of coloured glass which is then cut or etched away to create a multi-colour design in relief. An ancient technique rediscovered by Emile Gallé and popular with Art Nouveau and Art Deco glassmakers in the early 20thC.
candle slide: Small wooden slide designed to carry a candlestick.
Cardew, Michael (1901-83): English art potter, taught by Bernard Leach, and inspired by Oriental porcelain. Worked at the Winchcombe Pottery 1926-39.
Carlton House desk: A distinct type of writing desk which has a raised back with drawers which extend forward at the sides to create an 'enclosed' central writing area.
Carlton Ware: Brand name of Art Nouveau pottery made by Wiltshaw and Robinson, a Stoke-on-Trent pottery founded in 1897.
carousel figures: Horses and other animals from fairground carousels or roundabouts, usually classified as either 'jumpers' or 'standers'.
carriage clock: Originally one fitted with a device to ensure that the jolts common in the days of coach travel would not interfere with the oscillations of the balance spring. Now any small portable oblong clock of rectangular form, popular from the 19thC to the present day.
cartel clock: An 18thC French wall clock in the shape of a shield, often with a gilded bronze case and elaborately ornamented in rococo style.
cartouche: An ornate tablet or shield surrounded by scrollwork and foliage, often bearing a maker's name, inscription or coat-of-arms.
castelli: Maiolica from the Abruzzi region of Italy, noted for delicate landscapes painted by members of the Grue family.
Caughley: Shropshire factory, established c1750, producing porcelain very like that of Worcester, including early willow-pattern, often embellished by gilding.
celadon: Chinese stonewares with an opaque grey-green glaze, first made in the Sung dynasty and still made today, principally in Korea.
cellaret: Lidded container on legs designed to hold wine. The interior is often divided into sections for individual bottles.
centrepiece: Silver ornament, usually decorative rather than functional, designed to occupy the centre of a dining table.
Chaffers, Richard & Partners: Liverpool pottery manufacturer, operating around 1754-65, producing earthenwares resembling china and modelled on Worcester forms.
chaise longue: An elongated chair, the seat long enough to support the sitter's legs.
champlevé: Enamelling on copper or bronze, similar to cloisonné, in which a glass paste is applied to the hollowed-out design, fired and ground smooth.
character doll: One with a naturalistic face, especially laughing, crying, pouting, etc.
character jug: Earthenware jugs and sometimes mugs, widely made in 18th and 19thC, depicting a popular character, such as a politician, general, jockey or actor.
chest-on-chest: A chest of drawers supported on another chest of drawers, also known as a tallboy.
chesterfield: Type of large over-stuffed sofa introduced in late 19thC.
cheval mirror: Large toilet mirror in a frame with four legs, the mirror being pivoted and adjustable within the frame. Also known as a horse dressing glass and a psyche. Made c1750 onwards.
chiffonier: Generally a twin door cupboard with one or two drawers above and surmounted by shelves.
Chin dynasty: period in Chinese history AD1115-1260.
Chinese export porcelain: 16th to 18thC wares made in China specifically for export and often to European designs.
Chinese Imari: Chinese imitations of Japanese blue, red and gold painted Imari wares, made from the early 18thC.
Ch'ing dynasty: From 1644 to 1912, the period during which much decorated Chinese porcelain was exported to Europe.
chinoiserie: The fashion, prevailing in the late 18thC, for Chinese-style ornamentation on porcelain, wallpapers and fabrics, furniture and garden architecture.
chryselephantine: Originally made of gold and ivory, but now used for Art Deco statues made of ivory and another metal, typically bronze and very desirable.
claw and ball foot: A carved foot, shaped like a ball held in a talon , or claw.
Cliff, Clarice (1899-1972): Employed by A. J. Wilkinson Ltd, the pottery at Newport, Staffordshire, as artistic director in the 1930s. Designer of the colourful 'Bizarre' and 'Fantasque' ranges of mass-produced china.
clock garniture: A matching group of clock and vases or candelabra made for the mantel shelf. Often highly ornate.
cloisonné: Enamelling on metal with divisions in the design separated by lines of fine brass wire. A speciality of the Limoges region of France in the Middle Ages, and of Chinese craftsmen to the present day.
Coalport china: Porcelain manufactured at Coalbrookdale, Shropshire, from the 1790s, noted for the translucent felspathic wares produced from 1820 and the delicate colours of the figure groups.
coffer: In strict definition a coffer is a travelling trunk which is banded with metalwork and covered with leather or other material. However, the word tends to be used quite freely to describe chests of various kinds.
Colonial: An American object made during the period when the country consisted of 13 Colonies.
Commedia dell'Arte: Figures from traditional Italian theatre (Harlequin, Columbine, Scaramouche, Pantaloon) often depicted in porcelain groups in 18thC.
compound twist: In a wine glass stem, any air-twist made of multiple spirals; e.g. lace twist, gauze and multi-ply.
console table: Decorative side table with no back legs, being supported against the wall by brackets.
cordial glass: Smaller version of a wine glass, with a thick stem, heavy foot and small bowl; evolved 17thC for strong drink.
country furniture: General term for furniture made by provincial craftsmen; cottage furniture and especially that made of pine, oak, elm and the fruitwoods.

credenza: Used today to describe a type of side cabinet which is highly decorated and shaped. Originally it was an Italian sideboard used as a serving table.

crested china: Pottery decorated with colourful heraldic crests, first made by Goss but, by 1880, being produced in quantity by manufacturers throughout the UK and in Germany.

cup and cover: Carved decoration found on the bulbous turned legs of some Elizabethan furniture.

cut glass: Glass carved with revolving wheels and abrasive to create sharp-edged facets that reflect and refract light so as to sparkle and achieve a prismatic (rainbow) effect. Revived Bohemia 17thC, and common until superseded by pressed glass for utilitarian objects.

Cymric: The trade-name used by Liberty & Company for a mass produced range of silverware, inspired by Celtic art, introduced in 1899, and often incorporating enamelled pictorial plaques.

cypher: An impressed or painted mark on porcelain which gives the year of manufacture; each factory had its own set of codes; used principally mid to late 19thC.

davenport (1): Small writing desk with a sloping top and a series of real and false drawers below. Some have a writing surface which slides forward and rising compartments at the rear.

davenport (2): American term for a day-bed or reclining sofa with headrest.

Davenport (3): Important factory at Longport, Staffordshire, founded 1793 by John Davenport; originally manufactured earthenware, but noted from 1820 for very fine botanical wares and Imari style decoration.

day-bed: Couch with one sloped end to support the head and back whilst reclined. Either upholstered or caned. Made from 16thC until the mid-18thC. Also known in the US as a davenport.

Delft: Dutch tin glazed earthenwares named after the town of Delft, the principal production centre. 16thC Delft shows Chinese influence but by 17thC the designs are based on Dutch landscapes. Similar pottery made in England from the late 16thC is usually termed 'delftware'.

Della Robbia: Florentine Renaissance sculptor who invented technique of applying vitreous glaze to terracotta; English art pottery made at Birkenhead, late 19thC, in imitation of his work.

Denby: Stoneware made by Bourne & Son, at Denby, 19thC; also known as Bourne pottery.

Derby: Important porcelain factory founded 1756, producing very fine figure groups - often called English Meissen - as well as painted wares decorated with landscapes and botanical scenes.

die-stamping: Method of mass producing a design on metal by machine which passes sheet metal between a steel die and a drop hammer. Used for forming toys as well as stamping cutlery etc.

Dresser, Christopher (1835-1904): Influential English pottery and glass designer who was inspired by Japanese art and worked for Tiffany as well as the pottery firms of Ault, Linthorpe and Pilkington.

drop-in seat: Upholstered chair seat which is supported on the seat rails but which can be lifted out independently.

Du Paquier: Porcelain from Vienna, especially chinoiserie wares produced early 18thC.

écuelle: 17thC vessel, usually of silver, but also of ceramic for serving soup. Has a shallow, circular bowl with two handles and a domed cover. It often comes complete with a stand.

eglomisé: Painting on glass, associated with clock faces: often the reverse side of the glass is covered in gold or silver leaf through which a pattern is engraved and then painted black.

electroplate: The process of using electrical current to coat a base metal or alloy with silver, invented 1830s and gradually superseding Sheffield plate.

enamel (1): In ceramics, a second coloured but translucent glaze laid over the first glaze.

enamel (2): Coloured glass, applied to metal, ceramic or glass in paste form and then fired for decorative effect.

EPNS: Electroplated nickel silver; i.e. nickel alloy covered with a layer of silver using the electroplate process.

etched glass: Technique of cutting layers of glass away, using acid, much favoured by Art Nouveau and Art Deco glassmakers. Such sculpture in high relief is known as deep etched, and layers of multi-coloured glass were often treated in this way to make cameo glass.

fairings: Mould-made figure groups in cheap porcelain, produced in great quantity in the 19th and 20thC, especially in Germany; often humorous or sentimental. So called because they were sold, or given as prizes, at fairs.

famille jaune: 'Yellow family'; Chinese porcelain vessels in which yellow is the predominant ground colour.

famille noire: 'Black family'; Chinese porcelain in which black is the predominant ground colour.

famille rose: 'Pink family'; Chinese porcelain vessels with an enamel (overglaze) of pink to purple tones.

famille verte: 'Green family'; Chinese porcelain with a green enamel (overglaze), laid over yellows, blues, purples and iron red.

Fantasque: Name of a colourful range of household china designed by Clarice Cliff and manufactured in the 1930s by the Staffordshire pottery, A.J. Wilkinson Ltd.

fauteuil: French open-armed drawing room chair.

filigree: Lacy openwork of silver or gold thread, produced in large quantities since end 19thC.

flag bottom chair: Chair made with a rush seat.

flatware: Collective name for flat pottery, such as plates, trenchers and trays, as opposed to cups, vases and bowls.

fluted: A border that resembles a scalloped edge, used as a decoration on furniture, glass, silver and porcelain items.

frosted glass: Glass with a surface pattern made to resemble frost patterns or snow-crystals; common on pressed glass vessels for serving cold confections.

Fulda: Factory at Hessen that produced some of Germany's best faience in the mid-18thC; in the late 18thC turned to producing Meissen-style porcelain.

fusee: 18thC clockwork invention; a cone shaped drum, linked to the spring barrel by a length of gut or chain. The shape compensates for the declining strength of the mainspring thus ensuring constant timekeeping.

Gallé, Emile (1846-1904): Father of the French Art Nouveau movement and founder of a talented circle of designers based around Nancy. Simultaneously, in the 1880s, he designed delicate furniture embellished with marquetry and began experimenting with new glass techniques. In 1889, he developed cameo glass; in 1897 'marquetry in glass', or 'marquetrie de verre'. After his death, factories continued to produce his wares, signed Gallé but marked with a star, until the 1930s.

gilding: Process of applying thin gold foil to a surface. There are two methods. Oil gilding involves the use of linseed oil and is applied directly onto the woodwork. Water gilding requires the wood to be painted with gesso.

Glasgow School: Originally the name of the Glasgow School of Art at which Charles Rennie Mackintosh studied in the 1880s, and whose new buildings he designed in the 1890s. Now used to describe the style developed by Mackintosh and his followers, a simplified linear form of Art Nouveau highly influential on Continental work of the period.

Granite ware: A durable and inexpensive white earthenware, sold in the USA during the mid-1800s.

grisaille: Type of monochrome used to decorate furniture during the 18thC.

hall chair: Strongly constructed chair lacking intricate ornament and upholstery, being designed to stand in a hall to accommodate messengers and other callers in outdoor clothing. At the same time it had to be attractive enough to impress more important callers and was often carved with a crest or coat-of-arms for this purpose.

hallmark: Collective term for all the marks found on silver or gold consisting of an assay office, quality, date and maker's marks; sometimes the term is used only of the assay office mark.

hand pressed: Any glass object made in a hand operated press instead of a machine press.

handkerchief table: Table with a triangular top and a single triangular leaf. This arrangement enables it to fit into a corner when closed and form a square when opened.

hard paste: True porcelain made of china stone (petuntse) and kaolin; the formula was long known to, and kept secret by, Chinese potters but only discovered in the 1750s in England, from where it spread to the rest of Europe and the Americas.

harewood: Sycamore which has been stained a greenish colour is known as harewood. It is used mainly as an inlay wood and was known as silverwood in the 18thC.

Hirado: Japanese porcelain with figure and landscape painting in blue on a white body, often depicting boys at play, made exclusively for the Lords of Hirado, near Arita, mid-18th to mid-19thC.

hiramakie: Flat decoration in Japanese lacquerware, as opposed to carving or relief.

Hornby: manufacturers of clockwork and electric locomotives from c1910, best known today for the 'Dublo' range, introduced mid-1940s.

indianische Blumen: Indian flowers; painting on porcelain in the Oriental style, especially on mid-18thC Meissen and Höchst.

intaglio: Incised gem-stone, often set in a ring, used in antiquity and during the Renaissance as a seal. Any incised decoration; the opposite of carving in relief.

ironstone: Stoneware, patented 1813 by Charles James Mason, containing ground glassy slag, a by-product of iron smelting, for extra strength.

ivory porcelain: Development of 19thC, similar to parian but ivory coloured in biscuit form.

Jacobite: Wine glasses engraved with symbols of the Jacobites (supporters of Prince Charles Edward Stuart's claim to the English throne). Genuine examples date from 1746 to 1788. Countless later copies and forgeries exist.

Jumeau, Pierre François: Important French doll maker noted for 'Parisiennes', active 1842-99.

Kakiemon: Family of 17thC Japanese potters who produced wares decorated with flowers and figures on a white ground in distinctive colours: azure, yellow, turquoise and soft red. Widely imitated in Europe.

kashgai: Rugs woven by Iranian nomadic tribes, notable for the springy lustrous texture, and finely detailed rectilinear designs.

kelim: Flat woven rugs lacking a pile; also the flat woven fringe used to finish off the ends of a pile carpet.

kneehole desk: Writing desk with a space between the drawer pedestals for the user's legs.

knop (1): Knob, protuberance or swelling in the stem of a wine glass, of various forms which can be used as an aid to dating and provenance.

knop (2): In furniture, a swelling on an upright member.

Knox, Archibald (1864-1931): English designer of the Cymric range of silverware and Tudric pewter for Liberty's store in London, responsible for some 400 different designs.

Lalique, René (1860-1945): French designer of Art Nouveau jewellery in gold, silver and enamel, who founded his own workshop in Paris in 1885. After 1900 he turned to making figures in crystal and opalescent glass. From 1920 he emerged as the leading Art Deco glass maker, and his factory produced a huge range of designs.

lambing chair: Sturdy chair with a low seat traditionally used by shepherds at lambing time. It has tall enclosed sides for protection against draughts.

Lazy Susan: Another name for a dumb waiter.

Leach, Bernard (1887-1979): Father of English craft pottery who studied in China and Japan in order to master Oriental glazing techniques.

Lenci: Italian company manufacturing dolls with pressed felt faces in Turin in the 1920s, noted for the sideways glance of the painted eyes.

Liberty & Co.: Principal outlet for Art Nouveau designs in England. Arthur Lasenby Liberty (1843-1917) founded his furniture and drapery shop in 1875. Later he commissioned designs exclusive to his store, including Cymric silver and Tudric pewter, which gave rise to a distinctive 'Liberty style'.

linenfold: Carved decoration which resembles folded linen.

Liverpool: Important pottery production centre from the mid-18thC, noted for blue painted delftware punch bowls, and early porcelain produced by several different factories, now eagerly collected.

longcase clock: First made c1660 in England, a tall clock consisting of a case which houses the weights or pendulum and a hood housing the movement and dial. In U.S.A. also known as a tallcase clock.

lorgnette: A pair of opera glasses, or spectacles, mounted on a handle.

lowboy: A small dressing table, usually with a single frieze drawer or a small central shallow drawer flanked on either side by a deep drawer.

lyre clock: Early 19thC American pendulum clock, its shape resembling that of a lyre.

made up: A piece of furniture that has been put together from parts of other pieces of furniture.

majolica: Often used, in error, as an alternative spelling for maiolica; correctly, a richly-enamelled stoneware with high relief decoration developed by Minton, mid-19thC.

mantel clock: Clock provided with feet to stand on the mantelpiece.

Martinware: Art pottery made by the Martin brothers between 1873 and 1914, characterised by grotesque human and animal figures in stoneware.

medicine chest: Used by itinerant medics from 17thC, usually with compartments, labelled bottles, spoons and balances.

Meiji: Period in Japanese history 1868 to 1912, when the nation's art was much influenced by contact with the West, and much was made specifically for export.

mihrab: Prayer niche with a pointed arch; the motif which distinguishes a prayer rug from other types.

Mei ping: Chinese for cherry blossom, used to describe a tall vase, with high shoulders, small neck and narrow mouth, used to display flowering branches.

millefiori: Multi-coloured, or mosaic, glass, made since antiquity by fusing a number of coloured glass rods into a cane, and cutting off thin sections; much used to ornament paperweights.

Ming dynasty: Period in Chinese history from 1368 to 1644.
Minton: Pottery established by Thomas Minton, at Stoke-on-Trent, in late 18thC. Originally produced earthenwares and creamware; then, most famously, bone china. After 1850 the company produced fine copies of Renaissance maiolica and, in 1870, set up the Minton Art Pottery Studio in London as a training academy for young designers, producing fine Art Nouveau work.
Moorcroft, William (1872-1946): Staffordshire art potter, who worked for MacIntyre & Co. from 1898, and set up independently in 1913. Known for colourful vases with floral designs and his 'Florian' and 'Aurelian' wares.
Moore, Bernard: Founder of art pottery based in Longton, Staffordshire, c1900 specialising in unusual glaze effects.
Morris, William (1834-96): Regarded as the progenitor of the Art Nouveau style. The company Morris, Marshall and Faulkner (later simply Morris & Co.) was founded in 1861 to produce wallpaper, stained glass, chintz carpets and tapestries. The origins of his style can be traced to medieval Gothic, but his organic flowers and bird motifs encouraged later artists to seek inspiration for their designs in nature.
netsuke: Japanese carved toggles made to secure sagemono ('hanging things') to the obi (waist belt) from a cord; usually of ivory, lacquer, silver or wood, from the 16thC.
New Hall: Late 18thC potters' co-operative in Staffordshire making porcelain and bone china wares.
ormolu: Strictly, gilded bronze or brass but sometimes used loosely of any yellow metal. Originally used for furniture handles and mounts but, from the 18thC, for ink stands, candlesticks, clock cases, etc.
overlay: In cased glass, the top layer, usually engraved to reveal a different coloured layer beneath.
overmantel: Area above the shelf on a mantelpiece, often consisting of a mirror in an ornate frame, or some architectural feature in wood or stone.
over stuffed: Descriptive of upholstered furniture where the covering extends over the frame of the seat.
ovolo: Moulding of convex quarter-circle section. Sometimes found around the edges of drawers to form a small overlap onto the carcase.
papier mâché: moulded paper pulp, suitable for japanning and polishing, used for small articles such as trays, boxes, tea-caddies, and coasters.
Parisienne doll: French bisque head doll with a stuffed kid leather body, made by various manufacturers 1860s to 1880s.
pate: Crown of a doll's head into which the hair is stitched, usually of cork in the better quality dolls.
pâte-sur-pâte: 19thC Sèvres porcelain technique, much copied, of applying slip decoration to the body before firing.
Pembroke table: Small table with two short drop leaves along its length. Named after the Countess of Pembroke who is said to have been the first to order one. Also once known as a breakfast table.
percussion lock: Early 19thC firearm, one of the first to be fired by the impact of a sharp-nosed hammer on the cartridge cap.
pewter: Alloy of tin and lead; the higher the tin content the higher the quality; sometimes with small quantities of antimony added to make it hard with a highly polished surface.
pier glass: Mirror designed to be fixed to the pier, or wall, between two tall window openings, often partnered by a matching pier table. Made from mid-17thC.
Pilkington: Associated with the Lancashire glass factory, this pottery produced Art Nouveau ceramics in the early 20thC, remarkable for its iridescent and colourful glazes.
Pinxton: Soft-paste porcelain imitating Derby, made in Nottingham by William Billingsley, from c1800.
plate: Old fashioned term, still occasionally used, to describe gold and silver vessels; not to be confused with 'Sheffield plate', or plated vessels generally, in which silver is fused to a base metal alloy.
pole screen: Small adjustable screen mounted on a pole and designed to stand in front of an open fire to shield a lady's face from the heat.
portrait doll: One modelled on a well known figure.
poupard: Doll without legs, often mounted on a stick; popular in 19thC.
poured wax doll: One made by pouring molten wax on to a mould.
powder flask: Device for measuring out a precise quantity of priming powder made to be suspended from a musketeer's belt or bandolier and often ornately decorated. Sporting flasks are often made of antler and carved with hunting scenes.
powder horn: Cow horn hollowed out, blocked at the wide end with a wooden plug and fitted with a measuring device at the narrow end, used by musketeers for dispensing a precise quantity of priming powder.
pressed glass: Early 19thC invention, exploited rapidly in America, whereby mechanical pressure was used to form glassware in a mould, instead of using compressed air.
puzzle jug: Delftware form made from the 17thC, with several spouts and a syphon system, none of which will pour unless the others are blocked.
Qing: Alternative spelling of Ch'ing - the dynasty that ruled China from 1644 to 1916.
quarter clock: One which strikes the quarter and half hours as well as the full hours.
Quimper faience: From the factory in Brittany, France, established late 17thC and closely modelled on Rouen wares.
rack: Tall superstructure above a dresser.
refectory table: Modern term for the long dining tables of the 17thC and later.
regulator: Clock of great accuracy, thus sometimes used for controlling or checking other time pieces.
rosette: A round floral design ornament.
rummer/roemer: Originally 16th/17thC German wide bowled wine glass on a thick stem, decorated with prunts, on a base of concentric glass coils, often in green glass (waldglas). Widely copied throughout Europe in many forms.
sabre leg: Elegant curving leg associated with furniture of the Regency period but first appearing near the end of the 18thC. Also known as Trafalgar leg.
St. Cloud: Factory near Paris, famous for soft-paste porcelain in the first half of the 18thC, decorated in Kakiemon style and imitation blanc-de-chine.
salon chair: General term to describe a French or French style armchair.
satinwood: A moderately hard, yellow or light brown wood, with a very close grain, found in central and southern India, Coromandel, Ceylon and in the West Indies.
scent bottle: Small, portable flask of flattened pear shape, made of silver, rock crystal, porcelain or glass.
seal bottle: Wine bottles with an applied glass medallion or seal personalised with the owner's name, initials, coat-of-arms or a date. Produced from the early 17th to the mid-19thC when bottles were relatively expensive.
secrétaire bookcase: Secrétaire with a bookcase fitted above it.

SFBJ: Société de Fabrication de Bébés et Jouets; doll maker founded 1899 by merging the businesses of Jumeau, Bru and others. Products regarded as inferior to those of the original makers.
Sheraton revival: Descriptive of furniture produced in the style of Sheraton when his designs gained revived interest during the Edwardian period.
side boy: A long table made to place against a wall.
silver table: Small rectangular table designed for use in the dining room. They usually have a fretwork gallery.
Six Dynasties: Period in Chinese history AD265-589.
six-hour dial: One with only six divisions instead of twelve, often with the hours 1 - 6 in Roman numerals and 7 - 12 superimposed in Arabic numerals.
snuff box: Box made to contain snuff in silver, or any other material: early examples have an integral rasp and spoon, from 17thC.
sofa table: Type of drop leaf table which developed from the Pembroke table. It was designed to stand behind a sofa, so is long and thin with two short drop leaves at the ends and two drawers in the frieze.
softwood: One of two basic categories in which all timbers are classified. The softwoods are conifers which generally have leaves in the form of evergreen needles.
spelter: Zinc treated to look like bronze and much used as an inexpensive substitute in Art Nouveau appliqué ornament and Art Deco figures.
Steiff, Margarete: Maker of dolls and highly prized teddy bears, she first exhibited at Leipzig, 1903, but died 1909. The company she founded continued to mass produce toys, dolls and bears for export. Products can be identified by the 'Steiff' button trademark, usually in the ear.
stirrup cup: Silver cup, without handles, so-called because it was served, containing a suitable beverage, to huntsmen in the saddle, prior to their moving off. Often made in the shape of an animal's head.
Sung dynasty: Ruling Chinese dynasty from AD960-1279.
table clock: Early type of domestic clock, some say the predecessor of the watch, in which the dial is set vertically: often of drum shape.
tallboy: Chest of drawers raised upon another chest of drawers. Also known as a chest-on-chest.
T'ang dynasty: Period in Chinese history AD618-906 during which porcelain was first developed.
tazza: Wide but shallow bowl on a stem with a foot; ceramic and metal tazzas were made in antiquity and the form was revived by Venetian glassmakers in 15thC. Also made in silver from 16thC.
tea kettle: Silver, or other metal, vessel intended for boiling water at the table. Designed to sit over a spirit lamp, it sometimes had a rounded base instead of flat.
teapoy: Piece of furniture in the form of a tea caddy on legs, with a hinged lid opening to reveal caddies, mixing bowl and other tea drinking accessories.
tear: Tear-drop shaped air bubble in the stem of an early 18thC wine glass, from which the air-twist evolved.
tester: Wooden canopy over a bedstead which is supported on either two or four posts. It may extend fully over the bed and be known as a full tester, or only over the bedhead half and be known as a half tester.
tin glaze: Glassy white glaze of tin oxide; re-introduced to Europe in 14thC by Moorish potters; the characteristic glaze of delftware, faience and maiolica.
Toby jug: Originally a jug in the form of a man in a tricorn hat, first made by Ralph Wood of Burslem, mid-18thC; since produced in great quantity in many different forms.
transfer printed: Ceramic decoration technique perfected mid-18thC and used widely thereafter for mass produced wares. An engraved design is printed on to paper (the bat) using the ink consisting of glaze mixed with oil; the paper is then laid over the body of the vessel and burns off in firing, leaving an outline, usually in blue. Sometimes the outline was coloured in by hand.
trefoil: Three-cusped figure which resembles a symmetrical three-lobed leaf or flower.
tripod table: Descriptive of any table with a three-legged base but generally used to describe only small tables of this kind.
tsuba: Guard of a Japanese sword, usually consisting of an ornamented plate.
tulipwood: Yellow brown wood with reddish stripe imported from Central and South America and used as a veneer and for inlay and crossbanding. It is related to rosewood and kingwood.
Venetian glass: Fine soda glass and coloured glass blown and pinched into highly ornamented vessels of intricate form, made in Venice, and widely copied from 15thC.
verge escapement: Oldest form of escapement, found on clocks as early as AD1300 and still in use 1900. Consisting of a bar (the verge) with two flag shaped pallets that rock in and out of the teeth of the crown or escape wheel to regulate the movement.
vesta case: Ornate flat case of silver or other metal for carrying vestas, an early form of match. From mid-19thC.
vitrine: French display cabinet which is often of bombé or serpentine outline and ornately decorated with marquetry and ormolu.
waxjack: A stand for holding a coil of sealing wax, first used mid-1700s.
washstand: Stand designed to hold a basin for washing in the bedroom. Generally of two types. Either three or four uprights supporting a circular top to hold the basin and with a triangular shelf with a drawer. Or as a cupboard raised on four legs with a basin let into the top, sometimes with enclosing flaps. Also known as a basin stand.
Wedgwood: Pottery founded by Josiah Wedgwood (1730-95) at Stoke-on-Trent and noted for numerous innovations; especially creamware, basaltes, and pearlware; perhaps best known for jasperware, the blue stonewares decorated with white relief scenes from late 18thC.
Wellington chest: Distinct type of tall, narrow chest of drawers. They usually have either six or seven thin drawers one above the other and a hinged and lockable flap over one side to prevent them from opening. Made in the 19thC.
whatnot: Tall stand of four or five shelves and sometimes a drawer in addition. Some were made to stand in a corner. Used for the display of ornaments and known in Victorian times as an omnium.
WMF: Short for the Austrian Württembergische Metallwarenfabrik, one of the principal producers of Art Nouveau silver and silverplated objects, early 20thC.
yew: Hard, deep reddish brown wood used both as a veneer and solid. It is very resistant to woodworm and turns well.
Yuan dynasty: Period in Chinese history AD1280-1368 during which the art of underglaze painting was developed.

DIRECTORY OF SPECIALISTS

If you wish to be included in next year's directory, or if you have a change of address or telephone number, please advise Miller's Advertising Department by April 1996.

If you require a valuation for an item, it is advisable to check whether the dealer or specialist will carry out this service and if there is a charge. Please mention Miller's when making an enquiry. Having found a specialist who will carry out your valuation, it is best to send a photograph and description of the item to the specialist together with a stamped addressed envelope for the reply. A valuation by telephone is not possible. Most dealers are only too happy to help you with your enquiry – however, they are very busy people and consideration of the above points would be welcomed.

Architectural Antiques

Cheshire

Nostalgia, Elizabeth Durrant, 61 Shaw Heath, Stockport.
Tel: 0161 477 7706

Devon

Ashburton Marbles, Grate Hall, North Street, Ashburton, TQ13 7QD.
Tel: 01364 653189

Surrey

Drummonds of Bramley, Birtley Farm, Horsham Road, Bramley, Guildford, GU5 0LA.
Tel: 01483 898766

Arms & Militaria

Lincolnshire

Garth Vincent, The Old Manor House, Allington, Nr Grantham, NG32 2DH.
Tel: 01400 281358

Surrey

West Street Antiques, 63 West Street, Dorking.
Tel: 01306 883487

Sussex

Wallis & Wallis, West Street Auction Galleries, Lewes, BN7 2NJ.
Tel: 01273 480208

Warwickshire

James Wigington.
Tel: 01789 261418

West Midlands

Weller & Dufty Ltd, 141 Bromsgrove Street, Birmingham, B5 6RQ.
Tel: 0121 692 1414

Yorkshire

Andrew Spencer Bottomley, The Coach House, 173A Huddersfield Road, Thongsbridge, Holmfirth, Huddersfield, HD7 2TT.
Tel: 01484 685234

Barometers

Berkshire

Walker & Walker, Halfway Manor, Halfway, Nr Newbury.
Tel: 01488 658693 or 0831 147480

Devon

Barometer World, Quicksilver Barn, Merton, Okehampton, EX20 3DS.
Tel: 01805 603443
Barometers restoration

Wiltshire

P A Oxley, The Old Rectory, Cherhill, Calne, SN11 8UX.
Tel: 01249 816227

Books

London

Guide Emer, c/o 62 Menelik Road, West Hampstead, NW2 3RH.
Tel: 0171 435 5644
Directory.

Middlesex

John Ives, 5 Normanhurst Drive, Twickenham, TW1 1NA.
Tel: 0181 892 6265
Reference Books

Boxes & Treen

Somerset

Boxwood Antique Restorers, BAFRA, 67 High Street, Wincanton, BA9 9JZ.
Tel: 01963 33988
Cabinet making, polishing, carving, specialists in tortoiseshell, ivory and mother-of-pearl on boxes, caddies and furniture. See our main advertisement in the Boxes section.

Clocks and Watches

Cheshire

Coppelia Antiques, Holeford Lodge, Plumley Moor Road, Plumley.
Tel: 01565 722197

Essex

Its About Time, 863 London Road, Westcliff-on-Sea, SS0 952.
Tel: 01702 72574

Gloucestershire

Gerard Campbell, Maple House, Market Place, Lechlade-on-Thames, GL7 3AB.
Tel: 01367 252267

Jonathan Beech, Nurses Cottage, Ampney Crucis, Nr Cirencester, GL7 5RY.
Tel: 01285 851495

Humberside

Bell Antiques, 68A Harold Street, Grimsby, DN35 0HH.
Tel: 01472 695110

Time & Motion, 1 Beckside, Beverley, HU17 0PB.
Tel: 01482 881574

Kent

Derek Roberts Antiques, 24-25 Shipbourne Road, Tonbridge, TN10 3DN.
Tel: 01732 358986

The Old Clock Shop, 63 High Street, West Malling.
Tel: 01732 843246

Gem Antiques, 28 London Road, Sevenoaks, TN13 1AP.
Tel: 01732 743540

Lincolnshire

Pinfold Antiques, 3-5 Pinfold Lane, Rushington, NG34 9AD.
Tel: 01526 832057

London

The Clock Clinic Ltd, 85 Lower Richmond Road, SW5 1EU.
Tel: 0181 788 1407

Pieces of Time, 1-7 Davies Mews, W1Y 1AR.
Tel: 0171 629 2422

Roderick Antique Clocks, 23 Vicarage Gate, W8 4AA.
Tel: 0171 937 8517

Raffety, 34 Kensington Church Street, W8 4HA.
Tel: 0171 938 1100

Norfolk

K Lawson Antique Clocks, Scratby Garden Centre, Beach Road, Scratby, Gt Yarmouth, NR29 3AJ.
Tel: 01493 730950

Oxfordshire

Rosemary & Time, 42 Park Street, Thame.
Tel: 01844 216923

Surrey

Bryan Clisby, 86B Tilford Road, Farnham, TU9 8DS.
Tel: 01252 716436

The Clock Shop, 64 Church Street, Weybridge, KT13 8DL.
Tel: 01932 840407

The Old Clock Maker, Clavis, Manor Way, Knott Park, Oxshott, KT22 0HS.
Tel: 01372 843642

Sussex

Samuel Orr Antique Clocks, 36 High Street, Hurstpierpoint, Nr Brighton, BN6 9RG.
Tel: 01273 832081

Wiltshire

P A Oxley,
The Old Rectory,
Cherhill,
Calne, SN11 8UX.
Tel: 01249 816227

Allan Smith Clocks,
Amity Cottage,
162 Beechcroft Road,
Upper Stratton,
Swindon, SN2 6QE.
Tel: 01793 822977

Yorkshire

Brian Loomes,
Calf Haugh Farm,
Pateley Bridge,
HG3 5HW.
Tel: 01423 711163

Decorative Arts

Cleveland

Market Cross Jewellers,
160 Linthorpe Road,
Middlesborough,
TS1 3RB.
Tel: 01642 253939
Royal Doulton

Greater Manchester

A S Antiques,
26 Broad Street,
Pendleton,
Salford, M6 5BY.
Tel: 0161 737 5938

Hampshire

Bona Arts Decorative Ltd,
19 Princes Mead
Shopping Centre,
Farnborough, GU14 7TJ.
Tel: 01252
372188/544130

Kent

Peter Hearnden,
Corn Exchange Antiques
Centre, 64 The Pantiles,
Tunbridge Wells,
TN2 5TN.
Tel: 01892 539652

London

The Collector,
9 Church Street,
Marylebone, NW8 8DT.
Tel: 0171 706 4586
Royal Doulton

Rumours Decorative
Arts,
10 The Mall,
Upper Street,
Camden Passage,
Islington N1.
Tel: 01582 873561

Pieter Oosthuizen,
1st Floor,
Georgian Village,
Camden Passage, N1.
Tel: 0171 359 3322/376
3852

Sussex

Witney and Airault,
Prinny's Gallery,
3 Meeting House Lane,
The Lanes,
Brighton, BN1 1HB.
Tel: 01273 204554

Wales

Paul Gibbs Antiques,
25 Castle Street,
Conwy, Gwynedd,
LL32 8AY.
Tel: 01492 593429

Warwickshire

Rich Designs,
1 Shakespeare Street,
Stratford-upon-Avon,
CV37 6RN.
Tel: 01789 261612

Yorkshire

Muir Hewitt,
Halifax Antiques Centre,
Queens Road,
Gibbet Street,
Halifax,
HX1 4LR.
Tel: 01422 347377

Exporters

Humberside

Geoffrey Mole Antique
Exports,
400 Wincolmlee,
Hull.
Tel: 01482 327858

Somerset

M G R Exports,
Mike Read,
Station Road,
Bruton, BA10 0EH.
Tel: 01749 812460

Sussex

Lloyd Williams Antiques,
Anglo Am Warehouse,
2A Beach Road,
Eastbourne, BN22 7EX.
Tel: 01323 648661

Bexhill Antique Exporters,
56 Turkey Road,
Bexhill-on-Sea.
Tel: 01424 210182/
225103

Furniture

Cumbria

Anthemion,
Broughton Hall, Cartmel,
Grange-over-Sands,
LAU 7SH.
Tel: 015395 36295

Devon

McBains of Exeter,
Exeter Airport,
Clyst Honiton, EX5 2BA.
Tel: 01392 366261

Essex

F G Bruschweiler
(Antiques) Ltd,
41-67 Lower Lambricks,
Rayleigh,
SS6 7EN.
Tel: 01268 773761

Hampshire

Cedar Antiques Ltd,
High Street,
Hartley Wintney,
RG27 8NY.
Tel: 01252 843252

Hertfordshire

Collins Antiques,
Corner House,
Wheathampstead,
AL4 8AP.
Tel: 01582 833111

Kent

Linden Park Antiques,
7 Union Square,
The Pantiles,
Tunbridge Wells,
TN4 8HE.
Tel: 01892 538615

Sparks Antiques,
4 Manor Row,
High Street,
Tenterden, TN30 6HP.
Tel: 01580 766696

Flower House Antiques,
90 High Street,
Tenterden, TN30 6JB.
Tel: 01580 763764

Christine Antiques,
4-6 Ashford Road,
Tenterden, TN30 6AB.
Tel: 01580 764434

The Old Bakery
Antiques,
St David's Bridge,
Cranbrook, TN17 3HN.
Tel: 01580 713103
Oak & Country

Lincolnshire

Seaview Antiques,
Mr M Chalk,
Stanhope Road,
Horncastle.
Tel: 01507 524524

London

The Old Cinema,
160 Chiswick High Road,
W4 1PR.
Tel: 0181 995 4166

Oola Boola,
Robert Scales,
166 Tower Bridge Road,
SE1 3LS.
Tel: 0171 403 0794

Butchoff Antiques,
233 Westbourne Grove,
W11 2SE.
Tel: 0171 221 8174

Adams Rooms Ltd,
18-20 Ridgeway,
Wimbledon Village,
SW19 4QN.
Tel: 0181 946 7047

Furniture Cave,
533 Kings Road, SW10.
Tel: 0171 352 4229

Middlesex

Robert Phelps Ltd,
133-135 St Margaret's Rd,
East Twickenham,
TW1 1RG.
Tel: 0181 892 1778

Northamptonshire

Paul Hopwell Antiques,
30 High Street,
West Haddon, NN6 7AP.
Tel: 01788 510636
Oak & Country

Oxfordshire

Key Antiques,
11 Horse Fair,
Chipping Norton.
Tel: 01608 643777

Rupert Hitchcox,
The Garth,
Wards Grove,
Nr Chalgrove,
Oxford, OX9 7RW.
Tel: 01865 890241

John Charles Antiques,
John Ostroumoff,
20 High Street,
Wallingford, OX10 0BP.
Tel: 01491 825200

Somerset

The Granary Galleries,
Court House, Ash Priors,
Nr Bishops Lydeard,
Taunton, TA4 3NQ.
Tel: 01823 432402

Suffolk

Oswald Simpson,
Hall Street,
Long Melford.
Tel: 01787 377523
Oak & Country

Wrentham Antiques,
40-44 High Street,
Wrentham, NR34 7HB.
Tel: 01502 675583

Hubbard Antiques,
16 St Margaret's Green,
Ipswich, IP4 2BS.
Tel: 01473 226033

Surrey

John Hartley Antiques Ltd,
186 High Street,
Ripley, GU23 6BB.
Tel: 01483 224318

Ripley Antiques,
Heather Denham,
67 High Street,
Ripley.
Tel: 01483 224981

Anthony Welling,
Broadway Barn,
High Street,
Ripley, GU23 6AZ.
Tel: 01483 225384

Dorking Desk Shop,
41 West Street,
Dorking, RH4 1BU.
Tel: 01306 883327

Sussex

Dycheling Antiques,
34 High Street,
Ditchling,
Hassocks, BN6 8TA.
Tel: 01273 842929

Selecta International,
Paul Harland,
Trading Estate,
Bexhill Rd,
Woodingdean,
Brighton, BN2 6QT.
Tel: 01273 300628

Lakeside Ltd,
The Old Cement Works,
South Heighton,
Newhaven, BN9 0HS.
Tel: 01273 513326

Hadlow Down Antiques,
Hastingford Farm,
Hadlow Down,
Nr Uckfield, TN22 4DY.
Tel: 01825 830707
Oak & Country

Chichester House Antiques,
High Street,
Ditchling, BN6 8SY.
Tel: 01273 846615

British Antique Replicas Ltd,
School Close,
Queen Elizabeth Avenue,
Burgess Hill,
RH15 9RX.
Tel: 01444 245577

Sleeping Beauty,
Antique Beds,
212 Church Road,
Hove, BN3 2DT.
Tel: 01273 205115
Antique beds

International Furniture Exporters,
The Old Cement Works,
South Heighton,
Newhaven, BN9 0HS.
Tel: 01273 611251

Warwickshire

Apollo Antiques Ltd,
The Saltisford,
Birmingham Road,
Warwick, CV34 4TD.
Tel: 01926 494746

Don Spencer Antiques,
36A Market Place,
Warwick, CV34 4SH.
Tel: 01926 499857

West Midlands

Pierre of LP Antiques,
Short Acre Street,
Walsall.
Tel: 01922 746764

Martin Taylor Antiques,
140B Tettenhall Road,
Wolverhampton,
WV6 0BQ.
Tel: 01902 751166

Furniture & Exporters

Sussex

The Old Mint House,
High Street,
Pevensey,
Nr Eastbourne,
BN24 5LE.
Tel: 01323 762337

Glass

Avon

Somervale Antiques,
6 Radstock Road,
Midsomer Norton,
Bath, BA3 2AJ.
Tel: 01761 412686

London

Christine Bridge Antiques,
78 Castelnau,
SW13 9EX.
Tel: 0181 741 5501

West Midlands

David Hill,
Tel: 01384 70523
Reference books on glass - mail order only.

Marine

Devon

Temeraire,
11a Higher Street,
Brixham, TQ5 8HW.
Tel: 01803 851523

London

Thomas Mercer (Chronometers) Ltd,
32 Bury Street, St James,
SW1Y 6AU.
Tel: 0171 321 0353

Markets & Centres

Kent

The Weald Antiques Centre,
106 High Street,
Tenterden,
TN30 6HT.
Tel: 01580 762939

Lincolnshire

The Hemswell Antiques Centre,
Caenby Corner Estate,
Hemswell Cliff,
Gainsborough,
DN21 5TJ.
Tel: 01427 668389

London

The Old Cinema,
160 Chiswick High Road,
W4 1PR.
Tel: 0181 995 4166

Sussex

Bexhill Antiques Centre,
Old Town,
Bexhill.
Tel: 01424 210182

Mirrors

London

Hurlingham Antiques,
363 New Kings Road,
Fulham,
SW6 4RJ.
Tel: 0171 736 1095

Money Boxes

Yorkshire

John & Simon Haley,
89 Northgate,
Halifax, HX6 4NG.
Tel: 01422 822148

Oriental

Cornwall

Richfield Oriental Specialists Antiques,
C & TD Richfield,
104 Henver Road,
Newquay,
TR7 3BL.
Tel: 01637 871100
All aspects of Oriental works of art and ceramics.

Packers & Shippers

Avon

A J Williams (Shipping),
607 Sixth Avenue,
Central Park,
Petherton Road,
Hengrove, Bristol,
BS14 9B2.
Tel: 0117 989 2166

Dorset

Alan Franklin Transport,
26 Blackmoor Road,
Verwood, BH31 6BB.
Tel: 01202 826539

London

Hedley's Humpers,
Units 2,3 & 4,
97 Victoria Road,
NW10 6ND.
Tel: 0181 965 8733

Featherstons,
7 Ingate Place, SW8 3NS.
Fine Art: 0171 720 0422
Moving: 0171 720 8041

Middlesex

Vulcan International Services,
Unit 13/14 Ascot Road,
Clockhouse Lane,
Feltham, TW14 8QF.
Tel: 01784 244152

Somerset

Camion International Packing & Shipping,
Station Road,
Bruton, BA10 0EH.
Tel: 01749 813726

Paperweights

Cheshire

Sweetbriar Gallery,
Robin Hood Lane,
Helsby, WA6 9NH.
Tel: 01928 723851

Pianos

Avon

Piano Export,
Bridge Road, Kingswood,
Bristol, BS15 4PW.
Tel: 0117 956 8300

Kent

Period Piano Company,
Park Farm Oast,
Hareplain Road,
Biddenden, Nr Ashford,
TN27 8LJ.
Tel: 01580 291393
Specialist dealer and restorer of period pianos.

Pine

Cheshire

Richmond Galleries,
Watergate Building,
New Crane Street,
off Sealand Road,
Chester, CH1 4JE.
Tel: 01244 317602
Pine, country and Spanish furniture

Gloucestershire

Campden Country Pine Antiques,
High Street,
Chipping Campden,
GL55 6HN.
Tel: 01386 840315

Hampshire

The Pine Cellars,
39 Jewry Street,
Winchester, SO23 8RY.
Tel: 01962 867014

Ireland

Delvin Farm Antiques,
Gormonston, Co Meath.
Tel: 00 353 18412285

Old Court Pine (Alain Chawner),
Old Court, Collon,
Co Louth.
Tel: 00 353 41 26270

Honans Antiques,
Crowe Street,
Gort, County Galway.
Tel: 00 353 91 31407

Kent

Up Country,
The Old Corn Stores,
68 St John's Road,
Tunbridge Wells,
TN4 9PE.
Tel: 01892 523341

Antique & Design,
The Old Oast,
Hollow Lane,
Canterbury, CT1 3TG.
Tel: 01227 762871

The Warehouse,
29-30 Queens Gardens,
Worthington Street,
Dover, CT17 9AH.
Tel: 01304 242006

Lancashire

Enloc Antiques,
Birchenlee Mill,
Lenches Road,
Colne, BB8 8ET.
Tel: 01282 867101

Leicestershire

Hartwell Antiques,
152 Station Road,
Scraptoft, LE7 9UF.
Tel: 0116 241 6695

London

The Antique Warehouse,
9-14 Deptford Broadway,
SE8 4PA.
Tel: 0181 691 3062

Sussex

Ann Lingard,
Ropewalk Antiques,
Ropewalk,
Rye, TN31 7NA.
Tel: 01797 223486

Graham Price Antiques Ltd., Unit 4,
Chaucer Industrial Estate, Dittons Road,
Polegate,
BN26 6JD.
Tel: 01323 487167

Bob Hoare Pine Antiques,
Unit Q,
Phoenix Place,
North Street,
Lewes, BN7 2DQ.
Tel: 01273 480557

The Netherlands

Jacques van der Tol,
Antennestraat 34,
1322 A E Almere-Stad.
Tel: 00 31 3653 62050

Wales

Heritage Restorations,
Maes Y Glydfa,
Llanfair Caereinion,
Welshpool, SY21 0HD.
Tel: 01938 810384

The Pot Board,
30 King Street,
Carmarthen, SA31 1BS.
Tel: 01834 871276

Warwickshire

Cottage Pine Antiques,
19 Broad Street,
Brinklow, Nr Rugby,
CV23 0LS.
Tel: 01788 832673

Porcelain

Hampshire

Goss & Crested China Ltd,
62 Murray Road,
Horndean,
PO8 9JL.
Tel: 01705 597440
Goss & Crested.

London

Marion Langham,
Stand J30/31 Grays
Mews, Davies Street,
W1Y 1AR.
Tel: 0171 629 2511/
730 1002
Belleek.

Yorkshire

The Crested China Co,
Mr Taylor,
The Station House,
Driffield,
YO25 7PY.
Tel: 01377 257042
Goss & Crested.

Pottery

Buckinghamshire

Gillian Neale Antiques,
PO Box 247,
Aylesbury,
HP20 1JZ.
Tel: 01296 23754

Lancashire

Roy W Bunn Antiques,
34-36 Church Street,
Barnoldswick,
Colne, BB8 5UT.
Tel: 01282 813703

London

Jonathan Horne
(Antiques) Ltd,
66C Kensington Church
Street,
W8 4BY.
Tel: 0171 221 5658

Jacqueline Oosthuizen,
23 Cale Street,
Chelsea, SW3.
Tel: 0171 352 6071

Rogers de Rin,
76 Royal Hospital Road,
SW3 4HN.
Tel: 0171 352 9007
Wemyss.

M S Antiques,
25a Holland Street,
W8 4JF.
Tel: 0171 937 0793

Sue Norman,
Stand L4 Antiquarius,
135 King's Road, SW3.
Tel: 0171 352 7217

Valerie Howard,
2 Campden Street,
W8.
Tel: 0171 792 9702
Masons & Quimper.

Surrey

Special Auction Services,
Andrew Hilton,
The Coach House,
Midgham Park,
Reading, RG7 5UG.
Tel: 01734 712949

Antiques Arcadia,
22 Richmond Hill,
Richmond-on-Thames,
TW10 6QX.
Tel: 0181 940 2035

Pottery & Porcelain

Oxfordshire

Joanna C Glyn,
The Swan at Tetsworth
Antiques Centre,
High Street,
Tetsworth, OX9 7AB.
Tel: 01844 281777/351375
British Pottery & Porcelain 1740-1820

Publications

London

Antiques Trade Gazette,
17 Whitcomb Street,
WC2H 7PL.
Tel: 0171 930 9958

West Midlands

Antique Bulletin
HP Publishing,
2 Hampton Court Road,
Harborne,
Birmingham, B17 GAE.
Tel: 0121 428 2555

Restoration

Avon

Robert P Tandy, BAFRA,
Unit 5 Manor
Workshops, Manor Park,
West End, Nailsea,
Bristol, BS19 2DD.
Tel: 01275 856378

Stuart Bradbury,
M & S Bradbury, BAFRA,
The Barn, Hanham Lane,
Paulton, BS18 5PF.
Tel: 01761 418910

Colin Holcombe, BAFRA,
54 Alcove Road,
Fishponds,
Bristol, BS16 3DR.
Tel: 0117 965 1299

Lawrence Brass & Son,
BAFRA,
93-95 Walcot Street,
Bath, BA1 5BW.
Tel: 01225 464057

Bedfordshire

D M E Restoration Ltd,
BAFRA,
Duncan Michael Everitt,
11 Church Street,
Ampthill, MK45 2PL.
Tel: 01525 405819

Berkshire

Alpha (Antique)
Restorations, BAFRA,
Graham Childs,
High Street, Compton,
Newbury, RG16 0NL.
Tel: 01635 578245

Buckinghamshire

Wood Glorious Wood,
Ashwood,
41 Probemdall Avenue,
Aylesbury, HP21 8HZ.
Tel: 01296 437011

Cambridgeshire

Robert Williams, BAFRA,
Osborn's Farm,
32 Church Street,
Willingham, CB4 5HT.
Tel: 01954 260972

Cheshire

Anthony Allen
Antique Restorers &
Conservators, BAFRA,
Buxton Road, Newtown,
New Mills via Stockport,
SK12 3JS.
Tel: 01663 745274
Boulle, marquetry, walnut, oak, veneering, upholstery.

Cornwall

Graham Usher,
Fairhope Fine Furniture,
BAFRA,
Restoration & Courses,
5 Rose Terrace,
Mitchell, Nr Newquay,
TR8 5AU.
Tel: 01872 510551

Cumbria

Peter Hall & Son, BAFRA,
Danes Road, Staveley,
Nr Kendal, LA8 9PL.
Tel: 01539 821633

Devon

Tony Vernon, BAFRA,
15 Follett Road,
Topsham, EX3 0JP.
Tel: 01392 874635

Dan Bent, BAFRA,
Newholt,
Court Road,
Newton Ferrers,
Plymouth, PL8 1DE.
Tel: 01752 872831

Dorset

Michael Barrington,
BAFRA,
The Old Rectory,
Warmwell,
Dorchester, DT2 8HQ.
Tel: 01305 852104
18th & 19thC furniture, gilding, upholstery, antique metal work. Organ case work and pipe decoration, mechanical models, automatons and toys.

Richard Bolton, BAFRA,
Meadow Court,
Athelhampton House,
Nr Dorchester, DT2 7LG.
Tel: 01305 848346
All aspects of furniture restoration.

Philip Hawkins, BAFRA,
Glebe Barn,
Semley, Nr Shaftesbury,
SP7 9AP.
Tel: 01747 830830
Specialising in oak & country furniture

Tolpuddle Antique
Restorers, BAFRA,
Raymond Robertson,
The Stables,
Southover House,
Tolpuddle,
Dorchester, DT2 7HF.
Tel: 01305 848739

Essex

Clive Beardall, BAFRA,
104B High Street,
Maldon, CM9 7ET.
Tel: 01621 857890

Gloucestershire

Uedelhoven & Campion,
BAFRA,
Peter John Campion,
Well House, Gretton,
Cheltenham, GL54 5EP.
Tel: 01242 604403

Stephen Hill, BAFRA,
5 Cirencester Workshops,
Brewery Court,
Cirencester, GL7 1JH.
Tel: 01285 658817

Hunt & Lomas, BAFRA,
Christian Macduff Hunt,
Village Farm Workshops,
Preston Village,
Cirencester, GL7 5PR.
Tel: 01285 640111

Andrew Lelliott, BAFRA,
6 Tetbury Hill, Avening,
Tetbury, GL8 8LT.
Tel: 01453 835783
Furniture and clock cases, included on the Conservation Unit Register of the Museums and Galleries Commission.

Angus Stewart, BAFRA,
Sycamore Barn
Industrial Park,
Bourton-on-the-Water,
GL54 2HQ.
Tel: 01451 821611
Gilding, replacement mirror glass.

Alan Hessel, BAFRA
The Old Town Workshop,
St George's Close,
Moreton-in-Marsh,
GL56 0LP.
Tel: 01608 650026,
FAX: 01608 650026

Hampshire

BAFRA,
66 Gorran Avenue,
Rowner,
Gosport, PO13 0NF.
Tel: 01743 718162

Guy Bagshaw, BAFRA,
The Old Dairy,
Plain Farm,
East Tisted, Nr Alton,
GU34 3RT.
Tel: 01420 588362
Eclectic items, tutored weekends.

David C E Lewry,
BAFRA,
Wychelms,
66 Gorran Avenue,
Rowner, Gosport,
PO13 0NF.
Tel: 01329 286901
Furniture

Hertfordshire

Workshop Interiors,
6 Stanley Avenue,
Chiswell Green,
St Albans, AL2 3AB.
Tel: 01727 840456,
FAX: 01727 841705
Furniture, restoration, polishing, carving, turning, gilding and upholstery.

Charles Perry
Restorations Ltd,
John B Carr, BAFRA,
Praewood Farm,
Hemel Hempstead Road,
St Albans, AL3 6AA.
Tel: 01727 853487

Kent

Reflections Antique
Furniture Restoration,
The Old Pumping Station,
Pluckley Road,
Charing, TN27 0AH.
Tel: 01233 714044
Restoration, courses & security tagging.

Timothy Akers, BAFRA,
The Forge,
39 Chancery Lane,
Beckenham,
BR3 2NR.
Tel: 0181 650 9179
Longcase and bracket clocks, cabinet making, French polishing.

Bruce Luckhurst,
BAFRA,
Little Surrenden
Workshops,
Ashford Road,
Bethersden,
Nr Ashford,
TN26 3BG.
Tel: 01233 820589
One year course available.

Timothy Long Restoration,
BAFRA, St John's
Church, London Road,
Dunton Green,
Nr Sevenoaks,
TN13 2TE.
Tel: 01732 743368
Cabinet restoration, polishing, upholstery, brass and steel cabinet fittings.

Benedict Clegg,
BAFRA,
Rear of 20 Camden Road,
Tunbridge Wells,
TN1 2PT.
Tel: 01892 548095

Lincolnshire

E Czajkowski & Son,
96 Tor-O-Moor Road,
Woodhall Spa,
LN10 6SB.
Tel: 01526 352895
Restoration antique furniture, clocks and barometers.
Member of BAFRA, UKIC, registered with Museums and Galleries Commission.

London

Clifford Tracy, BAFRA,
6-40 Durnford Street,
Seven Sisters Road,
N15 5NQ.
Tel: 0181 800 4773

Titian Studio, BAFRA,
Rodrigo Titian,
318 Kensal Road,
W10 5BN.
Tel: 0181 960 6247
Carving, gilding, lacquer, painted furniture and French polishing.

Hope & Piaget,
Brian Duffy, BAFRA,
1K Leroy House,
436 Essex Road,
Islington, N1 3QP.
Tel: 0171 359 1400

Sebastian Giles
Furniture, BAFRA,
Sebastian Giles,
11 Junction Mews,
W2 1PN.
Tel: 0171 258 3721
Comprehensive.

Crawley Studios,
BAFRA,
Marie Louise Crawley,
39 Wood Vale,
SE23 3DS.
Tel: 0181 299 4121
Painted furniture, papier mâché, tôle ware, lacquer and gilding.

William Cook, BAFRA,
167 Battersea High Street,
SW11 3JS.
Tel: 0171 736 5329

Peter Binnington,
BAFRA,
68 Battersea High Street,
SW11 3HX.
Tel: 0171 223 9192
Marquetry, gilding, verre églomisé, period furniture.

Lucinda Compton,
Compton Hall
Restoration, BAFRA,
Unit A, 133 Riverside
Business Centre,
Haldane Place,
SW18 4UQ.
Tel: 0181 874 0762
Lacquer, gilding, painted furniture.

Lawrence Brass & Son,
BAFRA,
154 Sutherland Avenue,
Maida Vale, W9.
Tel: 01225 464057

Middlesex

Reginald W Dudman,
Antique Restorations,
BAFRA,
45 Windmill Road,
Brentford, TW8 0QQ.
Tel: 0181 568 5249
Oriental lacquer and japanning.

Norfolk

Mr R N Larwood, BAFRA
Fine Antique Restoration
& Conservation of
Furniture,
The Oaks,
Station Road, Larling,
Norwich, NR16 2QS.
Tel: 01953 717937

David Bartram, BAFRA,
The Raveningham
Centre, Castell Farm,
Beccles Road,
Raveningham,
NR14 6NU.
Tel: 01508 548721

Oxfordshire

Colin Piper Restoration
& Conservation, BAFRA,
Highfield House,
The Greens, Leafield,
Witney, OX8 5NP.
Tel: 01993 878593
Restoration and conservation of fine antique furniture, clocks and barometers.

Mark Griffin, BAFRA,
Byrebrook Studio,
Lower Farm, Northmoor,
Oxford, OX8 1AU.
Tel: 01865 300171

Alistair Frayling-Cork,
BAFRA,
2 Mill Lane,
Wallingford, OX10 0DH.
Tel: 01491 826221
Furniture restoration, stringed instruments, clock cases and brass fittings repaired.

Scotland

Trist & McBain, BAFRA,
9 Canongate Venture,
New Street,
Edinburgh,
EH8 8BH.
Tel: 0131 557 3828
Furniture, clocks, barometers,cane & rush seating.

Altyre - Traditional
Antique Restoration,
BAFRA,
Luigi Villani,
The Stables, Altyre
Estate,
Forres, IV36 0SH.
Tel: 01309 672572
Repairs and restoration of frames, furniture, sculptures, fittings, marble, etc. French polishing, gilding, marquetry.
Damage assessment and survey. Estimates, advice and lectures.

Shropshire

Richard Higgins, BAFRA,
The Old School,
Longnor, Nr Shrewsbury,
SY5 7PP.
Tel: 01743 718162
All fine furniture clocks, movements, dials and cases, casting, plating, boulle, gilding, lacquerwork, carving, period upholstery.

Somerset

Boxwood Antique
Restorers, BAFRA,
A K Stacey,
67 High Street,
Wincanton,
BA9 9JZ.
Tel: 01963 33988
Cabinet making, polishing, carving and specialists in tortoiseshell, ivory and mother-of-pearl on boxes, caddies and furniture. See our main advertisement in Boxes section.

Michael Durkee, BAFRA,
Castle House,
Units 1 & 3,
Bennetts Field Estate,
Wincanton,
BA9 9DT.
Tel: 01963 33884 (and
Fax)
Antique furniture.

Lawrence Brass & Son,
BAFRA,
93-95 Walcot Street,
Bath, BA1 5BW.
Tel: 01225 464057

Surrey

G & R Fraser-Sinclair &
Co, BAFRA,
11 Orchard Works,
Streeters Lane,
Beddington,
SM6 7ND.
Tel: 0181 669 5343

Stuart Hobbs, BAFRA,
Meath Paddock,
Meath Green Lane,
Horley,
RH6 8HZ.
Tel: 01293 782349
Furniture, clocks, barometers.

Michael Hedgecoe,
BAFRA,
21 Burrow Hill Green,
Chobham, Woking,
GU24 8QS.
Tel: 01276 858206

Timothy Naylor, BAFRA,
The Workshop,
2 Chertsey Road,
Chobham, Woking,
GU24 8NB.
Tel: 01276 855122

Simon Marsh, BAFRA,
The Old Butchers Shop,
High Street,
Bletchingley, RH1 4PA.
Tel: 01883 743350

Sussex

Thakeham Furniture,
BAFRA,
Timothy Chavasse,
Marehill Road,
Pulborough, RH20 2DY.
Tel: 01798 872006

Noel Pepperall, BAFRA,
Dairy Lane Cottage,
Walberton,
Arundel, BN18 0PT.
Tel: 01243 551282
Gilding, painted furniture.

Albert Plumb, BAFRA,
31 Whyke Lane,
Chichester,
PO19 2JS.
Tel: 01243 771212
Cabinet making, upholstery

Worcestershire

Phillip Slater, BAFRA
93 Hewell Road,
Barnt Green, Nr
Birmingham,
B45 8NL.
Tel: 0121 445 4942
Inlay work, marquetry.

Jeffrey Hall,
Malvern Studios,
BAFRA,
56 Cowleigh Road,
Malvern,
WR14 1QD.
Tel: 01684 574913

Yorkshire

Rodney F Kemble,
BAFRA,
16 Crag Vale Terrace,
Glusburn,
Nr Keighley,
BD20 8QU.
Tel: 01535
636954/633702
Furniture and small decorative items.

Lucinda Compton,
Compton Hall
Restoration,
BAFRA,
Manor House,
Marton-Le-Moor,
Ripon,
HG4 5AT.
Tel: 01423 324290
Lacquer, gilding, painted furniture.

Scientific Instruments

Scotland

Michael Bennett-Levy,
Monkton House,
Old Craighall,
Musselburgh,
Mid Lothian,
EH21 8SE.
Tel: 0131 665 5753

Services

Hampshire

Securikey Ltd,
P O Box 18,
Aldershot,
GU12 4SL.
Tel: 01252 311888/9

London

Just Brothers & Co,
Unit 3 Roeder House,
Vale Road,
N4 1NG.
Tel: 0181 880 2505

West Midlands

Retro Products,
174 Norton Road,
Stourbridge.
Tel: 01384 894042

Silver

Shropshire

Teme Valley Antiques,
1 The Bull Ring,
Ludlow,
SY8 1AD
Tel: 01584 874686

Sports & Games

Berkshire

Sir William Bentley
Billiards,
Standen Manor Farm,
Hungerford,
RG17 0RB.
Tel: 01488 681711/
01672 870629
Billiard tables

Hertfordshire

Hamilton Billiards &
Games Co,
Park Lane,
Knebworth.
Tel: 01438 811995
Billiard tables.

Somerset

Billiard Room Antiques,
The Old School,
Church Lane,
Chilcompton,
Bath,
BA3 4HP.
Tel: 01761 23283
Billiard tables.

Surrey

Academy Antiques,
5 Camp Hill Industrial
Estate,
West Byfleet,
KT14 6EW.
Tel: 01932 352067

Hampshire

Evans & Partridge,
Agriculture House,
High Street,
Stockbridge,
SO20 6HF.
Tel: 01264 810702
Fishing.

Kent

Garden House Antiques,
116-118 High Street,
Tenterden,
TN30 6HT.
Tel: 01580 763664
Fishing.

Reflections,
The Old Pumping Station,
Pluckley Road,
Charing,
TN27 0AH.
Tel: 01233 714044/
01303 261220
Buys vintage & antique fishing tackle.

Scotland

Timeless Tackle,
1 Blackwood Crescent,
Edinburgh,
EH9 1QZ.
Tel: 0131 667 1407
Fishing

Warwickshire

James Wigington,
Tel: 01789 261418
Fishing

Teddy Bears

Oxfordshire

Teddy Bears of Witney,
99 High Street,
Witney,
OX8 6LY.
Tel: 01993 702616

Toys

Sussex

Wallis & Wallis,
West Street Auction
Galleries,
Lewes.
BN7 2NJ
Tel: 01273 480208

Yorkshire

John & Simon Haley,
89 Northgate,
Halifax.
HX6 4NG
Tel: 01422 822148

Wine Antiques

Buckinghamshire

Christopher Sykes
Antiques,
The Old Parsonage,
Woburn,
MK17 9QM.
Tel: 01525 290259

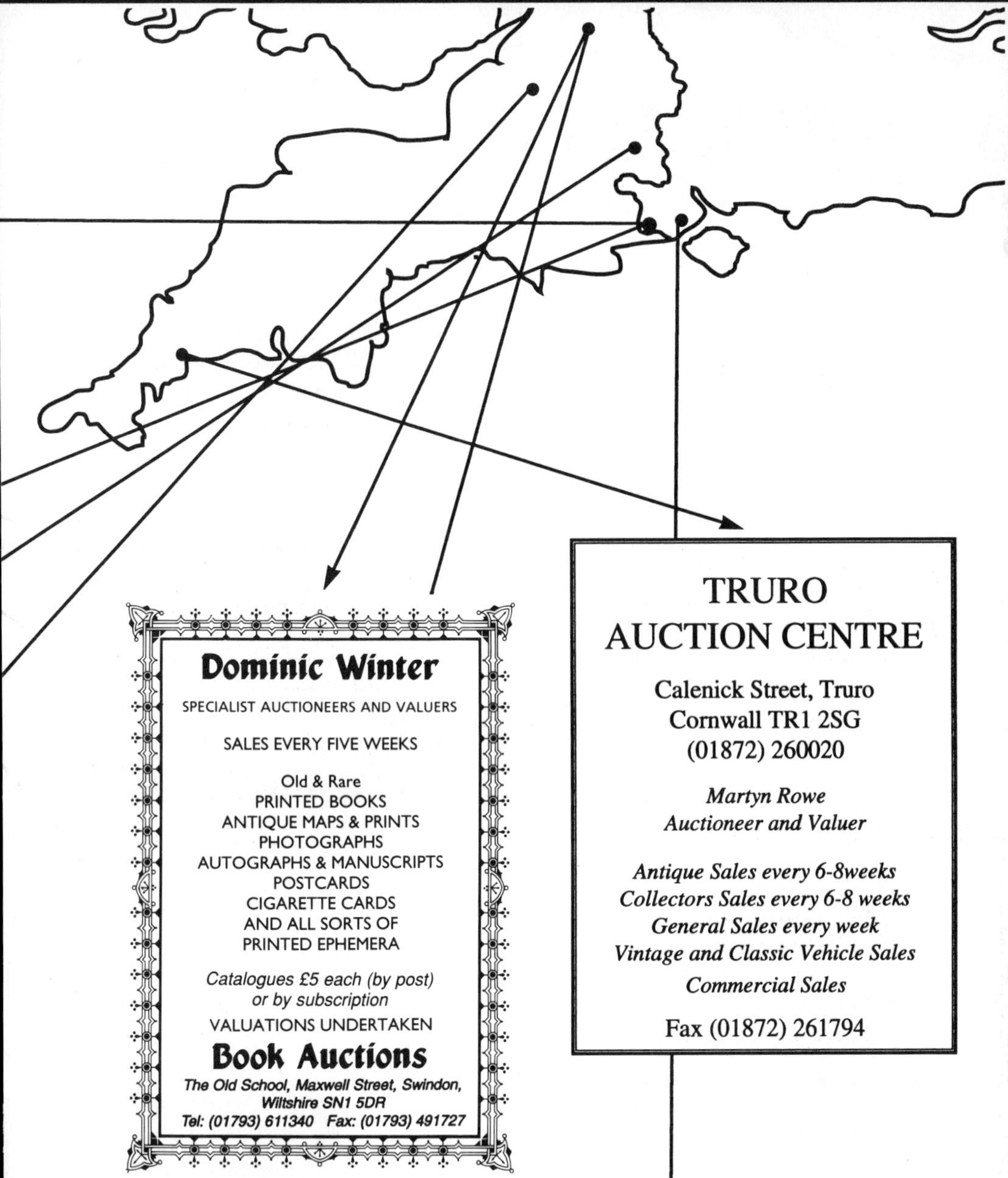

Dominic Winter

SPECIALIST AUCTIONEERS AND VALUERS

SALES EVERY FIVE WEEKS

Old & Rare
PRINTED BOOKS
ANTIQUE MAPS & PRINTS
PHOTOGRAPHS
AUTOGRAPHS & MANUSCRIPTS
POSTCARDS
CIGARETTE CARDS
AND ALL SORTS OF
PRINTED EPHEMERA

Catalogues £5 each (by post)
or by subscription

VALUATIONS UNDERTAKEN

Book Auctions

The Old School, Maxwell Street, Swindon,
Wiltshire SN1 5DR
Tel: (01793) 611340 Fax: (01793) 491727

TRURO AUCTION CENTRE

Calenick Street, Truro
Cornwall TR1 2SG
(01872) 260020

Martyn Rowe
Auctioneer and Valuer

Antique Sales every 6-8weeks
Collectors Sales every 6-8 weeks
General Sales every week
Vintage and Classic Vehicle Sales
Commercial Sales

Fax (01872) 261794

Kidson Trigg
CHARTERED SURVEYORS & AUCTIONEERS

WE OFFER A COMPREHENSIVE SERVICE TO BUYERS & SELLERS

* Large Monthly Auction Sales
* Quarterly Selected Fine Art Sales
* Periodic Specialist Sales
* *All Fully Catalogued* *
* Full house clearance service available
* On site sales of house contents arranged
* Valuations: full reports prepared for insurance, probate or family division
* Free verbal appraisals to prospective vendors in their own homes or at our salerooms

Unrestricted delivery times • Unlimited parking
Friendly helpful staff • Easy Access to motorways
(London M4 90 mins).

The Salerooms, Friars Farm, Sevenhampton, Highworth, Swindon, Wilts SN6 7PZ
Tel: 01793 861072/861000 Fax: 861105

GEORGE KIDNER
Fine Art Auctioneers and Valuers

The Old School
The Square • Pennington • Lymington
Hampshire • SO41 8GN
Telephone (01590) 670070

Auctioneers & Valuers of Fine Art, Antiques & Collectors' Items

The CANTERBURY AUCTION Galleries

KENT'S leading Independent Auctioneers and Valuers offer a fully professional yet personal service throughout the South East for the sale of Fine Art, Antiques and Collectors' Items. Detailed Valuations for Insurance, Probate, Family Division and Sale by Auction.

Member of the society SOFAA *of Fine Art Auctioneers*

40 STATION ROAD WEST, CANTERBURY, KENT, CT2 8AN
TELEPHONE 01227 763337. FAX 01227 456770

IBBETT MOSELY

125 High Street, SEVENOAKS 456731

A Regular Programme of Sales

of Antique, Victorian and Edwardian Furniture, Works of Art, Silver, Glass, Watches, China, Musical Instruments, Jewellery, etc. etc.

Held in our Saleroom at Sevenoaks.

Also valuations carried out for Probate, Insurance and Family Division.

Complete house clearances undertaken with personal supervision.

Storage facilities available for short periods pending sale.

Chattel Auctions and Valuations

JULIAN DAWSON
LEWES AUCTION ROOMS

Regular sales of
ANTIQUE FURNITURE AND EFFECTS

Weekly sales of
ANTIQUE & MODERN FURNITURE, BRIC-A-BRAC etc.
every Monday at 11 am

Auction Offices, 56 High Street. Lewes. Tel. Lewes 478221
Salerooms, Garden Street, Lewes, Sussex.

Lambert & Foster

TENTERDEN
Antique Auction Rooms

Monthly auction sales throughout the year

Sales and Valuation Advice always available

Wide range of other Auction Sales regularly conducted – yearly calendar available

102 High Street
Tenterden, Kent
(01580) 762083

Gorringes Auction Galleries

Member of the Society SOFAA of Fine Art Auctioneers

MONTHLY AUCTION SALES
Period Furniture, Porcelain, Glass, Objects of Vertu, Silver Plate
Jewellery, Books, Works of Art, Oriental Carpets
Valuations for Insurance, Probate, Family Division and Sale by Auction
Auction Sales conducted in Private Residences

15 NORTH STREET, LEWES, SUSSEX
Tel: (01273) 472503

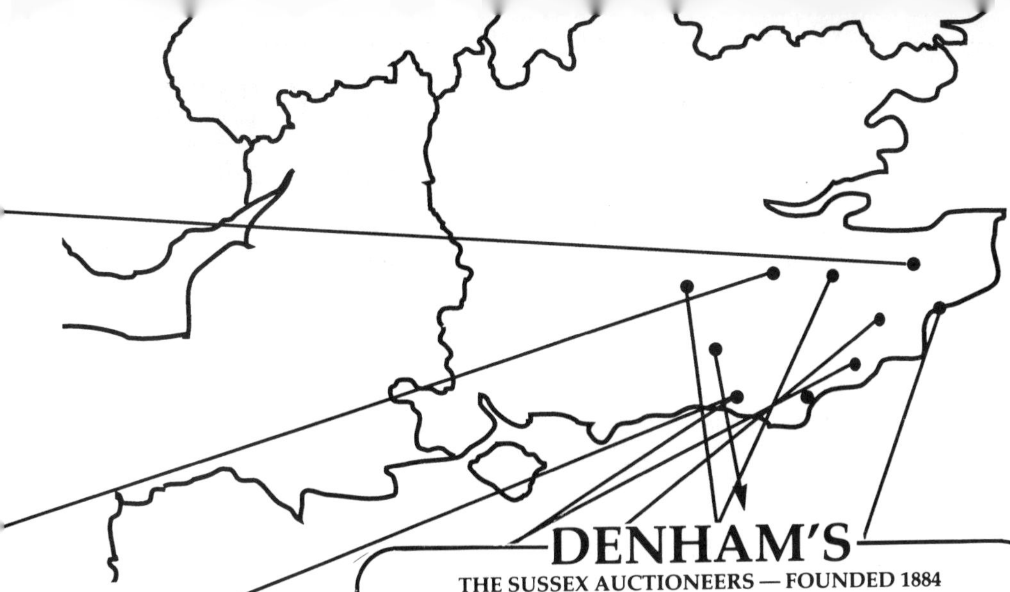

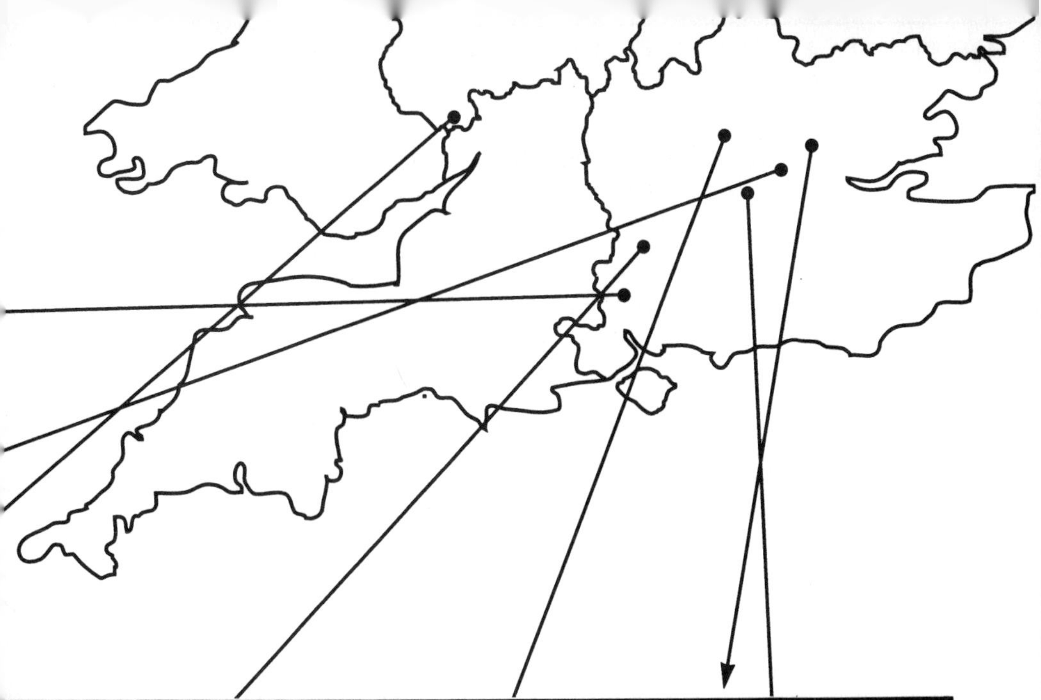

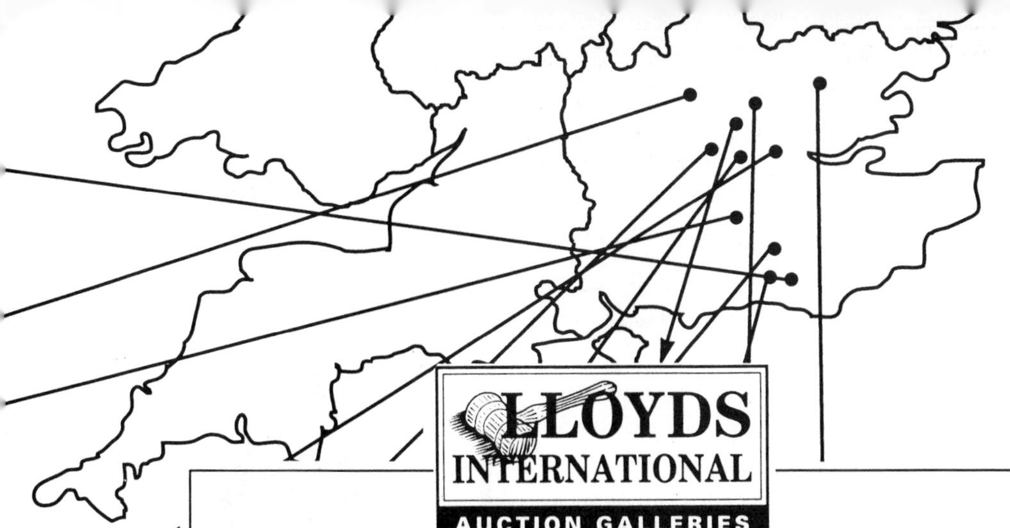

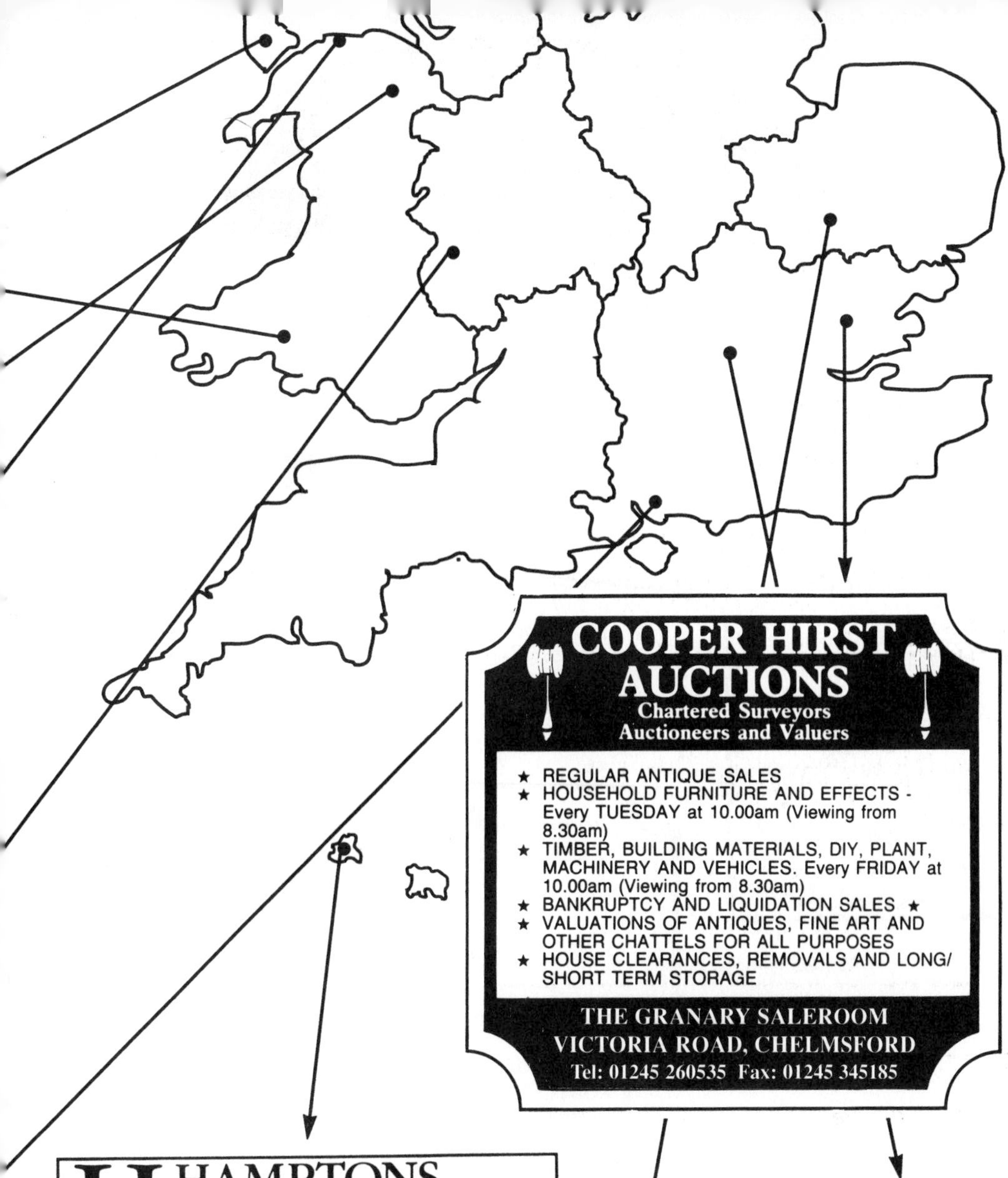

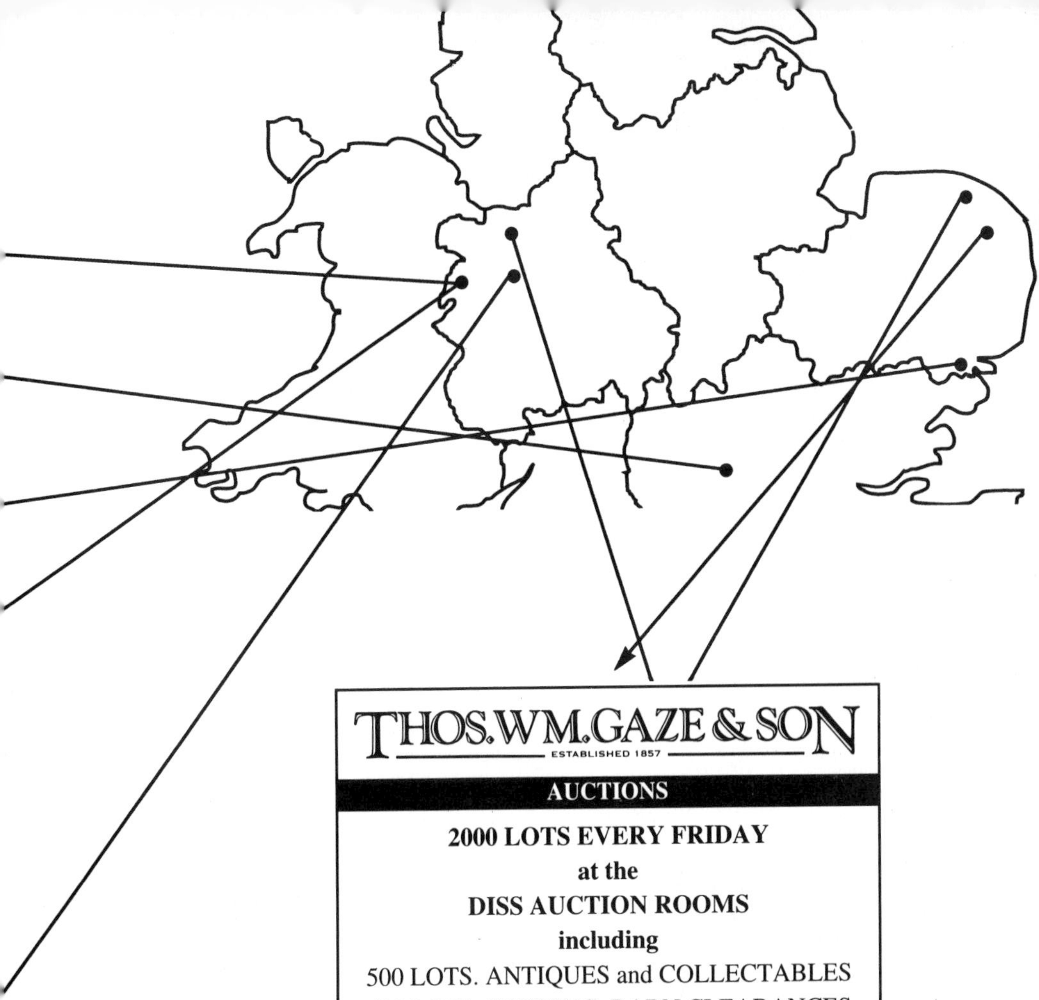

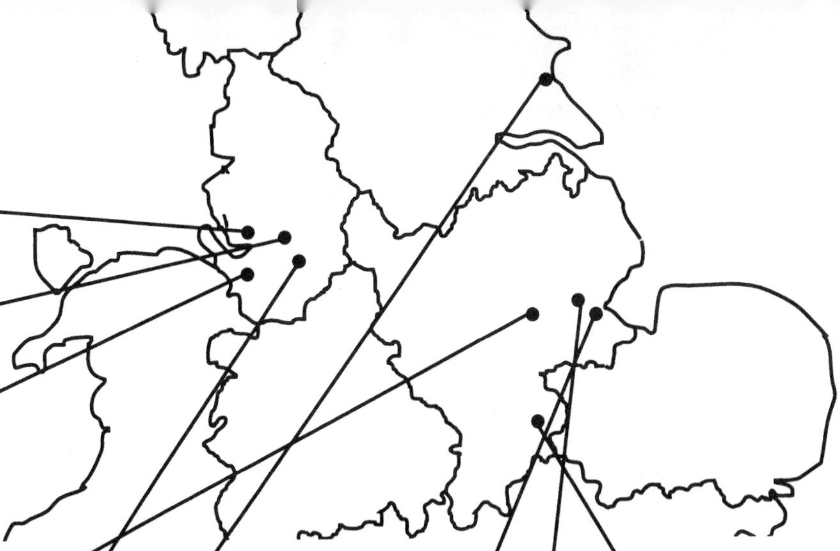

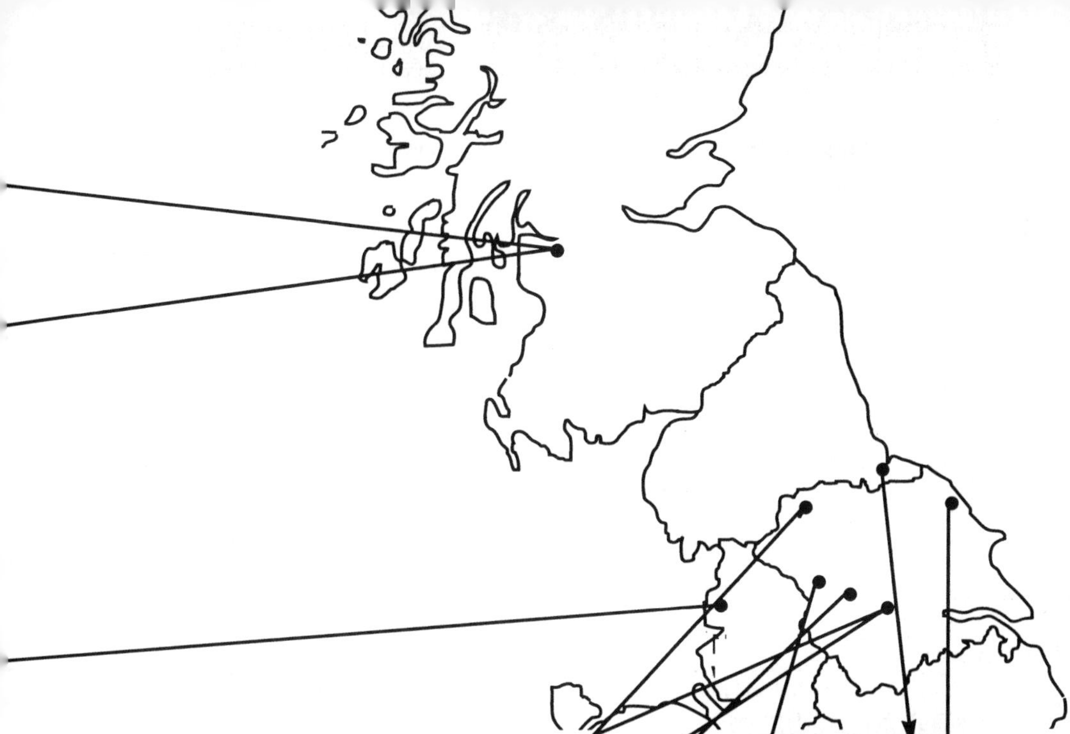

DIRECTORY OF AUCTIONEERS

Auctioneers who hold frequent sales should contact us for inclusion in the next Edition. Entries must be received by April 1996. There is no charge for this listing. Entries will be repeated in subsequent editions unless we are requested otherwise.

Avon

Aldridges, Bath,
The Auction Galleries,
130-132 Walcot Street,
Bath, BA1 5BG.
Tel: 01225 462830 & 462839

Bristol Auction Rooms,
St John's Place,
Apsley Road,
Clifton, Bristol, BS8 2ST.
Tel: 0117 973 7201

Clevedon Salerooms,
Herbert Road,
Clevedon, BS21 7ND.
Tel: 01275 876699

Gardiner Houlgate,
The Old Malthouse,
Comfortable Place,
Upper Bristol Road,
Bath, BA1 3AJ.
Tel: 01225 447933

Phillips,
1 Old King Street,
Bath, BA1 2JT.
Tel: 01225 310609

Phillips Fine Art Auctioneers,
71 Oakfield Road,
Clifton,
Bristol, BS8 2BE.
Tel: 0117 973 4052

Woodspring Auction Rooms,
Churchill Road,
Weston-super-Mare,
BS23 3HD.
Tel: 01934 628419

Bedfordshire

Wilson Peacock,
The Auction Centre,
26 Newnham Street,
Bedford, MK40 3JR.
Tel: 01234 266366

Berkshire

Chancellors, R. Elliott,
32 High Street,
Ascot, SL5 7HG.
Tel: 01344 872588

Dreweatt-Neate,
Donnington Priory,
Donnington,
Newbury,
RG13 2JE.
Tel: 01635 31234

Holloway's,
12 High Street,
Streatley, Reading.
Tel: 01491 872318

Martin & Pole,
12 Milton Road,
Wokingham.
Tel: 01734 790460

Shiplake Fine Art ,
31 Great Knollys Street,
Reading,
RG1 7HU.
Tel: 01734 594748

Buckinghamshire

Amersham Auction Rooms,
125 Station Road,
Amersham, HP7 0AH.
Tel: 01494 729292

Bourne End Auctions Rooms,
Station Approach,
Bourne End,
SL8 5QH.
Tel: 01628 531500

Hamptons,
10 Burkes Parade,
Beaconsfield, HP9 1PD.
Tel: 01494 672969

Wigley's,
Winslow Sale Room,
Market Square,
Winslow.
Tel: 01296 713011

Cheffins Grain & Comins,
2 Clifton Road,
Cambridge, CB2 4BW.
Tel: 01223 358721/213343

Goldsmiths,
15 Market Place,
Oundle.
Tel: 01832 272349

Grounds & Co,
2 Nene Quay,
Wisbech, PE13 1AG.
Tel: 01945 585041

Maxey & Son,
1-3 South Brink,
Wisbech, PE13 1RD.
Tel: 01945 584609

Phillips Auctioneers,
The Golden Rose, 17
Emmanuel Road,
Cambridge, CB1 1JW.
Tel: 01480 68144

Cheshire

Allen & Son, F W,
15/15a Station Road,
Cheadle Hulme,
SK8 5AF.
Tel: 0161 485 4121

Birchalls,
Cotebrook,
Tarporley, CW6 9DY.
Tel: 01829 760754

Birchalls,
Hatton Buildings,
Lightfoot Street, Hoole,
Chester.
Tel: 01244 328941

Dockree's,
224 Moss Lane, Bramhall,
Stockport, SK7 1BD.
Tel: 0161 485 1258

Highams Auctions,
Waterloo House,
Waterloo Road,
Stalybridge.
Tel: 0161 338 8698

Hilditch & Son, Andrew,
Hanover House,
1A The Square,
Sandbach, CW11 0AP.
Tel: 01270 762048/767246

Marshall & Co, Frank R,
Marshall House,
Church Hill,
Knutsford, WA16 6DH.
Tel: 01565 653284

Maxwell, John, of Wilmslow,
133A Woodford Road,
Woodford, SK7 1QD.
Tel: 0161 439 5182

Phillips North West,
New House,
150 Christleton Road,
Chester, CH3 5TD.
Tel: 01244 313936

Spencer, Henry Inc.,
Peter Wilson,
Victoria Gallery,
Market Street,
Nantwich.
Tel: 01270 623878

Wright Manley,
63 High Street,
Tarporley, CW6 0DR.
Tel: 01829 732151

Co. Durham

Denis Edkins,
Auckland Auction Room,
58 Kingsway,
Bishop Auckland,
DL14 7JF.
Tel: 01388 603095

Watson, & Son, Thomas,
Northumberland Street,
Darlington, DL3 7HJ.
Tel: 01325 462559/463485

Wingate Auction Co,
Station Lane,
Station Town, Wingate.
Tel: 01429 837245

Cornwall

David Lay, ASVA,
Auction House,
Alverton,
Penzance, TR18 4RE.
Tel: 01736 61414

Jeffery's,
5 Fore Street,
Lostwithiel,
PL22 0BP.
Tel: 01208 872245

Lambrays incorporating R J Hamm ASVA,
Polmorla Walk, The Platt,
Wadebridge, PL27 7AE.
Tel: 0120 881 3593

Lane & Son, W H,
65 Morrab Road,
Penzance, TR18 2QT.
Tel: 01736 61447

Phillips Cornwall,
Cornubia Hall,
Par, PL24 2AQ.
Tel: 0172 681 4047

Pooley and Rogers,
Regent Auction Rooms,
Abbey Street,
Penzance.
Tel: 01736 68814

Truro Auction Centre,
Calenick Street,
Truro.
Tel: 01872 260020

Cumbria

Cumbria Auction Rooms,
12 Lowther Street,
Carlisle, CA3 8DA.
Tel: 01228 25259

Hockney & Leigh,
The Auction Centre,
Grange-Over-Sands.
Tel: 015395 33316/33466

Mitchells,
Fairfield House,
Station Road,
Cockermouth,
CA13 9PY.
Tel: 01900 827800

Mossops & Co, Alfred,
Loughrigg Villa,
Kelsick Road,
Ambleside, .
Tel: 015394 33015

Thompson, James,
64 Main Street,
Kirkby,
Lonsdale, LA6 2AJ.
Tel: 015242 71555

Thomson, Roddick & Laurie,
24 Lowther Street,
Carlisle, CA3 8DA.
Tel: 01228 28939/39636

Derbyshire

Neales,
The Derby Saleroom,
Becket Street,
Derby, DE1 1HW.
Tel: 01332 343286

Richardson & Linnell Ltd,
The Auction Office, Cattle Market, Chequers Road,
Derby, DE21 6EP.
Tel: 01332 296369

Wheatcroft, Noel,
The Matlock Auction Gallery,
Old English Road,
Matlock, DE4 3LX.
Tel: 01629 584591

Devon

Bearnes,
Avenue Road,
Torquay, TQ2 5TG.
Tel: 01803 296277

Bonhams West Country,
Devon Fine Art Auction House, Dowell Street,
Honiton, EX14 8LX.
Tel: 01404 41872

Bowman, Michael J,
6 Haccombe House,
Netherton,
Newton Abbot,
TQ12 4SJ.
Tel: 01626 872890

Distin, Eric,
Chartered Surveyors,
2 Bretonside,
Plymouth.
Tel: 01752 663046 or 664841

Fenner & Co, Robin A, Fine Art & Antique Auctioneers,
The Stannary Gallery,
Drake Road,
Tavistock,
PL19 0AX.
Tel: 01822 617799/617800

Kings Auctioneers,
Pinnbrook Units, Venny Bridge, Pinhoe,
Exeter, EX4 8JX.
Tel: 01392 460644

Kingsbridge Auction Sales,
113 Fore Street,
Kingsbridge, TQ7 1BG.
Tel: 01548 856829

Phillips,
Alphin Brook Road,
Alphington,
Exeter, EX2 8TH.
Tel: 01392 439025

Potbury's,
High Street,
Sidmouth, EX10 8LN.
Tel: 01395 515555

Rendells,
Stone Park,
Ashburton, TQ13 7RH.
Tel: 01364 653017

Shobrook & Co, G S,
20 Western Approach,
Plymouth.
Tel: 01752 663341

Smale & Co, John,
11 High Street,
Barnstaple.
Tel: 01271 42000/42916

Sou'west Auctions,
Newport,
Barnstaple.
Tel: 01271 788581/850337

Spencer-Thomas, Martin,
Bicton Street Auction Rooms,
Exmouth, EX8 2RT.
Tel: 01395 267403

Taylors,
Honiton Galleries,
205 High Street,
Honiton, EX14 8LF.
Tel: 01404 42404

Ward & Chowen,
1 Church Lane,
Tavistock, PL19 8AA.
Tel: 01822 612458

Whitton & Laing,
32 Okehampton Street,
Exeter, EX4 1DY.
Tel: 01392 52621

Dorset

Cottees of Wareham,
The Market, East Street,
Wareham, BH20 4NR.
Tel: 01929 554915/552826

Dalkeith Auctions,
Dalkeith Hall, Dalkeith
Steps, Rear of 81 Old
Christchurch Road,
Bournemouth, BH1 1EW.
Tel: 01202 292905

House & Son,
Lansdowne House,
Christchurch Road,
Bournemouth, BH1 3JW.
Tel: 01202 556232

HY Duke & Son,
Weymouth Avenue,
Dorchester, DT1 1QS.
Tel: 01305 265080

HY Duke & Son,
The Weymouth Saleroom,
St Nicholas Street,
Weymouth.
Tel: 01305 761499

Morey & Sons, William,
The Saleroom,
St Michaels Lane,
Bridport, DT6 3RB.
Tel: 01308 422078

Riddetts of Bournemouth,
26 Richmond Hill,
The Square,
Bournemouth, BH2 6EJ.
Tel: 01202 555686

Southern Counties
Auctioneers,
Shaftesbury Livestock
Market, Christy's Lane,
Shaftesbury,
SP7 8PH.
Tel: 01747 851735

Stainer, Michael Ltd,
St Andrew's Hall,
Wolverton Road, Boscombe,
Bournemouth, BH7 6HT.
Tel: 01202 309999

Essex

Abridge Auction Rooms,
Market Place,
Abridge.
Tel: 01992 812107/813113

Baytree Auctions,
23 Broomhills Industrial
Estate,
Braintree, CM7 7RW.
Tel: 01376 328228

Black Horse Agencies
Ambrose,
149 High Road,
Loughton, IG10 4LZ.
Tel: 0181 502 3951

Brown, William H,
Paskell's Rooms,
11-14 East Hill,
Colchester, CO1 2QX.
Tel: 01206 868070

Cooper Hirst Auctions,
The Granary Saleroom,
Victoria Road,
Chelmsford, CM2 6LH.
Tel: 01245 260535

Grays Auction Rooms,
Ye Old Bake House,
Alfred Street,
Grays.
Tel: 01375 381181

Leigh Auction Rooms,
John Stacey & Sons,
88-90 Pall Mall,
Leigh-on-Sea.
Tel: 01702 77051

Saffron Walden Saleroom,
1 Market Street,
Saffron Walden, CB10 1JB.
Tel: 01799 513281

Trembath Welch,
The Old Town Hall,
Great Dunmow, CM6 1AU.
Tel: 01371 872117

Gloucestershire

Bruton, Knowles & Co,
111 Eastgate Street,
Gloucester, GL1 1PZ.
Tel: 01452 521267

Fraser Glennie & Partners,
The Old Rectory, Siddington,
Nr Cirencester, GL7 6HL.
Tel: 01285 659677

Hobbs & Chambers,
Market Place,
Cirencester, GL7 1QQ.
Tel: 01285 654736

Hobbs & Chambers,
15 Royal Crescent,
Cheltenham.
Tel: 01242 513722

Lawson, Ken, t/as
Specialised Postcard Auctions,
25 Gloucester Street,
Cirencester.
Tel: 01285 659057

Mallams,
26 Grosvenor Street,
Cheltenham, GL52 2SG.
Tel: 01242 235712

Moore, Allen & Innocent,
33 Castle Street,
Cirencester, GL7 1QD.
Tel: 01285 65183

Wotton Auction Rooms,
Tabernacle Road,
Wotton-under-Edge,
GL12 7EB.
Tel: 01453 844733

Greater Manchester

Capes Dunn & Co,
The Auction Galleries,
38 Charles Street,
Off Princess Street, M1 7DB.
Tel: 0161 273 6060/1911

Phillips,
Trinity House,
114 Washway Road,
Sale, M33 1RF.
Tel: 0161 962 9237

Hampshire

Andover Saleroom,
41A London Street,
Andover, SP10 2NY.
Tel: 01264 3648200

Basingstoke Auction Rooms,
82-84 Sarum Hill ,
Basingstoke, RG21 1ST.
Tel: 01256 840707

Evans & Partridge,
Agriculture House,
High Street,
Stockbridge, SO20 6HF.
Tel: 01264 810702

Fox & Sons,
5 & 7 Salisbury Street,
Fordingbridge, SP6 1AD.
Tel: 01425 652121

George Kidner,
The Old School,
The Square, Pennington,
Lymington, SO41 8GN.
Tel: 01590 670070

Jacobs & Hunt,
Lavant Street,
Petersfield, GU32 3EF.
Tel: 01730 62744/5

May & Son,
18 Bridge Street,
Andover, SP10 1BH.
Tel: 01264 323417

Nesbit & Co, D M,
7 Clarendon Road,
Southsea, PO5 2ED.
Tel: 01705 864321

Odiham Auction Sales,
The Eagle Works, Rear of
Hartley Wintney Garages,
High Street,
Hartley Wintney,
RG27 8PU.
Tel: 01252 844410

Phillips Fine Art
Auctioneers,
54 Southampton Road,
Ringwood, BH24 1JD.
Tel: 01425 473333

Phillips of Winchester,
The Red House,
Hyde Street,
Winchester, SO23 7DX.
Tel: 01962 862515

Romsey Auction Rooms,
86 The Hundred,
Romsey, SO51 8BX.
Tel: 01794 513331

Hereford

Morris Bricknell,
Stuart House,
Gloucester Road,
Ross-on-Wye,
HR9 5BU.
Tel: 01989 768320

Hereford & Worcs

Laney, Philip,
The Portland Room,
Portland Road,
Malvern, WR14 2TA.
Tel: 01684 893933

Russell Baldwin & Bright,
Ryelands Road,
Leominster, HR6 8NZ.
Tel: 01568 611166

Village Auctions,
Sychampton Community
Centre,
Ombersley.
Tel: 01905 421007

Williams, Richard,
2 High Street,
Pershore.
Tel: 01386 554031

Broadway Auctions,
41-43 High Street,
Broadway.
Tel: 01386 852456

Carless & Co,
58 Lowesmoor,
Worcester, WR1 2SE.
Tel: 01905 612449

Grant, Andrew,
St Mark's House,
St Mark's Close,
Worcester, WR5 3DJ.
Tel: 01905 357547

Griffiths & Co,
57 Foregate Street,
Worcester, WR1 1DZ.
Tel: 01905 26464

Hamptons,
Barnards Green Road,
Malvern.
Tel: 01684 892314

Phipps & Pritchard,
Bank Buildings,
Kidderminster,
DY10 1BU.
Tel: 01562 822244/6

Hertfordshire

Bayles,
Childs Farm, Cottered,
Buntingford.
Tel: 0176 381256

Brown & Merry,
Tring Market Auctions,
Brook Street,
Tring,
HP23 5EF.
Tel: 01442 826446

Hitchin Auctions Ltd,
The Corn Exchange,
Market Place,
Hitchin, SG5 1DY.
Tel: 01462 442151

Pickford, Andrew,
The Hertford Saleroom,
42 St Andrew Street,
Hertford, SG14 1JA.
Tel: 01992 583508

Sworder & Sons, G E,
15 Northgate End,
Bishops Stortford,
CM23 2ET.
Tel: 01279 651388

Vincent Auctions,
The Cranborne Rooms,
The Red Lion Public House,
The Great North Road,
Hatfield.
Tel: 01920 460417/01707
323908

Humberside

Baitson, Gilbert, FSVA,
The Edwardian Auction
Galleries, Wiltshire Road,
Hull, HU4 6PG.
Tel: 01482 500500

Dickinson Davy & Markham,
Wrawby Street,
Brigg,
DN20 8JJ.
Tel: 01652 653666

Evans & Sons, H,
1 St James's Street,
Hessle Road,
Hull, HU3 3DH.
Tel: 01482 23033

Isle of Wight

Phillips Fine Art Auctioneers,
Cross Street Salerooms,
Newport.
Tel: 01983 822031

Watson Bull & Porter,
Isle of Wight Auction Rooms,
79 Regent Street,
Shanklin,
PO37 7AP.
Tel: 01983 863441

Ways Auction House,
Garfield Road,
Ryde, PO33 2PT.
Tel: 01983 562255

Kent

Albert Andrews Auctions
& Sales,
Maiden Lane,
Crayford, DA1 4LX.
Tel: 01322 528868

Bracketts,
27-29 High Street,
Tunbridge Wells,
TN1 1UU.
Tel: 01892 533733

Canterbury Auction Galleries,
40 Station Road West,
Canterbury, CT2 8AN.
Tel: 01227 763337

Halifax Property Services,
Fine Art Department,
53 High Street,
Tenterden, TN30 6BG.
Tel: 01580 763200

Halifax Property Services,
15 Cattle Market,
Sandwich.
Tel: 01304 614369

Hall, Edwin,
Valley Antiques,
Lyminge, Folkestone.
Tel: 01303 862134

Hobbs Parker,
Romney House, Ashford
Market, Elwick Road,
Ashford, TN23 1PG.
Tel: 01233 622222

Hythe Auction Rooms,
35 Dymchurch Road,
Hythe, CT21 6JE.
Tel: 01303 237444/264155

Ibbett Mosely,
125 High Street,
Sevenoaks, TN13 1UT.
Tel: 01732 452246

Kent Sales, Giffords,
Holmesdale Road,
South Darenth.
Tel: 01322 864919

Lambert & Foster,
77 Commercial Road,
Paddock Wood, TN12 6DR.
Tel: 01892 832325

Lambert & Foster,
102 High Street,
Tenterden, TN30 6HT.
Tel: 01580 762083/763233

Mervyn Carey,
Twysden Cottage,
Benenden, Cranbrook.
Tel: 01580 240283

Norris, B J,
The Quest,
West Street, Harrietsham,
Maidstone, ME17 1JD.
Tel: 01622 859515

Phillips, Fine Art Auctioneers,
49 London Road,
Sevenoaks, TN13 1AR.
Tel: 01732 740310

Phillips Folkestone,
11 Bayle Parade,
Folkestone, CT20 1SQ.
Tel: 01303 455555

Town & Country House
Auctions,
North House, Oakley Road,
Bromley Common, BR2 8HG.
Tel: 0181 462 1735

Walter & Randall,
7-13 New Road,
Chatham, ME4 4QL.
Tel: 01634 841233

Wealden Auction Galleries
Desmond Judd,
23 Hendly Drive,
Cranbrook, TN17 3DY.
Tel: 01580 714522

Williams, Peter S, FSVA,
Orchard End,
Sutton Valence,
Maidstone, ME17 3LS.
Tel: 01622 842350

Lancashire

Edwards & Co Ltd, Charles,
4-8 Lynwood Road,
Blackburn, BB2 6HP.
Tel: 01254 691748

Entwistle Green,
The Galleries,
Kingsway, Ansdell,
Lytham St Annes,
FY8 1AB.
Tel: 01253 735442

Fairhurst & Son, Robt.,
39 Mawdsley Street,
Bolton.
Tel: 01204 28452/28453

Highams Auctions,
Southgate House,
Southgate Street,
Rhodes Bank, Oldham.
Tel: 0161 626 1021

Mills & Radcliffe Inc
D Murgatroyd & Son,
101 Union Street,
Oldham.
Tel: 0161 624 1072

Palamountain, David,
1-3 Osborne Grove,
Morecambe, LA4 4LP.
Tel: 01524 423941

Parkinson Son & Hamer
Auctions, J.R.,
The Auction Rooms,
Rochdale Road,
Bury.
Tel: 0161 761 1612/7372

Smythe's,
174 Victoria Road West,
Cleveleys.
Tel: 01253 854084

Warren & Wignall Ltd,
The Mill, Earnshaw Bridge,
Leyland Lane,
Leyland.
Tel: 01772 453252/451430

Wilkinson & Beighton
Auctioneers,
Woodhouse Green,
Thurcroft,
Rotherham.
Tel: 01743 231212

Leicestershire

Brown, William H,
The Warner Auction Rooms,
16/18 Halford Street,
Leicester, LE1 1JB.
Tel: 0116 251 9777

Churchgate Auctions,
The Churchgate Saleroom,
66 Churchgate,
Leicester.
Tel: 0116 262 1416

Gildings,
64 Roman Way,
Market Harborough,
LE16 7PQ.
Tel: 01858 410414

Noton Salerooms,
76 South Street,
Oakham.
Tel: 01572 722681

Stanley Auctions, David,
Stordon Grange,
Osgathorpe,
Loughborough.
Tel: 01530 222320

The Warner Auction Rooms
(William H. Brown),
16-18 Halford Street,
Leicester.
Tel: 0116 251 9777

Lincolnshire

Bourne Auction Rooms,
Spalding Road,
Bourne.
Tel: 01778 422686

Dowse & Son, A E,
89 Mary Street,
Scunthorpe.
Tel: 01724 842569/842039

Goldings,
The Grantham Auction
Rooms, Old Wharf Road,
Grantham, NG31 7AA.
Tel: 01476 65118

John H Walter,
1 Mint Lane,
Lincoln.
Tel: 01522 525454

Mawer & Son, Thomas,
63 Monks Road,
Lincoln, LN2 5HP.
Tel: 01522 524984

Spencer & Sons, Henry,
42 Silver Street,
Lincoln, LN2 1TA.
Tel: 01522 536666

Swain Auctions, Marilyn,
The Old Barracks,
Sandon Road,
Grantham,
NG31 9AS.
Tel: 01476 68861

London

Academy Auctioneers &
Valuers,
Northcote House,
Northcote Avenue,
Ealing, W5 3UR.
Tel: 0181 579 7466

Bonhams,
Montpelier Galleries,
Montpelier Street,
SW7 1HH.
Tel: 0171-584 9161

Bonhams,
Lots Road,
Chelsea,
SW10 0RN.
Tel: 0171 351 7111

Christie, Manson &
Woods Ltd,
8 King Street,
St James's,
SW1Y 6QT.
Tel: 0171 839 9060

Christie's Robson Lowe,
47 Duke Street,
St James's, SW1.
Tel: 0171 839 4034/5

Christie's South
(Kensington) Ltd,
85 Old Brompton Road,
SW7 3LD.
Tel: 0171 581 7611

Criterion Salerooms,
53 Essex Road,
Islington, N1 2BN.
Tel: 0171 359 5707

Dowell Lloyd & Co,
Putney Auction Galleries,
118 Putney Bridge Road,
SW15 2NQ.
Tel: 0181 788 7777

Forrest & Co,
79-85 Cobbold Road,
Leytonstone, E11 3NS.
Tel: 0181 534 2931

G.W.R. Auctions (Edmonton),
22 Bull Lane,
Edmonton, N18.
Tel: 0181 887 0525

Glendining's,
101 New Bond Street,
W1Y 9LG.
Tel: 0171 493 2445

Hamptons Fine Art
Auctioneers and Valuers,
6 Arlington Street,
SW1.
Tel: 0171 493 8222

Harmers of London,
91 New Bond Street,
W1.
Tel: 0171 629 0218

Hornsey Auctions Ltd,
54/56 High Street,
Hornsey, N8 7NX.
Tel: 0181 340 5334

Lots Road Chelsea Auction
Galleries,
71 Lots Road, Worldsend,
Chelsea, SW10 0RN.
Tel: 0171 351 7771

MacGregor Nash & Co,
Lodge House,
9-17 Lodge Lane,
North Finchley, N12 8JH.
Tel: 081 445 9000

Onslow's,
Metrostore,
Townmead Road, SW6 2RZ.
Tel: 0171 793 0240

Phillips,
Blenstock House,
7 Blenheim Street,
New Bond Street,
W1Y 0AS.
Tel: 0171 629 6602

Phillips,
10 Salem Road,
W2 4DL.
Tel: 0171 229 9090

Rippon Boswell & Co,
The Arcade,
South Kensington Station,
SW7 2NA.
Tel: 0171 589 4242

Rosebery's Fine Art Ltd,
Old Railway Booking Hall,
Station Road,
Crystal Palace,
SE19 2AZ.
Tel: 0181 778 4024

Sotheby's,
34-35 New Bond Street,
W1A 2AA.
Tel: 0171 493 8080

Southgate Auction Rooms,
55 High Street,
Southgate, N14 6LD.
Tel: 0181 886 7888

Stanley Gibbons Auctions Ltd,
399 Strand, WC2R 0LX.
Tel: 0171 836 8444

Thomas Moore,
217-219 Greenwich High Road, SE10.
Tel: 0181 858 7848

Town & Country House Auctions,
42A Nightingale Grove, SE13.
Tel: 0181 852 3145

Merseyside

Cato Crane & Co,
Liverpool Auction Rooms,
6 Stanhope Street,
Liverpool, L8 5RF.
Tel: 0151 709 5559

Hartley & Co,
12 & 14 Moss Street,
Liverpool.
Tel: 0151 263 6472/1865

Kingsley & Co,
3-5 The Quadrant, Hoylake,
Wirral.
Tel: 0151 632 5821

Outhwaite & Litherland,
Kingsway Galleries,
Fontenoy Street,
Liverpool, L3 2BE.
Tel: 0151 236 6561

Worralls,
13-15 Seel Street,
Liverpool, L1 4AU.
Tel: 0151 709 2950

Norfolk

Ewings,
Market Place, Reepham,
Norwich, NR10 4JJ.
Tel: 01603 870473

Gaze & Son, Thomas W M,
Diss Auction Rooms,
Roydon Road,
Diss, IP22 3LN.
Tel: 01379 650306

Hedge, Nigel F,
28B Market Place,
North Walsham,
NR28 9BS.
Tel: 01692 402881

Key, G A,
Aylsham Salerooms,
8 Market Place,
Aylsham, NR11 6EH.
Tel: 01263 733195

Northamptonshire

Corby & Co,
30-32 Brook Street,
Raunds.
Tel: 01933 623722

Heathcote Ball & Co,
Albion Auction Rooms,
Old Albion Brewery,
Commercial Street,
Northampton,
NN1 1PJ.
Tel: 01604 37263

Lowery's,
24 Bridge Street,
Northampton,
NN1 1NT.
Tel: 01604 21561

Merry's Auctioneers,
14 Bridge Street,
Northampton, NN1 1NJ.
Tel: 01604 32266

Nationwide Surveyors,
28 High Street,
Daventry.
Tel: 01327 312022

Southam & Sons,
Corn Exchange, Thrapston,
Kettering,
NN14 4JJ.
Tel: 01832 734486

Wilford Ltd, H,
Midland Road,
Wellingborough.
Tel: 01933 222760

Northumberland

Louis Johnson Auctioneers,
Oswald House,
63 Bridge Street,
Morpeth, NE61 1PQ
Tel: 01670 513025

Nottinghamshire

Arthur Johnson & Sons Ltd,
The Nottingham Auction Rooms, The Cattle Market,
Meadow Lane,
Nottingham,
NG2 3GY.
Tel: 0115 986 9128

Neales,
192-194 Mansfield Road,
Nottingham.
Tel: 0115 962 4141

Pye & Sons, John,
Corn Exchange,
Cattle Market, London Road,
Nottingham.
Tel: 0115 986 6261

Sheppard & Son, C B,
The Auction Galleries,
Chatsworth Street,
Sutton-in-Ashfield.
Tel: 01773 872419

Spencer and Sons, Henry (Phillips),
20 The Square,
Retford, DN22 6BX.
Tel: 01777 708633

Vennett-Smith, T,
11 Nottingham Road,
Gotham, Nottingham.
Tel: 0115 983 0541

Oxfordshire

Green & Co,
33 Market Place,
Wantage.
Tel: 01235 763561/2

Holloways,
49 Parsons Street,
Banbury, OX6 8PF.
Tel: 01295 253197

Mallams,
24 St Michael's Street,
Oxford, OX1 2EB.
Tel: 01865 241358

Messengers,
27 Sheep Street,
Bicester, OX6 7JF.
Tel: 01869 252901

Phillips,
39 Park End Street,
Oxford, OX1 1JD.
Tel: 01865 723524

Simmons & Sons,
32 Bell Street,
Henley-on-Thames,
RG9 2BH.
Tel: 01491 591111

Scotland

Christie's Scotland Ltd,
164-166 Bath Street,
Glasgow, G2 4TG.
Tel: 0141 332 8134

Fenton & Sons, B L ,
Forebank Auction Halls,
84 Victoria Road,
Dundee.
Tel: 01382 26227

Frasers Auctioneers,
8A Harbour Road,
Inverness, IV1 1SY.
Tel: 01463 232395

Hardie Ltd, William,
141 West Regent Street,
Glasgow, G2 2SG.
Tel: 0141 221 6780

Howe, J & J,
24 Commercial Street,
Alyth,
Perthshire.
Tel: 01828 632594

Loves Auction Rooms,
The Auction Galleries,
52-54 Canal Street,
Perth, PH2 8LF.
Tel: 01738 33337

Mainstreet Trading,
Mainstreet,
St Boswells, Melrose,
Roxburghshire.
Tel: 01835 823978

McTear & Co (Auctioneers & Valuers) Ltd, Robert,
Royal Exchange Salerooms,
6 North Court,
St Vincent Place,
Glasgow, G1 2DS.
Tel: 0141 221 4456

Milne, John,
9 North Silver Street,
Aberdeen.
Tel: 01224 639336

Paterson & Son, Robert,
8 Orchard Street, Paisley,
Renfrewshire, PA1 1UZ.
Tel: 0141 889 2435

Phillips Scotland,
65 George Street,
Edinburgh, EH2 2JL.
Tel: 0131 225 2266

Phillips Scotland,
207 Bath Street,
Glasgow, G2 4HD.
Tel: 0141 221 8377

Smellie & Sons Ltd, L S,
Within the Furniture Market,
Lower Auchingramont Road,
Hamilton, ML10 6BE.
Tel: 01698 282007

Sotheby's,
112 George Street,
Edinburgh.
Tel: 0131 226 7201

Thomson, Roddick & Laurie,
20 Murray Street,
Annan,
DG12 6EG.
Tel: 01461 202575

West Perthshire Auctions,
Dundas Street, Cowie,
Perthshire.
Tel: 01764 70613

Shropshire

Ludlow Antique Auctions Ltd,
29 Corve Street,
Ludlow, SY8 1DA.
Tel: 01584 875157

McCartneys,
25 Corve Street,
Ludlow.
Tel: 01584 872636

Mear & Co, Timothy,
Temeside Salerooms,
Ludford Bridge,
Ludlow,
SY8 1PE.
Tel: 01584 876081

Perry & Phillips,
Newmarket Salerooms,
Newmarket Buildings,
Listley Street,
Bridgnorth,
WV16 4AW.
Tel: 01746 762248

Somerset

Black Horse Agencies,
Alder King,
25 Market Place,
Wells.
Tel: 01749 73002

Cooper & Tanner,
Frome Auction Rooms,
Frome Market, Standerwick,
Nr Frome, BA11 2PY.
Tel: 01373 831010

Dores & Rees,
The Auction Mart,
Vicarage Street,
Frome.
Tel: 01373 462257

Fleming, John,
4 & 8 Fore Street,
Dulverton.
Tel: 01398 23597

Gribble Booth & Taylor,
13 The Parade,
Minehead,
TA24 5NL.
Tel: 01643 702281

Lawrences of Crewkerne,
South Street,
Crewkerne,
TA18 8AB.
Tel: 01460 73041

Richards,
The Town Hall,
The Square,
Axbridge,
BS26 2AR.
Tel: 01934 732969

The London Cigarette Card Co Ltd,
Sutton Road,
Somerton.
Tel: 01458 73452

Wellington Salerooms,
Mantle Street,
Wellington, TA21 8AR.
Tel: 01823 664815

Wells Auction Rooms,
66/68 Southover,
Wells.
Tel: 01749 678094

Staffordshire

Bagshaws,
17 High Street,
Uttoxeter, ST14 7HP.
Tel: 01889 562811

Hall & Lloyd,
South Street Auction Rooms,
Stafford,
ST16 2DZ.
Tel: 01785 58176

Louis Taylor Auctioneers & Valuers,
Britannia House,
10 Town Road, Hanley,
Stoke on Trent,
ST1 2QG.
Tel: 01782 214111

Wintertons Ltd,
Lichfield Auction Centre,
Wood End Lane, Fradley,
Lichfield,
WS13 8NF.
Tel: 01543 263256

Suffolk

Abbotts Auction Rooms,
Campsea Ashe,
Woodbridge,
IP13 0PS.
Tel: 01728 746323

ABC Auctions,
Central Avenue,
West Molesey.
Tel: 0181 941 5545

Boardman Fine Art,
Station Road Corner,
Haverhill, LB9 0EY.
Tel: 01440 730414

Brown, William H,
Ashford House,
Saxmundham.
Tel: 01728 603232

Diamond Mills & Co,
117 Hamilton Road,
Felixstowe, IP11 7BL.
Tel: 01394 282281

Lacy Scott,
Fine Art Department,
The Auction Centre,
10 Risbygate Street,
Bury St Edmunds, IP33 3AA.
Tel: 01284 763531

Neal Sons & Fletcher,
26 Church Street,
Woodbridge, IP12 1DP.
Tel: 01394 382263

Olivers,
Olivers Rooms,
Burkitts Lane,
Sudbury, CO10 6HB.
Tel: 01787 880305

Phillips,
Dover House, Wolsey Street,
Ipswich, IP1 1UD.
Tel: 01473 255137

Surrey

Chancellors,
74 London Road,
Kingston-upon-Thames,
KT2 6PX.
Tel: 0181 541 4139

Clarke Gammon,
The Guildford Auction
Rooms, Bedford Road,
Guildford, GU1 4SJ.
Tel: 01483 66458

Crows Auction Gallery,
Rear of Dorking Halls,
Reigate Road,
Dorking, RH4 1SG.
Tel: 01306 740382

Ewbank Fine Art,
Welbeck House, High Street,
Guildford, GU1 3JF.
Tel: 01483 232134

Hamptons,
Fine Art Auctioneers &
Valuers, 93 High Street,
Godalming, GU7 1AL.
Tel: 01483 423567

Lawrences Auctioneers,
Norfolk House,
80 High Street,
Bletchingley, RH1 4PA.
Tel: 01883 743323

Nicholson, John,
The Auction Rooms,
Longfield, Midhurst Road,
Fernhurst, GU27 3HA.
Tel: 01428 653727

Parkins,
18 Malden Road,
Cheam, SM3 8SD.
Tel: 0181 644 6633 & 6127

Phillips Fine Art Auctioneers,
Millmead,
Guildford.
Tel: 01483 504030

Richmond & Surrey Auctions,
Richmond Station,
Kew Road,
Old Railway Parcels Depot,
Richmond, TW9 2NA.
Tel: 0181 948 6677

Wentworth Auction Galleries,
21 Station Approach,
Virginia Water, GU25 4DW.
Tel: 01344 843711

Windibank, P F,
10-20 Reigate Road,
Dorking, RH4 1SG.
Tel: 01306 884556/876280

Sussex

Ascent Auction Galleries,
11-12 East Ascent,
St Leonards-on-Sea,
TN38 0DS.
Tel: 01424 420275

Bellman, John, Auctioneers,
New Pound Business Park,
Wisborough Green,
Billingshurst, RH14 0AY.
Tel: 01403 700858

Burstow & Hewett,
Abbey Auction Galleries and
Granary Salerooms,
Lower Lake,
Battle,
TN33 0AT.
Tel: 01424 772374

Cheney, Peter,
Western Road Auction
Rooms, Western Road,
Littlehampton,
BN17 5NP.
Tel: 01903 722264/713418

Clifford Dann Auction
Galleries,
20-21 High Street,
Lewes, BN7 2LN.
Tel: 01273 480111

Denham's,
Horsham Auction Galleries,
Warnham,
Horsham, RH12 3RZ.
Tel: 01403 255699/253837

Edgar Horn's,
Fine Art Auctioneers,
46-50 South Street,
Eastbourne, BN21 4XB.
Tel: 01323 410419

Ellis & Sons, R H,
44-46 High Street,
Worthing, BN11 1LL.
Tel: 01903 238999

Gorringes Auction Galleries,
Terminus Road,
Bexhill-on-Sea.
Tel: 01424 212994

Gorringes Auction Galleries,
15 North Street,
Lewes, BN7 2PD.
Tel: 01273 472503

Graves, Son & Pilcher,
71 Church Road,
Hove, BN3 2GL.
Tel: 01273 735266

Hove Auction Galleries,
1 Weston Road,
Hove.
Tel: 01273 736207

Lewes Auction Rooms
(Julian Dawson),
56 High Street,
Lewes, BN7 1XE.
Tel: 01273 478221

Nationwide,
Midhurst Auction Rooms,
West Street,
Midhurst, GU29 9NG.
Tel: 01730 812456

Phillips Fine Art
Auctioneers,
Baffins Hall, Baffins Lane,
Chichester, PO19 1UA.
Tel: 01243 787548

Raymond P Inman,
The Auction Galleries,
35 & 40 Temple Street,
Brighton,
BN1 3BH.
Tel: 01273 774777

Rye Auction Galleries,
Rock Channel,
Rye.
Tel: 01797 222124

Sotheby's Sussex,
Summers Place,
Billingshurst, RH14 9AD.
Tel: 01403 783933

Stride & Son,
Southdown House,
St John's Street,
Chichester, PO19 1XQ.
Tel: 01243 780207

Sussex Auction Galleries,
59 Perrymount Road,
Haywards Heath,
RH16 3DR.
Tel: 01444 414935

Wallis & Wallis,
West Street Auction
Galleries,
Lewes, BN7 2NJ.
Tel: 01273 480208

Watsons,
Heathfield Furniture
Salerooms,
The Market, Burwash Road,
Heathfield.
Tel: 01435 862132

Worthing Auction
Galleries Ltd,
31 Chatsworth Road,
Worthing, BN11 1LY.
Tel: 01903 205565

Tyne & Wear

Anderson & Garland
(Auctioneers),
Marlborough House,
Marlborough Crescent,
Newcastle-upon-Tyne,
NE1 4EE.
Tel: 0191 232 6278

Boldon Auction Galleries,
24a Front Street,
East Boldon, NE36 0SJ.
Tel: 0191 537 2630

Miller, Thomas N,
18-22 Gallowgate,
Newcastle-upon-Tyne,
NE1 4SN.
Tel: 0191 232 5617

Phillips North East,
St Mary's, Oakwellgate,
Gateshead, NE8 2AX.
Tel: 0191 477 6688

Sneddons,
Sunderland Auction Rooms,
30 Villiers Street,
Sunderland, SR1 1EJ.
Tel: 0191 514 5931

Warwickshire

Bigwood Auctioneers Ltd,
The Old School,
Tiddington,
Stratford-upon-Avon,
CV37 7AW.
Tel: 01789 269415

Locke & England,
Black Horse Agencies,
18 Guy Street,
Leamington Spa,
CV32 4RT.
Tel: 01926 889100

West Midlands

Biddle and Webb Ltd,
Ladywood Middleway,
Birmingham, B16 0PP.
Tel: 0121 455 8042

Cariss Residential,
20 High Street, Kings Heath,
Birmingham.
Tel: 0121 444 0088

Clare, Ronald E ,
Clare's Auction Rooms,
70 Park Street,
Birmingham.
Tel: 0121 643 0226

Fellows & Sons, Frank H ,
Augusta House,
19 Augusta Street, Hockley,
Birmingham, B18 6JA.
Tel: 0121 212 2131

Haywood, Giles,
The Auction House,
St John's Road,
Stourbridge, DY8 1EW.
Tel: 01384 370891

James & Lister Lea,
42 Bull Street,
Birmingham, B4 6AF.
Tel: 0121 200 1100

Phillips,
The Old House,
Station Road, Knowle,
Solihull, B93 0HT.
Tel: 01564 776151

Swash, Stuart FSVA,
Stamford House,
2 Waterloo Road,
Wolverhampton.
Tel: 01902 710626

Walker Barnett & Hill,
Waterloo Road Salerooms,
Clarence Street,
Wolverhampton, WV1 4DL.
Tel: 01902 773531

Weller & Dufty Ltd,
141 Bromsgrove Street,
Birmingham, B5 6RQ.
Tel: 0121 692 1414

Wiltshire

Aldridge & Son, Henry ,
Devizes Auction Rooms,
1 Wine Street,
Devizes, SN10 1AP.
Tel: 01380 729199

Dominic Winter Book
Auctions,
The Old School,
Maxwell Street,
Swindon, SN1 5DR.
Tel: 01793 611340

Hamptons,
20 High Street,
Marlborough, SN8 1AA.
Tel: 01672 516161

Kidson Trigg,
Friars Farm,
Sevenhampton,
Highworth,
Swindon,
SN6 7PZ.
Tel: 01793 861000/861072

Swindon Auction Rooms,
The Planks (off The Square),
Old Town,
Swindon,
SN3 1QP.
Tel: 01793 615915

Woolley & Wallis,
Salisbury Salerooms,
51-61 Castle Street,
Salisbury, SP1 3SU.
Tel: 01722 411422

Yorkshire

Audsley's Auctions
(C R Kemp BSc),
11 Morris Lane,
Kirkstall,
Leeds 5.
Tel: 0113 275 8787

Boulton & Cooper,
St Michaels House,
Market Place,
Malton, YO17 0LR.
Tel: 01653 696151

Brown, William H,
10 Regent Street,
Barnsley.
Tel: 01226 299221

Brown, William H ,
Stanilands Auction Room,
28 Nether Hall Road,
Doncaster.
Tel: 01302 367766

Chapman & Son, H C,
The Auction Mart,
North Street,
Scarborough,
YO11 1DL.
Tel: 01723 372424

Cundalls,
15 Market Place,
Malton,
YO17 0LP.
Tel: 01653 697820

Darwin & Sons, M W,
The Dales Furniture Hall,
Bedale.
Tel: 01677 422846

De Rome,
12 New John Street,
Westgate,
Bradford,
BD1 2QY.
Tel: 01274 734116

Dee Atkinson & Harrison,
The Exchange Saleroom,
Driffield.
Tel: 01377 253151

Eadon Lockwood & Riddle,
411 Petre Street,
Sheffield, S4 8LL.
Tel: 0114 261 8000

Eddisons,
Auction Rooms,
4-6 High Street,
Huddersfield,
HD1 2LS.
Tel: 01484 533151

GA Fine Art & Chattels,
Royal Auction Rooms,
Queen Street,
Scarborough.
Tel: 01723 353581

Geoffrey Summersgill ASVA,
8 Front Street, Acomb,
York.
Tel: 01904 791131

Hartley, Andrew,
Victoria Salerooms,
Little Lane,
Ilkley, LS29 8EA.
Tel: 01943 816363

Hutchinson Scott,
The Grange,
Marton-Le-Moor,
Ripon, HG4 5AT.
Tel: 01423 324264

Lithgow Sons & Partners,
The Antique House,
Station Road, Stokesley,
Middlesbrough,
TS9 7AB.
Tel: 01642 710158/710326

Malcolms No1 Auctioneers & Valuers,
The Chestnuts,
16 Park Avenue,
Sherburn-in-Elmet,
Nr Leeds, LS25 6EF.
Tel: 01977 684971

Matthews, Christopher,
23 Mount Street,
Harrogate,
HG2 8DQ.
Tel: 01423 871756

Morphets of Harrogate,
4-6 Albert Street,
Harrogate, HG1 1JL.
Tel: 01423 502282

Nationwide Fine Arts & Furniture,
27 Flowergate,
Whitby.
Tel: 01947 603433

Phillips Leeds,
17a East Parade,
Leeds, LS1 2BH.
Tel: 0113 2448011

Raby & Son, John H,
The Sale Rooms,
21 St Mary's Road,
Bradford 8,
BD8 7QL.
Tel: 01274 491121

Scarthingwell Auction Centre,
Scarthingwell,
Nr Tadcaster.
Tel: 01937 557955

Spencer & Sons Ltd, Henry,
1 St James' Row,
Sheffield, S1 1WZ.
Tel: 0114 272 8728

Stephenson & Son,
Livestock Centre, Murton,
York.
Tel: 01904 489731

Tennants,
The Auction Centre,
Harmby Road,
Leyburn,
DL8 5SG.
Tel: 01969 623780

Tennants,
34 Montpelier Parade,
Harrogate, HG1 2TG.
Tel: 01423 531661

Thompson's Auctioneers,
Dales Saleroom, The Dale Hall, Hampsthwaite,
Harrogate, HG3 2EG.
Tel: 01423 770741

Whitby Auction Rooms,
West End Saleroom,
The Paddock, Whitby.
Tel: 01947 603433

Windle & Co,
The Four Ashes, 535 Great Horton Road,
Bradford.
Tel: 01274 57299

Wales

Dodds Property World,
Victoria Auction Galleries,
9 Chester Street,
Mold, Clwyd, CH7 1EB.
Tel: 01352 752552

Evans & Co, E H,
Auction Sales Centre,
The Market Place, Kilgetty,
Dyfed, SA68 0UG.
Tel: 01834 812793 & 811151

Francis, Peter,
The Curiosity Saleroom,
19 King Street,
Carmarthen,
SA31 1BH.
Tel: 01267 233456

Morgan Evans & Co Ltd,
28-30 Church Street,
Llangefni, Anglesey,
Gwynedd,
LL77 7DU.
Tel: 01248 723303/77582

Morris Marshall & Poole,
10 Broad Street,
Newtown, Powys.
Tel: 01686 625900

Phillips in Wales Fine Art Auctioneers,
9-10 Westgate Street,
Cardiff, Glamorgan,
CF1 1DA.
Tel: 01222 396453

Players Auction Mart,
Players Industrial Estate,
Clydach,
Swansea.
Tel: 01792 846241

Rennies,
1 Agincourt Street,
Monmouth, NP5 3DZ.
Tel: 01600 712916

Rogers Jones & Co,
33 Abergele Road,
Colwyn Bay,
Clwyd, LL29 7RU.
Tel: 01492 532176

Wingett's Auction Gallery,
29 Holt Street, Wrexham,
Clwyd, LL13 8DH.
Tel: 01978 353553

Channel Islands

Hamptons, Martel,
Maides Ltd,
The Old Bank,
29 High Street,
St Peter Port,
Guernsey, GY1 4NY.
Tel: 01481 713463

Langlois Auctioneers & Valuers,
Westway Chambers,
39 Don Street,
St Helier,
Jersey, JE2 4TR.
Tel: 01534 22441

Francis, Peter,
The Curiosity Saleroom,
19 King Street,
Carmarthen,
SA31 1BH.
Tel: 01267 233456

Isle of Man

Chrystals Auctions,
Majestic Hotel,
Onchan.
Tel: 01624 673986

Isle of Man Chrystals Auctions,
Majestic Hotel,
Onchan.
Tel: 01624 673986

Ireland

James Adam & Sons,
26 St Stephen's Green,
Dublin 2.
Tel: 676 0261/661 3655

Christie's Dublin,
52 Waterloo Road,
Dublin.
Tel: 00 353 1 6680 585

Mealys,
Chatsworth Street,
Castle Comer,
Co. Kilkenny.
Tel: 00 353 564 1229

Morgans Auctions Ltd,
Duncrue Crescent,
Duncrue Road,
Belfast,
BT3 9BW.
Tel: 01232 771552

Temple Auctions Limited,
133 Carryduff Road,
Temple, Lisburn,
Co. Antrim,
BT27 6YL.
Tel: 01846 638777

Canada

Ritchie Inc., D & J
Auctioneers & Appraisers of Antiques & Fine Arts ,
288 King Street East,
Toronto, M5A 1K4.
Tel: (416) 364 1864

Waddingtons,
189 Queen Street East,
Toronto,
Ontario, M5A 1SZ .
Tel: (416) 362 1678

Germany

Sotheby's Berlin,
Palais amFestungsgraben,
Unter den Linden/Neue Wache D-10117 Berlin.
Tel: 49 (30) 394 3060

Hong Kong

Sotheby's,
309/310 Exchange Square Two, 8 Connaught Place,
Central,
Hong Kong.
Tel: 852 2524 8121

Italy

Christie's Rome,
Palazzo Massimo Lancellotti,
Piazza Navona 114.
Tel: (396) 687 2787

Sotheby's Rome,
Piazza d'Espana 90, 00186,
Rome.
Tel: 396 6841791/6781798

Monaco

Sotheby's Monaco,
BP 45-98001,
Monaco.
Tel: 93 30 8880

Christie's (Monaco),
S.A.M., Park Palace,
98000.
Tel: 010 339 325 1933

Netherlands

Sotheby's Amsterdam,
Rokin 102,
Amsterdam, 1012 KZ .
Tel: 31 (20) 627 5656

Switzerland

Christie's (International) S.A.,
8 Place de la Taconnerie,
1204 Geneva.
Tel: 010 4122 311 17 66

Sotheby's,
13 Quai du Mont Blanc,
CH-1201 Geneva.
Tel: 41 (22) 732 8585

U.S.A.

Butterfield & Butterfield,
220 San Bruno Avenue,
San Francisco, CA 94103.
Tel: 415 861 7500

Christie's East,
219 East 67th Street,
New York,
USA.
Tel: 001 212 546 1184

Don Treadway Gallery,
2128 Madison Road,
Cincinnati,
OH 45208.
Tel: 513 321 6742

Doyle Galleries, William,
175 East 87th Street,
New York, NY 10128.
Tel: 212 427 2730

Du Mouchelle Art Gallery,
409 East Jefferson Avenue,
Detroit, MI 48226.
Tel: 313 963 6255

Dunning's,
755 Church Road,
Elgin, IL 60123.
Tel: 708 741 3483

Freeman Fine Art Of Philadelphia Inc,
1808 Chestnut Street,
Philadelphia, PA 19103 USA.
Tel: 215 563 9275

Gene Harris Antiques,
203 S 18th Avenue,
Marshalltown, IA 50158.
Tel: 515 752 0600

Grogan & Co,
890 Commonwealth Avenue,
Boston, MA 2215.
Tel: 617 566 4100

Hanzel Galleries,
1120 S Michigan Avenue,
Chicago, IL 60605.
Tel: 312 922 6234

Hart Galleries,
2301 South Voss Road,
Houston, TX 77057.
Tel: 713 266 3500

Hindmans,
215 West Ohio Street,
Chicago,
Illinois 60610.
Tel: 0101 312 670 0010

Louisiana Auction Exchange,
2031 Government Street,
Baton Rouge, LA 70806.
Tel: 504 387 9777

Lubin Galleries,
30 West 26th Street,
New York, NY10010.
Tel: 212 929 0909

Luper Auction Galleries,
Box 5143,
Richmond, VA 23220.
Tel: 804 359 2493

Moran Auctioneers, John,
3202 E Foothill Boulevard,
Pasadena, CA 91107.
Tel: 818 793 1833

Morton M Goldberg,
547 Baronne Street,
New Orleans, LA 70113.
Tel: (504) 592 2300

Mystic Fine Arts,
47 Holmes Street,
Mystic, CT6355.
Tel: 203 572 8873

Neal Auction Co,
4038 Magazine Street,
New Orleans, LA 70115.
Tel: 504 899 5329

Northeast Auctions,
694 Lafayette Road,
Hampton, NH 3842.
Tel: 603 926 9800

Paul McInnis Inc Auction Gallery,
Route 88, 356 Exeter Road,
Hampton Falls,
New Hampshire, 03844.
Tel: 010 603 778 8989

Selkirk's,
4166 Olive Street,
St Louis, MO 63108.
Tel: 314 533 1700

Weschler & Son, Adam A,
909 E Street NW,
Washington, DC 20004.
Tel: 202 628 1281

Wolfs Gallery,
1239 W 6th Street,
Cleveland, OH 44113.
Tel: 216 575 9653

Eldred's,
Robert C Eldred Co Inc,
1475 Route 6A, East Dennis,
Massachusetts 02641 0796.
Tel: 0101 508 385 3116

Frank H Boos Gallery,
420 Enterprise Court,
Bloomfield Hills,
Michigan 48302.
Tel: 0101 810 332 1500

Lesley Hindman Auctioneers,
215 West Ohio Street,
Chicago,
Illinois,
IL 60610.
Tel: (312) 670 0010

Skinner Inc,
357 Main Street,
Boston,
MA 01740.
Tel: 0101 508 779 6241

Sloan's,
C G Sloan & Company Inc,
4920 Wyaconda Road,
North Bethesda,
MD 20852.
Tel: 0101 301 468 4911/ 669 5066

Sotheby's,
1334 York Avenue,
New York NY 10021.
Tel: 212 606 7000

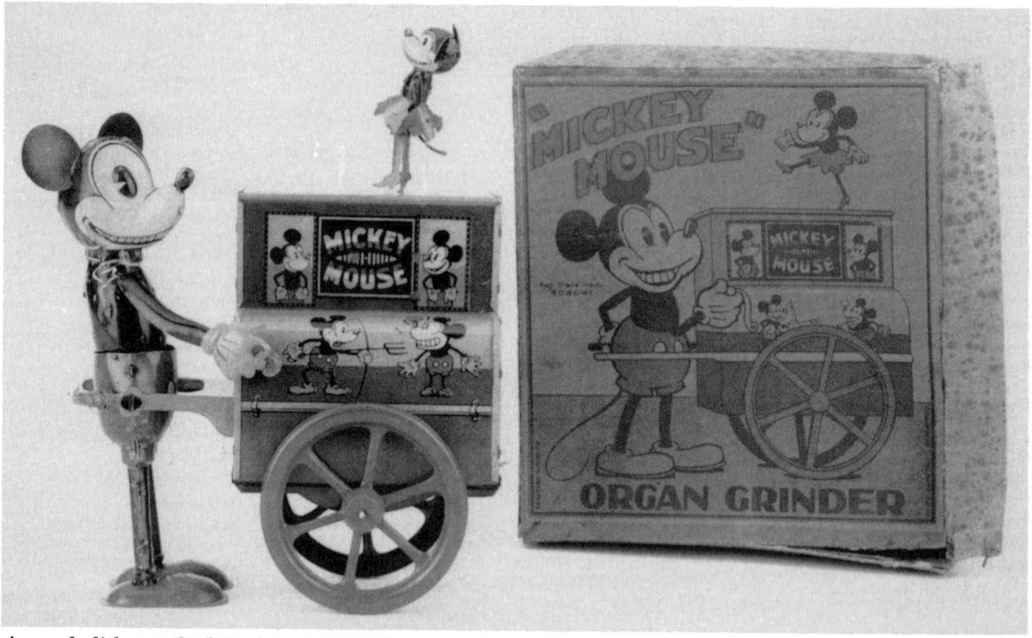

An early lithographed tinplate clockwork organ grinder, with Mickey Mouse cranking the organ, his head moves back and forth as Minnie Mouse dances on top of the organ to a 'rinky tink' tune, printed 'Made in Germany', probably by Distler, left arm missing, c1931, in original box, 8 by 6in (20 by 15cm).
£17,000–20,000 *CSK*

l. A Royal Quiet De Luxe portable typewriter, with gold-plated body and fittings, four-row keyboard, 1952, 11in (28cm) wide, in composition case and attached paper tag with printed address: 'The Pantechnicon, Heathfield Terrace' and manuscript inscription 'Mrs I Fleming 4, 23-2-73'.
£57,000–60,000 *CSK*

Ian Fleming commissioned this typewriter from the Royal Typewriter Company in New York in the spring of 1952, as a replacement for his old Imperial. The manuscript of the novel Casino Royale, *introducing 007 agent James Bond was typed on the machine.*

INDEX TO ADVERTISERS

INDEX

Italic page numbers denote information and pointer boxes.

D

E

G

H

I

J

K

L

1995
1996

EMER *Guide*

25th
Edition

Guide of French & European Antiques

Antique dealers, Art Galleries, Contemporary Art, Booksellers, Restorers, Auction Rooms, Experts, Museums

5 Guides EMER available separately	- France	100F
	- Europe	100F
	- Specialists	100F
	- Contemporary Art	80F
Or	- Flea Markets	20F
Complete Set	- 300F + (30F) p & p	

Edited by Edition Emer
47 Rue des Tournelles
75003 Paris, France
Tel:(1)42742715 Fax:(1)42740799
Credit Cards accepted.
Quote number & expiry date.

PIANO - EXPORT
TW & S SMALLRIDGE

Bridge Road, Kingswood, Bristol.
BS15 4PW England.

Telephone Bristol (0117) 956 8300
(International code 0044)

A telephone call is advisable before calling.
Open Monday-Friday

John Broadwood Square Piano c1860

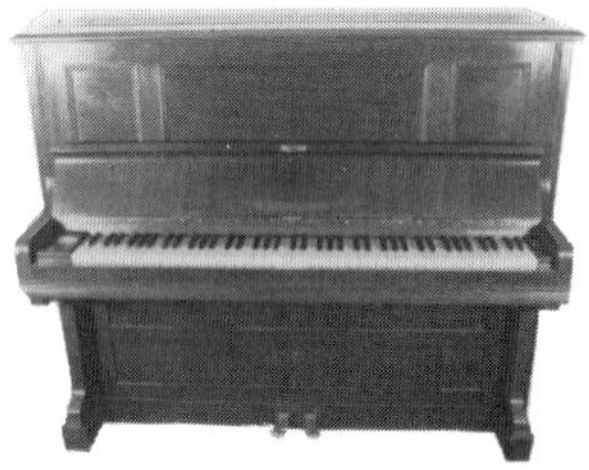

Bechstein Overstrung Rosewood Upright Piano c1913

SEE OUR MAIN COLOUR ADVERT ON PAGE 619

NEW

Miller's Collecting Books

Anyone who aquires books for pleasure will probably find something collectable on their shelves. This beautiful guide tells you how such finds can form the basis of a facinating collection. Illustrated with 450 fully captioned examples and a price range for every book shown. (£19.99)

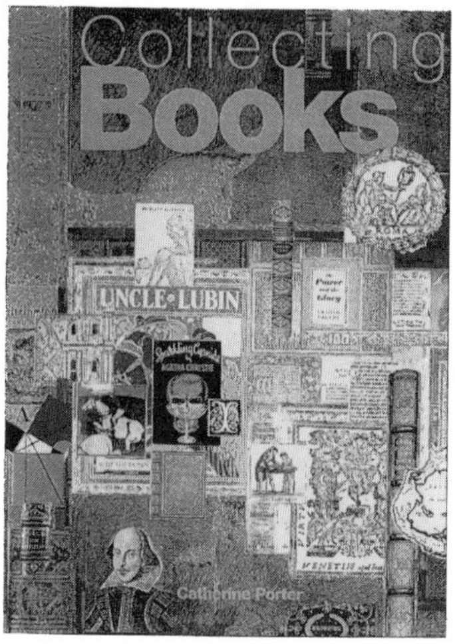

Available from
Cash Sales Dept.
Reed Book Services Limited
P.O. Box 5, Rushden, Northamptonshire NN10 6YX
Credit Card Hotline Tel: 01933 410511
Lines open from 9:00 to 5:00

Buxton

The 32nd Buxton Antiques Fair
11th - 18th May 1996
The Pavilion Gardens,
Buxton, Derbyshire

Surrey

The 28th Surrey Antiques Fair
5-8th October 1995
The Civic Hall, Guildford,
Surrey

Established Antiques Fairs of distinction and high repute offering pleasure to both lovers and collectors of craftsmanship and fine works of art.
For further information and complimentary tickets, please contact:

CULTURAL EXHIBITIONS LTD.
8 Meadrow, Godalming, Surrey
Telephone: Godalming (01483) 422562

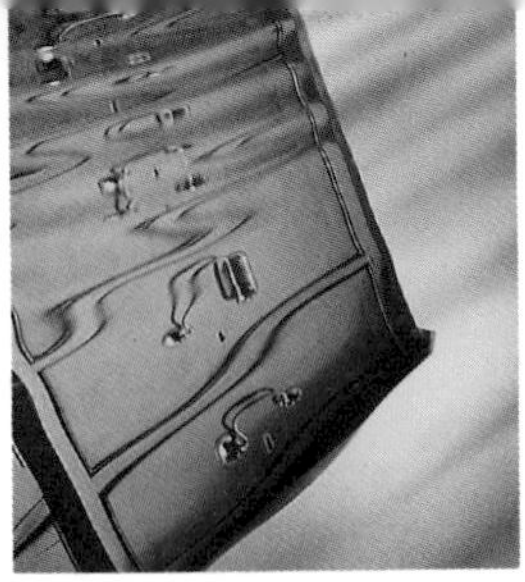

LAKESIDE
limited

Old Cement Works, South Heighton,
Newhaven, East Sussex BN9 0HS
Telephone 01273 513326 Facsimile 01273 515528

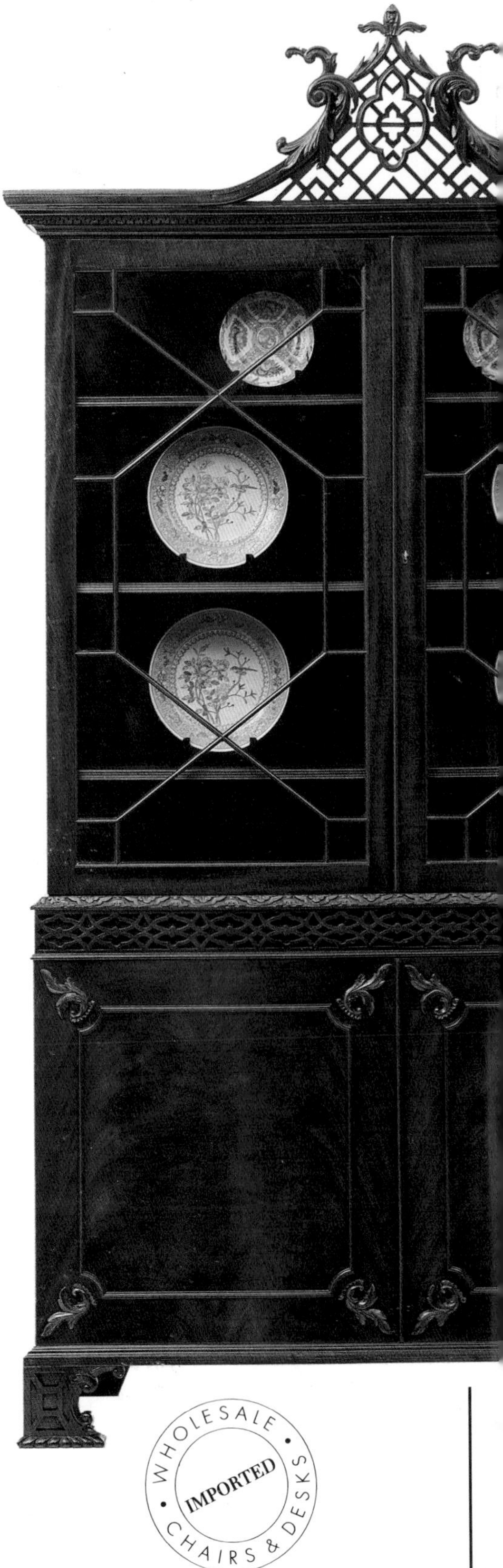

LAKESIDE FURNITURE FEATURES STRONG, CLASSIC DESIGNS WHETHER FOR THE AMERICAN OR EUROPEAN MARKET. USING ONLY OLD OR WELL SEASONED MATERIALS, THE HIGHEST QUALITY IS ASSURED.

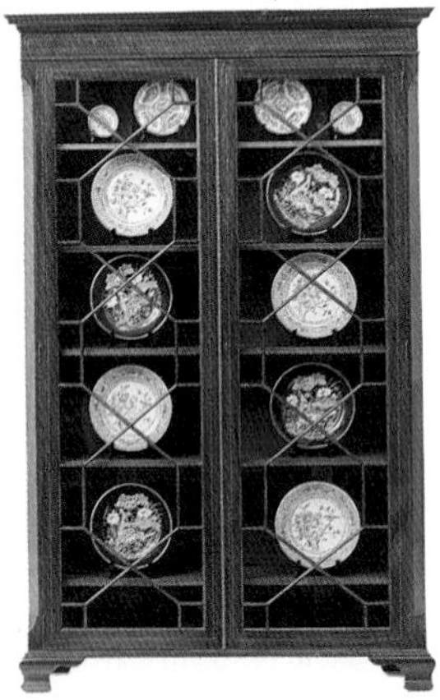

OUR SKILLED CRAFTSMAN MAKE EACH PIECE INDIVIDUALLY TO EXACT STANDARDS THERFORE WE CAN TAILOR TO SPECIFIC NEEDS. WE CAN ALSO MANUFACTURE CUSTOMISED DESIGNS IN A VARIETY OF MATERIALS.

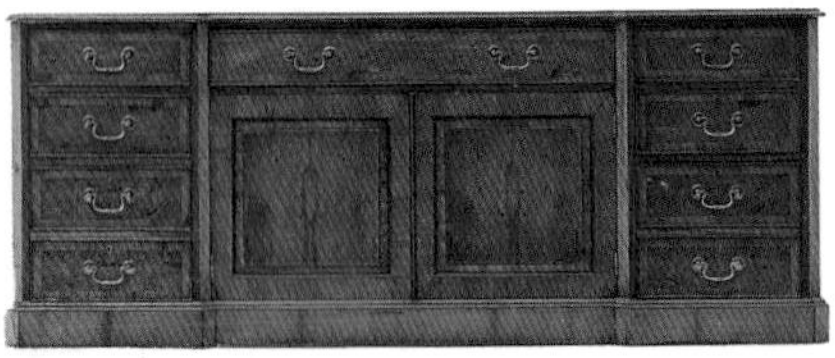

WE OFFER A FULLY COMPREHENSIVE SERVICE FROM CONSTRUCTION AND POLISHING TO UPHOLSTERY AND LEATHERING, CARRIED OUT BY OUR OWN CRAFTSMAN.

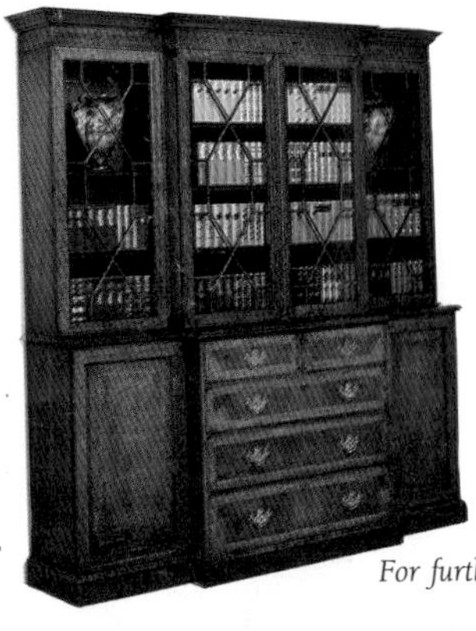

WHOLESALE • IMPORTED • CHAIRS & DESKS

For further fine examples of our furniture see our display ad on pages 14 & 15